OXFORD PHILOSOPHICAL TEXTS

DAVID HUME

A Treatise of
Human Nature

OXFORD PHILOSOPHICAL TEXTS

Series Editor: John Cottingham

The Oxford Philosophical Texts series consists of authoritative teaching editions of canonical texts in the history of philosophy from the ancient world down to modern times. Each volume provides a clear, well laid out text together with a comprehensive introduction by a leading specialist, giving the student detailed critical guidance on the intellectual context of the work and the structure and philosophical importance of the main arguments. Endnotes are supplied which provide further commentary on the arguments and explain unfamiliar references and terminology, and a full bibliography and index are also included.

The series aims to build up a definitive corpus of key texts in the Western philosophical tradition, which will form a reliable and enduring resource for students and teachers alike.

PUBLISHED IN THIS SERIES:

Berkeley *A Treatise concerning the Principles of Human Knowledge* (edited by Jonathan Dancy)
Berkeley *Three Dialogues between Hylas and Philonous* (edited by Jonathan Dancy)
Hume *An Enquiry concerning Human Understanding* (edited by Tom L. Beauchamp)
Hume *An Enquiry concerning the Principles of Morals* (edited by Tom L. Beauchamp)
Hume *A Treatise of Human Nature* (edited by David Fate Norton and Mary J. Norton)
Leibniz *Philosophical Texts* (edited by R. S. Woolhouse and Richard Francks)
Mill *Utilitarianism* (edited by Roger Crisp)

FORTHCOMING TITLES INCLUDE:

Frege *Philosophical Writings* (edited by Anthony Kenny)
Kant *Groundwork for the Metaphysics of Morals* (edited by Thomas E. Hill and Arnulf Zweig)
Kant *Prolegomena to Any Future Metaphysics* (edited by Günter Zöller)
Locke *An Essay concerning Human Understanding* (edited by S. Nicholas Jolley)
Spinoza *Ethics* (edited by G. H. R. Parkinson)

DAVID HUME

A Treatise of
Human Nature

EDITED BY
DAVID FATE NORTON
MARY J. NORTON

EDITOR'S INTRODUCTION BY
DAVID FATE NORTON

OXFORD
UNIVERSITY PRESS

OXFORD

UNIVERSITY PRESS

Great Clarendon Street, Oxford OX2 6DP

Oxford University Press is a department of the University of Oxford.
It furthers the University's objective of excellence in research, scholarship,
and education by publishing worldwide in

Oxford New York

Auckland Cape Town Dar es Salaam Hong Kong Karachi Kuala Lumpur
Madrid Melbourne Mexico City Nairobi New Delhi Shanghai Taipei Toronto

With offices in

Argentina Austria Brazil Chile Czech Republic France Greece
Guatemala Hungary Italy Japan South Korea Poland Portugal
Singapore Switzerland Thailand Turkey Ukraine Vietnam

Oxford is a registered trade mark of Oxford University Press
in the UK and in certain other countries

Published in the United States
by Oxford University Press Inc., New York

Editorial introduction and apparatus © David Fate Norton and Mary J. Norton 2000

British Library Cataloguing in Publication Data

Data available

Library of Congress Cataloging in Publication Data
Hume, David, 1711–1776.
A treatise of human nature / David Hume; edited by David Fate
Norton, Mary J. Norton; editor's introduction by David Fate Norton
(Oxford Philosophical Texts)
Includes bibliographical references and index.
1. Knowledge, Theory of.   I. Norton, David Fate.   II. Norton,
Mary J.   III. Title.   IV. Series.

B1485   2000   128—dc21   99-40916   CIP

ISBN 978-0-19-875172-4

22

Typeset by SNP Best-set Typesetter Ltd, Hong Kong

Contents

Contents

PART 2: THE TEXT

Contents

Contents

PART 1
Introductory Material

How to Use this Book

THIS volume contains the complete texts of Hume's *A Treatise of Human Nature* and of his *Abstract* of that work. To help you as you read Hume's texts, we have also provided an Editor's Introduction, Annotations, a Glossary, References, and an Index.

1. The Editor's Introduction begins with a brief account of Hume's life and writing. It then shows how each part of the *Treatise* (there are a total of ten such parts) contributes to the achievement of Hume's efforts to provide a comprehensive account of the workings, scope, and limits of the human mind. You may want to read the Editor's Introduction as a whole, or you may find it more useful to read the discussion of each part in conjunction with your reading of the corresponding part of the *Treatise*. At the end of this Introduction you will find suggestions for supplementary reading, including a list of Hume's other writings.

2. The Annotations anticipate questions you may have about the meaning of the text. Some annotations are explications of words or phrases whose meaning is crucial to an argument, others outline an argument, some refer you to relevant sections of the *Treatise*, and others relate what Hume says to what was said by some of his predecessors and contemporaries. The Annotations also include brief descriptive overviews of each of the parts and sections into which Hume divided the *Treatise*.

Wherever we have provided an annotation, we have marked the text with a superscript dagger, †. When you want to see what an annotation for a particular passage has to say, turn to the Annotations and look for the corresponding book, part, section, and paragraph number. Attention to the annotations will never serve as a substitute for a careful reading of Hume's text, but such attention may help you get your bearings or gain an overview of a complex work. Please remember that we do not suppose that our annotations or the other supporting materials are the last word on their subjects. Rather, these materials are intended to be part of a continuing dialogue in which you are an active participant when you read attentively and critically, aiming to develop your own insights into Hume's philosophy.

3. We urge you to look at the Glossary now, to read what we have said about its use and how it serves as a supplement to the Annotations, and then to scan a page or two of the entries found there. For example, note what we report about two words, *immediate*, and *vulgar*, which in the early eighteenth century had meanings significantly different from those they have today.

4. The References identify the individuals and books mentioned by Hume or by us.

5. The Index enables you to locate names and topics in the *Treatise*, the *Abstract*, the Editor's Introduction, and the Annotations.

These aids to reading the *Treatise* are an accessory to those Hume himself has provided. Even if you are studying only one portion of the *Treatise*, before you start take time to scan the Contents and read his Introduction. From the Contents you will get an overview of what his concerns are and how he plans to deal with them. From the Introduction you will gain a sense of his writing style, of how he develops his ideas, and of his intent to establish a kind of dialogue with his readers. Hume's brief *Abstract* of the *Treatise* may also help you understand his general goals and a central argument of Book 1. When you begin to study a particular section of the *Treatise*, notice how Hume builds up systematically to his conclusions. He often numbers the elements of arguments so that his readers can follow more easily. He regularly raises and responds to possible objections to his ideas. He reviews the approaches other writers have taken. He lays out thought experiments to test his hypotheses. Frequently, he summarizes his arguments at the end of one section or at the start of the next. Throughout, he refers the reader to those previous conclusions that provide a foundation for the current discussion. Remember, finally, that Hume saw himself as presenting a new science of human nature, and that the various parts of the *Treatise* are linked by this common purpose.

List of Abbreviations

Abs.	*An Abstract of* . . . A Treatise of Human Nature
Adv.	Advertisements to Book 1 and Book 3 of the *Treatise*
App.	Appendix to Vol. 3 of the *Treatise*. Passages first printed in the Appendix but now inserted in Book 1 are marked at the beginning and end by a superscript:^{App.}
Ed. Intro.	Editor's Introduction to the present volume
EHU	*An Enquiry concerning Human Understanding*
EPM	*An Enquiry concerning the Principles of Morals*
Intro.	Hume's Introduction to the *Treatise*
Letters	*The Letters of David Hume*
OED	*The Oxford English Dictionary*
Pref.	Preface to the *Abstract*

Introductory Material

Editor's Introduction

David Fate Norton

DAVID HUME'S *A Treatise of Human Nature* offers its readers a comprehensive and endlessly fascinating account of a topic of perennial interest, human nature itself. Hume begins the work by explaining why philosophy should follow what he calls the 'experimental method'. Then, after describing the basic elements of mind and thought, he goes on to explain the origin and nature of such fundamental concepts as space and time, cause and effect, necessity, external existence, and personal identity. Book 2 provides a ground-breaking account of the passions (of pride, humility, love, hatred, pity, and malice; of desire, aversion, grief, joy, hope, and fear) and an unforgettable discussion of the nature of human freedom. The third and final book articulates a challenging hypothesis about the origin and nature of moral distinctions, of the difference between virtue and vice. Throughout the whole, Hume attempts to balance the excitement produced by his novel and ingenious attempts to resolve a substantial set of profound philosophical issues, with his substantial doubts about our ability to do so.

Hume (1711–76) began working on *A Treatise of Human Nature* before his sixteenth birthday. By 1737, after ten years of more or less continuous effort, he had finished a draft of the work. Two years later, in January 1739, volume 1, 'Of the Understanding', and volume 2, 'Of the Passions', were published. 'Of Morals', the third and final volume of the work, was published in November 1740. Hume was never fully satisfied with the *Treatise*. Given the range of profound topics the work addresses and the youthfulness of its author, this dissatisfaction should not surprise us. However, it was not what he had said, but how he had said it, that bothered him. Hume later clarified or modified some of his conclusions, but he never abandoned the fundamental principles that direct and motivate the *Treatise*.

Hume's Early Years and Education

Hume was born in Edinburgh, Scotland's capital, on 26 April 1711. The years of his youth were divided between that city and Ninewells, his family's small land-holding at Chirnside, a village near the border with England.

Little is known about Hume's childhood. His father, Joseph, died when David was two; his mother, Katherine, never remarried, but, according to Hume, devoted herself to her three children. It was his mother who reported that young David was 'uncommonly wake-minded'—uncommonly acute, that is, in the local dialect of the period—and this report is consistent with all else we know of the young Hume.

Hume began studies at the University of Edinburgh in 1723, and apparently continued there through the spring of 1726. Like many students of the time, he did not take a degree. While at university he would have extended his reading in Latin literature and studied Greek. He would also have been expected to study logic (including theory of knowledge), metaphysics (including natural religion), and moral philosophy (including moral psychology or the theory of the passions), and probably studied elementary mathematics and attended lectures on world history. In addition, he followed a course of lectures and experiments in natural philosophy (such sciences as mechanics and hydraulics, for example) organized around the writings of Robert Boyle, whose use of the experimental method obviously impressed Hume. He also joined a private library (the Physiological Library), which gave him access to a wide range of books on the sciences then studied.[1]

Hume's father and maternal grandfather had both been lawyers. His own studious disposition, Hume tells us in his brief autobiography, led his family to suppose that he, too, would find the law a suitable profession. But he found in himself an 'unsurmountable aversion to every thing but the pursuits of philosophy and general learning', and thus while his family supposed he was reading law books, he was secretly reading two of his favourite authors, Cicero and Virgil.[2] After much study and reflection, he later reported, 'there seem'd to be open'd up to me a new Scene of Thought, which transported me beyond Measure, & made me, with an Ardor natural to young men, throw up every other Pleasure or Business to apply entirely to it. . . . I was infinitely happy in this Course of Life for some Months.' So avid was this pursuit of philosophy that Hume's health was undermined. The physician he consulted assured him that he was suffering only from 'the Disease of the Learned'. As Hume learned to study with more moderation his health improved.[3]

Hume's early philosophical reflections led him to the conclusion that the moral philosophy of the ancients was defective. It, like ancient natural philosophy, was too speculative; it depended 'more upon Invention than [on] Experience'. In putting together their theories of virtue and happiness, its authors had failed to give adequate attention to human nature, 'upon which every moral Conclusion must depend'. In contrast, Hume proposed to focus on human

---

[1] On Hume's knowledge of the science of his time, and of Boyle in particular, see Michael Barfoot, 'Hume and the Culture of Science in the Early Eighteenth Century', in M. A. Stewart (ed.), *Oxford Studies in the History of Philosophy* (Oxford: Clarendon Press, 1990), 151–90. To locate further studies on the many aspects of Hume discussed in this Introduction, see Roland Hall, *50 Years of Hume Scholarship* (Edinburgh: Edinburgh University Press, 1978), and Roland Hall and, later, William E. Morris, 'The Hume Literature . . .', *Hume Studies*, 4–7, 10–11, 13–14, 20– . For references to a more limited set of studies, see the Supplementary Reading at the end of this Introduction.

[2] *My Own Life*, a work first published in 1777. This brief autobiography is reprinted in *The Letters of David Hume* (hereafter *Letters*), ed. J. Y. T. Greig, 2 vols. (Oxford: Clarendon Press, 1932), 1:1–7, and in D. F. Norton (ed.), *The Cambridge Companion to Hume* (Cambridge: Cambridge University Press, 1993), 351–6.

[3] Letter of spring 1734; see *Letters*, 1:13–14. Hume's letter, which he called 'a kind of History of my Life', is also reprinted in Norton (ed.), *Cambridge Companion*, 345–50.

nature, making it the source from which he would derive the principles of moral philosophy.[4]

During the three years prior to his twenty-third birthday Hume 'collected the rude Materials for many Volumes'. However, he found it virtually impossible to put his ideas, ideas that he understood in broad outline, into an orderly, precise form. 'I had', he wrote, 'no Hopes of delivering my Opinions with such Elegance & Neatness, as to draw to me the Attention of the World, & I wou'd rather live & dye in Obscurity than produce them maim'd & imperfect. Such a miserable Disappointment I scarce ever remember to have heard of.' In this unhappy state Hume determined that he should put aside philosophy and take up a more active life. In the spring of 1734 he did so. Having been offered a job with a merchant located in Bristol, Hume left Scotland with the intention of losing himself and his disappointment in a new way of life.[5]

Hume's stay in Bristol was brief. The scene, he later reported, 'was totally unsuitable', and within a few months he was on his way to France, with the intention of pursuing his studies in a quiet place away from enquiring friends and family. He chose finally to settle in La Flèche, in Anjou, the site of the Jesuit seminary attended by Descartes in the early seventeenth century. We know little about Hume's life in France, but he clearly devoted much time to his *Treatise* for when he returned to England in September of 1737 he carried a manuscript of the work with him. The next year he spent in London revising his text (after conversations, surely, with others sharing his philosophical interests) and arranging for its publication.[6] In September 1738 he signed a contract to have the first two volumes of the *Treatise* published by John Noon. The completed volumes were offered for sale, anonymously, the following January.

The early sales of the *Treatise* were disappointing. So, too, were some of the reviews, which complained that the book, although showing signs of genius, was difficult to understand. In response, sometime in 1739 or early 1740 Hume prepared and published, again anonymously, his *Abstract* of the *Treatise*, a short work in which he undertook to explain what he called the chief argument of the *Treatise*.[7] During this same period he sent the manuscript of Book 3, 'Of Morals', to Francis Hutcheson, professor of moral philosophy at Glasgow University, and then revised his text in response to Hutcheson's criticisms.

---

[4] *Letters*, 1:14–16; Norton (ed.), *Cambridge Companion*, 346–8. On another occasion Hume complained that modern philosophers, because they have emphasized reason at the expense of feeling, have not 'treated Morals so well as the Antients'. See 'Hume's Early Memoranda', ed. E. C. Mossner, *Journal of the History of Ideas*, 9 (1948), 517.

[5] *Letters*, 1:14–17; Norton (ed.), *Cambridge Companion*, 349–50.

[6] Although during this time Hume was tempted to return to Scotland to visit family and friends, he did not do so, he said, because he could not overcome the shame he felt that, at age 26, he had no permanent position or any other success. How does it happen, he added, 'that we philosophers cannot as heartily despise the world, as it despises us?' (4 Mar. 1737; *Letters*, 1:24). Hume returned to Scotland only in Feb. 1739, soon after the first two volumes of the *Treatise* were published.

[7] This argument, summarized at *Abs.* 21 (at, that is, *Abstract*, para. 21), is discussed below, pp. I29–31.

Book 3, along with an Appendix to Book 1, was published at the end of 1740 by Thomas Longman.

A detailed account of Hume's early reading, of the wide-ranging reading that stimulated and helped to form the views expressed in the *Treatise*, is only now beginning to emerge. In addition to the authors already mentioned (Cicero, Virgil, Boyle, and Hutcheson), Hume says that in the three years ending in the spring of 1734 he had read 'most of the celebrated Books in Latin, French & English', and also learned Italian.[8] This breadth of study and reading do not necessarily distinguish Hume from other philosophers of his time, but it may suggest that, despite his obvious preference for what he called the 'experimental Method of Reasoning', no single writer or philosophical tradition can be relied upon to provide a comprehensive key to his thought. Hume's was an independent intellect struggling to come to grips with a wide range of complex philosophical problems and systems. Those only beginning to read his work should be wary of commentators who claim to unlock the secrets of Hume's thought by reference to one or two authors or to a single intellectual tradition.

A Treatise of Human Nature

In the two and a half centuries since the publication of the *Treatise* Hume has often, even routinely, been interpreted as a destructive sceptic. He has been taken, that is, as the philosopher whose principal achievement was to show that the empiricism of Locke and Berkeley, when taken to its logical conclusion, results in the denial of the reality of causes, objects, enduring selves, human freedom, and objective values, and who, moreover, delighted in this radically sceptical result. We can probably see how this inaccurate interpretation arose. Hume described himself as a sceptic at a time when sceptics were taken to be, as one reference work of his time put it, those who said that there is no real or certain knowledge of anything, and that we 'ought to Doubt of, and Disbelieve every thing'.[9] Hume's conception of his own scepticism is far more moderate; he insists, among other things, that our natures make it impossible for us to disbelieve many of the things some sceptics had claimed to doubt. Why was this explicit moderation generally overlooked by Hume's contemporaries and many later readers? Perhaps because Hume was also sceptical about religious matters. The *Treatise* makes little explicit comment about such issues, but it did

---

[8] *Letters*, 1:16; Norton (ed.), *Cambridge Companion*, 349. We know that Hume read such classical writers as Lucan, Lucretius, Seneca, Tacitus, and Plutarch; such popular English poets and essayists as John Milton, John Dryden, Matthew Prior, Daniel Defoe, Alexander Pope, Jonathan Swift, Joseph Addison, and Richard Steele; and such English philosophers as Francis Bacon, Thomas Hobbes, Isaac Newton, John Locke, the third Earl of Shaftesbury, Viscount Bolingbroke, Samuel Clarke, Anthony Collins, George Berkeley, Bernard de Mandeville, William Wollaston, and Joseph Butler. He also read such French writers as Michel de Montaigne, René Descartes, Pierre Gassendi, Blaise Pascal, Antoine Arnauld, Nicolas Malebranche, Nicolas Despréaux Boileau, Jacques Rohault, and Pierre Bayle; and such other continental figures as Niccolò Machiavelli, Hugo Grotius, and Samuel Pufendorf. To these well-known names one could add many others now obscure.

[9] John Harris, *Lexicon Technicum*, vol. 1 (1704), 'Sceptick'.

attack favourite doctrines of the religious (the immateriality of the soul, for example; see 1.4.5.17–21[10]), and it also took the then unorthodox step of attempting to solve philosophical problems without any appeal to religious principle or the benevolent character of the Deity. In several of his later works (*An Enquiry concerning Human Understanding*, *The Natural History of Religion*, and *Dialogues concerning Natural Religion*, for example) Hume was openly sceptical about many important aspects of religious belief. As a consequence, many of his contemporaries were motivated to denounce him as a dangerous infidel and to characterize all his philosophy as essentially destructive. These negative assessments have since been repeated by those who have failed, as many still do, to read Hume with care.

Whatever we may suppose accounts for this long-standing view that Hume is simply a destructive sceptic, the view is not supported by the text of the *Treatise*. The subtitle of this work tells us that it is 'an Attempt to introduce the experimental Method of Reasoning into Moral Subjects'. In the first paragraphs of his Introduction to his project Hume tells us that the application of the experimental method of reasoning to *natural* philosophy had produced important positive results. He then tells us that he intends the *Treatise* to make a similar, positive contribution to the other branch of philosophy, *moral* philosophy.[11] Our task here is to try to understand that positive contribution while yet recognizing that Hume saw himself as a kind of moderate sceptic.

For a start, Hume can be helpfully understood as what we might call a *post-sceptical* philosopher. That is, Hume's study of philosophy had convinced him that such important philosophers as Malebranche, Locke, Bayle, and Berkeley had already taken traditional metaphysics and epistemology to their sceptical conclusions. It was these earlier philosophers, and not Hume, who first argued that philosophy is unable to provide us with reliable accounts of the real natures and relations of things. It was Malebranche, a leading Cartesian philosopher of the late seventeenth century, who had argued that there are no true causes in nature, that our natural faculties are unable to establish that there is a material world, and that we know less about ourselves than we do about nature. It was Locke and his followers who had concluded that our knowledge of substances, whether material or immaterial, reduces to a vague *something, I know not what*. It was Bayle who had argued that every conceivable theory of space and time, and every philosophical system, is incoherent. It was Berkeley who had denied the existence of material objects. In addition, Hobbes, Mandeville, and others had denied that there are real moral distinctions. Granted, some of these arguments were mitigated by religious

---

[10] A reference of the form 1.4.5.17–21 is to the *Treatise*, to Book 1, Part 4, Sect. 5, paras. 17–21.

[11] In Hume's time philosophy had two distinctive branches. One, natural philosophy, included those subjects we now think of as the physical and natural sciences. The other, moral philosophy, focused on humans or human activity and included those subjects we would think of as the core of philosophy (theory of knowledge, metaphysics, and ethics, for example), as well as such subjects as psychology, political science, sociology, economics, and aesthetics (to use our terms), and important aspects of the study of religion.

commitments. Malebranche, for example, hypothesized that the activity of the Deity accounts for what we take to be natural causes and effects, and that the existence of the material world is established by the revealed word of God. But the fact remains: Hume's predecessors were, intentionally or otherwise, deeply sceptical about the *philosophical* grounds of our most basic beliefs.

Suggesting that Hume was a post-sceptical philosopher is not to suggest that he was not, in several important respects, a sceptic. He clearly did believe that human knowledge is limited in both scope and depth, and that philosophical claims are shot through with error and pretension. He had, however, no need to establish this obvious point. Well aware of the pervasive if often implicit scepticism of his predecessors, Hume concluded that the most important remaining task of philosophy, indeed, perhaps the only plausible remaining task, was to show how, given the apparent triumph of scepticism, we get on with our lives, including both our intellectual and our moral lives. His predecessors had thoroughly discredited the claim of humans to have sure and certain knowledge of the true nature of space, causal relations, external objects, mind, and moral differences. As Hume puts it in the Introduction to the *Treatise*, even ordinary people know that the philosophical enterprise is not going well, that the 'most trivial question' is a subject of debate, and that about the 'most momentous' questions we can reach no certain conclusion (Intro. 2).[12] The philosophy of the past had managed to produce only badly formed opinions for which an excess of zeal is shown. A change in method, Hume argues, will provide us with a new and sounder foundation—with a new science of human nature—on which all other sciences can rest.

THE EXPERIMENTAL METHOD AND THE SCIENCE OF HUMAN NATURE

In the Introduction to the *Treatise* Hume suggests that moral philosophy (see note 11 above) will be able to move beyond fruitless debate only if we change its focus. Instead of turning directly to particular issues currently debated in, say, metaphysics or ethics or politics, we should first focus our attention on the 'science of human nature', on, that is, the one branch of learning on which all other branches (or sciences) depend.[13] This means that before we attempt to settle the disputed issues in these other areas of study, we should become 'thoroughly acquainted with the extent and force of human understanding', and that we should also 'explain the nature of the ideas we employ, and of the operations we perform in our reasonings' (Intro. 4). Only when we know and understand the powers and operations of the human mind will we know what we can reasonably hope to understand about other subjects.

Hume also suggests that recent successes in natural philosophy have given us

[12] The reference is to Hume's Introduction to the *Treatise*, para. 2.

[13] In the present context, *science* denotes something like 'a methodically gathered and systematically organized set of facts, observations, and general principles regarding any specified subject' (cf. *OED* 4a). When using *science* in this sense, Hume is more likely to be referring to the sciences of morals or politics than to any of the physical sciences (biology, chemistry, physics) now typically comprehended by this term.

an important clue about how to proceed in our efforts to develop this foundational science of human nature. Early in the seventeenth century Francis Bacon
had argued that natural philosophers must actually observe and even test
nature if it is to be understood. Later natural philosophers did approach nature
in this way—they developed what by Hume's time was called the *experimental
method*—and, as a result, seemed to make great advances. Hume had studied
some of the great experimentalist natural philosophers, Boyle and Newton, for
example, and was impressed by their work. Given that the experimental
method had been so successful in natural philosophy, it seemed obvious to him
that we ought to use this same method to develop a new science of human
nature: 'the only solid foundation we can give to this science itself must be laid
on experience and observation' (Intro. 7).

Hume recognizes, however, that there are two limitations on this new
science. First, it, as much as the new natural philosophy, is limited in its scope.
Neither of the new kinds of science can hope to transcend experience.
Granted, we can hope to generalize from our observations, but we cannot
expect these generalizations to inform us of some higher level of reality beyond
the observable. This means that in moral philosophy we can hope to point out
how the mind works and what operations are within its scope or power. By
'tracing up our experiments to the utmost, and explaining all effects from the
simplest and fewest causes', we can try to make our new science as fundamental and comprehensive as possible. But we cannot hope to get behind the
scenes, so to speak, and discover *why* human nature and the mind are as they
are. As Hume sums up the matter, we should reject as 'presumptuous and
chimerical' any theory that claims to have gone beyond experience to 'discover
the ultimate original qualities of human nature' (Intro. 8).

In addition, we must recognize that there are differences between moral and
natural philosophy. The latter can often carry out what we now call laboratory
experiments. It can make experiments, as Hume puts it, 'purposely, with
premeditation, and after such a manner as to satisfy itself concerning every
particular difficulty which may arise'. In moral philosophy, Hume says, we
must be more passive. We must in this science make our experiments by means
of 'a cautious observation of human life, and take them as they appear in
the common course of the world, by men's behaviour in company, in affairs,
and in their pleasures'.[14] Notwithstanding these limitations, however, we may
hope 'to establish . . . a science, which will not be inferior in certainty, and
will be much superior in utility to any other of human comprehension' (Intro.
10). Hume's predecessors, by their intended and unintended scepticism, had
shown the limits of our knowledge and our own very real limitations. Hume,
accepting these limitations, attempts in the *Treatise* to articulate a new kind of
philosophy, an experience–based science of human nature.[15]

---

[14] Hume does occasionally make what appear to be deliberate, premeditated thought experiments. See e.g. the eight experiments described in 2.2.2.

[15] Hume often recast and revised his philosophical works, but his commitment to experience and
observation remained a central and unchanging component of his thought. See e.g. *Abs.* 2; *EHU*

Book 1: Of the Understanding

The first book of the *Treatise* is divided into four parts. In Part 1 Hume describes the basic components, the 'elements' as he calls them, of his philosophy. Part 2 focuses on our ideas of space and time. Part 3 discusses knowledge, probability, and belief in what Hume calls 'matter of fact', as well as our ideas of cause and effect and necessity. Part 4 takes up a wide range of topics: reason, belief in the existence of external objects, ancient and modern metaphysics, the nature of the soul or mind, personal identity, and various forms or kinds of scepticism.

Book 1 Part 1: The Elements of the Mental World

Many early modern philosophers were convinced that the immediate object of the mind is always something mental or internal to the mind.[16] In one respect, there is nothing surprising about this view. If the choice is between supposing that love or pain are internal and subjective, or external and objective, few would argue that they are external and objective. In another respect, this view is puzzling and contrary to common sense. When I think I see a tree, I think and act as if this tree is external and objective. I do not suppose the tree is something internal, a mere image or idea in my mind. And yet these philosophers said that the immediate object of the mind is always something internal to the mind. The philosophers' thesis was that, whenever we think we see an external object, the immediate object of our minds is a mental representation of that external object. Thus, when I think I see a tree, I am in fact experiencing only a mental representation of that tree.

These philosophers typically supposed that the ordinary person acts and talks as if he or she is directly aware of external objects or events. They also typically supposed that the ordinary person acts and talks as if there are external objects or events. The thesis was not about what ordinary people think they are aware of or what they think is real or external, nor was holding the thesis equivalent to denying that there are external objects.[17] The thesis was, rather, about how the mind works. Despite a number of disagreements about details, thoughtful analysis of the experience of perceiving and knowing the world had satisfied these philosophers that, whatever ordinary people believe about their experiences of trees or other external objects, the mind is acquainted with objects only through the mediation of mental representations which they called, typically, *ideas*.

4.2–13, 12.11; *EPM* 1.10; *Essays Moral, Political, and Literary*, ed. E. F. Miller, rev. edn. (Indianapolis: LibertyClassics, 1987), 231, 480.

[16] Locke, for example, explained that by the term 'idea' he meant 'whatsoever is the Object of the Understanding when a Man thinks . . . or whatever it is, which the Mind can be employ'd about in thinking' (*Essay concerning Human Understanding* 1.1.8), thus indicating that the immediate object of thought is always something mental. For references to other philosophers holding this view, see the annotation to 1.2.6.7.

[17] George Berkeley and Arthur Collier did deny that there are external, material objects, but even for them this denial constituted a second thesis, distinct from the claim that the immediate object of the mind is always an idea or perception.

Although Hume used a different vocabulary, he accepted this thesis about the immediate objects of the mind. 'Nothing', he says, 'is ever really present with [or to] the mind but its perceptions or impressions and ideas' (1.2.6.7). Moreover, his central concern in the *Treatise* is the mind, its operations, and those mental elements on which the mind operates or which it produces. This is not to say that the Hume of the *Treatise* shows no interest in the world beyond the mind. Indeed, he often speaks as if his interest were the external world. But his approach to the external world is inside-out. That is, he makes no effort to explain how the external world impinges on the mind through the senses, if that is what it does. Rather, he undertakes in *Treatise* 1 to explain something his predecessors had failed to explain, or even to see as needing explanation. He explains how it happens that we humans, beings whose minds are said to encounter nothing but the mental, come to believe that there is an external, non-mental world. He explains why it is that perfectly ordinary people—people who have never so much as heard a philosophical argument—think, talk, and act as though space, causes, and objects are external and objective.

This novel enterprise begins with a review, found in *Treatise* 1.1, of the 'elements' of the 'mental world' Hume has chosen to explore (1.1.4.6–7). *Perceptions* and *relations*, the elements on which he focuses, are basic features of all the philosophical explanations found in the *Treatise*.

PERCEPTIONS

We have already seen that Hume was convinced that the immediate object of the mind is always something mental or internal to the mind. Philosophers from Descartes to Locke and Berkeley had typically called these mental entities *ideas*. Hume revises this language. In his vocabulary *perceptions* are the immediate object of thought, but there are two fundamentally different types of perception, *impressions* and *ideas*.

Impressions include 'all our sensations, passions and emotions' and for starters can be said to enter the mind with greater force or vivacity than do ideas, the 'faint images' of impressions. Although Hume initially suggests that the difference between the two types of perception is simply the difference between actually experiencing something and later remembering that experience (1.1.1.1), we later learn that this particular difference is far from absolute. Ideas may on occasion be as forceful and vivacious as impressions (see, for example, 1.3.5).

Hume also says that our impressions and ideas are either simple or complex. Simple perceptions, those of particular colours or tastes, for example, 'admit of no distinction nor separation'. These perceptions are basic and unanalysable. In contrast, complex perceptions, impressions or ideas of Paris, for example, can be analysed or divided into constituent parts. Hume then argues that the real and fundamental difference between impressions and ideas is that the latter are causally dependent on the former. The 'first principle . . . in the science of human nature', he says, is that 'all our simple ideas proceed, either mediately or immediately, from their correspondent [resembling] impressions'. This important conclusion is supported by two facts. First, simple impressions and ideas are regularly found in resembling pairs; that is, it is typically the case that for each simple impression (the pain of a pinprick, say) there is subsequently a resembling simple idea (a recollection of this pain).[18] Such a 'constant conjunction' convinces Hume that the relationship between such resembling perceptions is a close one. Secondly, those who are unable to experience a given simple impression are unable to form an idea of that phenomenon. Those who have never eaten a pineapple (never had the impression of a pineapple) cannot form an idea of the taste of that fruit, while those lacking a particular sense organ are unable to form ideas of the qualities (colour, sound, smell) associated with that organ (1.1.1.2–12).

This discussion of impressions and ideas allows Hume quietly to position himself on a key issue in early modern philosophy, that concerning the source of such fundamental concepts as space and time, cause, or substance, and such principles as 'Every beginning of existence must have a cause'. The question was, Are these concepts and principles innate or learned? Is the human mind, prior to experience, provided in some way with important religious, metaphysical, moral, or mathematical concepts, or do we develop these concepts through experience? In opposition to those who said they are innate, Locke had argued there are no innate ideas or principles, and had then gone on to argue that the hypothesis of innate ideas is unnecessary because all our ideas and principles can be produced by experience.[19] Hume is in partial agreement with Locke on this matter. He agrees that our fundamental philosophical concepts (space, time, cause, and substance, for example) are the products of experience, and not innate. But Hume is far from satisfied with Locke's account of the origin of these concepts. Thus the *Treatise* includes an account of the origins of several fundamental ideas for which Locke and others, so Hume thought, had failed to give a convincing account. These include the ideas of space and time, of necessary connection or causal power, of external objects, of the self or personal identity, and of virtue and vice and justice and injustice, ideas whose detailed analysis is of central importance in the *Treatise*.[20]

---

[18] Hume's speculation about how one might form the idea of a previously unexperienced shade of blue (1.1.1.10–11) shows that some simple ideas may not be derived from exactly resembling simple impressions. But Hume takes his example to show that even this apparently anomalous idea of blue is ultimately derived from simple impressions (from impressions of the gradated set of blues most like it), and thus he can conclude that all simple ideas derive, either directly or indirectly, from simple impressions.

[19] Locke, after having argued that the theory of innate ideas or principles is unconvincing and incoherent (*Essay* 1.2–4), then undertakes to show how the mind, beginning as a 'white Paper . . . without any *Ideas*', comes to have its many different ideas, or how the 'Understanding may get all the *Ideas* it has, and by what ways and degrees they may come into the Mind' (*Essay* 2.1.1–2; see also 1.2.1, 28; 1.4.25).

[20] In the *Abstract* of the *Treatise* Hume argues that Locke's misuse of the term *idea* had led him to overstate the case against innate ideas. It is obvious, says Hume, that 'our stronger perceptions or

As Hume undertakes a brief but important '*Division of the subject*' at *Treatise* 1.1.2, he notes that our impressions are also of two kinds: *impressions of sensation* and *impressions of reflection*. Impressions of sensation, he says, arise 'in the soul originally, from unknown causes'. This is virtually all that the *Treatise* is ever to tell us about the origin of these impressions. The fact that Hume talks about *impressions of sensation*, or even about *sensations*, should not mislead us. How sensations arise and what their causes may be are not, Hume explicitly says, his concern. He is a moral philosopher. 'The examination of our sensations belongs more to anatomists and natural philosophers than to moral; and therefore shall not at present be enter'd upon'. This 'not at present' means, we learn, not in the *Treatise*, which is to say that there is in the entire work no theory of perception. That is, the *Treatise* offers no explanation of how external objects (assuming there are such objects) affect our sense organs and thus become causes of what are called impressions of sensation, nor is there any attempt to prove that there is or is not an external or material world.[21] On the other hand, there is an important and extensive discussion of how it is that we come to *believe* that there are enduring external objects (see especially 1.4.2), but this to Hume is an importantly different matter and must be recognized as such.

Impressions of reflection are what Hume calls *secondary impressions*, thus distinguishing them from impressions of sensation, or the *original impressions* with which experience begins. This is not to suggest that impressions of sensation are of more importance (they are not) than impressions of reflection, but only to emphasize that the latter impressions are 'deriv'd in a great measure from our ideas'. We feel such original impressions as heat or cold, thirst or hunger, those impressions, that is, that give us pleasure or pain. Of these impressions we then form ideas, and these ideas give rise to new and different secondary impressions. For example: I remember—I have an idea of—the intense facial pain I felt while walking into yesterday's bitterly cold wind. This idea of pain gives rise to a feeling of aversion, a strong inclination to avoid facing such a wind again. This new feeling, the feeling of aversion, is an impression of reflection.

Hume goes on to say that our secondary impressions may themselves be copied. When such an impression is copied, we have an idea of reflection, or what we might call a *secondary idea*. Presumably, if an idea of this kind gives rise to a further feeling, this would be a *tertiary impression*, and this in turn could be copied by a *tertiary idea*. Hume's discussion of this outcome may seem to

impressions are innate, and that natural affection, love of virtue, resentment, and all the other passions, arise immediately from nature' (*Abs.* 6).

[21] At 2.1.1.2 Hume repeats his refusal to be drawn into speculations about the physical causes of impressions of sensation. It is true, he suggests, that some of our impressions seem to 'depend upon natural and physical causes'. The examination of these, he goes on, 'wou'd lead me too far from my present subject, into the sciences of anatomy and natural philosophy. For this reason I shall here confine myself to those other impressions, which I have call'd *secondary* and *reflective* . . .'. See also 1.3.5.2.

highlight only a remote possibility, but in fact some of the key ideas he traces to their origins (the ideas of virtue and vice, for example) may be just such tertiary ideas. They are, according to Hume, ideas that arise from experience, but at a significant remove from impressions of sensation.

RELATIONS

Hume also distinguishes between two kinds of relation, natural and philosophical. The three *natural* relations, *resemblance, contiguity,* and *causation,* are in fact three forms or principles of natural association. If, for example, we see a portrait, its *resemblance* to the person portrayed may well naturally (involuntarily, that is) lead us to think of that person. If we think of the door to our home, an idea of the *contiguous* door frame and walls may involuntarily arise in the mind. If we perceive a particular *effect* (if we look out of the window and see that, although the sky is cloudless blue, everything in sight is soaking wet) we may well think of the *cause* of that effect (an earlier rain). In each of these cases there is said to be an 'associating quality' which connects two ideas in such a way that the experience of either idea 'naturally introduces the other' (1.1.4.1; 1.1.5.1).

In the *Treatise* Hume suggests that these three principles produce 'union or cohesion' among ideas, making it seem as if they are naturally associated by a force something like that of gravity or magnetism, forces that link physical objects together (1.1.4.6). In the *Abstract* he says that such naturally occurring associations will be seen to be of great importance in the science of human nature because, strictly speaking, they are 'the only links that bind the parts of the universe together, or connect us with any person or object exterior to ourselves. . . . they are really *to us* the cement of the universe, and all the operations of the mind must, in a great measure, depend on them'. He also suggests that if anything entitled him to be thought of as an innovator it was the use he had made 'of the principle of the association of ideas'. The human imagination, he notes, is free to join or separate ideas so as to make up virtually any combination it wishes. None the less, this freedom of the imagination is limited by the fact that 'there is a secret tie or union among particular ideas, which causes the mind to conjoin them more frequently together, and makes the one, upon its appearance, introduce the other' (*Abs. 35*).

As we have just seen, Hume finds that we have the ability or power to place, voluntarily and arbitrarily, any two ideas together, and then to ask in what respect(s) they are related. When we do this, we produce 'the ideas of *philosophical* relation'. According to Hume, there are seven such relations. Think, for example, of two apparently unrelated subjects never before compared together. Think of *Wiwaxia* (a marine life form, apparently extinct) and your personal indebtedness. We can ask whether our ideas of these subjects (1) *resemble* one another, or if they are (2) *identical,* (3) *contrary,* or (4) *contiguous.* We can also ask how they relate with respect to (5) *proportions of quantity* or (6) *degrees of any quality.* And we can even ask if the extinction of *Wiwaxia* is in fact the (7) *cause or effect* of your indebtedness (1.1.5).[22] As it happens, this particular set of comparisons is unlikely to provide significant insight into the subjects compared, but it does illustrate the extent to which we are free to explore possible relationships between any subjects or ideas whatsoever, including those that may never before have been thought of together. In calling such comparisons *philosophical relations* Hume was perhaps suggesting that just such imaginative comparisons are an essential component of the philosophical enterprise (1.1.3.4; 1.1.5).

ABSTRACT IDEAS

Hume concludes his review of the elements of his philosophy with an account of abstract or general ideas, of those ideas that represent kinds of thing (triangles or dogs, for example) and not just individuals. On this issue he explicitly adopts the theory of George Berkeley (see 1.1.7.1). According to this theory, abstract ideas do not represent generally (they do not represent kinds of thing) by being fundamentally indeterminate and for that reason equally representative of every member of the class of things they are said to exemplify. On the contrary, Berkeley insisted (and Hume agreed) that every idea is distinct or determinate. Consequently, the abstract idea of a triangle, for example, cannot be some idea so indistinct or indeterminate that, while yet being a triangle, is neither equilateral, isosceles, nor scalene. On the contrary, the abstract idea of a triangle is simply the idea of some particular and determinate plane figure bounded by three straight lines (the idea of some particular triangle) combined with a term, *triangle*, that refers to all triangles indiscriminately. The abstract idea of dog is formed by the idea of some particular dog (Rover, Spot, Toto) joined to a term, *dog*, that refers to all dogs indiscriminately. And so on.

Book 1 Part 2: The Ideas of Space and Time

The unstated goal of *Treatise* 1.2 is to explain how we come to have ideas of space and time, the ideas, so we implicitly believe, of two pervasive features of the world. Notice that it is our *ideas* of space and time, and not space and time themselves, that are the primary focus of Hume's attention.

From one perspective, Hume's views about our ideas of space and time are difficult to comprehend or appreciate. Philosophers began discussing the nature of space and time in classical times and continued this debate into the early eighteenth century and beyond. Thus, although Hume focuses on the *ideas* of space and time and in that sense intends to change the focus of this long-standing debate, he none the less learned much from his predecessors, and particularly from Pierre Bayle. In keeping with his robust philosophical scepticism, Bayle argued that, if space exists, it must derive from or be made up

---

[22] Note that three relations, resemblance, contiguity, and causation, may be either natural (the result of the involuntary associating quality) or philosophical (the result of a voluntary act of the mind).

of either (1) mathematical points; (2) minute and indivisible physical atoms; or (3) minute and infinitely divisible particles.[23] Against each of these possibilities Bayle raised what he supposed to be insurmountable objections. Space, he argued, cannot be made up of mathematical points, of physical atoms, or of particles. Therefore, space does not exist.[24]

Hume sidesteps this sceptical impasse about the existence of space *per se*. Satisfied that we have an idea of space, he undertakes to explain how we come to have that idea. As he has already concluded that all ideas derive from impressions (from sensations or feelings), it is reasonable to ask which impression or impressions give rise to this idea of space. In answering this question he seems to take cues from Bayle and the debate about space itself. At least, Hume argues that our idea of space cannot derive from a simple impression of an indivisible physical atom or infinitely divisible particle. We neither do nor can have simple impressions of those two kinds. But we do have compound impressions of an array of coloured or tangible mathematical points (the minimum visibles described at 1.2.3.15 and 1.2.4.2), and this experience is enough to give us the idea of space. It is able to do so because such an experience gives us the idea of a particular space, while the idea of space in general, the abstract idea of space to be accounted for, is an abstract idea of the sort Berkeley describes. The idea of space is nothing more than the idea of a particular space associated with the general term *space*, and in this way made to stand for all possible spaces.

Seen from a second perspective, Hume's conclusions about the ideas of space and time may be easier to appreciate. In *Treatise* 1.1 he had concluded that 'all our simple ideas proceed, either mediately or immediately, from their correspondent impressions'. Given this principle, he needs to show that the ideas of space and time derive, ultimately, from impressions of sensation. If there were simple impressions of space or time, this would be a relatively easy task. In that case, the idea of space would be nothing more than a copy of the impression of space, and the idea of time a copy of the impression of time. Hume is satisfied, however, that there are no simple impressions of space or time, and hence he has to determine which impressions do give rise to these ideas (1.2.3.1–7).

Here it may be helpful to compare Hume to Locke. Locke, satisfied that there are no innate ideas, had attempted to explain how we do come to have all our ideas, including the idea of space. His account of the idea of space is what we might call an *additive* one. That is, Locke supposes that we have simple impressions (to use Hume's term) of parts of extension, and that we reflectively combine these impressions. As we do so (as we add simple impression to simple impression) we produce the idea of length and, eventually, of extension in general. Hume, without explicitly mentioning this theory,

---

[23] A mathematical point has position without magnitude or parts; a physical atom is a body with magnitude, but it has no parts and is so small it cannot be divided; particles, although minutely small, are none the less divisible and even infinitely so.

[24] Bayle, *The Dictionary Historical and Critical* (hereafter, *Dictionary*), 'Zeno of Elea', nn. F–I.

repudiates it. He offers experimental evidence that our simplest impressions of physical objects (the smallest or minimum visibles, for example) are in fact of things both unextended and indivisible, although they are sensible (that is, they can be sensed because they are either coloured or tangible).[25] There are simple impressions of sight, but from these, given that they are impressions of unextended points, no merely additive process could produce dimension, extension, or the idea of space. On the other hand, vision does convey to us the impressions of these indivisible points arranged in one way or another. Imagine that against a dark background I see an arrangement or cluster of several unextended, brightly coloured points. Such a cluster appearance (what Hume describes as an order or manner of appearing) is the source of an idea of a particular space. The desk or table you now see can provide the same kind of experience, namely, the experience of numerous impressions of unextended and coloured points arranged in one manner or another. The 'idea of extension', Hume says, 'is nothing but a copy of these colour'd points, and of the manner of their appearance'. The arrangement of the coloured points, their *manner of appearing*, is a 'compound impression, which represents extension' in just the way that other compound impressions represent entire sets of resembling impressions—by being copied by an idea that is itself associated with a general term. Or, to put it differently, the idea of space Hume seeks to explain is the idea of space in general. Given that all ideas are particular or determinate, it follows that the idea of space in general is particular and determinate. It just is an idea that (*a*) copies a single compound impression and (*b*) is associated with a general term (*space* or *extension*) in such a way that one particular idea represents all such perceptions, just as the idea of a particular triangle or dog can be made to represent all possible (perceptions of) triangles or dogs (1.2.3.1–5, 15).[26]

Our idea of time is, with suitable modifications, accounted for in the same way. 'As 'tis from the disposition of visible and tangible objects we receive the idea of space, so from the succession of ideas and impressions we form the idea of time.' We have no simple impressions of time, and hence cannot form an idea of time by copying such impressions. But we can none the less form an idea of particular experiences of time—a particular succession of perceptions—and from this we can form the general or abstract idea of time. This abstract idea, Hume says, like all other abstract ideas, is represented in the imagination by a 'particular individual idea of a determinate quantity and

[25] To understand better what Hume means by an unextended coloured point, repeat his experiment: put a spot of ink on a piece of paper. Then, while looking at the spot, move away from it until it disappears. According to Hume, the moment before the spot disappears your impression of it will be as small as it can be (a *minimum visible*) and will be an unextended coloured point. See 1.2.1.4; 1.2.4.7.

[26] Although Hume in *Treatise* 1.2 says little to emphasize the fact, his account of the ideas of space and time gives to the imagination a significant and positive role. The imagination achieves what neither the senses nor reason can achieve. As will be seen, Hume also assigns the imagination a central role in the formation of other important ideas.

quality' joined to a term (in this case the term *time*) having general reference (1.2.3.6–7).[27]

Hume's conclusions in *Treatise* 1.2 leave virtually untouched the long-standing metaphysical puzzles about space and time. Neither do they directly overturn Bayle's radically sceptical conclusions about space. In this respect, Hume's conclusions appear to skirt these earlier discussions. This, I suggest, is exactly what he intended they should do. He intended to avoid these philosophical bogs. Focusing on 'the *appearances* of objects' rather than 'entering into disquisitions concerning their real nature and operations', he had a more sensible goal, that of giving an account of the origin and nature of our *ideas* of space and time (see 1.2.5.25–6 and Note 12).

Book 1 Part 3: *Knowledge, Probability, Belief, and Causation*

In *Treatise* 1.3 Hume reaches two fundamentally important conclusions. After first setting out what he takes to be the difference between 'knowledge' and 'probability', he argues that one highly important kind of belief, probable belief (belief in matter of fact or existence), is best described as an intense or lively *manner of conceiving* certain of our ideas. He then goes on to offer a comprehensive analysis of our ideas of cause and effect and of 'necessary connexion'— of the idea of necessity we have when we say that the occurrence of a given event or object, *C*, a cause, *necessarily* brings about or causes a given second event or object, *E*, an effect.

These are hard-won gains. According to Hume, previous philosophers had given little or no attention to belief as he here understands it, and thus he was entirely on his own. Furthermore, his novel account of belief and his novel account of the origin of our idea of necessary connexion are not only overlapping but also, at times, interchangeable. Finally, the search for the source of our idea of necessary connection proves to be a difficult one. Because our impressions of sensation never include an impression from which this idea of causal necessity is copied, Hume is forced to carry out his search in an indirect, even random, manner. His results amply justify his efforts, and ours to follow him.

RELATIONS REVISITED

Hume approaches the difference between knowledge and probability through a second discussion of philosophical relations. These relations, he argues, are of two kinds. The first kind includes *resemblance, proportion in quantity or number, degrees in any quality*, and *contrariety*; these relations 'depend entirely on the ideas, which we compare together'. The second kind includes the relations of *identity, relations of time and place*, and *causation*; these 'may be chang'd without any change in the ideas' (1.3.1.1) The precise distinction Hume means to make may be difficult to characterize, but for a start it is clear that the difference

---

[27] Hume argues that we cannot have the idea of a vacuum because that would be to have the idea of nothing, while having nothing as the object of thought would be to have no content before the mind—to have no perception at all—thus providing nothing for an idea to copy (see 1.2.5).

between the two types of relation does not, as some have supposed, reduce to the difference between a set of four logical, and another set of three factual or contingent, relations. Relations of the first type include *degrees in any quality*— as when one item in a related pair is heavier or more intensely blue than another (see also 1.1.5.7)—a decidedly factual or contingent matter, and hence we clearly need another description of the distinction Hume means to draw.

In saying that relations of the first type depend entirely on the ideas compared together, Hume appears to be suggesting that the difference between the two kinds of relation is the difference between relations that are *independent* of the manner or order in which perceptions are presented or considered, and relations that *depend* on this manner. To illustrate this contrast consider first two completely stable or unchanging ideas (two relata), X and Y. Hume tells us that whether these ideas come into the mind simultaneously, or X precedes Y by an instant or by a year, or Y precedes X by an instant or by a year, makes no relevant difference with respect to any relations of *resemblance, proportion in quantity or number, degrees in any quality*, or *contrariety* that hold, or do not hold, between these ideas. As long as the ideas compared together remain unchanged, these four relations remain constant. These relations are unaffected by any variation in the timing or order in which their relata are presented.

In contrast, Hume argues that the remaining three relations are affected by, and even determined by, the manner or order in which ideas or 'objects' come before the mind. Suppose that for many years A was always experienced just before B. In that case, we might well have been inclined to think that A is related to B as cause to effect. But if more recently we have experienced B just before A, we will no longer be inclined to think that A is the cause of B. Or, suppose that E and F were experienced simultaneously a year ago, but are now experienced at intervals of thirty days. In that case, we will think that E and F were temporally contiguous last year, but are temporally non-contiguous this year. Finally, if we experience T without interruption, we will be inclined to think that there is one and only object of type T, or that T (the object of our uninterrupted experience) is identical with itself. On the other hand, if our experience is interrupted so that we experience a series of resembling ideas (T, then T', then T'', and so on), we may be inclined to think that these distinct experiences are of distinct items of the same type and not experiences of one self-identical item. In other words, whether things come before the mind simultaneously, or one before the other, or uninterruptedly, makes a critical difference to the relations of *identity, time and place*, or *causation* attributed to them. It does so because, on Hume's account of the matter, these three relations are changed by variations in the timing or order in which the relata are presented.

In Hume's view there is another important difference between the two kinds of relation: the four relations of the first type provide a basis for certainty and knowledge. For Hume, this means that we discover by *intuition* that compared ideas are or are not resembling, contrary, or possessed of the same degree of a particular quality, and by *demonstration* their relative proportion or quantity. In this respect, Hume's position is similar to that of Locke. Locke had defined intuition as the immediate recognition of the similarity or dissimilarity of two ideas compared to one another. It is in this manner that we perceive that red is not blue or three is not two.[28] In addition, Locke had defined demonstration as a way of showing the agreement or disagreement of compared ideas by the use of still other ideas or proofs that have 'a constant, immutable, and visible connexion' with the ideas to be compared.[29] That is, we show that A = C by showing first that A = B is a constant and intuitively certain relationship; we then show that B = C is also such a constant and intuitively certain relationship; assuming that things equal to a third thing are equal to each other, we will in this way have demonstrated that A = C.

Locke had also ranked the forms of knowledge according to their degree of certainty. In this ranking, the highest form of knowledge, because it provides the greatest certainty, is *intuitive knowledge*, the knowledge obtained by intuition. The second form of knowledge is *demonstrative knowledge*, the knowledge obtained by demonstration. When Hume says that the relations of resemblance, contrariety, degrees in quality, and proportions in quantity or number can be 'the objects of knowledge and certainty', he is accepting this much of Locke's account of knowledge.[30] At the same time, he is also telling us something else of great importance: The remaining three relations, identity, contiguity, and causation, the relations that depend on the manner or order in which objects are presented to us, are never more than probable. As a consequence, although we may be thoroughly convinced that these relations will remain constant, we cannot be sure of that constancy. For that reason, our convictions about these relations never rise to the level of knowledge; they remain, at best, *probabilities*.[31]

---

[28] In intuition, according to Locke, 'the Mind perceives the Agreement or Disagreement of two *Ideas* immediately by themselves, without the intervention of any other' (*Essay* 4.2.1).

[29] In demonstration, according to Locke, 'the Mind perceives the Agreement or Disagreement of any *Ideas*, but not immediately' (*Essay* 4.2.2).

[30] Hume does not accept Locke's further suggestion that impressions of sensation count as *sensitive knowledge*; for Locke's view, see *Essay* 4.2.14.

[31] To illustrate: Suppose you have, one after the other, two temporally distinct but resembling impressions of sensation, T and T' (impressions of, say, either one florid green tennis ball presented twice, or of two such green balls presented one after the other). Suppose you then have, copied from these impressions, the ideas t and t', each the idea of a florid green tennis ball. Suppose finally that you find t and t' to be perfectly resembling. In these circumstances, you can be said to know that t and t' are resembling. That is, you can directly or intuitively compare the two ideas, and, as long as the ideas are unchanged, they will continue to be resembling. It may also be that the recognition of this resemblance produces in you the further conviction that T and T', although temporally distinct, were impressions of a single tennis ball and hence they and the ideas derived from them are in that sense identical. But this further conviction, however strong it may be, constitutes only a probability, for the fact is that the ideas t and t', although themselves exactly resembling, may none the less derive from the impressions of two distinct tennis balls. Whether they do or do not so derive is beside the point. The mere possibility is enough to show that your conviction fails to derive from those relationships said to provide *knowledge*, and thus must derive from one of the merely *probable* relationships. That is, the relation of identity initially appears to hold between t and t' not because these ideas are resembling, but because, as Hume puts it, of the manner or order in which T and T' were presented. To see

THE RELATION OF CAUSATION

Having concluded that the relations of identity, contiguity, and causation (or cause and effect) can never be more than probable, Hume goes on to argue that only one of these three relations, causation, provides the basis for a form of reasoning in so far as it carries us beyond present experience, or, 'beyond what is immediately present to the senses'. In contrast, the relations of identity and contiguity involve a merely passive reception of impressions and ideas. They require of the mind no 'exercise of the thought, or any action, properly speaking'. Thus, says Hume, 'we ought not to receive as reasoning any of the observations we may make concerning' identity or contiguity (1.3.2.2).

Causal reasoning, Hume says, is not only a true form of reasoning but even the most forceful of all such forms (1.3.7.5, Note 20). When we are engaged in such reasoning we are led to make inferences from an impression presently before the mind to an absent effect or cause. As Hume puts it, causal reasoning, and only causal reasoning, 'produces such a connexion, as to give us assurance from the existence or action of one object, that 'twas follow'd or preceded by any other existence or action' (1.3.2.2). This succinct remark can be seen to describe just those cases in which we infer either that some *no longer perceivable cause* (an earlier rain) has produced the effect now experienced (a thoroughly wet countryside), or that some now experienced cause (smoke in the kitchen) will produce a *not yet perceivable effect* (the shriek of the nearby smoke alarm).

In addition, we soon learn that causation is the only relation that produces the kind of belief that concerns Hume in this part of the *Treatise*. Hume does not here attempt to explain why we believe what we currently experience. The reason for this is clear: there is no need to explain the assurance accompanying our currently experienced impressions of sensation. Such impressions are lively and vivacious by nature and thus carry conviction with them.[32] Moreover, these impressions provide the model of the form of belief that Hume hopes to explain. He wants to explain, that is, why it is that we not only infer absent causes and effects, but also believe in them—why when the countryside is thoroughly wet we not only *think* or have the idea of falling rain, but also *believe* that rain has fallen, or why when we see smoke in the kitchen we dread the shriek of the smoke alarm. In general terms, his explanation of phenomena of

that this is so, imagine that you are now presented with a film showing that some other individuals experienced T and T′ simultaneously (they saw two balls at once behind the presenter's back). This new experience, although it will in no way change the ideas t and t′, will be enough to alter the relations thought to hold between them. These two ideas may still be thought to be exactly resembling, but it will be obvious that they are not identical in the relevant sense. For similar reasons, convictions about contiguity and causation will be found to be merely probable.

[32] Did causal or probable reasoning not include impressions as well as ideas (a 'mixture' of perceptions), it would not be believed. But did it contain only impressions—were there no ideas included in this reasoning—the result would, 'properly speaking, be sensation, not reasoning'. Hume then adds that it is 'necessary, that in all probable reasonings there be something present to the mind, either seen or remember'd; and that from this we infer something connected with it, which is not seen nor remember'd' (1.3.6.6.).

this sort is to suggest that causal reasoning turns our *ideas* of absent causes or effects into something like a *present impression* of those same causes or effects.

Hume's interest in the causal relation is closely related to his concern to understand probability, or that kind of belief on which so much of life and action depend (*Abs.* 4). He sees that the relation of causation produces such belief and seeks to understand both the causal relation, the connection between cause and effect, and the belief this relationship engenders. With these linked goals in mind, Hume asks what we mean by the term *causation*, and from what impression the idea of causation (of causal connection) is derived. He quickly concludes that this idea is not derived from the impression of some particular quality (such as motion or heat) found in all causes, for no single quality of this sort is so found (1.3.2.5). Neither do we have direct experience, in the form of an impression of sensation, of a causal link. If a moving billiard ball strikes a second ball, we *say* the first ball causes the second ball to move, but we never see or otherwise sense a direct causal link (a power, for example) between the two balls (*Abs.* 9–10). We see only the prior movement of the first ball, and the subsequent movement of the second ball.[33]

Perhaps, Hume suggests, our idea of causal connection is 'deriv'd from some *relation* among objects' or events. This proves to be an initially promising suggestion, for when he examines examples of what is taken to be a cause and its related effect, he in fairly short order finds two features that characterize this relation. He sees first that the cause and the effect are contiguous in time and, usually, space: a cause and its effect occur at about the same time and in about the same place.[34] He also sees that a cause always occurs prior to its effect, which is to say an effect always succeeds its cause. Contiguity and priority (or succession), Hume concludes, are two perceptible features of a causal relationship, but he also concludes that contiguity and priority are not by themselves enough to establish such a connection. There is another, more important aspect of the causal relation. When we say that one object or event is the cause of another object or event, we also think that the two objects or events are bound together in such a way that, if the cause occurs, the effect must follow, or if the effect is seen, the cause must have preceded it. In short, we think that causes necessarily produce their effects and thus that causes and effects are in that sense necessarily connected together. As Hume was to put this crucial point, when we say that objects are related as causes and effects, there is also 'a NECESSARY CONNEXION to be taken into consideration; and that relation is of much greater importance' than contiguity and priority (1.3.2.6–11; see also 2.3.1.18).

---

[33] Hume was later to say that the 'ultimate connexion of any objects' is not 'discoverable, either by our senses or reason, and that we can never penetrate so far into the essence and construction of bodies, as to perceive the principle, on which their mutual influence depends. 'Tis their constant union alone, with which we are acquainted; and 'tis from the constant union the necessity arises' (2.3.1.4; repeated, with minor modification, at *Abs.* 32; see also 1.3.14.24).

[34] Hume appears to hedge on the question of the necessity of spatial contiguity. He says that if the cause is not spatially contiguous to its effect, then it must be spatially contiguous to some intervening cause or chain of causes. But this suggests that the proximate cause of an effect must be spatially contiguous to that effect.

Hume's focus now shifts slightly, but importantly. He now wants to discover the source of this idea of necessary connection. Here, however, he encounters a substantial difficulty. Looking at the perceptible or objective features of examples of cause and effect, he is unable to find the impression that gives rise to the idea of necessary connection, the third and most important feature of the causal relation. Refusing to consider the suggestion that he has an idea that does not derive from some impression, and yet not able by a 'direct survey' to locate this impression, he decides to continue his enquiry in an indirect manner. He will, he says, 'beat about all the neighbouring fields' more or less at random, hoping by good fortune to come upon what he seeks, the source of this important idea (1.3.2.12–13). Hume's enquiry is not quite as disorganized as he suggests, for he is able to articulate several additional questions about necessary connection and the relation of cause and effect. Before he is finished, he has asked, and gone on to answer, seven such questions:

1. Why do we think that everything that begins to exist must necessarily have a cause? (1.3.2.14)
2. Why do we think that particular causes must necessarily have particular effects? (1.3.2.15)
3. What is the nature of the inference we draw from cause to effect or effect to cause? (1.3.2.15)
4. What is the nature of our belief in the causes or effects we infer? (1.3.2.15)
5. How does experience give rise to the view that everything that begins to exist must have a cause? (1.3.3.9)
6. Why, upon the present experience of a particular cause, do we infer that a particular effect is about to occur? (1.3.3.9)
7. Why do we think that instances of which we have not had experience must resemble those of which we have had experience, or that the course of nature continues always uniformly the same? (1.3.6.4)

CAUSES AND CAUSAL REASONING

In *Treatise* 1.3.3 Hume argues that the maxim *everything that begins to exist must have a cause*, a maxim presupposed by all moral and natural philosophy, is established neither by intuition nor by demonstration. As we have seen, Hume found that there are only three intuitive relations, resemblance, contrariety, or degrees of quality. The relation between a beginning of existence and a cause, whatever else it may be, is not one of these three relations. Consequently, this maxim cannot be known by intuition.[35] Furthermore, although demonstrative arguments have been offered in support of the maxim, Hume finds that these arguments are uniformly defective. Each such argument in one way or another presupposes exactly the point at issue: each presupposes that, in order to begin to exist, a thing or event must have a cause. We may very well *believe* that every

---

[35] Hume takes the maxim to be composed of two ideas, that of beginning to exist and that of being a cause, and asks, in effect, what relation holds between these ideas. Viewed in this way, he can see at once that the ideas are not related by resemblance, contrariety, or degrees of a quality.

beginning of existence must have a cause, but this belief is not the product of demonstrative reasoning. Given, then, that the maxim is neither intuitively nor demonstratively certain, it 'must necessarily', Hume concludes, 'arise from observation and experience'. Consequently, it may be useful to answer question (5), How does experience give rise to the view that everything that begins to exist must have a cause? This further question we can best answer, he suggests, by answering question (2), Why do we think that particular causes must necessarily have particular effects? and still another related to it, question (6), Why, upon the present experience of a particular cause, do we infer that a particular effect is about to occur?[36]

To answer these questions, Hume begins to look at our experience of cause and effect in a different way. He looks now at the mental elements included in those situations in which we infer that some event is a cause or an effect. He looks at the mental elements that make up an episode of causal reasoning. Which such elements, in what arrangement, characterize those situations in which we think that *A* is the cause of *B*? This new approach proves fruitful. He quickly discovers that each episode of causal reasoning includes, first, an impression of sense or memory that initiates this particular episode; secondly, a transition or inference; and thirdly, that mental element to which this inference directs us, namely, an enlivened or vivacious idea (an idea believed in) of an absent cause or effect. By the time he has analysed these three components, he has answers to several of the questions he has raised.

Given that causation is a philosophical as well as a natural relation, the mind may find itself considering causal patterns as mere hypotheses that produce no conviction. That is, I can hypothesize that some fictional event of which I have nothing more than an idea will bring about some future result of which I have another idea. I can imagine that some stranger will put a lottery ticket in my pocket, and then mysteriously cause that ticket to contain the winning numbers. But this fantasy will not result in conviction. I will not only not anticipate my winnings by buying a new car; I will not even check my pocket to see if the ticket is there. In contrast, if I see one billiard ball moving directly at another, I am convinced that the second ball will move after being struck. Whenever conviction of this sort is produced, Hume says, the process will have begun with 'an impression of the memory or senses', and not with ideas that are 'mere fictions of the imagination' (1.3.5.1–4). Such an impression of sense or memory is the first of the three mental elements found in an episode of causal reasoning.

What does an impression have that an idea lacks? Force and vivacity or intensity. How does this quality make a difference? To help us understand his answer to this question, Hume (in the *Abstract*) asks us to imagine Adam, this moment created in the full vigour of intellectual capacity, and deposited in a billiard parlour just in time to see a cue ball moving in the direction of an object ball.

---

[36] Or, equally, why, upon the present experience of a particular effect, do we believe that a particular cause has occurred? That we infer from either present causes or present effects is made clear at 1.3.8.14; App. 2; *Abs.* 10, 21.

We, familiar with the behaviour of billiard balls, see that the cue ball is about to strike an object ball, and anticipate that once this happens, the object ball will move. What does Adam anticipate? Nothing. Nothing at all. He has never seen a billiard ball before, and in fact now sees only a moving blob of colour. That this blob will strike another blob and cause it to move is beyond his wildest imagination. The hypothesis that this is what will happen carries no more conviction for him than does any other we might propose to him. Indeed, if the billiard table is very long, and we, while the cue ball is moving towards the object ball, ask Adam whether, on being struck, the object ball will move, or be swallowed up, he may well ask us what 'being struck' and 'move or be swallowed up' mean. On the other hand, if our newly created Adam has time, we can repeat the experiment. That is, we can hit a third ball into a fourth, and a fifth ball into a sixth, and so on. Before long Adam will likely anticipate that the moving cue ball will strike a resting ball and that this second ball will then move.

EXPERIENCE AND BELIEF

Generalizing from this example, we can answer two of the questions Hume has asked: questions (2), Why do we think that particular causes must necessarily have particular effects? and (6) Why, upon the present experience of a particular cause, do we infer that a particular effect is about to occur? The short answer to these questions is: Because of repeated experience. Adam repeatedly sees a moving ball striking a resting ball and the resting ball then begin to move. Once he has had these experiences, he begins to believe that the present movement of a first or moving ball will be followed by movement of a second, presently stationary, ball. Adam has watched as, time after time, a moving ball strikes a stationary ball, putting this second ball in motion. He watches as

A_1 strikes B_1, and then B_1 moves;
A_2 strikes B_2, and then B_2 moves;
A_3 strikes B_3, and then B_3 moves;
A_4 strikes B_4, and then B_4 moves;

I now strike A_5 in the direction of B_5. Adam, bored, turns his back and walks away. Without bothering to watch, he says, 'I know, B_5 is going to move.' Repeated experience, the constant conjunction of two impressions, has developed in Adam a kind of mental habit. Whenever he sees one billiard ball moving towards another, his mind, unbidden, leaps ahead, forming an idea of a future event—of an absent and future effect—and, moreover, he expects that absent and still future event to occur. He may not yet know our language well enough to say just what we would say, but Adam now believes that the movement of A_5 will cause the movement of B_5. Adam believes that this particular cause will have that particular effect.

But how, it will be asked, did we go from what Adam *expects* to what Adam *believes*? The answer lies in Hume's answers to two other questions he has raised. He has asked, remember, question (3), What is the nature of the inference we draw from cause to effect or effect to cause? The short answer to this question is: A transition or transfer of focus, brought about by repeated experience. When Adam turns away saying, 'I know, B_5 is going to move,' he reveals that he has begun to focus on the future. When I glimpse from my window the sun shining on a thoroughly wet countryside, I focus on what has already happened. Adam and I have transferred our focus from what we now see to an absent event. In Hume's terms, Adam has *inferred* future movement of the ball, a future effect; I have *inferred* past rain, a past cause. Transitions or inferences of this kind constitute the second mental element in an episode of causal reasoning.

There is, however, more to be said about this inference. Hume has also asked question (4), What is the nature of our belief in the causes or effects we infer? The answer he gives to this question comes in overlapping parts.

First, Hume says that belief in absent causes or effects is a feeling or sentiment. Precisely how to characterize this feeling presented Hume with a difficulty he was unable to resolve to his satisfaction, but he remained satisfied that the difference between merely conceiving that some event might happen, and believing that this event will happen, lies in the fact that the two perceptions *feel* different to us. Belief is a 'particular manner of forming an idea', a distinct 'manner of conception', or '*nothing but a peculiar feeling, different from the simple conception*' (1.3.7.6–7; App. 3). This feeling is 'particular' or 'peculiar' just in so far as it is more forceful or intense than a similar idea merely conceived.

Secondly, the inference that transfers our attention to an absent effect or cause in which we believe transfers our attention from an impression to an idea, and to ideas formed in the 'particular manner' just mentioned. The inference transfers our attention to a lively idea that *feels* different from an idea merely conceived. Indeed, Hume says that the belief we are trying to understand 'may be most accurately defin'd, A LIVELY IDEA RELATED TO OR ASSOCIATED WITH A PRESENT IMPRESSION' (1.3.7.5).

Thirdly, the inference itself plays a key role in the creation of belief. As our attention is transferred to the idea associated with some present impression, a portion of the force and liveliness of this impression is also transferred to the idea: '*when any impression becomes present to us, it not only transports the mind to such ideas as are related to it, but likewise communicates to them a share of its force and vivacity*' (1.3.8.2). Such enlivened ideas feel like impressions, which is presumably what Hume means when he tells us that 'all probable reasoning is nothing but a species of sensation' (1.3.8.12; see also 1.3.6.6). He means that probable or causal reasoning enlivens our ideas, giving them force and vivacity, and that once so enlivened they are in that respect virtually indistinguishable from impressions of sensation. In short, as a consequence of the kind of inference that characterizes causal reasoning, ideas are believed, or, perhaps more accurately, ideas become beliefs.[37] Moreover, as is clear, ideas enlivened in

---

[37] The force and vivacity transferred to an idea give that idea 'in a lesser degree the same effect' as 'those impressions, which are immediately present to the senses and perception. The effect, then, of

this way constitute the third and final mental element in an episode of causal reasoning.

When Adam's mind, unbidden, leaps ahead, forming an idea of a future event, B_5, and anticipating that B_5 will occur, Adam just is forming a belief of the kind Hume is explaining. What Adam has come to *expect* is exactly what Adam *believes*. Adam's 'mind runs by habit from the visible object of one ball moving towards another, to [an idea of] the usual effect of motion in the second ball. It not only conceives that motion, but *feels* something different in the conception of it' (*Abs.* 21). Adam is experiencing an impression (A_5) that brings to mind and transfers vivacity to a particular idea (B_5). When such a related set of mental events takes place, belief—belief in a matter of fact, in the existence of the absent effect—is produced.[38]

We, in our own way, were all newly created. That is, we have all had to start from scratch. We have all had to *learn* which objects to call causes and effects, and we have learned this by experience and only by experience. In our pasts many different items have been contiguous and immediately prior to, and constantly conjoined with, certain other items. These past constant conjunctions of what we take to be causes and effects have created a habit that links the relevant impressions and ideas. Consequently, if we now have an *impression* of some item (an event or an object) of type A, our minds are naturally and automatically led to have an *idea* of some item of type B and to believe that an item of type B is about to occur. And if we now have an *impression* of some item of type B, our minds are naturally and automatically led to have an *idea* of some item of type A, and to believe that an item of type A has previously occurred.

BELIEF IN THE UNIFORMITY OF NATURE

Hume's answers to question (1), Why do we think that everything that begins to exist must necessarily have a cause? and question (7), Why do we think that the course of nature continues always uniformly the same? have much in common. As we have noted, Hume in 1.3.3 canvasses and finds defective the demonstrative arguments purporting to show that everything that begins to exist must have a cause. He later points out that demonstrative arguments must also fail to show that '*the course of nature continues always uniformly the same*' or

---

belief is to raise up a simple idea to an equality with our impressions, and bestow on it a like influence on the passions. This effect it can only have by making an idea approach an impression in force and vivacity. . . . Belief, therefore, since it causes an idea to imitate the effects of the impressions, must make it resemble them in these qualities, and is nothing but *a more vivid and intense conception of any idea*' (1.3.10.3).

[38] Note that not only does Hume refer to these beliefs in absent effects or causes as beliefs in 'matter of fact', but that in *Treatise* 1.3, the Appendix, and the *Abstract* he typically uses the phrase 'matter of fact' to refer to just such absent causes or effects. He says, for example, that we 'can never be induc'd to believe any matter of fact, except where its cause, or its effect, direct or collateral, is present to us' (App. 2), and that 'all reasonings concerning *matter of fact* are founded on the relation of cause and effect' (*Abs.* 8; see also *Abs.* 21).

that the future will be like the past. Hume, in agreement with many other philosophers, holds that anything not formally inconsistent is conceivable, and that whatever is conceivable is possible. We cannot conceive that $2 = 3$, but we can conceive that the course of nature will change just as we know that it has, in some respects, changed in the past. We can conceive of compasses pointing to the south, as they would once have done. We can conceive of the sun rising in the west. We can conceive that even the most settled laws of nature may change. We can conceive that the future will not be like the past. 'We can', Hume says, 'at least conceive a change in the course of nature; which sufficiently proves, that such a change is not absolutely impossible,' and thus that its impossibility cannot be demonstrated (1.3.6.5). In the *Abstract* he is even clearer: 'What is possible can never be demonstrated to be false; and 'tis possible the course of nature may change, since we can conceive such a change' (*Abs.* 14). Hume is clearly convinced that *demonstrative reasoning* cannot show that the future will necessarily be like the past.[39]

Neither is it *probable reasoning* that convinces us of the uniformity of nature. Granted, experience leads us to suppose that every event has a cause and that the future will be like the past, and probable reasoning rests on experience. But if experience produces these important effects, it must do so, as Hume puts it, obliquely. No one, obviously, can have had experience of everything that has begun to exist, and thus no one, and no group of us, can claim direct evidence that everything that has already begun to exist has had a cause. It is equally obvious that no one can have had experience of the future, and thus, again, no one can claim to have direct evidence that the future will be like the past. Furthermore, we cannot show by probable arguments that the future will be like the past because all probable arguments rest on the assumption that the future will be like the past. We can only conclude that the future will be like the past if we first *assume* that the future will resemble the past (1.3.6.6–12; *Abs.* 14). The vitiating circularity of this assumption is obvious.

How then does experience give rise to the view that everything that begins to exist must have a cause and why do we think that the future will resemble the past?[40] As we have already seen, experience produces habits or expectations. Thus, just as repeated experiences of events of type *A* followed by events of type *B* produced in Adam a mental habit or tendency (Adam came to expect that *A*s would be followed by *B*s), so does the repeated experience of many

---

[39] Suppose we have come to believe that items of type *A* have always caused items of type *B*. Given Hume's account of relations, we can never *demonstrate* that what is possible (that *A*s at some future time will cease to cause *B*s) must be false because we cannot show that some different relation of *A*s and *B*s is contradictory or absurd. Even though *A*s and *B*s themselves remain entirely unchanged, three of their relations (identity, contiguity, and cause and effect) may be changed. That we can conceive of such changes in relations, without at the same time having to suppose that there have been changes in the ideas or objects related, shows that the relationships in question are not intuitive or demonstrative.

[40] These are questions (5) and (7) from the list found above.

kinds of constantly conjoined pairs produce in us more general habits or ten-dencies, including the tendency to suppose that any item we presently experi-ence had a cause, and the tendency to suppose that the constant conjunctions that we have experienced in the past will be experienced in the future. Experi-ence so works upon the mind (but upon the imagination, rather than the reason) that we extend our expectations well beyond the range of both actual and possible experience. We become so accustomed to linking what we call 'causes' and 'effects' that we become convinced that nothing could begin to exist without a cause. And, when our past experience is extensive and uniform, we become convinced that the future will resemble the past.

Hume also argues that, while we believe in the universality of causes and the uniformity of nature, we cannot prove either. Does everything that begins to exist have a cause? Is nature uniform? These are (distinct) questions of fact that possibly merit affirmative answers, but we humans cannot give reliable answers to them. Hume does not deny that every beginning of existence must have a cause or that nature is uniform. He does not take so dogmatic a position. He simply does not know the answers to these questions, and does not expect to learn these answers because neither reason nor experience is capable of provid-ing them. But while neither reason nor experience can answer these questions of fact, *custom*—Hume's name for 'every thing . . . which proceeds from a past repetition' (1.3.8.10)—leaves us believing in and acting on the universality of causes and the uniformity of nature. Custom is the true 'guide of life' that leads us to believe what reason and experience can neither prove nor disprove (1.3.8.8–14; *Abs.* 15–16). As we shall see, Hume will reach this same important conclusion on other occasions.

THE IDEA OF NECESSARY CONNECTION

Having followed Hume as he beat about the neighbouring fields, we can now return with him to the question whose answer he hoped to come upon: What is the source of our idea of necessary connection? From what impression is this idea copied?

Hume's initial survey satisfied him that this idea copies no single quality (such as motion or heat) found in every cause. He was also satisfied that our experience of causally related pairs gives us no direct experience, in the form of an impression of sensation, of a causal link. We see a moving ball strike a second ball, which then moves, but we never see or otherwise sense a direct causal link between the two balls. When we examine two objects related as cause and effect, we perceive in the objects only contiguity and priority or suc-cession, not a necessary connection. When we consider why it is that we say any two objects or events are causally related, we find that it is because they are contiguous, successive, and constantly conjoined, but no connection, power, or necessity is perceived in or between *the objects themselves*. Strictly speaking, in or about any two objects *A* and *B*, taken to be related as cause and effect, there is nothing that accounts for the causal inference we make when we experience just one of these objects.[41]

On the other hand, the constant conjunction of As and Bs does have an effect on the mind. Recall Adam learning about the behaviour of billiard balls. After Adam had experienced events of type A as contiguous, prior to, and constantly associated with events of type B, he came to *expect* a B whenever he experienced an A, and hence he automatically thought of a B on these occasions. Our experience is of the same form. No connection, power, or necessity is perceived between any given A and B, but, on the experience of an A, there is a felt expectation of a B. This felt expectation is not an impression of sensation; it is an impression of reflection or a secondary impression.[42] It is what Hume also calls a 'determination of the mind', and he unambiguously says that the idea of necessary connection is a copy of this feeling or determination. A constant conjunction, Hume writes, 'produces a new impression, and by that means' produces the idea of necessary connection. Following the repeated conjunction of As and Bs, we find 'that upon the appearance of one of the objects, the mind is *determin'd* by custom to consider its usual attendant, and to consider it in a stronger light upon account of its relation to the first object. 'Tis this impression, then, or *determination*, which affords me the idea of necessity' (1.3.14.1). Later, having noted that it is the observation of constant conjunctions that gives rise to the relevant 'determination of the mind', he says that necessity is 'an internal impression of the mind, or a determination to carry our thoughts from one object to another. Without considering it in this view, we can never arrive at the most distant notion of it, or be able to attribute it either to external or internal objects, to spirit or body, to causes or effects' (1.3.14.20; see also 2.3.1.4 and *Abs.* 32).

This conclusion, Hume well realizes, is shocking. 'What! the efficacy of causes lie in the determination of the mind!' Of all opinions imaginable, this, surely is 'the most violent' (1.3.14.24, 26). And yet, he insists, this conclusion is well founded and not unlike the widely held view that colours and sounds are found only in the mind, not in objects themselves. To become reconciled to the view that the idea of necessary connection derives from an impression of reflection, and not from an impression of a direct causal link between objects, Hume suggests that we should repeat until we are satisfied the arguments supporting these conclusions:

1. The inspection of any two events or objects, one of which is said necessarily to cause the other, never reveals a direct causal link or power that connects these items.
2. The idea of power or necessary connection arises from the constant conjunction of two events or objects, or two events or objects of the same type.
3. The repetition of a conjunction neither reveals nor causes anything new

---

[41] See above, pp. 127–8.
[42] On this distinction, see the discussion of impressions, p. 119.

in the events or objects said to be necessarily connected. But such a repetition does produce a 'customary transition' in the mind. It causes us to infer from the experience of one item of a customarily conjoined pair the second item in that pair.

4. This 'customary transition' is the source of an impression, namely, a felt determination of the mind. This determination is in turn the source of our idea of necessary connection—this determination copied, in the way that ideas copy impressions, is the idea of necessary connection.

5. It follows then that causal power and necessary connection are feelings of the mind, not qualities found in events or objects.[43]

Hume recognizes that his readers will have a deeply rooted propensity to think otherwise than he has concluded. He notes, however, that modern philosophers are widely agreed that humans are disposed to project their perceptions onto reality. Because sounds and smells and colours are uniformly associated with certain objects, we humans naturally or ordinarily suppose that these qualities are, in exactly the form they are experienced, in the objects with which they are associated. Ordinary humans think, to use Locke's language, that the ideas of secondary qualities (ideas of specific colours, sounds, and smells, for example) exactly and truly represent qualities inherent in objects themselves. Philosophers from Galileo to Locke and beyond had maintained that this is a mistake. They had argued that colour and several other qualities widely supposed to be in objects themselves are in fact only in the mind, and that we project these qualities from our minds onto objects. We put the green on the leaves and fragrance in the rose and then suppose these features are, in just this form, 'out there' on or in these objects. But however much the ordinary person may think that objects really are coloured or fragrant, this widely held philosophical theory says otherwise. The propensity or tendency to suppose that objects are really coloured or fragrant is both natural and extremely strong, but, according to these philosophers, it leads us to form mistaken beliefs about objects. This 'same propensity' to project, Hume argues, accounts for the fact that we suppose that causal necessity or power is in objects despite the fact that the only idea we have of necessity or power is copied from a determination found only in the mind (1.3.14.25).[44] In short, Hume insists that his account of our idea of necessary connection is analogous to, and no more shocking than, the widely held theory about primary and secondary qualities.

---

[43] Hume summarizes his conclusions by asking 'how often must we repeat to ourselves, *that* the simple view of any two objects or actions, however related, can never give us any idea of power, or of a connexion betwixt them: *that* this idea arises from the repetition of their union: *that* the repetition neither discovers nor causes any thing in the objects, but has an influence only on the mind, by that customary transition it produces: *that* this customary transition is, therefore, the same with the power and necessity; which are consequently qualities of perceptions, not of objects, and are internally felt by the soul, and not perceiv'd externally in bodies?' (1.3.14.24).

[44] Hume does not dogmatically deny that real but unknown causes exist in nature. He does, however, raise questions about the value and intelligibility of talk about such unknown causes; see in particular 1.3.14.27.

Book 1 Part 4: Forms of Scepticism

Treatise 1.4 is perhaps the most wide-ranging part of the *Treatise*. If it has a uni-fying theme, it is a sceptical one. In the course of his analyses Hume reiterates what some of his predecessors had collectively shown, namely, that neither reason nor the senses can demonstrate with certainty that there are enduring external objects and enduring selves. But *Treatise* 1.4 goes beyond this familiar point to a new sceptical conclusion. It is not just that reason and the senses cannot give us *certain knowledge* of the existence of external objects and selves. Reason and the senses cannot so much as produce *belief* in external objects and enduring selves; we have these fundamental beliefs because of the *imagination*, a faculty of doubtful reliability. Although our other faculties play a role in the process, it is the imagination that transforms some of our fleeting, insubstan-tial, and mind-dependent impressions into ideas of, and beliefs in, external objects—into ideas of entities that are enduring, substantial, and independent of the mind. And, as we learn in 1.4.6, it is because of the imagination that, despite the fact that we have no impression of any simple and enduring self underlying our perceptions, we form an idea of, and then believe in, such an enduring self.

EXTERNAL OBJECTS

Hume begins *Treatise* 1.4.2 by saying that it is pointless to ask whether there are external objects. That there are such objects is something 'we must take for granted'. We can, however, ask, '*What causes induce us to believe in the existence of body?*' Or, as we might put it, what makes us believe there are external objects? This question is seen to raise two related issues. First, why do we suppose that objects *endure* or that they continue to exist when they are not perceived? Sec-ondly, why do we suppose that objects are *external* to us, or that they are distinct from the mind and its perceptions?

The fundamental issue, Hume says, is which of three faculties, the *senses*, *reason*, or the *imagination*, produces our belief in the *distinct* (external) and *con-tinued* (enduring) existence of objects. Philosophers before him had argued that we know that there are continuing and external objects by means either of the senses or of reason. In contrast, Hume grants that we believe in external objects, but he doubts that this belief is due to either of these two competing favourites, sense or reason. These faculties may play some role in the formation of our belief in objects, but it is a third faculty, the imagination, that plays the decisive part.

The senses alone cannot account for our belief in objects because the senses do nothing more than provide us with impressions, while, for two reasons, impressions alone cannot be the source of our belief in objects. First, we suppose objects to exist for relatively long periods and continuously, and to exist independently of or outside the mind. In contrast, our impressions of sensation exist for only a matter of a few seconds, or, if they are supposed to have a longer existence, are obviously discontinuous. If we suppose these impressions are relatively *short-lived*, then, unlike objects, they lack endurance and are multiple. I have many such brief impressions of my watch, but I suppose myself to have only one watch, an object I believe without question to have existed continuously for many years.[45] If instead we suppose our impressions of sensation to be relatively *long-lived*, perhaps as long-lived as the objects we believe in, we must none the less grant that, unlike objects, impressions are discontinuous. Because my watch is at the bottom of a small basket, my impression of it has been turned off, so to speak, for several days, but the watch itself I believe to have existed continuously right up to the present moment.

Secondly, we suppose that objects exist separately from the mind. In contrast, impressions are elements of the mental world and 'never give us the least intimation of any thing beyond' themselves. That is, impressions themselves include no marks or signs indicating their origins. Even our impressions of sensation are experienced as feelings or sentiments and could only present themselves as separate or distinct objects if they were somehow at the same time able to present a distinct impression of the self to which the objects are believed to be external. This they never do. Granted, we have impressions that seem to derive from external objects, but a careful examination of these impressions shows them to be fundamentally indistinguishable from impressions of pain or colour, impressions that we suppose not to derive from or represent anything external: 'as far as the senses are judges, all perceptions are the same in the manner of their existence'. Taking these points together, we may 'conclude with certainty, that the opinion of a continu'd and of a distinct existence never arises from the senses' (1.4.2.3–13).

It is obvious as well, Hume goes on to suggest, that our belief in the existence of external objects is not dependent on reason. Philosophers have offered what they suppose to be convincing arguments in favour of external existence. Descartes had done so in Meditation 6, for example. But we readily see that these arguments are unnecessary to the belief they support, for they are known only to a relatively few individuals, while belief in external objects is universal. Furthermore, 'children, peasants, and the greatest part of mankind' make no distinction between impressions and external objects. They suppose that what they experience (what philosophers call impressions) are truly objects. This point of view is 'directly contrary' to that of reason and philosophy. Reason and philosophy tell us that our perceptions are, in crucial respects, all alike; they tell us 'that every thing, which appears to the mind, is nothing but a perception, and is interrupted, and dependent on the mind'. In contrast, ordinary persons 'attribute a distinct continu'd existence' to many of their impressions. Consequently, it cannot be reason that gives the ordinary person 'an assurance of the continu'd and distinct existence of body'; ordinary people believe in external objects without the least help from reason (1.4.2.14).

[45] Endurance is, of course, relative. The Precambrian shield we take to be significantly older than the bread constituting our morning toast, while that toast itself may exist much longer than still other things. The point is that the vast majority of the objects encountered at the common-sense level are taken to survive significantly longer than most perceptions.

How are we, then, to account for our belief in external objects? It must be, Hume argues, that the imagination, the third and last of the faculties to be considered, produces this belief, and that it does so by means of its responses to features unique to certain impressions. It is not, however, the involuntariness and relatively great force or intensity of sensations that accounts for our belief in external existence, for neither of these qualities is uniquely characteristic of the impressions taken to be caused by enduring, external objects. The pain caused by a fire is as involuntary and as intense as any other impression, and yet we do not suppose this pain to be in the fire and external to us. On the contrary, we come to suppose that there are continuing and external entities because of the way in which the imagination is affected by the *constancy* and the *coherence* of certain sets of impressions.

Some impressions, we find, always 'present themselves in the same uniform manner, and change not upon account of any interruption in my seeing or perceiving them'. I look from my window and have an impression of Mount Royal and of many trees and buildings. I look again a moment, a day, a year later, and these same items, in the same relationship to each other, appear again. Such *constancy* is a unique feature of all those impressions 'whose objects are suppos'd to have an external existence' (1.4.2.18). Hume grants, however, that this constancy is imperfect. The trees that I see from my window regularly undergo noticeable changes. So, too, although more slowly, the buildings I see, and even the mountain itself, appear to change. But through all these changes my impressions of these items preserve what Hume calls a *coherence* that contributes to our belief in the continuity of objects. One impression may be only similar to the preceding one, but the difference is so small that we take the two impressions to be identical. Or, if the difference between two impressions is still greater, it may none the less follow a previously experienced pattern. Returning to his room after an hour's absence, Hume found that his fire had changed. Before he left it was a cheerful blaze; when he returned it was no more than a few weakly glowing embers. But, having observed fires before, he is satisfied that the two states, despite their differences, are consistent with the burning of a single log. Impressions change, but they change in familiar and patterned ways that lead us to suppose that significantly different impressions have a single, external source (1.4.2.19).

Hume's account of the manner in which the constancy and coherence of mere impressions lead us to believe in the existence of continuing and external objects is lengthy and detailed. Central to this account is the claim that the coherence and constancy of certain sets of perceptions lead the imagination to suppose that these perceptions are produced by independently existing objects, and to attribute to these objects a degree of continuity unmatched by the perceptions that trigger our belief in them. These effects Hume explains by comparing the imagination to a boat that, once put in motion and given direction, continues on its course even when the oars are at rest. Because many individual impressions and ideas are experienced together in patterned ways, the imagination is, as it were, set on a course. Then, even when the pattern is disrupted, it continues on that course. When the pattern is disrupted (when some objects are not now experienced or available to be experienced) the imagination goes on thinking about these objects, or at least remaining ready to think about them. The mere sound of a squeaking hinge gives us an idea of the door to which the hinge is attached. The idea of the door is linked to that of a hall, to a stairs, to an entire house and garden, to a street, a town, a country, to a continent surrounded by the sea. A letter from a distant friend sets the imagination to making many of these same connections, and, once set in motion, the imagination tends to stay in motion. In addition, from the fact that a present impression so nearly resembles many previous ones, the imagination is led to suppose that objects have a continued existence. My impression of Mount Royal today is so like my past impressions of it, preserved as ideas in the memory, that I fail even to think of these as different perceptions. In consequence, I have formed the idea of one continuing mountain. It then happens that the force and vivacity of my present impression is transferred to this idea. At that point, and despite the fact that the relevant perceptions are both distinct from one another and fleeting, I *believe* in an independent and continuously existing object. In short, because of the imagination, we naturally believe the world is populated with objects having an independent and continuing existence.[46]

Hume concludes 1.4.2 with a critical look at two views regarding external existence. One of these, the theory of single existence, is the position of ordinary or unphilosophical persons. Those who take this view of the matter suppose that certain perceptions (impressions of sensation) and external objects are identical, so that objects themselves are supposed to be immediately before the mind: ''Tis certain, that almost all mankind, and even philosophers themselves, for the greatest part of their lives, take their perceptions to be their only objects, and suppose, that the very being, which is intimately present to the mind, is the real body or material existence.' It takes little effort, Hume argues, to show that this theory cannot be correct. Leaving both eyes open, press gently on one eyeball. The result: a double set of 'objects'. Or, move towards an object and it appears to become larger; move away, and it seems to grow smaller. Shapes, colours, and sounds are altered in the same way. It seems obvious, then, that objects and perceptions are not identical, and that the theory of single existence, despite being natural, is false. As Hume sums up the matter, 'a very little reflection and philosophy is sufficient to make us perceive the fallacy of that opinion [of single existence]. . . . when we compare experiments, and reason a little upon them, we quickly perceive, that the doctrine of the independent existence of our sensible perceptions is contrary to the plainest experience' (1.4.2.38, 44–5).

The alternative position, the theory of double existence, is the theory of modern philosophers. According to this view, there are existences of two kinds,

---

[46] About one-third (¶¶25–43) of this long section is given over to a further explanation of the way in which the imagination leads us to believe in objects.

mind-dependent perceptions and external, independent objects. In addition, the mind-dependent perceptions are said to be caused by, and to represent, the external objects. This theory, Hume argues, is no more satisfactory than the unsophisticated view it seeks to replace, and, in addition, depends for whatever plausibility it has on that same view. That is, were not philosophers already convinced that objects continue to exist even when not being perceived, they would not so much as think that there are objects distinct from, and the cause of, impressions. Why? Because once it is supposed, as modern philosophers suppose, that nothing is ever really present to the mind except perceptions, there are no grounds for suggesting that there are objects distinct from impressions.[47] The best that these modern philosophers can do is 'arbitrarily invent a new set of perceptions' that either exactly replicate those perceptions we already have, or else are nothing more than vague suppositions of things somehow distinct and different from our perceptions (1.4.2.56).

Hume begins *Treatise* 1.4.2 saying that we must take for granted the existence of objects. He closes the section on a more sceptical note. He is now, he says, 'inclin'd to repose no faith at all in my senses, or rather imagination'. Belief in external objects arises only because of certain commonplace qualities of the imagination (recall the comparison with a boat in motion), and certain features of perceptions (their coherence and constancy). These qualities and features may lead us to believe in the external and continuous existence of objects, but they fail to provide unassailable ground for that belief. Was Hume correct, then, to say that the existence of objects must be taken for granted? Is it indeed pointless to ask whether or not there are external objects? Generally speaking, these questions about external existence can be dismissed as pointless, for there is apparently no one who does not, most of the time, have an implicit faith in the existence of objects. But Hume also says that 'sceptical doubt arises naturally from a profound and intense reflection' on the question of external existence, and is, moreover, 'a malady, which can never be radically cur'd'. This malady is never, however, of long standing. We can never completely eliminate doubt in the existence of external objects, but such doubt is brief and those who feel it are soon again convinced that there are such objects (1.4.2.56–7).[48]

---

[47] Hume also argues that, once modern philosophers have supposed nothing is ever really present to the mind except perceptions, there would be no grounds for thinking that their imaginations *qua* philosophers could, 'directly and immediately', lead them to believe there are external objects (1.4.2.48). It is the ordinary person's world-view, and only this world-view, that includes the notion of externality and independence from which the imagination develops the idea of external and continuing objects. Modern philosophers, in contrast, insist that nothing is ever really present to the mind except perceptions, and that only what is present to the mind is experienced. If these philosophers hold themselves to this pure theory, they will have no notion of the external and no notion of the mind-independent, and hence could not so much as imagine that there are both perceptions in the mind and objects external to the mind. If these philosophers hold themselves to their theory, they, too, will have a theory of single existence, but this will be the idealist theory of Berkeley, a theory that says that ideas or perceptions are the only existences.

[48] Elsewhere Hume makes it clear that the total elimination of doubt would be far from a good thing. Long after our doubts have cooled, long after we have left the philosophical study (the place

ENDURING SELVES AND PERSONAL IDENTITY

At the outset of *Treatise* 1.4.5 ('Of the immateriality of the soul'), Hume tells us that an explanation of the 'intellectual world' (of the mind and its nature) will present fewer difficulties than did the account of our ideas of objects. Still, Hume's account of the idea we form of ourselves, or of our own personal identity, is in many ways similar to his account of the origin of our idea of objects.

Having in 1.4.5 concluded that we have no direct impression of an immaterial substance that unites our perceptions, Hume dismisses questions about the make-up of such a substance as unintelligible. In 1.4.6 ('Of personal identity'), he goes on to argue that the most we can hope to do is give a sensible answer to a question of this kind: what perceptions serve to produce, in each normal adult, an effective idea of a unified self to which all our diverse impressions and ideas are related? He begins by noting that some philosophers claim that we have continuous, direct impressions of our selves. These philosophers claim that at every moment each of us feels or intuits the existence, continuance, perfect identity, and simplicity of our self, with the result that each of us, at every moment, has an impression of her or his simple, unchanging self. If this claim is correct, then our idea of the self is nothing more than a copy of such impressions of the self.

This account of the matter, Hume says, is contrary to fact. If there were a direct impression of a simple and unchanging self, this impression would need to be simple and unchanging. But even when we reflect on our selves, even when we attempt to turn our attention onto such an impression of the self, we find that we encounter only a quick succession of ordinary impressions and ideas. However quick we may be, we can never catch an unattended self, as it were; it is never the self, but only some perception, that we encounter. Moreover, there are periods (during sleep, for example) when we appear to have no perceptions at all. Consequently, it is false to say that we at every moment intuit our selves. Whatever the philosophers may say, most of us find our selves to be 'nothing but a bundle or collection of different perceptions, which succeed each other with an inconceivable rapidity, and are in a perpetual flux and movement'. So far as we can determine by attending to our selves, the mind is, with one important exception, like a theatre with a constantly changing show. The exception? We have no information whatever about the putative 'theatre'. We only know there is a show (1.4.6.4).

What, then, gives us so vigorous an inclination to suppose that our successive perceptions are related to a single, underlying identity or self, and to suppose that this self has 'invariable and uninterrupted existence thro' the whole course of our lives?' (1.4.6.5). The answer lies in a correct understanding of how the mind works in matters relating to identity.

where these doubts reach their peak), the effect of these doubts remains to moderate our natural tendency to be rash and dogmatical. Moreover, if there is reason to doubt even so obvious a matter as the existence of objects, how much more reason must there be to doubt the dangerously rash and dogmatic claims of bigots and ideologues. See 1.4.1.5; 1.4.7.12–13; *EHU* 12.

Central to Hume's answer is his claim that, in this matter too, our minds commonly make a quite substantial mistake. Although our ideas of *identity* (of an identical object invariant through a succession of moments) and of *diversity* (of several different objects in succession) are entirely distinct, and even contrary to one another, we commonly confuse these ideas with one another. We take things that are in fact distinct to be identical. We do this because certain acts of the mind resemble one another and because these resembling acts of the mind come to be thought of as resembling perceptions. This confusion is then further compounded. We also suppose that our non-resembling perceptions, just as much as our resembling ones, are united by some underlying entity. We imagine ('feign' is Hume's term) 'some new and unintelligible principle' or entity—a self, a soul, a substance, or at least something 'unknown and mysterious'—that, somehow, holds together or unites these acts and perceptions (1.4.6.6–7).

The process just described should not be thought of as an elaborate form of conscious pretending. On the contrary, it is unconscious, automatic, and, for all practical purposes, universal. We each of us naturally enough say of ourselves that we are one person, thus suggesting that our multiple perceptions are united or connected by something that provides a 'real bond'. It is only after philosophical analysis that we come to realize that our perceptions are distinct existences, each different, distinguishable, and separable from every other perception. Philosophical analysis makes us realize that there is no 'real bond' between perceptions, and that we feel such a bond only because of the effects of the associating principles, resemblance, contiguity, and causation. That is, the three now familiar associating principles so relate our perceptions to one another that we seem to feel a real bond between them even though they are entirely distinct and separable. Much as a determination of the mind or a feeling of expectation is the source of the idea of necessary connection, so is what Hume calls a 'smooth and uninterrupted progress of the thought along a train of connected ideas' the source of the idea of the self. We find, then, that the idea of an identical self is another of the 'fictions' the mind naturally produces. The idea of an identical self has a source (it copies or is derived from one or more kinds of impression), but on closer inspection we again find the relevant impressions to be nothing like what we might have expected them to be. The impression bears little resemblance to the idea it engenders. As Hume puts it, 'identity is nothing really belonging to these different perceptions, and uniting them together; but is merely a quality, which we attribute to them, because of the union of their ideas in the imagination, when we reflect upon them' (1.4.6.16).

Sometime before November 1740 Hume became dissatisfied with his account of the origin of the idea of the self, and sceptical about finding a better one. In the Appendix to the third volume of the *Treatise* he reviews the explanation of the idea of personal identity found at 1.4.6. He is, he says, still satisfied that every idea is derived from an impression; that there is no direct and simple impression of self or substance; and hence that our idea of self cannot come from such a source. He is still satisfied that whatever is distinct is distinguishable; that whatever is distinguishable is separable by the thought or imagination; that whatever may be separated in thought may exist separately; and that these principles apply to our perceptions, which is to say that any perception may exist separately from any other perception and from the mind or any substance or subject of inhesion. He is still satisfied that nothing is ever present to the mind but perceptions, and that it is perceptions and only perceptions that form the self and that produce the feeling that gives rise to the idea of the self. He is still satisfied that these perceptions must be identical with this self and that we have no notion of a self beyond these perceptions. Just as philosophers have begun to accept the view 'that we have no idea of external substance, distinct from the ideas of particular qualities', so do we see 'that we have no notion of [internal or mental substance], distinct from the particular perceptions' (App. 11–19). But, he says, he now finds a serious defect in his account of how we come to think of our perceptions as bound together in 'a real simplicity and identity'. He is convinced, on the one hand, that if 'perceptions are distinct existences, [then] they form a whole only by being connected together'. He is also convinced, on the other hand, that 'no connexions among distinct existences are ever discoverable by human understanding'. And he cannot now see how to reconcile these two insights or 'principles', nor is he prepared to renounce either as false. The notion of personal identity arises from reflection on the way in which the past perceptions of the mind naturally introduce one another, but Hume is unable 'to explain the principles, that unite our successive perceptions in our thought or consciousness' or to discover any satisfactory theory of personal identity (App. 20–1). Candidly admitting that this issue is too difficult for him to solve, he holds out the hope that someone else may find a solution to it.

THE CONCLUSION OF BOOK 1

Having 'fully explain'd the nature of our judgment and understanding' (1.4.6.23), Hume pauses to take stock of his accomplishments. He is not encouraged by what he finds and wonders at his temerity in supposing he can push still further on his voyage of philosophical discovery. Has he not amply demonstrated that the human understanding is a frail and leaky craft, entirely unfit to navigate the vast ocean of human nature? Has he not also shown that his own understanding is equally frail? And has not his criticism of his intellectual peers cut him off from those who might otherwise have helped him? When he looks inward he sees the weakness of his powers; when he looks outward he foresees nothing but 'dispute, contradiction, anger, calumny and detraction' (1.4.7.2). How then can he possibly hope to provide a sound and fundamental science of human nature?

The problem, as Hume sees it, is that his own theory rests ultimately on nothing more than his own '*strong* propensity to consider objects *strongly* in that view, under which they appear to me' (1.4.7.3). Having shown, that is, that our beliefs are ultimately determined by the imagination, he must recognize that this same principle has determined his own views. Notwithstanding his typically human desire to know the real connections between things, he must recognize that those things that pass for causes are also the products of the imagination, and hence that his own theory is just such a product. This in itself would perhaps be no problem were it not that the 'memory, senses, and understanding' are all 'founded on the imagination', an 'inconstant and fallacious' faculty (1.4.7.3–4). In its commonplace and unreflective manifestations this faculty leads us to an inconsistent set of beliefs, including our beliefs in causes and objects. In its more reflective manifestations, the imagination not only leads us to question these same beliefs, but also to undercut and destroy them. We are faced, then, with a 'very dangerous dilemma'. We can rely on the commonplace properties of the imagination; these produce dubious, sometimes absurd, even dangerous, results. Or we can rely on the 'general and more establish'd properties of the imagination' (on, that is, 'the understanding'); in doing so, we would destroy the very beliefs on which our survival depends (1.4.7.4–7).

Hume attempts no resolution of this dilemma. But he does see that nature itself can dispel his philosophical gloom. In due course he leaves his study and goes on about his affairs. 'I dine, I play a game of back-gammon, I converse, and am merry with my friends,' reads his famous line (1.4.7.9). When he does so, he soon finds his doubts only a distant memory and he himself ready to abandon philosophy entirely. On reflection, however, he settles on a less radical course. He lets nature lead him out of his gloom, but he does not abandon philosophy. The urge to philosophize, he argues, is also natural, and engaging in philosophy is itself necessary if we are to overcome superstition and improve our understanding of the world. We may not only legitimately yield to, but should also cultivate, the urge to philosophize. At the same time he argues that we should acknowledge that none of our beliefs and opinions are beyond doubt. Those with positive theories should remember the human tendency to err and should thus embrace their theories and convictions with moderation. Those inclined to scepticism should for the same reason be moderate in their philosophical doubts. And such moderation should characterize not merely our philosophical views, but all our beliefs. 'In all the incidents of life', says Hume, 'we ought still to preserve our scepticism' (1.4.7.11). We cannot but accept many natural and commonplace beliefs, but we can none the less hope that our encounters with scepticism will leave each of us, even about these apparently unavoidable beliefs, less dogmatic and intolerant, and that this result will have a lasting and beneficial effect on society at large.

Book 2: Of the Passions

The fundamental goal of the *Treatise* is to provide us with a new science of human nature. In Hume's hands this science begins with the view that the immediate object of the mind is always a perception, an impression or an idea, internal to the mind. Book 1 explains at length the formation and role of some of these mental elements, certain important ideas (of space and time, cause and effect, necessary connection, external existence, personal identity) that are derived from impressions. Book 2 provides a detailed account of several secondary impressions, *impressions of reflection*, which are typically referred to as *passions*. Hume's object is to extend his science of human nature by providing an explanation of the formation and operation of these passions, an explanation that treats them as elements of mind. Consequently, his explanation makes no use of speculative physiology. Instead, he appeals to a few fundamental elements of human nature along with the operation of the principles of association as the basis for what he called an 'altogether . . . new and extraordinary' account of the passions (*Abs.* 30).

We can best begin by reviewing briefly what Hume means by the term *passion*, and how what he says about the passions fits into his science of human nature. Hume first discusses the passions in *Treatise* 1.1.2. He there distinguishes between impressions of sensation and impressions of reflection, but defers substantial discussion of the latter to *Treatise* 2. But even as he does so he suggests that:

(a) by the term *passion* he will usually refer to a set of 'secondary' or reflective impressions;

(b) many of these secondary impressions ('impressions of reflection') derive from ideas that copy certain bodily sensations, especially those of pleasure and pain;

(c) in addition to pride, hatred, compassion, etc., the passions include the desires.

Book 2 of the *Treatise* reaffirms these suggestions, and also tells us that:

(d) bodily pleasures and pains, either at the moment they are felt or when they are later recalled, give rise to many passions (2.1.1.2);

(e) the passions are of two fundamentally different kinds, the *productive*, or those that produce pleasure and pain (2.3.9.8), and the *responsive*, or those that are responses to pleasure and pain; the latter are the principal topic of *Treatise* 2;

(f) the responsive passions (which may be calm or violent, direct or indirect) are as open to systematic explanation as any of the phenomena of natural philosophy (2.1.3.6–7);

(g) certain fundamental features of human nature (sympathy, or the ability to communicate feelings, for example), in conjunction with the principles of association, are sufficient to account for the formation and operation of the responsive passions.

In addition, in the final part of *Treatise* 2 Hume argues that

(h) the will must be understood as a feeling, and not as a faculty (2.3.1);

(i) the view that the will can make uncaused choices is indefensible (2.3.1–3);

(*j*)   the passions, not reason, motivate us to action (2.3.3); moreover, some of the passions motivate us directly, while those that do not motivate directly either motivate indirectly or add force to existing motivations.

The significance of these views can be appreciated only when they are compared to those of some of Hume's predecessors. From ancient times many philosophers had characterized the passions as fundamentally negative and at odds with our better selves as represented by reason. Some supposed the passions to be natural elements of the human psyche, but saw them as essentially lawless or untamed forces ready to overpower reason, the rightful master of the soul, or as having already enslaved this putatively superior principle. Plato had suggested something along these lines, but Stoic writers, and especially those of the early modern period, went even further. They represented the passions as diseases that take illicit control of the mind or soul, and that are to be cured only by being eliminated, so that the ideal person is a person devoid of passion.[49]

In contrast, some early modern philosophers treated the passions as integral and positive features of human nature and human experience, and as features open to explanation by the new human sciences to which they ascribed. Descartes, for example, explicitly attempting to remedy previous failures to produce a comprehensive account of the passions, argues that the passions, by which he means the 'perceptions, sensations, or emotions of the soul', have an essentially physical cause, namely, the animal spirits. He also maintained that the passions have an essential and beneficial effect, that of moving us to want things and to act on those wants.[50] With the first of Descartes's theses Hume clearly disagreed, for he explains the passions by reference to elements of the mind rather than by appeal to the dubious physiology of animal spirits. But Hume did agree that the passions constitute an integral part of human nature, that they can be given a comprehensive explanation, and that their operation is both essential and beneficial.

At the beginning of *Treatise* 2 Hume reminds us that impressions are of two kinds, those of *sensation* and those of *reflection*. The impressions of reflection, he says, are the 'passions, and other emotions resembling them'. Without further ado, he proceeds to classify and analyse, at great length, these impressions of reflection. We eventually learn, however, that Hume distinguishes two fundamentally different kinds of passion: (1) the *productive* passions, or those passions whose operation produces pleasure or pain; and (2) the *responsive* passions, or those passions that arise in response to pain and pleasure.

THE PRODUCTIVE PASSIONS

It is only near the end of Book 2 that Hume draws our attention to the important difference between the productive and the responsive passions. Only then

---

[49]   For further details, see the annotation to 2.3.3.1.

[50]   Descartes, *The Passions of the Soul* 1.27–9, 36–40, in *The Philosophical Writings of Descartes*, trans. J. Cottingham, R. Stoothoff, D. Murdoch, and A. Kenny, 3 vols. (Cambridge: Cambridge University Press, 1985–91), 1:339, 342–3. On animal spirits, see the last annotation to 1.2.5.20 and the Glossary.

does he tell us that some of our passions arise 'from a natural impulse or instinct, which is perfectly unaccountable' and that passions of this kind (the desire to see enemies punished and friends happy, hunger and thirst, sexual appetite) 'produce' pleasure and pain, while the remaining passions are responses to pleasure and pain (2.3.9.8). Alerted by this remark, we find such productive passions discussed elsewhere in *Treatise* 2 and again in *Treatise* 3. When we do so, we soon come to understand what it is that is 'perfectly unaccountable' about this situation.

Consider, for example, Hume's explanation of love between the sexes. This particular passion is said to arise from the conjunction of three different passions. These include a responsive passion, 'the pleasing sensation arising from beauty', and two productive passions, 'the bodily appetite for generation [sexual appetite]; and a generous kindness' or desire for the happiness of our friends (2.2.11.1). He then suggests that these three passions work together, with beauty and the pleasure arising from beauty enhancing and even exciting both sexual appetite and benevolence (see 2.2.11.3–4).[51] In the end we do not know why we have the instincts we have, but we do understand how these instincts contribute to both our passional and our social experience. Consider also Hume's explanation of that 'love of truth, which was the first source' of the philosophical investigations he is pursuing (2.3.10.1). This passion, he says, is excited by some intellectual activities, but not by others. He then compares intellectual curiosity to the 'insatiable desire' some have to know 'the actions and circumstances of their neighbours' and suggests that each of these apparently distinctive desires derives ultimately from something 'implanted in human nature' (2.3.10.11). Moreover, the *Treatise* shows us that both forms of this curiosity contribute positively to human well-being. We see, then, that when Hume says that we cannot account for the natural instincts that give rise to the productive passions, he means only to emphasize that we cannot explain *why* we have these natural instincts or impulses. We can, however, say a great deal about how these passions work—we can describe and explain, for example, how custom, time, and distance affect such passions. We can also see that these instincts provide deep-seated and apparently universal motivations for human actions, and that some of them (our instinctive generosity and our interest in the activities of others, for example) play a significant role in the moral theory Hume outlines in *Treatise* 3.

THE RESPONSIVE PASSIONS

The responsive passions are impressions of reflection that arise in response to pain and pleasure. *Treatise* 2.1 and 2.2 discuss four responsive and indirect passions (pride, humility, love, and hatred) and also a number of other passions

---

[51] In *Treatise* 3 we learn that such enhancement can work both ways: 'An affection betwixt the sexes is a passion evidently implanted in human nature; and this passion not only appears in its peculiar symptoms, but also in inflaming every other principle of affection, and raising a stronger love from beauty, wit, kindness, than what wou'd otherwise flow from them' (3.2.1.12).

(anger, compassion, malice, and envy, for example) of the same type deriving from these four. *Treatise* 2.3.9 is principally concerned with several responsive and direct passions (sorrow, fear, and hope, for example). These discussions together provide a detailed account of the responsive passions.

Book 2 Part 1: The Indirect Passions of Pride and Humility

Although our passions, as perceptions or impressions, are simple and indefinable, there is much that can be said about them. Pride is 'that agreeable impression, which arises in the mind, when the view either of our virtue, beauty, riches or power makes us satisfy'd with ourselves', while humility is a disagreeable impression arising when these same characteristics make us dissatisfied with ourselves (2.1.7.8). The two passions are, as feelings, unlike or contrary. They have, however, the same *objects* and the same kinds of *cause*, and both depend upon one of the principles of association, resemblance.[52]

The object of pride or humility is always, according to Hume, that very individual who is feeling pride or humility. Hume calls those things in which we take pride (our personal qualities and our possessions, for example) the causes of pride. Such causes are *subjects* with particular *qualities* (a house that is beautiful, a character that is virtuous, or a body that is strong, for example).

In the course of sketching his account of the origin of pride and humility, Hume argues that the passions are dependent on qualities or principles that are inseparable from human nature and that cannot be explained by reference to other, more basic qualities. In the *Abstract* Hume suggests that 'all our passions are a kind of natural instincts, derived from nothing but the original constitution of the human mind', and that, in so far as they 'arise immediately from nature', are innate (*Abs.* 6). He insists, however, that it would be absurd to suppose that every cause of a passion such as pride has its effect because it corresponds to a unique and original instinct. We need not suppose that we have one instinct that makes us proud of a fine writing-desk and another that makes us proud of our tables and chairs. At least one of Hume's predecessors, Marin Cureau de la Chambre, had concluded that each of the passions corresponds to a distinctive motion of the animal spirits, but could give no systematic account of this fact. He seemed to offer nothing more than a loosely related bundle of explanatory hypotheses. Hume flatly rejects such *ad hoc* explanations of the passions. To explain the passions by appeal to a 'monstrous heap of principles', one for each passion, would be to fail in the science of human nature. Moral philosophy in general, and the theory of the passions in particular, ought to aim for the same economy of explanatory principle that characterizes astronomy and natural philosophy. The science of human nature must assume that the various causes of pride have a feature or features in common, and then look for such common elements.

[52] It is apparently because of this dependence on principles of association, especially resemblance, that Hume calls pride and humility (and also love and hatred) 'indirect passions'. As we will see, a cause of pride does not produce this pleasant passion directly, but indirectly or by means of resembling ideas and impressions.

What, then, accounts for the fact that we take pride in a seemingly unlimited range of things? Hume focuses on the principles of association. As thinking humans, we are unable to focus for any lengthy period on a single idea, but our thought does not jump from idea to idea in a purely random manner. As Hume had earlier explained, the mind, as it leaves one idea, takes up another that is related to the first by resemblance, contiguity, or cause and effect (see 1.1.4). He now points out that the mind is similarly affected by resembling impressions. The experience of one pleasant feeling or passion tends to lead us to experience others of the same general kind. The capriciousness of the mind means that our thoughts (ideas) and feelings (impressions) are fundamentally unstable, but the principles of association introduce and maintain a regularity amidst this constant change. As a consequence, very different causes (ideas of subjects and their qualities) can produce exactly resembling effects. My beautiful house, my virtuous character, my strong body, do not each produce a distinctive pleasure, but each does produce a pleasure, and each experience of such a pleasure, because it resembles the pleasure of pride, brings the pleasure of pride to mind. At the same time each of these items (my house, my character, my body), being mine, also brings to mind my idea of myself. In this way the association of impressions and the association of ideas work together to produce the passion of pride.

Having accepted these several suppositions and findings as correct, 'the true system' struck Hume, as he puts it, 'with an irresistible evidence', or force (2.1.5.5). That system, depending on a 'double relation of ideas and impressions', works like this: The causes of pride (certain subjects or entities) affect us by means of the ideas we have of them. Each such idea (whether of my beautiful house, my virtuous character, or my strong body) has an immediate effect upon me. The *subject* or entity of which I have an idea (the house, character, or body), because it is *mine*, brings to mind, by the *association of ideas*, the idea of *myself*. That is, the subject brings to mind the idea of precisely that individual who is always the object of pride. At the same time the *quality* of the subject or entity (the beauty, virtue, or strength of the subject), because it is a positive quality, gives me *pleasure*. This pleasure, by the *association of impressions*, brings to mind the resembling pleasure of pride. Thus from the experience of an idea having specific characteristics, I come to experience pride.

A schematic representation (see overleaf) of this account may be helpful: On Hume's account of the phenomenon, my feeling of pride in my beautiful house arises when a particular subject (my house) and quality (beauty) together excite an idea, *A*, of a beautiful house related to a 'correlative' idea of my self, or Idea *B*. Idea *A* also 'produces' Impression *A*, a distinct pleasure that, because it 'resembles' Impression *B*, pride, leads me to have Impression *B*. Idea *B* is 'connected' to Impression *B* as the object of this impression.[53]

[53] In this schema single lines with arrows indicate both causal and directional flow; the double line between Idea *B* and Impression *B* indicates what Hume calls a connection and describes as an essential, two-way connection. The schema suggests that the double relation of impressions and ideas (the relations represented by the two horizontal lines) is supplemented by the relations of ideas to

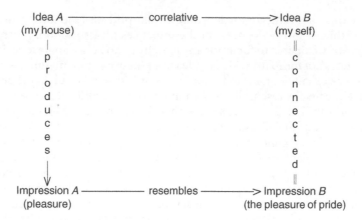

Once he has set out the basic features of his account of pride and humility, Hume turns his attention to some particular causes (virtue and vice, beauty and deformity, wealth and poverty) of these two indirect passions. By focusing on these causes he is able to carry out a series of tests of his theory. These tests confirm to his satisfaction that pride and humility depend upon the double relation of impressions and ideas he has outlined, but not without raising important questions that require attention—questions about the relation of pleasure to virtue and beauty, about the status of unexercised powers or capacities, and about sympathy.

THE 'VERY ESSENCE' OF VIRTUE AND BEAUTY

Hume's tests of his theory concerning the origin of pride and humility occupy five sections of Treatise 2.1. Two of these sections focus on virtue and vice and beauty and deformity. In his discussion of virtue (2.1.7) Hume argues that, according to certain accounts of the foundations of morality, we must say either that 'pleasure' is the 'very essence of virtue', or, what comes to the same thing, that 'satisfaction' constitutes the 'very nature and essence' of virtue. Pain, in contrast, constitutes the very essence of vice. In a related discussion of wit he says that the 'power of bestowing' pleasure is 'the very essence' of true wit, and the one thing that distinguishes it from the false wit that causes pain or 'uneasiness'. In his discussion of beauty (2.1.8) he says that pleasure and pain, or the 'power of producing' them, 'are not only necessary attendants of beauty and deformity, but constitute their very essence'.

Taken in isolation these remarks about the essence of virtue, beauty, and wit may suggest Hume thinks that virtue and beauty are nothing more than a certain kind of feeling, so that what we call *virtue* just is pleasure and nothing more, and that what we call *beauty* just is pleasure and nothing more. If we look

impressions (the relations represented by the vertical lines). In effect, the relevant relations are both doubled and redoubled.

carefully at Hume's other claims, we will see that this is not what he means. In the first place, a claim that virtue and beauty are identical with pleasure, or just are pleasure and nothing more, would appear to commit Hume to the view that virtue and beauty are indistinguishable from one another. But we can readily see that this is not his view. Virtue and beauty may each cause the same kind of feeling, namely, a pleasure that resembles the pleasure of pride, but on Hume's account the causes of this similar effect—virtue and beauty themselves—are clearly different. When virtue gives rise to pleasure and then pride it is always certain durable principles of an agent's mind (a benevolent intent, for example) that function as cause. When physical beauty gives rise to the same kind of pleasure, it is certain characteristics of the agent (the regular features of his face, for example) that function as cause. Given, then, that virtue and beauty are not identical with each other, it follows that they cannot be identical to that particular kind of feeling which they are both said to cause.

What, then, does Hume mean when he says that pleasure is the 'very essence' of virtue, beauty, and wit? He gives us an important clue. Speaking of pride and humility in general, he argues that these two passions are of such a nature that they always cause us to feel specific 'sensations, or . . . peculiar emotions'. So far as these two passions are concerned, he goes on, these peculiar feelings 'constitute their very being and essence' and consequently 'pride is a pleasant sensation, and humility a painful'. And what does this mean? It means that 'upon the removal of the pleasure and pain, there is in reality no pride nor humility' (2.1.5.4). It means, in other words, that the experience of certain forms of pleasure or pain is essential to the experience of pride and humility, or, to abandon Hume's vocabulary for our own, that the experience of certain kinds of feeling of pleasure and pain is a *necessary* (but not a *sufficient*) condition of the experience of pride or humility.

It is in this same sense, I suggest, that pleasure and pain constitute the 'very essence' of virtue and beauty. Hume does not mean that virtue and beauty just are pleasant or painful feelings and nothing more. He means, rather, that feeling a certain kind of pleasure is a necessary condition of the experience of virtue and beauty. As he says, 'if the power of producing pleasure and pain forms not the essence of beauty and deformity', these feelings 'are at least inseparable from the[se] qualities, and 'tis even difficult to consider them apart' (2.1.8.3). Hume grants that it is possible that virtue and beauty exist independently of human experience and human feelings. But, because our experience of these qualities is always accompanied by pleasure, it is beyond our ability to conceive of them as they are in themselves. We also come to treat this accompanying pleasure as an essential property of them. Indeed, as pleasure is the only invariant property of the experience of virtue, wit, or beauty, we come to think of pleasure as an essential part of these qualities.[54]

---

[54] In 1757 Hume published an abridged version of his account of the passions, a work now known as *A Dissertation on the Passions*. In this work he explicitly says that the pleasure and pain excited by certain features of mind 'are essential to vice and virtue' (2.6).

UNEXERCISED POWERS

If I own something that is beautiful or useful or novel, this item will give pleasure and, by the double relation of ideas and impressions, cause me to feel pride. We also find that we take pleasure and pride in wealth, the 'very essence' of which consists in the power it gives us of acquiring the pleasures and advantages of life (2.1.10.10). How, we ask, does mere wealth cause pride? Hume has earlier said that the 'distinction, which we often make betwixt a *power* and the *exercise* of it' is 'without foundation' (1.3.14.34), and thus talk of unexercised powers or capacities is really nonsense, and 'neither man nor any other being ought ever to be thought possest of any ability, unless it be exerted and put in action' (2.1.10.4). But now he suggests that an unexercised power of acquiring property can produce pride. Although it appears that Hume's theory has run aground on his own previous conclusion, he is unconcerned by this apparent inconsistency. He simply tells us that, while in a strict '*philosophical* way of thinking', talk of unexercised powers is nonsense, so far as the '*philosophy* of our passions' is concerned, we are pleased when we 'acquire an ability of procuring pleasure', and all that is left to do is to explain how this comes about.

The key to Hume's explanation, as we might have guessed, is experience. Suppose we have observed an individual, Doe, who has strong motives to perform a particular kind of act, *A*, and who typically acts on these motives. Suppose we have also observed a second individual, Rey, who has strong motives not to perform acts of type *A*, and who typically refrains from performing acts of this type. Given Hume's account of the effect of past experience on the mind, those who have experience of these individuals will expect Doe to perform an act of type *A*, and Rey to refrain from performing such an act. If we now further suppose that the performance of an act of type *A* will cause us significant harm, while refraining from such an act will be of significant benefit, we find that the present observation of Doe produces fear, and the present observation of Rey produces hope. Without any need to posit unexercised powers, we can see that expectations produce passions, and that particular expectations produce particular passions.[55]

To understand the relevance of this finding to the question raised (how does mere wealth cause pride?), we need only suppose that the person whose behaviour you have observed is yourself, and that you have observed yourself using your wealth to acquire things that give you pleasure—chocolate, clothes, computers, whatever. Knowing yourself to have wealth, and assuming there are no external constraints on your behaviour, you anticipate, with pleasure, that you will again use your wealth to acquire pleasing things. Your wealth arouses in you a particular kind of feeling, pleasure. That it is your wealth is enough to bring to mind your idea of yourself; that your wealth gives you this particular feeling, pleasure, is enough to arouse the resembling pleasure of pride. In short, by means of the double relation of impressions and ideas, your wealth becomes a cause of pride in yourself.

[55] For further discussion of experience and expectation, see above, pp. 131–5.

SYMPATHY

Hume also finds himself needing to explain what he calls a secondary cause of pride and humility. He needs to explain, that is, how the opinion others have of a person can cause pride or humility in that person. According to the theory presented in the early sections of *Treatise* 2.1, you experience pride when something of yours gives you a pleasure resembling the pleasure of pride. But in 2.1.11 ('Of the love of fame'), Hume takes note of a complicating phenomenon: being praised by others can cause or increase a person's pride. How is this possible? How does my esteem for you, triggered as it is by a pleasure I feel, give rise to your pride? Or how does it happen that your several praiseworthy qualities (your virtue, strength, or wealth) give you greater pride when they are noticed and approved by others? And why is it that pride and humility are more significantly affected by the praise or contempt of those we know and respect than by the praise or contempt of strangers? Each of these challenging phenomena—each of these 'secondary' causes of pride—is to be explained, Hume argues, by the operation of sympathy.

The first thing to notice about this explanation is that Hume does not, at least not in the *Treatise*, think of sympathy as a particular feeling. The word *sympathy* does not there designate the feeling we have for a close friend who is bereaved or in serious trouble. Hume would call that feeling *pity* or *compassion*, while *sympathy* is his name for a means or principle of communication (2.3.6.8)—his name for a general ability of humans to know and to experience as their own the sentiments or opinions of others. So vigorous and wide-ranging is this principle that its operation explains not only why appropriately situated individuals share sentiments and opinions, but also why larger groups and even whole nations share in this way.

A second thing to notice is that sympathy is not one of those unintelligible qualities or faculties scornfully dismissed at *Treatise* 1.4.3.10–11. Sympathy is a fundamental feature of human nature Hume has not previously mentioned, but it depends for its operation on that limited set of mental elements (perceptions and their relations) that form the basis of his explanations. Those already familiar with Hume's account of the relations holding between impressions and ideas and of the kind of belief that arises from experience will find few surprises in his explanation of the way in which sympathy works.

Imagine for the moment that you have recently heard some very good news, news that has made you exceptionally happy. Furthermore, your friends, when you meet them and even before you can say anything about your good news, recognize that you are elated, and themselves become infused with your happiness to such a degree that they, too, begin to feel happy. What has happened, according to Hume, is that your feeling of happiness has manifested itself in your appearance (through the expression on your face or other non-verbal clues) while your friends, seeing that happy appearance, have first thought of, and then experienced, the very same sentiment or passion you are experiencing. More generally stated, your news arouses an impression or particular passion in you. This passion in turn affects your appearance and behaviour. Those who encounter you perceive these outward signs of your passion. They perceive, for example, the brightness of your smile, the light in your eyes, or the eager pace of your walk. Your friends have, in other words, impressions of sensation of your external appearance, and these impressions of sensation, because they have in the past been associated with your friends' own feelings of happiness, bring to mind the idea of happiness. And this idea, once brought to mind in these circumstances, is readily converted into an impression: that is, it is given the forcefulness or vigour of an impression by, among other things, the impressions with which it is associated and by the lively sense of the self that is always present to each of us. Of course, neither you nor your friends are typically aware that this complex process is taking place, but according to Hume it does none the less take place, and with the effect that, more or less instantaneously upon encountering you, your friends find themselves feeling precisely the same passion that you are feeling.

The questions raised at the beginning of this section can now be answered. My esteem for you produces pride in you because my esteem is communicated to you and converted into pride. By the operation of sympathy, you feel the pleasure of my esteem. But then, because the object of my esteem is you, and because the pleasure of esteem resembles the pleasure of pride, you by association have both the idea of yourself and the pleasure of pride, the components essential to the experience of pride. By the same process, when I take notice of any of your praiseworthy qualities and feel esteem for you because of them, your pride is enhanced: again, my esteem, communicated to you, is converted into pride and added to the pride you already feel. Finally, pride and humility are more significantly affected by the praise or contempt of those we respect because we communicate more effectively with (have greater sympathy with) such individuals. According to Hume, we must know relatively well those we respect; we find, moreover, that we share with them significant interests and opinions. It happens, then, that the contempt of strangers is easier to bear than the contempt of family and friends because our sympathy with strangers is, in comparison, weaker. It is weaker because the associating relations (resemblance, contiguity, and cause and effect) linking us with strangers are weaker than those linking us with relatives or intimates (2.1.11.9–16).

Hume goes on to amplify his view by what may well be an analysis of his own behaviour. In late 1737 he admitted that despite his desire to see his family and friends after an absence of more than three years, he was reluctant to return to Scotland before he had accomplished something noteworthy.[56] In the meantime he had lived among strangers in both France and England. 'Suppose', he says in the *Treatise*, 'I am plac'd in a poor condition among strangers, and consequently am but lightly treated; I yet find myself easier in that situation, than when I was every day expos'd to the contempt of my kindred and countrymen' (2.1.11.17). Even at a distance his relatives may well

---

[56] Hume's remark is quoted in n. 6 above.

continue to feel contempt for him. And perhaps the strangers who are now his neighbours have the same negative reaction. But at least there are now two different sets of individuals who feel this contempt: there are now two distinct influences on him, and these influences do not unite as they would if the contempt were to come 'from persons who are at once both my neighbours and kindred'. Moreover, a person so circumstanced among strangers typically uses 'the greatest industry' to conceal his status, so that no one will suspect him 'to be of a family, much superior to his present fortune and way of living'. Consequently, those among whom this individual is living expect less of him. He may himself be disappointed with his condition, but his new neighbours show no signs of feeling this same disappointment because, not knowing his origins, they have no grounds for disappointment at seeing him in his present state. In short, by altering his circumstances, this individual is able to reduce or alter the role sympathy plays in determining the relative strength of his pride or humility. This, Hume concludes, is a further confirmation of his general thesis, namely, *'that the pleasure, which we receive from praise, arises from a communication of sentiments'* brought about by the operation of sympathy (2.1.11.17–19).

Book 2 Part 2: *The Indirect Passions of Love and Hatred*

In many respects, love and hatred (or esteem and contempt, as Hume also calls them) are similar to pride and humility, the principal subjects of *Treatise* 2.1. All four passions are indefinable, indirect passions. All take the idea of a person as their object. All are caused by precisely those qualities that produce pleasures or pains that resemble, but are yet distinct from, the four passions themselves. And all depend upon a double relation of impressions and ideas—on relations that bring to mind the impressions and ideas essential to the experience of such passions. There is, however, one fundamental difference. The object of pride and humility is always one's self, while the object of love and hatred is always some person other than one's self (2.2.1.2).

PASSIONS AND THE PRINCIPLES OF ASSOCIATION

Given the many similarities between these two sets of indirect passions, portions of *Treatise* 2.2 can be used to amplify and confirm the claim, first made in 2.1, that the principles of association, producing as they do a double relation of impressions and ideas, account for our experience of these passions. In 2.2.2, for example, Hume describes eight experiments that show how this set of double relations makes the indirect passions possible. While these may seem to be merely thought experiments, they are in fact descriptions of eight situations we could each easily enter into and of the passions we would experience were we to do so.

The eight experiments are not used to show which passions will be produced in the circumstances Hume describes. They are used, rather, to show that whether or not we feel the indirect passions depends upon the double relation of impressions and ideas. Hume notes, for example, that a beautiful, and for that reason pleasing, house, unrelated to (not possessed by) the person I happen to be with, produces no esteem for her. But let this same person come to possess this same house, so that the idea of the house not only gives pleasure, but is related to my idea of her, and I will at once feel esteem for her.

Consider a second example. If I esteem my brother because of some positive feature of his character, I find that I also feel pride in myself. Why does this happen? Because, Hume argues, the idea of my brother brings to mind the idea of myself, while the pleasure produced by the positive feature of his character resembles not only the pleasure of love, but also that of pride. In contrast, the positive features of my own character do not cause me to love my brother, a lack of response explained by the fact that my own positive qualities bring to mind the idea of myself, an idea so lively that it tends to overpower the related idea of my brother.

Looking back at his eight experiments, Hume is satisfied that each of them confirms his novel theory that the four passions discussed depend on the principles of association, or, more precisely, are produced by certain transitions that arise from a double relation of impressions and ideas (2.2.2.28). But, while clearly committed to explaining pride, humility, love, and hatred by means of the principles of association, Hume remained alert to apparent difficulties. At the beginning of 2.2.3, for example, he notes that many of the actions of other persons give us pleasure or pain, and hence are a source of love or hatred. As a general rule, we love or esteem those whose actions are of benefit to us, and hate or dislike those whose actions harm us. But a closer look at experience shows that our responses are more complicated than this general rule suggests. We sometimes continue to esteem individuals whose actions harm us, just as we dislike some of those who have done us no harm. How are these apparent anomalies to be explained? Only by appeal to the principles of association.

Hume notes that we tend to have no passional response to actions that were unintended or to those that are the result of constraints on the agent who has acted. Persons who harm us without intending to do so, or a judge, whose duty requires her to deliver a judgment that harms us, will not typically be hated as a result of these actions, or, if they are, the passion will be short-lived. Far from supposing that these reactions challenge his basic theory, Hume sees them as confirming it. He argues that our responses in these cases are explicable only on the assumption that there must be two associative relationships (one of ideas, the other of impressions) to produce any of the four indirect passions. If one of these two sets of associative relationships is lacking, so too will a passional response be lacking. Granted, we may learn of such weakened connections only after the fact (only after a passion has already been aroused), but when we see that an agent has injured us unintentionally, the relation of ideas that at first served to make her the object of our dislike or hatred is clearly weakened or severed, and our response is altered. It is only actions that are connected to some relatively long-lasting feature of an agent (only those actions connected with her character or intentions) that can set in motion the sequence of ideas that is sure to make that agent the object of our love or hatred. Actions unintentionally causing harm lack this connection and hence, when correctly understood, produce no passion. Analysis also shows that the actions of a judge or of others fulfilling their duties, although intended, are connected with the office or role of these agents, and not with the character and persons of the agents themselves. As a consequence, our passional responses to these agents are also altered. Similarly, persons who intend to help or harm us but who are unable to carry out their intended acts may still be the object of love or hatred. In these cases, the intent of the agent is alone enough to give pleasure or pain, and thus both a relation of impressions and a relation of ideas are set in motion, and a passion is produced.[57]

The principles of association also explain two other well-known phenomena: the fact that we feel a greater love for those we know well than for strangers (see 2.2.4), and the fact that we esteem the rich and powerful (2.2.5). We may readily see that certain strangers have qualities or possessions more noteworthy than those of our friends and family, and yet we typically love such intimates more than these strangers. Again, the theory of double relations provides the needed explanation. The oft-mentioned associative principles, resemblance, contiguity, and cause and effect, make it virtually certain that our ideas of our friends and family will be livelier than those of distant acquaintances or mere strangers. It is also likely that our friends and family will resemble us in temperament and disposition, a fact that facilitates the communication of sentiments by sympathy. In brief, friends and family, because closely connected to us, arouse both stronger impressions and livelier ideas than do strangers. It is no wonder, then, that we feel a greater esteem for such intimates than for any stranger.

Nothing, Hume says, has 'a greater tendency to give us an esteem for any person, than his power and riches' (2.2.5.1). At first glance, it may seem that we admire the wealthy or powerful simply because their possessions or capacities are in themselves pleasing, or because we see them as an expected source of benefit to ourselves. A closer look reveals that the situation is more complex than it seems, and that the principles of association, the source of the principle of sympathy, account for our regard of the wealthy. The possessions of the wealthy (their beautiful houses, for example) may be pleasurable, but they are not in themselves adequate to account for our esteem of their possessors. And only seldom do we have grounds for supposing that the wealthy will use their possessions to our advantage and pleasure, and thus self-interest (an expectation that we will benefit from these possessions) fails to account for the esteem we feel. Only sympathy, Hume concludes, can account for our esteem

---

[57] Hume later argues that all valid moral assessments are responses to, and assessments of, what he calls 'durable principles of the mind' (3.3.1.4). These relatively long-lasting principles or qualities (dispositions, we might call them) include motives of any sort: productive passions, desires, intentions, or qualities of character. They, and not actions or the consequences of actions, are the ultimate source of the moral sentiments by which we distinguish virtue from vice. See also 2.3.2.7; 3.2.1.2–8; and 3.3.1.5. For further discussion of Hume's view on this issue, see pp. 182–4 below.

of the wealthy: The possessions of the wealthy are assumed to be agreeable and to give pleasure to those who possess them. We who observe these wealthy and pleased individuals are, by the operation of sympathy, brought to feel the same pleasure they feel. That pleasure resembles the pleasure of esteem, and so produces in us (because of the double relation of impressions and ideas) the passion of esteem directed towards the idea of the person whose possession produced the pleasure we initially felt.

THE COMPOUND PASSIONS

Some passions are formed of a mixture of other, simpler passions; these Hume calls the compound passions. His account of them focuses principally on three pairs of contrary passions, benevolence and anger, respect and contempt, pity and malice, as well as on envy, and love between the sexes. We can usefully begin with Hume's descriptions of these eight passions. Then we will need to look at several variables—factors that play at most a small part in the arousal of pride, humility, love, and hatred, but which have a substantial and determining influence on the compound passions. This information in hand, we should be able to see why Hume on one occasion worries that his account may appear to be contradictory, and on another fears that he may appear to be arbitrarily appealing to a new principle to explain each new phenomenon he encounters (2.2.9.1, 11). What he has to say in response to these potential criticisms is sometimes difficult to understand, nor are we likely to be satisfied with some of his explanations even when we understand them, but it will still be clear that Hume intended his account to be not merely *ad hoc*, but a genuine contribution to a science of the passions.

First, brief descriptions of eight compound passions:

Benevolence and anger. The compound passion of benevolence is the desire of adding to the happiness of a person loved, while anger is the desire of adding to the misery of a person hated (2.2.6.3).

Pity, malice, and envy. Pity, malice, and envy are themselves moderately complex phenomena, but there is nothing intrinsically difficult about the definitions Hume gives of them. Pity or compassion resembles love and is a concern for the good or happiness of others, independently of any friendship that serves as the cause or source of this concern. Malice resembles hatred, and is a pleasure in the misery or sufferings of others, independently of any offence or injury that serves as the cause or source of this hostility (2.2.7.1; 2.2.8.1). Envy is excited by some pleasure of another person, a pleasure that person takes in a feature or possession supposed to be superior to my own similar feature or possession, and which for that reason produces pain in me. In so far as these passions resemble love and hatred, they can be expected to include desires (benevolence and anger) for the good or ill of those who are their objects (2.2.8.12).

Respect and contempt. Respect, says Hume, is a mixture of love and humility arising from the experience of the positive features or qualities of another person. Contempt, in contrast, is a mixture of hatred and pride arising from the experience of the negative features of another person (2.2.10.1–2).[58]

Love between the sexes. This passion, the '*amorous passion*', as Hume also calls it, is a mixture of three simpler 'impressions or passions, *viz*. the pleasing sensation arising from beauty; the bodily appetite for generation [sexual desire]; and a generous kindness or good-will' (2.2.11.1).

And now the several variables. Hume has no difficulty describing the compound passions. His difficulties begin when he recognizes that our passions, as affective responses, vary as our minds and circumstances vary. It is not unusual for two individuals to feel differently about some third person. Nor is it unusual for one individual to feel, at different times, both pity and malice towards the same person.

Not satisfied simply to note these obvious facts and to leave it at that, Hume undertakes to provide us with a systematic explanation of such affective variations. To put the point generally, he suggests that the apparent relativity of the passions is the product of the varying ways in which relevant objects and circumstances are experienced or portrayed by the imagination (2.2.9.1). We feel one passion rather than its contrary, and with one degree of intensity rather than another, because of variations in the relevant associative relations and in the subsequent operations of several well-entrenched dispositions of mind.

PASSIONS AND RELATIONS

As one might expect, Hume finds that the strength or liveliness of our pleasures and pains influences our passions. Pity, he argues, 'depends, in a great measure, on the contiguity, and even sight of the object' (2.2.7.4). This is apparently because the suffering of another, if near to hand and thus forceful, typically gives rise to compassion and benevolence, but if remote and thus weak, typically leaves us indifferent or even contemptuous (2.2.9.12). Similarly, envy of one's superiors, he observes, is especially dependent upon both resemblance and contiguity. It might be thought that the greater the difference between two persons, the greater the envy of the inferior will be. Not so. 'A common soldier bears no such envy to his general as to his sergeant or corporal', nor does a distinguished writer meet with as much jealousy from hacks and scribblers as from those authors whose abilities rival his own. Generally speaking, where ideas are not closely related, neither are the relevant pleasures and pains related or compared and envy fails to be produced (2.2.8.13). On the other hand, where there are resembling ideas or impressions, a compound passion is likely to result. As we saw above, love between the sexes depends upon resemblance, the resemblance of the desires arising from three sources: from the perception of

---

[58] Although Hume reserves the term *respect* for the compound resulting from the mixture of love and humility, he uses the term *contempt* to refer both to the compound of hatred and pride, and to the simple passion of hatred or dislike. In this short discussion of respect and contempt the term *contempt* refers only to the compound passion.

beauty; from kindness or goodwill; and from sexual appetite. These three desires are so much alike, says Hume, that it little matters which of them arises first, for whichever it is, the others are likely to follow (2.2.11.1–4).

DISPOSITIONS

As we have amply seen, Hume's account of the indirect passions depends heavily on the principles of association. These principles account for the fact that certain entities or their qualities are causes, and certain individuals are objects, of the four indirect passions (pride or love, humility or hatred). These same principles are essential to the communication of feelings by means of sympathy. If there were no other natural inclinations or dispositions at work, our passions would likely seem less capricious or unpredictable than they in fact are. But, as it happens, there are several additional dispositions, some without distinct names, that determine or influence the passions. These dispositions are here discussed under four headings: (1) comparison; (2) mental momentum and general rules; (3) projections and tendencies; and (4) attendant emotions.

Comparison. This principle Hume first introduces when pointing out several limitations of his theory: we 'judge of objects', he says, 'more from comparison than from their real and intrinsic merit' (2.1.6.4). Later he says that 'Every thing in this world is judg'd of by comparison' (2.1.11.18), that humans are so little 'govern'd by reason in their sentiments and opinions, that they always judge more of objects by comparison than from their intrinsic worth and value' (2.2.8.2), and that we 'naturally judge of every thing by comparison' (3.2.10.5). We are likely, in other words, to call a Shetland pony small and a Great Dane large even though the pony is the larger of the two. Or, if we are poor, we will think a sum of money important that, to a wealthy person, will seem inconsequential.

Comparison plays an equally important part in the formation of the passions. Given that we typically form our ideas of things by comparison, it follows that our estimate of our own happiness or misery will depend on our assessments of the happiness or misery of others: 'The misery of another gives us a more lively idea of our happiness, and his happiness of our misery. The former, therefore, produces delight; and the latter uneasiness' (2.2.8.8). Indeed, because comparison often causes us to reverse the opinion we would have formed from a non-comparative view of things, those features of others that would without comparison have given us pleasure give us pain because of comparison. It is comparison, for example, that causes us to feel pain and humility, rather than pleasure and esteem, when we hear of a friend's good fortune. Were we to confine our thoughts to our friend, hearing of his success would give us pleasure and lead to esteem of him. But comparison leads us to compare his good fortune with our own lack thereof, and the pain this causes us leads us to feel humility regarding ourselves.

Mental momentum and general rules. Hume first mentions what he describes as (but does not call) *mental momentum* in *Treatise* 1. Attempting to account for our idea of equality, he notes that nothing is more common than for the mind, once it has begun to proceed in any given manner, to continue 'even after the reason has ceas'd, which first determin'd it to begin' in that manner (1.2.4.24). Later in Book 1 he repeats his point more picturesquely, observing 'that the imagination, when set into any train of thinking, is apt to continue, even when its object fails it, and like a galley put in motion by the oars, carries on its course without any new impulse' (1.4.2.22). In the course of the *Treatise* we find this basic disposition displaying itself in a tendency to form general rules and in other ways that affect the nature or strength of our passions.

Our all-too-human tendency to form and use general rules is also first mentioned in *Treatise* 1. There Hume noted that once we have become accustomed to experiencing one object in conjunction with another, 'our imagination passes from the first to the second, by a natural transition, which precedes reflection, and which cannot be prevented by it' (1.3.13.8). This is a generally beneficial tendency, the very one that accounts for causal reasoning, but it is often carried too far. When it is, we form opinions that go well beyond the evidence available to us, even to the point of adopting prejudices. In his discussion of the compound passions, Hume again notes that this tendency to form general rules has a great influence on us, and he appeals to it in his explanation of particular passions. It explains, for example, the fact that we sometimes find ourselves feeling pity for a person who is not herself saddened. In such situations, instead of feeling what this person is feeling, we respond only to the adverse circumstances that would ordinarily cause her to be sad. She, perhaps because of great strength of mind, is not affected by these adverse circumstances, but our imagination, without waiting to discover all the facts of the situation, links our ideas of the circumstances to the idea of sadness and then, in its usual manner, converts that idea into the very sentiment we mistakenly suppose the person to be feeling (2.2.7.5; 2.2.8.5; see also 1.3.13.10; 2.1.9.13; and 3.2.2.24).

Projections and tendencies. The mind can also project passions into the future and thus receive by sympathy feelings that do not presently exist. In *Treatise* 1.3, in his account of our causal reasoning and the belief to which it gives rise, Hume emphasizes our tendency to project our feelings onto the world, and to form general rules that, in effect, predict the course the future will take. In Book 2 he notices that we not only predict the course of future events, but can, if aided by a forceful present experience, project ourselves into that future so successfully that we may now, by sympathy, feel passions that do not yet exist in the person who is the object of our attention or concern. Thus, observing a person who, although asleep, is in great and imminent danger, we find ourselves concerned for pains he does not feel, and 'sensible of pains and pleasures, which neither belong to ourselves, nor at the present instant have any real existence' (2.2.9.13).

Individual passions also have tendencies that influence our affective responses or feelings. Again, *Treatise* 1 provides precedents. There Hume notes that not only ideas, but also 'the actions of the mind', resemble one another (1.2.5.21). And of all relations, he later says, resemblance is the most likely to lead us into error, 'and that because it not only causes an association of ideas, but also of dispositions' (1.4.2.32). Now, in Book 2, having explained at length how many of our passions depend on a double relation of impressions and ideas, Hume explains that they also depend on 'the whole bent or tendency' of any of the passions that such a double relation initially arouses. That is, although a passion may be triggered by merely momentary sensations or pains or pleasures, passions are not to be understood as brief and transient phenomena present one moment and gone the next. Passions have both temporal dimension, and direction. This means that any two passions (pride and humility excepted) may have multiple 'impulses or directions' that are 'similar and correspondent' (2.2.9.2). Less abstractly, it means that many passions are conjoined with appetites or desires, and that passions so conjoined to desires will appear to have stronger and even unexpected tendencies.

This strengthening of passions conjoined with desires explains phenomena that would otherwise seem to be inconsistent with Hume's account of the indirect passions. Hume has previously told us that we typically feel pity in response to the suffering of those near to us, and indifference or even contempt in response to the suffering of those distant from us. But why, then, do we feel no compassion for a nearby business rival who goes bankrupt, and yet do feel compassion for a distant partner who meets the same fate? We can only explain these variable responses, Hume argues, by noting that the passions in question are determined by the fact that a set of resembling desires is strong enough to cause us to feel hatred and malice towards our rival, while another such set leads us to feel love and compassion towards our partner (2.2.9.9).

Attendant emotions. Hume explains that each of our impressions and ideas is disposed to arouse in us an emotion. These emotions are aroused so routinely that we cease to notice them, but by careful attention they can be detected. Curiously, Hume seems most interested in this discovery for its use in explaining an epistemological puzzle, the relativity of our judgements regarding the size of a given object. But he does explicitly note that his discovery must apply 'to virtue and vice, wit and folly, riches and poverty, happiness and misery, and other objects' that function as causes of the passions (2.2.8.4). He also invokes this discovery as part of his explanation of the fact that we keep at a distance those we think inferior to us. We cannot, he argues, encounter a rich person without feeling some faint touch of respect, nor a poor one without a faint touch of contempt. These two feelings, although faint, are directly contrary to each other. Consequently, if we find together in one place both the rich person and the poor one, their disproportion and the attendant contrariety of feeling will be noticed. It will be particularly noticed by the more superior of the two, for he or she will see the inferior person as ill-mannered (because presumptuous enough to approach a superior) and hence also an object of contempt, and will thus want to remain at a distance from this person (2.2.10.9–10).

At the beginning of his discussion of the compound passions, Hume advises his readers that his account of them will seem to lack the simplicity or elegance that characterizes his account of pride, humility, love, and hatred (2.2.6.2). In the course of the ensuing discussion he amply illustrates that his concern was well founded. He repeatedly finds it necessary to appeal to factors that were given little or no part to play in the production of the four simple passions, and so unexpectedly does he appeal to these factors that even he feared for the consistency and cogency of his account. This review of variables may not convince us that Hume's account of the compound passions is free of all loose ends, but it does show that his account is less disorganized than it may appear on first reading, and that the explanatory principles to which he appeals are generally grounded in his earlier discussions, especially those of Book 1. It also shows that Hume did not evade the complexities of our passional experience. He did not simply slice and twist that experience in order to make it fit neatly his elegant, associationist theory of the double relation of impressions and ideas. On the contrary, he often modified his theory to take into account what he supposed were well-founded observations about human experience.

Book 2 Part 3: *The Direct Passions and the Will*

At the beginning of *Treatise* 2.3 Hume says that understanding the passions depends on an understanding of the will which, although a feeling, is not, properly speaking, one of the passions. Consequently, he focuses first on the will, and then on the direct passions.

THE WILL AND ITS INFLUENCES

In contrast to a number of earlier philosophers, Hume maintains that the will is neither a distinct part or faculty of the mind nor a latent power of choice.[59] He means by the term *will*, he says, 'nothing but *the internal impression we feel and are conscious of, when we knowingly give rise to any new motion of our body, or new perception of our mind*' (2.3.1.2). This impression, also sometimes called *volition*, typically accompanies the direct passions. For example, the impression of will or volition is felt in conjunction with desire whenever the good which is the object of that desire is actually sought by means of 'any action of the mind or body' (2.3.9.7). This same impression of will or volition is felt in conjunction with aversion whenever the evil which is the object of aversion is knowingly avoided.

Hume says that his unorthodox description of the will frees him from traditional puzzles about the correct definition of this faculty. But he is unable to ignore the 'long disputed question concerning *liberty and necessity*' (2.3.1.2).

---

[59] Philosophers important to Hume and who treat the will as a faculty include Malebranche, *The Search after Truth* 1.2 (hereafter *Search*), trans. T. M. Lennon and P. J. Olscamp (Columbus, Ohio: State University Press, 1980), 4. Those who treat it as a faculty understood as a latent power include Locke, *Essay concerning Human Understanding* 2.21.5–7.

Earlier philosophers had in the course of a long and complicated debate come to focus on the will as a faculty that either does or does not have an undetermined liberty or freedom to choose or reject anything presented to it.

On one side of the issue were those who embraced what can be called a libertarian or indifferentist point of view: the view that the will is free in the sense that it is undetermined by anything but its own choice and thus has one form of 'liberty of indifference'. These libertarians did not deny that there are external forces or motives and that these necessarily determine the choices and actions of all those creatures (animals, most notably) that lack freedom of the will. But they did insist that the human will may sometimes remain completely indifferent to these influences and thus, however strong the influences may be, can retain its freedom in the form of an uninfluenced power of choice.[60] They insisted, in other words, that the human will is capable of uncaused actions or choices. On the other side of the issue were those who maintained that all choices of the human will are influenced in such a way that each such choice is the effect of some cause, and thus that any talk of uncaused choices or liberty of indifference is fundamentally unintelligible. This second set of writers typically argued that humans have a form of freedom, but they insisted that this freedom amounts only to the ability to act in accordance with our volitions, which are themselves influenced by our intellectual faculties or passions. Hume aligns himself with this second group by saying that human freedom extends no further than 'liberty of spontaneity', or freedom from coercion and physical constraint.[61]

Hume enters this long-standing dispute by raising and answering three questions:

1. Is the will indifferent to influence? That is, can uncaused choices or actions issue from the will? (2.3.1)
2. Why is it widely thought that the will is indifferent to influence or capable of uncaused choices or actions? (2.3.2)
3. Given that the will is not indifferent to influence, is it the understanding or the passions that influence it? (2.3.3)

1. *Is the will indifferent to influence?* Hume mounts a straightforward, systematic challenge to the libertarian claim that the will may be entirely indifferent to

---

[60] Luis de Molina, with whom this libertarian view is often associated, said that an agent is free (has liberty of indifference) if, all the necessary conditions of acting being in place, he 'can act or not act, or so perform one action that he is equally able to do the contrary' (*On Divine Foreknowledge, Concordia* 4). Leibniz, criticizing the views of a contemporary libertarian, William King, says that King supposes 'true freedom' to consist in 'an indifference . . . complete and absolute; so that, until the will has determined itself, there would be no reason for its determination . . . in choosing without reason one would cause what one chooses to be pleasing' (*Observations on* . . . The Origin of Evil, in *Theodicy*, ed. A. Farrer, trans. E. M. Huggard (London: Routledge, 1951), 406; for King's views, see his *Essay on the Origin of Evil*, trans. Edmund Law (London, 1731; fac. New York: Garland Press, 1978), 154–296).

[61] Anthony Collins, *A Philosophical Inquiry concerning Human Liberty* (London, 1717; fac. New York: Garland Press, 1978), provides a further helpful, contemporary perspective on these issues.

external influence or that it is a faculty from which uncaused actions or choices may issue. He begins by noting that all parties in this dispute agree that, because events in the physical world are connected together causally, there is no liberty or freedom in physical nature. Assuming the normal conditions in which billiards are played, a billiard ball sharply struck by moving balls must necessarily move, and any further balls struck by a moving cue ball are subject to the same necessity. As Anthony Collins put it, even clocks or other machines that seem to be capable of motion are, because they have neither sensory abilities or intelligence, 'subject to an *absolute, physical,* or *mechanical necessity*'.[62] Given agreement on this issue, the only question remaining, Hume suggests, concerns actions of the mind. Are they subject to this same kind of necessity or are they perhaps free of necessity?

To answer this question, Hume focuses on the idea of causal necessity. This idea does not, he reminds us, arise from sensory experience of a direct link between an object called a cause and some other object called the effect of that cause. Neither does it derive from some form of rational insight, an insight that reveals to us from the 'essence of bodies' just how they are necessarily connected together. Rather, as we saw in Book 1, it is only after we have experienced two objects in constant conjunction that we form the idea that they are causally related, and then only because the constant conjunction has produced 'a determination of the mind to pass from one object to its usual attendant' (2.3.1.4). In other words, we find ourselves entirely willing to say that physical nature is subject to necessity even though physical objects or events said to be causally related are perceived to be connected by nothing more than the relations of contiguity, succession, and constant conjunction. Consequently, if we find that these are precisely the relations holding in the moral world, we should be equally ready to grant that this same necessity characterizes this world.

Hume surveys the moral world, and finds that these same relations do hold in it. Motive, on the one hand, and volitions and actions, on the other, are just as regularly and constantly conjoined as a wide range of phenomena in the natural world. 'No union', he says, 'can be more constant and certain, than that of some actions with some motives and characters.' Of course, human behaviour may sometimes seem capricious, but the uncertainty or unpredictability of the moral world is no greater than that routinely observed in the physical world (2.3.1.12–16; *Abs.* 32). The fact to notice is that the experience of irregularities in the natural world never leads us to give up our belief that physical events are determined by causes. Granted, a perfect uniformity of experience provides greater evidence and higher probability than does less uniform experience, but, however mixed our experience, we never conclude that the actions of bodies are uncaused and the work of mere chance. We simply conclude that some events, some outcomes, are more probable than others.[63]

---

[62] Ibid., Preface, p. iii.

[63] Hume does not explicitly argue that we experience no direct tie or link between motive and volition, nor does he need to do so. If such a tie were experienced, it would itself show that the indifferentist position is mistaken.

We respond in the same way to experience of the moral world. A perfect uniformity of moral experience provides greater evidence than does less uniform experience, but, however mixed this experience may be, we never conclude that human actions, including acts of the will, are free in the sense of being uncaused or undetermined. Suppose for a moment that the will is a faculty or a distinct power of the mind. Now, if motives of type *A* (a particular kind of desire, for example) are always followed by actions of type *B* (an action of the will of the kind that results in the satisfaction of the desire specified), then we have, in Hume's terms, a *proof* that *A*-type motives cause *B*-type actions. If our experience is somewhat less uniform, we will be content to say that it is only *probable* that *A*-type motives cause *B*-type actions. If our experience lacks regularity or pattern, we will be content to say that we do not know what kind(s) of motive cause *B*-type actions, but this uncertainty will not leave us ready to say, nor will it force us to say, that these actions of the will are uncaused. We will not be able to say what the cause is, and we may even doubt our ability to find out what it is, but we will have no grounds for concluding that the choices of the will were indifferent or uncaused.

Hume further supports his view by pointing out that what is called *moral evidence* (that is, causal inferences based on the regular conjunctions of motives and actions) is widely and regularly mixed with *natural evidence* (that is, causal inferences based on the regular conjunctions of objects) to form a linked set of connections.[64] As he puts it:

when we consider how aptly *natural* and *moral* evidence cement together, and form only one chain of argument betwixt them, we shall make no scruple to allow, that they are of the same nature, and deriv'd from the same principles. A prisoner, who has neither money nor interest, discovers the impossibility of his escape, as well from the obstinacy of the gaoler, as from the walls and bars with which he is surrounded; and in all attempts for his freedom chooses rather to work upon the stone and iron of the one, than upon the inflexible nature of the other. (2.3.1.17)

Finally, it is useful to recall that Hume explicitly describes the will as a particular feeling, a feeling of volition, and not as a faculty (see 2.3.1.2). This is important because, given that the will is a feeling, it is even less likely to be outside the chain of cause and effect. Supposing the will to be a faculty, we might think it at least mildly plausible to suggest that it is indifferent to influence and thus able to make uncaused choices among the items presented to it; we can, perhaps, conceive of a *faculty* that stands thus aloof from causes. On the other hand, given that feelings in general are taken to be the effects of causes and can be readily explained as such effects, supposing the will to be a *feeling* makes it entirely implausible to suggest that it is free of causal or determining influence. If all other feelings are effects, what grounds could there be for supposing the feeling of volition is not also an effect? None comes readily to mind.

All things considered, then, we find no good reasons to think that, so far as

---

[64] Hume's understanding of causal inference (a transition, of attention and force or vivacity, from a present impression to an associated idea) is discussed above, pp. 131–7.

necessity is concerned, the moral world is different from the physical world. Our idea of necessity is derived from the experience of objects or events found to be contiguous, successive, and constantly conjoined. The events of the moral world are in this respect no different from those of the physical world. The events of both worlds also fall into patterns that give rise to the idea of necessary connection. They fall into patterns, that is, that lead us to conclude that, just as in the physical world *'whatever begins to exist must have a cause of existence'* (1.3.3.1), so too in the moral world whatever begins to exist must have a cause of existence. In short, each act of the will, each choice, must be supposed to have a cause.

2. *Why is it widely thought that the will is indifferent to influence or capable of uncaused choices or actions?* If there are no good reasons for supposing that the will has liberty of indifference and can thus operate outside the chain of cause and effect, why is this view so widely held? In general terms, because we are confused and because we are misled. Hume distinguishes three reasons. First, looking back after actions are completed, it seems to us that, prior to acting, these actions were not caused and necessary. In this, however, we are confused: we mistake *liberty of spontaneity* (the fact that we were not coerced or physically constrained) for *liberty of indifference*. Secondly, we *feel* that we have liberty of indifference. This, however, is a *'false sensation* or *experience'* and not a proof that such liberty exists. The feeling of necessity, we are reminded, is a determination in the mind of an intelligent being. The feeling of liberty amounts to little more than the absence of that determination, not evidence that nothing is influencing the will. We may think, for example, that our will was undetermined because we can imagine ourselves having made a different choice, or, on another occasion, we may actually make that contrary choice. But this does not prove that our will is indifferent and acting without cause or influence. On the contrary, it shows only that the 'desire of showing our liberty' can itself become an influence on the will.

Finally, Hume thinks that religious writers have taken an ill-founded interest in the matter of liberty. These writers claim that to suggest the will and its choices are part of a natural causal chain is to say that the choices of the will are necessary or determined, and to say that is to launch a dangerous attack on morality. If we do not have liberty of indifference, this argument goes, then we are essentially automatons without choice and without responsibility for the actions associated with us. Noting first that a view is not false simply because it is dangerous, Hume goes on to argue that these religious writers have things backward. It is their view, not his, that undermines morality. If my choices and the actions that follow them are not the effects of my deliberations or passions, in what sense am I responsible for them? If these choices are so free as to be uncaused, they appear not to be my choices. And if these choices and actions cannot reasonably be said to be mine, then moral assessments of them (moral praise, blame, reward, or punishment) will be entirely unwarranted. In other words, Hume argues that the libertarian theory that the will may act without causal influence eliminates all moral responsibility. It does so because it disconnects volitions from agents and their motives. As a result, choices (and the actions to which they lead), instead of being the effect of the deliberations or passions of an agent, become mere uncaused happenings lacking any moral or ethical significance.

3. *Given that the will is not indifferent to influence, is it the understanding or the passions that influence it?* Many of Hume's predecessors maintained that the human will is influenced by both reason and the passions. In contrast, Hume argues that reason can never by itself directly influence the will. He also explicitly rejects the closely related claims (*a*), that reason should direct the will, and (*b*), that we are virtuous only to the extent that our choices and actions conform to the direction of reason. Hume also rejected the commonplace view that reason can dispute with the passions over the direction of the will (2.3.3.1). By the early eighteenth century dozens of philosophers had written about the struggle between reason and the passions. Among those whose works Hume knew, Pascal had referred to 'the internal war of reason against the passions', while Bayle described human life as little more that 'a continual combat' between reason and the passions.[65] As might be expected, many moralists were concerned about which of these faculties should win this struggle. The neo-Stoics clearly favoured reason, even to the point of arguing that the mind should be purged of all passions. More moderate writers argued only that reason ought always to govern the passions. Some even granted that the passions, properly governed, could contribute positively to the virtuous life. Still others argued that reason is too slow and feeble to guide us, and hence that the passions must supplement reason. Malebranche, although satisfied that reason and the passions are in conflict, dismissed those who said that we should be guided only by reason: 'experience sufficiently shows us that things are not as reason says they should be, and it is ridiculous to philosophize against experience'.[66] Still, those who believed reason ought to control the passions were typically concerned that reason had in fact become passion's slave. As Bayle had pointed out, virtually every moralist from ancient times to the present had lamented the fact that reason is enslaved, and even Malebranche said that it is difficult to overcome the slavery to which the passions subject us because of our debased nature.[67]

In opposition to these commonplace claims, Hume argued that (1) because the passions alone influence the will, the passions and reason cannot be in conflict over the direction of the will; (2) because the will is not influenced by reason, reason obviously cannot be assigned direction of the will; (3) the subjection of reason to the passions, a subjection about which there had been such widespread lamentation, is perfectly natural and even commendable.

Hume undertakes to show first that reason alone cannot directly influence the will, and then that it cannot directly oppose the influence on the will that

---

[65] Blaise Pascal, *Pensées*, trans. A. J. Krailsheimer (Harmondsworth: Penguin, 1966), 410; Bayle, *Dictionary*, 'Helen', n. Y.

[66] Malebranche, *Search* 5.2, p. 342.

[67] Bayle, *Dictionary*, 'Helen', n. Y; 'Ovid', n. H; Malebranche, *Search* 5.2, p. 342.

the passions do have. The understanding, the faculty of reason, makes use of two kinds of reasoning, demonstrative and probable. It is generally agreed, Hume argues, that it is the prospect of pain or pleasure that arouses in us a desire to modify our circumstances. Such prospects arouse desires to bring about situations that enable us to avoid pain or obtain pleasure. Although both demonstrative and probable reasoning may contribute to our efforts to attain such ends, neither form of reasoning can by itself motivate us to seek any given end. Demonstrative reason, for example, may enable us to draw important conclusions. It may enable a merchant to sum up his accounts, thus leaving him prepared, should he be motivated to do so, to settle these. This form of reason may even enable us to draw conclusions regarding the relations of moral ideas—that truth-telling and virtue are compatible, for example. But, helpful though demonstrative reason may be, Hume insists that no one supposes it capable of motivating us to any particular end.

Much the same analysis applies to probable reasoning. This form of reasoning may enable us to know which course of action is most likely to bring about a given end, but, unless we are motivated to seek that end, this kind of information will be practically worthless. I know any number of nearby places at which I might buy a new car, but as I have no desire for a new car, this information has no significant effect on my behaviour. Whether or not I use this information depends on my desires or passions. They, and not the information, motivate me, a point that can be made, obviously, about all information. Probable reasoning also enables us to know how any given end is to be obtained, and information of this kind does affect subsequent choices and actions. But knowing which actions will produce which effects is not in itself enough to motivate us to undertake those actions in order to produce those effects: 'It can never in the least concern us to know,' Hume says, 'that such objects are causes, and such others effects, if both the causes and effects be indifferent to us' (2.3.3.3). Unless we have a prior interest in those causes and effects, we will make no use of the related information.

This analysis prepares the ground for what Hume calls a 'somewhat extraordinary' pronouncement, namely, that 'Reason is, and ought only to be the slave of the passions, and can never pretend to any other office than to serve and obey them' (2.3.3.4). The discoveries of reason, he has argued, never in themselves either produce or prevent the desires and volitions that lead to action. Notwithstanding the widespread talk about the war between reason and passion, reason and passion never come into direct conflict because they have substantially different roles to play. The passions alone determine our choices, while reason can only inform us about the relations of ideas or the connections between matters of fact. Moreover, so far as Hume is concerned, the fact that reason has only this subsidiary role to play is neither inappropriate nor lamentable. And so he concludes that reason not only is, but also ought to be, governed by the passions.

It would be a mistake, however, to ignore what Hume goes on to say. It is true that reason is merely the servant of the passions, but its role is by no means insignificant. As we have seen, reason informs the passions of the existence and natures of things, and of the steps to be taken if something is to be obtained or avoided. Reason serves, in effect, as the eyes and ears of the passions. Consequently, although reason cannot directly oppose the passions, it does have great influence on them. Our passions, we find, depend on particular judgements or beliefs, and these reason does have an important role in determining. Thus the alteration of a relevant belief may also result in an altered passion. If one of our passions, some desire, is founded on a mistaken belief that certain objects exist, or on a mistaken assessment of objects that do exist, it is reason that would inform us of these mistakes. When it has done so, we can expect the desire we previously felt to be altered or even extinguished. If we pursue some desired end by means that are defective or even counter-productive, it is only reason that can inform us of our mistake. When it has done so, we will find that our actions or desires have been changed. Thus, while Hume is notorious for having said that reason is and ought only to be the slave of the passions, it should not be forgotten that he balanced that striking remark with another: 'The moment we perceive the falshood of any supposition, or the insufficiency of any means our passions yield to our reason without any opposition' (2.3.3.7).

Hume concludes his discussion of the influences on the will by explaining why it is that so many have thought that reason and the passions are in conflict. Those who have made this mistake have failed to realize that we have both calm and violent passions. They have supposed, for example, that anger or hatred or intense desire and aversion are prototypical passions (they have supposed that passions are necessarily intense or violent) and thus have failed to recognize that our calm or virtually emotionless tendency towards benevolence (to mention only one example) is also a passion. Having made that mistake, they go on to the further mistake of supposing that reason and the passions are in conflict. The truth is, however, that the conflict is between the calm and violent passions. Our calm passions may directly influence the will, and in fact do so just as often and just as effectively as do any of the violent passions. It is this conflict between the calm and violent passions that is mistaken for a conflict between reason and the passions. However, the careful, perceptive philosopher will recognize this mistake for what it is and know that only the passions have a direct influence on our volitions.

THE DIRECT PASSIONS

The direct passions are of two kinds: (1) those which are direct responses to pain or pleasure or their expectation. The passions of this kind to which Hume gives the most attention are desire and aversion, grief and joy, hope and fear (2.3.1.1). And (2) those which are natural impulses or instincts producing pleasure and pain (the productive passions). As we have seen, the passions of this kind are 'desire of punishment to our enemies, and of happiness to our friends; hunger, lust, and a few other bodily appetites' (2.3.9.8). Hunger, for example, causes us to think of food as good, and thus to desire it.

In comparison with the indirect passions, the operation of the direct passions of the first kind is simple and straightforward. These passions, Hume says, are 'founded' on pleasure or good and pain or evil. By this he means that I will not experience a passion of this kind unless I am presented with something, some stimulus, that gives me pleasure or pain. Furthermore, the passion once aroused will cease to be felt (although perhaps not immediately) once the stimulus or cause is removed. But, while the cause of an indirect passion produces that passion only indirectly—only by producing a set of impressions and ideas that are the immediate cause of pride or love, for example—the stimulus of a direct passion may operate without this complex mediation. If I perceive something good, something that I believe will give me pleasure, that experience alone is enough to arouse desire, enough to cause me to feel the direct passion of desire. The perception of something evil, something painful, will arouse the feeling or direct passion of aversion.

Hume attempts to specify the factors, in the form of relations, that cause permutations of the direct passions. In general terms, the passions of joy, hope, grief, or fear derive directly from certain ideas, namely, our present ideas of specific past or future events or entities. If we are virtually assured of some good, we feel joy; if this same good is significantly less likely to come about, we feel hope. An evil that is certain to happen causes grief or sorrow; if uncertain, it causes fear (2.3.9.5–6). The nearness or remoteness of the cause of a direct passion is a factor in determining whether that passion will be violent or calm, whether it will, at one extreme, be a forceful, all-consuming feeling, or, at the other, be so soft and emotionless as to be almost unnoticeable (2.1.1.3; 2.3.4).

Why remoteness in time has a greater effect on the passions than does remoteness in space, and why, for example, distance in past time increases admiration more than the same distance in future time, may all be explained by reference to the properties of our ideas of time and space (2.3.7–8). The repeated or customary experience of some things results in inclinations and strong passions, while the repeated experience of other things reduces our interest in them, and results in weak passions. New experience, or novelty, agitates us, and thus it too may strengthen our passions (2.3.5). The imagination and the passions are so closely related that whatever affects the former also affects the latter—livelier ideas result in livelier passions. Thus our memories of recent experiences typically influence the passions more than those of older ones. So too do prospective pleasures or pains consistent with familiar experiences have a greater influence than do the prospects of unusual ones (2.3.6). In short, the relations of resemblance, contiguity, and cause and effect are also often found to determine, and thus to explain, direct passions of the first type. In contrast, those direct and productive passions that derive from natural impulses or instincts (from hunger, for example) are for that reason essentially independent of previous experience. Curiosity, or the love of truth, the subject of the closing section of *Treatise* 2, although a unique passion, is apparently just such a natural instinct. It is also, Hume says, 'the first source' of all his enquiries into human nature.

Book 3: Of Morals

'Of Morals', the third and final book of the *Treatise*, was published in November 1740, nearly two years after Books 1 and 2. In this book, as its title suggests, Hume is concerned with certain fundamental features of morality. More particularly, he undertakes to determine which kinds of perception enable us to make moral distinctions, and then to specify the circumstances in which these unique perceptions arise. The account he gives is intended to be part of the science of human nature discussed in the Introduction to the *Treatise* and to confirm and extend what has already been said about the understanding and the passions (3.1.1.1).

Hume begins his account of morality by reminding readers that we confront the world by means of perceptions. The stronger of these (sensations, passions, and feelings) he continues to call *impressions*. The weaker copies of these found in the memory and imagination he continues to call *ideas* (Advertisement to Book 3). From the fact that 'nothing is ever present to the mind but its perceptions', it follows that every operation of the mind, judgements about moral differences included, must be understood to be either an impression or an idea. As he says, 'To approve of one character, to condemn another, are only so many different perceptions.' Given this fact, Hume concludes that he can best begin his enquiry into morals with a precise question: Which kind of perception, impressions or ideas, enables us to distinguish between virtue and vice? (3.1.1.2–3).

Hume had at least two important and related reasons for wanting to answer this particular question. First, the long-standing debate about the foundations of morality was familiar to him. Participants in this debate had disputed whether morality is based on reason, on the will of God, on a moral sense, on convention and human need, or on some combination of these factors. Hume had mentioned this debate in Book 2, but he deferred substantial discussion of it to Book 3 (see 2.1.7.2). As it turns out, his answer to his question about impressions and ideas is an important part of an attempt to identify the foundations of morality: once he has concluded that moral differences are not distinguished by means of ideas, he can confidently assert that morality is not founded on reason.

Secondly, a principal goal of the *Treatise* is to trace the origin and development of certain kinds of ideas and impressions. *Treatise* 1 is centrally concerned with giving an account of the origin of, and of our belief in, several important ideas (of space and time, necessary connection, and external objects, for example). *Treatise* 2 is centrally concerned with giving an account of the origin of certain impressions of reflection (most of the passions and the will, for example). *Treatise* 3, by showing that moral differences are distinguished by impressions rather than ideas, continues this pattern. Having begun by showing that moral distinctions must depend on impressions (3.1.1), Hume goes on to argue that two unique impressions of reflection, the two moral sentiments—*approbation*, or a distinctive moral pleasure, and *disapprobation*, a distinctive moral pain—provide the basis for our moral distinctions (3.1.2).[68] In the rest of Book 3 Hume identifies and describes in substantial detail the circumstances in which these moral sentiments arise. These circumstances include what we might call the external conditions (the general environment in which humans live) and internal elements (the features of human nature and of individual humans).

Hume soon informs us that our unique moral sentiments arise in two significantly different sets of circumstances. This leads him to say that some virtues are *natural* and others are *artificial*. He argues that the natural virtues (the subject of *Treatise* 3.3) derive directly and immediately from human nature and have 'no dependance on [the] artifice or conventions of men' (3.3.1.1). In contrast, the artificial virtues (the subject of *Treatise* 3.2) do depend on human contrivance and on conventions that have developed over relatively long periods of time. These two kinds of virtue are alike, however, in their dependence on the operation of sympathy, the principle of communication first introduced in *Treatise* 2.[69]

Book 3 Part 1: The Source of Moral Distinctions

By 1740 several generations of early modern moralists had debated the question of the foundation of morality.[70] For many of these writers the fundamental issue had to do with the role of reason in morality. Those who championed reason, the rationalists, argued that morality, if it is not to be reduced to something merely relative or subjective, must be founded on reason. By this they meant, first, that the faculty of mind by which moral distinctions are recognized must be reason, for it is only this faculty that is capable of grasping the real and objective relations of things. Just as it is reason that grasps the eternal and immutable truths of mathematics, so it is reason that recognizes eternal and immutable moral differences. But the rationalists also said something more, something more difficult to understand. They said that morality is founded on *the reason of things*, on, that is, eternal and immutable principles that determine both the natures of all existing things (including all rational beings) and the relations between these things. They were saying, in other words, that moral distinctions are grounded on principles that pre-date the creation of the universe and that (because they are a part of his immutable nature) constrain the Deity himself.

As one such rationalist, John Balguy, put it, reason is '*a Faculty enabling us to perceive, either immediately or mediately, the Agreement or Disagreement of Ideas*'. Virtue or moral goodness is '*the Conformity of our Moral Actions to the Reasons of Things*'. For Balguy, then, a morally right action is an action that is consistent

---

[68] In the discussion that follows, I refer to the distinctive moral pleasure as *approbation*; the distinctive moral pain as *disapprobation*. In Book 3 Hume uses *disapprobation* in just this way, but he at least once (3.1.2.3) uses *approbation* to refer to non-moral pleasures.

[69] On sympathy, see above, pp. 155–7.

[70] For the names of some participants in this debate, see the first annotation to 2.1.7.2.

with the immutable natures of things and the 'real, unalterable, and eternal' relations between these natures.[71] Reason shows us that some actions are consistent with the real natures of agents and of those acted upon, as well as with the relations between them. These actions are right or virtuous. Reason also shows us that some actions are inconsistent with the real natures of agents and of those acted upon, as well as with the relations between them. These actions are wrong or, in the language of Hume's time, 'vicious'. Suppose, for example, an individual, Able, has acted generously towards two other individuals, Baker and Charles. In response, Baker shows gratitude, and Charles does not. According to Balguy, the response of Baker is consistent with the real generosity shown by Able. In consequence, we can say that the response of Baker is consistent with the real natures and relations of things and is accordingly a right or virtuous action. In contrast, the response of Charles is inconsistent with the generosity shown by Able. The response of Charles is inconsistent with the real natures and relations of things, and is for that reason a wrong or vicious action. Balguy also argues that the perception of these real natures and relations produces an obligation to act consistently with them, an obligation so strong and unshakeable that even the Deity himself is 'eternally subject' to the 'Rule of Action' it provides.[72]

THE FAILURE OF REASON

As we have seen, Hume begins his discussion of the foundations of morality by reminding us that 'nothing is ever present to the mind but its perceptions' (3.1.1.2). As perceptions are found in only two forms, impressions or ideas, he is brought directly to ask which of these two forms enables us to recognize moral differences and to make moral judgements. In raising this question, Hume directly confronts the rationalist account of moral foundations. He notes first that those who claim that morality amounts to a conformity with reason and certain unchanging relations of things also claim that moral distinctions can be traced to ideas and their relations, and thus that *reason alone* enables us to make moral distinctions. Then, drawing on important facts about our moral practice, Hume challenges the rationalists with a battery of arguments. These arguments are intended to show that moral distinctions are not the immediate or sole effect of reason, and that the grounds for claiming that morality rests solely on eternal and immutable relations are necessarily inadequate. To that end, he offers at least six arguments intended to show that morality is not founded on reason alone:

    1. The claims of the rationalists are inconsistent with the fact that the very act of making a moral distinction influences our behaviour. Moral distinctions directly and by themselves arouse passions and motivate us to action. In con-

---

[71] John Balguy, *The Foundation of Moral Goodness*, in 2 pts. (London, 1728–9; fac. New York: Garland Press, 1976), 30–3.

[72] Ibid., 32.

trast, reason has no direct influence on our passions or actions, a point established in *Treatise* 2.3.3.[73] Clearly, then, morality is not founded on reason alone (3.1.1.4–8).

2. The claims of the rationalists are inconsistent with the fact that our passions, volitions, and actions, those features of experience that constitute all or most of the moral domain, are not representative. That is, these features are 'compleat in themselves' and do not, as do ideas, stand in a relationship of representation to other perceptions, and hence cannot be said to be true or false. But reason is always and only concerned with just such relationships, either of ideas to ideas or of ideas to matter of fact, and with discovering which relationships are true and which false. Again, we see that morality cannot be founded on reason alone (3.1.1.9–10).

3. The fact that actions sometimes give rise to judgements that contradict previous judgements of reason, so that there are extended senses in which some actions may be said to be *unreasonable*, fails to show that morality is founded on reason. Choosing to act in a way that is inappropriate to some goal is often no more than an innocent mistake of fact, and hence such mistakes are clearly not the only source of immorality, nor are judgements about such mistakes always moral judgements. In addition, the rationalists presuppose, rather than explain, the distinction to which they appeal, namely the distinction between *mistakes of fact* and *mistakes of right* (3.1.1.11–14; see also 2.3.3.5–10).

4. The claims of the rationalists are inconsistent with the fact that moral assessments admit of degrees. We judge the theft of a piece of fruit to be far less reprehensible than the theft of a kingdom. So far as reason is concerned, the two crimes are equally inconsistent with the relations said to hold between owners and their property, and thus should, contrary to actual moral practice, be judged equally reprehensible (3.1.1.13).

5. The claim that reason alone is capable of making moral distinctions entails that such distinctions are either (*a*) some matter of fact discoverable by reason, or (*b*) derived from some distinctive relation of ideas. Experience shows that they are neither. First, as the rationalists insist that morality is capable of demonstration, they obviously do not suppose it to be a matter of fact, for no one supposes facts can be demonstrated. In addition, however closely we look at a morally charged action (at, that is, any action taken to be virtuous or vicious), we never discover virtue or vice to be features of the act *per se*. When, for example, we examine a case of wilful murder the most we discover are 'certain passions, motives, volitions, and thoughts' associated with the agent who performed the act. Hume grants that we learn about this action by means of certain impressions of sensation and that vice and virtue resemble colour or heat or other secondary qualities in one respect (our perceptions of these qualities are all in the mind), but he explicitly denies that virtue and vice

---

[73] See above, pp. 170–2.

are known or distinguished by means of impressions or ideas of sensation (3.1.1.17–18, 26).[74]

Secondly, there is no unique relation of ideas from which moral distinctions derive. The four relations of ideas that provide the basis for demonstration (these are resemblance, contrariety, degrees in quality, and proportions in quantity and number) are found to hold in both the natural and the moral worlds and are obviously not distinctive in the requisite sense. Moreover, if there were such a distinctive moral relation, it would need to fulfill two conditions, at least one of which is impossible to meet:

(*a*) The relation must be found to hold only between specific actions of the mind and specific external states of affairs. We find that we do not assign moral praise or blame to mere thoughts or ideas (to merely imagined acts, for example). This fact of moral experience shows that moral distinctions cannot derive from a relation of ideas. Moreover, were moral distinctions derived from relations of ideas, we would find ourselves making moral assessments of plants and animals. Experience shows that the behaviour of plants and animals, even that which closely parallels morally assessed human behaviour, is not morally assessed. It follows, then, that moral distinctions do not derive from relations of ideas.[75]

(*b*) The rationalist would need to show that this same relation, having eternally and immutably the same effect, necessarily holds for all rational creatures, the Deity included. Given that it has already been shown that connections between cause and effect are learned only through experience, it is clear that this condition cannot be met (3.1.1.19, 22–3).

6. Hume closes *Treatise* 3.1 by noting that every moral theory he has examined gives a flawed account of obligation. Each such theory begins with certain claims about what *is* the case (claims about the existence of the Deity or about human affairs, for example), and then without warning switches to claims about what *ought* or *ought not* to be the case. But, Hume objects, these new claims about what ought or ought not to be incorporate a relation entirely different from those that characterize the factual statements with which the theories begin. For that reason, this relation cannot be 'a deduction from [those] others, which are entirely different from it'(3.1.1.27). This criticism, although apparently not directed exclusively at the rationalists, does constitute a further objection to the claim that morality derives from reason alone.[76]

---

[74] Hume adds that the fact that virtue and vice are experienced only in the mind appears to have no practical consequences whatsoever. Given his commitment to the view that nothing is ever present to the mind but impressions and ideas, this lack of consequence is not surprising: moral perceptions are in this respect exactly like all other perceptions.

[75] 3.1.1.25 is clear on this point: If morality is dependent on relations of ideas, then animals and inanimate objects are morally charged (may be moral or immoral). Animals and inanimate objects are not morally charged. Therefore morality is not dependent on relations of ideas.

[76] There are many extensive discussions of this famous paragraph; to locate some of these, see the bibliographies cited in the Supplementary Reading.

MORAL SENTIMENTS

If it is not by means of ideas and reason that we distinguish or recognize virtue and vice, then, Hume concludes, it must be by means of impressions, by some form of sensation or feeling. Our examination of the morally charged act of wilful murder has already shown us, however, that moral qualities (vice and virtue) produce no impressions of sensation. Consequently, these qualities must make themselves known by means of certain impressions of reflection. The first question is, then, which impressions of reflection serve this function?

For a start we can say that virtue produces in observers an agreeable impression or feeling, a pleasure, while vice, in contrast, produces in observers a disagreeable impression or feeling, a pain. Moreover, virtue and vice are known by means of these impressions. As Hume puts it, 'virtue is distinguish'd by the pleasure, and vice by the pain, that any action, sentiment or character gives us by the mere view and contemplation' (3.1.2.11; see also 3.3.1.30). But, given that many things give rise to pleasure and pain and yet are not taken to be morally charged, clarification is needed. Hume begins to provide this clarification by insisting that the relevant feelings (approbation and disapprobation, the moral sentiments) are readily recognizable for what they are because they are unique feelings. They are, he says, '*particular* pains or pleasures' or sentiments of a 'particular kind'. That this is so, he further contends, means that explaining how it is that we come to feel these unique moral sentiments will be equivalent to understanding moral distinctions themselves. If we call a motive or action virtuous or vicious 'because its view causes a pleasure or uneasiness of a particular kind', then by giving an explanation of that distinctive pleasure or uneasiness we will, he says, 'sufficiently explain the vice or virtue' that causes them (3.1.2.3).

As a first step towards explaining the moral sentiments, Hume counters the suggestion that he is being inconsistent. In *Treatise* 3.1 he had established that animals and inanimate objects are not morally charged. But if it is true that virtue or vice are recognized by means of the pleasures or pains they cause, are we not forced to admit that animals and inanimate objects may be morally charged, may aptly be designated virtuous or vicious? Animals and objects also cause pleasure and pain, the effects by which virtue and vice are said to be known, and thus may reasonably, on Hume's own theory, be taken to be virtuous or vicious. In response, Hume makes three important claims.

1. There are many different kinds of pleasure and pain. The pleasure produced by good music, for example, is different from that produced by a good bottle of wine. Similarly, the kind of pleasure produced by the motives or actions of a person is clearly different from that produced by other kinds of entity.

2. It is only the qualities or actions of persons that give rise to pleasures or pains 'of that *peculiar* kind' which results in moral assessment.[77]

---

[77] At 3.1.2.5 Hume says only that virtue and vice must be found either in 'ourselves or others' (in persons), that they must excite pleasure or pain, and that they will consistently excite one of the four

3. Moral pleasures and pains, the moral sentiments, arise only in highly restricted circumstances. We do not experience one of these distinctive *moral* pains every time the actions of a person cause some form of pain. These very special sentiments are felt only when we abstract from or ignore our own self-interest. The motives and actions of an enemy may cause us substantial pain. But if we abstract from our selfish interests we may find these same motives and actions causing approbation, the distinctive moral pleasure, and thus leading us to judge this enemy to be honourable and virtuous.[78]

Imagine, then, that we observe a specific case of intentional killing. As a consequence of confronting this action, we first experience certain impressions of sensation. We see one person point a pistol at another, we hear shots; we see a person fall lifeless to the ground. In response to this extended action, according to Hume, we can expect to have a particular impression of reflection. We may, in fact, experience several such impressions, including shock or pity, but among these we can expect to find the distinctive impression of moral disapproval or disapprobation.[79] Only if that impression arises will we determine that the killing agent and the killing action are vicious or morally evil. Moreover, we make this determination just because we have this distinctive feeling: we will not need to make use of reason in order to *infer* that moral evil has been encountered. Should we ask why, in contrast, a leopard, seen to have deliberately stalked and killed a gazelle, is not said to be vicious, Hume will tell us that it is because that act, as it does not involve a human agent, does not arouse the distinctive sentiment of disapprobation. Hume does not attempt to explain why this should be the case; it is a fact of our nature that our moral sense is excited by certain features or actions of humans but not by the apparently analogous features of animals and plants.[80] But he does, by means of a discussion of the artificial and natural virtues, try to explain how the moral sense works.

indirect passions all of which (for humans) have persons (the self or 'some other person') for their objects (see 2.1.2.2; 2.2.1.2). In due course he refines his position, claiming (1), that it is only certain relatively durable mental qualities of persons (their intentions, motives, or character traits, for example) that give rise to the moral sentiments, and (2), that actions *per se* are neither virtuous nor vicious, but only the signs of virtue and vice (of virtuous or vicious qualities) in those who perform them. See 3.2.1.2–8, 3.3.1.3–5, and, from Hume's discussion of the passions, 2.2.3.3–8, 2.3.2.6–7.

[78] Hume sums up his account of the origin of the moral sentiments by saying 'that moral distinctions depend entirely on certain peculiar sentiments of pain and pleasure, and that whatever mental quality in ourselves or others gives us a satisfaction, by the survey or reflection, is of course virtuous; as every thing of this nature, that gives uneasiness, is vicious. Now since every quality in ourselves or others, which gives pleasure, always causes pride or love; as every one, that produces uneasiness, excites humility or hatred: It follows, that these two particulars are to be consider'd as equivalent, with regard to our mental qualities, *virtue* and the power of producing love or pride, *vice* and the power of producing humility or hatred. In every case, therefore, we must judge of the one by the other; and may pronounce any *quality* of the mind virtuous, which causes love or pride; and any one vicious, which causes hatred or humility' (3.3.1.3).

[79] Hume's theory does not entail that the hardened, vicious mind will feel disapprobation in such a case.

[80] Hume does not in the *Treatise* discuss the treatment of animals by humans.

Book 3 Part 2: The Artificial Virtues

Hume first mentions the debate over the foundations of morality in *Treatise* 2. There has been much interest, he says, in the question, *'Whether . . . moral distinctions be founded on natural and original principles, or arise from interest and education'*. Without going into detail or choosing sides in the debate, he there suggests that those who said that the alleged distinction between virtue and vice could be traced to self-interest and education had in effect claimed that morality itself has 'no foundation in nature' and is thus merely an arbitrary invention, a matter of convention or law.[81] In contrast, those who said that moral distinctions are founded on *'natural and original principles'* had in effect claimed that 'morality is something real, essential, and founded on nature', something neither arbitrary nor merely conventional (2.1.7.5).[82]

In *Treatise* 3 we learn that Hume thought both parties to this debate were partially correct. There is, he argues, a set of virtues (generosity and humaneness are examples) that are an essential part of human nature and that invariably accompany human experience. These, the subject of *Treatise* 3.3, he calls the *natural virtues*. There is another set of virtues (justice and promise-keeping are examples) that, although they derive from and are consistent with human nature, are conventions, the product of human contrivance. These are the *artificial virtues*.

Providing more detail, we can say of the natural virtues that

(*a*) they are original or inherent features of human nature;
(*b*) these inherent features are specific natural passions that have always motivated specific kinds of human behaviour;
(*c*) these motivating passions produce good on each occasion of their operation;
(*d*) these passions produce positive sentiments of moral approval whenever they are observed to motivate the behaviour of another human.

In contrast, we can say of the artificial virtues that

(*a*) they are not natural and inherent features of human nature;
(*b*) they have not always motivated or influenced human behaviour—they were unknown to humans living in their first, 'uncultivated state' (3.2.2.4). These virtues, although they derive ultimately from inherent features of human nature, and particularly from self-interest as it has been modified by a wide variety of contingent circumstances and necessities, have developed over the course of time in response to just such circumstances and necessities;

---

[81] Hume could have had in mind both egoists (Hobbes and Mandeville, for example) and religious voluntarists (Pufendorf, for example). Religious voluntarists maintain that morality is a free creation of the Deity, and that the Deity could equally well have created very different, even contrary, moral rules or conventions.

[82] Hume could have had in mind both rationalists (Clarke and Balguy, for example) and the moral sense philosophers (Shaftesbury and Hutcheson, for example).

(c) although the uniform practice of an artificial virtue (of justice, for example) appears to be absolutely necessary to the public good, the practice of this virtue may on any given occasion be contrary to both individual and public good. In such cases, the relevant virtuous acts produce only weak sentiments of approval.

Hume argues, in other words, that humans in their original condition had no need for the artificial virtues because their natural virtues or dispositions were adequate to maintain order in small, kinship-based units. But as human society became larger and more complex, circumstances changed (some material goods became scarce, for example), and these changes led to conflicts within or between the existing social units, conflicts that the natural virtues were unable to resolve. As a consequence, conventions regulating property and governance were (gradually) developed. Hume's account of the artificial virtues, found in *Treatise* 3.2, undertakes to explain three related matters: (1) the nature and origin of these conventions; (2) the development of morally significant motives adequate to produce actions conforming to these conventions; and (3) the fact that we have come to feel approbation (moral approval) in response to actions that conform to these conventions, and disapprobation (moral disapproval) in response to those that fail to conform to them.

MOTIVES AND MORAL QUALITIES

Hume begins his explanation of the artificial virtues with an important discussion of the relationship between the proximate causes (the motives) of an agent's actions and the moral character of that agent. He had previously suggested that the moral sentiments arise in response to the actions as well as the motives of human agents.[83] He now argues that actions themselves are lacking in moral character. Actions themselves may appear to be virtuous or vicious but they are so only by extension, only in so far as they are signs of 'certain principles in the mind and temper'. The 'principles' of which they are signs turn out to be the motives that cause agents to perform these same actions. Moreover, it is these underlying motives that are the object of our moral assessments. Thus, to say that a given individual is virtuous is to say that individual has motives of a distinct kind (3.2.1.2).[84]

In making this claim, Hume appears to align himself with a view held by many of his predecessors and contemporaries. In fact, moralists taking fundamentally different positions in the debate about the foundations of morality agree that the motives of individuals determine the moral character of the

---

[83] See above, pp. 179–80; and 3.1.1.10, 16, 26; 3.1.2.4.

[84] See also 2.3.3.3–5; 2.2.2.7. Elsewhere Hume indicates that these motives must be durable or relatively long-lasting features of the mind. We find that these morally relevant features include not only the passions, but also character, dispositions, and intentions.

actions performed by those individuals.[85] These moralists also agreed that an action has moral merit (is morally good) only if it has been produced by a benevolent or other-regarding motive. On this theory, an action motivated by self-interest is never, not even by extension, virtuous. Although such actions may in fact contribute to the public good, that is not enough to make them, or the agent who has performed them, virtuous. To be genuinely virtuous, an action must be performed out of a regard for others.[86] Given that Hume maintains that actions in themselves are always morally neutral, and that what appear to be virtuous actions derive their apparent virtue 'only from virtuous motives, and are consider'd merely as signs of those motives' (3.2.1.2–4), he too may be said to hold that actions are morally good only if motivated by a regard for others. We find, however, that Hume's position on this issue is substantially different from that of his older contemporaries. He never explicitly abandons the view that the moral quality of actions is determined by the motives that cause them, but, as we will see, he does grant that actions initially motivated by some forms of self-interest are, because of the operation of sympathy, regularly taken to be virtuous.

Hume also grants that other motives can mimic those original, virtuous motives that lead us to take some actions to be virtuous or vicious. Having concluded 'that no action can be virtuous, or morally good, unless there be in human nature some motive to produce it, distinct from the sense of its morality', Hume immediately asks if our 'sense of morality or duty' may not be sufficient to motivate us to perform a given action (3.2.1.7–8). He concedes that it may. For example, an individual who feels no gratitude and thus is not motivated by this feeling may none the less act as though he does have the feeling. He may be motivated by the desire to do what is expected of him. This is possible because, over a substantial period of time, some actions come to *appear* to be intrinsically virtuous. As a result, these actions may themselves motivate some individuals to mimic the effects of a more fundamental motive that they lack. But that this may happen presupposes, Hume insists, that a distinct and natural motive has already been at work. An action undertaken because it *appears* to be intrinsically virtuous has this *appearance* only because it resembles other actions that have previously been taken to be virtuous—only because it resembles actions

---

[85] Hume traced this view to Cicero, whom he found to have argued that it is 'on the Goodness or Badness of the Motives that the Virtue of the Action depends' (Letter to Hutcheson, 17 Sept. 1739; *Letters* 1:35). For Cicero's discussion, see *De finibus bonorum et malorum* [*About the Ends of Goods and Evils*] 4.16–17, 43–8. For further discussion of this issue, see the annotations to 3.2.1.2, 4.

[86] 'Actions which in Fact are exceedingly useful, shall appear void of *moral Beauty*, if we know they proceeded from no kind Intentions towards others' (Francis Hutcheson, *An Inquiry into the Original of our Ideas of Beauty and Virtue* 2.3.1 (fac. of 4th edn. Westmead, Hants: Gregg International Publishers, 1969), 167). 'But when an Agent has a view in any particular Action distinct from my Happiness, and that view is his *only Motive* to that Action, tho' that Action promote my Happiness . . . yet that Agent acquires no *Merit*' (John Gay, *Preliminary Dissertation concerning the Fundamental Principle of Virtue or Morality*, in William King, *Essay on the Origin of Evil* (London, 1731; fac. New York: Garland Press, 1978), p. xxvi).

that are taken to be virtuous because they have been produced by a virtuous motive. It is still the case that 'A virtuous motive . . . must precede the regard to the virtue,' the *apparent* virtue, that is, of the action in question (3.2.1.9).[87]

JUSTICE

Hume is now ready to discuss particular artificial virtues; he turns first to justice. Imagine, he begins, that an individual has borrowed a sum of money, having agreed to return this sum by some later date. This date has now been reached and the borrower asks, *'What reason or motive have I to restore the money?'* (3.2.1.9).[88] Sophisticated as we are, we could readily say that justice requires that one repay a loan when it is due. The example, however, is intended to direct our attention to the origins of justice. Imagine that the loan was made a long time ago and in what Hume calls humanity's rude or uncultivated original condition. Our likely reply, made in those circumstances, would completely baffle the borrower. What, a hypothetical Eve would have asked, do you mean by *justice*, and why in any case should one do what is just?[89] In this way Hume forces us to ask still another question: In such morally primitive circumstances what motive to repay the loan could there be? His answer to this question: Absolutely none.

Hume undertakes to establish this point by arguing (1) that there are exactly three original motives to action, (*a*) *self-love*, or a regard for one's private interest, (*b*) *general benevolence*, or a regard for the public interest, and (*c*) *private benevolence*, or a concern to do what benefits some other individual, and (2) that none of these original motives is a natural, universal motive to be just—that none of these original motives would motivate Eve to repay a loan. In support of this complex thesis he notes first that unbridled self-love appears to motivate more unjust acts than just ones.[90] He next notes that there is in human nature no general regard for public interest (our natural generosity is limited), nor

---

[87] The fact that the moral character of an action depends on the motives that produced it proves, Hume wrote to Hutcheson, 'that to every virtuous Action there must be a Motive or impelling Passion distinct from the Virtue, & that Virtue can never be the sole Motive to any Action' (Letter of 17 Sept. 1739; *Letters* 1:35). For further commentary on this point, see the annotation to 3.2.1.8.

[88] In Hume's account, the rules of justice have to do only with external goods or property (see 2.1.10.1; 3.2.2.7). This does not mean that he had no concern for the many other issues that we would suppose to be matters of justice and injustice. It only means he supposes these issues to fall within the scope of other virtues and vices. Thus, for example, a failure to respond to another person's suffering would be inhumane, while the failure to show respect for another person would be a vicious form of pride.

[89] Just as Adam would have found claims about the future behaviour of billiard balls unintelligible (see above, pp. 130–1), so too would Eve have found questions and claims about justice unintelligible.

[90] Hume also argues that, before the conventions of justice were developed, acting in accordance with the impartiality demanded by these conventions would have been seen to be vicious. In our original state, self-interest motivates us to act partially or selfishly. Moreover, the partiality we feel in that original state leads us to expect such partial behaviour, and to treat any significant deviation from this expectation as wrong: such partiality, he later says, has an influence not only on our 'behaviour and conduct in society, but even on our ideas of vice and virtue; so as to make us regard any remarkable transgression of such a degree of partiality . . . as vicious and immoral' (3.2.2.8).

does such a regard appear to be essential to acts of justice. And finally he notes that private benevolence is sometimes best served by violating the rules of justice. If Hume is correct, then there is no effective answer to the first question posed by Eve. In Eve's circumstances, there is no compelling reason or motive for her to repay the loan (3.2.1.9–17).

It is equally important to note that we could not effectively explain to Eve what we were talking about. Because there is no original and natural motive to be just, Eve will not be motivated to repay her loan. But even supposing that we could suddenly import into this uncultivated state a motive to be just, we still could not expect Eve to act justly because she would still not have the slightest idea what is meant by *justice*, and thus she would be unable to understand either explanations or exhortations regarding that virtue. As Hume puts it, in such morally primitive circumstances appeals to justice would have been 'perfectly unintelligible' and, indeed, 'wou'd never have been dream'd of' (3.2.1.9; 3.2.2.8). It is clear that, if morally uncultivated individuals could not so much as conceive of justice, they could not repay a loan because they supposed that was the just thing to do.

To conclude that a morally primitive person would neither understand what justice is, nor have an effective motivation to act justly, is to conclude that justice is an artificial virtue. It is to conclude that justice was unknown in humanity's original condition and has been constituted by conventions developed over a relatively long period of time. It is to conclude that, as Hume puts it, our 'sense of justice and injustice' (our sense that acting justly is the right way to act) 'is not deriv'd from nature, but arises artificially, tho' necessarily from education, and human conventions' (3.2.1.17).

Having reached this important conclusion, Hume turns his attention to two closely related questions. (1) How is it that humans have developed the conventions of justice? And (2) why is it that we treat the observance or neglect of these conventions as a *moral* issue—why do we include justice and injustice among the virtues and vices? (3.2.2.1, 23).

In response to his first question Hume emphasizes humanity's perilous condition. Of all animals, individual humans appear to have the fewest natural advantages in proportion to their needs and desires. Individually, humans are weak, inept, and in constant danger of losing whatever material goods they have gathered together. Only by joining forces could these deficiencies be remedied; only by forming societies could humans add substantially to their strength, their abilities, and their security. As it happens, however, society, *a convention-governed social unit*, was unknown to our most remote ancestors. Fortunately, the development and recognition of the advantages of such units depends upon an ineradicable feature of human nature: sexual appetite. Convention-governed social groups were not a part of our moral beginnings, but such groups emerged naturally enough as a consequence of the process of socialization that begins with sexual appetite and leads to the family, itself a social group (but not, in Hume's view, a convention-governed one). In the beginning, then, a powerful and entirely natural but amoral motive gave rise to small social groups (families) characterized by the kind of natural behaviour that gives rise to expectations and a substantial degree of routine cooperation.

This initial socialization soon enough led some of our ancestors to realize that the leading source of conflict among them arose from disputes about external goods, that it would be in the interest of each individual to reduce these conflicts, and that this end could be achieved by adopting conventions that stabilized the possession of these goods. Hume argues, in short, that the unreflective self-interest that characterizes the morally primitive state and that prevents the development of society was gradually restrained and redirected. But it was self-interest itself, enlightened and socialized self-interest, that brought about this important change and that made society possible. Nor, contrary to the claims of Hobbes and Locke, did the change take place all at once as individuals made explicit promises to one another. The initial conventions of justice were, rather, the result of individuals tacitly recognizing that they would each gain by accepting and following certain restraints regarding property, provided only that others would do the same thing (I refrain from stealing your sheep as long as you refrain from stealing mine). In fact, the restraints and expectations that produced the peace and order of society were articulated as explicit rules of property only after they had begun to have effect (3.2.2.1–22).

Assuming this answer to his question about the origins of justice is correct, what has Hume accomplished? For a start he has shown that justice is the product of a historical process dependent on implicit contrivance, and thus that it conforms to his concept of an artificial virtue. He has also shown that justice is not founded on the discovery, by reason, of eternal and immutable connections or relations of ideas. Justice arose because certain contingent conditions made it necessary to human well-being or survival. Had those conditions been different (had not material goods been in relatively short supply, for example) rules of property would not have been necessary for peace and order. Even now, were these conditions to change, justice would alter or wither away. And he has also confirmed that justice is not founded on ideas. The practice of justice gave rise to the relevant ideas, not vice versa. Only after conventions were tacitly developed by the practice of mutual restraint were the ideas of justice and injustice formed. The same must also be said of the subsidiary ideas of property, right, and obligation.

Hume himself sums up his accomplishment in a perhaps unexpected way. That portion of his answer just reviewed explains, he says, our '*natural* obligation to justice, *viz.* interest'. This appears to be Hume's way of saying he is satisfied that he has shown why, as the result of the gradual process he has described, individual humans have gained a motive to justice, namely, *enlightened* self-interest, that members of our species originally lacked, and also why these same individuals have come to feel that they ought to act justly. In short, he has explained how we as a species developed conventions to which we are now motivated to conform, and thus how we came to feel, when we find ourselves in particular circumstances, that (for self-interested or prudential reasons) we *ought* to conform to those conventions or to feel that we *ought* to act justly. That much, at least, we might have expected Hume to say. But he now tells us that he still needs to explain why it is that we treat the observance or neglect of the conventions of justice as a *moral* issue. He still needs, that is, to explain our '*moral* obligation' to justice (3.2.2.23).

Determining what Hume means by this comment is not easy. But given that he indicates that this '*moral* obligation' is 'the sentiment of right and wrong', he seems to be reminding us that the broader aim of *Treatise* 3 is to explain the origin of the distinctly moral sentiments, while at the same time telling us that he does not suppose that the foregoing historical account of justice provides a complete explanation of the fact that we feel the unique moral sentiments in response to just or unjust acts. Hume apparently sees the development of justice as passing through three stages and thus is here telling us that he has not yet explained the third and final stage.

What Hume supposes to have been our original or 'wild uncultivated state' (3.2.2.4) would have been stage 1 in the development of justice. In the part of *Treatise* 3.2.2 just reviewed he has explained our movement from this stage, wherein there were no conventions of justice and wherein any reference to such conventions would have been unintelligible, to stage 2. This second stage is characterized by the fact that the conventions that define and protect property have been developed. To say this is not only to say that individuals routinely respect each other's possessions, but also that they now have and understand the concept of justice and, along with it, the concept of property and the sense that it is appropriate to respect the property of others. The newly developed convention not only makes the concept of justice intelligible, but also gives this concept an action-guiding force. As Hume puts it, 'After this convention, concerning abstinence from the possessions of others, is enter'd into, and every one has acquir'd a stability in his possessions, there immediately arise the ideas of justice and injustice; as also those of *property, right*, and *obligation*' (3.2.2.11). Thus, while Eve, a stage 1 individual, was unable to understand our talk about justice, some of her descendants are entirely capable of understanding this concept. They also understand that being just means that one conforms one's behaviour to the conventions of justice, that conforming to these conventions is in one's best interest, and hence that this is the appropriate or prudent thing to do. To put this differently, humans in stage 2 have developed important new capabilities. They have developed and understand the conventions of justice; they have developed a motive (enlightened self-interest) to maintain these conventions; and they now feel a form of approval in response to actions that conform to these conventions and a form of disapproval in response to those that do not. Still remaining to be answered, however, is Hume's second question, why do acts of justice and injustice arouse the distinctive moral sentiments? The initial motive to justice is self-interest, not that regard for others (the 'first virtuous motive') which was earlier said to be an essential component of our moral approvals. Why, then, do we now give *moral* approval to acts of justice? Why, then, is there a stage 3, a stage in which we suppose we have a '*moral* obligation' to be just? (3.2.2.23).

Near the end of *Treatise* 3.2.2 Hume says that a complete answer to his second question depends upon later discussions found only in *Treatise* 3.3, but he none the less provides an enlightening sketch of his view of how it is that we come to attach *moral* significance to what is initially only a self-regarding or prudential concern that the conventions of justice be maintained. In the normal and slowly developing course of events, the societies made possible by the conventions of justice grew significantly larger and more complex. As a result, it became more difficult for an individual to see how her or his private interest was being served by adherence to the conventions now in place. As a result, some individuals began to disregard these conventions. Quite simply, they began to act unjustly, perhaps without even noticing that they were doing so. Other individuals, however, did invariably notice when these conventions were violated and they themselves were thereby harmed. Moreover, even when such unjust actions were remote and thus did not harm those who only observed them from a distance, these observers none the less disapproved of them. They did so, according to Hume, because they found such unjust behaviour 'prejudicial to human society, and pernicious to every one that approache[d] the person guilty of it' (3.2.2.24). In fact, even those individuals who acted unjustly found themselves made uneasy by their own unjust actions. Somehow a still further stage of development was reached. What had been initially a self-regarding concern that the conventions of justice be maintained (the situation in stage 2) became in addition an other-regarding concern that these conventions be followed (the situation in stage 3, the final stage and that which we ourselves are in).

Hume tells us that two features of human nature made this important moral development possible. The first feature is our tendency to establish general rules, and to give to these rules an inflexibility that can withstand even the pressures of self-interest. Once we have established the conventions that are to govern the possession and exchange of property, our sentiments may be influenced by these conventions even when they or their use conflicts with the self-interest that has produced them. Conventions having that kind of continuing force exercise at least a partial check on self-interest.

The second feature is sympathy. Hume recognizes that any particular act of justice may be contrary to both private and public good:

a single act of justice, consider'd in itself, may often be contrary to the public good; and 'tis only the concurrence of mankind, in a general scheme or system of action, which is advantageous. . . . if we examine all the questions, that come before any tribunal of justice, we shall find, that, considering each case apart, it wou'd as often be an instance of humanity to decide contrary to the laws of justice as conformable to them. Judges take from a poor man to give to a rich; they bestow on the dissolute the labour of the industrious; and put into the hands of the vicious the means of harming both themselves and others. The whole scheme, however, of law and justice is advantageous to the society and to every individual. (3.3.1.12)

Hume tells us, in other words, that only an unremitting commitment to the system of justice is beneficial to all concerned, and yet few would seem to have sufficient motive to maintain such a commitment. It is our inherent principle of communication, sympathy, that makes this commitment possible. Sympathy enables us to transcend our narrowly selfish interests and thus to feel approbation in response to actions that maintain the system of justice, and disapprobation in response to those that fail to give such support. It does so by enabling observers to feel the pleasures and pains produced in others affected by just or unjust acts that have no direct bearing on these observers. Hume argues at length that self-interest was 'the original motive to the *establishment* of justice', but he then goes on to insist we feel the moral sentiments in response to just and unjust actions only because of sympathy (3.2.2.24). If, for example, I observe that Jones is pained by the unjust action of Smith, then the operation of sympathy causes me to feel not only Jones's pain, but also the disesteem this pain has caused her to feel for Smith. More generally, as Hume later sums up the matter, just actions, once the conventions of justice are established, are '*naturally* attended with a strong sentiment of morals; which can proceed from nothing but our sympathy with the interests of society' (3.3.1.12). Our disposition to form and follow general rules and our ability to share sentiments with our fellow humans have enabled us to evolve to the point that we feel the distinctive moral sentiments in response to just or unjust actions.

ADDITIONAL ARTIFICIAL VIRTUES

Hume discusses four additional artificial virtues, promise-keeping; allegiance, or loyalty to government; treaty-keeping; and chastity. None of these virtues was found in stage 1, and the development of each has been dependent upon the needs and necessities of humankind. As we will see, the development and subsequent operation of each to some degree parallel the development and operation of justice.

Promise-keeping. If the keeping of promises were a natural virtue, Hume says in 3.2.5, then humans would have originally had a disposition to make and keep promises or contracts. But originally, he argues, humans did not so much as know what a promise was. Originally, there were no promises, and so there would have been no motive to honour them and, obviously, no moral sentiment felt in response to the keeping or breaking of them. It was only as our ancestors found that they as individuals needed the help of other individuals, and for that purpose needed also a means of securing future relations (particularly those having to do with external goods), that the concept and the practice of promising arose. That is, humans began to make simple contracts with one another: If you'll help me with my harvest today, then I'll help you with yours tomorrow. As this practice became commonplace and clearly understood, enlightened self-interest, and then sympathy, made the keeping of such promises a duty of the highest order. This is in effect to say that as the practice developed, individuals came to expect those who promised to keep their promises. They came first, for self-interested reasons, to approve of those who kept their promises and to disapprove of those who broke their promises. Later they came to feel approbation and disapprobation, the distinctive moral sentiments, in response to the keeping or breaking of promises.

Allegiance. Our sense of allegiance, according to Hume, builds on the virtues of justice and promise-keeping, and hence is clearly an artificial virtue. Society, our ancestors found, is necessary for our survival, and hence societies were formed. Because justice and promises were found to be necessary for the survival of society, conventions constituting them were developed and practised. But it was then found that our deep-seated tendency to put unreflective or short-term interests before enlightened or long-term interests threatened the very societies (especially larger, economically advanced ones) on which our well-being depends. To rectify this situation, to curb their own unruly tendencies, our ancestors invented and established governments (3.2.7). Either tacitly or, sometimes, in consequence of an explicit promise, they chose a governor whose task it was to enforce those conventions necessary for the existence of society. Moreover, whether the citizens of these newly emerged states came to recognize some head of state gradually and implicitly, or at some particular time explicitly promised to obey some particular governor, they did come to feel the duty of allegiance (3.2.8). They came to expect that those within the circle of their now *governed* society would conform to the laws of this society, and to feel that they ought to obey and be loyal to their ruler or state. Hume argues that it was at first enlightened self-interest that produced this sense of obligation, but that citizens came later to feel also the distinctive moral sentiments in response to actions showing or failing to show allegiance (see especially 3.2.10.3). He notes in particular that the 'uneasiness' aroused by 'seditious and disloyal actions' led early citizens (just as it now leads us) to take such actions to be vicious or morally wrong (3.2.8.7). In the end, then, our obligation to allegiance, like that to justice, has both a natural and a moral foundation (see 3.2.11.4).

Treaty-keeping. This virtue, the subject of 3.2.11, originates in circumstances similar to those that produce the convention of promising. Nations, like individuals, need one another's help and the security offered by contractual agreements. Consequently, rulers have learned to make promises, in the form of treaties, that bind whole nations. Hume notes, however, that treaties have not the same obligatory force as individual promises. There are also laws of nations, or implicit conventions governing the interactions of states. But because the self-interest of nations and rulers is relatively weakly implicated in the interactions between nations, both the natural and moral obligations to maintain the laws of nations or to honour treaties are weaker than the obligations of private individuals to keep their promises.

Chastity and modesty. Concerned lest his discussion of treaty-keeping suggest that the artificial virtues apply only erratically, Hume in 3.2.12 turns his attention to chastity and modesty. That chastity and modesty are widely taken to be women's virtues he supposes too obvious to require argument. He also supposes it widely understood that these virtues are conventional rather than natural. Consequently, Hume's goal is to show how our ideas of chastity and modesty 'arise from education, from the voluntary conventions of men, and from the interest of society' (3.2.12.2).

Earlier theorists had, like Hume, maintained that society derives ultimately from sexual union and the resulting family.[91] Hume notes, however, that the bond that maintains the traditional family unit is itself dependent upon the commitment of the male to this unit. He also notes that the connection between a male and his children is not as obvious as that between a female and those same children, and then goes on to argue that only if a male can be assured that he has fathered a particular child will he feel the parental bond that motivates him to contribute to the care of that child. It was in order to produce this bond and assurance that chastity came to be expected of women. If a woman permits herself to engage in sexual activity only with her husband, then a link, a conventional or artificial link, is created between her children and her husband. When that link is strong, the husband can be expected to contribute to the care of these children. The parallel virtue of modesty has been developed and inculcated because it reinforces this important link. The woman who not only is rigorously faithful to her husband, but also always appears to be chaste is said to strengthen the grounds for believing that her children are also her husband's children. As a consequence, the conventions to which women are expected to conform come in time to encompass matters having little or no connection with sexual activity. Where the interests of both individuals and society are so obviously involved, Hume adds, the development of such behaviour-guiding conventions is only a matter of time. And it is also only a matter of time until we find ourselves feeling the distinctive moral sentiments in response to chaste or unchaste behaviour. Human interests or needs give rise to the conventions regarding chastity and modesty, and then, once again, the operation of sympathy produces a *moral* concern for these conventions.

Book 3 Part 3: Natural Virtues and Natural Abilities

In comparison to his explanation of the artificial virtues, Hume's account of the natural virtues may seem uncomplicated. As we saw above (p. 181), the natural virtues are those founded on certain inherent features of human nature, features that have motivated human behaviour from its very beginning. At the outset of 3.3.1 Hume says that these 'entirely natural' virtues 'have no dependance on the artifice and contrivance of men'. Later in the same section he indicates that these virtues are natural passions or dispositions and that, in further contrast with the artificial virtues, they produce good on each occasion of their practice and a positive sentiment of approbation each time they are observed. Near the end of the section he says that, while all the artificial virtues contribute to the public good, and indeed exist only because they do so, some of

---

[91] For references to three such theorists, see the annotation to 3.2.2.4.

the natural virtues contribute only to the private good of those who possess them.

Hume does not in the *Treatise* provide his readers with a definitive list of the natural virtues. In 3.3.2 he assumes that a well-founded and well-modulated pride is a natural virtue. A section later he suggests that generosity, humanity, compassion, gratitude, friendship, fidelity, zeal, disinterestedness, and liberality are such virtues. At 3.3.4.7, while discussing natural abilities, he notes that industry, perseverance, patience, activity, vigilance, application, and constancy are useful virtues, and that prodigality, luxury, and irresolution are vicious (see also 3.3.1.24). But in fact Hume maintains that it is the *'grammarians'* (those charged with determining the meanings of words) who have the difficult chore of determining which qualities of mind deserve to be called virtues and which are only natural abilities. In contrast, his task, the task suited to a philosopher, is that of accounting for the sentiments of approbation or disapprobation aroused by such qualities (3.3.4.4).

Hume addresses this task by means of a review of many of the important conclusions of Books 2 and 3, a review that highlights the role sympathy has in the formation of moral sentiments. He begins by reminding us that:

(*a*) Humans are motivated principally by the effects of pleasure and pain, by, that is, desires and aversions, and such direct passions as grief, joy, hope, and fear (3.3.1.2).

(*b*) If the objects or qualities that produce pleasure and pain are related to us in specifiable ways (if we own them or if they are such qualities of ourselves as virtue or beauty), then they also cause one or more of the four indirect passions, pride, humility, love, or hatred (3.3.1.2).

(*c*) Moral distinctions depend on unique feelings of pleasure and pain, the moral sentiments, which are excited in response to 'mental qualit[ies] in ourselves or others' (3.3.1.3).

(*d*) These same mental qualities (such qualities of mind as character traits, dispositions, or intentions) also produce the four indirect passions. This fact leads to the conclusion that whatever qualities of mind produce love or pride may also be called virtues, while those that cause hatred or humility may also be called vices (3.3.1.3).

(*e*) Actions take on a moral character (are taken to be virtuous or vicious) only if they are produced by these relatively durable qualities of mind, and this because the moral sentiments are excited by actions only if these actions are themselves produced by, and hence the signs of, such durable qualities of mind (3.3.1.4–5).

(*f*) Those and only those relatively durable qualities of mind capable of producing the unique sentiment of approbation are virtues. Those and only those relatively durable qualities of mind capable of producing the unique sentiment of disapprobation are vices (3.3.1.5).

To discover why the moral sentiments arise only in response to 'mental qualities' and why moral assessments are of persons and not actions, we need to
look again, Hume says, at sympathy (3.3.1.6–7).

Hume begins this further investigation by reminding us that the minds of
individual humans are so much alike that we are naturally sympathetic, that we
naturally communicate passions and sentiments to one another. As we learned
in Book 2, it is this ability to communicate feelings that enables observers to be
pleased by precisely those objects (a beautiful house, for example) that please
those who possess them, or those qualities of mind (the virtue of being just, for
example) that please those who are affected by them. It is because of this same
ability to communicate that any durable quality of mind that benefits and thus
pleases another pleases those who observe this effect. We are pleased when a
father's affection, a durable quality of mind or character trait, leads him to care
for his children because his actions please these children and we by sympathy
share their pleasure. When we note that the sentiment we feel in these particular circumstances is the unique sentiment of approbation (a calm form of love
or esteem), and that it is just such qualities or traits as parental affection, recognized in just this way, that are identified as virtues, we begin to see why Hume
is ready to say that morality depends upon the principle of sympathy. When he
later argues that it is only by means of this principle that we are able to adopt
that general or impartial point of view that both makes possible and characterizes morality, we see why he supposes that 'the true origin of morals' will be
understood only when we understand the role played by sympathy (3.3.1.6–10;
3.3.3.2).

Hume's expanded discussion of sympathy includes a further important
claim. The qualities that give rise to the moral sentiments are of four kinds.
They are either

1. useful to those others who observe them; or
2. useful to the person who possesses them; or
3. immediately agreeable, without being useful, to those others who
   observe them;[92] or
4. immediately agreeable, without being useful, to the person who
   possesses them.

The principal concern of the middle sections of *Treatise* 3.3 (Sects. 2–5) is to
show that the approbation associated with the natural virtues and abilities
depends on the operation of sympathy and on qualities of these four kinds.

Hume's first illustration of his theory is intended to explain why it is that
a well-founded and well-modulated pride, here designated as 'greatness of
mind', is taken to be a virtue, while an excessive pride is taken to be a vice. The
key, we are told, is that individuals who are praised for their greatness of mind
are found to possess qualities that are immediately pleasing to observers (the

[92] Qualities are 'immediately agreeable' if they are agreeable directly or without any intermedi-
ary perception; a quality that pleases before we have had an opportunity to reflect on its potential
usefulness is directly or immediately pleasing in this sense.

third of the four types just listed). To show that this is the case Hume refers us to two previously discussed 'principles' or features of human nature, sympathy and comparison.[93] He then goes on to argue that, while comparison can sometimes cause us to envy and even despise those who are more able than ourselves, sympathy is the stronger principle. Because it is, we typically esteem such superior individuals. By the operation of sympathy the pleasure of their well-founded pride is conveyed to those who observe it. Thus conveyed, this pleasure is indistinguishable from those feelings of pleasure that constitute the moral sentiments. Thus conveyed, this pleasure is *approbation*. If on the other hand the pride we observe is not well founded or well modulated (suppose the observed individual to be in fact inferior to ourselves or arrogant and disdainful), we find that, because of the effects of comparison, we feel pain or *disapprobation*. Given that those mental qualities that excite approbation are designated virtues, and those that excite disapprobation are designated vices, it follows that a justly proportioned pride is a virtue, while an excessive pride is a vice. Hume also argues that a well-founded pride is a quality of the second type, a quality useful to the person who possesses it. Self-esteem, as we might call it, is an asset to those who possess it, and as such will be a source of pleasure to them. When this pleasure is conveyed to observers by the operation of sympathy it constitutes a further approbation of pride.[94]

Hume next undertakes the somewhat simpler task of showing why, on his theory, '*goodness*' or benevolence is taken to be a virtue (3.3.3.1). We find by experience that the generosity of individuals is normally confined to a narrow circle of family and friends. We also find that, even if an individual is generous only within that circle, so that we who are outside the circle obtain no benefit from the generosity we observe, sympathy causes us to be pleased with this generosity and to feel the sentiment of esteem or approbation. Hume grants that the nearness or remoteness of the persons benefited affects the intensity of our feeling of approbation, but this fact proves to be unimportant. Experience shows that we are able to overlook the intensity of our feelings in order to form a general and inalterable moral standard (see also 3.3.1.16). Moreover, benevolence is counted among the virtues not only because it is useful to others but also because it is pleasing to the person who possesses it. That is, because it pleases those who possess it, benevolence provides, by means of sympathy, a second source of the pleasure we feel in response to it. We find, then, that the processes that lead us to take greatness of mind to be a virtue also lead us to treat benevolence as one. This latter point is of especial interest to Hume. If we at least sometimes give our approbation to benevolence simply because it is

[93] For an account of comparison, see esp. 2.2.8.2, 6–20 and above p. 162; for sympathy, see esp. 2.1.11, 3.3.1.7–12, and above pp. 155–7.

[94] It is important to realize that Hume's primary interest here, as it often is in the *Treatise*, is descriptive, not normative. His observation of our moral practice had convinced him that pride, in the form of 'greatness of mind', is included among the natural virtues, and that excessive or unjustified pride is included among the vices. His goal is not to justify this moral practice, but to explain how it has come to be as it is.

pleasing to its possessor and without the least expectation of advantage to ourselves or others (see 3.3.3.4), then we can see that Hobbes and Mandeville, who deny just this possibility, are mistaken.

NATURAL ABILITIES

Many moralists, Hume says, suppose that the distinction between moral virtues and natural abilities is clear and of great significance. In contrast, Hume shows that, given his account of the foundation of morals, this claim is highly doubtful. There may be differences between virtues and abilities, but these differences are relatively slight and no greater than the differences between particular virtues. In addition, analysis shows that virtues and at least some natural abilities are alike in three important ways.

(a) Those natural abilities which are qualities of mind (good sense, for example) have the same general effect on observers that the virtues have: they produce esteem or approbation.

(b) One must have such abilities if one is to have a good reputation. The person who lacks, for example, good sense will scarcely be thought to be of good character.

(c) The natural abilities are by some said to be involuntary, leaving no room for freewill, while the virtues are allegedly voluntary. But this claim is false. At least some virtues (fortitude and magnanimity, for example) and their complementary vices seem to be (as we might put it) a part of our genetic endowment and beyond our control. On the other hand, some natural abilities (patience, for example) can be voluntarily developed. Finally, it is by no means clear that we feel approbation only in response to qualities that have been voluntarily embraced.

The more important point to be made is that we approve or esteem the natural abilities principally because they are useful to those who possess them. They enable their possessors to get on in the world, and thus give them pleasure. We as observers share this pleasure, and thus it is certain that we will, in the usual manner made possible by sympathy, feel approbation in response to these abilities. Natural defects are disapproved and often taken to be vices because they have the contrary effect. Natural defects cause pain in those who have them, and then cause uneasiness or disapprobation in those who observe and thus share this pain. We find, too, that some natural abilities (wit, for example) are esteemed because they are agreeable to others, and still others (good humour, for example) because they are agreeable to the person who possesses them. In each such case it is sympathy that accounts for the approbation and disapprobation of those who observe these several effects. In this respect, the virtues and natural abilities are exactly alike.

There are limits, however, to Hume's claims about the similarities between virtues and abilities. He grants that even such natural *intellectual* abilities as wit and good humour arouse sentiments of approbation that are both slightly different from and slightly weaker than those aroused by the virtues. These differences, he argues, are not great enough to establish that the natural abilities constitute a species separate from virtue. Problems arise for him, however, when he considers the natural *physical* abilities (such qualities as strength or beauty, for example). These qualities also produce pleasure or pain in so far as they are agreeable or useful to their possessors or to others. Consequently, they also arouse pleasure in observers by means of the operation of sympathy. But this pleasure, Hume insists, is distinctly different from our moral sentiments. For that reason, we do take physical abilities to constitute a species distinct from virtue. Unfortunately, Hume is unable to explain this crucial difference of feeling. 'There is', he unhelpfully concludes, 'something very inexplicable in this variation of our feelings; but 'tis what we have experience of with regard to all our passions and sentiments' (3.3.5.6).

THE CONCLUSION OF BOOK 3

In conclusion, Hume summarizes briefly his reasons for supposing that 'sympathy is the chief source of moral distinctions'. It is only because of sympathy, he reminds us, that we are able to feel approbation in response to actions contributing to the public good. Given that our approbation for acts of justice depends entirely on their 'tendency to the public good', it is clear that it is sympathy that accounts for our approbation of these acts (3.3.6.1). The same is true, *mutatis mutandis*, of the other artificial virtues. It is also sympathy that enables us to feel approbation in response to the agreeable and useful qualities of individuals, to, that is, just those qualities that we take to be virtues. Not satisfied with this summary, Hume goes on to suggest that his moral theory, relying as it does on sympathy, provides a new defence of the 'cause of virtue' (3.3.6.3). His theory agrees with that of Shaftesbury and Hutcheson in so far as they had found that our ability to make moral distinctions derives from original features of the human mind. The theory of the *Treatise*, by showing that the most important of these original features is sympathy and that sympathy is itself morally praiseworthy (because it is intrinsically other-regarding), represents, Hume believes, an advance on these earlier theories.

Aware that Hutcheson had criticized him for saying that justice is an artificial virtue, Hume goes on to note that even the artificial virtues are founded on inherent features of human nature. They are founded, first, on our deeply rooted self-interest, and then on our tendency to approve (because of the operation of sympathy) actions that contribute to the common good. These same considerations could be used to show that human happiness is dependent upon the practice of virtue. He could, in other words, go on to paint attractive pictures of morality. In doing so he would be encouraging his readers to be virtuous and would thus be evincing that 'Warmth in the Cause of Virtue' that Hutcheson had said he lacked. But 'reflections' of that sort would be ill placed in the work he has written. The moral philosopher, he replied in a letter to Hutcheson, must consider the human mind either as an Anatomist or as a Painter; either to discover its most secret Springs & Principles or to describe the Grace & Beauty of its Actions. I imagine it impossible to conjoin these two Views. Where you pull off the Skin, & display all the minute Parts, there appears something trivial, even in the noblest Attitudes & most vigorous Actions: Nor can you ever render the object graceful or engaging but by cloathing the Parts again with Skin & Flesh, & presenting only their bare Outside. An Anatomist, however, can give very good Advice to a Painter or Statuary: And in like manner, I am perswaded, that a Metaphysician may be very helpful to a Moralist; tho' I cannot easily conceive these two Characters united in the same Work. Any warm Sentiment of Morals, I am afraid, wou'd have the Air of Declamation amidst abstract Reasonings, & wou'd be esteem'd contrary to good Taste. And tho' I am much more ambitious of being esteem'd a Friend to Virtue, than a Writer of Taste; yet I must always carry the latter in my Eye, otherwise I must despair of ever being servic[e]able to Virtue.[95]

The Abstract *and the Early Reception of the* Treatise

Hume and many of his early readers were unhappy with the *Treatise*. Several journals reviewed the two volumes published in 1739, and most complained that the work was, where not clearly mistaken, difficult to comprehend. Hume, sensitive to this negative assessment of his literary capabilities, published in March 1740 the *Abstract* of the *Treatise*. This brief work is not an abridgement of the *Treatise*, but an attempt to make this long work clearer by outlining the 'CHIEF ARGUMENT' of *Treatise* 1 (*Abs.* title).[96] But even as he was publishing the *Abstract* Hume was telling Hutcheson that he was impatient to prepare a second edition of the *Treatise*, 'principally on Account of Alterations I intend to make in my Performance'.[97] Regrettably, no revised second edition was ever to appear. The first edition sold so poorly that, when its publishers died about 1760, dozens of copies were sold in bulk for a few pennies each. This lack of commercial success prevented Hume from preparing a revised edition of the *Treatise* and apparently led him to say, a few months before his death in 1776, that 'Never literary Attempt was more unfortunate than my Treatise of human Nature. It fell *dead-born from the Press*'.[98]

This lack of commercial success did not prevent Hume from making further

---

[95] Letter of 17 Sept. 1739; *Letters* 1:32–3; see also the final sentences of 3.3.6.

[96] This argument is discussed above, pp. 129–33. The *Abstract* was published anonymously and written as though the work of someone other than the author of the *Treatise* (Hume refers to himself as 'the Author' or by means of third-person pronouns), but some of his acquaintances knew that he had written the work. For brief accounts of the evidence that Hume is the author of the work, see J. M. Keynes and P. Sraffa, Introduction, *An Abstract of . . . A Treatise of Human Nature* (Cambridge: Cambridge University Press, 1938), pp. xxiii–xxxi; D. Raynor, 'The Authorship of the *Abstract* Revisited', *Hume Studies*, 19 (1993), 213–17; and D. F. Norton, 'More Evidence that Hume Wrote the *Abstract*', *Hume Studies*, 19 (1993), 217–22.

[97] Letter of 16 Mar. 1740; *Letters* 1:38.

[98] *My Own Life*, in *Letters*, 1:2; Norton (ed.), *Cambridge Companion*, 352.

efforts to present his philosophical discoveries. Even before he had published *Treatise* 3 he had formed the intention of making 'a new Tryal' in which the roles of practical moralist and abstract metaphysician would be made to 'agree a little better'.[99] True to his intent, he eventually recast his views into what he supposed a more palatable form, and as a result published three shorter works corresponding to the three books of the *Treatise*. These shorter works were *Philosophical Essays concerning the Human Understanding* (now known as *An Enquiry concerning Human Understanding*), first published in 1748; *An Enquiry concerning the Principles of Morals*, first published in 1751; and *Of the Passions* (now known as *A Dissertation on the Passions*), first published in 1757.

It must be noted that Hume preferred these recastings of the *Treatise* to the original work itself. He told a friend that he believed the first of them to

contain every thing of Consequence relating to the Understanding, which you woud meet with in the Treatise; & I give you my Advice against reading the latter. By shortening & simplifying the Questions, I really render them much more complete. . . . The philosophical Principles are the same in both: But I was carry'd away by the Heat of Youth & Invention to publish too precipitately. So vast an Undertaking, plan'd before I was one and twenty, & compos'd before twenty five, must necessarily be very defective. I have repented my Haste a hundred, & a hundred times.[100]

In addition, Hume took his second *Enquiry*, that concerning the principles of morals, to be 'of all my writings, historical, philosophical, or literary, incomparably the best', thus giving it clear preference over *Treatise* 3. Even more to the point, Hume tired of having his philosophical views and abilities judged on the basis of a youthful work he regretted publishing, and so he composed and included in his *Essays and Treatises on Several Subjects* (the authorized collection of his works) this notice:

Most of the principles and reasonings contained in this volume, were published in a work in three volumes, called *A Treatise of Human Nature*: A work which the author had projected before he left College, and which he wrote and published not long after. But not finding it successful, he was sensible of his error in going to the press too early, and he cast the whole anew in the following pieces; where some negligences in his former reasoning, and more in the expression, are, he hopes, corrected. Yet several writers, who have honoured the Author's Philosophy with answers, have taken care to direct all their batteries against that juvenile work, which the Author never acknowledged; and have affected to triumph in any advantages, which, they imagined, they had obtained over it: a practice very contrary to all rules of candour and fair-dealing, and a strong instance of those polemical artifices, which a bigotted zeal thinks itself authorised to employ. Henceforth, the Author desires, that the following pieces may alone be regarded as containing his philosophical sentiments and principles.[101]

---

[99] Letter of 17 Sept. 1739; *Letters*, 1:33.

[100] Letter of Mar.–Apr. 1751, to Gilbert Elliott of Minto; *Letters* 1:158; see also Hume's letter of Feb. 1754, to John Stewart; *Letters* 1:187.

[101] Cited from *An Enquiry concerning Human Understanding*, ed. T. L. Beauchamp, *Oxford Philosophical Texts* (Oxford: Oxford University Press, 1999), p. 84.

Despite this clear statement of preference, Hume's *Treatise* is still widely read and, by many readers, still considered the centrepiece of his philosophy. Nor is such a response unreasonable. Hume himself expressed conflicting opinions on the matter, suggesting that his later works clarify, but do not change his views. In addition, whatever may be the flaws of the *Treatise*, the views it expresses gave impetus and focus to the some of the most important philosophers of the late eighteenth century—Thomas Reid, Adam Smith, Immanuel Kant, and Jeremy Bentham, for example. It does not follow, however, that the *Treatise* is still widely read only because of its past importance. It is still read because it contains a multitude of important philosophical theses, many of which remain fresh and viable. It is still read because it provides us with fresh philosophical insights and, as Hume himself would appreciate, hours of intellectual pleasure. We can accept that Hume was disappointed with the *Treatise* and recognize that there may be differences between some of the views expressed in it and those found in his later works. But this should not deter us from reading and responding to this rich and rewarding philosophical classic.

Supplementary Reading

This bibliography provides information about Hume's writings and life, some brief remarks on how to learn more about his intellectual background, a short list of books that focus on Hume and some of the philosophical issues raised in the *Treatise*, and references to additional bibliographical aids.

1. HUME'S WRITINGS

A list of Hume's principal writings, in chronological order, with the year of first publication, but with the final title if a change of title occurred:

A. *Published in Hume's Lifetime*

A Treatise of Human Nature (1739–40).
An Abstract of . . . A Treatise of Human Nature (1740).
Essays, Moral and Political (1741 2, 1748).
An Enquiry concerning Human Understanding, first published as *Philosophical Essays concerning Human Understanding* (1748).
An Enquiry concerning the Principles of Morals (1751).
Political Discourses (1752).
Four Dissertations: 'The Natural History of Religion', 'Of the Passions' (later called 'A Dissertation on the Passions'), 'Of Tragedy', and 'Of the Standard of Taste' (1757).
The History of England (1754–62).

B. *Published Posthumously*

My Own Life (1777).
Dialogues concerning Natural Religion (1779).
Essays on Suicide and the Immortality of the Soul (1783).

C. *Current Editions*

Oxford University Press is currently publishing a critical edition of Hume's philosophical, political, and literary works. This edition is being edited by Tom L. Beauchamp, David Fate Norton, and M. A. Stewart; some volumes are not yet published. The most recent earlier edition of Hume's philosophical works is *The Philosophical Works of David Hume*, ed. T. H. Green and T. H. Grose, 4 vols. (London: 1882–6; fac. Darmstadt: Scientia Verlag, 1964). A current edition of Hume's essays: *Essays Moral, Political, and Literary*, ed. E. F. Miller, rev. edn. (Indianapolis: Liberty-Classics, 1987); of his history: *The History of England from the Invasion of Julius Caesar to the Revolution in 1688*, 6 vols. (Indianapolis: LibertyClassics, 1983–5).

Two items bearing on the *Treatise* and not included in the Green and Grose edition or the present volume are:

'Hume's Early Memoranda, 1729–1740', ed. E. C. Mossner, *Journal of the History of Ideas*, 9 (1948), 492–518. The dating of these notes is controversial, but all were probably made by the early 1740s.

A Letter from a Gentleman to his Friend in Edinburgh: Containing Some Observations on A Specimen of the Principles concerning Religion and Morality, said to be maintain'd in a Book lately publish'd, intituled, A Treatise of Human Nature, &c. (Edinburgh, 1745; fac. Edinburgh: Edinburgh University Press, 1967). This work, only partially by Hume and published without his permission, is based on a letter he sent to his friend Henry Home.

Three computer-readable editions of Hume's texts have been prepared. The most comprehensive of these is available in both disk and CD-ROM form in the Past Masters Series of the Intelex Corporation. This edition is based on editions of Hume's works prepared between 1825 and 1985. Hume's *Treatise* and two *Enquiries*, as edited by L. A. Selby-Bigge and revised by P. H. Nidditch, have been issued by Oxford University Press. Finally, HUMETEXT 1.0, prepared by Tom L. Beauchamp, David Fate Norton, and M. A. Stewart, is available from the Department of Philosophy, Georgetown University. This collection includes Hume's philosophical, political, and literary works, all prepared directly from eighteenth-century editions. These texts are not, however, critical editions.

2. HUME'S LIFE AND LETTERS

The most accessible introduction to Hume's life is his own brief autobiography, *My Own Life*, first published in 1777 and now available in many places, including the edition of his letters edited by J. Y. T. Greig listed just below and *The Cambridge Companion to Hume* listed in Section 4A of this bibliography.

A. *Biographies*

Burton, John Hill, *Life and Correspondence of David Hume* (Edinburgh, 1846; fac. New York: Garland, 1983).

Greig, J. Y. T., *David Hume* (Oxford: Clarendon Press, 1932).

Mossner, Ernest C., *The Life of David Hume*, 2nd edn. (Oxford: Clarendon Press, 1980).

B. *Collections of Letters by and to Hume*

Burton, John Hill (ed.), *Letters of Eminent Persons Addressed to David Hume* (Edinburgh, 1849; fac. Bristol: Thoemmes, 1989). At best only representative of the nearly 600 extant letters to Hume. For a reliable list of these letters, see the work by Greig and Beynon, Section 5B below.

The Letters of David Hume, ed. J. Y. T. Greig, 2 vols. (Oxford: Clarendon Press, 1932).

New Letters of David Hume, ed. Raymond Klibansky and Ernest C. Mossner (Oxford: Clarendon Press, 1954).

A new, comprehensive edition of Hume's correspondence is being prepared for Oxford University Press by David Raynor.

3. INTELLECTUAL BACKGROUND OF THE *TREATISE*

Hume read widely and responded, often critically, to the works he read. Cicero was one of his favourite classical authors; among classical philosophical writers, he was also familiar with Seneca, Lucretius, and Plutarch. In 1734 Hume claimed that he had in the previous three years read 'most of the celebrated Books in Latin, French & English' and also taught himself Italian. About a year before he finished Books 1 and 2 of the *Treatise*, he told a friend that the 'metaphysical parts' of the *Treatise* would be easier to understand following a reading of Malebranche's *Search after Truth*, Berkeley's *Principles of Human Knowledge*, the articles on Spinoza and Zeno in Bayle's *Dictionary*, and Descartes's *Meditations*. In the Introduction to the *Treatise* Hume alludes to the methodological innovations of such natural philosophers as Robert Boyle and Isaac Newton, and explicitly acknowledges the experimental moral philosophy of John Locke, Lord Shaftesbury, Francis Hutcheson, Joseph Butler, and Bernard Mandeville. In the course of the work he mentions or alludes to Thomas Hobbes, Antoine Arnauld, Anthony Collins, Blaise Pascal, Samuel Clarke, and many others, some of whom are mentioned in Ed. Intro., note 8.

For further information about these authors and their works, and the names of still further authors and books that apparently had an impact on Hume's early thinking, see the References. These include the names of all the authors to which reference is made in the *Treatise* and *Abstract* and in the editors' annotations to these works.

4. STUDIES OF HUME'S PHILOSOPHY

This guide to further reading mentions only a small part of the extensive literature on Hume and the *Treatise*. Note that most of the items found in Section 4A will themselves include a substantial guide to reading, while Section 5A lists more extensive bibliographies that will be of help to both beginning and advanced students of Hume.

A. *Introductory*

LAIRD, JOHN, *Hume's Philosophy of Human Nature* (London: Methuen, 1932).

MACNABB, D. G. C., *David Hume: His Theory of Knowledge and Morality*, 2nd edn. (London: Hutchinson, 1951).

—— 'Hume, David', *The Encyclopedia of Philosophy*, ed. Paul Edwards, 8 vols. (New York: Macmillan, 1967).

NORTON, DAVID FATE (ed.), *The Cambridge Companion to Hume* (Cambridge: Cambridge University Press, 1993).

PENELHUM, TERENCE, *David Hume: An Introduction to his Philosophical System* (West Lafayette: Purdue University Press, 1992).

SMITH, NORMAN [KEMP], 'The Naturalism of Hume', *Mind*, 14 (1905), 149–73, 335–47.

B. *Advanced Monographs*

ÁRDAL, PÁLL S., *Passion and Value in Hume's* Treatise, 2nd edn. (Edinburgh: Edinburgh University Press, 1989).

BAIER, ANNETTE C., *A Progress of Sentiments: Reflections on Hume's* Treatise (Cambridge, Mass.: Harvard University Press, 1991).

BEAUCHAMP, TOM L., and ROSENBERG, ALEXANDER, *Hume and the Problem of Causation* (New York: Oxford University Press, 1981).

BRICKE, JOHN, *Mind and Morality: An Examination of Hume's Moral Psychology* (Oxford: Oxford University Press, 1996).

FOGELIN, ROBERT J., *Hume's Skepticism in the* Treatise of Human Nature (London: Routledge, 1985).

FORBES, DUNCAN, *Hume's Philosophical Politics* (Cambridge: Cambridge University Press, 1975).

GARRETT, DON, *Cognition and Commitment in Hume's Philosophy* (New York: Oxford University Press, 1997).

LIVINGSTON, DONALD W., *Hume's Philosophy of Common Life* (Chicago: University of Chicago Press, 1984).

MACKIE, JOHN, *Hume's Moral Theory* (London: Routledge, 1980).

NORTON, DAVID FATE, *David Hume: Common Sense Moralist, Sceptical Metaphysician*, rev. edn. (Princeton: Princeton University Press, 1984).

OWEN, DAVID, *Hume's Reason* (Oxford: Oxford University Press, 1999).

RUSSELL, PAUL, *Freedom and Moral Sentiment: Hume's Way of Naturalizing Responsibility* (New York: Oxford University Press, 1995).

SMITH, NORMAN KEMP, *The Philosophy of David Hume* (London: Macmillan, 1940).

STEWART, JOHN B., *Opinion and Reform in Hume's Political Philosophy* (Princeton: Princeton University Press, 1992).

STROUD, BARRY, *Hume* (London: Routledge, 1977).

WRIGHT, JOHN P., *The Sceptical Realism of David Hume* (Manchester: Manchester University Press, 1983).

C. Advanced Anthologies

CHAPPELL, V. C. (ed.), *Hume: A Collection of Critical Essays* (New York: Doubleday, 1966).

LIVINGSTON, DONALD, and KING, JAMES (eds.), *Hume: A Re-evaluation* (New York: Fordham University Press, 1976).

NORTON, DAVID FATE, CAPALDI, NICHOLAS, and ROBISON, WADE (eds.), *McGill Hume Studies* (San Diego: Austin Hill Press, 1979).

STEWART, M. A. (ed.), *Studies in the Philosophy of the Scottish Enlightenment*, Oxford Studies in the History of Philosophy 1 (Oxford: Clarendon Press, 1990).

—— and WRIGHT, JOHN P. (eds.), *Hume and Hume's Connexions* (Edinburgh: Edinburgh University Press; University Park: Pennsylvania State University Press, 1995).

TWEYMAN, STANLEY (ed.), *David Hume: Critical Assessments*, 6 vols. (London: Routledge, 1995).

Hume Studies, a journal published twice yearly by the Hume Society, is a further source of important work on Hume.

5. BIBLIOGRAPHICAL AIDS

A. General

BEAUCHAMP, TOM L., 'Supplementary Reading', in *An Enquiry concerning the Principles of Morals*, Oxford Philosophical Texts (Oxford: Oxford University Press, 1997), 55–67.

—— 'Supplementary Reading', in *An Enquiry concerning Human Understanding*, Oxford Philosophical Texts (Oxford: Oxford University Press, 1999).

HALL, ROLAND, *50 Years of Hume Scholarship* (Edinburgh: Edinburgh University Press, 1978).

—— and later MORRIS, WILLIAM E., 'The Hume Literature . . .', *Hume Studies*, 4–7, 10–11, 13–14, 20. A supplement to Hall's *50 Years of Hume Scholarship*.

JESSOP, T. E., *A Bibliography of David Hume and of Scottish Philosophy, from Francis Hutcheson to Lord Balfour* (London: Brown & Son, 1938). A dated but still useful guide to Hume's publications.

The Philosopher's Index, ed. R. H. Lineback (Bowling Green, Ohio: Philosophy Documentation Center). Issued quarterly and annually in printed versions; also available in CD-ROM.

B. Specialized

The following may be useful for those intending to carry out advanced research on Hume and his work.

BEAUCHAMP, TOM L., 'Introduction: A History of the Enquiry on Morals', in David Hume, *An Enquiry concerning the Principles of Morals* (Oxford: Clarendon Press, 1998), xi–lxxx; 'Introduction: A History of the *Enquiry concerning Human Understanding*'; in David Hume, *An Enquiry concerning Human Understanding* (Oxford: Clarendon Press, 2000), xi–civ; and 'Introduction: A History of Two Dissertations', in David Hume, *A Dissertation on the Passions. The Natural History of Religion* (Oxford: Clarendon Press, 2006). These introductions include discussions of Hume's recasting of materials from the *Treatise* to form the *Enquiry concerning the Principles of Morals*, the *Enquiry concerning Human Understanding*; and the *Dissertation on the Passions*.

GREIG, J. Y. T., and BEYNON, HAROLD, *Calendar of Hume MSS. in the Possession of the Royal Society of Edinburgh* (Edinburgh: Royal Society of Edinburgh, 1932). Lists the greatest part of Hume's surviving correspondence and manuscripts.

IKEDA, SADAO, *Hume and the Eighteenth Century British Thought: An Annotated Catalogue*, 2 vols. (Tokyo: Chuo University Library, 1986, 1988). Includes a bibliography of the lifetime editions of Hume's works and information about works by other eighteenth-century British authors.

NORTON, DAVID FATE and NORTON, MARY J., *The David Hume Library* (Edinburgh: Edinburgh Bibliographical Society, 1996). An attempt to reconstruct a part of Hume's library.

A Note on the Texts of this Edition

The texts of this, the Oxford Philosophical Texts (OPT) edition of Hume's *Treatise* and *Abstract*, are those prepared for the Clarendon edition of *The Philosophical, Political, and Literary Works of David Hume*. As these texts are *critical texts* of the first editions of those works, they incorporate (1) Hume's corrections and manuscript amendments to the *Treatise* and *Abstract*; (2) the correction of typographical errors identified by both the previous and present editors of these works; and (3), the results of the present editors' efforts to eliminate certain orthographic and stylistic inconsistencies introduced by the printers of the first editions of these works.

A comprehensive record of the differences between the first-edition texts of the *Treatise* and *Abstract* and the critical versions of them printed here is set out in 'Editing the Texts of the the *Treatise*, the *Abstract*, and the *Letter from a Gentleman*', an essay included in vol. 2 of the Clarendon edition of these works, an edition now in press. This record and the relevant footnotes to it also identify and explain the relatively few substantive differences between the texts published here and the versions found in some of the earlier printings of the OPT edition. In addition, further study and consultation have led us to revise some decisions made, prior to January 2000, about the correct reading of the critical texts of these works.[1] Careful comparisons show that the OPT texts of the *Treatise* and *Abstract* are, with one exception, substantively and formally identical to those in the Clarendon edition of these works. The exception is the use, in the OPT texts, of the superscript obelisk (†) to indicate the existence of a relevant annotation in the Editors' Annotations found in Part 3 of this volume.

Beginning with the 11th impression of the OPT edition of the *Treatise* and *Abstract*, we have added in the right-hand margins the corresponding page numbers of the text of the earlier Oxford University Press edition of the *Treatise*, that published by L.A. Selby-Bigge in 1888, and lightly revised by P.H. Nidditch in 1978. An *SB* number on a line of the present edition indicates that at least a part of one word of that line occurs at the beginning of the first line of the Selby-Bigge page indicated.[2] There are two other things to keep in mind: (1) When a passage from the Appendix of the *Treatise* has been inserted into the

---

[1] See 'Substantive Differences between Two Texts of Hume's *Treatise*', in *Hume Studies*, 26 (2000), 245–77, and, for a complete list of corrections or revisions made to the earlier printings of the OPT edition, go to the McGill David Hume Collection website (http://digital library mcgill.ca/hume), and then click on 'Corrections to the OPT Treatise'.

[2] Because these *SB* numbers are now a part of these texts, we have omitted from this and all subsequent OPT editions the 'Guide to Parallel Paragraph and Page References in Oxford University Press Editions of Hume's *Treatise* and *Abstract*', a guide found on pages 623–33 of printings six through ten of the OPT edition.

main text of the work in accordance with Hume's instructions,[3] the *SB* numbers will not be continuous. This happens because Hume's Appendix was printed only at the end of the Selby-Bigge edition of the *Treatise* (on pages [623]–39), and because our edition of the *Treatise* numbers Hume's footnotes consecutively, 1–89, whereas the Selby-Bigge edition restarts numbering on each page on which a note or notes occur.

David and Mary Norton
Victoria, BC, Canada
January 2006

---

[3] These passages are marked, at their beginning and end, by a superscript abbreviation, App. For examples see Note 5, 1.2.4.22, and 1.2.4.31; for further details see page 565.

PART 2
The Text

A TREATISE OF HUMAN NATURE:

BEING AN ATTEMPT TO INTRODUCE
THE EXPERIMENTAL METHOD
OF REASONING
INTO MORAL SUBJECTS

Rara temporum felicitas, ubi sentire, quæ velis;
& quæ sentias, dicere licet.[†] TACITUS

Book 1.   *Of the Understanding*

ADVERTISEMENT

My design in the present work is sufficiently explain'd in the Introduction. *The reader must only observe, that all the subjects I have there plann'd out to myself, are not treated of in these two volumes. The subjects of the* Understanding *and* Passions *make a compleat chain of reasoning by themselves;*[†] *and I was willing to take advantage of this natural division, in order to try the taste of the public. If I have the good fortune to meet with success, I shall proceed to the examination of* Morals, Politics, *and* Criticism; *which will compleat this* Treatise of Human Nature. *The approbation of the public I consider as the greatest reward of my labours; but am determin'd to regard its judgment, whatever it be, as my best instruction.*

1   Nothing is more usual and more natural for those, who pretend to discover[†] any thing new to the world in philosophy and the sciences, than to insinuate the praises of their own systems, by decrying all those, which have been advanc'd before them.[†] And indeed were they content with lamenting that ignorance, which we still lie under in the most important questions, that can come before the tribunal of human reason, there are few, who have an acquaintance with the sciences, that wou'd not readily agree with them.[†] 'Tis easy for one of judgment and learning, to perceive the weak foundation even of those systems, which have obtain'd the greatest credit, and have carry'd their pretensions highest to accurate and profound reasoning. Principles taken upon trust, consequences lamely deduc'd from them, want of coherence in the parts, and of evidence in the whole, these are every where to be met with in the systems of the most eminent philosophers, and seem to have drawn disgrace upon philosophy itself.

2   Nor is there requir'd such profound knowledge to discover the present imperfect condition of the sciences, but even the rabble without doors may judge from the noise and clamour, which they hear, that all goes not well within.[†] There is nothing which is not the subject of debate, and in which men of learning are not of contrary opinions. The most trivial question escapes not our controversy, and in the most momentous we are not able to give any certain decision. Disputes are multiply'd, as if every thing was uncertain; and these disputes are manag'd with the greatest warmth, as if every thing was certain.[†] Amidst all this bustle 'tis not reason, which carries the prize, but eloquence; and no man needs ever despair of gaining proselytes to the most extravagant hypothesis, who has art enough to represent it in any favourable colours.[†] The victory is not gain'd by the men at arms, who manage the pike and the sword; but by the trumpeters, drummers, and musicians of the army.

3   From hence in my opinion arises that common prejudice against metaphysical reasonings of all kinds, even amongst those, who profess themselves scholars, and have a just value for every other part of literature.[†] By metaphysical reasonings, they do not understand those on any particular branch of science, but every kind of argument, which is any way abstruse, and requires some attention to be comprehended.[†] We have so often lost our labour in such researches, that we commonly reject them without hesitation, and resolve, if we must for ever be a prey to errors and delusions, that they shall at least be natural and entertaining. And indeed nothing but the most determin'd scepticism, along with a great degree of indolence, can justify this aversion to metaphysics.[†] For if truth be at all within the reach of human capacity, 'tis certain it must lie very deep and abstruse; and to hope we shall arrive at it without pains, while the greatest geniuses have fail'd with the utmost pains, must certainly be esteem'd suffi- ciently vain and presumptuous. I pretend to no such advantage in the philosophy

I am going to unfold, and wou'd esteem it a strong presumption against it, were it so very easy and obvious.

4   'Tis evident, that all the sciences have a relation, greater or less, to human nature; and that however wide any of them may seem to run from it, they still return back by one passage or another. Even *Mathematics*, *Natural Philosophy*,[†] and *Natural Religion*,[†] are in some measure dependent on the science of MAN;[†] since they lie under the cognizance of men, and are judg'd of by their powers and faculties. 'Tis impossible to tell what changes and improvements we might make in these sciences were we thoroughly acquainted with the extent and force of human understanding, and cou'd explain the nature of the ideas we employ, and of the operations we perform in our reasonings.[†] And these improvements are the more to be hop'd for in natural religion, as it is not content with instructing us in the nature of superior powers, but carries its views farther, to their disposition towards us,[†] and our duties towards them; and consequently we ourselves are not only the beings, that reason, but also one of the objects, concerning which we reason.

5   If therefore the sciences of Mathematics, Natural Philosophy, and Natural Religion, have such a dependence on the knowledge of man, what may be expected in the other sciences, whose connexion with human nature is more close and intimate?[†] The sole end of logic is to explain the principles and operations of our reasoning faculty, and the nature of our ideas:[†] Morals[†] and criticism[†] regard our tastes and sentiments: And politics[†] consider men as united in society, and dependent on each other. In these four sciences of *Logic*, *Morals*, *Criticism*, and *Politics*, is comprehended almost every thing, which it can any way import us[†] to be acquainted with, or which can tend either to the improvement or ornament of the human mind.   SB xvi

6   Here then is the only expedient, from which we can hope for success in our philosophical researches, to leave the tedious lingring method, which we have hitherto follow'd, and instead of taking now and then a castle or village on the frontier, to march up directly to the capital or center of these sciences, to human nature itself; which being once masters of, we may every where else hope for an easy victory. From this station we may extend our conquests over all those sciences, which more intimately concern human life, and may afterwards proceed at leisure to discover more fully those, which are the objects of pure curiosity. There is no question of importance, whose decision is not compriz'd in the science of man; and there is none, which can be decided with any certainty, before we become acquainted with that science. In pretending therefore to explain the principles of human nature, we in effect propose a compleat system of the sciences, built on a foundation almost entirely new, and the only one upon which they can stand with any security.

7   And as the science of man is the only solid foundation for the other sciences, so the only solid foundation we can give to this science itself must be laid on experience and observation. 'Tis no astonishing reflection to consider, that the application of experimental philosophy[†] to moral subjects shou'd come after that to natural at the distance of above a whole century; since we find in fact, that

4

there was about the same interval betwixt the origins of these sciences; and that reckoning from THALES to SOCRATES,[†] the space of time is nearly equal to that betwixt my LORD BACON and some late philosophers in *England*,[1] who have begun to put the science of man on a new footing, and have engag'd the attention, and excited the curiosity of the public. So true it is, that however other nations may rival us in poetry, and excel us in some other agreeable arts,[†] the improvements in reason and philosophy can only be owing to a land of toleration and of liberty. *SB xvii*

8   Nor ought we to think, that this latter improvement in the science of man will do less honour to our native country than the former in natural philosophy, but ought rather to esteem it a greater glory, upon account of the greater importance of that science, as well as the necessity it lay under of such a reformation. For to me it seems evident, that the essence of the mind being equally unknown to us with that of external bodies, it must be equally impossible to form any notion of its powers and qualities otherwise than from careful and exact experiments, and the observation of those particular effects, which result from its different circumstances and situations.[†] And tho' we must endeavour to render all our principles as universal as possible, by tracing up our experiments to the utmost,[†] and explaining all effects from the simplest and fewest causes, 'tis still certain we cannot go beyond experience; and any hypothesis, that pretends to discover the ultimate original qualities of human nature, ought at first to be rejected as presumptuous and chimerical.[†]

9   I do not think a philosopher, who wou'd apply himself so earnestly to the explaining the ultimate principles of the soul,[†] wou'd show himself a great master in that very science of human nature, which he pretends to explain, or very knowing in what is naturally satisfactory to the mind of man. For nothing is more certain, than that despair has almost the same effect upon us with enjoyment, and that we are no sooner acquainted with the impossibility of satisfying any desire, than the desire itself vanishes. When we see, that we have arriv'd at the utmost extent of human reason, we sit down contented; tho' we be perfectly satisfy'd in the main of our ignorance,[†] and perceive that we can give no reason for our most general and most refin'd principles, beside our experience of their reality; which is the reason of the mere vulgar,[†] and what it requir'd no study at first to have discover'd for the most particular and most extraordinary phænomenon. And as this impossibility of making any farther progress is enough to satisfy the reader, so the writer may derive a more delicate satisfaction from the free confession of his ignorance, and from his prudence in avoiding that error, into which so many have fallen, of imposing their conjectures and hypotheses on the world for the most certain principles. When this mutual contentment and satisfaction can be obtain'd betwixt the master and scholar, I know not what more we can require of our philosophy. *SB xviii*

10   But if this impossibility of explaining ultimate principles shou'd be esteem'd a defect in the science of man, I will venture to affirm, that 'tis a defect common

---

[1] Mr. *Locke*, my Lord *Shaftesbury*, Dr. *Mandeville*, Mr. *Hutcheson*, Dr. *Butler*, &c.[†] *SB xvii*

to it with all the sciences, and all the arts, in which we can employ ourselves, whether they be such as are cultivated in the schools of the philosophers, or practis'd in the shops of the meanest artizans. None of them can go beyond experience, or establish any principles which are not founded on that authority. Moral philosophy has, indeed, this peculiar disadvantage, which is not found in natural,[†] that in collecting its experiments, it cannot make them purposely, with *SB xix* premeditation, and after such a manner as to satisfy itself concerning every particular difficulty which may arise. When I am at a loss to know the effects of one body[†] upon another in any situation, I need only put them in that situation, and observe what results from it. But shou'd I endeavour to clear up after the same manner any doubt in moral philosophy, by placing myself in the same case with that which I consider, 'tis evident this reflection and premeditation wou'd so disturb the operation of my natural principles, as must render it impossible to form any just conclusion from the phænomenon.[†] We must therefore glean up our experiments in this science from a cautious observation of human life, and take them as they appear in the common course of the world, by men's behaviour in company, in affairs,[†] and in their pleasures. Where experiments of this kind are judiciously collected and compar'd, we may hope to establish on them a science, which will not be inferior in certainty, and will be much superior in utility to any other of human comprehension.

BOOK 1. *Of the* UNDERSTANDING

PART 1

Of ideas, their origin, composition, connexion, abstraction, &c.

Sect. 1. *Of the origin of our ideas*

1   All the perceptions† of the human mind resolve themselves into two distinct kinds, which I shall call IMPRESSIONS and IDEAS. The difference betwixt these consists in the degrees of force and liveliness,† with which they strike upon the mind, and make their way into our thought or consciousness. Those perceptions, which enter with most force and violence, we may name *impressions*; and under this name I comprehend all our sensations, passions and emotions, as they make their first appearance in the soul. By *ideas* I mean the faint images of these in thinking and reasoning; such as, for instance, are all the perceptions excited by the present discourse, excepting only, those which arise from the sight and touch, and excepting the immediate pleasure or uneasiness it may occasion. I believe it will not be very necessary to employ many words in explaining this distinction. Every one of himself will readily perceive the difference betwixt feeling and thinking. The common degrees of these are easily distinguish'd; tho' it is not impossible but in particular instances they may very nearly approach to each other. Thus in sleep, in a fever, in madness, or in any very violent emotions of soul, our ideas may approach to our impressions: As on the other hand it sometimes happens, that our impressions are so faint and low, that we cannot distinguish them from our ideas. But notwithstanding this near resemblance in a few instances, they are in general so very different, that no one can make a scruple to rank them under distinct heads, and assign to each a peculiar name to mark the difference.²

2   There is another division of our perceptions, which it will be convenient to observe, and which extends itself both to our impressions and ideas. This division is into SIMPLE and COMPLEX. Simple perceptions or impressions and ideas are such as admit of no distinction nor separation. The complex are the contrary to these, and may be distinguish'd into parts. Tho' a particular colour, taste, and smell† are qualities all united together in this apple, 'tis easy

---

² I here make use of these terms, *impression* and *idea*, in a sense different from what is usual, and I hope this liberty will be allow'd me. Perhaps I rather restore the word, *idea*, to its original sense, from which Mr. *Locke*† had perverted it, in making it stand for all our perceptions. By the term of *impression* I wou'd not be understood to express the manner, in which our lively perceptions are produc'd in the soul, but merely the perceptions themselves; for which there is no particular name either in the *English* or any other language, that I know of.

to perceive they are not the same, but are at least distinguishable from each other.

3   Having by these divisions given an order and arrangement to our objects,[†] we may now apply ourselves to consider with the more accuracy their qualities and relations. The first circumstance, that strikes my eye, is the great resemblance betwixt our impressions and ideas in every other particular, except their degree of force and vivacity. The one seem to be in a manner the reflection of the other; so that all the perceptions of the mind are double, and appear both as impres-   *SB 3* sions and ideas. When I shut my eyes and think of my chamber, the ideas I form are exact representations of the impressions I felt; nor is there any circumstance of the one, which is not to be found in the other. In running over my other perceptions, I find still the same resemblance and representation. Ideas and impressions appear always to correspond to each other. This circumstance seems to me remarkable, and engages my attention for a moment.

4   Upon a more accurate survey I find I have been carry'd away too far by the first appearance, and that I must make use of the distinction of perceptions into *simple* and *complex*, to limit this general decision, *that all our ideas and impressions are resembling.* I observe, that many of our complex ideas never had impressions, that corresponded to them, and that many of our complex impressions never are exactly copy'd in ideas. I can imagine to myself such a city as the *New Jerusalem*, whose pavement is gold and walls are rubies, tho' I never saw any such. I have seen *Paris*;[†] but shall I affirm I can form such an idea of that city, as will perfectly represent all its streets and houses in their real and just proportions?

5   I perceive, therefore, that tho' there is in general a great resemblance betwixt our *complex* impressions and ideas, yet the rule is not universally true, that they are exact copies of each other. We may next consider how the case stands with our *simple* perceptions. After the most accurate examination, of which I am capable, I venture to affirm, that the rule here holds without any exception, and that every simple idea has a simple impression, which resembles it; and every simple impression a correspondent idea.[†] That idea of red, which we form in the dark, and that impression, which strikes our eyes in sun-shine, differ only in degree, not in nature. That the case is the same with all our simple impressions and ideas, 'tis impossible to prove by a particular enumeration of them.[†] Every one may satisfy himself in this point by running over as many as he pleases.[†] But   *SB 4* if any one shou'd deny this universal resemblance, I know no way of convincing him, but by desiring him to show a simple impression, that has not a correspondent idea, or a simple idea, that has not a correspondent impression. If he does not answer this challenge,[†] as 'tis certain he cannot, we may from his silence and our own observation establish our conclusion.

6   Thus we find, that all simple ideas and impressions resemble each other; and as the complex are form'd from them, we may affirm in general, that these two species of perception are exactly correspondent. Having discover'd this relation, which requires no farther examination, I am curious to find some other of their

qualities. Let us consider how they stand with regard to their existence, and which of the impressions and ideas are causes, and which effects.

7   The *full* examination of this question is the subject of the present treatise;[†] and therefore we shall here content ourselves with establishing one general proposition, *that all our simple ideas in their first appearance are deriv'd from simple impressions, which are correspondent to them, and which they exactly represent.*

8   In seeking for phænomena to prove this proposition, I find only those of two kinds; but in each kind the phænomena are obvious, numerous, and conclusive. I first make myself certain, by a new review, of what I have already asserted, that every simple impression is attended with a correspondent idea, and every simple idea with a correspondent impression. From this constant conjunction[†] of resembling perceptions I immediately conclude, that there is a great connexion betwixt our correspondent impressions and ideas, and that the existence of the one has a considerable influence upon that of the other. Such a constant conjunction, in such an infinite number of instances, can never arise from chance; but clearly proves a dependence of the impressions on the ideas, or of the ideas on the impressions. That I may know on which side this dependence lies, I con- *SB 5* sider the order of their *first appearance*; and find by constant experience, that the simple impressions always take the precedence of their correspondent ideas, but never appear in the contrary order. To give a child an idea of scarlet or orange, of sweet or bitter, I present the objects, or in other words, convey to him these impressions; but proceed not so absurdly, as to endeavour to produce the impressions by exciting the ideas. Our ideas upon their appearance produce not their correspondent impressions, nor do we perceive any colour, or feel any sensation merely upon thinking of them. On the other hand we find, that any impression either of the mind or body is constantly follow'd by an idea, which resembles it, and is only different in the degrees of force and liveliness. The constant conjunction of our resembling perceptions, is a convincing proof, that the one are the causes of the other; and this priority of the impressions is an equal proof, that our impressions are the causes of our ideas, not our ideas of our impressions.

9   To confirm this I consider another plain and convincing phænomenon; which is, that wherever by any accident the faculties,[†] which give rise to any impressions, are obstructed in their operations, as when one is born blind or deaf; not only the impressions are lost, but also their correspondent ideas; so that there never appear in the mind the least traces of either of them. Nor is this only true, where the organs of sensation are entirely destroy'd, but likewise where they have never been put in action to produce a particular impression. We cannot form to ourselves a just idea of the taste of a pine-apple, without having actually tasted it.[†]

10   There is however one contradictory phænomenon, which may prove, that 'tis not absolutely impossible for ideas to go before their correspondent impressions. I believe it will readily be allow'd, that the several distinct ideas of colours, which

enter by the eyes, or those of sounds, which are convey'd by the hearing, are really different from each other, tho' at the same time resembling. Now if this be true of different colours, it must be no less so of the different shades of the same colour, that each of them produces a distinct idea, independent of the rest. For if this shou'd be deny'd, 'tis possible, by the continual gradation of shades, to run a colour insensibly into what is most remote from it;† and if you will not allow any of the means to be different, you cannot without absurdity deny the extremes† to be the same. Suppose therefore a person to have enjoy'd his sight for thirty years, and to have become perfectly well acquainted with colours of all kinds, excepting one particular shade of blue, for instance, which it never has been his fortune to meet with.† Let all the different shades of that colour, except that single one, be plac'd before him, descending gradually from the deepest to the lightest; 'tis plain, that he will perceive a blank, where that shade is wanting, and will be sensible, that there is a greater distance in that place betwixt the contiguous colours, than in any other. Now I ask, whether 'tis possible for him, from his own imagination, to supply this deficiency, and raise up to himself the idea of that particular shade, tho' it had never been convey'd to him by his senses? I believe there are few but will be of opinion that he can; and this may serve as a proof, that the simple ideas are not always deriv'd from the correspondent impressions; tho' the instance is so particular and singular, that 'tis scarce worth our observing, and does not merit that for it alone we shou'd alter our general maxim.†

11   But besides this exception, it may not be amiss to remark on this head, that the principle of the priority of impressions to ideas must be understood with another limitation, *viz.* that as our ideas are images of our impressions, so we can form secondary ideas, which are images of the primary; as appears from this very reasoning concerning them. This is not, properly speaking, an exception to the rule so much as an explanation of it. Ideas produce the images of themselves in new ideas; but as the first ideas are suppos'd to be deriv'd from impressions, it still remains true, that all our simple ideas proceed, either mediately or immediately, from their correspondent impressions.

12   This then is the first principle I establish in the science of human nature; nor ought we to despise it because of the simplicity of its appearance. For 'tis remarkable, that the present question concerning the precedency of our impressions or ideas, is the same with what has made so much noise in other terms,† when it has been disputed whether there be any *innate ideas*,† or whether all ideas be deriv'd from sensation and reflection. We may observe, that in order to prove the ideas of extension and colour not to be innate, philosophers do nothing but show, that they are convey'd by our senses. To prove the ideas of passion and desire not to be innate, they observe that we have a preceding experience of these emotions in ourselves. Now if we carefully examine these arguments, we shall find that they prove nothing but that ideas are preceded by other more lively perceptions, from which they are deriv'd, and which they represent. I hope this clear stating of the question will remove all disputes concerning it, and will render this principle of more use in our reasonings, than it seems hitherto to have been.

Sect. 2. *Division of the subject*

1 Since it appears, that our simple impressions are prior to their correspondent ideas, and that the exceptions are very rare, method[†] seems to require we shou'd examine our impressions, before we consider our ideas. Impressions may be divided into two kinds, those of SENSATION and those of REFLECTION. The first kind arises in the soul originally, from unknown causes.[†] The second is deriv'd in a great measure from our ideas, and that in the following order. An impression *SB 8* first strikes upon the senses, and makes us perceive heat or cold, thirst or hunger, pleasure or pain of some kind or other. Of this impression there is a copy taken by the mind, which remains after the impression ceases; and this we call an idea. This idea of pleasure or pain, when it returns upon the soul,[†] produces the new impressions of desire and aversion, hope and fear, which may properly be call'd impressions of reflection because deriv'd from it.[†] These again are copy'd by the memory and imagination, and become ideas; which perhaps in their turn give rise to other impressions and ideas. So that the impressions of reflection are only antecedent to their correspondent ideas; but posterior to those of sensation, and deriv'd from them. The examination of our sensations belongs more to anatomists and natural philosophers than to moral; and therefore shall not at present be enter'd upon.[†] And as the impressions of reflection, *viz.* passions, desires, and emotions, which principally deserve our attention, arise mostly from ideas, 'twill be necessary to reverse that method, which at first sight seems most natural; and in order to explain the nature and principles of the human mind, give a particular account of ideas, before we proceed to impressions. For this reason I have here chosen to begin with ideas.

Sect. 3. *Of the ideas of the memory and imagination*

1 We find by experience, that when any impression has been present with the mind, it again makes its appearance there as an idea; and this it may do after two different ways: Either when in its new appearance it retains a considerable degree of its first vivacity, and is somewhat intermediate betwixt an impression and an idea; or when it entirely loses that vivacity, and is a perfect idea.[†] The faculty, by which we repeat our impressions in the first manner, is call'd the MEMORY, and the other the IMAGINATION. 'Tis evident at first sight, that the ideas *SB 9* of the memory are much more lively and strong than those of the imagination, and that the former faculty paints its objects in more distinct colours, than any which are employ'd by the latter. When we remember any past event, the idea of it flows in upon the mind in a forcible manner; whereas in the imagination the perception is faint and languid, and cannot without difficulty be preserv'd by the mind steady and uniform for any considerable time. Here then is a sensible difference betwixt one species of ideas and another. But of this more fully hereafter.[3]

---

[3] Part 3. Sect. 5.[†]

2   There is another difference betwixt these two kinds of ideas, which is no less evident, namely that tho' neither the ideas of the memory nor imagination, neither the lively nor faint ideas can make their appearance in the mind, unless their correspondent impressions have gone before to prepare the way for them, yet the imagination is not restrain'd to the same order and form with the original impressions;[†] while the memory is in a manner ty'd down in that respect, without any power of variation.

3   'Tis evident, that the memory preserves the original form, in which its objects[†] were presented, and that wherever we depart from it in recollecting any thing, it proceeds from some defect or imperfection in that faculty. An historian may, perhaps, for the more convenient carrying on of his narration, relate an event before another, to which it was in fact posterior; but then he takes notice of this disorder, if he be exact; and by that means replaces the idea in its due position. 'Tis the same case in our recollection of those places and persons, with which we were formerly acquainted. The chief exercise of the memory is not to preserve the simple ideas, but their order and position. In short, this principle[†] is supported by such a number of common and vulgar phænomena, that we may spare ourselves the trouble of insisting on it any farther.

4   The same evidence follows us in our second principle, *of the liberty of the imagination to transpose and change its ideas.* The fables we meet with in poems and romances put this entirely out of question.[†] Nature there is totally confounded, and nothing mention'd but winged horses, fiery dragons, and monstrous giants. Nor will this liberty of the fancy[†] appear strange, when we consider, that all our ideas are copy'd from our impressions, and that there are not any two impressions which are perfectly inseparable.[†] Not to mention, that this is an evident consequence of the division of ideas into simple and complex.[†] Wherever the imagination perceives a difference among ideas, it can easily produce a separation.

SB 10

Sect. 4. *Of the connexion or association of ideas*

1 As all simple ideas may be separated by the imagination, and may be united again in what form it pleases, nothing wou'd be more unaccountable than the operations of that faculty, were it not guided by some universal principles, which render it, in some measure, uniform[†] with itself in all times and places. Were ideas entirely loose and unconnected, chance alone[†] wou'd join them; and 'tis impossible the same simple ideas shou'd fall regularly into complex ones (as they commonly do) without some bond of union among them, some associating quality, by which one idea naturally introduces another. This uniting principle among ideas is not to be consider'd as an inseparable connexion; for that has been already excluded from the imagination:[†] Nor yet are we to conclude, that without it the mind cannot join two ideas; for nothing is more free than that faculty: But we are only to regard it as a gentle force,[†] which commonly prevails,

and is the cause why, among other things, languages so nearly correspond to each other;[†] nature in a manner pointing out to every one those simple ideas, which are most proper to be united into a complex one. The qualities,[†] from which this association arises, and by which the mind is after this manner convey'd from one idea to another, are three, *viz.* RESEMBLANCE, CONTIGUITY in time or place, and CAUSE and EFFECT.   *SB 11*

2   I believe it will not be very necessary to prove, that these qualities produce an association among ideas, and upon the appearance of one idea naturally introduce another. 'Tis plain, that in the course of our thinking, and in the constant revolution of our ideas, our imagination runs easily from one idea to any other that *resembles* it, and that this quality alone is to the fancy a sufficient bond and association. 'Tis likewise evident, that as the senses, in changing their objects,[†] are necessitated to change them regularly, and take them as they lie *contiguous* to each other, the imagination must by long custom acquire the same method of thinking, and run along the parts of space and time in conceiving its objects.[†] As to the connexion, that is made by the relation of *cause and effect*, we shall have occasion afterwards[†] to examine it to the bottom, and therefore shall not at present insist upon it. 'Tis sufficient to observe, that there is no relation, which produces a stronger connexion in the fancy, and makes one idea more readily recal another, than the relation of cause and effect betwixt their objects.

3   That we may understand the full extent of these relations,[†] we must consider, that two objects are connected together in the imagination, not only when the one is immediately resembling, contiguous to, or the cause of the other, but also when there is interpos'd betwixt them a third object, which bears to both of them any of these relations. This may be carry'd on to a great length; tho' at the same time we may observe, that each remove considerably weakens the relation. Cousins in the fourth degree are connected by *causation*, if I may be allow'd to use that term; but not so closely as brothers, much less as child and parent. In general we may observe, that all the relations of blood depend upon cause and effect, and are esteem'd near or remote, according to the number of connecting causes interpos'd betwixt the persons.   *SB 12*

4   Of the three relations above-mention'd this of causation is the most extensive. Two objects may be consider'd as plac'd in this relation, as well when one is the cause of any of the actions or motions of the other, as when the former is the cause of the existence of the latter.[†] For as that action or motion is nothing but the object itself, consider'd in a certain light, and as the object continues the same[†] in all its different situations, 'tis easy to imagine how such an influence of objects upon one another may connect them in the imagination.

5   We may carry this farther, and remark, not only that two objects are connected by the relation of cause and effect, when the one produces a motion or any action in the other, but also when it has a power of producing it.[†] And this we may observe to be the source of all the relations of interest and duty, by which

men influence each other in society, and are plac'd in the ties of government and subordination. A master is such-a-one as by his situation, arising either from force or agreement, has a power of directing in certain particulars the actions of another, whom we call servant. A judge is one, who in all disputed cases can fix by his opinion the possession or property of any thing betwixt any members of the society. When a person is possess'd of any power, there is no more requir'd to convert it into action, but the exertion of the will; and *that* in every case is consider'd as possible, and in many as probable; especially in the case of authority, where the obedience of the subject is a pleasure and advantage to the superior.

6   These are therefore the principles of union or cohesion among our simple ideas, and in the imagination supply the place of that inseparable connexion, by which they are united in our memory. Here is a kind of ATTRACTION,[†] which in the mental world will be found to have as extraordinary effects as in the natural,   *SB 13* and to show itself in as many and as various forms. Its effects are every where conspicuous; but as to its causes, they are mostly unknown, and must be resolv'd into *original* qualities of human nature, which I pretend not to explain. Nothing is more requisite for a true philosopher, than to restrain the intemperate desire of searching into causes, and having establish'd any doctrine upon a sufficient number of experiments, rest contented with that, when he sees a farther examination wou'd lead him into obscure and uncertain speculations.[†] In that case his enquiry wou'd be much better employ'd in examining the effects than the causes of his principle.

7   Amongst the effects of this union or association of ideas, there are none more remarkable, than those complex ideas, which are the common subjects of our thoughts and reasoning, and generally arise from some principle of union among our simple ideas.[†] These complex ideas may be divided into RELATIONS, MODES, and SUBSTANCES. We shall briefly examine each of these in order, and shall subjoin some considerations concerning our *general* and *particular* ideas, before we leave the present subject, which may be consider'd as the elements of this philosophy.[†]

Sect. 5. *Of relations*

1   The word *relation* is commonly us'd in two senses considerably different from each other.[†] Either for that quality, by which two ideas are connected together in the imagination, and the one naturally introduces the other, after the manner above-explain'd;[†] or for that particular circumstance, in which, even upon the arbitrary union of two ideas in the fancy, we may think proper to compare them. In common language the former is always the sense, in which we use the word, *relation*; and 'tis only in philosophy, that we extend it to mean any particular   *SB 14* subject of comparison, without a connecting principle. Thus distance will be allow'd by philosophers to be a true relation, because we acquire an idea of it by the comparing of objects:[†] But in a common way we say, *that nothing can be more*

distant than such or such things from each other, nothing can have less relation; as if distance and relation were incompatible.

2   It may perhaps be esteem'd an endless task to enumerate all those qualities, which make objects admit of comparison, and by which the ideas of *philosophical* relation[†] are produc'd. But if we diligently consider them, we shall find that without difficulty they may be compriz'd under seven general heads, which may be consider'd as the sources of all *philosophical* relation.

3   1. The first is *resemblance*: And this is a relation, without which no philosophical relation can exist; since no objects will admit of comparison, but what have some degree of resemblance. But tho' resemblance be necessary to all philosophical relation, it does not follow, that it always produces a connexion or association of ideas. When a quality becomes very general, and is common to a great many individuals,[†] it leads not the mind directly to any one of them; but by presenting at once too great a choice, does thereby prevent the imagination from fixing on any single object.

4   2. *Identity* may be esteem'd a second species of relation. This relation I here consider as apply'd in its strictest sense to constant and unchangeable objects; without examining the nature and foundation of personal identity, which shall find its place afterwards.[†] Of all relations the most universal is that of identity, being common to every being, whose existence has any duration.

5   3. After identity the most universal and comprehensive relations are those of *space* and *time*, which are the sources of an infinite number of comparisons, such as *distant*, *contiguous*, *above*, *below*, *before*, *after*, &c.

6   4. All those objects, which admit of *quantity*, or *number*, may be compar'd in   *SB 15* that particular; which is another very fertile source of relation.

7   5. When any two objects possess the same *quality* in common, the *degrees*, in which they possess it, form a fifth species of relation. Thus of two objects, which are both heavy, the one may be either of greater, or less weight than the other. Two colours, that are of the same kind, may yet be of different shades, and in that respect admit of comparison.

8   6. The relation of *contrariety* may at first sight be regarded as an exception to the rule, *that no relation of any kind can subsist without some degree of resemblance*. But let us consider, that no two ideas are in themselves contrary, except those of existence and non-existence, which are plainly resembling, as implying both of them an idea of the object;[†] tho' the latter excludes the object from all times and places, in which it is suppos'd not to exist.

9   7. All other objects, such as fire and water, heat and cold, are only found to be contrary from experience, and from the contrariety of their *causes* or *effects*; which relation of cause and effect is a seventh philosophical relation, as well as a natural one. The resemblance imply'd in this relation, shall be explain'd afterwards.[†]

10   It might naturally be expected, that I shou'd join *difference* to the other relations. But that I consider rather as a negation of relation, than as any thing real or positive. Difference is of two kinds as oppos'd either to

identity or resemblance. The first is call'd a difference of *number*; the other of *kind.*†

Sect. 6. *Of modes and substances*

1   I wou'd fain ask those philosophers, who found so much of their reasonings on the distinction of substance and accident, and imagine we have clear ideas of each, whether the idea of *substance* be deriv'd from the impressions of sensation or reflection?† If it be convey'd to us by our senses, I ask, which of them; and after what manner? If it be perceiv'd by the eyes, it must be a colour; if by the ears, a sound; if by the palate, a taste; and so of the other senses. But I believe none will assert, that substance is either a colour, or a sound, or a taste. The idea of substance must therefore be deriv'd from an impression of reflection, if it really exist. But the impressions of reflection resolve themselves into our passions and emotions; none of which can possibly represent a substance. We have therefore no idea of substance, distinct from that of a collection of particular qualities, nor have we any other meaning when we either talk or reason concerning it.†   *SB 16*

2   The idea of a substance as well as that of a mode,† is nothing but a collection of simple ideas, that are united by the imagination, and have a particular name assign'd them, by which we are able to recal, either to ourselves or others, that collection. But the difference betwixt these ideas consists in this, that the particular qualities, which form a substance, are commonly referr'd to an unknown *something*, in which they are suppos'd to inhere; or granting this fiction† shou'd not take place, are at least suppos'd to be closely and inseparably connected by the relations of contiguity and causation. The effect of this is, that whatever new simple quality we discover to have the same connexion with the rest,† we immediately comprehend it among them, even tho' it did not enter into the first conception of the substance. Thus our idea of gold may at first be a yellow colour, weight, malleableness, fusibility; but upon the discovery of its dissolubility in *aqua regia*, we join that to the other qualities, and suppose it† to belong to the substance as much as if its idea had from the beginning made a part of the compound one. The principle of union being regarded as the chief part of the complex idea,† gives entrance to whatever quality afterwards occurs, and is equally comprehended by it, as are the others, which first presented themselves.

3   That this cannot take place in modes, is evident from considering their nature.   *SB 17* The simple ideas of which modes are form'd, either represent qualities, which are not united by contiguity and causation, but are dispers'd in different subjects; or if they be all united together, the uniting principle is not regarded as the foundation of the complex idea.† The idea of a dance is an instance of the first kind of modes; that of beauty of the second. The reason is obvious, why such complex ideas cannot receive any new idea, without changing the name, which distinguishes the mode.†

Sect. 7. *Of abstract ideas*

1   A very material question has been started concerning *abstract* or *general* ideas, *Whether they be general or particular in the mind's conception of them?* A great philosopher[4] has disputed the receiv'd opinion in this particular,[†] and has asserted, that all general ideas are nothing but particular ones, annex'd to a certain term, which gives them a more extensive signification, and makes them recal upon occasion other individuals,[†] which are similar to them. As I look upon this to be one of the greatest and most valuable discoveries that has been made of late years in the Republic of Letters,[†] I shall here endeavour to confirm it by some arguments, which I hope will put it beyond all doubt and controversy.

2   'Tis evident, that in forming most of our general ideas, if not all of them, we abstract from every particular degree of quantity and quality, and that an object ceases not to be of any particular species on account of every small alteration in its extension, duration and other properties. It may therefore be thought, that here is a plain dilemma, that decides concerning the nature of those abstract ideas, which have afforded so much speculation to philosophers. The abstract   *SB 18* idea of a man represents men of all sizes and all qualities; which 'tis concluded it cannot do, but either by representing at once all possible sizes and all possible qualities, or by representing no particular one at all. Now it having been esteem'd absurd to defend the former proposition, as implying an infinite capacity in the mind,[†] it has been commonly inferr'd in favour of the latter; and our abstract ideas have been suppos'd to represent no particular degree either of quantity or quality. But that this inference is erroneous,[†] I shall endeavour to make appear, *first*, by proving, that 'tis utterly impossible to conceive any quantity or quality, without forming a precise notion of its degrees: And *secondly* by showing, that tho' the capacity of the mind be not infinite, yet we can at once form a notion of all possible degrees of quantity and quality, in such a manner at least, as, however imperfect, may serve all the purposes of reflection and conversation.

3   To begin with the first proposition, *that the mind cannot form any notion of quantity or quality without forming a precise notion of the degrees of each*; we may prove this by the three following arguments. *First*, We have observ'd,[†] that whatever objects are different are distinguishable, and that whatever objects are distinguishable are separable by the thought and imagination. And we may here add, that these propositions are equally true in the *inverse*, and that whatever objects are separable are also distinguishable, and that whatever objects are distinguishable are also different. For how is it possible we can separate what is not distinguishable, or distinguish what is not different? In order therefore to know, whether abstraction implies a separation, we need only consider it in this view,[†] and examine, whether all the circumstances, which we abstract from in our general ideas, be such as are distinguishable and different from those, which we retain as essential parts of them. But 'tis evident at first sight, that the precise length of a line is not different nor distinguishable from the line itself; nor the   *SB 19*

---

[4] Dr. *Berkeley.*[†]   *SB 17*

precise degree of any quality from the quality. These ideas, therefore, admit no more of separation than they do of distinction and difference. They are consequently conjoin'd with each other in the conception; and the general idea of a line, notwithstanding all our abstractions and refinements, has in its appearance in the mind a precise degree of quantity and quality; however it may be made to represent others, which have different degrees of both.

4   *Secondly*, 'Tis confest, that no object can appear to the senses; or in other words, that no impression can become present to the mind, without being determin'd in its degrees both of quantity and quality.[†] The confusion, in which impressions are sometimes involv'd, proceeds only from their faintness and unsteadiness,[†] not from any capacity in the mind to receive any impression, which in its real existence has no particular degree nor proportion. That is a contradiction in terms; and even implies the flattest of all contradictions, *viz.* that 'tis possible for the same thing both to be and not to be.

5   Now since all ideas are deriv'd from impressions, and are nothing but copies and representations of them, whatever is true of the one must be acknowledg'd concerning the other. Impressions and ideas differ only in their strength and vivacity. The foregoing conclusion[†] is not founded on any particular degree of vivacity. It cannot therefore be affected by any variation in that particular. An idea is a weaker impression; and as a strong impression must necessarily have a determinate quantity and quality, the case must be the same with its copy or representative.

6   *Thirdly*, 'Tis a principle generally receiv'd in philosophy, that every thing in nature is individual, and that 'tis utterly absurd to suppose a triangle really existent, which has no precise proportion of sides and angles.[†] If this therefore be absurd in *fact and reality*, it must also be absurd in *idea*; since nothing of which we can form a clear and distinct idea is absurd and impossible. But to form the *SB 20* idea of an object, and to form an idea simply is the same thing; the reference of the idea to an object being an extraneous denomination, of which in itself it bears no mark or character. Now as 'tis impossible to form an idea of an object, that is possest of quantity and quality, and yet is possest of no precise degree of either; it follows, that there is an equal impossibility of forming an idea, that is not limited and confin'd in both these particulars. Abstract ideas are therefore in themselves individual, however they may become general in their representation. The image in the mind is only that of a particular object, tho' the application of it in our reasoning be the same, as if it were universal.

7   This application of ideas beyond their nature[†] proceeds from our collecting all their possible degrees of quantity and quality in such an imperfect manner as may serve the purposes of life, which is the second proposition I propos'd to explain.[†] When we have found a resemblance among several objects,[5] that often

---

[5App.] 'Tis evident, that even different simple ideas may have a similarity or resemblance to each *SB 637* other; nor is it necessary, that the point or circumstance of resemblance shou'd be distinct or separable from that in which they differ. *Blue* and *green* are different simple ideas, but are more resembling than *blue* and *scarlet*; tho' their perfect simplicity excludes all possibility of separation or distinction. 'Tis the same case with particular sounds, and tastes and smells. These admit of infinite

occur to us, we apply the same name to all of them, whatever differences we may observe in the degrees of their quantity and quality, and whatever other differences may appear among them. After we have acquir'd a custom of this kind,[†] the hearing of that name revives the idea of one of these objects, and makes the imagination conceive it with all its particular circumstances and proportions. But as the same word is suppos'd to have been frequently apply'd to other individuals, that are different in many respects from that idea, which is immediately present to the mind; the word not being able to revive the idea of all these individuals, only touches the soul, if I may be allow'd so to speak, and revives that custom, which we have acquir'd by surveying them. They are not really and in fact present to the mind, but only in power;[†] nor do we draw them all out distinctly in the imagination, but keep ourselves in a readiness to survey any of them, as we may be prompted by a present design or necessity. The word raises up an individual idea, along with a certain custom; and that custom produces any other individual one, for which we may have occasion. But as the production of all the ideas, to which the name may be apply'd, is in most cases impossible, we abridge that work by a more partial consideration, and find but few inconveniencies to arise in our reasoning from that abridgment.   *SB 21*

8   For this is one of the most extraordinary circumstances in the present affair, that after the mind has produc'd an individual idea, upon which we reason, the attendant custom, reviv'd by the general or abstract term, readily suggests any other individual, if by chance we form any reasoning, that agrees not with it. Thus shou'd we mention the word, *triangle*, and form the idea of a particular equilateral one to correspond to it, and shou'd we afterwards assert, *that the three angles of a triangle are equal to each other*, the other individuals of a scalenum and isosceles, which we over-look'd at first, immediately crowd in upon us,[†] and make us perceive the falshood of this proposition, tho' it be true with relation to that idea, which we had form'd. If the mind suggests not always these ideas upon occasion, it proceeds from some imperfection in its faculties; and such-a-one as is often the source of false reasoning and sophistry. But this is principally the case with those ideas which are abstruse and compounded. On other occasions the custom is more entire, and 'tis seldom we run into such errors.

9   Nay so entire is the custom, that the very same idea may be annext to several different words, and may be employ'd in different reasonings, without any danger of mistake. Thus the idea of an equilateral triangle of an inch perpendicular may serve us in talking of a *figure*, of a *rectilineal figure*, of a *regular figure*,[†] of a *triangle*, and of an *equilateral triangle*. All these terms, therefore, are in this case attended with the same idea; but as they are wont to be apply'd in a

---

resemblances upon the general appearance and comparison, without having any common circum-   *SB 637* stance the same. And of this we may be certain, even from the very abstract terms *simple idea*. They comprehend all simple ideas under them. These resemble each other in their simplicity. And yet from their very nature, which excludes all composition, this circumstance, in which they resemble, is not distinguishable nor separable from the rest. 'Tis the same case with all the degrees in any quality. They are all resembling, and yet the quality, in any individual, is not distinct from the degree.[App.]

greater or lesser compass, they excite their particular habits,[†] and thereby keep the mind in a readiness to observe, that no conclusion be form'd contrary to any ideas, which are usually compriz'd under them.   *SB 22*

10   Before those habits have become entirely perfect, perhaps the mind may not be content with forming the idea of only one individual, but may run over several, in order to make itself comprehend its own meaning, and the compass of that collection, which it intends to express by the general term. That we may fix the meaning of the word, *figure*, we may revolve in our mind the ideas of circles, squares, parallelograms, triangles of different sizes and proportions, and may not rest on one image or idea. However this may be, 'tis certain *that* we form the idea of individuals, whenever we use any general term; *that* we seldom or never can exhaust these individuals;[†] and *that* those, which remain, are only represented by means of that habit, by which we recal them, whenever any present occasion requires it. This then is the nature of our abstract ideas and general terms; and 'tis after this manner we account for the foregoing paradox, *that some ideas are particular in their nature, but general in their representation.*[†] A particular idea becomes general by being annex'd to a general term; that is, to a term, which from a customary conjunction has a relation to many other particular ideas, and readily recals them in the imagination.

11   The only difficulty, that can remain on this subject, must be with regard to that custom, which so readily recals every particular idea, for which we may have occasion, and is excited by any word or sound, to which we commonly annex it. The most proper method, in my opinion, of giving a satisfactory explication of this act of the mind, is by producing other instances, which are analogous to it, and other principles, which facilitate its operation. To explain the ultimate causes of our mental actions is impossible. 'Tis sufficient, if we can give any satisfactory account of them from experience and analogy.

12   *First* then I observe, that when we mention any great number, such as a thou-   *SB 23*
sand, the mind has generally no adequate idea of it, but only a power of producing such an idea, by its adequate idea of the decimals, under which the number is comprehended.[†] This imperfection, however, in our ideas, is never felt in our reasonings; which seems to be an instance parallel to the present one of universal ideas.

13   *Secondly*, We have several instances of habits, which may be reviv'd by one single word; as when a person, who has by rote any periods[†] of a discourse, or any number of verses, will be put in remembrance of the whole, which he is at a loss to recollect, by that single word or expression, with which they begin.

14   *Thirdly*, I believe every one, who examines the situation of his mind in reasoning, will agree with me, that we do not annex distinct and compleat ideas to every term we make use of, and that in talking of *government, church, negotiation, conquest*, we seldom spread out in our minds all the simple ideas, of which these complex ones are compos'd. 'Tis however observable, that notwithstanding this imperfection we may avoid talking nonsense on these subjects, and may perceive any repugnance among the ideas, as well as if we had a full comprehension of them. Thus if instead of saying, *that in war the weaker have always recourse to*

negotiation, we shou'd say, *that they have always recourse to conquest*, the custom, which we have acquir'd of attributing certain relations to ideas, still follows the words, and makes us immediately perceive the absurdity of that proposition;[†] in the same manner as one particular idea may serve us in reasoning concerning other ideas, however different from it in several circumstances.

15 · *Fourthly*, As the individuals are collected together, and plac'd under a general term with a view to that resemblance, which they bear to each other, this relation must facilitate their entrance in the imagination, and make them be suggested more readily upon occasion. And indeed if we consider the common progress of the thought, either in reflection or conversation, we shall find great reason *SB 24* to be satisfy'd in this particular. Nothing is more admirable, than the readiness, with which the imagination suggests its ideas, and presents them at the very instant, in which they become necessary or useful. The fancy runs from one end of the universe to the other in collecting those ideas, which belong to any subject. One wou'd think the whole intellectual world of ideas was at once subjected to our view, and that we did nothing but pick out such as were most proper for our purpose. There may not, however, be any present, beside those very ideas, that are thus collected by a kind of magical faculty in the soul,[†] which, tho' it be always most perfect in the greatest geniuses, and is properly what we call a genius, is however inexplicable by the utmost efforts of human understanding.

16 Perhaps these four reflections may help to remove all difficulties to the hypothesis I have propos'd[†] concerning abstract ideas, so contrary to that, which has hitherto prevail'd in philosophy. But to tell the truth I place my chief confidence in what I have already prov'd[†] concerning the impossibility of general ideas, according to the common method of explaining them. We must certainly seek some new system on this head, and there plainly is none beside what I have propos'd. If ideas be particular in their nature, and at the same time finite in their number, 'tis only by custom they can become general in their representation, and contain an infinite number of other ideas under them.

17 Before I leave this subject I shall employ the same principles to explain that *distinction of reason*,[†] which is so much talk'd of, and is so little understood, in the schools.[†] Of this kind is the distinction betwixt figure and the body figur'd; motion and the body mov'd. The difficulty of explaining this distinction arises from the principle above-explain'd, *that all ideas, which are different, are separable.*[†] For it follows from thence, that if the figure be different from the body, their ideas must be separable as well as distinguishable; if they be not *SB 25* different, their ideas can neither be separable nor distinguishable. What then is meant by a distinction of reason, since it implies neither a difference nor separation?

18 To remove this difficulty we must have recourse to the foregoing explication of abstract ideas. 'Tis certain that the mind wou'd never have dream'd of distinguishing a figure from the body figur'd, as being in reality neither distinguishable, nor different, nor separable; did it not observe, that even in this simplicity there might be contain'd many different resemblances and relations. Thus when

a globe of white marble is presented, we receive only the impression of a white colour dispos'd in a certain form, nor are we able to separate and distinguish the colour from the form. But observing afterwards a globe of black marble and a cube of white, and comparing them with our former object, we find two separate resemblances, in what formerly seem'd, and really is, perfectly inseparable. After a little more practice of this kind, we begin to distinguish the figure from the colour by a *distinction of reason*; that is, we consider the figure and colour together, since they are in effect the same and undistinguishable; but still view them in different aspects, according to the resemblances, of which they are susceptible. When we wou'd consider only the figure of the globe of white marble, we form in reality an idea both of the figure and colour, but tacitly carry our eye to its resemblance with the globe of black marble: And in the same manner, when we wou'd consider its colour only, we turn our view to its resemblance with the cube of white marble. By this means we accompany our ideas with a kind of reflection, of which custom renders us, in a great measure, insensible.[†] A person, who desires us to consider the figure of a globe of white marble without thinking on its colour, desires an impossibility; but his meaning is, that we shou'd consider the colour and figure together, but still keep in our eye the resemblance to the globe of black marble, or that to any other globe of whatever colour or substance.

PART 2

Of the ideas of space and time

Sect. 1. Of the infinite divisibility of our ideas of space and time

1   Whatever has the air of a paradox, and is contrary to the first and most unprejudic'd notions of mankind is often greedily embrac'd by philosophers, as showing the superiority of their science, which cou'd discover opinions so remote from vulgar conception.[†] On the other hand, any thing propos'd to us, which causes surprize and admiration, gives such a satisfaction to the mind, that it indulges itself in those agreeable emotions, and will never be perswaded that its pleasure is entirely without foundation. From these dispositions in philosophers and their disciples arises that mutual complaisance betwixt them; while the former furnish such plenty of strange and unaccountable opinions, and the latter so readily believe them. Of this mutual complaisance I cannot give a more evident instance than in the doctrine of infinite divisibility, with the examination of which I shall begin this subject of the ideas of space and time.

2   'Tis universally allow'd, that the capacity of the mind is limited,[†] and can never attain a full and adequate conception of infinity: And tho' it were not allow'd, 'twou'd be sufficiently evident from the plainest observation and experience. 'Tis also obvious, that whatever is capable of being divided *in infinitum*, must consist of an infinite number of parts, and that 'tis impossible to set any bounds to the number of parts, without setting bounds at the same time to the division. It requires scarce any induction[†] to conclude from hence, that the *idea*, which we form of any finite quality, is not infinitely divisible, but that by proper distinctions and separations we may run up this idea to inferior ones,[†] which will be perfectly simple and indivisible. In rejecting the infinite capacity of the mind, we suppose it may arrive at an end in the division of its ideas; nor are there any possible means of evading the evidence of this conclusion.[†]

3   'Tis therefore certain, that the imagination reaches a *minimum*, and may raise up to itself an idea, of which it cannot conceive any sub-division, and which cannot be diminish'd without a total annihilation.[†] When you tell me of the thousandth and ten thousandth part of a grain of sand, I have a distinct idea of these numbers and of their different proportions; but the images, which I form in my mind to represent the things themselves, are nothing different from each other, nor inferior to that image, by which I represent the grain of sand itself, which is suppos'd so vastly to exceed them. What consists of parts is distinguishable into them, and what is distinguishable is separable.[†] But whatever we may imagine of the thing, the idea of a grain of sand is not distinguishable, nor separable into twenty, much less into a thousand, ten thousand, or an infinite number of different ideas.

4   'Tis the same case with the impressions of the senses as with the ideas of the imagination. Put a spot of ink upon paper, fix your eye upon that spot, and retire to such a distance, that at last you lose sight of it; 'tis plain, that the moment before it vanish'd the image or impression was perfectly indivisible.† 'Tis not for want of rays of light striking on our eyes, that the minute parts of distant bodies convey not any sensible impression; but because they are remov'd beyond that distance, at which their impressions were reduc'd to a *minimum*, and were incapable of any farther diminution. A microscope or telescope, which renders them *SB 28* visible, produces not any new rays of light, but only spreads those, which always flow'd from them; and by that means both gives parts to impressions, which to the naked eye appear simple and uncompounded, and advances to a *minimum*, what was formerly imperceptible.

5   We may hence discover the error of the common opinion, that the capacity of the mind is limited on both sides, and that 'tis impossible for the imagination to form an adequate idea, of what goes beyond a certain degree of minuteness as well as of greatness. Nothing can be more minute, than some ideas, which we form in the fancy; and images, which appear to the senses; since these are ideas and images perfectly simple and indivisible. The only defect of our senses is, that they give us disproportion'd images of things, and represent as minute and uncompounded what is really great and compos'd of a vast number of parts. This mistake we are not sensible of; but taking the impressions of those minute objects, which appear to the senses, to be equal or nearly equal to the objects, and finding by reason, that there are other objects vastly more minute, we too hastily conclude, that these are inferior to any idea of our imagination or impression of our senses. This however is certain, that we can form ideas, which shall be no greater than the smallest atom of the animal spirits of an insect a thousand times less than a mite:† And we ought rather to conclude, that the difficulty lies in enlarging our conceptions so much as to form a just notion of a mite, or even of an insect a thousand times less than a mite. For in order to form a just notion of these animals, we must have a distinct idea representing every part of them; which, according to the system of infinite divisibility, is utterly impossible, and according to that of indivisible parts or atoms, is extremely difficult, by reason of the vast number and multiplicity of these parts.

Sect. 2. *Of the infinite divisibility of space and time*   *SB 29*

1   Wherever ideas are adequate representations of objects, the relations, contradictions and agreements of the ideas are all applicable to the objects;† and this we may in general observe to be the foundation of all human knowledge. But our ideas are adequate representations of the most minute parts of extension; and thro' whatever divisions and sub-divisions we may suppose these parts to be arriv'd at, they can never become inferior to some ideas, which we form. The plain consequence is, that whatever *appears* impossible and contradictory upon the comparison of these ideas, must be *really* impossible and contradictory, without any farther excuse or evasion.†

2   Every thing capable of being infinitely divided contains an infinite number of parts; otherwise the division wou'd be stopt short by the indivisible parts, which we shou'd immediately arrive at. If therefore any finite extension be infinitely divisible, it can be no contradiction to suppose, that a finite extension contains an infinite number of parts: And *vice versa*, if it be a contradiction to suppose, that a finite extension contains an infinite number of parts, no finite extension can be infinitely divisible.[†] But that this latter supposition is absurd, I easily convince myself by the consideration of my clear ideas. I first take the least idea I can form of a part of extension, and being certain that there is nothing more minute than this idea, I conclude, that whatever I discover by its means must be a real quality of extension. I then repeat this idea once, twice, thrice, *&c.* and find the compound idea of extension, arising from its repetition, always to augment, and become double, triple, quadruple, *&c.* till at last it swells up to a considerable bulk, greater or smaller, in proportion as I repeat more or less the same idea.[†] When I stop in the addition of parts, the idea of extension ceases to augment;   *SB 30* and were I to carry on the addition *in infinitum*, I clearly perceive, that the idea of extension must also become infinite. Upon the whole, I conclude, that the idea of an infinite number of parts is individually the same idea with[†] that of an infinite extension; that no finite extension is capable of containing an infinite number of parts; and consequently that no finite extension is infinitely divisible.[6]

3   I may subjoin another argument propos'd by a noted author,[7] which seems to me very strong and beautiful. 'Tis evident, that existence in itself belongs only to unity,[†] and is never applicable to number,[†] but on account of the unites, of which the number is compos'd. Twenty men may be said to exist; but 'tis only because one, two, three, four, *&c.* are existent; and if you deny the existence of the latter, that of the former falls of course. 'Tis therefore utterly absurd to suppose any number to exist, and yet deny the existence of unites; and as extension is always a number, according to the common sentiment of metaphysicians, and never resolves itself into any unite or indivisible quantity, it follows, that extension can never at all exist.[†] 'Tis in vain to reply, that any determinate quantity of extension is an unite; but such-a-one as admits of an infinite number of fractions, and is inexhaustible in its sub-divisions.[†] For by the same rule these twenty men *may be consider'd as an unite*. The whole globe of the earth, nay the whole universe *may be consider'd as an unite*. That term of unity is merely a fictitious denomination,[†] which the mind may apply to any quantity of objects it collects together; nor can such an unity any more exist alone than number can, as being in reality a true number. But the unity, which can exist alone, and whose   *SB 31* existence is necessary to that of all number, is of another kind, and must be perfectly indivisible, and incapable of being resolv'd into any lesser unity.

---

[6] It has been objected to me, that infinite divisibility supposes only an infinite number of *propor-*   *SB 30* *tional* not of *aliquot* parts,[†] and that an infinite number of proportional parts does not form an infinite extension. But this distinction is entirely frivolous. Whether these parts be call'd *aliquot* or *proportional*, they cannot be inferior to those minute parts we conceive; and therefore cannot form a less extension by their conjunction.   [7] Mons. *Malezieu.*[†]

4   All this reasoning takes place with regard to time;[†] along with an additional argument, which it may be proper to take notice of. 'Tis a property inseparable from time, and which in a manner constitutes its essence, that each of its parts succeeds another, and that none of them, however contiguous, can ever be co-existent.[†] For the same reason, that the year 1737 cannot concur with the present year 1738,[†] every moment must be distinct from, and posterior or antecedent to another. 'Tis certain then, that time, as it exists, must be compos'd of indivisible moments. For if in time we cou'd never arrive at an end of division, and if each moment, as it succeeds another, were not perfectly single and indivisible, there wou'd be an infinite number of co-existent moments, or parts of time; which I believe will be allow'd to be an arrant contradiction.

5   The infinite divisibility of space implies that of time, as is evident from the nature of motion. If the latter, therefore, be impossible, the former must be equally so.

6   I doubt not but it will readily be allow'd by the most obstinate defender of the doctrine of infinite divisibility, that these arguments are difficulties, and that 'tis impossible to give any answer to them which will be perfectly clear and satis-factory. But here we may observe, that nothing can be more absurd, than this custom of calling a *difficulty* what pretends to be a *demonstration*, and endeavour-ing by that means to elude its force and evidence.[†] 'Tis not in demonstrations as in probabilities, that difficulties can take place, and one argument counter-ballance another, and diminish its authority. A demonstration, if just, admits of no opposite difficulty; and if not just, 'tis a mere sophism, and consequently can never be a difficulty. 'Tis either irresistible, or has no manner of force. To talk therefore of objections and replies, and ballancing of arguments in such a ques-tion as this, is to confess, either that human reason is nothing but a play of words, or that the person himself, who talks so, has not a capacity equal to such subjects. Demonstrations may be difficult to be comprehended, because of the abstract-edness of the subject; but can never have any such difficulties as will weaken their authority, when once they are comprehended. *SB 32*

7   'Tis true, mathematicians are wont to say, that there are here equally strong arguments on the other side of the question, and that the doctrine of indivisible points is also liable to unanswerable objections.[†] Before I examine these argu-ments and objections in detail, I will here take them in a body, and endeavour by a short and decisive reasoning to prove at once, that 'tis utterly impossible they can have any just foundation.

8   'Tis an establish'd maxim in metaphysics, *that whatever the mind clearly con-ceives includes the idea of possible existence*, or in other words, *that nothing we imagine is absolutely impossible*.[†] We can form the idea of a golden mountain, and from thence conclude that such a mountain may actually exist.[†] We can form no idea of a mountain without a valley, and therefore regard it as impossible.[†]

9   Now 'tis certain we have an idea of extension; for otherwise why do we talk and reason concerning it?[†] 'Tis likewise certain, that this idea, as conceiv'd by the imagination, tho' divisible into parts or inferior ideas, is not infinitely divisi-

ble, nor consists of an infinite number of parts: For that exceeds the comprehension of our limited capacities. Here then is an idea of extension, which consists of parts or inferior ideas, that are perfectly indivisible: Consequently this idea implies no contradiction: Consequently 'tis possible for extension really to exist conformable to it:[†] And consequently all the arguments employ'd against the possibility of mathematical points are mere scholastick quibbles,[†] and unworthy of our attention.

10   These consequences we may carry one step farther, and conclude that all the pretended demonstrations for the infinite divisibility of extension are equally sophistical; since 'tis certain these demonstrations cannot be just without proving the impossibility of mathematical points; which 'tis an evident absurdity to pretend to.   *SB 33*

Sect. 3. *Of the other qualities of our ideas of space and time*

1   No discovery cou'd have been made more happily for deciding all controversies concerning ideas, than that above-mention'd,[†] that impressions always take the precedency of them, and that every idea, with which the imagination is furnish'd, first makes its appearance in a correspondent impression. These latter perceptions are all so clear and evident, that they admit of no controversy; tho' many of our ideas are so obscure, that 'tis almost impossible even for the mind, which forms them, to tell exactly their nature and composition. Let us apply this principle, in order to discover farther the nature of our ideas of space and time.

2   Upon opening my eyes, and turning them to the surrounding objects, I perceive many visible bodies; and upon shutting them again, and considering the distance betwixt these bodies, I acquire the idea of extension.[†] As every idea is deriv'd from some impression, which is exactly similar to it, the impressions similar to this idea of extension, must either be some sensations deriv'd from the sight, or some internal impressions arising from these sensations.

3   Our internal impressions[†] are our passions, emotions, desires and aversions; none of which, I believe, will ever be asserted to be the model, from which the idea of space is deriv'd. There remains therefore nothing but the senses, which can convey to us this original impression. Now what impression do our senses here convey to us? This is the principal question, and decides without appeal concerning the nature of the idea.[†]   *SB 34*

4   The table before me is alone sufficient by its view to give me the idea of extension. This idea, then, is borrow'd from, and represents some impression, which this moment appears to the senses. But my senses convey to me only the impressions of colour'd points,[†] dispos'd in a certain manner. If the eye is sensible of any thing farther, I desire it may be pointed out to me. But if it be impossible to show any thing farther, we may conclude with certainty, that the idea of extension is nothing but a copy of these colour'd points, and of the manner of their appearance.

5   Suppose that in the extended object, or composition of colour'd points, from which we first receiv'd the idea of extension, the points were of a purple colour; it follows, that in every repetition of that idea we wou'd not only place the points in the same order with respect to each other, but also bestow on them that precise colour, with which alone we are acquainted. But afterwards having experience of the other colours of violet, green, red, white, black, and of all the different compositions of these, and finding a resemblance in the disposition of colour'd points, of which they are compos'd, we omit the peculiarities of colour, as far as possible, and found an abstract idea merely on that disposition of points, or manner of appearance, in which they agree. Nay even when the resemblance is carry'd beyond the objects of one sense, and the impressions of touch are found to be similar to those of sight in the disposition of their parts; this does not hinder the abstract idea from representing both, upon account of their resemblance. All abstract ideas are really nothing but particular ones, consider'd in a certain light; but being annex'd to general terms, they are able to represent a vast variety, and to comprehend objects, which, as they are alike in some particulars, are in others vastly wide of each other.[†]

6   The idea of time, being deriv'd from the succession of our perceptions   *SB 35* of every kind, ideas as well as impressions, and impressions of reflection as well as of sensation, will afford us an instance of an abstract idea, which comprehends a still greater variety than that of space, and yet is represented in the fancy by some particular individual idea of a determinate quantity and quality.

7   As 'tis from the disposition of visible and tangible objects we receive the idea of space, so from the succession of ideas and impressions we form the idea of time, nor is it possible for time alone ever to make its appearance, or be taken notice of by the mind. A man in a sound sleep, or strongly occupy'd with one thought, is insensible of time; and according as his perceptions succeed each other with greater or less rapidity, the same duration appears longer or shorter to his imagination.[†] It has been remark'd by a great philosopher,[8] that our perceptions have certain bounds in this particular, which are fix'd by the original nature and constitution of the mind, and beyond which no influence of external objects on the senses is ever able to hasten or retard our thought. If you wheel about a burning coal with rapidity, it will present to the senses an image of a circle of fire;[†] nor will there seem to be any interval of time betwixt its revolutions; merely because 'tis impossible for our perceptions to succeed each other with the same rapidity, that motion may be communicated to external objects. Wherever we have no successive perceptions, we have no notion of time, even tho' there be a real succession in the objects. From these phænomena, as well as from many others, we may conclude, that time cannot make its appearance to the mind, either alone, or attended with a steady unchangeable object, but is always discover'd by some *perceivable* succession of changeable objects.

8   To confirm this we may add the following argument, which to me seems per-

---

[8] Mr. *Locke.*[†]

fectly decisive and convincing. 'Tis evident, that time or duration consists of different parts: For otherwise we cou'd not conceive a longer or shorter duration. 'Tis also evident, that these parts are not co-existent:[†] For that quality of the co-existence of parts belongs to extension, and is what distinguishes it from duration. Now as time is compos'd of parts, that are not co-existent; an unchangeable object, since it produces none but co-existent impressions, produces none that can give us the idea of time; and consequently that idea must be deriv'd from a succession of changeable objects, and time in its first appearance can never be sever'd from such a succession.

SB 36

9   Having therefore found, that time in its first appearance to the mind is always conjoin'd with a succession of changeable objects, and that otherwise it can never fall under our notice, we must now examine whether it can be *conceiv'd* without our conceiving any succession of objects, and whether it can alone form a distinct idea in the imagination.[†]

10   In order to know whether any objects, which are join'd in impression, be separable in idea, we need only consider, if they be different from each other; in which case, 'tis plain they may be conceiv'd apart. Every thing, that is different, is distinguishable; and every thing, that is distinguishable, may be separated, according to the maxims above-explain'd.[†] If on the contrary they be not different, they are not distinguishable; and if they be not distinguishable, they cannot be separated. But this is precisely the case with respect to time, compar'd with our successive perceptions. The idea of time is not deriv'd from a particular impression mix'd up with others, and plainly distinguishable from them; but arises altogether from the manner, in which impressions appear to the mind, without making one of the number.[†] Five notes play'd on a flute give us the impression and idea of time; tho' time be not a sixth impression, which presents itself to the hearing or any other of the senses. Nor is it a sixth impression, which the mind by reflection finds in itself. These five sounds making their appearance in this particular manner, excite no emotion in the mind, nor produce an affection of any kind, which being observ'd by it can give rise to a new idea. For *that* is necessary to produce a new idea of reflection, nor can the mind, by revolving over a thousand times all its ideas of sensation, ever extract from them any new original idea, unless nature has so fram'd its faculties, that it feels some new original impression arise from such a contemplation. But here it only takes notice of the *manner*, in which the different sounds make their appearance; and that it may afterwards consider without considering these particular sounds, but may conjoin it with any other objects.[†] The ideas of some objects it certainly must have, nor is it possible for it without these ideas ever to arrive at any conception of time; which since it appears not as any primary distinct impression, can plainly be nothing but different ideas, or impressions, or objects dispos'd in a certain manner, that is, succeeding each other.

SB 37

11   I know there are some who pretend, that the idea of duration is applicable in a proper sense to objects, which are perfectly unchangeable; and this I take to be the common opinion of philosophers as well as of the vulgar.[†] But to be convinc'd of its falsehood we need but reflect on the foregoing conclusion, that the

idea of duration is always deriv'd from a succession of changeable objects, and can never be convey'd to the mind by any thing stedfast and unchangeable. For it inevitably follows from thence, that since the idea of duration cannot be deriv'd from such an object, it can never in any propriety or exactness be apply'd to it, nor can any thing unchangeable be ever said to have duration. Ideas always represent the objects or impressions, from which they are deriv'd, and can never without a fiction represent or be apply'd to any other. By what fiction we apply the idea of time, even to what is unchangeable, and suppose, as is common, that duration is a measure of rest as well as of motion, we shall consider afterwards.[9]

12   There is another very decisive argument, which establishes the present doctrine concerning our ideas of space and time, and is founded only on that simple principle, *that our ideas of them are compounded of parts, which are indivisible*. This argument may be worth the examining.   *SB 38*

13   Every idea, that is distinguishable, being also separable, let us take one of those simple indivisible ideas, of which the compound one of *extension* is form'd, and separating it from all others, and considering it apart, let us form a judgment of its nature and qualities.

14   'Tis plain it is not the idea of extension. For the idea of extension consists of parts; and this idea, according to the supposition, is perfectly simple and indivisible. Is it therefore nothing? That is absolutely impossible. For as the compound idea of extension, which is real, is compos'd of such ideas; were these so many non-entities, there wou'd be a real existence compos'd of non-entities; which is absurd. Here therefore I must ask, *What is our idea of a simple and indivisible point?* No wonder if my answer appear somewhat new, since the question itself has scarce ever yet been thought of. We are wont to dispute concerning the nature of mathematical points, but seldom concerning the nature of their ideas.

15   The idea of space is convey'd to the mind by two senses, the sight and touch; nor does any thing ever appear extended, that is not either visible or tangible. That compound impression, which represents extension, consists of several lesser impressions, that are indivisible to the eye or feeling,[†] and may be call'd impressions of atoms or corpuscles endow'd with colour and solidity. But this is not all. 'Tis not only requisite, that these atoms shou'd be colour'd or tangible, in order to discover themselves to our senses; 'tis also necessary we shou'd preserve the idea of their colour or tangibility in order to comprehend them by our imagination. There is nothing but the idea of their colour or tangibility, which can render them conceivable by the mind. Upon the removal of the ideas of these sensible qualities, they are utterly annihilated to the thought or imagination.[†]   *SB 39*

16   Now such as the parts are, such is the whole. If a point be not consider'd as colour'd or tangible, it can convey to us no idea; and consequently the idea of

---

[9] Sect. 5.[†]   *SB 37*

extension, which is compos'd of the ideas of these points, can never possibly exist. But if the idea of extension really can exist, as we are conscious it does, its parts must also exist; and in order to that, must be consider'd as colour'd or tangible. We have therefore no idea of space or extension, but when we regard it as an object either of our sight or feeling.

17   The same reasoning will prove, that the indivisible moments of time must be fill'd with some real object or existence, whose succession forms the duration, and makes it be conceivable by the mind.

Sect. 4. *Objections answer'd*

1   Our system concerning space and time consists of two parts, which are intimately connected together. The first depends on this chain of reasoning. The capacity of the mind is not infinite; consequently no idea of extension or duration consists of an infinite number of parts or inferior ideas, but of a finite number, and these simple and indivisible: 'Tis therefore possible for space and time to exist conformable to this idea: And if it be possible, 'tis certain they actually do exist conformable to it; since their infinite divisibility is utterly impossible and contradictory.

2   The other part of our system is a consequence of this. The parts, into which the ideas of space and time resolve themselves, become at last indivisible; and these indivisible parts, being nothing in themselves, are inconceivable when not fill'd with something real and existent. The ideas of space and time are therefore no separate or distinct ideas, but merely those of the manner or order, in which *SB 40* objects exist: Or, in other words, 'tis impossible to conceive either a vacuum and extension without matter,[†] or a time, when there was no succession or change in any real existence. The intimate connexion betwixt these parts of our system is the reason why we shall examine together the objections, which have been urg'd against both of them, beginning with those against the finite divisibility of extension.

3   1. The first of these objections, which I shall take notice of, is more proper to prove this connexion and dependance of the one part upon the other, than to destroy either of them. It has often been maintain'd in the schools, that extension must be divisible, *in infinitum*, because the system of mathematical points is absurd; and that system is absurd, because a mathematical point is a non-entity, and consequently can never by its conjunction with others form a real existence.[†] This wou'd be perfectly decisive, were there no medium[†] betwixt the infinite divisibility of matter, and the non-entity of mathematical points. But there is evidently a medium, *viz.* the bestowing a colour or solidity on these points; and the absurdity of both the extremes is a demonstration of the truth and reality of this medium. The system of *physical* points,[†] which is another medium, is too absurd to need a refutation. A real extension, such as a physical point is suppos'd to be, can never exist without parts, different from each other; and wherever objects are different, they are distinguishable and separable by the imagination.

4   2. The second objection is deriv'd from the necessity there wou'd be of *penetration*,[†] if extension consisted of mathematical points. A simple and indivisible atom, that touches another, must necessarily penetrate it; for 'tis impossible it can touch it by its external parts, from the very supposition of its perfect simplicity, which excludes all parts. It must therefore touch it intimately, and in its whole essence, *secundum se, tota, & totaliter*;[†] which is the very definition of penetration. But penetration is impossible:[†] Mathematical points are of consequence equally impossible.   SB 41

5   I answer this objection by substituting a juster idea of penetration. Suppose two bodies containing no void within their circumference,[†] to approach each other, and to unite in such a manner that the body, which results from their union, is no more extended than either of them; 'tis this we must mean when we talk of penetration. But 'tis evident this penetration is nothing but the annihilation of one of these bodies, and the preservation of the other, without our being able to distinguish particularly which is preserv'd and which annihilated. Before the approach we have the idea of two bodies. After it we have the idea only of one. 'Tis impossible for the mind to preserve any notion of difference betwixt two bodies of the same nature existing in the same place at the same time.

6   Taking then penetration in this sense, for the annihilation of one body upon its approach to another, I ask any one, if he sees a necessity, that a colour'd or tangible point shou'd be annihilated upon the approach of another colour'd or tangible point? On the contrary, does he not evidently perceive, that from the union of these points there results an object, which is compounded and divisible, and may be distinguish'd into two parts, of which each preserves its existence distinct and separate, notwithstanding its contiguity to the other? Let him aid his fancy by conceiving these points to be of different colours, the better to prevent their coalition and confusion. A blue and a red point may surely lie contiguous without any penetration or annihilation. For if they cannot, what possibly can become of them? Whether will the red or the blue be annihilated? Or if these colours unite into one, what new colour will they produce by their union?

7   What chiefly gives rise to these objections, and at the same time renders it so difficult to give a satisfactory answer to them, is the natural infirmity and unsteadiness both of our imagination and senses, when employ'd on such minute objects. Put a spot of ink upon paper, and retire to such a distance, that the spot becomes altogether invisible;[†] you will find, that upon your return and nearer approach the spot first becomes visible by short intervals; and afterwards becomes always visible; and afterwards acquires only a new force in its colouring without augmenting its bulk; and afterwards, when it has encreas'd to such a degree as to be really extended, 'tis still difficult for the imagination to break it into its component parts, because of the uneasiness it finds in the conception of such a minute object as a single point. This infirmity affects most of our reasonings on the present subject, and makes it almost impossible to answer in an intelligible manner, and in proper expressions, many questions which may arise concerning it.   SB 42

8   3. There have been many objections drawn from the *mathematics* against the indivisibility of the parts of extension; tho' at first sight that science seems rather favourable to the present doctrine; and if it be contrary in its *demonstrations*, 'tis perfectly conformable in its *definitions*. My present business then must be to defend the definitions, and refute the demonstrations.

9   A surface is *defin'd* to be length and breadth without depth: A line to be length without breadth or depth: A point to be what has neither length, breadth nor depth.[†] 'Tis evident, that all this is perfectly unintelligible upon any other supposition than that of the composition of extension by indivisible points or atoms. How else cou'd any thing exist without length, without breadth, or without depth?

10   Two different answers, I find, have been made to this argument; neither of which is in my opinion satisfactory. The *first* is, that the objects of geometry, those surfaces, lines and points, whose proportions and positions it examines, are mere ideas in the mind; and not only never did, but never can exist in nature.[†] They never did exist; for no one will pretend to draw a line or make a surface entirely conformable to the definition: They never can exist; for we may produce demonstrations from these very ideas to prove, that they are impossible.   *SB 43*

11   But can any thing be imagin'd more absurd and contradictory than this reasoning? Whatever can be conceiv'd by a clear and distinct idea necessarily implies the possibility of existence;[†] and he who pretends to prove the impossibility of its existence by any argument deriv'd from the clear idea, in reality asserts, that we have no clear idea of it, because we have a clear idea. 'Tis in vain to search for a contradiction in any thing that is distinctly conceiv'd by the mind. Did it imply any contradiction, 'tis impossible it cou'd ever be conceiv'd.

12   There is therefore no medium betwixt allowing at least the possibility of indivisible points, and denying their idea; and 'tis on this latter principle, that the *second* answer to the foregoing argument[†] is founded. It has been pretended,[10] that tho' it be impossible to conceive a length without any breadth, yet by an abstraction without a separation, we can consider the one without regarding the other; in the same manner as we may think of the length of the way betwixt two towns, and overlook its breadth. The length is inseparable from the breadth both in nature and in our minds; but this excludes not a partial consideration, and a *distinction of reason*, after the manner above-explain'd.[†]

13   In refuting this answer I shall not insist on the argument, which I have already sufficiently explain'd,[†] that if it be impossible for the mind to arrive at a *minimum* in its ideas, its capacity must be infinite, in order to comprehend the infinite number of parts, of which its idea of any extension wou'd be compos'd. I shall here endeavour to find some new absurdities in this reasoning.

14   A surface terminates a solid; a line terminates a surface; a point terminates a line;[†] but I assert, that if the *ideas* of a point, line or surface were not indivisible,

[10]   *L'Art de penser.*[†]

'tis impossible we shou'd ever conceive these terminations. For let these ideas be   SB 44
suppos'd infinitely divisible; and then let the fancy endeavour to fix itself on the
idea of the last surface, line or point; it immediately finds this idea to break into
parts; and upon its seizing the last of these parts, it loses its hold by a new division, and so on *in infinitum*, without any possibility of its arriving at a concluding
idea. The number of fractions bring it no nearer the last division, than the first
idea it form'd. Every particle eludes the grasp by a new fraction; like quick-
silver, when we endeavour to seize it. But as in fact there must be something,
which terminates the idea of every finite quantity; and as this terminating idea
cannot itself consist of parts or inferior ideas; otherwise it wou'd be the last of its
parts, which finish'd the idea, and so on;[†] this is a clear proof, that the ideas of
surfaces, lines and points admit not of any division; those of surfaces in depth; of
lines in breadth and depth; and of points in any dimension.

15   The *schoolmen* were so sensible of the force of this argument, that some of
them maintain'd, that nature has mix'd among those particles of matter, which
are divisible *in infinitum*, a number of mathematical points, in order to give a termination to bodies; and others eluded the force of this reasoning by a heap of
unintelligible cavils and distinctions.[†] Both these adversaries equally yield the
victory. A man who hides himself, confesses as evidently the superiority of his
enemy, as another, who fairly delivers his arms.

16   Thus it appears, that the definitions of mathematics destroy the pretended demonstrations; and that if we have the idea of indivisible points,
lines and surfaces conformable to the definition, their existence is certainly possible: But if we have no such idea, 'tis impossible we can ever conceive the termination of any figure; without which conception there can be no geometrical
demonstration.

17   But I go farther, and maintain, that none of these demonstrations can have
sufficient weight to establish such a principle, as this of infinite divisibility; and   SB 45
that because with regard to such minute objects, they are not properly demonstrations, being built on ideas, which are not exact, and maxims, which are not
precisely true. When geometry decides any thing concerning the proportions of
quantity, we ought not to look for the utmost *precision* and exactness.[†] None of its
proofs extend so far. It takes the dimensions and proportions of figures justly;
but roughly, and with some liberty. Its errors are never considerable; nor wou'd
it err at all, did it not aspire to such an absolute perfection.

18   I first ask mathematicians, what they mean when they say one line or surface is
EQUAL to, or GREATER, or LESS than another? Let any of them give an answer, to
whatever sect he belongs, and whether he maintains the composition of extension by indivisible points, or by quantities divisible *in infinitum*. This question
will embarrass both of them.

19   There are few or no mathematicians, who defend the hypothesis of indivisible
points; and yet these have the readiest and justest answer to the present question.
They need only reply, that lines or surfaces are equal, when the numbers of
points in each are equal; and that as the proportion of the numbers varies, the
proportion of the lines and surfaces is also vary'd. But tho' this answer be *just*, as

well as obvious; yet I may affirm, that this standard of equality is entirely *useless*, and that it never is from such a comparison we determine objects to be equal or unequal with respect to each other. For as the points, which enter into the composition of any line or surface, whether perceiv'd by the sight or touch, are so minute and so confounded with each other, that 'tis utterly impossible for the mind to compute their number, such a computation will never afford us a standard, by which we may judge of proportions. No one will ever be able to determine by an exact numeration, that an inch has fewer points than a foot, or a foot fewer than an ell or any greater measure; for which reason we seldom or never consider this as the standard of equality or inequality.

20   As to those, who imagine, that extension is divisible *in infinitum*, 'tis impossible they can make use of this answer, or fix the equality of any line or surface by a numeration of its component parts. For since, according to their hypothesis, the least as well as greatest figures contain an infinite number of parts; and since infinite numbers, properly speaking, can neither be equal nor unequal with respect to each other; the equality or inequality of any portions of space can never depend on any proportion in the number of their parts. 'Tis true, it may be said, that the inequality of an ell and a yard consists in the different numbers of the feet, of which they are compos'd; and that of a foot and a yard in the number of the inches. But as that quantity we call an inch in the one is suppos'd equal to what we call an inch in the other, and as 'tis impossible for the mind to find this equality by proceeding *in infinitum* with these references to inferior quantities; 'tis evident, that at last we must fix some standard of equality different from an enumeration of the parts. *SB 46*

21   There are some,[11] who pretend, that equality is best defin'd by *congruity*, and that any two figures are equal, when upon the placing of one upon the other, all their parts correspond to and touch each other. In order to judge of this definition let us consider, that since equality is a relation, it is not, strictly speaking, a property in the figures themselves, but arises merely from the comparison, which the mind makes betwixt them. If it consists, therefore, in this imaginary application and mutual contact of parts, we must at least have a distinct notion of these parts, and must conceive their contact. Now 'tis plain, that in this conception we wou'd run up these parts to the greatest minuteness, which can possibly be conceiv'd; since the contact of large parts wou'd never render the figures equal. But the minutest parts we can conceive are mathematical points; and consequently this standard of equality is the same with that deriv'd from the equality of the number of points; which we have already determin'd to be a just but an useless standard. We must therefore look to some other quarter for a solution of the present difficulty. *SB 47*

22   ^{App.}There are many philosophers, who refuse to assign any standard of *equality*, but assert, that 'tis sufficient to present two objects, that are equal, in order to give us a just notion of this proportion.[†] All definitions, say they, are fruitless, without the perception of such objects; and where we perceive such objects, we *SB 637*

---

[11]   See Dr. *Barrow*'s mathematical lectures.[†]   *SB 46*

35

no longer stand in need of any definition. To this reasoning I entirely agree; and assert, that the only useful notion of equality, or inequality, is deriv'd from the whole united appearance and the comparison of particular objects. For^{App.} 'tis   *SB 47* evident, that the eye, or rather the mind is often able at one view to determine the proportions of bodies, and pronounce them equal to, or greater or less than each other, without examining or comparing the number of their minute parts. Such judgments are not only common, but in many cases certain and infallible. When the measure of a yard and that of a foot are presented, the mind can no more question, that the first is longer than the second, than it can doubt of those principles, which are the most clear and self-evident.

23   There are therefore three proportions, which the mind distinguishes in the general appearance of its objects, and calls by the names of *greater*, *less* and *equal*. But tho' its decisions concerning these proportions be sometimes infallible, they are not always so; nor are our judgments of this kind more exempt from doubt and error, than those on any other subject. We frequently correct our first opinion by a review and reflection; and pronounce those objects to be equal, which at first we esteem'd unequal; and regard an object as less, tho' before it appear'd greater than another. Nor is this the only correction, which these judgments of our senses undergo; but we often discover our error by a juxta-position of the objects; or where that is impracticable, by the use of some common and invariable measure, which being successively apply'd to each, informs us of their different proportions. And even this correction is susceptible of a new correction, and of different degrees of exactness, according to the nature of the instrument, by which we measure the bodies, and the care which we employ in the comparison.

24   When therefore the mind is accustom'd to these judgments and their corrections, and finds that the same proportion which makes two figures have in the eye that appearance, which we call *equality*, makes them also correspond to each   *SB 48* other, and to any common measure, with which they are compar'd, we form a mix'd notion of equality deriv'd both from the looser and stricter methods of comparison. But we are not content with this. For as sound reason convinces us that there are bodies *vastly* more minute than those, which appear to the senses; and as a false reason wou'd perswade us, that there are bodies *infinitely* more minute; we clearly perceive, that we are not possess'd of any instrument or art of measuring, which can secure us from all error and uncertainty. We are sensible, that the addition or removal of one of these minute parts, is not discernible either in the appearance or measuring; and as we imagine, that two figures, which were equal before, cannot be equal after this removal or addition, we therefore suppose some imaginary standard of equality, by which the appearances and measuring are exactly corrected, and the figures reduc'd entirely to that proportion. This standard is plainly imaginary. For as the very idea of equality is that of such a particular appearance corrected by juxta-position or a common measure, the notion of any correction beyond what we have instruments and art to make, is a mere fiction of the mind, and useless as well as incomprehensible. But tho' this standard be only imaginary, the fiction however is very

natural;[†] nor is any thing more usual, than for the mind to proceed after this manner with any action, even after the reason has ceas'd, which first determin'd it to begin. This appears very conspicuously with regard to time; where tho' 'tis evident we have no exact method of determining the proportions of parts, not even so exact as in extension, yet the various corrections of our measures, and their different degrees of exactness, have given us an obscure and implicit notion of a perfect and entire equality. The case is the same in many other subjects. A musician finding his ear become every day more delicate, and correcting himself by reflection and attention, proceeds with the same act of the mind, even when the subject fails him, and entertains a notion of a compleat *tierce* or *octave*, without being able to tell whence he derives his standard. A painter forms the same fiction with regard to colours. A mechanic with regard to motion. To the one *light* and *shade*; to the other *swift* and *slow* are imagin'd to be capable of an exact comparison and equality beyond the judgments of the senses.

SB 49

25   We may apply the same reasoning to CURVE and RIGHT lines. Nothing is more apparent to the senses, than the distinction betwixt a curve and a right line; nor are there any ideas we more easily form than the ideas of these objects. But however easily we may form these ideas, 'tis impossible to produce any definition of them, which will fix the precise boundaries betwixt them. When we draw lines upon paper or any continu'd surface, there is a certain order, by which the lines run along from one point to another, that they may produce the entire impression of a curve or right line; but this order is perfectly unknown, and nothing is observ'd but the united appearance.[†] Thus even upon the system of indivisible points, we can only form a distant notion of some unknown standard to these objects.[†] Upon that of infinite divisibility we cannot go even this length; but are reduc'd merely to the general appearance, as the rule by which we determine lines to be either curve or right ones. But tho' we can give no perfect definition of these lines, nor produce any very exact method of distinguishing the one from the other; yet this hinders us not from correcting the first appearance by a more accurate consideration, and by a comparison with some rule, of whose rectitude from repeated trials we have a greater assurance. And 'tis from these corrections, and by carrying on the same action of the mind, even when its reason fails us, that we form the loose idea of a perfect standard to these figures, without being able to explain or comprehend it.[†]

26   'Tis true, mathematicians pretend they give an exact definition of a right line, when they say, *it is the shortest way betwixt two points*.[†] But in the *first* place I observe, that this is more properly the discovery of one of the properties of a right line, than a just definition of it. For I ask any one, if upon mention of a right line he thinks not immediately on such a particular appearance, and if 'tis not by accident only that he considers this property? A right line can be comprehended alone; but this definition is unintelligible without a comparison with other lines, which we conceive to be more extended. In common life 'tis establish'd as a maxim, that the streightest way is always the shortest; which wou'd be as absurd as to say, the shortest way is always the shortest, if our idea of a right line was not different from that of the shortest way betwixt two points.

SB 50

27   *Secondly*, I repeat what I have already establish'd,[†] that we have no precise idea of equality and inequality, shorter and longer, more than of a right line or a curve; and consequently that the one can never afford us a perfect standard for the other. An exact idea can never be built on such as are loose and undeterminate.

28   The idea of a *plane surface* is as little susceptible of a precise standard as that of a right line; nor have we any other means of distinguishing such a surface, than its general appearance. 'Tis in vain, that mathematicians represent a plane surface as produc'd by the flowing of a right line.[†] 'Twill immediately be objected, that our idea of a surface is as independent of this method of forming a surface, as our idea of an ellipse is of that of a cone; that the idea of a right line is no more precise than that of a plane surface; that a right line may flow irregularly, and by that means form a figure quite different from a plane;[†] and that therefore we must suppose it to flow along two right lines, parallel to each other, and on the same plane; which is a description, that explains a thing by itself, and returns in a circle.

29   It appears, then, that the ideas which are most essential to geometry, *viz.* those of equality and inequality, of a right line and a plane surface, are far from being exact and determinate, according to our common method of conceiving them.   *SB 51* Not only we are incapable of telling, if the case be in any degree doubtful, when such particular figures are equal; when such a line is a right one, and such a surface a plane one; but we can form no idea of that proportion,[†] or of these figures, which is firm and invariable. Our appeal is still to the weak and fallible judgment, which we make from the appearance of the objects, and correct by a compass or common measure; and if we join the supposition of any farther correction, 'tis of such-a-one as is either useless or imaginary. In vain shou'd we have recourse to the common topic, and employ the supposition of a deity, whose omnipotence may enable him to form a perfect geometrical figure, and describe a right line without any curve or inflexion. As the ultimate standard of these figures is deriv'd from nothing but the senses and imagination, 'tis absurd to talk of any perfection beyond what these faculties can judge of; since the true perfection of any thing consists in its conformity to its standard.

30   Now since these ideas are so loose and uncertain, I wou'd fain ask any mathematician what infallible assurance he has, not only of the more intricate and obscure propositions of his science, but of the most vulgar and obvious principles? How can he prove to me, for instance, that two right lines cannot have one common segment? Or that 'tis impossible to draw more than one right line betwixt any two points? Shou'd he tell me, that these opinions are obviously absurd, and repugnant to our clear ideas; I wou'd answer, that I do not deny, where two right lines incline upon each other with a sensible angle, but 'tis absurd to imagine them to have a common segment.[†] But supposing these two lines to approach at the rate of an inch in twenty leagues, I perceive no absurdity in asserting, that upon their contact they become one.[†] For, I beseech you, by what rule or standard do you judge, when you assert, that the line, in which I have suppos'd them to concur, cannot make the same right line with those two,   *SB 52*

that form so small an angle betwixt them? You must surely have some idea of a right line, to which this line does not agree. Do you therefore mean, that it takes not the points in the same order and by the same rule, as is peculiar and essential to a right line? If so, I must inform you, that besides that in judging after this manner you allow, that extension is compos'd of indivisible points (which, perhaps, is more than you intend) besides this, I say, I must inform you, that neither is this the standard from which we form the idea of a right line; nor, if it were, is there any such firmness in our senses or imagination, as to determine when such an order is violated or preserv'd. The original standard of a right line is in reality nothing but a certain general appearance; and 'tis evident right lines may be made to concur with each other, and yet correspond to this standard, tho' corrected by all the means either practicable or imaginable.

31   ^{App.}To whatever side mathematicians turn, this dilemma still meets them. If   *SB 638*
they judge of equality, or any other proportion, by the accurate and exact standard, *viz.* the enumeration of the minute indivisible parts, they both employ a standard, which is useless in practice, and actually establish the indivisibility of extension, which they endeavour to explode. Or if they employ, as is usual, the inaccurate standard, deriv'd from a comparison of objects, upon their general appearance, corrected by measuring and juxta-position; their first principles, tho' certain and infallible, are too coarse to afford any such subtile inferences as they commonly draw from them. The first principles are founded on the imagination and senses: The conclusion, therefore, can never go beyond, much less contradict these faculties.^{App.}

32   This may open our eyes a little, and let us see, that no geometrical demonstra-   *SB 52*
tion for the infinite divisibility of extension can have so much force as what we naturally attribute to every argument, which is supported by such magnificent pretensions. At the same time we may learn the reason, why geometry fails of evidence in this single point, while all its other reasonings command our fullest assent and approbation. And indeed it seems more requisite to give the reason of this exception, than to show, that we really must make such an exception, and regard all the mathematical arguments for infinite divisibility as utterly sophistical. For 'tis evident, that as no idea of quantity is infinitely divisible, there cannot be imagin'd a more glaring absurdity, than to endeavour to prove, that quantity itself admits of such a division; and to prove this by means of ideas, which are directly opposite in that particular. And as this absurdity is very glaring in itself, so there is no argument founded on it, which is not attended with a new absurdity, and involves not an evident contradiction.

33   I may give as instances those arguments for infinite divisibility, which are   *SB 53*
deriv'd from the *point of contact*. I know there is no mathematician, who will not refuse to be judg'd by the diagrams he describes upon paper, these being loose draughts, as he will tell us, and serving only to convey with greater facility certain ideas, which are the true foundation of all our reasoning. This I am satisfy'd with, and am willing to rest the controversy merely upon these ideas. I desire therefore our mathematician to form, as accurately as possible, the ideas of a circle and a right line; and I then ask, if upon the conception of their contact he

can conceive them as touching in a mathematical point, or if he must necessarily imagine them to concur for some space?[†] Which-ever side he chooses, he runs himself into equal difficulties. If he affirms, that in tracing these figures in his imagination, he can imagine them to touch only in a point, he allows the possibility of that idea, and consequently of the thing. If he says, that in his conception of the contact of those lines he must make them concur, he thereby acknowledges the fallacy of geometrical demonstrations, when carry'd beyond a certain degree of minuteness; since 'tis certain he has such demonstrations against the concurrence of a circle and a right line; that is, in other words, he can prove an idea, *viz.* that of concurrence, to be *incompatible* with two other ideas, *viz.* those of a circle and right line; tho' at the same time he acknowledges these ideas to be *inseparable*.

Sect. 5. *The same subject continu'd*

1   If the second part of my system be true, *that the idea of space or extension is nothing but the idea of visible or tangible points distributed in a certain order;*[†] it follows, that we can form no idea of a vacuum, or space, where there is nothing visible or tangible. This gives rise to three objections, which I shall examine   *SB 54* together, because the answer I shall give to one is a consequence of that which I shall make use of for the others.

2   *First*, It may be said, that men have disputed for many ages concerning a vacuum and a plenum,[†] without being able to bring the affair to a final decision; and philosophers, even at this day, think themselves at liberty to take party on either side,[†] as their fancy leads them. But whatever foundation there may be for a controversy concerning the things themselves, it may be pretended, that the very dispute is decisive concerning the idea, and that 'tis impossible men cou'd so long reason about a vacuum, and either refute or defend it, without having a notion of what they refuted or defended.[†]

3   *Secondly*, If this argument shou'd be contested, the reality or at least possibility of the *idea* of a vacuum may be prov'd by the following reasoning. Every idea is possible, which is a necessary and infallible consequence of such as are possible. Now tho' we allow the world to be at present a plenum, we may easily conceive it to be depriv'd of motion; and this idea will certainly be allow'd possible. It must also be allow'd possible, to conceive the annihilation of any part of matter by the omnipotence of the deity, while the other parts remain at rest.[†] For as every idea, that is distinguishable, is separable by the imagination; and as every idea, that is separable by the imagination, may be conceiv'd to be separately existent; 'tis evident, that the existence of one particle of matter, no more implies the existence of another, than a square figure in one body implies a square figure in every one. This being granted, I now demand what results from the concurrence of these two possible ideas of *rest* and *annihilation*, and what must we conceive to follow upon the annihilation of all the air and subtile matter[†] in the chamber, supposing the walls to remain the same, without any motion or alteration? There are some metaphysicians, who answer, that since matter and extension are the

same, the annihilation of one necessarily implies that of the other;[†] and there
being now no distance[†] betwixt the walls of the chamber, they touch each other;
in the same manner as my hand touches the paper, which is immediately before
me. But tho' this answer be very common, I defy these metaphysicians to conceive the matter according to their hypothesis, or imagine the floor and roof, with
all the opposite sides of the chamber, to touch each other, while they continue in
rest, and preserve the same position.[†] For how can the two walls, that run from
south to north, touch each other, while they touch the opposite ends of two
walls, that run from east to west? And how can the floor and roof ever meet,
while they are separated by the four walls, that lie in a contrary position? If you
change their position, you suppose a motion. If you conceive any thing betwixt
them, you suppose a new creation. But keeping strictly to the two ideas of *rest*
and *annihilation*, 'tis evident, that the idea, which results from them, is not that
of a contact of parts, but something else; which is concluded to be the idea of a
vacuum.

SB 55

4   The *third* objection carries the matter still farther, and not only asserts, that
the idea of a vacuum is real and possible, but also necessary and unavoidable.
This assertion is founded on the motion we observe in bodies, which, 'tis
maintain'd, wou'd be impossible and inconceivable without a vacuum, into
which one body must move in order to make way for another.[†] I shall not enlarge
upon this objection, because it principally belongs to natural philosophy, which
lies without our present sphere.

5   In order to answer these objections, we must take the matter pretty deep, and
consider the nature and origin of several ideas, lest we dispute without understanding perfectly the subject of the controversy. 'Tis evident the idea of darkness is no positive idea,[†] but merely the negation of light, or more properly
speaking, of colour'd and visible objects. A man, who enjoys his sight, receives
no other perception from turning his eyes on every side, when entirely depriv'd
of light, than what is common to him with one born blind; and 'tis certain such-
a-one has no idea either of light or darkness. The consequence of this is, that 'tis
not from the mere removal of visible objects we receive the impression of extension without matter; and that the idea of utter darkness can never be the same
with that of vacuum.[†]

SB 56

6   Suppose again a man to be supported in the air, and to be softly convey'd along
by some invisible power; 'tis evident he is sensible of nothing,[†] and never
receives the idea of extension, nor indeed any idea, from this invariable motion.
Even supposing he moves his limbs to and fro, this cannot convey to him that
idea. He feels in that case a certain sensation or impression, the parts of which
are successive to each other, and may give him the idea of time: But certainly
are not dispos'd in such a manner, as is necessary to convey the idea of space or
extension.

7   Since then it appears, that darkness and motion, with the utter removal of
every thing visible and tangible, can never give us the idea of extension without
matter, or of a vacuum; the next question is, whether they can convey this idea,
when mix'd with something visible and tangible?

8   'Tis commonly allow'd by philosophers, that all bodies, which discover themselves to the eye, appear as if painted on a plane surface,[†] and that their different degrees of remoteness from ourselves are discover'd more by reason than by the senses.[†] When I hold up my hand before me, and spread my fingers, they are separated as perfectly by the blue colour of the firmament, as they cou'd be by any visible object, which I cou'd place betwixt them. In order, therefore, to know whether the sight can convey the impression and idea of a vacuum, we must suppose, that amidst an entire darkness, there are luminous bodies presented to us, whose light discovers only these bodies themselves, without giving us any impression of the surrounding objects.

9   We must form a parallel supposition concerning the objects of our feeling.   *SB 57*
'Tis not proper to suppose a perfect removal of all tangible objects: We must allow something to be perceiv'd by the feeling; and after an interval and motion of the hand or other organ of sensation, another object of the touch to be met with; and upon leaving that, another; and so on, as often as we please. The question is, whether these intervals do not afford us the idea of extension without body?

10   To begin with the first case; 'tis evident, that when only two luminous bodies appear to the eye, we can perceive, whether they be conjoin'd or separate; whether they be separated by a great or small distance; and if this distance varies, we can perceive its encrease or diminution, with the motion of the bodies. But as the distance is not in this case any thing colour'd or visible, it may be thought that there is here a vacuum or pure extension, not only intelligible to the mind, but obvious to the very senses.

11   This is our natural and most familiar way of thinking; but which we shall learn to correct by a little reflection. We may observe, that when two bodies present themselves, where there was formerly an entire darkness, the only change, that is discoverable, is in the appearance of these two objects, and that all the rest continues to be as before, a perfect negation of light, and of every colour'd or visible object. This is not only true of what may be said to be remote from these bodies, but also of the very distance, which is interpos'd betwixt them; *that* being nothing but darkness, or the negation of light; without parts, without composition, invariable and indivisible. Now since this distance causes no perception different from what a blind man receives from his eyes, or what is convey'd to us in the darkest night, it must partake of the same properties: And as blindness and darkness afford us no ideas of extension, 'tis impossible that the dark and undistinguishable distance betwixt two bodies can ever produce that idea.

12   The sole difference betwixt an absolute darkness and the appearance of two or   *SB 58*
more visible luminous objects consists, as I said, in the objects themselves, and in the manner they affect our senses. The angles, which the rays of light flowing from them, form with each other;[†] the motion that is requir'd in the eye, in its passage from one to the other;[†] and the different parts of the organs, which are affected by them;[†] these produce the only perceptions, from which we can judge

of the distance. But as these perceptions are each of them simple and indivisible, they can never give us the idea of extension.

13   We may illustrate this by considering the sense of feeling, and the imaginary distance or interval interpos'd betwixt tangible or solid objects. I suppose two cases, *viz.* that of a man supported in the air, and moving his limbs to and fro, without meeting any thing tangible; and that of a man, who feeling something tangible, leaves it, and after a motion, of which he is sensible, perceives another tangible object; and I then ask, wherein consists the difference betwixt these two cases? No one will make any scruple to affirm, that it consists merely in the perceiving those objects, and that the sensation, which arises from the motion, is in both cases the same: And as that sensation is not capable of conveying to us an idea of extension, when unaccompany'd with some other perception, it can no more give us that idea, when mix'd with the impressions of tangible objects; since that mixture produces no alteration upon it.

14   But tho' motion and darkness, either alone, or attended with tangible and visible objects, convey no idea of a vacuum or extension without matter, yet they are the causes why we falsly imagine we can form such an idea.[†] For there is a close relation betwixt that motion and darkness, and a real extension, or composition of visible and tangible objects.

15   *First,* We may observe, that two visible objects appearing in the midst of utter darkness, affect the senses in the same manner, and form the same angle by the rays, which flow from them, and meet in the eye, as if the distance betwixt them were fill'd with visible objects, that give us a true idea of extension. The sensation of motion is likewise the same, when there is nothing tangible interpos'd betwixt two bodies, as when we feel a compounded body, whose different parts are plac'd beyond each other.

16   *Secondly,* We find by experience, that two bodies, which are so plac'd as to affect the senses in the same manner with two others, that have a certain extent of visible objects interpos'd betwixt them, are capable of receiving the same extent, without any sensible impulse or penetration, and without any change on that angle, under which they appear to the senses. In like manner, where there is one object, which we cannot feel after another without an interval, and the perceiving of that sensation we call motion in our hand or organ of sensation; experience shows us, that 'tis possible the same objects may be felt with the same sensation of motion, along with the interpos'd impression of solid and tangible objects, attending the sensation. That is, in other words, an invisible and intangible distance may be converted into a visible and tangible one, without any change on the distant objects.

17   *Thirdly,* We may observe, as another relation betwixt these two kinds of distance, that they have nearly the same effects on every natural phænomenon. For as all qualities, such as heat, cold, light, attraction, *&c.* diminish in proportion to the distance;[†] there is but little difference observ'd, whether this distance be mark'd out by compounded and sensible objects, or be known only by the manner, in which the distant objects affect the senses.

18   Here then are three relations betwixt that distance, which conveys the idea of extension, and that other, which is not fill'd with any colour'd or solid object. The distant objects affect the senses in the same manner, whether separated by the one distance or the other; the second species of distance is found capable of receiving the first; and they both equally diminish the force of every quality.

19   These relations betwixt the two kinds of distance will afford us an easy reason, *SB 60* why the one has so often been taken for the other, and why we imagine we have an idea of extension without the idea of any object either of the sight or feeling. For we may establish it as a general maxim in this science of human nature, that wherever there is a close relation betwixt two ideas, the mind is very apt to mistake them, and in all its discourses and reasonings to use the one for the other. This phænomenon occurs on so many occasions, and is of such consequence, that I cannot forbear stopping a moment to examine its causes. I shall only premise, that we must distinguish exactly betwixt the phænomenon itself, and the causes, which I shall assign for it; and must not imagine from any uncertainty in the latter, that the former is also uncertain. The phænomenon may be real, tho' my explication be chimerical. The falshood of the one is no consequence of that of the other; tho' at the same time we may observe, that 'tis very natural for us to draw such a consequence; which is an evident instance of that very principle, which I endeavour to explain.

20   When I receiv'd the relations of *resemblance, contiguity* and *causation*, as principles of union among ideas, without examining into their causes,[†] 'twas more in prosecution of my first maxim, that we must in the end rest contented with experience,[†] than for want of something specious and plausible, which I might have display'd on that subject. 'Twou'd have been easy to have made an imaginary dissection of the brain,[†] and have shown, why upon our conception of any idea, the animal spirits[†] run into all the contiguous traces, and rouze up the other ideas, that are related to it. But tho' I have neglected any advantage, which I might have drawn from this topic in explaining the relations of ideas, I am afraid I must here have recourse to it, in order to account for the mistakes that arise from these relations. I shall therefore observe, that as the mind is endow'd with a power of exciting any idea it pleases; whenever it dispatches the spirits into that *SB 61* region of the brain, in which the idea is plac'd; these spirits always excite the idea, when they run precisely into the proper traces, and rummage that cell, which belongs to the idea. But as their motion is seldom direct, and naturally turns a little to the one side or the other; for this reason the animal spirits, falling into the contiguous traces, present other related ideas in lieu of that, which the mind desir'd at first to survey. This change we are not always sensible of; but continuing still the same train of thought, make use of the related idea, which is presented to us, and employ it in our reasoning, as if it were the same with what we demanded. This is the cause of many mistakes and sophisms in philosophy; as will naturally be imagin'd, and as it wou'd be easy to show, if there was occasion.

21   Of the three relations above-mention'd, that of resemblance is the most fertile

source of error; and indeed there are few mistakes in reasoning, which do not borrow largely from that origin. Resembling ideas are not only related together, but the actions of the mind, which we employ in considering them, are so little different, that we are not able to distinguish them. This last circumstance is of great consequence; and we may in general observe, that wherever the actions of the mind in forming any two ideas are the same or resembling, we are very apt to confound these ideas, and take the one for the other.[†] Of this we shall see many instances in the progress of this treatise.[†] But tho' resemblance be the relation, which most readily produces a mistake in ideas, yet the others of causation and contiguity may also concur in the same influence. We might produce the figures of poets and orators, as sufficient proofs of this, were it as usual, as it is reasonable, in metaphysical subjects to draw our arguments from that quarter. But lest metaphysicians shou'd esteem this below their dignity, I shall borrow a proof from an observation, which may be made on most of their own discourses, *viz.* that 'tis usual for men to use words for ideas,[†] and to talk instead of thinking in their reasonings. We use words for ideas, because they are commonly so closely connected, that the mind easily mistakes them. And this likewise is the reason, why we substitute the idea of a distance, which is not consider'd either as visible or tangible, in the room of extension,[†] which is nothing but a composition of visible or tangible points dispos'd in a certain order. In causing this mistake there concur both the relations of *causation* and *resemblance*. As the first species of distance is found to be convertible into the second, 'tis in this respect a kind of cause;[†] and the similarity of their manner of affecting the senses, and diminishing every quality, forms the relation of resemblance.

SB 62

22   After this chain of reasoning and explication of my principles, I am now prepar'd to answer all the objections that have been offer'd, whether deriv'd from *metaphysics* or *mechanics*.[†] The frequent disputes concerning a vacuum, or extension without matter, prove not the reality of the idea, upon which the dispute turns;[†] there being nothing more common, than to see men deceive themselves in this particular; especially when by means of any close relation, there is another idea presented, which may be the occasion of their mistake.

23   We may make almost the same answer to the second objection, deriv'd from the conjunction of the ideas of rest and annihilation.[†] When every thing is annihilated in the chamber, and the walls continue immoveable, the chamber must be conceiv'd much in the same manner as at present, when the air that fills it, is not an object of the senses. This annihilation leaves to the *eye*, that fictitious distance, which is discover'd by the different parts of the organ, that are affected, and by the degrees of light and shade; and to the *feeling*, that which consists in a sensation of motion in the hand, or other member of the body. In vain shou'd we search any farther. On which-ever side we turn this subject, we shall find that these are the only impressions such an object can produce after the suppos'd annihilation; and it has already been remark'd,[†] that impressions can give rise to no ideas, but to such as resemble them.

SB 63

24   Since a body interpos'd betwixt two others may be suppos'd to be annihilated,

without producing any change upon such as lie on each hand of it, 'tis easily conceiv'd, how it may be created anew, and yet produce as little alteration. Now the
motion of a body has much the same effect as its creation.[†] The distant bodies are
no more affected in the one case, than in the other. This suffices to satisfy the
imagination, and proves there is no repugnance in such a motion. Afterwards
experience comes in play to perswade us that two bodies, situated in the manner
above-describ'd, have really such a capacity of receiving body betwixt them, and
that there is no obstacle to the conversion of the invisible and intangible distance
into one that is visible and tangible. However natural that conversion may seem,
we cannot be sure it is practicable, before we have had experience of it.

25   Thus I seem to have answer'd the three objections above-mention'd;[†] tho' at
the same time I am sensible, that few will be satisfy'd with these answers, but will
immediately propose new objections and difficulties. 'Twill probably be said,
that my reasoning makes nothing to the matter in hand, and that I explain only
the manner in which objects affect the senses, without endeavouring to account
for their real nature and operations.[†] Tho' there be nothing visible or tangible
interpos'd betwixt two bodies, yet we find *by experience*, that the bodies may be
plac'd in the same manner, with regard to the eye, and require the same motion
of the hand in passing from one to the other, as if divided by something visible
and tangible. This invisible and intangible distance is also found *by experience* to
contain a capacity of receiving body, or of becoming visible and tangible. Here is
the whole of my system; and in no part of it have I endeavour'd to explain the
cause, which separates bodies after this manner, and gives them a capacity of   *SB 64*
receiving others betwixt them, without any impulse or penetration.

26   I answer this objection, by pleading guilty, and by confessing that my intention never was to penetrate into the nature of bodies, or explain the secret causes
of their operations. For besides that this belongs not to my present purpose, I am
afraid, that such an enterprize is beyond the reach of human understanding, and
that we can never pretend to know body otherwise than by those external properties, which discover themselves to the senses. As to those who attempt any
thing farther, I cannot approve of their ambition, till I see, in some one instance
at least, that they have met with success. But at present I content myself with
knowing perfectly the manner in which objects affect my senses, and their connexions with each other, as far as experience informs me of them. This suffices
for the conduct of life; and this also suffices for my philosophy, which pretends
only to explain the nature and causes of our perceptions, or impressions
and ideas.[12]

[12App.] As long as we confine our speculations to the *appearances* of objects to our senses, without   *SB 638*
entering into disquisitions concerning their real nature and operations, we are safe from all difficulties, and can never be embarrass'd by any question. Thus, if it be ask'd, whether the invisible and
intangible distance, interpos'd betwixt two objects, be something or nothing: 'Tis easy to answer,
that it is *something*, viz. a property of the objects, which affect the *senses* after such a particular
manner. If it be ask'd, whether two objects, having such a distance betwixt them, touch or not: It
may be answer'd, that this depends upon the definition of the word, *touch*. If objects be said to
touch, when there is nothing *sensible* interpos'd betwixt them, these objects touch: If objects be said

27   I shall conclude this subject of extension with a paradox, which will easily be explain'd from the foregoing reasoning. This paradox is, that if you are pleas'd to give to the invisible and intangible distance, or in other words, to the capacity of becoming a visible and tangible distance, the name of a vacuum, extension and matter are the same, and yet there is a vacuum. If you will not give it that name, motion is possible in a plenum, without any impulse *in infinitum*, without returning in a circle, and without penetration. But however we may express ourselves, we must always confess, that we have no idea of any real extension without filling it with sensible objects, and conceiving its parts as visible or tangible.

28   As to the doctrine, that time is nothing but the manner, in which some real objects exist; we may observe, that 'tis liable to the same objections as the similar doctrine with regard to extension. If it be a sufficient proof, that we have the idea   *SB 65* of a vacuum, because we dispute and reason concerning it;[†] we must for the same reason have the idea of time without any changeable existence; since there is no subject of dispute more frequent and common. But that we really have no such idea, is certain. For whence shou'd it be deriv'd? Does it arise from an impression of sensation or of reflection? Point it out distinctly to us, that we may know its nature and qualities. But if you cannot point out *any such impression*, you may be certain you are mistaken, when you imagine you have *any such idea*.

29   But tho' it be impossible to show the impression, from which the idea of time without a changeable existence is deriv'd; yet we can easily point out those appearances, which make us fancy we have that idea. For we may observe, that there is a continual succession of perceptions in our mind; so that the idea of time being for ever present with us; when we consider a stedfast object at five-a-clock, and regard the same at six; we are apt to apply to it that idea in the same manner as if every moment were distinguish'd by a different position, or an alteration of the object. The first and second appearances of the object, being compar'd with the succession of our perceptions, seem equally remov'd as if the object had really chang'd. To which we may add, what experience shows us, that the object was susceptible of such a number of changes betwixt these appearances; as also that the unchangeable or rather fictitious duration has the same

to touch, when their *images* strike contiguous parts of the eye, and when the hand *feels* both objects   *SB 639* successively, without any interpos'd motion, these objects do not touch. The appearances of objects to our senses are all consistent; and no difficulties can ever arise, but from the obscurity of the terms we make use of.

2   If we carry our enquiry beyond the appearances of objects to the senses, I am afraid, that most of our conclusions will be full of scepticism and uncertainty. Thus, if it be ask'd, whether or not the invisible and intangible distance be always full of *body*, or of something that by an improvement of our organs might become visible or tangible, I must acknowledge, that I find no very decisive arguments on either side; tho' I am inclin'd to the contrary opinion, as being more suitable to vulgar and popular notions.[†] If the *Newtonian* philosophy be rightly understood, it will be found to mean no more. A vacuum is asserted: That is, bodies are said to be plac'd after such a manner, as to receive bodies betwixt them, without impulsion or penetration. The real nature of this position of bodies is unknown. We are only acquainted with its effects on the senses, and its power of receiving body. Nothing is more suitable to that philosophy,[†] than a modest scepticism to a certain degree, and a fair confession of ignorance in subjects, that exceed all human capacity.[App.]

effect upon every quality, by encreasing or diminishing it, as that succession, which is obvious to the senses. From these three relations we are apt to confound our ideas, and imagine we can form the idea of a time and duration, without any change or succession.

Sect. 6. *Of the idea of existence, and of external existence* *SB 66*

1   It may not be amiss, before we leave this subject, to explain the ideas of *existence* and of *external existence*; which have their difficulties, as well as the ideas of space and time. By this means we shall be the better prepar'd for the examination of knowledge and probability,[†] when we understand perfectly all those particular ideas, which may enter into our reasoning.

2   There is no impression nor idea of any kind, of which we have any consciousness or memory, that is not conceiv'd as existent;[†] and 'tis evident, that from this consciousness the most perfect idea and assurance of *being*[†] is deriv'd. From hence we may form a dilemma, the most clear and conclusive that can be imagin'd, *viz.* that since we never remember any idea or impression without attributing existence to it, the idea of existence must either be deriv'd from a distinct impression, conjoin'd with every perception or object of our thought, or must be the very same with the idea of the perception or object.

3   As this dilemma is an evident consequence of the principle, that every idea arises from a similar impression, so our decision betwixt the propositions of the dilemma is no more doubtful. So far from there being any distinct impression, attending every impression and every idea, that I do not think there are any two distinct impressions, which are inseparably conjoin'd. Tho' certain sensations may at one time be united, we quickly find they admit of a separation, and may be presented apart. And thus, tho' every impression and idea we remember be consider'd as existent, the idea of existence is not deriv'd from any particular impression.[†]

4   The idea of existence, then, is the very same with the idea of what we conceive to be existent. To reflect on any thing simply, and to reflect on it as existent, are nothing different from each other.[†] That idea, when conjoin'd with the idea of *SB 67* any object, makes no addition to it. Whatever we conceive, we conceive to be existent. Any idea we please to form is the idea of a being; and the idea of a being is any idea we please to form.

5   Whoever opposes this, must necessarily point out that distinct impression, from which the idea of entity[†] is deriv'd, and must prove, that this impression is inseparable from every perception we believe to be existent. This we may without hesitation conclude to be impossible.

6   Our foregoing reasoning[13] concerning the *distinction* of ideas without any real *difference* will not here serve us in any stead. That kind of distinction is founded on the different resemblances, which the same simple idea may have to several different ideas. But no object can be presented resembling some object with

---

[13] Part 1. Sect. 7.[†]

respect to its existence, and different from others in the same particular; since every object, that is presented, must necessarily be existent.

7   A like reasoning will account for the idea of *external existence*. We may observe, that 'tis universally allow'd by philosophers, and is besides pretty obvious of itself, that nothing is ever really present with the mind but its perceptions or impressions and ideas, and that external objects become known to us only by those perceptions they occasion.† To hate, to love, to think, to feel, to see; all this is nothing but to perceive.

8   Now since nothing is ever present to the mind but perceptions, and since all ideas are deriv'd from something antecedently present to the mind; it follows, that 'tis impossible for us so much as to conceive or form an idea of any thing specifically different† from ideas and impressions. Let us fix our attention out of ourselves as much as possible:† Let us chace our imagination to the heavens, or to the utmost limits of the universe; we never really advance a step beyond ourselves, nor can conceive any kind of existence, but those perceptions, which have appear'd in that narrow compass. This is the universe of the imagination, nor have we any idea but what is there produc'd.   *SB 68*

9   The farthest we can go towards a conception of external objects, when suppos'd *specifically* different from our perceptions, is to form a relative idea of them, without pretending to comprehend the related objects. Generally speaking we do not suppose them specifically different; but only attribute to them different relations, connexions and durations. But of this more fully hereafter.[14]

---

[14] Part 4. Sect. 2.†

PART 3

Of knowledge and probability

Sect. 1. *Of knowledge*

1 There are seven different kinds of philosophical relation,[15] viz. *resemblance, identity, relations of time and place, proportion in quantity or number, degrees in any quality, contrariety*, and *causation*. These relations may be divided into two classes; into such as depend entirely on the ideas, which we compare together, and such as may be chang'd without any change in the ideas.[†] 'Tis from the idea of a triangle, that we discover the relation of equality,[†] which its three angles bear to two right ones; and this relation is invariable, as long as our idea remains the same. On the contrary, the relations of *contiguity* and *distance*[†] betwixt two objects may be chang'd merely by an alteration of their place, without any change on the objects themselves or on their ideas; and the place depends on a hundred different accidents, which cannot be foreseen by the mind. 'Tis the same case with *identity* and *causation*.[†] Two objects, tho' perfectly resembling each other, and even appearing in the same place at different times, may be numerically different: And as the power, by which one object produces another, is never discoverable merely from their ideas, 'tis evident *cause and effect* are relations, of which we receive information from experience, and not from any abstract reasoning or reflection. There is no single phænomenon, even the most simple, which can be accounted for from the qualities of the objects, as they appear to us; or which we cou'd foresee without the help of our memory and experience.

2 It appears, therefore, that of these seven philosophical relations, there remain only four, which depending solely upon ideas, can be the objects of knowledge and certainty.[†] These four are *resemblance, contrariety, degrees in quality*, and *proportions in quantity or number*. Three of these relations are discoverable at first sight, and fall more properly under the province of intuition than demonstration.[†] When any objects *resemble* each other, the resemblance will at first strike the eye, or rather the mind; and seldom requires a second examination. The case is the same with *contrariety*, and with the *degrees of any quality*. No one can once doubt but existence and non–existence destroy each other, and are perfectly incompatible and contrary. And tho' it be impossible to judge exactly of the degrees of any quality, such as colour, taste, heat, cold, when the difference betwixt them is very small; yet 'tis easy to decide, that any of them is superior or inferior to another, when their difference is considerable. And this decision we always pronounce at first sight, without any enquiry or reasoning.

---

[15] Part 1. Sect. 5.

3   We might proceed, after the same manner, in fixing the *proportions of quantity or number*, and might at one view observe a superiority or inferiority betwixt any numbers, or figures; especially where the difference is very great and remarkable. As to equality or any exact proportion, we can only guess at it from a single consideration; except in very short numbers, or very limited portions of extension; which are comprehended in an instant, and where we perceive an impossibility of falling into any considerable error. In all other cases we must settle the proportions with some liberty, or proceed in a more *artificial* manner.[†]

4   I have already observ'd,[†] that geometry, or the *art*, by which we fix the proportions of figures; tho' it much excels both in universality and exactness, the loose judgments of the senses and imagination; yet never attains a perfect precision   *SB 71* and exactness. Its first principles are still drawn from the general appearance of the objects; and that appearance can never afford us any security, when we examine the prodigious minuteness of which nature is susceptible. Our ideas seem to give a perfect assurance, that no two right lines can have a common segment; but if we consider these ideas, we shall find, that they always suppose a sensible inclination of the two lines, and that where the angle they form is extremely small, we have no standard of a right line so precise as to assure us of the truth of this proposition.[†] 'Tis the same case with most of the primary decisions of the mathematics.[†]

5   There remain, therefore, algebra and arithmetic as the only sciences, in which we can carry on a chain of reasoning to any degree of intricacy, and yet preserve a perfect exactness and certainty. We are possest of a precise standard, by which we can judge of the equality and proportion of numbers; and according as they correspond or not to that standard, we determine their relations, without any possibility of error. When two numbers are so combin'd, as that the one has always an unite answering to every unite of the other, we pronounce them equal; and 'tis for want of such a standard of equality in extension, that geometry can scarce be esteem'd a perfect and infallible science.

6   But here it may not be amiss to obviate a difficulty, which may arise from my asserting, that tho' geometry falls short of that perfect precision and certainty, which are peculiar to arithmetic and algebra, yet it excels the imperfect judgments of our senses and imagination. The reason why I impute any defect to geometry, is, because its original and fundamental principles are deriv'd merely from appearances; and it may perhaps be imagin'd, that this defect must always attend it, and keep it from ever reaching a greater exactness in the comparison of objects or ideas, than what our eye or imagination alone is able to attain. I own that this defect so far attends it, as to keep it from ever aspiring to a full certainty: *SB 72* But since these fundamental principles depend on the easiest and least deceitful appearances, they bestow on their consequences a degree of exactness, of which these consequences are singly incapable. 'Tis impossible for the eye to determine the angles of a chiliagon[†] to be equal to 1996 right angles, or make any conjecture, that approaches this proportion; but when it determines, that right lines cannot concur; that we cannot draw more than one right line betwixt two given points; its mistakes can never be of any consequence. And this is the nature and

use of geometry, to run us up to† such appearances, as, by reason of their simplicity, cannot lead us into any considerable error.

7   I shall here take occasion to propose a second observation concerning our demonstrative reasonings, which is suggested by the same subject of the mathematics. 'Tis usual with mathematicians, to pretend, that those ideas, which are their objects, are of so refin'd and spiritual a nature, that they fall not under the conception of the fancy, but must be comprehended by a pure and intellectual view, of which the superior faculties of the soul are alone capable.† The same notion runs thro' most parts of philosophy, and is principally made use of to explain our abstract ideas, and to show how we can form an idea of a triangle, for instance, which shall neither be an isosceles nor scalenum, nor be confin'd to any particular length and proportion of sides. 'Tis easy to see, why philosophers are so fond of this notion of some spiritual and refin'd perceptions; since by that means they cover many of their absurdities, and may refuse to submit to the decisions of clear ideas, by appealing to such as are obscure and uncertain. But to destroy this artifice,† we need but reflect on that principle so oft insisted on,† *that all our ideas are copy'd from our impressions*. For from thence we may immediately conclude, that since all impressions are clear and precise, the ideas, which are copy'd from them, must be of the same nature, and can never, but from our fault, contain any thing so dark and intricate. An idea is by its very nature   *SB 73* weaker and fainter than an impression; but being in every other respect the same, cannot imply any very great mystery. If its weakness render it obscure, 'tis our business to remedy that defect, as much as possible, by keeping the idea steady and precise; and till we have done so, 'tis in vain to pretend to reasoning and philosophy.

Sect. 2. *Of probability; and of the idea of cause and effect*

1   This is all I think necessary to observe concerning those four relations, which are the foundation of science;† but as to the other three, which depend not upon the idea, and may be absent or present even while *that* remains the same, 'twill be proper to explain them more particularly. These three relations are *identity*, *the situations in time and place*,† and *causation*.

2   All kinds of reasoning consist in nothing but a *comparison*, and a discovery of those relations, either constant or inconstant, which two or more objects bear to each other. This comparison we may make, either when both the objects are present to the senses, or when neither of them is present, or when only one. When both the objects are present to the senses along with the relation, we call *this* perception rather than reasoning; nor is there in this case any exercise of the thought, or any action, properly speaking, but a mere passive admission of the impressions thro' the organs of sensation.† According to this way of thinking, we ought not to receive as reasoning any of the observations we may make concerning *identity*, and the *relations of time and place*; since in none of them the mind can go beyond what is immediately present to the senses, either

to discover the real existence or the relations of objects.[†] 'Tis only *causation*, which produces such a connexion, as to give us assurance from the existence or action of one object, that 'twas follow'd or preceded by any other existence or action; nor can the other two relations be ever made use of in reasoning, except so far as they either affect or are affected by it. There is nothing in any objects to perswade us, that they are either always *remote* or always *contiguous*; and when from experience and observation we discover, that their relation in this particular is invariable, we always conclude there is some secret *cause*, which separates or unites them. The same reasoning extends to *identity*. We readily suppose an object may continue individually the same, tho' several times absent from and present to the senses; and ascribe to it an identity, notwithstanding the interruption of the perception, whenever we conclude, that if we had kept our eye or hand constantly upon it, it wou'd have convey'd an invariable and uninterrupted perception.[†] But this conclusion beyond the impressions of our senses can be founded only on the connexion of *cause and effect*; nor can we otherwise have any security, that the object is not chang'd upon us, however much the new object may resemble that which was formerly present to the senses. Whenever we discover such a perfect resemblance, we consider, whether it be common in that species of objects; whether possibly or probably any cause cou'd operate in producing the change and resemblance; and according as we determine concerning these causes and effects, we form our judgment concerning the identity of the object.

SB 74

3   Here then it appears, that of those three relations, which depend not upon the mere ideas,[†] the only one, that can be trac'd beyond[†] our senses, and informs us of existences and objects, which we do not see or feel, is *causation*. This relation, therefore, we shall endeavour to explain fully before we leave the subject of the understanding.

4   To begin regularly, we must consider the idea of *causation*, and see from what origin it is deriv'd. 'Tis impossible to reason justly, without understanding perfectly the idea concerning which we reason; and 'tis impossible perfectly to understand any idea, without tracing it up to its origin, and examining that primary impression, from which it arises. The examination of the impression bestows a clearness on the idea; and the examination of the idea bestows a like clearness on all our reasoning.

SB 75

5   Let us therefore cast our eye on any two objects, which we call cause and effect, and turn them on all sides, in order to find that impression, which produces an idea of such prodigious consequence.[†] At first sight I perceive, that I must not search for it in any of the particular *qualities* of the objects; since, which-ever of these qualities I pitch on, I find some object, that is not possest of it, and yet falls under the denomination of cause or effect.[†] And indeed there is nothing existent, either externally or internally, which is not to be consider'd either as a cause or an effect; tho' 'tis plain there is no one quality, which universally belongs to all beings, and gives them a title to that denomination.

6   The idea, then, of causation must be deriv'd from some *relation* among

objects; and that relation we must now endeavour to discover. I find in the first place, that whatever objects are consider'd as causes or effects, are *contiguous*; and that nothing can operate in a time or place, which is ever so little remov'd from those of its existence. Tho' distant objects may sometimes seem productive of each other, they are commonly found upon examination to be link'd by a chain of causes, which are contiguous among themselves, and to the distant objects; and when in any particular instance we cannot discover this connexion, we still presume it to exist. We may therefore consider the relation of CONTIGUITY as essential to that of causation;[†] at least may suppose it such, according to the general opinion, till we can find a more proper occasion[16] to clear up this matter, by examining what objects are or are not susceptible of juxta-position and conjunction.

7   The second relation I shall observe as essential to causes and effects, is not so universally acknowledg'd, but is liable to some controversy. 'Tis that of PRIORITY of time in the cause before the effect. Some pretend that 'tis not absolutely necessary a cause shou'd precede its effect; but that any object or action, in the very first moment of its existence, may exert its productive quality, and give rise to another object or action, perfectly co-temporary with itself.[†] But beside that experience in most instances seems to contradict this opinion, we may establish the relation of priority by a kind of inference or reasoning. 'Tis an establish'd maxim both in natural and moral philosophy, that an object, which exists for any time in its full perfection without producing another, is not its sole cause;[†] but is assisted by some other principle, which pushes it from its state of inactivity, and makes it exert that energy, of which it was secretly possest. Now if any cause may be perfectly co-temporary with its effect, 'tis certain, according to this maxim, that they must all of them be so; since any one of them, which retards its operation for a single moment, exerts not itself at that very individual time, in which it might have operated; and therefore is no proper cause.[†] The consequence of this wou'd be no less than the destruction of that succession of causes, which we observe in the world; and indeed, the utter annihilation of time. For if one cause were co-temporary with its effect, and this effect with *its* effect, and so on, 'tis plain there wou'd be no such thing as succession, and all objects must be co-existent.

8   If this argument appear satisfactory, 'tis well. If not, I beg the reader to allow me the same liberty, which I have us'd in the preceding case,[†] of supposing it such. For he shall find, that the affair is of no great importance.

9   Having thus discover'd or suppos'd the two relations of *contiguity* and *succession* to be essential to causes and effects, I find I am stopt short, and can proceed no farther in considering any single instance of cause and effect. Motion in one body is regarded upon impulse[†] as the cause of motion in another. When we consider these objects with the utmost attention, we find only that the one body approaches the other; and that the motion of it precedes that of the other, but without any sensible interval.[†] 'Tis in vain to rack ourselves with *farther* thought

[16] Part 4. Sect. 5.[†]

and reflection upon this subject. We can go no *farther* in considering this particular instance.

10   Shou'd any one leave this instance,[†] and pretend to define a cause, by saying
it is something productive of another, 'tis evident he wou'd say nothing. For
what does he mean by *production*? Can he give any definition of it, that will not
be the same with that of causation? If he can; I desire it may be produc'd. If
he cannot; he here runs in a circle, and gives a synonimous term instead of a
definition.

11   Shall we then rest contented with these two relations of contiguity and succession, as affording a compleat idea of causation? By no means. An object may
be contiguous and prior to another, without being consider'd as its cause. There
is a NECESSARY CONNEXION to be taken into consideration; and that relation is of
much greater importance, than any of the other two above-mention'd.

12   Here again I turn the object on all sides, in order to discover the nature of this
necessary connexion, and find the impression, or impressions, from which its
idea may be deriv'd. When I cast my eye on the *known qualities* of objects, I
immediately discover that the relation of cause and effect depends not in the
least on *them*. When I consider their *relations*,[†] I can find none but those of contiguity and succession; which I have already regarded as imperfect and unsatisfactory. Shall the despair of success make me assert, that I am here possest of an
idea, which is not preceded by any similar impression? This wou'd be too strong
a proof of levity and inconstancy; since the contrary principle has been already
so firmly establish'd,[†] as to admit of no farther doubt; at least, till we have more
fully examin'd the present difficulty.

13   We must, therefore, proceed like those, who being in search of any thing, that   *SB 78*
lies conceal'd from them, and not finding it in the place they expected, beat about
all the neighbouring fields, without any certain view or design, in hopes their
good fortune will at last guide them to what they search for. 'Tis necessary for us
to leave the direct survey of this question concerning the nature of that *necessary
connexion*, which enters into our idea of cause and effect; and endeavour to find
some other questions, the examination of which will perhaps afford a hint, that
may serve to clear up the present difficulty.[†] Of these questions there occur two,
which I shall proceed to examine, *viz.*

14   *First*, For what reason we pronounce it *necessary*, that every thing whose existence has a beginning, shou'd also have a cause?[†]

15   *Secondly*, Why we conclude, that such particular causes must *necessarily* have
such particular effects; and what is the nature of that *inference* we draw from the
one to the other, and of the *belief* we repose in it?[†]

16   I shall only observe before I proceed any farther, that tho' the ideas of cause
and effect be deriv'd from the impressions of reflection as well as from those of
sensation, yet for brevity's sake, I commonly mention only the latter as the origin
of these ideas; tho' I desire that whatever I say of them may also extend to the
former. Passions are connected with their objects and with one another; no less
than external bodies are connected together.[†] The same relation, then, of cause
and effect, which belongs to one, must be common to all of them.

Sect. 3. *Why a cause is always necessary*

1 To begin with the first question concerning the necessity of a cause: 'Tis a general maxim in philosophy, that *whatever begins to exist, must have a cause of existence*. This is commonly taken for granted in all reasonings, without any proof given or demanded.† 'Tis suppos'd to be founded on intuition,† and to be one of those maxims, which tho' they may be deny'd with the lips, 'tis impossible for men in their hearts really to doubt of. But if we examine this maxim by the idea of knowledge above-explain'd,† we shall discover in it no mark of any such intuitive certainty; but on the contrary shall find, that 'tis of a nature quite foreign to that species of conviction.   *SB 79*

2   All certainty arises from the comparison of ideas, and from the discovery of such relations as are unalterable, so long as the ideas continue the same. These relations are *resemblance, proportions in quantity and number, degrees of any quality*, and *contrariety*; none of which are imply'd in this proposition, *whatever has a beginning has also a cause of existence*. That proposition therefore is not intuitively certain. At least any one, who wou'd assert it to be intuitively certain, must deny these to be the only infallible relations, and must find some other relation of that kind to be imply'd in it; which it will then be time enough to examine.

3   But here is an argument, which proves at once, that the foregoing proposition† is neither intuitively nor demonstrably certain. We can never demonstrate† the necessity of a cause to every new existence, or new modification of existence, without showing at the same time the impossibility there is, that any thing can ever begin to exist without some productive principle; and where the latter proposition cannot be prov'd, we must despair of ever being able to prove the former. Now that the latter proposition is utterly incapable of a demonstrative proof, we may satisfy ourselves by considering, that as all distinct ideas are separable from each other, and as the ideas of cause and effect are evidently distinct, 'twill be easy for us to conceive any object to be non-existent this moment, and existent the next, without conjoining to it the distinct idea of a cause or productive principle. The separation, therefore, of the idea of a cause from that of a   *SB 80* beginning of existence, is plainly possible for the imagination; and consequently the actual separation of these objects is so far possible, that it implies no contradiction nor absurdity; and is therefore incapable of being refuted by any reasoning from mere ideas; without which 'tis impossible to demonstrate the necessity of a cause.

4   Accordingly we shall find upon examination, that every demonstration, which has been produc'd for the necessity of a cause, is fallacious and sophistical. All the points of time and place, say some philosophers,[17] in which we can suppose any object to begin to exist, are in themselves equal; and unless there be some cause, which is peculiar to one time and to one place, and which by that means determines and fixes the existence, it must remain in eternal suspence; and the object can never begin to be, for want of something to fix its beginning.

---

[17] Mr. *Hobbes*.†

But I ask; Is there any more difficulty in supposing the time and place to be fix'd without a cause, than to suppose the existence to be determin'd in that manner? The first question that occurs on this subject is always, *whether* the object shall exist or not? The next, *when* and *where* it shall begin to exist? If the removal of a cause be intuitively absurd in the one case, it must be so in the other: And if that absurdity be not clear without a proof in the one case, it will equally require one in the other. The absurdity, then, of the one supposition can never be a proof of that of the other; since they are both upon the same footing, and must stand or fall by the same reasoning.

5   The second argument,[18] which I find us'd on this head, labours under an equal difficulty. Every thing, 'tis said, must have a cause; for if any thing wanted a cause, *it* wou'd produce *itself*; that is, exist before it existed; which is impossible. But this reasoning is plainly unconclusive; because it supposes, that in our denial of a cause we still grant what we expressly deny, *viz.* that there must be a cause; which therefore is taken to be the object itself; and *that*, no doubt, is an evident contradiction. But to say that any thing is produc'd, or to express myself more properly, comes into existence, without a cause, is not to affirm, that 'tis itself its own cause; but on the contrary in excluding all external causes, excludes *a fortiori* the thing itself, which is created. An object, that exists absolutely without any cause, certainly is not its own cause; and when you assert, that the one follows from the other, you suppose the very point in question, and take it for granted, that 'tis utterly impossible any thing can ever begin to exist without a cause, but that upon the exclusion of one productive principle, we must still have recourse to another.   *SB 81*

6   'Tis exactly the same case with the third argument,[19] which has been employ'd to demonstrate the necessity of a cause. Whatever is produc'd without any cause, is produc'd by *nothing*; or in other words, has nothing for its cause.[†] But nothing can never be a cause, no more than it can be something, or equal to two right angles. By the same intuition, that we perceive nothing not to be equal to two right angles, or not to be something, we perceive, that it can never be a cause; and consequently must perceive, that every object has a real cause of its existence.

7   I believe it will not be necessary to employ many words in showing the weakness of this argument, after what I have said of the foregoing.[†] They are all of them founded on the same fallacy, and are deriv'd from the same turn of thought. 'Tis sufficient only to observe, that when we exclude all causes we really do exclude them, and neither suppose nothing nor the object itself to be the causes of the existence; and consequently can draw no argument from the absurdity of these suppositions to prove the absurdity of that exclusion. If every thing must have a cause, it follows, that upon the exclusion of other causes we must accept of the object itself or of nothing as causes. But 'tis the very point in question, whether every thing must have a cause or not; and therefore, according to all just reasoning, it ought never to be taken for granted.   *SB 82*

---

[18] Dr. *Clarke* and others.[†]   [19] Mr. *Locke*.[†]   *SB 80–1*

8   They are still more frivolous, who say, that every effect must have a cause, because 'tis imply'd in the very idea of effect.† Every effect necessarily presupposes a cause; effect being a relative term, of which cause is the correlative. But this does not prove, that every being must be preceded by a cause; no more than it follows, because every husband must have a wife, that therefore every man must be marry'd. The true state of the question is, whether every object, which begins to exist, must owe its existence to a cause; and this I assert neither to be intuitively nor demonstratively certain, and hope to have prov'd it sufficiently by the foregoing arguments.

9   Since it is not from knowledge or any scientific reasoning,† that we derive the opinion of† the necessity of a cause to every new production, that opinion must necessarily arise from observation and experience. The next question, then, shou'd naturally be, *How experience gives rise to such a principle?* But as I find it will be more convenient to sink this question in the following, *Why we conclude, that such particular causes must necessarily have such particular effects, and why we form an inference from one to another?*† we shall make that the subject of our future enquiry.† 'Twill, perhaps, be found in the end, that the same answer will serve for both questions.

Sect. 4. *Of the component parts of our reasonings concerning cause and effect*

1   Tho' the mind in its reasonings from causes or effects carries its view beyond those objects, which it sees or remembers, it must never lose sight of them entirely, nor reason merely upon its own ideas, without some mixture of impressions, or at least of ideas of the memory, which are equivalent to impressions. When we infer effects from causes, we must establish the existence of these   *SB 83* causes; which we have only two ways of doing, either by an immediate perception† of our memory or senses, or by an inference from other causes; which causes again we must ascertain in the same manner, either by a present impression, or by an inference from *their* causes, and so on, till we arrive at some object, which we see or remember. 'Tis impossible for us to carry on our inferences *in infinitum*; and the only thing, that can stop them, is an impression of the memory† or senses, beyond which there is no room for doubt or enquiry.

2   To give an instance of this, we may choose any point of history, and consider for what reason we either believe or reject it. Thus we believe that CÆSAR was kill'd in the senate-house on the *ides* of *March*; and that because this fact is establish'd on the unanimous testimony of historians, who agree to assign this precise time and place to that event. Here are certain characters and letters present either to our memory or senses; which characters we likewise remember to have been us'd as the signs of certain ideas; and these ideas were either in the minds of such as were immediately present at that action, and receiv'd the ideas directly from its existence; or they were deriv'd from the testimony of others, and that again from another testimony, by a visible gradation, till we arrive at those who were eye-witnesses and spectators of the event.† 'Tis obvious all this chain of

argument or connexion of causes and effects, is at first founded on those characters or letters, which are seen or remember'd, and that without the authority either of the memory or senses our whole reasoning wou'd be chimerical and without foundation. Every link of the chain wou'd in that case hang upon another; but there wou'd not be any thing fix'd to one end of it, capable of sustaining the whole; and consequently there wou'd be no belief nor evidence. And this actually is the case with all *hypothetical* arguments, or reasonings upon a supposition; there being in them, neither any present impression, nor belief of a real existence.

3   I need not observe, that 'tis no just objection to the present doctrine, that we *SB 84* can reason upon our past conclusions or principles, without having recourse to those impressions, from which they first arose. For even supposing these impressions shou'd be entirely effac'd from the memory, the conviction they produc'd may still remain; and 'tis equally true, that all reasonings concerning causes and effects are originally deriv'd from some impression; in the same manner, as the assurance of a demonstration proceeds always from a comparison of ideas, tho' it may continue after the comparison is forgot.

Sect. 5. *Of the impressions of the senses and memory*

1   In this kind of reasoning, then, from causation, we employ materials, which are of a mix'd and heterogeneous nature, and which, however connected, are yet essentially different from each other. All our arguments concerning causes and effects consist both of an impression of the memory or senses, and of the idea of that existence, which produces the object of the impression, or is produc'd by it.[†] Here therefore we have three things to explain, viz. *First*, The original impression. *Secondly*, The transition to the idea of the connected cause or effect. *Thirdly*, The nature and qualities of that idea.

2   As to those *impressions*, which arise from the *senses*, their ultimate cause is, in my opinion, perfectly inexplicable by human reason, and 'twill always be impossible to decide with certainty, whether they arise immediately from the object,[†] or are produc'd by the creative power of the mind,[†] or are deriv'd from the author of our being.[†] Nor is such a question any way material to our present purpose. We may draw inferences from the coherence of our perceptions, whether they be true or false; whether they represent nature justly, or be mere illusions of the senses.[†]

3   When we search for the characteristic, which distinguishes the *memory* from *SB 85* the imagination, we must immediately perceive, that it cannot lie in the simple ideas it presents to us; since both these faculties borrow their simple ideas from the impressions, and can never go beyond these original perceptions. These faculties are as little distinguish'd from each other by the arrangement of their complex ideas. For tho' it be a peculiar property of the memory to preserve the original order and position of its ideas, while the imagination transposes and changes them, as it pleases; yet this difference is not sufficient to distinguish them in their operation, or make us know the one from the other; it being

impossible to recal the past impressions, in order to compare them with our present ideas, and see whether their arrangement be exactly similar. Since therefore the memory is known, neither by the order of its *complex* ideas, nor the nature of its *simple* ones; it follows, that the difference betwixt it and the imagination lies in its superior force and vivacity. A man may indulge his fancy in feigning any past scene of adventures;[†] nor wou'd there be any possibility of distinguishing this from a remembrance of a like kind, were not the ideas of the imagination fainter and more obscure.

4   [App]It frequently happens, that when two men have been engag'd in any scene   *SB 627* of action, the one shall remember it much better than the other, and shall have all the difficulty in the world to make his companion recollect it. He runs over several circumstances in vain; mentions the time, the place, the company, what   *SB 628* was said, what was done on all sides; till at last he hits on some lucky circumstance, that revives the whole, and gives his friend a perfect memory of every thing. Here the person that forgets receives at first all the ideas from the discourse of the other, with the same circumstances of time and place; tho' he considers them as mere fictions of the imagination. But as soon as the circumstance is mention'd, that touches the memory, the very same ideas now appear in a new light, and have, in a manner, a different feeling from what they had before. Without any other alteration, beside that of the feeling, they become immediately ideas of the memory,[†] and are assented to.

5   Since, therefore, the imagination can represent all the same objects that the memory can offer to us, and since those faculties are only distinguish'd by the different *feeling* of the ideas they present, it may be proper to consider what is the nature of that feeling. And here I believe every one will readily agree with me, that the ideas of the memory are more *strong* and *lively* than those of the fancy.[App] A painter, who intended to represent a passion or emotion of any kind,   *SB 85* wou'd endeavour to get a sight of a person actuated by a like emotion, in order to enliven his ideas, and give them a force and vivacity superior to what is found in those, which are mere fictions of the imagination. The more recent this memory is, the clearer is the idea; and when after a long interval he wou'd return to the contemplation of his object, he always finds its idea to be much decay'd,[†] if not wholly obliterated. We are frequently in doubt concerning the ideas of the memory, as they become very weak and feeble; and are at a loss to determine whether any image proceeds from the fancy or the memory, when it is not drawn in such lively colours as distinguish that latter faculty. I think I remember such an event, says one; but am not sure. A long tract of time has almost worn it out of   *SB 86* my memory, and leaves me uncertain whether or not it be the pure offspring of my fancy.

6   And as an idea of the memory, by losing its force and vivacity, may degenerate to such a degree, as to be taken for an idea of the imagination; so on the other hand an idea of the imagination may acquire such a force and vivacity, as to pass for an idea of the memory, and counterfeit its effects on the belief and judgment. This is noted in the case of liars; who by the frequent repetition of their lies,

come at last to believe and remember them, as realities; custom and habit having in this case, as in many others, the same influence on the mind as nature, and infixing the idea with equal force and vigour.

7   Thus it appears, that the *belief* or *assent*, which always attends the memory and senses, is nothing but the vivacity of those perceptions they present; and that this alone distinguishes them from the imagination. To believe is in this case to feel an immediate impression of the senses, or a repetition of that impression in the memory. 'Tis merely the force and liveliness of the perception, which constitutes the first act of the judgment,[†] and lays the foundation of that reasoning, which we build upon it, when we trace the relation of cause and effect.

Sect. 6. *Of the inference from the impression to the idea*

1   'Tis easy to observe, that in tracing this relation,[†] the inference we draw from cause to effect, is not deriv'd merely from a survey of these particular objects,[†] and from such a penetration into their essences as may discover the dependance of the one upon the other. There is no object, which implies the existence of any other if we consider these objects in themselves, and never look beyond the ideas which we form of them. Such an inference wou'd amount to knowledge, and *SB 87* wou'd imply the absolute contradiction and impossibility of conceiving any thing different. But as all distinct ideas are separable, 'tis evident there can be no impossibility of that kind. When we pass from a present impression to the idea of any object, we might possibly have separated the idea from the impression, and have substituted any other idea in its room.

2   'Tis therefore by EXPERIENCE only, that we can infer the existence of one object from that of another.[†] The nature of experience is this. We remember to have had frequent instances of the existence of one species of objects; and also remember, that the individuals of another species of objects have always attended them, and have existed in a regular order of contiguity and succession with regard to them. Thus we remember to have seen that species of object we call *flame*, and to have felt that species of sensation we call *heat*. We likewise call to mind their constant conjunction in all past instances. Without any farther ceremony, we call the one *cause* and the other *effect*, and infer the existence of the one from that of the other.[†] In all those instances, from which we learn the conjunction of particular causes and effects, both the causes and effects have been perceiv'd by the senses, and are remember'd: But in all cases, wherein we reason concerning them, there is only one perceiv'd or remember'd, and the other is supply'd in conformity to our past experience.

3   Thus in advancing we have insensibly[†] discover'd a new relation[†] betwixt cause and effect, when we least expected it, and were entirely employ'd upon another subject. This relation is their CONSTANT CONJUNCTION. Contiguity and succession are not sufficient to make us pronounce any two objects to be cause and effect, unless we perceive, that these two relations are preserv'd in several instances. We may now see the advantage of quitting the direct survey of this

relation,† in order to discover the nature of that *necessary connexion*, which makes so essential a part of it. There are hopes, that by this means we may at last arrive at our propos'd end; tho' to tell the truth, this new-discover'd relation of a constant conjunction seems to advance us but very little in our way. For it implies no more than this, that like objects have always been plac'd in like relations of contiguity and succession; and it seems evident, at least at first sight, that by this means we can never discover any new idea, and can only multiply, but not enlarge the objects of our mind.† It may be thought, that what we learn not from one object, we can never learn from a hundred, which are all of the same kind, and are perfectly resembling in every circumstance. As our senses show us in one instance two bodies, or motions, or qualities in certain relations of succession and contiguity; so our memory presents us only with a multitude of instances, wherein we always find like bodies, motions, or qualities in like relations. From the mere repetition of any past impression, even to infinity, there never will arise any new original idea, such as that of a necessary connexion; and the number of impressions has in this case no more effect than if we confin'd ourselves to one only. But tho' this reasoning seems just and obvious; yet as it wou'd be folly to despair too soon, we shall continue the thread of our discourse; and having found, that after the discovery of the constant conjunction of any objects, we always draw an inference from one object to another, we shall now examine the nature of that inference, and of the transition from the impression to the idea. Perhaps 'twill appear in the end, that the necessary connexion depends on the inference, instead of the inference's depending on the necessary connexion.†

SB 88

4   Since it appears, that the transition from an impression present to the memory or senses to the idea of an object, which we call cause or effect, is founded on past *experience*, and on our remembrance of their *constant conjunction*, the next question is, whether experience produces the idea by means of the understanding or imagination; whether we are determin'd by reason to make the transition, or by a certain association and relation of perceptions? If reason determin'd us, it wou'd proceed upon that principle, *that instances, of which we have had no experience,*† *must resemble those, of which we have had experience, and that the course of nature continues always uniformly the same.* In order therefore to clear up this matter, let us consider all the arguments, upon which such a proposition may be suppos'd to be founded; and as these must be deriv'd either from *knowledge* or *probability*, let us cast our eye on each of these degrees of evidence, and see whether they afford any just conclusion of this nature.

SB 89

5   Our foregoing method of reasoning† will easily convince us, that there can be no *demonstrative* arguments to prove, *that those instances, of which we have had no experience, resemble those, of which we have had experience.* We can at least conceive a change in the course of nature; which sufficiently proves, that such a change is not absolutely impossible. To form a clear idea of any thing, is an undeniable argument for its possibility, and is alone a refutation of any pretended demonstration against it.

6   Probability, as it discovers not† the relations of ideas, consider'd as such, but

only those of objects, must in some respects be founded on the impressions of our memory and senses, and in some respects on our ideas. Were there no mixture of any impression in our probable reasonings, the conclusion wou'd be entirely chimerical: And were there no mixture of ideas, the action of the mind, in observing the relation, wou'd, properly speaking, be sensation, not reasoning.[†] 'Tis therefore necessary, that in all probable reasonings there be something present to the mind, either seen or remember'd; and that from this we infer something connected with it, which is not seen nor remember'd.

7   The only connexion or relation of objects, which can lead us beyond the immediate impressions of our memory and senses, is that of cause and effect; and that because 'tis the only one, on which we can found a just inference from one object to another.[†] The idea of cause and effect is deriv'd from *experience*,   *SB 90* which informs us, that such particular objects, in all past instances, have been constantly conjoin'd with each other: And as an object similar to one of these is suppos'd to be immediately present in its impression, we thence presume on the existence of one similar to its usual attendant.[†] According to this account of things, which is, I think, in every point unquestionable, probability is founded on the presumption of a resemblance betwixt those objects, of which we have had experience, and those, of which we have had none; and therefore 'tis impossible this presumption can arise from probability.[†] The same principle cannot be both the cause and effect of another; and this is, perhaps, the only proposition concerning that relation, which is either intuitively or demonstratively certain.

8   Shou'd any one think to elude this argument; and without determining whether our reasoning on this subject be deriv'd from demonstration or probability, pretend that all conclusions from causes and effects are built on solid reasoning: I can only desire, that this reasoning may be produc'd, in order to be expos'd to our examination. It may, perhaps, be said, that after experience of the constant conjunction of certain objects, we reason in the following manner. Such an object is always found to produce another. 'Tis impossible it cou'd have this effect, if it was not endow'd with a power of production. The power necessarily implies the effect; and therefore there is a just foundation for drawing a conclusion from the existence of one object to that of its usual attendant. The past production implies a power: The power implies a new production: And the new production is what we infer from the power and the past production.

9   'Twere easy for me to show the weakness of this reasoning, were I willing to make use of those observations, I have already made,[†] that the idea of *production* is the same with that of *causation*, and that no existence certainly and demonstratively implies a power in any other object; or were it proper to anticipate what   *SB 91* I shall have occasion to remark afterwards[†] concerning the idea we form of *power* and *efficacy*. But as such a method of proceeding may seem either to weaken my system, by resting one part of it on another, or to breed a confusion in my reasoning, I shall endeavour to maintain my present assertion without any such assistance.

10   It shall therefore be allow'd for a moment, that the production of one object

by another in any one instance implies a power; and that this power is connected with its effect. But it having been already prov'd,[†] that the power lies not in the sensible qualities of the cause; and there being nothing but the sensible qualities present to us; I ask, why in other instances you presume that the same power still exists, merely upon the appearance of these qualities?[†] Your appeal to past experience decides nothing in the present case; and at the utmost can only prove, that that very object, which produc'd any other, was at that very instant endow'd with such a power; but can never prove, that the same power must continue in the same object or collection of sensible qualities; much less, that a like power is always conjoin'd with like sensible qualities.[†] Shou'd it be said, that we have experience, that the same power continues united with the same object, and that like objects are endow'd with like powers, I wou'd renew my question, *Why from this experience we form any conclusion beyond those past instances, of which we have had experience?* If you answer this question in the same manner as the preceding, your answer gives still occasion to a new question of the same kind, even *in infinitum*; which clearly proves, that the foregoing reasoning[†] had no just foundation.

11　　　Thus not only our reason fails us in the discovery of the *ultimate connexion* of causes and effects, but even after experience has inform'd us of their *constant conjunction*, 'tis impossible for us to satisfy ourselves by our reason, why we shou'd extend that experience beyond those particular instances, which have fallen under our observation. We suppose, but are never able to prove, that there must be a resemblance betwixt those objects, of which we have had experience, and those which lie beyond the reach of our discovery. *SB 92*

12　　　We have already taken notice[†] of certain relations, which make us pass from one object to another, even tho' there be no reason to determine us to that transition; and this we may establish for a general rule, that wherever the mind constantly and uniformly makes a transition without any reason, it is influenc'd by these relations. Now this is exactly the present case. Reason can never show us the connexion of one object with another, tho' aided by experience, and the observation of their constant conjunction in all past instances. When the mind, therefore, passes from the idea or impression of one object to the idea or belief of another, it is not determin'd by reason, but by certain principles, which associate together the ideas of these objects, and unite them in the imagination.[†] Had ideas no more union in the fancy than objects seem to have to the understanding, we cou'd never draw any inference from causes to effects, nor repose belief in any matter of fact.[†] The inference, therefore, depends solely on the union of ideas.

13　　　The principles of union among ideas, I have reduc'd to three general ones,[†] and have asserted, that the idea or impression of any object naturally introduces the idea of any other object, that is resembling, contiguous to, or connected with it. These principles I allow to be neither the *infallible* nor the *sole* causes of an union among ideas. They are not the infallible causes. For one may fix his attention during some time on any one object without looking farther. They are not the sole causes. For the thought has evidently a very irregular motion in running along its objects, and may leap from the heavens to the earth, from one end of the creation to the other, without any certain method or order.[†] But tho' I allow this weakness in these three relations, and this irregularity in the imagination; yet I assert that the only *general* principles, which associate ideas, are resemblance, *SB 93* contiguity and causation.

14   There is indeed a principle of union among ideas, which at first sight may be esteem'd different from any of these, but will be found at the bottom to depend on the same origin. When every individual of any species of objects is found by experience to be constantly united with an individual of another species, the appearance of any new individual of either species naturally conveys the thought to its usual attendant. Thus because such a particular idea is commonly annex'd to such a particular word,[†] nothing is requir'd but the hearing of that word to produce the correspondent idea; and 'twill scarce be possible for the mind, by its utmost efforts, to prevent that transition. In this case it is not absolutely necessary, that upon hearing such a particular sound, we shou'd reflect on any past experience, and consider what idea has been usually connected with the sound. The imagination of itself supplies the place of this reflection,[†] and is so accustom'd to pass from the word to the idea, that it interposes not a moment's delay betwixt the hearing of the one, and the conception of the other.

15   But tho' I acknowledge this to be a true principle of association among ideas, I assert it to be the very same with that betwixt the ideas of cause and effect, and to be an essential part in all our reasonings from that relation. We have no other notion of cause and effect, but that of certain objects, which have been *always conjoin'd* together, and which in all past instances have been found inseparable. We cannot penetrate into the reason of the conjunction. We only observe the thing itself, and always find that from the constant conjunction the objects acquire an union in the imagination. When the impression of one becomes present to us, we immediately form an idea of its usual attendant; and consequently we may establish this as one part of the definition of an opinion or belief, *that 'tis an idea related to or associated with a present impression.*

16   Thus tho' causation be a *philosophical* relation, as implying contiguity, succes- *SB 94* sion, and constant conjunction, yet 'tis only so far as it is a *natural* relation,[†] and produces an union among our ideas, that we are able to reason upon it, or draw any inference from it.

Sect. 7. *Of the nature of the idea or belief*

1   The idea of an object[†] is an essential part of the belief of it, but not the whole. We conceive many things, which we do not believe. In order then to discover more fully the nature of belief, or the qualities of those ideas we assent to,[†] let us weigh the following considerations.

2   'Tis evident, that all reasonings from causes or effects terminate in conclusions, concerning matter of fact; that is, concerning the existence of objects or of their qualities.[†] 'Tis also evident, that the idea of existence is nothing

different from the idea of any object, and that when after the simple conception of any thing we wou'd conceive it as existent, we in reality make no addition to or alteration on our first idea. Thus when we affirm, that God is existent, we simply form the idea of such a being, as he is represented to us; nor is the existence, which we attribute to him, conceiv'd by a particular idea, which we join to the idea of his other qualities, and can again separate and distinguish from them. But I go farther; and not content with asserting, that the conception of the existence of any object is no addition to the simple conception of it, I likewise maintain,[†] that the belief of the existence joins no new ideas to those, which compose the idea of the object. When I think of God, when I think of him as existent, and when I believe him to be existent, my idea of him neither encreases nor diminishes. But as 'tis certain there is a great difference betwixt the simple conception of the existence of an object, and the belief of it, and as this difference lies not in the parts or composition of the idea, which we conceive; it follows, that it must lie in the *manner*, in which we conceive it.[†] *SB 95*

3　　Suppose a person present with me, who advances propositions, to which I do not assent, *that* Cæsar *dy'd in his bed, that silver is more fusible than lead*, or *mercury heavier than gold*; 'tis evident, that notwithstanding my incredulity, I clearly understand his meaning, and form all the same ideas, which he forms. My imagination is endow'd with the same powers as his; nor is it possible for him to conceive any idea, which I cannot conceive; or conjoin any, which I cannot conjoin. I therefore ask, wherein consists the difference betwixt believing and disbelieving any proposition? The answer is easy with regard to propositions, that are prov'd by intuition or demonstration. In that case, the person, who assents, not only conceives the ideas according to the proposition, but is necessarily determin'd to conceive them in that particular manner, either immediately or by the interposition of other ideas.[†] Whatever is absurd is unintelligible; nor is it possible for the imagination to conceive any thing contrary to a demonstration. But as in reasonings from causation, and concerning matters of fact, this absolute necessity[†] cannot take place, and the imagination is free to conceive both sides of the question, I still ask, *Wherein consists the difference betwixt incredulity and belief?* since in both cases the conception of the idea is equally possible and requisite.

4　　'Twill not be a satisfactory answer to say, that a person, who does not assent to a proposition you advance; after having conceiv'd the object in the same manner with you; immediately conceives it in a different manner, and has different ideas of it. This answer is unsatisfactory; not because it contains any falshood, but because it discovers not all the truth. 'Tis confest, that in all cases, wherein we dissent from any person, we conceive both sides of the question; but as we can believe only one, it evidently follows, that the belief must make some difference *SB 96* betwixt that conception to which we assent, and that from which we dissent. We may mingle, and unite, and separate, and confound, and vary our ideas in a hundred different ways; but till there appears some principle,[†] which fixes one of these different situations, we have in reality no opinion: And this principle, as it plainly makes no addition to our precedent ideas,[†] can only change the *manner* of our conceiving them.

5   All the perceptions of the mind are of two kinds, *viz.* impressions and ideas, which differ from each other only in their different degrees of force and vivacity.[†] Our ideas are copy'd from our impressions, and represent them in all their parts. When you wou'd any way vary the idea of a particular object, you can only encrease or diminish its force and vivacity. If you make any other change on it, it represents a different object or impression. The case is the same as in colours. A particular shade of any colour may acquire a new degree of liveliness or brightness without any other variation. But when you produce any other variation, 'tis no longer the same shade or colour. So that as belief does nothing but vary the manner, in which we conceive any object, it can only bestow on our ideas an additional force and vivacity. An opinion, therefore, or belief may be most accurately defin'd, A LIVELY IDEA RELATED TO OR ASSOCIATED WITH A PRESENT IMPRESSION.[20]

6   Here are the heads of those arguments,[†] which lead us to this conclusion.   *SB 97* When we infer the existence of an object from that of others, some object must always be present either to the memory or senses, in order to be the foundation of our reasoning; since the mind cannot run up with[†] its inferences *in infinitum*. Reason can never satisfy us that the existence of any one object does ever imply that of another; so that when we pass from the impression of one to the idea or belief of another, we are not determin'd by reason, but by custom or a principle of association. But belief is somewhat more than a simple idea. 'Tis a particular

---

[20] We may here take occasion to observe a very remarkable error, which being frequently incul-   *SB 96* cated in the schools, has become a kind of establish'd maxim, and is universally receiv'd by all logicians. This error consists in the vulgar division of the acts of the understanding, into *conception*, *judgment* and *reasoning*, and in the definitions we give of them.[†] Conception is defin'd to be the simple survey of one or more ideas: Judgment to be the separating or uniting of different ideas: Reasoning to be the separating or uniting of different ideas by the interposition of others, which show the relation they bear to each other. But these distinctions and definitions are faulty in very considerable articles. For *first*, 'tis far from being true, that in every judgment, which we form, we unite two different ideas; since in that proposition, *God is*, or indeed any other, which regards existence, the idea of existence is no distinct idea, which we unite with that of the object, and which is capable of forming a compound idea by the union. *Secondly*, As we can thus form a proposition,   *SB 97* which contains only one idea, so we may exert our reason without employing more than two ideas, and without having recourse to a third to serve as a medium betwixt them. We infer a cause immediately from its effect; and this inference is not only a true species of reasoning, but the strongest of all others, and more convincing than when we interpose another idea to connect the two extremes. What we may in general affirm concerning these three acts of the understanding, is, that taking them in a proper light, they all resolve themselves into the first, and are nothing but particular ways of conceiving our objects. Whether we consider a single object, or several; whether we dwell on these objects, or run from them to others; and in whatever form or order we survey them, the act of the mind exceeds not a simple conception; and the only remarkable difference, which occurs on this occasion, is, when we join belief to the conception, and are perswaded of the truth of what we conceive. This act of the mind has never yet been explain'd by any philosopher; and therefore I am at liberty to propose my hypothesis concerning it; which is, that 'tis only a strong and steady conception of any idea, and such as approaches in some measure to an immediate impression.

manner of forming an idea: And as the same idea can only be vary'd by a variation of its degrees of force and vivacity; it follows upon the whole, that belief is a lively idea produc'd by a relation to a present impression, according to the foregoing definition.

7   ^{App.}This operation of the mind, which forms the belief of any matter of fact,   *SB 628*
seems hitherto to have been one of the greatest mysteries of philosophy; tho' no one has so much as suspected, that there was any difficulty in explaining it.[†] For my part I must own, that I find a considerable difficulty in the case; and that even when I think I understand the subject perfectly, I am at a loss for terms to express my meaning. I conclude, by an induction which seems to me very evident, that an opinion or belief is nothing but an idea, that is different from a fiction, not in the nature, or the order of its parts, but in the *manner* of its being conceiv'd. But when I wou'd explain this *manner*, I scarce find any word that fully answers the   *SB 629*
case, but am oblig'd to have recourse to every one's feeling, in order to give him a perfect notion of this operation of the mind. An idea assented to *feels* different from a fictitious idea, that the fancy alone presents to us: And this different feeling I endeavour to explain by calling it a superior *force*, or *vivacity*, or *solidity*, or *firmness*, or *steadiness*. This variety of terms, which may seem so unphilosophical,[†] is intended only to express that act of the mind, which renders realities more present to us than fictions, causes them to weigh more in the thought, and gives them a superior influence on the passions and imagination. Provided we agree about the thing, 'tis needless to dispute about the terms. The imagination has the command over all its ideas, and can join, and mix, and vary them in all the ways possible. It may conceive objects with all the circumstances of place and time. It may set them, in a manner, before our eyes in their true colours, just as they might have existed. But as it is impossible, that that faculty can ever, of itself, reach belief, 'tis evident, that belief consists not in the nature and order of our ideas, but in the manner of their conception, and in their feeling to the mind. I confess, that 'tis impossible to explain perfectly this feeling or manner of conception. We may make use of words, that express something near it. But its true and proper name is *belief*, which is a term that every one sufficiently understands in common life. And in philosophy we can go no farther, than assert, that it is something *felt* by the mind, which distinguishes the ideas of the judgment[†] from the fictions of the imagination. It gives them more force and influence; makes them appear of greater importance; infixes them in the mind; and renders them the governing principles of all our actions.^{App.}

8   This definition[†] will also be found to be entirely conformable to every one's   *SB 97*
feeling and experience. Nothing is more evident, than that those ideas, to which we assent, are more strong, firm, and vivid, than the loose reveries of a castle-builder. If one person sits down to read a book as a romance, and another as a true history, they plainly receive the same ideas, and in the same order; nor does the   *SB 98*
incredulity of the one, and the belief of the other hinder them from putting the very same sense upon their author.[†] His words produce the same ideas in both; tho' his testimony has not the same influence on them. The latter has a more lively conception of all the incidents. He enters deeper into the concerns of the

persons: Represents to himself their actions, and characters, and friendships, and enmities: He even goes so far as to form a notion of their features, and air, and person. While the former, who gives no credit to the testimony of the author, has a more faint and languid conception of all these particulars; and except on account of the style and ingenuity of the composition, can receive little entertainment from it.

Sect. 8. *Of the causes of belief*

1   Having thus explain'd the nature of belief, and shown that it consists in a lively idea related to a present impression; let us now proceed to examine from what principles it is deriv'd, and what bestows the vivacity on the idea.

2   I wou'd willingly establish it as a general maxim in the science of human nature, *that when any impression becomes present to us, it not only transports the mind to such ideas as are related to it, but likewise communicates to them a share of its force and vivacity*. All the operations of the mind depend in a great measure on its disposition, when it performs them; and according as the spirits[†] are more or less elevated, and the attention more or less fix'd, the action will always have more or less vigour and vivacity. When therefore any object is presented, which elevates and enlivens the thought, every action,[†] to which the mind applies itself, will be more strong and vivid, as long as that disposition continues. Now 'tis evident the continuance of the disposition depends entirely on the objects, about which the mind is employ'd; and that any new object naturally gives a new direction to the spirits, and changes the disposition; as on the contrary, when the mind fixes constantly on the same object, or passes easily and insensibly along related objects, the disposition has a much longer duration. Hence it happens, that when the mind is once enliven'd by a present impression, it proceeds to form a more lively idea of the related objects, by a natural transition of the disposition from the one to the other. The change of the objects is so easy, that the mind is scarce sensible of it, but applies itself to the conception of the related idea with all the force and vivacity it acquir'd from the present impression.

SB 99

3   If in considering the nature of relation, and that facility of transition, which is essential to it, we can satisfy ourselves concerning the reality of this phænomenon, 'tis well: But I must confess I place my chief confidence in experience to prove so material a principle. We may, therefore, observe, as the first experiment[†] to our present purpose, that upon the appearance of the picture of an absent friend, our idea of him is evidently enliven'd by the *resemblance*, and that every passion, which that idea occasions, whether of joy or sorrow, acquires new force and vigour. In producing this effect there concur both a relation and a present impression. Where the picture bears him no resemblance, or at least was not intended for him,[†] it never so much as conveys our thought to him: And where it is absent, as well as the person; tho' the mind may pass from the thought of the one to that of the other; it feels its idea to be rather weaken'd than enliven'd by that transition. We take a pleasure in viewing the picture of a friend, when 'tis set

before us; but when 'tis remov'd, rather choose to consider him directly, than by reflection in an image, which is equally distant and obscure.

4   The ceremonies of the *Roman Catholic* religion may be consider'd as experiments of the same nature.[†] The devotees of that strange superstition usually plead in excuse of the mummeries,[†] with which they are upbraided, that they feel the good effect of those external motions, and postures, and actions, in enlivening their devotion, and quickening their fervour, which otherwise wou'd decay away, if directed entirely to distant and immaterial objects. We shadow out the objects of our faith, say they, in sensible types and images,[†] and render them more present to us by the immediate presence of these types, than 'tis possible for us to do, merely by an intellectual view and contemplation. Sensible objects have always a greater influence on the fancy than any other; and this influence they readily convey to those ideas, to which they are related, and which they resemble. I shall only infer from these practices, and this reasoning, that the effect of resemblance in enlivening the idea is very common; and as in every case a resemblance and a present impression must concur,[†] we are abundantly supply'd with experiments to prove the reality of the foregoing principle.[†]

SB 100

5   We may add force to these experiments by others of a different kind, in considering the effects of *contiguity*, as well as of *resemblance*. 'Tis certain, that distance diminishes the force of every idea, and that upon our approach to any object; tho' it does not discover itself to our senses; it operates upon the mind with an influence that imitates an immediate impression. The thinking on any object readily transports the mind to what is contiguous; but 'tis only the actual presence of an object, that transports it with a superior vivacity. When I am a few miles from home, whatever relates to it touches me more nearly than when I am two hundred leagues distant; tho' even at that distance the reflecting on any thing in the neighbourhood of my friends and family naturally produces an idea of them. But as in this latter case, both the objects of the mind are ideas; notwithstanding there is an easy transition betwixt them; that transition alone is not able to give a superior vivacity to any of the ideas, for want of some immediate impression.[21]

6   No one can doubt but causation has the same influence as the other two relations of resemblance and contiguity. Superstitious people are fond of the relics of saints and holy men, for the same reason that they seek after types and images, in order to enliven their devotion, and give them a more intimate and

SB 101

[21App.] *Naturane nobis, inquit, datum dicam, an errore quodam, ut, cum ea loca videamus, in quibus memoria dignos viros acceperimus multum esse versatos, magis moveamur, quam siquando eorum ipsorum aut facta audiamus aut scriptum aliquod legamus? Velut ego nunc moveor. Venit enim mihi Platonis in mentem, quem accepimus primum hic disputare solitum: Cujus etiam illi hortuli propinqui non memoriam solum mihi afferunt, sed ipsum videntur in conspectu meo hic ponere. Hic Speusippus, hic Xenocrates, hic ejus auditor Polemo; cujus ipsa illa sessio fuit, quam videmus. Equidem etiam curiam nostram, Hostiliam dico, non hanc novam, quæ mihi minor esse videtur postquam est major, solebam intuens Scipionem, Catonem, Lælium, nostrum vero in primis avum cogitare. Tanta vis admonitionis inest in locis; ut non sine causa ex his memoriæ ducta sit disciplina.*[†] Cicero de Finibus, lib. 5.[App.]

SB 630

strong conception of those exemplary lives, which they desire to imitate. Now 'tis evident, one of the best relicts a devotee cou'd procure, wou'd be the handy-work of a saint; and if his cloaths and furniture are ever to be consider'd in this light, 'tis because they were once at his disposal, and were mov'd and affected by him; in which respect they are to be consider'd as imperfect effects, and as connected with him by a shorter chain of consequences than any of those, from which we learn the reality of his existence. This phænomenon clearly proves, that a present impression with a relation of causation may enliven any idea, and consequently produce belief or assent, according to the precedent definition of it.[†]

7   But why need we seek for other arguments to prove, that a present impression with a relation or transition of the fancy may enliven any idea, when this very instance of our reasonings from cause and effect will alone suffice to that purpose? 'Tis certain we must have an idea of every matter of fact, which we believe. 'Tis certain, that this idea arises only from a relation to a present impression. 'Tis certain, that the belief super-adds nothing to the idea, but only changes our manner of conceiving it, and renders it more strong and lively. The present conclusion concerning the influence of relation is the immediate consequence of all these steps; and every step appears to me sure and infallible. There enters nothing into this operation of the mind but a present impression, a lively idea, and a relation or association in the fancy betwixt the impression and idea; so that there can be no suspicion of mistake.

8   In order to put this whole affair in a fuller light, let us consider it as a question in natural philosophy, which we must determine by experience and observation. I suppose there is an object presented, from which I draw a certain conclusion,   *SB 102* and form to myself ideas, which I am said to believe or assent to. Here 'tis evident, that however that object, which is present to my senses, and that other, whose existence I infer by reasoning, may be thought to influence each other by their particular powers or qualities; yet as the phænomenon of belief, which we at present examine, is merely internal, these powers and qualities, being entirely unknown, can have no hand in producing it.[†] 'Tis the present impression, which is to be consider'd as the true and real cause of the idea, and of the belief which attends it. We must therefore endeavour to discover by experiments the particular qualities, by which 'tis enabled to produce so extraordinary an effect.

9   *First* then I observe, that the present impression has not this effect by its own proper power and efficacy, and when consider'd alone, as a single perception, limited to the present moment. I find, that an impression, from which, on its first appearance, I can draw no conclusion, may afterwards become the foundation of belief, when I have had experience of its usual consequences. We must in every case have observ'd the same impression in past instances, and have found it to be constantly conjoin'd with some other impression.[†] This is confirm'd by such a multitude of experiments, that it admits not of the smallest doubt.

10   From a *second* observation I conclude, that the belief, which attends the present impression, and is produc'd by a number of past impressions and conjunctions; that this belief, I say, arises immediately, without any new operation of

the reason or imagination. Of this I can be certain, because I never am conscious of any such operation, and find nothing in the subject, on which it can be founded. Now as we call every thing CUSTOM, which proceeds from a past repetition, without any new reasoning or conclusion, we may establish it as a certain truth, that all the belief, which follows upon any present impression, is deriv'd solely from that origin.[†] When we are accustom'd to see two impressions conjoin'd together, the appearance or idea of the one immediately carries us to the idea of the other.   *SB 103*

11   Being fully satisfy'd on this head, I make a *third* set of experiments, in order to know, whether any thing be requisite, beside the customary transition, towards the production of this phænomenon of belief. I therefore change the first impression into an idea; and observe, that tho' the customary transition to the correlative idea[†] still remains, yet there is in reality no belief nor perswasion. A present impression, then, is absolutely requisite to this whole operation;[†] and when after this I compare an impression with an idea, and find that their only difference consists in their different degrees of force and vivacity, I conclude upon the whole, that belief is a more vivid and intense conception of an idea, proceeding from its relation to a present impression.

12   Thus all probable reasoning is nothing but a species of sensation.[†] 'Tis not solely in poetry and music, we must follow our taste and sentiment, but likewise in philosophy. When I am convinc'd of any principle, 'tis only an idea, which strikes more strongly upon me. When I give the preference to one set of arguments above another, I do nothing but decide from my feeling concerning the superiority of their influence. Objects have no discoverable connexion together; nor is it from any other principle but custom operating upon the imagination, that we can draw any inference from the appearance of one to the existence of another.

13   'Twill here be worth our observation, that the past experience, on which all our judgments concerning cause and effect depend, may operate on our mind in such an insensible manner as never to be taken notice of, and may even in some measure be unknown to us. A person, who stops short in his journey upon meeting a river in his way, foresees the consequences of his proceeding forward; and his knowledge of these consequences is convey'd to him by past experience, which informs him of such certain conjunctions of causes and effects. But can we think, that on this occasion he reflects on any past experience, and calls to   *SB 104* remembrance instances, that he has seen or heard of, in order to discover the effects of water on animal bodies? No surely; this is not the method, in which he proceeds in his reasoning. The idea of sinking is so closely connected with that of water, and the idea of suffocating with that of sinking, that the mind makes the transition without the assistance of the memory. The custom operates before we have time for reflection. The objects seem so inseparable, that we interpose not a moment's delay in passing from the one to the other. But as this transition proceeds from experience, and not from any primary connexion betwixt the ideas,[†] we must necessarily acknowledge, that experience may produce a belief

and a judgment of causes and effects by a secret operation, and without being once thought of. This removes all pretext, if there yet remains any, for asserting that the mind is convinc'd by reasoning of that principle, *that instances of which we have no experience, must necessarily resemble those, of which we have.*† For we here find, that the understanding or imagination can draw inferences from past experience, without reflecting on it; much more without forming any principle concerning it, or reasoning upon that principle.

14   In general we may observe, that in all the most establish'd and uniform conjunctions of causes and effects, such as those of gravity, impulse, solidity, *&c.*† the mind never carries its view expressly to consider any past experience: Tho' in other associations of objects, which are more rare and unusual, it may assist the custom and transition of ideas by this reflection. Nay we find in some cases, that the reflection produces the belief without the custom; or more properly speaking, that the reflection† produces the custom in an *oblique* and *artificial* manner. I explain myself. 'Tis certain, that not only in philosophy, but even in common life, we may attain the knowledge of a particular cause merely by one experiment, provided it be made with judgment, and after a careful removal of all foreign and superfluous circumstances.† Now as after one experiment of this *SB 105* kind, the mind, upon the appearance either of the cause or the effect, can draw an inference concerning the existence of its correlative; and as a habit can never be acquir'd merely by one instance; it may be thought, that belief cannot in this case be esteem'd the effect of custom. But this difficulty will vanish, if we consider, that tho' we are here suppos'd to have had only one experiment of a particular effect, yet we have many millions to convince us of this principle; *that like objects, plac'd in like circumstances, will always produce like effects*; and as this principle has establish'd itself by a sufficient custom, it bestows an evidence and firmness on any opinion, to which it can be apply'd. The connexion of the ideas is not habitual after one experiment; but this connexion is comprehended under another principle, that is habitual; which brings us back to our hypothesis. In all cases we transfer our experience to instances, of which we have no experience, either *expressly* or *tacitly*, either *directly* or *indirectly*.

15   I must not conclude this subject without observing, that 'tis very difficult to talk of the operations of the mind with perfect propriety† and exactness; because common language has seldom made any very nice distinctions among them, but has generally call'd by the same term all such as nearly resemble each other. And as this is a source almost inevitable of obscurity and confusion in the author; so it may frequently give rise to doubts and objections in the reader, which otherwise he wou'd never have dream'd of. Thus my general position, that an opinion or belief is *nothing but a strong and lively idea deriv'd from a present impression related to it*, may be liable to the following objection, by reason of a little ambiguity in those words *strong and lively.*† It may be said, that not only an impression may give rise to reasoning, but that an idea may also have the same influence; especially upon my principle, *that all our ideas are deriv'd from correspondent impressions.* For suppose I form at present an idea, of which I have forgot the

correspondent impression, I am able to conclude from this idea, that such an
impression did once exist; and as this conclusion is attended with belief, it may
be ask'd, from whence are the qualities of force and vivacity deriv'd, which constitute this belief? And to this I answer very readily, *from the present idea*. For as
this idea is not here consider'd, as the representation of any absent object, but as
a real perception in the mind, of which we are intimately conscious, it must be
able to bestow on whatever is related to it the same quality, call it *firmness*, or
solidity, or *force*, or *vivacity*, with which the mind reflects upon it, and is assur'd
of its present existence.[†] The idea here supplies the place of an impression, and
is entirely the same, so far as regards our present purpose.

16   Upon the same principles we need not be surpriz'd to hear of the remembrance of an idea; that is, of the idea of an idea, and of its force and vivacity
superior to the loose conceptions of the imagination. In thinking of our past
thoughts we not only delineate out the objects, of which we were thinking,
but also conceive the action of the mind in the meditation, that certain *je-ne-
scai-quoi*, of which 'tis impossible to give any definition or description, but
which every one sufficiently understands. When the memory offers an idea of
this, and represents it as past, 'tis easily conceiv'd how that idea may have more
vigour and firmness, than when we think of a past thought, of which we have no
remembrance.

17   After this any one will understand how we may form the idea of an impression
and of an idea, and how we may believe the existence of an impression and of
an idea.

Sect. 9. *Of the effects of other relations and other habits*

1   However convincing the foregoing arguments[†] may appear, we must not rest
contented with them, but must turn the subject on every side, in order to find
some new points of view, from which we may illustrate and confirm such extraordinary, and such fundamental principles. A scrupulous hesitation to receive
any new hypothesis is so laudable a disposition in philosophers, and so necessary
to the examination of truth, that it deserves to be comply'd with, and requires
that every argument be produc'd, which may tend to their satisfaction, and every
objection remov'd, which may stop them in their reasoning.

2   I have often observ'd,[†] that, beside cause and effect, the two relations of
resemblance and contiguity, are to be consider'd as associating principles of
thought, and as capable of conveying the imagination from one idea to another. I
have also observ'd,[†] that when of two objects connected together by any of these
relations, one is immediately present to the memory or senses, not only the mind
is convey'd to its correlative by means of the associating principle; but likewise
conceives it with an additional force and vigour, by the united operation of that
principle, and of the present impression. All this I have observ'd, in order to
confirm by analogy, my explication of our judgments concerning cause and
effect. But this very argument may, perhaps, be turn'd against me, and instead of
a confirmation of my hypothesis, may become an objection to it. For it may be

said, that if all the parts of that hypothesis be true, viz. *that* these three species of relation are deriv'd from the same principles; *that* their effects in enforcing and enlivening our ideas are the same; and *that* belief is nothing but a more forcible and vivid conception of an idea; it shou'd follow, that that action of the mind may not only be deriv'd from the relation of cause and effect, but also from those of contiguity and resemblance. But as we find by experience, that belief arises only from causation, and that we can draw no inference from one object to another, except they be connected by this relation, we may conclude, that there is some error in that reasoning, which leads us into such difficulties.

3   This is the objection; let us now consider its solution. 'Tis evident, that whatever is present to the memory, striking upon the mind with a vivacity, which   *SB 108* resembles an immediate impression, must become of considerable moment in all the operations of the mind, and must easily distinguish itself above the mere fictions of the imagination. Of these impressions or ideas of the memory we form a kind of system, comprehending whatever we remember to have been present, either to our internal perception or senses; and every particular of that system, join'd to the present impressions, we are pleas'd to call a *reality*.† But the mind stops not here. For finding, that with this system of perceptions, there is another connected by custom, or if you will, by the relation of cause or effect, it proceeds to the consideration of their ideas; and as it feels that 'tis in a manner necessarily determin'd to view these particular ideas, and that the custom or relation, by which it is determin'd, admits not of the least change, it forms them into a new system, which it likewise dignifies with the title of *realities*.† The first of these systems is the object of the memory and senses; the second of the judgment.

4   'Tis this latter principle, which peoples the world, and brings us acquainted with such existences, as by their removal in time and place, lie beyond the reach of the senses and memory. By means of it I paint the universe in my imagination, and fix my attention on any part of it I please. I form an idea of *Rome*, which I neither see nor remember; but which is connected with such impressions as I remember to have receiv'd from the conversation and books of travellers and historians. This idea of *Rome* I place in a certain situation on the idea of an object, which I call the globe. I join to it the conception of a particular government, and religion, and manners. I look backward and consider its first foundation; its several revolutions, successes, and misfortunes. All this, and every thing else, which I believe, are nothing but ideas; tho' by their force and settled order, arising from custom and the relation of cause and effect, they distinguish themselves from the other ideas, which are merely the offspring of the imagination.

5   As to the influence of contiguity and resemblance, we may observe, that if the   *SB 109* contiguous and resembling objects be comprehended in this system of realities, there is no doubt but these two relations will assist that of cause and effect, and infix the related idea with more force in the imagination. This I shall enlarge upon presently.† Mean while I shall carry my observation a step farther, and assert, that even where the related object is but feign'd, the relation will serve to

enliven the idea, and encrease its influence. A poet, no doubt, will be the better able to form a strong description of the *Elysian* fields,[†] that he prompts his imagination by the view of a beautiful meadow or garden; as at another time he may by his fancy place himself in the midst of these fabulous regions, that by the feign'd contiguity he may enliven his imagination.

6   But tho' I cannot altogether exclude the relations of resemblance and contiguity from operating on the fancy in this manner, 'tis observable that, when single,[†] their influence is very feeble and uncertain. As the relation of cause and effect is requisite to perswade us of any real existence, so is this perswasion requisite to give force to these other relations. For where upon the appearance of an impression we not only feign another object, but likewise arbitrarily, and of our mere good-will and pleasure give it a particular relation to the impression, this can have but a small effect upon the mind; nor is there any reason, why, upon the return of the same impression, we shou'd be determin'd to place the same object in the same relation to it. There is no manner of necessity for the mind to feign any resembling and contiguous objects;[†] and if it feigns such, there is as little necessity for it always to confine itself to the same, without any difference or variation. And indeed such a fiction is founded on so little reason, that nothing but pure *caprice* can determine the mind to form it; and that principle being fluctuating and uncertain, 'tis impossible it can ever operate with any considerable degree of force and constancy. The mind foresees and anticipates the   *SB 110* change; and even from the very first instant feels the looseness of its actions, and the weak hold it has of its objects. And as this imperfection is very sensible in every single instance, it still encreases by experience and observation, when we compare the several instances we may remember, and form a *general rule* against the reposing any assurance in those momentary glimpses of light, which arise in the imagination from a feign'd resemblance and contiguity.

7   The relation of cause and effect has all the opposite advantages. The objects it presents are fixt and unalterable. The impressions of the memory never change in any considerable degree; and each impression draws along with it a precise idea, which takes its place in the imagination, as something solid and real, certain and invariable. The thought is always determin'd to pass from the impression to the idea, and from that particular impression to that particular idea, without any choice or hesitation.

8   But not content with removing this objection, I shall endeavour to extract from it a proof of the present doctrine. Contiguity and resemblance have an effect much inferior to causation; but still have some effect, and augment the conviction of any opinion, and the vivacity of any conception. If this can be prov'd in several new instances, beside what we have already observ'd, 'twill be allow'd no inconsiderable argument, that belief is nothing but a lively idea related to a present impression.

9   To begin with contiguity; it has been remark'd among the *Mahometans* as well as *Christians*, that those *pilgrims*, who have seen *Mecca* or the *Holy Land* are ever after more faithful and zealous believers, than those who have not had that advantage. A man, whose memory presents him with a lively image of the

Red-Sea, and the *Desert*, and *Jerusalem*, and *Galilee*, can never doubt of any miraculous events, which are related either by *Moses* or the *Evangelists*.[†] The lively idea of the places passes by an easy transition to the facts, which are *SB 111* suppos'd to have been related to them by contiguity, and encreases the belief by encreasing the vivacity of the conception. The remembrance of these fields and rivers has the same influence on the vulgar as a new argument; and from the same causes.

10   We may form a like observation concerning *resemblance*. We have remark'd,[†] that the conclusion, which we draw from a present object to its absent cause or effect, is never founded on any qualities, which we observe in that object, consider'd in itself; or, in other words, that 'tis impossible to determine, otherwise than by experience, what will result from any phænomenon, or what has preceded it. But tho' this be so evident in itself, that it seem'd not to require any proof; yet some philosophers have imagin'd that there is an apparent cause for the communication of motion, and that a reasonable man might immediately infer the motion of one body from the impulse of another, without having recourse to any past observation.[†] That this opinion is false will admit of an easy proof. For if such an inference may be drawn merely from the ideas of body, of motion, and of impulse, it must amount to a demonstration, and must imply the absolute impossibility of any contrary supposition. Every effect, then, beside the communication of motion, implies a formal contradiction; and 'tis impossible not only that it can exist, but also that it can be conceiv'd. But we may soon satisfy ourselves of the contrary, by forming a clear and consistent idea of one body's moving upon another, and of its rest[†] immediately upon the contact; or of its returning back in the same line, in which it came; or of its annihilation; or circular or elliptical motion: And in short, of an infinite number of other changes, which we may suppose it to undergo. These suppositions are all consistent and natural;[†] and the reason, why we imagine the communication of motion to be more consistent and natural not only than those suppositions, but also than any other natural effect, is founded on the relation of *resemblance* betwixt the cause *SB 112* and effect, which is here united to experience, and binds the objects in the closest and most intimate manner to each other, so as to make us imagine them to be absolutely inseparable. Resemblance, then, has the same or a parallel influence with experience; and as the only immediate effect of experience is to associate our ideas together, it follows, that all belief arises from the association of ideas, according to my hypothesis.

11   'Tis universally allow'd by the writers on optics, that the eye at all times sees an equal number of physical points, and that a man on the top of a mountain has no larger an image presented to his senses, than when he is coop'd up in the narrowest court or chamber.[†] 'Tis only by experience that he infers the greatness of the object from some peculiar qualities of the image; and this inference of the judgment he confounds with sensation, as is common on other occasions. Now 'tis evident, that the inference of the judgment is here much more lively than what is usual in our common reasonings, and that a man has a more vivid conception of the vast extent of the ocean from the image he receives by the eye,

when he stands on the top of a high promontory, than merely from hearing the roaring of the waters. He feels a more sensible pleasure from its magnificence; which is a proof of a more lively idea: And he confounds his judgment with sensation; which is another proof of it. But as the inference is equally certain and immediate in both cases, this superior vivacity of our conception in one case can proceed from nothing but this, that in drawing an inference from the sight, beside the customary conjunction, there is also a resemblance betwixt the image and the object we infer; which strengthens the relation, and conveys the vivacity of the impression to the related idea with an easier and more natural movement.

12   No weakness of human nature is more universal and conspicuous than what we commonly call CREDULITY, or a too easy faith in the testimony of others; and this weakness is also very naturally accounted for from the influence of resem-   *SB 113* blance. When we receive any matter of fact upon human testimony, our faith arises from the very same origin as our inferences from causes to effects, and from effects to causes; nor is there any thing but our *experience* of the governing principles of human nature, which can give us any assurance of the veracity of men. But tho' experience be the true standard of this, as well as of all other judgments, we seldom regulate ourselves entirely by it; but have a remarkable propensity to believe whatever is reported, even concerning apparitions, enchantments, and prodigies, however contrary to daily experience and observation. The words or discourses of others have an intimate connexion with certain ideas in their mind; and these ideas have also a connexion with the facts or objects, which they represent. This latter connexion is generally much overrated, and commands our assent beyond what experience will justify; which can proceed from nothing beside the resemblance betwixt the ideas and the facts. Other effects only point out their causes in an oblique manner; but the testimony of men does it directly, and is to be consider'd as an image as well as an effect. No wonder, therefore, we are so rash in drawing our inferences from it, and are less guided by experience in our judgments concerning it, than in those upon any other subject.

13   As resemblance, when conjoin'd with causation, fortifies our reasonings; so the want of it in any very great degree is able almost entirely to destroy them. Of this there is a remarkable instance in the universal carelessness and stupidity of men with regard to a future state,[†] where they show as obstinate an incredulity, as they do a blind credulity on other occasions. There is not indeed a more ample matter of wonder to the studious, and of regret to the pious man, than to observe the negligence of the bulk of mankind concerning their approaching condition; and 'tis with reason, that many eminent theologians have not scrupled to affirm, that tho' the vulgar have no formal principles of infidelity, yet they are really infi-   *SB 114* dels in their hearts, and have nothing like what we can call a belief of the eternal duration of their souls.[†] For let us consider on the one hand what divines have display'd with such eloquence concerning the importance of eternity; and at the same time reflect, that tho' in matters of rhetoric we ought to lay our account

with some exaggeration, we must in this case allow, that the strongest figures[†] are infinitely inferior to the subject: And after this let us view on the other hand the prodigious security of men in this particular: I ask, if these people really believe what is inculcated on[†] them, and what they pretend to affirm; and the answer is obviously in the negative. As belief is an act of the mind arising from custom, 'tis not strange the want of resemblance shou'd overthrow what custom has established, and diminish the force of the idea, as much as that latter principle encreases it. A future state is so far remov'd from our comprehension, and we have so obscure an idea of the manner, in which we shall exist after the dissolution of the body, that all the reasons we can invent, however strong in themselves, and however much assisted by education, are never able with slow imaginations to surmount this difficulty, or bestow a sufficient authority and force on the idea. I rather choose to ascribe this incredulity to the faint idea we form of our future condition, deriv'd from its want of resemblance to the present life, than to that deriv'd from its remoteness. For I observe, that men are every where concern'd about what may happen after their death, provided it regard this world; and that there are few to whom their name, their family, their friends, and their country are in any period of time entirely indifferent.

14   And indeed the want of resemblance in this case[†] so entirely destroys belief, that except those few, who upon cool reflection on the importance of the subject, have taken care by repeated meditation to imprint in their minds the arguments for a future state, there scarce are any, who believe the immortality of the soul[†]   *SB 115* with a true and establish'd judgment; such as is deriv'd from the testimony of travellers and historians. This appears very conspicuously wherever men have occasion to compare the pleasures and pains, the rewards and punishments of this life with those of a future; even tho' the case does not concern themselves, and there is no violent passion to disturb their judgment. The *Roman Catholics* are certainly the most zealous of any sect in the christian world; and yet you'll find few among the more sensible people of that communion, who do not blame the *Gunpowder-treason*,[†] and the massacre of St. *Bartholomew*,[†] as cruel and barbarous, tho' projected or executed against those very people, whom without any scruple they condemn to eternal and infinite punishments. All we can say in excuse for this inconsistency is, that they really do not believe what they affirm concerning a future state; nor is there any better proof of it than the very inconsistency.

15   We may add to this a remark, that in matters of religion men take a pleasure in being terrify'd, and that no preachers are so popular, as those who excite the most dismal and gloomy passions. In the common affairs of life, where we feel and are penetrated with the solidity[†] of the subject, nothing can be more disagreeable than fear and terror; and 'tis only in dramatic performances and in religious discourses, that they ever give pleasure. In these latter cases the imagination reposes itself indolently[†] on the idea; and the passion, being soften'd by the want of belief in the subject, has no more than the agreeable effect of enlivening the mind, and fixing the attention.

16   The present hypothesis will receive additional confirmation, if we examine the effects of other kinds of custom, as well as of other relations. To understand this we must consider, that custom, to which I attribute all belief and reasoning, may operate upon the mind in invigorating an idea after two several ways. For supposing that in all past experience we have found two objects to have been always conjoin'd together, 'tis evident, that upon the appearance of one of these *SB 116* objects in an impression, we must from custom make an easy transition to the idea of that object, which usually attends it; and by means of the present impression and easy transition must conceive that idea in a stronger and more lively manner, than we do any loose floating image of the fancy.[†] But let us next suppose, that a mere idea alone, without any of this curious and almost artificial preparation, shou'd frequently make its appearance in the mind, this idea must by degrees acquire a facility and force; and both by its firm hold and easy introduction distinguish itself from any new and unusual idea. This is the only particular, in which these two kinds of custom agree; and if it appear, that their effects on the judgment are similar and proportionable, we may certainly conclude, that the foregoing explication of that faculty is satisfactory.[†] But can we doubt of this agreement in their influence on the judgment, when we consider the nature and effects of EDUCATION?

17   All those opinions and notions of things, to which we have been accustom'd from our infancy, take such deep root, that 'tis impossible for us, by all the powers of reason and experience, to eradicate them; and this habit not only approaches in its influence, but even on many occasions prevails over that which arises from the constant and inseparable union of causes and effects. Here we must not be contented with saying, that the vividness of the idea produces the belief: We must maintain that they are individually the same.[†] The frequent repetition of any idea infixes it in the imagination; but cou'd never possibly of itself produce belief, if that act of the mind was, by the original constitution of our natures, annex'd only to a reasoning and comparison of ideas. Custom may lead us into some false comparison of ideas. This is the utmost effect we can conceive of it. But 'tis certain it cou'd never supply the place of[†] that comparison, nor produce any act of the mind, which naturally belong'd to that principle.

18   A person, that has lost a leg or an arm by amputation, endeavours for a long *SB 117* time afterwards to serve himself with them. After the death of any one, 'tis a common remark of the whole family, but especially of the servants, that they can scarce believe him to be dead, but still imagine him to be in his chamber or in any other place, where they were accustom'd to find him. I have often heard in conversation, after talking of a person, that is any way celebrated, that one, who has no acquaintance with him, will say, *I have never seen such-a-one, but almost fancy I have; so often have I heard talk of him.* All these are parallel instances.

19   If we consider this argument from *education* in a proper light, 'twill appear very convincing; and the more so, that 'tis founded on one of the most common phænomena, that is any where to be met with. I am perswaded, that upon examination we shall find more than one half of those opinions, that prevail among mankind, to be owing to education, and that the principles, which are thus

implicitly embrac'd, over-ballance those, which are owing either to abstract reasoning or experience. As liars, by the frequent repetition of their lies, come at last to remember them; so the judgment, or rather the imagination, by the like means, may have ideas so strongly imprinted on it, and conceive them in so full a light, that they may operate upon the mind in the same manner with those, which the senses, memory or reason present to us. But as education is an artificial and not a natural cause, and as its maxims are frequently contrary to reason, and even to themselves in different times and places, it is never upon that account recogniz'd by philosophers; tho' in reality it be built almost on the same foundation of custom and repetition as our experience or reasonings from causes and effects.[22]

Sect. 10. *Of the influence of belief* SB 118

1 But tho' education be disclaim'd by philosophy,† as a fallacious ground of assent to any opinion, it prevails nevertheless in the world, and is the cause why all systems, upon whatever convincing arguments they may be founded, are apt to be rejected at first as new and unusual. This perhaps will be the fate of what I have here advanc'd concerning *belief*, and our reasonings from causes to effects; and tho' the proofs I have produc'd appear to me perfectly conclusive, I expect not to make many proselytes to my opinion. Men will scarce ever be perswaded, that effects of such consequence can flow from principles, which are seemingly so inconsiderable, and that the far greatest part of our reasonings with all our actions and passions can be deriv'd from nothing but custom and habit. To obviate this objection, I shall here anticipate a little what wou'd more properly fall under our consideration afterwards, when we come to treat of the passions and the sense of beauty.†

2 Nature has implanted in the human mind a perception of good or evil, or in other words, of pain and pleasure, as the chief spring and moving principle of all its actions.† But pain and pleasure have two ways of making their appearance in the mind; of which the one has effects very different from the other. They may either appear in impression to the actual feeling and experience, or only in idea, as at present when I mention them. 'Tis evident the influence of these upon our actions is far from being equal. Impressions always actuate the soul, and that in the highest degree; but 'tis not every idea which has the same effect. Nature has proceeded with caution in this case, and seems to have carefully avoided the SB 119

---

[22] In general we may observe, that as our assent to all probable reasonings is founded on the SB 117 vivacity of ideas, it resembles many of those whimsies and prejudices, which are rejected under the opprobrious character of being the offspring of the imagination. By this expression it appears that the word, *imagination*, is commonly us'd in two different senses; and tho' nothing be more contrary to true philosophy, than this inaccuracy, yet in the following reasonings I have often been oblig'd to SB 118 fall into it. When I oppose the imagination to the memory, I mean the faculty, by which we form our fainter ideas. When I oppose it to reason, I mean the same faculty, excluding only our demonstrative and probable reasonings. When I oppose it to neither, 'tis indifferent whether it be taken in the larger or more limited sense, or at least the context will sufficiently explain the meaning.†

inconveniencies of two extremes. Did impressions alone influence the will, we shou'd every moment of our lives be subject to the greatest calamities; because, tho' we foresaw their approach, we shou'd not be provided by nature with any principle of action, which might impel us to avoid them. On the other hand, did every idea influence our actions, our condition wou'd not be much mended. For such is the unsteadiness and activity of thought, that the images of every thing, especially of goods and evils, are always wandering in the mind; and were it mov'd by every idle conception of this kind, it wou'd never enjoy a moment's peace and tranquillity.

3   Nature has, therefore, chosen a medium, and has neither bestow'd on every idea of good and evil the power of actuating the will, nor yet has entirely excluded them from this influence. Tho' an idle fiction has no efficacy, yet we find by experience, that the ideas of those objects, which we believe either are or will be existent, produce in a lesser degree the same effect with those impressions, which are immediately present to the senses and perception. The effect, then, of belief is to raise up a simple idea to an equality with our impressions, and bestow on it a like influence on the passions. This effect it can only have by making an idea approach an impression in force and vivacity. For as the different degrees of force make all the original difference betwixt an impression and an idea, they must of consequence be the source of all the differences in the effects of these perceptions, and their removal, in whole or in part, the cause of every new resemblance they acquire. Wherever we can make an idea approach the impressions in force and vivacity, it will likewise imitate them in its influence on the mind; and *vice versa*, where it imitates them in that influence, as in the present case, this must proceed from its approaching them in force and vivacity. Belief, therefore, since it causes an idea to imitate the effects of the impressions, must make it resemble them in these qualities, and is nothing but *a more vivid and*   *SB 120* *intense conception of any idea*. This, then, may both serve as an additional argument for the present system, and may give us a notion after what manner our reasonings from causation are able to operate on the will and passions.

4   As belief is almost absolutely requisite to the exciting our passions, so the passions in their turn are very favourable to belief; and not only such facts as convey agreeable emotions, but very often such as give pain, do upon that account become more readily the objects of faith and opinion. A coward, whose fears are easily awaken'd, readily assents to every account of danger he meets with; as a person of a sorrowful and melancholy disposition is very credulous of every thing, that nourishes his prevailing passion.[†] When any affecting object is presented, it gives the alarm, and excites immediately a degree of its proper passion; especially in persons who are naturally inclin'd to that passion. This emotion passes by an easy transition to the imagination; and diffusing itself over our idea of the affecting object, makes us form that idea with greater force and vivacity, and consequently assent to it, according to the precedent system. Admiration and surprize have the same effect as the other passions; and accordingly we may observe, that among the vulgar, quacks and projectors meet with a more easy faith[†] upon account of their magnificent pretensions, than if they kept them-

selves within the bounds of moderation. The first astonishment, which naturally attends their miraculous relations, spreads itself over the whole soul, and so vivifies and enlivens the idea, that it resembles the inferences we draw from experience. This is a mystery, with which we may be already a little acquainted, and which we shall have farther occasion to be let into in the progress of this treatise.†

5   After this account of the influence of belief on the passions, we shall find less difficulty in explaining its effects on the imagination, however extraordinary they may appear. 'Tis certain we cannot take pleasure in any discourse, where our judgment gives no assent to those images which are presented to our fancy. *SB 121* The conversation of those, who have acquir'd a habit of lying, tho' in affairs of no moment, never gives any satisfaction; and that because those ideas they present to us, not being attended with belief, make no impression upon the mind. Poets themselves, tho' liars by profession,† always endeavour to give an air of truth to their fictions; and where that is totally neglected, their performances, however ingenious, will never be able to afford much pleasure. In short, we may observe, that even when ideas have no manner of influence on the will and passions, truth and reality are still requisite, in order to make them entertaining to the imagination.

6   But if we compare together all the phænomena that occur on this head, we shall find, that truth, however necessary it may seem in all works of genius, has no other effect than to procure an easy reception for the ideas, and to make the mind acquiesce in them with satisfaction, or at least without reluctance. But as this is an effect, which may easily be suppos'd to flow from that solidity and force, which, according to my system, attend those ideas that are establish'd by reasonings from causation; it follows, that all the influence of belief upon the fancy may be explain'd from that system. Accordingly we may observe, that wherever that influence arises from any other principles beside truth or reality, they supply its place, and give an equal entertainment to the imagination. Poets have form'd what they call a poetical system of things,† which tho' it be believ'd neither by themselves nor readers, is commonly esteem'd a sufficient foundation for any fiction. We have been so much accustom'd to the names of MARS, JUPITER, VENUS,† that in the same manner as education infixes any opinion, the constant repetition of these ideas makes them enter into the mind with facility, and prevail upon the fancy, without influencing the judgment. In like manner tragedians always borrow their fable, or at least the names of their principal actors, from some known passage in history; and that not in order to deceive the *SB 122* spectators; for they will frankly confess, that truth is not in any circumstance inviolably observ'd; but in order to procure a more easy reception into the imagination for those extraordinary events, which they represent. But this is a precaution, which is not requir'd of comic poets, whose personages and incidents, being of a more familiar kind, enter easily into the conception, and are receiv'd without any such formality, even tho' at first sight they be known to be fictitious, and the pure offspring of the fancy.

7   This mixture of truth and falshood in the fables of tragic poets not only serves

our present purpose, by showing, that the imagination can be satisfy'd without any absolute belief or assurance; but may in another view be regarded as a very strong confirmation of this system.[†] 'Tis evident, that poets make use of this artifice of borrowing the names of their persons, and the chief events of their poems, from history, in order to procure a more easy reception for the whole, and cause it to make a deeper impression on the fancy and affections. The several incidents of the piece acquire a kind of relation by being united into one poem or representation; and if any of these incidents be an object of belief, it bestows a force and vivacity on the others, which are related to it. The vividness of the first conception diffuses itself along the relations, and is convey'd, as by so many pipes or canals,[†] to every idea that has any communication with the primary one. This, indeed, can never amount to a perfect assurance; and that because the union among the ideas is, in a manner, accidental: But still it approaches so near, in its influence, as may convince us, that they are deriv'd from the same origin. Belief must please the imagination by means of the force and vivacity which attends it; since every idea, which has force and vivacity, is found to be agreeable to that faculty.

8   To confirm this we may observe, that the assistance is mutual betwixt the judgment and fancy, as well as betwixt the judgment and passion; and that belief not only gives vigour to the imagination, but that a vigorous and strong imagina-   *SB 123*
tion is of all talents the most proper to procure belief and authority. 'Tis difficult for us to withhold our assent from what is painted out to us in all the colours of eloquence; and the vivacity produc'd by the fancy is in many cases greater than that which arises from custom and experience. We are hurry'd away by the lively imagination of our author or companion; and even he himself is often a victim to his own fire and genius.

9   Nor will it be amiss to remark, that as a lively imagination very often degenerates into madness or folly, and bears it a great resemblance in its operations; so they[†] influence the judgment after the same manner, and produce belief from the very same principles. When the imagination, from any extraordinary ferment of the blood and spirits, acquires such a vivacity as disorders all its powers and faculties, there is no means of distinguishing betwixt truth and falshood; but every loose fiction or idea, having the same influence as the impressions of the memory, or the conclusions of the judgment, is receiv'd on the same footing, and operates with equal force on the passions.[†] A present impression and a customary transition are now no longer necessary to enliven our ideas. Every chimera of the brain is as vivid and intense as any of those inferences, which we formerly dignify'd with the name of conclusions concerning matters of fact, and sometimes as the present impressions of the senses.

10   [App.]We may observe the same effect of poetry in a lesser degree; and this is   *SB 630*
common both to poetry and madness, that the vivacity they bestow on the ideas is not deriv'd from the particular situations or connexions of the objects of these ideas, but from the present temper and disposition of the person. But how great

soever the pitch may be, to which this vivacity rises, 'tis evident, that in poetry it never has the same *feeling* with that which arises in the mind, when we reason, tho' even upon the lowest species of probability.[†] The mind can easily distinguish betwixt the one and the other; and whatever emotion the poetical enthusiasm may give to the spirits, 'tis still the mere phantom of belief or perswasion. The case is the same with the idea, as with the passion it occasions. There is no passion of the human mind but what may arise from poetry; tho' at the same time the *feelings* of the passions are very different when excited by poetical fictions, from what they are when they arise from belief and reality. A passion, which is disagreeable in real life, may afford the highest entertainment in a tragedy, or epic poem. In the latter case it lies not with that weight upon us: It feels less firm and solid: And has no other than the agreeable effect of exciting the spirits, and rouzing the attention. The difference in the passions is a clear proof of a like difference in those ideas, from which the passions are deriv'd. Where the vivacity arises from a customary conjunction with a present impression; tho' the imagination may not, in appearance, be so much mov'd; yet there is always something more forcible and real in its actions, than in the fervours of poetry and eloquence. The force of our mental actions in this case, no more than in any other, is not to be measur'd by the apparent agitation of the mind.[†] A poetical description may have a more sensible effect on the fancy, than an historical narration. It may collect more of those circumstances, that form a compleat image or picture. It may seem to set the object before us in more lively colours. But still the ideas it presents are different to the *feeling* from those, which arise from the memory and the judgment. There is something weak and imperfect amidst all that seeming vehemence of thought and sentiment, which attends the fictions of poetry.

11   We shall afterwards have occasion to remark both the resemblances and differences betwixt a poetical enthusiasm, and a serious conviction.[†] In the mean time I cannot forbear observing, that the great difference in their feeling proceeds in some measure from reflection and *general rules*.[†] We observe, that the vigour of conception, which fictions receive from poetry and eloquence, is a circumstance merely accidental, of which every idea is equally susceptible; and that such fictions are connected with nothing that is real. This observation makes us only lend ourselves, so to speak, to the fiction: But causes the idea to feel very different from the external establish'd perswasions founded on memory and custom. They are somewhat of the same kind: But the one is much inferior to the other, both in its causes and effects.

12   A like reflection on *general rules* keeps us from augmenting our belief upon every encrease of the force and vivacity of our ideas. Where an opinion admits of no doubt, or opposite probability, we attribute to it a full conviction; tho' the want of resemblance, or contiguity, may render its force inferior to that of other opinions. 'Tis thus the understanding corrects the appearances of the senses, and makes us imagine, that an object at twenty foot distance seems even to the eye as large as one of the same dimensions at ten.[App.]

Sect. 11. *Of the probability of chances*

1   But in order to bestow on this system[†] its full force and evidence, we must carry our eye from it a moment to consider its consequences, and explain from the same principles some other species of reasoning, which are deriv'd from the same origin.

2   Those philosophers, who have divided human reason into *knowledge* and *probability*, and have defin'd the first to be *that evidence, which arises from the comparison of ideas*, are oblig'd to comprehend all our arguments from causes or effects under the general term of *probability*.[†] But tho' every one be free to use his terms in what sense he pleases; and accordingly in the precedent part of this discourse, I have follow'd this method of expression; 'tis however certain, that in common discourse we readily affirm, that many arguments from causation exceed probability, and may be receiv'd as a superior kind of evidence. One wou'd appear ridiculous, who wou'd say, that 'tis only probable the sun will rise to-morrow,[†] or that all men must dye;[†] tho' 'tis plain we have no farther assurance of these facts, than what experience affords us. For this reason, 'twou'd perhaps be more convenient, in order at once to preserve the common signification of words, and mark the several degrees of evidence, to distinguish human reason into three kinds, viz. *that from knowledge, from proofs, and from probabilities*.[†] By knowledge, I mean the assurance arising from the comparison of ideas. By proofs, those arguments, which are deriv'd from the relation of cause and effect, and which are entirely free from doubt and uncertainty. By probability, that evidence, which is still attended with uncertainty. 'Tis this last species of reasoning, I proceed to examine.

3   Probability or reasoning from conjecture may be divided into two kinds, *viz.* that which is founded on *chance*, and that which arises from *causes*. We shall consider each of these in order.

4   The idea of cause and effect is deriv'd from experience, which presenting us with certain objects constantly conjoin'd with each other, produces such a habit of surveying them in that relation, that we cannot without a sensible violence[†] survey them in any other. On the other hand, as chance is nothing real in itself, and, properly speaking, is merely the negation of a cause,[†] its influence on the mind is contrary to that of causation; and 'tis essential to it, to leave the imagination perfectly indifferent, either to consider the existence or non-existence of that object, which is regarded as contingent. A cause traces the way to our thought, and in a manner forces us to survey such certain objects, in such certain relations. Chance can only destroy this determination of the thought, and leave the mind in its native situation of indifference; in which, upon the absence of a cause, 'tis instantly re-instated.

5   Since therefore an entire indifference is essential to chance, no one chance can possibly be superior to another, otherwise than as it is compos'd of a superior number of equal chances. For if we affirm that one chance can, after any other manner, be superior to another, we must at the same time affirm, that there is something, which gives it the superiority, and determines the event rather

to that side than the other: That is, in other words, we must allow of a cause, and destroy the supposition of chance; which we had before establish'd.[†] A perfect and total indifference is essential to chance, and one total indifference can never in itself be either superior or inferior to another. This truth is not peculiar to my system, but is acknowledg'd by every one, that forms calculations concerning chances.[†]

6   And here 'tis remarkable, that tho' chance and causation be directly contrary, yet 'tis impossible for us to conceive this combination of chances, which is requisite to render one hazard superior to another, without supposing a mixture of causes among the chances, and a conjunction of necessity in some particulars, *SB 126* with a total indifference in others. Where nothing limits the chances, every notion, that the most extravagant fancy can form, is upon a footing of equality; nor can there be any circumstance to give one the advantage above another. Thus unless we allow, that there are some causes to make the dice fall, and preserve their form in their fall, and lie upon some one of their sides, we can form no calculation concerning the laws of hazard.[†] But supposing these causes to operate, and supposing likewise all the rest to be indifferent and to be determin'd by chance, 'tis easy to arrive at a notion of a superior combination of chances. A dye, that has four sides mark'd with a certain number of spots, and only two with another, affords us an obvious and easy instance of this superiority. The mind is here limited by the causes to such a precise number and quality of the events; and at the same time is undetermin'd in its choice of any particular event.

7   Proceeding then in that reasoning, wherein we have advanc'd three steps; *that* chance is merely the negation of a cause, and produces a total indifference in the mind; *that* one negation of a cause and one total indifference can never be superior or inferior to another; and *that* there must always be a mixture of causes among the chances, in order to be the foundation of any reasoning: We are next to consider what effect a superior combination of chances can have upon the mind, and after what manner it influences our judgment and opinion. Here we may repeat all the same arguments we employ'd[†] in examining that belief, which arises from causes; and may prove after the same manner, that a superior number of chances produces our assent neither by *demonstration* nor *probability*. 'Tis indeed evident, that we can never by the comparison of mere ideas make any discovery, which can be of consequence in this affair, and that 'tis impossible to prove with certainty, that any event must fall on that side where there is a superior number of chances. To suppose in this case any certainty, were to overthrow what we have establish'd concerning the opposition of chances,[†] and their *SB 127* perfect equality and indifference.

8   Shou'd it be said, that tho' in an opposition of chances 'tis impossible to determine with *certainty*, on which side the event will fall, yet we can pronounce with certainty, that 'tis more likely and probable, 'twill be on that side where there is a superior number of chances, than where there is an inferior: Shou'd this be said, I wou'd ask, what is here meant by *likelihood and probability*? The likelihood and probability of chances is a superior number of equal chances; and consequently

when we say 'tis likely the event will fall on the side, which is superior, rather than on the inferior, we do no more than affirm, that where there is a superior number of chances there is actually a superior, and where there is an inferior there is an inferior; which are identical propositions, and of no consequence.[†] The question is, by what means a superior number of equal chances operates upon the mind, and produces belief or assent;[†] since it appears, that 'tis neither by arguments deriv'd from demonstration, nor from probability.

9   In order to clear up this difficulty, we shall suppose a person to take a dye, form'd after such a manner as that four of its sides are mark'd with one figure, or one number of spots, and two with another; and to put this dye into the box with an intention of throwing it: 'Tis plain, he must conclude the one figure to be more probable than the other, and give the preference to that which is inscrib'd on the greatest number of sides. He in a manner believes, that this will lie uppermost; tho' still with hesitation and doubt, in proportion to the number of chances, which are contrary:[†] And according as these contrary chances diminish, and the superiority encreases on the other side, his belief acquires new degrees of stability and assurance. This belief arises from an operation of the mind upon the simple and limited object before us; and therefore its nature will be the more easily discover'd and explain'd. We have nothing but one single dye to contemplate, in order to comprehend one of the most curious operations of the understanding.   *SB 128*

10   This dye form'd as above, contains three circumstances worthy of our attention. *First*, Certain causes, such as gravity, solidity, a cubical figure, *&c.* which determine it to fall, to preserve its form in its fall, and to turn up one of its sides. *Secondly*, A certain number of sides, which are suppos'd indifferent. *Thirdly*, A certain figure, inscrib'd on each side. These three particulars form the whole nature of the dye, so far as relates to our present purpose; and consequently are the only circumstances regarded by the mind in its forming a judgment concerning the result of such a throw. Let us, therefore, consider gradually and carefully what must be the influence of these circumstances on the thought and imagination.

11   *First*, We have already observ'd,[†] that the mind is determin'd by custom to pass from any cause to its effect, and that upon the appearance of the one, 'tis almost impossible for it not to form an idea of the other. Their constant conjunction in past instances has produc'd such a habit in the mind, that it always conjoins them in its thought, and infers the existence of the one from that of its usual attendant. When it considers the dye as no longer supported by the box, it cannot without violence regard it as suspended in the air; but naturally places it on the table,[†] and views it as turning up one of its sides. This is the effect of the intermingled causes, which are requisite to our forming any calculation concerning chances.

12   *Secondly*, 'Tis suppos'd, that tho' the dye be necessarily determin'd to fall, and turn up one of its sides, yet there is nothing to fix the particular side, but that this is determin'd entirely by chance. The very nature and essence of chance is a negation of causes, and the leaving the mind in a perfect indifference among

those events, which are suppos'd contingent. When therefore the thought is determin'd by the causes to consider the dye as falling and turning up one of its *SB 129* sides, the chances present all these sides as equal, and make us consider every one of them, one after another, as alike probable and possible.[†] The imagination passes from the cause, *viz.* the throwing of the dye, to the effect, *viz.* the turning up one of the six sides; and feels a kind of impossibility both of stopping short in the way, and of forming any other idea. But as all these six sides are incompatible, and the dye cannot turn up above one at once, this principle directs us not to consider all of them at once as lying uppermost; which we look upon as impossible: Neither does it direct us with its entire force to any particular side; for in that case this side wou'd be consider'd as certain and inevitable; but it directs us to the whole six sides after such a manner as to divide its force equally among them.[†] We conclude in general, that some one of them must result from the throw: We run all of them over in our minds: The determination of the thought is common to all; but no more of its force falls to the share of any one, than what is suitable to its proportion with the rest. 'Tis after this manner the original impulse,[†] and consequently the vivacity of thought, arising from the causes, is divided and split in pieces by the intermingled chances.

13   We have already seen the influence of the two first qualities of the dye, *viz.* the *causes*, and the *number* and *indifference* of the sides, and have learn'd how they give an impulse to the thought, and divide that impulse into as many parts as there are unites in the number of sides. We must now consider the effects of the *third* particular, *viz.* the *figures* inscrib'd on each side. 'Tis evident, that where several sides have the same figure inscrib'd on them, they must concur in their influence on the mind, and must unite upon one image or idea of a figure all those divided impulses, that were dispers'd over the several sides, upon which that figure is inscrib'd.[†] Were the question only what side will be turn'd up, these are all perfectly equal, and no one cou'd ever have any advantage above another. But as the question is concerning the figure, and as the same figure is presented *SB 130* by more than one side; 'tis evident, that the impulses belonging to all these sides must re-unite in that one figure, and become stronger and more forcible by the union. Four sides are suppos'd in the present case to have the same figure inscrib'd on them, and two to have another figure. The impulses of the former are, therefore, superior to those of the latter. But as the events are contrary, and 'tis impossible both these figures can be turn'd up; the impulses likewise become contrary, and the inferior destroys the superior, as far as its strength goes.[†] The vivacity of the idea is always proportionable to the degrees of the impulse or tendency to the transition; and belief is the same with the vivacity of the idea, according to the precedent doctrine.

Sect. 12. *Of the probability of causes*

1   What I have said concerning the probability of chances can serve to no other purpose, than to assist us in explaining the probability of causes; since 'tis commonly allow'd by philosophers, that what the vulgar call chance is nothing but a

secret and conceal'd cause.[†] That species of probability, therefore, is what we must chiefly examine.

2   The probabilities of causes are of several kinds; but are all deriv'd from the same origin, viz. *the association of ideas to a present impression.* As the habit, which produces the association, arises from the frequent conjunction of objects, it must arrive at its perfection by degrees, and must acquire new force from each instance, that falls under our observation. The first instance has little or no force: The second makes some addition to it: The third becomes still more sensible; and 'tis by these slow steps, that our judgment arrives at a full assurance. But before it attains this pitch of perfection, it passes thro' several inferior degrees, and in all of them is only to be esteem'd a presumption or probability. The gra-   *SB 131* dation, therefore, from probabilities to proofs is in many cases insensible; and the difference betwixt these kinds of evidence is more easily perceiv'd in the remote degrees, than in the near and contiguous.

3   'Tis worthy of remark on this occasion, that tho' the species of probability here explain'd be the first in order, and naturally takes place before any entire proof can exist, yet no one, who is arriv'd at the age of maturity, can any longer be acquainted with it.[†] 'Tis true, nothing is more common than for people of the most advanc'd knowledge to have attain'd only an imperfect experience of many particular events; which naturally produces only an imperfect habit and transition: But then we must consider, that the mind, having form'd another observation[†] concerning the connexion of causes and effects, gives new force to its reasoning from that observation; and by means of it can build an argument on one single experiment, when duly prepar'd and examin'd. What we have found once to follow from any object, we conclude will for ever follow from it; and if this maxim be not always built upon as certain, 'tis not for want of a sufficient number of experiments, but because we frequently meet with instances to the contrary; which leads us to the second species of probability, where there is a *contrariety* in our experience and observation.[†]

4   'Twou'd be very happy for men in the conduct of their lives and actions, were the same objects always conjoin'd together, and we had nothing to fear but the mistakes of our own judgment, without having any reason to apprehend the uncertainty of nature. But as 'tis frequently found, that one observation is contrary to another, and that causes and effects follow not in the same order, of which we have had experience, we are oblig'd to vary our reasoning on account of this uncertainty, and take into consideration the contrariety of events.[†] The first question, that occurs on this head, is concerning the nature and causes of the contrariety.

5   The vulgar, who take things according to their first appearance, attribute the   *SB 132* uncertainty of events to such an uncertainty in the causes, as makes them often fail of their usual influence, tho' they meet with no obstacle nor impediment in their operation.[†] But philosophers observing, that almost in every part of nature there is contain'd a vast variety of springs and principles, which are hid, by reason of their minuteness or remoteness, find that 'tis at least possible the con-

trariety of events may not proceed from any contingency in the cause, but from the secret operation of contrary causes. This possibility is converted into certainty by farther observation, when they remark,[†] that upon an exact scrutiny, a contrariety of effects always betrays a contrariety of causes, and proceeds from their mutual hindrance and opposition. A peasant can give no better reason for the stopping of any clock or watch than to say, that commonly it does not go right: But an artizan easily perceives, that the same force in the spring or pendulum has always the same influence on the wheels; but fails of its usual effect, perhaps by reason of a grain of dust, which puts a stop to the whole movement. From the observation of several parallel instances, philosophers form a maxim, that the connexion betwixt all causes and effects is equally necessary, and that its seeming uncertainty in some instances proceeds from the secret opposition of contrary causes.

6   But however philosophers and the vulgar may differ in their explication of the contrariety of events, their inferences from it are always of the same kind, and founded on the same principles. A contrariety of events in the past may give us a kind of hesitating belief for the future after two several ways. *First,* By producing an imperfect habit and transition from the present impression to the related idea. When the conjunction of any two objects is frequent, without being entirely constant, the mind is determin'd to pass from one object to the other; but not with so entire a habit, as when the union is uninterrupted, and all the instances we have ever met with are uniform and of a piece. We find from common experience, in our actions as well as reasonings, that a constant perseverance in any course of life produces a strong inclination and tendency to continue for the future; tho' there are habits of inferior degrees of force, proportion'd to the inferior degrees of steadiness and uniformity in our conduct.   *SB 133*

7   There is no doubt but this principle[†] sometimes takes place, and produces those inferences we draw from contrary phænomena; tho' I am perswaded, that upon examination we shall not find it to be the principle, that most commonly influences the mind in this species of reasoning. When we follow only the habitual determination of the mind, we make the transition without any reflection, and interpose not a moment's delay betwixt the view of one object and the belief of that, which is often found to attend it. As the custom depends not upon any deliberation, it operates immediately, without allowing any time for reflection. But this method of proceeding we have but few instances of in our probable reasonings;[†] and even fewer than in those, which are deriv'd from the uninterrupted conjunction of objects. In the former species of reasoning we commonly take knowingly into consideration the contrariety of past events; we compare the different sides of the contrariety, and carefully weigh the experiments, which we have on each side: Whence we may conclude, that our reasonings of this kind arise not *directly* from the habit, but in an *oblique* manner; which we must now endeavour to explain.

8   'Tis evident, that when an object is attended with contrary effects, we judge of them only by our past experience, and always consider those as possible, which

we have observ'd to follow from it. And as past experience regulates our judgment concerning the possibility of these effects, so it does that concerning their probability; and that effect, which has been the most common, we always esteem the most likely. Here then are two things to be consider'd, *viz.* the *reasons* which determine us to make the past a standard for the future, and the *manner* how we extract a single judgment from a contrariety of past events.   *SB 134*

9   *First,* We may observe, that the supposition, *that the future resembles the past,* is not founded on arguments of any kind, but is deriv'd entirely from habit, by which we are determin'd to expect for the future the same train of objects, to which we have been accustom'd. This habit or determination to transfer the past to the future is full and perfect; and consequently the first impulse of the imagination in this species of reasoning is endow'd with the same qualities.

10   But, *secondly,* when in considering past experiments we find them of a contrary nature, this determination, tho' full and perfect in itself, presents us with no steady object, but offers us a number of disagreeing images in a certain order and proportion. The first impulse, therefore, is here broke into pieces, and diffuses itself over all those images, of which each partakes an equal share of that force and vivacity, that is deriv'd from the impulse.† Any of these past events may again happen; and we judge, that when they do happen, they will be mix'd in the same proportion as in the past.

11   If our intention, therefore, be to consider the proportions of contrary events in a great number of instances, the images presented by our past experience must remain in their *first form,* and preserve their first proportions.† Suppose, for instance, I have found by long observation, that of twenty ships, which go to sea, only nineteen return. Suppose I see at present twenty ships that leave the port: I transfer my past experience to the future, and represent to myself nineteen of these ships as returning in safety, and one as perishing. Concerning this there can be no difficulty. But as we frequently run over those several ideas of past events, in order to form a judgment concerning one single event, which appears uncertain; this consideration must change the *first form* of our ideas, and draw together the divided images presented by experience; since 'tis to *it* we refer the determination of that particular event, upon which we reason. Many of   *SB 135* these images are suppos'd to concur, and a superior number to concur on one side. These agreeing images unite together, and render the idea more strong and lively, not only than a mere fiction of the imagination, but also than any idea, which is supported by a lesser number of experiments. Each new experiment is as a new stroke of the pencil, which bestows an additional vivacity on the colours, without either multiplying or enlarging the figure. This operation of the mind has been so fully explain'd† in treating of the probability of chance, that I need not here endeavour to render it more intelligible. Every past experiment may be consider'd as a kind of chance; it being uncertain to us, whether the object will exist conformable to one experiment or another: And for this reason every thing that has been said on the one subject is applicable to both.

12   Thus upon the whole, contrary experiments produce an imperfect belief, either by weakening the habit, or by dividing and afterwards joining in different

parts, that *perfect* habit, which makes us conclude in general, that instances, of which we have no experience, must necessarily resemble those of which we have.

13   To justify still farther this account of the second species of probability, where we reason with knowledge and reflection from a contrariety of past experiments, I shall propose the following considerations, without fearing to give offence by that air of subtility, which attends them. Just reasoning ought still, perhaps, to retain its force, however subtile;[†] in the same manner as matter preserves its solidity in the air, and fire, and animal spirits, as well as in the grosser and more sensible forms.

14   *First*, We may observe, that there is no probability so great as not to allow of a contrary possibility; because otherwise 'twou'd cease to be a probability, and wou'd become a certainty. That probability of causes, which is most extensive, and which we at present examine, depends on a contrariety of experiments; and 'tis evident an experiment in the past proves at least a possibility for the future.

15   *Secondly*, The component parts of this possibility and probability are of the same nature, and differ in number only, but not in kind. It has been observ'd,[†] that all single chances are entirely equal, and that the only circumstance, which can give any event, that is contingent, a superiority over another, is a superior number of chances. In like manner, as the uncertainty of causes is discover'd by experience, which presents us with a view of contrary events, 'tis plain, that when we transfer the past to the future, the known to the unknown, every past experiment has the same weight, and that 'tis only a superior number of them, which can throw the ballance on any side. The possibility, therefore, which enters into every reasoning of this kind, is compos'd of parts, which are of the same nature both among themselves, and with those, that compose the opposite probability. *SB 136*

16   *Thirdly*, We may establish it as a certain maxim, that in all moral as well as natural phænomena, wherever any cause consists of a number of parts, and the effect encreases or diminishes, according to the variation of that number, the effect, properly speaking, is a compounded one, and arises from the union of the several effects, that proceed from each part of the cause.[†] Thus because the gravity of a body encreases or diminishes by the encrease or diminution of its parts, we conclude that each part contains this quality and contributes to the gravity of the whole.[†] The absence or presence of a part of the cause is attended with that of a proportionable part of the effect. This connexion or constant conjunction sufficiently proves the one part to be the cause of the other. As the belief, which we have of any event, encreases or diminishes according to the number of chances or past experiments, 'tis to be consider'd as a compounded effect, of which each part arises from a proportionable number of chances or experiments.

17   Let us now join these three observations, and see what conclusion we can draw from them. To every probability there is an opposite possibility. This possibility is compos'd of parts, that are entirely of the same nature with those of

the probability; and consequently have the same influence on the mind and *SB 137* understanding. The belief, which attends the probability, is a compounded effect, and is form'd by the concurrence of the several effects, which proceed from each part of the probability. Since therefore each part of the probability contributes to the production of the belief, each part of the possibility must have the same influence on the opposite side; the nature of these parts being entirely the same. The contrary belief, attending the possibility, implies a view of a certain object, as well as the probability does an opposite view. In this particular both these degrees of belief are alike. The only manner then, in which the superior number of similar component parts in the one can exert its influence, and prevail above the inferior in the other, is by producing a stronger and more lively view of its object. Each part presents a particular view; and all these views uniting together produce one general view, which is fuller and more distinct by the greater number of causes or principles, from which it is deriv'd.

18   The component parts of the probability and possibility, being alike in their nature, must produce like effects; and the likeness of their effects consists in this, that each of them presents a view of a particular object. But tho' these parts be alike in their nature, they are very different in their quantity and number; and this difference must appear in the effect as well as the similarity. Now as the view they present is in both cases full and entire, and comprehends the object in all its parts, 'tis impossible that in this particular there can be any difference; nor is there any thing but a superior vivacity in the probability, arising from the concurrence of a superior number of views, which can distinguish these effects.

19   Here is almost the same argument in a different light. All our reasonings concerning the probability of causes are founded on the transferring of past to future. The transferring of any past experiment to the future is sufficient to give *SB 138* us a view of the object; whether that experiment be single, or combin'd with others of the same kind; whether it be entire,[†] or oppos'd by others of a contrary kind. Suppose, then, it acquires both these qualities of combination and opposition, it loses not upon that account its former power of presenting a view of the object, but only concurs with and opposes other experiments, that have a like influence. A question, therefore, may arise concerning the manner both of the concurrence and opposition. As to the *concurrence*, there is only the choice left betwixt these two hypotheses. *First,* That the view of the object, occasion'd by the transference of each past experiment, preserves itself entire,[†] and only multiplies the number of views. Or, *secondly,* that it runs into the other similar and correspondent views, and gives them a superior degree of force and vivacity. But that the first hypothesis is erroneous, is evident from experience, which informs us, that the belief, attending any reasoning, consists in one conclusion, not in a multitude of similar ones, which wou'd only distract the mind, and in many cases wou'd be too numerous to be comprehended distinctly by any finite capacity. It remains, therefore, as the only reasonable opinion, that these similar views run into each other, and unite their forces; so as to produce a stronger and clearer view, than what arises from any one alone. This is the manner, in which past

experiments concur, when they are transferr'd to any future event. As to the manner of their *opposition*, 'tis evident, that as the contrary views are incompatible with each other, and 'tis impossible the object can at once exist conformable to both of them, their influence becomes mutually destructive, and the mind is determin'd to the superior only with that force, which remains after substracting the inferior.

20   I am sensible how abstruse all this reasoning must appear to the generality of readers, who not being accustom'd to such profound reflections on the intellectual faculties of the mind, will be apt to reject as chimerical whatever strikes not in with the common receiv'd notions, and with the easiest and most obvious *SB 139* principles of philosophy. And no doubt there are some pains requir'd to enter into these arguments; tho' perhaps very little are necessary to perceive the imperfection of every vulgar hypothesis on this subject, and the little light, which philosophy can yet afford us in such sublime and such curious speculations. Let men be once fully perswaded of these two principles, *that there is nothing in any object, consider'd in itself, which can afford us a reason for drawing a conclusion beyond it*; and, *that even after the observation of the frequent or constant conjunction of objects, we have no reason to draw any inference concerning any object beyond those of which we have had experience*; I say, let men be once fully convinc'd of these two principles, and this will throw them so loose[†] from all common systems, that they will make no difficulty of receiving any, which may appear the most extraordinary. These principles we have found to be sufficiently convincing, even with regard to our most certain reasonings from causation: But I shall venture to affirm, that with regard to these conjectural or probable reasonings they still acquire a new degree of evidence.

21   *First*, 'Tis obvious, that in reasonings of this kind, 'tis not the object presented to us, which, consider'd in itself, affords us any reason to draw a conclusion concerning any other object or event. For as this latter object is suppos'd uncertain, and as the uncertainty is deriv'd from a conceal'd contrariety of causes in the former, were any of the causes plac'd in the known qualities of that object, they wou'd no longer be conceal'd, nor wou'd our conclusion be uncertain.

22   But, *secondly*, 'tis equally obvious in this species of reasoning, that if the transference of the past to the future were founded merely on a conclusion of the understanding, it cou'd never occasion any belief or assurance. When we transfer contrary experiments to the future, we can only repeat these contrary experiments with their particular proportions; which cou'd not produce assurance in *SB 140* any single event, upon which we reason, unless the fancy melted together all those images that concur, and extracted from them one single idea or image, which is intense and lively in proportion to the number of experiments from which it is deriv'd, and their superiority above their antagonists.[†] Our past experience presents no determinate object; and as our belief, however faint, fixes itself on a determinate object, 'tis evident, that the belief arises not merely from the transference of past to future, but from some operation of the *fancy* conjoin'd with it. This may lead us to conceive the manner, in which that faculty enters into all our reasonings.

23   I shall conclude this subject with two reflections, which may deserve our attention. The *first* may be explain'd after this manner. When the mind forms a reasoning concerning any matter of fact, which is only probable, it casts its eye backward upon past experience, and transferring it to the future, is presented with so many contrary views of its object, of which those that are of the same kind uniting together, and running into one act of the mind, serve to fortify and enliven it. But suppose that this multitude of views or glimpses of an object proceeds not from experience, but from a voluntary act of the imagination; this effect does not follow, or at least, follows not in the same degree. For tho' custom and education produce belief by such a repetition, as is not deriv'd from experience, yet this requires a long tract of time, along with a very frequent and *undesign'd*[†] repetition. In general we may pronounce, that a person, who wou'd *voluntarily* repeat any idea in his mind,[23] tho' supported by one past experience, wou'd be no more inclin'd to believe the existence of its object, than if he had contented himself with one survey of it. Beside the effect of design; each act of the mind, being separate and independent, has a separate influence, and joins not its force with that of its fellows. Not being united by any common object, producing them, they have no relation to each other; and consequently make no transition or union of forces. This phænomenon we shall understand better afterwards.[†]

SB 141

24   My *second* reflection is founded on those large probabilities, which the mind can judge of, and the minute differences it can observe betwixt them. When the chances or experiments on one side amount to ten thousand, and on the other to ten thousand and one, the judgment gives the preference to the latter, upon account of that superiority; tho' 'tis plainly impossible for the mind to run over every particular view, and distinguish the superior vivacity of the image arising from the superior number, where the difference is so inconsiderable. We have a parallel instance in the affections. 'Tis evident, according to the principles above-mention'd,[†] that when an object produces any passion in us, which varies according to the different quantity of the object; I say, 'tis evident, that the passion, properly speaking, is not a simple emotion, but a compounded one, of a great number of weaker passions, deriv'd from a view of each part of the object. For otherwise 'twere impossible the passion shou'd encrease by the encrease of these parts. Thus a man, who desires a thousand pound, has in reality a thousand or more desires, which uniting together, seem to make only one passion; tho' the composition evidently betrays itself upon every alteration of the object, by the preference he gives to the larger number, if superior only by an unite. Yet nothing can be more certain, than that so small a difference wou'd not be discernible in the passions, nor cou'd render them distinguishable from each other. The difference, therefore, of our conduct in preferring the greater number depends not upon our passions, but upon custom, and *general rules*. We have found in a multitude of instances, that the augmenting the numbers of any sum augments the passion, where the numbers are precise and the difference sen-

---

[23] Sects. 9, 10.[†]

SB 140

sible. The mind can perceive from its immediate feeling, that three guineas produce a greater passion than two; and *this* it transfers to larger numbers, because of the resemblance; and by a general rule assigns to a thousand guineas, a stronger passion than to nine hundred and ninety nine. These general rules we shall explain presently.[†]

25   But beside these two species of probability, which are deriv'd from an *imperfect* experience and from *contrary* causes, there is a third arising from ANALOGY,[†] which differs from them in some material circumstances. According to the hypothesis above-explain'd,[†] all kinds of reasoning from causes or effects are founded on two particulars, *viz.* the constant conjunction of any two objects in all past experience, and the resemblance of a present object to any one of them. The effect of these two particulars is, that the present object invigorates and enlivens the imagination; and the resemblance, along with the constant union, conveys this force and vivacity to the related idea; which we are therefore said to believe, or assent to. If you weaken either the union or resemblance, you weaken the principle of transition, and of consequence that belief, which arises from it. The vivacity of the first impression cannot be fully convey'd to the related idea, either where the conjunction of their objects is not constant, or where the present impression does not perfectly resemble any of those, whose union we are accustom'd to observe. In those probabilities of chance and causes above-explain'd,[†] 'tis the constancy of the union, which is diminish'd; and in the probability deriv'd from analogy, 'tis the resemblance only, which is affected. Without some degree of resemblance, as well as union, 'tis impossible there can be any reasoning: But as this resemblance admits of many different degrees, the reasoning becomes proportionably more or less firm and certain. An experiment loses of its force, when transferr'd to instances, which are not exactly resembling; tho' 'tis evident it may still retain as much as may be the foundation of probability, as long as there is any resemblance remaining.

Sect. 13. *Of unphilosophical probability*

1   All these kinds of probability are receiv'd[†] by philosophers, and allow'd to be reasonable foundations of belief and opinion. But there are others, that are deriv'd from the same principles, tho' they have not had the good fortune to obtain the same sanction. The *first* probability of this kind may be accounted for thus. The diminution of the union,[†] and of the resemblance, as above-explain'd,[†] diminishes the facility of the transition, and by that means weakens the evidence; and we may farther observe, that the same diminution of the evidence will follow from a diminution of the impression, and from the shading of those colours, under which it appears to the memory or senses. The argument, which we found on any matter of fact we remember, is more or less convincing, according as the fact is recent or remote; and tho' the difference in these degrees of evidence be not receiv'd by philosophy as solid and legitimate; because in that case an argument must have a different force to-day, from what it shall have a month hence; yet notwithstanding the opposition of philosophy, 'tis certain, this

circumstance has a considerable influence on the understanding, and secretly changes the authority of the same argument, according to the different times, in which it is propos'd to us. A greater force and vivacity in the impression naturally conveys a greater to the related idea; and 'tis on the degrees of force and vivacity, that the belief depends, according to the foregoing system.†

2   There is a *second* difference, which we may frequently observe in our degrees of belief and assurance, and which never fails to take place, tho' disclaim'd by philosophers. An experiment, that is recent and fresh in the memory, affects us more than one that is in some measure obliterated; and has a superior influence on the judgment, as well as on the passions. A lively impression produces more *SB 144* assurance than a faint one; because it has more original force to communicate to the related idea, which thereby acquires a greater force and vivacity. A recent observation has a like effect; because the custom and transition is there more entire, and preserves better the original force in the communication. Thus a drunkard, who has seen his companion die of a debauch, is struck with that instance for some time, and dreads a like accident for himself: But as the memory of it decays away by degrees, his former security returns, and the danger seems less certain and real.

3   I add, as a *third* instance of this kind, that tho' our reasonings from proofs and from probabilities be considerably different from each other, yet the former species of reasoning often degenerates insensibly into the latter, by nothing but the multitude of connected arguments. 'Tis certain, that when an inference is drawn immediately from an object, without any intermediate cause or effect, the conviction is much stronger, and the perswasion more lively, than when the imagination is carry'd thro' a long chain of connected arguments, however infallible the connexion of each link may be esteem'd.† 'Tis from the original impression, that the vivacity of all the ideas is deriv'd, by means of the customary transition of the imagination; and 'tis evident this vivacity must gradually decay in proportion to the distance, and must lose somewhat in each transition. Sometimes this distance has a greater influence than even contrary experiments wou'd have; and a man may receive a more lively conviction from a probable reasoning, which is close and immediate, than from a long chain of consequences, tho' just and conclusive in each part. Nay 'tis seldom such reasonings produce any conviction; and one must have a very strong and firm imagination to preserve the evidence† to the end, where it passes thro' so many stages.

4   But here it may not be amiss to remark a very curious phænomenon, which the present subject suggests to us. 'Tis evident there is no point of antient history, of *SB 145* which we can have any assurance, but by passing thro' many millions of causes and effects, and thro' a chain of arguments of almost an immeasurable length. Before the knowledge of the fact cou'd come to the first historian, it must be convey'd thro' many mouths; and after it is committed to writing, each new copy is a new object, of which the connexion with the foregoing is known only by experience and observation. Perhaps, therefore, it may be concluded from the precedent reasoning, that the evidence of all antient history must now be lost; or at

least, will be lost in time, as the chain of causes encreases, and runs on to a greater length. But as it seems contrary to common sense to think, that if the Republic of Letters,[†] and the art of printing continue on the same footing as at present, our posterity, even after a thousand ages,[†] can ever doubt if there has been such a man as JULIUS CÆSAR; this may be consider'd as an objection to the present system. If belief consisted only in a certain vivacity, convey'd from an original impression, it wou'd decay by the length of the transition, and must at last be utterly extinguish'd: And *vice versa*, if belief on some occasions be not capable of such an extinction; it must be something different from that vivacity.

5   Before I answer this objection I shall observe, that from this topic there has been borrow'd a very celebrated argument against the *Christian Religion;*[†] but with this difference, that the connexion betwixt each link of the chain in human testimony has been there suppos'd not to go beyond probability, and to be liable to a degree of doubt and uncertainty. And indeed it must be confest, that in this manner of considering the subject, (which however is not a true one) there is no history or tradition, but what must in the end lose all its force and evidence. Every new probability diminishes the original conviction; and however great that conviction may be suppos'd, 'tis impossible it can subsist under such re-iterated diminutions. This is true in general; tho' we shall find afterwards,²⁴ that there is one very memorable exception, which is of vast consequence in the present subject of the understanding.   *SB 146*

6   Mean while to give a solution of the preceding objection upon the supposi-tion, that historical evidence amounts at first to an entire proof; let us consider, that tho' the links are innumerable, that connect any original fact with the present impression, which is the foundation of belief; yet they are all of the same kind, and depend on the fidelity of printers and copists. One edition passes into another, and that into a third, and so on, till we come to that volume we peruse at present. There is no variation in the steps. After we know one, we know all of them; and after we have made one, we can have no scruple as to the rest. This cir-cumstance alone preserves the evidence of history, and will perpetuate the memory of the present age to the latest posterity. If all the long chain of causes and effects, which connect any past event with any volume of history, were com-pos'd of parts different from each other, and which 'twere necessary for the mind distinctly to conceive, 'tis impossible we shou'd preserve to the end any belief or evidence. But as most of these proofs are perfectly resembling, the mind runs easily along them, jumps from one part to another with facility, and forms but a confus'd and general notion of each link. By this means a long chain of argument, has as little effect in diminishing the original vivacity, as a much shorter wou'd have, if compos'd of parts, which were different from each other, and of which each requir'd a distinct consideration.

7   A *fourth* unphilosophical species of probability is that deriv'd from *general rules*, which we rashly form to ourselves, and which are the source of what we

----

²⁴ Part 4. Sect. 1.[†]

properly call PREJUDICE.[†] An *Irishman* cannot have wit, and a *Frenchman* cannot have solidity;[†] for which reason, tho' the conversation of the former in any instance be visibly very agreeable, and of the latter very judicious, we have entertain'd such a prejudice against them, that they must be dunces or fops[†] in spite of sense and reason. Human nature is very subject to errors of this kind; and perhaps this nation[†] as much as any other.

SB 147

8   Shou'd it be demanded why men form general rules, and allow them to influence their judgment, even contrary to present observation and experience, I shou'd reply, that in my opinion it proceeds from those very principles, on which all judgments concerning causes and effects depend. Our judgments concerning cause and effect are deriv'd from habit and experience; and when we have been accustom'd to see one object united to another, our imagination passes from the first to the second, by a natural transition, which precedes reflection, and which cannot be prevented by it. Now 'tis the nature of custom not only to operate with its full force, when objects are presented, that are exactly the same with those to which we have been accustom'd; but also to operate in an inferior degree, when we discover such as are similar; and tho' the habit loses somewhat of its force by every difference, yet 'tis seldom entirely destroy'd, where any considerable circumstances remain the same. A man, who has contracted a custom of eating fruit by the use of pears or peaches, will satisfy himself with melons, where he cannot find his favourite fruit; as one, who has become a drunkard by the use of red wines, will be carry'd almost with the same violence to white, if presented to him. From this principle I have accounted for[†] that species of probability, deriv'd from analogy, where we transfer our experience in past instances to objects which are resembling, but are not exactly the same with those concerning which we have had experience. In proportion as the resemblance decays, the probability diminishes; but still has some force as long as there remain any traces of the resemblance.

9   This observation we may carry farther; and may remark, that tho' custom be the foundation of all our judgments, yet sometimes it has an effect on the imagination in opposition to the judgment, and produces a contrariety in our sentiments concerning the same object. I explain myself. In almost all kinds of causes there is a complication of circumstances, of which some are essential, and others superfluous; some are absolutely requisite to the production of the effect, and others are only conjoin'd by accident. Now we may observe, that when these superfluous circumstances are numerous, and remarkable, and frequently conjoin'd with the essential, they have such an influence on the imagination, that even in the absence of the latter they carry us on to the conception of the usual effect, and give to that conception a force and vivacity, which make it superior to the mere fictions of the fancy. We may correct this propensity by a reflection on the nature of those circumstances; but 'tis still certain, that custom takes the start, and gives a biass to the imagination.

SB 148

10   To illustrate this by a familiar instance, let us consider the case of a man, who being hung out from a high tower in a cage of iron cannot forbear trembling, when he surveys the precipice below him, tho' he knows himself to be perfectly

secure from falling, by his experience of the solidity of the iron, which supports him; and tho' the ideas of fall and descent, and harm and death, be deriv'd solely from custom and experience.[†] The same custom goes beyond the instances, from which it is deriv'd, and to which it perfectly corresponds; and influences his ideas of such objects as are in some respect resembling, but fall not precisely under the same rule. The circumstances of depth and descent strike so strongly upon him, that their influence cannot be destroy'd by the contrary circumstances of support and solidity, which ought to give him a perfect security. His imagination runs away with its object, and excites a passion proportion'd to it. That passion returns back upon the imagination and enlivens the idea; which lively idea has a new influence on the passion, and in its turn augments its force and violence; and both his fancy and affections, thus mutually supporting each other, cause the whole to have a very great influence upon him.   *SB 149*

11   But why need we seek for other instances, while the present subject of unphilosophical probabilities offers us so obvious an one, in the opposition betwixt the judgment and imagination arising from these effects of custom? According to my system, all reasonings[†] are nothing but the effects of custom; and custom has no influence, but by enlivening the imagination, and giving us a strong conception of any object. It may, therefore, be concluded, that our judgment and imagination can never be contrary, and that custom cannot operate on the latter faculty after such a manner, as to render it opposite to the former.[†] This difficulty we can remove after no other manner, than by supposing the influence of general rules. We shall afterwards[25] take notice of some general rules, by which we ought to regulate our judgment concerning causes and effects; and these rules are form'd on the nature of our understanding, and on our experience of its operations in the judgments we form concerning objects. By them we learn to distinguish the accidental circumstances from the efficacious causes; and when we find that an effect can be produc'd without the concurrence of any particular circumstance, we conclude that that circumstance makes not a part of the efficacious cause, however frequently conjoin'd with it. But as this frequent conjunction necessarily makes it have some effect on the imagination, in spite of the opposite conclusion from general rules, the opposition of these two principles produces a contrariety in our thoughts, and causes us to ascribe the one inference to our judgment, and the other to our imagination. The general rule is attributed to our judgment; as being more extensive and constant. The exception to the imagination; as being more capricious and uncertain.

12   Thus our general rules are in a manner set in opposition to each other. When an object appears, that resembles any cause in very considerable circumstances,   *SB 150*
the imagination naturally carries us to a lively conception of the usual effect, tho' the object be different in the most material and most efficacious circumstances from that cause. Here is the first influence of general rules. But when we take a review of this act of the mind, and compare it with the more general and authentic operations of the understanding, we find it to be of an irregular

[25] Sect. 15.[†]   *SB 149*

nature, and destructive of all the most establish'd principles of reasoning; which is the cause of our rejecting it. This is a second influence of general rules, and implies the condemnation of the former. Sometimes the one, sometimes the other prevails, according to the disposition and character of the person. The vulgar are commonly guided by the first, and wise men by the second. Mean while the sceptics may here have the pleasure of observing a new and signal contradiction in our reason, and of seeing all philosophy ready to be subverted by a principle of human nature, and again sav'd by a new direction of the very same principle. The following of general rules is a very unphilosophical species of probability; and yet 'tis only by following them that we can correct this, and all other unphilosophical probabilities.

13   Since we have instances, where general rules operate on the imagination even contrary to the judgment, we need not be surpriz'd to see their effects encrease, when conjoin'd with that latter faculty, and to observe that they bestow on the ideas they present to us a force superior to what attends any other. Every one knows, there is an indirect manner of insinuating praise or blame, which is much less shocking than the open flattery or censure of any person. However he may communicate his sentiments by such secret insinuations, and make them known with equal certainty as by the open discovery of them, 'tis certain that their influence is not equally strong and powerful. One who lashes me with conceal'd strokes of satire, moves not my indignation to such a degree, as if he flatly told me I was a fool and coxcomb; tho' I equally understand his meaning, as if he did. *SB 151* This difference is to be attributed to the influence of general rules.

14   Whether a person openly abuses me, or slyly intimates his contempt, in neither case do I immediately perceive his sentiment or opinion; and 'tis only by signs, that is, by its effects, I become sensible of it.[†] The only difference, then, betwixt these two cases consists in this, that in the open discovery of his sentiments he makes use of signs, which are general and universal; and in the secret intimation employs such as are more singular and uncommon. The effect of this circumstance is, that the imagination, in running from the present impression to the absent idea, makes the transition with greater facility, and consequently conceives the object with greater force, where the connexion is common and universal, than where it is more rare and particular. Accordingly we may observe, that the open declaration of our sentiments is call'd the taking off the mask, as the secret intimation of our opinions is said to be the veiling of them. The difference betwixt an idea produc'd by a general connexion, and that arising from a particular one is here compar'd to the difference betwixt an impression and an idea. This difference in the imagination has a suitable effect on the passions; and this effect is augmented by another circumstance. A secret intimation of anger or contempt shows that we still have some consideration for the person, and avoid the directly abusing him. This makes a conceal'd satire less disagreeable; but still this depends on the same principle. For if an idea were not more feeble, when only intimated, it wou'd never be esteem'd a mark of greater respect to proceed in this method than in the other.

15   Sometimes scurrility is less displeasing than delicate satire, because it revenges us in a manner for the injury at the very time it is committed, by affording us a just reason to blame and contemn the person, who injures us. But this phænomenon likewise depends upon the same principle. For why do we *SB 152* blame all gross and injurious language, unless it be, because we esteem it contrary to good-breeding and humanity? And why is it contrary, unless it be more shocking than any delicate satire? The rules of good-breeding condemn whatever is openly disobliging, and gives a sensible pain and confusion to those, with whom we converse. After this is once establish'd, abusive language is universally blam'd, and gives less pain upon account of its coarseness and incivility, which render the person despicable, that employs it. It becomes less disagreeable, merely because originally it is more so; and 'tis more disagreeable, because it affords an inference by general and common rules, that are palpable and undeniable.

16   To this explication of the different influence of open and conceal'd flattery or satire, I shall add the consideration of another phænomenon, which is analogous to it. There are many particulars in the point of honour[†] both of men and women, whose violations, when open and avow'd, the world never excuses, but which it is more apt to overlook, when the appearances are sav'd, and the transgression is secret and conceal'd. Even those, who know with equal certainty, that the fault is committed, pardon it more easily, when the proofs seem in some measure oblique and equivocal, than when they are direct and undeniable. The same idea is presented in both cases, and, properly speaking, is equally assented to by the judgment; and yet its influence is different, because of the different manner, in which it is presented.

17   Now if we compare these two cases, of the *open* and *conceal'd* violations of the laws of honour, we shall find, that the difference betwixt them consists in this, that in the first case the sign, from which we infer the blameable action, is single, and suffices alone to be the foundation of our reasoning and judgment; whereas in the latter the signs are numerous, and decide little or nothing when alone and unaccompany'd with many minute circumstances, which are almost imperceptible. But 'tis certainly true, that any reasoning is always the more convincing, *SB 153* the more single and united it is to the eye, and the less exercise it gives to the imagination to collect all its parts, and run from them to the correlative idea, which forms the conclusion. The labour of the thought disturbs the regular progress of the sentiments, as we shall observe presently.[26] The idea strikes not on us with such vivacity; and consequently has no such influence on the passions and imagination.

18   From the same principles we may account for those observations of the Cardinal DE RETZ, *that there are many things, in which the world wishes to be deceiv'd*; and *that it more easily excuses a person in acting than in talking contrary to the decorum of his profession and character.*[†] A fault in words is commonly more open

---

[26] Part 4. Sect. 1.[†]

and distinct than one in actions, which admit of many palliating excuses, and decide not so clearly concerning the intention and views of the actor.

19   Thus it appears upon the whole, that every kind of opinion or judgment, which amounts not to knowledge, is deriv'd entirely from the force and vivacity of the perception, and that these qualities constitute in the mind, what we call the BELIEF of the existence of any object. This force and this vivacity are most conspicuous in the memory; and therefore our confidence in the veracity of that faculty is the greatest imaginable, and equals in many respects the assurance of a demonstration. The next degree[†] of these qualities is that deriv'd from the relation of cause and effect; and this too is very great, especially when the conjunction is found by experience to be perfectly constant, and when the object, which is present to us, exactly resembles those, of which we have had experience. But below this degree of evidence there are many others, which have an influence on the passions and imagination, proportion'd to that degree of force and vivacity, which they communicate to the ideas. 'Tis by habit we make the transition from cause to effect; and 'tis from some present impression we borrow that vivacity, which we diffuse over the correlative idea. But when we have not observ'd a sufficient number of instances, to produce a strong habit; or when these instances are contrary to each other; or when the resemblance is not exact; or the present impression is faint and obscure; or the experience in some measure obliterated from the memory; or the connexion dependent on a long chain of objects; or the inference deriv'd from general rules, and yet not conformable to them: In all these cases the evidence diminishes by the diminution of the force and intenseness of the idea. This therefore is the nature of the judgment and probability.   *SB 154*

20   What principally gives authority to this system is, beside the undoubted arguments, upon which each part is founded, the agreement of these parts, and the necessity of one to explain another. The belief, which attends our memory,[†] is of the same nature with that, which is deriv'd from our judgments: Nor is there any difference betwixt that judgment, which is deriv'd from a constant and uniform connexion of causes and effects, and that which depends upon an interrupted and uncertain. 'Tis indeed evident, that in all determinations, where the mind decides from contrary experiments, 'tis first divided within itself, and has an inclination to either side in proportion to the number of experiments we have seen and remember. This contest is at last determin'd to the advantage of that side, where we observe a superior number of these experiments; but still with a diminution of force in the evidence correspondent to the number of the opposite experiments. Each possibility, of which the probability is compos'd, operates separately upon the imagination; and 'tis the larger collection of possibilities, which at last prevails, and that with a force proportionable to its superiority. All these phænomena lead directly to the precedent system; nor will it ever be possible upon any other principles to give a satisfactory and consistent explication of them. Without considering these judgments as the effects of custom on the imagination, we shall lose ourselves in perpetual contradiction and absurdity.   *SB 155*

Sect. 14. *Of the idea of necessary connexion*

1 Having thus explain'd the manner, *in which we reason beyond our immediate impressions, and conclude that such particular causes must have such particular effects;*† we must now return upon our footsteps to examine that question, which first occur'd to us,[27] and which we dropt in our way,† viz. *What is our idea of necessity, when we say that two objects are necessarily connected together?* Upon this head I repeat what I have often had occasion to observe,† that as we have no idea, that is not deriv'd from an impression, we must find some impression, that gives rise to this idea of necessity, if we assert we have really such an idea. In order to this I consider, in what objects necessity is commonly suppos'd to lie; and finding that it is always ascrib'd to causes and effects, I turn my eye to two objects suppos'd to be plac'd in that relation; and examine them in all the situations, of which they are susceptible. I immediately perceive, that they are *contiguous* in time and place, and that the object we call cause *precedes* the other we call effect. In no one instance can I go any farther, nor is it possible for me to discover any third relation betwixt these objects. I therefore enlarge my view to comprehend several instances; where I find like objects always existing in like relations of contiguity and succession. At first sight this seems to serve but little to my purpose. The reflection on several instances only repeats the same objects; and therefore can never give rise to a new idea. But upon farther enquiry I find, that the repetition is not in every particular the same, but produces a new impression, and by that means the idea, which I at present examine. For after a frequent repetition, I find, that upon the appearance of one of the objects, the mind is *determin'd* by custom to consider its usual attendant, and to consider it in a stronger light upon account of its relation to the first object. 'Tis this impression, then, or *determination*, which affords me the idea of necessity.   *SB 156*

2   I doubt not but these consequences will at first sight be receiv'd without difficulty, as being evident deductions from principles, which we have already establish'd,† and which we have often employ'd in our reasonings. This evidence both in the first principles, and in the deductions, may seduce us unwarily into the conclusion, and make us imagine it contains nothing extraordinary, nor worthy of our curiosity. But tho' such an inadvertence may facilitate the reception of this reasoning, 'twill make it be the more easily forgot; for which reason I think it proper to give warning, that I have just now examin'd one of the most sublime questions in philosophy, viz. *that concerning the power and efficacy of causes;* where all the sciences seem so much interested. Such a warning will naturally rouze up the attention of the reader, and make him desire a more full account of my doctrine, as well as of the arguments, on which it is founded. This request is so reasonable, that I cannot refuse complying with it; especially as I am hopeful that these principles, the more they are examin'd, will acquire the more force and evidence.

3   There is no question, which on account of its importance, as well as difficulty,

---

[27] Sect. 2.†   *SB 155*

has caus'd more disputes both among antient and modern philosophers, than this concerning the efficacy of causes, or that quality which makes them be follow'd by their effects.[†] But before they enter'd upon these disputes, methinks it wou'd not have been improper to have examin'd what idea we have of that efficacy, which is the subject of the controversy. This is what I find principally wanting in their reasonings, and what I shall here endeavour to supply.

4   I begin with observing that the terms of *efficacy, agency, power, force, energy, necessity, connexion,* and *productive quality,* are all nearly synonimous; and therefore 'tis an absurdity to employ any of them in defining the rest. By this observation we reject at once all the vulgar definitions, which philosophers have given of power and efficacy;[†] and instead of searching for the idea in these definitions, must look for it in the impressions, from which it is originally deriv'd. If it be a compound idea, it must arise from compound impressions. If simple, from simple impressions. *SB 157*

5   I believe the most general and most popular explication of this matter,[28] is to say, that finding from experience, that there are several new productions in matter, such as the motions and variations of body, and concluding that there must somewhere be a power capable of producing them, we arrive at last by this reasoning at the idea of power and efficacy. But to be convinc'd that this explication is more popular than philosophical, we need but reflect on two very obvious principles. *First,* That reason alone can never give rise to any original idea,[†] and *secondly,* that reason, as distinguish'd from experience, can never make us conclude, that a cause or productive quality is absolutely requisite to every beginning of existence.[†] Both these considerations have been sufficiently explain'd; and therefore shall not at present be any farther insisted on.

6   I shall only infer from them, that since reason can never give rise to the idea of efficacy, that idea must be deriv'd from experience, and from some particular instances of this efficacy, which make their passage into the mind by the common channels of sensation or reflection. Ideas always represent their objects or impressions; and *vice versa,* there are some objects necessary to give rise to every idea. If we pretend, therefore, to have any just idea of this efficacy, we must produce some instance, wherein the efficacy is plainly discoverable to the mind, and its operations obvious to our consciousness or sensation. By the refusal of this, we acknowledge, that the idea is impossible and imaginary; since the principle of innate ideas, which alone can save us from this dilemma, has been already refuted, and is now almost universally rejected in the learned world.[†] Our present business, then, must be to find some natural production, where the operation and efficacy of a cause can be clearly conceiv'd and comprehended by the mind, without any danger of obscurity or mistake. *SB 158*

7   In this research we meet with very little encouragement from that prodigious diversity, which is found in the opinions of those philosophers, who have pretended to explain the secret force and energy of causes.[29] There are some, who

----

[28] See Mr. *Locke*; chapter of power.[†]   *SB 157*
[29] See Father *Malebranche*, Book 6. Part 2. chap. 3, and the illustrations upon it.[†]   *SB 158*

maintain, that bodies operate by their substantial form; others, by their accidents or qualities; several, by their matter and form; some, by their form and accidents; others, by certain virtues and faculties distinct from all this.[†] All these sentiments again are mix'd and vary'd in a thousand different ways; and form a strong presumption, that none of them have any solidity or evidence, and that the supposition of an efficacy in any of the known qualities of matter is entirely without foundation. This presumption must encrease upon us, when we consider, that these principles of substantial forms, and accidents, and faculties, are not in reality any of the known properties of bodies, but are perfectly unintelligible and inexplicable. For 'tis evident philosophers wou'd never have had recourse to such obscure and uncertain principles had they met with any satisfaction in such as are clear and intelligible; especially in such an affair as this, which must be an object of the simplest understanding, if not of the senses. Upon the whole, we may conclude, that 'tis impossible in any one instance to show the principle, in which the force and agency of a cause is plac'd; and that the most refin'd and most vulgar understandings are equally at a loss in this particular. If any one think proper to refute this assertion, he need not put himself to the trouble of inventing any long reasonings; but may at once show us an instance of a cause, where we discover the power or operating principle. This defiance we are oblig'd frequently to make use of, as being almost the only means of proving a negative in philosophy.[†]   *SB 159*

8   The small success, which has been met with in all the attempts to fix this power,[†] has at last oblig'd philosophers to conclude, that the ultimate force and efficacy of nature is perfectly unknown to us, and that 'tis in vain we search for it in all the known qualities of matter.[†] In this opinion they are almost unanimous; and 'tis only in the inference they draw from it, that they discover any difference in their sentiments. For some of them, as the *Cartesians* in particular, having establish'd it as a principle, that we are perfectly acquainted with the essence of matter, have very naturally inferr'd, that it is endow'd with no efficacy, and that 'tis impossible for it of itself to communicate motion, or produce any of those effects, which we ascribe to it. As the essence of matter consists in extension, and as extension implies not actual motion, but only mobility; they conclude, that the energy, which produces the motion, cannot lie in the extension.[†]

9   This conclusion leads them into another, which they regard as perfectly unavoidable. Matter, say they, is in itself entirely inactive, and depriv'd of any power, by which it may produce, or continue, or communicate motion: But since these effects are evident to our senses, and since the power, that produces them, must be plac'd somewhere, it must lie in the DEITY, or that divine being, who contains in his nature all excellency and perfection. 'Tis the deity, therefore, who is the prime mover of the universe, and who not only first created matter, and gave it its original impulse, but likewise by a continu'd exertion of omnipotence, supports its existence, and successively bestows on it all those motions, and configurations, and qualities, with which it is endow'd.

10   This opinion is certainly very curious, and well worth our attention; but 'twill   *SB 160*
appear superfluous to examine it in this place, if we reflect a moment on our

present purpose in taking notice of it. We have establish'd it as a principle, that as all ideas are deriv'd from impressions, or some precedent *perceptions*, 'tis impossible we can have any idea of power and efficacy, unless some instances can be produc'd, wherein this power *is perceiv'd* to exert itself. Now as these instances can never be discover'd in body, the *Cartesians*, proceeding upon their principle of innate ideas, have had recourse to a supreme spirit or deity, whom they consider as the only active being in the universe, and as the immediate cause of every alteration in matter.[†] But the principle of innate ideas being allow'd to be false, it follows, that the supposition of a deity can serve us in no stead, in accounting for that idea of agency, which we search for in vain in all the objects, which are presented to our senses, or which we are internally conscious of in our own minds. For if every idea be deriv'd from an impression, the idea of a deity proceeds from the same origin; and if no impression, either of sensation or reflection, implies any force or efficacy, 'tis equally impossible to discover or even imagine any such active principle in the deity. Since these philosophers, therefore, have concluded, that matter cannot be endow'd with any efficacious principle, because 'tis impossible to discover in it such a principle; the same course of reasoning shou'd determine them to exclude it from the supreme being. Or if they esteem that opinion absurd and impious, as it really is, I shall tell them how they may avoid it; and that is, by concluding from the very first, that they have no adequate idea of power or efficacy in any object; since neither in body nor spirit, neither in superior nor inferior natures, are they able to discover one single instance of it.

11   The same conclusion is unavoidable upon the hypothesis of those, who maintain the efficacy of second causes, and attribute a derivative, but a real power and energy to matter. For as they confess, that this energy lies not in any of the *SB 161* known qualities of matter, the difficulty still remains concerning the origin of its idea. If we have really an idea of power, we may attribute power to an unknown quality: But as 'tis impossible, that that idea can be deriv'd from such a quality, and as there is nothing in known qualities, which can produce it; it follows that we deceive ourselves, when we imagine we are possest of any idea of this kind, after the manner we commonly understand it. All ideas are deriv'd from, and represent impressions. We never have any impression, that contains any power or efficacy. We never therefore have any idea of power.

12   [App.]Some have asserted, that we feel an energy, or power, in our own mind;[†] and *SB 632* that having in this manner acquir'd the idea of power, we transfer that quality to matter, where we are not able immediately to discover it. The motions of our body, and the thoughts and sentiments of our mind, (say they) obey the will; nor do we seek any farther to acquire a just notion of force or power. But to convince us how fallacious this reasoning is, we need only consider, that the will being here consider'd as a cause, has no more a discoverable connexion with its effects, than any material cause has with its proper effect. So far from perceiving the connexion betwixt an act of volition, and a motion of the body; 'tis allow'd that no effect is more inexplicable from the powers and essence of thought and matter. Nor is the empire of the will over our mind more intelligible. The effect

is there distinguishable and separable from the cause, and cou'd not be foreseen without the experience of their constant conjunction. We have command over our mind to a certain degree, but beyond *that* lose all empire over it: And 'tis evidently impossible to fix any precise bounds to our authority, where we consult not experience. In short, the actions of the mind are, in this respect, the same with those of matter. We perceive only their constant conjunction; nor can we ever reason beyond it. No internal impression has an apparent energy, more than external objects have. Since, therefore, matter is confess'd by philosophers to operate by an unknown force, we shou'd in vain hope to attain an idea of force by consulting our own minds.[30App.]   *SB 633*

13   It has been establish'd[†] as a certain principle, that general or abstract ideas are   *SB 161* nothing but individual ones taken in a certain light, and that, in reflecting on any object, 'tis as impossible to exclude from our thought all particular degrees of quantity and quality as from the real nature of things. If we be possest, therefore, of any idea of power in general, we must also be able to conceive some particular species of it; and as power cannot subsist alone, but is always regarded as an attribute of some being or existence, we must be able to place this power in some particular being, and conceive that being as endow'd with a real force and energy, by which such a particular effect necessarily results from its operation. We must distinctly and particularly conceive the connexion betwixt the cause and effect, and be able to pronounce, from a simple view of the one, that it must be follow'd or preceded by the other. This is the true manner of conceiving a particular power in a particular body: And a general idea being impossible without an individual; where the latter is impossible, 'tis certain the former can never exist. Now nothing is more evident, than that the human mind cannot form such an idea of two objects, as to conceive any connexion betwixt them, or comprehend distinctly that power or efficacy, by which they are united. Such a connexion wou'd amount to a demonstration, and wou'd imply the absolute   *SB 162* impossibility for the one object not to follow, or to be conceiv'd not to follow upon the other: Which kind of connexion has already been rejected[†] in all cases. If any one is of a contrary opinion, and thinks he has attain'd a notion of power in any particular object, I desire he may point out to me that object. But till I meet with such-a-one, which I despair of, I cannot forbear concluding, that since we can never distinctly conceive how any particular power can possibly reside in any particular object, we deceive ourselves in imagining we can form any such general idea.

14   Thus upon the whole we may infer, that when we talk of any being, whether of a superior or inferior nature, as endow'd with a power or force, proportion'd to any effect; when we speak of a necessary connexion betwixt objects, and

---

[30App.] The same imperfection attends our ideas of the deity; but this can have no effect either on   *SB 633* religion or morals. The order of the universe proves an omnipotent mind; that is, a mind whose will is *constantly attended* with the obedience of every creature and being. Nothing more is requisite to give a foundation to all the articles of religion, nor is it necessary we shou'd form a distinct idea of the force and energy of the supreme being.[App.]

suppose, that this connexion depends upon an efficacy or energy, with which any of these objects are endow'd; in all these expressions, *so apply'd*, we have really no distinct meaning, and make use only of common words, without any clear and determinate ideas. But as 'tis more probable, that these expressions do here lose their true meaning by being *wrong apply'd*, than that they never have any meaning; 'twill be proper to bestow another consideration on this subject, to see if possibly we can discover the nature and origin of those ideas, we annex to them.

15   Suppose two objects to be presented to us, of which the one is the cause and the other the effect; 'tis plain, that from the simple consideration of one, or both these objects we never shall perceive the tie, by which they are united, or be able certainly to pronounce, that there is a connexion betwixt them. 'Tis not, therefore, from any one instance, that we arrive at the idea of cause and effect, of a necessary connexion of power, of force, of energy, and of efficacy. Did we never see any but particular conjunctions of objects, entirely different from each other, we shou'd never be able to form any such ideas.

16   But again; suppose we observe several instances, in which the same objects are   *SB 163*
always conjoin'd together, we immediately conceive a connexion betwixt them, and begin to draw an inference from one to another. This multiplicity of resembling instances, therefore, constitutes the very essence of power or connexion, and is the source, from which the idea of it arises. In order, then, to understand the idea of power, we must consider that multiplicity; nor do I ask more to give a solution of that difficulty, which has so long perplex'd us. For thus I reason. The repetition of perfectly similar instances can never *alone* give rise to an original idea, different from what is to be found in any particular instance, as has been observ'd,[†] and as evidently follows from our fundamental principle, *that all ideas are copy'd from impressions*. Since therefore the idea of power is a new original idea, not to be found in any one instance, and which yet arises from the repetition of several instances, it follows, that the repetition *alone* has not that effect, but must either *discover* or *produce* something new, which is the source of that idea. Did the repetition neither discover nor produce any thing new, our ideas might be multiply'd by it, but wou'd not be enlarg'd above what they are upon the observation of one single instance.[†] Every enlargement, therefore, (such as the idea of power or connexion) which arises from the multiplicity of similar instances, is copy'd from some effects of the multiplicity, and will be perfectly understood by understanding these effects. Wherever we find any thing new to be discover'd or produc'd by the repetition, there we must place the power, and must never look for it in any other object.

17   But 'tis evident, in the *first* place, that the repetition of like objects in like relations of succession and contiguity *discovers* nothing new in any one of them; since we can draw no inference from it, nor make it a subject either of our demonstrative or probable reasonings; as has been already prov'd.[31] Nay suppose   *SB 164*
we cou'd draw an inference, 'twou'd be of no consequence in the present case;

---

[31] Sect. 6.[†]   *SB 163*

110

since no kind of reasoning can give rise to a new idea, such as this of power is; but wherever we reason, we must antecedently be possest of clear ideas, which may be the objects of our reasoning. The conception always precedes the understanding; and where the one is obscure, the other is uncertain; where the one fails, the other must fail also.

18   *Secondly*, 'Tis certain that this repetition of similar objects in similar situations *produces* nothing new either in these objects, or in any external body. For 'twill readily be allow'd, that the several instances we have of the conjunction of resembling causes and effects are in themselves entirely independent, and that the communication of motion, which I see result at present from the shock of two billiard-balls, is totally distinct from that which I saw result from such an impulse a twelve-month ago. These impulses have no influence on each other. They are entirely divided by time and place; and the one might have existed and communicated motion, tho' the other never had been in being.

19   There is, then, nothing new either discover'd or produc'd in any objects by their constant conjunction, and by the uninterrupted resemblance of their relations of succession and contiguity. But 'tis from this resemblance, that the ideas of necessity, of power, and of efficacy, are deriv'd. These ideas, therefore, represent not any thing, that does or can belong to the objects, which are constantly conjoin'd. This is an argument, which, in every view we can examine it, will be found perfectly unanswerable. Similar instances are still the first source of our idea of power or necessity; at the same time that they have no influence by their similarity either on each other, or on any external object. We must, therefore, turn ourselves to some other quarter to seek the origin of that idea.

20   Tho' the several resembling instances, which give rise to the idea of power,   *SB 165* have no influence on each other, and can never produce any new quality *in the object*, which can be the model of that idea, yet the *observation* of this resemblance produces a new impression *in the mind*, which is its real model. For after we have observ'd the resemblance in a sufficient number of instances, we immediately feel a determination of the mind to pass from one object to its usual attendant, and to conceive it in a stronger light upon account of that relation. This determination is the only effect of the resemblance; and therefore must be the same with power or efficacy, whose idea is deriv'd from the resemblance.[†] The several instances of resembling conjunctions lead us into the notion of power and necessity. These instances are in themselves totally distinct from each other, and have no union but in the mind, which observes them, and collects their ideas. Necessity, then, is the effect of this observation, and is nothing but an internal impression of the mind, or a determination to carry our thoughts from one object to another. Without considering it in this view, we can never arrive at the most distant notion of it, or be able to attribute it either to external or internal objects, to spirit or body, to causes or effects.

21   The necessary connexion betwixt causes and effects is the foundation of our inference from one to the other. The foundation of our inference is the transition arising from the accustom'd union. These are, therefore, the same.

22   The idea of necessity arises from some impression. There is no impression

convey'd by our senses, which can give rise to that idea. It must, therefore, be deriv'd from some internal impression, or impression of reflection. There is no internal impression, which has any relation[†] to the present business, but that propensity, which custom produces, to pass from an object to the idea of its usual attendant. This therefore is the essence of necessity. Upon the whole, necessity is something, that exists in the mind, not in objects; nor is it possible for us ever to form the most distant idea of it, consider'd as a quality in bodies. Either we have no idea of necessity, or necessity is nothing but that determination of the thought to pass from causes to effects and from effects to causes, according to their experienc'd union.

SB 166

23   Thus as the necessity, which makes two times two equal to four, or three angles of a triangle equal to two right ones, lies only in the act of the understanding, by which we consider and compare these ideas; in like manner the necessity or power, which unites causes and effects, lies in the determination of the mind to pass from the one to the other.[†] The efficacy or energy of causes is neither plac'd in the causes themselves, nor in the deity, nor in the concurrence of these two principles; but belongs entirely to the soul, which considers the union of two or more objects in all past instances. 'Tis here that the real power of causes is plac'd, along with their connexion and necessity.

24   I am sensible, that of all the paradoxes, which I have had, or shall hereafter have occasion to advance in the course of this treatise, the present one is the most violent, and that 'tis merely by dint of solid proof and reasoning I can ever hope it will have admission, and overcome the inveterate prejudices of mankind. Before we are reconcil'd to this doctrine, how often must we repeat to ourselves, *that* the simple view of any two objects or actions, however related, can never give us any idea of power, or of a connexion betwixt them: *that* this idea arises from the repetition of their union: *that* the repetition neither discovers nor causes any thing in the objects, but has an influence only on the mind, by that customary transition it produces: *that* this customary transition is, therefore, the same with the power and necessity; which are consequently qualities of perceptions, not of objects, and are internally felt by the soul, and not perceiv'd externally in bodies? There is commonly an astonishment attending every thing extraordinary; and this astonishment changes immediately into the highest degree of esteem or contempt, according as we approve or disapprove of the subject. I am much afraid, that tho' the foregoing reasoning appears to me the shortest and most decisive imaginable; yet with the generality of readers the biass of the mind will prevail, and give them a prejudice against the present doctrine.

SB 167

25   This contrary biass is easily accounted for. 'Tis a common observation, that the mind has a great propensity to spread itself on external objects, and to conjoin with them any internal impressions, which they occasion, and which always make their appearance at the same time that these objects discover themselves to the senses.[†] Thus as certain sounds and smells are always found to attend certain visible objects, we naturally imagine a conjunction, even in place,

betwixt the objects and qualities, tho' the qualities be of such a nature as to admit of no such conjunction, and really exist no where. But of this more fully here-after.[32] Mean while 'tis sufficient to observe, that the same propensity is the reason, why we suppose necessity and power to lie in the objects we consider, not in our mind, that considers them; notwithstanding it is not possible for us to form the most distant idea of that quality, when it is not taken for the determination of the mind, to pass from the idea of an object to that of its usual attendant.

26   But tho' this be the only reasonable account we can give of necessity, the contrary notion is so riveted in the mind from the principles above-mention'd,[†] that I doubt not but my sentiments will be treated by many as extravagant and ridiculous. What! the efficacy of causes lie in the determination of the mind![†] As if causes did not operate entirely independent of the mind, and wou'd not continue their operation, even tho' there was no mind existent to contemplate them, or reason concerning them. Thought may well depend on causes for its operation, but not causes on thought. This is to reverse the order of nature, and make that secondary, which is really primary. To every operation there is a power proportion'd; and this power must be plac'd on the body, that operates. If we remove the power from one cause, we must ascribe it to another: But to remove it from all causes, and bestow it on a being, that is no ways related to the cause or effect, but by perceiving them, is a gross absurdity, and contrary to the most certain principles of human reason.   *SB 168*

27   I can only reply to all these arguments, that the case is here much the same, as if a blind man shou'd pretend to find a great many absurdities in the supposition, that the colour of scarlet is not the same with the sound of a trumpet, nor light the same with solidity.[†] If we have really no idea of a power or efficacy in any object, or of any real connexion betwixt causes and effects, 'twill be to little purpose to prove, that an efficacy is necessary in all operations. We do not understand our own meaning in talking so, but ignorantly confound ideas, which are entirely distinct from each other. I am, indeed, ready to allow, that there may be several qualities both in material and immaterial objects, with which we are utterly unacquainted; and if we please to call these *power* or *efficacy*, 'twill be of little consequence to the world. But when, instead of meaning these unknown qualities, we make the terms of power and efficacy signify something, of which we have a clear idea, and which is incompatible with those objects, to which we apply it, obscurity and error begin then to take place, and we are led astray by a false philosophy. This is the case, when we transfer the determination of the thought to external objects, and suppose any real intelligible connexion betwixt them; that being a quality, which can only belong to the mind that considers them.

28   As to what may be said, that the operations of nature are independent of our thought and reasoning, I allow it; and accordingly have observ'd,[†] that objects bear to each other the relations of contiguity and succession; that like objects

---

[32] Part 4. Sect. 5.[†]   *SB 167*

may be observ'd in several instances to have like relations; and that all this is independent of, and antecedent to the operations of the understanding. But if we go any farther, and ascribe a power or necessary connexion to these objects; this is what we can never observe in them, but must draw the idea of it from what we feel internally in contemplating them. And this I carry so far, that I am ready to convert my present reasoning into an instance of it, by a subtility, which it will not be difficult to comprehend.

29   When any object is presented to us, it immediately conveys to the mind a lively idea of that object, which is usually found to attend it; and this determination of the mind forms the necessary connexion of these objects. But when we change the point of view, from the objects to the perceptions; in that case the impression is to be consider'd as the cause, and the lively idea as the effect; and their necessary connexion is that new determination, which we feel to pass from the idea of the one to that of the other. The uniting principle among our internal perceptions is as unintelligible as that among external objects, and is not known to us any other way than by experience. Now the nature and effects of experience have been already sufficiently examin'd and explain'd. It never gives us any insight into the internal structure or operating principle of objects, but only accustoms the mind to pass from one to another.

30   'Tis now time to collect all the different parts of this reasoning, and by joining them together form an exact definition of the relation of cause and effect, which makes the subject of the present enquiry. This order wou'd not have been excusable, of first examining our inference from the relation before we had explain'd the relation itself, had it been possible to proceed in a different method. But as the nature of the relation depends so much on that of the inference, we have been oblig'd to advance in this seemingly preposterous manner,† and make use of terms before we were able exactly to define them, or fix their meaning. We shall now correct this fault by giving a precise definition of cause and effect.

31   There may two definitions be given of this relation, which are only different, by their presenting a different view of the same object, and making us consider it either as a *philosophical* or as a *natural* relation;† either as a comparison of two ideas, or as an association betwixt them. We may define a CAUSE to be "An object precedent and contiguous to another, and where all the objects resembling the former are plac'd in like relations of precedency and contiguity to those objects, that resemble the latter." If this definition be esteem'd defective, because drawn from objects foreign to the cause, we may substitute this other definition in its place, *viz.* "A CAUSE is an object precedent and contiguous to another, and so united with it, that the idea of the one determines the mind to form the idea of the other, and the impression of the one to form a more lively idea of the other." Shou'd this definition also be rejected for the same reason, I know no other remedy, than that the persons, who express this delicacy,† shou'd substitute a juster definition in its place. But for my part I must own my incapacity for such an undertaking. When I examine with the utmost accuracy those objects, which are commonly denominated causes and effects, I find, in considering a single instance, that the one object is precedent and contiguous to the other; and in

enlarging my view to consider several instances, I find only, that like objects are constantly plac'd in like relations of succession and contiguity. Again, when I consider the influence of this constant conjunction, I perceive, that such a relation can never be an object of reasoning, and can never operate upon the mind, but by means of custom, which determines the imagination to make a transition from the idea of one object to that of its usual attendant, and from the impression of one to a more lively idea of the other. However extraordinary these sentiments may appear, I think it fruitless to trouble myself with any farther enquiry or reasoning upon the subject, but shall repose myself on them as on establish'd maxims.

32   'Twill only be proper, before we leave this subject, to draw some corollaries   *SB 171* from it, by which we may remove several prejudices and popular errors, that have very much prevail'd in philosophy. *First*, We may learn from the foregoing doctrine, that all causes are of the same kind, and that in particular there is no foundation for that distinction, which we sometimes make betwixt efficient causes, and causes *sine qua non*; or betwixt efficient causes, and formal, and material, and exemplary, and final causes.[†] For as our idea of efficiency is deriv'd from the constant conjunction of two objects, wherever this is observ'd, the cause is efficient; and where it is not, there can never be a cause of any kind. For the same reason we must reject the distinction betwixt *cause* and *occasion*,[†] when suppos'd to signify any thing essentially different from each other. If constant conjunction be imply'd in what we call occasion, 'tis a real cause. If not, 'tis no relation at all, and cannot give rise to any argument or reasoning.

33   *Secondly*, The same course of reasoning will make us conclude, that there is but one kind of *necessity*, as there is but one kind of cause, and that the common distinction betwixt *moral* and *physical* necessity is without any foundation in nature.[†] This clearly appears from the precedent explication of necessity. 'Tis the constant conjunction of objects, along with the determination of the mind, which constitutes a physical necessity: And the removal of these is the same thing with *chance*. As objects must either be conjoin'd or not, and as the mind must either be determin'd or not to pass from one object to another, 'tis impossible to admit of any medium betwixt chance and an absolute necessity. In weakening this conjunction and determination you do not change the nature of the necessity; since even in the operation of bodies, these have different degrees of constancy and force, without producing a different species of that relation.

34   The distinction, which we often make betwixt *power* and the *exercise* of it, is equally without foundation.[†]

35   *Thirdly*, We may now be able fully to overcome all that repugnance, which 'tis   *SB 172* so natural for us to entertain against the foregoing reasoning,[†] by which we endeavour'd to prove, that the necessity of a cause to every beginning of existence is not founded on any arguments either demonstrative or intuitive. Such an opinion will not appear strange after the foregoing definitions.[†] If we define a cause to be, *An object precedent and contiguous to another, and where all the objects resembling the former are plac'd in a like relation of priority and contiguity to those objects, that resemble the latter*; we may easily conceive, that there is no absolute

nor metaphysical necessity, that every beginning of existence shou'd be attended with such an object. If we define a cause to be, *An object precedent and contiguous to another, and so united with it in the imagination, that the idea of the one determines the mind to form the idea of the other, and the impression of the one to form a more lively idea of the other*; we shall make still less difficulty of assenting to this opinion. Such an influence on the mind is in itself perfectly extraordinary and incomprehensible; nor can we be certain of its reality, but from experience and observation.

36　　　　I shall add as a *fourth* corollary, that we can never have reason to believe that any object exists, of which we cannot form an idea. For as all our reasonings concerning existence are deriv'd from causation, and as all our reasonings concerning causation are deriv'd from the experienc'd conjunction of objects, not from any reasoning or reflection, the same experience must give us a notion of these objects, and must remove all mystery from our conclusions. This is so evident, that 'twou'd scarce have merited our attention, were it not to obviate certain objections of this kind, which might arise against the following reasonings[†] concerning *matter* and *substance*. I need not observe, that a full knowledge of the object is not requisite, but only of those qualities of it, which we believe to exist.

Sect. 15. *Rules by which to judge of causes and effects*

1　　　According to the precedent doctrine,[†] there are no objects, which by the mere survey, without consulting experience, we can determine to be the causes of any other; and no objects, which we can certainly determine in the same manner not to be the causes. Any thing may produce any thing. Creation, annihilation, motion, reason, volition; all these may arise from one another, or from any other object we can imagine. Nor will this appear strange, if we compare two principles explain'd above,[†] *that the constant conjunction of objects determines their causation*, and *that properly speaking, no objects are contrary to each other, but existence and non-existence.*[33] Where objects are not contrary, nothing hinders them from having that constant conjunction, on which the relation of cause and effect totally depends.[†]

2　　　Since therefore 'tis possible for all objects to become causes or effects to each other, it may be proper to fix some general rules, by which we may know when they really are so.

3　　　1. The cause and effect must be contiguous in space and time.

4　　　2. The cause must be prior to the effect.

5　　　3. There must be a constant union betwixt the cause and effect. 'Tis chiefly this quality, that constitutes the relation.

6　　　4. The same cause always produces the same effect, and the same effect never arises but from the same cause.[†] This principle we derive from experience, and is the source of most of our philosophical reasonings. For when by any clear

---

[33] Part 1. Sect. 5.[†]

experiment we have discover'd the causes or effects of any phænomenon, we immediately extend our observation to every phænomenon of the same kind, without waiting for that constant repetition, from which the first idea of this relation is deriv'd.

7   5. There is another principle, which hangs upon this, *viz.* that where several different objects produce the same effect, it must be by means of some quality, which we discover to be common amongst them.[†] For as like effects imply like causes, we must always ascribe the causation to the circumstance, wherein we discover the resemblance.

8   6. The following principle is founded on the same reason. The difference in the effects of two resembling objects must proceed from that particular, in which they differ.[†] For as like causes always produce like effects, when in any instance we find our expectation to be disappointed, we must conclude that this irregularity proceeds from some difference in the causes.

9   7. When any object encreases or diminishes with the encrease or diminution of its cause, 'tis to be regarded as a compounded effect, deriv'd from the union of the several different effects, which arise from the several different parts of the cause.[†] The absence or presence of one part of the cause is here suppos'd to be always attended with the absence or presence of a proportionable part of the effect. This constant conjunction sufficiently proves, that the one part is the cause of the other. We must, however, beware not to draw such a conclusion from a few experiments. A certain degree of heat gives pleasure; if you diminish that heat, the pleasure diminishes; but it does not follow, that if you augment it beyond a certain degree, the pleasure will likewise augment; for we find that it degenerates into pain.

10   8. The eighth and last rule I shall take notice of is, that an object, which exists for any time in its full perfection without any effect, is not the sole cause of that effect, but requires to be assisted by some other principle, which may forward its influence and operation.[†] For as like effects necessarily follow from like causes, and in a contiguous time and place, their separation for a moment shows, that these causes are not compleat ones.

11   Here is all the LOGIC[†] I think proper to employ in my reasoning; and perhaps even this was not very necessary, but might have been supply'd by the natural principles of our understanding. Our scholastic head-pieces and logicians show no such superiority above the mere vulgar in their reason and ability, as to give us any inclination to imitate them in delivering a long system of rules and precepts to direct our judgment, in philosophy.[†] All the rules of this nature are very easy in their invention, but extremely difficult in their application; and even experimental philosophy,[†] which seems the most natural and simple of any, requires the utmost stretch of human judgment. There is no phænomenon in nature, but what is compounded and modify'd by so many different circumstances, that in order to arrive at the decisive point, we must carefully separate whatever is superfluous, and enquire by new experiments, if every particular circumstance of the first experiment was essential to it. These new experiments are liable to a discussion of the same kind; so that the utmost constancy is requir'd to make us

persevere in our enquiry, and the utmost sagacity to choose the right way among so many that present themselves. If this be the case even in natural philosophy, how much more in moral, where there is a much greater complication of circumstances, and where those views and sentiments, which are essential to any action of the mind, are so implicit and obscure, that they often escape our strictest attention, and are not only unaccountable in their causes, but even unknown in their existence? I am much afraid, lest the small success I meet with in my enquiries will make this observation bear the air of an apology rather than of boasting.

12   If any thing can give me security in this particular, 'twill be the enlarging the sphere of my experiments as much as possible; for which reason it may be proper in this place to examine the reasoning faculty of brutes, as well as that of human creatures.   *SB 176*

Sect. 16. *Of the reason of animals*

1   Next to the ridicule of denying an evident truth, is that of taking much pains to defend it; and no truth appears to me more evident, than that beasts are endow'd with thought and reason as well as men. The arguments are in this case so obvious, that they never escape the most stupid and ignorant.†

2   We are conscious, that we ourselves, in adapting means to ends, are guided by reason and design, and that 'tis not ignorantly nor casually we perform those actions, which tend to self-preservation, to the obtaining pleasure, and avoiding pain. When therefore we see other creatures, in millions of instances, perform like actions, and direct them to like ends, all our principles of reason and probability carry us with an invincible force to believe the existence of a like cause. 'Tis needless in my opinion to illustrate this argument by the enumeration of particulars. The smallest attention will supply us with more than are requisite. The resemblance betwixt the actions of animals and those of men is so entire in this respect, that the very first action of the first animal we shall please to pitch on, will afford us an incontestable argument for the present doctrine.

3   This doctrine is as useful as it is obvious, and furnishes us with a kind of touchstone, by which we may try every system in this species of philosophy. 'Tis from the resemblance of the external actions of animals to those we ourselves perform, that we judge their internal likewise to resemble ours; and the same principle of reasoning, carry'd one step farther, will make us conclude that since our internal actions resemble each other, the causes, from which they are deriv'd, must also be resembling. When any hypothesis, therefore, is advanc'd to explain   *SB 177* a mental operation, which is common to men and beasts, we must apply the same hypothesis to both; and as every true hypothesis will abide this trial, so I may venture to affirm, that no false one will ever be able to endure it. The common defect of those systems, which philosophers have employ'd to account for the actions of the mind, is, that they suppose such a subtility and refinement of thought, as not only exceeds the capacity of mere animals, but even of children and the common people in our own species;† who are notwithstanding suscep-

tible of the same emotions and affections as persons of the most accomplish'd genius and understanding. Such a subtility is a clear proof of the falshood, as the contrary simplicity of the truth, of any system.

4   Let us therefore put our present system concerning the nature of the understanding to this decisive trial, and see whether it will equally account for the reasonings of beasts as for those of the human species.

5   Here we must make a distinction betwixt those actions of animals, which are of a vulgar nature, and seem to be on a level with their common capacities, and those more extraordinary instances of sagacity, which they sometimes discover for their own preservation, and the propagation of their species. A dog, that avoids fire and precipices, that shuns strangers, and caresses his master, affords us an instance of the first kind. A bird, that chooses with such care and nicety the place and materials of her nest, and sits upon her eggs for a due time, and in a suitable season, with all the precaution, that a chymist is capable of in the most delicate projection, furnishes us with a lively instance of the second.

6   As to the former actions, I assert they proceed from a reasoning, that is not in itself different, nor founded on different principles, from that which appears in human nature. 'Tis necessary in the *first* place, that there be some impression   *SB 178* immediately present to their memory or senses, in order to be the foundation of their judgment. From the tone of voice the dog infers his master's anger, and foresees his own punishment. From a certain sensation affecting his smell, he judges his game not to be far distant from him.

7   *Secondly*, The inference he draws from the present impression is built on experience, and on his observation of the conjunction of objects in past instances. As you vary this experience, he varies his reasoning. Make a beating follow upon one sign or motion for some time, and afterwards upon another; and he will successively draw different conclusions, according to his most recent experience.

8   Now let any philosopher make a trial, and endeavour to explain that act of the mind, which we call *belief*, and give an account of the principles, from which it is deriv'd, independent of the influence of custom on the imagination, and let his hypothesis be equally applicable to beasts as to the human species; and after he has done this, I promise to embrace his opinion. But at the same time I demand as an equitable condition, that if my system be the only one, which can answer to all these terms, it may be receiv'd as entirely satisfactory and convincing. And that 'tis the only one, is evident almost without any reasoning. Beasts certainly never perceive any real connexion among objects. 'Tis therefore by experience they infer one from another. They can never by any arguments form a general conclusion, that those objects, of which they have had no experience, resemble those of which they have.[†] 'Tis therefore by means of custom alone, that experience operates upon them. All this was sufficiently evident with respect to man. But with respect to beasts there cannot be the least suspicion of mistake; which must be own'd to be a strong confirmation, or rather an invincible proof of my system.

9   Nothing shows more the force of habit in reconciling us to any phænomenon, than this, that men are not astonish'd at the operations of their own reason, at the same time, that they admire the *instinct* of animals, and find a difficulty in explaining it, merely because it cannot be reduc'd to the very same principles. To consider the matter aright, reason is nothing but a wonderful and unintelligible instinct in our souls,[†] which carries us along a certain train of ideas, and endows them with particular qualities, according to their particular situations and relations. This instinct, 'tis true, arises from past observation and experience; but can any one give the ultimate reason, why past experience and observation produces such an effect, any more than why nature alone shou'd produce it? Nature may certainly produce whatever can arise from habit: Nay, habit is nothing but one of the principles of nature, and derives all its force from that origin.

SB 179

PART 4

Of the sceptical and other systems of philosophy

Sect. 1. *Of scepticism with regard to reason*

1   In all demonstrative sciences the rules are certain and infallible; but when we apply them, our fallible and uncertain faculties are very apt to depart from them, and fall into error. We must, therefore, in every reasoning form a new judgment, as a check or controul on our first judgment or belief; and must enlarge our view to comprehend a kind of history of all the instances, wherein our understanding has deceiv'd us, compar'd with those, wherein its testimony was just and true. Our reason must be consider'd as a kind of cause, of which truth is the natural effect; but such-a-one as by the irruption of other causes, and by the inconstancy of our mental powers, may frequently be prevented. By this means all knowledge degenerates into probability; and this probability is greater or less, according to our experience of the veracity or deceitfulness of our understanding, and according to the simplicity or intricacy of the question.[†]

2   There is no algebraist nor mathematician so expert in his science, as to place entire confidence in any truth immediately upon his discovery of it, or regard it as any thing, but a mere probability. Every time he runs over his proofs, his confidence encreases; but still more by the approbation of his friends; and is rais'd to its utmost perfection by the universal assent and applauses of the learned world. Now 'tis evident, that this gradual encrease of assurance is nothing but the addition of new probabilities, and is deriv'd from the constant union of causes and effects, according to past experience and observation.

3   In accompts of any length or importance, merchants seldom trust to the infallible certainty of numbers for their security; but by the artificial structure of the accompts, produce a probability beyond what is deriv'd from the skill and experience of the accomptant. For that is plainly of itself some degree of probability; tho' uncertain and variable, according to the degrees of his experience and length of the accompt. Now as none will maintain, that our assurance in a long numeration exceeds probability, I may safely affirm, that there scarce is any proposition concerning numbers, of which we can have a fuller security. For 'tis easily possible, by gradually diminishing the numbers, to reduce the longest series of addition to the most simple question, which can be form'd, to an addition of two single numbers; and upon this supposition we shall find it impracticable to show the precise limits of knowledge and of probability, or discover that particular number, at which the one ends and the other begins. But knowledge and probability are of such contrary and disagreeing natures, that they cannot well run insensibly into each other, and that because they will not divide, but must be either entirely present, or entirely absent.[†] Besides, if any single

121

addition were certain, every one wou'd be so, and consequently the whole or total sum; unless the whole can be different from all its parts. I had almost said, that this was certain; but I reflect, that it must reduce *itself*, as well as every other reasoning, and from knowledge degenerate into probability.

4   Since therefore all knowledge resolves itself into probability, and becomes at last of the same nature with that evidence, which we employ in common life, we must now examine this latter species of reasoning, and see on what foundation it stands.

5   In every judgment, which we can form concerning probability, as well as concerning knowledge, we ought always to correct the first judgment, deriv'd *SB 182* from the nature of the object, by another judgment, deriv'd from the nature of the understanding. 'Tis certain a man of solid sense and long experience ought to have, and usually has, a greater assurance in his opinions, than one that is foolish and ignorant, and that our sentiments have different degrees of authority, even with ourselves, in proportion to the degrees of our reason and experience. In the man of the best sense and longest experience, this authority is never entire; since even such-a-one must be conscious of many errors in the past, and must still dread the like for the future. Here then arises a new species of probability to correct and regulate the first, and fix its just standard and proportion. As demonstration is subject to the controul of probability, so is probability liable to a new correction by a reflex act of the mind,[†] wherein the nature of our understanding, and our reasoning from the first probability become our objects.

6   Having thus found in every probability, beside the original uncertainty inherent in the subject, a new uncertainty deriv'd from the weakness of that faculty, which judges, and having adjusted these two together, we are oblig'd by our reason to add a new doubt deriv'd from the possibility of error in the estimation we make of the truth and fidelity of our faculties.[†] This is a doubt, which immediately occurs to us, and of which, if we wou'd closely pursue our reason, we cannot avoid giving a decision. But this decision, tho' it shou'd be favourable to our preceding judgment, being founded only on probability, must weaken still farther our first evidence, and must itself be weaken'd by a fourth doubt of the same kind, and so on *in infinitum*; till at last there remain nothing of the original probability, however great we may suppose it to have been, and however small the diminution by every new uncertainty. No finite object can subsist under a decrease repeated *in infinitum*; and even the vastest quantity, which can enter into human imagination, must in this manner be reduc'd to nothing. Let our first *SB 183* belief be never so strong, it must infallibly perish by passing thro' so many new examinations, of which each diminishes somewhat of its force and vigour. When I reflect on the natural fallibility of my judgment, I have less confidence in my opinions, than when I only consider the objects concerning which I reason; and when I proceed still farther, to turn the scrutiny against every successive estimation I make of my faculties, all the rules of logic require a continual diminution, and at last a total extinction of belief and evidence.

7   Shou'd it here be ask'd me, whether I sincerely assent to this argument, which I seem to take such pains to inculcate, and whether I be really one of those sceptics, who hold that all is uncertain, and that our judgment is not in *any* thing possest of *any* measures of truth and falshood;[†] I shou'd reply, that this question is entirely superfluous, and that neither I, nor any other person was ever sincerely and constantly of that opinion. Nature, by an absolute and uncontroulable necessity has determin'd us to judge as well as to breathe and feel; nor can we any more forbear viewing certain objects in a stronger and fuller light, upon account of their customary connexion with a present impression, than we can hinder ourselves from thinking as long as we are awake, or seeing the surrounding bodies, when we turn our eyes towards them in broad sun-shine. Whoever has taken the pains to refute the cavils of this *total* scepticism, has really disputed without an antagonist, and endeavour'd by arguments to establish a faculty, which nature has antecedently implanted in the mind, and render'd unavoidable.

8   My intention then in displaying so carefully the arguments of that fantastic sect,[†] is only to make the reader sensible of the truth of my hypothesis, *that all our reasonings concerning causes and effects are deriv'd from nothing but custom; and that belief is more properly an act of the sensitive, than of the cogitative part of our natures.*[†] I have here prov'd, that the very same principles, which make us form a decision upon any subject, and correct that decision by the consideration of our genius and capacity,[†] and of the situation of our mind, when we examin'd that subject; I say, I have prov'd, that these same principles, when carry'd farther, and apply'd to every new reflex judgment, must, by continually diminishing the original evidence, at last reduce it to nothing, and utterly subvert all belief and opinion. If belief, therefore, were a simple act of the thought, without any peculiar manner of conception, or the addition of a force and vivacity, it must infallibly destroy itself, and in every case terminate in a total suspence of judgment. But as experience will sufficiently convince any one, who thinks it worth while to try, that tho' he can find no error in the foregoing arguments,[†] yet he still continues to believe, and think, and reason as usual, he may safely conclude, that his reasoning and belief is some sensation or peculiar manner of conception, which 'tis impossible for mere ideas and reflections to destroy.

SB 184

9   But here, perhaps, it may be demanded, how it happens, even upon my hypothesis, that these arguments above-explain'd produce not a total suspence of judgment, and after what manner the mind ever retains a degree of assurance in any subject? For as these new probabilities, which by their repetition perpetually diminish the original evidence, are founded on the very same principles, whether of thought or sensation, as the primary judgment, it may seem unavoidable, that in either case they must equally subvert it, and by the opposition, either of contrary thoughts or sensations, reduce the mind to a total uncertainty. I suppose, there is some question propos'd to me, and that after revolving over the impressions of my memory and senses, and carrying my thoughts from them to such objects, as are commonly conjoin'd with them, I feel a stronger and more

forcible conception on the one side, than on the other. This strong conception forms my first decision. I suppose, that afterwards I examine my judgment itself, and observing from experience, that 'tis sometimes just and sometimes erroneous, I consider it as regulated by contrary principles or causes, of which some *SB 185* lead to truth, and some to error; and in ballancing these contrary causes, I diminish by a new probability the assurance of my first decision. This new probability is liable to the same diminution as the foregoing, and so on, *in infinitum.* 'Tis therefore demanded, *How it happens, that even after all we retain a degree of belief, which is sufficient for our purpose, either in philosophy or common life?*

10   I answer, that after the first and second decision; as the action of the mind becomes forc'd and unnatural, and the ideas faint and obscure; tho' the principles of judgment, and the ballancing of opposite causes be the same as at the very beginning; yet their influence on the imagination, and the vigour they add to, or diminish from the thought, is by no means equal. Where the mind reaches not its objects with easiness and facility, the same principles have not the same effect as in a more natural conception of the ideas; nor does the imagination feel a sensation, which holds any proportion with that which arises from its common judgments and opinions. The attention is on the stretch: The posture of the mind is uneasy; and the spirits being diverted from their natural course, are not govern'd in their movements by the same laws, at least not to the same degree, as when they flow in their usual channel.[†]

11   If we desire similar instances, 'twill not be very difficult to find them. The present subject of metaphysics will supply us abundantly. The same argument, which wou'd have been esteem'd convincing in a reasoning concerning history or politics, has little or no influence in these abstruser subjects, even tho' it be perfectly comprehended; and that because there is requir'd a study and an effort of thought, in order to its being comprehended: And this effort of thought disturbs the operation of our sentiments, on which the belief depends. The case is the same in other subjects. The straining of the imagination always hinders the regular flowing of the passions and sentiments. A tragic poet, that wou'd repre- *SB 186* sent his heroes as very ingenious and witty in their misfortunes, wou'd never touch the passions.[†] As the emotions of the soul prevent any subtile reasoning and reflection, so these latter actions of the mind are equally prejudicial to the former.[†] The mind, as well as the body, seems to be endow'd with a certain precise degree of force and activity, which it never employs in one action, but at the expence of all the rest. This is more evidently true, where the actions are of quite different natures; since in that case the force of the mind is not only diverted, but even the disposition chang'd, so as to render us incapable of a sudden transition from one action to the other, and still more of performing both at once. No wonder, then, the conviction, which arises from a subtile reasoning, diminishes in proportion to the efforts, which the imagination makes to enter into the reasoning, and to conceive it in all its parts. Belief, being a lively conception, can never be entire, where it is not founded on something natural and easy.

12   This I take to be the true state of the question, and cannot approve of that

expeditious way, which some take with the sceptics,[†] to reject at once all their arguments without enquiry or examination. If the sceptical reasonings be strong, say they, 'tis a proof, that reason may have some force and authority: If weak, they can never be sufficient to invalidate all the conclusions of our understanding. This argument is not just; because the sceptical reasonings, were it possible for them to exist, and were they not destroy'd by their subtility, wou'd be successively both strong and weak, according to the successive dispositions of the mind. Reason first appears in possession of the throne, prescribing laws, and imposing maxims, with an absolute sway and authority. Her enemy,[†] therefore, is oblig'd to take shelter under her protection, and by making use of rational arguments to prove the fallaciousness and imbecility of reason, produces, in a manner, a patent under her hand and seal.[†] This patent has at first an authority, proportion'd to the present and immediate authority of reason, from which it is deriv'd. But as it is suppos'd to be contradictory to reason, it gradually diminishes the force of that governing power, and its own at the same time; till at last they both vanish away into nothing, by a regular and just diminution. The sceptical and dogmatical reasons[†] are of the same kind, tho' contrary in their operation and tendency; so that where the latter is strong, it has an enemy of equal force in the former to encounter; and as their forces were at first equal, they still continue so, as long as either of them subsists; nor does one of them lose any force in the contest, without taking as much from its antagonist. 'Tis happy, therefore, that nature breaks the force of all sceptical arguments in time, and keeps them from having any considerable influence on the understanding. Were we to trust entirely to their self-destruction, that can never take place, till they have first subverted all conviction, and have totally destroy'd human reason.

SB 187

Sect. 2. *Of scepticism with regard to the senses*

1   Thus the sceptic still continues to reason and believe, even tho' he asserts, that he cannot defend his reason by reason; and by the same rule he must assent to the principle concerning the existence of body, tho' he cannot pretend by any arguments of philosophy to maintain its veracity. Nature has not left this to his choice, and has doubtless esteem'd it an affair of too great importance to be trusted to our uncertain reasonings and speculations. We may well ask, *What causes induce us to believe in the existence of body?* but 'tis in vain to ask, *Whether there be body or not?* That is a point, which we must take for granted in all our reasonings.

2   The subject, then, of our present enquiry is concerning the *causes* which induce us to believe in the existence of body: And my reasonings on this head I shall begin with a distinction, which at first sight may seem superfluous, but which will contribute very much to the perfect understanding of what follows. We ought to examine apart those two questions, which are commonly confounded together, *viz.* why we attribute a CONTINU'D existence to objects, even when they are not present to the senses; and why we suppose them to have an

SB 188

existence DISTINCT from the mind and perception?[†] Under this last head I comprehend their situation as well as relations, their *external* position as well as the *independence* of their existence and operation. These two questions concerning the continu'd and distinct existence of body are intimately connected together. For if the objects of our senses continue to exist, even when they are not perceiv'd, their existence is of course independent of and distinct from the perception; and *vice versa*, if their existence be independent of the perception and distinct from it, they must continue to exist, even tho' they be not perceiv'd.[†] But tho' the decision of the one question decides the other; yet that we may the more easily discover the principles of human nature, from whence the decision arises, we shall carry along with us this distinction, and shall consider, whether it be the *senses*, *reason*, or the *imagination*, that produces the opinion of a *continu'd* or of a *distinct* existence. These are the only questions, that are intelligible on the present subject. For as to the notion of external existence, when taken for something specifically different from our perceptions, we have already shown its absurdity.[34]

3   To begin with the SENSES, 'tis evident these faculties are incapable of giving rise to the notion of the *continu'd* existence of their objects, after they no longer appear to the senses. For that is a contradiction in terms,[†] and supposes that the senses continue to operate, even after they have ceas'd all manner of operation. These faculties, therefore, if they have any influence in the present case, must produce the opinion of a distinct, not of a continu'd existence; and in order to that, must present their impressions either as images and representations, or as these very distinct and external existences.[†]   *SB 189*

4   That our senses offer not their impressions as the images of something *distinct*, or *independent*, and *external*, is evident; because they convey to us nothing but a single perception, and never give us the least intimation of any thing beyond. A single perception can never produce the idea of a double existence,[†] but by some inference either of the reason or imagination. When the mind looks farther than what immediately appears to it, its conclusions can never be put to the account of[†] the senses; and it certainly looks farther, when from a single perception it infers a double existence, and supposes the relations of resemblance and causation betwixt them.[†]

5   If our senses, therefore, suggest any idea of distinct existences, they must convey the impressions as those very existences, by a kind of fallacy and illusion. Upon this head we may observe, that all sensations are felt by the mind, such as they really are, and that when we doubt, whether they present themselves as distinct objects, or as mere impressions, the difficulty is not concerning their nature, but concerning their relations and situation.[†] Now if the senses presented our impressions as external to, and independent of ourselves, both the objects and ourselves must be obvious to our senses, otherwise they cou'd not be compar'd by these faculties. The difficulty, then, is how far we are *ourselves* the objects of our senses.

---

[34] Part 2. Sect. 6.[†]   *SB 188*

6   'Tis certain there is no question in philosophy more abstruse than that concerning identity, and the nature of the uniting principle, which constitutes a person.† So far from being able by our senses merely to determine this question, we must have recourse to the most profound metaphysics to give a satisfactory answer to it; and in common life 'tis evident these ideas of self and person are never very fix'd nor determinate. 'Tis absurd, therefore, to imagine the senses   *SB 190* can ever distinguish betwixt ourselves and external objects.

7   Add to this, that every impression, external and internal, passions, affections, sensations, pains and pleasures, are originally on the same footing; and that whatever other differences we may observe among them, they appear, all of them, in their true colours, as impressions or perceptions. And indeed, if we consider the matter aright, 'tis scarce possible it shou'd be otherwise, nor is it conceivable that our senses shou'd be more capable of deceiving us in the situation and relations, than in the nature of our impressions. For since all actions and sensations of the mind are known to us by consciousness,† they must necessarily appear in every particular what they are, and be what they appear. Every thing that enters the mind, being in *reality* a perception, 'tis impossible any thing shou'd to *feeling* appear different. This were to suppose, that even where we are most intimately conscious, we might be mistaken.

8   But not to lose time in examining, whether 'tis possible for our senses to deceive us, and represent our perceptions as distinct from ourselves, that is as *external* to and *independent* of us; let us consider whether they really do so, and whether this error proceeds from an immediate sensation, or from some other causes.

9   To begin with the question concerning *external* existence, it may perhaps be said, that setting aside the metaphysical question of the identity of a thinking substance, our own body evidently belongs to us; and as several impressions appear exterior to the body, we suppose them also exterior to ourselves. The paper, on which I write at present, is beyond my hand. The table is beyond the paper. The walls of the chamber beyond the table. And in casting my eye towards the window, I perceive a great extent of fields and buildings beyond my chamber. From all this it may be inferr'd, that no other faculty is requir'd, beside the senses, to convince us of the external existence of body. But to prevent this infer-   *SB 191* ence, we need only weigh the three following considerations. *First*, That, properly speaking, 'tis not our body we perceive, when we regard our limbs and members, but certain impressions, which enter by the senses; so that the ascribing a real and corporeal existence to these impressions, or to their objects, is an act of the mind as difficult to explain, as that which we examine at present. *Secondly*, Sounds, and tastes, and smells, tho' commonly regarded by the mind as continu'd independent qualities, appear not to have any existence in extension, and consequently cannot appear to the senses as situated externally to the body. The reason, why we ascribe a place to them, shall be consider'd afterwards.[35] *Thirdly*, Even our sight informs us not of distance or outness (so to speak)

---

[35] Sect. 5.†

immediately and without a certain reasoning and experience, as is acknowledg'd by the most rational philosophers.[†]

10   As to the *independency* of our perceptions on ourselves, this can never be an object of the senses;[†] but any opinion we form concerning it, must be deriv'd from experience and observation: And we shall see afterwards,[†] that our conclusions from experience are far from being favourable to the doctrine of the independency of our perceptions. Mean while we may observe that when we talk of real distinct existences, we have commonly more in our eye their independency than external situation in place, and think an object has a sufficient reality,[†] when its being is uninterrupted, and independent of the incessant revolutions,[†] which we are conscious of in ourselves.

11   Thus to resume what I have said concerning the senses; they give us no notion of continu'd existence, because they cannot operate beyond the extent, in which they really operate. They as little produce the opinion of a distinct existence, because they neither can offer it to the mind as represented, nor as original. To offer it as represented, they must present both an object and an image. To make it appear as original, they must convey a falsehood; and this falsehood must lie in the relations and situation: In order to which they must be able to compare the object with ourselves; and even in that case they do not, nor is it possible they shou'd, deceive us. We may, therefore, conclude with certainty, that the opinion of a continu'd and of a distinct existence never arises from the senses. *SB 192*

12   To confirm this we may observe, that there are three different kinds of impressions convey'd by the senses.[†] The first are those of the figure, bulk, motion and solidity of bodies. The second those of colours, tastes, smells, sounds, heat and cold. The third are the pains and pleasures, that arise from the application of objects to our bodies, as by the cutting of our flesh with steel, and such like. Both philosophers and the vulgar suppose the first of these to have a distinct continu'd existence. The vulgar only regard the second as on the same footing. Both philosophers and the vulgar, again, esteem the third to be merely perceptions; and consequently interrupted and dependent beings.[†]

13   Now 'tis evident, that, whatever may be our philosophical opinion, colours, sounds, heat and cold, as far as appears to the senses, exist after the same manner with motion and solidity, and that the difference we make betwixt them in this respect, arises not from the mere perception.[†] So strong is the prejudice for the distinct continu'd existence of the former qualities, that when the contrary opinion[†] is advanc'd by modern philosophers, people imagine they can almost refute it from their feeling and experience, and that their very senses contradict this philosophy. 'Tis also evident, that colours, sounds, *&c.* are originally on the same footing with the pain that arises from steel, and pleasure that proceeds from a fire; and that the difference betwixt them is founded neither on perception nor reason, but on the imagination. For as they are confest to be, both of them, nothing but perceptions arising from the particular configurations and *SB 193* motions of the parts of body, wherein possibly can their difference consist? Upon the whole, then, we may conclude, that as far as the senses are judges, all perceptions are the same in the manner of their existence.

14   We may also observe in this instance of sounds and colours, that we can attribute a distinct continu'd existence to objects without ever consulting REASON, or weighing our opinions by any philosophical principles. And indeed, whatever convincing arguments philosophers may fancy they can produce to establish the belief of objects independent of the mind, 'tis obvious these arguments are known but to very few, and that 'tis not by them, that children, peasants, and the greatest part of mankind are induc'd to attribute objects to some impressions, and deny them to others.[†] Accordingly we find, that all the conclusions, which the vulgar form on this head, are directly contrary to those, which are confirm'd by philosophy. For philosophy informs us, that every thing, which appears to the mind, is nothing but a perception, and is interrupted, and dependent on the mind; whereas the vulgar confound perceptions and objects, and attribute a distinct continu'd existence to the very things they feel or see.[†] This sentiment, then, as it is entirely unreasonable,[†] must proceed from some other faculty than the understanding. To which we may add, that as long as we take our perceptions and objects to be the same, we can never infer the existence of the one from that of the other, nor form any argument from the relation of cause and effect; which is the only one that can assure us of matter of fact. Even after we distinguish our perceptions from our objects, 'twill appear presently,[†] that we are still incapable of reasoning from the existence of one to that of the other: So that upon the whole our reason neither does, nor is it possible it ever shou'd, upon any supposition, give us an assurance of the continu'd and distinct existence of body. That opinion must be entirely owing to the IMAGINATION;[†] which must now be the subject of our enquiry.

15   Since all impressions are internal and perishing existences, and appear as such, the notion of their distinct and continu'd existence must arise from a concurrence of some of their qualities with the qualities of the imagination; and since this notion does not extend to all of them, it must arise from certain qualities peculiar to some impressions. 'Twill therefore be easy for us to discover these qualities by a comparison of the impressions, to which we attribute a distinct and continu'd existence, with those, which we regard as internal and perishing.   *SB 194*

16   We may observe, then, that 'tis neither upon account of the involuntariness of certain impressions, as is commonly suppos'd, nor of their superior force and violence,[†] that we attribute to them a reality, and continu'd existence, which we refuse to others, that are voluntary or feeble. For 'tis evident our pains and pleasures, our passions and affections, which we never suppose to have any existence beyond our perception, operate with greater violence, and are equally involuntary, as the impressions of figure and extension, colour and sound, which we suppose to be permanent beings. The heat of a fire,[†] when moderate, is suppos'd to exist in the fire; but the pain, which it causes upon a near approach, is not taken to have any being except in the perception.

17   These vulgar opinions, then, being rejected, we must search for some other hypothesis, by which we may discover those peculiar qualities in our impressions, which makes us attribute to them a distinct and continu'd existence.

18   After a little examination, we shall find, that all those objects, to which we attribute a continu'd existence, have a peculiar *constancy*,[†] which distinguishes them from the impressions, whose existence depends upon our perception. These mountains, and houses, and trees,[†] which lie at present under my eye, have always appear'd to me in the same order; and when I lose sight of them by shutting my eyes or turning my head, I soon after find them return upon me without the least alteration. My bed and table, my books and papers, present themselves in the same uniform manner, and change not upon account of any interruption in my seeing or perceiving them. This is the case with all the impressions, whose objects are suppos'd to have an external existence; and is the case with no other impressions, whether gentle or violent, voluntary or involuntary. *SB 195*

19   This constancy, however, is not so perfect as not to admit of very considerable exceptions. Bodies often change their position and qualities, and after a little absence or interruption may become hardly knowable. But here 'tis observable, that even in these changes they preserve a *coherence*, and have a regular dependence on each other; which is the foundation of a kind of reasoning from causation, and produces the opinion of their continu'd existence. When I return to my chamber after an hour's absence, I find not my fire in the same situation, in which I left it: But then I am accustom'd in other instances to see a like alteration produc'd in a like time, whether I am present or absent, near or remote. This coherence, therefore, in their changes is one of the characteristics of external objects, as well as their constancy.

20   Having found that the opinion of the continu'd existence of body depends on the COHERENCE and CONSTANCY of certain impressions, I now proceed to examine after what manner these qualities give rise to so extraordinary an opinion.[†] To begin with the coherence; we may observe, that tho' those internal impressions, which we regard as fleeting and perishing,[†] have also a certain coherence or regularity in their appearances, yet 'tis of somewhat a different nature, from that which we discover in bodies. Our passions are found by experience to have a mutual connexion with and dependance on each other; but on no occasion is it necessary to suppose, that they have existed and operated, when they were not perceiv'd, in order to preserve the same dependance and connexion, of which we have had experience. The case is not the same with relation to external objects. Those require a continu'd existence, or otherwise lose, in a great measure, the *SB 196* regularity of their operation. I am here seated in my chamber with my face to the fire; and all the objects, that strike my senses, are contain'd in a few yards around me. My memory, indeed, informs me of the existence of many objects; but then this information extends not beyond their past existence, nor do either my senses or memory give any testimony to the continuance of their being. When therefore I am thus seated, and revolve over these thoughts, I hear on a sudden a noise as of a door turning upon its hinges; and a little after see a porter, who advances towards me. This gives occasion to many new reflections and reasonings. First, I never have observ'd, that this noise cou'd proceed from any thing but the motion of a door; and therefore conclude, that the present phænomenon is a contradiction to all past experience, unless the door, which I remember on

the other side of the chamber, be still in being. Again, I have always found, that a human body was possest of a quality, which I call gravity, and which hinders it from mounting in the air, as this porter must have done to arrive at my chamber, unless the stairs I remember be not annihilated by my absence. But this is not all. I receive a letter, which upon opening I perceive by the hand-writing and sub-scription to have come from a friend, who says he is two hundred leagues distant. 'Tis evident I can never account for this phænomenon, conformable to my ex-perience in other instances, without spreading out in my mind the whole sea and continent betwixt us, and supposing the effects and continu'd existence of posts[†] and ferries, according to my memory and observation. To consider these phænomena of the porter and letter in a certain light, they are contradictions to[†] common experience, and may be regarded as objections to those maxims, which we form concerning the connexions of causes and effects. I am accustom'd to hear such a sound, and see such an object in motion at the same time. I have not receiv'd in this particular instance both these perceptions. These observations are contrary, unless I suppose that the door still remains, and that it was open'd   *SB 197* without my perceiving it: And this supposition, which was at first entirely arbi-trary and hypothetical,[†] acquires a force and evidence by its being the only one, upon which I can reconcile these contradictions.[†] There is scarce a moment of my life, wherein there is not a similar instance presented to me, and I have not occasion to suppose the continu'd existence of objects, in order to connect their past and present appearances, and give them such an union with each other, as I have found by experience to be suitable to their particular natures and circum-stances. Here then I am naturally led to regard the world, as something real and durable, and as preserving its existence, even when it is no longer present to my perception.

21   But tho' this conclusion from the coherence of appearances may seem to be of the same nature with our reasonings concerning causes and effects;[†] as being deriv'd from custom, and regulated by past experience; we shall find[†] upon examination, that they are at the bottom considerably different from each other, and that this inference arises from the understanding, and from custom in an indirect and oblique manner. For 'twill readily be allow'd, that since nothing is ever really present to the mind, besides its own perceptions, 'tis not only impos-sible, that any habit shou'd ever be acquir'd otherwise than by the regular suc-cession of these perceptions, but also that any habit shou'd ever exceed that degree of regularity. Any degree, therefore, of regularity in our perceptions, can never be a foundation for us to infer a greater degree of regularity in some objects, which are not perceiv'd; since this supposes a contradiction, *viz.* a habit acquir'd by what was never present to the mind. But 'tis evident, that whenever we infer the continu'd existence of the objects of sense from their coherence, and the frequency of their union, 'tis in order to bestow on the objects a greater regularity than what is observ'd in our mere perceptions. We remark a con-nexion betwixt two kinds of objects in their past appearance to the senses, but are   *SB 198* not able to observe this connexion to be perfectly constant, since the turning about of our head, or the shutting of our eyes is able to break it. What then do we

suppose in this case, but that these objects still continue their usual connexion, notwithstanding their apparent interruption, and that the irregular appearances are join'd by something, of which we are insensible? But as all reasoning concerning matters of fact arises only from custom, and custom can only be the effect of repeated perceptions, the extending of custom and reasoning beyond the perceptions can never be the direct and natural effect of the constant repetition and connexion, but must arise from the co-operation of some other principles.

22   I have already observ'd,[36] in examining the foundation of mathematics, that the imagination, when set into any train of thinking, is apt to continue, even when its object fails it, and like a galley put in motion by the oars, carries on its course without any new impulse. This I have assign'd† for the reason, why, after considering several loose standards of equality, and correcting them by each other, we proceed to imagine so correct and exact a standard of that relation, as is not liable to the least error or variation. The same principle makes us easily entertain this opinion of the continu'd existence of body. Objects have a certain coherence even as they appear to our senses; but this coherence is much greater and more uniform, if we suppose the objects to have a continu'd existence; and as the mind is once in the train of observing an uniformity among objects, it naturally continues, till it renders the uniformity as compleat as possible. The simple supposition of their continu'd existence suffices for this purpose, and gives us a notion of a much greater regularity among objects, than what they have when we look no farther than our senses.

23   But whatever force we may ascribe to this principle, I am afraid 'tis too weak to support alone so vast an edifice, as is that of the continu'd existence of all exter- *SB 199* nal bodies; and that we must join the *constancy*† of their appearance to the *coherence*, in order to give a satisfactory account of that opinion. As the explication of this will lead me into a considerable compass of very profound reasoning; I think it proper, in order to avoid confusion, to give a short sketch or abridgment of my system, and afterwards draw out all its parts in their full compass. This inference from the constancy of our perceptions, like the precedent from their coherence, gives rise to the opinion of the *continu'd* existence of body, which is prior to that of its *distinct* existence, and produces that latter principle.

24   When we have been accustom'd to observe a constancy in certain impressions, and have found, that the perception of the sun or ocean, for instance, returns upon us after an absence or annihilation with like parts and in a like order, as at its first appearance, we are not apt to regard these interrupted perceptions as different, (which they really are) but on the contrary consider them as individually the same, upon account of their resemblance. But as this interruption of their existence is contrary to their perfect identity, and makes us regard the first impression as annihilated, and the second as newly created, we find ourselves somewhat at a loss, and are involv'd in a kind of contradiction. In order to free ourselves

---

[36] Part 2. Sect. 4.†   *SB 198*

from this difficulty, we disguise, as much as possible, the interruption, or rather remove it entirely, by supposing that these interrupted perceptions are connected by a real existence, of which we are insensible. This supposition, or idea of continu'd existence, acquires a force and vivacity from the memory of these broken impressions, and from that propensity, which they give us, to suppose them the same; and according to the precedent reasoning,[†] the very essence of belief consists in the force and vivacity of the conception.

25   In order to justify this system, there are four things requisite. *First*, To explain the *principium individuationis*, or principle of identity.[†] *Secondly*, Give a reason,   *SB 200* why the resemblance of our broken and interrupted perceptions induces us to attribute an identity to them.[†] *Thirdly*, Account for that propensity, which this illusion gives, to unite these broken appearances by a continu'd existence.[†] *Fourthly* and lastly, Explain that force and vivacity of conception, which arises from the propensity.[†]

26   *First*, As to the principle of individuation;[†] we may observe, that the view of any one object is not sufficient to convey the idea of identity. For in that proposition, *an object is the same with itself*, if the idea express'd by the word, *object*, were no ways distinguish'd from that meant by *itself*, we really shou'd mean nothing, nor wou'd the proposition contain a predicate and a subject, which however are imply'd in this affirmation.[†] One single object conveys the idea of unity, not that of identity.[†]

27   On the other hand, a multiplicity of objects can never convey this idea, however resembling they may be suppos'd.[†] The mind always pronounces the one not to be the other, and considers them as forming two, three, or any determinate number of objects, whose existences are entirely distinct and independent.

28   Since then both number and unity are incompatible with the relation of identity, it must lie in something that is neither of them.[†] But to tell the truth, at first sight this seems utterly impossible. Betwixt unity and number there can be no medium; no more than betwixt existence and non–existence. After one object is suppos'd to exist, we must either suppose another also to exist; in which case we have the idea of number: Or we must suppose it not to exist; in which case the first object remains at unity.

29   To remove this difficulty, let us have recourse to the idea of time or duration. I have already observ'd,[37] that time, in a strict sense, implies succession, and that when we apply its idea to any unchangeable object, 'tis only by a fiction of the imagination, by which the unchangeable object is suppos'd to participate of the   *SB 201* changes of the co–existent objects, and in particular of that of our perceptions. This fiction of the imagination almost universally takes place; and 'tis by means of it, that a single object, plac'd before us, and survey'd for any time without our discovering in it any interruption or variation, is able to give us a notion of identity. For when we consider any two points of this time,[†] we may place them in

---

37 Part 2. Sect. 5.[†]   *SB 200*

different lights: We may either survey them at the very same instant; in which case they give us the idea of number, both by themselves and by the object; which must be multiply'd,[†] in order to be conceiv'd at once, as existent in these two different points of time: Or on the other hand, we may trace the succession of time by a like succession of ideas, and conceiving first one moment, along with the object then existent, imagine afterwards a change in the time without any *variation* or *interruption* in the object; in which case it gives us the idea of unity.[†] Here then is an idea, which is a medium betwixt unity and number; or more properly speaking, is either of them, according to the view, in which we take it: And this idea we call that of identity. We cannot, in any propriety of speech, say, that an object is the same with itself, unless we mean, that the object existent at one time is the same with itself existent at another. By this means we make a difference, betwixt the idea meant by the word, *object*, and that meant by *itself*, without going the length of number,[†] and at the same time without restraining ourselves to a strict and absolute unity.[†]

30   Thus the principle of individuation is nothing but the *invariableness* and *uninterruptedness*[†] of any object, thro' a suppos'd variation of time, by which the mind can trace it in the different periods of its existence, without any break of the view,[†] and without being oblig'd to form the idea of multiplicity or number.

31   I now proceed to explain the *second* part of my system,[†] and show why the constancy of our perceptions makes us ascribe to them a perfect numerical *SB 202* identity, tho' there be very long intervals betwixt their appearance, and they have only one of the essential qualities of identity, viz. *invariableness.* That I may avoid all ambiguity and confusion on this head, I shall observe, that I here account for the opinions and belief of the vulgar with regard to the existence of body; and therefore must entirely conform myself to their manner of thinking and of expressing themselves. Now we have already observ'd,[†] that however philosophers may distinguish betwixt the objects and perceptions of the senses; which they suppose co-existent and resembling; yet this is a distinction, which is not comprehended by the generality of mankind, who as they perceive only one being, can never assent to the opinion of a double existence and representation.[†] Those very sensations, which enter by the eye or ear, are with them the true objects, nor can they readily conceive that this pen or paper, which is immediately perceiv'd, represents another, which is different from, but resembling it. In order, therefore, to accommodate myself to their notions, I shall at first suppose, that there is only a single existence, which I shall call indifferently *object* or *perception*, according as it shall seem best to suit my purpose, understanding by both of them what any common man means by a hat, or shoe, or stone, or any other impression, convey'd to him by his senses. I shall be sure to give warning,[†] when I return to a more philosophical way of speaking and thinking.

32   To enter, therefore, upon the question concerning the source of the error and deception with regard to identity, when we attribute it to our resembling perceptions, notwithstanding their interruption; I must here recal an observation,

which I have already prov'd and explain'd.[38] Nothing is more apt to make us mistake one idea for another, than any relation betwixt them, which associates them together in the imagination, and makes it pass with facility from one to the other. Of all relations, that of resemblance is in this respect the most efficacious; *SB 203* and that because it not only causes an association of ideas, but also of dispositions, and makes us conceive the one idea by an act or operation of the mind, similar to that by which we conceive the other. This circumstance I have observ'd[†] to be of great moment; and we may establish it for a general rule, that whatever ideas place the mind in the same disposition or in similar ones, are very apt to be confounded. The mind readily passes from one to the other, and perceives not the change without a strict attention, of which, generally speaking, 'tis wholly incapable.

33   In order to apply this general maxim, we must first examine the disposition of the mind in viewing any object which preserves a perfect identity,[†] and then find some other object, that is confounded with it, by causing a similar disposition. When we fix our thought on any object, and suppose it to continue the same for some time; 'tis evident we suppose the change to lie only in the time, and never exert ourselves to produce any new image or idea of the object. The faculties of the mind repose themselves in a manner, and take no more exercise, than what is necessary to continue that idea, of which we were formerly possest, and which subsists without variation or interruption. The passage from one moment to another is scarce felt, and distinguishes not itself by a different perception or idea, which may require a different direction of the spirits, in order to its conception.

34   Now what other objects, beside identical ones, are capable of placing the mind in the same disposition, when it considers them, and of causing the same uninterrupted passage of the imagination from one idea to another? This question is of the last importance. For if we can find any such objects, we may certainly conclude, from the foregoing principle,[†] that they are very naturally confounded with identical ones, and are taken for them in most of our reasonings. But tho' this question be very important, 'tis not very difficult nor doubtful. For I imme- *SB 204* diately reply, that a succession of related objects places the mind in this disposition, and is consider'd with the same smooth and uninterrupted progress of the imagination, as attends the view of the same invariable object. The very nature and essence of relation is to connect our ideas with each other, and upon the appearance of one, to facilitate the transition to its correlative. The passage betwixt related ideas is, therefore, so smooth and easy, that it produces little alteration on the mind, and seems like the continuation of the same action; and as the continuation of the same action is an effect of the continu'd view of the same object, 'tis for this reason we attribute sameness to every succession of related objects. The thought slides along the succession with equal facility, as if it consider'd only one object; and therefore confounds the succession with the identity.

[38] Part 2. Sect. 5.[†]   *SB 202*

35   We shall afterwards[†] see many instances of this tendency of relation to make
us ascribe an *identity* to *different* objects; but shall here confine ourselves to the
present subject. We find by experience, that there is such a *constancy* in almost all
the impressions of the senses, that their interruption produces no alteration
on them, and hinders them not from returning the same in appearance and in
situation as at their first existence. I survey the furniture of my chamber; I shut
my eyes, and afterwards open them; and find the new perceptions to resemble
perfectly those, which formerly struck my senses. This resemblance is observ'd
in a thousand instances, and naturally connects together our ideas of these interrupted perceptions by the strongest relation, and conveys the mind with an easy
transition from one to another. An easy transition or passage of the imagination,
along the ideas of these different and interrupted perceptions, is almost the same
disposition of mind with that in which we consider one constant and uninterrupted perception. 'Tis therefore very natural for us to mistake the one for the
other.[39]

36   The persons, who entertain this opinion concerning the identity of our   *SB 205*
resembling perceptions, are in general all the unthinking and unphilosophical
part of mankind, (that is, all of us, at one time or other) and consequently such as
suppose their perceptions to be their only objects, and never think of a double
existence internal and external, representing and represented. The very image,
which is present to the senses, is with us the real body; and 'tis to these interrupted images we ascribe a perfect identity. But as the interruption of the
appearance seems contrary to the identity, and naturally leads us to regard these
resembling perceptions as different from each other, we here find ourselves at a
loss how to reconcile such opposite opinions. The smooth passage of the imagination along the ideas of the resembling perceptions makes us ascribe to them a
perfect identity. The interrupted manner of their appearance makes us consider
them as so many resembling, but still distinct beings, which appear after certain
intervals. The perplexity arising from this contradiction produces a propension
to unite these broken appearances by the fiction of a continu'd existence, which
is the *third* part of that hypothesis I propos'd to explain.[†]

37   Nothing is more certain from experience, than that any contradiction either to
the sentiments or passions gives a sensible uneasiness, whether it proceeds from
without or from within; from the opposition of external objects, or from the
combat of internal principles. On the contrary, whatever strikes in with the

---

[39] This reasoning, it must be confest, is somewhat abstruse, and difficult to be comprehended;   *SB 204–5*
but it is remarkable, that this very difficulty may be converted into a proof of the reasoning. We may
observe, that there are two relations, and both of them resemblances, which contribute to our mis-
taking the succession of our interrupted perceptions for an identical object. The first is, the resemblance of the perceptions: The second is the resemblance, which the act of the mind in surveying a
succession of resembling objects bears to that in surveying an identical object. Now these resemblances we are apt to confound with each other; and 'tis natural we shou'd, according to this very
reasoning. But let us keep them distinct, and we shall find no difficulty in conceiving the precedent
argument.[†]

natural propensities, and either externally forwards their satisfaction, or internally concurs with their movements, is sure to give a sensible pleasure. Now *SB 206* there being here an opposition betwixt the notion of the identity of resembling perceptions, and the interruption of their appearance, the mind must be uneasy in that situation, and will naturally seek relief from the uneasiness. Since the uneasiness arises from the opposition of two contrary principles, it must look for relief by sacrificing the one to the other. But as the smooth passage of our thought along our resembling perceptions makes us ascribe to them an identity, we can never without reluctance yield up that opinion. We must, therefore, turn to the other side, and suppose that our perceptions are no longer interrupted, but preserve a continu'd as well as an invariable existence, and are by that means entirely the same. But here the interruptions in the appearance of these perceptions are so long and frequent, that 'tis impossible to overlook them; and as the *appearance* of a perception in the mind and its *existence* seem at first sight entirely the same, it may be doubted, whether we can ever assent to so palpable a contradiction, and suppose a perception to exist without being present to the mind. In order to clear up this matter, and learn how the interruption in the appearance of a perception implies not necessarily an interruption in its existence, 'twill be proper to touch upon some principles, which we shall have occasion to explain more fully afterwards.[40]

38   We may begin with observing, that the difficulty in the present case is not concerning the matter of fact, or whether the mind forms such a conclusion concerning the continu'd existence of its perceptions, but only concerning the manner in which the conclusion is form'd, and principles from which it is deriv'd. 'Tis certain, that almost all mankind, and even philosophers themselves, for the greatest part of their lives, take their perceptions to be their only objects, and suppose, that the very being, which is intimately present to the mind, is the real body or material existence. 'Tis also certain, that this very perception or *SB 207* object is suppos'd to have a continu'd uninterrupted being, and neither to be annihilated by our absence, nor to be brought into existence by our presence. When we are absent from it, we say it still exists, but that we do not feel, we do not see it. When we are present, we say we feel, or see it. Here then may arise two questions; *First*, How we can satisfy ourselves in supposing a perception to be absent from the mind without being annihilated? *Secondly*, After what manner we conceive an object to become present to the mind, without some new creation of a perception or image;[†] and what we mean by this *seeing*, and *feeling*, and *perceiving*?

39   As to the first question; we may observe, that what we call a *mind*, is nothing but a heap or collection of different perceptions, united together by certain relations, and suppos'd, tho' falsly, to be endow'd with a perfect simplicity and identity.[†] Now as every perception is distinguishable from another, and may be consider'd as separately existent; it evidently follows, that there is no absurdity

[40] Sect. 6.[†]   *SB 206*

in separating any particular perception from the mind; that is, in breaking off all its relations, with that connected mass of perceptions, which constitute a thinking being.

40   The same reasoning affords us an answer to the second question. If the name of *perception* renders not this separation from a mind absurd and contradictory, the name of *object*, standing for the very same thing, can never render their conjunction impossible. External objects are seen, and felt, and become present to the mind; that is, they acquire such a relation to a connected heap of perceptions, as to influence them very considerably in augmenting their number by present reflections and passions, and in storing the memory with ideas. The same continu'd and uninterrupted being may, therefore, be sometimes present to the mind, and sometimes absent from it, without any real or essential change in the being itself. An interrupted appearance to the senses implies not necessarily an interruption in the existence. The supposition of the continu'd existence of sen-   *SB 208* sible objects or perceptions involves no contradiction. We may easily indulge our inclination to that supposition. When the exact resemblance of our perceptions makes us ascribe to them an identity, we may remove the seeming interruption by feigning a continu'd being, which may fill those intervals, and preserve a perfect and entire identity to our perceptions.

41   But as we here not only *feign* but *believe* this continu'd existence, the question is, *From whence arises such a belief?* and this question leads us to the *fourth* member of this system.† It has been prov'd already,† that belief in general consists in nothing, but the vivacity of an idea; and that an idea may acquire this vivacity by its relation to some present impression. Impressions are naturally the most vivid perceptions of the mind; and this quality is in part convey'd by the relation to every connected idea. The relation causes a smooth passage from the impression to the idea, and even gives a propensity to that passage. The mind falls so easily from the one perception to the other, that it scarce perceives the change, but retains in the second a considerable share of the vivacity of the first. It is excited by the lively impression; and this vivacity is convey'd to the related idea, without any great diminution in the passage, by reason of the smooth transition and the propensity of the imagination.

42   But suppose, that this propensity arises from some other principle, besides that of relation; 'tis evident it must still have the same effect, and convey the vivacity from the impression to the idea. Now this is exactly the present case. Our memory presents us with a vast number of instances of perceptions perfectly resembling each other, that return at different distances of time, and after considerable interruptions. This resemblance gives us a propension to consider these interrupted perceptions as the same; and also a propension to connect them by a continu'd existence, in order to justify this identity, and avoid the contradiction, in which the interrupted appearance of these perceptions seems   *SB 209* necessarily to involve us. Here then we have a propensity to feign the continu'd existence of all sensible objects; and as this propensity arises from some lively impressions of the memory, it bestows a vivacity on that fiction; or in other words, makes us believe the continu'd existence of body. If sometimes we ascribe

a continu'd existence to objects, which are perfectly new to us, and of whose constancy and coherence we have no experience, 'tis because the manner, in which they present themselves to our senses, resembles that of constant and coherent objects; and this resemblance is a source of reasoning and analogy, and leads us to attribute the same qualities to the similar objects.

43   I believe an intelligent reader will find less difficulty to assent to this system, than to comprehend it fully and distinctly, and will allow, after a little reflection, that every part carries its own proof along with it. 'Tis indeed evident, that as the vulgar *suppose* their perceptions to be their only objects, and at the same time *believe* the continu'd existence of matter, we must account for the origin of the belief upon that supposition. Now upon that supposition, 'tis a false opinion that any of our objects, or perceptions, are identically the same after an interruption; and consequently the opinion of their identity can never arise from reason, but must arise from the imagination. The imagination is seduc'd into such an opinion only by means of the resemblance of certain perceptions; since we find they are only our resembling perceptions, which we have a propension to suppose the same. This propension to bestow an identity on our resembling perceptions, produces the fiction of a continu'd existence; since that fiction, as well as the identity, is really false, as is acknowledg'd by all philosophers,[†] and has no other effect than to remedy the interruption of our perceptions, which is the only circumstance that is contrary to their identity. In the last place this propension causes belief by means of the present impressions of the memory; since without the remembrance of former sensations, 'tis plain we never shou'd have any belief of the continu'd existence of body. Thus in examining all these parts, we find that each of them is supported by the strongest proofs; and that all of them together form a consistent system, which is perfectly convincing. A strong propensity or inclination alone, without any present impression, will sometimes cause a belief or opinion. How much more when aided by that circumstance? *SB 210*

44   But tho' we are led after this manner, by the natural propensity of the imagination, to ascribe a continu'd existence to those sensible objects or perceptions, which we find to resemble each other in their interrupted appearance; yet a very little reflection and philosophy is sufficient to make us perceive the fallacy of that opinion. I have already observ'd,[†] that there is an intimate connexion betwixt those two principles, of a *continu'd* and of a *distinct* or *independent* existence, and that we no sooner establish the one than the other follows, as a necessary consequence. 'Tis the opinion of a continu'd existence, which first takes place, and without much study or reflection draws the other along with it, wherever the mind follows its first and most natural tendency. But when we compare experiments, and reason a little upon them, we quickly perceive, that the doctrine of the independent existence of our sensible perceptions is contrary to the plainest experience. This leads us backward upon our footsteps to perceive our error in attributing a continu'd existence to our perceptions, and is the origin of many very curious opinions, which we shall here endeavour to account for.

45   'Twill first be proper to observe a few of those experiments, which convince us, that our perceptions are not possest of any independent existence. When we press one eye with a finger, we immediately perceive all the objects to become double, and one half of them to be remov'd from their common and natural position.[†] But as we do not attribute a continu'd existence to both these perceptions, *SB 211* and as they are both of the same nature, we clearly perceive, that all our perceptions are dependent on our organs, and the disposition of our nerves and animal spirits. This opinion is confirm'd by the seeming encrease and diminution of objects, according to their distance; by the apparent alterations in their figure; by the changes in their colour and other qualities from our sickness and distempers; and by an infinite number of other experiments of the same kind;[†] from all which we learn, that our sensible perceptions are not possest of any distinct or independent existence.

46   The natural consequence of this reasoning shou'd be, that our perceptions have no more a continu'd than an independent existence; and indeed philosophers have so far run into this opinion, that they change their system, and distinguish, (as we shall do for the future[†]) betwixt perceptions and objects, of which the former are suppos'd to be interrupted, and perishing, and different at every different return;[†] the latter to be uninterrupted, and to preserve a continu'd existence and identity. But however philosophical this new system may be esteem'd, I assert that 'tis only a palliative remedy, and that it contains all the difficulties of the vulgar system, with some others, that are peculiar to itself. There are no principles either of the understanding or fancy, which lead us directly to embrace this opinion of the double existence of perceptions and objects, nor can we arrive at it but by passing thro' the common hypothesis of the identity and continuance of our interrupted perceptions. Were we not first perswaded, that our perceptions are our only objects, and continue to exist even when they no longer make their appearance to the senses, we shou'd never be led to think, that our perceptions and objects are different, and that our objects alone preserve a continu'd existence. *The latter hypothesis has no primary recommendation either to reason or the imagination, but acquires all its influence on the imagination from the former.* This proposition contains two parts, which we shall *SB 212* endeavour to prove as distinctly and clearly, as such abstruse subjects will permit.

47   As to the first part of the proposition, *that this philosophical hypothesis has no primary recommendation, either to reason or the imagination,* we may soon satisfy ourselves with regard to *reason* by the following reflections. The only existences, of which we are certain, are perceptions, which being immediately present to us by consciousness, command our strongest assent, and are the first foundation of all our conclusions. The only conclusion we can draw from the existence of one thing to that of another, is by means of the relation of cause and effect, which shows, that there is a connexion betwixt them, and that the existence of one is dependent on that of the other. The idea of this relation is deriv'd from past experience, by which we find, that two beings are constantly conjoin'd together, and are always present at once to the mind. But as no beings

are ever present to the mind but perceptions; it follows that we may observe a conjunction or a relation of cause and effect betwixt different perceptions, but can never observe it betwixt perceptions and objects. 'Tis impossible, therefore, that from the existence or any of the qualities of the former, we can ever form any conclusion concerning the existence of the latter, or ever satisfy our reason in this particular.

48　　'Tis no less certain, that this philosophical system has no primary recommendation to the *imagination*, and that that faculty wou'd never, of itself, and by its original tendency, have fallen upon such a principle. I confess it will be somewhat difficult to prove this to the full satisfaction of the reader; because it implies a negative, which in many cases will not admit of any positive proof. If any one wou'd take the pains to examine this question, and wou'd invent a system, to account for the direct origin of this opinion from the imagination, we shou'd be able, by the examination of that system, to pronounce a certain judgment in the present subject. Let it be taken for granted, that our perceptions are broken, and *SB 213* interrupted, and however like, are still different from each other; and let any one upon this supposition show why the fancy, directly and immediately, proceeds to the belief of another existence, resembling these perceptions in their nature, but yet continu'd, and uninterrupted, and identical; and after he has done this to my satisfaction, I promise to renounce my present opinion. Mean while I cannot forbear concluding, from the very abstractedness and difficulty of the first supposition,[†] that 'tis an improper subject for the fancy to work upon. Whoever wou'd explain the origin of the *common* opinion concerning the continu'd and distinct existence of body, must take the mind in its *common* situation, and must proceed upon the supposition, that our perceptions are our only objects, and continue to exist even when they are not perceiv'd. Tho' this opinion be false, 'tis the most natural of any, and has alone any primary recommendation to the fancy.

49　　As to the second part of the proposition, *that the philosophical system acquires all its influence on the imagination from the vulgar one*; we may observe, that this is a natural and unavoidable consequence of the foregoing conclusion, *that it has no primary recommendation to reason or the imagination.* For as the philosophical system is found by experience to take hold of many minds, and in particular of all those, who reflect ever so little on this subject, it must derive all its authority from the vulgar system; since it has no original authority of its own. The manner, in which these two systems, tho' directly contrary, are connected together, may be explain'd, as follows.

50　　The imagination naturally runs on in this train of thinking. Our perceptions are our only objects: Resembling perceptions are the same, however broken or interrupted in their appearance: This appearing interruption is contrary to the identity: The interruption consequently extends not beyond the appearance, and the perception or object really continues to exist, even when absent from us: Our sensible perceptions have, therefore, a continu'd and uninterrupted exis-　*SB 214* tence. But as a little reflection destroys this conclusion, that our perceptions have a continu'd existence, by showing that they have a dependent one, 'twou'd naturally be expected, that we must altogether reject the opinion, that there is such a thing in nature as a continu'd existence, which is preserv'd even when it no longer appears to the senses. The case, however, is otherwise. Philosophers are so far from rejecting the opinion of a continu'd existence upon rejecting that of the independence and continuance of our sensible perceptions, that tho' all sects agree in the latter sentiment, the former, which is, in a manner, its necessary consequence, has been peculiar to a few extravagant sceptics;[†] who after all maintain'd that opinion in words only, and were never able to bring themselves sincerely to believe it.

51   There is a great difference betwixt such opinions as we form after a calm and profound reflection, and such as we embrace by a kind of instinct or natural impulse, on account of their suitableness and conformity to the mind. If these opinions become contrary, 'tis not difficult to foresee which of them will have the advantage. As long as our attention is bent upon the subject, the philosophical and study'd principle may prevail; but the moment we relax our thoughts, nature will display herself, and draw us back to our former opinion. Nay she has sometimes such an influence, that she can stop our progress, even in the midst of our most profound reflections, and keep us from running on with all the consequences of any philosophical opinion. Thus tho' we clearly perceive the dependence and interruption of our perceptions, we stop short in our career, and never upon that account reject the notion of an independent and continu'd existence. That opinion has taken such deep root in the imagination, that 'tis impossible ever to eradicate it, nor will any strain'd metaphysical conviction of the dependence of our perceptions be sufficient for that purpose.

52   But tho' our natural and obvious principles here prevail above our study'd   *SB 215*
reflections, 'tis certain there must be some struggle and opposition in the case; at least so long as these reflections retain any force or vivacity. In order to set ourselves at ease in this particular, we contrive a new hypothesis, which seems to comprehend both these principles of reason and imagination. This hypothesis is the philosophical one of the double existence of perceptions and objects; which pleases our reason, in allowing, that our dependent perceptions are interrupted and different; and at the same time is agreeable to the imagination, in attributing a continu'd existence to something else, which we call *objects*. This philosophical system, therefore, is the monstrous offspring of two principles, which are contrary to each other, which are both at once embrac'd by the mind, and which are unable mutually to destroy each other. The imagination tells us, that our resembling perceptions have a continu'd and uninterrupted existence, and are not annihilated by their absence. Reflection tells us, that even our resembling perceptions are interrupted in their existence, and different from each other. The contradiction betwixt these opinions we elude by a new fiction, which is conformable to the hypotheses both of reflection and fancy, by ascribing these contrary qualities to different existences; the *interruption* to perceptions, and the *continuance* to objects. Nature is obstinate, and will not quit the field, however strongly attack'd by reason; and at the same time reason is so clear in the point, that there is no possibility of disguising her. Not being able to reconcile these two enemies, we endeavour to set ourselves at ease as much as possible, by suc-

cessively granting to each whatever it demands, and by feigning a double existence, where each may find something, that has all the conditions it desires. Were we fully convinc'd, that our resembling perceptions are continu'd, and identical, and independent, we shou'd never run into this opinion of a double existence; since we shou'd find satisfaction in our first supposition, and wou'd not look beyond. Again, were we fully convinc'd, that our perceptions are dependent, *SB 216* and interrupted, and different, we shou'd be as little inclin'd to embrace the opinion of a double existence; since in that case we shou'd clearly perceive the error of our first supposition of a continu'd existence, and wou'd never regard it any farther. 'Tis therefore from the intermediate situation of the mind,† that this opinion arises, and from such an adherence to these two contrary principles, as makes us seek some pretext to justify our receiving both; which happily at last is found in the system of a double existence.

53   Another advantage of this philosophical system is its similarity to the vulgar one; by which means we can humour our reason for a moment, when it becomes troublesome and sollicitous; and yet upon its least negligence or inattention, can easily return to our vulgar and natural notions. Accordingly we find, that philosophers neglect not this advantage; but immediately upon leaving their closets, mingle with the rest of mankind in those exploded opinions, that our perceptions are our only objects, and continue identically and uninterruptedly the same in all their interrupted appearances.

54   There are other particulars of this system, wherein we may remark its dependence on the fancy, in a very conspicuous manner. Of these, I shall observe the two following. *First*, We suppose external objects to resemble internal perceptions. I have already shown,† that the relation of cause and effect can never afford us any just conclusion from the existence or qualities of our perceptions to the existence of external continu'd objects; And I shall farther add, that even tho' they cou'd afford such a conclusion, we shou'd never have any reason to infer, that our objects resemble our perceptions. That opinion, therefore, is deriv'd from nothing but the quality of the fancy above-explain'd,† *that it borrows all its ideas from some precedent perceptions.* We never can conceive any thing but perceptions, and therefore must make every thing resemble them.

55   *Secondly*, As we suppose our objects in general to resemble our perceptions, so *SB 217* we take it for granted, that every particular object resembles that perception, which it causes. The relation of cause and effect determines us to join the other of resemblance; and the ideas of these existences being already united together in the fancy by the former relation, we naturally add the latter to compleat the union. We have a strong propensity to compleat every union by joining new relations to those which we have before observ'd betwixt any ideas, as we shall have occasion to observe presently.[41]

56   Having thus given an account of all the systems both popular and philosophical, with regard to external existences, I cannot forbear giving vent to a certain sentiment, which arises upon reviewing those systems. I begun† this subject with

---

[41] Sect. 5.†

premising, that we ought to have an implicit faith in our senses, and that this wou'd be the conclusion, I shou'd draw from the whole of my reasoning. But to be ingenuous, I feel myself *at present* of a quite contrary sentiment, and am more inclin'd to repose no faith at all in my senses, or rather imagination, than to place in it such an implicit confidence. I cannot conceive how such trivial qualities of the fancy,[†] conducted by such false suppositions, can ever lead to any solid and rational system. They are the coherence and constancy of our perceptions, which produce the opinion of their continu'd existence; tho' these qualities of perceptions have no perceivable connexion with such an existence.[†] The constancy of our perceptions has the most considerable effect, and yet is attended with the greatest difficulties. 'Tis a gross illusion to suppose, that our resembling perceptions are numerically the same; and 'tis this illusion, which leads us into the opinion, that these perceptions are uninterrupted, and are still existent, even when they are not present to the senses. This is the case with our popular system. And as to our philosophical one, 'tis liable to the same difficulties; and is over-and-above loaded with this absurdity, that it at once denies and establishes the vulgar supposition. Philosophers deny our resembling perceptions to be identically the same, and uninterrupted; and yet have so great a propensity to believe them such, that they arbitrarily invent a new set of perceptions, to which they attribute these qualities. I say, a new set of perceptions: For we may well suppose in general, but 'tis impossible for us distinctly to conceive, objects to be in their nature any thing but exactly the same with perceptions.[†] What then can we look for from this confusion of groundless and extraordinary opinions but error and falshood? And how can we justify to ourselves any belief we repose in them? *SB 218*

57   This sceptical doubt, both with respect to reason and the senses, is a malady, which can never be radically cur'd, but must return upon us every moment, however we may chace it away, and sometimes may seem entirely free from it. 'Tis impossible upon any system to defend either our understanding or senses; and we but expose them farther when we endeavour to justify them in that manner. As the sceptical doubt arises naturally from a profound and intense reflection on those subjects, it always encreases, the farther we carry our reflections, whether in opposition or conformity to it. Carelessness and in-attention alone can afford us any remedy.[†] For this reason I rely entirely upon them; and take it for granted, whatever may be the reader's opinion at this present moment, that an hour hence he will be perswaded there is both an external and internal world; and going upon that supposition, I intend to examine some general systems both antient and modern,[†] which have been propos'd of both, before I proceed to a more particular enquiry concerning our impressions.[†] This will not, perhaps, in the end be found foreign to our present purpose.[†]

Sect. 3. *Of the antient philosophy*   *SB 219*

1   Several moralists have recommended it as an excellent method of becoming acquainted with our own hearts, and knowing our progress in virtue, to recollect our dreams in a morning, and examine them with the same rigour, that we

wou'd our most serious and most deliberate actions.[†] Our character is the same throughout, say they, and appears best where artifice, fear, and policy have no place, and men can neither be hypocrites with themselves nor others. The generosity, or baseness of our temper, our meekness or cruelty, our courage or pusillanimity, influence the fictions of the imagination with the most unbounded liberty, and discover themselves in the most glaring colours. In like manner, I am perswaded, there might be several useful discoveries made from a criticism of the fictions of the antient philosophy, concerning *substances*, and *substantial forms*, and *accidents*, and *occult qualities*; which, however unreasonable and capricious, have a very intimate connexion with the principles of human nature.

2   'Tis confest by the most judicious philosophers, that our ideas of bodies are nothing but collections form'd by the mind of the ideas of the several distinct sensible qualities, of which objects are compos'd, and which we find to have a constant union with each other.[†] But however these qualities may in themselves be entirely distinct, 'tis certain we commonly regard the compound, which they form, as ONE thing, and as continuing the SAME under very considerable alterations. The acknowledg'd composition is evidently contrary to this suppos'd *simplicity*, and the variation to the *identity*. It may, therefore, be worth while to consider the *causes*, which make us almost universally fall into such evident contradictions, as well as the *means* by which we endeavour to conceal them.[†]

3   'Tis evident, that as the ideas of the several distinct *successive* qualities of objects are united together by a very close relation, the mind, in looking along the succession,[†] must be carry'd from one part of it to another by an easy transition, and will no more perceive the change, than if it contemplated the same unchangeable object. This easy transition is the effect, or rather essence of relation; and as the imagination readily takes one idea for another, where their influence on the mind is similar; hence it proceeds, that any such succession of related qualities is readily consider'd as one continu'd object, existing without any variation. The smooth and uninterrupted progress of the thought, being alike in both cases, readily deceives the mind, and makes us ascribe an identity to the changeable succession of connected qualities.

    SB 220

4   But when we alter our method of considering the succession, and instead of tracing it gradually thro' the successive points of time, survey at once any two distinct periods of its duration, and compare the different conditions of the successive qualities;[†] in that case the variations, which were insensible when they arose gradually, do now appear of consequence, and seem entirely to destroy the identity. By this means there arises a kind of contrariety in our method of thinking, from the different points of view, in which we survey the object, and from the nearness or remoteness of those instants of time, which we compare together. When we gradually follow an object in its successive changes, the smooth progress of the thought makes us ascribe an identity to the succession; because 'tis by a similar act of the mind we consider an unchangeable object. When we compare its situation after a considerable change the progress of the

thought is broke; and consequently we are presented with the idea of diversity: In order to reconcile which contradictions the imagination is apt to feign something unknown and invisible, which it supposes to continue the same under all these variations; and this unintelligible something it calls a *substance,* or *original and first matter.*

5   We entertain a like notion with regard to the *simplicity* of substances, and from   *SB 221*
like causes. Suppose an object perfectly simple and indivisible to be presented, along with another object, whose *co-existent* parts are connected together by a strong relation, 'tis evident the actions of the mind, in considering these two objects, are not very different. The imagination conceives the simple object at once, with facility, by a single effort of thought, without change or variation. The connexion of parts in the compound object has almost the same effect, and so unites the object within itself, that the fancy feels not the transition in passing from one part to another. Hence the colour, taste, figure, solidity, and other qualities, combin'd in a peach or melon, are conceiv'd to form *one thing*; and that on account of their close relation, which makes them affect the thought in the same manner, as if perfectly uncompounded. But the mind rests not here. Whenever it views the object in another light, it finds that all these qualities are different, and distinguishable, and separable from each other; which view of things being destructive of its primary and more natural notions, obliges the imagination to feign an unknown something, or *original* substance and matter, as a principle of union or cohesion among these qualities, and as what may give the compound object a title to be call'd one thing, notwithstanding its diversity and composition.

6   The peripatetic philosophy† asserts the *original* matter to be perfectly homogeneous in all bodies, and considers fire, water, earth, and air, as of the very same substance; on account of their gradual revolutions and changes into each other. At the same time it assigns to each of these species of objects a distinct *substantial form,* which it supposes to be the source of all those different qualities they possess, and to be a new foundation of simplicity and identity to each particular species.† All depends on our manner of viewing the objects. When we look along the insensible changes of bodies,† we suppose all of them to be of the same substance or essence. When we consider their sensible differences, we attribute to   *SB 222*
each of them a substantial and essential difference. And in order to indulge ourselves in both these ways of considering our objects, we suppose all bodies to have at once a substance and a substantial form.

7   The notion of *accidents* is an unavoidable consequence of this method of thinking with regard to substances and substantial forms;† nor can we forbear looking upon colours, sounds, tastes, figures, and other properties of bodies, as existences, which cannot subsist apart, but require a subject of inhesion to sustain and support them. For having never discover'd any of these sensible qualities, where, for the reasons above-mention'd,† we did not likewise fancy a substance to exist; the same habit, which makes us infer a connexion betwixt cause and effect, makes us here infer a dependance of every quality on the

unknown substance. The custom of imagining a dependance has the same effect as the custom of observing it wou'd have. This conceit, however, is no more reasonable than any of the foregoing. Every quality being a distinct thing from another, may be conceiv'd to exist apart, and may exist apart, not only from every other quality, but from that unintelligible chimera of a substance.

8   But these philosophers carry their fictions still farther in their sentiments concerning *occult qualities*,[†] and both suppose a substance supporting, which they do not understand, and an accident supported, of which they have as imperfect an idea. The whole system, therefore, is entirely incomprehensible, and yet is deriv'd from principles as natural as any of those above-explain'd.

9   In considering this subject we may observe a gradation of three opinions, that rise above each other, according as the persons, who form them, acquire new degrees of reason and knowledge. These opinions are that of the vulgar, that of a false philosophy, and that of the true; where we shall find upon enquiry, that the true philosophy approaches nearer to the sentiments of the vulgar, than to *SB 223* those of a mistaken knowledge. 'Tis natural for men, in their common and careless way of thinking, to imagine they perceive a connexion betwixt such objects as they have constantly found united together; and because custom has render'd it difficult to separate the ideas, they are apt to fancy such a separation to be in itself impossible and absurd. But philosophers, who abstract from the effects of custom, and compare the ideas of objects, immediately perceive the falshood of these vulgar sentiments, and discover that there is no known connexion among objects. Every different object appears to them entirely distinct and separate; and they perceive, that 'tis not from a view of the nature and qualities of objects we infer one from another, but only when in several instances we observe them to have been constantly conjoin'd. But these philosophers, instead of drawing a just inference from this observation, and concluding, that we have no idea of power or agency, separate from the mind, and belonging to causes; I say, instead of drawing this conclusion, they frequently search for the qualities, in which this agency consists, and are displeas'd with every system, which their reason suggests to them, in order to explain it. They have sufficient force of genius to free them from the vulgar error, that there is a natural and perceivable connexion betwixt the several sensible qualities and actions of matter; but not sufficient to keep them from ever seeking for this connexion in matter, or causes. Had they fallen upon the just conclusion, they wou'd have return'd back to the situation of the vulgar, and wou'd have regarded all these disquisitions with indolence and indifference. At present they seem to be in a very lamentable condition, and such as the poets have given us but a faint notion of in their descriptions of the punishments of *Sisyphus* and *Tantalus*.[†] For what can be imagin'd more tormenting, than to seek with eagerness, what for ever flies us; and seek for it in a place, where 'tis impossible it can ever exist?

10   But as nature seems to have observ'd a kind of justice and compensation in *SB 224* every thing, she has not neglected philosophers more than the rest of the creation; but has reserv'd them a consolation amidst all their disappointments and

afflictions. This consolation principally consists in their invention of the words *faculty* and *occult quality*. For it being usual, after the frequent use of terms, which are really significant and intelligible, to omit the idea, which we wou'd express by them, and to preserve only the custom, by which we recal the idea at pleasure; so it naturally happens, that after the frequent use of terms, which are wholly insignificant and unintelligible, we fancy them to be on the same footing with the precedent, and to have a secret meaning, which we might discover by reflection. The resemblance of their appearance deceives the mind, as is usual, and makes us imagine a thorough resemblance and conformity. By this means these philosophers set themselves at ease, and arrive at last, by an illusion, at the same indifference, which the people attain by their stupidity, and true philosophers by their moderate scepticism. They need only say, that any phænomenon, which puzzles them, arises from a faculty or an occult quality, and there is an end of all dispute and enquiry upon the matter.

11 But among all the instances, wherein the Peripatetics have shown they were guided by every trivial propensity of the imagination, no one is more remarkable than their *sympathies*, *antipathies*, and *horrors of a vacuum*.[†] There is a very remarkable inclination in human nature, to bestow on external objects the same emotions, which it observes in itself; and to find every where those ideas, which are most present to it. This inclination, 'tis true, is suppress'd by a little reflection, and only takes place in children, poets, and the antient philosophers. It appears in children, by their desire of beating the stones, which hurt them: In poets, by their readiness to personify every thing: And in the antient philosophers, by these fictions of sympathy and antipathy. We must pardon children, because of their age; poets, because they profess to follow implicitly the suggestions of their fancy: But what excuse shall we find to justify our philosophers in so signal a weakness? *SB 225*

Sect. 4. *Of the modern philosophy*

1 But here it may be objected, that the imagination, according to my own confession, being the ultimate judge of all systems of philosophy, I am unjust in blaming the antient philosophers for making use of that faculty, and allowing themselves to be entirely guided by it in their reasonings. In order to justify myself, I must distinguish in the imagination betwixt the principles which are permanent, irresistible, and universal; such as the customary transition from causes to effects, and from effects to causes: And the principles, which are changeable, weak, and irregular; such as those I have just now taken notice of.[†] The former are the foundation of all our thoughts and actions, so that upon their removal human nature must immediately perish and go to ruin. The latter are neither unavoidable to mankind, nor necessary, or so much as useful in the conduct of life; but on the contrary are observ'd only to take place in weak minds, and being opposite to the other principles of custom and reasoning, may easily be subverted by a due contrast and opposition. For this reason the former are receiv'd by philosophy, and the latter rejected. One who concludes somebody

to be near him, when he hears an articulate voice in the dark, reasons justly and naturally; tho' that conclusion be deriv'd from nothing but custom, which infixes and enlivens the idea of a human creature, on account of his usual conjunction with the present impression. But one, who is tormented he knows not why, with the apprehension of spectres in the dark, may, perhaps, be said to reason, and to reason naturally too: But then it must be in the same sense, that a malady is said to be natural; as arising from natural causes, tho' it be contrary to health, the most agreeable and most natural situation of man. *SB 226*

2   The opinions of the antient philosophers, their fictions of substance and accident, and their reasonings concerning substantial forms and occult qualities, are like the spectres in the dark, and are deriv'd from principles, which, however common, are neither universal nor unavoidable in human nature. The *modern philosophy*† pretends to be entirely free from this defect, and to arise only from the solid, permanent, and consistent principles of the imagination. Upon what grounds this pretension is founded must now be the subject of our enquiry.

3   The fundamental principle of that philosophy is the opinion concerning colours, sounds, tastes, smells, heat and cold; which it asserts to be nothing but impressions in the mind, deriv'd from the operation of external objects, and without any resemblance to the qualities of the objects. Upon examination, I find only one of the reasons commonly produc'd for this opinion to be satisfactory, *viz.* that deriv'd from the variations of those impressions, even while the external object, to all appearance, continues the same. These variations depend upon several circumstances. Upon the different situations of our health: A man in a malady feels a disagreeable taste in meats, which before pleas'd him the most.† Upon the different complexions and constitutions of men:† That seems bitter to one, which is sweet to another. Upon the difference of their external situation and position: Colours reflected from the clouds change according to the distance of the clouds, and according to the angle they make with the eye and luminous body.† Fire also communicates the sensation of pleasure at one distance, and that of pain at another.† Instances of this kind are very numerous and frequent.

4   The conclusion drawn from them, is likewise as satisfactory as can possibly be imagin'd. 'Tis certain, that when different impressions of the same sense arise from any object, every one of these impressions has not a resembling quality existent in the object. For as the same object cannot, at the same time, be endow'd with different qualities of the same sense, and as the same quality cannot resemble impressions entirely different; it evidently follows, that many of our impressions have no external model or archetype.† Now from like effects we presume like causes.† Many of the impressions of colour, sound, &c. are confest to be nothing but internal existences,† and to arise from causes, which no way resemble them. These impressions are in appearance nothing different from the other impressions of colour, sound, &c. We conclude, therefore, that they are, all of them, deriv'd from a like origin. *SB 227*

5   This principle being once admitted, all the other doctrines of that philosophy

seem to follow by an easy consequence. For upon the removal of sounds, colours, heat, cold, and other sensible qualities, from the rank of continu'd independent existences, we are reduc'd merely to what are call'd primary qualities, as the only *real* ones, of which we have any adequate notion. These primary qualities are extension and solidity, with their different mixtures and modifications; figure, motion, gravity, and cohesion. The generation, encrease, decay, and corruption of animals and vegetables, are nothing but changes of figure and motion; as also the operations of all bodies on each other; of fire, of light, water, air, earth, and of all the elements and powers of nature.[†] One figure and motion produces another figure and motion; nor does there remain in the material universe any other principle, either active or passive, of which we can form the most distant idea.

6   I believe many objections might be made to this system: But at present I shall confine myself to one, which is in my opinion very decisive. I assert, that instead of explaining the operations of external objects by its means, we utterly annihilate all these objects, and reduce ourselves to the opinions of the most extravagant scepticism concerning them.[†] If colours, sounds, tastes, and smells be merely perceptions, nothing we can conceive is possest of a real, continu'd, and independent existence; not even motion, extension and solidity, which are the primary qualities chiefly insisted on. *SB 228*

7   To begin with the examination of motion; 'tis evident this is a quality altogether inconceivable alone, and without a reference to some other object. The idea of motion necessarily supposes that of a body moving. Now what is our idea of the moving body, without which motion is incomprehensible? It must resolve itself into the idea of extension or of solidity; and consequently the reality of motion depends upon that of these other qualities.

8   This opinion, which is universally acknowledg'd concerning motion, I have prov'd[†] to be true with regard to extension; and have shown that 'tis impossible to conceive extension, but as compos'd of parts, endow'd with colour or solidity. The idea of extension is a compound idea; but as it is not compounded of an infinite number of parts or inferior ideas, it must at last resolve itself into such as are perfectly simple and indivisible. These simple and indivisible parts, not being ideas of extension, must be non–entities, unless conceiv'd as colour'd or solid. Colour is excluded from any real existence. The reality, therefore, of our idea of extension depends upon the reality of that of solidity, nor can the former be just while the latter is chimerical. Let us, then, lend our attention to the examination of the idea of solidity.

9   The idea of solidity is that of two objects, which being impell'd by the utmost force, cannot penetrate each other; but still maintain a separate and distinct existence. Solidity, therefore, is perfectly incomprehensible alone, and without the conception of some bodies, which are solid, and maintain this separate and distinct existence. Now what idea have we of these bodies? The ideas of colours, sounds, and other secondary qualities are excluded. The idea of motion depends on that of extension, and the idea of extension on that of solidity. 'Tis impossible, therefore, that the idea of solidity can depend on either of them. For that wou'd be to run in a circle, and make one idea depend on another, while at *SB 229*

the same time the latter depends on the former. Our modern philosophy, there-fore, leaves us no just nor satisfactory idea of solidity; nor consequently of matter.

10   This argument will appear entirely conclusive to every one that comprehends it; but because it may seem abstruse and intricate to the generality of readers, I hope to be excus'd, if I endeavour to render it more obvious by some variation of the expression. In order to form an idea of solidity, we must conceive two bodies pressing on each other without any penetration; and 'tis impossible to arrive at this idea, when we confine ourselves to one object, much more without conceiv-ing any. Two non-entities cannot exclude each other from their places; because they never possess any place,[†] nor can be endow'd with any quality. Now I ask, what idea do we form of these bodies or objects, to which we suppose solidity to belong? To say, that we conceive them merely as solid, is to run on *in infinitum*.[†] To affirm, that we paint them out to ourselves as extended, either resolves all into a false idea, or returns in a circle. Extension must necessarily be consider'd either as colour'd, which is a false idea; or as solid, which brings us back to the first question. We may make the same observation concerning mobility and figure; and upon the whole must conclude, that after the exclusion of colours, sounds, heat and cold from the rank of external existences, there remains nothing, which can afford us a just and consistent idea of body.

11   Add to this, that, properly speaking, solidity or impenetrability is nothing, but an impossibility of annihilation, as has been already observ'd:[42] For which reason   *SB 230* 'tis the more necessary for us to form some distinct idea of that object, whose annihilation we suppose impossible. An impossibility of being annihilated cannot exist, and can never be conceiv'd to exist, by itself; but necessarily requires some object or real existence, to which it may belong. Now the difficulty still remains, how to form an idea of this object or existence, without having recourse to the secondary and sensible qualities.

12   Nor must we omit on this occasion our accustom'd method of examining ideas by considering those impressions, from which they are deriv'd. The impressions, which enter by the sight and hearing, the smell and taste, are affirm'd by modern philosophy to be without any resembling objects;[†] and consequently the idea of solidity, which is suppos'd to be real, can never be deriv'd from any of these senses. There remains, therefore, the feeling as the only sense, that can convey the impression, which is original to the idea of solidity; and indeed we naturally imagine, that we feel the solidity of bodies, and need but touch any object in order to perceive this quality. But this method of thinking is more popular than philosophical; as will appear from the following reflections.

13   *First*, 'Tis easy to observe, that tho' bodies are felt by means of their solidity, yet the feeling is a quite different thing from the solidity; and that they have not the least resemblance to each other. A man, who has the palsey[†] in one hand, has as perfect an idea of impenetrability, when he observes that hand to be supported

---

[42] Part 2. Sect. 4.[†]   *SB 229*

by the table, as when he feels the same table with the other hand. An object, that presses upon any of our members, meets with resistance; and that resistance, by the motion it gives to the nerves and animal spirits, conveys a certain sensation to the mind; but it does not follow, that the sensation, motion, and resistance are any ways resembling.[†]

14   *Secondly*, The impressions of touch are simple impressions, except when   *SB 231* consider'd with regard to their extension; which makes nothing to the present purpose:[†] And from this simplicity I infer, that they neither represent solidity, nor any real object.[†] For let us put two cases, *viz.* that of a man, who presses a stone, or any solid body, with his hand, and that of two stones, which press each other; 'twill readily be allow'd, that these two cases are not in every respect alike, but that in the former there is conjoin'd with the solidity, a feeling or sensation, of which there is no appearance in the latter. In order, therefore, to make these two cases alike, 'tis necessary to remove some part of the impression, which the man feels by his hand, or organ of sensation; and that being impossible in a simple impression, obliges us to remove the whole, and proves that this whole impression has no archetype or model in external objects. To which we may add, that solidity necessarily supposes two bodies, along with contiguity and impulse; which being a compound object, can never be represented by a simple impression. Not to mention, that tho' solidity continues always invariably the same, the impressions of touch change every moment upon us; which is a clear proof that the latter are not representations of the former.

15   Thus there is a direct and total opposition betwixt our reason and our senses; or more properly speaking, betwixt those conclusions we form from cause and effect, and those that perswade us of the continu'd and independent existence of body. When we reason from cause and effect, we conclude, that neither colour, sound, taste, nor smell have a continu'd and independent existence. When we exclude these sensible qualities there remains nothing in the universe, which has such an existence.

Sect. 5. *Of the immateriality of the soul*   *SB 232*

1   Having found such contradictions and difficulties in every system concerning external objects, and in the idea of matter, which we fancy so clear and determinate, we shall naturally expect still greater difficulties and contradictions in every hypothesis concerning our internal perceptions, and the nature of the mind, which we are apt to imagine so much more obscure, and uncertain. But in this we shou'd deceive ourselves. The intellectual world, tho' involv'd in infinite obscurities, is not perplex'd with any such contradictions, as those we have discover'd in the natural.[†] What is known concerning it, agrees with itself; and what is unknown, we must be contented to leave so.

2   'Tis true, wou'd we hearken to certain philosophers, they promise to diminish our ignorance;[†] but I am afraid 'tis at the hazard of running us into contradictions, from which the subject is of itself exempted. These philosophers are the curious reasoners concerning the material or immaterial substances, in which

they suppose our perceptions to inhere. In order to put a stop to these endless cavils on both sides, I know no better method, than to ask these philosophers in a few words, *What they mean by substance and inhesion?* And after they have answer'd this question, 'twill then be reasonable, and not till then, to enter seriously into the dispute.

3   This question we have found impossible to be answer'd with regard to matter and body: But besides that in the case of the mind, it labours under all the same difficulties, 'tis burthen'd with some additional ones, which are peculiar to that subject. As every idea is deriv'd from a precedent impression, had we any idea of the substance of our minds, we must also have an impression of it; which is very difficult, if not impossible, to be conceiv'd. For how can an impression represent   *SB 233* a substance, otherwise than by resembling it?[†] And how can an impression resemble a substance, since, according to this philosophy, it is not a substance, and has none of the peculiar qualities or characteristics of a substance?

4   But leaving the question of *What may or may not be?* for that other *What actually is?* I desire those philosophers, who pretend that we have an idea of the substance of our minds, to point out the impression that produces it, and tell distinctly after what manner that impression operates, and from what object it is deriv'd. Is it an impression of sensation or of reflection? Is it pleasant, or painful, or indifferent? Does it attend us at all times, or does it only return at intervals? If at intervals, at what times principally does it return, and by what causes is it produc'd?

5   If instead of answering these questions, any one shou'd evade the difficulty, by saying, that the definition of a substance is *something which may exist by itself;*[†] and that this definition ought to satisfy us: Shou'd this be said, I shou'd observe, that this definition agrees to every thing, that can possibly be conceiv'd; and never will serve to distinguish substance from accident, or the soul from its perceptions. For thus I reason. Whatever is clearly conceiv'd may exist; and whatever is clearly conceiv'd, after any manner, may exist after the same manner. This is one principle, which has been already acknowledg'd.[†] Again, every thing, which is different, is distinguishable, and every thing which is distinguishable, is separable by the imagination. This is another principle.[†] My conclusion from both is, that since all our perceptions are different from each other, and from every thing else in the universe, they are also distinct and separable, and may be consider'd as separately existent, and may exist separately, and have no need of any thing else to support their existence. They are, therefore, substances, as far as this definition explains a substance.

6   Thus neither by considering the first origin of ideas, nor by means of a defini-   *SB 234* tion are we able to arrive at any satisfactory notion of substance; which seems to me a sufficient reason for abandoning utterly that dispute concerning the materiality and immateriality of the soul, and makes me absolutely condemn even the question itself. We have no perfect idea of any thing but of a perception. A substance is entirely different from a perception. We have, therefore, no idea of a substance. Inhesion in something is suppos'd to be requisite to support the existence of our perceptions. Nothing appears requisite to support the

existence of a perception. We have, therefore, no idea of inhesion. What possibility then of answering that question, *Whether perceptions inhere in a material or immaterial substance*, when we do not so much as understand the meaning of the question?

7   There is one argument commonly employ'd for the immateriality of the soul, which seems to me remarkable.[†] Whatever is extended consists of parts; and whatever consists of parts is divisible, if not in reality, at least in the imagination. But 'tis impossible any thing divisible can be *conjoin'd* to a thought or perception, which is a being altogether inseparable and indivisible. For supposing such a conjunction, wou'd the indivisible thought exist on the left or on the right hand of this extended divisible body? On the surface or in the middle? On the back- or fore-side of it? If it be conjoin'd with the extension, it must exist somewhere within its dimensions. If it exist within its dimensions, it must either exist in one particular part; and then that particular part is indivisible, and the perception is conjoin'd only with it, not with the extension: Or if the thought exists in every part, it must also be extended, and separable, and divisible, as well as the body; which is utterly absurd and contradictory. For can any one conceive a passion of a yard in length, a foot in breadth, and an inch in thickness? Thought, therefore, and extension are qualities wholly incompatible, and never can incorporate together into one subject.   *SB 235*

8   This argument affects not the question concerning the *substance* of the soul, but only that concerning its *local conjunction*[†] with matter; and therefore it may not be improper to consider in general what objects are, or are not susceptible of a local conjunction. This is a curious question, and may lead us to some discoveries of considerable moment.

9   The first notion of space and extension is deriv'd solely from the senses of sight and feeling; nor is there any thing, but what is colour'd or tangible, that has parts dispos'd after such a manner, as to convey that idea. When we diminish or encrease a relish,[†] 'tis not after the same manner that we diminish or encrease any visible object; and when several sounds strike our hearing at once, custom and reflection alone make us form an idea of the degrees of the distance and contiguity of those bodies, from which they are deriv'd. Whatever marks the place of its existence either must be extended, or must be a mathematical point, without parts or composition. What is extended must have a particular figure, as square, round, triangular; none of which will agree to a desire,[†] or indeed to any impression or idea, except of these two senses above-mention'd. Neither ought a desire, tho' indivisible, to be consider'd as a mathematical point. For in that case 'twou'd be possible, by the addition of others, to make two, three, four desires, and these dispos'd and situated in such a manner, as to have a determinate length, breadth and thickness; which is evidently absurd.

10   'Twill not be surprizing after this, if I deliver a maxim, which is condemn'd by several metaphysicians,[†] and is esteem'd contrary to the most certain principles of human reason. This maxim is *that an object may exist, and yet be no where*: And I assert, that this is not only possible, but that the greatest part of beings do and must exist after this manner. An object may be said to be no where, when its parts

are not so situated with respect to each other, as to form any figure or quantity;   *SB 236*
nor the whole with respect to other bodies so as to answer to our notions of contiguity or distance. Now this is evidently the case with all our perceptions and
objects,[†] except those of the sight and feeling. A moral reflection cannot be
plac'd on the right or on the left hand of a passion, nor can a smell or sound
be either of a circular or a square figure. These objects and perceptions, so
far from requiring any particular place, are absolutely incompatible with it,
and even the imagination cannot attribute it to them. And as to the absurdity
of supposing them to be no where, we may consider, that if the passions and sentiments appear to the perception to have any particular place, the idea of extension might be deriv'd from them, as well as from the sight and touch; contrary
to what we have already establish'd.[†] If they *appear* not to have any particular
place, they may possibly *exist* in the same manner; since whatever we conceive is
possible.

11   'Twill not now be necessary to prove, that those perceptions, which are
simple, and exist no where, are incapable of any conjunction in place with matter
or body, which is extended and divisible; since 'tis impossible to found a relation
but on some common quality.[43] It may be better worth our while to remark, that
this question of the local conjunction of objects does not only occur in meta
physical disputes concerning the nature of the soul, but that even in common
life we have every moment occasion to examine it. Thus supposing we consider a
fig at one end of the table, and an olive at the other, 'tis evident, that in forming
the complex ideas of these substances, one of the most obvious is that of their
different relishes; and 'tis as evident, that we incorporate and conjoin these
qualities with such as are colour'd and tangible. The bitter taste of the one, and
sweet of the other are suppos'd to lie in the very visible body, and to be separated
from each other by the whole length of the table. This is so notable and so natural
an illusion, that it may be proper to consider the principles, from which it is   *SB 237*
deriv'd.

12   Tho' an extended object be incapable of a conjunction in place with another,
that exists without any place or extension, yet are they susceptible of many other
relations.[†] Thus the taste and smell of any fruit are inseparable from its other
qualities of colour and tangibility; and which-ever of them be the cause or effect,
'tis certain they are always co-existent. Nor are they only co-existent in general,
but also co-temporary in their appearance in the mind; and 'tis upon the application of the extended body to our senses we perceive its particular taste and smell.
These relations, then, of *causation*, and *contiguity in the time of their appearance*,
betwixt the extended object and the quality, which exists without any particular
place, must have such an effect on the mind, that upon the appearance of one it
will immediately turn its thought to the conception of the other. Nor is this all.
We not only turn our thought from one to the other upon account of their relation, but likewise endeavour to give them a new relation, *viz.* that of *a conjunction
in place*, that we may render the transition more easy and natural. For 'tis a

[43] Part 1. Sect. 5.[†]   *SB 236*

quality, which I shall often have occasion to remark in human nature, and shall explain more fully in its proper place,[†] that when objects are united by any relation, we have a strong propensity to add some new relation to them, in order to compleat the union. In our arrangement of bodies we never fail to place such as are resembling, in contiguity to each other, or at least in correspondent points of view: Why? but because we feel a satisfaction in joining the relation of contiguity to that of resemblance, or the resemblance of situation to that of qualities. The effects of this propensity have been already observ'd[44] in that resemblance, which we so readily suppose betwixt particular impressions and their external causes. But we shall not find a more evident effect of it, than in the present   *SB 238* instance, where from the relations of causation and contiguity in time betwixt two objects, we feign likewise that of a conjunction in place, in order to strengthen the connexion.

13   But whatever confus'd notions we may form of an union in place betwixt an extended body, as a fig, and its particular taste, 'tis certain that upon reflection we must observe in this union something altogether unintelligible and contradictory. For shou'd we ask ourselves one obvious question, *viz.* if the taste, which we conceive to be contain'd in the circumference of the body, is in every part of it or in one only, we must quickly find ourselves at a loss, and perceive the impossibility of ever giving a satisfactory answer. We cannot reply, that 'tis only in one part: For experience convinces us, that every part has the same relish. We can as little reply, that it exists in every part: For then we must suppose it figur'd and extended; which is absurd and incomprehensible. Here then we are influenc'd by two principles directly contrary to each other, *viz.* that *inclination* of our fancy by which we are determin'd to incorporate the taste with the extended object,[†] and our *reason*, which shows us the impossibility of such an union. Being divided betwixt these opposite principles, we renounce neither one nor the other, but involve the subject in such confusion and obscurity, that we no longer perceive the opposition. We suppose, that the taste exists within the circumference of the body, but in such a manner, that it fills the whole without extension, and exists entire in every part without separation. In short, we use in our most familiar way of thinking, that scholastic principle, which, when crudely propos'd, appears so shocking, of *totum in toto & totum in qualibet parte:*[†] Which is much the same, as if we shou'd say, that a thing is in a certain place, and yet is not there.

14   All this absurdity proceeds from our endeavouring to bestow a place on what is utterly incapable of it; and that endeavour again arises from our inclination to   *SB 239* compleat an union, which is founded on causation, and a contiguity of time, by attributing to the objects a conjunction in place. But if ever reason be of sufficient force to overcome prejudice, 'tis certain, that in the present case it must prevail. For we have only this choice left, either to suppose that some beings exist without any place; or that they are figur'd and extended; or that when they are

---

[44] Sect. 2, towards the end.[†]   *SB 237*

incorporated with extended objects, the whole is in the whole, and the whole in every part. The absurdity of the two last suppositions proves sufficiently the veracity of the first. Nor is there any fourth opinion. For as to the supposition of their existence in the manner of mathematical points,[†] it resolves itself into the second opinion, and supposes, that several passions may be plac'd in a circular figure, and that a certain number of smells, conjoin'd with a certain number of sounds, may make a body of twelve cubic inches; which appears ridiculous upon the bare mentioning of it.

15   But tho' in this view of things we cannot refuse to condemn the materialists, who conjoin all thought with extension;[†] yet a little reflection will show us equal reason for blaming their antagonists,[†] who conjoin all thought with a simple and indivisible substance. The most vulgar philosophy[†] informs us, that no external object can make itself known to the mind immediately, and without the interposition of an image or perception. That table, which just now appears to me, is only a perception, and all its qualities are qualities of a perception. Now the most obvious of all its qualities is extension. The perception consists of parts. These parts are so situated, as to afford us the notion of distance and contiguity; of length, breadth, and thickness. The termination of these three dimensions is what we call figure. This figure is moveable, separable, and divisible. Mobility, and separability are the distinguishing properties of extended objects. And to cut short all disputes, the very idea of extension is copy'd from nothing but an impression, and consequently must perfectly agree to it. To say the idea of extension agrees to any thing, is to say it is extended.[†]   *SB 240*

16   The free-thinker[†] may now triumph in his turn; and having found there are impressions and ideas really extended, may ask his antagonists, how they can incorporate a simple and indivisible subject with an extended perception? All the arguments of theologians[†] may here be retorted upon them. Is the indivisible subject, or immaterial substance, if you will, on the left or on the right hand of the perception? Is it in this particular part, or in that other? Is it in every part without being extended? Or is it entire in any one part without deserting the rest? 'Tis impossible to give any answer to these questions, but what will both be absurd in itself, and will account for the union of our indivisible perceptions with an extended substance.[†]

17   This gives me an occasion to take anew into consideration the question concerning the substance of the soul; and tho' I have condemn'd[†] that question as utterly unintelligible, yet I cannot forbear proposing some farther reflections concerning it. I assert, that the doctrine of the immateriality, simplicity, and indivisibility of a thinking substance is a true atheism,[†] and will serve to justify all those sentiments, for which *Spinoza* is so universally infamous.[†] From this topic, I hope at least to reap one advantage, that my adversaries will not have any pretext to render the present doctrine odious by their declamations, when they see that they can be so easily retorted on them.[†]

18   The fundamental principle of the atheism of *Spinoza* is the doctrine of the simplicity of the universe, and the unity of that substance, in which he supposes

both thought and matter to inhere. There is only one substance, says he, in the world; and that substance is perfectly simple and indivisible, and exists every where, without any local presence. Whatever we discover externally by sensation; whatever we feel internally by reflection; all these are nothing but modifications of that one, simple, and necessarily existent being, and are not possest of any separate or distinct existence. Every passion of the soul; every configuration of matter, however different and various, inhere in the same substance, and preserve in themselves their characters of distinction, without communicating them to that subject, in which they inhere. The same *substratum*, if I may so speak, supports the most different modifications, without any difference in itself; and varies them, without any variation. Neither time, nor place, nor all the diversity of nature are able to produce any composition or change in its perfect simplicity and identity. *SB 241*

19   I believe this brief exposition of the principles of that famous atheist will be sufficient for the present purpose, and that without entering farther into these gloomy and obscure regions, I shall be able to show, that this hideous hypothesis is almost the same with that of the immateriality of the soul, which has become so popular. To make this evident, let us remember,[45] that as every idea is deriv'd from a preceding perception, 'tis impossible our idea of a perception, and that of an object or external existence can ever represent what are specifically different from each other. Whatever difference we may suppose betwixt them, 'tis still incomprehensible to us; and we are oblig'd either to conceive an external object merely as a relation without a relative,[†] or to make it the very same with a perception or impression.

20   The consequence I shall draw from this may, at first sight, appear a mere sophism; but upon the least examination will be found solid and satisfactory. I say then, that since we may suppose, but never can conceive a specific difference betwixt an object and impression; any conclusion we form concerning the connexion and repugnance[†] of impressions, will not be known certainly to be applicable to objects; but that on the other hand, whatever conclusions of this kind we form concerning objects, will most certainly be applicable to impressions. The reason is not difficult. As an object is suppos'd to be different from an impression, we cannot be sure, that the circumstance, upon which we found our *SB 242*
reasoning, is common to both, supposing we form the reasoning upon the impression. 'Tis still possible, that the object may differ from it in that particular. But when we first form our reasoning concerning the object, 'tis beyond doubt, that the same reasoning must extend to the impression: And that because the quality of the object, upon which the argument is founded, must at least be conceiv'd by the mind; and cou'd not be conceiv'd, unless it were common to an impression; since we have no idea but what is deriv'd from that origin. Thus we may establish it as a certain maxim, that we can never, by any principle, but by an irregular kind of reasoning from experience,[46] discover a connexion or repugnance betwixt objects, which extends not to impressions; tho' the inverse propo-

---

[45] Part 2. Sect. 6.[†]   [46] Such as that of Sect. 2,[†] from the coherence of our perceptions.   *SB 241–2*

sition may not be equally true, that all the discoverable relations of impressions are common to objects.

21   To apply this to the present case; there are two different systems of beings presented, to which I suppose myself under a necessity of assigning some substance, or ground of inhesion.† I observe first the universe of objects or of body: The sun, moon and stars; the earth, seas, plants, animals, men, ships, houses, and other productions either of art or nature. Here *Spinoza* appears, and tells me, that these are only modifications; and that the subject, in which they inhere, is simple, uncompounded, and indivisible. After this I consider the other system of beings, *viz.* the universe of thought, or my impressions and ideas. There I observe another sun, moon and stars; an earth, and seas, cover'd and inhabited by plants and animals; towns, houses, mountains, rivers; and in short every thing I can discover or conceive in the first system. Upon my enquiring concerning these, theologians present themselves, and tell me, that these also are modifications, and modifications of one simple, uncompounded, and indivisible substance. Immediately upon which I am deafen'd with the noise of a hundred voices, that treat the first hypothesis with detestation and scorn, and the second *SB 243* with applause and veneration. I turn my attention to these hypotheses to see what may be the reason of so great a partiality; and find that they have the same fault of being unintelligible, and that as far as we can understand them, they are so much alike, that 'tis impossible to discover any absurdity in one, which is not common to both of them. We have no idea of any quality in an object, which does not agree to, and may not represent a quality in an impression; and that because all our ideas are deriv'd from our impressions. We can never, therefore, find any repugnance betwixt an extended object as a modification, and a simple uncompounded essence, as its substance, unless that repugnance takes place equally betwixt the perception or impression of that extended object, and the same uncompounded essence. Every idea of a quality in an object passes thro' an impression; and therefore every *perceivable* relation, whether of connexion or repugnance, must be common both to objects and impressions.

22   But tho' this argument, consider'd in general, seems evident beyond all doubt and contradiction, yet to make it more clear and sensible,† let us survey it in detail; and see whether all the absurdities, which have been found in the system of *Spinoza*, may not likewise be discover'd in that of theologians.[47]

23   *First*, It has been said against *Spinoza*, according to the scholastic way of talking, rather than thinking,† that a mode, not being any distinct or separate existence, must be the very same with its substance, and consequently the extension of the universe, must be in a manner identify'd with that simple, uncompounded essence, in which the universe is suppos'd to inhere.† But this, it may be pretended, is utterly impossible and inconceivable unless the indivisible substance expand itself, so as to correspond to the extension, or the extension contract itself, so as to answer to the indivisible substance. This argument seems just, as far as we can understand it; and 'tis plain nothing is requir'd, but a change *SB 244*

---

[47] See *Bayle*'s dictionary, article of *Spinoza*.†   *SB 243*

in the terms, to apply the same argument to our extended perceptions, and the simple essence of the soul; the ideas of objects and perceptions being in every respect the same, only attended with the supposition of a difference, that is unknown and incomprehensible.

24   *Secondly*, It has been said, that we have no idea of substance, which is not applicable to matter; nor any idea of a distinct substance, which is not applicable to every distinct portion of matter.[†] Matter, therefore, is not a mode but a substance, and each part of matter is not a distinct mode, but a distinct substance. I have already prov'd,[†] that we have no perfect idea of substance; but that taking it for *something, that can exist by itself*, 'tis evident every perception is a substance, and every distinct part of a perception a distinct substance: And consequently the one hypothesis labours under the same difficulties in this respect with the other.

25   *Thirdly*, It has been objected to the system of one simple substance in the universe, that this substance being the support or *substratum* of every thing, must at the very same instant be modify'd into forms, which are contrary and incompatible.[†] The round and square figures are incompatible in the same substance at the same time. How then is it possible, that the same substance can at once be modify'd into that square table, and into this round one? I ask the same question concerning the impressions of these tables; and find that the answer is no more satisfactory in one case than in the other.

26   It appears, then, that to whatever side we turn, the same difficulties follow us, and that we cannot advance one step towards the establishing the simplicity and immateriality of the soul, without preparing the way for a dangerous and irrecoverable atheism.[†] 'Tis the same case, if instead of calling thought a *modification* of the soul, we shou'd give it the more antient, and yet more modish name of an *action*.[†] By an action we mean much the same thing, as what is commonly   *SB 245* call'd an *abstract mode*; that is, something, which, properly speaking, is neither distinguishable, nor separable from its substance, and is only conceiv'd by a distinction of reason, or an abstraction.[†] But nothing is gain'd by this change of the term of *modification*, for that of *action*; nor do we free ourselves from one single difficulty by its means; as will appear from the two following reflections.

27   *First*, I observe, that the word, *action*, according to this explication of it, can never justly be apply'd to any perception, as deriv'd from a mind or thinking substance.[†] Our perceptions are all really different, and separable, and distinguishable from each other, and from every thing else, which we can imagine; and therefore 'tis impossible to conceive, how they can be the action or abstract mode of any substance. The instance of motion, which is commonly made use of to show after what manner perception depends, as an action, upon its substance, rather confounds than instructs us. Motion to all appearance induces no real nor essential change on the body, but only varies its relation to other objects. But betwixt a person in the morning walking in a garden with company, agreeable to him; and a person in the afternoon enclos'd in a dungeon, and full of terror, despair, and resentment, there seems to be a radical difference, and of quite another kind, than what is produc'd on a body by the change of its situation. As

we conclude from the distinction and separability of their ideas, that external objects have a separate existence from each other; so when we make these ideas themselves our objects, we must draw the same conclusion concerning *them*, according to the precedent reasoning.[†] At least it must be confest, that having no idea of the substance of the soul, 'tis impossible for us to tell how it can admit of such differences, and even contrarieties of perception without any fundamental change; and consequently can never tell in what sense perceptions are actions of that substance. The use, therefore, of the word, *action*, unaccompany'd with any meaning, instead of that of *modification*, makes no addition to our knowledge, nor is of any advantage to the doctrine of the immateriality of the soul.

SB 246

28   I add in the *second* place, that if it brings any advantage to that cause, it must bring an equal to the cause of atheism. For do our theologians pretend to make a monopoly of the word, *action*, and may not the atheists likewise take possession of it, and affirm that plants, animals, men, *&c.* are nothing but particular actions of one simple universal substance, which exerts itself from a blind and absolute necessity? This you'll say is utterly absurd. I own 'tis unintelligible; but at the same time assert, according to the principles above-explain'd,[†] that 'tis impossible to discover any absurdity in the supposition, that all the various objects in nature are actions of one simple substance, which absurdity will not be applicable to a like supposition concerning impressions and ideas.

29   From these hypotheses concerning the *substance* and *local conjunction* of our perceptions, we may pass to another, which is more intelligible than the former, and more important than the latter, *viz.* concerning the *cause* of our perceptions. Matter and motion, 'tis commonly said in the schools, however vary'd, are still matter and motion, and produce only a difference in the position and situation of objects.[†] Divide a body as often as you please, 'tis still body. Place it in any figure, nothing ever results but figure, or the relation of parts. Move it in any manner, you still find motion or a change of relation. 'Tis absurd to imagine, that motion in a circle, for instance, shou'd be nothing but merely motion in a circle; while motion in another direction, as in an ellipse, shou'd also be a passion or moral reflection: That the shocking of two globular particles shou'd become a sensation of pain, and that the meeting of two triangular ones shou'd afford a pleasure. Now as these different shocks, and variations, and mixtures are the only changes, of which matter is susceptible, and as these never afford us any idea of thought or perception, 'tis concluded to be impossible, that thought can ever be caus'd by matter.

SB 247

30   Few have been able to withstand the seeming evidence of this argument; and yet nothing in the world is more easy than to refute it. We need only reflect on what has been prov'd at large,[†] that we are never sensible of any connexion betwixt causes and effects, and that 'tis only by our experience of their constant conjunction, we can arrive at any knowledge of this relation. Now as all objects, which are not contrary, are susceptible of a constant conjunction, and as no real objects are contrary; I have inferr'd from these principles,[48] that to consider the

---

[48] Part 3. Sect. 15.[†]

matter *a priori*, any thing may produce any thing, and that we shall never discover a reason, why any object may or may not be the cause of any other, however great, or however little the resemblance may be betwixt them. This evidently destroys the precedent reasoning[†] concerning the cause of thought or perception. For tho' there appear no manner of connexion betwixt motion or thought, the case is the same with all other causes and effects. Place one body of a pound weight on one end of a lever, and another body of the same weight on another end; you will never find in these bodies any principle of motion dependent on their distances from the center, more than of thought and perception. If you pretend, therefore, to prove *a priori*, that such a position of bodies can never cause thought; because turn it which way you will, 'tis nothing but a position of bodies; you must by the same course of reasoning conclude, that it can never produce motion; since there is no more apparent connexion in the one case than in the other. But as this latter conclusion is contrary to evident experience, and as 'tis possible we may have a like experience in the operations of the mind, and may perceive a constant conjunction of thought and motion; you reason too hastily, when from the mere consideration of the ideas, you conclude that 'tis impossible motion can ever produce thought, or a different position of parts give rise to a different passion or reflection. Nay 'tis not only possible we may have such an experience, but 'tis certain we have it; since every one may perceive, that the different dispositions of his body change his thoughts and sentiments. And shou'd it be said, that this depends on the union of soul and body; I wou'd answer, that we must separate the question concerning the substance of the mind from that concerning the cause of its thought; and that confining ourselves to the latter question we find by the comparing their ideas, that thought and motion are different from each other, and by experience, that they are constantly united; which being all the circumstances, that enter into the idea of cause and effect, when apply'd to the operations of matter, we may certainly conclude, that motion may be, and actually is, the cause of thought and perception.

SB 248

31   There seems only this dilemma left us in the present case; either to assert, that nothing can be the cause of another, but where the mind can perceive the connexion in its idea of the objects: Or to maintain, that all objects, which we find constantly conjoin'd, are upon that account to be regarded as causes and effects. If we choose the first part of the dilemma, these are the consequences. *First*, We in reality affirm, that there is no such thing in the universe as a cause or productive principle, not even the deity himself; since our idea of that supreme being is deriv'd from particular impressions, none of which contain any efficacy, nor seem to have *any* connexion with *any* other existence. As to what may be said, that the connexion betwixt the idea of an infinitely powerful being, and that of any effect, which he wills, is necessary and unavoidable; I answer, that we have no idea of a being endow'd with any power, much less of one endow'd with infinite power. But if we will change expressions, we can only define power by connexion; and then in saying, that the idea of an infinitely powerful being is connected with that of every effect, which he wills, we really do no more than assert, that a

SB 249

being, whose volition is connected with every effect, is connected with every effect; which is an identical proposition, and gives us no insight into the nature of this power or connexion. But, *secondly*, supposing, that the deity were the great and efficacious principle, which supplies the deficiency of all causes,† this leads us into the grossest impieties and absurdities. For upon the same account, that we have recourse to him in natural operations, and assert that matter cannot of itself communicate motion, or produce thought, *viz.* because there is no apparent connexion betwixt these objects; I say, upon the very same account, we must acknowledge that the deity is the author of all our volitions and perceptions; since they have no more apparent connexion either with one another, or with the suppos'd but unknown substance of the soul. This agency of the supreme being we know to have been asserted by several philosophers[49] with relation to all the actions of the mind, except volition, or rather an inconsiderable part of volition; tho' 'tis easy to perceive, that this exception is a mere pretext, to avoid the dangerous consequences of that doctrine.† If nothing be active but what has an apparent power, thought is in no case any more active than matter; and if this inactivity must make us have recourse to a deity, the supreme being is the real cause of all our actions, bad as well as good, vicious as well as virtuous.

32   Thus we are necessarily reduc'd to the other side of the dilemma, *viz.* that all objects, which are found to be constantly conjoin'd, are upon that account only to be regarded as causes and effects. Now as all objects, which are not contrary, are susceptible of a constant conjunction, and as no real objects are contrary; it follows, that for aught we can determine by the mere ideas, any thing may be the *SB 250* cause or effect of any thing; which evidently gives the advantage to the materialists above their antagonists.

33   To pronounce, then, the final decision upon the whole; the question concerning the substance of the soul is absolutely unintelligible: All our perceptions are not susceptible of a local union, either with what is extended or unextended; there being some of them of the one kind, and some of the other:† And as the constant conjunction of objects constitutes the very essence† of cause and effect, matter and motion may often be regarded as the causes of thought, as far as we have any notion of that relation.

34   'Tis certainly a kind of indignity to philosophy, whose sovereign authority ought every where to be acknowledg'd, to oblige her on every occasion to make apologies for her conclusions, and justify herself to every particular art and science, which may be offended at her. This puts one in mind of a king arraign'd for high-treason against his subjects. There is only one occasion, when philosophy will think it necessary and even honourable to justify herself, and that is, when religion may seem to be in the least offended; whose rights are as dear to her as her own, and are indeed the same. If any one, therefore, shou'd imagine

[49] As Father *Malebranche* and other *Cartesians.*†   *SB 249*

that the foregoing arguments are any ways dangerous to religion, I hope the following apology will remove his apprehensions.[†]

35   There is no foundation for any conclusion *a priori*, either concerning the operations or duration of any object, of which 'tis possible for the human mind to form a conception. Any object may be imagin'd to become entirely inactive, or to be annihilated in a moment; and 'tis an evident principle, *that whatever we can imagine, is possible*. Now this is no more true of matter, than of spirit; of an extended compounded substance, than of a simple and unextended. In both cases the metaphysical arguments for the immortality of the soul are equally inconclusive;[†] and in both cases the moral arguments and those deriv'd from the analogy of nature are equally strong and convincing. If my philosophy, therefore, makes no addition to the arguments for religion, I have at least the satisfaction to think it takes nothing from them, but that every thing remains precisely as before.   *SB 251*

Sect. 6. *Of personal identity*

1   There are some philosophers, who imagine we are every moment intimately conscious of what we call our SELF; that we feel its existence and its continuance in existence; and are certain, beyond the evidence of a demonstration, both of its perfect identity and simplicity.[†] The strongest sensation, the most violent passion, say they, instead of distracting us from this view, only fix it the more intensely, and make us consider their influence on *self* either by their pain or pleasure. To attempt a farther proof of this were to weaken its evidence; since no proof can be deriv'd from any fact, of which we are so intimately conscious; nor is there any thing, of which we can be certain, if we doubt of this.

2   Unluckily all these positive assertions are contrary to that very experience, which is pleaded for them, nor have we any idea of *self*, after the manner it is here explain'd. For from what impression cou'd this idea be deriv'd? This question 'tis impossible to answer without a manifest contradiction and absurdity; and yet 'tis a question, which must necessarily be answer'd, if we wou'd have the idea of self pass for clear and intelligible. It must be some one impression, that gives rise to every real idea. But self or person is not any one impression, but that to which our several impressions and ideas are suppos'd to have a reference. If any impression gives rise to the idea of self, that impression must continue invariably the same, thro' the whole course of our lives; since self is suppos'd to exist after that manner. But there is no impression constant and invariable. Pain and plea-   *SB 252* sure, grief and joy, passions and sensations succeed each other, and never all exist at the same time. It cannot, therefore, be from any of these impressions, or from any other, that the idea of self is deriv'd; and consequently there is no such idea.[†]

3   But farther, what must become of all our particular perceptions upon this hypothesis? All these are different, and distinguishable, and separable from each other, and may be separately consider'd, and may exist separately, and have no need of any thing to support their existence. After what manner, therefore, do

164

they belong to self; and how are they connected with it? For my part, when I enter most intimately into what I call *myself*, I always stumble on some particular perception or other, of heat or cold, light or shade, love or hatred, pain or pleasure.† I never can catch *myself* at any time without a perception, and never can observe any thing but the perception. When my perceptions are remov'd for any time, as by sound sleep; so long am I insensible of *myself*, and may truly be said not to exist.† And were all my perceptions remov'd by death, and cou'd I neither think, nor feel, nor see, nor love, nor hate after the dissolution of my body, I shou'd be entirely annihilated, nor do I conceive what is farther requisite to make me a perfect non-entity. If any one upon serious and unprejudic'd reflection, thinks he has a different notion of *himself*, I must confess I can reason no longer with him. All I can allow him is, that he may be in the right as well as I, and that we are essentially different in this particular. He may, perhaps, perceive something simple and continu'd, which he calls *himself*; tho' I am certain there is no such principle in me.

4   But setting aside some metaphysicians of this kind,† I may venture to affirm of the rest of mankind, that they are nothing but a bundle or collection of different perceptions, which succeed each other with an inconceivable rapidity, and are in a perpetual flux and movement. Our eyes cannot turn in their sockets without varying our perceptions. Our thought is still more variable than our sight; and all *SB 253* our other senses and faculties contribute to this change; nor is there any single power of the soul, which remains unalterably the same, perhaps for one moment. The mind is a kind of theatre, where several perceptions successively make their appearance; pass, re-pass, glide away, and mingle in an infinite variety of postures and situations. There is properly no *simplicity* in it at one time, nor *identity* in different; whatever natural propension we may have to imagine that simplicity and identity. The comparison of the theatre must not mislead us. They are the successive perceptions only, that constitute the mind; nor have we the most distant notion of the place, where these scenes are represented, or of the materials, of which it is compos'd.

5   What then gives us so great a propension to ascribe an identity to these successive perceptions, and to suppose ourselves possest of an invariable and uninterrupted existence thro' the whole course of our lives? In order to answer this question, we must distinguish betwixt personal identity, as it regards our thought or imagination, and as it regards our passions or the concern we take in ourselves. The first is our present subject;† and to explain it perfectly we must take the matter pretty deep, and account for that identity, which we attribute to plants and animals; there being a great analogy betwixt it, and the identity of a self or person.

6   We have a distinct idea of an object, that remains invariable and uninterrupted thro' a suppos'd variation of time; and this idea we call that of *identity* or *sameness*.† We have also a distinct idea of several different objects existing in succession, and connected together by a close relation; and this to an accurate view affords as perfect a notion of *diversity*, as if there was no manner of relation among the objects. But tho' these two ideas of identity, and a succession of

related objects be in themselves perfectly distinct, and even contrary, yet 'tis certain, that in our common way of thinking they are generally confounded with each other. That action of the imagination, by which we consider the uninter- *SB 254* rupted and invariable object, and that by which we reflect on the succession of related objects, are almost the same to the feeling, nor is there much more effort of thought requir'd in the latter case than in the former. The relation facilitates the transition of the mind from one object to another, and renders its passage as smooth as if it contemplated one continu'd object. This resemblance is the cause of the confusion and mistake, and makes us substitute the notion of identity, instead of that of related objects. However at one instant we may consider the related succession as variable or interrupted, we are sure the next to ascribe to it a perfect identity, and regard it as invariable and uninterrupted. Our propensity to this mistake is so great from the resemblance above-mention'd, that we fall into it before we are aware; and tho' we incessantly correct ourselves by reflec- tion, and return to a more accurate method of thinking, yet we cannot long sustain our philosophy, or take off this biass from the imagination.† Our last resource is to yield to it, and boldly assert that these different related objects are in effect the same, however interrupted and variable. In order to justify to our- selves this absurdity, we often feign some new and unintelligible principle, that connects the objects together, and prevents their interruption or variation. Thus we feign the continu'd existence of the perceptions of our senses, to remove the interruption; and run into† the notion of a *soul*, and *self*, and *substance*, to disguise the variation. But we may farther observe, that where we do not give rise to such a fiction, our propension to confound identity with relation is so great, that we are apt to imagine something unknown and mysterious, connecting the parts, beside their relation;[50] and this I take to be the case with regard to the identity we *SB 255* ascribe to plants and animals. And even when this does not take place, we still feel a propensity to confound these ideas, tho' we are not able fully to satisfy our- selves in that particular, nor find any thing invariable and uninterrupted to justify our notion of identity.

7   Thus the controversy concerning identity is not merely a dispute of words.† For when we attribute identity, in an improper sense, to variable or interrupted objects, our mistake is not confin'd to the expression, but is commonly attended with a fiction, either of something invariable and uninterrupted, or of some- thing mysterious and inexplicable, or at least with a propensity to such fictions. What will suffice to prove this hypothesis to the satisfaction of every fair enquirer, is to show from daily experience and observation, that the objects, which are variable or interrupted, and yet are suppos'd to continue the same, are such only as consist of a succession of parts, connected together by resemblance, contiguity, or causation. For as such a succession answers evidently to our notion

---

[50] If the reader is desirous to see how a great genius may be influenc'd by these seemingly trivial *SB 254* principles of the imagination, as well as the mere vulgar, let him read my Lord *Shaftesbury*'s rea- sonings concerning the uniting principle of the universe, and the identity of plants and animals. See his *Moralists*: or *Philosophical Rhapsody*.†

of diversity, it can only be by mistake we ascribe to it an identity; and as the relation of parts, which leads us into this mistake, is really nothing but a quality, which produces an association of ideas, and an easy transition of the imagination from one to another, it can only be from the resemblance, which this act of the mind bears to that, by which we contemplate one continu'd object, that the error arises. Our chief business, then, must be to prove, that all objects, to which we ascribe identity, without observing their invariableness and uninterruptedness, are such as consist of a succession of related objects.

8   In order to this, suppose any mass of matter, of which the parts are contiguous and connected, to be plac'd before us; 'tis plain we must attribute a perfect identity to this mass, provided all the parts continue uninterruptedly and invariably the same, whatever motion or change of place we may observe either in the whole or in any of the parts. But supposing some very *small* or *inconsiderable* part to be added to the mass, or substracted from it; tho' this absolutely destroys the identity of the whole, strictly speaking; yet as we seldom think so accurately, we scruple not to pronounce a mass of matter the same, where we find so trivial an alteration. The passage of the thought from the object before the change to the object after it, is so smooth and easy, that we scarce perceive the transition, and are apt to imagine, that 'tis nothing but a continu'd survey of the same object. *SB 256*

9   There is a very remarkable circumstance, that attends this experiment; which is, that tho' the change of any considerable part in a mass of matter destroys the identity of the whole, yet we must measure the greatness of the part, not absolutely, but by its *proportion* to the whole.[†] The addition or diminution of a mountain wou'd not be sufficient to produce a diversity in a planet; tho' the change of a very few inches wou'd be able to destroy the identity of some bodies. 'Twill be impossible to account for this, but by reflecting that objects operate upon the mind, and break or interrupt the continuity of its actions not according to their real greatness, but according to their proportion to each other: And therefore, since this interruption makes an object cease to appear the same, it must be the uninterrupted progress of the thought, which constitutes the imperfect identity.

10   This may be confirm'd by another phænomenon. A change in any considerable part of a body destroys its identity; but 'tis remarkable, that where the change is produc'd *gradually* and *insensibly* we are less apt to ascribe to it the same effect. The reason can plainly be no other, than that the mind, in following the successive changes of the body, feels an easy passage from the surveying its condition in one moment to the viewing of it in another, and at no particular time perceives any interruption in its actions. From which continu'd perception, it ascribes a continu'd existence and identity to the object.

11   But whatever precaution we may use in introducing the changes gradually, and making them proportionable to the whole, 'tis certain, that where the changes are at last observ'd to become considerable, we make a scruple of ascribing identity to such different objects. There is, however, another artifice, by which we may induce the imagination to advance a step farther; and that is, *SB 257*

by producing a reference of the parts to each other, and a combination to some *common end* or purpose. A ship, of which a considerable part has been chang'd by frequent reparations, is still consider'd as the same; nor does the difference of the materials hinder us from ascribing an identity to it. The common end, in which the parts conspire, is the same under all their variations, and affords an easy transition of the imagination from one situation of the body to another.[†]

12   But this is still more remarkable, when we add a *sympathy*[†] of parts to their *common end*, and suppose that they bear to each other, the reciprocal relation of cause and effect in all their actions and operations. This is the case with all animals and vegetables; where not only the several parts have a reference to some general purpose, but also a mutual dependance on, and connexion with each other. The effect of so strong a relation is, that tho' every one must allow, that in a very few years both vegetables and animals endure a *total* change, yet we still attribute identity to them, while their form, size, and substance are entirely alter'd. An oak, that grows from a small plant to a large tree, is still the same oak; tho' there be not one particle of matter, or figure of its parts the same. An infant becomes a man, and is sometimes fat, sometimes lean, without any change in his identity.

13   We may also consider the two following phænomena, which are remarkable in their kind. The *first* is, that tho' we commonly be able to distinguish pretty exactly betwixt numerical and specific identity,[†] yet it sometimes happens, that we confound them, and in our thinking and reasoning employ the one for the other. Thus a man, who hears a noise, that is frequently interrupted and renew'd, says, it is still the same noise; tho' 'tis evident the sounds have only a specific identity or resemblance, and there is nothing numerically the same, but the cause, which produc'd them. In like manner it may be said without breach of the propriety of language, that such a church, which was formerly of brick, fell to ruin, and that the parish rebuilt the same church of free-stone, and according to modern architecture. Here neither the form nor materials are the same, nor is there any thing common to the two objects, but their relation to the inhabitants of the parish; and yet this alone is sufficient to make us denominate them the same. But we must observe, that in these cases the first object is in a manner annihilated before the second comes into existence; by which means, we are never presented in any one point of time with the idea of difference and multiplicity; and for that reason are less scrupulous in calling them the same. *SB 258*

14   *Secondly*, We may remark, that tho' in a succession of related objects, it be in a manner requisite, that the change of parts be not sudden nor entire, in order to preserve the identity, yet where the objects are in their nature changeable and inconstant, we admit of a more sudden transition, than wou'd otherwise be consistent with that relation. Thus as the nature of a river consists in the motion and change of parts; tho' in less than four and twenty hours these be totally alter'd; this hinders not the river from continuing the same during several ages. What is natural and essential to any thing is, in a manner, expected; and what is expected

makes less impression, and appears of less moment, than what is unusual and extraordinary. A considerable change of the former kind seems really less to the imagination, than the most trivial alteration of the latter; and by breaking less the continuity of the thought, has less influence in destroying the identity.

15   We now proceed to explain the nature of *personal identity*, which has become   *SB 259* so great a question in philosophy, especially of late years in *England*,[†] where all the abstruser sciences are study'd with a peculiar ardour and application. And here 'tis evident, the same method of reasoning must be continu'd, which has so successfully explain'd the identity of plants, and animals, and ships, and houses, and of all the compounded and changeable productions either of art or nature. The identity, which we ascribe to the mind of man, is only a fictitious one, and of a like kind with that which we ascribe to vegetables and animal bodies. It cannot, therefore, have a different origin, but must proceed from a like operation of the imagination upon like objects.

16   But lest this argument shou'd not convince the reader; tho' in my opinion perfectly decisive; let him weigh the following reasoning, which is still closer and more immediate. 'Tis evident, that the identity, which we attribute to the human mind, however perfect we may imagine it to be, is not able to run the several different perceptions into one, and make them lose their characters of distinction and difference, which are essential to them. 'Tis still true, that every distinct perception, which enters into the composition of the mind, is a distinct existence, and is different, and distinguishable, and separable from every other perception, either co-temporary or successive. But, as, notwithstanding this distinction and separability, we suppose the whole train of perceptions to be united by identity, a question naturally arises concerning this relation of identity; whether it be something that really binds our several perceptions together, or only associates their ideas in the imagination? That is, in other words, whether in pronouncing concerning the identity of a person, we observe some real bond among his perceptions, or only feel one among the ideas we form of them? This question we might easily decide, if we wou'd recollect what has been already prov'd at large,[†] that the understanding never observes any real connexion among objects, and   *SB 260* that even the union of cause and effect, when strictly examin'd, resolves itself into a customary association of ideas. For from thence it evidently follows, that identity is nothing really belonging to these different perceptions, and uniting them together; but is merely a quality, which we attribute to them, because of the union of their ideas in the imagination, when we reflect upon them. Now the only qualities, which can give ideas an union in the imagination, are these three relations above-mention'd.[†] These are the uniting principles in the ideal world,[†] and without them every distinct object is separable by the mind, and may be separately consider'd, and appears not to have any more connexion with any other object, than if disjoin'd by the greatest difference and remoteness. 'Tis, therefore, on some of these three relations of resemblance, contiguity and causation, that identity depends; and as the very essence of these relations consists in their producing an easy transition of ideas; it follows, that our notions of per-

sonal identity, proceed entirely from the smooth and uninterrupted progress of the thought along a train of connected ideas, according to the principles above-explain'd.[†]

17   The only question, therefore, which remains, is, by what relations this uninterrupted progress of our thought is produc'd, when we consider the successive existence of a mind or thinking person? And here 'tis evident we must confine ourselves to resemblance and causation, and must drop contiguity, which has little or no influence in the present case.

18   To begin with *resemblance*; suppose we cou'd see clearly into the breast of another, and observe that succession of perceptions, which constitutes his mind or thinking principle, and suppose that he always preserves the memory of a considerable part of past perceptions; 'tis evident, that nothing cou'd more contribute to the bestowing a relation on this succession amidst all its variations. For what is the memory but a faculty, by which we raise up the images of past perceptions? And as an image necessarily resembles its object, must not the frequent *SB 261* placing of these resembling perceptions in the chain of thought, convey the imagination more easily from one link to another, and make the whole seem like the continuance of one object? In this particular, then, the memory not only discovers the identity, but also contributes to its production, by producing the relation of resemblance among the perceptions. The case is the same whether we consider ourselves or others.

19   As to *causation*; we may observe, that the true idea of the human mind, is to consider it as a system of different perceptions or different existences, which are link'd together by the relation of cause and effect, and mutually produce, destroy, influence, and modify each other.[†] Our impressions give rise to their correspondent ideas; and these ideas in their turn produce other impressions. One thought chaces another, and draws after it a third, by which it is expell'd in its turn. In this respect, I cannot compare the soul more properly to any thing than to a republic or commonwealth, in which the several members are united by the reciprocal ties of government and subordination, and give rise to other persons, who propagate the same republic in the incessant changes of its parts. And as the same individual republic may not only change its members, but also its laws and constitutions; in like manner the same person may vary his character and disposition, as well as his impressions and ideas, without losing his identity. Whatever changes he endures, his several parts are still connected by the relation of causation. And in this view our identity with regard to the passions serves to corroborate that with regard to the imagination, by the making our distant perceptions influence each other, and by giving us a present concern for our past or future pains or pleasures.

20   As memory alone acquaints us with the continuance and extent of this succession of perceptions, 'tis to be consider'd, upon that account chiefly, as the source of personal identity. Had we no memory, we never shou'd have any notion of causation, nor consequently of that chain of causes and effects, which constitute *SB 262* our self or person. But having once acquir'd this notion of causation from the memory, we can extend the same chain of causes, and consequently the identity

of our persons beyond our memory, and can comprehend times, and circumstances, and actions, which we have entirely forgot, but suppose in general to have existed. For how few of our past actions are there, of which we have any memory? Who can tell me, for instance, what were his thoughts and actions on the first of *January* 1715, the 11th of *March* 1719, and the 3d of *August* 1733? Or will he affirm, because he has entirely forgot the incidents of these days, that the present self is not the same person with the self of that time; and by that means overturn all the most establish'd notions of personal identity? In this view, therefore, memory does not so much *produce* as *discover* personal identity, by showing us the relation of cause and effect among our different perceptions. 'Twill be incumbent on those, who affirm that memory produces entirely our personal identity, to give a reason why we can thus extend our identity beyond our memory.†

21   The whole of this doctrine leads us to a conclusion, which is of great importance in the present affair, *viz.* that all the nice and subtile questions concerning personal identity can never possibly be decided, and are to be regarded rather as grammatical than as philosophical difficulties. Identity depends on the relations of ideas; and these relations produce identity, by means of that easy transition they occasion. But as the relations, and the easiness of the transition may diminish by insensible degrees, we have no just standard, by which we can decide any dispute concerning the time, when they acquire or lose a title to the name of identity. All the disputes concerning the identity of connected objects are merely verbal, except so far as the relation of parts gives rise to some fiction or imaginary principle of union, as we have already observ'd.†

22   What I have said concerning the first origin and uncertainty of our notion   *SB 263*
of identity, as apply'd to the human mind, may be extended with little or no variation to that of *simplicity*. An object, whose different co-existent parts are bound together by a close relation, operates upon the imagination after much the same manner as one perfectly simple and indivisible, and requires not a much greater stretch of thought in order to its conception. From this similarity of operation we attribute a simplicity to it, and feign a principle of union as the support of this simplicity, and the center of all the different parts and qualities of the object.

23   Thus we have finish'd our examination of the several systems of philosophy, both of the intellectual and natural world; and in our miscellaneous way of reasoning have been led into several topics; which will either illustrate and confirm some preceding part of this discourse, or prepare the way for our following opinions. 'Tis now time to return to a more close examination of our subject, and to proceed in the accurate anatomy of human nature,† having fully explain'd the nature of our judgment and understanding.

Sect. 7. *Conclusion of this book*

1   But before I launch out into those immense depths of philosophy, which lie before me, I find myself inclin'd to stop a moment in my present station, and to ponder that voyage, which I have undertaken, and which undoubtedly requires

the utmost art and industry to be brought to a happy conclusion. Methinks I am like a man, who having struck on many shoals, and having narrowly escap'd ship-wreck in passing a small frith, has yet the temerity to put out to sea in the same leaky weather-beaten vessel, and even carries his ambition so far as to think *SB 264* of compassing the globe under these disadvantageous circumstances. My memory of past errors and perplexities, makes me diffident for the future. The wretched condition, weakness, and disorder of the faculties, I must employ in my enquiries, encrease my apprehensions. And the impossibility of amending or correcting these faculties, reduces me almost to despair, and makes me resolve to perish on the barren rock, on which I am at present, rather than venture myself upon that boundless ocean, which runs out into immensity. This sudden view of my danger strikes me with melancholy; and as 'tis usual for that passion, above all others, to indulge itself; I cannot forbear feeding my despair, with all those desponding reflections, which the present subject furnishes me with in such abundance.

2   I am first affrighted and confounded with that forlorn solitude, in which I am plac'd in my philosophy, and fancy myself some strange uncouth monster, who not being able to mingle and unite in society, has been expell'd all human commerce,[†] and left utterly abandon'd and disconsolate. Fain wou'd I run into the crowd for shelter and warmth; but cannot prevail with myself to mix with such deformity.[†] I call upon others to join me, in order to make a company apart; but no one will hearken to me. Every one keeps at a distance, and dreads that storm, which beats upon me from every side. I have expos'd myself to the enmity of all metaphysicians, logicians, mathematicians, and even theologians; and can I wonder at the insults I must suffer? I have declar'd my disapprobation of their systems; and can I be surpriz'd, if they shou'd express a hatred of mine and of my person? When I look abroad, I foresee on every side, dispute, contradiction, anger, calumny and detraction. When I turn my eye inward, I find nothing but doubt and ignorance. All the world conspires to oppose and contradict me; tho' such is my weakness, that I feel all my opinions loosen and fall of themselves, when unsupported by the approbation of others. Every step I take is with *SB 265* hesitation, and every new reflection makes me dread an error and absurdity in my reasoning.

3   For with what confidence can I venture upon such bold enterprizes, when beside those numberless infirmities peculiar to myself, I find so many which are common to human nature? Can I be sure, that in leaving all establish'd opinions I am following truth; and by what criterion shall I distinguish her, even if fortune shou'd at last guide me on her foot-steps? After the most accurate and exact of my reasonings, I can give no reason why I shou'd assent to it; and feel nothing but a *strong* propensity to consider objects *strongly* in that view, under which they appear to me. Experience is a principle, which instructs me in the several conjunctions of objects for the past. Habit is another principle, which determines me to expect the same for the future; and both of them conspiring to operate upon the imagination, make me form certain ideas in a more intense and lively manner, than others, which are not attended with the same advantages. Without

this quality,[†] by which the mind enlivens some ideas beyond others (which seemingly is so trivial, and so little founded on reason) we cou'd never assent to any argument, nor carry our view beyond those few objects, which are present to our senses. Nay, even to these objects we cou'd never attribute any existence, but what was dependent on the senses; and must comprehend them entirely in that succession of perceptions, which constitutes our self or person. Nay farther, even with relation to that succession, we cou'd only admit of those perceptions, which are immediately present to our consciousness, nor cou'd those lively images, with which the memory presents us, be ever receiv'd as true pictures of past perceptions. The memory, senses, and understanding are, therefore, all of them founded on the imagination, or the vivacity of our ideas.

4   No wonder a principle[†] so inconstant and fallacious shou'd lead us into errors, when implicitly follow'd (as it must be) in all its variations. 'Tis this principle, *SB 266* which makes us reason from causes and effects; and 'tis the same principle, which convinces us of the continu'd existence of external objects, when absent from the senses. But tho' these two operations be equally natural and necessary in the human mind, yet in some circumstances they are directly contrary,[51] nor is it possible for us to reason justly and regularly from causes and effects, and at the same time believe the continu'd existence of matter. How then shall we adjust those principles together? Which of them shall we prefer? Or in case we prefer neither of them, but successively assent to both, as is usual among philosophers, with what confidence can we afterwards usurp that glorious title,[†] when we thus knowingly embrace a manifest contradiction?

5   This contradiction wou'd be more excusable, were it compensated by any degree of solidity and satisfaction in the other parts of our reasoning.[52] But the case is quite contrary. When we trace up the human understanding to its first principles, we find it to lead us into such sentiments, as seem to turn into ridicule all our past pains and industry, and to discourage us from future enquiries. Nothing is more curiously enquir'd after by the mind of man, than the causes of every phænomenon; nor are we content with knowing the immediate causes, but push on our enquiries, till we arrive at the original and ultimate principle. We wou'd not willingly stop before we are acquainted with that energy in the cause, by which it operates on its effect; that tie, which connects them together; and that efficacious quality, on which the tie depends. This is our aim in all our studies and reflections: And how must we be disappointed, when we learn, that this connexion, tie, or energy lies merely in ourselves, and is nothing but that determination of the mind, which is acquir'd by custom, and causes us to make a transition from an object to its usual attendant, and from the impression of one to the lively idea of the other? Such a discovery not only cuts off all hope of ever *SB 267* attaining satisfaction, but even prevents our very wishes; since it appears, that when we say we desire to know the ultimate and operating principle, as something, which resides in the external object, we either contradict ourselves, or talk without a meaning.

---

[51] Sect. 4.[†]   [52] Part 3. Sect. 14.[†]   *SB 266*

6   This deficiency in our ideas is not, indeed, perceiv'd in common life, nor are we sensible,[†] that in the most usual conjunctions of cause and effect we are as ignorant of the ultimate principle, which binds them together, as in the most unusual and extraordinary. But this[†] proceeds merely from an illusion of the imagination; and the question is, how far we ought to yield to these illusions. This question is very difficult, and reduces us to a very dangerous dilemma, which-ever way we answer it. For if we assent to every trivial suggestion of the fancy; beside that these suggestions are often contrary to each other; they lead us into such errors, absurdities, and obscurities, that we must at last become asham'd of our credulity. Nothing is more dangerous to reason than the flights of the imagination, and nothing has been the occasion of more mistakes among philosophers.[†] Men of bright fancies may in this respect be compar'd to those angels, whom the scripture represents as covering their eyes with their wings.[†] This has already appear'd in so many instances, that we may spare ourselves the trouble of enlarging upon it any farther.

7   But on the other hand, if the consideration of these instances makes us take a resolution to reject all the trivial suggestions of the fancy, and adhere to the understanding, that is, to the general and more establish'd properties of the imagination;[†] even this resolution, if steadily executed, wou'd be dangerous, and attended with the most fatal consequences. For I have already shown,[53] that the understanding, when it acts alone, and according to its most general principles, entirely subverts itself, and leaves not the lowest degree of evidence in any proposition, either in philosophy or common life. We save ourselves from this *SB 268* total scepticism only by means of that singular and seemingly trivial property of the fancy, by which we enter with difficulty into remote views of things, and are not able to accompany them with so sensible an impression, as we do those, which are more easy and natural. Shall we, then, establish it for a general maxim, that no refin'd or elaborate reasoning is ever to be receiv'd? Consider well the consequences of such a principle. By this means you cut off entirely all science and philosophy: You proceed upon one singular quality of the imagination, and by a parity of reason must embrace all of them: And you expressly contradict yourself; since this maxim must be built on the preceding reasoning, which will be allow'd to be sufficiently refin'd and metaphysical. What party, then, shall we choose among these difficulties? If we embrace this principle, and condemn all refin'd reasoning, we run into the most manifest absurdities.[†] If we reject it in favour of these reasonings, we subvert entirely the human understanding. We have, therefore, no choice left but betwixt a false reason and none at all. For my part, I know not what ought to be done in the present case. I can only observe what is commonly done; which is, that this difficulty is seldom or never thought of; and even where it has once been present to the mind, is quickly forgot, and leaves but a small impression behind it. Very refin'd reflections have little or no influence upon us; and yet we do not, and cannot establish it for a rule, that they ought not to have any influence; which implies a manifest contradiction.

[53] Sect. 1.[†]   *SB 267*

8   But what have I here said, that reflections very refin'd and metaphysical have little or no influence upon us? This opinion I can scarce forbear retracting, and condemning from my present feeling and experience. The *intense* view of these manifold contradictions and imperfections in human reason has so wrought upon me, and heated my brain, that I am ready to reject all belief and reasoning, and can look upon no opinion even as more probable or likely than another. Where am I, or what? From what causes do I derive my existence,   *SB 269* and to what condition shall I return? Whose favour shall I court, and whose anger must I dread? What beings surround me? and on whom have I any influence, or who have any influence on me? I am confounded with all these questions, and begin to fancy myself in the most deplorable condition imaginable, inviron'd with the deepest darkness, and utterly depriv'd of the use of every member and faculty.

9   Most fortunately it happens, that since reason is incapable of dispelling these clouds, nature herself suffices to that purpose, and cures me of this philosophical melancholy and delirium, either by relaxing this bent of mind, or by some avocation, and lively impression of my senses, which obliterate all these chimeras. I dine, I play a game of back-gammon, I converse, and am merry with my friends; and when after three or four hour's amusement, I wou'd return to these speculations, they appear so cold, and strain'd, and ridiculous, that I cannot find in my heart to enter into them any farther.

10   Here then I find myself absolutely and necessarily determin'd to live, and talk, and act like other people in the common affairs of life.[†] But notwithstanding that my natural propensity, and the course of my animal spirits and passions reduce me to this indolent belief in the general maxims of the world,[†] I still feel such remains of my former disposition, that I am ready to throw all my books and papers into the fire, and resolve never more to renounce the pleasures of life for the sake of reasoning and philosophy. For these are my sentiments in that splenetic humour,[†] which governs me at present. I may, nay I must yield to the current of nature, in submitting to my senses and understanding; and in this blind submission I show most perfectly my sceptical disposition and principles.[†] But does it follow, that I must strive against the current of nature, which leads me to indolence and pleasure; that I must seclude myself, in some measure,   *SB 270* from the commerce and society of men, which is so agreeable; and that I must torture my brain with subtilities and sophistries, at the very time that I cannot satisfy myself concerning the reasonableness of so painful an application, nor have any tolerable prospect of arriving by its means at truth and certainty? Under what obligation do I lie of making such an abuse of time? And to what end can it serve either for the service of mankind, or for my own private interest? No: If I must be a fool, as all those who reason or believe any thing *certainly* are, my follies shall at least be natural and agreeable. Where I strive against my inclination, I shall have a good reason for my resistance; and will no more be led a wandering into such dreary solitudes, and rough passages, as I have hitherto met with.

11   These are the sentiments of my spleen and indolence; and indeed I must

confess, that philosophy has nothing to oppose to them, and expects a victory more from the returns of a serious good-humour'd disposition, than from the force of reason and conviction. In all the incidents of life we ought still to preserve our scepticism. If we believe, that fire warms, or water refreshes, 'tis only because it costs us too much pains to think otherwise. Nay if we are philosophers, it ought only to be upon sceptical principles, and from an inclination, which we feel to the employing ourselves after that manner. Where reason is lively, and mixes itself with some propensity, it ought to be assented to. Where it does not, it never can have any title to operate upon us.

12   At the time, therefore, that I am tir'd with amusement and company, and have indulg'd a *reverie* in my chamber, or in a solitary walk by a river-side, I feel my mind all collected within itself,[†] and am naturally *inclin'd* to carry my view into all those subjects, about which I have met with so many disputes in the course of my reading and conversation. I cannot forbear having a curiosity to be acquainted with the principles of moral good and evil, the nature and foundation *SB 271* of government, and the cause of those several passions and inclinations, which actuate and govern me.[†] I am uneasy to think I approve of one object, and disapprove of another; call one thing beautiful, and another deform'd; decide concerning truth and falshood, reason and folly, without knowing upon what principles I proceed. I am concern'd for the condition of the learned world, which lies under such a deplorable ignorance in all these particulars. I feel an ambition to arise in me of contributing to the instruction of mankind, and of acquiring a name by my inventions and discoveries. These sentiments spring up naturally in my present disposition; and shou'd I endeavour to banish them, by attaching myself to any other business or diversion, I *feel* I shou'd be a loser in point of pleasure; and this is the origin of my philosophy.

13   But even suppose this curiosity and ambition shou'd not transport me into speculations without the sphere of common life, it wou'd necessarily happen, that from my very weakness I must be led into such enquiries. 'Tis certain, that superstition is much more bold in its systems and hypotheses than philosophy; and while the latter contents itself with assigning new causes and principles to the phænomena, which appear in the visible world, the former opens a world of its own, and presents us with scenes, and beings, and objects, which are altogether new.[†] Since therefore 'tis almost impossible for the mind of man to rest, like those of beasts, in that narrow circle of objects, which are the subject of daily conversation and action, we ought only to deliberate concerning the choice of our guide, and ought to prefer that which is safest and most agreeable. And in this respect I make bold to recommend philosophy, and shall not scruple to give it the preference to superstition of every kind or denomination. For as superstition arises naturally and easily from the popular opinions of mankind, it seizes more strongly on the mind, and is often able to disturb us in the conduct of our *SB 272* lives and actions. Philosophy on the contrary, if just, can present us only with mild and moderate sentiments; and if false and extravagant, its opinions are merely the objects of a cold and general speculation, and seldom go so far as to interrupt the course of our natural propensities. The CYNICS[†] are an extra-

ordinary instance of philosophers, who from reasonings purely philosophical ran into as great extravagancies of conduct as any *Monk* or *Dervise* that ever was in the world. Generally speaking, the errors in religion are dangerous; those in philosophy only ridiculous.

14   I am sensible, that these two cases of the strength and weakness of the mind will not comprehend all mankind, and that there are in *England*, in particular, many honest gentlemen, who being always employ'd in their domestic affairs, or amusing themselves in common recreations, have carry'd their thoughts very little beyond those objects, which are every day expos'd to their senses. And indeed, of such as these I pretend not to make philosophers, nor do I expect them either to be associates in these researches or auditors of these discoveries. They do well to keep themselves in their present situation; and instead of refining them into philosophers, I wish we cou'd communicate to our founders of systems, a share of this gross earthy mixture,† as an ingredient, which they commonly stand much in need of, and which wou'd serve to temper those fiery particles, of which they are compos'd. While a warm imagination is allow'd to enter into philosophy, and hypotheses embrac'd merely for being specious and agreeable, we can never have any steady principles, nor any sentiments, which will suit with common practice and experience. But were these hypotheses once remov'd, we might hope to establish a system or set of opinions, which if not true (for that, perhaps, is too much to be hop'd for) might at least be satisfactory to the human mind, and might stand the test of the most critical examination. Nor shou'd we despair of attaining this end, because of the many chimerical systems, which *SB 273* have successively arisen and decay'd away among men, wou'd we consider the shortness of that period, wherein these questions have been the subjects of enquiry and reasoning. Two thousand years with such long interruptions, and under such mighty discouragements are a small space of time to give any tolerable perfection to the sciences; and perhaps we are still in too early an age of the world to discover any principles, which will bear the examination of the latest posterity. For my part, my only hope is, that I may contribute a little to the advancement of knowledge, by giving in some particulars a different turn to the speculations of philosophers, and pointing out to them more distinctly those subjects, where alone they can expect assurance and conviction. Human Nature is the only science of man; and yet has been hitherto the most neglected. 'Twill be sufficient for me, if I can bring it a little more into fashion; and the hope of this serves to compose my temper from that spleen, and invigorate it from that indolence, which sometimes prevail upon me. If the reader finds himself in the same easy disposition, let him follow me in my future speculations. If not, let him follow his inclination, and wait the returns of application and good humour. The conduct of a man, who studies philosophy in this careless manner, is more truly sceptical than that of one, who feeling in himself an inclination to it, is yet so over-whelm'd with doubts and scruples, as totally to reject it. A true sceptic will be diffident of his philosophical doubts, as well as of his philosophical conviction; and will never refuse any innocent satisfaction, which offers itself, upon account of either of them.

15   Nor is it only proper we shou'd in general indulge our inclination in the most elaborate philosophical researches, notwithstanding our sceptical principles, but also that we shou'd yield to that propensity, which inclines us to be positive and certain in *particular points*, according to the light, in which we survey them in any *particular instant*. 'Tis easier to forbear all examination and enquiry, than to   *SB 274* check ourselves in so natural a propensity, and guard against that assurance, which always arises from an exact and full survey of an object. On such an occasion we are apt not only to forget our scepticism, but even our modesty too; and make use of such terms as these, *'tis evident, 'tis certain, 'tis undeniable*; which a due deference to the public ought, perhaps, to prevent. I may have fallen into this fault after the example of others; but I here enter a *caveat* against any objections, which may be offer'd on that head; and declare that such expressions were extorted from me by the present view of the object, and imply no dogmatical spirit, nor conceited idea of my own judgment, which are sentiments that I am sensible can become no body, and a sceptic still less than any other.

The end of the first BOOK.

A TREATISE OF HUMAN NATURE:

BEING AN ATTEMPT TO INTRODUCE
THE EXPERIMENTAL METHOD
OF REASONING
INTO MORAL SUBJECTS

Rara temporum felicitas, ubi sentire, quæ velis;
& quæ sentias, dicere licet.[†] TACITUS

Book 2.   *Of the Passions*

BOOK 2.   *Of the PASSIONS*

PART 1

Of pride and humility

Sect. 1.   *Division of the subject*

1   As all the perceptions of the mind may be divided into *impressions* and *ideas*, so the impressions admit of another division into *original* and *secondary*. This division of the impressions is the same with that which I formerly made use of when I distinguish'd them into impressions of *sensation* and *reflection*.[54] Original impressions or impressions of sensation are such as without any antecedent perception arise in the soul, from the constitution of the body, from the animal spirits,[†] or from the application of objects to the external organs.[†] Secondary, or reflective impressions are such as proceed from some of these original ones, either immediately or by the interposition of its idea.[†] Of the first kind are all the impressions of the senses, and all bodily pains and pleasures: Of the second are the passions, and other emotions resembling them.

2   'Tis certain, that the mind, in its perceptions, must begin somewhere; and that since the impressions precede their correspondent ideas, there must be some impressions, which without any introduction make their appearance in the soul. As these depend upon natural and physical causes, the examination of them wou'd lead me too far from my present subject, into the sciences of anatomy and natural philosophy.[†] For this reason I shall here confine myself to those other impressions, which I have call'd *secondary* and *reflective*, as arising either from the original impressions, or from their ideas. Bodily pains and pleasures are the source of many passions, both when felt and consider'd by the mind; but arise originally in the soul, or in the body, which-ever you please to call it, without any preceding thought or perception. A fit of the gout produces a long train of passions, as grief, hope, fear; but is not deriv'd immediately from any affection[†] or idea.

3   The reflective impressions may be divided into two kinds, *viz.* the *calm* and the *violent*. Of the first kind is the sense of beauty and deformity in action, composition, and external objects. Of the second are the passions of love and hatred, grief and joy, pride and humility. This division is far from being exact. The raptures of poetry and music frequently rise to the greatest height; while those other impressions, properly call'd *passions*, may decay into so soft an emotion, as to become, in a manner, imperceptible. But as in general the passions are more

---

[54]   Book 1. Part 1. Sect. 2.[†]

violent than the emotions arising from beauty and deformity, these impressions have been commonly distinguish'd from each other.[†] The subject of the human mind being so copious and various, I shall here take advantage of this vulgar and specious division, that I may proceed with the greater order; and having said all I thought necessary concerning our ideas,[†] shall now explain those violent emotions or passions, their nature, origin, causes, and effects.

4   When we take a survey of the passions, there occurs a division of them into *direct* and *indirect*. By direct passions I understand such as arise immediately from good or evil, from pain or pleasure. By indirect such as proceed from the same principles, but by the conjunction of other qualities.[†] This distinction I cannot at present justify or explain any farther.[†] I can only observe in general, that under the indirect passions I comprehend pride, humility, ambition, vanity, love, hatred, envy, pity, malice, generosity, with their dependants. And under the direct passions, desire, aversion, grief, joy, hope, fear, despair and security. I shall begin with the former.   *SB 277*

Sect. 2.   *Of pride and humility; their objects and causes*

1   The passions of PRIDE and HUMILITY being simple and uniform impressions, 'tis impossible we can ever, by a multitude of words, give a just definition of them, or indeed of any of the passions.[†] The utmost we can pretend to is a description of them, by an enumeration of such circumstances, as attend them: But as these words, *pride* and *humility*, are of general use, and the impressions they represent the most common of any, every one, of himself, will be able to form a just idea of them, without any danger of mistake. For which reason, not to lose time upon preliminaries, I shall immediately enter upon the examination of these passions.

2   'Tis evident, that pride and humility, tho' directly contrary, have yet the same OBJECT. This object is self, or that succession of related ideas and impressions, of which we have an intimate memory and consciousness.[†] Here the view always fixes when we are actuated by either of these passions. According as our idea of ourself is more or less advantageous, we feel either of those opposite affections, and are elated by pride, or dejected with humility. Whatever other objects may be comprehended by the mind, they are always consider'd with a view to ourselves; otherwise they wou'd never be able either to excite these passions, or produce the smallest encrease or diminution of them. When self enters not into the consideration, there is no room either for pride or humility.

3   But tho' that connected succession of perceptions, which we call *self*, be always the object of these two passions, 'tis impossible it can be their CAUSE, or be sufficient alone to excite them. For as these passions are directly contrary, and   *SB 278* have the same object in common; were their object also their cause; it cou'd never produce any degree of the one passion, but at the same time it must excite an equal degree of the other; which opposition and contrariety must destroy both. 'Tis impossible a man can at the same time be both proud and humble; and where he has different reasons for these passions, as frequently happens, the pas-

sions either take place alternately; or if they encounter, the one annihilates the other, as far as its strength goes, and the remainder only of that, which is superior, continues to operate upon the mind.† But in the present case neither of the passions cou'd ever become superior; because supposing it to be the view only of ourself, which excited them, that being perfectly indifferent to either, must produce both in the very same proportion; or in other words, can produce neither. To excite any passion, and at the same time raise an equal share of its antagonist, is immediately to undo what was done, and must leave the mind at last perfectly calm and indifferent.

4   We must, therefore, make a distinction betwixt the cause and the object of these passions; betwixt that idea, which excites them, and that to which they direct their view, when excited. Pride and humility, being once rais'd, immediately turn our attention to ourself, and regard that as their ultimate and final object; but there is something farther requisite in order to raise them: Something, which is peculiar to one of the passions, and produces not both in the very same degree. The first idea,† that is presented to the mind, is that of the cause or productive principle. This excites the passion, connected with it; and that passion, when excited, turns our view to another idea, which is that of self. Here then is a passion plac'd betwixt two ideas, of which the one produces it, and the other is produc'd by it. The first idea, therefore, represents the *cause*, the second the *object* of the passion.

5   To begin with the causes of pride and humility; we may observe, that their
most obvious and remarkable property is the vast variety of *subjects*,† on which they may be plac'd. Every valuable quality of the mind, whether of the imagination, judgment, memory or disposition; wit, good-sense, learning, courage, justice, integrity; all these are the causes of pride; and their opposites of humility. Nor are these passions confin'd to the mind, but extend their view to the body likewise. A man may be proud of his beauty, strength, agility, good mein, address in dancing, riding, fencing, and of his dexterity in any manual business or manufacture. But this is not all. The passions looking farther, comprehend whatever objects are in the least ally'd or related to us. Our country, family, children, relations, riches, houses, gardens, horses, dogs, cloaths; any of these may become a cause either of pride or of humility.

6   From the consideration of these causes, it appears necessary we shou'd make a new distinction in the causes of the passion, betwixt that *quality*, which operates, and the *subject*, on which it is plac'd. A man, for instance, is vain of a beautiful house, which belongs to him, or which he has himself built and contriv'd. Here the object of the passion is himself, and the cause is the beautiful house: Which cause again is sub-divided into two parts, *viz.* the quality, which operates upon the passion, and the subject, in which the quality inheres. The quality is the beauty, and the subject is the house, consider'd as his property or contrivance. Both these parts are essential, nor is the distinction vain and chimerical.† Beauty, consider'd merely as such, unless plac'd upon something related to us, never produces any pride or vanity; and the strongest relation alone, without beauty, or something else in its place, has as little influence on that passion.

Since, therefore, these two particulars are easily separated, and there is a necessity for their conjunction, in order to produce the passion, we ought to consider them as component parts of the cause; and infix in our minds an exact idea of this distinction.

Sect. 3. *Whence these objects and causes are deriv'd* *SB 280*

1 Being so far advanc'd as to observe a difference betwixt the *object* of the passions and their *cause*, and to distinguish in the cause the *quality*, which operates on the passions, from the *subject*, in which it inheres; we now proceed to examine what determines each of them to be what it is, and assigns such a particular object, and quality, and subject to these affections. By this means we shall fully understand the origin of pride and humility.

2   'Tis evident in the first place, that these passions are determin'd[†] to have self for their *object*, not only by a natural but also by an original property.[†] No one can doubt but this property is *natural* from the constancy and steadiness of its operations. 'Tis always self, which is the object of pride and humility; and whenever the passions look beyond, 'tis still with a view to ourselves, nor can any person or object otherwise have any influence upon us.

3   That this proceeds from an *original* quality or primary impulse,[†] will likewise appear evident, if we consider that 'tis the distinguishing characteristic of these passions. Unless nature had given some original qualities to the mind, it cou'd never have any secondary ones; because in that case it wou'd have no foundation for action, nor cou'd ever begin to exert itself. Now these qualities, which we must consider as original, are such as are most inseparable from the soul, and can be resolv'd into no other: And such is the quality, which determines the object of pride and humility.

4   We may, perhaps, make it a greater question, whether the *causes*, that produce the passion, be as *natural* as the object, to which it is directed, and whether all that vast variety proceeds from caprice or from the constitution of the mind?[†] This doubt we shall soon remove, if we cast our eye upon human nature, and *SB 281* consider that in all nations and ages, the same objects still give rise to pride and humility; and that upon the view even of a stranger, we can know pretty nearly, what will either encrease or diminish his passions of this kind. If there be any variation in this particular, it proceeds from nothing but a difference in the tempers and complexions of men; and is besides very inconsiderable. Can we imagine it possible, that while human nature remains the same, men will ever become entirely indifferent to their power, riches, beauty or personal merit, and that their pride and vanity will not be affected by these advantages?

5   But tho' the causes of pride and humility be plainly *natural*, we shall find upon examination, that they are not *original*, and that 'tis utterly impossible they shou'd each of them be adapted to these passions by a particular provision, and primary constitution of nature.[†] Beside their prodigious number, many of them are the effects of art, and arise partly from the industry, partly from the caprice,

and partly from the good fortune of men. Industry produces houses, furniture, cloaths. Caprice determines their particular kinds and qualities. And good fortune frequently contributes to all this, by discovering the effects that result from the different mixtures and combinations of bodies. 'Tis absurd, therefore, to imagine, that each of these was foreseen and provided for by nature, and that every new production of art, which causes pride or humility; instead of adapting itself to the passions by partaking of some general quality, that naturally operates on the mind; is itself the object of an original principle, which till then lay conceal'd in the soul, and is only by accident at last brought to light. Thus the first mechanic, that invented a fine scritoire, produc'd pride in him, who became possest of it, by principles different from those, which made him proud of handsome chairs and tables. As this appears evidently ridiculous, we must conclude, that each cause of pride and humility is not adapted to the passions by a distinct original quality; but that there are some one or more circumstances common to *SB 282* all of them, on which their efficacy depends.

6   Besides, we find in the course of nature, that tho' the effects be many, the principles, from which they arise, are commonly but few and simple, and that 'tis the sign of an unskilful naturalist to have recourse to a different quality,[†] in order to explain every different operation. How much more must this be true with regard to the human mind, which being so confin'd a subject may justly be thought incapable of containing such a monstrous heap of principles, as wou'd be necessary to excite the passions of pride and humility, were each distinct cause adapted to the passions by a distinct set of principles?

7   Here, therefore, moral philosophy is in the same condition as natural, with regard to astronomy before the time of *Copernicus*. The antients, tho' sensible of that maxim, *that nature does nothing in vain*,[†] contriv'd such intricate systems of the heavens,[†] as seem'd inconsistent with true philosophy, and gave place at last to something more simple and natural. To invent without scruple a new principle to every new phænomenon, instead of adapting it to the old; to overload our hypotheses with a variety of this kind; are certain proofs, that none of these principles is the just one, and that we only desire, by a number of falshoods, to cover our ignorance of the truth.

Sect. 4. *Of the relations of impressions and ideas*

1   Thus we have establish'd two truths without any obstacle or difficulty, *that 'tis from natural principles this variety of causes excites pride and humility*, and *that 'tis not by a different principle each different cause is adapted to its passion*. We shall now proceed to enquire how we may reduce these principles to a lesser number, and find among the causes something common, on which their influence depends.

2   In order to this we must reflect on certain properties of human nature, which *SB 283* tho' they have a mighty influence on every operation both of the understanding and passions, are not commonly much insisted on by philosophers. The *first* of

these is the association of ideas, which I have so often observ'd and explain'd.[†] 'Tis impossible for the mind to fix itself steadily upon one idea for any considerable time; nor can it by its utmost efforts ever arrive at such a constancy. But however changeable our thoughts may be, they are not entirely without rule and method in their changes. The rule, by which they proceed, is to pass from one object to what is resembling, contiguous to, or produc'd by it. When one idea is present to the imagination, any other, united by these relations, naturally follows it, and enters with more facility by means of that introduction.

3   The *second* property I shall observe in the human mind is a like association of impressions. All resembling impressions[†] are connected together, and no sooner one arises than the rest immediately follow. Grief and disappointment give rise to anger, anger to envy, envy to malice, and malice to grief again, till the whole circle be compleated. In like manner our temper, when elevated with joy, naturally throws itself into love, generosity, pity, courage, pride, and the other resembling affections. 'Tis difficult for the mind, when actuated by any passion, to confine itself to that passion alone, without any change or variation. Human nature is too inconstant to admit of any such regularity. Changeableness is essential to it. And to what can it so naturally change as to affections or emotions, which are suitable to the temper, and agree with that set of passions, which then prevail? 'Tis evident, then, there is an attraction or association among impressions, as well as among ideas; tho' with this remarkable difference, that ideas are associated by resemblance, contiguity, and causation; and impressions only by resemblance.

4   In the *third* place, 'tis observable of these two kinds of association,[†] that they very much assist and forward each other, and that the transition is more easily made where they both concur in the same object. Thus a man, who, by any injury from another, is very much discompos'd and ruffled in his temper, is apt to find a hundred subjects of discontent, impatience, fear, and other uneasy passions; especially if he can discover these subjects in or near the person, who was the cause of his first passion. Those principles, which forward the transition of ideas, here concur with those, which operate on the passions; and both uniting in one action, bestow on the mind a double impulse. The new passion, therefore, must arise with so much greater violence, and the transition to it must be render'd so much more easy and natural.

5   Upon this occasion I may cite the authority of an elegant writer,[†] who expresses himself in the following manner. "As the fancy[†] delights in every thing that is great, strange, or beautiful, and is still more pleased the more it finds of these perfections in the *same* object, so is it capable of receiving a new satisfaction by the assistance of another sense. Thus any continued sound, as the musick of birds, or a fall of water, awakens every moment the mind of the beholder, and makes him more attentive to the several beauties of the place that lye before him. Thus if there arises a fragrancy of smells or perfumes, they heighten the pleasures of the imagination, and make even the colours and verdure of the landskip appear more agreeable; for the ideas of both senses recommend each other, and are pleasanter together than when they enter the mind separately: As

SB 284

the different colours of a picture, when they are well disposed, set off one another, and receive an additional beauty from the advantage of their situation." In this phænomenon we may remark the association both of impressions and ideas, as well as the mutual assistance they lend each other.

Sect. 5. *Of the influence of these relations on pride and humility* SB 285

1   These principles[†] being establish'd on unquestionable experience, I begin to consider how we shall apply them, by revolving over all the causes of pride and humility, whether these causes be regarded, as the qualities, that operate, or as the subjects,[†] on which the qualities are plac'd. In examining these *qualities* I immediately find many of them to concur in producing the sensation of pain and pleasure, independent of those affections, which I here endeavour to explain. Thus the beauty of our person, of itself, and by its very appearance, gives pleasure, as well as pride; and its deformity, pain as well as humility. A magnificent feast delights us, and a sordid one displeases. What I discover to be true in some instances, I *suppose* to be so in all; and take it for granted at present, without any farther proof, that every cause of pride, by its peculiar qualities, produces a separate pleasure, and of humility a separate uneasiness.

2   Again, in considering the *subjects*, to which these qualities adhere, I make a new *supposition*, which also appears probable from many obvious instances, *viz.* that these subjects are either parts of ourselves, or something nearly related to us. Thus the good and bad qualities of our actions and manners constitute virtue and vice,[†] and determine our personal character, than which nothing operates more strongly on these passions. In like manner, 'tis the beauty or deformity[†] of our person, houses, equipage, or furniture, by which we are render'd either vain or humble. The same qualities, when transferr'd to subjects, which bear us no relation, influence not in the smallest degree either of these affections.

3   Having thus in a manner suppos'd two properties of the causes of these affections, *viz.* that the *qualities* produce a separate pain or pleasure, and that the *subjects*, on which the qualities are plac'd, are related to self; I proceed to examine SB 286 the passions themselves, in order to find something in them, correspondent to the suppos'd properties of their causes. *First*, I find, that the peculiar object of pride and humility is determin'd by an original and natural instinct, and that 'tis absolutely impossible, from the primary constitution of the mind, that these passions shou'd ever look beyond self,[†] or that individual person, of whose actions and sentiments each of us is intimately conscious. Here at last the view always rests, when we are actuated by either of these passions; nor can we, in that situation of mind, ever lose sight of this object. For this I pretend not to give any reason; but consider such a peculiar direction of the thought as an original quality.

4   The *second* quality, which I discover in these passions, and which I likewise consider as an original quality, is their sensations, or the peculiar emotions[†] they excite in the soul, and which constitute their very being and essence.[†] Thus pride is a pleasant sensation, and humility a painful; and upon the removal of

the pleasure and pain, there is in reality no pride nor humility. Of this our very feeling convinces us; and beyond our feeling, 'tis here in vain to reason or dispute.

5   If I compare, therefore, these two *establish'd* properties of the passions, *viz.* their object, which is self, and their sensation, which is either pleasant or painful, to the two *suppos'd* properties of the causes, *viz.* their relation to self, and their tendency to produce a pain or pleasure, independent of the passion; I immediately find, that taking these suppositions to be just, the true system breaks in upon me with an irresistible evidence. That cause, which excites the passion, is related to the object, which nature has attributed to the passion; the sensation, which the cause separately produces, is related to the sensation of the passion: From this double relation of ideas and impressions, the passion is deriv'd.[†] The one idea is easily converted into its correlative; and the one impression into that, *SB 287* which resembles and corresponds to it: With how much greater facility must this transition be made, where these movements mutually assist each other, and the mind receives a double impulse[†] from the relations both of its impressions and ideas?

6   That we may comprehend this the better, we must suppose, that nature has given to the organs of the human mind,[†] a certain disposition fitted to produce a peculiar impression or emotion, which we call *pride*: To this emotion she has assign'd a certain idea, *viz.* that of *self*, which it never fails to produce. This contrivance of nature is easily conceiv'd. We have many instances of such a situation of affairs. The nerves of the nose and palate are so dispos'd, as in certain circumstances to convey such peculiar sensations to the mind: The sensations of lust and hunger always produce in us the idea of those peculiar objects, which are suitable to each appetite. These two circumstances are united in pride. The organs are so dispos'd as to produce the passion; and the passion, after its production, naturally produces a certain idea. All this needs no proof.[†] 'Tis evident we never shou'd be possest of that passion, were there not a disposition of mind proper for it; and 'tis as evident, that the passion always turns our view to ourselves, and makes us think of our own qualities and circumstances.

7   This being fully comprehended, it may now be ask'd, *Whether nature produces the passion immediately, of herself; or whether she must be assisted by the co-operation of other causes?* For 'tis observable, that in this particular her conduct is different in the different passions and sensations. The palate must be excited by an external object, in order to produce any relish: But hunger arises internally, without the concurrence of any external object. But however the case may stand with other passions and impressions, 'tis certain, that pride requires the assistance of some foreign object, and that the organs, which produce it, exert not themselves like the heart and arteries, by an original internal movement. For *first*, daily *SB 288* experience convinces us, that pride requires certain causes to excite it, and languishes when unsupported by some excellency in the character, in bodily accomplishments, in cloaths, equipage or fortune. *Secondly*, 'tis evident pride wou'd be perpetual, if it arose immediately from nature; since the object is always the same, and there is no disposition of body peculiar to pride, as there is to thirst

and hunger. *Thirdly*, Humility is in the very same situation with pride; and therefore, either must, upon this supposition, be perpetual likewise, or must destroy the contrary passion from the very first moment; so that none of them cou'd ever make its appearance. Upon the whole, we may rest satisfy'd with the foregoing conclusion, that pride must have a cause, as well as an object, and that the one has no influence without the other.

8   The difficulty, then, is only to discover this cause, and find what it is that gives the first motion to pride, and sets those organs in action, which are naturally fitted to produce that emotion. Upon my consulting experience, in order to resolve this difficulty, I immediately find a hundred different causes, that produce pride; and upon examining these causes, I suppose, what at first I perceive to be probable, that all of them concur in two circumstances; which are, that of themselves they produce an impression, ally'd to the passion, and are plac'd on a subject, ally'd to the object of the passion. When I consider after this the nature of *relation*, and its effects both on the passions and ideas, I can no longer doubt, upon these suppositions, that 'tis the very principle,[†] which gives rise to pride, and bestows motion on those organs, which being naturally dispos'd to produce that affection, require only a first impulse or beginning to their action. Any thing, that gives a pleasant sensation, and is related to self, excites the passion of pride, which is also agreeable, and has self for its object.

9   What I have said of pride is equally true of humility. The sensation of humility is uneasy, as that of pride is agreeable; for which reason the separate sensation, arising from the causes, must be revers'd,[†] while the relation to self continues the same. Tho' pride and humility are directly contrary in their effects, and in their sensations, they have notwithstanding the same object; so that 'tis requisite only to change the relation of impressions,[†] without making any change upon that of ideas. Accordingly we find, that a beautiful house, belonging to ourselves, produces pride; and that the same house, still belonging to ourselves, produces humility, when by any accident its beauty is chang'd into deformity, and thereby the sensation of pleasure, which corresponded to pride, is transform'd into pain, which is related to humility. The double relation betwixt the ideas and impressions subsists in both cases, and produces an easy transition from the one emotion to the other.

10   In a word, nature has bestow'd a kind of attraction on certain impressions and ideas, by which one of them, upon its appearance, naturally introduces its correlative.[†] If these two attractions or associations of impressions and ideas concur on the same object, they mutually assist each other, and the transition of the affections and of the imagination is made with the greatest ease and facility. When an idea produces an impression, related to an impression, which is connected with an idea, related to the first idea, these two impressions must be in a manner inseparable, nor will the one in any case be unattended with the other. 'Tis after this manner, that the particular causes of pride and humility are determin'd. The quality, which operates on the passion, produces separately an impression resembling it; the subject, to which the quality adheres, is related to self, the object of the passion: No wonder the

SB 289

whole cause, consisting of a quality and of a subject, does so unavoidably give rise to the passion.

11   To illustrate this hypothesis, we may compare it to that, by which I have already explain'd the belief attending the judgments, which we form from causation.[†] I have observ'd, that in all judgments of this kind, there is always   *SB 290* a present impression, and a related idea; and that the present impression gives a vivacity to the fancy, and the relation conveys this vivacity, by an easy transition, to the related idea. Without the present impression, the attention is not fix'd, nor the spirits excited.[†] Without the relation, this attention rests on its first object, and has no farther consequence. There is evidently a great analogy betwixt that hypothesis, and our present one of an impression and idea, that transfuse themselves into another impression and idea by means of their double relation: Which analogy must be allow'd to be no despicable proof of both hypotheses.

Sect. 6. *Limitations of this system*

1 But before we proceed farther in this subject, and examine particularly all the causes of pride and humility, 'twill be proper to make some limitations to the general system, *that all agreeable objects, related to ourselves, by an association of ideas and of impressions, produce pride, and disagreeable ones, humility*: And these limitations are deriv'd from the very nature of the subject.

2   1. Suppose an agreeable object to acquire a relation to self, the first passion, that appears on this occasion, is joy;[†] and this passion discovers itself upon a slighter relation than pride and vain-glory.[†] We may feel joy upon being present at a feast, where our senses are regal'd with delicacies of every kind: But 'tis only the master of the feast, who, beside the same joy, has the additional passion of self-applause and vanity. 'Tis true, men sometimes boast of a great entertainment, at which they have only been present; and by so small a relation convert their pleasure into pride: But, however, this must in general be own'd, that joy arises from a more inconsiderable relation than vanity, and that many things,   *SB 291* which are too foreign to produce pride, are yet able to give us a delight and pleasure. The reason of the difference may be explain'd thus. A relation is requisite to joy, in order to approach the object to us, and make it give us any satisfaction. But beside this, which is common to both passions, 'tis requisite to pride, in order to produce a transition from one passion to another, and convert the satisfaction into vanity. As it[†] has a double task to perform, it must be endow'd with double force and energy. To which we may add, that where agreeable objects bear not a very close relation to ourselves, they commonly do to some other person; and this latter relation not only excels, but even diminishes, and sometimes destroys the former, as we shall see afterwards.[55]

3   Here then is the first limitation, we must make to our general position, *that*

---

[55] Part 2. Sect. 4.[†]

every thing related to us, which produces pleasure or pain, produces likewise pride or humility. There is not only a relation requir'd, but a close one, and a closer than is requir'd to joy.

4   2. The second limitation is, that the agreeable or disagreeable object be not only closely related, but also peculiar to ourselves, or at least common to us with a few persons. 'Tis a quality observable in human nature, and which we shall endeavour to explain afterwards,[†] that every thing, which is often presented, and to which we have been long accustom'd, loses its value in our eyes, and is in a little time despis'd and neglected. We likewise judge of objects more from comparison than from their real and intrinsic merit;[†] and where we cannot by some contrast enhance their value, we are apt to overlook even what is essentially good in them. These qualities of the mind have an effect upon joy as well as pride; and 'tis remarkable, that goods, which are common to all mankind, and have become familiar to us by custom, give us little satisfaction; tho' perhaps of a more excellent kind, than those on which, for their singularity, we set a much higher value.   *SB 292*
But tho' this circumstance operates on both these passions, it has a much greater influence on vanity. We are rejoic'd for many goods, which, on account of their frequency, give us no pride. Health, when it returns after a long absence, affords us a very sensible satisfaction; but is seldom regarded as a subject of vanity, because 'tis shar'd with such vast numbers.

5   The reason, why pride is so much more delicate in this particular than joy, I take to be, as follows. In order to excite pride, there are always two objects we must contemplate, *viz.* the *cause* or that object which produces pleasure; and self, which is the real object of the passion. But joy has only one object necessary to its production, *viz.* that which gives pleasure; and tho' it be requisite, that this bear some relation to self, yet that is only requisite in order to render it agreeable; nor is self, properly speaking, the object of this passion. Since, therefore, pride has in a manner two objects, to which it directs our view; it follows, that where neither of them have any singularity, the passion must be more weaken'd upon that account, than a passion, which has only one object. Upon comparing ourselves with others, as we are every moment apt to do, we find we are not in the least distinguish'd; and upon comparing the object we possess, we discover still the same unlucky circumstance. By two comparisons so disadvantageous the passion must be entirely destroy'd.

6   3. The third limitation is, that the pleasant or painful object be very discernible and obvious, and that not only to ourselves, but to others also. This circumstance, like the two foregoing, has an effect upon joy, as well as pride. We fancy ourselves more happy, as well as more virtuous or beautiful, when we appear so to others; but are still more ostentatious of our virtues than of our pleasures. This proceeds from causes, which I shall endeavour to explain afterwards.[†]

7   4. The fourth limitation is deriv'd from the inconstancy of the cause of these   *SB 293*
passions, and from the short duration of its connexion with ourselves. What is casual and inconstant gives but little joy, and less pride. We are not much

satisfy'd with the thing itself; and are still less apt to feel any new degrees of self-satisfaction upon its account. We foresee and anticipate its change by the imagination; which makes us little satisfy'd with the thing: We compare it to ourselves, whose existence is more durable; by which means its inconstancy appears still greater. It seems ridiculous to infer an excellency in ourselves from an object, which is of so much shorter duration, and attends us during so small a part of our existence. 'Twill be easy to comprehend the reason, why this cause operates not with the same force in joy as in pride; since the idea of self is not so essential to the former passion as to the latter.

8   5. I may add as a fifth limitation, or rather enlargement of this system, that *general rules* have a great influence upon pride and humility, as well as on all the other passions. Hence we form a notion of different ranks of men, suitable to the power or riches they are possest of; and this notion we change not upon account of any peculiarities of the health or temper of the persons, which may deprive them of all enjoyment in their possessions. This may be accounted for from the same principles, that explain'd[†] the influence of general rules on the understanding. Custom readily carries us beyond the just bounds in our passions, as well as in our reasonings.

9   It may not be amiss to observe on this occasion, that the influence of general rules and maxims on the passions very much contributes to facilitate the effects of all the principles, which we shall explain in the progress of this treatise. For 'tis evident, that if a person full-grown, and of the same nature with ourselves, were on a sudden transported into our world,[†] he wou'd be very much embarrass'd with every object, and wou'd not readily find what degree of love or hatred, pride or humility, or any other passion he ought to attribute to it. The passions are often vary'd by very inconsiderable principles;[†] and these do not always play with a perfect regularity, especially on the first trial. But as custom and practice have brought to light all these principles, and have settled the just value of every thing; this must certainly contribute to the easy production of the passions, and guide us, by means of general establish'd maxims, in the proportions we ought to observe in preferring one object to another. This remark may, perhaps, serve to obviate difficulties, that may arise concerning some causes, which I shall hereafter ascribe[†] to particular passions, and which may be esteem'd too refin'd to operate so universally and certainly, as they are found to do.   *SB 294*

10   I shall close this subject with a reflection deriv'd from these five limitations. This reflection is, that the persons, who are proudest, and who in the eye of the world have most reason for their pride, are not always the happiest; nor the most humble always the most miserable, as may at first sight be imagin'd from this system. An evil[†] may be real, tho' its cause has no relation to us: It may be real, without being peculiar: It may be real, without showing itself to others: It may be real, without being constant: And it may be real, without falling under the general rules. Such evils as these will not fail to render us miserable, tho' they have little tendency to diminish pride: And perhaps the most real and the most solid evils of life will be found of this nature.

Sect. 7. *Of vice and virtue*

1   Taking these limitations along with us, let us proceed to examine the causes of pride and humility; and see, whether in every case we can discover the double relations, by which they operate on the passions. If we find that all these causes are related to self, and produce a pleasure or uneasiness separate from the passion, there will remain no farther scruple with regard to the present system. We shall principally endeavour to prove the latter point; the former being in a manner self-evident.

SB 295

2   To begin with VICE and VIRTUE, which are the most obvious causes of these passions; 'twou'd be entirely foreign to my present purpose to enter upon the controversy, which of late years has so much excited the curiosity of the public, *Whether these moral distinctions be founded on natural and original principles, or arise from interest and education?*† The examination of this I reserve for the following book;† and in the mean time shall endeavour to show, that my system maintains its ground upon either of these hypotheses; which will be a strong proof of its solidity.

3   For granting that morality had no foundation in nature, it must still be allow'd, that vice and virtue, either from self-interest or the prejudices of education, produce in us a real pain and pleasure; and this we may observe to be strenuously asserted by the defenders of that hypothesis.† Every passion, habit, or turn of character (say they) which has a tendency to our advantage or prejudice, gives a delight or uneasiness; and 'tis from thence the approbation or disapprobation arises. We easily gain from the liberality of others, but are always in danger of losing by their avarice: Courage defends us, but cowardice lays us open to every attack: Justice is the support of society, but injustice, unless check'd, wou'd quickly prove its ruin: Humility exalts, but pride mortifies us. For these reasons the former qualities are esteem'd virtues, and the latter regarded as vices. Now since 'tis granted there is a delight or uneasiness still attending merit or demerit of every kind, this is all that is requisite for my purpose.

4   But I go farther, and observe, that this moral hypothesis and my present system not only agree together, but also that, allowing the former to be just, 'tis an absolute and invincible proof of the latter. For if all morality be founded on the pain or pleasure, which arises from the prospect of any loss or advantage, that may result from our own characters, or from those of others, all the effects of morality must be deriv'd from the same pain or pleasure, and among the rest, the passions of pride and humility. The very essence of virtue, according to this hypothesis, is to produce pleasure, and that of vice to give pain. The virtue and vice must be part of our character in order to excite pride or humility. What farther proof can we desire for the double relation of impressions and ideas?

SB 296

5   The same unquestionable argument may be deriv'd from the opinion of those, who maintain that morality is something real, essential, and founded on nature.† The most probable hypothesis, which has been advanc'd to explain the distinction betwixt vice and virtue, and the origin of moral rights and obligations, is,

that from a primary constitution of nature certain characters and passions, by the very view and contemplation, produce a pain, and others in like manner excite a pleasure.[†] The uneasiness and satisfaction are not only inseparable from vice and virtue, but constitute their very nature and essence.[†] To approve of a character is to feel an original delight upon its appearance. To disapprove of it is to be sensible of an uneasiness.[†] The pain and pleasure, therefore, being the primary causes of vice and virtue, must also be the causes of all their effects, and consequently of pride and humility, which are the unavoidable attendants of that distinction.

6   But supposing this hypothesis of moral philosophy shou'd be allow'd to be false, 'tis still evident, that pain and pleasure, if not the causes of vice and virtue, are at least inseparable from them. A generous and noble character affords a satisfaction even in the survey; and when presented to us, tho' only in a poem or fable, never fails to charm and delight us. On the other hand cruelty and treachery displease from their very nature; nor is it possible ever to reconcile us to these qualities, either in ourselves or others. Thus one hypothesis of morality *SB 297* is an undeniable proof of the foregoing system,[†] and the other at worst agrees with it.

7   But pride and humility arise not from these qualities alone of the mind, which, according to the vulgar systems of ethicks,[†] have been comprehended as parts of moral duty, but from any other that has a connexion with pleasure and uneasiness. Nothing flatters our vanity more than the talent of pleasing by our wit, good humour, or any other accomplishment; and nothing gives us a more sensible mortification than a disappointment in any attempt of that nature. No one has ever been able to tell what *wit* is, and to show why such a system of thought must be receiv'd under that denomination, and such another rejected. 'Tis only by taste we can decide concerning it, nor are we possest of any other standard, upon which we can form a judgment of this kind. Now what is this *taste*, from which true and false wit in a manner receive their being, and without which no thought can have a title to either of these denominations? 'Tis plainly nothing but a sensation of pleasure from true wit, and of uneasiness from false, without our being able to tell the reasons of that pleasure or uneasiness. The power of bestowing these opposite sensations is, therefore, the very essence of true and false wit;[†] and consequently the cause of that pride or humility, which arises from them.

8   There may, perhaps, be some, who being accustom'd to the style of the schools and pulpit, and having never consider'd human nature in any other light, than that in which *they* place it, may here be surpriz'd to hear me talk of virtue as exciting pride, which they look upon as a vice; and of vice as producing humility, which they have been taught to consider as a virtue.[†] But not to dispute about words, I observe, that by *pride* I understand that agreeable impression, which arises in the mind, when the view either of our virtue, beauty, riches or power makes us satisfy'd with ourselves: And that by *humility* I mean the opposite impression. 'Tis evident the former impression is not always vicious, nor the latter virtuous. The most rigid morality allows us to receive a pleasure from *SB 298*

reflecting on a generous action; and 'tis by none esteem'd a virtue to feel any fruitless remorses upon the thoughts of past villainy and baseness. Let us, therefore, examine these impressions, consider'd in themselves; and enquire into their causes, whether plac'd on the mind or body, without troubling ourselves at present with that merit or blame, which may attend them.

Sect. 8. *Of beauty and deformity*

1   Whether we consider the body as a part of ourselves, or assent to those philosophers, who regard it as something external,[†] it must still be allow'd to be near enough connected with us to form one of these double relations, which I have asserted to be necessary to the causes of pride and humility. Wherever, therefore, we can find the other relation of impressions to join to this of ideas, we may expect with assurance either of these passions, according as the impression is pleasant or uneasy. But *beauty* of all kinds gives us a peculiar delight and satisfaction; as *deformity* produces pain, upon whatever subject it may be plac'd, and whether survey'd in an animate or inanimate object. If the beauty or deformity, therefore, be plac'd upon our own bodies, this pleasure or uneasiness must be converted into pride or humility, as having in this case all the circumstances requisite to produce a perfect transition of impressions and ideas.[†] These opposite sensations are related to the opposite passions. The beauty or deformity is closely related to self, the object of both these passions. No wonder, then, our own beauty becomes an object of pride, and deformity of humility.

2   But this effect of personal and bodily qualities is not only a proof of the present system, by showing that the passions arise not in this case without all the circumstances I have requir'd, but may be employ'd as a stronger and more convincing argument. If we consider all the hypotheses, which have been form'd either by philosophy or common reason, to explain the difference betwixt beauty and deformity, we shall find that all of them resolve into this, that beauty is such an order and construction of parts, as either by the *primary constitution* of our nature, by *custom*, or by *caprice*, is fitted to give a pleasure and satisfaction to the soul.[†] This is the distinguishing character of beauty, and forms all the difference betwixt it and deformity, whose natural tendency is to produce uneasiness.[†] Pleasure and pain, therefore, are not only necessary attendants of beauty and deformity, but constitute their very essence.[†] And indeed, if we consider, that a great part of the beauty, which we admire either in animals or in other objects, is deriv'd from the idea of convenience and utility,[†] we shall make no scruple to assent to this opinion. That shape, which produces strength, is beautiful in one animal; and that which is a sign of agility in another. The order and convenience of a palace are no less essential to its beauty, than its mere figure and appearance. In like manner the rules of architecture require, that the top of a pillar shou'd be more slender than its base, and that because such a figure conveys to us the idea of security, which is pleasant; whereas the contrary form gives us the apprehension of danger, which is uneasy.[†] From innumerable instances of this kind, as well as from considering that beauty like wit, cannot be defin'd, but is discern'd

SB 299

only by a taste or sensation, we may conclude, that beauty is nothing but a form, which produces pleasure, as deformity is a structure of parts, which conveys pain; and since the power of producing pain and pleasure makes in this manner the essence of beauty and deformity, all the effects of these qualities must be deriv'd from the sensation; and among the rest pride and humility, which of all their effects are the most common and remarkable.

3   This argument I esteem just and decisive; but in order to give greater author- *SB 300* ity to the present reasoning, let us suppose it false for a moment, and see what will follow. 'Tis certain, then, that if the power of producing pleasure and pain forms not the essence of beauty and deformity, the sensations are at least inseparable from the qualities, and 'tis even difficult to consider them apart. Now there is nothing common to natural and moral beauty, (both of which are the causes of pride) but this power of producing pleasure; and as a common effect supposes always a common cause,[†] 'tis plain the pleasure must in both cases be the real and influencing cause of the passion. Again; there is nothing originally different betwixt the beauty of our bodies and the beauty of external and foreign objects, but that the one has a near relation to ourselves, which is wanting in the other. This original difference, therefore, must be the cause of all their other differences, and among the rest, of their different influence upon the passion of pride, which is excited by the beauty of our person, but is not affected in the least by that of foreign and external objects. Placing, then, these two conclusions together, we find they compose the preceding system betwixt them, *viz.* that pleasure, as a related or resembling impression, when plac'd on a related object, by a natural transition, produces pride; and its contrary, humility. This system, then, seems already sufficiently confirm'd by experience; tho' we have not yet exhausted all our arguments.

4   'Tis not the beauty of the body alone that produces pride, but also its strength and force. Strength is a kind of power; and therefore the desire to excel in strength is to be consider'd as an inferior species of *ambition*.[†] For this reason the present phænomenon[†] will be sufficiently accounted for, in explaining that passion.

5   Concerning all other bodily accomplishments we may observe in general, that whatever in ourselves is either useful, beautiful, or surprizing, is an object of pride; and its contrary, of humility. Now 'tis obvious, that every thing useful, *SB 301* beautiful or surprizing, agrees in producing a separate pleasure, and agrees in nothing else. The pleasure, therefore, with the relation to self must be the cause of the passion.

6   Tho' it shou'd be question'd, whether beauty be not something real, and different from the power of producing pleasure, it can never be disputed, that as surprize is nothing but a pleasure arising from novelty, it is not, properly speaking, a quality in any object, but merely a passion or impression in the soul.[†] It must, therefore, be from that impression, that pride by a natural transition arises. And it arises so naturally, that there is nothing *in us or belonging to us*, which produces surprize, that does not at the same time excite that other passion. Thus we are vain of the surprizing adventures we have met with, the

escapes we have made, and dangers we have been expos'd to. Hence the origin of vulgar lying; where men without any interest, and merely out of vanity, heap up a number of extraordinary events, which are either the fictions of their brain, or if true, have at least no connexion with themselves. Their fruitful invention supplies them with a variety of adventures; and where that talent is wanting, they appropriate such as belong to others, in order to satisfy their vanity.

7　　In this phænomenon are contain'd two curious experiments, which if we compare them together, according to the known rules,[†] by which we judge of cause and effect in anatomy, natural philosophy, and other sciences, will be an undeniable argument for that influence of the double relations above-mention'd.[†] By one of these experiments we find, that an object produces pride merely by the interposition of pleasure; and that because the quality, by which it produces pride, is in reality nothing but the power of producing pleasure. By the other experiment we find, that the pleasure produces the pride by a transition along related ideas; because when we cut off that relation the passion is immediately destroy'd. A surprizing adventure, in which we have been ourselves engag'd, is related to us, and by that means produces pride: But the　*SB 302* adventures of others, tho' they may cause pleasure, yet for want of this relation of ideas, never excite that passion. What farther proof can be desir'd for the present system?

8　　There is only one objection to this system with regard to our body; which is, that tho' nothing be more agreeable than health, and more painful than sickness, yet commonly men are neither proud of the one, nor mortify'd with the other. This will easily be accounted for, if we consider the *second* and *fourth* limitations,[†] propos'd to our general system. It was observ'd, that no object ever produces pride or humility, if it has not something *peculiar* to ourself; as also, that every cause of that passion must be in some measure *constant*, and hold some proportion to the duration of ourself, which is its object. Now as health and sickness vary incessantly to all men, and there is none, who is *solely* or *certainly* fix'd in either, these accidental blessings and calamities are in a manner separated from us, and are never consider'd as connected with our being and existence. And that this account is just appears hence, that wherever a malady of any kind is so rooted in our constitution, that we no longer entertain any hopes of recovery, from that moment it becomes an object of humility; as is evident in old men, whom nothing mortifies more than the consideration of their age and infirmities. They endeavour, as long as possible, to conceal their blindness and deafness, their rheums and gouts; nor do they ever confess them without reluctance and uneasiness. And tho' young men are not asham'd of every head-ach or cold they fall into, yet no topic is so proper to mortify human pride, and make us entertain a mean opinion of our nature, than this, that we are every moment of our lives subject to such infirmities. This sufficiently proves that bodily pain and sickness are in themselves proper causes of humility; tho' the custom of estimating every thing by comparison more than by its intrinsic worth and value, makes us overlook these calamities, which we find to be incident to every one, and　*SB 303* causes us to form an idea of our merit and character independent of them.

9   We are asham'd of such maladies as affect others, and are either dangerous or disagreeable to them. Of the epilepsy; because it gives a horror to every one present:† Of the itch; because it is infectious:† Of the king's-evil;† because it commonly goes to posterity. Men always consider the sentiments of others in their judgment of themselves. This has evidently appear'd† in some of the foregoing reasonings; and will appear still more evidently, and be more fully explain'd afterwards.†

Sect. 9. *Of external advantages and disadvantages*

1   But tho' pride and humility have the qualities of our mind and body, that is *self*, for their natural and more immediate causes, we find by experience, that there are many other objects, which produce these affections, and that the primary one† is, in some measure, obscur'd and lost by the multiplicity of foreign and extrinsic. We found a vanity upon houses, gardens, equipages, as well as upon personal merit and accomplishments; and tho' these external advantages be in themselves widely distant from thought of a person, yet they considerably influence even a passion, which is directed to that as its ultimate object. This happens when external objects acquire any particular relation to ourselves, and are associated or connected with us. A beautiful fish in the ocean, an animal in a desart, and indeed any thing that neither belongs, nor is related to us, has no manner of influence on our vanity, whatever extraordinary qualities it may be endow'd with, and whatever degree of surprize and admiration it may naturally occasion. It must be some way associated with us in order to touch our pride. Its idea must hang, in a manner, upon that of ourselves; and the transition from the one to the other must be easy and natural.   *SB 304*

2   But here 'tis remarkable, that tho' the relation of *resemblance* operates upon the mind in the same manner as contiguity and causation, in conveying us from one idea to another, yet 'tis seldom a foundation either of pride or of humility. If we resemble a person in any of the valuable parts of his character, we must, in some degree, possess the quality, in which we resemble him; and this quality we always choose to survey directly in ourselves rather than by reflection in another person, when we wou'd found upon it any degree of vanity. So that tho' a likeness may occasionally produce that passion by suggesting a more advantageous idea of ourselves, 'tis there the view fixes at last, and the passion finds its ultimate and final cause.

3   There are instances, indeed, wherein men show a vanity in resembling a great man in his countenance, shape, air, or other minute circumstances, that contribute not in any degree to his reputation; but it must be confess'd, that this extends not very far, nor is of any considerable moment in these affections. For this I assign the following reason. We can never have a vanity of resembling in trifles any person, unless he be possess'd of very shining qualities, which give us a respect and veneration for him. These qualities, then, are, properly speaking, the causes of our vanity, by means of their relation to ourselves. Now after what manner are they related to ourselves? They are parts of the

person we value, and consequently connected with these trifles; which are also suppos'd to be parts of him. These trifles are connected with the resembling qualities in us; and these qualities in us, being parts, are connected with the whole; and by that means form a chain of several links betwixt ourselves and the shining qualities of the person we resemble. But besides that this multitude of relations must weaken the connexion; 'tis evident the mind, in passing from the shining qualities to the trivial ones, must by that contrast the better perceive the minuteness of the latter, and be in some measure asham'd of the comparison and resemblance.   *SB 305*

4   The relation, therefore, of contiguity, or that of causation, betwixt the cause and object of pride and humility, is alone requisite to give rise to these passions; and these relations are nothing else but qualities, by which the imagination is convey'd from one idea to another. Now let us consider what effect these can possibly have upon the mind, and by what means they become so requisite to the production of the passions. 'Tis evident, that the association of ideas operates in so silent and imperceptible a manner, that we are scarce sensible of it, and discover it more by its effects than by any immediate feeling or perception. It produces no emotion, and gives rise to no new impression of any kind,[†] but only modifies those ideas, of which the mind was formerly possess'd, and which it cou'd recal upon occasion. From this reasoning, as well as from undoubted experience, we may conclude, that an association of ideas, however necessary, is not alone sufficient to give rise to any passion.

5   'Tis evident, then, that when the mind feels the passion either of pride or humility upon the appearance of a related object, there is, beside the relation or transition of thought, an emotion or original impression produc'd by some other principle. The question is, whether the emotion first produc'd be the passion itself, or some other impression related to it? This question we cannot be long in deciding. For besides all the other arguments, with which this subject abounds, it must evidently appear, that the relation of ideas, which experience shows to be so requisite a circumstance to the production of the passion, wou'd be entirely superfluous, were it not to second a relation of affections,[†] and facilitate the transition from one impression to another. If nature produc'd immediately the passion of pride or humility, it wou'd be compleated in itself, and wou'd require no farther addition or encrease from any other affection. But supposing the first emotion to be only related to pride or humility, 'tis easily conceiv'd to what   *SB 306* purpose the relation of objects may serve, and how the two different associations, of impressions and ideas, by uniting their forces, may assist each other's operation. This is not only easily conceiv'd, but I will venture to affirm 'tis the only manner, in which we can conceive this subject. An easy transition of ideas, which, of itself, causes no emotion, can never be necessary, or even useful to the passions, but by forwarding the transition betwixt some related impressions. Not to mention, that the same object causes a greater or smaller degree of pride, not only in proportion to the encrease or decrease of its qualities, but also to the distance or nearness of the relation; which is a clear argument for the transition of affections along the relation of ideas; since every change in the relation

produces a proportionable change in the passion. Thus one part of the preceding system, concerning the relations of ideas is a sufficient proof of the other, concerning that of impressions; and is itself so evidently founded on experience, that 'twou'd be lost time to endeavour farther to prove it.

6 This will appear still more evidently in particular instances. Men are vain of the beauty of their country, of their county, of their parish.[†] Here the idea of beauty plainly produces a pleasure. This pleasure is related to pride. The object or cause of this pleasure is, by the supposition,[†] related to self, or the object of pride. By this double relation of impressions and ideas, a transition is made from the one impression to the other.

7 Men are also vain of the temperature of the climate, in which they were born; of the fertility of their native soil; of the goodness of the wines, fruits or victuals, produc'd by it; of the softness or force of their language; with other particulars of that kind. These objects have plainly a reference to the pleasures of the senses, and are originally consider'd as agreeable to the feeling, taste or hearing. How is it possible they cou'd ever become objects of pride, except by means of that transition above-explain'd?[†]

8 There are some, that discover a vanity of an opposite kind, and affect to depreciate their own country, in comparison of those, to which they have travell'd. These persons find, when they are at home, and surrounded with their countrymen, that the strong relation betwixt them and their own nation is shar'd with so many, that 'tis in a manner lost to them; whereas their distant relation to a foreign country, which is form'd by their having seen it and liv'd in it, is augmented by their considering how few there are who have done the same. For this reason they always admire the beauty, utility and rarity of what is abroad, above what is at home. *SB 307*

9 Since we can be vain of a country, climate or any inanimate object, which bears a relation to us, 'tis no wonder we are vain of the qualities of those, who are connected with us by blood or friendship. Accordingly we find, that the very same qualities, which in ourselves produce pride, produce also in a lesser degree the same affection, when discover'd in persons related to us. The beauty, address, merit, credit and honours of their kindred are carefully display'd by the proud, as some of the most considerable sources of their vanity.

10 As we are proud of riches in ourselves, so to satisfy our vanity we desire that every one, who has any connexion with us, shou'd likewise be possest of them, and are asham'd of any one, that is mean or poor, among our friends and relations. For this reason we remove the poor as far from us as possible; and as we cannot prevent poverty in some distant collaterals,[†] and our forefathers are taken to be our nearest relations; upon this account every one affects to be of a good family, and to be descended from a long succession of rich and honourable ancestors.

11 I have frequently observ'd, that those, who boast of the antiquity of their families, are glad when they can join this circumstance, that their ancestors for many generations have been uninterrupted proprietors of the same portion of

SB 308

land,[†] and that their family has never chang'd its possessions, or been transplanted into any other county or province. I have also observ'd, that 'tis an additional subject of vanity, when they can boast, that these possessions have been transmitted thro' a descent compos'd entirely of males, and that the honours and fortune have never past thro' any female. Let us endeavour to explain these phænomena by the foregoing system.[†]

12   'Tis evident, that when any one boasts of the antiquity of his family, the subjects of his vanity are not merely the extent of time and number of ancestors, but also their riches and credit, which are suppos'd to reflect a lustre on himself on account of his relation to them. He first considers these objects; is affected by them in an agreeable manner; and then returning back to himself, thro' the relation of parent and child, is elevated with the passion of pride, by means of the double relation of impressions and ideas. Since therefore the passion depends on these relations, whatever strengthens any of the relations must also encrease the passion, and whatever weakens the relations must diminish the passion. Now 'tis certain the identity of the possession[†] strengthens the relation of ideas arising from blood and kindred, and conveys the fancy with greater facility from one generation to another, from the remotest ancestors to their posterity, who are both their heirs and their descendants. By this facility the impression is transmitted more entire, and excites a greater degree of pride and vanity.

13   The case is the same with the transmission of the honours and fortune thro' a succession of males without their passing thro' any female. 'Tis a quality of human nature, which we shall consider afterwards,[56] that the imagination naturally turns to whatever is important and considerable; and where two objects are presented to it, a small and a great one, usually leaves the former, and dwells entirely upon the latter. As in the society of marriage, the male sex has the advantage above the female,[†] the husband first engages our attention; and whether we *SB 309* consider him directly, or reach him by passing thro' related objects, the thought both rests upon him with greater satisfaction, and arrives at him with greater facility than his consort. 'Tis easy to see, that this property must strengthen the child's relation to the father, and weaken that to the mother. For as all relations[†] are nothing but a propensity to pass from one idea to another, whatever strengthens the propensity strengthens the relation; and as we have a stronger propensity to pass from the idea of the children to that of the father, than from the same idea to that of the mother, we ought to regard the former relation as the closer and more considerable. This is the reason why children commonly bear their father's name, and are esteem'd to be of nobler or baser birth, according to *his* family. And tho' the mother shou'd be possest of a superior spirit and genius to the father, as often happens, the *general rule* prevails, notwithstanding the exception, according to the doctrine above-explain'd.[†] Nay even when a superiority of any kind is so great, or when any other reasons have such an effect, as to make the children rather represent the mother's family than the father's, the general rule

---

[56] Part 2. Sect. 2.[†]   *SB 308*

still retains such an efficacy that it weakens the relation, and makes a kind of break in the line of ancestors. The imagination runs not along them with facility, nor is able to transfer the honour and credit of the ancestors to their posterity of the same name and family so readily, as when the transition is conformable to the general rules, and passes from father to son, or from brother to brother.

Sect. 10. *Of property and riches*

1   But the relation, which is esteem'd the closest, and which of all others produces most commonly the passion of pride, is that of *property*. This relation 'twill be impossible for me fully to explain before I come to treat of justice and the other *SB 310* moral virtues.[†] 'Tis sufficient to observe on this occasion, that property may be defin'd, *such a relation betwixt a person and an object as permits him, but forbids any other, the free use and possession of it, without violating the laws of justice and moral equity.*[†] If justice, therefore, be a virtue, which has a natural and original influence on the human mind, property may be look'd upon as a particular species of *causation*;[†] whether we consider the liberty it gives the proprietor to operate as he please upon the object, or the advantages, which he reaps from it. 'Tis the same case, if justice, according to the system of certain philosophers, shou'd be esteem'd an artificial and not a natural virtue.[†] For then honour, and custom, and civil laws supply the place of natural conscience, and produce, in some degree, the same effects. This in the mean time is certain, that the mention of the property naturally carries our thought to the proprietor, and of the proprietor to the property; which being a proof of a perfect relation of ideas is all that is requisite to our present purpose. A relation of ideas, join'd to that of impressions, always produces a transition of affections; and therefore, whenever any pleasure or pain arises from an object, connected with us by property, we may be certain, that either pride or humility must arise from this conjunction of relations; if the foregoing system[†] be solid and satisfactory. And whether it be so or not, we may soon satisfy ourselves by the most cursory view of human life.

2   Every thing belonging to a vain man is the best that is any where to be found. His houses, equipage, furniture, cloaths, horses, hounds, excel all others in his conceit; and 'tis easy to observe, that from the least advantage in any of these, he draws a new subject of pride and vanity. His wine, if you'll believe him, has a finer flavour than any other; his cookery is more exquisite; his table more orderly; his servants more expert; the air, in which he lives, more healthful; the soil he cultivates more fertile; his fruits ripen earlier and to greater perfection: Such a *SB 311* thing is remarkable for its novelty; such another for its antiquity: This is the workmanship of a famous artist; that belong'd once to such a prince or great man: All objects, in a word, that are useful, beautiful or surprizing, or are related to such, may, by means of property, give rise to this passion. These agree in giving pleasure, and agree in nothing else. This alone is common to them; and therefore must be the quality that produces the passion, which is their common effect. As every new instance is a new argument, and as the instances are here

without number, I may venture to affirm, that scarce any system was ever so fully prov'd by experience, as that which I have here advanc'd.

3   If the property of any thing, that gives pleasure either by its utility, beauty or novelty, produces also pride by a double relation of impressions and ideas; we need not be surpriz'd, that the power of acquiring this property, shou'd have the same effect. Now riches are to be consider'd as the power of acquiring the property of what pleases; and 'tis only in this view they have any influence on the passions. Paper[†] will, on many occasions, be consider'd as riches, and that because it may convey the power of acquiring money: And money is not riches, as it is a metal endow'd with certain qualities of solidity, weight and fusibility; but only as it has a relation to the pleasures and conveniencies of life. Taking then this for granted, which is in itself so evident, we may draw from it one of the strongest arguments I have yet employ'd to prove the influence of the double relations on pride and humility.

4   It has been observ'd[†] in treating of the understanding, that the distinction, which we sometimes make betwixt a *power* and the *exercise* of it, is entirely frivolous, and that neither man nor any other being ought ever to be thought possest of any ability, unless it be exerted and put in action. But tho' this be strictly true in a just and *philosophical* way of thinking, 'tis certain it is not the *philosophy* of our passions; but that many things operate upon them by means of the idea and supposition of power, independent of its actual exercise. We are pleas'd when we acquire an ability of procuring pleasure, and are displeas'd when another acquires a power of giving pain. This is evident from experience; but in order to give a just explication of the matter, and account for this satisfaction and uneasiness, we must weigh the following reflections.   *SB 312*

5   'Tis evident the error of distinguishing power from its exercise proceeds not entirely from the scholastic doctrine of *free-will*,[†] which, indeed, enters very little into common life, and has but small influence on our vulgar and popular ways of thinking. According to that doctrine, motives deprive us not of free-will, nor take away our power of performing or forbearing any action. But according to common notions a man has no power, where very considerable motives lie betwixt him and the satisfaction of his desires, and determine him to forbear what he wishes to perform. I do not think I have fallen into my enemy's power, when I see him pass me in the streets with a sword by his side, while I am unprovided of any weapon. I know that the fear of the civil magistrate is as strong a restraint as any of iron, and that I am in as perfect safety as if he were chain'd or imprison'd. But when a person acquires such an authority over me, that not only there is no external obstacle to his actions; but also that he may punish or reward me as he pleases, without any dread of punishment in his turn, I then attribute a full power to him, and consider myself as his subject or vassal.

6   Now if we compare these two cases, that of a person, who has very strong motives of interest or safety to forbear any action, and that of another, who lies under no such obligation, we shall find, according to the philosophy explain'd in the foregoing book,[†] that the only *known* difference betwixt them lies in this, that in the former case we conclude from *past experience*, that the person never will

perform that action, and in the latter, that he possibly or probably will perform it.[†] Nothing is more fluctuating and inconstant on many occasions, than the will $SB\,313$ of man; nor is there any thing but strong motives, which can give us an absolute certainty in pronouncing concerning any of his future actions. When we see a person free from these motives, we suppose a possibility either of his acting or forbearing; and tho' in general we may conclude him to be determin'd by motives and causes, yet this removes not the uncertainty of our judgment concerning these causes, nor the influence of that uncertainty on the passions.[†] Since therefore we ascribe a power of performing an action to every one, who has no very powerful motive to forbear it, and refuse it to such as have; it may justly be concluded, that *power* has always a reference to its *exercise*, either actual or probable, and that we consider a person as endow'd with any ability when we find from past experience, that 'tis probable, or at least possible he may exert it. And indeed, as our passions always regard the real existence of objects,[†] and we always judge of this reality from past instances; nothing can be more likely of itself, without any farther reasoning, than that power consists in the possibility or probability of any action, as discover'd by experience and the practice of the world.

7   Now 'tis evident, that wherever a person is in such a situation with regard to me, that there is no very powerful motive to deter him from injuring me, and consequently 'tis *uncertain* whether he will injure me or not, I must be uneasy in such a situation, and cannot consider the possibility or probability of that injury without a sensible concern. The passions are not only affected by such events as are certain and infallible, but also in an inferior degree by such as are possible and contingent. And tho' perhaps I never really feel any harm, and discover by the event, that, philosophically speaking, the person never had any power of harming me; since he did not exert any; this prevents not my uneasiness from the preceding uncertainty. The agreeable passions may here operate as well as the uneasy, and convey a pleasure when I perceive a good to become either possible or probable by the possibility or probability of another's bestowing it on me, $SB\,314$ upon the removal of any strong motives, which might formerly have hinder'd him.

8   But we may farther observe, that this satisfaction encreases, when any good approaches in such a manner that it is in one's *own* power to take or leave it, and there neither is any physical impediment, nor any very strong motive to hinder our enjoyment. As all men desire pleasure, nothing can be more probable, than its existence when there is no external obstacle to the producing it, and men perceive no danger in following their inclinations. In that case their imagination easily anticipates the satisfaction, and conveys the same joy, as if they were perswaded of its real and actual existence.[†]

9   But this accounts not sufficiently for the satisfaction, which attends riches. A miser receives delight from his money; that is, from the *power* it affords him of procuring all the pleasures and conveniencies of life, tho' he knows he has enjoy'd his riches for forty years without ever employing them; and consequently cannot conclude by any species of reasoning, that the real existence of

these pleasures is nearer, than if he were entirely depriv'd of all his possessions.[†] But tho' he cannot form any such conclusion in a way of reasoning concerning the nearer approach of the pleasure, 'tis certain he *imagines* it to approach nearer, whenever all external obstacles are remov'd, along with the more powerful motives of interest and danger, which oppose it. For farther satisfaction on this head I must refer to my account of the will, where I shall explain that false sensation of liberty,[57] which makes us imagine we can perform any thing, that is not very dangerous or destructive. Whenever any other person is under no strong obligations of interest to forbear any pleasure, we judge from *experience*, that the pleasure will exist, and that he will probably obtain it. But when ourselves are in that situation, we judge from an *illusion of the fancy*, that the pleasure is still closer and more immediate. The will seems to move easily every way, and casts a shadow or image of itself, even to that side, on which it did not settle.[†] By means of this image the enjoyment seems to approach nearer to us, and gives us the same lively satisfaction, as if it were perfectly certain and unavoidable. *SB 315*

10 'Twill now be easy to draw this whole reasoning to a point, and to prove, that when riches produce any pride or vanity in their possessors, as they never fail to do, 'tis only by means of a double relation of impressions and ideas. The very essence of riches consists in the power of procuring the pleasures and conveniencies of life.[†] The very essence of this power consists in the probability of its exercise, and in its causing us to anticipate, by a *true* or *false* reasoning, the real existence of the pleasure.[†] This anticipation of pleasure is, in itself, a very considerable pleasure; and as its cause is some possession or property, which we enjoy, and which is thereby related to us, we here clearly see all the parts of the foregoing system[†] most exactly and distinctly drawn out before us.

11 For the same reason, that riches cause pleasure and pride, and poverty excites uneasiness and humility, power must produce the former emotions, and slavery the latter.[†] Power or an authority over others makes us capable of satisfying all our desires; as slavery, by subjecting us to the will of others, exposes us to a thousand wants, and mortifications.

12 'Tis here worth observing, that the vanity of power, or shame of slavery, are much augmented by the consideration of the persons, over whom we exercise our authority, or who exercise it over us. For supposing it possible to frame statues of such an admirable mechanism, that they cou'd move and act in obedience to the will; 'tis evident the possession of them wou'd give pleasure and pride, but not to such a degree, as the same authority, when exerted over sensible and rational creatures, whose condition, being compar'd to our own, makes it seem more agreeable and honourable. Comparison is in every case a sure method of augmenting our esteem of any thing.[†] A rich man feels the felicity of his condition better by opposing it to that of a beggar. But there is a peculiar advantage in power, by the contrast, which is, in a manner, presented to us, betwixt ourselves and the person we command. The comparison is obvious and natural: The imagination finds it in the very subject: The passage of the thought to its *SB 316*

---

[57] Part 3. Sect. 2.[†] *SB 314*

conception is smooth and easy. And that this circumstance has a considerable effect in augmenting its influence, will appear afterwards[†] in examining the nature of *malice* and *envy*.

Sect. 11. *Of the love of fame*

1   But beside these original causes of pride and humility, there is a secondary one in the opinions of others, which has an equal influence on the affections. Our reputation, our character, our name are considerations of vast weight and importance; and even the other causes of pride; virtue, beauty and riches; have little influence, when not seconded by the opinions and sentiments of others. In order to account for this phænomenon 'twill be necessary to take some compass, and first explain the nature of *sympathy*.

2   No quality of human nature is more remarkable, both in itself and in its consequences, than that propensity we have to sympathize with others, and to receive by communication their inclinations and sentiments, however different from, or even contrary to our own. This is not only conspicuous in children, who implicitly embrace every opinion propos'd to them; but also in men of the greatest judgment and understanding, who find it very difficult to follow their own reason or inclination, in opposition to that of their friends and daily companions. To this principle we ought to ascribe the great uniformity we may observe in the humours and turn of thinking of those of the same nation; and 'tis much more probable, that this resemblance arises from sympathy, than from any influence of the soil and climate, which, tho' they continue invariably the same, are not able to preserve the character of a nation the same for a century together. A good-natur'd man finds himself in an instant of the same humour with his company; and even the proudest and most surly take a tincture from their countrymen and acquaintance. A chearful countenance infuses a sensible complacency and serenity into my mind; as an angry or sorrowful one throws a sudden damp upon me. Hatred, resentment, esteem, love, courage, mirth and melancholy; all these passions I feel more from communication than from my own natural temper and disposition. So remarkable a phænomenon merits our attention, and must be trac'd up to its first principles.   *SB 317*

3   When any affection is infus'd by sympathy, it is at first known only by its effects, and by those external signs in the countenance and conversation, which convey an idea of it.[†] This idea is presently converted into an impression, and acquires such a degree of force and vivacity, as to become the very passion itself, and produce an equal emotion, as any original affection.[†] However instantaneous this change of the idea into an impression may be, it proceeds from certain views and reflections, which will not escape the strict scrutiny of a philosopher, tho' they may the person himself, who makes them.

4   'Tis evident, that the idea, or rather impression of ourselves is always intimately present with us, and that our consciousness gives us so lively a conception of our own person, that 'tis not possible to imagine, that any thing can in this

particular go beyond it.[†] Whatever object, therefore, is related to ourselves must be conceiv'd with a like vivacity of conception, according to the foregoing principles;[†] and tho' this relation shou'd not be so strong as that of causation, it must still have a considerable influence. Resemblance and contiguity are relations not to be neglected; especially when by an inference from cause and effect, and by the observation of external signs, we are inform'd of the real existence of the object, which is resembling or contiguous.

SB 318

5   Now 'tis obvious, that nature has preserv'd a great resemblance among all human creatures, and that we never remark any passion or principle in others, of which, in some degree or other, we may not find a parallel in ourselves. The case is the same with the fabric of the mind, as with that of the body. However the parts may differ in shape or size, their structure and composition are in general the same. There is a very remarkable resemblance, which preserves itself amidst all their variety; and this resemblance must very much contribute to make us enter into the sentiments of others, and embrace them with facility and pleasure. Accordingly we find, that where, beside the general resemblance of our natures, there is any peculiar similarity in our manners, or character, or country, or language, it facilitates the sympathy. The stronger the relation is betwixt ourselves and any object, the more easily does the imagination make the transition, and convey to the related idea the vivacity of conception, with which we always form the idea of our own person.

6   Nor is resemblance the only relation, which has this effect, but receives new force from other relations, that may accompany it. The sentiments of others have little influence, when far remov'd from us, and require the relation of contiguity, to make them communicate themselves entirely. The relations of blood, being a species of causation, may sometimes contribute to the same effect; as also acquaintance, which operates in the same manner with education and custom; as we shall see more fully afterwards.[58] All these relations, when united together, convey the impression or consciousness of our own person to the idea of the sentiments or passions of others, and makes us conceive them in the strongest and most lively manner.

7   It has been remark'd[†] in the beginning of this treatise, that all ideas are borrow'd from impressions, and that these two kinds of perceptions differ only in the degrees of force and vivacity, with which they strike upon the soul. The component parts of ideas and impressions are precisely alike. The manner and order of their appearance may be the same. The different degrees of their force and vivacity are, therefore, the only particulars, that distinguish them: And as this difference may be remov'd, in some measure, by a relation betwixt the impressions and ideas, 'tis no wonder an idea of a sentiment or passion, may by this means be so enliven'd as to become the very sentiment or passion. The lively idea of any object always approaches its impression;[†] and 'tis certain we may feel sickness and pain from the mere force of imagination, and make a malady real by

SB 319

---

[58] Part 2. Sect. 4.[†]

SB 318

often thinking of it. But this is most remarkable in the opinions and affections;[†] and 'tis there principally that a lively idea is converted into an impression. Our affections depend more upon ourselves, and the internal operations of the mind, than any other impressions; for which reason they arise more naturally from the imagination, and from every lively idea we form of them. This is the nature and cause of sympathy; and 'tis after this manner we enter so deep into the opinions and affections of others, whenever we discover them.

8   What is principally remarkable in this whole affair is the strong confirmation these phænomena give to the foregoing system[†] concerning the understanding, and consequently to the present one concerning the passions; since these are analogous to each other. 'Tis indeed evident, that when we sympathize with the passions and sentiments of others, these movements appear at first in *our* mind as mere ideas, and are conceiv'd to belong to another person, as we conceive any other matter of fact. 'Tis also evident, that the ideas of the affections of others are converted into the very impressions they represent,[†] and that the passions arise in conformity to the images we form of them. All this is an object of the plainest experience, and depends not on any hypothesis of philosophy. *SB 320* That science can only be admitted to explain the phænomena; tho' at the same time it must be confest, they are so clear of themselves, that there is but little occasion to employ it. For besides the relation of cause and effect, by which we are convinc'd of the reality of the passion, with which we sympathize; besides this, I say, we must be assisted by the relations of resemblance and contiguity, in order to feel the sympathy in its full perfection. And since these relations can entirely convert an idea into an impression, and convey the vivacity of the latter into the former, so perfectly as to lose nothing of it in the transition, we may easily conceive how the relation of cause and effect alone, may serve to strengthen and enliven an idea. In sympathy there is an evident conversion of an idea into an impression. This conversion arises from the relation of objects to ourself. Ourself is always intimately present to us. Let us compare all these circumstances, and we shall find, that sympathy is exactly correspondent to the operations of our understanding; and even contains something more surprizing and extraordinary.[†]

9   'Tis now time to turn our view from the general consideration of sympathy, to its influence on pride and humility, when these passions arise from praise and blame, from reputation and infamy. We may observe, that no person is ever prais'd by another for any quality, which wou'd not, if real, produce, of itself, a pride in the person possest of it. The elogiums either turn upon his power, or riches, or family, or virtue; all of which are subjects of vanity, that we have already explain'd and accounted for.[†] 'Tis certain, then, that if a person consider'd himself in the same light, in which he appears to his admirer, he wou'd first receive a separate pleasure, and afterwards a pride or self-satisfaction, according to the hypothesis above-explain'd.[†] Now nothing is more natural than for us to embrace the opinions of others in this particular; both from *sympathy*, which renders all their sentiments intimately present to us; and from *reasoning*, which makes us regard their judgment, as a kind of argument for what they *SB 321*

affirm. These two principles of authority[†] and sympathy influence almost all our opinions; but must have a peculiar influence, when we judge of our own worth and character. Such judgments are always attended with passion;[59] and nothing tends more to disturb our understanding, and precipitate us into any opinions, however unreasonable, than their connexion with passion; which diffuses itself over the imagination, and gives an additional force to every related idea. To which we may add, that being conscious of great partiality in our own favour, we are peculiarly pleas'd with any thing, that confirms the good opinion we have of ourselves, and are easily shock'd with whatever opposes it.

10   All this appears very probable in theory; but in order to bestow a full certainty on this reasoning, we must examine the phænomena of the passions, and see if they agree with it.

11   Among these phænomena we may esteem it a very favourable one to our present purpose, that tho' fame in general be agreeable, yet we receive a much greater satisfaction from the approbation of those, whom we ourselves esteem and approve of, than of those, whom we hate and despise. In like manner we are principally mortify'd with the contempt of persons, upon whose judgment we set some value, and are, in a great measure, indifferent about the opinions of the rest of mankind. But if the mind receiv'd from any original instinct a desire of fame, and aversion to infamy, fame and infamy wou'd influence us without distinction; and every opinion, according as it were favourable or unfavourable, wou'd equally excite that desire or aversion. The judgment of a fool is the judgment of another person, as well as that of a wise man, and is only inferior in its influence on our own judgment.

12   We are not only better pleas'd with the approbation of a wise man than with that of a fool, but receive an additional satisfaction from the former, when 'tis obtain'd after a long and intimate acquaintance. This is accounted for after the   *SB 322* same manner.

13   The praises of others never give us much pleasure, unless they concur with our own opinion, and extol us for those qualities, in which we chiefly excel. A mere soldier little values the character of eloquence: A gownman of courage:[†] A bishop of humour: Or a merchant of learning. Whatever esteem a man may have for any quality, abstractedly consider'd; when he is conscious he is not possest of it; the opinions of the whole world will give him little pleasure in that particular, and that because they never will be able to draw his own opinion after them.

14   Nothing is more usual than for men of good families, but narrow circumstances, to leave their friends and country, and rather seek their livelihood by mean and mechanical employments among strangers, than among those, who are acquainted with their birth and education. We shall be unknown, say they, where we go. No body will suspect from what family we are sprung. We shall be remov'd from all our friends and acquaintance, and our poverty and meanness will by that means sit more easy upon us.[†] In examining these sentiments, I find they afford many very convincing arguments for my present purpose.

[59] Book 1. Part 3. Sect. 10.[†]   *SB 321*

15   *First*, We may infer from them, that the uneasiness of being contemn'd depends on sympathy, and that sympathy depends on the relation of objects to ourselves; since we are most uneasy under the contempt of persons, who are both related to us by blood, and contiguous in place. Hence we seek to diminish this sympathy and uneasiness by separating these relations,[†] and placing ourselves in a contiguity to strangers, and at a distance from relations.

16   *Secondly*, We may conclude, that relations are requisite to sympathy, not absolutely consider'd as relations, but by their influence in converting our ideas of the sentiments of others into the very sentiments, by means of the association betwixt the idea of their persons, and that of our own. For here the relations of kindred and contiguity both subsist;[†] but not being united in the same persons, they contribute in a less degree to the sympathy. *SB 323*

17   *Thirdly*, This very circumstance of the diminution of sympathy by the separation of relations[†] is worthy of our attention. Suppose I am plac'd in a poor condition among strangers, and consequently am but lightly treated; I yet find myself easier in that situation, than when I was every day expos'd to the contempt of my kindred and countrymen.[†] Here I feel a double contempt; from my relations, but they are absent; from those about me, but they are strangers. This double contempt is likewise strengthen'd by the two relations of kindred and contiguity. But as the persons are not the same, who are connected with me by those two relations, this difference of ideas separates the impressions arising from the contempt, and keeps them from running into each other. The contempt of my neighbours has a certain influence; as has also that of my kindred: But these influences are distinct, and never unite; as when the contempt proceeds from persons who are at once both my neighbours and kindred. This phænomenon is analogous to the system of pride and humility above-explain'd,[†] which may seem so extraordinary to vulgar apprehensions.

18   *Fourthly*, A person in these circumstances naturally conceals his birth from those among whom he lives, and is very uneasy, if any one suspects him to be of a family, much superior to his present fortune and way of living. Every thing in this world is judg'd of by comparison. What is an immense fortune for a private gentleman is beggary for a prince. A peasant wou'd think himself happy in what cannot afford necessaries for a gentleman. When a man has either been accustom'd to a more splendid way of living, or thinks himself entitled to it by his birth and quality, every thing below is disagreeable and even shameful; and 'tis with the greatest industry he conceals his pretensions to a better fortune. Here he himself knows his misfortunes; but as those, with whom he lives, are ignorant of them, he has the disagreeable reflection and comparison suggested only by his own thoughts, and never receives it by a sympathy with others; which must contribute very much to his ease and satisfaction. *SB 324*

19   If there be any objections to this hypothesis, *that the pleasure, which we receive from praise, arises from a communication of sentiments*, we shall find, upon examination, that these objections, when taken in a proper light, will serve to confirm it. Popular fame may be agreeable even to a man, who despises the vulgar; but 'tis

because their multitude gives them additional weight and authority. Plagiaries are delighted with praises, which they are conscious they do not deserve; but this is a kind of castle-building,[†] where the imagination amuses itself with its own fictions, and strives to render them firm and stable by a sympathy with the sentiments of others. Proud men are most shock'd with contempt, tho' they do not most readily assent to it; but 'tis because of the opposition betwixt the passion, which is natural to them, and that receiv'd by sympathy. A violent lover[†] in like manner is very much displeas'd when you blame and condemn his love; tho' 'tis evident your opposition can have no influence, but by the hold it takes of himself, and by his sympathy with you. If he despises you, or perceives you are in jest, whatever you say has no effect upon him.

Sect. 12. *Of the pride and humility of animals*

1   Thus in whatever light we consider this subject, we may still observe, that the causes of pride and humility correspond exactly to our hypothesis, and that nothing can excite either of these passions, unless it be both related to ourselves, and produces a pleasure or pain independent of the passion. We have not only prov'd, that a tendency to produce pleasure or pain is common to all the causes of pride or humility, but also that 'tis the only thing, which is common; and consequently is the quality, by which they operate.[†] We have farther prov'd, that the most considerable causes of these passions are really nothing but the power of producing either agreeable or uneasy sensations; and therefore that all their effects, and amongst the rest, pride and humility, are deriv'd solely from that origin. Such simple and natural principles, founded on such solid proofs, cannot fail to be receiv'd by philosophers, unless oppos'd by some objections, that have escap'd me.   *SB 325*

2   'Tis usual with anatomists to join their observations and experiments on human bodies to those on beasts,[†] and from the agreement of these experiments to derive an additional argument for any particular hypothesis. 'Tis indeed certain, that where the structure of parts in brutes is the same as in men, and the operation of these parts also the same, the causes of that operation cannot be different, and that whatever we discover to be true of the one species, may be concluded without hesitation to be certain of the other. Thus tho' the mixture of humours[†] and the composition of minute parts may justly be presum'd to be somewhat different in men from what it is in mere animals; and therefore any experiment we make upon the one concerning the effects of medicines will not always apply to the other; yet as the structure of the veins and muscles, the fabric and situation of the heart, of the lungs, the stomach, the liver and other parts, are the same or nearly the same in all animals, the very same hypothesis, which in one species explains muscular motion,[†] the progress of the chyle,[†] the circulation of the blood, must be applicable to every one; and according as it agrees or disagrees with the experiments we may make in any species of creatures, we may draw a proof of its truth or falshood on the whole. Let us, therefore, apply this

method of enquiry, which is found so just and useful in reasonings concerning ~~SB 326~~
the body, to our present anatomy of the mind, and see what discoveries we can
make by it.

3　　　In order to this we must first show the correspondence of *passions* in men and
animals, and afterwards compare the *causes*, which produce these passions.

4　　　'Tis plain, that almost in every species of creatures, but especially of the
nobler kind,[†] there are many evident marks of pride and humility. The very port
and gait of a swan, or turkey, or peacock show the high idea he has entertain'd of
himself, and his contempt of all others. This is the more remarkable, that in the
two last species of animals, the pride always attends the beauty, and is discover'd
in the male only. The vanity and emulation of nightingales in singing have
been commonly remark'd; as likewise that of horses in swiftness, of hounds in
sagacity and smell, of the bull and cock in strength, and of every other animal in
his particular excellency.[†] Add to this, that every species of creatures, which
approach so often to man, as to familiarize themselves with him, show an evident
pride in his approbation, and are pleas'd with his praises and caresses, independent of every other consideration. Nor are they the caresses of every one
without distinction, which give them this vanity, but those principally of the
persons they know and love; in the same manner as that passion is excited in
mankind. All these are evident proofs, that pride and humility are not merely
human passions, but extend themselves over the whole animal creation.

5　　　The *causes* of these passions are likewise much the same in beasts as in us,
making a just allowance for our superior knowledge and understanding. Thus
animals have little or no sense of virtue or vice;[†] they quickly lose sight of the
relations of blood; and are incapable of that of right and property:[†] For which
reason the causes of their pride and humility must lie solely in the body, and can
never be plac'd either in the mind or external objects.[†] But so far as regards the
body, the same qualities cause pride in the animal as in the human kind; and 'tis
on beauty, strength, swiftness or some other useful or agreeable quality that this ~~SB 327~~
passion is always founded.

6　　　The next question is, whether, since those passions are the same, and arise
from the same causes thro' the whole creation, the *manner*, in which the causes
operate, be also the same? According to all rules of analogy,[†] this is justly to be
expected; and if we find upon trial, that the explication of these phænomena,
which we make use of in one species, will not apply to the rest, we may presume
that that explication, however specious, is in reality without foundation.

7　　　In order to decide this question, let us consider, that there is evidently the
same *relation* of ideas, and deriv'd from the same causes, in the minds of animals
as in those of men. A dog, that has hid a bone, often forgets the place; but when
brought to it, his thought passes easily to what he formerly conceal'd, by means
of the contiguity, which produces a relation among his ideas. In like manner,
when he has been heartily beat in any place, he will tremble on his approach to it,
even tho' he discover no signs of any present danger.[†] The effects of resemblance
are not so remarkable; but as that relation makes a considerable ingredient in
causation, of which all animals show so evident a judgment, we may conclude

that the three relations of resemblance, contiguity and causation operate in the same manner upon beasts as upon human creatures.

8   There are also instances of the relation of impressions, sufficient to convince us, that there is an union of certain affections with each other in the inferior species of creatures as well as in the superior, and that their minds are frequently convey'd thro' a series of connected emotions. A dog, when elevated with joy, runs naturally into love and kindness,[†] whether of his master or of the sex.[†] In like manner, when full of pain and sorrow, he becomes quarrelsome and ill-natur'd; and that passion, which at first was grief, is by the smallest occasion converted into anger.

9   Thus all the internal principles, that are necessary in us to produce either   *SB 328* pride or humility, are common to all creatures; and since the causes, which excite these passions, are likewise the same, we may justly conclude, that these causes operate after the same *manner* thro' the whole animal creation. My hypothesis is so simple, and supposes so little reflection and judgment, that 'tis applicable to every sensible creature; which must not only be allow'd to be a convincing proof of its veracity, but, I am confident, will be found an objection to every other system.

PART 2

Of love and hatred

Sect. 1. *Of the objects and causes of love and hatred*

1   'Tis altogether impossible to give any definition of the passions of LOVE and HATRED; and that because they produce merely a simple impression, without any mixture or composition. 'Twou'd be as unnecessary to attempt any description of them, drawn from their nature, origin, causes and objects; and that both because these are the subjects of our present enquiry, and because these passions of themselves are sufficiently known from our common feeling and experience. This we have already observ'd[†] concerning pride and humility, and here repeat it concerning love and hatred; and indeed there is so great a resemblance betwixt these two sets of passions, that we shall be oblig'd to begin with a kind of abridgment of our reasonings concerning the former, in order to explain the latter.

2   As the immediate *object* of pride and humility is self or that identical person, of whose thoughts, actions, and sensations we are intimately conscious;[†] so the *object* of love and hatred is some other person, of whose thoughts, actions, and sensations we are not conscious. This is sufficiently evident from experience. Our love and hatred are always directed to some sensible being[†] external to us; and when we talk of *self-love*, 'tis not in a proper sense,[†] nor has the sensation it produces any thing in common with that tender emotion, which is excited by a friend or mistress. 'Tis the same case with hatred. We may be mortify'd by our own faults and follies; but never feel any anger or hatred, except from the injuries of others.

3   But tho' the object of love and hatred be always some other person, 'tis plain that the object is not, properly speaking, the *cause* of these passions, or alone sufficient to excite them.[†] For since love and hatred are directly contrary in their sensation, and have the same object in common, if that object were also their cause, it wou'd produce these opposite passions in an equal degree; and as they must, from the very first moment, destroy each other, none of them wou'd ever be able to make its appearance. There must, therefore, be some cause different from the object.

4   If we consider the causes of love and hatred, we shall find they are very much diversify'd, and have not many things in common.[†] The virtue, knowledge, wit, good sense, good humour of any person, produce love and esteem; as the opposite qualities, hatred and contempt.[†] The same passions arise from bodily accomplishments, such as beauty, force, swiftness, dexterity; and from their contraries; as likewise from the external advantages and disadvantages of family, possessions, cloaths, nation and climate. There is not one of these

214

objects, but what by its different qualities may produce love and esteem, or hatred and contempt.

5   From the view of these causes we may derive a new distinction betwixt the *quality* that operates, and the *subject* on which it is plac'd.[†] A prince, that is possess'd of a stately palace, commands the esteem of the people upon that account; and that *first*, by the beauty of the palace, and *secondly*, by the relation of property, which connects it with him. The removal of either of these destroys the passion; which evidently proves that the cause is a compounded one.

6   'Twou'd be tedious to trace the passions of love and hatred, thro' all the observations which we have form'd[†] concerning pride and humility, and which are equally applicable to both sets of passions. 'Twill be sufficient to *remark* in general, that the object of love and hatred is evidently some thinking person; and that the sensation of the former passion is always agreeable, and of the latter uneasy. We may also *suppose* with some show of probability, *that the cause of both these passions is always related to a thinking being*, and *that the cause of the former produces a separate pleasure, and of the latter a separate uneasiness.*[†]   *SB 331*

7   One of these suppositions, *viz.* that the cause of love and hatred must be related to a person or thinking being, in order to produce these passions, is not only probable, but too evident to be contested. Virtue and vice, when consider'd in the abstract; beauty and deformity, when plac'd on inanimate objects; poverty and riches, when belonging to a third person, excite no degree of love or hatred, esteem or contempt towards those, who have no relation to them. A person looking out at a window, sees me in the street, and beyond me a beautiful palace, with which I have no concern: I believe none will pretend, that this person will pay me the same respect, as if I were owner of the palace.

8   'Tis not so evident at first sight, that a relation of impressions[†] is requisite to these passions, and that because in the transition the one impression is so much confounded with the other, that they become in a manner undistinguishable. But as in pride and humility, we have easily been able to make the separation, and to prove, that every cause of these passions produces a separate pain or pleasure,[†] I might here observe the same method with the same success, in examining particularly the several causes of love and hatred. But as I hasten to a full and decisive proof of these systems, I delay this examination for a moment:[†] And in the mean time shall endeavour to convert to my present purpose all my reasonings concerning pride and humility, by an argument that is founded on unquestionable experience.

9   There are few persons, that are satisfy'd with their own character, or genius, or fortune, who are not desirous of showing themselves to the world, and of acquiring the love and approbation of mankind. Now 'tis evident, that the very same qualities and circumstances, which are the causes of pride or self-esteem, are also the causes of vanity or the desire of reputation; and that we always put to view those particulars with which in ourselves we are best satisfy'd. But if love and esteem were not produc'd by the same qualities as pride, according as these qualities are related to ourselves or others, this method of proceeding wou'd be very absurd, nor cou'd men expect a correspondence in the sentiments of every   *SB 332*

other person, with those they themselves have entertain'd. 'Tis true, few can form exact systems of the passions, or make reflections on their general nature and resemblances. But without such a progress in philosophy, we are not subject to many mistakes in this particular, but are sufficiently guided by common experience, as well as by a kind of *presensation*;[†] which tells us what will operate on others, by what we feel immediately in ourselves. Since then the same qualities that produce pride or humility, cause love or hatred; all the arguments that have been employ'd[†] to prove, that the causes of the former passions excite a pain or pleasure independent of the passion, will be applicable with equal evidence to the causes of the latter.

Sect. 2. *Experiments to confirm this system*

1   Upon duly weighing these arguments, no one will make any scruple to assent to that conclusion I draw from them, concerning the transition along related impressions and ideas, especially as 'tis a principle, in itself, so easy and natural. But that we may place this system beyond doubt both with regard to love and hatred, pride and humility, 'twill be proper to make some new experiments upon all these passions, as well as to recal a few of those observations, which I have formerly touch'd upon.[†]

2   In order to make these experiments, let us suppose I am in company with a   *SB 333*
person, whom I formerly regarded without any sentiments either of friendship or enmity. Here I have the natural and ultimate object of all these four passions plac'd before me. Myself am the proper object of pride or humility; the other person of love or hatred.

3   Regard now with attention the nature of these passions, and their situation with respect to each other. 'Tis evident here are four affections, plac'd, as it were, in a square or regular connexion with, and distance from each other. The passions of pride and humility, as well as those of love and hatred, are connected together by the identity of their object, which to the first set of passions is self, to the second some other person. These two lines of communication or connexion form two opposite sides of the square. Again, pride and love are agreeable passions; hatred and humility uneasy. This similitude of sensation betwixt pride and love, and that betwixt humility and hatred, form a new connexion, and may be consider'd as the other two sides of the square. Upon the whole, pride is connected with humility, love with hatred, by their objects or ideas: Pride with love, humility with hatred, by their sensations or impressions.[†]

4   I say then, that nothing can produce any of these passions without bearing it a double relation, *viz.* of ideas to the object of the passion, and of sensation to the passion itself. This we must prove by our experiments.

5   *First Experiment.* To proceed with the greater order in these experiments, let us first suppose, that being plac'd in the situation above-mention'd, *viz.* in company with some other person, there is an object presented, that has no relation either of impressions or ideas to any of these passions. Thus suppose we

regard together an ordinary stone, or other common object, belonging to neither of us, and causing of itself no emotion, or independent pain and pleasure: 'Tis evident such an object will produce none of these four passions. Let us try it upon each of them successively. Let us apply it to love, to hatred, to humility, to *SB 334* pride; none of them ever arises in the smallest degree imaginable. Let us change the object, as oft as we please; provided still we choose one, that has neither of these two relations. Let us repeat the experiment in all the dispositions, of which the mind is susceptible. No object, in the vast variety of nature, will, in any disposition, produce any passion without these relations.

6   *Second Experiment.* Since an object, that wants both these relations can never produce any passion, let us bestow on it only one of these relations; and see what will follow. Thus suppose, I regard a stone or any common object, that belongs either to me or my companion, and by that means acquires a relation of ideas to the object of the passions: 'Tis plain, that to consider the matter *a priori*, no emotion of any kind can reasonably be expected. For besides, that a relation of ideas operates secretly and calmly on the mind,[†] it bestows an equal impulse towards the opposite passions of pride and humility, love and hatred, according as the object belongs to ourselves or others; which opposition of the passions must destroy both, and leave the mind perfectly free from any affection or emotion.[†] This reasoning *a priori* is confirm'd by experience. No trivial or vulgar object, that causes not a pain or pleasure, independent of the passion, will ever, by its property or other relations, either to ourselves or others, be able to produce the affections of pride or humility, love or hatred.

7   *Third Experiment.* 'Tis evident, therefore, that a relation of ideas is not able alone to give rise to these affections. Let us now remove this relation, and in its stead place a relation of impressions, by presenting an object, which is agreeable or disagreeable, but has no relation either to ourself or companion; and let us observe the consequences. To consider the matter first *a priori*, as in the preceding experiment; we may conclude, that the object will have a small, but an uncertain connexion with these passions. For besides, that this relation is not a cold and imperceptible one,[†] it has not the inconvenience of the relation of ideas, nor *SB 335* directs us with equal force to two contrary passions, which by their opposition destroy each other. But if we consider, on the other hand, that this transition from the sensation to the affection is not forwarded by any principle, that produces a transition of ideas; but, on the contrary, that tho' the one impression be easily transfus'd into the other, yet the change of objects[†] is suppos'd contrary to all the principles, that cause a transition of that kind; we may from thence infer, that nothing will ever be a steady or durable cause of any passion, that is connected with the passion merely by a relation of impressions. What our reason wou'd conclude from analogy, after ballancing these arguments, wou'd be, that an object, which produces pleasure or uneasiness, but has no manner of connexion either with ourselves or others, may give such a turn to the disposition, as that it may naturally fall into pride or love, humility or hatred, and search for other objects, upon which, by a double relation, it can found these affections;[†]

but that an object, which has only one of these relations, tho' the most advantageous one, can never give rise to any constant and establish'd passion.

8 Most fortunately all this reasoning is found to be exactly conformable to experience, and the phænomena of the passions. Suppose I were travelling with a companion thro' a country, to which we are both utter strangers; 'tis evident, that if the prospects be beautiful, the roads agreeable, and the inns commodious, this may put me into good humour both with myself and fellow-traveller. But as we suppose, that this country has no relation either to myself or friend, it can never be the immediate cause of pride or love; and therefore if I found not the passion on some other object, that bears either of us a closer relation, my emotions are rather to be consider'd as the overflowings of an elevate or humane disposition, than as an establish'd passion. The case is the same where the object produces uneasiness.

9 *Fourth Experiment.* Having found, that neither an object without any relation $SB\,336$ of ideas or impressions, nor an object, that has only one relation, can ever cause pride or humility, love or hatred; reason alone may convince us, without any farther experiment, that whatever has a double relation must necessarily excite these passions; since 'tis evident they must have some cause. But to leave as little room for doubt as possible, let us renew our experiments, and see whether the event in this case answers our expectation. I choose an object, such as virtue, that causes a separate satisfaction: On this object I bestow a relation to self; and find, that from this disposition of affairs, there immediately arises a passion. But what passion? That very one of pride, to which this object bears a double relation. Its idea is related to that of self, the object of the passion: The sensation it causes resembles the sensation of the passion. That I may be sure I am not mistaken in this experiment, I remove first one relation; then another; and find, that each removal destroys the passion, and leaves the object perfectly indifferent. But I am not content with this. I make a still farther trial; and instead of removing the relation, I only change it for one of a different kind. I suppose the virtue to belong to my companion, not to myself; and observe what follows from this alteration. I immediately perceive the affections to wheel about, and leaving pride, where there is only one relation, *viz.* of impressions, fall to the side of love, where they are attracted by a double relation of impressions and ideas. By repeating the same experiment, in changing anew the relation of ideas, I bring the affections back to pride; and by a new repetition I again place them at love or kindness. Being fully convinc'd of the influence of this relation, I try the effects of the other; and by changing virtue for vice, convert the pleasant impression, which arises from the former, into the disagreeable one, which proceeds from the latter. The effect still answers expectation. Vice, when plac'd on another, excites, by means of its double relations, the passion of hatred, instead of love, which for the same reason arises from virtue. To continue the $SB\,337$ experiment, I change anew the relation of ideas, and suppose the vice to belong to myself. What follows? What is usual. A subsequent change of the passion from hatred to humility. This humility I convert into pride by a new change of the impression; and find after all that I have compleated the round,[†] and have

by these changes brought back the passion to that very situation, in which I first found it.

10   But to make the matter still more certain, I alter the object; and instead of vice and virtue, make the trial upon beauty and deformity, riches and poverty, power and servitude. Each of these objects runs the circle of the passions in the same manner, by a change of their relations: And in whatever order we proceed, whether thro' pride, love, hatred, humility, or thro' humility, hatred, love, pride, the experiment is not in the least diversify'd. Esteem and contempt, indeed, arise on some occasions instead of love and hatred; but these are at the bottom the same passions, only diversify'd by some causes, which we shall explain afterwards.†

11   *Fifth Experiment.* To give greater authority to these experiments, let us change the situation of affairs as much as possible, and place the passions and objects in all the different positions, of which they are susceptible. Let us suppose, beside the relations above-mention'd,† that the person, along with whom I make all these experiments, is closely connected with me either by blood or friendship. He is, we shall suppose, my son or brother, or is united to me by a long and familiar acquaintance. Let us next suppose, that the cause of the passion acquires a double relation of impressions and ideas to this person; and let us see what the effects are of all these complicated attractions and relations.

12   Before we consider what they are in fact, let us determine what they ought to be, conformable to my hypothesis. 'Tis plain, that, according as the impression is either pleasant or uneasy, the passion of love or hatred must arise towards the person, who is thus connected to the cause of the impression by these double relations, which I have all along requir'd. The virtue of a brother must make me love him; as his vice or infamy must excite the contrary passion. But to judge only from the situation of affairs, I shou'd not expect, that the affections wou'd rest there, and never transfuse themselves into any other impression.† As there is here a person, who by means of a double relation is the object of my passion, the very same reasoning leads me to think the passion will be carry'd farther. The person has a relation of ideas to myself, according to the supposition; the passion, of which he is the object, by being either agreeable or uneasy, has a relation of impressions to pride or humility. 'Tis evident, then, that one of these passions must arise from the love or hatred.

SB 338

13   This is the reasoning I form in conformity to my hypothesis; and am pleas'd to find upon trial that every thing answers exactly to my expectation. The virtue or vice of a son or brother not only excites love or hatred, but by a new transition, from similar causes, gives rise to pride or humility. Nothing causes greater vanity than any shining quality in our relations; as nothing mortifies us more than their vice or infamy. This exact conformity of experience to our reasoning is a convincing proof of the solidity of that hypothesis, upon which we reason.

14   *Sixth Experiment.* This evidence will be still augmented, if we reverse the experiment, and preserving still the same relations, begin only with a different passion. Suppose, that instead of the virtue or vice of a son or brother, which causes first love or hatred, and afterwards pride or humility, we place these good

or bad qualities on ourselves, without any immediate connexion with the person, who is related to us: Experience shows us, that by this change of situation the whole chain is broke, and that the mind is not convey'd from one passion to another, as in the preceding instance.[†] We never love or hate a son or brother for the virtue or vice we discern in ourselves; tho' 'tis evident the same qualities in him give us a very sensible pride or humility. The transition from pride or humility to love or hatred is not so natural as from love or hatred to pride or humility. This may at first sight be esteem'd contrary to my hypothesis; since the relations of impressions and ideas are in both cases precisely the same. Pride and humility are impressions related to love and hatred. Myself am related to the person. It shou'd, therefore, be expected, that like causes must produce like effects, and a perfect transition arise from the double relation, as in all other cases. This difficulty we may easily solve by the following reflections.

SB 339

15   'Tis evident, that as we are at all times intimately conscious of ourselves,[†] our sentiments and passions, their ideas must strike upon us with greater vivacity than the ideas of the sentiments and passions of any other person. But every thing, that strikes upon us with vivacity, and appears in a full and strong light, forces itself, in a manner, into our consideration, and becomes present to the mind on the smallest hint and most trivial relation. For the same reason, when it is once present, it engages the attention, and keeps it from wandering to other objects, however strong may be their relation to our first object. The imagination passes easily from obscure to lively ideas, but with difficulty from lively to obscure. In the one case the relation is aided by another principle: In the other case, 'tis oppos'd by it.

16   Now I have observ'd,[†] that those two faculties of the mind, the imagination and passions, assist each other in their operation, when their propensities are similar, and when they act upon the same object. The mind has always a propensity to pass from a passion to any other related to it; and this propensity is forwarded when the object of the one passion is related to that of the other. The two impulses concur with each other, and render the whole transition more smooth and easy. But if it shou'd happen, that while the relation of ideas, strictly speaking, continues the same, its influence, in causing a transition of the imagination, shou'd no longer take place, 'tis evident its influence on the passions must also cease, as being dependent entirely on that transition. This is the reason why pride or humility is not transfus'd into love or hatred with the same ease, that the latter passions are chang'd into the former. If a person be my brother I am his likewise: But tho' the relations be reciprocal, they have very different effects on the imagination. The passage is smooth and open from the consideration of any person related to us to that of ourself, of whom we are every moment conscious. But when the affections are once directed to ourself, the fancy passes not with the same facility from that object to any other person, how closely so ever connected with us. This easy or difficult transition of the imagination operates upon the passions, and facilitates or retards their transition; which is a clear proof, that these two faculties of the passions and imagination are

SB 340

connected together, and that the relations of ideas have an influence upon the affections. Besides innumerable experiments that prove this, we here find, that even when the relation remains; if by any particular circumstance its usual effect upon the fancy in producing an association or transition of ideas, is prevented; its usual effect upon the passions, in conveying us from one to another, is in like manner prevented.

17   Some may, perhaps, find a contradiction betwixt this phænomenon and that of sympathy, where the mind passes easily from the idea of ourselves to that of any other object related to us.[†] But this difficulty will vanish, if we consider that in sympathy our own person is not the object of any passion, nor is there any thing, that fixes our attention on ourselves; as in the present case, where we are suppos'd to be actuated with pride or humility. Ourself, independent of the perception of every other object, is in reality nothing:[†] For which reason we must turn our view to external objects; and 'tis natural for us to consider with most attention such as lie contiguous to us, or resemble us. But when self is the object   *SB 341* of a passion, 'tis not natural to quit the consideration of it, till the passion be exhausted; in which case the double relations of impressions and ideas can no longer operate.

18   *Seventh Experiment.* To put this whole reasoning to a farther trial, let us make a new experiment; and as we have already seen[†] the effects of related passions and ideas, let us here suppose an identity of passions along with a relation of ideas; and let us consider the effects of this new situation. 'Tis evident a transition of the passions from the one object to the other is here in all reason to be expected; since the relation of ideas is suppos'd still to continue, and an identity of impressions must produce a stronger connexion, than the most perfect resemblance, that can be imagin'd. If a double relation, therefore, of impressions and ideas is able to produce a transition from one to the other, much more an identity of impressions with a relation of ideas. Accordingly we find, that when we either love or hate any person, the passions seldom continue within their first bounds; but extend themselves towards all the contiguous objects, and comprehend the friends and relations of him we love or hate. Nothing is more natural than to bear a kindness to one brother on account of our friendship for another, without any farther examination of his character. A quarrel with one person gives us a hatred for the whole family, tho' entirely innocent of that, which displeases us. Instances of this kind are every where to be met with.

19   There is only one difficulty in this experiment, which it will be necessary to account for, before we proceed any farther. 'Tis evident, that tho' all passions pass easily from one object to another related to it, yet this transition is made with greater facility, where the more considerable object is first presented, and the lesser follows it, than where this order is revers'd, and the lesser takes the precedence. Thus 'tis more natural for us to love the son upon account of the father, than the father upon account of the son; the servant for the master, than   *SB 342* the master for the servant; the subject for the prince, than the prince for the subject. In like manner we more readily contract a hatred against a whole family,

where our first quarrel is with the head of it, than where we are displeas'd with a son, or servant, or some inferior member. In short, our passions, like other objects, descend with greater facility than they ascend.

20   That we may comprehend, wherein consists the difficulty of explaining this phænomenon, we must consider, that the very same reason, which determines the imagination to pass from remote to contiguous objects, with more facility than from contiguous to remote, causes it likewise to change with more ease, the less for the greater, than the greater for the less. Whatever has the greatest influence is most taken notice of; and whatever is most taken notice of, presents itself most readily to the imagination. We are more apt to over-look in any subject, what is trivial, than what appears of considerable moment; but especially if the latter takes the precedence, and first engages our attention. Thus if any accident makes us consider the *Satellites* of *Jupiter*,† our fancy is naturally determin'd to form the idea of that planet; but if we first reflect on the principal planet, 'tis more natural for us to overlook its attendants. The mention of the provinces of any empire conveys our thought to the seat of the empire; but the fancy returns not with the same facility to the consideration of the provinces. The idea of the servant makes us think of the master; that of the subject carries our view to the prince. But the same relation has not an equal influence in conveying us back again. And on this is founded that reproach of *Cornelia* to her sons, that they ought to be asham'd she shou'd be more known by the title of the daughter of *Scipio*, than by that of the mother of the *Gracchi*.† This was, in other words, exhorting them to render themselves as illustrious and famous as their grand-father, otherwise the imagination of the people, passing from her who was inter-mediate, and plac'd in an equal relation to both, wou'd always leave them, and   *SB 343* denominate her by what was more considerable and of greater moment. On the same principle is founded that common custom of making wives† bear the name of their husbands, rather than husbands that of their wives; as also the ceremony of giving the precedency to those, whom we honour and respect.† We might find many other instances to confirm this principle, were it not already sufficiently evident.

21   Now since the fancy finds the same facility in passing from the lesser to the greater, as from remote to contiguous, why does not this easy transition of ideas assist the transition of passions in the former case, as well as in the latter?† The virtues of a friend or brother produce first love, and then pride; because in that case the imagination passes from remote to contiguous, according to its propensity. Our own virtues produce not first pride, and then love to a friend or brother; because the passage in that case wou'd be from contiguous to remote, contrary to its propensity. But the love or hatred of an inferior causes not readily any passion to the superior, tho' that be the natural propensity of the imagination: While the love or hatred of a superior, causes a passion to the infe-rior, contrary to its propensity. In short, the same facility of transition operates not in the same manner upon superior and inferior as upon contiguous and remote. These two phænomena appear contradictory, and require some atten-tion to be reconcil'd.

22   As the transition of ideas is here made contrary to the natural propensity of the imagination, that faculty must be over-power'd by some stronger principle of another kind; and as there is nothing ever present to the mind but impressions and ideas, this principle must necessarily lie in the impressions. Now it has been observ'd,[†] that impressions or passions are connected only by their resemblance, and that where any two passions place the mind in the same or in similar dispositions, it very naturally passes from the one to the other: As on the contrary, a repugnance in the dispositions produces a difficulty in the transition of the pas-   *SB 344* sions. But 'tis observable, that this repugnance may arise from a difference of degree as well as of kind; nor do we experience a greater difficulty in passing suddenly from a small degree of love to a small degree of hatred, than from a small to a great degree of either of these affections. A man, when calm or only moderately agitated, is so different, in every respect, from himself, when disturb'd with a violent passion, that no two persons can be more unlike;[†] nor is it easy to pass from the one extreme to the other, without a considerable interval betwixt them.

23   The difficulty is not less, if it be not rather greater, in passing from the strong passion to the weak, than in passing from the weak to the strong, provided the one passion upon its appearance destroys the other, and they do not both of them exist at once.[†] But the case is entirely alter'd, when the passions unite together, and actuate the mind at the same time. A weak passion, when added to a strong, makes not so considerable a change in the disposition, as a strong when added to a weak; for which reason there is a closer connexion betwixt the great degree and the small, than betwixt the small degree and the great.

24   The degree of any passion depends upon the nature of its object; and an affection directed to a person, who is considerable in our eyes, fills and possesses the mind much more than one, which has for its object a person we esteem of less consequence.[†] Here then the contradiction betwixt the propensities of the imagination and passion displays itself. When we turn our thought to a great and a small object, the imagination finds more facility in passing from the small to the great, than from the great to the small; but the affections find a greater difficulty: And as the affections are a more powerful principle than the imagination, no wonder they prevail over it, and draw the mind to their side. In spite of the difficulty of passing from the idea of great to that of little, a passion directed to the former, produces always a similar passion towards the latter; when the great and   *SB 345* little are related together. The idea of the servant conveys our thought most readily to the master; but the hatred or love of the master produces with greater facility anger or good-will to the servant. The strongest passion in this case takes the precedence;[†] and the addition of the weaker making no considerable change on the disposition, the passage is by that means render'd more easy and natural betwixt them.

25   As in the foregoing experiment[†] we found, that a relation of ideas, which, by any particular circumstance, ceases to produce its usual effect of facilitating the transition of ideas, ceases likewise to operate on the passions; so in the present experiment we find the same property of the impressions. Two different degrees

of the same passion are surely related together; but if the smaller be first present, it has little or no tendency to introduce the greater; and that because the addition of the great to the little, produces a more sensible alteration on the temper, than the addition of the little to the great. These phænomena, when duly weigh'd, will be found convincing proofs of this hypothesis.

26   And these proofs will be confirm'd, if we consider the manner in which the mind here reconciles the contradiction,[†] I have observ'd betwixt the passions and the imagination. The fancy passes with more facility from the less to the greater, than from the greater to the less: But on the contrary a violent passion produces more easily a feeble, than that does a violent.[†] In this opposition the passion in the end prevails over the imagination; but 'tis commonly by comply-ing with it, and by seeking another quality, which may counter-ballance that principle, from whence the opposition arises. When we love the father or master of a family, we little think of his children or servants. But when these are present with us, or when it lies any ways in our power to serve them, the nearness and contiguity in this case encreases their magnitude, or at least removes that oppo-sition, which the fancy makes to the transition of the affections. If the imagina-tion finds a difficulty in passing from greater to less, it finds an equal facility in passing from remote to contiguous, which brings the matter to an equality, and leaves the way open from the one passion to the other. *SB 346*

27   *Eighth Experiment.* I have observ'd[†] that the transition from love or hatred to pride or humility, is more easy than from pride or humility to love or hatred; and that the difficulty, which the imagination finds in passing from contiguous to remote, is the cause why we scarce have any instance of the latter transition of the affections. I must, however, make one exception, *viz.* when the very cause of the pride and humility is plac'd in some other person.[†] For in that case the im-agination is necessitated to consider the person, nor can it possibly confine its view to ourselves. Thus nothing more readily produces kindness and affection to any person, than his approbation of our conduct and character: As on the other hand, nothing inspires us with a stronger hatred, than his blame or contempt. Here 'tis evident, that the original passion is pride or humility, whose object is self; and that this passion is transfus'd into love or hatred, whose object is some other person, notwithstanding the rule I have already establish'd,[†] *that the im-agination passes with difficulty from contiguous to remote.* But the transition in this case is not made merely on account of the relation betwixt ourselves and the person; but because that very person is the real cause of our first passion, and of consequence is intimately connected with it. 'Tis his approbation that produces pride; and disapprobation, humility. No wonder, then, the imagination returns back again attended with the related passions of love and hatred. This is not a contradiction, but an exception to the rule; and an exception that arises from the same reason with the rule itself.

28   Such an exception as this is, therefore, rather a confirmation of the rule.[†] And indeed, if we consider all the eight experiments I have explain'd, we shall find that the same principle appears in all of them, and that 'tis by means of a transi-tion arising from a double relation of impressions and ideas, pride and humility, *SB 347*

224

love and hatred are produc'd. An object without a relation,[60] or with but one,[61] never produces either of these passions; and 'tis found that the passion always varies in conformity to the relation.[62] Nay we may observe, that where the relation, by any particular circumstance, has not its usual effect of producing a transition either of ideas or of impressions, it ceases to operate upon the passions, and gives rise neither to pride nor love, humility nor hatred.[63] This rule we find still to hold good, even under the appearance of its contrary; and as relation is frequently experienc'd to have no effect; which upon examination is found to proceed from some particular circumstance, that prevents the transition; so even in instances, where that circumstance, tho' present, prevents not the transition, 'tis found to arise from some other circumstance, which counter-ballances it.[64] Thus not only the variations resolve themselves into the general principle, but even the variations of these variations.

Sect. 3. *Difficulties solv'd*

1   After so many and such undeniable proofs drawn from daily experience and observation, it may seem superfluous to enter into a particular examination of all the causes of love and hatred. I shall, therefore, employ the sequel of this part, *First*, In removing some difficulties, concerning particular causes of these passions.[†] *Secondly*, In examining the compound affections, which arise from the mixture of love and hatred with other emotions.[†]

2   Nothing is more evident, than that any person acquires our kindness, or is *SB 348* expos'd to our ill-will,[†] in proportion to the pleasure or uneasiness we receive from him, and that the passions keep pace exactly with the sensations in all their changes and variations. Whoever can find the means either by his services, his beauty, or his flattery, to render himself useful or agreeable to us, is sure of our affections: As on the other hand, whoever harms or displeases us never fails to excite our anger or hatred.[†] When our own nation is at war with any other, we detest them under the character of cruel, perfidious, unjust and violent: But always esteem ourselves and allies equitable, moderate, and merciful. If the general of our enemies be successful, 'tis with difficulty we allow him the figure and character of a man.[†] He is a sorcerer: He has a communication with dæmons; as is reported of *Oliver Cromwell*,[†] and the Duke of *Luxembourg*:[†] He is bloody-minded, and takes a pleasure in death and destruction. But if the success be on our side, our commander has all the opposite good qualities, and is a pattern of virtue, as well as of courage and conduct. His treachery we call policy: His cruelty is an evil inseparable from war. In short, every one of his faults we either endeavour to extenuate, or dignify it with the name of that virtue, which approaches it. 'Tis evident the same method of thinking runs thro' common life.

---

[60] First Experiment.   [61] Second and Third Experiments.   *SB 347*
[62] Fourth Experiment.   [63] Sixth Experiment.
[64] Seventh and Eighth Experiments.

3   There are some, who add another condition, and require not only that the pain and pleasure arise from the person, but likewise that it arise knowingly, and with a particular design and intention.† A man, who wounds and harms us by accident, becomes not our enemy upon that account, nor do we think ourselves bound by any ties of gratitude to one, who does us any service after the same manner. By the intention we judge of the actions, and according as that is good or bad, they become causes of love or hatred.

4   But here we must make a distinction.† If that quality in another, which pleases or displeases, be constant and inherent in his person and character, it will cause love or hatred independent of the intention: But otherwise a knowledge and design is requisite, in order to give rise to these passions. One that is disagreeable by his deformity† or folly is the object of our aversion, tho' nothing be more certain, than that he has not the least intention of displeasing us by these qualities. But if the uneasiness proceed not from a quality, but an action, which is produc'd and annihilated in a moment, 'tis necessary, in order to produce some relation, and connect this action sufficiently with the person, that it be deriv'd from a particular fore-thought and design. 'Tis not enough, that the action arise from the person, and have him for its immediate cause and author. This relation alone is too feeble and inconstant to be a foundation for these passions. It reaches not the sensible and thinking part, and neither proceeds from any thing *durable* in him, nor leaves any thing behind it; but passes in a moment, and is as if it had never been. On the other hand, an intention shows certain qualities, which remaining after the action is perform'd, connect it with the person, and facilitate the transition of ideas from one to the other. We can never think of him without reflecting on these qualities; unless repentance and a change of life have produc'd an alteration in that respect: In which case the passion is likewise alter'd. This therefore is one reason, why an intention is requisite to excite either love or hatred. *SB 349*

5   But we must farther consider, that an intention, besides its strengthening the relation of ideas, is often necessary to produce a relation of impressions, and give rise to pleasure and uneasiness. For 'tis observable, that the principal part of an injury is the contempt and hatred, which it shows in the person, that injures us; and without that, the mere harm gives us a less sensible uneasiness. In like manner, a good office is agreeable, chiefly because it flatters our vanity, and is a proof of the kindness and esteem of the person, who performs it. The removal of the intention, removes the mortification in the one case, and vanity in the other; and must of course cause a remarkable diminution in the passions of love and hatred. *SB 350*

6   I grant, that these effects of the removal of design, in diminishing the relations of impressions and ideas, are not entire, nor able to remove every degree of these relations. But then I ask, if the removal of design be able entirely to remove the passions of love and hatred? Experience, I am sure, informs us of the contrary, nor is there any thing more certain, than that men often fall into a violent anger for injuries, which they themselves must own to be entirely involuntary and accidental. This emotion, indeed, cannot be of long continuance; but still is

sufficient to show, that there is a natural connexion betwixt uneasiness and anger, and that the relation of impressions will operate upon a very small relation of ideas.[†] But when the violence of the impression is once a little abated, the defect of the relation begins to be better felt; and as the character of a person is no wise interested in such injuries as are casual and involuntary, it seldom happens that on their account, we entertain a lasting enmity.

7   To illustrate this doctrine by a parallel instance, we may observe, that not only the uneasiness, which proceeds from another by accident, has but little force to excite our passion, but also that which arises from an acknowledg'd necessity and duty. One that has a real design of harming us, proceeding not from hatred and ill-will, but from justice and equity, draws not upon him our anger, if we be in any degree reasonable; notwithstanding he is both the cause, and the knowing cause of our sufferings. Let us examine a little this phænomenon.

8   'Tis evident in the first place, that this circumstance is not decisive; and tho' it may be able to diminish the passions, 'tis seldom it can entirely remove them. How few criminals are there, who have no ill-will to the person, that accuses them, or to the judge, that condemns them, even tho' they be conscious of their own deserts? In like manner our antagonist in a law-suit, and our competitor for any office, are commonly regarded as our enemies; tho' we must acknowledge, if we wou'd but reflect a moment, that their motive is entirely as justifiable as our own.   *SB 351*

9   Besides we may consider, that when we receive harm from any person, we are apt to imagine him criminal, and 'tis with extreme difficulty we allow of his justice and innocence. This is a clear proof, that, independent of the opinion of iniquity,[†] any harm or uneasiness has a natural tendency to excite our hatred, and that afterwards we seek for reasons upon which we may justify and establish the passion. Here the idea of injury produces not the passion, but arises from it.

10   Nor is it any wonder that passion shou'd produce the opinion of injury; since otherwise it must suffer a considerable diminution, which all the passions avoid as much as possible.[†] The removal of injury may remove the anger, without proving that the anger arises only from the injury.[†] The harm and the justice are two contrary objects,[†] of which the one has a tendency to produce hatred, and the other love; and 'tis according to their different degrees, and our particular turn of thinking, that either of the objects prevails, and excites its proper passion.

Sect. 4. *Of the love of relations*

1   Having given[†] a reason, why several actions, that cause a real pleasure or uneasiness, excite not any degree, or but a small one, of the passion of love or hatred towards the actors; 'twill be necessary to show, wherein consists the pleasure or uneasiness of many objects,[†] which we find by experience to produce these passions.

2   According to the preceding system[†] there is always requir'd a double relation of impressions and ideas betwixt the cause and effect, in order to produce either

love or hatred. But tho' this be universally true, 'tis remarkable that the passion of love may be excited by only one *relation* of a different kind, *viz.* betwixt ourselves and the object;[†] or more properly speaking, that this relation is always attended with both the others.[†] Whoever is united to us by any connexion is always sure of a share of our love, proportion'd to the connexion, without enquiring into his other qualities. Thus the relation of blood produces the strongest tie the mind is capable of in the love of parents to their children, and a lesser degree of the same affection, as the relation lessens. Nor has consanguinity alone this effect, but any other relation without exception. We love our countrymen, our neighbours, those of the same trade, profession, and even name with ourselves. Every one of these relations is esteem'd some tie, and gives a title to a share of our affection.

3   There is another phænomenon, which is parallel to this, *viz.* that *acquaintance*, without any kind of relation,[†] gives rise to love and kindness. When we have contracted a habitude and intimacy with any person; tho' in frequenting his company we have not been able to discover any very valuable quality, of which he is possess'd; yet we cannot forbear preferring him to strangers, of whose superior merit we are fully convinc'd. These two phænomena of the effects of relation and acquaintance will give mutual light to each other, and may be both explain'd from the same principle.

4   Those, who take a pleasure in declaiming against human nature, have observ'd, that man is altogether insufficient to support himself; and that when you loosen all the holds, which he has of external objects, he immediately drops down into the deepest melancholy and despair. From this, say they, proceeds that continual search after amusement in gaming, in hunting, in business; by which we endeavour to forget ourselves, and excite our spirits from the languid state, into which they fall, when not sustain'd by some brisk and lively emotion.[†] To this method of thinking I so far agree, that I own the mind to be insufficient, of itself, to its own entertainment, and that it naturally seeks after foreign objects, which may produce a lively sensation, and agitate the spirits. On the appearance of such an object it awakes, as it were, from a dream: The blood flows with a new tide: The heart is elevated: And the whole man acquires a vigour, which he cannot command in his solitary and calm moments. Hence company is naturally so rejoicing, as presenting the liveliest of all objects, *viz.* a rational and thinking being like ourselves, who communicates to us all the actions of his mind; makes us privy to his inmost sentiments and affections; and lets us see, in the very instant of their production, all the emotions, which are caus'd by any object. Every lively idea is agreeable, but especially that of a passion, because such an idea becomes a kind of passion, and gives a more sensible agitation to the mind, than any other image or conception.

5   This being once admitted, all the rest is easy. For as the company of strangers is agreeable to us for *a short time*, by enlivening our thought; so the company of our relations and acquaintance must be peculiarly agreeable, because it has this effect in a greater degree, and is of more *durable* influence. Whatever is related

to us is conceiv'd in a lively manner by the easy transition from ourselves to the related object. Custom also, or acquaintance facilitates the entrance, and strengthens the conception of any object. The first case is parallel to our reasonings from cause and effect;[†] the second to education.[†] And as reasoning and education concur only in producing a lively and strong idea of any object; so is this the only particular, which is common to relation and acquaintance. This must, therefore, be the influencing quality, by which they produce all their common effects;[†] and love or kindness being one of these effects, it must be from the force and liveliness of conception, that the passion is deriv'd. Such a conception is peculiarly agreeable, and makes us have an affectionate regard for every thing, that produces it, when the proper object of kindness and good-will.

6   'Tis obvious, that people associate together according to their particular   *SB 354*
tempers and dispositions, and that men of gay tempers naturally love the gay; as the serious bear an affection to the serious. This not only happens, where they remark this resemblance betwixt themselves and others, but also by the natural course of the disposition, and by a certain sympathy, which always arises betwixt similar characters. Where they remark the resemblance, it operates after the manner of a relation, by producing a connexion of ideas. Where they do not remark it, it operates by some other principle; and if this latter principle be similar to the former, it must be receiv'd as a confirmation of the foregoing reasoning.[†]

7   The idea of ourselves is always intimately present to us, and conveys a sensible degree of vivacity to the idea of any other object, to which we are related. This lively idea changes by degrees into a real impression; these two kinds of perception being in a great measure the same, and differing only in their degrees of force and vivacity. But this change must be produc'd with the greater ease, that our natural temper[†] gives us a propensity to the same impression, which we observe in others, and makes it arise upon any slight occasion. In that case resemblance converts the idea into an impression, not only by means of the relation, and by transfusing the original vivacity into the related idea; but also by presenting such materials as take fire from the least spark. And as in both cases a love or affection arises from the resemblance, we may learn that a sympathy with others is agreeable only by giving an emotion to the spirits, since an easy sympathy and correspondent emotions are alone common to *relation*, *acquaintance*, and *resemblance*.

8   The great propensity men have to pride may be consider'd as another similar phænomenon.[†] It often happens, that after we have liv'd a considerable time in any city; however at first it might be disagreeable to us; yet as we become familiar with the objects, and contract an acquaintance, tho' merely with the streets and buildings, the aversion diminishes by degrees, and at last changes into the op-   *SB 355*
posite passion. The mind finds a satisfaction and ease in the view of objects, to which it is accustom'd, and naturally prefers them to others, which, tho', perhaps, in themselves more valuable, are less known to it. By the same quality of the mind we are seduc'd into a good opinion of ourselves, and of all objects, that

belong to us. They appear in a stronger light; are more agreeable; and consequently fitter subjects of pride and vanity, than any other.

9   It may not be amiss, in treating of the affection we bear our acquaintance and relations, to observe some pretty curious phænomena, which attend it. 'Tis easy to remark in common life, that children esteem their relation to their mother to be weaken'd, in a great measure, by her second marriage, and no longer regard her with the same eye, as if she had continu'd in her state of widow-hood.[†] Nor does this happen only, when they have felt any inconveniencies from her second marriage, or when her husband is much her inferior; but even without any of these considerations, and merely because she has become part of another family. This also takes place with regard to the second marriage of a father; but in a much less degree: And 'tis certain the ties of blood are not so much loosen'd in the latter case as by the marriage of a mother. These two phænomena are remarkable in themselves, but much more so when compar'd.

10   In order to produce a perfect relation betwixt two objects, 'tis requisite, not only that the imagination be convey'd from one to the other by resemblance, contiguity or causation, but also that it return back from the second to the first with the same ease and facility. At first sight this may seem a necessary and unavoidable consequence. If one object resemble another, the latter object must necessarily resemble the former. If one object be the cause of another, the second object is effect to its cause. 'Tis the same case with contiguity: And therefore the relation being always reciprocal, it may be thought, that the return of the imagination from the second to the first must also, in every case, be equally natural as its passage from the first to the second. But upon farther examination we shall easily discover our mistake. For supposing the second object, beside its reciprocal relation to the first, to have also a strong relation to a third object; in that case the thought, passing from the first object to the second, returns not back with the same facility, tho' the relation continues the same; but is readily carry'd on to the third object, by means of the new relation, which presents itself, and gives a new impulse to the imagination. This new relation, therefore, weakens the tie betwixt the first and second objects. The fancy is by its very nature wavering and inconstant; and considers always two objects as more strongly related together, where it finds the passage equally easy both in going and returning, than where the transition is easy only in one of these motions. The double motion is a kind of a double tie, and binds the objects together in the closest and most intimate manner.

SB 356

11   The second marriage of a mother breaks not the relation of child and parent; and that relation suffices to convey my imagination from myself to her with the greatest ease and facility. But after the imagination is arriv'd at this point of view, it finds its object to be surrounded with so many other relations, which challenge its regard,[†] that it knows not which to prefer, and is at a loss what new object to pitch upon. The ties of interest and duty bind her to another family, and prevent that return of the fancy from her to myself, which is necessary to support the union. The thought has no longer the vibration,[†] requisite to set it perfectly at ease, and indulge its inclination to change. It goes with facility, but returns with

difficulty; and by that interruption finds the relation much weaken'd from what it wou'd be were the passage open and easy on both sides.

12   Now to give a reason, why this effect follows not in the same degree upon the second marriage of a father: We may reflect on what has been prov'd already,[†] that tho' the imagination goes easily from the view of a lesser object to that of a *SB 357* greater, yet it returns not with the same facility from the greater to the less. When my imagination goes from myself to my father, it passes not so readily from him to his second wife, nor considers him as entering into a different family, but as continuing the head of that family, of which I am myself a part. His superiority prevents the easy transition of the thought from him to his spouse, but keeps the passage still open for a return to myself along the same relation of child and parent. He is not sunk in the new relation he acquires; so that the double motion or vibration of thought is still easy and natural. By this indulgence of the fancy in its inconstancy, the tie of child and parent still preserves its full force and influence.

13   A mother thinks not her tie to a son weaken'd, because 'tis shar'd with her husband: Nor a son his with a parent, because 'tis shar'd with a brother. The third object is here related to the first, as well as to the second; so that the imagination goes and comes along all of them with the greatest facility.

Sect. 5. *Of our esteem for the rich and powerful*

1   Nothing has a greater tendency to give us an esteem for any person, than his power and riches; or a contempt, than his poverty and meanness: And as esteem and contempt are to be consider'd as species of love and hatred, 'twill be proper in this place to explain these phænomena.

2   Here it happens most fortunately, that the greatest difficulty is not to discover a principle capable of producing such an effect, but to choose the chief and predominant among several, that present themselves. The *satisfaction* we take in the riches of others, and the *esteem* we have for the possessors may be ascrib'd to three different causes. *First*, To the objects they possess; such as houses, gardens, equipages; which, being agreeable in themselves, necessarily produce *SB 358* a sentiment of pleasure in every one, that either considers or surveys them. *Secondly*, To the expectation of advantage from the rich and powerful by our sharing their possessions. *Thirdly*, To sympathy, which makes us partake of the satisfaction of every one, that approaches us. All these principles may concur in producing the present phænomenon. The question is, to which of them we ought principally to ascribe it?

3   'Tis certain, that the first principle, *viz*. the reflection on agreeable objects, has a greater influence, than what, at first sight, we may be apt to imagine. We seldom reflect on what is beautiful or ugly, agreeable or disagreeable, without an emotion of pleasure or uneasiness; and tho' these sensations appear not much in our common indolent way of thinking, 'tis easy, either in reading or conversation, to discover them. Men of wit always turn the discourse on subjects that are entertaining to the imagination; and poets never present any objects but such as

are of the same nature. Mr. *Philips* has chosen *Cyder* for the subject of an excellent poem.[†] Beer wou'd not have been so proper, as being neither so agreeable to the taste nor eye. But he wou'd certainly have preferr'd wine to either of them, cou'd his native country have afforded him so agreeable a liquor. We may learn from thence, that every thing, which is agreeable to the senses, is also in some measure agreeable to the fancy, and conveys to the thought an image of that satisfaction, which it gives by its real application to the bodily organs.

4   But tho' these reasons may induce us to comprehend this delicacy of the imagination among the causes of the respect, which we pay the rich and powerful, there are many other reasons, that may keep us from regarding it as the sole or principal. For as the ideas of pleasure can have an influence only by means of their vivacity, which makes them approach impressions, 'tis most natural those ideas shou'd have that influence, which are favour'd by most circumstances, and *SB 359* have a natural tendency to become strong and lively; such as our ideas of the passions and sensations of any human creature. Every human creature resembles ourselves, and by that means has an advantage above any other object, in operating on the imagination.

5   Besides, if we consider the nature of that faculty, and the great influence which all relations have upon it, we shall easily be perswaded, that however the ideas of the pleasant wines, music, or gardens, which the rich man enjoys, may become lively and agreeable, the fancy will not confine itself to them, but will carry its view to the related objects; and in particular, to the person, who possesses them. And this is the more natural, that the pleasant idea or image produces here a passion towards the person, by means of his relation to the object; so that 'tis unavoidable but he must enter into the original conception, since he makes the object of the derivative passion.[†] But if he enters into the original conception, and is consider'd as enjoying these agreeable objects, 'tis *sympathy*, which is properly the cause of the affection; and the *third* principle is more powerful and universal than the *first*.[†]

6   Add to this, that riches and power alone, even tho' unemploy'd, naturally cause esteem and respect: And consequently these passions arise not from the idea of any beautiful or agreeable objects. 'Tis true; money implies a kind of representation of such objects, by the power it affords of obtaining them; and for that reason may still be esteem'd proper to convey those agreeable images, which may give rise to the passion. But as this prospect is very distant, 'tis more natural for us to take a contiguous object, *viz.* the satisfaction, which this power affords the person, who is possest of it. And of this we shall be farther satisfy'd, if we consider, that riches represent the goods of life, only by means of the will; which employs them; and therefore imply in their very nature an idea of the person, and cannot be consider'd without a kind of sympathy with his sensations and *SB 360* enjoyments.

7   This we may confirm by a reflection, which to some will, perhaps, appear too subtile and refin'd. I have already observ'd,[†] that power, as distinguish'd from its exercise, has either no meaning at all, or is nothing but a possibility or probabil-

ity of existence; by which any object approaches to reality, and has a sensible influence on the mind. I have also observ'd,[†] that this approach, by an illusion of the fancy, appears much greater, when we ourselves are possest of the power, than when it is enjoy'd by another; and that in the former case the objects seem to touch upon the very verge of reality, and convey almost an equal satisfaction, as if actually in our possession. Now I assert, that where we esteem a person upon account of his riches, we must enter into this sentiment of the proprietor, and that without such a sympathy the idea of the agreeable objects, which they give him the power to produce, wou'd have but a feeble influence upon us. An avaritious man is respected for his money, tho' he scarce is possest of a *power*; that is, there scarce is a *probability* or even *possibility* of his employing it in the acquisition of the pleasures and conveniencies of life.[†] To himself alone this power seems perfect and entire; and therefore we must receive his sentiments by sympathy, before we can have a strong intense idea of these enjoyments, or esteem him upon account of them.

8   Thus we have found, that the *first* principle, viz. *the agreeable idea of those objects, which riches afford the enjoyment of;* resolves itself in a great measure into the *third*, and becomes a *sympathy* with the person we esteem or love. Let us now examine the *second* principle, viz. *the agreeable expectation of advantage*, and see what force we may justly attribute to it.

9   'Tis obvious, that tho' riches and authority undoubtedly give their owner a power of doing us service, yet this power is not to be consider'd as on the same footing with that, which they afford him, of pleasing himself, and satisfying his own appetites. Self-love[†] approaches the power and exercise very near each other in the latter case; but in order to produce a similar effect in the former, we must suppose a friendship and good-will to be conjoin'd with the riches. Without that circumstance 'tis difficult to conceive on what we can found our hope of advantage from the riches of others, tho' there is nothing more certain, than that we naturally esteem and respect the rich, even before we discover in them any such favourable disposition towards us.   *SB 361*

10   But I carry this farther, and observe, not only that we respect the rich and powerful, where they show no inclination to serve us, but also when we lie so much out of the sphere of their activity, that they cannot even be suppos'd to be endow'd with that power. Prisoners of war are always treated with a respect suitable to their condition;[†] and 'tis certain riches go very far towards fixing the condition of any person. If birth and quality enter for a share, this still affords us an argument of the same kind. For what is it we call a man of birth, but one who is descended from a long succession of rich and powerful ancestors, and who acquires our esteem by his relation to persons whom we esteem? His ancestors, therefore, tho' dead, are respected, in some measure, on account of their riches, and consequently without any kind of expectation.

11   But not to go so far as prisoners of war and the dead to find instances of this disinterested esteem for riches, let us observe with a little attention those phænomena that occur to us in common life and conversation. A man, who is

himself of a competent fortune, upon coming into a company of strangers, naturally treats them with different degrees of respect and deference, as he is inform'd of their different fortunes and conditions; tho' 'tis impossible he can ever propose, and perhaps wou'd not accept of any advantage from them. A traveller is always admitted into company, and meets with civility, in proportion as his train and equipage speak him a man of great or moderate fortune. In short, the different ranks of men are, in a great measure, regulated by riches, and that with regard to superiors as well as inferiors, strangers as well as acquaintance.

12   There is, indeed, an answer to these arguments, drawn from the influence of *general rules.*[†] It may be pretended, that being accustom'd to expect succour and protection from the rich and powerful, and to esteem them upon that account, we extend the same sentiments to those, who resemble them in their fortune, but from whom we can never hope for any advantage. The general rule still prevails, and by giving a bent to the imagination draws along the passion, in the same manner as if its proper object were real and existent.

13   But that this principle does not here take place, will easily appear, if we consider, that in order to establish a general rule, and extend it beyond its proper bounds, there is requir'd a certain uniformity in our experience, and a great superiority of those instances, which are conformable to the rule, above the contrary. But here the case is quite otherwise. Of a hundred men of credit and fortune I meet with, there is not, perhaps, one from whom I can expect advantage; so that 'tis impossible any custom can ever prevail in the present case.

14   Upon the whole, there remains nothing, which can give us an esteem for power and riches, and a contempt for meanness and poverty, except the principle of *sympathy*, by which we enter into the sentiments of the rich and poor, and partake of their pleasure and uneasiness. Riches give satisfaction to their possessor; and this satisfaction is convey'd to the beholder by the imagination, which produces an idea resembling the original impression in force and vivacity. This agreeable idea or impression is connected with love, which is an agreeable passion. It proceeds from a thinking conscious being, which is the very object of love. From this relation of impressions, and identity of ideas, the passion arises, according to my hypothesis.

15   The best method of reconciling us to this opinion is to take a general survey of the universe, and observe the force of sympathy thro' the whole animal creation, and the easy communication of sentiments from one thinking being to another. In all creatures, that prey not upon others, and are not agitated with violent passions, there appears a remarkable desire of company, which associates them together, without any advantages they can ever propose to reap from their union. This is still more conspicuous in man, as being the creature of the universe, who has the most ardent desire of society, and is fitted for it by the most advantages. We can form no wish, which has not a reference to society. A perfect solitude is, perhaps, the greatest punishment we can suffer. Every pleasure languishes when enjoy'd apart from company, and every pain becomes more cruel and intolerable. Whatever other passions we may be actuated by; pride, ambition, avarice,

curiosity, revenge or lust; the soul or animating principle of them all is sympathy; nor wou'd they have any force, were we to abstract entirely from the thoughts and sentiments of others. Let all the powers and elements of nature conspire to serve and obey one man: Let the sun rise and set at his command: The sea and rivers roll as he pleases, and the earth furnish spontaneously whatever may be useful or agreeable to him: He will still be miserable, till you give him some one person at least, with whom he may share his happiness, and whose esteem and friendship he may enjoy.

16   This conclusion from a general view of human nature, we may confirm by particular instances, wherein the force of sympathy is very remarkable. Most kinds of beauty are deriv'd from this origin; and tho' our first object be some senseless inanimate piece of matter, 'tis seldom we rest there, and carry not our view to its influence on sensible and rational creatures.[†] A man, who shows us any house or building, takes particular care among other things to point out the convenience of the apartments,[†] the advantages of their situation, and the little room lost in the stairs, anti-chambers and passages;[†] and indeed 'tis evident, the *SB 364* chief part of the beauty consists in these particulars. The observation of convenience gives pleasure, since convenience is a beauty. But after what manner does it give pleasure? 'Tis certain our own interest is not in the least concern'd; and as this is a beauty of interest, not of form, so to speak, it must delight us merely by communication, and by our sympathizing with the proprietor of the lodging. We enter into his interest by the force of imagination, and feel the same satisfaction, that the objects naturally occasion in him.

17   This observation extends to tables, chairs, scritoires, chimneys, coaches, sadles, ploughs, and indeed to every work of art;[†] it being an universal rule, that their beauty is chiefly deriv'd from their utility, and from their fitness for that purpose, to which they are destin'd. But this is an advantage, that concerns only the owner, nor is there any thing but sympathy, which can interest the spectator.

18   'Tis evident, that nothing renders a field more agreeable than its fertility, and that scarce any advantages of ornament or situation will be able to equal this beauty. 'Tis the same case with particular trees and plants, as with the field on which they grow. I know not but a plain, overgrown with furze and broom, may be, in itself, as beautiful as a hill cover'd with vines or olive-trees; tho' it will never appear so to one, who is acquainted with the value of each. But this is a beauty merely of imagination, and has no foundation in what appears to the senses. Fertility and value have a plain reference to use; and that to riches, joy, and plenty; in which, tho' we have no hope of partaking, yet we enter into them by the vivacity of the fancy, and share them, in some measure, with the proprietor.

19   There is no rule in painting more reasonable than that of ballancing the figures, and placing them with the greatest exactness on their proper centers of gravity.[†] A figure, which is not justly ballanc'd, is disagreeable; and that because it conveys the ideas of its fall, of harm, and of pain: Which ideas are painful, *SB 365* when by sympathy they acquire any degree of force and vivacity.

20   Add to this, that the principal part of personal beauty is an air of health and vigour, and such a construction of members as promises strength and activity. This idea of beauty cannot be accounted for but by sympathy.

21   In general we may remark, that the minds of men are mirrors to one another, not only because they reflect each other's emotions, but also because those rays of passions, sentiments and opinions may be often reverberated, and may decay away by insensible degrees.[†] Thus the pleasure, which a rich man receives from his possessions, being thrown upon[†] the beholder, causes a pleasure and esteem; which sentiments again, being perceiv'd and sympathiz'd with, encrease the pleasure of the possessor; and being once more reflected, become a new foundation for pleasure and esteem in the beholder. There is certainly an original satisfaction in riches deriv'd from that power, which they bestow, of enjoying all the pleasures of life; and as this is their very nature and essence, it must be the first source of all the passions, which arise from them. One of the most considerable of these passions is that of love or esteem in others, which therefore proceeds from a sympathy with the pleasure of the possessor. But the possessor has also a secondary satisfaction in riches arising from the love and esteem he acquires by them, and this satisfaction is nothing but a second reflection of that original pleasure, which proceeded from himself. This secondary satisfaction or vanity becomes one of the principal recommendations of riches, and is the chief reason, why we either desire them for ourselves, or esteem them in others. Here then is a third rebound of the original pleasure; after which 'tis difficult to distinguish the images and reflections, by reason of their faintness and confusion.

Sect. 6. *Of benevolence and anger* *SB 366*

1   Ideas may be compar'd to the extension and solidity of matter, and impressions, especially reflective ones, to colours, tastes, smells and other sensible qualities. Ideas never admit of a total union, but are endow'd with a kind of impenetrability, by which they exclude each other, and are capable of forming a compound by their conjunction, not by their mixture.[†] On the other hand, impressions and passions are susceptible of an entire union; and like colours, may be blended so perfectly together, that each of them may lose itself, and contribute only to vary that uniform impression, which arises from the whole. Some of the most curious phænomena of the human mind are deriv'd from this property of the passions.

2   In examining those ingredients, which are capable of uniting with love and hatred, I begin to be sensible, in some measure, of a misfortune, that has attended every system of philosophy, with which the world has been yet acquainted. 'Tis commonly found, that in accounting for the operations of nature by any particular hypothesis; among a number of experiments, that quadrate exactly with the principles we wou'd endeavour to establish; there is always some phænomenon, which is more stubborn, and will not so easily bend to our purpose.[†] We need not be surpriz'd, that this shou'd happen in natural

philosophy. The essence and composition of external bodies are so obscure, that we must necessarily, in our reasonings, or rather conjectures concerning them, involve ourselves in contradictions and absurdities. But as the perceptions of the mind are perfectly known,[†] and I have us'd all imaginable caution in forming conclusions concerning them, I have always hop'd to keep clear of those contradictions, which have attended every other system.[†] Accordingly the difficulty, which I have at present in my eye, is no-wise contrary to my system; but only departs a little from that simplicity, which has been hitherto its principal force and beauty.

SB 367

3   The passions of love and hatred are always follow'd by, or rather conjoin'd with benevolence and anger. 'Tis this conjunction, which chiefly distinguishes these affections from pride and humility. For pride and humility are pure emotions in the soul, unattended with any desire, and not immediately exciting us to action.[†] But love and hatred are not compleated within themselves, nor rest in that emotion, which they produce, but carry the mind to something farther. Love is always follow'd by a desire of the happiness of the person belov'd, and an aversion to his misery: As hatred produces a desire of the misery and an aversion to the happiness of the person hated. So remarkable a difference betwixt these two sets of passions of pride and humility, love and hatred, which in so many other particulars correspond to each other, merits our attention.

4   The conjunction of this desire and aversion with love and hatred may be accounted for by two different hypotheses.[†] The first is, that love and hatred have not only a *cause*, which excites them, *viz.* pleasure and pain; and an *object*, to which they are directed, *viz.* a person or thinking being;[†] but likewise an *end*, which they endeavour to attain, *viz.* the happiness or misery of the person belov'd or hated; all which views, mixing together, make only one passion. According to this system, love is nothing but the desire of happiness to another person, and hatred that of misery. The desire and aversion constitute the very nature of love and hatred. They are not only inseparable but the same.

5   But this is evidently contrary to experience. For tho' 'tis certain we never love any person without desiring his happiness, nor hate any without wishing his misery, yet these desires arise only upon the ideas of the happiness or misery of our friend or enemy being presented by the imagination, and are not absolutely essential to love and hatred. They are the most obvious and natural sentiments of these affections, but not the only ones. The passions may express themselves in a hundred ways, and may subsist a considerable time, without our reflecting on the happiness or misery of their objects;[†] which clearly proves, that these desires are not the same with love and hatred, nor make any essential part of them.

SB 368

6   We may, therefore, infer, that benevolence and anger are passions different from love and hatred, and only conjoin'd with them, by the original constitution of the mind.[†] As nature has given to the body certain appetites and inclinations, which she encreases, diminishes, or changes according to the situation of the fluids or solids; she has proceeded in the same manner with the mind. According as we are possess'd with love or hatred, the correspondent desire of the happiness or misery of the person, who is the object of these passions, arises in the

mind, and varies with each variation of these opposite passions. This order of things, abstractedly consider'd, is not necessary. Love and hatred might have been unattended with any such desires, or their particular connexion might have been entirely revers'd. If nature had so pleas'd, love might have had the same effect as hatred, and hatred as love. I see no contradiction in supposing a desire of producing misery annex'd to love, and of happiness to hatred. If the sensation of the passion and desire be opposite, nature cou'd have alter'd the sensation without altering the tendency of the desire, and by that means made them compatible with each other.

Sect. 7. *Of compassion*

1 But tho' the desire of the happiness or misery of others, according to the love or hatred we bear them, be an arbitrary and original instinct implanted in our nature, we find it may be counterfeited[†] on many occasions, and may arise from secondary principles. *Pity* is a concern for, and *malice*[†] a joy in the misery of others, without any friendship or enmity to occasion this concern or joy. We pity even strangers, and such as are perfectly indifferent to us: And if our ill-will to another proceed from any harm or injury, it is not, properly speaking, malice, but revenge. But if we examine these affections of pity and malice we shall find them to be secondary ones, arising from original affections, which are vary'd by some particular turn of thought and imagination. *SB 369*

2   'Twill be easy to explain the passion of *pity*, from the precedent reasoning concerning *sympathy*.[†] We have a lively idea of every thing related to us. All human creatures are related to us by resemblance. Their persons, therefore, their interests, their passions, their pains and pleasures must strike upon us in a lively manner, and produce an emotion similar to the original one; since a lively idea is easily converted into an impression. If this be true in general, it must be more so of affliction and sorrow. These have always a stronger and more lasting influence than any pleasure or enjoyment.

3   A spectator of a tragedy passes thro' a long train of grief, terror, indignation, and other affections, which the poet represents in the persons he introduces. As many tragedies end happily, and no excellent one can be compos'd without some reverses of fortune, the spectator must sympathize with all these changes, and receive the fictitious joy as well as every other passion. Unless, therefore, it be asserted, that every distinct passion is communicated by a distinct original quality, and is not deriv'd from the general principle of sympathy above-explain'd,[†] it must be allow'd, that all of them arise from that principle. To except any one in particular must appear highly unreasonable.[†] As they are all first present in the mind of one person, and afterwards appear in the mind of another; and as the manner of their appearance, first as an idea, then as an impression, is in every case the same, the transition must arise from the same principle. I am at least sure, that this method of reasoning wou'd be consider'd as certain, either in natural philosophy or common life. *SB 370*

4   Add to this, that pity depends, in a great measure, on the contiguity, and even sight of the object; which is a proof, that 'tis deriv'd from the imagination. Not to mention that women and children are most subject to pity,[†] as being most guided by that faculty.[†] The same infirmity, which makes them faint at the sight of a naked sword, tho' in the hands of their best friend, makes them pity extremely those, whom they find in any grief or affliction. Those philosophers,[†] who derive this passion from I know not what subtile reflections on the instability of fortune, and our being liable to the same miseries we behold, will find this observation contrary to them among a great many others, which it were easy to produce.

5   There remains only to take notice of a pretty remarkable phænomenon of this passion; which is, that the communicated passion of sympathy[†] sometimes acquires strength from the weakness of its original, and even arises by a transition from affections, which have no existence. Thus when a person obtains any honourable office, or inherits a great fortune, we are always the more rejoic'd for his prosperity, the less sense he seems to have of it, and the greater equanimity and indifference he shows in its enjoyment. In like manner a man, who is not dejected by misfortunes, is the more lamented on account of his patience; and if that virtue extends so far as utterly to remove all sense of uneasiness, it still farther encreases our compassion. When a person of merit falls into what is vulgarly esteem'd a great misfortune, we form a notion of his condition; and carrying our fancy from the cause to the usual effect, first conceive a lively idea of his sorrow, and then feel an impression of it, entirely over-looking that greatness of mind, which elevates him above such emotions, or only considering it so far as to encrease our admiration, love and tenderness for him. We find from experience, *SB 371* that such a degree of passion is usually connected with such a misfortune; and tho' there be an exception in the present case, yet the imagination is affected by the *general rule*, and makes us conceive a lively idea of the passion, or rather feel the passion itself, in the same manner, as if the person were really actuated by it. From the same principles we blush for the conduct of those, who behave themselves foolishly before us; and that tho' they show no sense of shame, nor seem in the least conscious of their folly. All this proceeds from sympathy; but 'tis of a partial kind, and views its objects only on one side,[†] without considering the other, which has a contrary effect, and wou'd entirely destroy that emotion, which arises from the first appearance.

6   We have also instances, wherein an indifference and insensibility under misfortune encreases our concern for the misfortunate, even tho' the indifference proceed not from any virtue and magnanimity. 'Tis an aggravation[†] of a murder, that it was committed upon persons asleep and in perfect security; as historians readily observe of any infant prince,[†] who is captive in the hands of his enemies, that he is the more worthy of compassion the less sensible he is of his miserable condition. As we ourselves are here acquainted with the wretched situation of the person,[†] it gives us a lively idea and sensation of sorrow, which is the passion that *generally* attends it; and this idea becomes still more lively, and the sensation

more violent by a contrast with that security and indifference, which we observe in the person himself. A contrast of any kind never fails to affect the imagination, especially when presented by the subject; and 'tis on the imagination that pity entirely depends.†

Sect. 8. *Of malice and envy*

SB 372

1   We must now proceed to account for the passion of *malice*,† which imitates the effects of hatred, as pity does those of love; and gives us a joy in the sufferings and miseries of others, without any offence or injury on their part.

2   So little are men govern'd by reason in their sentiments and opinions, that they always judge more of objects by comparison than from their intrinsic worth and value. When the mind considers, or is accustom'd to, any degree of perfection, whatever falls short of it, tho' really esteemable, has notwithstanding the same effect upon the passions, as what is defective and ill. This is an *original* quality of the soul,† and similar to what we have every day experience of in our bodies. Let a man heat one hand and cool the other; the same water will, at the same time, seem both hot and cold, according to the disposition of the different organs. A small degree of any quality, succeeding a greater, produces the same sensation, as if less than it really is, and even sometimes as the opposite quality. Any gentle pain, that follows a violent one, seems as nothing, or rather becomes a pleasure; as on the other hand a violent pain, succeeding a gentle one, is doubly grievous and uneasy.

3   This no one can doubt of with regard to our passions and sensations. But there may arise some difficulty with regard to our ideas and objects. When an object augments or diminishes to the eye or imagination from a comparison with others, the image and idea of the object are still the same, and are equally extended in the *retina*, and in the brain or organ of perception. The eyes refract the rays of light, and the optic nerves convey the images to the brain in the very same manner, whether a great or small object has preceded; nor does even the imagination alter the dimensions of its object on account of a comparison with others. The question then is, how from the same impression and the same idea SB 373 we can form such different judgments concerning the same object, and at one time admire its bulk, and at another despise its littleness? This variation in our judgments must certainly proceed from a variation in some perception; but as the variation lies not in the immediate impression or idea of the object, it must lie in some other impression, that accompanies it.

4   In order to explain this matter, I shall just touch upon two principles, one of which shall be more fully explain'd in the progress of this treatise; the other has been already accounted for.† I believe it may safely be establish'd for a general maxim, that no object is presented to the senses, nor image form'd in the fancy, but what is accompany'd with some emotion or movement of spirits proportion'd to it; and however custom may make us insensible of this sensation, and cause us to confound it with the object or idea, 'twill be easy, by careful and exact experiments, to separate and distinguish them. For to instance only in the cases

of extension and number; 'tis evident, that any very bulky object, such as the ocean, an extended plain, a vast chain of mountains, a wide forest; or any very numerous collection of objects, such as an army, a fleet, a crowd, excites in the mind a sensible emotion; and that the admiration, which arises on the appearance of such objects, is one of the most lively pleasures, which human nature is capable of enjoying. Now as this admiration encreases or diminishes by the encrease or diminution of the objects, we may conclude, according to our foregoing principles,[65] that 'tis a compound effect, proceeding from the conjunction of the several effects, which arise from each part of the cause. Every part, then, of extension, and every unite of number has a separate emotion attending it, when conceiv'd by the mind; and tho' that emotion be not always agreeable, yet by its conjunction with others, and by its agitating the spirits to a just pitch, it contributes to the production of admiration, which is always agreeable. If this be allow'd with respect to extension and number, we can make no difficulty with respect to virtue and vice, wit and folly, riches and poverty, happiness and misery, and other objects of that kind, which are always attended with an evident emotion. $SB 374$

5   The second principle I shall take notice of is that of our adherence to *general rules*; which has such a mighty influence on the actions and understanding, and is able to impose on the very senses. When an object is found by experience to be always accompany'd with another; whenever the first object appears, tho' chang'd in very material circumstances; we naturally fly to the conception of the second, and form an idea of it in as lively and strong a manner, as if we had inferr'd its existence by the justest and most authentic conclusion of our understanding. Nothing can undeceive us, not even our senses, which, instead of correcting this false judgment, are often perverted by it, and seem to authorize its errors.

6   The conclusion I draw from these two principles, join'd to the influence of comparison above-mention'd,[†] is very short and decisive. Every object is attended with some emotion proportion'd to it; a great object with a great emotion, a small object with a small emotion. A great *object*, therefore, succeeding a small one makes a great *emotion* succeed a small one. Now a great emotion succeeding a small one becomes still greater, and rises beyond its ordinary proportion. But as there is a certain degree of an emotion, which commonly attends every magnitude of an object; when the emotion encreases, we naturally imagine that the object has likewise encreas'd.[†] The effect conveys our view to its usual cause, a certain degree of emotion to a certain magnitude of the object; nor do we consider, that comparison may change the emotion without changing any thing in the object. Those, who are acquainted with the metaphysical part of optics,[†] and know how we transfer the judgments and conclusions of the under- $SB 375$ standing to the senses, will easily conceive this whole operation.

7   But leaving this new discovery of an impression, that secretly attends every idea; we must at least allow of that principle, from whence the discovery arose,

---

[65] Book 1. Part 3. Sect. 15. $SB 373$

that objects appear greater or less by a comparison with others. We have so many instances of this, that it is impossible we can dispute its veracity; and 'tis from this principle I derive the passions of malice and envy.

8   'Tis evident we must receive a greater or less satisfaction or uneasiness from reflecting on our own condition and circumstances, in proportion as they appear more or less fortunate or unhappy, in proportion to the degrees of riches, and power, and merit, and reputation, which we think ourselves possest of. Now as we seldom judge of objects from their intrinsic value, but form our notions of them from a comparison with other objects; it follows, that according as we observe a greater or less share of happiness or misery in others, we must make an estimate of our own, and feel a consequent pain or pleasure. The misery of another gives us a more lively idea of our happiness, and his happiness of our misery. The former, therefore, produces delight; and the latter uneasiness.

9   Here then is a kind of pity reverst, or contrary sensations arising in the beholder, from those which are felt by the person, whom he considers. In general we may observe, that in all kinds of comparison an object makes us always receive from another, to which it is compar'd, a sensation contrary to what arises from itself in its direct and immediate survey. A small object makes a great one appear still greater. A great object makes a little one appear less. Deformity of itself produces uneasiness; but makes us receive new pleasure by its contrast with a beautiful object, whose beauty is augmented by it; as on the other hand, beauty, which of itself produces pleasure, makes us receive a new pain by the contrast with any thing ugly, whose deformity it augments. The case, therefore, *SB 376* must be the same with happiness and misery. The direct survey of another's pleasure naturally gives us pleasure, and therefore produces pain when compar'd with our own. His pain, consider'd in itself, is painful to us, but augments the idea of our own happiness, and gives us pleasure.

10   Nor will it appear strange, that we may feel a reverst sensation from the happiness and misery of others; since we find the same comparison may give us a kind of malice against ourselves, and make us rejoice for our pains, and grieve for our pleasures. Thus the prospect of past pain is agreeable, when we are satisfy'd with our present condition; as on the other hand our past pleasures give us uneasiness, when we enjoy nothing at present equal to them. The comparison being the same, as when we reflect on the sentiments of others, must be attended with the same effects.

11   Nay a person may extend this malice against himself, even to his present fortune, and carry it so far as designedly to seek affliction, and encrease his pains and sorrows. This may happen upon two occasions. *First*, Upon the distress and misfortune of a friend, or person dear to him. *Secondly*, Upon the feeling any remorses for a crime, of which he has been guilty. 'Tis from the principle of comparison that both these irregular appetites for evil arise. A person, who indulges himself in any pleasure, while his friend lies under affliction, feels the reflected uneasiness from his friend more sensibly by a comparison with the original pleasure, which he himself enjoys. This contrast, indeed, ought also to enliven the present pleasure. But as grief is here suppos'd to be the predominant

passion, every addition falls to that side, and is swallow'd up in it, without operating in the least upon the contrary affection. 'Tis the same case with those
penances, which men inflict on themselves for their past sins and failings. When
a criminal reflects on the punishment he deserves, the idea of it is magnify'd by a
comparison with his present ease and satisfaction; which forces him, in a
manner, to seek uneasiness, in order to avoid so disagreeable a contrast.   *SB 377*

12   This reasoning will account for the origin of *envy* as well as of malice. The
only difference betwixt these passions lies in this, that envy is excited by some
present enjoyment of another, which by comparison diminishes our idea of our
own: Whereas malice is the unprovok'd desire of producing evil to another, in
order to reap a pleasure from the comparison. The enjoyment, which is the
object of envy, is commonly superior to our own. A superiority naturally seems
to overshade us, and presents a disagreeable comparison. But even in the case
of an inferiority, we still desire a greater distance, in order to augment still more
the idea of ourself.† When this distance diminishes, the comparison is less to our
advantage; and consequently gives us less pleasure, and is even disagreeable.
Hence arises that species of envy, which men feel, when they perceive their inferiors approaching or overtaking them in the pursuits of glory or happiness. In
this envy we may see the effects of comparison twice repeated. A man, who compares himself to his inferior, receives a pleasure from the comparison: And when
the inferiority decreases by the elevation of the inferior, what shou'd only have
been a decrease of pleasure, becomes a real pain, by a new comparison with its
preceding condition.

13   'Tis worthy of observation concerning that envy, which arises from a superiority in others, that 'tis not the great disproportion betwixt ourself and another,
which produces it; but on the contrary, our proximity. A common soldier bears
no such envy to his general as to his sergeant or corporal; nor does an eminent
writer meet with so great jealousy in common hackney scriblers, as in authors,
that more nearly approach him. It may, indeed, be thought, that the greater the
disproportion is, the greater must be the uneasiness from the comparison. But
we may consider on the other hand, that the great disproportion cuts off the
relation, and either keeps us from comparing ourselves with what is remote from   *SB 378*
us, or diminishes the effects of the comparison. Resemblance and proximity
always produce a relation of ideas; and where you destroy these ties, however
other accidents may bring two ideas together; as they have no bond or connecting quality to join them in the imagination; 'tis impossible they can remain long
united, or have any considerable influence on each other.

14   I have observ'd† in considering the nature of ambition, that the great feel a
double pleasure in authority from the comparison of their own condition with
that of their slaves; and that this comparison has a double influence, because 'tis
natural, and presented by the subject. When the fancy, in the comparison of
objects, passes not easily from the one object to the other, the action of the mind
is, in a great measure, broke, and the fancy, in considering the second object,
begins, as it were, upon a new footing. The impression, which attends every
object, seems not greater in that case by succeeding a less of the same kind; but

these two impressions are distinct, and produce their distinct effects, without any communication together. The want of relation in the ideas breaks the relation of the impressions, and by such a separation prevents their mutual operation and influence.

15   To confirm this we may observe, that the proximity in the degree of merit is not alone sufficient to give rise to envy, but must be assisted by other relations. A poet is not apt to envy a philosopher, or a poet of a different kind, of a different nation, or of a different age. All these differences prevent or weaken the comparison, and consequently the passion.

16   This too is the reason, why all objects appear great or little, merely by a comparison with those of the same species. A mountain neither magnifies nor diminishes a horse in our eyes; but when a *Flemish* and a *Welsh* horse are seen together,[†] the one appears greater and the other less, than when view'd apart.

17   From the same principle we may account for that remark of historians, that   *SB 379* any party in a civil war always choose to call in a foreign enemy at any hazard rather than submit to their fellow-citizens. *Guicciardin* applies this remark to the wars in *Italy*,[†] where the relations betwixt the different states are, properly speaking, nothing but of name, language, and contiguity. Yet even these relations, when join'd with superiority, by making the comparison more natural, make it likewise more grievous, and cause men to search for some other superiority, which may be attended with no relation, and by that means may have a less sensible influence on the imagination. The mind quickly perceives its several advantages and disadvantages; and finding its situation to be most uneasy, where superiority is conjoin'd with other relations, seeks its repose as much as possible, by their separation, and by breaking that association of ideas, which renders the comparison so much more natural and efficacious. When it cannot break the association, it feels a stronger desire to remove the superiority; and this is the reason why travellers are commonly so lavish of their praises to the *Chinese* and *Persians*, at the same time, that they depreciate those neighbouring nations, which may stand upon a foot of rivalship with their native country.

18   These examples from history and common experience are rich and curious; but we may find parallel ones in the arts, which are no less remarkable. Shou'd an author compose a treatise, of which one part was serious and profound, another light and humorous, every one wou'd condemn so strange a mixture, and wou'd accuse him of the neglect of all rules of art and criticism.[†] These rules of art are founded on the qualities of human nature; and the quality of human nature, which requires a consistency in every performance, is that which renders the mind incapable of passing in a moment from one passion and disposition to a quite different one. Yet this makes us not blame Mr. *Prior* for joining his *Alma* and his *Solomon* in the same volume;[†] tho' that admirable poet has succeeded   *SB 380* perfectly well in the gaiety of the one, as well as in the melancholy of the other. Even supposing the reader shou'd peruse these two compositions without any interval, he wou'd feel little or no difficulty in the change of passions: Why, but because he considers these performances as entirely different, and by this break

in the ideas, breaks the progress of the affections, and hinders the one from influencing or contradicting the other?

19   An heroic and burlesque design, united in one picture, wou'd be monstrous; tho' we place two pictures of so opposite a character in the same chamber, and even close by each other, without any scruple or difficulty.

20   In a word, no ideas can affect each other, either by comparison, or by the passions they separately produce, unless they be united together by some relation, which may cause an easy transition of the ideas, and consequently of the emotions or impressions, attending the ideas; and may preserve the one impression in the passage of the imagination to the object of the other. This principle is very remarkable, because it is analogous to what we have observ'd[†] both concerning the *understanding* and the *passions*. Suppose two objects to be presented to me, which are not connected by any kind of relation. Suppose that each of these objects separately produces a passion; and that these two passions are in themselves contrary: We find from experience, that the want of relation in the objects or ideas hinders the natural contrariety of the passions, and that the break in the transition of the thought removes the affections from each other, and prevents their opposition. 'Tis the same case with comparison; and from both these phænomena we may safely conclude, that the relation of ideas must forward the transition of impressions; since its absence alone is able to prevent it, and to separate what naturally shou'd have operated upon each other. When the absence of an object or quality removes any usual or natural effect, we may certainly conclude that its presence contributes to the production of the effect.

Sect. 9. *Of the mixture of benevolence and anger with compassion and malice*

SB 381

1   Thus we have endeavour'd[†] to account for *pity* and *malice*. Both these affections arise from the imagination, according to the light, in which it places its object. When our fancy considers directly the sentiments of others, and enters deep into them, it makes us sensible of all the passions it surveys, but in a particular manner of grief or sorrow. On the contrary, when we compare the sentiments of others to our own, we feel a sensation directly opposite to the original one, *viz.* a joy from the grief of others, and a grief from their joy. But these are only the first foundations of the affections of pity and malice. Other passions are afterwards confounded with them. There is always a mixture of love or tenderness with pity, and of hatred or anger with malice. But it must be confess'd, that this mixture seems at first sight to be contradictory to my system.[†] For as pity is an uneasiness, and malice a joy, arising from the misery of others, pity shou'd naturally, as in all other cases, produce hatred; and malice, love. This contradiction I endeavour to reconcile, after the following manner.

2   In order to cause a transition of passions, there is requir'd a double relation of impressions and ideas, nor is one relation sufficient to produce this effect. But that we may understand the full force of this double relation, we must consider,

that 'tis not the present sensation alone or momentary pain or pleasure, which determines the character of any passion, but the whole bent or tendency of it[†] from the beginning to the end. One impression may be related to another, not only when their sensations are resembling, as we have all along suppos'd in the preceding cases; but also when their impulses or directions are similar and correspondent.[†] This cannot take place with regard to pride and humility; because these are only pure sensations, without any direction or tendency to action.[†] We are, therefore, to look for instances of this peculiar relation of impressions only in such affections, as are attended with a certain appetite or desire; such as those of love and hatred.

SB 382

3   Benevolence or the appetite, which attends love, is a desire of the happiness of the person belov'd, and an aversion to his misery; as anger or the appetite, which attends hatred, is a desire of the misery of the person hated, and an aversion to his happiness. A desire, therefore, of the happiness of another, and aversion to his misery, are similar to benevolence; and a desire of his misery and aversion to his happiness are correspondent to anger. Now pity is a desire of happiness to another, and aversion to his misery; as malice is the contrary appetite. Pity, then, is related to benevolence; and malice to anger: And as benevolence has been already found[†] to be connected with love, by a natural and original quality, and anger with hatred; 'tis by this chain the passions of pity and malice are connected with love and hatred.

4   This hypothesis is founded on sufficient experience. A man, who from any motive has entertain'd a resolution of performing an action, naturally runs into every other view or motive, which may fortify that resolution, and give it authority and influence on the mind. To confirm us in any design, we search for motives drawn from interest, from honour, from duty. What wonder, then, that pity and benevolence, malice, and anger, being the same desires arising from different principles, shou'd so totally mix together as to be undistinguishable? As to the connexion betwixt benevolence and love, anger and hatred, being *original* and primary,[†] it admits of no difficulty.

5   We may add to this another experiment,[†] *viz.* that benevolence and anger, and consequently love and hatred, arise when our happiness or misery have any dependance on the happiness or misery of another person, without any farther relation. I doubt not but this experiment will appear so singular as to excuse us for stopping a moment to consider it.

SB 383

6   Suppose, that two persons of the same trade shou'd seek employment in a town, that is not able to maintain both, 'tis plain the success of one is perfectly incompatible with that of the other, and that whatever is for the interest of either is contrary to that of his rival, and so *vice versa*. Suppose again, that two merchants, tho' living in different parts of the world, shou'd enter into co-partnership together, the advantage or loss of one becomes immediately the advantage or loss of his partner, and the same fortune necessarily attends both. Now 'tis evident, that in the first case, hatred always follows upon the contrariety of interests; as in the second, love arises from their union. Let us consider to what principle we can ascribe these passions.

7   'Tis plain they arise not from the double relations of impressions and ideas, if we regard only the present sensation. For taking the first case of rivalship; tho' the pleasure and advantage of an antagonist necessarily causes my pain and loss, yet to counter-ballance this, his pain and loss causes my pleasure and advantage; and supposing him to be unsuccessful, I may by this means receive from him a superior degree of satisfaction.† In the same manner the success of a partner rejoices me, but then his misfortunes afflict me in an equal proportion; and 'tis easy to imagine, that the latter sentiment may in many cases preponderate. But whether the fortune of a rival or partner be good or bad, I always hate the former and love the latter.

8   This love of a partner cannot proceed from the relation or connexion† betwixt us; in the same manner as I love a brother or countryman. A rival has almost as close a relation to me as a partner. For as the pleasure of the latter causes my pleasure, and his pain my pain; so the pleasure of the former causes my pain, and his pain my pleasure. The connexion, then, of cause and effect is the same in both cases; and if in the one case, the cause and effect have a farther relation of resemblance, they have that of contrariety in the other; which, being also a species of resemblance, leaves the matter pretty equal.   *SB 384*

9   The only explication, then, we can give of this phænomenon is deriv'd from that principle of a parallel direction above-mention'd.† Our concern for our own interest gives us a pleasure in the pleasure, and a pain in the pain of a partner, after the same manner as by sympathy we feel a sensation correspondent to those, which appear in any person, who is present with us. On the other hand, the same concern for our interest makes us feel a pain in the pleasure, and a pleasure in the pain of a rival; and in short the same contrariety of sentiments as arises from comparison and malice. Since, therefore, a parallel direction of the affections, proceeding from interest, can give rise to benevolence or anger, no wonder the same parallel direction, deriv'd from sympathy and from comparison, shou'd have the same effect.

10   In general we may observe, that 'tis impossible to do good to others, from whatever motive, without feeling some touches of kindness and good-will towards 'em; as the injuries we do, not only cause hatred in the person, who suffers them, but even in ourselves. These phænomena, indeed, may in part be accounted for from other principles.

11   But here there occurs a considerable objection, which 'twill be necessary to examine before we proceed any farther. I have endeavour'd† to prove, that power and riches, or poverty and meanness; which give rise to love or hatred, without producing any original pleasure or uneasiness; operate upon us by means of a secondary sensation deriv'd from a sympathy with that pain or satisfaction, which they produce in the person, who possesses them. From a sympathy with his pleasure there arises love; from that with his uneasiness, hatred. But 'tis a maxim, which I have just now establish'd,† and which is absolutely necessary to the explication of the phænomena of pity and malice, *That 'tis not the present sensation or momentary pain or pleasure, which determines the character*   *SB 385* *of any passion, but the general bent or tendency of it from the beginning to the end.*

For this reason, pity or a sympathy with pain produces love, and that because it interests us in the fortunes of others, good or bad, and gives us a secondary sensation correspondent to the primary;[†] in which it has the same influence with love and benevolence. Since then this rule holds good in one case, why does it not prevail throughout, and why does sympathy in uneasiness ever produce any passion beside good-will and kindness? Is it becoming a philosopher to alter his method of reasoning, and run from one principle to its contrary, according to the particular phænomenon, which he wou'd explain?

12   I have mention'd[†] two different causes, from which a transition of passion may arise, *viz.* a double relation of ideas and impressions, and what is similar to it, a conformity in the tendency and direction of any two desires, which arise from different principles. Now I assert, that when a sympathy with uneasiness is weak, it produces hatred or contempt by the former cause; when strong, it produces love or tenderness by the latter. This is the solution of the foregoing difficulty, which seems so urgent;[†] and this is a principle founded on such evident arguments, that we ought to have establish'd it, even tho' it were not necessary to the explication of any phænomenon.

13   'Tis certain, that sympathy is not always limited to the present moment, but that we often feel by communication the pains and pleasures of others, which are not in being, and which we only anticipate by the force of imagination. For supposing I saw a person perfectly unknown to me, who, while asleep in the fields, was in danger of being trod under foot by horses, I shou'd immediately run to his assistance; and in this I shou'd be actuated by the same principle of sympathy, which makes me concern'd for the present sorrows of a stranger. The bare mention of this is sufficient. Sympathy being nothing but a lively idea converted into an impression, 'tis evident, that, in considering the future possible or probable condition of any person, we may enter into it with so vivid a conception as to make it our own concern; and by that means be sensible of pains and pleasures, which neither belong to ourselves, nor at the present instant have any real existence. *SB 386*

14   But however we may look forward to the future in sympathizing with any person, the extending of our sympathy depends in a great measure upon our sense of his present condition. 'Tis a great effort of imagination, to form such lively ideas even of the present sentiments of others as to feel these very sentiments; but 'tis impossible we cou'd extend this sympathy to the future, without being aided by some circumstance in the present, which strikes upon us in a lively manner. When the present misery of another has any strong influence upon me, the vivacity of the conception is not confin'd merely to its immediate object, but diffuses its influence over all the related ideas, and gives me a lively notion of all the circumstances of that person, whether past, present, or future; possible, probable or certain. By means of this lively notion I am interested in them; take part with them; and feel a sympathetic motion in my breast, conformable to whatever I imagine in his. If I diminish the vivacity of the first conception, I diminish that of the related ideas; as pipes can convey no more water than what arises at the fountain. By this diminution I destroy the future

prospect, which is necessary to interest me perfectly in the fortune of another. I may feel the present impression, but carry my sympathy no farther, and never transfuse the force of the first conception into my ideas of the related objects. If it be another's misery, which is presented in this feeble manner, I receive it by communication, and am affected with all the passions related to it: But as I am not so much interested as to concern myself in his good fortune, as well as his bad, I never feel the extensive sympathy,[†] nor the passions related to *it*.

15   Now in order to know what passions are related to these different kinds of sympathy, we must consider, that benevolence is an original pleasure[†] arising from the pleasure of the person belov'd, and a pain proceeding from his pain: From which correspondence of impressions there arises a subsequent desire of his pleasure, and aversion to his pain. In order, then, to make a passion run parallel with benevolence, 'tis requisite we shou'd feel these double impressions, correspondent to those of the person, whom we consider; nor is any one of them alone sufficient for that purpose. When we sympathize only with one impression, and that a painful one, this sympathy is related to anger and to hatred, upon account of the uneasiness it conveys to us. But as the extensive or limited sympathy depends upon the force of the first sympathy;[†] it follows, that the passion of love or hatred depends upon the same principle. A strong impression, when communicated, gives a double tendency of the passions; which is related to benevolence and love by a similarity of direction; however painful the first impression might have been. A weak impression, that is painful, is related to anger and hatred by the resemblance of sensations. Benevolence, therefore, arises from a great degree of misery, or any degree strongly sympathiz'd with: Hatred or contempt from a small degree, or one weakly sympathiz'd with; which is the principle I intended to prove and explain.

16   Nor have we only our reason to trust to for this principle, but also experience. A certain degree of poverty produces contempt; but a degree beyond causes compassion and good-will. We may under-value a peasant or servant; but when the misery of a beggar appears very great, or is painted in very lively colours, we sympathize with him in his afflictions, and feel in our heart evident touches of pity and benevolence. The same object causes contrary passions according to its different degrees. The passions, therefore, must depend upon principles, that operate in such certain degrees,[†] according to my hypothesis. The encrease of the sympathy has evidently the same effect as the encrease of the misery.

17   A barren or desolate country always seems ugly and disagreeable, and commonly inspires us with contempt for the inhabitants. This deformity, however, proceeds in a great measure from a sympathy with the inhabitants, as has been already observ'd;[†] but it is only a weak one, and reaches no farther than the immediate sensation, which is disagreeable. The view of a city in ashes conveys benevolent sentiments; because we there enter so deep into the interests of the miserable inhabitants, as to wish for their prosperity, as well as feel their adversity.

18   But tho' the force of the impression generally produces pity and benevolence, 'tis certain, that by being carry'd too far it ceases to have that effect. This,

SB 387

SB 388

perhaps, may be worth our notice. When the uneasiness is either small in itself, or remote from us, it engages not the imagination, nor is able to convey an equal concern for the future and contingent good, as for the present and real evil. Upon its acquiring greater force, we become so interested in the concerns of the person, as to be sensible both of his good and bad fortune; and from that compleat sympathy[†] there arises pity and benevolence. But 'twill easily be imagin'd, that where the present evil strikes with more than ordinary force, it may entirely engage our attention, and prevent that double sympathy, above-mention'd.[†] Thus we find, that tho' every one, but especially women,[†] are apt to contract a kindness for criminals, who go to the scaffold, and readily imagine them to be uncommonly handsome and well-shap'd; yet one, who is present at the cruel execution of the rack, feels no such tender emotions; but is in a manner overcome with horror,[†] and has no leisure to temper this uneasy sensation by any opposite sympathy.

19   But the instance, which makes the most clearly for my hypothesis, is that wherein by a change of the objects we separate the double sympathy even from a middling degree of the passion; in which case we find, that pity, instead of producing love and tenderness as usual, always gives rise to the contrary affection. When we observe a person in misfortunes, we are affected with pity and love; but the author of that misfortune becomes the object of our strongest hatred, and is the more detested in proportion to the degree of our compassion. Now for what reason shou'd the same passion of pity produce love to the person, who suffers the misfortune, and hatred to the person, who causes it; unless it be because in the latter case the author bears a relation only to the misfortune; whereas in considering the sufferer we carry our view on every side, and wish for his prosperity, as well as are sensible of his affliction? *SB 389*

20   I shall just observe, before I leave the present subject, that this phænomenon of the double sympathy, and its tendency to cause love, may contribute to the production of the kindness, which we naturally bear our relations and acquaintance.[†] Custom and relation make us enter deeply into the sentiments of others; and whatever fortune we suppose to attend them, is render'd present to us by the imagination, and operates as if originally our own. We rejoice in their pleasures, and grieve for their sorrows, merely from the force of sympathy. Nothing that concerns them is indifferent to us; and as this correspondence of sentiments is the natural attendant of love, it readily produces that affection.

Sect. 10. *Of respect and contempt*

1   There now remains only to explain the passions of *respect* and *contempt*,[†] along with the *amorous* affection,[†] in order to understand all the passions which have any mixture of love or hatred. Let us begin with respect and contempt.

2   In considering the qualities and circumstances of others, we may either regard them as they really are in themselves; or may make a comparison betwixt them and our own qualities and circumstances; or may join these two methods *SB 390*

of consideration. The good qualities of others, from the first point of view, produce love; from the second, humility; and from the third, respect; which is a mixture of these two passions. Their bad qualities, after the same manner, cause either hatred, or pride, or contempt, according to the light in which we survey them.

3　　That there is a mixture of pride in contempt, and of humility in respect, is, I think, too evident, from their very feeling or appearance, to require any particular proof. That this mixture arises from a tacit comparison of the person contemn'd or respected with ourselves is no less evident. The same man may cause either respect, love, or contempt by his condition and talents, according as the person, who considers him, from his inferior becomes his equal or superior. In changing the point of view, tho' the object may remain the same, its proportion to ourselves entirely alters; which is the cause of an alteration in the passions. These passions, therefore, arise from our observing the proportion; that is, from a comparison.

4　　I have already observ'd,[†] that the mind has a much stronger propensity to pride than to humility, and have endeavour'd, from the principles of human nature, to assign a cause for this phænomenon. Whether my reasoning be receiv'd or not, the phænomenon is undisputed, and appears in many instances. Among the rest, 'tis the reason why there is a much greater mixture of pride in contempt, than of humility in respect, and why we are more elevated with the view of one below us, than mortify'd with the presence of one above us. Contempt or scorn has so strong a tincture of pride, that there scarce is any other passion discernible: Whereas in esteem or respect, love makes a more considerable ingredient than humility. The passion of vanity is so prompt, that it rouzes at the least call; while humility requires a stronger impulse to make it exert itself.

5　　But here it may reasonably be ask'd, why this mixture takes place only in some *SB 391* cases, and appears not on every occasion? All those objects,[†] which cause love, when plac'd on another person, are the causes of pride, when transferr'd to ourselves; and consequently ought to be causes of humility, as well as love, while they belong to others, and are only compar'd to those, which we ourselves possess. In like manner every quality, which, by being directly consider'd, produces hatred, ought always to give rise to pride by comparison, and by a mixture of these passions of hatred and pride ought to excite contempt or scorn. The difficulty then is, why any objects ever cause pure love or hatred, and produce not always the mixt passions of respect and contempt.

6　　I have suppos'd[†] all along, that the passions of love and pride, and those of humility and hatred are similar in their sensations, and that the two former are always agreeable, and the two latter painful. But tho' this be universally true, 'tis observable, that the two agreeable, as well as the two painful passions, have some differences, and even contrarieties, which distinguish them. Nothing invigorates and exalts the mind equally with pride and vanity; tho' at the same time love or tenderness is rather found to weaken and infeeble it. The same difference is observable betwixt the uneasy passions. Anger and hatred bestow a new force on all our thoughts and actions; while humility and shame deject and discourage us. Of these qualities of the passions, 'twill be necessary to form a distinct idea. Let us remember, that pride and hatred invigorate the soul; and love and humility infeeble it.

7 From this it follows, that tho' the conformity betwixt love and pride in the agreeableness of their sensation makes them always be excited by the same objects, yet this other contrariety is the reason, why they are excited in very different degrees. Genius and learning are *pleasant* and *magnificent* objects, and by both these circumstances are adapted to pride and vanity; but have a relation to love by their pleasure only. Ignorance and simplicity are *disagreeable* and *mean*, which in the same manner gives them a double connexion with humility, and a single one with hatred. We may, therefore, consider it as certain, that tho' the same object always produces love and pride, humility and hatred, according to its different situations, yet it seldom produces either the two former or the two latter passions in the same proportion. *SB 392*

8 'Tis here we must seek for a solution of the difficulty above-mention'd,[†] why any object ever excites pure love or hatred, and does not always produce respect or contempt, by a mixture of humility or pride. No quality in another gives rise to humility by comparison, unless it wou'd have produc'd pride by being plac'd in ourselves; and *vice versa* no object excites pride by comparison, unless it wou'd have produc'd humility by the direct survey. This is evident, objects always produce by *comparison* a sensation directly contrary to their *original* one. Suppose, therefore, an object to be presented, which is peculiarly fitted to produce love, but imperfectly to excite pride; this object, belonging to another, gives rise directly to a great degree of love, but to a small one of humility by comparison; and consequently that latter passion is scarce felt in the compound, nor is able to convert the love into respect. This is the case with good nature, good humour, facility, generosity, beauty, and many other qualities. These have a peculiar aptitude to produce love in others; but not so great a tendency to excite pride in ourselves: For which reason the view of them, as belonging to another person, produces pure love, with but a small mixture of humility and respect. 'Tis easy to extend the same reasoning to the opposite passions.

9 Before we leave this subject, it may not be amiss to account for a pretty curious phænomenon, *viz.* why we commonly keep at a distance such as we contemn, and allow not our inferiors to approach too near even in place and situation. It *SB 393* has already been observ'd,[†] that almost every kind of idea is attended with some emotion, even the ideas of number and extension, much more those of such objects as are esteem'd of consequence in life, and fix our attention. 'Tis not with entire indifference we can survey either a rich man or a poor one, but must feel some faint touches, at least, of respect in the former case, and of contempt in the latter. These two passions are contrary to each other; but in order to make this contrariety be felt, the objects must be some way related; otherwise the affections are totally separate and distinct, and never encounter. The relation takes place wherever the persons become contiguous;[†] which is a general reason why

we are uneasy at seeing such disproportion'd objects, as a rich man and a poor one, a nobleman and a porter, in that situation.

10   This uneasiness, which is common to every spectator, must be more sensible to the superior; and that because the near approach of the inferior is regarded as a piece of ill-breeding, and shows that he is not sensible of the disproportion, and is no way affected by it. A sense of superiority in another breeds in all men an inclination to keep themselves at a distance from him, and determines them to redouble the marks of respect and reverence, when they are oblig'd to approach him; and where they do not observe that conduct, 'tis a proof they are not sensible of his superiority. From hence too it proceeds, that any great *difference* in the degrees of any quality is call'd a *distance* by a common metaphor,[†] which, however trivial it may appear, is founded on natural principles of the imagination. A great difference inclines us to produce a distance. The ideas of distance and difference are, therefore, connected together. Connected ideas are readily taken for each other; and this is in general the source of the metaphor, as we shall have occasion to observe afterwards.[†]

Sect. 11. *Of the amorous passion, or love betwixt the sexes* SB 394

1   Of all the compound passions, which proceed from a mixture of love and hatred with other affections, no one better deserves our attention, than that love, which arises betwixt the sexes, as well on account of its force and violence, as those curious principles of philosophy, for which it affords us an uncontestable argument. 'Tis plain, that this affection, in its most natural state, is deriv'd from the conjunction of three different impressions or passions, *viz.* the pleasing sensation arising from beauty; the bodily appetite for generation; and a generous kindness or good-will. The origin of kindness from beauty may be explain'd from the foregoing reasoning.[†] The question is how the bodily appetite is excited by it.

2   The appetite of generation, when confin'd to a certain degree, is evidently of the pleasant kind, and has a strong connexion with all the agreeable emotions. Joy, mirth, vanity, and kindness are all incentives to this desire; as well as music, dancing, wine, and good cheer. On the other hand, sorrow, melancholy, poverty, humility are destructive of it. From this quality 'tis easily conceiv'd why it shou'd be connected with the sense of beauty.

3   But there is another principle that contributes to the same effect. I have observ'd[†] that the parallel direction of the desires is a real relation, and no less than a resemblance in their sensation, produces a connexion among them. That we may fully comprehend the extent of this relation, we must consider, that any principal desire may be attended with subordinate ones, which are connected with it, and to which if other desires are parallel, they are by that means related to the principal one. Thus hunger may oft be consider'd as the primary inclination of the soul,[†] and the desire of approaching the meat[†] as the secondary one; SB 395 since 'tis absolutely necessary to the satisfying that appetite. If an object, therefore, by any separate qualities, inclines us to approach the meat, it naturally

encreases our appetite; as on the contrary, whatever inclines us to set our victuals at a distance, is contradictory to hunger, and diminishes our inclination to them. Now 'tis plain that beauty has the first effect, and deformity the second:[†] Which is the reason why the former gives us a keener appetite for our victuals, and the latter is sufficient to disgust us at the most savoury dish, that cookery has invented. All this is easily applicable to the appetite for generation.

4   From these two relations, *viz.* resemblance and a parallel desire, there arises such a connexion betwixt the sense of beauty, the bodily appetite, and benevolence, that they become in a manner inseparable: And we find from experience, that 'tis indifferent which of them advances first; since any of them is almost sure to be attended with the related affections. One, who is inflam'd with lust, feels at least a momentary kindness towards the object of it, and at the same time fancies her more beautiful than ordinary; as there are many, who begin with kindness and esteem for the wit and merit of the person, and advance from that to the other passions. But the most common species of love is that which first arises from beauty, and afterwards diffuses itself into kindness and into the bodily appetite. Kindness or esteem, and the appetite to generation, are too remote to unite easily together. The one is, perhaps, the most refin'd passion of the soul; the other the most gross and vulgar. The love of beauty is plac'd in a just medium betwixt them, and partakes of both their natures: From whence it proceeds, that 'tis so singularly fitted to produce both.

5   This account of love is not peculiar to my system, but is unavoidable on any hypothesis. The three affections, which compose this passion, are evidently distinct, and has each of them its distinct object.[†] 'Tis certain, therefore, that 'tis only by their relation they produce each other. But the relation of passions is not alone sufficient. 'Tis likewise necessary, there shou'd be a relation of ideas. The beauty of one person never inspires us with love for another. This then is a sensible proof of the double relation of impressions and ideas. From one instance so evident as this we may form a judgment of the rest.   *SB 396*

6   This may also serve in another view to illustrate what I have insisted on concerning the origin of pride and humility, love and hatred. I have observ'd,[†] that tho' self be the object of the first set of passions, and some other person of the second, yet these objects cannot alone be the causes of the passions; as having each of them a relation to two contrary affections, which must from the very first moment destroy each other. Here then is the situation of the mind, as I have already describ'd it.[†] It has certain organs naturally fitted to produce a passion; that passion, when produc'd, naturally turns the view to a certain object. But this not being sufficient to produce the passion, there is requir'd some other emotion, which by a double relation of impressions and ideas may set these principles in action, and bestow on them their first impulse. This situation is still more remarkable with regard to the appetite of generation. Sex is not only the object, but also the cause of the appetite.[†] We not only turn our view to it, when actuated by that appetite; but the reflecting on it suffices to excite the appetite. But as this cause loses its force by too great frequency, 'tis necessary it shou'd be quicken'd by some new impulse; and that impulse we find to arise from the

beauty of the *person*; that is, from a double relation of impressions and ideas. Since this double relation is necessary where an affection has both a distinct cause, and object, how much more so, where it has only a distinct object, without any determinate cause?

Sect. 12. *Of the love and hatred of animals*

SB 397

1 But to pass from the passions of love and hatred, and from their mixtures and compositions, as they appear in man, to the same affections, as they display themselves in brutes; we may observe, not only that love and hatred are common to the whole sensitive creation, but likewise that their causes, as above-explain'd,† are of so simple a nature, that they may easily be suppos'd to operate on mere animals. There is no force of reflection or penetration requir'd. Every thing is conducted by springs and principles, which are not peculiar to man, or any one species of animals.† The conclusion from this is obvious in favour of the foregoing system.

2   Love in animals, has not for its only object animals of the same species, but extends itself farther, and comprehends almost every sensible and thinking being. A dog naturally loves a man above his own species, and very commonly meets with a return of affection.

3   As animals are but little susceptible either of the pleasures or pains of the imagination, they can judge of objects only by the sensible good or evil, which they produce, and from *that* must regulate their affections towards them. Accordingly we find, that by benefits or injuries we produce their love or hatred; and that by feeding and cherishing any animal, we quickly acquire his affections; as by beating and abusing him we never fail to draw on us his enmity and ill-will.

4   Love in beasts is not caus'd so much by relation, as in our species;† and that because their thoughts are not so active as to trace relations, except in very obvious instances. Yet 'tis easy to remark, that on some occasions it has a considerable influence upon them. Thus acquaintance, which has the same effect as relation, always produces love in animals either to men or to each other. For the same reason any likeness among them is the source of affection. An ox confin'd SB 398 to a park with horses, will naturally join their company, if I may so speak, but always leaves it to enjoy that of his own species, where he has the choice of both.

5   The affection of parents to their young proceeds from a peculiar instinct in animals, as well as in our species.

6   'Tis evident, that *sympathy*, or the communication of passions, takes place among animals, no less than among men. Fear, anger, courage and other affections are frequently communicated from one animal to another, without their knowledge of that cause, which produc'd the original passion. Grief likewise is receiv'd by sympathy; and produces almost all the same consequences, and excites the same emotions as in our species. The howlings and lamentations of a dog produce a sensible concern in his fellows. And 'tis remarkable, that tho' almost all animals use in play the same member, and nearly the same action as in

fighting; a lion, a tyger, a cat their paws; an ox his horns; a dog his teeth; a horse his heels: Yet they most carefully avoid harming their companion, even tho' they have nothing to fear from his resentment; which is an evident proof of the sense brutes have of each other's pain and pleasure.

7   Every one has observ'd how much more dogs are animated when they hunt in a pack, than when they pursue their game apart; and 'tis evident this can proceed from nothing but from sympathy. 'Tis also well known to hunters, that this effect follows in a greater degree, and even in too great a degree, where two packs, that are strangers to each other, are join'd together. We might, perhaps, be at a loss to explain this phænomenon, if we had not experience of a similar in ourselves.

8   Envy and malice are passions very remarkable in animals. They are perhaps more common than pity; as requiring less effort of thought and imagination.

PART 3

Of the will and direct passions

Sect. 1. *Of liberty and necessity*

1 We come now to explain the *direct* passions,[†] or the impressions, which arise immediately from good or evil, from pain or pleasure. Of this kind are, *desire* and *aversion*, *grief* and *joy*, *hope* and *fear*.

2 Of all the immediate effects of pain and pleasure, there is none more remarkable than the WILL; and tho', properly speaking, it be not comprehended among the passions, yet as the full understanding of its nature and properties, is necessary to the explanation of them, we shall here make it the subject of our enquiry. I desire it may be observ'd, that by the *will*, I mean nothing but *the internal impression we feel and are conscious of, when we knowingly give rise to any new motion of our body, or new perception of our mind*. This impression, like the preceding ones of pride and humility, love and hatred, 'tis impossible to define,[†] and needless to describe any farther; for which reason we shall cut off all those definitions and distinctions, with which philosophers are wont to perplex rather than clear up this question; and entering at first upon the subject, shall examine that long disputed question concerning *liberty and necessity*; which occurs so naturally in treating of the will.[†]

3 'Tis universally acknowledg'd, that the operations of external bodies are necessary, and that in the communication of their motion, in their attraction, and mutual cohesion, there are not the least traces of indifference or liberty.[†] Every *SB 400* object is determin'd by an absolute fate to a certain degree and direction of its motion, and can no more depart from that precise line, in which it moves, than it can convert itself into an angel, or spirit, or any superior substance. The actions, therefore, of matter are to be regarded as instances of necessary actions; and whatever is in this respect on the same footing with matter, must be acknowledg'd to be necessary. That we may know whether this be the case with the actions of the mind, we shall begin with examining matter, and considering on what the idea of a necessity in its operations is founded, and why we conclude one body or action to be the infallible cause of another.

4 It has been observ'd[†] already, that in no single instance the ultimate connexion of any objects is discoverable, either by our senses or reason, and that we can never penetrate so far into the essence and construction of bodies, as to perceive the principle, on which their mutual influence depends. 'Tis their constant union alone, with which we are acquainted; and 'tis from the constant union the necessity arises. If objects had not an uniform and regular conjunction with each other, we shou'd never arrive at any idea of cause and effect; and even after all, the necessity, which enters into that idea, is nothing but a determination of the

mind to pass from one object to its usual attendant, and infer the existence of one from that of the other. Here then are two particulars, which we are to consider as essential to necessity, *viz.* the constant *union* and the *inference* of the mind; and wherever we discover these we must acknowledge a necessity. As the actions of matter have no necessity, but what is deriv'd from these circumstances, and it is not by any insight into the essence of bodies we discover their connexion, the absence of this insight, while the union and inference remain, will never, in any case, remove the necessity. 'Tis the observation of the union, which produces the inference; for which reason it might be thought sufficient, if we prove a constant union in the actions of the mind,[†] in order to establish the inference, along with the necessity of these actions. But that I may bestow a greater force on my reasoning, I shall examine these particulars apart, and shall first prove from experience, that our actions have a constant union with our motives, tempers, and circumstances, before I consider the inferences we draw from it.

SB 401

5   To this end a very slight and general view of the common course of human affairs will be sufficient. There is no light, in which we can take them, that does not confirm this principle. Whether we consider mankind according to the difference of sexes, ages, governments, conditions, or methods of education; the same uniformity and regular operation of natural principles are discernible. Like causes still produce like effects;[†] in the same manner as in the mutual action of the elements and powers of nature.

6   There are different trees, which regularly produce fruit, whose relish is different from each other; and this regularity will be admitted as an instance of necessity and causes in external bodies. But are the products of *Guienne* and of *Champagne*[†] more regularly different than the sentiments, actions, and passions of the two sexes, of which the one are distinguish'd by their force and maturity, the other by their delicacy and softness?

7   Are the changes of our body from infancy to old age more regular and certain than those of our mind and conduct? And wou'd a man be more ridiculous, who wou'd expect that an infant of four years old will raise a weight of three hundred pound, than one, who from a person of the same age, wou'd look for a philosophical reasoning, or a prudent and well-concerted action?

8   We must certainly allow, that the cohesion of the parts of matter arises from natural and necessary principles, whatever difficulty we may find in explaining them: And for a like reason we must allow, that human society is founded on like principles; and our reason in the latter case, is better than even that in the former; because we not only observe, that men *always* seek society, but can also explain the principles, on which this universal propensity is founded.[†] For is it more certain, that two flat pieces of marble will unite together, than that two young savages of different sexes will copulate? Do the children arise from this copulation more uniformly, than does the parents care for their safety and preservation? And after they have arriv'd at years of discretion by the care of their parents, are the inconveniencies attending their separation more certain than their foresight of these inconveniencies, and their care of avoiding them by a close union and confederacy?

SB 402

9   The skin, pores, muscles, and nerves of a day-labourer are different from those of a man of quality: So are his sentiments, actions and manners. The different stations of life[†] influence the whole fabric, external and internal; and these different stations arise necessarily, because uniformly, from the necessary and uniform principles of human nature. Men cannot live without society, and cannot be associated without government.[†] Government makes a distinction of property, and establishes the different ranks of men.[†] This produces industry, traffic, manufactures, law-suits, war, leagues, alliances, voyages, travels, cities, fleets, ports, and all those other actions and objects, which cause such a diversity, and at the same time maintain such an uniformity in human life.

10   Shou'd a traveller, returning from a far country, tell us, that he had seen a climate in the fiftieth degree of northern latitude, where all the fruits ripen and come to perfection in the winter, and decay in the summer, after the same manner as in *England* they are produc'd and decay in the contrary seasons, he wou'd find few so credulous as to believe him. I am apt to think a traveller wou'd meet with as little credit, who shou'd inform us of people exactly of the same character with those in *Plato*'s *Republic*[†] on the one hand, or those in *Hobbes*'s *Leviathan*[†] on the other. There is a general course of nature in human actions, as well as in the operations of the sun and the climate. There are also characters peculiar to different nations and particular persons, as well as common to mankind. The knowledge of these characters is founded on the observation of an uniformity in the actions,[†] that flow from them; and this uniformity forms the very essence[†] of necessity.

SB 403

11   I can imagine only one way of eluding this argument, which is by denying that uniformity of human actions, on which it is founded. As long as actions have a constant union and connexion with the situation and temper of the agent, however we may in words refuse to acknowledge the necessity, we really allow the thing. Now some may, perhaps, find a pretext to deny this regular union and connexion. For what is more capricious than human actions? What more inconstant than the desires of man? And what creature departs more widely, not only from right reason, but from his own character and disposition? An hour, a moment is sufficient to make him change from one extreme to another, and overturn what cost the greatest pain and labour to establish. Necessity is regular and certain. Human conduct is irregular and uncertain.[†] The one, therefore, proceeds not from the other.

12   To this I reply, that in judging of the actions of men we must proceed upon the same maxims, as when we reason concerning external objects.[†] When any phænomena are constantly and invariably conjoin'd together, they acquire such a connexion in the imagination, that it passes from one to the other, without any doubt or hesitation. But below this there are many inferior degrees of evidence and probability, nor does one single contrariety of experiment entirely destroy all our reasoning.[†] The mind ballances the contrary experiments, and deducting the inferior from the superior, proceeds with that degree of assurance or evidence, which remains. Even when these contrary experiments are entirely equal, we remove not the notion of causes and necessity; but supposing that the usual

contrariety proceeds from the operation of contrary and conceal'd causes, we conclude, that the chance or indifference lies only in our judgment on account of our imperfect knowledge, not in the things themselves, which are in every case equally necessary, tho' to appearance not equally constant or certain. No union can be more constant and certain, than that of some actions with some motives and characters; and if in other cases the union is uncertain, 'tis no more than what happens in the operations of body, nor can we conclude any thing from the one irregularity, which will not follow equally from the other.

13   'Tis commonly allow'd that mad-men have no liberty.[†] But were we to judge by their actions, these have less regularity and constancy than the actions of wise-men, and consequently are farther remov'd from necessity. Our way of thinking in this particular is, therefore, absolutely inconsistent; but is a natural consequence of these confus'd ideas and undefin'd terms, which we so commonly make use of in our reasonings, especially on the present subject.

14   We must now show, that as the *union* betwixt motives and actions has the same constancy, as that in any natural operations, so its influence on the understanding is also the same, in *determining* us to infer the existence of one from that of another.[†] If this shall appear, there is no known circumstance, that enters into the connexion and production of the actions of matter, that is not to be found in all the operations of the mind; and consequently we cannot, without a manifest absurdity, attribute necessity to the one, and refuse it to the other.

15   There is no philosopher, whose judgment is so riveted to this fantastical system of liberty, as not to acknowledge the force of *moral evidence*, and both in speculation and practice proceed upon it, as upon a reasonable foundation. Now moral evidence is nothing but a conclusion concerning the actions of men, deriv'd from the consideration of their motives, temper and situation. Thus when we see certain characters or figures describ'd upon paper, we infer that the person, who produc'd them, wou'd affirm such facts, the death of *Cæsar*, the success of *Augustus*, the cruelty of *Nero*;[†] and remembring many other concurrent testimonies we conclude, that those facts were once really existent, and that so many men, without any interest, wou'd never conspire to deceive us; especially since they must, in the attempt, expose themselves to the derision of all their contemporaries, when these facts were asserted to be recent and universally known. The same kind of reasoning runs thro' politics, war, commerce, œconomy, and indeed mixes itself so entirely in human life, that 'tis impossible to act or subsist a moment without having recourse to it. A prince, who imposes a tax upon his subjects, expects their compliance. A general, who conducts an army, makes account of a certain degree of courage. A merchant looks for fidelity and skill in his factor or super-cargo. A man, who gives orders for his dinner, doubts not of the obedience of his servants. In short, as nothing more nearly interests us than our own actions and those of others, the greatest part of our reasonings is employ'd in judgments concerning them. Now I assert, that whoever reasons after this manner, does *ipso facto* believe the actions of the will to arise from necessity, and that he knows not what he means, when he denies it.

16   All those objects, of which we call the one *cause* and the other *effect*, consider'd in themselves, are as distinct and separate from each other, as any two things in nature, nor can we ever, by the most accurate survey of them, infer the existence of the one from that of the other.[†] 'Tis only from experience and the observation of their constant union, that we are able to form this inference; and even after all, the inference is nothing but the effects of custom on the imagination. We must not here be content with saying, that the idea of cause and effect arises from objects constantly united; but must affirm, that 'tis the very same with the idea of these objects, and that the *necessary connexion* is not discover'd by a conclusion of the understanding, but is merely a perception of the mind.[†] *SB 406* Wherever, therefore, we observe the same union, and wherever the union operates in the same manner upon the belief and opinion, we have the idea of causes and necessity, tho' perhaps we may avoid those expressions. Motion in one body in all past instances, that have fallen under our observation, is follow'd upon impulse by motion in another. 'Tis impossible for the mind to penetrate farther. From this constant union it *forms* the idea of cause and effect, and by its influence *feels* the necessity. As there is the same constancy, and the same influence in what we call moral evidence, I ask no more. What remains can only be a dispute of words.

17   And indeed, when we consider how aptly *natural* and *moral* evidence cement together, and form only one chain of argument betwixt them, we shall make no scruple to allow, that they are of the same nature, and deriv'd from the same principles.[†] A prisoner, who has neither money nor interest, discovers the impossibility of his escape, as well from the obstinacy of the goaler, as from the walls and bars with which he is surrounded; and in all attempts for his freedom chooses rather to work upon the stone and iron of the one, than upon the inflexible nature of the other. The same prisoner, when conducted to the scaffold, foresees his death as certainly from the constancy and fidelity of his guards as from the operation of the ax or wheel. His mind runs along a certain train of ideas: The refusal of the soldiers to consent to his escape, the action of the executioner; the separation of the head and body; bleeding, convulsive motions, and death. Here is a connected chain of natural causes and voluntary actions; but the mind feels no difference betwixt them in passing from one link to another; nor is less certain of the future event than if it were connected with the present impressions of the memory and senses by a train of causes cemented together by what we are pleas'd to call a *physical necessity*. The same experienc'd union has the same effect on the mind, whether the united objects be motives, volitions and *SB 407* actions; or figure and motion. We may change the names of things; but their nature and their operation on the understanding never change.

18   I dare be positive no one will ever endeavour to refute these reasonings otherwise than by altering my definitions, and assigning a different meaning to the terms of *cause*, and *effect*, and *necessity*, and *liberty*, and *chance*. According to my definitions, necessity makes an essential part of causation; and consequently liberty, by removing necessity, removes also causes, and is the very same thing

with chance. As chance is commonly thought to imply a contradiction, and is at least directly contrary to experience,[†] there are always the same arguments against liberty or free-will. If any one alters the definitions, I cannot pretend to argue with him, till I know the meaning he assigns to these terms.

Sect. 2. *The same subject continu'd*

1　I believe we may assign the three following reasons for the prevalence of the doctrine of liberty, however absurd it may be in one sense, and unintelligible in any other. *First*, After we have perform'd any action; tho' we confess we were influenc'd by particular views and motives; 'tis difficult for us to perswade ourselves we were govern'd by necessity, and that 'twas utterly impossible for us to have acted otherwise; the idea of necessity seeming to imply something of force, and violence, and constraint, of which we are not sensible. Few are capable of distinguishing betwixt the liberty of *spontaneity*,[†] as it is call'd in the schools, and the liberty of *indifference*;[†] betwixt that which is oppos'd to violence,[†] and that which means a negation of necessity and causes. The first is even the most common sense of the word; and as 'tis only that species of liberty, which it concerns us to preserve, our thoughts have been principally turn'd towards it, and have almost universally confounded it with the other.　　　*SB 408*

2　*Secondly*, There is a *false sensation* or *experience* even of the liberty of indifference; which is regarded as an argument for its real existence. The necessity of any action, whether of matter or of the mind, is not properly a quality in the agent,[†] but in any thinking or intelligent being, who may consider the action, and consists in the determination of his thought to infer its existence from some preceding objects: As liberty or chance, on the other hand, is nothing but the want of that determination, and a certain looseness, which we feel in passing or not passing from the idea of one to that of the other. Now we may observe, that tho' in reflecting on human actions we seldom feel such a looseness or indifference, yet it very commonly happens, that in performing the actions themselves we are sensible of something like it: And as all related or resembling objects are readily taken for each other, this has been employ'd as a demonstrative or even an intuitive proof of human liberty.[†] We feel that our actions are subject to our will on most occasions, and imagine we feel that the will itself is subject to nothing; because when by a denial of it we are provok'd to try, we feel that it[†] moves easily every way, and produces an image of itself even on that side, on which it did not settle. This image or faint motion, we perswade ourselves, cou'd have been compleated into the thing itself; because, shou'd that be deny'd, we find, upon a second trial, that it can. But these efforts are all in vain; and whatever capricious and irregular actions we may perform; as the desire of showing our liberty is the sole motive of our actions; we can never free ourselves from the bonds of necessity.[†] We may imagine we feel a liberty within ourselves; but a spectator can commonly infer our actions from our motives and character; and even where he cannot, he concludes in general, that he might, were he perfectly acquainted with every circumstance of our situation and temper, and the most secret springs　　　*SB 409* of our complexion and disposition. Now this is the very essence of necessity, according to the foregoing doctrine.†

3   A *third* reason why the doctrine of liberty has generally been better receiv'd in the world, than its antagonist, proceeds from *religion*, which has been very unnecessarily interested in this question. There is no method of reasoning more common, and yet none more blameable, than in philosophical debates to endeavour to refute any hypothesis by a pretext of its dangerous consequences to religion and morality.† When any opinion leads us into absurdities, 'tis certainly false; but 'tis not certain an opinion is false, because 'tis of dangerous consequence. Such topics,† therefore, ought entirely to be foreborn, as serving nothing to the discovery of truth, but only to make the person of an antagonist odious. This I observe in general, without pretending to draw any advantage from it. I submit myself frankly to an examination of this kind, and dare venture to affirm, that the doctrine of necessity, according to my explication of it, is not only innocent, but even advantageous to religion and morality.

4   I define necessity two ways, conformable to the two definitions of *cause*, of which it makes an essential part. I place it either in the constant union and conjunction of like objects, or in the inference of the mind from the one to the other. Now necessity, in both these senses, has universally, tho' tacitly, in the schools, in the pulpit, and in common life, been allow'd to belong to the will of man, and no one has ever pretended to deny, that we can draw inferences concerning human actions, and that those inferences are founded on the experienc'd union of like actions with like motives and circumstances. The only particular in which any one can differ from me, is either, that perhaps he will refuse to call this *necessity*. But as long as the meaning is understood, I hope the word can do no harm. Or   *SB 410* that he will maintain there is something else in the operations of matter. Now whether it be so or not is of no consequence to religion, whatever it may be to natural philosophy. I may be mistaken in asserting, that we have no idea of any other connexion in the actions of body, and shall be glad to be farther instructed on that head: But sure I am, I ascribe nothing to the actions of the mind, but what must readily be allow'd of. Let no one, therefore, put an invidious construction on my words, by saying simply, that I assert the necessity of human actions, and place them on the same footing with the operations of senseless matter. I do not ascribe to the will that unintelligible necessity, which is suppos'd to lie in matter. But I ascribe to matter, that intelligible quality, call it necessity or not, which the most rigorous orthodoxy does or must allow to belong to the will. I change, therefore, nothing in the receiv'd systems, with regard to the will, but only with regard to material objects.

5   Nay I shall go farther, and assert, that this kind of necessity is so essential to religion and morality, that without it there must ensue an absolute subversion of both, and that every other supposition is entirely destructive to all laws both *divine* and *human*. 'Tis indeed certain, that as all human laws are founded on rewards and punishments, 'tis suppos'd as a fundamental principle, that these motives have an influence on the mind, and both produce the good and prevent the evil actions. We may give to this influence what name we please;

but as 'tis usually conjoin'd with the action, common sense requires it shou'd be esteem'd a cause, and be look'd upon as an instance of that necessity, which I wou'd establish.

6   This reasoning is equally solid, when apply'd to *divine* laws, so far as the deity is consider'd as a legislator, and is suppos'd to inflict punishment and bestow rewards with a design to produce obedience. But I also maintain, that even where he acts not in his magisterial capacity, but is regarded as the avenger of crimes *SB 411* merely on account of their odiousness and deformity, not only 'tis impossible, without the necessary connexion of cause and effect in human actions, that punishments cou'd be inflicted compatible with justice and moral equity; but also that it cou'd ever enter into the thoughts of any reasonable being to inflict them. The constant and universal object of hatred or anger is a person or creature endow'd with thought and consciousness; and when any criminal or injurious actions excite that passion, 'tis only by their relation to the person or connexion with him. But according to the doctrine of liberty or chance, this connexion is reduc'd to nothing,[†] nor are men more accountable for those actions, which are design'd and premeditated, than for such as are the most casual and accidental. Actions are by their very nature temporary and perishing; and where they proceed not from some cause in the characters and disposition of the person, who perform'd them, they infix not themselves upon him, and can neither redound to his honour, if good, nor infamy, if evil. The action itself may be blameable; it may be contrary to all the rules of morality and religion: But the person is not responsible for it; and as it proceeded from nothing in him, that is durable or constant, and leaves nothing of that nature behind it, 'tis impossible he can, upon its account, become the object of punishment or vengeance. According to the hypothesis of liberty, therefore, a man is as pure and untainted, after having committed the most horrid crimes, as at the first moment of his birth, nor is his character any way concern'd in his actions; since they are not deriv'd from it, and the wickedness of the one can never be us'd as a proof of the depravity of the other. 'Tis only upon the principles of necessity, that a person acquires any merit or demerit from his actions, however the common opinion may incline to the contrary.

7   But so inconsistent are men with themselves, that tho' they often assert, that necessity utterly destroys all merit and demerit either towards mankind or superior powers, yet they continue still to reason upon these very principles of *SB 412* necessity in all their judgments concerning this matter. Men are not blam'd for such evil actions as they perform ignorantly and casually, whatever may be their consequences. Why? But because the causes of these actions are only momentary, and terminate in them alone. Men are less blam'd for such evil actions, as they perform hastily and unpremeditately, than for such as proceed from thought and deliberation. For what reason? But because a hasty temper, tho' a constant cause in the mind, operates only by intervals, and infects not the whole character. Again, repentance wipes off every crime, especially if attended with an evident reformation of life and manners. How is this to be accounted for? But by asserting that actions render a person criminal, merely as they are proofs of

criminal passions or principles in the mind; and when by any alteration of these principles they cease to be just proofs, they likewise cease to be criminal. But according to the doctrine of *liberty* or *chance* they never were just proofs, and consequently never were criminal.

8   Here then I turn to my adversary, and desire him to free his own system from these odious consequences before he charge them upon others. Or if he rather chooses, that this question shou'd be decided by fair arguments before philosophers, than by declamations before the people, let him return to what I have advanc'd[†] to prove that liberty and chance are synonimous; and concerning the nature of moral evidence and the regularity of human actions. Upon a review of these reasonings, I cannot doubt of an entire victory; and therefore having prov'd,[†] that all actions of the will have particular causes, I proceed to explain[†] what these causes are, and how they operate.

Sect. 3. *Of the influencing motives of the will*   *SB 413*

1   Nothing is more usual in philosophy, and even in common life, than to talk of the combat of passion and reason, to give the preference to reason, and assert that men are only so far virtuous as they conform themselves to its dictates.[†] Every rational creature, 'tis said, is oblig'd to regulate his actions by reason; and if any other motive or principle challenge the direction of his conduct, he ought to oppose it, till it be entirely subdu'd, or at least brought to a conformity with that superior principle. On this method of thinking the greatest part of moral philosophy, antient and modern, seems to be founded; nor is there an ampler field, as well for metaphysical arguments, as popular declamations, than this suppos'd pre-eminence of reason above passion. The eternity, invariableness, and divine origin of the former have been display'd to the best advantage: The blindness, unconstancy, and deceitfulness of the latter have been as strongly insisted on. In order to show the fallacy of all this philosophy, I shall endeavour to prove *first*, that reason alone can never be a motive to any action of the will; and *secondly*, that it can never oppose passion in the direction of the will.

2   The understanding exerts itself after two different ways, as it judges from demonstration or probability;[†] as it regards the abstract relations of our ideas, or those relations of objects, of which experience only gives us information. I believe it scarce will be asserted, that the first species of reasoning alone is ever the cause of any action. As its proper province is the world of ideas, and as the will always places us in that of realities, demonstration and volition seem, upon that account, to be totally remov'd, from each other. Mathematics, indeed, are useful in all mechanical operations, and arithmetic in almost every art and profession: But 'tis not of themselves they have any influence. Mechanics are the art   *SB 414* of regulating the motions of bodies *to some design'd end or purpose*; and the reason why we employ arithmetic in fixing the proportions of numbers, is only that we may discover the proportions of their influence and operation. A merchant is desirous of knowing the sum total of his accounts with any person: Why? But that he may learn what sum will have the same *effects* in paying his debt, and

going to market, as all the particular articles taken together. Abstract or demonstrative reasoning, therefore, never influences any of our actions, but only as it directs our judgment concerning causes and effects; which leads us to the second operation of the understanding.

3   'Tis obvious, that when we have the prospect of pain or pleasure from any object, we feel a consequent emotion of aversion or propensity,[†] and are carry'd to avoid or embrace what will give us this uneasiness or satisfaction. 'Tis also obvious, that this emotion rests not here, but making us cast our view on every side, comprehends whatever objects are connected with its original one by the relation of cause and effect. Here then reasoning takes place to discover this relation; and according as our reasoning varies, our actions receive a subsequent variation. But 'tis evident in this case, that the impulse arises not from reason, but is only directed by it. 'Tis from the prospect of pain or pleasure that the aversion or propensity arises towards any object: And these emotions extend themselves to the causes and effects of that object, as they are pointed out to us by reason and experience. It can never in the least concern us to know, that such objects are causes, and such others effects, if both the causes and effects be indifferent to us. Where the objects themselves do not affect us, their connexion can never give them any influence; and 'tis plain, that as reason is nothing but the discovery of this connexion, it cannot be by its means that the objects are able to affect us.

4   Since reason alone can never produce any action, or give rise to volition, I infer, that the same faculty is as incapable of preventing volition, or of disputing the preference with any passion or emotion.[†] This consequence is necessary. 'Tis impossible reason cou'd have the latter effect of preventing volition, but by giving an impulse in a contrary direction to our passion; and that impulse, had it operated alone, wou'd have been able to produce volition. Nothing can oppose or retard the impulse of passion, but a contrary impulse; and if this contrary impulse ever arises from reason, that latter faculty must have an original influence on the will, and must be able to cause, as well as hinder any act of volition. But if reason has no original influence, 'tis impossible it can withstand any principle, which has such an efficacy, or ever keep the mind in suspence a moment. Thus it appears, that the principle, which opposes our passion, cannot be the same with reason, and is only call'd so in an improper sense. We speak not strictly and philosophically when we talk of the combat of passion and of reason. Reason is, and ought only to be the slave of the passions, and can never pretend to any other office than to serve and obey them. As this opinion may appear somewhat extraordinary,[†] it may not be improper to confirm it by some other considerations.

SB 415

5   A passion is an original existence, or, if you will, modification of existence, and contains not any representative quality, which renders it a copy of any other existence or modification. When I am angry, I am actually possest with the passion, and in that emotion have no more a reference to any other object, than when I am thirsty, or sick, or more than five foot high. 'Tis impossible, therefore,

that this passion can be oppos'd by, or be contradictory to truth and reason; since this contradiction consists in the disagreement of ideas, consider'd as copies, with those objects, which they represent.[†]

6   What may at first occur on this head, is, that as nothing can be contrary to truth or reason, except what has a reference to it, and as the judgments of our understanding only have this reference, it must follow, that passions can be con-   SB 416
trary to reason only so far as they are *accompany'd* with some judgment or opinion.[†] According to this principle, which is so obvious and natural, 'tis only in two senses, that any affection can be call'd unreasonable. *First*, When a passion, such as hope or fear, grief or joy, despair or security, is founded on the supposi-tion of the existence of objects, which really do not exist. *Secondly*, When in exerting any passion in action, we choose means insufficient for the design'd end, and deceive ourselves in our judgment of causes and effects. Where a passion is neither founded on false suppositions, nor chooses means insuf-ficient for the end, the understanding can neither justify nor condemn it. 'Tis not contrary to reason to prefer the destruction of the whole world to the scratching of my finger.[†] 'Tis not contrary to reason for me to choose my total ruin, to prevent the least uneasiness of an *Indian* or person wholly unknown to me. 'Tis as little contrary to reason to prefer even my own acknowledg'd lesser good to my greater, and have a more ardent affection for the former than the latter. A trivial good may, from certain circumstances, produce a desire superior to what arises from the greatest and most valuable enjoyment; nor is there any thing more extraordinary in this, than in mechanics to see one pound weight raise up a hundred by the advantage of its situation. In short, a passion must be accompany'd with some false judgment, in order to its being unreasonable; and even then 'tis not the passion, properly speaking, which is unreasonable, but the judgment.

7   The consequences are evident. Since a passion can never, in any sense, be call'd unreasonable, but when founded on a false supposition, or when it chooses means insufficient for the design'd end, 'tis impossible, that reason and passion can ever oppose each other, or dispute for the government of the will and actions. The moment we perceive the falshood of any supposition, or the insufficiency of any means our passions yield to our reason without any opposition. I may desire   SB 417
any fruit as of an excellent relish; but whenever you convince me of my mistake, my longing ceases. I may will the performance of certain actions as means of obtaining any desir'd good; but as my willing of these actions is only secondary, and founded on the supposition, that they are causes of the propos'd effect; as soon as I discover the falshood of that supposition, they must become indifferent to me.

8   'Tis natural for one, that does not examine objects with a strict philosophic eye, to imagine, that those actions of the mind are entirely the same, which produce not a different sensation, and are not immediately distinguishable to the feeling and perception. Reason, for instance, exerts itself without producing any sensible emotion; and except in the more sublime disquisitions of philosophy, or

in the frivolous subtilities of the schools, scarce ever conveys any pleasure or uneasiness. Hence it proceeds, that every action of the mind, which operates with the same calmness and tranquillity, is confounded with reason by all those, who judge of things from the first view and appearance. Now 'tis certain, there are certain calm desires and tendencies, which, tho' they be real passions, produce little emotion in the mind, and are more known by their effects than by the immediate feeling or sensation. These desires are of two kinds; either certain instincts originally implanted in our natures, such as benevolence and resentment, the love of life, and kindness to children; or the general appetite to good, and aversion to evil, consider'd merely as such. When any of these passions are calm, and cause no disorder in the soul, they are very readily taken for the determinations of reason, and are suppos'd to proceed from the same faculty, with that, which judges of truth and falshood. Their nature and principles have been suppos'd the same, because their sensations are not evidently different.

9   Beside these calm passions, which often determine the will, there are certain violent emotions of the same kind,[†] which have likewise a great influence on that faculty. When I receive any injury from another, I often feel a violent passion of resentment, which makes me desire his evil and punishment, independent of all considerations of pleasure and advantage to myself. When I am immediately threaten'd with any grievous ill, my fears, apprehensions, and aversions rise to a great height, and produce a sensible emotion.   *SB 418*

10   The common error of metaphysicians[†] has lain in ascribing the direction of the will entirely to one of these principles, and supposing the other to have no influence. Men often act knowingly against their interest: For which reason the view of the greatest possible good does not always influence them. Men often counter-act a violent passion in prosecution of their interests and designs: 'Tis not therefore the present uneasiness alone, which determines them. In general we may observe, that both these principles operate on the will; and where they are contrary, that either of them prevails, according to the *general* character or *present* disposition of the person. What we call strength of mind, implies the prevalence of the calm passions above the violent; tho' we may easily observe, there is no man so constantly possess'd of this virtue, as never on any occasion to yield to the sollicitations of passion and desire.[†] From these variations of temper proceeds the great difficulty of deciding concerning the actions and resolutions of men, where there is any contrariety of motives and passions.

Sect. 4. *Of the causes of the violent passions*

1   There is not in philosophy a subject of more nice speculation than this of the different *causes* and *effects* of the calm and violent passions. 'Tis evident passions influence not the will in proportion to their violence,[†] or the disorder they occasion in the temper; but on the contrary, that when a passion has once become a settled principle of action, and is the predominant inclination of the soul, it commonly produces no longer any sensible agitation. As repeated custom and its own force have made every thing yield to it, it directs the actions and conduct   *SB 419*

without that opposition and emotion, which so naturally attend every momentary gust of passion. We must, therefore, distinguish betwixt a calm and a weak passion; betwixt a violent and a strong one. But notwithstanding this, 'tis certain, that when we wou'd govern a man, and push him to any action, 'twill commonly be better policy to work upon the violent than the calm passions, and rather take him by his inclination, than what is vulgarly call'd his *reason*.[†] We ought to place the object in such particular situations as are proper to encrease the violence of the passion. For we may observe, that all depends upon the situation of the object, and that a variation in this particular will be able to change the calm and the violent passions into each other. Both these kinds of passions pursue good, and avoid evil;[†] and both of them are encreas'd or diminish'd by the encrease or diminution of the good or evil. But herein lies the difference betwixt them: The same good, when near, will cause a violent passion, which, when remote, produces only a calm one. As this subject belongs very properly to the present question concerning the will, we shall here examine it to the bottom, and shall consider some of those circumstances and situations of objects, which render a passion either calm or violent.

2   'Tis a remarkable property of human nature, that any emotion, which attends a passion, is easily converted into it, tho' in their natures they be originally different from, and even contrary to each other. 'Tis true; in order to make a perfect union among passions, there is always requir'd a double relation of impressions and ideas; nor is one relation sufficient for that purpose. But tho' this be confirm'd by undoubted experience, we must understand it with its proper limitations, and must regard the double relation, as requisite only to make one passion produce another. When two passions are already produc'd by their separate causes, and are both present in the mind, they readily mingle and unite, tho' they have but one relation, and sometimes without any. The predominant passion swallows up the inferior, and converts it into itself. The spirits, when once excited, easily receive a change in their direction; and 'tis natural to imagine this change will come from the prevailing affection. The connexion is in many respects closer betwixt any two passions, than betwixt any passion and indifference.

SB 420

3   When a person is once heartily in love, the little faults and caprices of his mistress, the jealousies and quarrels, to which that commerce is so subject; however unpleasant and related to anger and hatred; are yet found to give additional force to the prevailing passion. 'Tis a common artifice of politicians, when they wou'd affect any person very much by a matter of fact, of which they intend to inform him, first to excite his curiosity; delay as long as possible the satisfying it; and by that means raise his anxiety and impatience to the utmost, before they give him a full insight into the business. They know that his curiosity will precipitate him into the passion they design to raise, and assist the object in its influence on the mind. A soldier advancing to the battle, is naturally inspir'd with courage and confidence, when he thinks on his friends and fellow-soldiers; and is struck with fear and terror, when he reflects on the enemy. Whatever new emotion, therefore, proceeds from the former naturally encreases the courage; as the same

emotion, proceeding from the latter, augments the fear; by the relation of ideas, and the conversion of the inferior emotion into the predominant. Hence it is that in martial discipline, the uniformity and lustre of our habit, the regularity of our figures and motions, with all the pomp and majesty of war, encourage ourselves and allies;[†] while the same objects in the enemy strike terror into us, tho' agreeable and beautiful in themselves.

4   Since passions, however independent, are naturally transfus'd into each other,   *SB 421*
if they are both present at the same time; it follows, that when good or evil is plac'd in such a situation, as to cause any particular emotion, beside its direct passion of desire or aversion, that latter passion must acquire new force and violence.

5   This happens, among other cases, whenever any object excites contrary passions. For 'tis observable that an opposition of passions commonly causes a new emotion in the spirits, and produces more disorder, than the concurrence of any two affections of equal force. This new emotion is easily converted into the predominant passion, and encreases its violence, beyond the pitch it wou'd have arriv'd at had it met with no opposition. Hence we naturally desire what is forbid, and take a pleasure in performing actions, merely because they are unlawful. The notion of duty, when opposite to the passions, is seldom able to overcome them; and when it fails of that effect, is apt rather to encrease them, by producing an opposition in our motives and principles.

6   The same effect follows whether the opposition arises from internal motives or external obstacles. The passion commonly acquires new force and violence in both cases. The efforts, which the mind makes to surmount the obstacle, excite the spirits and enliven the passion.

7   Uncertainty has the same influence as opposition. The agitation of the thought; the quick turns it makes from one view to another; the variety of passions, which succeed each other, according to the different views: All these produce an agitation in the mind, and transfuse themselves into the predominant passion.

8   There is not in my opinion any other natural cause, why security diminishes the passions, than because it removes that uncertainty, which encreases them. The mind, when left to itself, immediately languishes; and in order to preserve its ardour, must be every moment supported by a new flow of passion. For the   *SB 422*
same reason, despair, tho' contrary to security, has a like influence.

9   'Tis certain nothing more powerfully animates any affection, than to conceal some part of its object by throwing it into a kind of shade, which at the same time that it shows enough to pre-possess us in favour of the object, leaves still some work for the imagination. Besides that obscurity is always attended with a kind of uncertainty; the effort, which the fancy makes to compleat the idea, rouzes the spirits, and gives an additional force to the passion.

10   As despair and security, tho' contrary to each other, produce the same effects; so absence is observ'd to have contrary effects, and in different circumstances either encreases or diminishes our affections. The *Duc de la Rochefoucault* has very well observ'd, that absence destroys weak passions, but encreases strong; as

the wind extinguishes a candle, but blows up a fire.† Long absence naturally weakens our idea, and diminishes the passion: But where the idea is so strong and lively as to support itself, the uneasiness, arising from absence, encreases the passion, and gives it new force and violence.

Sect. 5. *Of the effects of custom*

1   But nothing has a greater effect both to encrease and diminish our passions, to convert pleasure into pain, and pain into pleasure, than custom and repetition. Custom has two *original* effects upon the mind, in bestowing a *facility* in the performance of any action or the conception of any object;† and afterwards a *tendency* or *inclination* towards it; and from these we may account for all its other effects, however extraordinary.

2   When the soul applies itself to the performance of any action, or the conception of any object, to which it is not accustom'd, there is a certain unpliableness in the faculties, and a difficulty of the spirit's moving in their new direction. As   *SB 423* this difficulty excites the spirits, 'tis the source of wonder, surprize, and of all the emotions, which arise from novelty; and is in itself very agreeable, like every thing, which enlivens the mind to a moderate degree. But tho' surprize be agreeable in itself, yet as it puts the spirits in agitation, it not only augments our agreeable affections, but also our painful, according to the foregoing principle,† *that every emotion, which precedes or attends a passion, is easily converted into it.* Hence every thing, that is new, is most affecting, and gives us either more pleasure or pain, than what, strictly speaking, naturally belongs to it. When it often returns upon us, the novelty wears off; the passions subside; the hurry of the spirits is over; and we survey the objects with greater tranquillity.

3   By degrees the repetition produces a facility, which is another very powerful principle of the human mind, and an infallible source of pleasure, where the facility goes not beyond a certain degree. And here 'tis remarkable that the pleasure, which arises from a moderate facility, has not the same tendency with that which arises from novelty, to augment the painful, as well as the agreeable affections. The pleasure of facility does not so much consist in any ferment of the spirits, as in their orderly motion; which will sometimes be so powerful as even to convert pain into pleasure, and give us a relish in time for what at first was most harsh and disagreeable.

4   But again, as facility converts pain into pleasure, so it often converts pleasure into pain, when it is too great, and renders the actions of the mind so faint and languid, that they are no longer able to interest and support it. And indeed, scarce any other objects become disagreeable thro' custom; but such as are naturally attended with some emotion or affection, which is destroy'd by the too frequent repetition. One can consider the clouds, and heavens, and trees, and stones, however frequently repeated, without ever feeling any aversion. But   *SB 424* when the fair sex, or music, or good cheer, or any thing, that naturally ought to be agreeable, becomes indifferent, it easily produces the opposite affection.†

5   But custom not only gives a facility to perform any action, but likewise an

inclination and tendency towards it, where it is not entirely disagreeable, and can never be the object of inclination. And this is the reason why custom encreases all *active* habits, but diminishes *passive*, according to the observation of a late eminent philosopher.[†] The facility takes off from the force of the passive habits by rendering the motion of the spirits faint and languid. But as in the active, the spirits are sufficiently supported of themselves, the tendency of the mind gives them new force, and bends them more strongly to the action.

Sect. 6. *Of the influence of the imagination on the passions*

1   'Tis remarkable, that the imagination and affections have a close union together, and that nothing, which affects the former, can be entirely indifferent to the latter. Wherever our ideas of good or evil acquire a new vivacity, the passions become more violent; and keep pace with the imagination in all its variations. Whether this proceeds from the principle above-mention'd,[†] *that any attendant emotion is easily converted into the predominant*, I shall not determine. 'Tis sufficient for my present purpose, that we have many instances to confirm this influence of the imagination upon the passions.

2   Any pleasure, with which we are acquainted, affects us more than any other, which we own to be superior, but of whose nature we are wholly ignorant. Of the one we can form a particular and determinate idea: The other we conceive under the general notion of pleasure; and 'tis certain, that the more general and universal any of our ideas are, the less influence they have upon the imagination. A general idea, tho' it be nothing but a particular one consider'd in a certain view,[†] is commonly more obscure; and that because no particular idea, by which we represent a general one, is ever fix'd or determinate, but may easily be chang'd for other particular ones, which will serve equally in the representation. *SB 425*

3   There is a noted passage in the history of *Greece*, which may serve for our present purpose. *Themistocles* told the *Athenians*, that he had form'd a design, which wou'd be highly useful to the public, but which 'twas impossible for him to communicate to them without ruining the execution, since its success depended entirely on the secrecy with which it shou'd be conducted. The *Athenians*, instead of granting him full power to act as he thought fitting, order'd him to communicate his design to *Aristides*, in whose prudence they had an entire confidence, and whose opinion they were resolv'd blindly to submit to. The design of *Themistocles* was secretly to set fire to the fleet of all the *Grecian* commonwealths, which was assembled in a neighbouring port, and which being once destroy'd, wou'd give the *Athenians* the empire of the sea without any rival. *Aristides* return'd to the assembly, and told them, that nothing cou'd be more advantageous than the design of *Themistocles*; but at the same time that nothing cou'd be more unjust: Upon which the people unanimously rejected the project.[†]

4   A late celebrated historian[66] admires this passage of antient history, as one of

---

[66] Mons. *Rollin*.[†]

the most singular that is any where to be met with. *Here,* says he, *they are not philosophers, to whom 'tis easy in their schools to establish the finest maxims and most sublime rules of morality, who decide that interest ought never to prevail above justice. 'Tis a whole people interested in the proposal, which is made to them, who consider it as of importance to the public good, and who notwithstanding reject it unanimously, and without hesitation, merely because it is contrary to justice.* For my part I see nothing so extraordinary in this proceeding of the *Athenians.* The same reasons, which render it so easy for philosophers to establish these sublime maxims, tend, in part, to diminish the merit of such a conduct in that people. Philosophers never ballance betwixt profit and honesty, because their decisions are general, and neither their passions nor imaginations are interested in the objects. And tho' in the present case the advantage was immediate to the *Athenians,* yet as it was known only under the general notion of advantage, without being conceiv'd by any particular idea, it must have had a less considerable influence on their imaginations, and have been a less violent temptation, than if they had been acquainted with all its circumstances: Otherwise 'tis difficult to conceive, that a whole people, unjust and violent as men commonly are, shou'd so unanimously have adher'd to justice, and rejected any considerable advantage.

SB 426

5   Any satisfaction, which we lately enjoy'd, and of which the memory is fresh and recent, operates on the will with more violence, than another of which the traces are decay'd, and almost obliterated. From whence does this proceed, but that the memory in the first case assists the fancy, and gives an additional force and vigour to its conceptions? The image of the past pleasure being strong and violent, bestows these qualities on the idea of the future pleasure, which is connected with it by the relation of resemblance.

6   A pleasure, which is suitable to the way of life, in which we are engag'd, excites more our desires and appetites than another, which is foreign to it. This phænomenon may be explain'd from the same principle.

7   Nothing is more capable of infusing any passion into the mind, than eloquence, by which objects are represented in their strongest and most lively colours. We may of ourselves acknowledge, that such an object is valuable, and such another odious; but till an orator excites the imagination, and gives force to these ideas, they may have but a feeble influence either on the will or the affections.

SB 427

8   But eloquence is not always necessary. The bare opinion of another, especially when enforc'd with passion, will cause an idea of good or evil to have an influence upon us, which wou'd otherwise have been entirely neglected. This proceeds from the principle of sympathy or communication; and sympathy, as I have already observ'd,[†] is nothing but the conversion of an idea into an impression by the force of imagination.

9   'Tis remarkable, that lively passions commonly attend a lively imagination. In this respect, as well as others, the force of the passion depends as much on the temper of the person, as the nature or situation of the object.

10   I have already observ'd,[†] that belief is nothing but a lively idea related to a present impression. This vivacity is a requisite circumstance to the exciting all

our passions, the calm as well as the violent; nor has a mere fiction of the imagination any considerable influence upon either of them. 'Tis too weak to take any hold of the mind, or be attended with emotion.

Sect. 7. *Of contiguity and distance in space and time*

1   There is an easy reason, why every thing contiguous to us, either in space or time, shou'd be conceiv'd with a peculiar force and vivacity, and excel every other object, in its influence on the imagination. Ourself is intimately present to us,[†] and whatever is related to self must partake of that quality. But where an object is so far remov'd as to have lost the advantage of this relation, why, as it is farther remov'd, its idea becomes still fainter and more obscure, wou'd, perhaps, require a more particular examination.

2   'Tis obvious, that the imagination can never totally forget the points of space and time, in which we are existent; but receives such frequent advertisements of them from the passions and senses, that however it may turn its attention to foreign and remote objects, it is necessitated every moment to reflect on the present. 'Tis also remarkable, that in the conception of those objects, which we regard as real and existent, we take them in their proper order and situation, and never leap from one object to another, which is distant from it, without running over, at least in a cursory manner, all those objects, which are interpos'd betwixt them. When we reflect, therefore, on any object distant from ourselves, we are oblig'd not only to reach it at first by passing thro' all the intermediate space betwixt ourselves and the object, but also to renew our progress every moment; being every moment recall'd to the consideration of ourselves and our present situation. 'Tis easily conceiv'd, that this interruption must weaken the idea by breaking the action of the mind, and hindering the conception from being so intense and continu'd, as when we reflect on a nearer object. The *fewer* steps we make to arrive at the object, and the *smoother* the road is, this diminution of vivacity is less sensibly felt, but still may be observ'd more or less in proportion to the degrees of distance and difficulty.

SB 428

3   Here then we are to consider two kinds of objects, the contiguous and remote; of which the former, by means of their relation to ourselves, approach an impression in force and vivacity; the latter by reason of the interruption in our manner of conceiving them, appear in a weaker and more imperfect light. This is their effect on the imagination. If my reasoning be just, they must have a proportionable effect on the will and passions. Contiguous objects must have an influence much superior to the distant and remote. Accordingly we find in common life, that men are principally concern'd about those objects, which are not much remov'd either in space or time, enjoying the present, and leaving what is afar off to the care of chance and fortune.[†] Talk to a man of his condition thirty years hence, and he will not regard you. Speak of what is to happen to-morrow, and he will lend you attention. The breaking of a mirror gives us more concern

SB 429

when at home, than the burning of a house, when abroad, and some hundred leagues distant.

4   But farther; tho' distance both in space and time has a considerable effect on the imagination, and by that means on the will and passions, yet the consequence of a removal in *space* are much inferior to those of a removal in *time*. Twenty years are certainly but a small distance of time in comparison of what history and even the memory of some may inform them of, and yet I doubt if a thousand leagues, or even the greatest distance of place this globe can admit of, will so remarkably weaken our ideas, and diminish our passions. A *West-India* merchant will tell you, that he is not without concern about what passes in *Jamaica*; tho' few extend their views so far into futurity, as to dread very remote accidents.

5   The cause of this phænomenon must evidently lie in the different properties of space and time. Without having recourse to metaphysics, any one may easily observe, that space or extension consists of a number of co-existent parts dispos'd in a certain order, and capable of being at once present to the sight or feeling. On the contrary, time or succession, tho' it consists likewise of parts, never presents to us more than one at once; nor is it possible for any two of them ever to be co-existent.[†] These qualities of the objects have a suitable effect on the imagination. The parts of extension being susceptible of an union to the senses, acquire an union in the fancy; and as the appearance of one part excludes not another, the transition or passage of the thought thro' the contiguous parts is by that means render'd more smooth and easy. On the other hand, the incompatibility of the parts of time in their real existence separates them in the imagination, and makes it more *difficult* for that faculty to trace any long succession or series of events. Every part must appear single and alone, nor can regularly have entrance into the fancy without banishing what is   *SB 430* suppos'd to have been immediately precedent. By this means any distance in time causes a greater interruption in the thought than an equal distance in space, and consequently weakens more considerably the idea, and consequently the passions; which depend in a great measure, on the imagination, according to my system.

6   There is another phænomenon of a like nature with the foregoing, viz. *the superior effects of the same distance in futurity above that in the past*. This difference with respect to the will is easily accounted for. As none of our actions can alter the past, 'tis not strange it shou'd never determine the will. But with respect to the passions the question is yet entire, and well worth the examining.

7   Besides the propensity to a gradual progression thro' the points of space and time, we have another peculiarity in our method of thinking, which concurs in producing this phænomenon. We always follow the succession of time in placing our ideas, and from the consideration of any object pass more easily to that, which follows immediately after it, than to that which went before it. We may learn this, among other instances, from the order, which is always observ'd in historical narrations. Nothing but an absolute necessity can oblige an historian to

break the order of time, and in his *narration* give the precedence to an event, which was in *reality* posterior to another.

8   This will easily be apply'd to the question in hand, if we reflect on what I have before observ'd,[†] that the present situation of the person is always that of the imagination, and that 'tis from thence we proceed to the conception of any distant object. When the object is past, the progression of the thought in passing to it from the present is contrary to nature, as proceeding from one point of time to that which is preceding, and from that to another preceding, in opposition to the natural course of the succession. On the other hand, when we turn our thought to a future object, our fancy flows along the stream of time, and arrives at the object by an order, which seems most natural, passing always from one point of time to that which is immediately posterior to it. This *easy* progression of ideas favours the imagination, and makes it conceive its object in a stronger and fuller light, than when we are continually oppos'd in our passage, and are oblig'd to overcome the difficulties arising from the natural propensity of the fancy. A small degree of distance in the past has, therefore, a greater effect, in interrupting and weakening the conception, than a much greater in the future. From this effect of it on the imagination is deriv'd its influence on the will and passions.   *SB 431*

9   There is another cause, which both contributes to the same effect, and proceeds from the same quality of the fancy, by which we are determin'd to trace the succession of time by a similar succession of ideas. When from the present instant we consider two points of time equally distant in the future and in the past, 'tis evident, that, abstractedly consider'd, their relation to the present is almost equal. For as the future will *sometime* be present, so the past was *once* present. If we cou'd, therefore, remove this quality of the imagination, an equal distance in the past and in the future, wou'd have a similar influence. Nor is this only true, when the fancy remains fix'd, and from the present instant surveys the future and the past; but also when it changes its situation, and places us in different periods of time. For as on the one hand, in supposing ourselves existent in a point of time interpos'd betwixt the present instant and the future object, we find the future object approach to us, and the past retire, and become more distant: So on the other hand, in supposing ourselves existent in a point of time interpos'd betwixt the present and the past, the past approaches to us, and the future becomes more distant. But from the property of the fancy above-mention'd[†] we rather choose to fix our thought on the point of time interpos'd betwixt the present and the future, than on that betwixt the present and the past.   *SB 432* We advance, rather than retard our existence; and following what seems the natural succession of time, proceed from past to present, and from present to future. By which means we conceive the future as flowing every moment nearer us, and the past as retiring. An equal distance, therefore, in the past and in the future, has not the same effect on the imagination; and that because we consider the one as continually encreasing, and the other as continually diminishing. The fancy anticipates the course of things, and surveys the object in that condition, to which it tends, as well as in that, which is regarded as the present.

Sect. 8. *The same subject continu'd*

1 Thus we have accounted for three phænomena, which seem pretty remarkable. Why distance weakens the conception and passion: Why distance in time has a greater effect than that in space: And why distance in past time has still a greater effect than that in future. We must now consider three phænomena, which seem to be, in a manner, the reverse of these: Why a very great distance encreases our esteem and admiration for an object: Why such a distance in time encreases it more than that in space: And a distance in past time more than that in future. The curiousness of the subject will, I hope, excuse my dwelling on it for some time.

2 To begin with the first phænomenon, why a great distance encreases our esteem and admiration for an object; 'tis evident, that the mere view and contemplation of any greatness, whether successive or extended, enlarges the soul, and gives it a sensible delight and pleasure. A wide plain, the ocean, eternity, a succession of several ages; all these are entertaining objects, and excel every thing, however beautiful, which accompanies not its beauty with a suitable greatness. Now when any very distant object is presented to the imagination, *SB 433* we naturally reflect on the interpos'd distance, and by that means, conceiving something great and magnificent, receive the usual satisfaction. But as the fancy passes easily from one idea to another related to it, and transports to the second all the passions excited by the first, the admiration, which is directed to the distance, naturally diffuses itself over the distant object. Accordingly we find, that 'tis not necessary the object shou'd be actually distant from us, in order to cause our admiration; but that 'tis sufficient, if, by the natural association of ideas, it conveys our view to any considerable distance. A great traveller, tho' in the same chamber, will pass for a very extraordinary person; as a *Greek* medal, even in our cabinet, is always esteem'd a valuable curiosity. Here the object, by a natural transition, conveys our view to the distance; and the admiration, which arises from that distance, by another natural transition, returns back to the object.

3 But tho' every great distance produces an admiration for the distant object, a distance in time has a more considerable effect than that in space. Antient busts and inscriptions are more valu'd than *Japan* tables:† And not to mention the *Greeks* and *Romans*, 'tis certain we regard with more veneration the old *Chaldeans* and *Egyptians*, than the modern *Chinese* and *Persians*, and bestow more fruitless pains to clear up the history and chronology of the former,† than it wou'd cost us to make a voyage, and be certainly inform'd of the character, learning and government of the latter. I shall be oblig'd to make a digression in order to explain this phænomenon.

4 'Tis a quality very observable in human nature, that any opposition, which does not entirely discourage and intimidate us, has rather a contrary effect, and inspires us with a more than ordinary grandeur and magnanimity. In collecting our force to overcome the opposition, we invigorate the soul, and give it an elevation with which otherwise it wou'd never have been acquainted. Compliance, by *SB 434*

rendering our strength useless, makes us insensible of it; but opposition awakens and employs it.

5   This is also true in the inverse. Opposition not only enlarges the soul; but the soul, when full of courage and magnanimity, in a manner seeks opposition.

> *Spumantemque dari pecora inter inertia votis*
> *Optat aprum, aut fulvum descendere monte leonem.*[†]

6   Whatever supports and fills the passions is agreeable to us; as on the contrary, what weakens and infeebles them is uneasy. As opposition has the first effect, and facility the second, no wonder the mind, in certain dispositions, desires the former, and is averse to the latter.

7   These principles have an effect on the imagination as well as on the passions. To be convinc'd of this we need only consider the influence of *heights* and *depths* on that faculty. Any great elevation of place communicates a kind of pride or sublimity of imagination, and gives a fancy'd superiority over those that lie below; and, *vice versa*, a sublime and strong imagination conveys the idea of ascent and elevation. Hence it proceeds, that we associate, in a manner, the idea of whatever is good with that of height, and evil with lowness. Heaven is suppos'd to be above, and hell below. A noble genius is call'd an elevate and sublime one. *Atque udam spernit humum fugiente penna.*[†] On the contrary, a vulgar and trivial conception is styl'd indifferently low or mean. Prosperity is denominated ascent, and adversity descent. Kings and princes are suppos'd to be plac'd at the top of human affairs; as peasants and day-labourers are said to be in the lowest stations. These methods of thinking, and of expressing ourselves, are not of so little consequence as they may appear at first sight.

8   'Tis evident to common sense, as well as philosophy, that there is no natural nor essential difference betwixt high and low, and that this distinction arises only from the gravitation of matter, which produces a motion from the one to the other. The very same direction, which in this part of the globe is call'd *ascent*, is denominated *descent* in our antipodes; which can proceed from nothing but the contrary tendency of bodies. Now 'tis certain, that the tendency of bodies, continually operating upon our senses, must produce, from custom, a like tendency in the fancy, and that when we consider any object situated in an ascent, the idea of its weight gives us a propensity to transport it from the place, in which it is situated, to the place immediately below it, and so on, till we come to the ground, which equally stops the body and our imagination. For a like reason we feel a difficulty in mounting, and pass not without a kind of reluctance from the inferior to that which is situated above it; as if our ideas acquir'd a kind of gravity from their objects. As a proof of this, do we not find, that the facility, which is so much study'd in music and poetry, is call'd the *fall* or *cadency* of the harmony or period; the idea of facility communicating to us that of descent, in the same manner as descent produces a facility?[†]

9   Since the imagination, therefore, in running from low to high, finds an opposition in its internal qualities and principles, and since the soul, when elevated with joy and courage, in a manner seeks opposition, and throws itself with

SB 435

alacrity into any scene of thought or action, where its courage meets with matter to nourish and employ it; it follows, that every thing, which invigorates and enlivens the soul, whether by touching the passions or imagination, naturally conveys to the fancy this inclination for ascent, and determines it to run against the natural stream of its thoughts and conceptions. This aspiring progress of the imagination suits the present disposition of the mind; and the difficulty, instead of extinguishing its vigour and alacrity, has the contrary effect, of sustaining and encreasing it. Virtue, genius, power, and riches are for this reason associated with height and sublimity; as poverty, slavery, and folly are conjoin'd with descent and lowness. Were the case the same with us as *Milton* represents it to be with the angels, to whom *descent is adverse*, and who *cannot sink without labour and compulsion*, this order of things wou'd be entirely inverted;[†] as appears hence, that the very nature of ascent and descent is deriv'd from the difficulty and propensity, and consequently every one of their effects proceeds from that origin. *SB 436*

10   All this is easily apply'd to the present question, why a considerable distance in time produces a greater veneration for the distant objects than a like removal in space. The imagination moves with more difficulty in passing from one portion of time to another, than in a transition thro' the parts of space; and that because space or extension appears united to our senses, while time or succession is always broken and divided. This difficulty, when join'd with a small distance, interrupts and weakens the fancy: But has a contrary effect in a great removal. The mind, elevated by the vastness of its object, is still farther elevated by the difficulty of the conception; and being oblig'd every moment to renew its efforts in the transition from one part of time to another, feels a more vigorous and sublime disposition, than in a transition thro' the parts of space, where the ideas flow along with easiness and facility. In this disposition, the imagination, passing, as is usual, from the consideration of the distance to the view of the distant objects, gives us a proportionable veneration for it; and this is the reason why all the relicts of antiquity are so precious in our eyes, and appear more valuable than what is brought even from the remotest parts of the world.

11   The third phænomenon I have remark'd will be a full confirmation of this. 'Tis not every removal in time, which has the effect of producing veneration and esteem. We are not apt to imagine our posterity will excel us, or equal our ancestors. This phænomenon is the more remarkable, because any distance in futurity weakens not our ideas so much as an equal removal in the past. Tho' a removal in the past, when very great, encreases our passions beyond a like removal in the future, yet a small removal has a greater influence in diminishing them. *SB 437*

12   In our common way of thinking we are plac'd in a kind of middle station betwixt the past and future; and as our imagination finds a kind of difficulty in running along the former, and a facility in following the course of the latter, the difficulty conveys the notion of ascent, and the facility of the contrary. Hence we imagine our ancestors to be, in a manner, mounted above us, and our posterity to lie below us. Our fancy arrives not at the one without effort, but easily reaches the other: Which effort weakens the conception, where the distance is small; but enlarges and elevates the imagination, when attended with a suitable object. As

on the other hand, the facility assists the fancy in a small removal, but takes off from its force when it contemplates any considerable distance.

13   It may not be improper, before we leave this subject of the will, to resume, in a few words, all that has been said concerning it, in order to set the whole more distinctly before the eyes of the reader. What we commonly understand by *passion* is a violent and sensible emotion of mind, when any good or evil is presented, or any object, which, by the original formation of our faculties, is fitted to excite an appetite. By *reason* we mean affections of the very same kind with the former; but such as operate more calmly, and cause no disorder in the temper: Which tranquillity leads us into a mistake concerning them, and causes us to regard them as conclusions only of our intellectual faculties.[†] Both the *causes* and *effects* of these violent and calm passions are pretty variable, and depend, in a great measure, on the peculiar temper and disposition of every individual. Generally speaking, the violent passions have a more powerful influence on the will; tho' 'tis often found, that the calm ones, when corroborated by reflection, and seconded by resolution, are able to controul them in their most furious move-   *SB 438* ments. What makes this whole affair more uncertain, is, that a calm passion may easily be chang'd into a violent one, either by a change of temper, or of the circumstances and situation of the object, as by the borrowing of force from any attendant passion, by custom, or by exciting the imagination. Upon the whole, this struggle of passion and of reason, as it is call'd,[†] diversifies human life, and makes men so different not only from each other, but also from themselves in different times. Philosophy can only account for a few of the greater and more sensible events of this war; but must leave all the smaller and more delicate revolutions, as dependent on principles too fine and minute for her comprehension.

Sect. 9. *Of the direct passions*

1   'Tis easy to observe, that the passions, both direct and indirect, are founded on pain and pleasure, and that in order to produce an affection of any kind, 'tis only requisite to present some good or evil. Upon the removal of pain and pleasure there immediately follows a removal of love and hatred, pride and humility, desire and aversion, and of most of our reflective or secondary impressions.

2   The impressions, which arise from good and evil most naturally, and with the least preparation are the *direct* passions of desire and aversion, grief and joy, hope and fear, along with volition. The mind by an *original* instinct tends to unite itself with the good, and to avoid the evil, tho' they be conceiv'd merely in idea, and be consider'd as to exist in any future period of time.

3   But supposing that there is an immediate impression of pain or pleasure, and *that* arising from an object related to ourselves or others, this does not prevent the propensity or aversion, with the consequent emotions, but by concurring with certain dormant principles of the human mind, excites the new impres-   *SB 439* sions of pride or humility, love or hatred. That propensity, which unites us to the

object, or separates us from it, still continues to operate, but in conjunction with the *indirect* passions, which arise from a double relation of impressions and ideas.[†]

4 These indirect passions, being always agreeable or uneasy, give in their turn additional force to the direct passions, and encrease our desire and aversion to the object. Thus a suit of fine cloaths produces pleasure from their beauty; and this pleasure produces the direct passions, or the impressions of volition and desire. Again, when these cloaths are consider'd as belonging to ourself, the double relation conveys to us the sentiment of pride, which is an indirect passion; and the pleasure, which attends that passion, returns back to the direct affections, and gives new force to our desire or volition, joy or hope.

5 When good is certain or probable, it produces JOY. When evil is in the same situation there arises GRIEF or SORROW.

6 When either good or evil is uncertain, it gives rise to FEAR or HOPE, according to the degrees of uncertainty on the one side or the other.

7 DESIRE arises from good consider'd simply, and AVERSION is deriv'd from evil. The WILL exerts itself, when either the good or the absence of the evil may be attain'd by any action of the mind or body.

8 Beside good and evil, or in other words, pain and pleasure, the direct passions frequently arise from a natural impulse or instinct, which is perfectly unaccountable. Of this kind is the desire of punishment to our enemies, and of happiness to our friends; hunger, lust, and a few other bodily appetites. These passions, properly speaking, produce good and evil, and proceed not from them, like the other affections.[†]

9 None of the direct affections seem to merit our particular attention, except hope and fear, which we shall here endeavour to account for. 'Tis evident, that the very same event, which by its certainty wou'd produce grief or joy, gives always rise to fear or hope, when only probable and uncertain. In order, therefore, to understand the reason why this circumstance makes such a considerable difference, we must reflect on what I have already advanc'd[†] in the preceding book concerning the nature of probability. *SB 440*

10 Probability arises from an opposition of contrary chances or causes, by which the mind is not allow'd to fix on either side, but is incessantly tost from one to another, and at one moment is determin'd to consider an object as existent, and at another moment as the contrary. The imagination or understanding, call it which you please, fluctuates betwixt the opposite views; and tho' perhaps it may be oftner turn'd to the one side than the other, 'tis impossible for it, by reason of the opposition of causes or chances, to rest on either. The *pro* and *con* of the question alternately prevail; and the mind, surveying the object in its opposite principles, finds such a contrariety as utterly destroys all certainty and establish'd opinion.

11 Suppose, then, that the object, concerning whose reality we are doubtful, is an object either of desire or aversion, 'tis evident, that, according as the mind turns itself either to the one side or the other, it must feel a momentary impression of

joy or sorrow. An object, whose existence we desire, gives satisfaction, when we reflect on those causes, which produce it; and for the same reason excites grief or uneasiness from the opposite consideration:[†] So that as the understanding, in all probable questions, is divided betwixt the contrary points of view, the affections must in the same manner be divided betwixt opposite emotions.

12   Now if we consider the human mind, we shall find, that with regard to the passions, 'tis not of the nature of a wind-instrument of music, which in running over all the notes immediately loses the sound after the breath ceases; but rather resembles a string-instrument, where after each stroke the vibrations still retain some sound, which gradually and insensibly decays. The imagination is *SB 441* extremely quick and agile; but the passions are slow and restive: For which reason, when any object is presented, that affords a variety of views to the one, and emotions to the other; tho' the fancy may change its views with great celerity; each stroke will not produce a clear and distinct note of passion, but the one passion will always be mixt and confounded with the other.[†] According as the probability inclines to good or evil, the passion of joy or sorrow predominates in the composition: Because the nature of probability is to cast a superior number of views or chances on one side; or, which is the same thing, a superior number of returns of one passion; or since the dispers'd passions are collected into one, a superior degree of that passion. That is, in other words, the grief and joy being intermingled with each other, by means of the contrary views of the imagination, produce by their union the passions of hope and fear.

13   Upon this head there may be started a very curious question concerning that contrariety of passions, which is our present subject. 'Tis observable, that where the objects of contrary passions are presented at once, beside the encrease of the predominant passion (which has been already explain'd,[†] and commonly arises at their first shock or rencounter) it sometimes happens, that both the passions exist successively, and by short intervals; sometimes, that they destroy each other, and neither of them takes place; and sometimes that both of them remain united in the mind. It may, therefore, be ask'd, by what theory we can explain these variations, and to what general principle we can reduce them?

14   When the contrary passions arise from objects entirely different, they take place alternately, the want of relation[†] in the ideas separating the impressions from each other, and preventing their opposition. Thus when a man is afflicted for the loss of a law-suit, and joyful for the birth of a son, the mind running from the agreeable to the calamitous object, with whatever celerity it may perform this *SB 442* motion, can scarcely temper the one affection with the other, and remain betwixt them in a state of indifference.

15   It more easily attains that calm situation, when the same event is of a mixt nature, and contains something adverse and something prosperous in its different circumstances. For in that case, both the passions, mingling with each other by means of the relation, become mutually destructive, and leave the mind in perfect tranquillity.

16   But suppose, in the third place, that the object is not a compound of good or evil, but is consider'd as probable or improbable in any degree; in that case I

assert, that the contrary passions will both of them be present at once in the soul, and instead of destroying and tempering each other, will subsist together, and produce a third impression or affection by their union.[†] Contrary passions are not capable of destroying each other, except when their contrary movements exactly rencounter, and are opposite in their direction, as well as in the sensation they produce. This exact rencounter depends upon the relations of those ideas, from which they are deriv'd, and is more or less perfect, according to the degrees of the relation. In the case of probability the contrary chances are so far related, that they determine concerning the existence or non–existence of the same object. But this relation is far from being perfect; since some of the chances lie on the side of existence, and others on that of non–existence; which are objects altogether incompatible. 'Tis impossible by one steady view to survey the opposite chances, and the events dependent on them; but 'tis necessary, that the imagination shou'd run alternately from the one to the other. Each view of the imagination produces its peculiar passion, which decays away by degrees, and is follow'd by a sensible vibration after the stroke.[†] The incompatibility of the views keeps the passions from shocking in a direct line, if that expression may be allow'd; and yet their relation is sufficient to mingle their fainter emotions. 'Tis after this manner that hope and fear arise from the different mixture of these opposite passions of grief and joy, and from their imperfect union and conjunction. *SB 443*

17   Upon the whole, contrary passions succeed each other alternately, when they arise from different objects: They mutually destroy each other, when they proceed from different parts of the same: And they subsist both of them, and mingle together, when they are deriv'd from the contrary and incompatible chances or possibilities, on which any one object depends. The influence of the relations of ideas is plainly seen in this whole affair. If the objects of the contrary passions be totally different, the passions are like two opposite liquors in different bottles, which have no influence on each other. If the objects be intimately connected, the passions are like an *alcali* and an *acid*, which, being mingled, destroy each other. If the relation be more imperfect, and consists in the contradictory views of the same object, the passions are like oil and vinegar, which, however mingled, never perfectly unite and incorporate.

18   As the hypothesis concerning hope and fear carries its own evidence along with it, we shall be the more concise in our proofs. A few strong arguments are better than many weak ones.

19   The passions of fear and hope may arise when the chances are equal on both sides, and no superiority can be discover'd in the one above the other. Nay, in this situation the passions are rather the strongest, as the mind has then the least foundation to rest upon, and is toss'd with the greatest uncertainty. Throw in a superior degree of probability to the side of grief, you immediately see that passion diffuse itself over the composition, and tincture it into fear. Encrease the probability, and by that means the grief, the fear prevails still more and more, till at last it runs insensibly, as the joy continually diminishes, into pure grief. After you have brought it to this situation, diminish the grief, after the same manner

that you encreas'd it; by diminishing the probability on that side, you'll see the   *SB 444*
passion clear every moment, till it changes insensibly into hope; which again
runs, after the same manner, by slow degrees, into joy, as you encrease that part
of the composition by the encrease of the probability. Are not these as plain
proofs, that the passions of fear and hope are mixtures of grief and joy, as in
optics 'tis a proof, that a colour'd ray of the sun passing thro' a prism, is a composition of two others, when, as you diminish or encrease the quantity of either,
you find it prevail proportionably more or less in the composition? I am sure
neither natural nor moral philosophy admits of stronger proofs.

20   Probability is of two kinds, either when the object is really in itself uncertain,
and to be determin'd by chance; or when, tho' the object be already certain, yet
'tis uncertain to our judgment, which finds a number of proofs on each side of
the question. Both these kinds of probability cause fear and hope; which can
only proceed from that property, in which they agree, *viz.* the uncertainty and
fluctuation they bestow on the imagination by that contrariety of views, which is
common to both.

21   'Tis a probable good or evil, that commonly produces hope or fear; because
probability, being a wavering and unconstant method of surveying an object,
causes naturally a like mixture and uncertainty of passion. But we may observe,
that wherever from other causes this mixture can be produc'd, the passions of
fear and hope will arise, even tho' there be no probability; which must be allow'd
to be a convincing proof of the present hypothesis.

22   We find that an evil, barely conceiv'd as *possible*, does sometimes produce fear;
especially if the evil be very great. A man cannot think of excessive pains and
tortures without trembling, if he be in the least danger of suffering them.[†] The
smallness of the probability is compensated by the greatness of the evil; and the
sensation is equally lively, as if the evil were more probable. One view or glimpse
of the former, has the same effect as several of the latter.

23   But they are not only possible evils, that cause fear, but even some allow'd to be   *SB 445*
impossible; as when we tremble on the brink of a precipice, tho' we know ourselves to be in perfect security,[†] and have it in our choice whether we will advance
a step farther. This proceeds from the immediate presence of the evil, which
influences the imagination in the same manner as the certainty of it wou'd do;
but being encounter'd by the reflection on our security, is immediately retracted,
and causes the same kind of passion, as when from a contrariety of chances contrary passions are produc'd.

24   Evils, that are *certain*, have sometimes the same effect in producing fear, as the
possible or impossible. Thus a man in a strong prison well-guarded, without
the least means of escape, trembles at the thought of the rack, to which he is
sentenc'd. This happens only when the certain evil is terrible and confounding;
in which case the mind continually rejects it with horror, while it continually
presses in upon the thought. The evil is there fix'd and establish'd, but the mind
cannot endure to fix upon it; from which fluctuation and uncertainty there arises
a passion of much the same appearance with fear.

25 But 'tis not only where good or evil is uncertain, as to its *existence*, but also as to its *kind*, that fear or hope arises. Let one be told by a person, whose veracity he cannot doubt of, that one of his sons is suddenly kill'd, 'tis evident the passion this event wou'd occasion, wou'd not settle into pure grief, till he got certain information, which of his sons he had lost. Here there is an evil certain, but the kind of it uncertain: Consequently the fear we feel on this occasion is without the least mixture of joy, and arises merely from the fluctuation of the fancy betwixt its objects. And tho' each side of the question produces here the same passion, yet that passion cannot settle, but receives from the imagination a tremulous and unsteady motion, resembling in its cause, as well as in its sensation, the mixture and contention of grief and joy.

26 From these principles we may account for a phænomenon in the passions, *SB 446* which at first sight seems very extraordinary, *viz.* that surprize is apt to change into fear, and every thing that is unexpected affrights us. The most obvious conclusion from this is, that human nature is in general pusillanimous; since upon the sudden appearance of any object we immediately conclude it to be an evil, and without waiting till we can examine its nature, whether it be good or bad, are at first affected with fear. This I say is the most obvious conclusion; but upon farther examination we shall find that the phænomenon is otherwise to be accounted for. The suddenness and strangeness of an appearance naturally excite a commotion in the mind, like every thing for which we are not prepar'd, and to which we are not accustom'd. This commotion, again, naturally produces a curiosity or inquisitiveness, which being very violent, from the strong and sudden impulse of the object, becomes uneasy, and resembles in its fluctuation and uncertainty, the sensation of fear or the mix'd passions of grief and joy. This image of fear naturally converts into the thing itself, and gives us a real apprehension of evil, as the mind always forms its judgments more from its present disposition than from the nature of its objects.

27 Thus all kinds of uncertainty have a strong connexion with fear, even tho' they do not cause any opposition of passions by the opposite views and considerations they present to us. A person, who has left his friend in any malady, will feel more anxiety upon his account, than if he were present, tho' perhaps he is not only incapable of giving him assistance, but likewise of judging of the event of his sickness. In this case, tho' the principal object of the passion, *viz.* the life or death of his friend, be to him equally uncertain when present as when absent; yet there are a thousand little circumstances of his friend's situation and condition, the knowledge of which fixes the idea, and prevents that fluctuation and uncertainty so near ally'd to fear. Uncertainty is, indeed, in one respect as *SB 447* near ally'd to hope as to fear, since it makes an essential part in the composition of the former passion; but the reason, why it inclines not to that side, is, that uncertainty alone is uneasy, and has a relation of impressions to the uneasy passions.

28 'Tis thus our uncertainty concerning any minute circumstance relating to a person encreases our apprehensions of his death or misfortune. *Horace* has remark'd this phænomenon.

Ut assidens implumibus pullis avis
Serpentium allapsus timet,
Magis relictis; non, ut adsit, auxili
Latura plus præsentibus.†

29   But this principle of the connexion of fear with uncertainty I carry farther, and observe that any doubt produces that passion, even tho' it presents nothing to us on any side but what is good and desireable. A virgin, on her bridal-night goes to bed full of fears and apprehensions, tho' she expects nothing but pleasure of the highest kind, and what she has long wish'd for. The newness and greatness of the event, the confusion of wishes and joys, so embarrass the mind, that it knows not on what passion to fix itself; from whence arises a fluttering or unsettledness of the spirits, which being, in some degree, uneasy, very naturally degenerates into fear.

30   Thus we still find, that whatever causes any fluctuation or mixture of passions, with any degree of uneasiness, always produces fear, or at least a passion so like it, that they are scarcely to be distinguish'd.

31   I have here confin'd myself to the examination of hope and fear in their most simple and natural situation, without considering all the variations they may receive from the mixture of different views and reflections. *Terror, consternation, astonishment, anxiety*, and other passions of that kind, are nothing but different species and degrees of fear. 'Tis easy to imagine how a different situation of the object, or a different turn of thought, may change even the sensation of a passion; and this may in general account for all the particular subdivisions of the other affections, as well as of fear. Love may show itself in the shape of *tenderness, friendship, intimacy, esteem, good-will*, and in many other appearances; which at the bottom are the same affections, and arise from the same causes, tho' with a small variation, which it is not necessary to give any particular account of. 'Tis for this reason I have all along confin'd myself to the principal passion.   *SB 448*

32   The same care of avoiding prolixity is the reason why I wave the examination of the will and direct passions, as they appear in animals; since nothing is more evident, than that they are of the same nature, and excited by the same causes as in human creatures. I leave this to the reader's own observation; desiring him at the same time to consider the additional force this bestows on the present system.

Sect. 10. *Of curiosity, or the love of truth*

1   But methinks we have been not a little inattentive to run over so many different parts of the human mind, and examine so many passions, without taking once into the consideration that love of truth, which was the first source of all our enquiries. 'Twill therefore be proper, before we leave this subject, to bestow a few reflections on that passion, and show its origin in human nature. 'Tis an affection of so peculiar a kind, that 'twou'd have been impossible to have treated of it

under any of those heads, which we have examin'd, without danger of obscurity and confusion.

2   Truth is of two kinds, consisting either in the discovery of the proportions of ideas,[†] consider'd as such, or in the conformity of our ideas of objects to their real existence. 'Tis certain, that the former species of truth, is not desir'd merely as truth, and that 'tis not the justness of our conclusions, which alone gives the   *SB 449* pleasure. For these conclusions are equally just, when we discover the equality of two bodies by a pair of compasses, as when we learn it by a mathematical demonstration; and tho' in the one case the proofs be demonstrative, and in the other only sensible, yet generally speaking, the mind acquiesces with equal assurance in the one as in the other.[†] And in an arithmetical operation, where both the truth and the assurance are of the same nature, as in the most profound algebraical problem, the pleasure is very inconsiderable, if rather it does not degenerate into pain: Which is an evident proof, that the satisfaction, which we sometimes receive from the discovery of truth, proceeds not from it, merely as such, but only as endow'd with certain qualities.

3   The first and most considerable circumstance requisite to render truth agreeable, is the genius and capacity, which is employ'd in its invention and discovery. What is easy and obvious is never valu'd; and even what is *in itself* difficult, if we come to the knowledge of it without difficulty, and without any stretch of thought or judgment, is but little regarded. We love to trace the demonstrations of mathematicians; but shou'd receive small entertainment from a person, who shou'd barely inform us of the proportions of lines and angles, tho' we repos'd the utmost confidence both in his judgment and veracity. In this case 'tis sufficient to have ears to learn the truth. We never are oblig'd to fix our attention or exert our genius; which of all other exercises of the mind is the most pleasant and agreeable.

4   But tho' the exercise of genius be the principal source of that satisfaction we receive from the sciences, yet I doubt, if it be alone sufficient to give us any considerable enjoyment. The truth we discover must also be of some importance. 'Tis easy to multiply algebraical problems to infinity, nor is there any end in the discovery of the proportions of conic sections; tho' few mathematicians take any pleasure in these researches, but turn their thoughts to what is more useful   *SB 450* and important. Now the question is, after what manner this utility and importance operate upon us? The difficulty on this head arises from hence, that many philosophers have consum'd their time, have destroy'd their health, and neglected their fortune, in the search of such truths, as they esteem'd important and useful to the world, tho' it appear'd from their whole conduct and behaviour, that they were not endow'd with any share of public spirit, nor had any concern for the interests of mankind. Were they convinc'd, that their discoveries were of no consequence, they wou'd entirely lose all relish for their studies, and that tho' the consequences be entirely indifferent to them; which seems to be a contradiction.

5   To remove this contradiction, we must consider, that there are certain desires and inclinations, which go no farther than the imagination, and are rather the

faint shadows and images of passions, than any real affections. Thus, suppose a man, who takes a survey of the fortifications of any city; considers their strength and advantages, natural or acquir'd; observes the disposition and contrivance of the bastions, ramparts, mines, and other military works; 'tis plain, that in proportion as all these are fitted to attain their ends, he will receive a suitable pleasure and satisfaction. This pleasure, as it arises from the utility, not the form of the objects, can be no other than a sympathy with the inhabitants, for whose security all this art is employ'd; tho' 'tis possible, that this person, as a stranger or an enemy, may in his heart have no kindness for them, or may even entertain a hatred against them.

6 It may indeed be objected, that such a remote sympathy is a very slight foundation for a passion, and that so much industry and application, as we frequently observe in philosophers, can never be deriv'd from so inconsiderable an original. But here I return to what I have already remark'd,[†] that the pleasure of study consists chiefly in the action of the mind, and the exercise of the genius and understanding in the discovery or comprehension of any truth. If the importance of the truth be requisite to compleat the pleasure, 'tis not on account of any considerable addition, which of itself it brings to our enjoyment, but only because 'tis, in some measure, requisite to fix our attention. When we are careless and inattentive, the same action of the understanding has no effect upon us, nor is able to convey any of that satisfaction, which arises from it, when we are in another disposition. *SB 451*

7 But beside the action of the mind, which is the principal foundation of the pleasure, there is likewise requir'd a degree of success in the attainment of the end, or the discovery of that truth we examine. Upon this head I shall make a general remark, which may be useful on many occasions, *viz.* that where the mind pursues any end with passion; tho' that passion be not deriv'd originally from the end, but merely from the action and pursuit; yet by the natural course of the affections, we acquire a concern for the end itself, and are uneasy under any disappointment we meet with in the pursuit of it.[†] This proceeds from the relation and parallel direction of the passions above-mention'd.[†]

8 To illustrate all this by a familiar instance, I shall observe, that there cannot be two passions more nearly resembling each other, than those of hunting and philosophy, whatever disproportion may at first sight appear betwixt them. 'Tis evident, that the pleasure of hunting consists in the action of the mind and body; the motion, the attention, the difficulty, and the uncertainty. 'Tis evident likewise, that these actions must be attended with an idea of utility, in order to their having any effect upon us. A man of the greatest fortune, and the farthest remov'd from avarice, tho' he takes a pleasure in hunting after patridges and pheasants, feels no satisfaction in shooting crows and magpies; and that because he considers the first as fit for the table, and the other as entirely useless. Here 'tis certain, that the utility or importance of itself causes no real passion, but is only requisite to support the imagination; and the same person, who over-looks a ten times greater profit in any other subject, is pleas'd to bring home half a dozen woodcocks or plovers, after having employ'd several hours in hunting after *SB 452*

them. To make the parallel betwixt hunting and philosophy more compleat, we may observe, that tho' in both cases the end of our action may in itself be despis'd, yet in the heat of the action we acquire such an attention to this end, that we are very uneasy under any disappointments, and are sorry when we either miss our game, or fall into any error in our reasoning.[†]

9   If we want another parallel to these affections, we may consider the passion of gaming, which affords a pleasure from the same principles as hunting and philosophy. It has been remark'd, that the pleasure of gaming arises not from interest alone; since many leave a sure gain for this entertainment: Neither is it deriv'd from the game alone; since the same persons have no satisfaction, when they play for nothing: But proceeds from both these causes united, tho' separately they have no effect.[†] 'Tis here, as in certain chymical preparations, where the mixture of two clear and transparent liquids produces a third, which is opaque and colour'd.

10   The interest, which we have in any game, engages our attention, without which we can have no enjoyment, either in that or in any other action. Our attention being once engag'd, the difficulty, variety, and sudden reverses of fortune, still farther interest us; and 'tis from that concern our satisfaction arises. Human life is so tiresome a scene, and men generally are of such indolent dispositions, that whatever amuses them, tho' by a passion mixt with pain, does in the main give them a sensible pleasure.[†] And this pleasure is here encreas'd by the nature of the objects, which being sensible, and of a narrow compass, are enter'd into with facility, and are agreeable to the imagination.

11   The same theory, that accounts for the love of truth in mathematics and   *SB 453* algebra, may be extended to morals, politics, natural philosophy, and other studies, where we consider not the abstract relations of ideas, but their real connexions and existence. But beside the love of knowledge, which displays itself in the sciences, there is a certain curiosity implanted in human nature,[†] which is a passion deriv'd from a quite different principle. Some people have an insatiable desire of knowing the actions and circumstances of their neighbours, tho' their interest be no way concern'd in them, and they must entirely depend on others for their information; in which case there is no room for study or application. Let us search for the reason of this phænomenon.

12   It has been prov'd at large,[†] that the influence of belief is at once to enliven and infix any idea in the imagination, and prevent all kind of hesitation and uncertainty about it. Both these circumstances are advantageous. By the vivacity of the idea we interest the fancy, and produce, tho' in a lesser degree, the same pleasure, which arises from a moderate passion. As the vivacity of the idea gives pleasure, so its certainty prevents uneasiness, by fixing one particular idea in the mind, and keeping it from wavering in the choice of its objects. 'Tis a quality of human nature, which is conspicuous on many occasions, and is common both to the mind and body, that too sudden and violent a change is unpleasant to us, and that however any objects may in themselves be indifferent, yet their alteration gives uneasiness. As 'tis the nature of doubt to cause a variation in the thought, and transport us suddenly from one idea to another, it must of consequence be

the occasion of pain. This pain chiefly takes place, where interest, relation, or the greatness and novelty of any event interests us in it. 'Tis not every matter of fact, of which we have a curiosity to be inform'd; neither are they such only as we have an interest to know. 'Tis sufficient if the idea strikes on us with such force, and concerns us so nearly, as to give us an uneasiness in its instability and inconstancy. A stranger, when he arrives first at any town, may be entirely indifferent about knowing the history and adventures of the inhabitants; but as he becomes farther acquainted with them, and has liv'd any considerable time among them, he acquires the same curiosity as the natives. When we are reading the history of a nation, we may have an ardent desire of clearing up any doubt or difficulty, that occurs in it; but become careless in such researches, when the ideas of these events are, in a great measure, obliterated.

The end of the second BOOK.

A TREATISE OF HUMAN NATURE:

BEING AN ATTEMPT TO INTRODUCE
THE EXPERIMENTAL METHOD
OF REASONING
INTO MORAL SUBJECTS

—Duræ semper virtutis amator,
Quære quid est virtus,
et posce exemplar honesti. [†] LUCAN

Book 3. *Of Morals*

With an Appendix.
Wherein some Passages of the foregoing Volumes
are Illustrated and Explain'd.

ADVERTISEMENT

I think it proper to inform the public, that tho' this be a third volume of the Treatise of Human Nature, *yet 'tis in some measure independent of the other two, and requires not that the reader shou'd enter into all the abstract reasonings contain'd in them.* † *I am hopeful it may be understood by ordinary readers, with as little attention as is usually given to any books of reasoning. It must only be observ'd, that I continue to make use of the terms,* impressions *and* ideas, *in the same sense as formerly;* † *and that by* impressions *I mean our stronger perceptions, such as our sensations, affections and sentiments; and by* ideas *the fainter perceptions, or the copies of these in the memory and imagination.*

BOOK 3. *Of* MORALS

PART 1

Of virtue and vice in general

Sect. 1. *Moral distinctions not deriv'd from reason*

1 There is an inconvenience which attends all abstruse reasoning, that it may silence, without convincing an antagonist, and requires the same intense study to make us sensible of its force, that was at first requisite for its invention. When we leave our closet, and engage in the common affairs of life, its conclusions seem to vanish, like the phantoms of the night on the appearance of the morning; and 'tis difficult for us to retain even that conviction, which we had attain'd with difficulty. This is still more conspicuous in a long chain of reasoning, where we must preserve to the end the evidence of the first propositions, and where we often lose sight of all the most receiv'd maxims, either of philosophy or common life. I am not, however, without hopes, that the present system of philosophy will acquire new force as it advances; and that our reasonings concerning *morals* will corroborate whatever has been said concerning the *understanding* and the *passions*.† Morality is a subject that interests us above all others: We fancy the peace of society to be at stake in every decision concerning it; and 'tis evident, that this concern must make our speculations appear more real and solid, than where the subject is, in a great measure, indifferent to us. What affects us, we conclude can never be a chimera; and as our passion is engag'd on the one side or the other, we naturally think that the question lies within human comprehension; which, in other cases of this nature, we are apt to entertain some doubt of. Without this advantage I never shou'd have ventur'd upon a third volume of such abstruse philosophy, in an age, wherein the greatest part of men seem agreed to convert reading into an amusement, and to reject every thing that requires any considerable degree of attention to be comprehended.†

2 It has been observ'd,† that nothing is ever present to the mind but its perceptions; and that all the actions of seeing, hearing, judging, loving, hating, and thinking, fall under this denomination. The mind can never exert itself in any action, which we may not comprehend under the term of *perception*; and consequently that term is no less applicable to those judgments, by which we distinguish moral good and evil, than to every other operation of the mind. To approve of one character, to condemn another, are only so many different perceptions.

3 Now as perceptions resolve themselves into two kinds, viz. *impressions*

and *ideas*,[†] this distinction gives rise to a question, with which we shall open up our present enquiry concerning morals, *Whether 'tis by means of our* ideas *or* impressions *we distinguish betwixt vice and virtue, and pronounce an action blameable or praise-worthy?* This will immediately cut off all loose discourses and declamations, and reduce us to something precise and exact on the present subject.

4   Those who affirm that virtue is nothing but a conformity to reason; that there are eternal fitnesses and unfitnesses of things, which are the same to every rational being that considers them; that the immutable measures of right and wrong impose an obligation, not only on human creatures, but also on the deity himself:[†] All these systems concur in the opinion, that morality, like truth, is discern'd merely by ideas, and by their juxta-position and comparison. In   *SB 457* order, therefore, to judge of these systems, we need only consider, whether it be possible, from reason alone,[†] to distinguish betwixt moral good and evil, or whether there must concur some other principles to enable us to make that distinction.

5   If morality had naturally no influence on human passions and actions, 'twere in vain to take such pains to inculcate it; and nothing wou'd be more fruitless than that multitude of rules and precepts, with which all moralists abound. Philosophy is commonly divided into *speculative* and *practical*; and as morality is always comprehended under the latter division, 'tis suppos'd to influence our passions and actions, and to go beyond the calm and indolent judgments of the understanding.[†] And this is confirm'd by common experience, which informs us, that men are often govern'd by their duties, and are deter'd from some actions by the opinion of injustice, and impell'd to others by that of obligation.

6   Since morals, therefore, have an influence on the actions and affections, it follows, that they cannot be deriv'd from reason; and that because reason alone, as we have already prov'd,[†] can never have any such influence. Morals excite passions, and produce or prevent actions. Reason of itself is utterly impotent in this particular. The rules of morality, therefore, are not conclusions of our reason.

7   No one, I believe, will deny the justness of this inference; nor is there any other means of evading it, than by denying that principle, on which it is founded. As long as it is allow'd, that reason has no influence on our passions and actions, 'tis in vain to pretend, that morality is discover'd only by a deduction of reason. An active principle can never be founded on an inactive; and if reason be inactive in itself, it must remain so in all its shapes and appearances, whether it exerts itself in natural or moral subjects, whether it considers the powers of external bodies, or the actions of rational beings.

8   It wou'd be tedious to repeat all the arguments, by which I have prov'd,[67]   *SB 458* that reason is perfectly inert, and can never either prevent or produce any action or affection. 'Twill be easy to recollect what has been said upon that subject. I shall only recal[†] on this occasion one of these arguments, which I shall

---

[67] Book 2. Part 3. Sect. 3.

endeavour to render still more conclusive, and more applicable to the present subject.

9   Reason is the discovery of truth or falshood. Truth or falshood consists in an agreement or disagreement either to the *real* relations of ideas, or to *real* existence and matter of fact. Whatever, therefore, is not susceptible of this agreement or disagreement, is incapable of being true or false, and can never be an object of our reason. Now 'tis evident our passions, volitions, and actions, are not susceptible of any such agreement or disagreement; being original facts and realities, compleat in themselves, and implying no reference to other passions, volitions, and actions. 'Tis impossible, therefore, they can be pronounc'd either true or false, and be either contrary or conformable to reason.[†]

10   This argument is of double advantage to our present purpose. For it proves *directly*, that actions do not derive their merit from a conformity to reason, nor their blame from a contrariety to it;[†] and it proves the same truth more *indirectly*, by showing us, that as reason can never immediately prevent or produce any action by contradicting or approving of it, it cannot be the source of the distinction betwixt moral good and evil, which are found to have that influence.[†] Actions may be laudable or blameable; but they cannot be reasonable or unreasonable: Laudable or blameable, therefore, are not the same with reasonable or unreasonable. The merit and demerit of actions frequently contradict, and sometimes controul our natural propensities. But reason has no such influence. Moral distinctions, therefore, are not the offspring of reason. Reason is wholly inactive, and can never be the source of so active a principle as conscience, or a sense of morals.

11   But perhaps it may be said, that tho' no will or action can be immediately con-   *SB 459* tradictory to reason, yet we may find such a contradiction in some of the attendants of the action, that is, in its causes or effects. The action may cause a judgment, or may be *obliquely* caus'd by one, when the judgment concurs with a passion; and by an abusive way of speaking, which philosophy will scarce allow of, the same contrariety may, upon that account, be ascrib'd to the action.[†] How far this truth or falshood may be the source of morals, 'twill now be proper to consider.

12   It has been observ'd,[†] that reason, in a strict and philosophical sense, can have an influence on our conduct only after two ways: Either when it excites a passion by informing us of the existence of something which is a proper object of it; or when it discovers the connexion of causes and effects, so as to afford us means of exerting any passion. These are the only kinds of judgment, which can accompany our actions, or can be said to produce them in any manner; and it must be allow'd, that these judgments may often be false and erroneous. A person may be affected with passion, by supposing a pain or pleasure to lie in an object, which has no tendency to produce either of these sensations, or which produces the contrary to what is imagin'd. A person may also take false measures for the attaining his end, and may retard, by his foolish conduct, instead of forwarding the execution of any project. These false judgments may be thought to affect the passions and actions, which are connected with them, and may be said to render

them unreasonable, in a figurative and improper way of speaking. But tho' this be acknowledg'd, 'tis easy to observe, that these errors are so far from being the source of all immorality, that they are commonly very innocent, and draw no manner of guilt upon the person who is so unfortunate as to fall into them. They extend not beyond a mistake of *fact*, which moralists have not generally suppos'd criminal, as being perfectly involuntary. I am more to be lamented than blam'd, if I am mistaken with regard to the influence of objects in producing pain or pleasure, or if I know not the proper means of satisfying my desires. No one can ever regard such errors as a defect in my moral character. A fruit, for instance, that is really disagreeable, appears to me at a distance, and thro' mistake I fancy it to be pleasant and delicious. Here is one error. I choose certain means of reaching this fruit, which are not proper for my end. Here is a second error; nor is there any third one, which can ever possibly enter into our reasonings concerning actions. I ask, therefore, if a man, in this situation, and guilty of these two errors, is to be regarded as vicious and criminal, however unavoidable they might have been? Or if it be possible to imagine, that such errors are the sources of all immorality?

SB 460

13 And here it may be proper to observe, that if moral distinctions be deriv'd from the truth or falshood of those judgments, they must take place wherever we form the judgments; nor will there be any difference, whether the question be concerning an apple or a kingdom, or whether the error be avoidable or unavoidable. For as the very essence of morality is suppos'd to consist in an agreement or disagreement to reason, the other circumstances are entirely arbitrary, and can never either bestow on any action the character of virtuous or vicious, or deprive it of that character. To which we may add, that this agreement or disagreement, not admitting of degrees, all virtues and vices wou'd of course be equal.†

14 Shou'd it be pretended, that tho' a mistake of *fact* be not criminal, yet a mistake of *right* often is; and that this may be the source of immorality: I wou'd answer, that 'tis impossible such a mistake can ever be the original source of immorality, since it supposes a real right and wrong; that is, a real distinction in morals, independent of these judgments. A mistake, therefore, of right may become a species of immorality; but 'tis only a secondary one, and is founded on some other, antecedent to it.†

15 As to those judgments which are the *effects* of our actions, and which, when false, give occasion to pronounce the actions contrary to truth and reason; we may observe, that our actions never cause any judgment, either true or false, in ourselves, and that 'tis only on others they have such an influence. 'Tis certain, that an action, on many occasions, may give rise to false conclusions in others; and that a person, who thro' a window sees any lewd behaviour of mine with my neighbour's wife, may be so simple as to imagine she is certainly my own. In this respect my action resembles somewhat a lye or falshood; only with this difference, which is material, that I perform not the action with any intention of giving rise to a false judgment in another, but merely to satisfy my lust and passion. It causes, however, a mistake and false judgment by accident; and the

SB 461

falshood of its effects may be ascrib'd, by some odd figurative way of speaking, to the action itself. But still I can see no pretext of reason for asserting, that the tendency to cause such an error is the first spring or original source of all immorality.[68]†

16   Thus upon the whole, 'tis impossible, that the distinction betwixt moral good and evil, can be made by reason; since that distinction has an influence upon our   *SB 462*

---

[68] One might think it were entirely superfluous to prove this, if a late author, who has had the   *SB 461*
good fortune to obtain some reputation, had not seriously affirm'd, that such a falshood is the foundation of all guilt and moral deformity.† That we may discover the fallacy of his hypothesis, we need only consider, that a false conclusion is drawn from an action, only by means of an obscurity of natural principles, which makes a cause be secretly interrupted in its operation, by contrary causes, and renders the connexion betwixt two objects uncertain and variable.† Now, as a like uncertainty and variety of causes take place, even in natural objects, and produce a like error in our judgment, if that tendency to produce error were the very essence of vice and immorality, it shou'd follow, that even inanimate objects might be vicious and immoral.

2   'Tis in vain to urge, that inanimate objects act without liberty and choice.† For as liberty and choice are not necessary to make an action produce in us an erroneous conclusion, they can be, in no respect, essential to morality; and I do not readily perceive, upon this system, how they can ever come to be regarded by it. If the tendency to cause error be the origin of immorality, that tendency and immorality wou'd in every case be inseparable.

3   Add to this, that if I had us'd the precaution of shutting the windows, while I indulg'd myself in those liberties with my neighbour's wife, I shou'd have been guilty of no immorality; and that because my action, being perfectly conceal'd, wou'd have had no tendency to produce any false conclusion.

4   For the same reason, a thief, who steals in by a ladder at a window, and takes all imaginable care to   *SB 462*
cause no disturbance, is in no respect criminal. For either he will not be perceiv'd, or if he be, 'tis impossible he can produce any error, nor will any one, from these circumstances, take him to be other than what he really is.

5   'Tis well known, that those who are squint-sighted,† do very readily cause mistakes in others, and that we imagine they salute or are talking to one person, while they address themselves to another. Are they therefore, upon that account, immoral?

6   Besides, we may easily observe, that in all those arguments there is an evident reasoning in a circle. A person who takes possession of *another*'s goods, and uses them as his *own*, in a manner declares them to be his own; and this falshood is the source of the immorality of injustice. But is property, or right, or obligation, intelligible, without an antecedent morality?†

7   A man that is ungrateful to his benefactor, in a manner affirms, that he never receiv'd any favours from him. But in what manner? Is it because 'tis his duty to be grateful? But this supposes, that there is some antecedent rule of duty and morals. Is it because human nature is generally grateful, and makes us conclude, that a man who does any harm never receiv'd any favour from the person he harm'd? But human nature is not so generally grateful, as to justify such a conclusion. Or if it were, is an exception to a general rule in every case criminal, for no other reason than because it is an exception?

8   But what may suffice entirely to destroy this whimsical system is, that it leaves us under the same difficulty to give a reason why truth is virtuous and falshood vicious, as to account for the merit or turpitude of any other action. I shall allow, if you please, that all immorality is deriv'd from this suppos'd falshood in action, provided you can give me any plausible reason, why such a falshood is immoral. If you consider rightly of the matter, you will find yourself in the same difficulty as at the beginning.

9   This last argument is very conclusive; because, if there be not an evident merit or turpitude annex'd to this species of truth or falshood, it can never have any influence upon our actions. For, who ever thought of forbearing any action, because others might possibly draw false conclusions from it? Or, who ever perform'd any, that he might give rise to true conclusions?

actions, of which reason alone is incapable. Reason and judgment may, indeed, be the mediate cause of an action, by prompting, or by directing a passion:[†] But it is not pretended, that a judgment of this kind, either in its truth or falshood, is attended with virtue or vice. And as to the judgments, which are caus'd by our actions, they can still less bestow those moral qualities on the actions, which are their causes.

SB 463

17   But to be more particular, and to show, that those eternal immutable fitnesses and unfitnesses of things cannot be defended by sound philosophy, we may weigh the following considerations.

18   If the thought and understanding were alone capable of fixing the boundaries of right and wrong, the character of virtuous and vicious either must lie in some relations of objects, or must be a matter of fact, which is discover'd by our reasoning. This consequence is evident. As the operations of human understanding divide themselves into two kinds, the comparing of ideas, and the inferring of matter of fact; were virtue discover'd by the understanding; it must be an object of one of these operations, nor is there any third operation of the understanding, which can discover it. There has been an opinion very industriously propagated by certain philosophers, that morality is susceptible of demonstration; and tho' no one has ever been able to advance a single step in those demonstrations; yet 'tis taken for granted, that this science may be brought to an equal certainty with geometry or algebra.[†] Upon this supposition, vice and virtue must consist in some relations; since 'tis allow'd on all hands, that no matter of fact is capable of being demonstrated.[†] Let us, therefore, begin with examining this hypothesis, and endeavour, if possible, to fix those moral qualities, which have been so long the objects of our fruitless researches. Point out distinctly the relations, which constitute morality or obligation, that we may know wherein they consist, and after what manner we must judge of them.

19   If you assert, that vice and virtue consist in relations susceptible of certainty and demonstration, you must confine yourself to those *four* relations, which alone admit of that degree of evidence; and in that case you run into absurdities, from which you will never be able to extricate yourself. For as you make the very essence of morality to lie in the relations, and as there is no one of these relations but what is applicable, not only to an irrational, but also to an inanimate object; it follows, that even such objects must be susceptible of merit or demerit. *Resemblance, contrariety, degrees in quality*, and *proportions in quantity and number;*[†] all these relations belong as properly to matter, as to our actions, passions, and volitions. 'Tis unquestionable, therefore, that morality lies not in any of these relations, nor the sense of it in their discovery.[69]

SB 464

---

[69] As a proof, how confus'd our way of thinking on this subject commonly is, we may observe, that those who assert, that morality is demonstrable, do not say, that morality lies in the relations, and that the relations are distinguishable by reason. They only say, that reason can discover such an action, in such relations, to be virtuous, and such another vicious. It seems they thought it sufficient, if they cou'd bring the word, *relation*, into the proposition, without troubling themselves whether it was to the purpose or not.[†] But here, I think, is plain argument. Demonstrative reason discovers only relations. But that reason, according to this hypothesis, discovers also vice and

20   Shou'd it be asserted, that the sense of morality consists in the discovery of some relation, distinct from these, and that our enumeration was not compleat, when we comprehended all demonstrable relations under four general heads: To this I know not what to reply, till some one be so good as to point out to me this new relation. 'Tis impossible to refute a system, which has never yet been explain'd. In such a manner of fighting in the dark, a man loses his blows in the air, and often places them where the enemy is not present.

21   I must, therefore, on this occasion, rest contented with requiring the two following conditions of any one that wou'd undertake to clear up this system. *First,* As moral good and evil belong only to the actions of the mind, and are deriv'd from our situation with regard to external objects, the relations, from which these moral distinctions arise, must lie only betwixt internal actions, and exter-   *SB 465* nal objects, and must not be applicable either to internal actions, compar'd among themselves, or to external objects, when plac'd in opposition to other external objects.[†] For as morality is suppos'd to attend certain relations, if these relations cou'd belong to internal actions consider'd singly, it wou'd follow, that we might be guilty of crimes in ourselves, and independent of our situation, with respect to the universe: And in like manner, if these moral relations cou'd be apply'd to external objects, it wou'd follow, that even inanimate beings wou'd be susceptible of moral beauty and deformity. Now it seems difficult to imagine, that any relation can be discover'd betwixt our passions, volitions and actions, compar'd to external objects, which relation might not belong either to these passions and volitions, or to these external objects, compar'd among *themselves*.

22   But it will be still more difficult to fulfil the *second* condition, requisite to justify this system. According to the principles of those who maintain an abstract rational difference betwixt moral good and evil, and a natural fitness and unfitness of things, 'tis not only suppos'd, that these relations, being eternal and immutable, are the same, when consider'd by every rational creature, but their *effects* are also suppos'd to be necessarily the same; and 'tis concluded they have no less, or rather a greater, influence in directing the will of the deity, than in governing the rational and virtuous of our own species.[†] These two particulars are evidently distinct. 'Tis one thing to know virtue, and another to conform the will to it. In order, therefore, to prove, that the measures of right and wrong are eternal laws, *obligatory* on every rational mind, 'tis not sufficient to show the relations upon which they are founded: We must also point out the connexion betwixt the relation and the will; and must prove that this connexion is so necessary, that in every well-dispos'd mind, it must take place and have its influence; tho' the difference betwixt these minds be in other respects immense and infinite. Now besides what I have already prov'd,[†] that even in human nature no   *SB 466*

virtue. These moral qualities, therefore, must be relations. When we blame any action, in any situation, the whole complicated object, of action and situation, must form certain relations, wherein the essence of vice consists. This hypothesis is not otherwise intelligible. For what does reason discover, when it pronounces any action vicious? Does it discover a relation or a matter of fact? These questions are decisive, and must not be eluded.   *SB 464*

relation can ever alone produce any action; besides this, I say, it has been shown,[†] in treating of the understanding, that there is no connexion of cause and effect, such as this is suppos'd to be, which is discoverable otherwise than by experience, and of which we can pretend to have any security by the simple consideration of the objects. All beings in the universe, consider'd in themselves, appear entirely loose and independent of each other. 'Tis only by experience we learn their influence and connexion; and this influence we ought never to extend beyond experience.

23   Thus it will be impossible to fulfil the *first* condition requisite to the system of eternal rational measures of right and wrong; because it is impossible to show those relations, upon which such a distinction may be founded: And 'tis as impossible to fulfil the *second* condition; because we cannot prove *a priori*, that these relations, if they really existed and were perceiv'd, wou'd be universally forcible and obligatory.

24   But to make these general reflections more clear and convincing, we may illustrate them by some particular instances, wherein this character of moral good or evil is the most universally acknowledg'd. Of all crimes that human creatures are capable of committing, the most horrid and unnatural is ingratitude, especially when it is committed against parents, and appears in the more flagrant instances of wounds and death.[†] This is acknowledg'd by all mankind, philosophers as well as the people; the question only arises among philosophers, whether the guilt or moral deformity of this action be discover'd by demonstrative reasoning, or be felt by an internal sense, and by means of some sentiment, which the reflecting on such an action naturally occasions? This question will soon be decided against the former opinion, if we can show the same relations in other objects, without the notion of any guilt or iniquity attending them. Reason or science is nothing but the comparing of ideas, and the discovery of their relations; and if the same relations have different characters, it must evidently *SB 467* follow, that those characters are not discover'd merely by reason. To put the affair, therefore, to this trial, let us choose any inanimate object, such as an oak or elm; and let us suppose, that by the dropping of its seed, it produces a sapling below it, which springing up by degrees, at last overtops and destroys the parent tree: I ask, if in this instance there be wanting any relation, which is discoverable in parricide or ingratitude? Is not the one tree the cause of the other's existence; and the latter the cause of the destruction of the former, in the same manner as when a child murders his parent? 'Tis not sufficient to reply, that a choice or will is wanting. For in the case of parricide, a will does not give rise to any *different* relations, but is only the cause from which the action is deriv'd; and consequently produces the *same* relations, that in the oak or elm arise from some other principles. 'Tis a will or choice, that determines a man to kill his parent; and they are the laws of matter and motion, that determine a sapling to destroy the oak, from which it sprung. Here then the same relations have different causes; but still the relations are the same: And as their discovery is not in both cases attended with a notion of immorality, it follows, that that notion does not arise from such a discovery.

25   But to choose an instance, still more resembling; I wou'd fain ask any one, why incest in the human species is criminal, and why the very same action, and the same relations in animals have not the smallest moral turpitude and deformity?[†] If it be answer'd, that this action is innocent in animals, because they have not reason sufficient to discover its turpitude; but that man, being endow'd with that faculty, which *ought* to restrain him to his duty, the same action instantly becomes criminal to him; shou'd this be said, I wou'd reply, that this is evidently arguing in a circle. For before reason can perceive this turpitude, the turpitude must exist; and consequently is independent of the decisions of our reason, and is their object more properly than their effect. According to this system, then, *SB 468* every animal that has sense, and appetite, and will; that is, every animal, must be susceptible of all the same virtues and vices, for which we ascribe praise and blame to human creatures. All the difference is, that our superior reason may serve to discover the vice or virtue, and by that means may augment the blame or praise: But still this discovery supposes a separate being in these moral distinctions, and a being, which depends only on the will and appetite, and which, both in thought and reality, may be distinguish'd from the reason. Animals are susceptible of the same relations, with respect to each other, as the human species, and therefore wou'd also be susceptible of the same morality, if the essence of morality consisted in these relations. Their want of a sufficient degree of reason may hinder them from perceiving the duties and obligations of morality, but can never hinder these duties from existing; since they must antecedently exist, in order to their being perceiv'd. Reason must find them, and can never produce them. This argument deserves to be weigh'd, as being, in my opinion, entirely decisive.

26   Nor does this reasoning only prove, that morality consists not in any relations, that are the objects of science; but if examin'd, will prove with equal certainty, that it consists not in any *matter of fact*, which can be discover'd by the understanding. This is the *second* part of our argument; and if it can be made evident, we may conclude, that morality is not an object of reason. But can there be any difficulty in proving, that vice and virtue are not matters of fact, whose existence we can infer by reason? Take any action allow'd to be vicious: Wilful murder, for instance. Examine it in all lights, and see if you can find that matter of fact, or real existence, which you call *vice*. In which-ever way you take it, you find only certain passions, motives, volitions, and thoughts. There is no other matter of fact in the case. The vice entirely escapes you, as long as you consider the object. You never can find it, till you turn your reflection into your own breast, and find *SB 469* a sentiment of disapprobation, which arises in you, towards this action.[†] Here is a matter of fact; but 'tis the object of feeling, not of reason. It lies in yourself, not in the object. So that when you pronounce any action or character to be vicious, you mean nothing, but that from the constitution of your nature you have a feeling or sentiment of blame from the contemplation of it. Vice and virtue, therefore, may be compar'd to sounds, colours, heat and cold, which, according to modern philosophy, are not qualities in objects, but perceptions in the mind:[†] And this discovery in morals, like that other in physics, is to be regarded as a

considerable advancement of the speculative sciences; tho', like that too, it has little or no influence on practice. Nothing can be more real, or concern us more, than our own sentiments of pleasure and uneasiness; and if these be favourable to virtue, and unfavourable to vice, no more can be requisite to the regulation of our conduct and behaviour.

27   I cannot forbear adding to these reasonings an observation, which may, perhaps, be found of some importance. In every system of morality, which I have hitherto met with, I have always remark'd, that the author proceeds for some time in the ordinary way of reasoning, and establishes the being of a God, or makes observations concerning human affairs; when of a sudden I am surpriz'd to find, that instead of the usual copulations of propositions, *is*, and *is not*, I meet with no proposition that is not connected with an *ought*, or an *ought not*.[†] This change is imperceptible; but is, however, of the last consequence. For as this *ought*, or *ought not*, expresses some new relation or affirmation, 'tis necessary that it shou'd be observ'd and explain'd; and at the same time that a reason shou'd be given, for what seems altogether inconceivable, how this new relation can be a deduction from others, which are entirely different from it.[†] But as authors do not commonly use this precaution, I shall presume to recommend it to the reader; and am perswaded, that this small attention wou'd subvert all the vulgar systems of morality, and let us see, that the distinction of vice and virtue is not founded merely on the relations of objects, nor is perceiv'd by reason.

SB 470

Sect. 2. *Moral distinctions deriv'd from a moral sense*

1   Thus the course of the argument leads us to conclude, that since vice and virtue are not discoverable merely by reason, or the comparison of ideas, it must be by means of some impression or sentiment they occasion, that we are able to mark the difference betwixt them. Our decisions concerning moral rectitude and depravity are evidently perceptions; and as all perceptions are either impressions or ideas, the exclusion of the one is a convincing argument for the other.[†] Morality, therefore, is more properly felt than judg'd of;[†] tho' this feeling or sentiment is commonly so soft and gentle, that we are apt to confound it with an idea, according to our common custom of taking all things for the same, which have any near resemblance to each other.[†]

2   The next question is, of what nature are these impressions, and after what manner do they operate upon us? Here we cannot remain long in suspense, but must pronounce the impression arising from virtue, to be agreeable, and that proceeding from vice to be uneasy. Every moment's experience must convince us of this. There is no spectacle so fair and beautiful as a noble and generous action; nor any which gives us more abhorrence than one that is cruel and treacherous. No enjoyment equals the satisfaction we receive from the company of those we love and esteem; as the greatest of all punishments is to be oblig'd to pass our lives with those we hate or contemn. A very play or romance may afford us

instances of this pleasure, which virtue conveys to us; and pain, which arises
from vice.[†]

3   Now since the distinguishing impressions, by which moral good or evil is
known, are nothing but *particular* pains or pleasures; it follows, that in all
enquiries concerning these moral distinctions, it will be sufficient to show the
principles, which make us feel a satisfaction or uneasiness from the survey of any
character, in order to satisfy us why the character is laudable or blameable. An
action, or sentiment, or character is virtuous or vicious; why? because its view
causes a pleasure or uneasiness of a particular kind. In giving a reason, therefore,
for the pleasure or uneasiness, we sufficiently explain the vice or virtue. To have
the sense of virtue, is nothing but to *feel* a satisfaction of a particular kind from
the contemplation of a character. The very *feeling* constitutes our praise or
admiration.[†] We go no farther; nor do we enquire into the cause of the satisfaction.[†] We do not infer a character to be virtuous, because it pleases: But in feeling
that it pleases after such a particular manner, we in effect feel that it is virtuous.[†]
The case is the same as in our judgments concerning all kinds of beauty, and
tastes, and sensations.[†] Our approbation is imply'd in the immediate pleasure
they convey to us.

4   I have objected[†] to the system, which establishes eternal rational measures of
right and wrong, that 'tis impossible to show, in the actions of reasonable creatures, any relations, which are not found in external objects; and therefore, if
morality always attended these relations, 'twere possible for inanimate matter to
become virtuous or vicious. Now it may, in like manner, be objected to the
present system, that if virtue and vice be determin'd by pleasure and pain, these
qualities must, in every case, arise from the sensations; and consequently any
object, whether animate or inanimate, rational or irrational, might become
morally good or evil, provided it can excite a satisfaction or uneasiness. But tho'
this objection seems to be the very same, it has by no means the same force, in the
one case as in the other. For, *first*, 'tis evident, that under the term *pleasure*, we
comprehend sensations, which are very different from each other,[†] and which
have only such a distant resemblance, as is requisite to make them be express'd
by the same abstract term. A good composition of music and a bottle of good
wine equally produce pleasure; and what is more, their goodness is determin'd
merely by the pleasure. But shall we say upon that account, that the wine is harmonious, or the music of a good flavour? In like manner an inanimate object, and
the character or sentiments of any person may, both of them, give satisfaction;
but as the satisfaction is different, this keeps our sentiments concerning them
from being confounded, and makes us ascribe virtue to the one, and not to the
other. Nor is every sentiment of pleasure or pain, which arises from characters
and actions, of that *peculiar* kind, which makes us praise or condemn. The good
qualities of an enemy are hurtful to us; but may still command our esteem and
respect. 'Tis only when a character is consider'd in general, without reference to
our particular interest, that it causes such a feeling or sentiment, as denominates
it morally good or evil. 'Tis true, those sentiments, from interest and morals, are

303

apt to be confounded, and naturally run into one another. It seldom happens, that we do not think an enemy vicious, and can distinguish betwixt his opposition to our interest and real villainy or baseness. But this hinders not, but that the sentiments are, in themselves, distinct; and a man of temper and judgment may preserve himself from these illusions. In like manner, tho' 'tis certain a musical voice is nothing but one that naturally gives a *particular* kind of pleasure; yet 'tis difficult for a man to be sensible, that the voice of an enemy is agreeable, or to allow it to be musical. But a person of a fine ear, who has the command of himself, can separate these feelings, and give praise to what deserves it.

5   *Secondly*, We may call to remembrance the preceding system of the passions, SB 473 in order to remark a still more considerable difference among our pains and pleasures. Pride and humility, love and hatred are excited, when there is any thing presented to us, that both bears a relation to the object of the passion, and produces a separate sensation related to the sensation of the passion.† Now virtue and vice are attended with these circumstances. They must necessarily be plac'd either in ourselves or others, and excite either pleasure or uneasiness; and therefore must give rise to one of these four passions; which clearly distinguishes them from the pleasure and pain arising from inanimate objects, that often bear no relation to us: And this is, perhaps, the most considerable effect that virtue and vice have upon the human mind.

6   It may now be ask'd *in general*, concerning this pain or pleasure, that distinguishes moral good and evil, *From what principles is it deriv'd, and whence does it arise in the human mind?* To this I reply, *first*, that 'tis absurd to imagine, that in every particular instance, these sentiments are produc'd by an *original* quality and *primary* constitution.† For as the number of our duties is, in a manner, infinite, 'tis impossible that our original instincts shou'd extend to each of them, and from our very first infancy impress on the human mind all that multitude of precepts, which are contain'd in the compleatest system of ethics. Such a method of proceeding is not conformable to the usual maxims, by which nature is conducted, where a few principles produce all that variety we observe in the universe, and every thing is carry'd on in the easiest and most simple manner. 'Tis necessary, therefore, to abridge these primary impulses, and find some more general principles, upon which all our notions of morals are founded.

7   But in the *second* place, shou'd it be ask'd, whether we ought to search for these principles in *nature*, or whether we must look for them in some other origin? I wou'd reply, that our answer to this question depends upon the defini- SB 474 tion of the word, *nature*, than which there is none more ambiguous and equivocal.† If *nature* be oppos'd to miracles, not only the distinction betwixt vice and virtue is natural, but also every event, which has ever happen'd in the world, *excepting those miracles, on which our religion is founded*. In saying, then, that the sentiments of vice and virtue are natural in this sense, we make no very extraordinary discovery.

8   But *nature* may also be oppos'd to rare and unusual; and in this sense of the word, which is the common one, there may often arise disputes concerning what is natural or unnatural; and one may in general affirm, that we are not possess'd

of any very precise standard, by which these disputes can be decided. Frequent and rare depend upon the number of examples we have observ'd; and as this number may gradually encrease or diminish, 'twill be impossible to fix any exact boundaries betwixt them. We may only affirm on this head, that if ever there was any thing, which cou'd be call'd natural in this sense, the sentiments of morality certainly may; since there never was any nation of the world, nor any single person in any nation, who was utterly depriv'd of them, and who never, in any instance, show'd the least approbation or dislike of manners.[†] These sentiments are so rooted in our constitution and temper, that without entirely confounding the human mind by disease or madness, 'tis impossible to extirpate and destroy them.

9   But *nature* may also be oppos'd to artifice,[†] as well as to what is rare and unusual; and in this sense it may be disputed, whether the notions of virtue be natural or not. We readily forget, that the designs, and projects, and views of men are principles as necessary in their operation as heat and cold, moist and dry: But taking them to be free and entirely our own, 'tis usual for us to set them in opposition to the other principles of nature. Shou'd it, therefore, be demanded, whether the sense of virtue be natural or artificial, I am of opinion, *SB 475* that 'tis impossible for me at present to give any precise answer to this question. Perhaps it will appear afterwards,[†] that our sense of some virtues is artificial, and that of others natural. The discussion of this question will be more proper, when we enter upon an exact detail of each particular vice and virtue.[70]

10   Mean while it may not be amiss to observe from these definitions of *natural* and *unnatural*, that nothing can be more unphilosophical than those systems, which assert, that virtue is the same with what is natural, and vice with what is unnatural.[†] For in the first sense of the word, *nature*, as oppos'd to miracles, both vice and virtue are equally natural; and in the second sense, as oppos'd to what is unusual, perhaps virtue will be found to be the most unnatural. At least it must be own'd, that heroic virtue, being as unusual, is as little natural as the most brutal barbarity. As to the third sense of the word, 'tis certain, that both vice and virtue are equally artificial, and out of nature. For however it may be disputed, whether the notion of a merit or demerit in certain actions be natural or artificial, 'tis evident, that the actions themselves are artificial, and are perform'd with a certain design and intention; otherwise they cou'd never be rank'd under any of these denominations.[†] 'Tis impossible, therefore, that the character of natural and unnatural can ever, in any sense, mark the boundaries of vice and virtue.

11   Thus we are still brought back to our first position, that virtue is distinguish'd by the pleasure, and vice by the pain, that any action, sentiment or character gives us by the mere view and contemplation. This decision is very commodious; because it reduces us to this simple question, *Why any action or sentiment upon the general view or survey, gives a certain satisfaction or uneasiness?* in order to show

---

[70] In the following discourse *natural* is also oppos'd sometimes to *civil*, sometimes to *moral*.[†] The opposition will always discover the sense, in which it is taken.

the origin of its moral rectitude or depravity, without looking for any incompre-   *SB 476* hensible relations and qualities, which never did exist in nature, nor even in our imagination, by any clear and distinct conception. I flatter myself I have executed a great part of my present design by a state of the question, which appears to me so free from ambiguity and obscurity.

PART 2

Of justice and injustice

Sect. 1. *Justice, whether a natural or artificial virtue?*

1 I have already hinted,[†] that our sense of every kind of virtue is not natural; but that there are some virtues, that produce pleasure and approbation by means of an artifice or contrivance, which arises from the circumstances and necessities of mankind. Of this kind I assert *justice* to be; and shall endeavour to defend this opinion by a short, and, I hope, convincing argument, before I examine[†] the nature of the artifice, from which the sense of that virtue is deriv'd.

2   'Tis evident, that when we praise any actions, we regard only the motives that produc'd them, and consider the actions as signs or indications of certain principles in the mind and temper.[†] The external performance has no merit. We must look within[†] to find the moral quality. This we cannot do directly; and therefore fix our attention on actions, as on external signs. But these actions are still consider'd as signs; and the ultimate object of our praise and approbation is the motive, that produc'd them.

3   After the same manner, when we require any action, or blame a person for not performing it, we always suppose, that one in that situation shou'd be influenc'd by the proper motive of that action, and we esteem it vicious in him to be regardless of it. If we find, upon enquiry, that the virtuous motive was still powerful over his breast, tho' check'd in its operation by some circumstances unknown to us, we retract our blame, and have the same esteem for him, as if he had actually perform'd the action, which we require of him.

SB 478

4   It appears, therefore, that all virtuous actions derive their merit only from virtuous motives, and are consider'd merely as signs of those motives. From this principle I conclude, that the first virtuous motive, which bestows a merit on any action, can never be a regard to the virtue of that action, but must be some other natural motive or principle. To suppose, that the mere regard to the virtue of the action, may be the first motive, which produc'd the action, and render'd it virtuous, is to reason in a circle. Before we can have such a regard, the action must be really virtuous; and this virtue must be deriv'd from some virtuous motive: And consequently the virtuous motive must be different from the regard to the virtue of the action.[†] A virtuous motive is requisite to render an action virtuous. An action must be virtuous, before we can have a regard to its virtue. Some virtuous motive, therefore, must be antecedent to that regard.

5   Nor is this merely a metaphysical subtility; but enters into all our reasonings in common life, tho' perhaps we may not be able to place it in such distinct philosophical terms. We blame a father for neglecting his child. Why? because it shows a want of natural affection, which is the duty of every parent. Were not

natural affection a duty, the care of children cou'd not be a duty; and 'twere impossible we cou'd have the duty in our eye[†] in the attention we give to our off-spring. In this case, therefore, all men suppose a motive to the action distinct from a sense of duty.

6   Here is a man, that does many benevolent actions; relieves the distress'd, comforts the afflicted, and extends his bounty even to the greatest strangers. No character can be more amiable and virtuous. We regard these actions as proofs of the greatest humanity. This humanity bestows a merit on the actions. A regard to this merit is, therefore, a secondary consideration, and deriv'd from the antecedent principle of humanity, which is meritorious and laudable.

7   In short, it may be establish'd as an undoubted maxim, *that no action can be*   SB 479
virtuous, or morally good, unless there be in human nature some motive to produce it,
distinct from the sense of its morality.

8   But may not the sense of morality or duty produce an action, without any other motive? I answer, It may: But this is no objection to the present doctrine. When any virtuous motive or principle is common in human nature, a person, who feels his heart devoid of that principle, may hate himself upon that account, and may perform the action without the motive, from a certain sense of duty, in order to acquire by practice, that virtuous principle, or at least, to disguise to himself, as much as possible, his want of it. A man that really feels no gratitude in his temper, is still pleas'd to perform grateful actions, and thinks he has, by that means, fulfill'd his duty. Actions are at first only consider'd as signs of motives: But 'tis usual, in this case, as in all others, to fix our attention on the signs, and neglect, in some measure, the thing signify'd. But tho', on some occasions, a person may perform an action merely out of regard to its moral obligation, yet still this supposes in human nature some distinct principles, which are capable of producing the action, and whose moral beauty renders the action meritorious.[†]

9   Now to apply all this to the present case; I suppose a person to have lent me a sum of money, on condition that it be restor'd in a few days; and also suppose, that after the expiration of the term agreed on, he demands the sum: I ask, *What reason or motive have I to restore the money?* It will, perhaps, be said, that my regard to justice, and abhorrence of villainy and knavery, are sufficient reasons for me, if I have the least grain of honesty, or sense of duty and obligation. And this answer, no doubt, is just and satisfactory to man in his civiliz'd state, and when train'd up according to a certain discipline and education. But in his rude and more *natural* condition, if you are pleas'd to call such a condition natural,[†] this answer wou'd be rejected as perfectly unintelligible and sophistical. For one   SB 480
in that situation wou'd immediately ask you, *Wherein consists this honesty and justice, which you find in restoring a loan, and abstaining from the property of others?*[†]
It does not surely lie in the external action. It must, therefore, be plac'd in the motive, from which the external action is deriv'd. This motive can never be a regard to the honesty of the action. For 'tis a plain fallacy to say, that a virtuous motive is requisite to render an action honest, and at the same time that a regard

to the honesty is the motive of the action. We can never have a regard to the virtue of an action, unless the action be antecedently virtuous. No action can be virtuous, but so far as it proceeds from a virtuous motive. A virtuous motive, therefore, must precede the regard to the virtue; and 'tis impossible, that the virtuous motive and the regard to the virtue can be the same.

10   'Tis requisite, then, to find some motive to acts of justice and honesty, distinct from our regard to the honesty; and in this lies the great difficulty. For shou'd we say, that a concern for our private interest or reputation is the legitimate motive to all honest actions; it wou'd follow, that wherever that concern ceases, honesty can no longer have place. But 'tis certain, that self-love, when it acts at its liberty, instead of engaging us to honest actions, is the source of all injustice and violence; nor can a man ever correct those vices, without correcting and restraining the *natural* movements of that appetite.[†]

11   But shou'd it be affirm'd, that the reason or motive of such actions is the *regard to public interest*, to which nothing is more contrary than examples of injustice and dishonesty; shou'd this be said, I wou'd propose the three following considerations, as worthy of our attention. *First*, public interest is not naturally attach'd to the observation of the rules of justice; but is only connected with it, after an artificial convention for the establishment of these rules, as shall be shown more at large hereafter.[†] *Secondly*, if we suppose, that the loan was secret, and that it is necessary for the interest of the person, that the money be restor'd in the same manner (as when the lender wou'd conceal his riches), in that case the example ceases, and the public is no longer interested in the actions of the borrower;[†] tho' I suppose there is no moralist, who will affirm, that the duty and obligation ceases. *Thirdly*, experience sufficiently proves, that men, in the ordinary conduct of life, look not so far as the public interest, when they pay their creditors, perform their promises, and abstain from theft, and robbery, and injustice of every kind. That is a motive too remote and too sublime to affect the generality of mankind, and operate with any force in actions so contrary to private interest as are frequently those of justice and common honesty.

SB 481

12   In general, it may be affirm'd, that there is no such passion in human minds, as the love of mankind, merely as such, independent of personal qualities, of services, or of relation to ourself. 'Tis true, there is no human, and indeed no sensible, creature, whose happiness or misery does not, in some measure, affect us, when brought near to us, and represented in lively colours: But this proceeds merely from sympathy,[†] and is no proof of such an universal affection to mankind, since this concern extends itself beyond our own species. An affection betwixt the sexes is a passion evidently implanted in human nature; and this passion not only appears in its peculiar symptoms, but also in inflaming every other principle of affection, and raising a stronger love from beauty, wit, kindness, than what wou'd otherwise flow from them. Were there an universal love among all human creatures, it wou'd appear after the same manner. Any degree of a good quality wou'd cause a stronger affection than the same degree of a bad quality wou'd cause hatred; contrary to what we find by experience.

Men's tempers are different, and some have a propensity to the tender, and others to the rougher, affections: But in the main, we may affirm, that man in general, or human nature, is nothing but the object both of love and hatred,   *SB 482* and requires some other cause, which by a double relation of impressions and ideas, may excite these passions.[†] In vain wou'd we endeavour to elude this hypothesis. There are no phænomena that point out any such kind affection to men, independent of their merit, and every other circumstance. We love company in general; but 'tis as we love any other amusement. An *Englishman* in *Italy* is a friend: A *Europæan* in *China*; and perhaps a man wou'd be belov'd as such, were we to meet him in the moon. But this proceeds only from the relation to ourselves; which in these cases gathers force by being confin'd to a few persons.

13   If public benevolence, therefore, or a regard to the interests of mankind, cannot be the original motive to justice, much less can *private benevolence*, or a *regard to the interests of the party concern'd*, be this motive. For what if he be my enemy, and has given me just cause to hate him? What if he be a vicious man, and deserves the hatred of all mankind? What if he be a miser, and can make no use of what I wou'd deprive him of? What if he be a profligate debauchee, and wou'd rather receive harm than benefit from large possessions? What if I be in necessity, and have urgent motives to acquire something for my family? In all these cases, the original motive to justice wou'd fail; and consequently the justice itself, and along with it all property, right, and obligation.[†]

14   A rich man lies under a moral obligation to communicate to those in necessity a share of his superfluities. Were private benevolence the original motive to justice, a man wou'd not be oblig'd to leave others in the possession of more than he is oblig'd to give them. At least the difference wou'd be very inconsiderable. Men generally fix their affections more on what they are possess'd of, than on what they never enjoy'd: For this reason, it wou'd be greater cruelty to dispossess a man of any thing, than not to give it him. But who will assert, that this is the only foundation of justice?[†]

15   Besides, we must consider, that the chief reason, why men attach themselves   *SB 483* so much to their possessions is, that they consider them as their property, and as secur'd to them inviolably by the laws of society. But this is a secondary consideration, and dependent on the preceding notions of justice and property.[†]

16   A man's property is suppos'd to be fenc'd against every mortal, in every possible case. But private benevolence towards the proprietor is, and ought to be, weaker in some persons, than in others: And in many, or indeed in most persons, must absolutely fail. Private benevolence, therefore, is not the original motive of justice.[†]

17   From all this it follows, that we have naturally[†] no real or universal motive for observing the laws of equity, but the very equity and merit of that observance; and as no action can be equitable or meritorious, where it cannot arise from some separate motive, there is here an evident sophistry and reasoning in a circle. Unless, therefore, we will allow, that nature has establish'd a sophistry, and

render'd it necessary and unavoidable, we must allow, that the sense of justice and injustice is not deriv'd from nature, but arises artificially, tho' necessarily from education, and human conventions.

18   I shall add, as a corollary to this reasoning, that since no action can be laudable or blameable, without some motives or impelling passions, distinct from the sense of morals,[†] these distinct passions must have a great influence on that sense. 'Tis according to their general force in human nature, that we blame or praise. In judging of the beauty of animal bodies, we always carry in our eye the œconomy of a certain species; and where the limbs and features observe that proportion, which is common to the species, we pronounce them handsome and beautiful. In like manner we always consider the *natural* and *usual* force of the passions, when we determine concerning vice and virtue; and if the passions depart very much from the common measures on either side, they are always disapprov'd as vicious. A man naturally loves his children better than his nephews, his nephews better than his cousins, his cousins better than strangers, where *SB 484* every thing else is equal. Hence arise our common measures of duty, in preferring the one to the other. Our sense of duty always follows the common and natural course of our passions.[†]

19   To avoid giving offence, I must here observe, that when I deny justice to be a natural virtue, I make use of the word, *natural*, only as oppos'd to *artificial*.[†] In another sense of the word; as no principle of the human mind is more natural than a sense of virtue; so no virtue is more natural than justice. Mankind is an inventive species; and where an invention is obvious and absolutely necessary, it may as properly be said to be natural as any thing that proceeds immediately from original principles, without the intervention of thought or reflection. Tho' the rules of justice be *artificial*, they are not *arbitrary*. Nor is the expression improper to call them *laws of nature*;[†] if by *natural* we understand what is common to any species, or even if we confine it to mean what is inseparable from the species.

Sect. 2. *Of the origin of justice and property*

1   We now proceed to examine two questions, viz. *concerning the manner, in which the rules of justice are establish'd by the artifice of men*; and *concerning the reasons, which determine us to attribute to the observance or neglect of these rules a moral beauty and deformity*. These questions will appear afterwards to be distinct. We shall begin with the former.[†]

2   Of all the animals, with which this globe is peopled, there is none towards whom nature seems, at first sight, to have exercis'd more cruelty than towards man, in the numberless wants and necessities, with which she has loaded him, and in the slender means, which she affords to the relieving these necessities. In other creatures these two particulars generally compensate each other. If we consider the lion as a voracious and carnivorous animal, we shall easily discover *SB 485* him to be very necessitous; but if we turn our eye to his make and temper, his

agility, his courage, his arms, and his force, we shall find, that his advantages hold proportion with his wants. The sheep and ox are depriv'd of all these advantages; but their appetites are moderate, and their food is of easy purchase. In man alone, this unnatural conjunction of infirmity, and of necessity, may be observ'd in its greatest perfection. Not only the food, which is requir'd for his sustenance, flies his search and approach, or at least requires his labour to be produc'd, but he must be possess'd of cloaths and lodging, to defend him against the injuries of the weather; tho' to consider him only in himself, he is provided neither with arms, nor force, nor other natural abilities, which are in any degree answerable to so many necessities.[†]

3   'Tis by society alone he is able to supply his defects, and raise himself up to an equality with his fellow-creatures, and even acquire a superiority above them. By society all his infirmities are compensated; and tho' in that situation his wants multiply every moment upon him, yet his abilities are still more augmented, and leave him in every respect more satisfy'd and happy, than 'tis possible for him, in his savage and solitary condition, ever to become. When every individual person labours apart, and only for himself, his force is too small to execute any considerable work; his labour being employ'd in supplying all his different necessities, he never attains a perfection in any particular art; and as his force and success are not at all times equal, the least failure in either of these particulars must be attended with inevitable ruin and misery. Society provides a remedy for these *three* inconveniencies. By the conjunction of forces, our power is augmented: By the partition of employments, our ability encreases: And by mutual succour we are less expos'd to fortune and accidents. 'Tis by this additional *force*, *ability*, and *security*, that society becomes advantageous.[†]

4   But in order to form society, 'tis requisite not only that it be advantageous, but
also that men be sensible of its advantages; and 'tis impossible, in their wild uncultivated state, that by study and reflection alone, they shou'd ever be able to attain this knowledge. Most fortunately, therefore, there is conjoin'd to those necessities, whose remedies are remote and obscure, another necessity, which having a present and more obvious remedy, may justly be regarded as the first and original principle of human society. This necessity is no other than that natural appetite betwixt the sexes, which unites them together, and preserves their union,[†] till a new tye takes place in their concern for their common offspring.[†] This new concern becomes also a principle of union betwixt the parents and offspring, and forms a more numerous society; where the parents govern by the advantage of their superior strength and wisdom, and at the same time are restrain'd in the exercise of their authority by that natural affection, which they bear their children. In a little time, custom and habit operating on the tender minds of the children, makes them sensible of the advantages, which they may reap from society, as well as fashions them by degrees for it, by rubbing off those rough corners and untoward affections, which prevent their coalition.

5   For it must be confest, that however the circumstances of human nature may render an union necessary, and however those passions of lust and natural affection may seem to render it unavoidable; yet there are other particulars in our

natural temper, and in our *outward circumstances*, which are very incommodious, and are even contrary to the requisite conjunction. Among the former, we may justly esteem our *selfishness* to be the most considerable. I am sensible, that, generally speaking, the representations of this quality have been carry'd much too far; and that the descriptions, which certain philosophers[†] delight so much to form of mankind in this particular, are as wide of nature as any accounts of monsters, which we meet with in fables and romances. So far from thinking, that men have no affection for any thing beyond themselves, I am of opinion, that tho' it be rare to meet with one, who loves any single person better than himself; yet 'tis as rare to meet with one, in whom all the kind affections, taken together, do not over-ballance all the selfish. Consult common experience: Do you not see, that tho' the whole expence of the family be generally under the direction of the master of it, yet there are few that do not bestow the largest part of their fortunes on the pleasures of their wives, and the education of their children, reserving the smallest portion for their own proper use and entertainment? This is what we may observe concerning such as have those endearing ties; and may presume, that the case wou'd be the same with others, were they plac'd in a like situation.

6   But tho' this generosity must be acknowledg'd to the honour of human nature, we may at the same time remark, that so noble an affection, instead of fitting men for large societies, is almost as contrary to them, as the most narrow selfishness. For while each person loves himself better than any other single person, and in his love to others bears the greatest affection to his relations and acquaintance, this must necessarily produce an opposition of passions, and a consequent opposition of actions; which cannot but be dangerous to the new-establish'd union.[†]

7   'Tis however worth while to remark, that this contrariety of passions wou'd be attended with but small danger, did it not concur with a peculiarity in our *outward circumstances*, which affords it an opportunity of exerting itself. There are three different species of goods, which we are possess'd of; the internal satisfaction of our mind, the external advantages of our body, and the enjoyment of such possessions as we have acquir'd by our industry and good fortune.[†] We are perfectly secure in the enjoyment of the first. The second may be ravish'd from us, but can be of no advantage to him who deprives us of them. The last only are both expos'd to the violence of others, and may be transferr'd without suffering any loss or alteration; while at the same time, there is not a sufficient quantity of them to supply every one's desires and necessities. As the improvement, therefore, of these goods is the chief advantage of society, so the *instability* of their possession, along with their *scarcity*, is the chief impediment.[†]

8   In vain shou'd we expect to find, in *uncultivated nature*, a remedy to this inconvenience; or hope for any inartificial principle of the human mind, which might controul those partial affections, and make us overcome the temptations arising from our circumstances. The idea of justice can never serve to this purpose, or be taken for a natural principle, capable of inspiring men with an equitable conduct towards each other. That virtue, as it is now understood, wou'd never

have been dream'd of among rude and savage men.[†] For the notion of injury or injustice implies an immorality or vice committed against some other person: And as every immorality is deriv'd from some defect or unsoundness of the passions, and as this defect must be judg'd of, in a great measure, from the ordinary course of nature in the constitution of the mind; 'twill be easy to know, whether we be guilty of any immorality, with regard to others, by considering the natural, and usual force of those several affections, which are directed towards them. Now it appears, that in the original frame of our mind, our strongest attention is confin'd to ourselves; our next is extended to our relations and acquaintance; and 'tis only the weakest which reaches to strangers and indifferent persons. This partiality, then, and unequal affection, must not only have an influence on our behaviour and conduct in society, but even on our ideas of vice and virtue; so as to make us regard any remarkable transgression of such a degree of partiality, either by too great an enlargement, or contraction of the affections, as vicious and immoral.[†] This we may observe in our common judgments concerning actions, where we blame a person, who either centers all his affections in his family, or is so regardless of them, as, in any opposition of interest, to give the preference to a stranger, or mere chance acquaintance. From all which it follows, that our natural uncultivated ideas of morality, instead of providing a remedy for the partiality of our affections, do rather conform themselves to that partiality, and give it an additional force and influence.

SB 489

9   The remedy, then, is not deriv'd from nature, but from *artifice*; or more properly speaking, nature provides a remedy in the judgment and understanding, for what is irregular and incommodious in the affections. For when men, from their early education in society, have become sensible of the infinite advantages that result from it, and have besides acquir'd a new affection to company and conversation; and when they have observ'd, that the principal disturbance in society arises from those goods, which we call external, and from their looseness and easy transition from one person to another; they must seek for a remedy, by putting these goods, as far as possible, on the same footing with the fix'd and constant advantages of the mind and body. This can be done after no other manner, than by a convention enter'd into by all the members of the society to bestow stability on the possession of those external goods, and leave every one in the peaceable enjoyment of what he may acquire by his fortune and industry. By this means, every one knows what he may safely possess; and the passions are restrain'd in their partial and contradictory motions. Nor is such a restraint contrary to these passions; for if so, it cou'd never be enter'd into, nor maintain'd; but it is only contrary to their heedless and impetuous movement. Instead of departing from our own interest, or from that of our nearest friends, by abstaining from the possessions of others, we cannot better consult both these interests, than by such a convention; because it is by that means we maintain society, which is so necessary to their well-being and subsistence, as well as to our own.

10   This convention is not of the nature of a *promise*: For even promises themselves, as we shall see afterwards, arise from human conventions.[†] It is only a

SB 490

general sense of common interest; which sense all the members of the society express to one another, and which induces them to regulate their conduct by certain rules. I observe, that it will be for my interest to leave another in the possession of his goods, *provided* he will act in the same manner with regard to me. He is sensible of a like interest in the regulation of his conduct. When this common sense of interest is mutually express'd, and is known to both, it produces a suitable resolution and behaviour. And this may properly enough be call'd a convention or agreement betwixt us, tho' without the interposition of a promise; since the actions of each of us have a reference to those of the other, and are perform'd upon the supposition, that something is to be perform'd on the other part. Two men, who pull the oars of a boat, do it by an agreement or convention, tho' they have never given promises to each other. Nor is the rule concerning the stability of possession the less deriv'd from human conventions, that it arises gradually, and acquires force by a slow progression, and by our repeated experience of the inconveniencies of transgressing it. On the contrary, this experience assures us still more, that the sense of interest has become common to all our fellows, and gives us a confidence of the future regularity of their conduct: And 'tis only on the expectation of this, that our moderation and abstinence are founded. In like manner are languages gradually establish'd by human conventions without any promise. In like manner do gold and silver become the common measures of exchange, and are esteem'd sufficient payment for what is of a hundred times their value.

11   After this convention, concerning abstinence from the possessions of others, is enter'd into, and every one has acquir'd a stability in his possessions, there immediately arise the ideas of justice and injustice; as also those of *property*, *right*, and *obligation*. The latter are altogether unintelligible without first understanding the former. Our property is nothing but those goods, whose constant possession is establish'd by the laws of society; that is, by the laws of justice. Those, therefore, who make use of the words *property*, or *right*, or *obligation*, before they have explain'd the origin of justice, or even make use of them in that explication, are guilty of a very gross fallacy, and can never reason upon any solid foundation.† A man's property is some object related to him. This relation is not natural, but moral, and founded on justice. 'Tis very preposterous, therefore, to imagine, that we can have any idea of property, without fully comprehending the nature of justice, and showing its origin in the artifice and contrivance of men. The origin of justice explains that of property. The same artifice gives rise to both. As our first and most natural sentiment of morals is founded on the nature of our passions, and gives the preference to ourselves and friends, above strangers; 'tis impossible there can be naturally any such thing as a fix'd right or property, while the opposite passions of men impel them in contrary directions, and are not restrain'd by any convention or agreement.

12   No one can doubt, that the convention for the distinction of property, and for the stability of possession, is of all circumstances the most necessary to the establishment of human society, and that after the agreement for the fixing and observing of this rule, there remains little or nothing to be done towards

SB 491

settling a perfect harmony and concord. All the other passions, beside this of interest, are either easily restrain'd, or are not of such pernicious consequence, when indulg'd. *Vanity* is rather to be esteem'd a social passion, and a bond of union among men. *Pity* and *love* are to be consider'd in the same light. And as to *envy* and *revenge*, tho' pernicious, they operate only by intervals, and are directed against particular persons, whom we consider as our superiors or enemies. This avidity alone, of acquiring goods and possessions for ourselves *SB 492* and our nearest friends, is insatiable, perpetual, universal, and directly destructive of society. There scarce is any one, who is not actuated by it; and there is no one, who has not reason to fear from it, when it acts without any restraint, and gives way to its first and most natural movements. So that upon the whole, we are to esteem the difficulties in the establishment of society, to be greater or less, according to those we encounter in regulating and restraining this passion.

13   'Tis certain, that no affection of the human mind has both a sufficient force, and a proper direction to counter-ballance the love of gain, and render men fit members of society, by making them abstain from the possessions of others. Benevolence to strangers is too weak for this purpose; and as to the other passions, they rather inflame this avidity, when we observe, that the larger our possessions are, the more ability we have of gratifying all our appetites. There is no passion, therefore, capable of controuling the interested affection, but the very affection itself, by an alteration of its direction. Now this alteration must necessarily take place upon the least reflection; since 'tis evident, that the passion is much better satisfy'd by its restraint, than by its liberty, and that by preserving society, we make much greater advances in the acquiring possessions, than by running into the solitary and forlorn condition, which must follow upon violence and an universal licence. The question, therefore, concerning the wickedness or goodness of human nature, enters not in the least into that other question concerning the origin of society; nor is there any thing to be consider'd but the degrees of men's sagacity or folly. For whether the passion of self-interest be esteem'd vicious or virtuous, 'tis all a case; since itself alone restrains it: So that if it be virtuous, men become social by their virtue; if vicious, their vice has the same effect.[†]

14   Now as 'tis by establishing the rule for the stability of possession, that this *SB 493* passion[†] restrains itself; if that rule be very abstruse, and of difficult invention; society must be esteem'd, in a manner, accidental, and the effect of many ages. But if it be found, that nothing can be more simple and obvious than that rule; that every parent, in order to preserve peace among his children, must establish it; and that these first rudiments of justice must every day be improv'd, as the society enlarges: If all this appear evident, as it certainly must, we may conclude, that 'tis utterly impossible for men to remain any considerable time in that savage condition, which precedes society; but that his very first state and situation may justly be esteem'd social. This, however, hinders not, but that philosophers may, if they please, extend their reasoning to the suppos'd *state of nature;*[†]

provided they allow it to be a mere philosophical fiction, which never had, and never cou'd have any reality. Human nature being compos'd of two principal parts, which are requisite in all its actions, the affections and understanding; 'tis certain, that the blind motions of the former, without the direction of the latter, incapacitate men for society: And it may be allow'd us to consider separately the effects, that result from the separate operations of these two component parts of the mind. The same liberty may be permitted to moral, which is allow'd to natural philosophers; and 'tis very usual with the latter to consider any motion as compounded and consisting of two parts separate from each other, tho' at the same time they acknowledge it to be in itself uncompounded and inseparable.

15   This *state of nature*, therefore, is to be regarded as a mere fiction, not unlike that of the *golden age*,[†] which poets have invented; only with this difference, that the former is describ'd as full of war, violence and injustice; whereas the latter is painted out to us, as the most charming and most peaceable condition, that can possibly be imagin'd. The seasons, in that first age of nature, were so temperate, if we may believe the poets, that there was no necessity for men to provide themselves with cloaths and houses as a security against the violence of heat and cold.   *SB 494* The rivers flow'd with wine and milk: The oaks yielded honey; and nature spontaneously produc'd her greatest delicacies.[†] Nor were these the chief advantages of that happy age. The storms and tempests were not alone remov'd from nature; but those more furious tempests were unknown to human breasts, which now cause such uproar, and engender such confusion. Avarice, ambition, cruelty, selfishness, were never heard of: Cordial affection, compassion, sympathy, were the only movements, with which the human mind was yet acquainted. Even the distinction of *mine* and *thine* was banish'd from that happy race of mortals, and carry'd with them the very notions of property and obligation, justice and injustice.

16   This, no doubt, is to be regarded as an idle fiction; but yet deserves our attention, because nothing can more evidently show the origin of those virtues, which are the subjects of our present enquiry. I have already observ'd, that justice takes its rise from human conventions; and that these are intended as a remedy to some inconveniencies, which proceed from the concurrence of certain *qualities* of the human mind with the *situation* of external objects. The qualities of the mind are *selfishness* and *limited generosity*: And the situation of external objects is their *easy change*, join'd to their *scarcity* in comparison of the wants and desires of men. But however philosophers may have been bewilder'd in those speculations, poets have been guided more infallibly, by a certain taste or common instinct, which in most kinds of reasoning goes farther than any of that art and philosophy, with which we have been yet acquainted. They easily perceiv'd, if every man had a tender regard for another, or if nature supply'd abundantly all our wants and desires, that the jealousy of interest, which justice supposes, cou'd no longer have place; nor wou'd there be any occasion for those distinctions and limits of property and possession, which at present are in use among mankind. Encrease

to a sufficient degree the benevolence of men, or the bounty of nature, and you *SB 495* render justice useless, by supplying its place with much nobler virtues, and more valuable blessings. The selfishness of men is animated by the few possessions we have, in proportion to our wants; and 'tis to restrain this selfishness, that men have been oblig'd to separate themselves from the community, and to distinguish betwixt their own goods and those of others.

17   Nor need we have recourse to the fictions of poets to learn this; but beside the reason of the thing, may discover the same truth by common experience and observation. 'Tis easy to remark, that a cordial affection renders all things common among friends; and that marry'd people in particular mutually lose their property, and are unacquainted with the *mine* and *thine*, which are so necessary, and yet cause such disturbance in human society. The same effect arises from any alteration in the circumstances of mankind; as when there is such a plenty of any thing as satisfies all the desires of men: In which case the distinction of property is entirely lost, and every thing remains in common. This we may observe with regard to air and water, tho' the most valuable of all external objects; and may easily conclude, that if men were supply'd with every thing in the same abundance, or if *every one* had the same affection and tender regard for *every one* as for himself; justice and injustice wou'd be equally unknown among mankind.

18   Here then is a proposition, which, I think may be regarded as certain, *that 'tis only from the selfishness and confin'd generosity of man, along with the scanty provision nature has made for his wants, that justice derives its origin.* If we look backward we shall find, that this proposition bestows an additional force on some of those observations, which we have already made on this subject.

19   *First,* we may conclude from it, that a regard to public interest, or a strong extensive benevolence, is not our first and original motive for the observation of the rules of justice;[†] since 'tis allow'd, that if men were endow'd with such a *SB 496* benevolence, these rules wou'd never have been dreamt of.

20   *Secondly,* we may conclude from the same principle, that the sense of justice is not founded on reason, or on the discovery of certain connexions and relations of ideas, which are eternal, immutable, and universally obligatory.[†] For since it is confest, that such an alteration as that above-mention'd, in the temper and circumstances of mankind, wou'd entirely alter our duties and obligations, 'tis necessary upon the common system, *that the sense of virtue is deriv'd from reason,* to show the change which this must produce in the relations and ideas. But 'tis evident, that the only cause, why the extensive generosity of man, and the perfect abundance of every thing, wou'd destroy the very idea of justice, is because they render it useless; and that, on the other hand, his confin'd benevolence, and his necessitous condition, give rise to that virtue, only by making it requisite to the public interest, and to that of every individual. 'Twas therefore a concern for our own, and the public interest, which made us establish the laws of justice; and nothing can be more certain, than that it is not any relation of ideas, which gives us this concern, but our impressions and sentiments, without which every thing in nature is perfectly indifferent to us, and can never in the least

affect us. The sense of justice, therefore, is not founded on our ideas, but on our impressions.

21   *Thirdly*, we may farther confirm the foregoing proposition, *that those impressions, which give rise to this sense of justice, are not natural to the mind of man, but arise from artifice and human conventions.* For since any considerable alteration of temper and circumstances destroys equally justice and injustice; and since such an alteration has an effect only by changing our own and the public interest; it follows, that the first establishment of the rules of justice depends on these different interests. But if men pursu'd the public interest naturally, and with a hearty affection, they wou'd never have dream'd of restraining each other by these rules; and if they pursu'd their own interest, without any precaution, they wou'd run head-long into every kind of injustice and violence. These rules, therefore, are artificial, and seek their end in an oblique and indirect manner; nor is the interest, which gives rise to them, of a kind that cou'd be pursu'd by the natural and inartificial passions of men.   *SB 497*

22   To make this more evident, consider, that tho' the rules of justice are establish'd merely by interest, their connexion with interest is somewhat singular, and is different from what may be observ'd on other occasions. A single act of justice is frequently contrary to *public interest*; and were it to stand alone, without being follow'd by other acts, may, in itself, be very prejudicial to society. When a man of merit, of a beneficent disposition, restores a great fortune to a miser, or a seditious bigot, he has acted justly and laudably, but the public is a real sufferer. Nor is every single act of justice, consider'd apart, more conducive to private interest, than to public; and 'tis easily conceiv'd how a man may impoverish himself by a signal instance of integrity, and have reason to wish, that with regard to that single act, the laws of justice were for a moment suspended in the universe. But however single acts of justice may be contrary, either to public or private interest, 'tis certain, that the whole plan or scheme is highly conducive, or indeed absolutely requisite, both to the support of society, and the well-being of every individual. 'Tis impossible to separate the good from the ill. Property must be stable, and must be fix'd by general rules. Tho' in one instance the public be a sufferer, this momentary ill is amply compensated by the steady prosecution of the rule, and by the peace and order, which it establishes in society. And even every individual person must find himself a gainer, on ballancing the account; since, without justice, society must immediately dissolve, and every one must fall into that savage and solitary condition, which is infinitely worse than the worst situation that can possibly be suppos'd in society. When therefore men have had experience enough to observe, that whatever may be the consequence of any single act of justice, perform'd by a single person, yet the whole system of actions, concurr'd in by the whole society, is infinitely advantageous to the whole, and to every part; it is not long before justice and property take place. Every member of society is sensible of this interest: Every one expresses this sense to his fellows, along with the resolution he has taken of squaring his actions by it, on condition that others will do the same. No more is requisite to induce any one of them to perform an act of justice, who has the first opportunity. This becomes an   *SB 498*

example to others. And thus justice establishes itself by a kind of convention or agreement; that is, by a sense of interest, suppos'd to be common to all, and where every single act is perform'd in expectation that others are to perform the like. Without such a convention, no one wou'd ever have dream'd, that there was such a virtue as justice, or have been induc'd to conform his actions to it. Taking any single act, my justice may be pernicious in every respect; and 'tis only upon the supposition, that others are to imitate my example, that I can be induc'd to embrace that virtue; since nothing but this combination can render justice advantageous, or afford me any motives to conform my self to its rules.

23   We come now to the *second* question we propos'd, viz. *Why we annex the idea of virtue to justice, and of vice to injustice?*[†] This question will not detain us long after the principles, which we have already establish'd.[†] All we can say of it at present will be dispatch'd in a few words: And for farther satisfaction, the reader must wait till we come to the *third* part of this book. The *natural* obligation to justice, *viz.* interest, has been fully explain'd; but as to the *moral* obligation, or the sentiment of right and wrong, 'twill first be requisite to examine the natural virtues, before we can give a full and satisfactory account of it.[†]

24   After men have found by experience, that their selfishness and confin'd generosity, acting at their liberty, totally incapacitate them for society; and at the same time have observ'd, that society is necessary to the satisfaction of those very passions, they are naturally induc'd to lay themselves under the restraint of such rules, as may render their commerce more safe and commodious. To the imposition then, and observance of these rules, both in general, and in every particular instance, they are at first mov'd only by a regard to interest; and this motive, on the first formation of society, is sufficiently strong and forcible. But when society has become numerous, and has encreas'd to a tribe or nation, this interest is more remote; nor do men so readily perceive, that disorder and confusion follow upon every breach of these rules, as in a more narrow and contracted society. But tho' in our own actions we may frequently lose sight of that interest, which we have in maintaining order, and may follow a lesser and more present interest, we never fail to observe the prejudice we receive, either mediately or immediately, from the injustice of others; as not being in that case either blinded by passion, or byass'd by any contrary temptation. Nay when the injustice is so distant from us, as no way to affect our interest, it still displeases us; because we consider it as prejudicial to human society, and pernicious to every one that approaches the person guilty of it. We partake of their uneasiness by *sympathy*; and as every thing, which gives uneasiness in human actions, upon the general survey, is call'd *vice*, and whatever produces satisfaction, in the same manner, is denominated *virtue*; this is the reason why the sense of moral good and evil follows upon justice and injustice. And tho' this sense, in the present case, be deriv'd only from contemplating the actions of others, yet we fail not to extend it even to our own actions. The *general rule* reaches beyond those instances, from which it arose; while at the same time we naturally *sympathize* with others in the sentiments they entertain of us. Thus *self-interest* is the original motive to the

establishment of justice: But a *sympathy* with *public* interest is the source of the *moral* approbation, which attends that virtue. This latter principle of sympathy is too weak to controul our passions; but has sufficient force to influence our taste, and give us the sentiments of approbation or blame.

25   Tho' this progress of the sentiments be *natural*, and even necessary, 'tis certain, that it is here forwarded by the artifice of politicians, who, in order to govern men more easily, and preserve peace in human society, have endeavour'd to produce an esteem for justice, and an abhorrence of injustice. This, no doubt, must have its effect; but nothing can be more evident, than that the matter has been carry'd too far by certain writers on morals, who seem to have employ'd their utmost efforts to extirpate all sense of virtue from among mankind. Any artifice of politicians may assist nature in the producing of those sentiments, which she suggests to us, and may even on some occasions, produce alone an approbation or esteem for any particular action; but 'tis impossible it shou'd be the sole cause of the distinction we make betwixt vice and virtue. For if nature did not aid us in this particular, 'twou'd be in vain for politicians to talk of *honourable* or *dishonourable, praise-worthy* or *blameable.*† These words wou'd be perfectly unintelligible, and wou'd no more have any idea annex'd to them, than if they were of a tongue perfectly unknown to us. The utmost politicians can perform, is, to extend the natural sentiments beyond their original bounds; but still nature must furnish the materials, and give us some notion of moral distinctions.

26   As public praise and blame encrease our esteem for justice; so private education and instruction contribute to the same effect. For as parents easily observe, that a man is the more useful, both to himself and others, the greater degree of probity and honour he is endow'd with; and that those principles have greater force, when custom and education assist interest and reflection: For these reasons they are induc'd to inculcate on their children, from their earliest infancy, the principles of probity, and teach them to regard the observance of those rules, by which society is maintain'd, as worthy and honourable, and their violation as base and infamous. By this means the sentiments of honour may take root in their tender minds, and acquire such firmness and solidity, that they may fall little short of those principles, which are the most essential to our natures, and the most deeply radicated in our internal constitution.

27   What farther contributes to encrease their solidity, is the interest of our reputation, after the opinion, *that a merit or demerit attends justice or injustice*, is once firmly establish'd among mankind. There is nothing, which touches us more nearly than our reputation, and nothing on which our reputation more depends than our conduct, with relation to the property of others. For this reason, every one, who has any regard to his character, or who intends to live on good terms with mankind, must fix an inviolable law to himself, never, by any temptation, to be induc'd to violate those principles, which are essential to a man of probity and honour.

28   I shall make only one observation before I leave this subject, *viz.* that tho' I assert, that in the *state of nature*, or that imaginary state, which preceded society,

there be neither justice nor injustice, yet I assert not, that it was allowable, in such a state, to violate the property of others.[†] I only maintain, that there was no such thing as property; and consequently cou'd be no such thing as justice or injustice. I shall have occasion to make a similar reflection with regard to *promises*, when I come to treat of them;[†] and I hope this reflection, when duly weigh'd, will suffice to remove all odium from the foregoing opinions, with regard to justice and injustice.

Sect. 3. *Of the rules, which determine property*

1   Tho' the establishment of the rule, concerning the stability of possession, be not only useful, but even absolutely necessary to human society, it can never serve to any purpose, while it remains in such general terms. Some method must be *SB 502* shown, by which we may distinguish what particular goods are to be assign'd to each particular person, while the rest of mankind are excluded from their possession and enjoyment. Our next business, then, must be to discover the reasons which modify this general rule, and fit it to the common use and practice of the world.

2   'Tis obvious, that those reasons are not deriv'd from any utility or advantage, which either the *particular* person or the public may reap from his enjoyment of any *particular* goods, beyond what wou'd result from the possession of them by any other person. 'Twere better, no doubt, that every one were possess'd of what is most suitable to him, and proper for his use: But besides, that this relation of fitness may be common to several at once, 'tis liable to so many controversies, and men are so partial and passionate in judging of these controversies, that such a loose and uncertain rule wou'd be absolutely incompatible with the peace of human society. The convention concerning the stability of possession is enter'd into, in order to cut off all occasions of discord and contention; and this end wou'd never be attain'd, were we allow'd to apply this rule differently in every particular case, according to every particular utility, which might be discover'd in such an application. Justice, in her decisions, never regards the fitness or unfitness of objects to particular persons, but conducts herself by more extensive views. Whether a man be generous, or a miser, he is equally well receiv'd by her, and obtains with the same facility a decision in his favours, even for what is entirely useless to him.[†]

3   It follows, therefore, that the general rule, *that possession must be stable*, is not apply'd by particular judgments, but by other general rules, which must extend to the whole society, and be inflexible either by spite or favour. To illustrate this, I propose the following instance. I first consider men in their savage and solitary condition; and suppose, that being sensible of the misery of that *SB 503* state, and foreseeing the advantages that wou'd result from society, they seek each other's company, and make an offer of mutual protection and assistance. I also suppose, that they are endow'd with such sagacity as immediately to perceive, that the chief impediment to this project of society and partnership lies in the avidity and selfishness of their natural temper; to remedy which, they

enter into a convention for the stability of possession, and for mutual restraint and forbearance. I am sensible, that this method of proceeding is not altogether natural; but besides that I here only suppose those reflections to be form'd at once, which in fact arise insensibly and by degrees; besides this, I say, 'tis very possible, that several persons, being by different accidents separated from the societies, to which they formerly belong'd, may be oblig'd to form a new society among themselves;† in which case they are entirely in the situation above-mention'd.

4   'Tis evident, then, that their first difficulty, in this situation, after the general convention for the establishment of society, and for the constancy of possession, is, how to separate their possessions, and assign to each his particular portion, which he must for the future inalterably enjoy. This difficulty will not detain them long; but it must immediately occur, as the most natural expedient, that every one continue to enjoy what he is at present master of, and that property or constant possession be conjoin'd to the immediate possession. Such is the effect of custom, that it not only reconciles us to any thing we have long enjoy'd, but even gives us an affection for it, and makes us prefer it to other objects, which may be more valuable, but are less known to us. What has long lain under our eye, and has often been employ'd to our advantage, *that* we are always the most unwilling to part with; but can easily live without possessions, which we never have enjoy'd, and are not accustom'd to. 'Tis evident, therefore, that men wou'd easily acquiesce in this expedient, *that every one continue to enjoy what he is at present possess'd of*; and this is the reason, why they wou'd so naturally agree in preferring it.[71]   *SB 504*

---

[71] No questions in philosophy are more difficult, than when a number of causes present themselves for the same phænomenon, to determine which is the principal and predominant. There seldom is any very precise argument to fix our choice, and men must be contented to be guided by a kind of taste or fancy, arising from analogy, and a comparison of similar instances. Thus, in the present case, there are, no doubt, motives of public interest for most of the rules, which determine property; but still I suspect, that these rules are principally fix'd by the imagination, or the more frivolous properties of our thought and conception. I shall continue to explain these causes, leaving it to the reader's choice, whether he will prefer those deriv'd from public utility, or those deriv'd from the imagination. We shall begin with the right of the present possessor.

2   'Tis a quality, which I have already observ'd in human nature,[a] that when two objects appear in a close relation to each other, the mind is apt to ascribe to them an additional relation, in order to compleat the union; and this inclination is so strong, as often to make us run into errors (such as that of the conjunction of thought and matter) if we find that they can serve to that purpose. Many of our impressions are incapable of place or local position;† and yet those very impressions we suppose to have a local conjunction with the impressions of sight and touch, merely because they are conjoin'd by causation, and are already united in the imagination. Since, therefore, we can feign a new relation, and even an absurd one, in order to compleat any union, 'twill easily be imagin'd, that if there be any relations, which depend on the mind, 'twill readily conjoin them to any preceding relation, and unite, by a new bond, such objects as have already an union in the fancy. Thus for instance, we never fail, in our arrangement of bodies, to place those which are *resembling* in *contiguity* to each other, or at least in *correspondent* points of view; because we feel a satisfaction in joining the relation of contiguity to that of resemblance, or the resemblance of situation to that of qualities. And this is easily accounted for from the known properties of human nature.† When the mind is determin'd to join certain objects, but undetermin'd in its choice of the particular objects, it naturally turns its eye

5   But we may observe, that tho' the rule of the assignment of property to the   *SB 505*
present possessor be natural, and by that means useful, yet its utility extends not
beyond the first formation of society; nor wou'd any thing be more pernicious,
than the constant observance of it; by which restitution wou'd be excluded, and
every injustice wou'd be authoriz'd and rewarded. We must, therefore, seek for
some other circumstance, that may give rise to property after society is once
establish'd; and of this kind, I find four most considerable, *viz.* OCCUPATION, PRE-
SCRIPTION, ACCESSION, and SUCCESSION. We shall briefly examine each of these,
beginning with *occupation.*[†]

6   The possession of all external goods is changeable and uncertain; which is one
of the most considerable impediments to the establishment of society, and is the
reason why, by universal agreement, express or tacit, men restrain themselves by
what we now call the rules of justice and equity. The misery of the condition,
which precedes this restraint, is the cause why we submit to that remedy as
quickly as possible; and this affords an easy reason, why we annex the idea of
property to the first possession, or to *occupation.* Men are unwilling to leave
property in suspence, even for the shortest time, or open the least door to violence and disorder. To which we may add, that the first possession always
engages the attention most; and did we neglect it, there wou'd be no colour of
reason for assigning property to any succeeding possession.[72]

7   There remains nothing, but to determine exactly, what is meant by posses-   *SB 506*
sion; and this is not so easy as may at first sight be imagin'd. We are said to be in
possession of any thing, not only when we immediately touch it, but also when
we are so situated with respect to it, as to have it in our power to use it; and may
move, alter, or destroy it, according to our present pleasure or advantage. This
relation, then, is a species of cause and effect; and as property is nothing but a

---

to such as are related together. They are already united in the mind: They present themselves at the   *SB 504*
same time to the conception; and instead of requiring any new reason for their conjunction, it
wou'd require a very powerful reason to make us over-look this natural affinity. This we shall have
occasion to explain more fully afterwards, when we come to treat of *beauty.*[†] In the mean time, we
may content ourselves with observing, that the same love of order and uniformity, which arranges
the books in a library, and the chairs in a parlour, contributes to the formation of society, and to the
well-being of mankind, by modifying the general rule concerning the stability of possession. As
property forms a relation betwixt a person and an object, 'tis natural to found it on some preceding
relation; and as property is nothing but a constant possession, secur'd by the laws of society, 'tis   *SB 505*
natural to add it to the present possession, which is a relation that resembles it. For this also has its
influence. If it be natural to conjoin all sorts of relations, 'tis more so, to conjoin such relations as are
resembling, and are related together.
                              [a] Book 1. Part 4. Sect. 5.[†]   *SB 504*

[72] Some philosophers account for the right of occupation, by saying, that every one has a prop-   *SB 505*
erty in his own labour; and when he joins that labour to any thing, it gives him the property of the
whole:[†] But, 1. There are several kinds of occupation, where we cannot be said to join our labour to
the object we acquire: As when we possess a meadow by grazing our cattle upon it. 2. This accounts
for the matter by means of *accession*; which is taking a needless circuit.[†] 3. We cannot be said to join
our labour to any thing but in a figurative sense. Properly speaking, we only make an alteration on it   *SB 506*
by our labour. This forms a relation betwixt us and the object; and thence arises the property,
according to the preceding principles.[†]

stable possession,[†] deriv'd from the rules of justice, or the conventions of men, 'tis to be consider'd as the same species of relation. But here we may observe, that as the power of using any object becomes more or less certain, according as the interruptions we may meet with are more or less probable; and as this probability may encrease by insensible degrees; 'tis in many cases impossible to determine when possession begins or ends; nor is there any certain standard, by which we can decide such controversies. A wild boar, that falls into our snares, is deem'd to be in our possession, if it be impossible for him to escape. But what do we mean by impossible? How do we separate this impossibility from an improbability? And how distinguish that exactly from a probability? Mark the precise limits of the one and the other, and show the standard, by which we may decide all disputes that may arise, and, as we find by experience, frequently do arise upon this subject?[73]

---

[73] If we seek a solution of these difficulties in reason and public interest, we never shall find satisfaction; and if we look for it in the imagination, 'tis evident, that the qualities, which operate upon that faculty, run so insensibly and gradually into each other, that 'tis impossible to give them any precise bounds or termination. The difficulties on this head must encrease, when we consider, that our judgment alters very sensibly, according to the subject, and that the same power and proximity will be deem'd possession in one case, which is not esteem'd such in another. A person, who has hunted a hare to the last degree of weariness, wou'd look upon it as an injustice for another to rush in before him, and seize his prey. But the same person, advancing to pluck an apple,[†] that hangs within his reach, has no reason to complain, if another, more alert, passes him, and takes possession. What is the reason of this difference, but that immobility, not being natural to the hare, but the effect of industry, forms in that case a strong relation with the hunter, which is wanting in the other?   *SB 507*

2   Here then it appears, that a certain and infallible power of enjoyment, without touch or some other sensible relation, often produces not property: And I farther observe, that a sensible relation, without any present power, is sometimes sufficient to give a title to any object. The sight of a thing is seldom a considerable relation, and is only regarded as such, when the object is hidden, or very obscure; in which case we find, that the view alone conveys a property; according to that maxim, *that even a whole continent belongs to the nation, which first discover'd it.* 'Tis however remarkable, that both in the case of discovery and that of possession, the first discoverer and possessor must join to the relation an intention of rendering himself proprietor, otherwise the relation will not have its effect; and that because the connexion in our fancy betwixt the property and the relation is not so great, but that it requires to be help'd by such an intention.

3   From all these circumstances, 'tis easy to see how perplex'd many questions may become concerning the acquisition of property by occupation; and the least effort of thought may present us with instances, which are not susceptible of any reasonable decision. If we prefer examples, which are real, to such as are feign'd, we may consider the following one, which is to be met with in almost every writer,[†] that has treated of the laws of nature.

4   Two *Grecian* colonies, leaving their native country, in search of new seats, were inform'd that a city near them was deserted by its inhabitants. To know the truth of this report, they dispatch'd at once two messengers, one from each colony; who finding on their approach, that their information   *SB 508* was true, begun a race together with an intention to take possession of the city, each of them for his countrymen. One of these messengers, finding that he was not an equal match for the other, launch'd his spear at the gates of the city, and was so fortunate as to fix it there before the arrival of his companion. This produc'd a dispute betwixt the two colonies, which of them was the proprietor of the empty city; and this dispute still subsists among philosophers. For my part I find the dispute impossible to be decided, and that because the whole question hangs upon the fancy, which in this case is not possess'd of any precise or determinate standard, upon which it can give sentence.

8   But such disputes may not only arise concerning the real existence of prop-   *SB 507*
erty and possession, but also concerning their extent; and these disputes
are often susceptible of no decision, or can be decided by no other faculty than
the imagination. A person who lands on the shore of a small island, that is desart
and uncultivated, is deem'd its possessor from the very first moment, and
acquires the property of the whole; because the object is there bounded and cir-
cumscrib'd in the fancy, and at the same time is proportion'd to the new possessor. The same person landing on a desart island, as large as *Great Britain*,
extends his property no farther than his immediate possession; tho' a numerous
colony are esteem'd the proprietors of the whole from the instant of their
debarkment.[†]

9   But it often happens, that the title of first possession becomes obscure thro'
time; and that 'tis impossible to determine many controversies, which may arise
concerning it. In that case long possession or *prescription*[†] naturally takes place,   *SB 508*
and gives a person a sufficient property in any thing he enjoys. The nature of
human society admits not of any great accuracy; nor can we always remount to
the first origin of things, in order to determine their present condition. Any considerable space of time sets objects at such a distance, that they seem, in a
manner, to lose their reality, and have as little influence on the mind, as if they
never had been in being.[†] A man's title, that is clear and certain at present, will
seem obscure and doubtful fifty years hence, even tho' the facts, on which it is
founded, shou'd be prov'd with the greatest evidence and certainty. The same
facts have not the same influence after so long an interval of time.[†] And this may
be receiv'd as a convincing argument for our preceding doctrine with regard to
property and justice.[†] Possession during a long tract of time conveys a title to any
object. But as 'tis certain, that, however every thing be produc'd in time, there is   *SB 509*
nothing real, that is produc'd by time; it follows, that property being produc'd by
time, is not any thing real in the objects, but is the offspring of the sentiments, on
which alone time is found to have any influence.[74†]

5   To make this evident, let us consider, that if these two persons had been simply members of the   *SB 508*
colonies, and not messengers or deputies, their actions wou'd not have been of any consequence;
since in that case their relation to the colonies wou'd have been but feeble and imperfect. Add to
this, that nothing determin'd them to run to the gates rather than the walls, or any other part of the
city, but that the gates, being the most obvious and remarkable part, satisfy the fancy best in taking
them for the whole; as we find by the poets, who frequently draw their images and metaphors from
them. Besides we may consider, that the touch or contact of the one messenger is not properly possession, no more than the piercing the gates with a spear; but only forms a relation; and there is a
relation, in the other case, equally obvious, tho' not, perhaps, of equal force. Which of these relations, then, conveys a right and property, or whether any of them be sufficient for that effect, I leave
to the decision of such as are wiser than myself.

[74] Present possession is plainly a relation betwixt a person and an object; but is not sufficient to   *SB 509*
counter-ballance the relation of first possession, unless the former be long and uninterrupted: In
which case the relation is encreas'd on the side of the present possession, by the extent of time, and
diminish'd on that of first possession, by the distance.[†] This change in the relation produces a consequent change in the property.

10   We acquire the property of objects by *accession*, when they are connected in an intimate manner with objects that are already our property, and at the same time are inferior to them. Thus the fruits of our garden, the offspring of our cattle, and the work of our slaves, are all of them esteem'd our property, even before possession. Where objects are connected together in the imagination, they are apt to be put on the same footing, and are commonly suppos'd to be endow'd with the same qualities. We readily pass from one to the other, and make no difference in our judgments concerning them; especially if the latter be inferior to the former.[75]

[75] This source of property can never be explain'd but from the imagination; and one may affirm, that the causes are here unmix'd. We shall proceed to explain them more particularly, and illustrate them by examples from common life and experience.

2   It has been observ'd above,† that the mind has a natural propensity to join relations, especially resembling ones, and finds a kind of fitness and uniformity in such an union. From this propensity are deriv'd these laws of nature, *that upon the first formation of society, property always follows the present possession*; and afterwards, *that it arises from first or from long possession*. Now we may easily observe, that relation is not confin'd merely to one degree; but that from an object, that is related to us, we acquire a relation to every other object, which is related to it, and so on, till the thought loses the chain by too long a progress. However the relation may weaken by each remove, 'tis not immediately destroy'd; but frequently connects two objects by means of an intermediate one, which is related to both. And this principle is of such force as to give rise to the right of *accession*, and causes us to acquire the property not only of such objects as we are immediately possess'd of, but also of such as are closely connected with them.

3   Suppose a *German*, a *Frenchman*, and a *Spaniard* to come into a room, where there are plac'd upon the table three bottles of wine, *Rhenish*, *Burgundy*, and *Port*; and suppose they shou'd fall a quarrelling about the division of them; a person, who was chosen for umpire, wou'd naturally, to show his impartiality, give every one the product of his own country: And this from a principle,† which, in some measure, is the source of those laws of nature, that ascribe property to occupation, prescription and accession.   *SB 510*

4   In all these cases, and particularly that of accession, there is first a *natural* union betwixt the idea of the person and that of the object, and afterwards a new and *moral* union produc'd by that right or property, which we ascribe to the person. But here there occurs a difficulty, which merits our attention, and may afford us an opportunity of putting to trial that singular method of reasoning, which has been employ'd on the present subject. I have already observ'd,† that the imagination passes with greater facility from little to great, than from great to little, and that the transition of ideas is always easier and smoother in the former case than in the latter. Now as the right of accession arises from the easy transition of ideas, by which related objects are connected together, it shou'd naturally be imagin'd, that the right of accession must encrease in strength, in proportion as the transition of ideas is perform'd with greater facility. It may, therefore, be thought, that when we have acquir'd the property of any small object, we shall readily consider any great object related to it as an accession, and as belonging to the proprietor of the small one; since the transition is in that case very easy from the small object to the great one, and shou'd connect them together in the closest manner. But in fact the case is always found to be otherwise. The empire of *Great Britain* seems to draw along with it the dominion of the *Orkneys*, the *Hebrides*, the isle of *Man*, and the isle of *Wight*; but the authority over those lesser islands does not naturally imply any title to *Great Britain*. In short, a small object naturally follows a great one as its accession; but a great one is never suppos'd to belong to the proprietor of a small one related to it, merely on account of that property and relation. Yet in this latter case the transition of ideas is smoother from the proprietor to the small object, which is his property, and from the small object to the great one, than in the former case from the proprietor to the great object, and from the great one to the small. It may therefore be thought, that these

phænomena are objections to the foregoing hypothesis,[†] *that the ascribing of property to accession is nothing but an effect of the relations of ideas, and of the smooth transition of the imagination.*

5   'Twill be easy to solve this objection, if we consider the agility and unsteadiness of the imagination, with the different views, in which it is continually placing its objects. When we attribute to a person a property in two objects, we do not always pass from the person to one object, and from that to the other related to it. The objects being here to be consider'd as the property of the person, we are apt to join them together, and place them in the same light. Suppose, therefore, a great and a small object to be related together; if a person be strongly related to the great object, he will likewise be strongly related to both the objects, consider'd together, because he is related to the most considerable part. On the contrary, if he be only related to the small object, he will not be strongly related to both, consider'd together, since his relation lies only with the most trivial part, which is not apt to strike us in any great degree, when we consider the whole. And this is the reason, why small objects become accessions to great ones, and not great to small.   *SB 511*

6   'Tis the general opinion of philosophers and civilians,[†] that the sea is incapable of becoming the property of any nation; and that because 'tis impossible to take possession of it, or form any such distinct relation with it, as may be the foundation of property. Where this reason ceases, property immediately takes place. Thus the most strenuous advocates for the liberty of the seas universally allow, that friths and bays naturally belong as an accession to the proprietors of the surrounding continent. These have properly no more bond or union with the land, than the *Pacific* ocean wou'd have; but having an union in the fancy, and being at the same time *inferior*, they are of course regarded as an accession.

7   The property of rivers, by the laws of most nations,[†] and by the natural turn of our thought, is attributed to the proprietors of their banks, excepting such vast rivers as the *Rhine* or the *Danube*, which seem too large to the imagination to follow as an accession to the property of the neighbouring fields. Yet even these rivers are consider'd as the property of that nation, thro' whose dominions they run; the idea of a nation being of a suitable bulk to correspond with them, and bear them such a relation in the fancy.

8   The accessions, which are made to lands bordering upon rivers, follow the land, say the civilians, provided they be made by what they call *alluvion*,[†] that is, insensibly and imperceptibly; which are circumstances that mightily assist the imagination in the conjunction. Where there is any considerable portion torn at once from one bank, and join'd to another, it becomes not his property, whose land it falls on, till it unite with the land, and till the trees or plants have spread their roots into both. Before that, the imagination does not sufficiently join them.

9   There are other cases, which somewhat resemble this of accession, but which, at the bottom, are considerably different, and merit our attention. Of this kind is the conjunction of the properties of different persons, after such a manner as not to admit of *separation*. The question is, to whom the united mass must belong?

10   Where this conjunction is of such a nature as to admit of *division*, but not of *separation*,[†] the decision is natural and easy. The whole mass must be suppos'd to be common betwixt the proprietors of the several parts, and afterwards must be divided according to the proportions of these parts. But   *SB 512* here I cannot forbear taking notice of a remarkable subtility of the *Roman* law, in distinguishing betwixt *confusion* and *commixtion*. Confusion is an union of two bodies, such as different liquors, where the parts become entirely undistinguishable. Commixtion is the blending of two bodies, such as two bushels of corn, where the parts remain separate in an obvious and visible manner. As in the latter case the imagination discovers not so entire an union as in the former, but is able to trace and preserve a distinct idea of the property of each; this is the reason, why the *civil* law, tho' it establish'd an entire community in the case of *confusion*, and after that a proportional division, yet in the case of *commixtion*, supposes each of the proprietors to maintain a distinct right; however necessity may at last force them to submit to the same division.

11   *Quod si frumentum Titii frumento tuo mistum fuerit: siquidem ex voluntate vestra, commune est: quia singula corpora, id est, singula grana, quæ cujusque propria fuerunt, ex consensu vestro communicata sunt. Quod si casu id mistum fuerit, vel Titius id miscuerit sine tua voluntate, non videtur commune esse; quia singula corpora in sua substantia durant. Sed nec magis istis casibus commune sit frumentum quam grex intelligitur esse communis, si pecora Titii tuis pecoribus mista fuerint. Sed si ab alterutro vestrûm*

11   The right of *succession*[†] is a very natural one, from the presum'd consent of *SB 510* the parent or near relation, and from the general interest of mankind, which requires, that men's possessions shou'd pass to those, who are dearest to them, in order to render them more industrious and frugal. Perhaps these causes are *SB 511* seconded by the influence of *relation*, or the association of ideas, by which we are naturally directed to consider the son after the parent's decease, and ascribe to him a title to his father's possessions. Those goods must become the property *SB 512* of some body: But *of whom* is the question. Here 'tis evident the person's children naturally present themselves to the mind; and being already connected to those possessions by means of their deceas'd parent, we are apt to connect *SB 513*

---

totum id frumentum retineatur, in rem quidem actio pro modo frumenti cujusque competit. Arbitrio autem judicis continetur, ut ipse æstimet quale cujusque frumentum fuerit.[†] Inst. Lib. 2. Tit. 1. ¶28.

12   Where the properties of two persons are united after such a manner as neither to admit of *division* nor *separation*, as when one builds a house on another's ground, in that case, the whole must belong to one of the proprietors: And here I assert, that it naturally is conceiv'd to belong to the proprietor of the most considerable part. For however the compound object may have a relation to two different persons, and carry our view at once to both of them, yet as the most considerable part principally engages our attention, and by the strict union draws the inferior along it; for this reason, the whole bears a relation to the proprietor of that part, and is regarded as his property. The only difficulty is, what we shall be pleas'd to call the most considerable part, and most attractive to the imagination.

13   This quality depends on several different circumstances, which have little connexion with each other. One part of a compound object may become more considerable than another, either because it is more constant and durable; because it is of greater value; because it is more obvious and remarkable; because it is of greater extent; or because its existence is more separate and independent. 'Twill be easy to conceive, that, as these circumstances may be conjoin'd and oppos'd in all the different ways, and according to all the different degrees, which can be imagin'd, there will result *SB 513* many cases, where the reasons on both sides are so equally ballanc'd, that 'tis impossible for us to give any satisfactory decision. Here then is the proper business of municipal laws, to fix what the principles of human nature have left undetermin'd.

14   The superficies yields to the soil, says the civil law: The writing to the paper: The canvas to the picture.[†] These decisions do not well agree together, and are a proof of the contrariety of those principles, from which they are deriv'd.

15   But of all the questions of this kind the most curious is that, which for so many ages divided the disciples of *Proculus* and *Sabinus*.[†] Suppose a person shou'd make a cup from the metal of another, or a ship from his wood, and suppose the proprietor of the metal or wood shou'd demand his goods, the question is, whether he acquires a title to the cup or ship? *Sabinus* maintain'd the affirmative, and asserted that the substance or matter is the foundation of all the qualities; that it is incorruptible and immortal, and therefore superior to the form, which is casual and dependent. On the other hand, *Proculus* observ'd, that the form is the most obvious and remarkable part, and that from it bodies are denominated of this or that particular species. To which he might have added, that the matter or substance is in most bodies so fluctuating and uncertain, that 'tis utterly impossible to trace it in all its changes. For my part, I know not from what principles such a controversy can be certainly determin'd. I shall therefore content my self with observing, that the decision of *Tribonian*[†] seems to me pretty ingenious; that the cup belongs to the proprietor of the metal, because it can be brought back to its first form: But that the ship belongs to the author of its form for a contrary reason. But however ingenious this reason may seem, it plainly depends upon the fancy, which by the possibility of such a reduction, finds a closer connexion and relation betwixt a cup and the proprietor of its metal, than betwixt a ship and the proprietor of its wood, where the substance is more fix'd and unalterable.

them still farther by the relation of property. Of this there are many parallel instances.[76]

Sect. 4. *Of the transference of property by consent* SB 514

1   However useful, or even necessary, the stability of possession may be to human society, 'tis attended with very considerable inconveniencies. The relation of fitness or suitableness ought never to enter into consideration, in distributing the properties of mankind; but we must govern ourselves by rules, which are more general in their application, and more free from doubt and uncertainty. Of this kind is *present* possession upon the first establishment of society; and afterwards *occupation, prescription, accession,* and *succession.*[†] As these depend very much on chance, they must frequently prove contradictory both to men's wants and desires; and persons and possessions must often be very ill adjusted. This is a grand inconvenience, which calls for a remedy. To apply one directly, and allow every man to seize by violence what he judges to be fit for him, wou'd destroy society; and therefore the rules of justice seek some medium betwixt a rigid stability, and this changeable and uncertain adjustment. But there is no medium better than that obvious one, that possession and property shou'd always be stable, except when the proprietor agrees to bestow them on some other person. This rule can have no ill consequence, in occasioning wars and dissentions; since the proprietor's consent, who alone is concern'd, is taken along in the alienation: And it may serve to many good purposes in adjusting property to persons. Different parts of the earth produce different commodities; and not only so, but different men both are by nature fitted for different employments, and attain to greater perfection in any one, when they confine themselves to it alone. All this requires a mutual exchange and commerce; for which reason the translation of property by consent is founded on a law of nature,[†] as well as its stability without such a consent.

2   So far is determin'd by a plain utility and interest. But perhaps 'tis from more   SB 515
trivial reasons, that *delivery*, or a sensible transference of the object is commonly requir'd by civil laws, and also by the laws of nature, according to most authors, as a requisite circumstance in the translation of property.[†] The property of an object, when taken for something real, without any reference to morality, or the

---

[76] In examining the different titles to authority in government, we shall meet with many reasons   SB 513
to convince us, that the right of succession depends, in a great measure, on the imagination. Mean while I shall rest contented with observing one example, which belongs to the present subject. Suppose that a person die without children, and that a dispute arises among his relations concerning his inheritance; 'tis evident, that if his riches be deriv'd partly from his father, partly from his mother, the most natural way of determining such a dispute, is, to divide his possessions, and assign each part to the family, from whence it is deriv'd. Now as the person is suppos'd to have been once the full and entire proprietor of those goods; I ask, what is it makes us find a certain equity and natural reason in this partition, except it be the imagination? His affection to these families does not depend upon his possessions; for which reason his consent can never be presum'd precisely for such a partition. And as to the public interest, it seems not to be in the least concern'd on the one side or the other.

sentiments of the mind, is a quality perfectly insensible, and even inconceivable; nor can we form any distinct notion, either of its stability or translation. This imperfection of our ideas is less sensibly felt with regard to its stability, as it engages less our attention, and is easily past over by the mind, without any scrupulous examination. But as the translation of property from one person to another is a more remarkable event, the defect of our ideas becomes more sensible on that occasion, and obliges us to turn ourselves on every side in search of some remedy. Now as nothing more enlivens any idea than a present impression, and a relation betwixt that impression and the idea;[†] 'tis natural for us to seek some false light from this quarter. In order to aid the imagination in conceiving the transference of property, we take the sensible object, and actually transfer its possession to the person, on whom we wou'd bestow the property. The suppos'd resemblance of the actions, and the presence of this sensible delivery, deceive the mind, and make it fancy, that it conceives the mysterious transition of the property. And that this explication of the matter is just, appears hence, that men have invented a *symbolical* delivery, to satisfy the fancy, where the real one is impracticable. Thus the giving the keys of a granary is understood to be the delivery of the corn contain'd in it: The giving of stone and earth represents the delivery of a mannor. This is a kind of superstitious practice in civil laws, and in the laws of nature, resembling the *Roman Catholic* superstitions in religion. As the *Roman Catholics* represent the inconceivable mysteries of the *Christian* religion, and render them more present to the mind, by a taper, or habit, or grimace, which is *SB 516* suppos'd to resemble them; so lawyers and moralists have run into like inventions for the same reason, and have endeavour'd by those means to satisfy themselves concerning the transference of property by consent.

Sect. 5. *Of the obligation of promises*

1   That the rule of morality, which enjoins the performance of promises, is not *natural*, will sufficiently appear from these two propositions, which I proceed to prove, viz. *that a promise wou'd not be intelligible, before human conventions had establish'd it*; and *that even if it were intelligible, it wou'd not be attended with any moral obligation.*

2   I say, *first*, that a promise is not intelligible naturally, nor antecedent to human conventions; and that a man, unacquainted with society, cou'd never enter into any engagements with another, even tho' they cou'd perceive each other's thoughts by intuition. If promises be natural and intelligible, there must be some act of the mind attending these words, *I promise*; and on this act of the mind must the obligation depend. Let us, therefore, run over all the faculties of the soul, and see which of them is exerted in our promises.

3   The act of the mind, exprest by a promise, is not a *resolution* to perform any thing: For that alone never imposes any obligation. Nor is it a *desire* of such a performance: For we may bind ourselves without such a desire, or even with an aversion, declar'd and avow'd. Neither is it the *willing* of that action, which we promise to perform: For a promise always regards some future time, and the will

has an influence only on present actions.[†] It follows, therefore, that since the act of the mind, which enters into a promise, and produces its obligation, is neither the resolving, desiring, nor willing any particular performance, it must necessarily be the *willing* of that *obligation*, which arises from the promise.[†] Nor is this only a conclusion of philosophy; but is entirely conformable to our common ways of thinking and of expressing ourselves, when we say that we are bound by our own consent, and that the obligation arises from our mere will and pleasure. The only question, then, is, whether there be not a manifest absurdity in supposing this act of the mind, and such an absurdity as no man cou'd fall into, whose ideas are not confounded by prejudice and the fallacious use of language? *SB 517*

4   All morality depends upon our sentiments; and when any action, or quality of the mind, pleases us *after a certain manner*, we say it is virtuous; and when the neglect, or non-performance of it, displeases us *after a like manner*, we say that we lie under an obligation to perform it. A change of the obligation supposes a change of the sentiment; and a creation of a new obligation supposes some new sentiment to arise. But 'tis certain we can naturally no more change our own sentiments, than the motions of the heavens; nor by a single act of our will, that is, by a promise, render any action agreeable or disagreeable, moral or immoral; which, without that act, wou'd have produc'd contrary impressions, or have been endow'd with different qualities. It wou'd be absurd, therefore, to will any new obligation, that is, any new sentiment of pain or pleasure; nor is it possible, that men cou'd naturally fall into so gross an absurdity. A promise, therefore, is *naturally* something altogether unintelligible, nor is there any act of the mind belonging to it.[77]

5   But, *secondly*, if there was any act of the mind belonging to it, it cou'd not *naturally* produce any obligation. This appears evidently from the foregoing reasoning. A promise creates a new obligation. A new obligation supposes new *SB 518*

---

[77] Were morality discoverable by reason, and not by sentiment, 'twou'd be still more evident, *SB 517*
that promises cou'd make no alteration upon it. Morality is suppos'd to consist in relation. Every new imposition of morality, therefore, must arise from some new relation of objects; and consequently the will cou'd not produce *immediately* any change in morals, but cou'd have that effect only by producing a change upon the objects. But as the moral obligation of a promise is the pure effect of the will, without the least change in any part of the universe; it follows, that promises have no *natural* obligation.

2   Shou'd it be said, that this act of the will being in effect a new object, produces new relations and new duties; I wou'd answer, that this is a pure sophism, which may be detected by a very moderate share of accuracy and exactness. To will a new obligation, is to will a new relation of objects; and *SB 518*
therefore, if this new relation of objects were form'd by the volition itself, we shou'd in effect will the volition; which is plainly absurd and impossible. The will has here no object to which it cou'd tend; but must return upon itself *in infinitum*. The new obligation depends upon new relations. The new relations depend upon a new volition. The new volition has for its object a new obligation, and consequently new relations, and consequently a new volition; which volition again has in view a new obligation, relation, and volition, without any termination. 'Tis impossible, therefore, we cou'd ever will a new obligation; and consequently 'tis impossible the will cou'd ever accompany a promise, or produce a new obligation of morality.

sentiments to arise. The will never creates new sentiments. There cou'd not naturally, therefore, arise any obligation from a promise, even supposing the mind cou'd fall into the absurdity of willing that obligation.

6   The same truth may be prov'd still more evidently by that reasoning, which prov'd justice in general to be an artificial virtue.[†] No action can be requir'd of us as our duty, unless there be implanted in human nature some actuating passion or motive, capable of producing the action. This motive cannot be the sense of duty. A sense of duty supposes an antecedent obligation: And where an action is not requir'd by any natural passion, it cannot be requir'd by any natural obligation; since it may be omitted without proving any defect or imperfection in the mind and temper, and consequently without any vice. Now 'tis evident we have no motive leading us to the performance of promises, distinct from a sense of duty. If we thought, that promises had no moral obligation, we never shou'd feel any inclination to observe them. This is not the case with the natural virtues.[†] Tho' there was no obligation to relieve the miserable, our humanity wou'd lead us to it; and when we omit that duty, the immorality of the omission arises from its being a proof, that we want the natural sentiments of humanity. A father knows it to be his duty to take care of his children: But he has also a natural   *SB 519* inclination to it. And if no human creature had that inclination, no one cou'd lie under any such obligation. But as there is naturally no inclination to observe promises, distinct from a sense of their obligation; it follows, that fidelity is no natural virtue, and that promises have no force, antecedent to human conventions.

7   If any one dissent from this, he must give a regular proof of these two propositions, viz. *that there is a peculiar act of the mind, annext to promises*; and *that consequent to this act of the mind, there arises an inclination to perform, distinct from a sense of duty*. I presume, that it is impossible to prove either of these two points; and therefore I venture to conclude, that promises are human inventions, founded on the necessities and interests of society.

8   In order to discover these necessities and interests, we must consider the same qualities of human nature, which we have already found[†] to give rise to the preceding laws of society. Men being naturally selfish, or endow'd only with a confin'd generosity, they are not easily induc'd to perform any action for the interest of strangers, except with a view to some reciprocal advantage, which they had no hope of obtaining but by such a performance. Now as it frequently happens, that these mutual performances cannot be finish'd at the same instant, 'tis necessary, that one party be contented to remain in uncertainty, and depend upon the gratitude of the other for a return of kindness. But so much corruption is there among men, that, generally speaking, this becomes but a slender security; and as the benefactor is here suppos'd to bestow his favours with a view to self-interest, this both takes off from the obligation, and sets an example of selfishness, which is the true mother of ingratitude. Were we, therefore, to follow the natural course of our passions and inclinations, we shou'd perform but few actions for the advantage of others, from disinterested views; because we are naturally very

limited in our kindness and affection: And we shou'd perform as few of that kind, out of a regard to interest; because we cannot depend upon their gratitude. Here then is the mutual commerce of good offices in a manner lost among mankind, and every one reduc'd to his own skill and industry for his well-being and subsistence. The invention of the law of nature, concerning the *stability* of possession, has already render'd men tolerable to each other; that of the *transference* of property and possession by consent has begun to render them mutually advantageous: But still these laws, however strictly observ'd, are not sufficient to render them so serviceable to each other, as by nature they are fitted to become. Tho' possession be *stable*, men may often reap but small advantage from it, while they are possess'd of a greater quantity of any species of goods than they have occasion for, and at the same time suffer by the want of others. The *transference* of property, which is the proper remedy for this inconvenience, cannot remedy it entirely; because it can only take place with regard to such objects as are *present* and *individual*, but not to such as are *absent* or *general*. One cannot transfer the property of a particular house, twenty leagues distant; because the consent cannot be attended with delivery,[†] which is a requisite circumstance. Neither can one transfer the property of ten bushels of corn, or five hogsheads of wine, by the mere expression and consent; because these are only general terms, and have no direct relation to any particular heap of corn, or barrels of wine. Besides, the commerce of mankind is not confin'd to the barter of commodities, but may extend to services and actions, which we may exchange to our mutual interest and advantage. Your corn is ripe to-day; mine will be so to-morrow. 'Tis profitable for us both, that I shou'd labour with you to-day, and that you shou'd aid me to-morrow. I have no kindness for you, and know you have as little for me. I will not, therefore, take any pains upon your account; and shou'd I labour with you upon my own account, in expectation of a return, I know I shou'd be disappointed, and that I shou'd in vain depend upon your gratitude. Here then I leave you to labour alone: You treat me in the same manner. The seasons change; and both of us lose our harvests for want of mutual confidence and security.[†]

9   All this is the effect of the natural and inherent principles and passions of human nature; and as these passions and principles are inalterable, it may be thought, that our conduct, which depends on them, must be so too, and that 'twou'd be in vain, either for moralists or politicians, to tamper with us, or attempt to change the usual course of our actions, with a view to public interest. And indeed, did the success of their designs depend upon their success in correcting the selfishness and ingratitude of men, they wou'd never make any progress, unless aided by omnipotence, which is alone able to new-mould the human mind, and change its character in such fundamental articles.[†] All they can pretend to, is, to give a new direction to those natural passions, and teach us that we can better satisfy our appetites in an oblique and artificial manner, than by their headlong and impetuous motion. Hence I learn to do a service to another, without bearing him any real kindness; because I foresee, that he will return my service, in expectation of another of the same kind, and in order to

SB 520

SB 521

maintain the same correspondence of good offices with me or with others. And accordingly, after I have serv'd him, and he is in possession of the advantage arising from my action, he is induc'd to perform his part, as foreseeing the consequences of his refusal.

10   But tho' this self-interested commerce of men begins to take place, and to predominate in society, it does not entirely abolish the more generous and noble intercourse of friendship and good offices. I may still do services to such persons as I love, and am more particularly acquainted with, without any prospect of advantage; and they may make me a return in the same manner, without any view but that of recompensing my past services. In order, therefore, to distinguish those two different sorts of commerce, the interested and the disinterested, *SB 522* there is a *certain form of words* invented for the former, by which we bind ourselves to the performance of any action. This form of words constitutes what we call a *promise*, which is the sanction of the interested commerce of mankind. When a man says *he promises any thing*, he in effect expresses a *resolution* of performing it; and along with that, by making use of this *form of words*, subjects himself to the penalty of never being trusted again in case of failure. A resolution is the natural act of the mind, which promises express: But were there no more than a resolution in the case, promises wou'd only declare our former motives, and wou'd not create any new motive or obligation. They are the conventions of men, which create a new motive, when experience has taught us, that human affairs wou'd be conducted much more for mutual advantage, were there certain *symbols* or *signs* instituted, by which we might give each other security of our conduct in any particular incident. After these signs are instituted, whoever uses them is immediately bound by his interest to execute his engagements, and must never expect to be trusted any more, if he refuse to perform what he promis'd.

11   Nor is that knowledge, which is requisite to make mankind sensible of this interest in the *institution* and *observance* of promises, to be esteem'd superior to the capacity of human nature, however savage and uncultivated. There needs but a very little practice of the world, to make us perceive all these consequences and advantages. The shortest experience of society discovers them to every mortal; and when each individual perceives the same sense of interest in all his fellows, he immediately performs his part of any contract, as being assur'd, that they will not be wanting in theirs. All of them, by concert, enter into a scheme of actions, calculated for common benefit, and agree to be true to their word; nor is there any thing requisite to form this concert or convention, but that every one have a sense of interest in the faithful fulfilling of engagements, and express that sense to other members of the society. This immediately causes that interest to *SB 523* operate upon them; and interest is the *first* obligation to the performance of promises.[†]

12   Afterwards a sentiment of morals concurs with interest, and becomes a new obligation upon mankind. This sentiment of morality, in the performance of promises, arises from the same principles as that in the abstinence from the property of others. *Public interest*, *education*, and *the artifices of politicians*, have

the same effect in both cases. The difficulties, that occur to us, in supposing a moral obligation to attend promises, we either surmount or elude. For instance; the expression of a resolution is not commonly suppos'd to be obligatory; and we cannot readily conceive how the making use of a certain form of words shou'd be able to cause any material difference. Here, therefore, we *feign* a new act of the mind, which we call the *willing* an obligation; and on this we suppose the morality to depend. But we have prov'd already,[†] that there is no such act of the mind, and consequently that promises impose no natural obligation.

13   To confirm this, we may subjoin some other reflections concerning that will, which is suppos'd to enter into a promise, and to cause its obligation. 'Tis evident, that the will alone is never suppos'd to cause the obligation, but must be express'd by words or signs, in order to impose a tye upon any man.[†] The expression being once brought in as subservient to the will, soon becomes the principal part of the promise; nor will a man be less bound by his word, tho' he secretly give a different direction to his intention, and withhold himself both from a resolution, and from willing an obligation. But tho' the expression makes on most occasions the whole of the promise, yet it does not always so; and one, who shou'd make use of any expression, of which he knows not the meaning, and which he uses without any intention of binding himself, wou'd not certainly be bound by it. Nay, tho' he knows its meaning, yet if he uses it in jest only, and with   *SB 524* such signs as show evidently he has no serious intention of binding himself, he wou'd not lie under any obligation of performance; but 'tis necessary, that the words be a perfect expression of the will, without any contrary signs. Nay, even this we must not carry so far as to imagine, that one, whom, by our quickness of understanding, we conjecture, from certain signs, to have an intention of deceiving us, is not bound by his expression or verbal promise, if we accept of it; but must limit this conclusion to those cases, where the signs are of a different kind from those of deceit. All these contradictions are easily accounted for, if the obligation of promises be merely a human invention for the convenience of society; but will never be explain'd, if it be something *real* and *natural*, arising from any action of the mind or body.

14   I shall farther observe, that since every new promise imposes a new obligation of morality on the person who promises, and since this new obligation arises from his will; 'tis one of the most mysterious and incomprehensible operations that can possibly be imagin'd, and may even be compar'd to *transubstantiation*,[†] or *holy orders*,[78] where a certain form of words, along with a certain intention, changes entirely the nature of an external object, and even of a human creature. But tho' these mysteries be so far alike, 'tis very remarkable, that they differ widely in other particulars, and that this difference may be regarded as a strong proof of the difference of their origins. As the obligation of promises is an invention for the interest of society, 'tis warp'd into as many different forms as that interest requires, and even runs into direct contradictions, rather than

---

[78] I mean so far, as holy orders are suppos'd to produce the *indelible character*.[†] In other respects they are only a legal qualification.

lose sight of its object. But as those other monstrous doctrines are mere priestly inventions, and have no public interest in view, they are less disturb'd in their progress by new obstacles; and it must be own'd, that, after the first absurdity, they follow more directly the current of reason and good sense. Theologians clearly perceiv'd, that the external form of words, being mere sound, requires an intention to make them have any efficacy; and that this intention being once consider'd as a requisite circumstance, its absence must equally prevent the effect, whether avow'd or conceal'd, whether sincere or deceitful. Accordingly they have commonly determin'd, that the intention of the priest makes the sacrament, and that when he secretly withdraws his intention, he is highly criminal in himself; but still destroys the baptism, or communion, or holy orders.[†] The terrible consequences of this doctrine were not able to hinder its taking place;[†] as the inconvenience of a similar doctrine, with regard to promises, have prevented that doctrine from establishing itself. Men are always more concern'd about the present life than the future;[†] and are apt to think the smallest evil, which regards the former, more important than the greatest, which regards the latter.

SB 525

15   We may draw the same conclusion, concerning the origin of promises, from the *force*, which is suppos'd to invalidate all contracts, and to free us from their obligation. Such a principle is a proof, that promises have no natural obligation, and are mere artificial contrivances for the convenience and advantage of society. If we consider aright of the matter, force is not essentially different from any other motive of hope or fear, which may induce us to engage our word, and lay ourselves under any obligation. A man, dangerously wounded, who promises a competent sum to a surgeon to cure him, wou'd certainly be bound to performance; tho' the case be not so much different from that of one, who promises a sum to a robber, as to produce so great a difference in our sentiments of morality, if these sentiments were not built entirely on public interest and convenience.

Sect. 6. *Some farther reflections concerning justice and injustice*

SB 526

1   We have now run over the three fundamental laws of nature, *that of the stability of possession, of its transference by consent*, and *of the performance of promises*.[†] 'Tis on the strict observance of these three laws, that the peace and security of human society entirely depend; nor is there any possibility of establishing a good correspondence among men, where these are neglected. Society is absolutely necessary for the well-being of men; and these are as necessary to the support of society. Whatever restraint they may impose on the passions of men, they are the real offspring of those passions, and are only a more artful and more refin'd way of satisfying them. Nothing is more vigilant and inventive than our passions; and nothing is more obvious, than the convention for the observance of these rules. Nature has, therefore, trusted this affair entirely to the conduct of men, and has not plac'd in the mind any peculiar original principles, to determine us to a set of actions, into which the other principles of our frame and constitution were

sufficient to lead us. And to convince us the more fully of this truth, we may here stop a moment, and from a review of the preceding reasonings may draw some new arguments, to prove that these laws, however necessary, are entirely artificial, and of human invention; and consequently that justice is an artificial, and not a natural virtue.

2   1. The first argument I shall make use of is deriv'd from the vulgar definition of justice. Justice is commonly defin'd to be *a constant and perpetual will of giving every one his due*. In this definition 'tis suppos'd, that there are such things as right and property, independent of justice, and antecedent to it; and that they wou'd have subsisted, tho' men had never dreamt of practising such a virtue. I   *SB 527* have already observ'd,[†] in a cursory manner, the fallacy of this opinion, and shall here continue to open up a little more distinctly my sentiments on that subject.

3   I shall begin with observing, that this quality, which we call *property*, is like many of the imaginary qualities of the *peripatetic* philosophy,[†] and vanishes upon a more accurate inspection into the subject, when consider'd apart from our moral sentiments. 'Tis evident property does not consist in any of the sensible qualities of the object. For these may continue invariably the same, while the property changes. Property, therefore, must consist in some relation of the object.[†] But 'tis not in its relation with regard to other external and inanimate objects. For these may also continue invariably the same, while the property changes. This quality, therefore, consists in the relations of objects to intelligent and rational beings. But 'tis not the external and corporeal relation, which forms the essence of property. For that relation may be the same betwixt inanimate objects, or with regard to brute creatures; tho' in those cases it forms no property. 'Tis, therefore, in some internal relation, that the property consists; that is, in some influence, which the external relations of the object have on the mind and actions.[†] Thus the external relation, which we call *occupation* or first possession, is not of itself imagin'd to be the property of the object, but only to cause its property. Now 'tis evident, this external relation causes nothing in external objects, and has only an influence on the mind, by giving us a sense of duty in abstaining from that object, and in restoring it to the first possessor. These actions are properly what we call *justice*; and consequently 'tis on that virtue that the nature of property depends, and not the virtue on the property.

4   If any one, therefore, wou'd assert, that justice is a natural virtue, and injustice a natural vice, he must assert, that abstracting from the notions of *property*, and *right*, and *obligation*, a certain conduct and train of actions, in certain external   *SB 528* relations of objects, has naturally a moral beauty or deformity, and causes an original pleasure or uneasiness. Thus the restoring a man's goods to him is consider'd as virtuous, not because nature has annex'd a certain sentiment of pleasure to such a conduct, with regard to the property of others, but because she has annex'd that sentiment to such a conduct, with regard to those external objects, of which others have had the first or long possession, or which they have receiv'd by the consent of those, who have had first or long possession. If nature has

given us no such sentiment, there is not, naturally, nor antecedent to human conventions, any such thing as property. Now, tho' it seems sufficiently evident, in this dry and accurate consideration of the present subject, that nature has annex'd no pleasure or sentiment of approbation to such a conduct; yet that I may leave as little room for doubt as possible, I shall subjoin a few more arguments to confirm my opinion.

5   *First*, If nature had given us a pleasure of this kind, it wou'd have been as evident and discernible as on every other occasion; nor shou'd we have found any difficulty to perceive, that the consideration of such actions, in such a situation, gives a certain pleasure and a sentiment of approbation. We shou'd not have been oblig'd to have recourse to notions of property in the definition of justice, and at the same time make use of the notions of justice in the definition of property. This deceitful method of reasoning is a plain proof, that there are contain'd in the subject some obscurities and difficulties, which we are not able to surmount, and which we desire to evade by this artifice.

6   *Secondly*, Those rules, by which property, right, and obligation are determin'd, have in them no marks of a natural origin, but many of artifice and contrivance. They are too numerous to have proceeded from nature:[†] They are changeable by human laws: And have all of them a direct and evident tendency to public good, and the support of society. This last circumstance is remarkable upon two accounts. *First*, because, tho' the cause of the establishment of   *SB 529* these laws had been a *regard* for the public good, as much as the public good is their natural tendency, they wou'd still have been artificial, as being purposely contriv'd and directed to a certain end. *Secondly*, because, if men had been endow'd with such a strong regard for public good, they wou'd never have restrain'd themselves by these rules;[†] so that the laws of justice arise from natural principles in a manner still more oblique and artificial. 'Tis self-love which is their real origin; and as the self-love of one person is naturally contrary to that of another, these several interested passions are oblig'd to adjust themselves after such a manner as to concur in some system of conduct and behaviour. This system, therefore, comprehending the interest of each individual, is of course advantageous to the public; tho' it be not intended for that purpose by the inventors.

7   2. In the second place we may observe, that all kinds of vice and virtue run insensibly into each other, and may approach by such imperceptible degrees as will make it very difficult, if not absolutely impossible, to determine when the one ends, and the other begins; and from this observation we may derive a new argument for the foregoing principle.[†] For whatever may be the case, with regard to all kinds of vice and virtue, 'tis certain, that rights, and obligations, and property, admit of no such insensible gradation, but that a man either has a full and perfect property, or none at all; and is either entirely oblig'd to perform any action, or lies under no manner of obligation. However civil laws may talk of a perfect *dominion*, and of an imperfect,[†] 'tis easy to observe, that this arises from a fiction, which has no foundation in reason, and can never enter into our notions

of natural justice and equity. A man that hires a horse, tho' but for a day, has as full a right to make use of it for that time, as he whom we call its proprietor has to make use of it any other day; and 'tis evident, that however the use may be bounded in time or degree, the right itself is not susceptible of any such grada- *SB 530* tion, but is absolute and entire, so far as it extends. Accordingly we may observe, that this right both arises and perishes in an instant; and that a man entirely acquires the property of any object by occupation, or the consent of the proprietor; and loses it by his own consent; without any of that insensible gradation, which is remarkable in other qualities and relations. Since, therefore, this is the case with regard to property, and rights, and obligations, I ask, how it stands with regard to justice and injustice? After whatever manner you answer this question, you run into inextricable difficulties. If you reply, that justice and injustice admit of degree, and run insensibly into each other, you expressly contradict the foregoing position, that obligation and property are not susceptible of such a gradation. These depend entirely upon justice and injustice, and follow them in all their variations. Where the justice is entire, the property is also entire: Where the justice is imperfect, the property must also be imperfect. And *vice versa*, if the property admit of no such variations, they must also be incompatible with justice. If you assent, therefore, to this last proposition, and assert, that justice and injustice are not susceptible of degrees, you in effect assert, that they are not *naturally* either vicious or virtuous; since vice and virtue, moral good and evil, and indeed all *natural* qualities, run insensibly into each other, and are, on many occasions, undistinguishable.

8   And here it may be worth while to observe, that tho' abstract reasoning, and the general maxims of philosophy and law establish this position, *that property, and right, and obligation admit not of degrees*, yet in our common and negligent way of thinking, we find great difficulty to entertain that opinion, and do even *secretly* embrace the contrary principle. An object must either be in the possession of one person or another. An action must either be perform'd or not. The necessity there is of choosing one side in these dilemmas, and the impossibility *SB 531* there often is of finding any just medium, oblige us, when we reflect on the matter, to acknowledge, that all property and obligation are entire. But on the other hand, when we consider the origin of property and obligation, and find that they depend on public utility, and sometimes on the propensities of the imagination, which are seldom entire on any side; we are naturally inclin'd to imagine, that these moral relations† admit of an insensible gradation. Hence it is, that in references, where the consent of the parties leaves the referees† entire masters of the subject, they commonly discover so much equity and justice on both sides, as induces them to strike a medium, and divide the difference betwixt the parties. Civil judges, who have not this liberty, but are oblig'd to give a decisive sentence on some one side, are often at a loss how to determine, and are necessitated to proceed on the most frivolous reasons in the world. Half rights and obligations, which seem so natural in common life, are perfect absurdities in their tribunals; for which reason they are often oblig'd to take half arguments for whole ones, in order to terminate the affair one way or other.

9   3. The third argument of this kind I shall make use of may be explain'd thus. If we consider the ordinary course of human actions, we shall find, that the mind restrains not itself by any general and universal rules; but acts on most occasions as it is determin'd by its present motives and inclination. As each action is a particular individual event, it must proceed from particular principles, and from our immediate situation within ourselves, and with respect to the rest of the universe. If on some occasions we extend our motives beyond those very circumstances, which gave rise to them, and form something like *general rules* for our conduct, 'tis easy to observe, that these rules are not perfectly inflexible, but allow of many exceptions. Since, therefore, this is the ordinary course of human actions, we may conclude, that the laws of justice, being universal and perfectly inflexible, can never be deriv'd from nature, nor be the immediate offspring of any natural motive or inclination. No action can be either morally good or evil, unless there be some natural passion or motive to impel us to it, or deter us from it;[†] and 'tis evident, that the morality must be susceptible of all the same variations, which are natural to the passion. Here are two persons, who dispute for an estate; of whom one is rich, a fool, and a batchelor; the other poor, a man of sense, and has a numerous family: The first is my enemy; the second my friend.[†] Whether I be actuated in this affair by a view to public or private interest, by friendship or enmity, I must be induc'd to do my utmost to procure the estate to the latter. Nor wou'd any consideration of the right and property of the persons be able to restrain me, were I actuated only by natural motives, without any combination or convention with others. For as all property depends on morality; and as all morality depends on the ordinary course of our passions and actions; and as these again are only directed by particular motives; 'tis evident, such a partial conduct must be suitable to the strictest morality, and cou'd never be a violation of property. Were men, therefore, to take the liberty of acting with regard to the laws of society, as they do in every other affair, they wou'd conduct themselves, on most occasions, by particular judgments, and wou'd take into consideration the characters and circumstances of the persons, as well as the general nature of the question. But 'tis easy to observe, that this wou'd produce an infinite confusion in human society, and that the avidity and partiality of men wou'd quickly bring disorder into the world, if not restrain'd by some general and inflexible principles. 'Twas, therefore, with a view to this inconvenience, that men have establish'd these principles, and have agreed to restrain themselves by general rules, which are unchangeable by spite and favour, and by particular views of private or public interest. These rules, then, are artificially invented for a certain purpose, and are contrary to the common principles of human nature, which *SB 533* accommodate themselves to circumstances, and have no stated invariable method of operation.

10   Nor do I perceive how I can easily be mistaken in this matter. I see evidently, that when any man imposes on himself general inflexible rules in his conduct with others, he considers certain objects as their property, which he supposes to be sacred and inviolable. But no proposition can be more evident, than that property is perfectly unintelligible without first supposing justice and injustice; and

that these moral qualities are as unintelligible, unless we have motives, independent of the morality, to impel us to just actions, and deter us from unjust ones. Let those motives, therefore, be what they will, they must accommodate themselves to circumstances, and must admit of all the variations, which human affairs, in their incessant revolutions, are susceptible of. They are consequently a very improper foundation for such rigid inflexible rules as the laws of nature; and 'tis evident these laws can only be deriv'd from human conventions, when men have perceiv'd the disorders that result from following their natural and variable principles.

11 Upon the whole, then, we are to consider this distinction betwixt justice and injustice, as having two different foundations, *viz.* that of *self-interest*, when men observe, that 'tis impossible to live in society without restraining themselves by certain rules; and that of *morality*, when this interest is once observ'd to be common to all mankind, and men receive a pleasure from the view of such actions as tend to the peace of society, and an uneasiness from such as are contrary to it. 'Tis the voluntary convention and artifice of men, which makes the first interest take place; and therefore those laws of justice are so far to be consider'd as *artificial*. After that interest is once establish'd and acknowledg'd, the sense of morality in the observance of these rules follows *naturally*, and of itself; tho' 'tis certain, that it is also augmented by a new *artifice*, and that the public instructions of politicians, and the private education of parents, contribute to the giving us a sense of honour and duty in the strict regulation of our actions with regard to the properties of others.[†] *SB 534*

Sect. 7. *Of the origin of government*

1 Nothing is more certain, than that men are, in a great measure, govern'd by interest, and that even when they extend their concern beyond themselves, 'tis not to any great distance; nor is it usual for them, in common life, to look farther than their nearest friends and acquaintance.[†] 'Tis no less certain, that 'tis impossible for men to consult their interest in so effectual a manner, as by an universal and inflexible observance of the rules of justice, by which alone they can preserve society, and keep themselves from falling into that wretched and savage condition, which is commonly represented as the *state of nature*. And as this interest, which all men have in the upholding of society, and the observation of the rules of justice, is great, so is it palpable and evident, even to the most rude and uncultivated of human race; and 'tis almost impossible for any one, who has had experience of society, to be mistaken in this particular. Since, therefore, men are so sincerely attach'd to their interest, and their interest is so much concern'd in the observance of justice, and this interest is so certain and avow'd; it may be ask'd, how any disorder can ever arise in society, and what principle there is in human nature so *powerful* as to overcome so strong a passion, or so *violent* as to obscure so clear a knowledge?

2 It has been observ'd,[†] in treating of the passions, that men are mightily govern'd by the imagination, and proportion their affections more to the light,

under which any object appears to them, than to its real and intrinsic value. What strikes upon them with a strong and lively idea commonly prevails above *SB 535* what lies in a more obscure light; and it must be a great superiority of value, that is able to compensate this advantage. Now as every thing, that is contiguous to us, either in space or time, strikes upon us with such an idea, it has a proportional effect on the will and passions, and commonly operates with more force than any object, that lies in a more distant and obscure light.[†] Tho' we may be fully convinc'd, that the latter object excels the former, we are not able to regulate our actions by this judgment; but yield to the sollicitations of our passions, which always plead in favour of whatever is near and contiguous.

3   This is the reason why men so often act in contradiction to their known interest; and in particular why they prefer any trivial advantage, that is present, to the maintenance of order in society, which so much depends on the observance of justice. The consequences of every breach of equity seem to lie very remote, and are not able to counter-ballance any immediate advantage, that may be reap'd from it. They are, however, nevertheless real for being remote; and as all men are, in some degree, subject to the same weakness, it necessarily happens, that the violations of equity must become very frequent in society, and the commerce of men, by that means, be render'd very dangerous and uncertain. You have the same propension, that I have, in favour of what is contiguous above what is remote. You are, therefore, naturally carry'd to commit acts of injustice as well as I. Your example both pushes me forward in this way by imitation, and also affords me a new reason for any breach of equity, by showing me, that I shou'd be the cully of my integrity, if I alone shou'd impose on myself a severe restraint amidst the licentiousness of others.

4   This quality, therefore, of human nature, not only is very dangerous to society, but also seems, on a cursory view, to be incapable of any remedy. The remedy can only come from the consent of men; and if men be incapable of themselves to prefer remote to contiguous, they will never consent to any thing, *SB 536* which wou'd oblige them to such a choice, and contradict, in so sensible a manner, their natural principles and propensities. Whoever chooses the means, chooses also the end; and if it be impossible for us to prefer what is remote, 'tis equally impossible for us to submit to any necessity, which wou'd oblige us to such a method of acting.

5   But here 'tis observable, that this infirmity of human nature becomes a remedy to itself, and that the provision we make against our negligence about remote objects, proceeds merely from our natural inclination to that negligence. When we consider any objects at a distance, all their minute distinctions vanish, and we always give the preference to whatever is in itself preferable, without considering its situation and circumstances. This gives rise to what in an improper sense we call *reason*,[†] which is a principle, that is often contradictory to those propensities that display themselves upon the approach of the object. In reflecting on any action, which I am to perform a twelve-month hence, I always resolve to prefer the greater good, whether at that time it will be more contiguous or remote; nor does any difference in that particular make a difference in my

present intentions and resolutions. My distance from the final determination makes all those minute differences vanish, nor am I affected by any thing, but the general and more discernible qualities of good and evil. But on my nearer approach, those circumstances, which I at first over-look'd, begin to appear, and have an influence on my conduct and affections. A new inclination to the present good springs up, and makes it difficult for me to adhere inflexibly to my first purpose and resolution. This natural infirmity I may very much regret, and I may endeavour, by all possible means, to free myself from it. I may have recourse to study and reflection within myself; to the advice of friends; to frequent meditation, and repeated resolution: And having experienc'd how ineffectual all these are, I may embrace with pleasure any other expedient, by which I may impose a   *SB 537* restraint upon myself, and guard against this weakness.

6   The only difficulty, therefore, is to find out this expedient, by which men cure their natural weakness, and lay themselves under the necessity of observing the laws of justice and equity, notwithstanding their violent propension to prefer contiguous to remote. 'Tis evident such a remedy can never be effectual without correcting this propensity; and as 'tis impossible to change or correct any thing material in our nature,[†] the utmost we can do is to change our circumstances and situation, and render the observance of the laws of justice our nearest interest, and their violation our most remote. But this being impracticable with respect to all mankind, it can only take place with respect to a few, whom we thus immediately interest in the execution of justice. These are the persons, whom we call civil magistrates, kings and their ministers, our governors and rulers, who being indifferent persons to the greatest part of the state, have no interest, or but a remote one, in any act of injustice; and being satisfy'd with their present condition, and with their part in society, have an immediate interest in every execution of justice, which is so necessary to the upholding of society. Here then is the origin of civil government and allegiance. Men are not able radically to cure, either in themselves or others, that narrowness of soul, which makes them prefer the present to the remote. They cannot change their natures. All they can do is to change their situation, and render the observance of justice the immediate interest of some particular persons, and its violation their more remote. These persons, then, are not only induc'd to observe those rules in their own conduct, but also to constrain others to a like regularity, and enforce the dictates of equity thro' the whole society. And if it be necessary, they may also interest others more immediately in the execution of justice, and create a number of officers, civil and military, to assist them in their government.

7   But this execution of justice, tho' the principal, is not the only advantage   *SB 538* of government. As violent passion hinders men from seeing distinctly the interest they have in an equitable behaviour towards others; so it hinders them from seeing that equity itself, and gives them a remarkable partiality in their own favours. This inconvenience is corrected in the same manner as that above-mention'd.[†] The same persons, who execute the laws of justice, will also decide all controversies concerning them; and being indifferent to the greatest

part of the society, will decide them more equitably than every one wou'd in his own case.

8   By means of these two advantages, in the *execution* and *decision* of justice, men acquire a security against each other's weakness and passion, as well as against their own, and under the shelter of their governors, begin to taste at ease the sweets of society and mutual assistance. But government extends farther its beneficial influence; and not contented to protect men in those conventions they make for their mutual interest, it often obliges them to make such conventions, and forces them to seek their own advantage, by a concurrence in some common end or purpose. There is no quality in human nature, which causes more fatal errors in our conduct, than that which leads us to prefer whatever is present to the distant and remote, and makes us desire objects more according to their situation than their intrinsic value. Two neighbours may agree to drain a meadow, which they possess in common; because 'tis easy for them to know each other's mind; and each must perceive, that the immediate consequence of his failing in his part, is, the abandoning the whole project. But 'tis very difficult, and indeed impossible, that a thousand persons shou'd agree in any such action; it being difficult for them to concert so complicated a design, and still more difficult for them to execute it; while each seeks a pretext to free himself of the trouble and expence, and wou'd lay the whole burden on others. Political society easily remedies both these inconveniencies. Magistrates find an immediate interest in the interest of any considerable part of their subjects. They need consult no body but themselves to form any scheme for the promoting of that interest. And as the failure of any one piece in the execution is connected, tho' not immediately, with the failure of the whole, they prevent that failure, because they find no interest in it, either immediate or remote. Thus bridges are built; harbours open'd; ramparts rais'd; canals form'd; fleets equip'd; and armies disciplin'd; every where, by the care of government, which, tho' compos'd of men subject to all human infirmities, becomes, by one of the finest and most subtile inventions imaginable, a composition, that is, in some measure, exempted from all these infirmities.

SB 539

Sect. 8. *Of the source of allegiance*

1   Tho' government be an invention very advantageous, and even in some circumstances absolutely necessary to mankind; it is not necessary in all circumstances, nor is it impossible for men to preserve society for some time, without having recourse to such an invention. Men, 'tis true, are always much inclin'd to prefer present interest to distant and remote; nor is it easy for them to resist the temptation of any advantage, that they may immediately enjoy, in apprehension of an evil, that lies at a distance from them: But still this weakness is less conspicuous, where the possessions, and the pleasures of life are few, and of little value, as they always are in the infancy of society. An *Indian* is but little tempted to dispossess another of his hut, or to steal his bow, as being already provided of the same

advantages; and as to any superior fortune, which may attend one above another in hunting and fishing, 'tis only casual and temporary, and will have but small tendency to disturb society.[†] And so far am I from thinking with some philosophers, that men are utterly incapable of society without government,[†] that I assert the first rudiments of government to arise from quarrels, not among men of the same society, but among those of different societies. A less degree of riches will suffice to this latter effect, than is requisite for the former. Men fear nothing from public war and violence but the resistance they meet with, which, because they share it in common, seems less terrible; and because it comes from strangers, seems less pernicious in its consequences, than when they are expos'd singly against one whose commerce is advantageous to them, and without whose society 'tis impossible they can subsist. Now foreign war to a society without government necessarily produces civil war. Throw any considerable goods among men, they instantly fall a quarrelling, while each strives to get possession of what pleases him, without regard to the consequences. In a foreign war the most considerable of all goods, life and limbs, are at stake; and as every one shuns dangerous posts, seizes the best arms, seeks excuse for the slightest wounds, the rules of society, which may be well enough observ'd, while men were calm, can now no longer take place, when they are in such commotion.

SB 540

2 This we find verify'd in the *American* tribes, where men live in concord and amity among themselves without any establish'd government; and never pay submission to any of their fellows, except in time of war, when their captain enjoys a shadow of authority, which he loses after their return from the field, and the establishment of peace with the neighbouring tribes.[†] This authority, however, instructs them in the advantages of government, and teaches them to have recourse to it, when either by the pillage of war, by commerce, or by any fortuitous inventions, their riches and possessions have become so considerable as to make them forget, on every emergence, the interest they have in the preservation of peace and justice. Hence we may give a plausible reason, among others, why all governments are at first monarchical, without any mixture and variety; and why republics arise only from the abuses of monarchy and despotic power. Camps are the true mothers of cities;[†] and as war cannot be administred, by reason of the suddenness of every exigency, without some authority in a single person, the same kind of authority naturally takes place in that civil government, which succeeds the military. And this reason I take to be more natural, than the common one deriv'd from patriarchal government, or the authority of a father, which is said first to take place in one family, and to accustom the members of it to the government of a single person.[†] The state of society without government is one of the most natural states of men, and may subsist with the conjunction of many families, and long after the first generation.[†] Nothing but an encrease of riches and possessions cou'd oblige men to quit it; and so barbarous and uninstructed are all societies on their first formation, that many years must elapse before these cou'd encrease to such a degree, as to disturb men in the enjoyment of peace and concord.

SB 541

3 But tho' it be possible for men to maintain a small uncultivated society

without government, 'tis impossible they shou'd maintain a society of any kind without justice, and the observance of those three fundamental laws concerning the stability of possession, its translation by consent, and the performance of promises. These are, therefore, antecedent to government, and are suppos'd to impose an obligation before the duty of allegiance to civil magistrates has once been thought of. Nay, I shall go farther, and assert, that government, *upon its first establishment*, wou'd naturally be suppos'd to derive its obligation from those laws of nature, and, in particular, from that concerning the performance of promises. When men have once perceiv'd the necessity of government to maintain peace, and execute justice, they wou'd naturally assemble together, wou'd choose magistrates, determine their power, and *promise* them obedience. As a promise is suppos'd to be a bond or security already in use, and attended with a moral obligation, 'tis to be consider'd as the original sanction of government, and as the source of the first obligation to obedience. This reasoning appears so natural, that it has become the foundation of our fashionable system of politics, *SB 542* and is in a manner the creed of a party[†] amongst us, who value themselves, with reason, on the soundness of their philosophy, and their liberty of thought. *All men*, say they, *are born free and equal: Government and superiority can only be establish'd by consent: The consent of men, in establishing government, imposes on them a new obligation, unknown to the laws of nature. Men, therefore, are bound to obey their magistrates, only because they promise it; and if they had not given their word, either expressly or tacitly, to preserve allegiance, it wou'd never have become a part of their moral duty.*[†] This conclusion, however, when carry'd so far as to comprehend government in all its ages and situations, is entirely erroneous;[†] and I maintain, that tho' the duty of allegiance be at first grafted on the obligation of promises, and be for some time supported by that obligation, yet as soon as the advantages of government are fully known and acknowledg'd, it immediately takes root of itself, and has an original obligation and authority, independent of all contracts. This is a principle of moment, which we must examine with care and attention, before we proceed any farther.

4   'Tis reasonable for those philosophers, who assert justice to be a natural virtue, and antecedent to human conventions, to resolve all civil allegiance into the obligation of a promise, and assert that 'tis our own consent alone, which binds us to any submission to magistracy.[†] For as all government is plainly an invention of men, and the origin of most governments is known in history, 'tis necessary to mount higher, in order to find the source of our political duties, if we wou'd assert them to have any *natural* obligation of morality. These philosophers, therefore, quickly observe, that society is as antient as the human species, and those three fundamental laws of nature as antient as society: So that taking advantage of the antiquity, and obscure origin of these laws, they first deny them to be artificial and voluntary inventions of men, and then seek to ingraft on them those other duties, which are more plainly artificial. But being once undeceiv'd in this particular, and having found that *natural*, as well as *civil* *SB 543* justice, derives its origin from human conventions, we shall quickly perceive, how fruitless it is to resolve the one into the other, and seek, in the laws of nature,

a stronger foundation for our political duties than interest, and human conventions; while these laws themselves are built on the very same foundation. On which-ever side we turn this subject, we shall find, that these two kinds of duty are exactly on the same footing, and have the same source both of their *first invention* and *moral obligation*. They are contriv'd to remedy like inconveniencies, and acquire their moral sanction in the same manner, from their remedying those inconveniencies. These are two points, which we shall endeavour to prove as distinctly as possible.

5   We have already shown,† that men *invented* the three fundamental laws of nature, when they observ'd the necessity of society to their mutual subsistance, and found, that 'twas impossible to maintain any correspondence together, without some restraint on their natural appetites. The same self-love, therefore, which renders men so incommodious to each other, taking a new and more convenient direction, produces the rules of justice, and is the *first* motive of their observance. But when men have observ'd, that tho' the rules of justice be sufficient to maintain any society, yet 'tis impossible for them, of themselves, to observe those rules, in large and polish'd societies; they establish government, as a new invention to attain their ends, and preserve the old, or procure new advantages, by a more strict execution of justice. So far, therefore, our *civil* duties are connected with our *natural*, that the former are invented chiefly for the sake of the latter; and that the principal object of government is to constrain men to observe the laws of nature. In this respect, however, that law of nature, concerning the performance of promises, is only compriz'd along with the rest; and its exact observance is to be consider'd as an effect of the institution of government, and not the obedience to government as an effect of the obligation of a promise. Tho' the object of our civil duties be the enforcing of our natural, yet the *first* motive of the invention, as well as the performance of both, is nothing but self-interest:[79] And since there is a separate interest in the obedience to government, from that in the performance of promises, we must also allow of a separate obligation. To obey the civil magistrate is requisite to preserve order and concord in society. To perform promises is requisite to beget mutual trust and confidence in the common offices of life. The ends, as well as the means, are perfectly distinct; nor is the one subordinate to the other.   *SB 544*

6   To make this more evident, let us consider, that men will often bind themselves by promises to the performance of what it wou'd have been their interest to perform, independent of these promises; as when they wou'd give others a fuller security, by super-adding a new obligation of interest to that which they formerly lay under. The interest in the performance of promises, besides its moral obligation, is general, avow'd, and of the last consequence in life. Other interests may be more particular and doubtful; and we are apt to entertain a greater suspicion, that men may indulge their humour, or passion, in acting contrary to them. Here, therefore, promises come naturally in play, and are often requir'd for fuller satisfaction and security. But supposing those other interests

[79] First in time, not in dignity or force.

to be as general and avow'd as the interest in the performance of a promise, they will be regarded as on the same footing, and men will begin to repose the same confidence in them. Now this is exactly the case with regard to our civil duties, or obedience to the magistrate; without which no government cou'd subsist, nor any peace or order be maintain'd in large societies, where there are so many possessions on the one hand, and so many wants, real or imaginary, on the other. Our civil duties, therefore, must soon detach themselves from our promises, and acquire a separate force and influence. The interest in both is of the very same kind: 'Tis general, avow'd, and prevails in all times and places. There is, then, no *SB 545* pretext of reason for founding the one upon the other; while each of them has a foundation peculiar to itself. We might as well resolve the obligation to abstain from the possessions of others, into the obligation of a promise, as that of allegiance. The interests are not more distinct in the one case than the other. A regard to property is not more necessary to natural society, than obedience is to civil society or government; nor is the former society more necessary to the being of mankind, than the latter to their well-being and happiness. In short, if the performance of promises be advantageous, so is obedience to government: If the former interest be general, so is the latter: If the one interest be obvious and avow'd, so is the other. And as these two rules are founded on like obligations of interest, each of them must have a peculiar authority, independent of the other.

7   But 'tis not only the *natural* obligations of interest, which are distinct in promises and allegiance; but also the *moral* obligations[†] of honour and conscience: Nor does the merit or demerit of the one depend in the least upon that of the other. And indeed, if we consider the close connexion there is betwixt the natural and moral obligations, we shall find this conclusion to be entirely unavoidable. Our interest is always engag'd on the side of obedience to magistracy; and there is nothing but a great present advantage, that can lead us to rebellion, by making us over-look the remote interest, which we have in the preserving of peace and order in society. But tho' a present interest may thus blind us with regard to our own actions, it takes not place with regard to those of others; nor hinders them from appearing in their true colours, as highly prejudicial to our own interest, or at least to that of the public, which we partake of by *sympathy*. This naturally gives us an uneasiness, in considering such seditious and disloyal actions, and makes us attach to them the idea of vice and moral deformity. 'Tis the same principle, which causes us to disapprove of all kinds of private injustice, and in particular of the breach of promises. We blame all *SB 546* treachery and breach of faith; because we consider, that the freedom and extent of human commerce depend entirely on a fidelity with regard to promises. We blame all disloyalty to magistrates; because we perceive, that the execution of justice, in the stability of possession, its translation by consent, and the performance of promises, is impossible, without submission to government. As there are here two interests entirely distinct from each other, they must give rise to two moral obligations, equally separate and independant. Tho' there was no such thing as a promise in the world, government wou'd still be necessary in all large

349

and civiliz'd societies; and if promises had only their own proper obligation, without the separate sanction of government, they wou'd have but little efficacy in such societies. This separates the boundaries of our public and private duties, and shows that the latter are more dependant on the former, than the former on the latter. *Education*, and *the artifice of politicians*, concur in bestowing a farther morality on loyalty, and branding all rebellion with a greater degree of guilt and infamy. Nor is it a wonder, that politicians shou'd be very industrious in inculcating such notions, where their interest is so particularly concern'd.[†]

8   Lest those arguments shou'd not appear entirely conclusive (as I think they are) I shall have recourse to authority, and shall prove, from the universal consent of mankind, that the obligation of submission to government is not deriv'd from any promise of the subjects. Nor need any one wonder, that tho' I have all along endeavour'd to establish my system on pure reason, and have scarce ever cited the judgment even of philosophers or historians on any article, I shou'd now appeal to popular authority, and oppose the sentiments of the rabble to any philosophical reasoning. For it must be observ'd, that the opinions of men, in this case, carry with them a peculiar authority, and are, in a great measure, infallible. The distinction of moral good and evil is founded on the pleasure or pain, which results from the view of any sentiment, or character; and as that pleasure   *SB 547* or pain cannot be unknown to the person who feels it, it follows, that there is just so much vice or virtue in any character, as every one places in it, and that 'tis impossible in this particular we can ever be mistaken.[80] And tho' our judgments concerning the *origin* of any vice or virtue, be not so certain as those concerning their *degrees*; yet, since the question in this case regards not any philosophical origin of an obligation, but a plain matter of fact, 'tis not easily conceiv'd how we can fall into an error. A man, who acknowledges himself to be bound to another, for a certain sum, must certainly know whether it be by his own bond, or that of his father; whether it be of his mere good-will, or for money lent him; and under what conditions, and for what purposes he has bound himself. In like manner, it being certain, that there is a moral obligation to submit to government, because every one thinks so; it must be as certain, that this obligation arises not from a promise; since no one, whose judgment has not been led astray by too strict adherence to a system of philosophy, has ever yet dreamt of ascribing it to that origin. Neither magistrates nor subjects have form'd this idea of our civil duties.

9   We find, that magistrates are so far from deriving their authority, and the obligation to obedience in their subjects, from the foundation of a promise or original contract, that they conceal, as far as possible, from their people, especially from the vulgar, that they have their origin from thence. Were this the

---

[80] This proposition must hold strictly true, with regard to every quality, that is determin'd merely by sentiment. In what sense we can talk either of a *right* or a *wrong* taste in morals, eloquence, or beauty, shall be consider'd afterwards.[†] In the mean time, it may be observ'd, that there is such an uniformity in the *general* sentiments of mankind, as to render such questions of but small importance.

sanction of government, our rulers wou'd never receive it tacitly, which is the utmost that can be pretended; since what is given tacitly and insensibly can never have such influence on mankind, as what is perform'd expressly and openly. A tacit promise is, where the will is signify'd by other more diffuse signs than those of speech; but a will there must certainly be in the case, and that can never escape the person's notice, who exerted it, however silent or tacit. But were you to ask the far greatest part of the nation, whether they had ever consented to the authority of their rulers, or promis'd to obey them, they wou'd be inclin'd to think very strangely of you; and wou'd certainly reply, that the affair depended not on their consent, but that they were born to such an obedience. In consequence of this opinion, we frequently see them imagine such persons to be their natural rulers, as are at that time depriv'd of all power and authority, and whom no man, however foolish, wou'd voluntarily choose;[†] and this merely because they are in that line, which rul'd before, and in that degree of it, which us'd to succeed; tho' perhaps in so distant a period, that scarce any man alive cou'd ever have given any promise of obedience. Has a government, then, no authority over such as these, because they never consented to it, and wou'd esteem the very attempt of such a free choice a piece of arrogance and impiety? We find by experience, that it punishes them very freely for what it calls treason and rebellion, which, it seems, according to this system, reduces itself to common injustice. If you say, that by dwelling in its dominions, they in effect consented to the establish'd government; I answer, that this can only be, where they think the affair depends on their choice, which few or none, beside those philosophers, have ever yet imagin'd. It never was pleaded as an excuse for a rebel, that the first act he perform'd, after he came to years of discretion, was to levy war against the sovereign of the state; and that while he was a child he cou'd not bind himself by his own consent, and having become a man, show'd plainly, by the first act he perform'd, that he had no design to impose on himself any obligation to obedience. We find, on the contrary, that civil laws punish this crime at the same age as any other, which is criminal, of itself, without our consent; that is, when the person is come to the full use of reason: Whereas to this crime they ought in justice to allow some intermediate time, in which a tacit consent at least might be suppos'd. To which we may add, that a man living under an absolute government, wou'd owe it no allegiance; since, by its very nature, it depends not on consent. But as that is as *natural* and *common* a government as any, it must certainly occasion some obligation; and 'tis plain from experience, that men, who are subjected to it, do always think so. This is a clear proof, that we do not commonly esteem our allegiance to be deriv'd from our consent or promise; and a farther proof is, that when our promise is upon any account expressly engag'd, we always distinguish exactly betwixt the two obligations, and believe the one to add more force to the other, than in a repetition of the same promise. Where no promise is given, a man looks not on his faith as broken in private matters, upon account of rebellion; but keeps those two duties of honour and allegiance perfectly distinct and separate. As the uniting of them was thought by these philosophers a very subtile invention, this is a convincing proof, that 'tis not a true one; since no man

SB 548

SB 549

can either give a promise, or be restrain'd by its sanction and obligation unknown to himself.

Sect. 9. *Of the measures of allegiance*

1 Those political writers, who have had recourse to a promise, or original contract, as the source of our allegiance to government, intended to establish a principle, which is perfectly just and reasonable; tho' the reasoning, upon which they endeavour'd to establish it, was fallacious and sophistical. They wou'd prove, that our submission to government admits of exceptions, and that an egregious tyranny in the rulers is sufficient to free the subjects from all ties of allegiance.[†] Since men enter into society, say they, and submit themselves to government, by their free and voluntary consent, they must have in view certain advantages, *SB 550* which they propose to reap from it, and for which they are contented to resign their native liberty. There is, therefore, something mutual engag'd on the part of the magistrate, *viz.* protection and security; and 'tis only by the hopes he affords of these advantages, that he can ever perswade men to submit to him. But when instead of protection and security, they meet with tyranny and oppression, they are freed from their promises, (as happens in all conditional contracts) and return to that state of liberty, which preceded the institution of government. Men wou'd never be so foolish as to enter into such engagements as shou'd turn entirely to the advantage of others, without any view of bettering their own condition. Whoever proposes to draw any profit from our submission, must engage himself, either expressly or tacitly, to make us reap some advantage from his authority; nor ought he to expect, that without the performance of his part we will ever continue in obedience.

2 I repeat it: This conclusion is just, tho' the principles be erroneous; and I flatter myself, that I can establish the same conclusion on more reasonable principles. I shall not take such a compass, in establishing our political duties, as to assert, that men perceive the advantages of government; that they institute government with a view to those advantages; that this institution requires a promise of obedience; which imposes a moral obligation to a certain degree, but being conditional, ceases to be binding, whenever the other contracting party performs not his part of the engagement. I perceive, that a promise itself arises entirely from human conventions, and is invented with a view to a certain interest.[†] I seek, therefore, some such interest more immediately connected with government, and which may be at once the original motive to its institution, and the source of our obedience to it. This interest I find to consist in the security and protection, which we enjoy in political society, and which we can never attain, when perfectly free and independent.[†] As interest, therefore, is the immediate *SB 551* sanction of government, the one can have no longer being than the other; and whenever the civil magistrate carries his oppression so far as to render his authority perfectly intolerable, we are no longer bound to submit to it. The cause ceases; the effect must cease also.

3   So far the conclusion is immediate and direct, concerning the *natural* obligation which we have to allegiance. As to the *moral* obligation, we may observe, that the maxim wou'd here be false, that *when the cause ceases, the effect must cease also.* For there is a principle of human nature, which we have frequently taken notice of, that men are mightily addicted to *general rules,*[†] and that we often carry our maxims beyond those reasons, which first induc'd us to establish them. Where cases are similar in many circumstances, we are apt to put them on the same footing, without considering, that they differ in the most material circumstances, and that the resemblance is more apparent than real. It may, therefore, be thought, that in the case of allegiance our moral obligation of duty will not cease, even tho' the natural obligation of interest, which is its cause, has ceas'd; and that men may be bound by *conscience* to submit to a tyrannical government against their own and the public interest. And indeed, to the force of this argument I so far submit, as to acknowledge, that general rules commonly extend beyond the principles, on which they are founded; and that we seldom make any exception to them, unless that exception have the qualities of a general rule, and be founded on very numerous and common instances. Now this I assert to be entirely the present case. When men submit to the authority of others, 'tis to procure themselves some security against the wickedness and injustice of men, who are perpetually carry'd, by their unruly passions, and by their present and immediate interest, to the violation of all the laws of society. But as this imperfection is inherent in human nature, we know that it must attend men in all their states and conditions; and that those, whom we choose for rulers, do not immediately become of a superior nature to the rest of mankind, upon account of their superior power and authority. What we expect from them depends not on a change of their nature but of their situation, when they acquire a more immediate interest in the preservation of order and the execution of justice. But besides that this interest is only more immediate in the execution of justice among their subjects, not in disputes betwixt themselves and their subjects; besides this, I say, we may often expect, from the irregularity of human nature, that they will neglect even this immediate interest, and be transported by their passions into all the excesses of cruelty and ambition. Our general knowledge of human nature, our observation of the past history of mankind, our experience of present times; all these causes must induce us to open the door to exceptions, and must make us conclude, that we may resist the more violent effects of supreme power, without any crime or injustice.

SB 552

4   Accordingly we may observe, that this is both the general practice and principle of mankind, and that no nation, that cou'd find any remedy, ever yet suffer'd the cruel ravages of a tyrant, or were blam'd for their resistance.[†] Those who took up arms against *Dionysius*[†] or *Nero,*[†] or *Philip* the Second,[†] have the favour of every reader in the perusal of their history; and nothing but the most violent perversion of common sense can ever lead us to condemn them. 'Tis certain, therefore, that in all our notions of morals we never entertain such an absurdity as that of passive obedience,[†] but make allowances for resistance in the more

flagrant instances of tyranny and oppression. The general opinion of mankind has some authority in all cases; but in this of morals 'tis perfectly infallible. Nor is it less infallible, because men cannot distinctly explain the principles, on which it is founded. Few persons can carry on this train of reasoning: "Government is a mere human invention for the interest of society. Where the tyranny of the governor removes this interest, it also removes the natural obligation to obedience. The moral obligation is founded on the natural, and therefore must cease *SB 553* where *that* ceases; especially where the subject is such as makes us foresee very many occasions wherein the natural obligation may cease, and causes us to form a kind of general rule for the regulation of our conduct in such occurrences." But tho' this train of reasoning be too subtile for the vulgar, 'tis certain, that all men have an implicit notion of it, and are sensible, that they owe obedience to government merely on account of the public interest; and at the same time, that human nature is so subject to frailties and passions, as may easily pervert this institution, and change their governors into tyrants and public enemies. If the sense of interest were not our original motive to obedience, I wou'd fain ask, what other principle is there in human nature capable of subduing the natural ambition of men, and forcing them to such a submission?[†] Imitation and custom are not sufficient. For the question still recurs, what motive first produces those instances of submission, which we imitate, and that train of actions, which produces the custom? There evidently is no other principle than interest; and if interest first produces obedience to government, the obligation to obedience must cease, whenever the interest ceases, in any great degree, and in a considerable number of instances.

Sect. 10. *Of the objects of allegiance*

1   But tho', on some occasions, it may be justifiable, both in sound politics and morality, to resist supreme power, 'tis certain, that in the ordinary course of human affairs nothing can be more pernicious and criminal; and that besides the convulsions, which always attend revolutions, such a practice tends directly to the subversion of all government, and the causing an universal anarchy and confusion among mankind. As numerous and civiliz'd societies cannot subsist without government, so government is entirely useless without an exact obedi- *SB 554* ence. We ought always to weigh the advantages, which we reap from authority, against the disadvantages; and by this means we shall become more scrupulous of putting in practice the doctrine of resistance. The common rule requires submission; and 'tis only in cases of grievous tyranny and oppression, that the exception can take place.

2   Since then such a blind submission is commonly due to magistracy, the next question is, *To whom it is due, and whom we are to regard as our lawful magistrates?* In order to answer this question, let us recollect what we have already establish'd concerning the origin of government and political society.[†] When men have once experienc'd the impossibility of preserving any steady order in society, while every one is his own master, and violates or observes the laws of society, accord-

ing to his present interest or pleasure, they naturally run into the invention of government, and put it out of their own power, as far as possible, to transgress the rules of justice. Government, therefore, arises from the voluntary convention of men; and 'tis evident, that the same convention, which establishes government, will also determine the persons who are to govern, and will remove all doubt and ambiguity in this particular. And the voluntary consent of men must here have the greater efficacy, that the authority of the magistrate does *at first* stand upon the foundation of a promise of the subjects,[†] by which they bind themselves to obedience; as in every other contract or engagement. The same promise, then, which binds them to obedience, ties them down to a particular person, and makes him the object of their allegiance.

3   But when government has been establish'd on this footing for some considerable time, and the separate interest, which we have in submission, has produc'd a separate sentiment of morality, the case is entirely alter'd, and a promise is no longer able to determine the particular magistrate; since it is no longer consider'd as the foundation of government. We naturally suppose ourselves born to submission; and imagine, that such particular persons have a right to command, as we on our part are bound to obey. These notions of right and obligation are deriv'd from nothing but the *advantage* reapt from government, which gives us a repugnance to practise resistance ourselves, and makes us displeas'd with any instance of it in others. But here 'tis remarkable, that in this new state of affairs, the original sanction of government, which is *interest*, is not admitted to determine the persons, whom we are to obey, as the original sanction did at first, when affairs were on the footing of a *promise*. A *promise* fixes and determines the persons, without any uncertainty: But 'tis evident, that if men were to regulate their conduct in this particular, by the view of a peculiar *interest*, either public or private, they wou'd involve themselves in endless confusion, and wou'd render all government, in a great measure, ineffectual. The private interest of every one is different; and tho' the public interest in itself be always one and the same, yet it becomes the source of as great dissentions, by reason of the different opinions of particular persons concerning it. The same interest, therefore, which causes us to submit to magistracy, makes us renounce itself in the choice of our magistrates, and binds us down to a certain form of government, and to particular persons, without allowing us to aspire to the utmost perfection in either. The case is here the same as in that law of nature concerning the stability of possession.[†] 'Tis highly advantageous, and even absolutely necessary to society, that possession shou'd be stable; and this leads us to the establishment of such a rule: But we find, that were we to follow the same advantage, in assigning particular possessions to particular persons, we shou'd disappoint our end, and perpetuate the confusion, which that rule is intended to prevent. We must, therefore, proceed by general rules, and regulate ourselves by general interests, in modifying the law of nature concerning the stability of possession. Nor need we fear, that our attachment to this law will diminish upon account of the seeming frivolousness of those interests, by which it is determin'd. The impulse of the mind is deriv'd from a very strong interest; and those other more minute interests serve

SB 555

SB 556

only to direct the motion, without adding any thing to it, or diminishing from it. 'Tis the same case with government. Nothing is more advantageous to society than such an invention; and this interest is sufficient to make us embrace it with ardour and alacrity; tho' we are oblig'd afterwards to regulate and direct our devotion to government by several considerations, which are not of the same importance, and to choose our magistrates without having in view any particular advantage from the choice.

4   The *first* of those principles I shall take notice of, as a foundation of the right of magistracy, is that which gives authority to almost all the establish'd governments of the world: I mean, *long possession* in any one form of government, or succession of princes. 'Tis certain, that if we remount to the first origin of every nation, we shall find, that there scarce is any race of kings, or form of a commonwealth, that is not primarily founded on usurpation and rebellion, and whose title is not at first worse than doubtful and uncertain. Time alone gives solidity to their right; and operating gradually on the minds of men, reconciles them to any authority, and makes it seem just and reasonable. Nothing causes any sentiment to have a greater influence upon us than custom, or turns our imagination more strongly to any object. When we have been long accustom'd to obey any set of men, that general instinct or tendency, which we have to suppose a moral obligation attending loyalty, takes easily this direction, and chooses that set of men for its objects. 'Tis interest which gives the general instinct; but 'tis custom which gives the particular direction.

5   And here 'tis observable, that the same length of time has a different influence on our sentiments of morality, according to its different influence on the mind.   SB 557
We naturally judge of every thing by comparison; and since in considering the fate of kingdoms and republics, we embrace a long extent of time, a small duration has not in this case a like influence on our sentiments, as when we consider any other object. One thinks he acquires a right to a horse, or a suit of cloaths, in a very short time; but a century is scarce sufficient to establish any new government, or remove all scruples in the minds of the subjects concerning it. Add to this, that a shorter period of time will suffice to give a prince a title to any additional power he may usurp, than will serve to fix his right, where the whole is an usurpation. The kings of *France* have not been possess'd of absolute power for above two reigns;[†] and yet nothing will appear more extravagant to *Frenchmen* than to talk of their liberties. If we consider what has been said concerning *accession*,[†] we shall easily account for this phænomenon.

6   When there is no form of government establish'd by *long* possession, the *present* possession is sufficient to supply its place, and may be regarded as the *second* source of all public authority. Right to authority is nothing but the constant possession of authority, maintain'd by the laws of society and the interests of mankind; and nothing can be more natural than to join this constant possession to the present one, according to the principles above-mention'd.[†] If the same principles did not take place with regard to the property of private persons, 'twas because these principles were counter-ballanc'd by very strong considerations of interest; when we observ'd, that all restitution wou'd by that means be

prevented, and every violence be authoriz'd and protected. And tho' the same motives may seem to have force, with regard to public authority, yet they are oppos'd by a contrary interest;[†] which consists in the preservation of peace, and the avoiding of all changes, which, however they may be easily produc'd in private affairs, are unavoidably attended with bloodshed and confusion, where the public is interested.

7   Any one, who finding the impossibility of accounting for the right of the *SB 558* present possessor, by any receiv'd system of ethics, shou'd resolve to deny absolutely that right, and assert, that it is not authoriz'd by morality, wou'd be justly thought to maintain a very extravagant paradox, and to shock the common sense and judgment of mankind.[†] No maxim is more conformable, both to prudence and morals, than to submit quietly to the government, which we find establish'd in the country where we happen to live, without enquiring too curiously into its origin and first establishment. Few governments will bear being examin'd so rigorously. How many kingdoms are there at present in the world, and how many more do we find in history, whose governors have no better foundation for their authority than that of present possession? To confine ourselves to the *Roman* and *Grecian* empire; is it not evident, that the long succession of emperors, from the dissolution of the *Roman* liberty, to the final extinction of that empire by the *Turks*,[†] cou'd not so much as pretend to any other title to the empire? The election of the senate was a mere form, which always follow'd the choice of the legions; and these were almost always divided in the different provinces, and nothing but the sword was able to terminate the difference. 'Twas by the sword, therefore, that every emperor acquir'd, as well as defended his right; and we must either say, that all the known world, for so many ages, had no government, and ow'd no allegiance to any one, or must allow, that the right of the stronger, in public affairs, is to be receiv'd as legitimate, and authoriz'd by morality, when not oppos'd by any other title.

8   The right of *conquest* may be consider'd as a *third* source of the title of sovereigns. This right resembles very much that of present possession; but has rather a superior force, being seconded by the notions of glory and honour, which we ascribe to *conquerors*, instead of the sentiments of hatred and detestation, which attend *usurpers*. Men naturally favour those they love; and therefore are more apt to ascribe a right to successful violence, betwixt one sovereign and another, than *SB 559* to the successful rebellion of a subject against his sovereign.[81]

9   When neither long possession, nor present possession, nor conquest take place, as when the first sovereign, who founded any monarchy, dies; in that case, the right of *succession* naturally prevails in their stead, and men are commonly induc'd to place the son of their late monarch on the throne, and suppose him to inherit his father's authority. The presum'd consent of the father, the

---

[81] It is not here asserted, that *present possession* or *conquest* are sufficient to give a title against *long possession* and *positive laws*: But only that they have some force, and will be able to cast the ballance where the titles are otherwise equal, and will even be sufficient *sometimes* to sanctify the weaker title. What degree of force they have is difficult to determine. I believe all moderate men will allow, that they have great force in all disputes concerning the rights of princes.

imitation of the succession to private families, the interest, which the state has in choosing the person, who is most powerful, and has the most numerous followers; all these reasons lead men to prefer the son of their late monarch to any other person.[82]

10   These reasons have some weight; but I am perswaded, that to one, who considers impartially of the matter, 'twill appear, that some principles of the imagination[†] concur with those views of justice and interest. The royal authority seems to be connected with the young prince even in his father's life-time, by the natural transition of the thought; and still more after his death: So that nothing is more natural than to compleat this union by a new relation, and by putting him actually in possession of what seems so naturally to belong to him.

11   To confirm this we may weigh the following phænomena, which are pretty curious in their kind. In elective monarchies the right of succession has no place by the laws and settled custom; and yet its influence is so natural, that 'tis impossible entirely to exclude it from the imagination, and render the subjects indif-   *SB 560* ferent to the son of their deceas'd monarch. Hence in some governments of this kind, the choice commonly falls on one or other of the royal family; and in some governments they are all excluded. Those contrary phænomena proceed from the same principle. Where the royal family is excluded, 'tis from a refinement in politics, which makes people sensible of their propensity to choose a sovereign in that family, and gives them a jealousy of their liberty, lest their new monarch, aided by this propensity, shou'd establish his family, and destroy the freedom of elections for the future.

12   The history of *Artaxerxes*, and the younger *Cyrus*,[†] may furnish us with some reflections to the same purpose. *Cyrus* pretended a right to the throne above his elder brother, because he was born after his father's accession. I do not pretend, that this reason was valid. I wou'd only infer from it, that he wou'd never have made use of such a pretext, were it not for the qualities of the imagination above-mention'd,[†] by which we are naturally inclin'd to unite by a new relation whatever objects we find already united. *Artaxerxes* had an advantage above his brother, as being the eldest son, and the first in succession: But *Cyrus* was more closely related to the royal authority, as being begot after his father was invested with it.

13   Shou'd it here be pretended, that the view of convenience may be the source of all the right of succession, and that men gladly take advantage of any rule, by which they can fix the successor of their late sovereign, and prevent that anarchy and confusion, which attends all new elections: To this I wou'd answer, that perhaps this motive may contribute somewhat to the effect; but, that without another principle, 'tis impossible such a motive shou'd take place. The interest of a nation requires, that the succession to the crown shou'd be fix'd one way or other; but 'tis the same thing to its interest in what way it be fix'd:[†] So that if the

---

[82] To prevent mistakes I must observe, that this case of succession is not the same with that of   *SB 559* hereditary monarchies, where custom has fix'd the right of succession. These depend upon the principle of long possession above-explain'd.

relation of blood had not an effect independent of public interest, it wou'd never have been regarded, without a positive law; and 'twou'd have been impossible, that so many positive laws of different nations cou'd ever have concurr'd precisely in the same views and intentions.

14   This leads us to consider the *fifth* source of authority, viz. *positive laws*; when the legislature establishes a certain form of government and succession of princes. At first sight it may be thought, that this must resolve into some of the preceding titles of authority. The legislative power, whence the positive law is deriv'd, must either be establish'd by original contract, long possession, present possession, conquest, or succession; and consequently the positive law must derive its force from some of these principles. But here 'tis remarkable, that tho' a positive law can only derive its force from these principles, yet it acquires not all the force of the principle from whence it is deriv'd, but loses considerably in the transition; as it is natural to imagine. For instance; a government is establish'd for many centuries on a certain system of laws, forms, and methods of succession. The legislative power, establish'd by this long succession, changes all on a sudden the whole system of government, and introduces a new constitution in its stead. I believe few of the subjects will think themselves bound to comply with this alteration, unless it have an evident tendency to the public good: But will think themselves still at liberty to return to the antient government. Hence the notion of *fundamental laws*; which are suppos'd to be inalterable by the will of the sovereign: And of this nature the *Salic* law† is understood to be in *France*. How far these fundamental laws extend is not determin'd in any government; nor is it possible it ever shou'd. There is such an insensible gradation from the most material laws to the most trivial, and from the most antient laws to the most modern, that 'twill be impossible to set bounds to the legislative power, and determine how far it may innovate in the principles of government. That is the work more of imagination and passion than of reason.

15   Whoever considers the history of the several nations of the world; their revolutions, conquests, encrease, and diminution; the manner in which their particular governments are establish'd, and the successive right transmitted from one person to another, will soon learn to treat very lightly all disputes concerning the rights of princes, and will be convinc'd, that a strict adherence to any general rules, and the rigid loyalty to particular persons and families, on which some people set so high a value, are virtues that hold less of reason, than of bigotry and superstition. In this particular, the study of history confirms the reasonings of true philosophy; which, showing us the original qualities of human nature, teaches us to regard the controversies in politics as incapable of any decision in most cases, and as entirely subordinate to the interests of peace and liberty. Where the public good does not evidently demand a change; 'tis certain, that the concurrence of all those titles, *original contract*, *long possession*, *present possession*, *succession*, and *positive laws*, forms the strongest title to sovereignty, and is justly regarded as sacred and inviolable. But when these titles are mingled and oppos'd in different degrees, they often occasion perplexity; and are less capable of solution from the arguments of lawyers and philosophers, than from

the swords of the soldiery. Who shall tell me, for instance, whether *Germanicus*, or *Drusus*, ought to have succeeded *Tiberius*,[†] had he dy'd while they were both alive, without naming any of them for his successor? Ought the right of adoption to be receiv'd as equivalent to that of blood in a nation, where it had the same effect in private families, and had already, in two instances, taken place in the public? Ought *Germanicus* to be esteem'd the eldest son, because he was born before *Drusus*; or the younger, because he was adopted after the birth of his brother? Ought the right of the elder to be regarded in a nation, where the eldest brother had no advantage in the succession to private families? Ought the *Roman* empire at that time to be esteem'd hereditary, because of two examples; or ought it, even so early, to be regarded as belonging to the stronger, or the present possessor, as being founded on so recent an usurpation? Upon whatever principles we may pretend to answer these and such like questions, I am afraid we shall never be able to satisfy an impartial enquirer, who adopts no party in political controversies, and will be satisfy'd with nothing but sound reason and philosophy.

SB 563

16   But here an *English* reader will be apt to enquire concerning that famous *revolution*,[†] which has had such a happy influence on our constitution, and has been attended with such mighty consequences. We have already remark'd,[†] that in the case of enormous tyranny and oppression, 'tis lawful to take arms even against supreme power; and that as government is a mere human invention for mutual advantage and security, it no longer imposes any obligation, either natural or moral, when once it ceases to have that tendency. But tho' this *general* principle be authoriz'd by common sense, and the practice of all ages, 'tis certainly impossible for the laws, or even for philosophy, to establish any *particular* rules, by which we may know when resistance is lawful; and decide all controversies, which may arise on that subject. This may not only happen with regard to supreme power; but 'tis possible, even in some constitutions, where the legislative authority is not lodg'd in one person, that there may be a magistrate so eminent and powerful, as to oblige the laws to keep silence in this particular. Nor wou'd this silence be an effect only of their *respect*, but also of their *prudence*; since 'tis certain, that in the vast variety of circumstances, which occur in all governments, a particular exercise of power, in so great a magistrate, may at one time be beneficial to the public, which at another time wou'd be pernicious and tyrannical. But notwithstanding this silence of the laws in limited monarchies, 'tis certain, that the people still retain the right of resistance; since 'tis impossible, even in the most despotic governments, to deprive them of it. The same necessity of self-preservation, and the same motive of public good, give them the same liberty in the one case as in the other. And we may farther observe, that in such mix'd governments, the cases, wherein resistance is lawful, must occur much oftener, and greater indulgence be given to the subjects to defend themselves by force of arms, than in arbitrary governments. Not only where the chief magistrate enters into measures, in themselves, extremely pernicious to the public, but even when he wou'd encroach on the other parts of the constitution,

SB 564

and extend his power beyond the legal bounds, it is allowable to resist and dethrone him; tho' such resistance and violence may, in the general tenor of the laws, be deem'd unlawful and rebellious.[†] For besides that nothing is more essential to public interest, than the preservation of public liberty; 'tis evident, that if such a mix'd government be once suppos'd to be establish'd, every part or member of the constitution must have a right of self-defence, and of maintaining its antient bounds against the encroachment of every other authority. As matter wou'd have been created in vain, were it depriv'd of a power of resistance, without which no part of it cou'd preserve a distinct existence, and the whole might be crowded up into a single point: So 'tis a gross absurdity to suppose, in any government, a right without a remedy, or allow, that the supreme power is shar'd with the people, without allowing, that 'tis lawful for them to defend their share against every invader. Those, therefore, who wou'd seem to respect our free government, and yet deny the right of resistance, have renounc'd all pretensions to common sense, and do not merit a serious answer.

17   It does not belong to my present purpose to show, that these general principles are applicable to the late *revolution*; and that all the rights and privileges, which ought to be sacred to a free nation, were at that time threaten'd with the utmost danger. I am better pleas'd to leave this controverted subject, if it really admits of controversy; and to indulge myself in some philosophical reflections, which naturally arise from that important event. *SB 565*

18   *First*, We may observe, that shou'd the *lords* and *commons*[†] in our constitution, without any reason from public interest, either depose the king in being, or after his death exclude the prince, who, by laws and settled custom, ought to succeed, no one wou'd esteem their proceedings legal, or think themselves bound to comply with them. But shou'd the king, by his unjust practices, or his attempts for a tyrannical and despotic power, justly forfeit his legal authority, it then not only becomes morally lawful and suitable to the nature of political society to dethrone him; but what is more, we are apt likewise to think, that the remaining members of the constitution acquire a right of excluding his next heir, and of choosing whom they please for his successor. This is founded on a very singular quality of our thought and imagination. When a king forfeits his authority, his heir ought naturally to remain in the same situation, as if the king were remov'd by death; unless by mixing himself in the tyranny, he forfeit it for himself. But tho' this may seem reasonable, we easily comply with the contrary opinion. The deposition of a king, in such a government as ours, is certainly an act beyond all common authority, and an illegal assuming a power for public good, which, in the ordinary course of government, can belong to no member of the constitution. When the public good is so great and so evident as to justify the action, the commendable use of this licence causes us naturally to attribute to the *parliament* a right of using farther licences; and the antient bounds of the laws being once transgress'd with approbation, we are not apt to be so strict in confining ourselves precisely within their limits. The mind naturally runs on with any train of action, which it has begun;[†] nor do we commonly make any scruple concerning our duty, after the first action of any kind, which we perform. Thus at the

revolution, none who thought the deposition of the father justifiable, esteem'd   *SB 566*
themselves to be confin'd to his infant son; tho' had that unhappy monarch dy'd innocent at that time, and had his son, by any accident, been convey'd beyond seas, there is no doubt but a regency wou'd have been appointed till he shou'd come to age, and cou'd be restor'd to his dominions. As the slightest properties of the imagination have an effect on the judgments of the people, it shows the wisdom of the laws and of the parliament to take advantage of such properties, and to choose the magistrates either in or out of a line, according as the vulgar will most naturally attribute authority and right to them.

19   *Secondly*, Tho' the accession of the *Prince* of *Orange* to the throne might at first give occasion to many disputes, and his title be contested, it ought not now to appear doubtful, but must have acquir'd a sufficient authority from those three princes, who have succeeded him upon the same title.[†] Nothing is more usual, tho' nothing may, at first sight, appear more unreasonable, than this way of thinking. Princes often *seem* to acquire a right from their successors, as well as from their ancestors; and a king, who during his life-time might justly be deem'd an usurper, will be regarded by posterity as a lawful prince, because he has had the good fortune to settle his family on the throne, and entirely change the antient form of government. *Julius Cæsar* is regarded as the first *Roman* emperor; while *Sulla* and *Marius*, whose titles were really the same as his, are treated as tyrants and usurpers.[†] Time and custom give authority to all forms of government, and all successions of princes; and that power, which at first was founded only on injustice and violence, becomes in time legal and obligatory. Nor does the mind rest there; but returning back upon its footsteps, transfers to their predecessors and ancestors that right, which it naturally ascribes to the posterity, as being related together, and united in the imagination. The present king of *France* makes *Hugh Capet* a more lawful prince than *Cromwell*;[†] as the establish'd liberty of the *Dutch* is no inconsiderable apology for their obstinate   *SB 567*
resistance to *Philip* the Second.[†]

Sect. 11. *Of the laws of nations*

1   When civil government has been establish'd over the greatest part of mankind, and different societies have been form'd contiguous to each other, there arises a new set of duties among the neighbouring states, suitable to the nature of that commerce, which they carry on with each other. Political writers tell us, that in every kind of intercourse, a body politic is to be consider'd as one person;[†] and indeed this assertion is so far just, that different nations, as well as private persons, require mutual assistance; at the same time that their selfishness and ambition are perpetual sources of war and discord. But tho' nations in this particular resemble individuals, yet as they are very different in other respects, no wonder they regulate themselves by different maxims, and give rise to a new set of rules, which we call the *laws of nations*.[†] Under this head we may comprize the sacredness of the persons of ambassadors, the declaration of war, the abstaining

from poison'd arms, with other duties of that kind,[†] which are evidently calculated for the commerce, that is peculiar to different societies.

2 But tho' these rules be super-added to the laws of nature, the former do not entirely abolish the latter; and one may safely affirm, that the three fundamental rules of justice, the stability of possession, its transference by consent, and the performance of promises, are duties of princes, as well as of subjects. The same interest produces the same effect in both cases. Where possession has no stability, there must be perpetual war. Where property is not transferr'd by consent, there can be no commerce. Where promises are not observ'd, there can be no leagues nor alliances. The advantages, therefore, of peace, commerce, and *SB 568* mutual succour, make us extend to different kingdoms the same notions of justice, which take place among individuals.

3 There is a maxim very current in the world, which few politicians are willing to avow, but which has been authoriz'd by the practice of all ages, *that there is a system of morals calculated for princes, much more free than that which ought to govern private persons.*[†] 'Tis evident this is not to be understood of the lesser *extent* of public duties and obligations; nor will any one be so extravagant as to assert, that the most solemn treaties ought to have no force among princes.[†] For as princes do actually form treaties among themselves, they must propose some advantage from the execution of them; and the prospect of such advantage for the future must engage them to perform their part, and must establish that law of nature. The meaning, therefore, of this political maxim is, that tho' the morality of princes has the same *extent*, yet it has not the same *force* as that of private persons, and may lawfully be transgress'd from a more trivial motive. However shocking such a proposition may appear to certain philosophers, 'twill be easy to defend it upon those principles, by which we have accounted for the origin of justice and equity.

4 When men have found by experience, that 'tis impossible to subsist without society, and that 'tis impossible to maintain society, while they give free course to their appetites; so urgent an interest quickly restrains their actions, and imposes an obligation to observe those rules, which we call the *laws of justice.*[†] This obligation of interest rests not here; but by the necessary course of the passions and sentiments, gives rise to the moral obligation of duty;[†] while we approve of such actions as tend to the peace of society, and disapprove of such as tend to its disturbance. The same *natural* obligation of interest takes place among independent kingdoms, and gives rise to the same *morality*; so that no one of ever so corrupt morals will approve of a prince, who voluntarily, and of his own accord, *SB 569* breaks his word, or violates any treaty. But here we may observe, that tho' the intercourse of different states be advantageous, and even sometimes necessary, yet it is not so necessary nor advantageous as that among individuals, without which 'tis utterly impossible for human nature ever to subsist. Since, therefore, the *natural* obligation to justice, among different states, is not so strong as among individuals, the *moral* obligation, which arises from it, must partake of its weakness; and we must necessarily give a greater indulgence to a prince or minister,

who deceives another; than to a private gentleman, who breaks his word of honour.

5   Shou'd it be ask'd, *What proportion these two species of morality bear to each other?* I wou'd answer, that this is a question, to which we can never give any precise answer; nor is it possible to reduce to numbers the proportion, which we ought to fix betwixt them. One may safely affirm, that this proportion finds itself, without any art or study of men; as we may observe on many other occasions. The practice of the world goes farther in teaching us the degrees of our duty, than the most subtile philosophy, which was ever yet invented. And this may serve as a convincing proof, that all men have an implicit notion of the foundation of those moral rules concerning natural and civil justice, and are sensible, that they arise merely from human conventions, and from the interest, which we have in the preservation of peace and order. For otherwise the diminution of the interest wou'd never produce a relaxation of the morality, and reconcile us more easily to any transgression of justice among princes and republics, than in the private commerce of one subject with another.

Sect. 12. *Of chastity and modesty*   SB 570

1   If any difficulty attend this system concerning the laws of nature and nations, 'twill be with regard to the universal approbation or blame, which follows their observance or transgression, and which some may not think sufficiently explain'd from the general interests of society. To remove, as far as possible, all scruples of this kind, I shall here consider another set of duties, *viz.* the *modesty* and *chastity* which belong to the fair sex: And I doubt not but these virtues will be found to be still more conspicuous instances of the operation of those principles, which I have insisted on.

2   There are some philosophers, who attack the female virtues with great vehemence, and fancy they have gone very far in detecting popular errors, when they can show, that there is no foundation in nature for all that exterior modesty, which we require in the expressions, and dress, and behaviour of the fair sex.[†] I believe I may spare myself the trouble of insisting on so obvious a subject, and may proceed, without farther preparation, to examine after what manner such notions arise from education, from the voluntary conventions of men, and from the interest of society.

3   Whoever considers the length and feebleness of human infancy, with the concern which both sexes naturally have for their offspring, will easily perceive, that there must be an union of male and female for the education of the young, and that this union must be of considerable duration. But in order to induce the men to impose on themselves this restraint, and undergo chearfully all the fatigues and expences, to which it subjects them, they must believe, that the children are their own, and that their natural instinct is not directed to a wrong object, when they give a loose to love and tenderness. Now if we examine the structure of the human body, we shall find, that this security is very difficult to be attain'd on our part; and that since, in the copulation of the sexes, the princi-   SB 571

ple of generation goes from the man to the woman, an error may easily take place on the side of the former, tho' it be utterly impossible with regard to the latter. From this trivial and anatomical observation is deriv'd that vast difference betwixt the education and duties of the two sexes.

4   Were a philosopher to examine the matter *a priori*, he wou'd reason after the following manner. Men are induc'd to labour for the maintenance and education of their children, by the perswasion that they are really their own; and therefore 'tis reasonable, and even necessary, to give them some security in this particular. This security cannot consist entirely in the imposing of severe punishments on any transgressions of conjugal fidelity on the part of the wife; since these public punishments cannot be inflicted without legal proof, which 'tis difficult to meet with in this subject. What restraint, therefore, shall we impose on women, in order to counter-ballance so strong a temptation as they have to infidelity? There seems to be no restraint possible, but in the punishment of bad fame or reputation; a punishment, which has a mighty influence on the human mind, and at the same time is inflicted by the world upon surmizes, and conjectures, and proofs, that wou'd never be receiv'd in any court of judicature. In order, therefore, to impose a due restraint on the female sex, we must attach a peculiar degree of shame to their infidelity, above what arises merely from its injustice, and must bestow proportionable praises on their chastity.

5   But tho' this be a very strong motive to fidelity, our philosopher wou'd quickly discover, that it wou'd not alone be sufficient to that purpose. All human creatures, especially the female sex, are apt to over-look remote motives in favour of any present temptation:[†] The temptation is here the strongest imaginable: Its approaches are insensible and seducing: And a woman easily finds, or flatters herself she shall find, certain means of securing her reputation, and preventing *SB 572* all the pernicious consequences of her pleasures. 'Tis necessary, therefore, that, beside the infamy attending such licences, there shou'd be some preceding backwardness or dread, which may prevent their first approaches, and may give the female sex a repugnance to all expressions, and postures, and liberties, that have an immediate relation to that enjoyment.

6   Such wou'd be the reasonings of our speculative philosopher: But I am perswaded, that if he had not a perfect knowledge of human nature, he wou'd be apt to regard them as mere chimerical speculations, and wou'd consider the infamy attending infidelity, and backwardness to all its approaches, as principles that were rather to be wish'd than hop'd for in the world. For what means, wou'd he say, of perswading mankind, that the transgressions of conjugal duty are more infamous than any other kind of injustice, when 'tis evident they are more excusable, upon account of the greatness of the temptation? And what possibility of giving a backwardness to the approaches of a pleasure, to which nature has inspir'd so strong a propensity; and a propensity that 'tis absolutely necessary in the end to comply with, for the support of the species?

7   But speculative reasonings, which cost so much pains to philosophers, are often form'd by the world naturally, and without reflection: As difficulties, which seem unsurmountable in theory, are easily got over in practice. Those,

who have an interest in the fidelity of women, naturally disapprove of their infidelity, and all the approaches to it. Those, who have no interest, are carry'd along with the stream, and are also apt to be affected with sympathy for the general interests of society. Education takes possession of the ductile minds of the fair sex in their infancy. And when a general rule of this kind is once establish'd, men are apt to extend it beyond those principles, from which it first arose. Thus batchelors, however debauch'd, cannot choose but be shock'd with any instance of lewdness or impudence in women. And tho' all these maxims have a plain reference to generation, yet women past child-bearing have no more privi- *SB 573* lege in this respect, than those who are in the flower of their youth and beauty. Men have undoubtedly an implicit notion, that all these ideas of modesty and decency have a regard to generation; since they impose not the same laws, *with the same force*, on the male sex, where that reason takes not place. The exception is there obvious and extensive, and founded on a remarkable difference, which produces a clear separation and disjunction of ideas. But as the case is not the same with regard to the different ages of women, for this reason, tho' men know, that these notions are founded on the public interest, yet the general rule carries us beyond the original principle, and makes us extend the notions of modesty over the whole sex, from their earliest infancy to their extremest old-age and infirmity.

8   Courage, which is the point of honour among men, derives its merit, in a great measure, from artifice, as well as the chastity of women; tho' it has also some foundation in nature, as we shall see afterwards.[†]

9   As to the obligations which the male sex lie under, with regard to chastity, we may observe, that according to the general notions of the world, they bear nearly the same proportion to the obligations of women, as the obligations of the law of nations do to those of the law of nature.[†] 'Tis contrary to the interest of civil society, that men shou'd have an *entire* liberty of indulging their appetites in venereal enjoyment: But as this interest is weaker than in the case of the female sex, the moral obligation, arising from it, must be proportionably weaker. And to prove this we need only appeal to the practice and sentiments of all nations and ages.

PART 3

Of the other virtues and vices

Sect. 1. Of the origin of the natural virtues and vices

1   We come now to the examination of such virtues and vices as are entirely natural, and have no dependance on the artifice and contrivance of men. The examination of these will conclude this system of morals.

2   The chief spring or actuating principle of the human mind is pleasure or pain;[†] and when these sensations are remov'd, both from our thought and feeling, we are, in a great measure, incapable of passion or action, of desire or volition. The most immediate effects of pleasure and pain are the propense and averse motions of the mind; which are diversify'd into volition, into desire and aversion, grief and joy, hope and fear, according as the pleasure or pain changes its situation, and becomes probable or improbable, certain or uncertain, or is consider'd as out of our power for the present moment.[†] But when along with this, the objects, that cause pleasure or pain, acquire a relation to ourselves or others; they still continue to excite desire and aversion, grief and joy: But cause, at the same time, the indirect passions of pride or humility, love or hatred, which in this case have a double relation of impressions and ideas to the pain or pleasure.[†]

3   We have already observ'd,[†] that moral distinctions depend entirely on certain peculiar sentiments of pain and pleasure, and that whatever mental quality in ourselves or others gives us a satisfaction, by the survey or reflection, is of course virtuous; as every thing of this nature, that gives uneasiness, is vicious. Now since every quality in ourselves or others, which gives pleasure, always causes pride or love; as every one, that produces uneasiness, excites humility or hatred: It follows, that these two particulars are to be consider'd as equivalent, with regard to our mental qualities, *virtue* and the power of producing love or pride, *vice* and the power of producing humility or hatred. In every case, therefore, we must judge of the one by the other; and may pronounce any *quality* of the mind virtuous, which causes love or pride; and any one vicious, which causes hatred or humility.[†]

4   If any *action* be either virtuous or vicious, 'tis only as a sign of some quality or character. It must depend upon durable principles of the mind, which extend over the whole conduct, and enter into the personal character. Actions themselves, not proceeding from any constant principle, have no influence on love or hatred, pride or humility; and consequently are never consider'd in morality.[†]

5   This reflection is self-evident, and deserves to be attended to, as being of the utmost importance in the present subject. We are never to consider any single

action in our enquiries concerning the origin of morals; but only the quality or character from which the action proceeded. These alone are *durable* enough to affect our sentiments concerning the person. Actions are, indeed, better indications of a character than words, or even wishes and sentiments; but 'tis only so far as they are such indications, that they are attended with love or hatred, praise or blame.

6   To discover the true origin of morals, and of that love or hatred, which arises from mental qualities, we must take the matter pretty deep, and compare some principles, which have been already examin'd and explain'd.

7   We may begin with considering anew the nature and force of *sympathy*.[†] The minds of all men are similar in their feelings and operations; nor can any one be actuated by any affection, of which all others are not, in some degree, suscep-   *SB 576* tible. As in strings equally wound up, the motion of one communicates itself to the rest; so all the affections readily pass from one person to another, and beget correspondent movements in every human creature. When I see the *effects* of passion in the voice and gesture of any person, my mind immediately passes from these effects to their causes, and forms such a lively idea of the passion, as is presently converted into the passion itself. In like manner, when I perceive the *causes* of any emotion, my mind is convey'd to the effects, and is actuated with a like emotion. Were I present at any of the more terrible operations of surgery, 'tis certain, that even before it begun, the preparation of the instruments, the laying of the bandages in order, the heating of the irons,[†] with all the signs of anxiety and concern in the patient and assistants, wou'd have a great effect upon my mind, and excite the strongest sentiments of pity and terror. No passion of another discovers itself immediately to the mind. We are only sensible of its causes or effects. From *these* we infer the passion: And consequently *these* give rise to our sympathy.

8   Our sense of beauty depends very much on this principle; and where any object has a tendency to produce pleasure in its possessor, it is always regarded as beautiful;[†] as every object, that has a tendency to produce pain, is disagreeable and deform'd. Thus the conveniency of a house, the fertility of a field, the strength of a horse, the capacity, security, and swift-sailing of a vessel, form the principal beauty of these several objects. Here the object, which is denominated beautiful, pleases only by its tendency to produce a certain effect. That effect is the pleasure or advantage of some other person. Now the pleasure of a stranger, for whom we have no friendship, pleases us only by sympathy. To this principle, therefore, is owing the beauty, which we find in every thing that is useful. How considerable a part this is of beauty will easily appear upon reflection. Wherever an object has a tendency to produce pleasure   *SB 577* in the possessor, or in other words, is the proper *cause* of pleasure, it is sure to please the spectator, by a delicate sympathy with the possessor. Most of the works of art are esteem'd beautiful, in proportion to their fitness for the use of man, and even many of the productions of nature derive their beauty from that source. Handsome and beautiful, on most occasions, is not an absolute but a

relative quality, and pleases us by nothing but its tendency to produce an end that is agreeable.[83]

9   The same principle produces, in many instances, our sentiments of morals, as well as those of beauty. No virtue is more esteem'd than justice, and no vice more detested than injustice; nor are there any qualities, which go farther to the fixing the character, either as amiable or odious. Now justice is a moral virtue, merely because it has that tendency to the good of mankind; and, indeed, is nothing but an artificial invention to that purpose. The same may be said of allegiance, of the laws of nations, of modesty, and of good-manners.[†] All these are mere human contrivances for the interest of society. The inventors of them had chiefly in view their own interest. But we carry our approbation of them into the most distant countries and ages, and much beyond our own interest. And since there is a very strong sentiment of morals, which has always attended them, we must allow, that the reflecting on the tendency of characters and mental qualities, is sufficient to give us the sentiments of approbation and blame. Now as the means to an end can only be agreeable, where the end is agreeable; and as the good of society, where our own interest is not concern'd, or that of our friends, pleases only by sympathy: It follows, that sympathy is the source of the esteem, which we pay to all the artificial virtues.[†]

10   Thus it appears, *that* sympathy is a very powerful principle in human nature, *that* it has a great influence on our taste of beauty, and *that* it produces our sentiment of morals in all the artificial virtues. From thence we may presume, that it *SB 578* also gives rise to many of the other virtues; and that qualities acquire our approbation, because of their tendency to the good of mankind. This presumption must become a certainty, when we find that most of those qualities, which we *naturally* approve of, have actually that tendency, and render a man a proper member of society: While the qualities, which we *naturally* disapprove of, have a contrary tendency, and render any intercourse with the person dangerous or disagreeable. For having found, that such tendencies have force enough to produce the strongest sentiment of morals, we can never reasonably, in these cases, look for any other cause of approbation or blame; it being an inviolable maxim in philosophy, that where any particular cause is sufficient for an effect, we ought to rest satisfy'd with it, and ought not to multiply causes without necessity.[†] We have happily attain'd experiments[†] in the artificial virtues, where the tendency of qualities to the good of society, is the *sole* cause of our approbation, without any suspicion of the concurrence of another principle. From thence we learn the force of that principle. And where that principle may take place, and the quality approv'd of is really beneficial to society, a true philosopher will never require any other principle to account for the strongest approbation and esteem.

11   That many of the natural virtues have this tendency to the good of society,

---

[83] *Decentior equus cujus astricta sunt ilia; sed idem velocior. Pulcher aspectu sit athleta, cujus lacertos* *SB 577* *exercitatio expressit; idem certamini paratior. Nunquam vero* species *ab* utilitate *dividitur. Sed hoc quidem discernere, modici judicii est.*[†] *Quinct.* lib. 8.

no one can doubt of. Meekness, beneficence, charity, generosity, clemency, moderation, equity, bear the greatest figure among the moral qualities, and are commonly denominated the *social* virtues, to mark their tendency to the good of society. This goes so far, that some philosophers[†] have represented all moral distinctions as the effect of artifice and education, when skilful politicians endeavour'd to restrain the turbulent passions of men, and make them operate to the public good, by the notions of honour and shame. This system, however, is not consistent with experience. For, *first*, there are other virtues and vices beside those which have this tendency to the public advantage and loss. *Secondly*, had   *SB 579* not men a natural sentiment of approbation and blame, it cou'd never be excited by politicians; nor wou'd the words *laudable* and *praise-worthy*, *blameable* and *odious*, be any more intelligible, than if they were a language perfectly unknown to us, as we have already observ'd.[†] But tho' this system be erroneous, it may teach us, that moral distinctions arise, in a great measure, from the tendency of qualities and characters to the interest of society, and that 'tis our concern for that interest, which makes us approve or disapprove of them. Now we have no such extensive concern for society but from sympathy; and consequently 'tis that principle, which takes us so far out of ourselves, as to give us the same pleasure or uneasiness in characters which are useful or pernicious to society, as if they had a tendency to our own advantage or loss.

12   The only difference betwixt the natural virtues and justice lies in this, that the good, which results from the former, arises from every single act, and is the object of some natural passion: Whereas a single act of justice, consider'd in itself, may often be contrary to the public good; and 'tis only the concurrence of mankind, in a general scheme or system of action, which is advantageous. When I relieve persons in distress, my natural humanity is my motive; and so far as my succour extends, so far have I promoted the happiness of my fellow-creatures. But if we examine all the questions, that come before any tribunal of justice, we shall find, that, considering each case apart, it wou'd as often be an instance of humanity to decide contrary to the laws of justice as conformable to them. Judges take from a poor man to give to a rich; they bestow on the dissolute the labour of the industrious; and put into the hands of the vicious the means of harming both themselves and others. The whole scheme, however, of law and justice is advantageous to the society and to every individual; and 'twas with a view to this advantage, that men, by their voluntary conventions, establish'd it. After it is once establish'd by these conventions, it is *naturally* attended with a strong sentiment of morals; which can proceed from nothing   *SB 580* but our sympathy with the interests of society.[†] We need no other explication of that esteem, which attends such of the natural virtues, as have a tendency to the public good.

13   I must farther add, that there are several circumstances, which render this hypothesis much more probable with regard to the natural than the artificial virtues. 'Tis certain, that the imagination is more affected by what is particular, than by what is general;[†] and that the sentiments are always mov'd with difficulty, where their objects are, in any degree, loose and undetermin'd: Now every

particular act of justice is not beneficial to society, but the whole scheme or system: And it may not, perhaps, be any individual person, for whom we are concern'd, who receives benefit from justice, but the whole society alike. On the contrary, every particular act of generosity, or relief of the industrious and indigent, is beneficial; and is beneficial to a particular person, who is not undeserving of it. 'Tis more natural, therefore, to think, that the tendencies of the latter virtue will affect our sentiments, and command our approbation, than those of the former; and therefore, since we find, that the approbation of the former arises from their tendencies, we may ascribe, with better reason, the same cause to the approbation of the latter. In any number of similar effects, if a cause can be discover'd for one, we ought to extend that cause to all the other effects, which can be accounted for by it:[†] But much more, if these other effects be attended with peculiar circumstances, which facilitate the operation of that cause.

14   Before I proceed farther, I must observe two remarkable circumstances in this affair, which may seem objections to the present system. The first may be thus explain'd. When any quality, or character, has a tendency to the good of mankind, we are pleas'd with it, and approve of it; because it presents the lively idea of pleasure; which idea affects us by sympathy, and is itself a kind of pleasure. But as this sympathy is very variable, it may be thought, that our sentiments of morals must admit of all the same variations. We sympathize more with *SB 581* persons contiguous to us, than with persons remote from us: With our acquaintance, than with strangers: With our countrymen, than with foreigners. But notwithstanding this variation of our sympathy, we give the same approbation to the same moral qualities in *China* as in *England*. They appear equally virtuous, and recommend themselves equally to the esteem of a judicious spectator. The sympathy varies without a variation in our esteem. Our esteem, therefore, proceeds not from sympathy.

15   To this I answer: The approbation of moral qualities most certainly is not deriv'd from reason, or any comparison of ideas; but proceeds entirely from a moral taste, and from certain sentiments of pleasure or disgust, which arise upon the contemplation and view of particular qualities or characters. Now 'tis evident, that these sentiments, whence-ever they are deriv'd, must vary according to the distance or contiguity of the objects;[†] nor can I feel the same lively pleasure from the virtues of a person, who liv'd in *Greece* two thousand years ago, that I feel from the virtues of a familiar friend and acquaintance. Yet I do not say, that I esteem the one more than the other: And therefore, if the variation of the sentiment, without a variation of the esteem, be an objection, it must have equal force against every other system, as against that of sympathy. But to consider the case aright, it has no force at all; and 'tis the easiest matter in the world to account for it. Our situation, with regard both to persons and things, is in continual fluctuation; and a man, that lies at a distance from us, may, in a little time, become a familiar acquaintance. Besides, every particular man has a peculiar position with regard to others; and 'tis impossible we cou'd ever converse together on any reasonable terms, were each of us to consider characters and persons, only as they appear from his peculiar point of view. In order, therefore,

to prevent those continual *contradictions*, and arrive at a more *stable* judgment of things, we fix on some *steady* and *general* points of view; and always, in our thoughts, place ourselves in them, whatever may be our present situation. In like manner, external beauty is determin'd merely by pleasure; and 'tis evident, a beautiful countenance cannot give so much pleasure, when seen at the distance of twenty paces, as when it is brought nearer us. We say not, however, that it appears to us less beautiful: Because we know what effect it will have in such a position, and by that reflection we correct its momentary appearance. *SB 582*

16   In general, all sentiments of blame or praise are variable, according to our situation of nearness or remoteness, with regard to the person blam'd or prais'd, and according to the present disposition of our mind. But these variations we regard not in our general decisions, but still apply the terms expressive of our liking or dislike, in the same manner, as if we remain'd in one point of view. Experience soon teaches us this method of correcting our sentiments, or at least, of correcting our language, where the sentiments are more stubborn and inalterable. Our servant, if diligent and faithful, may excite stronger sentiments of love and kindness than *Marcus Brutus*, as represented in history; but we say not upon that account, that the former character is more laudable than the latter. We know, that were we to approach equally near to that renown'd patriot, he wou'd command a much higher degree of affection and admiration.† Such corrections are common with regard to all the senses; and indeed 'twere impossible we cou'd ever make use of language, or communicate our sentiments to one another, did we not correct the momentary appearances of things, and overlook our present situation.

17   'Tis therefore from the influence of characters and qualities, upon those who have an intercourse with any person, that we blame or praise him. We consider not whether the persons, affected by the qualities, be our acquaintance or strangers, countrymen or foreigners. Nay, we over-look our own interest in those general judgments; and blame not a man for opposing us in any of our *SB 583* pretensions, when his own interest is particularly concern'd. We make allowance for a certain degree of selfishness in men; because we know it to be inseparable from human nature, and inherent in our frame and constitution. By this reflection we correct those sentiments of blame, which so naturally arise upon any opposition.†

18   But however the general principle of our blame or praise may be corrected by those other principles, 'tis certain, they are not altogether efficacious, nor do our passions often correspond entirely to the present theory. 'Tis seldom men heartily love what lies at a distance from them, and what no way redounds to their particular benefit; as 'tis no less rare to meet with persons, who can pardon another any opposition he makes to their interest, however justifiable that opposition may be by the general rules of morality. Here we are contented with saying, that reason requires such an impartial conduct, but that 'tis seldom we can bring ourselves to it, and that our passions do not readily follow the determination of our judgment.† This language will be easily understood, if we consider what we formerly said† concerning that *reason*, which is able to oppose our

372

passion; and which we have found to be nothing but a general calm determination of the passions, founded on some distant view or reflection. When we form our judgments of persons, merely from the tendency of their characters to our own benefit, or to that of our friends, we find so many contradictions to our sentiments in society and conversation, and such an uncertainty from the incessant changes of our situation, that we seek some other standard of merit and demerit, which may not admit of so great variation. Being thus loosen'd from our first station, we cannot afterwards fix ourselves so commodiously by any means as by a sympathy with those, who have any commerce with the person we consider. This is far from being as lively as when our own interest is concern'd, or that of our particular friends; nor has it such an influence on our love and hatred: But being equally conformable to our calm and general principles, 'tis said to have an equal authority over our reason, and to command our judgment and opinion. We blame equally a bad action, which we read of in history, with one perform'd in our neighbourhood the other day: The meaning of which is, that we know from reflection, that the former action wou'd excite as strong sentiments of disapprobation as the latter, were it plac'd in the same position.†   *SB 584*

19   I now proceed to the *second* remarkable circumstance, which I propos'd to take notice of. Where a person is possess'd of a character, that in its natural tendency is beneficial to society, we esteem him virtuous, and are delighted with the view of his character, even tho' particular accidents prevent its operation, and incapacitate him from being serviceable to his friends and country. Virtue in rags is still virtue;† and the love, which it procures, attends a man into a dungeon or desart, where the virtue can no longer be exerted in action, and is lost to all the world. Now this may be esteem'd an objection to the present system. Sympathy interests us in the good of mankind; and if sympathy were the source of our esteem for virtue, that sentiment of approbation cou'd only take place, where the virtue actually attain'd its end, and was beneficial to mankind. Where it fails of its end, 'tis only an imperfect means; and therefore can never acquire any merit from that end. The goodness of an end can bestow a merit on such means alone as are compleat, and actually produce the end.

20   To this we may reply, that where any object, in all its parts, is fitted to attain any agreeable end, it naturally gives us pleasure, and is esteem'd beautiful, even tho' some external circumstances be wanting to render it altogether effectual.† 'Tis sufficient if every thing be compleat in the object itself. A house, that is contriv'd with great judgment for all the commodities of life, pleases us upon that account; tho' perhaps we are sensible, that no one will ever dwell in it. A   *SB 585* fertile soil, and a happy climate, delight us by a reflection on the happiness which they wou'd afford the inhabitants, tho' at present the country be desart and uninhabited. A man, whose limbs and shape promise strength and activity, is esteem'd handsome, tho' condemn'd to perpetual imprisonment. The imagination has a set of passions belonging to it, upon which our sentiments of beauty much depend. These passions are mov'd by degrees of liveliness and strength, which are inferior to *belief,* and independent of the real existence of their objects. Where a character is, in every respect, fitted to be beneficial to society, the imag-

ination passes easily from the cause to the effect, without considering that there are still some circumstances wanting to render the cause a compleat one. *General rules* create a species of probability, which sometimes influences the judgment, and always the imagination.[†]

21   'Tis true, when the cause is compleat, and a good disposition is attended with good fortune, which renders it really beneficial to society, it gives a stronger pleasure to the spectator, and is attended with a more lively sympathy. We are more affected by it; and yet we do not say that it is more virtuous, or that we esteem it more. We know, that an alteration of fortune may render the benevolent disposition entirely impotent; and therefore we separate, as much as possible, the fortune from the disposition. The case is the same, as when we correct the different sentiments of virtue, which proceed from its different distances from ourselves. The passions do not always follow our corrections; but these corrections serve sufficiently to regulate our abstract notions, and are alone regarded, when we pronounce in general concerning the degrees of vice and virtue.

22   'Tis observ'd by critics, that all words or sentences, which are difficult to the pronunciation, are disagreeable to the ear.[†] There is no difference, whether a man hear them pronounc'd, or read them silently to himself. When I run over a book with my eye, I imagine I hear it all; and also, by the force of imagination, enter into the uneasiness, which the delivery of it wou'd give the speaker. The uneasiness is not real; but as such a composition of words has a natural tendency to produce it, this is sufficient to affect the mind with a painful sentiment, and render the style harsh and disagreeable. 'Tis a similar case, where any real quality is, by accidental circumstances, render'd impotent, and is depriv'd of its natural influence on society.   *SB 586*

23   Upon these principles we may easily remove any contradiction, which may appear to be betwixt the *extensive sympathy*, on which our sentiments of virtue depend, and that *limited generosity* which I have frequently observ'd to be natural to men, and which justice and property suppose, according to the precedent reasoning. My sympathy with another may give me the sentiment of pain and disapprobation, when any object is presented, that has a tendency to give him uneasiness; tho' I may not be willing to sacrifice any thing of my own interest, or cross any of my passions, for his satisfaction. A house may displease me by being ill-contriv'd for the convenience of the owner; and yet I may refuse to give a shilling towards the rebuilding of it. Sentiments must touch the heart, to make them controul our passions: But they need not extend beyond the imagination, to make them influence our taste. When a building seems clumsy and tottering to the eye, it is ugly and disagreeable; tho' we be fully assur'd of the solidity of the workmanship. 'Tis a kind of fear, which causes this sentiment of disapprobation; but the passion is not the same with that which we feel, when oblig'd to stand under a wall, that we really think tottering and insecure.[†] The *seeming tendencies* of objects affect the mind: And the emotions they excite are of a like species with those, which proceed from the *real consequences* of objects, but their feeling is different.[†] Nay, these emotions are so different in their feeling, that they may often

374

be contrary, without destroying each other; as when the fortifications of a city belonging to an enemy are esteem'd beautiful upon account of their strength, tho' we cou'd wish that they were entirely destroy'd. The imagination adheres to the *general* views of things, and distinguishes betwixt the feelings they produce, and those which arise from our particular and momentary situation. *SB 587*

24 If we examine the panegyrics that are commonly made of great men, we shall find, that most of the qualities, which are attributed to them, may be divided into two kinds, *viz.* such as make them perform their part in society; and such as render them serviceable to themselves, and enable them to promote their own interest. Their *prudence, temperance, frugality, industry, assiduity, enterprize, dexterity*, are celebrated, as well as their *generosity* and *humanity*. If we ever give an indulgence to any quality, that disables a man from making a figure in life, 'tis to that of *indolence*, which is not suppos'd to deprive one of his parts and capacity, but only suspends their exercise; and that without any inconvenience to the person himself, since 'tis, in some measure, from his own choice. Yet indolence is always allow'd to be a fault, and a very great one, if extreme: Nor do a man's friends ever acknowledge him to be subject to it, but in order to save his character in more material articles. He cou'd make a figure, say they, if he pleas'd to give application: His understanding is sound, his conception quick, and his memory tenacious; but he hates business, and is indifferent about his fortune. And this a man sometimes may make even a subject of vanity; tho' with the air of confessing a fault: Because he may think, that this incapacity for business implies much more noble qualities; such as a philosophical spirit, a fine taste, a delicate wit, or a relish for pleasure and society. But take any other case: Suppose a quality, that without being an indication of any other good qualities, incapacitates a man *always* for business, and is destructive to his interest; such as a blundering understanding, and a wrong judgment of every thing in life; inconstancy and irresolution; or a want of address in the management of men and business: These are all allow'd to be imperfections in a character; and many men wou'd rather acknowledge the greatest crimes, than have it suspected, that they are, in any degree, subject to them. *SB 588*

25 'Tis very happy, in our philosophical researches, when we find the same phænomenon diversify'd by a variety of circumstances; and by discovering what is common among them, can the better assure ourselves of the truth of any hypothesis we may make use of to explain that phænomenon. Were nothing esteem'd virtue but what were beneficial to society, I am perswaded, that the foregoing explication of the moral sense ought still to be receiv'd, and that upon sufficient evidence: But this evidence must grow upon us, when we find other kinds of virtue, which will not admit of any explication except from that hypothesis. Here is a man, who is not remarkably defective in his social qualities; but what principally recommends him is his dexterity in business, by which he has extricated himself from the greatest difficulties, and conducted the most delicate affairs with a singular address and prudence. I find an esteem for him immediately to arise in me: His company is a satisfaction to me; and before I have any

farther acquaintance with him, I wou'd rather do him a service than another, whose character is in every other respect equal, but is deficient in that particular. In this case, the qualities that please me are all consider'd as useful to the person, and as having a tendency to promote his interest and satisfaction. They are only regarded as means to an end, and please me in proportion to their fitness for that end. The end, therefore, must be agreeable to me. But what makes the end agreeable? The person is a stranger: I am no way interested in him, nor lie under any obligation to him: His happiness concerns not me, farther than the happiness of every human, and indeed of every sensible creature: That is, it affects me only by sympathy. From that principle, whenever I discover his happiness and good, whether in its causes or effects, I enter so deeply into it, that it gives me a sensible emotion. The appearance of qualities, that have a *tendency* to promote it, have an agreeable effect upon my imagination, and command my love and esteem.   *SB 589*

26   This theory may serve to explain, why the same qualities, in all cases, produce both pride and love, humility and hatred; and the same man is always virtuous or vicious, accomplish'd or despicable to others, who is so to himself.[†] A person, in whom we discover any passion or habit, which originally is only incommodious to himself, becomes always disagreeable to us, merely on its account; as on the other hand, one whose character is only dangerous and disagreeable to others, can never be satisfy'd with himself, as long as he is sensible of that disadvantage. Nor is this observable only with regard to characters and manners, but may be remark'd even in the most minute circumstances. A violent cough in another gives us uneasiness; tho' in itself it does not in the least affect us. A man will be mortify'd, if you tell him he has a stinking breath; tho' 'tis evidently no annoyance to himself. Our fancy easily changes its situation; and either surveying ourselves as we appear to others, or considering others as they feel themselves, makes us enter, by that means, into sentiments, which no way belong to us, and in which nothing but sympathy is able to interest us. And this sympathy we sometimes carry so far, as even to be displeas'd with a quality commodious to us, merely because it displeases others, and renders us disagreeable in their eyes; tho' perhaps we never can have any interest in rendering ourselves agreeable to them.

27   There have been many systems of morality advanc'd by philosophers in all ages; but if they are strictly examin'd, they may be reduc'd to two, which alone merit our attention. Moral good and evil are certainly distinguish'd by our *sentiments*, not by *reason*:[†] But these sentiments may arise either from the mere species or appearance of characters and passions, or from reflections on their tendency to the happiness of mankind, and of particular persons.[†] My opinion is, that both these causes are intermix'd in our judgments of morals; after the same manner as they are in our decisions concerning most kinds of external beauty: Tho' I am also of opinion, that reflections on the tendencies of actions have by far the greatest influence, and determine all the great lines of our duty. There are, however, instances, in cases of less moment, wherein this immediate taste or sentiment produces our approbation. Wit, and a certain easy and disen-   *SB 590*

gag'd behaviour, are qualities *immediately agreeable* to others, and command their love and esteem. Some of these qualities produce satisfaction in others by particular *original* principles of human nature, which cannot be accounted for: Others may be resolv'd into principles, which are more general. This will best appear upon a particular enquiry.

28   As some qualities acquire their merit from their being *immediately agreeable* to others, without any tendency to public interest; so some are denominated virtuous from their being *immediately agreeable* to the person himself, who possesses them. Each of the passions and operations of the mind has a particular feeling, which must be either agreeable or disagreeable. The first is virtuous, the second vicious. This particular feeling constitutes the very nature of the passion; and therefore needs not be accounted for.

29   But however directly the distinction of vice and virtue may seem to flow from the immediate pleasure or uneasiness, which particular qualities cause to ourselves or others; 'tis easy to observe, that it has also a considerable dependence on the principle of *sympathy* so often insisted on. We approve of a person, who is possess'd of qualities *immediately agreeable* to those, with whom he has any commerce; tho' perhaps we ourselves never reap'd any pleasure from them. We also approve of one, who is possess'd of qualities, that are *immediately agreeable* to himself; tho' they be of no service to any mortal. To account for this we must have recourse to the foregoing principles.[†]

30   Thus, to take a general review of the present hypothesis: Every quality of the   *SB 591* mind is denominated *virtuous*, which gives pleasure by the mere survey; as every quality, which produces pain, is call'd *vicious*. This pleasure and this pain may arise from four different sources. For we reap a pleasure from the view of a character, which is naturally fitted to be useful to others, or to the person himself, or which is agreeable to others, or to the person himself. One may, perhaps, be surpriz'd, that amidst all these interests and pleasures, we shou'd forget our own, which touch us so nearly on every other occasion. But we shall easily satisfy ourselves on this head, when we consider, that every particular person's pleasure and interest being different, 'tis impossible men cou'd ever agree in their sentiments and judgments, unless they chose some common point of view, from which they might survey their object, and which might cause it to appear the same to all of them. Now in judging of characters, the only interest or pleasure, which appears the same to every spectator, is that of the person himself, whose character is examin'd; or that of persons, who have a connexion with him. And tho' such interests and pleasures touch us more faintly than our own, yet being more constant and universal, they counter-ballance the latter even in practice, and are alone admitted in speculation as the standard of virtue and morality. They alone produce that particular feeling or sentiment, on which moral distinctions depend.

31   As to the good or ill desert of virtue or vice, 'tis an evident consequence of the sentiments of pleasure or uneasiness. These sentiments produce love or hatred; and love or hatred, by the original constitution of human passion, is attended with benevolence or anger; that is, with a desire of making happy the person we

love, and miserable the person we hate. We have treated of this more fully on another occasion.[†]

Sect. 2. *Of greatness of mind*

SB 592

1   It may now be proper to illustrate this general system of morals, by applying it to particular instances of virtue and vice, and showing how their merit or demerit arises from the four sources here explain'd.[†] We shall begin with examining the passions of *pride* and *humility*, and shall consider the vice or virtue that lies in their excesses or just proportion. An excessive pride or over-weaning conceit of ourselves is always esteem'd vicious, and is universally hated; as modesty, or a just sense of our weakness, is esteem'd virtuous, and procures the good-will of every one. Of the four sources of moral distinctions, this is to be ascrib'd to the *third*, viz. the immediate agreeableness and disagreeableness of a quality to others, without any reflections on the tendency of that quality.

2   In order to prove this, we must have recourse to two principles, which are very conspicuous in human nature. The *first* of these is the *sympathy*, and communication of sentiments and passions above-mention'd.[†] So close and intimate is the correspondence of human souls, that no sooner any person approaches me, than he diffuses on me all his opinions, and draws along my judgment in a greater or lesser degree. And tho', on many occasions, my sympathy with him goes not so far as entirely to change my sentiments, and way of thinking; yet it seldom is so weak as not to disturb the easy course of my thought, and give an authority to that opinion, which is recommended to me by his assent and approbation. Nor is it any way material upon what subject he and I employ our thoughts. Whether we judge of an indifferent person, or of my own character, my sympathy gives equal force to his decision: And even his sentiments of his own merit make me consider him in the same light, in which he regards himself.

3   This principle of sympathy is of so powerful and insinuating a nature, that it   SB 593 enters into most of our sentiments and passions, and often takes place under the appearance of its contrary. For 'tis remarkable, that when a person opposes me in any sentiment, which I am strongly bent upon, and rouzes up my passion by contradiction, I have always a degree of sympathy with him, nor does my commotion proceed from any other origin. We may here observe an evident conflict or rencounter of opposite principles and passions. On the one side there is that passion or sentiment, which is natural to me; and 'tis observable, that the stronger this passion is, the greater is the commotion. There must also be some passion or sentiment on the other side; and this passion can proceed from nothing but sympathy. The sentiments of others can never affect us, but by becoming, in some measure, our own; in which case they operate upon us, by opposing and encreasing our passions, in the very same manner, as if they had been originally deriv'd from our own temper and disposition. While they remain conceal'd in the minds of others, they can never have any influence upon us: And even when they are known, if they went no farther than the imagination, or con-

ception; that faculty is so accustom'd to objects of every different kind, that a mere idea, tho' contrary to our sentiments and inclinations, wou'd never alone be able to affect us.

4   The *second* principle I shall take notice of is that of *comparison*, or the variation of our judgments concerning objects, according to the proportion they bear to those with which we compare them. We judge more of objects by comparison, than by their intrinsic worth and value; and regard every thing as mean, when set in opposition to what is superior of the same kind. But no comparison is more obvious than that with ourselves; and hence it is that on all occasions it takes place, and mixes with most of our passions. This kind of comparison is directly contrary to sympathy in its operation, as we have observ'd in treating of *compassion* and *malice. In all kinds of comparison an object makes us always receive from*   SB 594 *another, to which it is compar'd, a sensation contrary to what arises from itself in its direct and immediate survey. The direct survey of another's pleasure naturally gives us pleasure, and therefore produces pain when compar'd with our own. His pain, consider'd in itself, is painful to us, but augments the idea of our own happiness, and gives us pleasure.*[84]

5   Since then those principles of sympathy, and a comparison with ourselves, are directly contrary, it may be worth while to consider, what general rules can be form'd, beside the particular temper of the person, for the prevalence of the one or the other. Suppose I am now in safety at land, and wou'd willingly reap some pleasure from this consideration: I must think on the miserable condition of those who are at sea in a storm, and must endeavour to render this idea as strong and lively as possible, in order to make me more sensible of my own happiness. But whatever pains I may take, the comparison will never have an equal efficacy, as if I were really on the shore, and saw a ship at a distance, tost by a tempest, and in danger every moment of perishing on a rock or sand-bank.[85] But suppose this idea to become still more lively. Suppose the ship to be driven so near me, that I can perceive distinctly the horror, painted on the countenance of the seamen and passengers, hear their lamentable cries, see the dearest friends give their last adieu, or embrace with a resolution to perish in each other's arms: No man has so savage a heart as to reap any pleasure from such a spectacle, or withstand the motions of the tenderest compassion and sympathy. 'Tis evident, therefore, there is a medium in this case; and that if the idea be too faint, it has no influence   SB 595 by comparison; and on the other hand, if it be too strong, it operates on us entirely by sympathy, which is the contrary to comparison.[†] Sympathy being the conversion of an idea into an impression, demands a greater force and vivacity in the idea than is requisite to comparison.

6   All this is easily apply'd to the present subject. We sink very much in our own

---

[84] Book 2. Part 2. Sect. 8.[†]   SB 594
[85] *Suave mari magno turbantibus æquora ventis*
    E terra magnum alterius spectare laborem;
    Non quia vexari quemquam est jucunda voluptas,
    Sed quibus ipse malis careas quia cernere suav' est.[†] *Lucret.*

eyes, when in the presence of a great man, or one of a superior genius; and this humility makes a considerable ingredient in that *respect*, which we pay our superiors, according to our foregoing reasonings on that passion.[86] Sometimes even envy and hatred arise from the comparison; but in the greatest part of men, it rests at respect and esteem. As sympathy has such a powerful influence on the human mind, it causes pride to have, in some measure, the same effect as merit; and by making us enter into those elevated sentiments, which the proud man entertains of himself, presents that comparison, which is so mortifying and disagreeable. Our judgment does not entirely accompany him in the flattering conceit, in which he places himself; but still is so shaken as to receive the idea it presents, and to give it an influence above the loose conceptions of the imagination. A man, who, in an idle humour, wou'd form a notion of a person of a merit very much superior to his own, wou'd not be mortify'd by that fiction: But when a man, whom we are really perswaded to be of inferior merit, is presented to us; if we observe in him any extraordinary degree of pride and self-conceit; the firm perswasion he has of his own merit, takes hold of the imagination, and diminishes us in our own eyes, in the same manner, as if he were really possess'd of all the good qualities which he so liberally attributes to himself. Our idea is here precisely in that medium, which is requisite to make it operate on us by comparison. Were it accompany'd with belief, and did the person appear to have the same merit, which he assumes to himself, it wou'd have a contrary effect, and *SB 596* wou'd operate on us by sympathy. The influence of that principle wou'd then be superior to that of comparison, contrary to what happens where the person's merit seems below his pretensions.

7   The necessary consequence of these principles is, that pride, or an overweaning conceit of ourselves, must be vicious; since it causes uneasiness in all men, and presents them every moment with a disagreeable comparison. 'Tis a trite observation in philosophy, and even in common life and conversation, that 'tis our own pride, which makes us so much displeas'd with the pride of other people; and that vanity becomes insupportable to us merely because we are vain.[†] The gay naturally associate themselves with the gay, and the amorous with the amorous: But the proud never can endure the proud, and rather seek the company of those who are of an opposite disposition. As we are, all of us, proud in some degree, pride is universally blam'd and condemn'd by all mankind; as having a natural tendency to cause uneasiness in others by means of comparison. And this effect must follow the more naturally, that those, who have an ill-grounded conceit of themselves, are for ever making those comparisons, nor have they any other method of supporting their vanity. A man of sense and merit is pleas'd with himself, independent of all foreign considerations: But a fool must always find some person, that is more foolish, in order to keep himself in good humour with his own parts and understanding.

---

[86] Book 2. Part 2. Sect. 10.   *SB 595*

8   But tho' an over-weaning conceit of our own merit be vicious and disagreeable, nothing can be more laudable, than to have a value for ourselves, where we really have qualities that are valuable. The utility and advantage of any quality to ourselves is a source of virtue, as well as its agreeableness to others; and 'tis certain, that nothing is more useful to us in the conduct of life, than a due degree of pride, which makes us sensible of our own merit, and gives us a confidence *SB 597* and assurance in all our projects and enterprizes. Whatever capacity any one may be endow'd with, 'tis entirely useless to him, if he be not acquainted with it, and form not designs suitable to it. 'Tis requisite on all occasions to know our own force; and were it allowable to err on either side, 'twou'd be more advantageous to over-rate our merit, than to form ideas of it, below its just standard. Fortune commonly favours the bold and enterprizing; and nothing inspires us with more boldness than a good opinion of ourselves.

9   Add to this, that tho' pride, or self-applause, be sometimes disagreeable to others, 'tis always agreeable to ourselves; as on the other hand, modesty, tho' it give pleasure to every one, who observes it, produces often uneasiness in the person endow'd with it. Now it has been observ'd,† that our own sensations determine the vice and virtue of any quality, as well as those sensations, which it may excite in others.

10   Thus self-satisfaction and vanity may not only be allowable, but requisite in a character. 'Tis, however, certain, that good-breeding and decency require that we shou'd avoid all signs and expressions, which tend directly to show that passion. We have, all of us, a wonderful partiality for ourselves, and were we always to give vent to our sentiments in this particular, we shou'd mutually cause the greatest indignation in each other, not only by the immediate presence of so disagreeable a subject of comparison, but also by the contrariety of our judgments. In like manner, therefore, as we establish the *laws of nature*, in order to secure property in society, and prevent the opposition of self-interest; we establish the *rules of good-breeding*, in order to prevent the opposition of men's pride, and render conversation agreeable and inoffensive. Nothing is more disagreeable than a man's over-weaning conceit of himself: Every one almost has a strong propensity to this vice: No one can well distinguish *in himself* betwixt the vice *SB 598* and virtue, or be certain, that his esteem of his own merit is well-founded: For these reasons, all direct expressions of this passion are condemn'd; nor do we make any exception to this rule in favour of men of sense and merit. They are not allow'd to do themselves justice openly, in words, no more than other people; and even if they show a reserve and secret doubt in doing themselves justice in their own thoughts, they will be more applauded. That impertinent, and almost universal propensity of men, to over-value themselves, has given us such a *prejudice* against self-applause, that we are apt to condemn it, by a *general rule*, wherever we meet with it; and 'tis with some difficulty we give a privilege to men of sense, even in their most secret thoughts. At least, it must be own'd, that some disguise in this particular is absolutely requisite; and that if we harbour pride in our breasts, we must carry a fair outside, and have the appearance of modesty and

mutual deference in all our conduct and behaviour. We must, on every occasion, be ready to prefer others to ourselves; to treat them with a kind of deference, even tho' they be our equals; to seem always the lowest and least in the company, where we are not very much distinguish'd above them: And if we observe these rules in our conduct, men will have more indulgence for our secret sentiments, when we discover them in an oblique manner.

11   I believe no one, who has any practice of the world, and can penetrate into the inward sentiments of men, will assert, that the humility, which good-breeding and decency require of us, goes beyond the outside, or that a thorough sincerity in this particular is esteem'd a real part of our duty. On the contrary, we may observe, that a genuine and hearty pride, or self-esteem, if well conceal'd and well founded, is essential to the character of a man of honour, and that there is no quality of the mind, which is more indispensibly requisite to procure the esteem and approbation of mankind. There are certain deferences and mutual submis-   *SB 599*
sions, which custom requires of the different ranks of men towards each other; and whoever exceeds in this particular, if thro' interest, is accus'd of meanness; if thro' ignorance, of simplicity. 'Tis necessary, therefore, to know our rank and station in the world, whether it be fix'd by our birth, fortune, employments, talents or reputation. 'Tis necessary to feel the sentiment and passion of pride in conformity to it, and to regulate our actions accordingly. And shou'd it be said, that prudence may suffice to regulate our actions in this particular, without any real pride, I wou'd observe, that here the object of prudence is to conform our actions to the general usage and custom; and that 'tis impossible those tacit airs of superiority shou'd ever have been establish'd and authoriz'd by custom, unless men were generally proud, and unless that passion were generally approv'd, when well-grounded.

12   If we pass from common life and conversation to history, this reasoning acquires new force, when we observe, that all those great actions and sentiments, which have become the admiration of mankind, are founded on nothing but pride and self-esteem. *Go*, says *Alexander* the Great to his soldiers, when they refus'd to follow him to the *Indies*, *go tell your countrymen, that you left Alexander compleating the conquest of the world*. This passage was always particularly admir'd by the prince of *Conde*, as we learn from *St. Evremond. Alexander*, said that prince, "abandon'd by his soldiers, among barbarians, not yet fully subdu'd, felt in himself such a dignity and right of empire, that he cou'd not believe it pos-sible any one cou'd refuse to obey him. Whether in *Europe* or in *Asia*, among *Greeks* or *Persians*, all was indifferent to him: Wherever he found men, he fancy'd he had found subjects."†

13   In general we may observe, that whatever we call *heroic virtue*, and admire under the character of greatness and elevation of mind, is either nothing but a steady and well-establish'd pride and self-esteem, or partakes largely of that passion. Courage, intrepidity, ambition, love of glory, magnanimity, and all the   *SB 600*
other shining virtues of that kind, have plainly a strong mixture of self-esteem in them, and derive a great part of their merit from that origin. Accordingly we find, that many religious declaimers decry those virtues as purely pagan and

natural, and represent to us the excellency of the *Christian* religion, which places humility in the rank of virtues, and corrects the judgment of the world, and even of philosophers, who so generally admire all the efforts of pride and ambition.[†] Whether this virtue of humility has been rightly understood, I shall not pretend to determine.[†] I am content with the concession, that the world naturally esteems a well-regulated pride, which secretly animates our conduct, without breaking out into such indecent expressions of vanity, as may offend the vanity of others.

14   The merit of pride or self-esteem is deriv'd from two circumstances, *viz.* its utility and its agreeableness to ourselves; by which it capacitates us for business, and, at the same time, gives us an immediate satisfaction. When it goes beyond its just bounds, it loses the first advantage, and even becomes prejudicial; which is the reason why we condemn an extravagant pride and ambition, however regulated by the decorums of good-breeding and politeness. But as such a passion is still agreeable, and conveys an elevated and sublime sensation to the person, who is actuated by it, the sympathy with that satisfaction diminishes considerably the blame, which naturally attends its dangerous influence on his conduct and behaviour. Accordingly we may observe, that an excessive courage and magnanimity, especially when it displays itself under the frowns of fortune, contributes, in a great measure, to the character of a hero, and will render a person the admiration of posterity; at the same time, that it ruins his affairs, and leads him into dangers and difficulties, with which otherwise he wou'd never have been acquainted.

15   Heroism, or military glory, is much admir'd by the generality of mankind. They consider it as the most sublime kind of merit. Men of cool reflection are not so sanguine in their praises of it. The infinite confusions and disorder, which   *SB 601* it has caus'd in the world, diminish much of its merit in their eyes. When they wou'd oppose the popular notions on this head, they always paint out the evils, which this suppos'd virtue has produc'd in human society; the subversion of empires, the devastation of provinces, the sack of cities. As long as these are present to us, we are more inclin'd to hate than admire the ambition of heroes. But when we fix our view on the person himself, who is the author of all this mischief, there is something so dazling in his character, the mere contemplation of it so elevates the mind, that we cannot refuse it our admiration. The pain, which we receive from its tendency to the prejudice of society, is over-power'd by a stronger and more immediate sympathy.

16   Thus our explication of the merit or demerit, which attends the degrees of pride or self-esteem, may serve as a strong argument for the preceding hypothesis, by showing the effects of those principles above-explain'd in all the variations of our judgments concerning that passion. Nor will this reasoning be advantageous to us only by showing, that the distinction of vice and virtue arises from the *four* principles of the *advantage* and of the *pleasure* of the *person himself,* and of *others*: But may also afford us a strong proof of some under-parts of that hypothesis.

17   No one, who duly considers of this matter, will make any scruple of allowing,

at any piece of ill-breeding, or any expression of pride and haughtiness, is displeasing to us, merely because it shocks our own pride, and leads us by sympathy into a comparison, which causes the disagreeable passion of humility. Now as an insolence of this kind is blam'd even in a person who has always been civil to ourselves in particular; nay, in one, whose name is only known to us in history; it follows, that our disapprobation proceeds from a sympathy with others, and from the reflection, that such a character is highly displeasing and odious to every one, who converses or has any intercourse with the person possest of it. We sympathize with those people in their uneasiness; and as their uneasiness proceeds in part from a sympathy with the person who insults them, we may here observe a double rebound of the sympathy; which is a principle very similar to what we have observ'd on another occasion.[87]

SB 602

Sect. 3. *Of goodness and benevolence*

1   Having thus explain'd the origin of that praise and approbation, which attends every thing we call *great* in human affections; we now proceed to give an account of their *goodness*, and show whence its merit is deriv'd.

2   When experience has once given us a competent knowledge of human affairs, and has taught us the proportion they bear to human passion, we perceive, that the generosity of men is very limited, and that it seldom extends beyond their friends and family, or, at most, beyond their native country. Being thus acquainted with the nature of man, we expect not any impossibilities from him; but confine our view to that narrow circle, in which any person moves, in order to form a judgment of his moral character. When the natural tendency of his passions leads him to be serviceable and useful within his sphere, we approve of his character, and love his person, by a sympathy with the sentiments of those, who have a more particular connexion with him. We are quickly oblig'd to forget our own interest in our judgments of this kind, by reason of the perpetual contradictions, we meet with in society and conversation, from persons that are not plac'd in the same situation, and have not the same interest with ourselves. The only point of view, in which our sentiments concur with those of others, is, when we consider the tendency of any passion to the advantage or harm of those, who have any immediate connexion or intercourse with the person possess'd of it. And tho' this advantage or harm be often very remote from ourselves, yet sometimes 'tis very near us, and interests us strongly by sympathy. This concern we readily extend to other cases, that are resembling; and when these are very remote, our sympathy is proportionably weaker, and our praise or blame fainter and more doubtful. The case is here the same as in our judgments concerning external bodies.[†] All objects seem to diminish by their distance: But tho' the appearance of objects to our senses be the original standard, by which we judge of them, yet we do not say, that they actually diminish by the distance; but cor-

SB 603

---

[87] Book 2. Part 2. Sect. 5.[†]

SB 602

recting the appearance by reflection, arrive at a more constant and establish'd judgment concerning them. In like manner, tho' sympathy be much fainter than our concern for ourselves, and a sympathy with persons remote from us much fainter than that with persons near and contiguous; yet we neglect all these differences in our calm judgments concerning the characters of men. Besides, that we ourselves often change our situation in this particular, we every day meet with persons, who are in a different situation from ourselves, and who cou'd never converse with us on any reasonable terms, were we to remain constantly in that situation and point of view, which is peculiar to us. The intercourse of sentiments, therefore, in society and conversation, makes us form some general inalterable standard, by which we may approve or disapprove of characters and manners. And tho' the *heart* does not always take part with those general notions, or regulate its love and hatred by them, yet are they sufficient for discourse, and serve all our purposes in company, in the pulpit, on the theatre,[†] and in the schools.

3   From these principles we may easily account for that merit, which is commonly ascrib'd to *generosity, humanity, compassion, gratitude, friendship, fidelity, zeal, disinterestedness, liberality*, and all those other qualities, which form the character of good and benevolent. A propensity to the tender passions makes a *SB 604* man agreeable and useful in all the parts of life; and gives a just direction to all his other qualities, which otherwise may become prejudicial to society. Courage and ambition, when not regulated by benevolence, are fit only to make a tyrant and public robber. 'Tis the same case with judgment and capacity, and all the qualities of that kind. They are indifferent in themselves to the interests of society, and have a tendency to the good or ill of mankind, according as they are directed by these other passions.

4   As love is *immediately agreeable* to the person, who is actuated by it, and hatred *immediately disagreeable*; this may also be a considerable reason, why we praise all the passions that partake of the former, and blame all those that have any considerable share of the latter. 'Tis certain we are infinitely touch'd with a tender sentiment, as well as with a great one. The tears naturally start in our eyes at the conception of it; nor can we forbear giving a loose to the same tenderness towards the person who exerts it. All this seems to me a proof, that our approbation has, in those cases, an origin different from the prospect of utility and advantage, either to ourselves or others. To which we may add, that men naturally, without reflection, approve of that character, which is most like their own. The man of a mild disposition and tender affections, in forming a notion of the most perfect virtue, mixes in it more of benevolence and humanity, than the man of courage and enterprize, who naturally looks upon a certain elevation of mind as the most accomplish'd character. This must evidently proceed from an *immediate* sympathy, which men have with characters similar to their own. They enter with more warmth into such sentiments, and feel more sensibly the pleasure, which arises from them.

5   'Tis remarkable, that nothing touches a man of humanity more than any instance of extraordinary delicacy in love or friendship, where a person is

attentive to the smallest concerns of his friend, and is willing to sacrifice to them the most considerable interest of his own. Such delicacies have little influence on society; because they make us regard the greatest trifles: But they are the more engaging, the more minute the concern is, and are a proof of the highest merit in any one, who is capable of them. The passions are so contagious, that they pass with the greatest facility from one person to another, and produce correspondent movements in all human breasts. Where friendship appears in very signal instances, my heart catches the same passion, and is warm'd by those warm sentiments, that display themselves before me. Such agreeable movements must give me an affection to every one that excites them. This is the case with every thing that is agreeable in any person. The transition from pleasure to love is easy: But the transition must here be still more easy; since the agreeable sentiment, which is excited by sympathy, is love itself; and there is nothing requir'd but to change the object. SB 605

6   Hence the peculiar merit of benevolence in all its shapes and appearances. Hence even its weaknesses are virtuous and amiable; and a person, whose grief upon the loss of a friend were excessive, wou'd be esteem'd upon that account. His tenderness bestows a merit, as it does a pleasure, on his melancholy.

7   We are not, however, to imagine, that all the angry passions are vicious, tho' they are disagreeable. There is a certain indulgence due to human nature in this respect. Anger and hatred are passions inherent in our very frame and constitution. The want of them, on some occasions, may even be a proof of weakness and imbecility. And where they appear only in a low degree, we not only excuse them because they are natural; but even bestow our applauses on them, because they are inferior to what appears in the greatest part of mankind.

8   Where these angry passions rise up to cruelty, they form the most detested of all vices. All the pity and concern which we have for the miserable sufferers by this vice, turns against the person guilty of it, and produces a stronger hatred than we are sensible of on any other occasion. SB 606

9   Even when the vice of inhumanity rises not to this extreme degree, our sentiments concerning it are very much influenc'd by reflections on the harm that results from it. And we may observe in general, that if we can find any quality in a person, which renders him incommodious to those, who live and converse with him, we always allow it to be a fault or blemish, without any farther examination. On the other hand, when we enumerate the good qualities of any person, we always mention those parts of his character, which render him a safe companion, an easy friend, a gentle master, an agreeable husband, or an indulgent father. We consider him with all his relations in society; and love or hate him, according as he affects those, who have any immediate intercourse with him. And 'tis a most certain rule, that if there be no relation of life, in which I cou'd not wish to stand to a particular person, his character must so far be allow'd to be perfect. If he be as little wanting to himself as to others, his character is entirely perfect. This is the ultimate test of merit and virtue.

Sect. 4. *Of natural abilities*

1   No distinction is more usual in all systems of ethics, than that betwixt *natural
abilities* and *moral virtues*; where the former are plac'd on the same footing with
bodily endowments, and are suppos'd to have no merit or moral worth annex'd to
them.[†] Whoever considers the matter accurately, will find, that a dispute upon
this head wou'd be merely a dispute of words,[†] and that tho' these qualities are
not altogether of the same kind, yet they agree in the most material circumstances. They are both of them equally mental qualities: And both of them
equally produce pleasure; and have of course an equal tendency to procure the   *SB 607*
love and esteem of mankind. There are few, who are not as jealous of their character, with regard to sense and knowledge, as to honour and courage; and much
more than with regard to temperance and sobriety. Men are even afraid of
passing for good-natur'd; lest *that* shou'd be taken for want of understanding:
And often boast of more debauches than they have been really engag'd in, to
give themselves airs of fire and spirit. In short, the figure a man makes in the
world, the reception he meets with in company, the esteem paid him by his
acquaintance; all these advantages depend almost as much upon his good sense
and judgment, as upon any other part of his character. Let a man have the best
intentions in the world, and be the farthest from all injustice and violence, he will
never be able to make himself be much regarded, without a moderate share, at
least, of parts and understanding. Since then natural abilities, tho', perhaps,
inferior, yet are on the same footing, both as to their causes and effects, with
those qualities which we call moral virtues, why shou'd we make any distinction
betwixt them?

2   Tho' we refuse to natural abilities the title of virtues, we must allow, that
they procure the love and esteem of mankind; that they give a new lustre to
the other virtues; and that a man possess'd of them is much more entitled to
our good-will and services, than one entirely void of them. It may, indeed, be
pretended, that the sentiment of approbation, which those qualities produce,
besides its being *inferior*, is also somewhat *different* from that, which attends
the other virtues. But this, in my opinion, is not a sufficient reason for excluding
them from the catalogue of virtues. Each of the virtues, even benevolence,
justice, gratitude, integrity, excites a different sentiment or feeling in the
spectator. The characters of *Cæsar*[†] and *Cato*,[†] as drawn by *Sallust*,[†] are both
of them virtuous, in the strictest sense of the word; but in a different way:
Nor are the sentiments entirely the same, which arise from them. The one
produces love; the other esteem: The one is amiable; the other awful:[†] We   *SB 608*
cou'd wish to meet with the one character in a friend; the other character
we wou'd be ambitious of in ourselves. In like manner, the approbation,
which attends natural abilities, may be somewhat different to the feeling
from that, which arises from the other virtues, without making them entirely
of a different species. And indeed we may observe, that the natural abilities,
no more than the other virtues, produce not, all of them, the same kind of

approbation. Good sense and genius beget esteem: Wit and humour excite love.[88]

3   Those, who represent the distinction betwixt natural abilities and moral virtues as very material, may say, that the former are entirely involuntary, and have therefore no merit attending them, as having no dependance on liberty and free-will.[†] But to this I answer, *first*, that many of those qualities, which all moralists, especially the antients, comprehend under the title of moral virtues, are equally involuntary and necessary, with the qualities of the judgment and imagination.[†] Of this nature are constancy, fortitude, magnanimity; and, in short, all the qualities which form the *great* man. I might say the same, in some degree, of the others; it being almost impossible for the mind to change its character in any considerable article, or cure itself of a passionate or splenetic temper, when they are natural to it. The greater degree there is of these blameable qualities, the more vicious they become, and yet they are the less voluntary. *Secondly*, I wou'd have any one give me a reason, why virtue and vice may not be involuntary, as well as beauty and deformity. These moral distinctions arise from the natural distinctions of pain and pleasure; and when we receive those feelings from the general consideration of any quality or character, we denominate it vicious or virtuous. Now I believe no one will assert, that a quality can never produce pleasure or pain to the person who considers it, unless it be perfectly voluntary in the person who possesses it. *Thirdly*, As to free-will, we have shown that it has no place with regard to the actions, no more than the qualities of men.[†] It is not a just consequence, that what is voluntary is free. Our actions are more voluntary than our judgments; but we have not more liberty in the one than in the other.   *SB 609*

4   But tho' this distinction betwixt voluntary and involuntary be not sufficient to justify the distinction betwixt natural abilities and moral virtues, yet the former distinction will afford us a plausible reason, why moralists have invented the latter. Men have observ'd, that tho' natural abilities and moral qualities be in the main on the same footing, there is, however, this difference betwixt them, that the former are almost invariable by any art or industry; while the latter, or at least, the actions, that proceed from them, may be chang'd by the motives of reward and punishment, praise and blame.[†] Hence legislators, and divines, and moralists, have principally apply'd themselves to the regulating these voluntary actions, and have endeavour'd to produce additional motives for being virtuous in that particular. They knew, that to punish a man for folly, or exhort him to be prudent and sagacious, wou'd have but little effect; tho' the same punishments and exhortations, with regard to justice and injustice, might have a considerable influence. But as men, in common life and conversation, do not carry those ends

---

[88] Love and esteem are at the bottom the same passions, and arise from like causes.[†] The qualities, that produce both, are agreeable, and give pleasure. But where this pleasure is severe and serious; or where its object is great, and makes a strong impression; or where it produces any degree of humility and awe: In all these cases, the passion, which arises from the pleasure, is more properly denominated esteem than love. Benevolence attends both: But is connected with love in a more eminent degree.   *SB 608*

in view, but naturally praise or blame whatever pleases or displeases them, they do not seem much to regard this distinction, but consider prudence under the character of virtue as well as benevolence, and penetration as well as justice. Nay, we find, that all moralists, whose judgment is not perverted by a strict adherence to a system, enter into the same way of thinking; and that the antient moralists in particular made no scruple of placing prudence at the head of the cardinal virtues.† There is a sentiment of esteem and approbation, which may be excited, *SB 610* in some degree, by any faculty of the mind, in its perfect state and condition; and to account for this sentiment is the business of *philosophers*. It belongs to *grammarians*† to examine what qualities are entitled to the denomination of *virtue*; nor will they find, upon trial, that this is so easy a task, as at first sight they may be apt to imagine.

5   The principal reason why natural abilities are esteem'd, is because of their tendency to be useful to the person, who is possess'd of them. 'Tis impossible to execute any design with success, where it is not conducted with prudence and discretion; nor will the goodness of our intentions alone suffice to procure us a happy issue to our enterprizes. Men are superior to beasts principally by the superiority of their reason;† and they are the degrees of the same faculty, which set such an infinite difference betwixt one man and another. All the advantages of art are owing to human reason; and where fortune is not very capricious, the most considerable part of these advantages must fall to the share of the prudent and sagacious.

6   When it is ask'd, whether a quick or a slow apprehension be most valuable? whether one, that at first view penetrates into a subject, but can perform nothing upon study; or a contrary character, which must work out every thing by dint of application? whether a clear head, or a copious invention? whether a profound genius, or a sure judgment? in short, what character, or peculiar understanding, is more excellent than another? 'tis evident we can answer none of these questions, without considering which of those qualities capacitates a man best for the world, and carries him farthest in any of his undertakings.

7   There are many other qualities of the mind, whose merit is deriv'd from the same origin. *Industry, perseverance, patience, activity, vigilance, application, constancy*, with other virtues of that kind, which 'twill be easy to recollect, are esteem'd valuable upon no other account, than their advantage in the conduct of *SB 611* life. 'Tis the same case with *temperance, frugality, œconomy, resolution*: As on the other hand, *prodigality, luxury, irresolution, uncertainty*, are vicious, merely because they draw ruin upon us, and incapacitate us for business and action.

8   As wisdom and good-sense are valu'd, because they are *useful* to the person possess'd of them; so *wit* and *eloquence* are valu'd, because they are *immediately agreeable* to others. On the other hand, *good humour* is lov'd and esteem'd, because it is *immediately agreeable* to the person himself. 'Tis evident, that the conversation of a man of wit is very satisfactory; as a chearful good-humour'd companion diffuses a joy over the whole company, from a sympathy with his gaiety. These qualities, therefore, being agreeable, they naturally beget love and esteem, and answer to all the characters of virtue.

9   'Tis difficult to tell, on many occasions, what it is that renders one man's conversation so agreeable and entertaining, and another's so insipid and distasteful.
As conversation is a transcript of the mind as well as books, the same qualities,
which render the one valuable, must give us an esteem for the other. This we
shall consider afterwards.† In the mean time it may be affirm'd in general, that all
the merit a man may derive from his conversation (which, no doubt, may be very
considerable) arises from nothing but the pleasure it conveys to those who are
present.

10   In this view, *cleanliness* is also to be regarded as a virtue; since it naturally
renders us agreeable to others, and is a very considerable source of love and
affection. No one will deny, that a negligence in this particular is a fault; and as
faults are nothing but smaller vices, and this fault can have no other origin than
the uneasy sensation, which it excites in others, we may in this instance, seemingly so trivial, clearly discover the origin of the moral distinction of vice and
virtue in other instances.

11   Besides all those qualities, which render a person lovely or valuable, there is   *SB 612*
also a certain *je-ne-sçai-quoi* of agreeable and handsome, that concurs to the same
effect. In this case, as well as in that of wit and eloquence, we must have recourse
to a certain sense,† which acts without reflection, and regards not the tendencies
of qualities and characters. Some moralists account for all the sentiments of
virtue by this sense.† Their hypothesis is very plausible. Nothing but a particular
enquiry can give the preference to any other hypothesis. When we find, that
almost all the virtues have such particular tendencies; and also find, that these
tendencies are sufficient alone to give a strong sentiment of approbation:† We
cannot doubt, after this, that qualities are approv'd of, in proportion to the
advantage, which results from them.

12   The *decorum* or *indecorum*† of a quality, with regard to the age, or character,
or station, contributes also to its praise or blame.† This decorum depends, in a
great measure, upon experience. 'Tis usual to see men lose their levity, as they
advance in years. Such a degree of gravity, therefore, and such years, are connected together in our thoughts. When we observe them separated in any
person's character, this imposes a kind of violence on our imagination, and is
disagreeable.

13   That faculty of the soul, which, of all others, is of the least consequence to the
character, and has the least virtue or vice in its several degrees, at the same time,
that it admits of a great variety of degrees, is the *memory*. Unless it rise up to that
stupendous height as to surprize us, or sink so low as, in some measure, to affect
the judgment, we commonly take no notice of its variations, nor ever mention
them to the praise or dispraise of any person. 'Tis so far from being a virtue to
have a good memory, that men generally affect to complain of a bad one;† and
endeavouring to perswade the world, that what they say is entirely of their own
invention, sacrifice it to the praise of genius and judgment. Yet to consider the
matter abstractedly, 'twou'd be difficult to give a reason, why the faculty of   *SB 613*
recalling past ideas with truth and clearness, shou'd not have as much merit in it,
as the faculty of placing our present ideas in such an order, as to form true propo-

sitions and opinions. The reason of the difference certainly must be, that the memory is exerted without any sensation of pleasure or pain; and in all its middling degrees serves almost equally well in business and affairs. But the least variations in the judgment are sensibly felt in their consequences; while at the same time that faculty is never exerted in any eminent degree, without an extraordinary delight and satisfaction. The sympathy with this utility and pleasure bestows a merit on the understanding; and the absence of it makes us consider the memory as a faculty very indifferent to blame or praise.

14   Before I leave this subject of *natural abilities*, I must observe, that, perhaps, one source of the esteem and affection, which attends them, is deriv'd from the *importance* and *weight*, which they bestow on the person possess'd of them. He becomes of greater consequence in life. His resolutions and actions affect a greater number of his fellow-creatures. Both his friendship and enmity are of moment. And 'tis easy to observe, that whoever is elevated, after this manner, above the rest of mankind, must excite in us the sentiments of esteem and approbation. Whatever is important engages our attention, fixes our thought, and is contemplated with satisfaction. The histories of kingdoms are more interesting than domestic stories: The histories of great empires more than those of small cities and principalities: And the histories of wars and revolutions more than those of peace and order. We sympathize with the persons that suffer, in all the various sentiments which belong to their fortunes. The mind is occupy'd by the multitude of the objects, and by the strong passions, that display themselves. And this occupation or agitation of the mind is commonly agreeable and amusing. The same theory accounts for the esteem and regard we pay to men of extraordinary parts and abilities. The good and ill of multitudes are *SB 614* connected with their actions. Whatever they undertake is important, and challenges our attention. Nothing is to be over-look'd and despis'd, that regards them. And where any person can excite these sentiments, he soon acquires our esteem; unless other circumstances of his character render him odious and disagreeable.

Sect. 5. *Some farther reflections concerning the natural abilities*

1   It has been observ'd,[†] in treating of the passions, that pride and humility, love and hatred, are excited by any advantages or disadvantages of the *mind*, *body*, or *fortune*; and that these advantages or disadvantages have that effect by producing a separate impression of pain or pleasure. The pain or pleasure, which arises from the general survey or view of any action or quality of the *mind*, constitutes[†] its vice or virtue, and gives rise to our approbation or blame, which is nothing but a fainter and more imperceptible love or hatred. We have assign'd[†] four different sources of this pain and pleasure; and in order to justify more fully that hypothesis, it may here be proper to observe, that the advantages or disadvantages of the *body* and of *fortune*, produce a pain or pleasure from the very same principles. The tendency of any object to be *useful* to the person possess'd of it, or to others; to convey *pleasure* to him or to others; all these circumstances convey an

immediate pleasure to the person, who considers the object, and command his love and approbation.

2   To begin with the advantages of the *body*; we may observe a phænomenon, which might appear somewhat trivial and ludicrous, if any thing cou'd be trivial, which fortify'd a conclusion of such importance, or ludicrous, which was employ'd in a philosophical reasoning. 'Tis a general remark, that those we call good *women's men*,[†] who have either signaliz'd themselves by their amorous exploits, or whose make of body promises any extraordinary vigour of that kind, *SB 615* are well receiv'd by the fair sex, and naturally engage the affections even of those, whose virtue prevents any design of ever giving employment to those talents. Here 'tis evident, that the ability of such a person to give enjoyment, is the real source of that love and esteem he meets with among the females; at the same time that the women, who love and esteem him, have no prospect of receiving that enjoyment themselves, and can only be affected by means of their sympathy with one, that has a commerce of love with him. This instance is singular, and merits our attention.

3   Another source of the pleasure we receive from considering bodily advantages, is their utility to the person himself, who is possess'd of them. 'Tis certain, that a considerable part of the beauty of men, as well as of other animals, consists in such a conformation of members, as we find by experience to be attended with strength and agility, and to capacitate the creature for any action or exercise.[†] Broad shoulders, a lank belly, firm joints, taper legs; all these are beautiful in our species, because they are signs of force and vigour, which being advantages we naturally sympathize with, they convey to the beholder a share of that satisfaction they produce in the possessor.

4   So far as to the *utility*, which may attend any quality of the body. As to the immediate *pleasure*, 'tis certain, that an air of health, as well as of strength and agility, makes a considerable part of beauty; and that a sickly air in another is always disagreeable, upon account of that idea of pain and uneasiness, which it conveys to us. On the other hand, we are pleas'd with the regularity of our own features, tho' it be neither useful to ourselves nor others; and 'tis necessary for us, in some measure, to set ourselves at a distance, to make it convey to us any satisfaction. We commonly consider ourselves as we appear in the eyes of others, and sympathize with the advantageous sentiments they entertain with regard to us.

5   How far the advantages of *fortune* produce esteem and approbation from the *SB 616* same principles, we may satisfy ourselves by reflecting on our precedent reasoning on that subject. We have observ'd,[†] that our approbation of those, who are possess'd of the advantages of fortune, may be ascrib'd to three different causes. *First*, To that immediate pleasure, which a rich man gives us, by the view of the beautiful cloaths, equipage, gardens, or houses, which he possesses. *Secondly*, To the advantage, which we hope to reap from him by his generosity and liberality. *Thirdly*, To the pleasure and advantage, which he himself reaps from his possessions, and which produce an agreeable sympathy in us. Whether we ascribe our esteem of the rich and great to one or all of these causes, we may clearly see the

traces of those principles, which give rise to the sense of vice and virtue. I believe most people, at first sight, will be inclin'd to ascribe our esteem of the rich to self-interest, and the prospect of advantage. But as 'tis certain, that our esteem or deference extends beyond any prospect of advantage to ourselves, 'tis evident, that that sentiment must proceed from a sympathy with those, who are dependent on the person we esteem and respect, and who have an immediate connexion with him. We consider him as a person capable of contributing to the happiness or enjoyment of his fellow-creatures, whose sentiments, with regard to him, we naturally embrace. And this consideration will serve to justify my hypothesis in preferring the *third* principle to the other two, and ascribing our esteem of the rich to a sympathy with the pleasure and advantage, which they themselves receive from their possessions.[†] For as even the other two principles cannot operate to a due extent, or account for all the phænomena, without having recourse to a sympathy of one kind or other; 'tis much more natural to choose that sympathy, which is immediate and direct, than that which is remote and indirect. To which we may add, that where the riches or power are very great, and render the person considerable and important in the world, the esteem attending them, may, in part, be ascrib'd to another source, distinct from these three, *viz.* their interesting the mind by a prospect of the multitude, and importance of their consequences: Tho', in order to account for the operation of this principle, we must also have recourse to *sympathy*; as we have observ'd[†] in the preceding section. *SB 617*

6   It may not be amiss, on this occasion, to remark the flexibility of our sentiments, and the several changes they so readily receive from the objects, with which they are conjoin'd. All the sentiments of approbation, which attend any particular species of objects, have a great resemblance to each other, tho' deriv'd from different sources; and, on the other hand, those sentiments, when directed to different objects, are different to the feeling, tho' deriv'd from the same source.[†] Thus the beauty of all visible objects causes a pleasure pretty much the same, tho' it be sometimes deriv'd from the mere *species* and appearance of the objects; sometimes from sympathy, and an idea of their utility. In like manner, whenever we survey the actions and characters of men, without any particular interest in them, the pleasure, or pain, which arises from the survey (with some minute differences) is, in the main, of the same kind, tho' perhaps there be a great diversity in the causes, from which it is deriv'd. On the other hand, a convenient house, and a virtuous character, cause not the same feeling of approbation; even tho' the source of our approbation be the same, and flow from sympathy and an idea of their utility. There is something very inexplicable in this variation of our feelings; but 'tis what we have experience of with regard to all our passions and sentiments.

Sect. 6. *Conclusion of this book*   *SB 618*

1   Thus upon the whole I am hopeful, that nothing is wanting to an accurate proof of this system of ethics. We are certain, that sympathy is a very powerful

principle in human nature. We are also certain, that it has a great influence on our sense of beauty, when we regard external objects, as well as when we judge of morals. We find, that it has force sufficient to give us the strongest sentiments of approbation, when it operates alone, without the concurrence of any other principle; as in the cases of justice, allegiance, chastity, and good-manners.[†] We may observe, that all the circumstances requisite for its operation are found in most of the virtues; which have, for the most part, a tendency to the good of society, or to that of the person possess'd of them. If we compare all these circumstances, we shall not doubt, that sympathy is the chief source of moral distinctions; especially when we reflect, that no objection can be rais'd against this hypothesis in one case, which will not extend to all cases. Justice is certainly approv'd of for no other reason, than because it has a tendency to the public good: And the public good is indifferent to us, except so far as sympathy interests us in it. We may presume the like with regard to all the other virtues, which have a like tendency to the public good. They must derive all their merit from our sympathy with those, who reap any advantage from them: As the virtues, which have a tendency to the good of the person possess'd of them, derive their merit from our sympathy with him.[†]

2   Most people will readily allow, that the useful qualities of the mind are virtuous, because of their utility. This way of thinking is so natural, and occurs on so many occasions, that few will make any scruple of admitting it. Now this being once admitted, the force of sympathy must necessarily be acknowledg'd. Virtue is consider'd as means to an end. Means to an end are only valu'd so far as the end is valu'd. But the happiness of strangers affects us by sympathy alone. To that principle, therefore, we are to ascribe the sentiment of approbation, which arises from the survey of all those virtues, that are useful to society, or to the person possess'd of them. These form the most considerable part of morality. *SB 619*

3   Were it proper in such a subject to bribe the reader's assent, or employ any thing but solid argument, we are here abundantly supply'd with topics to engage the affections. All lovers of virtue (and such we all are in speculation, however we may degenerate in practice) must certainly be pleas'd to see moral distinctions deriv'd from so noble a source, which gives us a just notion both of the *generosity* and *capacity* of our nature. It requires but very little knowledge of human affairs to perceive, that a sense of morals is a principle inherent in the soul, and one of the most powerful that enters into the composition. But this sense must certainly acquire new force, when reflecting on itself, it approves of those principles, from whence it is deriv'd, and finds nothing but what is great and good in its rise and origin. Those who resolve the sense of morals into original instincts of the human mind, may defend the cause of virtue with sufficient authority;[†] but want the advantage, which those possess, who account for that sense by an extensive sympathy with mankind.[†] According to the latter system, not only virtue must be approv'd of, but also the sense of virtue: And not only that sense, but also the principles, from whence it is deriv'd. So that nothing is presented on any side, but what is laudable and good.

4   This observation may be extended to justice, and the other virtues of that kind. Tho' justice be artificial, the sense of its morality is natural. 'Tis the combination of men, in a system of conduct, which renders any act of justice beneficial to society. But when once it has that tendency, we *naturally* approve of it;[†]   *SB 620* and if we did not so, 'tis impossible any combination or convention cou'd ever produce that sentiment.

5   Most of the inventions of men are subject to change. They depend upon humour and caprice. They have a vogue for a time, and then sink into oblivion. It may, perhaps, be apprehended, that if justice were allow'd to be a human invention, it must be plac'd on the same footing. But the cases are widely different. The interest, on which justice is founded, is the greatest imaginable, and extends to all times and places. It cannot possibly be serv'd by any other invention. It is obvious, and discovers itself on the very first formation of society. All these causes render the rules of justice stedfast and immutable; at least, as immutable as human nature. And if they were founded on original instincts, cou'd they have any greater stability?

6   The same system may help us to form a just notion of the *happiness*, as well as of the *dignity* of virtue, and may interest every principle of our nature in the embracing and cherishing that noble quality. Who indeed does not feel an accession of alacrity in his pursuits of knowledge and ability of every kind, when he considers, that beside the advantages, which immediately result from these acquisitions, they also give him a new lustre in the eyes of mankind, and are universally attended with esteem and approbation? And who can think any advantages of fortune a sufficient compensation for the least breach of the *social* virtues, when he considers, that not only his character with regard to others, but also his peace and inward satisfaction entirely depend upon his strict observance of them; and that a mind will never be able to bear its own survey, that has been wanting in its part to mankind and society? But I forbear insisting on this subject. Such reflections require a work apart, very different from the genius of the present. The anatomist ought never to emulate the painter; nor in his accurate dissections and portraitures of the smaller parts of the human body, pretend to give his figures any graceful and engaging attitude or expression. There is   *SB 621* even something hideous, or at least minute in the views of things, which he presents; and 'tis necessary the objects shou'd be set more at a distance, and be more cover'd up from sight, to make them engaging to the eye and imagination. An anatomist, however, is admirably fitted to give advice to a painter;[†] and 'tis even impracticable to excel in the latter art, without the assistance of the former. We must have an exact knowledge of the parts, their situation and connexion, before we can design with any elegance or correctness. And thus the most abstract speculations concerning human nature, however cold and unentertaining, become subservient to *practical morality*; and may render this latter science more correct in its precepts, and more perswasive in its exhortations.

APPENDIX

1   There is nothing I wou'd more willingly lay hold of, than an opportunity of confessing my errors; and shou'd esteem such a return to truth and reason to be more honourable than the most unerring judgment. A man, who is free from mistakes, can pretend to no praises, except from the justness of his understanding: But a man, who corrects his mistakes, shows at once the justness of his understanding, and the candour and ingenuity of his temper. I have not yet been so fortunate as to discover any very considerable mistakes in the reasonings deliver'd in the preceding volumes,[†] except on one article:[†] But I have found by experience, that some of my expressions have not been so well chosen, as to guard against all mistakes in the readers; and 'tis chiefly to remedy this defect, I have subjoin'd the following appendix.

2   We can never be induc'd to believe any matter of fact, except where its cause, or its effect, direct or collateral, is present to us; but what the nature is of that belief, which arises from the relation of cause and effect, few have had the curiosity to ask themselves. In my opinion, this dilemma is inevitable. Either the belief is some new idea, such as that of *reality* or *existence*, which we join to the simple conception of an object, or it is merely a peculiar *feeling* or *sentiment*. That it is not a new idea, annex'd to the simple conception, may be evinc'd from these two arguments. *First*, We have no abstract idea of existence, distinguishable and separable from the idea of particular objects.[†] 'Tis impossible, therefore, that this idea of existence can be annex'd to the idea of any object, or form the difference betwixt a simple conception and belief. *Secondly*, The mind has the command over all its ideas, and can separate, unite, mix, and vary them, as it pleases;[†] so that if belief consisted merely in a new idea, annex'd to the conception, it wou'd be in a man's power to believe what he pleas'd. We may, therefore, conclude, that belief consists merely in a certain feeling or sentiment; in something, that depends not on the will, but must arise from certain determinate causes and principles, of which we are not masters. When we are convinc'd of any matter of fact, we do nothing but conceive it, along with a certain feeling, different from what attends the mere *reveries* of the imagination. And when we express our incredulity concerning any fact, we mean, that the arguments for the fact produce not that feeling. Did not the belief consist in a sentiment different from our mere conception, whatever objects were presented by the wildest imagination, wou'd be on an equal footing with the most establish'd truths founded on history and experience. There is nothing but the feeling, or sentiment, to distinguish the one from the other.

3   This, therefore, being regarded as an undoubted truth, *that belief is nothing but a peculiar feeling, different from the simple conception*, the next question, that naturally occurs, is, *What is the nature of this feeling, or sentiment, and whether it be analogous to any other sentiment of the human mind?* This question is important. For if it be not analogous to any other sentiment, we must despair of explaining

396

its causes, and must consider it as an original principle of the human mind. If it be analogous, we may hope to explain its causes from analogy, and trace it up to more general principles. Now that there is a greater firmness and solidity in the conceptions, which are the objects of conviction and assurance, than in the loose and indolent reveries of a castle-builder, every one will readily own. They strike upon us with more force; they are more present to us; the mind has a firmer hold of them, and is more actuated and mov'd by them. It acquiesces in them; and, in a manner, fixes and reposes itself on them. In short, they approach nearer to the impressions, which are immediately present to us; and are therefore analogous to *SB 625* many other operations of the mind.

4 There is not, in my opinion, any possibility of evading this conclusion, but by asserting, that belief, beside the simple conception, consists in some impression or feeling, distinguishable from the conception. It does not modify the conception, and render it more present and intense: It is only annex'd to it, after the same manner that *will* and *desire* are annex'd to particular conceptions of good and pleasure. But the following considerations will, I hope, be sufficient to remove this hypothesis. *First*, It is directly contrary to experience, and our immediate consciousness. All men have ever allow'd reasoning to be merely an operation of our thoughts or ideas; and however those ideas may be vary'd to the feeling, there is nothing ever enters into our *conclusions* but ideas, or our fainter conceptions. For instance; I hear at present a person's voice, whom I am acquainted with; and this sound comes from the next room. This impression of my senses immediately conveys my thoughts to the person, along with all the surrounding objects. I paint them out to myself as existent at present, with the same qualities and relations, that I formerly knew them possess'd of. These ideas take faster hold of my mind, than the ideas of an enchanted castle. They are different to the feeling; but there is no distinct or separate impression attending them. 'Tis the same case when I recollect the several incidents of a journey, or the events of any history. Every particular fact is there the object of belief. Its idea is modify'd differently from the loose reveries of a castle-builder: But no distinct impression attends every distinct idea, or conception of matter of fact. This is the subject of plain experience. If ever this experience can be disputed on any occasion, 'tis when the mind has been agitated with doubts and difficulties; and afterwards, upon taking the object in a new point of view, or being presented with a new argument, fixes and reposes itself in one settled conclusion and belief. In this case there is a feeling distinct and separate from the conception.[†] *SB 626* The passage from doubt and agitation to tranquillity and repose, conveys a satisfaction and pleasure to the mind. But take any other case. Suppose I see the legs and thighs of a person in motion, while some interpos'd object conceals the rest of his body. Here 'tis certain, the imagination spreads out the whole figure. I give him a head and shoulders, and breast and neck. These members I conceive and believe him to be possess'd of. Nothing can be more evident, than that this whole operation is perform'd by the thought or imagination alone. The transition is immediate. The ideas presently strike us. Their customary connexion with the present impression, varies them and modifies them in a certain manner, but

produces no act of the mind, distinct from this peculiarity of conception. Let any one examine his own mind, and he will evidently find this to be the truth.

5   *Secondly*, Whatever may be the case, with regard to this distinct impression, it must be allow'd, that the mind has a firmer hold, or more steady conception of what it takes to be matter of fact, than of fictions. Why then look any farther, or multiply suppositions without necessity?†

6   *Thirdly*, We can explain the *causes* of the firm conception, but not those of any separate impression. And not only so, but the causes of the firm conception exhaust the whole subject, and nothing is left to produce any other effect. An inference concerning a matter of fact is nothing but the idea of an object, that has been frequently conjoin'd, or is associated with a present impression. This is the whole of it. Every part is requisite to explain, from analogy, the more steady conception; and nothing remains capable of producing any distinct impression.

7   *Fourthly*, The *effects* of belief, in influencing the passions and imagination, can all be explain'd from the firm conception; and there is no occasion to have recourse to any other principle. These arguments, with many others, enumerated in the foregoing volumes, sufficiently prove, that belief only modifies the *SB 627* idea or conception; and renders it different to the feeling, without producing any distinct impression.

8   Thus upon a general view of the subject, there appear to be two questions of importance, which we may venture to recommend to the consideration of philosophers, *Whether there be any thing to distinguish belief from the simple conception beside the feeling or sentiment?* And, *Whether this feeling be any thing but a firmer conception, or a faster hold, that we take of the object?*

9   If, upon impartial enquiry, the same conclusion, that I have form'd, be assented to by philosophers, the next business is to examine the analogy, which there is betwixt belief, and other acts of the mind, and find the cause of the firmness and strength of conception: And this I do not esteem a difficult task. The transition from a present impression, always enlivens and strengthens any idea. When any object is presented, the idea of its usual attendant immediately strikes us, as something real and solid. 'Tis *felt*, rather than conceiv'd, and approaches the impression, from which it is deriv'd, in its force and influence. This I have prov'd at large.† I cannot add any new arguments; tho' perhaps my reasoning on this whole question, concerning cause and effect, wou'd have been more convincing, had the following passages been inserted in the places, which I have mark'd for them. I have added a few illustrations on other points, where I thought it necessary.†

---

10   I had entertain'd some hopes, that however deficient our theory of the intellec- *SB 633* tual world might be, it wou'd be free from those contradictions, and absurdities, which seem to attend every explication, that human reason can give of the material world.† But upon a more strict review of the section concerning *personal*

identity,[†] I find myself involv'd in such a labyrinth, that, I must confess, I neither know how to correct my former opinions, nor how to render them consistent. If this be not a good *general* reason for scepticism, 'tis at least a sufficient one (if I were not already abundantly supply'd) for me to entertain a diffidence and modesty in all my decisions. I shall propose the arguments on both sides, beginning with those that induc'd me to deny the strict and proper identity and simplicity of a self or thinking being.[†]

11   When we talk of *self* or *substance*, we must have an idea annex'd to these terms, otherwise they are altogether unintelligible. Every idea is deriv'd from preceding impressions; and we have no impression of self or substance, as something simple and individual. We have, therefore, no idea of them in that sense.

12   Whatever is distinct, is distinguishable; and whatever is distinguishable, is   *SB 634* separable by the thought or imagination. All perceptions are distinct. They are, therefore, distinguishable, and separable, and may be conceiv'd as separately existent, and may exist separately, without any contradiction or absurdity.

13   When I view this table and that chimney, nothing is present to me but particular perceptions, which are of a like nature with all the other perceptions. This is the doctrine of philosophers. But this table, which is present to me, and that chimney, may and do exist separately. This is the doctrine of the vulgar, and implies no contradiction. There is no contradiction, therefore, in extending the same doctrine to all the perceptions.

14   In general, the following reasoning seems satisfactory. All ideas are borrow'd from preceding perceptions. Our ideas of objects, therefore, are deriv'd from that source. Consequently no proposition can be intelligible or consistent with regard to objects, which is not so with regard to perceptions. But 'tis intelligible and consistent to say, that objects exist distinct and independent, without any common *simple* substance or subject of inhesion. This proposition, therefore, can never be absurd with regard to perceptions.

15   When I turn my reflection on *myself*, I never can perceive this *self* without some one or more perceptions; nor can I ever perceive any thing but the perceptions. 'Tis the composition of these, therefore, which forms the self.

16   We can conceive a thinking being to have either many or few perceptions. Suppose the mind to be reduc'd even below the life of an oyster. Suppose it to have only one perception, as of thirst or hunger.[†] Consider it in that situation. Do you conceive any thing but merely that perception? Have you any notion of *self* or *substance*? If not, the addition of other perceptions can never give you that notion.

17   The annihilation, which some people suppose to follow upon death, and which entirely destroys this self, is nothing but an extinction of all particu-   *SB 635* lar perceptions; love and hatred, pain and pleasure, thought and sensation. These therefore must be the same with self; since the one cannot survive the other.

18   Is *self* the same with *substance*? If it be, how can that question have place, concerning the subsistence of self, under a change of substance?[†] If they be distinct,

what is the difference betwixt them? For my part, I have a notion of neither, when conceiv'd distinct from particular perceptions.

19   Philosophers begin to be reconcil'd to the principle, *that we have no idea of external substance, distinct from the ideas of particular qualities.* This must pave the way for a like principle with regard to the mind, *that we have no notion of it, distinct from the particular perceptions.*

20   So far I seem to be attended with sufficient evidence. But having thus loosen'd all our particular perceptions,[†] when I proceed to explain the principle of connexion,[89] which binds them together, and makes us attribute to them a real simplicity and identity; I am sensible, that my account is very defective, and that nothing but the seeming evidence of the precedent reasonings[†] cou'd have induc'd me to receive it. If perceptions are distinct existences, they form a whole only by being connected together. But no connexions among distinct existences are ever discoverable by human understanding. We only *feel* a connexion or a determination of the thought, to pass from one object to another. It follows, therefore, that the thought alone finds personal identity, when reflecting on the train of past perceptions, that compose a mind, the ideas of them are felt to be connected together, and naturally introduce each other.[†] However extraordinary this conclusion may seem, it need not surprize us. Most philosophers seem inclin'd to think, that personal identity *arises* from consciousness; and consciousness is nothing but a reflected thought or perception.[†] The present philosophy, therefore, has so far a promising aspect. But all my hopes vanish, when I come to explain the principles, that unite our successive perceptions in our thought or consciousness. I cannot discover any theory, which gives me satisfaction on this head.   *SB 636*

21   In short there are two principles, which I cannot render consistent; nor is it in my power to renounce either of them, viz. *that all our distinct perceptions are distinct existences,* and *that the mind never perceives any real connexion among distinct existences.* Did our perceptions either inhere in something simple and individual, or did the mind perceive some real connexion among them, there wou'd be no difficulty in the case. For my part, I must plead the privilege of a sceptic, and confess, that this difficulty is too hard for my understanding. I pretend not, however, to pronounce it absolutely insuperable. Others, perhaps, or myself, upon more mature reflection, may discover some hypothesis, that will reconcile those contradictions.

22   I shall also take this opportunity of confessing two other errors[†] of less importance, which more mature reflection has discover'd to me in my reasoning. The first may be found in Book 1, pages 42–3, where I say, that the distance betwixt two bodies is known, among other things, by the angles, which the rays of light flowing from the bodies make with each other. 'Tis certain, that these angles are not known to the mind, and consequently can never discover the distance. The second error may be found in Book 1, page 67, where I say, that two ideas of the same object can only be different by their different degrees of force and

---

[89] Book 1, pp. 169–70.[†]   *SB 635*

vivacity. I believe there are other differences among ideas, which cannot properly be comprehended under these terms. Had I said, that two ideas of the same object can only be different by their different *feeling*, I shou'd have been nearer the truth.

FINIS.

AN ABSTRACT OF A BOOK

LATELY PUBLISHED;

ENTITULED,

A TREATISE OF HUMAN NATURE, &c.

WHEREIN THE

CHIEF ARGUMENT OF THAT BOOK

IS FARTHER

ILLUSTRATED AND EXPLAINED

PREFACE

1   *My expectations in this small performance may seem somewhat extraordinary, when I declare that my intentions are to render a larger work more intelligible to ordinary capacities, by abridging it.†* *'Tis however certain, that those who are not accustomed to abstract reasoning, are apt to lose the thread of argument, where it is drawn out to a great length, and each part fortified with all the arguments, guarded against all the objections, and illustrated with all the views, which occur to a writer in the diligent survey of his subject. Such Readers will more readily apprehend a chain of reasoning, that is more single and concise, where the chief propositions only are linkt on to each other, illustrated by some simple examples, and confirmed by a few of the more forcible arguments. The parts lying nearer together can better be compared, and the connexion be more easily traced from the first principles to the last conclusion.*

2   *The work, of which I here present the Reader with an abstract, has been complained of as obscure and difficult to be comprehended,† and I am apt to think, that this proceeded as much from the length as from the abstractedness of the argument. If I have remedied this inconvenience in any degree, I have attained my end. The book seemed to me to have such an air of singularity, and novelty as claimed the attention of the public; especially if it be found, as the Author† seems to insinuate, that were his philosophy received, we must alter from the foundation the greatest part of the sciences. Such bold attempts are always advantageous in the Republic of Letters, because they* *shake off the yoke of authority, accustom men to think for themselves, give new hints, which men of genius may carry farther, and by the very opposition, illustrate points, wherein no one before suspected any difficulty.*

3   *The Author must be contented to wait with patience for some time before the learned world can agree in their sentiments of his performance. 'Tis his misfortune, that he cannot make an* appeal to the people, *who in all matters of common reason and eloquence are found so infallible a tribunal. He must be judged by the* FEW, *whose verdict is more apt to be corrupted by partiality and prejudice, especially as no one is a proper judge in these subjects, who has not often thought of them; and* such *are apt to form to themselves systems of their own, which they resolve not to relinquish.† I hope the Author will excuse me for intermeddling in this affair, since my aim is only to encrease his auditory, by removing some difficulties, which have kept many from apprehending his meaning.*

4   *I have chosen one simple argument, which I have carefully traced from the beginning to the end. This is the only point I have taken care to finish. The rest is only hints of particular passages, which seemed to me curious and remarkable.*

An Abstract of a Book lately Published, entituled,
A Treatise of Human Nature, &c.

1   This book seems to be wrote upon the same plan with several other works that have had a great vogue of late years in *England*. The philosophical spirit, which has been so much improved all over *Europe* within these last fourscore years,[†] has been carried to as great a length in this kingdom as in any other. Our writers seem even to have started a new kind of philosophy, which promises more both to the entertainment and advantage of mankind, than any other with which the world has been yet acquainted. Most of the philosophers of antiquity, who treated of human nature, have shewn more of a delicacy of sentiment, a just sense of morals, or a greatness of soul, than a depth of reasoning and reflection. They content themselves with representing the common sense of mankind in the strongest lights, and with the best turn of thought and expression, without following out steadily a chain of propositions, or forming the several truths into a regular science. But 'tis at least worth while to try if the science of *man* will not admit of the same accuracy which several parts of natural philosophy are found susceptible of. There seems to be all the reason in the world to imagine that it may be carried to the greatest degree of exactness. If, in exam- ining several phænomena, we find that they resolve themselves into one common principle, and can trace this principle into another, we shall at last arrive at those few simple principles, on which all the rest depend. And tho' we can never arrive at the ultimate principles,[†] 'tis a satisfaction to go as far as our faculties will allow us.

2   This seems to have been the aim of our late philosophers, and, among the rest, of this author. He proposes to anatomize human nature[†] in a regular manner, and promises to draw no conclusions but where he is authorized by experience. He talks with contempt of hypotheses; and insinuates, that such of our countrymen as have banished them from moral philosophy, have done a more signal service to the world, than *my Lord Bacon*, whom he considers as the father of experimental physicks. He mentions, on this occasion, *Mr. Locke, my Lord Shaftesbury, Dr. Mandeville, Mr. Hutcheson, Dr. Butler*, who, tho' they differ in many points among themselves, seem all to agree in founding their accurate disquisitions of human nature entirely upon experience.[†]

3   Beside the satisfaction of being acquainted with what most nearly concerns us, it may be safely affirmed, that almost all the sciences are comprehended in the science of human nature, and are dependent on it. *The sole end of* logic *is to explain the principles and operations of our reasoning faculty, and the nature of our ideas;* morals and criticism *regard our tastes and sentiments; and* politics *consider men as united in society, and dependent on each other.*[†] This treatise therefore of human nature seems intended for a system of the sciences. The author has

finished what regards logic, and has laid the foundation of the other parts in his account of the passions.[†]

4   The celebrated *Monsieur Leibnitz* has observed[†] it to be a defect in the common systems of logic, that they are very copious when they explain the operations of the understanding in the forming of demonstrations, but are too concise when they treat of probabilities, and those other measures of evidence on which life and action entirely depend[†], and which are our guides even in most of our philosophical speculations. In this censure, he comprehends the *Essay on Human Understanding*, *Le Recherche de la verité*, and *L'Art de penser*.[†] The author of the *Treatise of Human Nature* seems to have been sensible of this defect in these philosophers, and has endeavoured, as much as he can, to supply it. As his book contains a great number of speculations very new and remarkable, it will be impossible to give the reader a just notion of the whole. We shall therefore chiefly confine ourselves to his explication of our reasonings from cause and effect. If we can make this intelligible to the reader, it may serve as a specimen of the whole. *SB 647*

5   Our author begins with some definitions.[†] He calls a *perception* whatever can be present to the mind, whether we employ our senses, or are actuated with passion, or exercise our thought and reflection. He divides our perceptions into two kinds, *viz. impressions* and *ideas*. When we feel a passion or emotion of any kind, or have the images of external objects conveyed by our senses; the perception of the mind is what he calls an *impression*, which is a word that he employs in a new sense. When we reflect on a passion or an object which is not present, this perception is an *idea*. *Impressions*, therefore, are our lively and strong perceptions; *ideas* are the fainter and weaker. This distinction is evident; as evident as that betwixt feeling and thinking.

6   The first proposition he advances, is, that all our ideas, or weak perceptions, are derived from our impressions, or strong perceptions, and that we can never think of any thing which we have not seen without us, or felt in our own minds.[†] This proposition seems to be equivalent to that which *Mr. Locke* has taken such pains to establish, *viz. that no ideas are innate*.[†] Only it may be observed, as an inaccuracy of that famous philosopher, that he comprehends all our perceptions under the term of idea, in which sense it is false, that we have no innate ideas. For it is evident our stronger perceptions or impressions are innate, and that natural affection, love of virtue, resentment, and all the other passions, arise immediately from nature. I am perswaded, who-ever would take the question in this light, would be easily able to reconcile all parties. *Father Malebranche* would find himself at a loss to point out any thought of the mind, which did not represent something antecedently felt by it, either internally, or by means of the external senses, and must allow, that however we may compound, and mix, and augment, and diminish our ideas, they are all derived from these sources.[†] *Mr. Locke*, on the other hand, would readily acknowledge, that all our passions are a kind of natural instinct, derived from nothing but the original constitution of the human mind. *SB 648*

7   Our author thinks, that "no discovery could have been made more happily for

deciding all controversies concerning ideas, than this, that impressions always take the precedency of them, and that every idea, with which the imagination is furnished, first makes its appearance in a correspondent impression. These latter perceptions are all so clear and evident, that they admit of no controversy; tho' many of our ideas are so obscure, that 'tis almost impossible even for the mind, which forms them, to tell exactly their nature and composition."[†] Accordingly, wherever any idea is ambiguous, he has always recourse to the impression, which must render it clear and precise. And when he suspects that any philosophical term has no idea annexed to it (as is too common) he always asks *from what impression that pretended idea is derived?* And if no impression can be produced, he concludes that the term is altogether insignificant. 'Tis after this manner he examines our idea of *substance* and *essence*; and it were to be wished, that this rigorous method were more practised in all philosophical debates.[†]

SB 649

8   'Tis evident, that all reasonings concerning *matter of fact*[†] are founded on the relation of cause and effect, and that we can never infer the existence of one object from another, unless they be connected together, either mediately or immediately. In order therefore to understand these reasonings, we must be perfectly acquainted with the idea of a cause; and in order to that, must look about us to find something that is the cause of another.[†]

9   Here is a billiard-ball[†] lying on the table, and another ball moving towards it with rapidity. They strike; and the ball, which was formerly at rest, now acquires a motion. This is as perfect an instance of the relation of cause and effect as any which we know, either by sensation or reflection. Let us therefore examine it. 'Tis evident, that the two balls touched one another before the motion was communicated, and that there was no interval betwixt the shock and the motion. *Contiguity* in time and place is therefore a requisite circumstance to the operation of all causes. 'Tis evident likewise, that the motion, which was the cause, is prior to the motion, which was the effect. *Priority* in time is therefore another requisite circumstance in every cause.[†] But this is not all. Let us try any other balls of the same kind in a like situation, and we shall always find, that the impulse of the one produces motion in the other. Here therefore is a *third* circumstance, *viz.* that of a *constant conjunction* betwixt the cause and effect.[†] Every object like the cause, produces always some object like the effect. Beyond these three circumstances of contiguity, priority, and constant conjunction, I can discover nothing in this cause. The first ball is in motion; touches the second; immediately the second is in motion: and when I try the experiment with the same or like balls, in the same or like circumstances, I find, that upon the motion and touch of the one ball, motion always follows in the other. In whatever shape I turn this matter, and however I examine it, I can find nothing farther.

SB 650

10   This is the case when both the cause and effect are present to the senses. Let us now see upon what our inference is founded, when we conclude from the one that the other has existed or will exist.[†] Suppose I see a ball moving in a streight line towards another, I immediately conclude, that they will shock, and that the second will be in motion. This is the inference from cause to effect; and of this nature are all our reasonings in the conduct of life: on this is founded

all our belief in history: and from hence is derived all philosophy, excepting only geometry and arithmetic.[†] If we can explain the inference from the shock of two balls, we shall be able to account for this operation of the mind in all instances.

11   Were a man, such as *Adam*, created in the full vigour of understanding, without experience, he would never be able to infer motion in the second ball from the motion and impulse of the first. It is not any thing that reason sees in the cause, which makes us *infer* the effect. Such an inference, were it possible, would amount to a demonstration, as being founded merely on the comparison of ideas.[†] But no inference from cause to effect amounts to a demonstration. Of which there is this evident proof. The mind can always *conceive* any effect to follow from any cause, and indeed any event to follow upon another: whatever we *conceive* is possible,[†] at least in a metaphysical sense: but wherever a demonstration takes place, the contrary is impossible, and implies a contradiction. There is no demonstration, therefore, for any conjunction of cause and effect. And this is *SB 651* a principle, which is generally allowed by philosophers.

12   It would have been necessary, therefore, for *Adam* (if he was not inspired)[†] to have had *experience* of the effect, which followed upon the impulse of these two balls. He must have seen, in several instances, that when the one ball struck upon the other, the second always acquired motion. If he had seen a sufficient number of instances of this kind, whenever he saw the one ball moving towards the other, he would always conclude without hesitation, that the second would acquire motion. His understanding would anticipate his sight, and form a conclusion suitable to his past experience.

13   It follows, then, that all reasonings concerning cause and effect are founded on experience, and that all reasonings from experience are founded on the supposition, that the course of nature will continue uniformly the same. We conclude, that like causes, in like circumstances, will always produce like effects. It may now be worth while to consider, what determines us to form a conclusion of such infinite consequence.[†]

14   'Tis evident, that *Adam* with all his science, would never have been able to *demonstrate*, that the course of nature must continue uniformly the same, and that the future must be conformable to the past. What is possible can never be demonstrated to be false; and 'tis possible the course of nature may change, since we can conceive such a change. Nay, I will go farther, and assert, that he could not so much as prove by any *probable* arguments, that the future must be conformable to the past. All probable arguments are built on the supposition, that there is this conformity betwixt the future and the past, and therefore can never prove it.[†] This conformity is a *matter of fact*, and if it must be proved, will admit of no proof but from experience. But our experience in the past can be a proof of nothing for the future, but upon a supposition, that there is a resemblance *SB 652* betwixt them. This therefore is a point, which can admit of no proof at all, and which we take for granted without any proof.

15   We are determined by CUSTOM alone to suppose the future conformable to the past.[†] When I see a billiard-ball moving towards another, my mind is immedi-

ately carried by habit to the usual effect, and anticipates my sight by conceiving the second ball in motion. There is nothing in these objects, abstractly considered, and independent of experience, which leads me to form any such conclusion: and even after I have had experience of many repeated effects of this kind, there is no argument, which determines me to suppose, that the effect will be conformable to past experience. The powers, by which bodies operate, are entirely unknown. We perceive only their sensible qualities: and what *reason* have we to think, that the same powers will always be conjoined with the same sensible qualities?

16   'Tis not, therefore, reason, which is the guide of life, but custom.† That alone determines the mind, in all instances, to suppose the future conformable to the past. However easy this step may seem, reason would never, to all eternity, be able to make it.

17   This is a very curious discovery, but leads us to others, that are still more curious. *When I see a billiard-ball moving towards another, my mind is immediately carried by habit to the usual effect, and anticipates my sight by conceiving the second ball in motion.* But is this all? Do I nothing but CONCEIVE the motion of the second ball? No surely. I also BELIEVE that it will move. What then is this *belief*? And how does it differ from the simple conception of any thing? Here is a new question unthought of by philosophers.†

18   When a demonstration convinces me of any proposition, it not only makes me conceive the proposition, but also makes me sensible, that 'tis impossible to conceive any thing contrary. What is demonstratively false implies a contradiction; and what implies a contradiction cannot be conceived.† But with regard to any matter of fact, however strong the proof may be from experience, I can always conceive the contrary,† tho' I cannot always believe it. The belief, therefore, makes some difference betwixt the conception to which we assent, and that to which we do not assent. *SB 653*

19   To account for this, there are only two hypotheses.† It may be said, that belief joins some new idea to those which we may conceive without assenting to them. But this hypothesis is false. For *first*, no such idea can be produced. When we simply conceive an object, we conceive it in all its parts. We conceive it as it might exist, tho' we do not believe it to exist. Our belief of it would discover no new qualities. We may paint out the entire object in imagination without believing it. We may set it, in a manner, before our eyes, with every circumstance of time and place. 'Tis the very object conceived as it might exist; and when we believe it, we can do no more.

20   *Secondly*, The mind has a faculty of joining all ideas together, which involve not a contradiction; and therefore if belief consisted in some idea, which we add to the simple conception, it would be in a man's power, by adding this idea to it, to believe any thing, which he can conceive.

21   Since therefore belief implies a conception, and yet is something more; and since it adds no new idea to the conception; it follows, that it is a different MANNER of conceiving† an object; *something* that is distinguishable to the feeling, and depends not upon our will, as all our ideas do. My mind runs by habit from

the visible object of one ball moving towards another, to the usual effect of motion in the second ball. It not only conceives that motion, but *feels* something different in the conception of it from a mere reverie of the imagination. The presence of this visible object, and the constant conjunction of that particular effect, render the idea different to the *feeling* from those loose ideas, which come into the mind without any introduction. This conclusion seems a little surprizing; but we are led into it by a chain of propositions, which admit of no doubt. To ease the reader's memory I shall briefly resume them. No matter of fact can be proved but from its cause or its effect. Nothing can be known to be the cause of another but by experience. We can give no reason for extending to the future our experience in the past; but are entirely determined by custom, when we conceive an effect to follow from its usual cause. But we also believe an effect to follow, as well as conceive it. This belief joins no new idea to the conception. It only varies the manner of conceiving, and makes a difference to the feeling or sentiment. Belief, therefore, in all matters of fact arises only from custom, and is an idea conceived in a peculiar *manner*. *SB 654*

22   Our author proceeds to explain the manner or feeling, which renders belief different from a loose conception. He seems sensible, that 'tis impossible by words to describe this feeling, which every one must be conscious of in his own breast. He calls it sometimes a *stronger* conception, sometimes a more *lively*, a more *vivid*, a *firmer*, or a more *intense* conception.[†] And indeed, whatever name we may give to this feeling, which constitutes belief, our author thinks it evident, that it has a more forcible effect on the mind than fiction and mere conception. This he proves by its influence on the passions and on the imagination; which are only moved by truth or what is taken for such.[†] Poetry, with all its art, can never cause a passion, like one in real life. It fails in the original conception of its objects, which never *feel* in the same manner as those which command our belief and opinion.[†]

23   Our author presuming, that he had sufficiently proved, that the ideas we assent to are different to the feeling from the other ideas, and that this feeling is more firm and lively than our common conception, endeavours in the next place to explain the cause of this lively feeling by an analogy with other acts of the mind.[†] His reasoning seems to be curious; but could scarce be rendered intelligible, or at least probable to the reader, without a long detail, which would exceed the compass I have prescribed to myself. *SB 655*

24   I have likewise omitted many arguments, which he adduces to prove that belief consists merely in a peculiar feeling or sentiment. I shall only mention one. Our past experience is not always uniform. Sometimes one effect follows from a cause, sometimes another: In which case we always believe, that that will exist which is most common.[†] I see a billiard-ball moving towards another. I cannot distinguish whether it moves upon its axis, or was struck so as to skim along the table. In the first case, I know it will not stop after the shock. In the second it may stop. The first is most common, and therefore I lay my account[†] with that effect. But I also conceive the other effect, and conceive it as possible, and as connected with the cause. Were not the one conception differ-

ent in the feeling or sentiment from the other, there would be no difference betwixt them.

25   We have confined ourselves in this whole reasoning to the relation of cause and effect, as discovered in the motions and operations of matter. But the same reasoning extends to the operations of the mind.[†] Whether we consider the influence of the will in moving our body, or in governing our thought, it may safely be affirmed, that we could never foretel the effect, merely from the consideration of the cause, without experience. And even after we have experience of these effects, 'tis custom alone, not reason, which determines us to make it the standard of our future judgments. When the cause is presented, the mind, from habit, immediately passes to the conception and belief of the usual effect. This belief is something different from the conception. It does not, however, join any new idea to it. It only makes it be felt differently, and renders it stronger and more lively.   *SB 656*

26   Having dispatcht this material point concerning the nature of the inference from cause and effect, our author returns upon his footsteps, and examines anew the idea of that relation.[†] In the considering of motion communicated from one ball to another, we could find nothing but contiguity, priority in the cause, and constant conjunction. But, beside these circumstances, 'tis commonly supposed, that there is a necessary connexion betwixt the cause and effect, and that the cause possesses something, which we call a *power*, or *force*, or *energy*.[†] The question is, what idea is annexed to these terms? If all our ideas or thoughts be derived from our impressions, this power must either discover itself to our senses, or to our internal feeling. But so little does any *power* discover itself to the senses in the operations of matter, that the *Cartesians* have made no scruple to assert, that matter is utterly deprived of energy, and that all its operations are performed merely by the energy of the supreme Being. But the question still recurs, *What idea have we of energy or power even in the supreme Being?* All our idea of a Deity (according to those who deny innate ideas) is nothing but a composition of those ideas, which we acquire from reflecting on the operations of our own minds.[†] Now our own minds afford us no more notion of energy than matter does. When we consider our will or volition *a priori*, abstracting from experience, we are never able to infer any effect from it. And when we take the assistance of experience, it only shows us objects contiguous, successive, and   *SB 657* constantly conjoined.[†] Upon the whole, then, either we have no idea at all of force and energy, and these words are altogether insignificant, or they can mean nothing but that determination of the thought, acquired by habit, to pass from the cause to its usual effect.[†] But who-ever would thoroughly understand this must consult the author himself. 'Tis sufficient, if I can make the learned world apprehend, that there is some difficulty in the case, and that who-ever solves the difficulty must say some thing very new and extraordinary; as new as the difficulty itself.

27   By all that has been said the reader will easily perceive, that the philosophy contained in this book is very sceptical, and tends to give us a notion of the imperfections and narrow limits of human understanding. Almost all reasoning

is there reduced to experience;[†] and the belief, which attends experience, is explained to be nothing but a peculiar sentiment, or lively conception produced by habit. Nor is this all. When we believe any thing of *external* existence, or suppose an object to exist a moment after it is no longer perceived, this belief is nothing but a sentiment of the same kind.[†] Our author insists upon several other sceptical topics;[†] and upon the whole concludes, that we assent to our faculties, and employ our reason only because we cannot help it. Philosophy would render us entirely *Pyrrhonian*, were not nature too strong for it.[†]

28   I shall conclude the logics of this author with an account of two opinions, which seem to be peculiar to himself, as indeed are most of his opinions. He asserts, that the soul, as far as we can conceive it, is nothing but a system or train of different perceptions, those of heat and cold, love and anger, thoughts and sensations; all united together, but without any perfect simplicity or identity.[†] *Des Cartes* maintained that thought was the essence of the mind;[†] not this thought or that thought, but thought in general. This seems to be absolutely unintelligible, since every thing, that exists, is particular: And therefore it must be our several particular perceptions, that compose the mind. I say, *compose* the mind, not *belong* to it. The mind is not a substance, in which the perceptions inhere. That notion is as unintelligible as the *Cartesian*, that thought or perception in general is the essence of the mind. We have no idea of substance of any kind, since we have no idea but what is derived from some impression, and we have no impression of any substance either material or spiritual.[†] We know nothing but particular qualities and perceptions.[†] As our idea of any body, a peach, for instance, is only that of a particular taste, colour, figure, size, consistence, *&c.* So our idea of any mind is only that of particular perceptions, without the notion of any thing we call substance, either simple or compound.

SB 658

29   The second principle, which I proposed to take notice of, is with regard to geometry. Having denied the infinite divisibility of extension, our author finds himself obliged to refute those mathematical arguments, which have been adduced for it;[†] and these indeed are the only ones of any weight. This he does by denying geometry to be a science exact enough to admit of conclusions so subtle as those which regard infinite divisibility.[†] His arguments may be thus explained. All geometry is founded on the notions of equality and inequality, and therefore according as we have or have not an exact standard of those relations, the science itself will or will not admit of great exactness.[†] Now there is an exact standard of equality, if we suppose that quantity is composed of indivisible points. Two lines are equal when the numbers of the points, that compose them, are equal, and when there is a point in one corresponding to a point in the other. But tho' this standard be exact, 'tis useless; since we can never compute the number of points in any line. It is besides founded on the supposition of finite divisibility, and therefore can never afford any conclusion against it.[†] If we reject this standard of equality, we have none that has any pretensions to exactness. I find two that are commonly made use of. Two lines above a yard, for instance, are

SB 659

said to be equal, when they contain any inferior quantity, as an inch, an equal number of times. But this runs in a circle. For the quantity we call an inch in the one is supposed to be *equal* to what we call an inch in the other: And the question still is, by what standard we proceed when we judge them to be equal; or, in other words, what we mean when we say they are equal. If we take still inferior quantities, we go on *in infinitum*. This therefore is no standard of equality.[†] The greatest part of philosophers, when asked what they mean by equality, say, that the word admits of no definition, and that it is sufficient to place before us two equal bodies, such as two diameters of a circle, to make us understand that term.[†] Now this is taking the *general appearance* of the objects for the standard of that proportion, and renders our imagination and senses the ultimate judges of it.[†] But such a standard admits of no exactness, and can never afford any conclusion contrary to the imagination and senses. Whether this reasoning be just or not, must be left to the learned world to judge. 'Twere certainly to be wished, that some expedient were fallen upon to reconcile philosophy and common sense, which with regard to the question of infinite divisibility have waged most cruel wars with each other.

30   We must now proceed to give some account of the second volume of this work, which treats of the PASSIONS. 'Tis of more easy comprehension than the first; but contains opinions, that are altogether as new and extraordinary. The author begins with *pride* and *humility*. He observes, that the objects which excite these passions, are very numerous, and seemingly very different from each other. Pride or self-esteem may arise from the qualities of the mind; wit, good-sense, *SB 660* learning, courage, integrity: from those of the body; beauty, strength, agility, good mein, address in dancing, riding, fencing: from external advantages; country, family, children, relations, riches, houses, gardens, horses, dogs, cloaths.[†] He afterwards proceeds to find out that common circumstance, in which all these objects agree, and which causes them to operate on the passions.[†] His theory likewise extends to love and hatred, and other affections.[†] As these questions, tho' curious, could not be rendered intelligible without a long discourse, we shall here omit them.

31   It may perhaps be more acceptable to the reader to be informed of what our author says concerning *free-will*. He has laid the foundation of his doctrine in what he said concerning cause and effect, as above-explained.[†] " 'Tis universally acknowledged, that the operations of external bodies are necessary, and that in the communication of their motion, in their attraction, and mutual cohesion, there are not the least traces of indifference or liberty." ----- "Whatever therefore is in this respect on the same footing with matter, must be acknowledged to be necessary. That we may know whether this be the case with the actions of the mind, we may examine matter, and consider on what the idea of a necessity in its operations is founded, and why we conclude one body or action to be the infallible cause of another.

32   "It has been observed already, that in no single instance the ultimate connexion of any objects is discoverable, either by our senses or reason, and that we can

415

never penetrate so far into the essence and construction of bodies, as to perceive the principle, on which their mutual influence is founded. 'Tis their constant union alone, with which we are acquainted; and 'tis from the constant union the necessity arises, when the mind is determined to pass from one object to its usual attendant, and infer the existence of one from that of the other. Here then are *SB 661* two particulars, which we are to regard as essential to *necessity, viz.* the constant *union* and the *inference* of the mind; and wherever we discover these we must acknowledge a necessity."[†] Now nothing is more evident than the constant union of particular actions with particular motives. If all actions be not constantly united with their proper motives, this uncertainty is no more than what may be observed every day in the actions of matter, where by reason of the mixture and uncertainty of causes, the effect is often variable and uncertain. Thirty grains of opium will kill any man that is not accustomed to it; tho' thirty grains of rhubarb will not always purge him.[†] In like manner the fear of death will always make a man go twenty paces out of his road; tho' it will not always make him do a bad action.

33   And as there is often a constant conjunction of the actions of the will with their motives, so the inference from the one to the other is often as certain as any reasoning concerning bodies: and there is always an inference proportioned to the constancy of the conjunction. On this is founded our belief in witnesses, our credit in history, and indeed all kinds of moral evidence, and almost the whole conduct of life.

34   Our author pretends, that this reasoning puts the whole controversy in a new light, by giving a new definition of necessity.[†] And, indeed, the most zealous advocates for free-will must allow this union and inference with regard to human actions. They will only deny, that this makes the whole of necessity. But then they must shew, that we have an idea of something else in the actions of matter; which, according to the foregoing reasoning, is impossible.

35   Thro' this whole book, there are great pretensions to new discoveries in philosophy; but if any thing can entitle the author to so glorious a name as that of an *inventor*, 'tis the use he makes of the principle of the association of ideas, which *SB 662* enters into most of his philosophy. Our imagination has a great authority over our ideas; and there are no ideas that are different from each other, which it cannot separate, and join, and compose into all the varieties of fiction.[†] But notwithstanding the empire of the imagination, there is a secret tie or union among particular ideas, which causes the mind to conjoin them more frequently together, and makes the one, upon its appearance, introduce the other. Hence arises what we call the *apropos* of discourse:[†] hence the connexion of writing: and hence that thread, or chain of thought, which a man naturally supports even in the loosest *reverie*. These principles of association are reduced to three, *viz. Resemblance*; a picture naturally makes us think of the man it was drawn for. *Contiguity*; when *St. Dennis* is mentioned, the idea of *Paris* naturally occurs.[†] *Causation*; when we think of the son, we are apt to carry our attention to the father.[†] 'Twill be easy to conceive of what vast consequence these principles must be in the science of human nature, if we consider, that so far as regards the mind,

these are the only links that bind the parts of the universe together, or connect us with any person or object exterior to ourselves. For as it is by means of thought only that any thing operates upon our passions, and as these are the only ties of our thoughts, they are really *to us* the cement of the universe, and all the operations of the mind must, in a great measure, depend on them.

FINIS

PART 3
Supplementary Material

Editors' Annotations

Annotations are signalled in the text by a dagger,[†]. There are several types of annotation:

1. *Textual summaries.* The annotations to each part and section of the *Treatise* begin with a summary, intended to be descriptive rather than interpretative, of that part or section of the text. Although they cannot serve as a substitute for careful study of the text, these summaries provide new readers with a general sense of what Hume was trying to do. They may also help those more familiar with the text to see or recall broader outlines of the *Treatise.*

2. *Translations.* Translations are provided for the Latin phrases and quotations used by Hume. These translations are from the editions listed in the References, unless otherwise noted.

3. *Amplified cross-references.* Hume occasionally provided notes to direct readers to relevant discussions found elsewhere in the *Treatise.* More often he simply mentions that something has been discussed above or below without indicating where. We have supplied the locations of such cross-references whenever their target is more than a few paragraphs away.

4. *Amplified references.* Our annotations amplify Hume's usually sketchy notes by adding authors' names, titles of books, or other information. For brief additional information on the persons or books mentioned in Hume's notes or our Annotations, see References.

5. *Explications of difficult words and phrases.* Hume uses many words and phrases in ways that are unusual by today's standards. When we think that some readers might need to have these terms explained in order not to misunderstand a particular sentence or argument, we have marked the term with the usual sign ([†]) and given an explanation in these annotations. Some words or phrases are used by Hume in archaic or obsolete senses that, although unlikely to create serious misunderstanding, will be of interest to the careful reader. The meanings of these words and phrases are included in the Glossary. There are also Glossary entries for many important words that are used in more than one sense. Glossary entries are not marked in the text.

6. *Explications of difficult passages.* The *Treatise* abounds with arguments: many are relatively clear, but some are not and may give pause even to those familiar with the work. We restate or outline, briefly and in ordinary language, the passages that have seemed difficult to us or to students we have consulted. Our goal is not to provide a definitive reading of these texts, but rather to help readers see what is at issue in them.

7. *Allusions to other writers.* Hume often mentions the views of others without identifying the authors or works to which he alludes. This casual approach to previous discussions was not uncommon in his time—perhaps it was taken for granted that contemporary readers would make the needed connections. To help present-day readers, we have suggested authors and books, usually from those that Hume is known or thought to have read, that reflect the issues he raises. These suggestions are neither definitive nor complete. Whenever possible, our references to these works are to parts or chapters, with, when the additional information is needed to pinpoint a location, volume and page numbers of the editions cited in the References included in square brackets. Thus the reference 'Locke, *Essay* 2.8.8' is to book 2, chapter 8, section 8 of John Locke's *An Essay concerning Human Understanding*, while 'Malebranche, *Search* 1.10 [48–53]', refers to a book

421

and chapter number in Malebranche's *The Search after Truth*, and also provides, in brackets, the relevant page numbers in the edition cited in the References.

Because of concerns about the length of these annotations, references are made to Hume's later works (see pp. 1101–2) on only a few occasions and then only when these have a direct bearing on the meaning of the *Treatise*. Readers will be able to link the *Treatise* to these later works by a judicious use of the indexes provided here and in other Oxford University Press editions of Hume's works.

While preparing the Editor's Introduction and these Supplementary Materials we have received help from both students and colleagues. We gratefully acknowledge this help, and extend special thanks to Tom Beauchamp, Jack Davidson, David Davies, Emilio Mazza, Knud Haakonssen, Jane McIntyre, and David Owen, as well as to Peter Momtchiloff, Angela Griffin, and Laurien Berkeley of Oxford University Press.

Annotations to the *Treatise*

BOOK 1. OF THE UNDERSTANDING

Title-page

Rara . . . licet] The rare good fortune of an age in which we may feel what we wish and say what we feel (Tacitus, *Histories* 1.1).

Advertisement

The subjects . . . themselves] The first two volumes of the *Treatise*, on the understanding and the passions, appeared in January 1739; the third and final volume, on morals, was published in November 1740. All three volumes were published anonymously.

Introduction

Finding philosophy to be characterized by zealous and seemingly fruitless debate, Hume suggests that the time has come for a different approach. Instead of focusing on the particular issues arising in, say, metaphysics or ethics or political science, we should direct our attention to the science of human nature in order to understand what ideas are and how we use them, and how we understand or reason. With this goal in mind, Hume suggests that moral philosophy should adopt the experimental method, the same method that had, in the previous hundred years, enabled natural philosophy (the study of physical nature) to make important advances. This new science will not be able to carry out laboratory experiments, nor can we expect it to discover the ultimate principles of human nature. But if we rely on 'experience and observation' we can hope to establish 'a science, which will not be inferior in certainty, and will be much superior in utility to any other of human comprehension' (¶10). (For further discussion of the Introduction to the *Treatise*, see Ed. Intro., I14–15.)

1 pretend to discover] claim to discover; no suggestion of imaginary activity is intended.
   than to insinuate . . . them] Hume is talking about those who hope to promote their own systems by criticizing earlier ones. For examples of this behaviour, see Francis Bacon, *Advancement of Learning* 1; and René Descartes, *Meditations* 1. (For further information about books and their authors or the other individuals mentioned in these annotations, see the References.
   there are few . . . them] Individuals familiar with the sciences will readily agree with those who point out their defects. In Hume's time any branch of knowledge, systematically treated, was a science. In ¶5 of this section, for example, he includes among the sciences not only natural philosophy and mathematics, but also natural religion, logic, morals, politics, and criticism.
2 but even the rabble . . . within] A *rabble* is a disorderly crowd of ordinary people. Hume portrays this crowd as listening outside an imaginary hall within which 'men of

learning' are dogmatically debating issues in the 'sciences'. Hume turns the tables here: the scholars, not the crowd, are the source of the 'noise and clamour'.

2 **Disputes . . . certain**] On the one hand, the magnitude of the controversy suggests that there is no end of unanswered questions; on the other hand, the heated manner in which combatants argue their positions indicates that they believe they have definitive answers to all these questions.

Amidst . . . colours] Reason loses out to those with the rhetorical ability to make hypotheses appear to be true even when they are not.

3 **common prejudice . . . literature**] Hume contrasts metaphysics with learning in general. By 'metaphysical reasonings' he means the discussion of such issues as the nature of existence, the nature of space, of cause and effect, of objects, of the soul or mind, of identity, of freedom, and of virtue. The *Treatise* has much to say that is relevant to these issues. Isaac Watts, one of the most popular writers of Hume's time, was also concerned that metaphysics had been treated as a thing to scorn and even to sneer at (*Brief Scheme of Ontology*, Preface [318]).

By metaphysical . . . comprehended] Those who are prejudiced against metaphysical arguments do not think of them as arguments on a particular subject, but merely as arguments that are abstruse or difficult to understand. Hume describes his own philosophy as abstruse (3.1.1.1), and, at the end of this paragraph, as not 'easy and obvious'.

can justify . . . metaphysics] Hume's ironical point is that the aversion to metaphysics is not justified.

4 *Natural Philosophy*] the form of enquiry that focuses on physical nature, or what we now think of as the natural sciences.

Natural Religion] This is the form of enquiry that, as its name suggests, uses only our natural abilities (reason and the senses) to discover the nature of the Deity or deities and to delineate our religious and moral duties. In contrast, *revealed religion*, as its name suggests, is allegedly known through some form of divine revelation.

science of man] what Hume usually calls the 'science of human nature', that is, the systematic study and description of human nature.

'**Tis impossible . . . reasonings**] The goal of the *Treatise* is to acquaint us with the matters mentioned.

disposition towards us] both the attitude of the superior beings towards us, and the manner in which these beings have ordered things with respect to humanity.

5 **other sciences . . . intimate**] The sciences of mathematics, natural philosophy, and natural religion are, Hume argues, dependent upon our understanding of human nature. We can expect, then, that the sciences of logic, morals, politics, and criticism, because their subject-matter is intimately linked to aspects of human nature, will prove to be even more dependent upon our understanding of that same nature.

The sole end of logic . . . ideas] Note that Hume's conception of logic is a broad one, roughly equivalent to what many philosophers would now call epistemology.

Morals] ethics and ethical theory; the science having to do with the conduct of life. See also 3.1.1.1.

criticism] In the early 18th c. criticism was the art of judging any kind of writing or discourse.

politics] the science concerned with the governing and regulating of states.

import us] be important to us.

7 **experimental philosophy**] a form of philosophy that relies on experiment and observation to determine the laws of nature or the properties or behaviour of things.

century . . . Socrates] Hume implicitly accepts the view of Cicero (*Academica* 1.4) that

Socrates was the first to turn philosophy to an investigation of moral issues and suggests that he did so about 100 years after Thales' speculations about the ultimate nature of the physical world. It is thus reasonable, Hume suggests, that the experimental method should be applied to moral philosophy a century after its introduction, about 1600, by Francis Bacon.

n. 1 **Mr.** *Locke . . . Butler*, &c.] Of the five philosophers listed, John Locke, author of *An Essay concerning Human Understanding* (1690), was the earliest. For the dates and relevant publications of these figures, see the References. At *Abs.* 2 Hume notes that, although these five philosophers 'differ in many points among themselves', they 'seem all to agree in founding their accurate disquisitions of human nature entirely upon experience'.

other agreeable arts] painting, architecture, or music, for example.

8 **experiments . . . situations**] In the early 18th c. experiments were not necessarily thought of as activities carried out in laboratories, or even as tests carried out in carefully controlled conditions. The terms *observation*, *experience*, and *experiment* were often used interchangeably. As a result Hume and his contemporaries may take relatively simple observations of human behaviour (observing the concern of parents for their children, for example) to be experiments.

by tracing . . . utmost] following the course of experiments as far as this can take us.

and any hypothesis . . . chimerical] Hume wants us to push our researches about causes and principles as far as we can, but he also wants us to be contented with what experience can reveal to us (see also 1.1.7.11). It is a mistake, he argues, to speculate about the 'ultimate original qualities of human nature' because qualities of that sort are beyond the reach of our faculties and experience, and because unfounded, fanciful speculation about them will end in fruitless, rancorous debate. Hume's caution in this regard is like that of the experimental natural philosophers; see e.g. Newton, *Principia* 3 [2:543–7].

9 **soul**] Hume often uses the terms *soul* and *mind* interchangeably to mean that which, in humans, thinks or acts. See e.g. 1.1.2.

we sit down . . . ignorance] Locke had recommended that we be willing 'to sit down in a quiet Ignorance of those Things, which, upon Examination, are found to be beyond the reach of our Capacities' (*Essay* 1.1.4). A similar view is expressed by Arnauld and Nicole in an earlier work that Hume had read, *Logic; or, The Art of Thinking* (often called *The Port-Royal Logic*); see 4.1 [230].

vulgar] The vulgar (ordinary, unphilosophical individuals) 'take things according to their first appearance' (1.3.12.5). Hume says that this 'unthinking and unphilosophical part of mankind' includes 'all of us, at one time or other' (1.4.2.36).

10 **in natural**] in natural philosophy.

body] object or material thing, not (necessarily) an animate human body.

'tis evident . . . phænomenon] Once we realized we were part of an experiment, we could not or would not act in a normal manner. Consequently, the experiment in question would not be a reliable indicator of normal behaviour.

affairs] business.

Book 1 Part 1. *Of ideas, their origin, composition, connexion, abstraction, &c.*

In *Treatise* 1.1 Hume reviews what he calls the 'elements' of his philosophy (1.1.4.6). The basic elements of this world are *perceptions* and their *relations*. It is important to understand these elements, for particular perceptions (objects of feeling and thought) and their relations (connections and comparisons) are the principal subject-matter of the remaining nine parts of the *Treatise*. (For further discussion of *Treatise* 1.1, see Ed. Intro., I16–21.)

Book 1 Part 1 Sect. 1. *Of the origin of our ideas*

Hume tells us that our perceptions are of two kinds, *impressions* and *ideas*. Impressions appear first and are generally more intense than ideas. If we feel a pain, our perception is an impression. If we remember this same pain, then our perception is an idea. We also learn that perceptions (impressions and ideas) may be *simple* (those that cannot be further divided) and *complex* (those made up of combinations of simple perceptions). Any given impression may have a resembling idea, while every simple idea derives, either directly or indirectly, from a resembling and temporally prior simple impression.

1 **perceptions**] Hume regularly uses the term *perception* to refer to whatever mental element is the focus of attention when one thinks, feels, perceives, desires, etc. When he talks about what we might call *sense perception*, Hume typically speaks of *sensations* or of *impressions of sensation*; see also 2.1.1.1–2. Hume, like many other early modern philosophers, is convinced 'that nothing is ever really present [to] the mind but its perceptions or impressions and ideas, and that external objects become known to us only by those perceptions' they seem to cause (1.2.6.7).
force and liveliness] strength and intensity. The *Treatise* uses a number of different terms, usually in combinations of two, to describe the difference between impressions and ideas. In addition to having more *force* and *liveliness*, impressions are said to have more *vivacity, violence, vigour, firmness, intensity,* and *solidity,* and are said to be more *vivid, forcible,* and *real.* Hume again discusses the meaning of *force, liveliness, vivacity,* etc. at 1.3.7.7 and 1.3.8.15. Later in the present paragraph he says that the difference between impressions and ideas can be understood as the 'difference betwixt feeling and thinking'. Feeling or sensing (having impressions) is typically a more intense or forceful experience than is remembering or imagining (having ideas of) those impressions.
n. 2 *idea* . . . Mr. *Locke*] Locke uses the term *idea* 'to stand for whatsoever is the Object of the Understanding when a Man thinks . . . or whatever it is, which the Mind can be employ'd about in thinking' (*Essay* 1.1.8).
2 **colour . . . smell**] These are simple perceptions; a specific set of them, united in a particular way, results in the complex perception of an apple. See also ¶4 of this section and 1.1.3.4.
3 **objects**] here, the objects of this study, namely, the two kinds of perception, impressions and ideas.
4 *New Jerusalem . . . Paris*] The first allusion is to a symbolical holy city mentioned in the Christian scriptures; see Rev. 21:2. The idea of the New Jerusalem is a complex idea for which there is no corresponding complex impression. Hume suggests that his present complex idea of the real city of Paris, even though based on previous impressions, cannot exactly copy all the many features of that city.
5 **correspondent idea**] resembling idea.
That the case . . . them] The point cannot be proven by reviewing all simple perceptions because the number of these is unlimited.
running over . . . pleases] Hume encourages his readers to consult their own experiences regarding the matters he is discussing; in this way he would make experimentalists of each of us.
answer this challenge] Hume often issues such challenges; see also, for example, 1.2.3.4; 1.2.5.3; 1.2.6.5; 1.3.14.7, 13, 31; 1.3.16.8; 1.4.2.48; 1.4.5.4; 1.4.6.3.

7 **present treatise**] Hume could be referring only to Book 1, 'Of the Understanding', but it seems more likely that he has the entire *Treatise* in mind.

8 **constant conjunction**] This important relation is discussed at length in *Treatise* 1.3.4–8 and 14; see also Ed. Intro., I31–7.

9 **faculties**] here, the senses.
pine-apple . . . tasted it] Locke, *Essay* 2.1.6, takes it as given that a person who had never eaten 'a Pine-Apple' would not know the taste of this fruit.

10 **to run . . . from it**] gradually to change a colour into a distinctively different colour.
means . . . extremes] The 'means' are the interim shades of colour in the continuum just discussed; the 'extremes' of this continuum are the 'remote' colours at the ends of the continuum.
excepting one . . . meet with] Note that Hume's argument assumes that the number of colours, or shades of a colour, is limited.
maxim] that is, the maxim at ¶7 of this section. By not altering his maxim simply because he had discovered one contrary phenomenon, Hume practises Newton's fourth rule: '*In experimental philosophy we are to look upon propositions inferred by general induction from phenomena as accurately or very nearly true, notwithstanding any contrary hypotheses that may be imagined, till such time as other phenomena occur, by which they may either be made more accurate, or liable to exceptions*' (*Principia* 3 [2:400]).

12 **noise in other terms**] contentious debate.
innate ideas] A key document in the debate about innate ideas was Locke's *Essay* 1.2–4. Hume's proposed solution to the controversy depends heavily upon the significantly different meaning that he, in contrast to Locke, assigns to the term *idea*. On this issue, see also *Abs.* 6 and Ed. Intro., I18.

Book 1 Part 1 Sect. 2. *Division of the subject*

Impressions can be sorted another way: there are *impressions of sensation* or 'sensations', and *impressions of reflection* or 'passions, desires, and emotions'. The question of how our sensations arise (of the causes of our sensations) should be left to the natural philosophers. Our impressions of reflection derive largely from ideas. For this reason ideas will be studied first, in Book 1; impressions of reflection are the topic of Book 2.

1 **method**] following the proper or most useful order or sequence.
The first . . . causes] Hume takes the view that, although we believe that our impressions of sensation are caused by external objects, the grounds for this belief are suspect. See also 1.3.5.2, and esp. 1.4.2.
returns upon the soul] comes again into the mind.
because deriv'd from it] that is, because derived from reflection when reflection is understood as a sequence of events that begins with (1) an impression of sensation that is copied by (2) a corresponding idea that in turn gives rise to (3) a further perception, namely, an impression of reflection. Pain (a primary impression or impression of sensation), if remembered or reflected upon (copied and brought again to mind in the form of an idea), can produce fear (a secondary impression, or impression of reflection).
and therefore . . . upon] Hume never does attempt to explain the physiology of sensation (see also 1.2.5.26; 2.1.1.2). Neither does he accept any of the several available hypotheses about the origin of sensations (see 1.3.5.2). He simply accepts that we have what he calls *impressions of sensation* while explicitly disclaiming any interest in

explaining the process by which these impressions are produced. In this regard his phi-losophy differs significantly from that of several of his predecessors to whom he had paid careful attention. See e.g. Descartes, *Passions of the Soul* 1.35–6; Malebranche, *Search* 1.10 [48–53]; and on at least one occasion (*Essay* 2.8), Locke.

Book 1 Part 1 Sect. 3. *Of the ideas of the memory and imagination*

If an impression reappears in the mind after an absence, it does so either as an idea of the *memory* or an idea of the *imagination*. Ideas of the memory more or less replicate both the form and order of the impressions they copy, especially the form of simple impressions, and they retain some of the force or intensity of their originals. In comparison with ideas of the memory, ideas of the imagination are weaker representations of the impressions they copy. In addition, because the imagination is free to transform and reorder its elements, and thus produce new complex ideas, the ideas of the imagination often depart from the form and order of the impressions they copy.

1 **perfect idea**] an idea that has no force or vivacity.
   n. 3 Part 3. Sect. 5] See 1.3.5.3–6.
2 **yet the imagination . . . impressions**] In so far as ideas appear to represent a sequence of events or a spatial arrangement, the imagination can reorder them in any way it wishes. We can even imagine, for example, that the events of last Tuesday came after those of last Wednesday, or that the sun rises in the west.
3 **objects**] The *objects* of the memory (and of the imagination) are ideas.
   this principle] The principle is that 'the memory preserves the original form, in which its objects were presented'.
4 **The fables . . . question**] The fables illustrate and confirm the second principle.
   fancy] imagination. Hume often uses *fancy* and *imagination* interchangeably.
   and that . . . inseparable] Although Hume does not here say so, the principle that each of our impressions is completely separable from every other impression is of central importance to many arguments found in the *Treatise* (see e.g. 1.2.1.3; 1.4.6.16).
   Not to mention . . . complex] Given that complex ideas are made up of simple ones, themselves derived from simple impressions, it follows (1) that the mind (the imagina-tion) can manipulate ideas, and (2) that complex ideas may be broken down into their constituent parts (on this point, see 1.2.1.3). We learn in the next section that the imagi-nation is not completely at liberty to transpose or alter ideas.

Book 1 Part 1 Sect. 4. *Of the connexion or association of ideas*

In this section we learn that the imagination, although free, is given some guidance by nature. There are at least three principles of *association*, principles that, in spite of the freedom the imagination has, may produce 'union or cohesion' (¶6) among certain ideas—may cause these ideas to arrange themselves in organized patterns. Thus, if there is a *resemblance* between one idea and another, thinking of the one adds to the likelihood that we will think of the other. The same effect results from thinking of ideas whose perceptions were characterized by either *contiguity* or a *cause and effect* relationship. Among the most important effects of these principles of association are our complex ideas of *relations*, *substances*, and *modes*. (On the principles of association, see also Ed. Intro., I20–1, 51, 57–60.)

1 **render it . . . uniform**] make it consistent with.
   chance alone] Hume later (1.3.11) argues that chance is not something positive or real

that can act as a cause. Thus 'chance alone' could not account for the association of ideas.

already excluded . . . imagination] See 1.1.3.

force] As will be seen in ¶6 of this section, Hume is thinking about a force in the 'mental world' (in the mind) analogous to the forces of gravity or magnetism in the physical world.

languages . . . each other] Hume, familiar only with European languages, was, along with many other Europeans of his time, impressed by the conceptual and semantic similarities within that limited group of languages.

qualities] here, the features or characteristics of perceptions.

2 senses . . . objects] Hume here accepts, presumably for purposes of illustration, the common-sense view that our senses make us aware of physical objects.

imagination . . . objects] Here and in the following sentences Hume returns to using the term *objects* to refer to the *ideas* with which the imagination is concerned.

occasion afterwards] The relation of cause and effect is discussed at length in 1.3, esp. Sects. 2–7, 14–15.

3 these relations] The *relations* of which Hume is now speaking correspond to the *qualities* mentioned in ¶1 of this section. The three relations are resemblance, contiguity in time and place, and cause and effect.

4 Two objects . . . latter] Hume argues that, of the three relations mentioned, the relation of causation is the most widely found because a given cause may be the cause of some feature (movement, for example) of an effect and also the cause of the existence of that same effect.

continues the same] continues to be the same object.

5 power of producing it] the ability or capacity to produce an effect, although not yet exercised. For further discussions of the distinction between power and its exercise, see 1.3.14.34; 2.1.10.4–12; 2.2.5.7.

6 ATTRACTION] *Attraction* was a name given to the forces, gravity or magnetism, for example, by which a body draws to itself another body distant from it. John Keill said that 'we may call the Endeavour of Bodies to approach one another, *Attraction*; by which word we do not mean to determine the Cause of that Action ' (*Introduction to Natural Philosophy* 2; see also Newton, *Principia* 1.11 [1:192]).

Nothing . . . uncertain speculations] On this point, see also Intro. 8; 1.1.7.11; and Ed. Intro., l12–15, 45–6.

7 Amongst . . . ideas] Hume notes that the principles of association produce our complex ideas of many of the things we think about—of such things as external objects and even of causation itself.

elements of this philosophy] Perceptions (impressions and ideas) and relations are the building-blocks of the philosophical explanations Hume provides in the remainder of the *Treatise*.

Book 1 Part 1 Sect. 5. *Of relations*

The word *relation* is typically thought to have two meanings. In the more common sense, *relation* refers to that *quality* which so connects two ideas that the one 'naturally introduces the other' (¶1). Such *natural relations* (resemblance, contiguity, cause and effect) were described in 1.1.4. In contrast, there are *philosophical relations*, or the kind of relation produced when two ideas are arbitrarily or voluntarily compared. Seven such philosophical relations are identified: *resemblance, identity, space and time* (sometimes called *contiguity*), *quantity or number, degrees of quality, contrariety,* and *cause and effect.* (For further discussion of relations, see Ed. Intro., I20–1.)

1 **The word . . . other**] Hume goes on to modify what he says is a widely held distinction. Several of his predecessors had distinguished, as he does, between 'natural' and
'philosophical' (also 'arbitrary' or 'voluntary') relations, but with a different result.
Whereas Hume counts as natural those *relations of ideas* that result from the operation
of the principles of association, and as philosophical those resulting from an arbitrary
or voluntary decision to compare ideas, these predecessors focused on the *relations of
things* themselves. They distinguished between what they saw to be the natural or real
relations of particular things (of father and son, for example) and a contrasting voluntary relation (of husband and wife, for example). For a summary view of the position
Hume has modified, see Chambers, *Cyclopædia,* 'Relation', 'Association,' 'Comparison', and Watts, *Brief Scheme of Ontology,* chs. 1, 7.
above-explained] See 1.1.4.
Thus distance . . . objects] Compare Locke, *Essay* 2.13.3: 'This Space considered
barely in length between any two Beings, without considering any thing else between
them, is called *Distance.*'

2 *philosophical* **relation**] Hume normally calls those voluntary relations under discussion in this section *philosophical relations.* In contrast, those relations resulting from the
operation of the natural, associative principles described in 1.1.4 are called *natural*
relations. Notice that *resemblance, contiguity,* and *cause and effect* are both natural and
philosophical relations.

3 **individuals**] individual entities of any sort.

4 **personal identity . . . afterwards**] See esp. 1.4.6.

8 **as implying . . . object**] Hume's point is that even to think of something as not existing one must first have some conception or idea of that thing.

9 **explain'd afterwards**] See 1.3.9.10–15 and 1.3.13.11–13.

10 **Difference . . . kind**] Two objects so alike as to be indistinguishable manifest *difference
in number* (because the one is not the other), but not *difference of kind* (because they are
alike or of the same kind). Any set of different but indistinguishable objects manifests
the relation of *resemblance.* In contrast, a single object may be said to be without *difference of number* just because it is identical with itself. Any such single object manifests
the relation of *identity.* For more on number and identity, see 1.4.2.26–9; 1.4.6.6–13.

Book 1 Part 1 Sect. 6. *Of modes and substances*

Hume notes that some philosophers take the distinction between *substances* (or substrata)
and *modes* (or modifications of a substance; also called accidents or qualities) to be very
important, but these philosophers do not satisfactorily account for their idea of substance
as substratum. Our only idea of substance is of an 'unknown something' in which a collection of qualities is supposed to be united, and to which a unique name is attached. In
spite of its shortcomings, however, this concept of an unknown something is important,
for it allows us to treat as one thing a set of qualities that may be expanded by the discovery of a new quality. A mode is different from a substance. The qualities of a mode are not
supposed to be united in a substratum, and thus any change in the collection of qualities
making up a mode has the effect of creating a new or different mode.

1 **I wou'd fain ask . . . reflection**] The philosophers who placed the most emphasis on
the notions of substance and mode or accident were the scholastics. For these philoso-

phers, each existing thing is composed of an underlying substratum (*primary substance*) which, having received an essential form (*secondary substance*), is then further modified by several additional, non-essential features (called variously *modes, accidents, properties, attributes,* or *qualities*) that are said to inhere in the substance. Thus an apple consists of such a substratum modified by the essential form, apple, and such specific accidents or properties as colour, shape, weight, taste, texture, etc. Many early modern philosophers were critical of this scholastic vocabulary; see e.g. Hobbes, *Leviathan* 4.46; Malebranche, *Elucidations* 15 [658].

We have . . . concerning it] Hume here and in the following paragraph offers a brief criticism of the views of those who claim that the accidents or qualities of things exist or inhere in a substratum or substance. His principal point is that we experience only the accidents or qualities of things; substance itself is never experienced and hence there is no clear idea of it. Locke had made exactly this point, and claimed that the term *substance* refers merely to an obscure *something* (what we might call a *logical subject*) underlying the set of particular qualities an object is perceived to have. We have clear ideas of the colour, shape, weight, taste, and texture of the apple we are eating, but of its substance we can only say that it is 'something, I know not what' (*Essay* 2.13.18–19; 2.23.1–4, 37). Hume returns to the issue of substance and our conception of it at 1.4.3; see also *Abs.* 28.

2 mode] a modification of a substance or substances, and always dependent for its existence on the substance or substances of which it is a mode (the word was used interchangeably with *accident* and *quality*). Hume goes on to explain what he conceives to be the principal difference between our ideas of substances and modes, given that both are no more than collections of simple ideas united by the imagination and given distinct names.

fiction] an invention, but not necessarily a voluntary or arbitrary invention. The fiction of 'an unknown *something*' is apparently the product of the associative principles of the imagination, and in that sense is natural, although perhaps not unavoidable; see also 1.4.3.1, 4–8; 1.4.4.2.

with the rest] with the other qualities already taken to characterize a substance or some particular kind of thing such as gold.

it] the newly discovered quality, namely, solubility in aqua regia.

the complex idea] the complex idea of the substance, that is.

3 the uniting . . . idea] Whatever it is that may unite the component ideas of a mode, it is never supposed that these ideas are united by an 'unknown *something*' in which qualities 'are suppos'd to inhere' (¶2 of this section).

The reason . . . mode] Hume has compared two kinds of complex idea: those treated as substances, and those treated only as modes. Those treated as substances may have added to them a 'new simple quality' without becoming new complex ideas. If we add the quality, 'dissolubility in *aqua regia*' (¶2 of this section), to our complex idea of a particular substance, gold, the idea still remains an idea of gold. In contrast, if we add the quality, singing, to our complex idea of a particular mode, dance, we produce a new mode, the revue.

Book 1 Part 1 Sect. 7. *Of abstract ideas*

Hume begins by crediting George Berkeley with discovering that abstract or general ideas are merely the ideas of individual things (of a particular plane figure bounded by three straight lines, for example) associated with a term or name ('triangle') that refers to all figures having exactly these characteristics. Hume undertakes to confirm this view by showing that it is impossible that we could have an idea that, by being appropriately indistinct, could be an idea of each one of the individuals represented by an abstract idea. He first argues that we cannot conceive of things without conceiving of them as having distinct qualities. He then argues that abstract ideas of the sort Berkeley describes meet all our conceptual needs. Later he argues that the view *'that all ideas, which are different, are separable'* is consistent with a further kind of abstraction, namely, distinctions of reason, or distinctions (as between an object and its shape, for example) that entail no real separation (¶17). Because we are able to form abstract ideas of such things as colour and shape, we can in time focus on a particular body without attending to the shape or colour of that body, even though we can have no experience of a body distinct from its shape or colour.

1 n. 4 *Dr. Berkeley*] George Berkeley, *Principles*, Introduction 6–20.
   receiv'd opinion . . . particular] widely held opinion on this issue. What Hume calls the received opinion is the account of abstract or general ideas offered by such philosophers as Pierre Gassendi and John Locke. Locke's view is that these ideas are 'Fictions and Contrivances of the Mind' formed only when one has learned to consider the idea of a triangle in such an abstract and comprehensive way that one thinks of a triangle, but does not think of any particular triangle, for any particular triangle would be of some particular form—equilateral or scalene, for example. The general idea of a triangle must, Locke says, be 'all and none of these at once' (*Essay* 4.7.9; Locke's theory is set out most fully in *Essay* 3.3. For Gassendi's view, see *Logic* 1.4). Chambers outlines the controversy, reporting first on the received or 'standing opinion', and then sketching the view of a recent 'eminent and ingenious Author, Dean *Berkeley*', who in effect had denied there are any ideas of the sort Locke had posited and had thus 'gone a good way towards . . . setting philosophy on a new footing' (*Cyclopædia*, 'Abstraction'). For Berkeley's criticisms of the received opinion, see his *New Theory of Vision* 122–5 and *Principles*, Introduction 6–20.
   individuals] individuals of the sort represented by general or abstract ideas: individual triangles, individual humans, etc.
   Republic of Letters] the 'learned world', as Hume says at 1.3.14.6. That informal community of the learned, a community constituted by, we might say, scholars and the reading public along with their conversations and such material items as books, journals, and manuscripts.

2 **Now it having . . . mind**] It has been argued that if abstract ideas are supposed to represent all individuals of a certain class (all triangles, for example), then it would follow that any mind, having such an idea, would need an unlimited power of imagining. No human mind has such a power. Consequently, this particular view of abstraction (the first alternative) has been dismissed as untenable.
   But that . . . erroneous] Hume intends to show that the second of the two alternatives, namely, that our abstract ideas represent no particular degree of quantity or quality, is also false.

3 **have observ'd**] See 1.1.3.4.
   in this view] from this perspective.

4 *Secondly . . .* **quality**] Gassendi had argued that all perceptions have determinate or particular quantity or quality (*Logic* 1.4). Locke had granted that 'the *Ideas first* in the Mind, 'tis evident, are those of particular Things', from which, gradually, a relatively few general ideas are formed (*Essay* 4.7.9; see also 3.3.1). At *Principles*, Introduction 10, Berkeley articulates the view Hume adopts; see also *Dialogues* 1 [1:192].

The confusion . . . unsteadiness] That some impressions may seem featureless is not the result of an ability of the mind to entertain featureless perceptions, but, rather, a consequence of the faintness of these impressions.

5 foregoing conclusion] See ¶4 of this section.

6 *Thirdly . . . angles*] See e.g. *Search* 3.2.6 [232], where Malebranche, in the midst of proposing a theory of perception and abstraction very different from those of Locke or Hume, says 'that every creature is a particular being'. Locke insists that, in one sense, abstract ideas (as he understands them) are imperfect: what abstract ideas portray or represent (a triangle that is at once both all triangles and no particular triangle, for example) cannot exist, for everything that exists is a particular and individuated thing (*Essay* 4.7.9; see also 3.3.1).

7 This application . . . nature] the use, that is, of individuated or particularized ideas as general ideas that represent entire classes of things.

propos'd to explain] See this section, ¶2.

a custom of this kind] a habit of applying the same name to objects that resemble each other even though these objects differ to some degree.

They are . . . power] Hume is speaking of the set of individual perceptions that are not actually in the mind at a given moment, but which then come to mind when one hears or uses the term with which ideas belonging to that set have been associated. Hearing the word *triangle*, for example, may bring to mind any of the countless, distinct geometrical figures belonging to the class, triangle.

8 crowd in upon us] come to mind.

9 *regular figure*] both equilateral and equiangular.

they excite . . . habits] arouse particular dispositions of mind.

10 exhaust these individuals] list or consider all the individual items that are referred to by the general term.

foregoing paradox . . . *representation*] The reference is to ¶6 of this section.

12 *First . . . comprehended*] Hume is saying that the mind does not, in response to hearing the term *a thousand*, conceive of a thousand individual items. Rather, it understands that four digits are required to represent this term. But this inability to conceive of the thousand individuals does not prevent us from reasoning adequately about them.

13 has by rote any periods] has memorized portions of a work.

14 that proposition] the second proposition, *that in war the weaker have always recourse to conquest.*

15 magical . . . soul] here, a faculty of the mind beyond explanation, and hence slightly mysterious.

16 have propos'd] earlier in this section, esp. ¶¶7–10.

already prov'd] earlier in this section, esp. ¶2–6.

17 *distinction of reason*] a distinction between two qualities or attributes (between the shape and the colour of a single object, for example) that cannot exist apart, but which can allegedly be conceived apart. Arnauld and Nicole say that 'when, in the case of a single thing having different attributes, we think of one attribute without thinking of the other', we make a distinction of reason (*Logic* 1.5 [38]). Others who discuss distinctions of reason include Descartes, *Meditations*, *Replies* 1; *Principles of Philosophy* 1.60–3, 2.8; and Berkeley, *Principles*, Introduction 10.

in the schools] in the universities, especially the medieval ones. Hume may also have had in mind such textbooks as the *Logic* of Arnauld and Nicole.

The difficulty . . . *separable*] Hume notes that he has claimed '*that all ideas, which are different, are separable'* (see 1.1.3.4 and ¶3 of this section). Here he argues that, if this principle is true, then we should be able to separate the idea of the shape of a body from the idea of the body itself, in conformity to what are called *distinctions of reason.* But, as we cannot so separate body and figure (and many other pairs of ideas), it appears that either the principle is false, or that we need to reconsider the nature of distinctions of reason. Hume chooses the latter option.

18 of which custom . . . insensible] Because of the frequency of the experience we cease to notice it.

Book 1 Part 2. *Of the ideas of space and time*

Hume devotes the bulk of this part of the *Treatise* to explaining the origin of our ideas of space and time. He begins by noting that it is widely agreed that the 'capacity of the mind is limited' (1.2.1.2), and goes on to say that it cannot be the case that our ideas of space and time consist of 'an infinite number of parts or inferior ideas' (1.2.4.1). These ideas must consist of a finite number of parts that are 'simple and indivisible' (1.2.1.2). He then argues that the simple, indivisible, and unextended parts that make up the general idea of space would be inconceivable were they not coloured or tangible. Because they are coloured or tangible, we can experience an array of them in such a way as to be given the idea of space, or of the 'manner or order, in which objects exist' (1.2.4.2). An analogous account is given of the idea of time. He also argues that space and time themselves must be composed of parts that are fundamentally like the constituent parts of their respective ideas. In Sections 4 and 5 Hume anticipates and answers objections to his view. In Section 5 he takes up the much disputed question of whether or not there can be a vacuum or void. His conclusion: whatever may be true in fact, we have no *idea* of a void. Near the close of this section Hume insists that his 'intention never was to penetrate into the nature of bodies, or explain the secret causes of their operations'. Such an undertaking is 'beyond the reach of human understanding' (1.2.5.26). Section 6 considers the nature and origin of our ideas of existence and external existence. (For further discussion of *Treatise* 1.2, see Ed. Intro., I21–4.)

Book 1 Part 2 Sect. 1. *Of the infinite divisibility of our ideas of space and time*

Hume notes that it is widely agreed that the human mind has a limited capacity and is unable to form an adequate conception of infinity—of either the infinitely large or the infinitely small. It follows, he argues, that *ideas* themselves must have a minimum size. Indeed, there is experimental proof that perceptions have a minimum size: perceptions smaller than a certain minimum simply cannot be experienced, and hence do not exist. Moreover, as nothing in nature can be more minute than such minimal ideas, it follows that we do have ideas that, despite some defects, adequately represent the most minute natural phenomena.

1 Whatever . . . conception] At *Abs.* 29 Hume underscores this point by saying that philosophy and common sense have, with 'regard to the question of infinite divisibility . . . waged most cruel wars with each other'.
2 'Tis universally . . . limited] Other early modern moral and natural philosophers who argue that the human mind is significantly limited include Descartes, *Meditations* 3; *Principles of Philosophy* 3.2; Hobbes, *Leviathan* 1.3; Pascal, *Pensées* 199; Arnauld and Nicole, *Logic* 4.8 (9th axiom); Rohault, *System of Natural Philosophy* 1.21.3; Malebranche, *Search* 2.3.1.4; Locke, *Essay* 2.17.15; Bayle, *Dictionary*, 'Zeno of Elea', n. G; Keill, *An Introduction to Natural Philosophy* [62]; Berkeley, *Principles*, Introduction 4.

It requires . . . induction] It requires little attention to particulars in order to reach a general conclusion. For the one other use of the term *induction* in the *Treatise*, see 1.3.7.7.

run up . . . inferior ones] analyse or reduce to lesser, constituent ideas or parts.

In rejecting . . . conclusion] The same evidence and principles that lead us to conclude that the human mind cannot encompass the infinitely large also lead to the conclusion that it cannot conceive the infinitely small. Our conceptions, or ideas, have both an upper and a lower limit.

3 'Tis therefore . . . annihilation] Berkeley had said, 'For, whatever may be said of extension in abstract, it is certain, sensible extension is not infinitely divisible. There is a *minimum tangible*, and a *minimum visible*, beyond which sense cannot perceive' (*New Theory of Vision* 54; see also *Principles* 1.127–32 and Locke, *Essay* 2.15.9). In this context, minima (minimums) are 'the smallest quantities attainable in any given case' (Chambers, *Cyclopædia*, 'Minima').

What consists . . . separable] See the last annotation to 1.1.3.4.

4 Put a spot . . . indivisible] Hume shows us how to experience a minimum visible, or what he takes to be a coloured point that is indivisible and unextended (having position but no spatial extension or dimension). He later (1.2.3) argues that it is from the experience of a cluster of these points that we derive the idea of space or extension.

5 atom . . . animal spirits . . . mite] In the early 18th c. an atom was taken to be 'a Corpuscle, or Part, or Particle of Matter so minute or small as to be indivisible' (Bailey, *Dictionary*). On animal spirits, see the annotation to 1.2.5.20. The mite was given new attention following the publication of a drawing of one such insect, greatly enlarged, in Robert Hooke's *Micrographia* of 1665. Jacques Rohault had concluded that we lack the capacity to form ideas commensurate with the smallest parts of a mite (*System of Natural Philosophy* 1.21.3).

Book 1 Part 2 Sect. 2. *Of the infinite divisibility of space and time*

An *adequate idea*, according to Hume, is an idea that accurately represents an object. He next argues that if particular ideas adequately represent particular objects, then these ideas must reveal the nature of the objects they represent. He goes on to suggest that, from the repetition of the smallest possible idea of extension, itself representing the most minute possible being, the mind can produce a compound idea of extension. This compound idea must be made up of indivisible units. Similar arguments are used to show that our idea of time is also made up of indivisible units. The fact that we can and must conceive of space and time as being made up of simple and indivisible units, coupled with certain other principles, leads Hume to conclude that space and time themselves are composed of indivisible units.

1 Wherever ideas . . . objects] Hume's account of adequate ideas is similar to that sketched by Gassendi (*Logic* 1.1 [84]), then more fully articulated by Locke, who said that adequate ideas are those 'which perfectly represent those Archetypes [original entities], which the Mind supposes them taken from' (*Essay* 2.31.1).

But our ideas . . . evasion] Having in 1.2.1 established that nothing could be smaller than our smallest ideas, Hume now concludes that there is a perfect correspondence between our smallest ideas and the most minute parts of extension. It follows, he claims, that the relations of those things represented by these ideas must conform to the relations of the ideas themselves. This claim may be compared with his later remarks about his intentions in this part of the *Treatise*; see 1.2.5.25–6.

2 **If . . . divisible**] In opposition to the Aristotelian view that an infinitely divisible entity is only *potentially* infinite, Bayle had written, 'if matter is divisible *in infinitum*, it actually contains an infinite number of parts, and is not therefore an infinite in power [potentially], but an infinite which really and actually exists' (*Dictionary*, 'Zeno of Elea', n. F); see also Ed. Intro., I21–2.

I then repeat . . . idea] Compare Locke, *Essay* 2.13.1–4, where the compounding of ideas leading to the formation of the idea of space is described.

is individually the same idea with] is identical to.

n. 6 *aliquot* parts] Aliquot parts are parts that are contained a certain number of times, without remainder, in the whole they compose—as 2 is contained 3 times in 6. Who it was that raised this objection to Hume is unknown.

3 **n. 7 Mons. *Malezieu***] Nicholas de Malezieu, author of *Elements of Geometry*.

unity] here, an individual thing, or unit. Hume also uses 'unite' with the same meaning.

number] that which results when two or more units of a like kind are assembled or collected together; an aggregate. Hume goes on to say that the attenuated ('fictitious') reality of an aggregate depends entirely on the existence of the individual things or units of which it is composed. See Berkeley, *Principles* 1.120, for a similar claim.

and as extension . . . exist] Hume claims that many metaphysicians hold, at the same time and inconsistently, that extension is an aggregate of units and that, because any putative unit is divisible into further units, there are no such units. Metaphysicians taking this view are discussed by Bayle, *Dictionary*, 'Zeno of Elea', n. I.

'Tis in vain . . . sub-divisions] Compare Bayle: 'It would be vain for you to claim that infinity has no parts, which must necessarily be false with respect to all infinite numbers, since [any] number includes essentially several [units]' (*Dictionary*, 'Zeno of Elea', n. I). **That term . . . denomination**] The term 'unity' used in that way refers to a merely fictitious unit—to an aggregate, rather than a true unit.

4 **takes place . . . time**] applies also to time.

and that none . . . co-existent] The claim that the parts of time cannot coexist, and hence must be indivisible, is also made by Bayle; see *Dictionary*, 'Zeno of Elea', n. F.

1738] In *My Own Life* Hume says that he 'came over to London in 1737' after having spent three years in France, during which he wrote the *Treatise*. In 1738 he was living in London and revising the text he had prepared in France.

6 **calling a *difficulty* . . . evidence**] Samuel Clarke attempted to avoid criticism by granting that there were some 'difficulties' with his view of infinite divisibility. Anthony Collins objected to Clarke's position in much the same way that Hume does. For both Clarke and Collins, see Clarke, *Works*, 2: 525; 3: 814, 849–50, 855.

7 **'Tis true . . . objections**] Arnauld and Nicole, for example, had argued that any atom said to be indivisible must either be extended or unextended. If it is extended, it has parts (a left and a right side, for example) and is thus divisible; if it is not extended, then it cannot be a composite part of extension, for no two unextended points or atoms added together make an extension (*Logic* 4.1 [231–2]). See also Bayle, *Dictionary*, 'Zeno of Elea', n. G. In contrast, Hume undertakes to show how two or more unextended points can give rise to the idea of extension.

8 **maxim in metaphysics . . . *impossible***] See e.g. Descartes, who writes, 'Existence is contained in the idea or concept of every single thing, since we cannot conceive of anything except as existing' (*Meditations*, Reply to Objection 2, Axiom 10).

We can form . . . exist] The compound idea of a fictitious golden mountain is dis-

cussed by Hobbes (*Human Nature* 3.4 [4:11]) and Gassendi (*Logic* 1.3); Gassendi's position is in turn considered by Arnauld and Nicole *(Logic* 1.1–2).
We can form . . . impossible] Descartes argues that we cannot consistently conceive of a mountain without a valley; see *Meditations 5.*
9 Now 'tis certain . . . concerning it] Contrast, however, 1.2.5.2, 22.
conformable to it] in a form consistent with this idea of extension.
mathematical points . . . quibbles] Mathematical points are for Hume indivisible and unextended coloured points, the minimum visibles of 1.2.1.4; see also 1.2.3.4; 1.2.4.3. For references to scholastic arguments against the existence of mathematical points, see Bayle, *Dictionary,* 'Zeno of Elea', n. G.

Book 1 Part 2 Sect. 3. *Of the other qualities of our ideas of space and time*

Hume first argues that the ideas of space and time are, like all ideas, derived from impressions. Neither, however, is derived from a single, corresponding *simple* impression. The idea of space is derived from the impressions of sets of minimum visibles (of indivisible and unextended but visible mathematical points) arranged at intervals from one another. He then argues that the abstract idea of time is derived from a succession of indivisible perceptions, and that we cannot conceive of time without experiencing of a succession of objects.

1 above-mention'd] See 1.1.1.7.
2 extension] Hume freely interchanges the terms *space* and *extension.*
3 internal impressions] also called 'impressions of reflection'; see 1.1.2.
This is . . . idea] That is, the answer to this question definitively decides what we can say about the idea of extension. Hume argues that, given that all simple ideas derive from simple impressions, and that our idea of extension does not derive from impressions of reflection, it follows that the idea of extension must derive from some impression(s) of sensation. If this (these) can be identified, we will then understand our idea of extension.
4 colour'd points] These are the unextended, immaterial, and indivisible mathematical points discussed at 1.2.1.4; 1.2.2.9; see also ¶15 of this section and 1.4.4.8.
5 All abstract ideas . . . other] Hume's account of abstract ideas and of the distinctions of reason that permit us to ignore the colour of the points we experience is found in 1.1.7; esp. ¶¶1, 17–18.
7 A man . . . imagination] The example is found in Locke, *Essay* 2.14.4. Hume's views on succession as it bears on the formation of the idea of time appear to owe much to Locke's discussion in 2.14.
n. 8 Mr. *Locke*] See *Essay* 2.14, esp. 7–15, for the bounds or limits Hume mentions.
wheel . . . fire] rotate rapidly a fiery object fastened to the end of a rope or wire. The resulting visual phenomenon is described by Rohault, *System of Natural Philosophy* 1.35, and Chambers, *Cyclopædia,* 'Visible'. Locke, *Essay* 2.14.8, discusses the phenomenon more generally.
8 not co-existent] See 1.2.2.4.
9 Having therefore . . . imagination] Hume asks if, having once formed the idea of time through the experience of a succession of changing objects, we can then conceive of time without such a succession, and if we can think of this one idea, time, in isolation from all other ideas.

10 **above-explain'd.**] See 1.1.3.4 and 1.1.7.3.

without . . . number] without being a distinguishable entity among a set of entities.

conjoin it . . . objects] join the relevant *manner*—the succession of perceptions that give rise to the idea of time—to other successions of perceptions.

11 **I know . . . vulgar**] According to Chambers, the Epicureans (Gassendi, for example) and Corpuscularians (Robert Boyle, for example) conceived of time as something like the succession, one after the other, from eternity to eternity, of uniquely temporal particles. Thus time was conceived to be independent of change in ordinary entities or of the succession of our ideas. Other philosophers, Chambers says, supposed that there is an absolute time, flowing in an eternal, unchanging sequence, that is the only true measure of duration. Time so conceived could readily be applied to unchanging objects (*Cyclopædia*, 'Time').

n. 9 Sect. 5] See 1.2.5.29.

15 **feeling**] sense of touch.

annihilated . . . imagination] If these atoms have no sensory properties, they are effectively non-existent to us; see also 1.4.4.8. Berkeley (*Principles* 1.9–10) had made much of this point in his criticism of the putative distinction between primary and secondary qualities.

Book 1 Part 2 Sect. 4. *Objections answer'd*

Hume has argued that indivisible and unextended mathematical points constitute the parts of space and time, and that our ideas of space and time are derived from complex impressions of such points. He now considers three objections to his theory: (1) such mathematical points are non-entities, or nothing, and hence cannot make up a 'real existence' such as space; (2) such points, lacking dimension, would always completely penetrate one another, and thus would necessarily fail to provide a basis for space or the idea of space; (3) such points are contrary to many essential features of mathematics. Hume counters each of these objections. Responding to the third of them involves him in an extensive discussion of equality, and leads him to conclude that geometry, because it lacks any precise standard of equality, is an art, and not an exact science. (On geometry, see also 1.3.1.4.)

2 **a vacuum . . . matter**] a void, or a space devoid of all matter. For further discussion of our conception of a vacuum, see 1.2.5.

3 **It has often . . . existence**] Bayle reports that 'Infinite divisibility is the hypothesis that Aristotle embrac'd, and it is the one of almost all philosophy professors in all universities for several centuries' (*Dictionary*, 'Zeno of Elea', n. G).

no medium] no middle ground or alternative position.

The system of *physical* points] the theory that extension or space is made up of indivisible *material* units. Hume finds this theory to be absurd because physical atoms necessarily have parts and hence are not indivisible, while he argues that his theory of mathematical points (which, although coloured or tangible, are *immaterial*) provides a satisfactory alternative to all earlier and unsatisfactory accounts of space. For further discussion of these theories, see Ed. Intro., I21–4.

4 **the necessity . . . *penetration***] the necessity there would be of any two contiguous points occupying precisely the same space. Such a consequence is said to follow because the points in question are by definition dimensionless and without parts (they have no sides or limits to keep themselves apart) and hence if they did touch they

would penetrate. They would, that is, meld intimately together in one place. See also the Glossary, penetration (1).

secundum se, tota, & totaliter] according to itself, totally and completely.

But penetration is impossible] That is, distinct things do not and cannot meld together as the theory suggests.

5 **Suppose two bodies . . . circumference**] Suppose two bodies each containing no empty spaces; suppose, in other words, two completely solid bodies.

7 **Put a spot . . . invisible**] Hume is pointing out further features of the experiment first mentioned at 1.2.1.4.

9 **A surface . . . line . . . point . . . depth**] These are standard definitions of Euclidean geometry. A line was also said to be formed by the motion of a point. See e.g. Harris, *Lexicon Technicum* 1, 'Line'.

10 **are mere ideas . . . in nature**] Bayle, for example, says that mathematicians admit that length without breadth and breadth without depth 'cannot exist outside our minds', and that mathematical objects are mere 'fictions that can never have any existence' (*Dictionary*, 'Zeno of Elea', n. G; 'Zeno the Epicurean', n. D); see also the annotation to Note 10.

11 **Whatever . . . existence**] For a less restrictive version of this principle, see 1.2.2.8. Hume's claim here closely parallels an axiom found in the *Logic* of Arnauld and Nicole: '*At least possible existence is contained in the idea of everything which we conceive clearly and distinctly*' (4.7 [250]).

12 **foregoing argument**] The argument found in ¶9 of this section.

n. 10 *L'Art de penser*] *Logic; or, The Art of Thinking* 1.5. The authors of this work (Arnauld and Nicole) argue that geometers, having taken body extended in length, breadth, and thickness as their subject, have attempted to gain a better understanding of this subject by first considering it in relation to one dimension, length; then in relation to two dimensions, area; and then in three dimensions, solidity. This, they go on, 'shows how ridiculous is the argument of some skeptics who try to call into question the certainty of geometry, on the grounds that it presupposes lines and surfaces which are not found in nature. For geometers by no means assume that there are lines without width or surfaces without depth. They only think that it is possible to consider the length without paying attention to the width. This is indubitable, just as when, in measuring the distance from one city to another, we measure only the length of a path without bothering with its width' (1.5 [37–8]).

above-explain'd.] See 1.1.7.17–18.

13 **sufficiently explain'd**] See 1.2.1.

14 **A surface . . . line**] Hume is again repeating standard Euclidean views.

But . . . and so on] Hume's restatement of his argument might itself be restated: Assume a line AB, said to be terminated at B by point p. If points are infinitely divisible, then AB cannot be terminated by p, but must be said to be terminated by p^*, or that part of p making up a smaller point and nearest the termination of AB. But if points are infinitely divisible, then AB cannot be terminated by p^*, but must be said to be terminated by p^{**}, or that part of p^* making up a smaller point and nearest the termination of AB. But if points are infinitely divisible, then . . . and so on.

15 **The *schoolmen* . . . distinctions**] Hume is paraphrasing Bayle; see *Dictionary*, 'Zeno of Elea', n. G.

17 **When geometry . . . exactness**] The argument of the remaining portion of 1.2.4 is briefly summarized in *Abs.* 29. Hume there reports that, having 'denied the infinite divisibility of extension', he finds it necessary 'to refute those mathematical

arguments, which have been adduced for it' and that he does this 'by denying geometry to be a science exact enough to admit of conclusions so subtile as those which regard infinite divisibility'.

21 n. 11 mathematical lectures] *The Usefulness of Mathematical Learning Explained and Demonstrated*, a set of lectures by Isaac Barrow. The suggestion that congruity best defines equality is found in Lecture 11.

22 There are . . . proportion] Butler argued that all attempts to define 'similitude or equality' would be confusing. 'Yet', he said, 'there is no difficulty at all in ascertaining the idea. For as, upon two triangles being compared or viewed together, there arises to the mind the idea of similitude; or upon twice two and four, the idea of equality' ('Of Personal Identity', in *Works*, 1:307; see also Chambers, *Cyclopædia*, 'Judgment').

24 the fiction . . . natural] This is only the first of several *natural* fictions to which Hume calls attention. In general terms, such natural fictions are ideas that, although they take us beyond experience, are none the less the involuntary result of experience and the usual processes of the mind. In contrast, the fictions of the poet or dramatist might be called *artificial* fictions; these arise voluntarily, or, to use Hume's language, as the result of contrivance or design. For more on *fictions*, see the Glossary.

25 but this order . . . appearance] In spite of what the mathematicians say, our experiences are limited to what we can perceive.
distant notion . . . objects] See *Abs.* 29 for additional discussion of the useless or inadequate standard of equality derived from the notion of indivisible (mathematical) points.
that we form . . . comprehend it] In short, we *imagine* there is a perfect standard of equality, and act as though there is such a standard, but no such standard has been, or is likely to be, articulated.

26 'Tis true . . . *two points*] Again, Hume is repeating standard Euclidean views.

27 already establish'd] This section, ¶¶18 ff.

28 that mathematicians . . . line] This standard view of the mathematicians is stated thus by Chambers: 'The origin of all *Magnitude* is a point, which, though void of parts itself, yet its flux [motion] forms a line, the flux of that a surface, and [the motion] of that a body' (*Cyclopædia*, 'Magnitude').
that a right line . . . plane] That a flowing line would produce a plane surface only if it flowed always in the same plane was well known to Hume's contemporaries. Harris (*Lexicon Technicum* 1, 'Surface') had said that 'a *Plane Surface* or *Superficies*, is made by the Motion of a *Right Line* [a straight line] always keeping in the same Plane'. Hume's additional claim is that such a definition is circular because it uses the notion *plane* to define a *plane surface*.

29 that proportion] equality.

30 that two right lines . . . segment] According to Euclidean geometry, if what *appear* to be two straight lines have a common segment, then either the two are in fact one straight line, or one is not a straight line; if two straight lines intersect, they do so at a single dimensionless point, and have no length in common; if two straight lines fail always to touch one another, they are parallel. On the use of *but* in 'but 'tis absurd', see the Glossary.
twenty leagues . . . one] The length of a league was never standardized, but 20 leagues would equal about 50 miles (80 km.). Imagine you are looking down a set of railroad tracks that in fact converge at the rate of 1 inch in 50 miles (2.5 cm. in 80 km.). Assuming the tracks are 4 feet (120 cm.) apart where you stand, they will touch one another after 2,400 miles (3,840 km.). How is it known, Hume goes on, that the two

apparently converging lines do not form (for some distance, at least) one single line? On what grounds could you argue that the two lines will touch at only one dimensionless and indivisible point, and not form a single line for some measurable distance?

33 and I then ask . . . space] Even were we only to imagine a circle touching a straight line, we would likely always imagine some segment of the two lines to be in common. If we do not so imagine, if we do succeed in imagining the two as touching only at a single dimensionless point, then we have in effect conceded that there are indivisible mathematical points.

Book 1 Part 2 Sect. 5. *The same subject continu'd*

If it is true *'that the idea of space or extension is nothing but the idea of visible or tangible points distributed in a certain order'* (¶1), then it follows that no idea of a vacuum or a void (of a space in which there is nothing visible or tangible) is possible. Hume considers three objections to this conclusion: (1) we dispute concerning a vacuum, and hence must have an idea of it; (2) the idea of a vacuum can be derived from ideas known to be possible; (3) the idea of a vacuum is necessary to explain motion. He also explains why, contrary to fact, we think we have the idea of a vacuum. Near the end of the section, Hume grants that he has explained 'only the manner in which objects affect the senses, without endeavouring to account for their real nature and operations', and adds that it was never his intention 'to penetrate into the nature of bodies, or explain the secret causes of their operations' (¶¶25–6).

1 *that . . . order*] See 1.2.3.4–5.

2 *First . . . vacuum . . . plenum*] Philosophers had long debated whether the cosmos or universe could include any completely empty spaces (voids or vacuums) or whether it is completely full (a plenum). The Aristotelians maintained that nature abhors a vacuum. The Cartesians (Descartes and his followers) argued that the essence of matter is extension, and thus were committed to the view that every part of space or extension just is matter, and that the universe is full of matter, or a plenum. In contrast, such philosophers as Gassendi, Boyle, and Newton argued that the universe can and does include empty spaces, and that there are experimental proofs of this fact.
to take party . . . side] to take sides.
it may be pretended . . . defended] Locke says that 'those who dispute for or against a *Vacuum*, do thereby confess, they have distinct *Ideas* of *Vacuum* and *Plenum*' (*Essay* 2.13.21). Hume returns to this issue in ¶22 of this section; see also 1.2.2.9.

3 It must . . . rest] Rohault, a Cartesian and committed to the doctrine of a plenum (see ¶2 of this section), refused to speculate about the answer to the question 'Whether God could not by his Omnipotence make a *Vacuum*, by annihilating all the Air in a Room, and hindring any more from coming in its Place?' He was, however, willing to answer the question, what would *'we conceive* [to] follow, if God should annihilate all the Air in a Room, and not suffer any other to enter in its Place?' The answer, he said, explicitly ignoring what might happen outside the chamber, is 'that the Walls would approach one another so near, that there would remain no Space betwixt them' (*System of Natural Philosophy* 1.8). Descartes, *Principles of Philosophy* 2.18, raises a similar question about a 'vessel', and gives the same answer: 'the sides of the vessel would . . . have to be in contact'. The remainder of Hume's paragraph assumes that his readers are aware of this discussion. Keill, *Introduction to Natural Philosophy* 2, raises objections to the Cartesian arguments against the existence of a vacuum, but leaves

the issue of the real nature of space, whether 'actually extended in itself', or arising 'from the Relation of Bodies existing in it', to be disputed by metaphysicians.

3 **subtile matter**] or *materia subtilis*; the name given by Descartes to fine, continuously agitated particles, supposed to fill the heavens or any space from which all grosser matter, including air, has been removed or evacuated.

There are some . . . other] Descartes and his followers would give this answer.

distance] *Distance* is another term for *extension* and, for the Cartesians, *matter*.

I defy . . . position] Rohault (see above) obviously did not suppose the walls would remain where they had originally been.

4 **This assertion . . . another**] The claim that without a void motion would be impossible dates from the ancient atomists. See Lucretius, *Nature of Things* 1.330 ff. Newton argued that if there were no empty spaces not even the heaviest bodies could fall, and that for the motion of the planets and comets to be 'regular, and lasting, it is necessary the celestial spaces be void of all matter' (*Principia* 3 Props. 6, 10, as found in Chambers, *Cyclopædia*, 'Vacuum').

5 **'Tis evident . . . positive idea**] In contrast, Locke had insisted that even an idea that appears to be caused by a privation (the idea of darkness, shadow, or cold, for example) is 'a real *positive Idea* in the Understanding' (*Essay* 2.8.1–2).

The consequence . . . vacuum] Hume here completes the first stage of an argument intended to show that no sensory experience, and no manner of deprivation of sensory experience, can produce the idea of a vacuum or void. His first claim is that complete visual deprivation—the experience of complete darkness—does not produce the idea of a void.

6 **sensible of nothing**] completely deprived of tactile sensations.

8 **'Tis commonly . . . surface**] Chambers reports that 'In bodies, the *superficies* [that is, surface] is all that presents itself to the eye' (*Cyclopædia*, 'Superficies').

degrees of remoteness . . . senses] Whether distance is perceived immediately or inferred after experience had been widely discussed in conjunction with a question raised by William Molyneux: Would a person, born blind, and then enabled to see, be able to distinguish immediately, by sight, two very different three-dimensional objects (a sphere from a cube, for example)? Those who answered in the negative were of the opinion that judgement of distance by sight is *learned* rather than instinctive or natural. They were of the opinion, to use Hume's terms, that distance is 'discover'd more by reason than the senses'. See e.g. Locke, *Essay* 2.9.8.

12 **The angles . . . each other**] In the Appendix to the *Treatise* Hume wrote: 'I shall also take this opportunity of confessing two other errors of less importance, which more mature reflection has discover'd to me in my reasoning. The first may be found in Book 1, pages 42–3, where I say, that the distance betwixt two bodies is known, among other things, by the angles, which the rays of light flowing from the bodies make with each other. 'Tis certain, that these angles are not known to the mind, and consequently can never discover the distance'. (¶22) Efforts to explain the perception of distance by means of rays of light and angles are found in Descartes, *Optics* 6 [1:170–2]; Malebranche, *Search* 1.9.3; Rohault, *System of Natural Philosophy* 1.32.14; Chambers, *Cyclopædia*, 'Visible'. Berkeley, *New Theory of Vision* 3–15, had argued that the view Hume repudiates is unsatisfactory.

the motion . . . other] Berkeley had argued that a noticeable feeling is associated with a change of the eyes' point of focus. As we look at nearer things our eyes turn in; as we look at more distant things, they turn out, and this turning is felt by us (*New Theory of Vision* 16–17).

and the different . . . by them] Chambers had explained how the parts of the eye may be affected: 'the eye disposes itself differently, according to the different distances it is to see, *viz.* for remote objects the pupil is dilated, and the crystalline brought nearer the retina, and the whole eye made more globous [spherical]' (*Cyclopædia*, 'Visible').

14 But tho' motion . . . idea] Although Hume does not use the term *fiction* in the ensuing discussion, he there appears to describe how another *natural fiction* arises. See the annotation to 1.2.4.24.

17 For as all qualities . . . distance] Newton's law of universal gravitation holds that gravity is inversely proportional to distance. John Keill had demonstrated that the effects of such qualities as light, heat, cold, and odour similarly vary in proportion to the distance of the source from the affected organ (*Introduction to Natural Philosophy* 1).

20 When I receiv'd . . . causes] See 1.1.4.

maxim . . . experience] See Intro. 8–9; 1.1.4.6.

imaginary dissection of the brain] Such a dissection would have been contrary to the maxim just mentioned and to Hume's expressed intent (1.1.2) to leave physiological theorizing to the anatomists. That he speaks of an 'imaginary dissection' could have reminded some of his readers of Matthew Prior's humorous poem *Alma; or, The Progress of the Mind* (a work Hume mentions at 2.2.8.18), where such an imaginary dissection is also hypothesized:

> Here, RICHARD, how could I explain,
> The various Lab'rinths of the Brain? . . .
> I could demonstrate every Pore,
> Where Mem'ry lays up all her Store;
> And to an Inch compute the Station,
> 'Twixt Judgment, and Imagination.
> O Friend! I could display much Learning,
> At least to Men of small Discerning. . . .
> Could I but see thy Head dissected!

> (3.151–81)

Philosophers whose work Hume knew and who attempt to explain many phenomena of the mind by speculations about animal spirits (see the next annotation) and brain traces include Descartes (see esp. *Passions of the Soul* 1.7 ff.) and Malebranche (see *Search* 2.1.5; 2.2.2).

animal spirits] Chambers describes animal spirits as 'an exceedingly thin, subtile, moveable fluid juice or humour separated from the blood in the cortex of the brain, hence received into the minute fibres of the medulla, and by them discharged into the nerves, by which it is conveyed through every part of the body, to be the instrument of sensation, muscular motion, *&c*'. Although he grants that the 'existence of the *animal spirits*' is controversial, Chambers contends that they provide the best explanation of bodily motion and function: 'the infinite use they are of in the animal œconomy, and the exceedingly lame account we should have of any of the animal functions without them, will still keep the greatest part of the world on their side' (*Cyclopædia*, 'Spirit'). In contrast to Chambers's claim, by 1733 George Cheyne was arguing that the theory of animal spirits is as useless as Ptolemy's astronomy; see ch. 9 of Cheyne's *English Malady*. See also the Glossary entry on animal spirits.

21 Resembling ideas . . . other] We may be confused not only because certain ideas resemble one another, but also because these ideas are produced by operations that

resemble one another. In the present case, this helps to explain how we confuse our well-founded idea of extension with a fictitious notion of an unseeable and intangible distance, and thereby appear to give distinct meaning to the word *vacuum*. On resembling operations, see also 1.4.2.32; 1.4.6.7; a similar phenomenon is reported at 1.3.8.2.

21 Of this . . . treatise] See e.g. 1.4.2.35, 42–4, 56; 1.4.5.12; 1.4.6.6; 3.1.2.1.

words for ideas] Hume holds that words are meaningless unless they refer to, or are regularly associated with, particular and clear ideas distinct from them. See also 1.1.7.14; 1.3.14.14; and App.11. For related views on this topic, see e.g. Spinoza, *Ethics* 2, Post. 49; Arnauld and Nicole, *Logic* 1.11; Rohault, *System of Natural Philosophy* 1.4; Locke, *Essay* 3.2.7; 3.10.4; Berkeley, *Alciphron*, Dial. 7.

room of extension] in place of the idea of extension.

As the first . . . cause] We mistakenly substitute the idea of *distance*, derived from the experience of empty spaces between objects, for the idea of *extension*, derived from the experience of an array of tangible or visible points and the true source of the idea of extension. We make this mistake because the two kinds of experience resemble one another in important ways.

22 *mechanics*] here, a part of *natural philosophy*. See ¶4 of this section.

The frequent disputes . . . turns] See ¶2 of this section.

23 rest and annihilation] See ¶3 of this section.

already been remark'd] See 1.1.1.3–7. Hume's earlier, more precise claim is that *simple* impressions give rise to, and resemble, *simple* ideas.

24 Now the motion . . . creation] See ¶4 of this section. Hume's remark is reminiscent of the Cartesian view that what appears to be motion is effectively continuous re-creation (by the Deity) in a set of different locations. See Descartes, *Meditations* 3; *Principles of Philosophy* 2.36, 42; Malebranche, *Elucidations* 15 [660].

25 above-mention'd] See ¶¶2–4 of this section.

'Twill . . . operations] As we find in the following paragraph, this possible objection aptly reflects one goal of *Treatise* 1, namely, to explain the manner in which we are affected by what we *take* to be physical objects, without any intent to explain the physical causes of this experience—without attempting to explain, that is, 'the real nature and operations' of bodies themselves. See also the last annotation to 1.1.2.1.

n. 12.2 tho' I am inclin'd . . . notions] Hume does not know the answer to the question raised in the previous sentence, but he is more inclined to believe, as ordinary people do, that there are vacuums (that there are empty spaces) even though we have no idea of a vacuum. As he goes on to say, he is not convinced that, even with better sensory abilities, we would see that space is always filled with body, nor does he suppose that our perceptions provide a definitive measure of what there is.

n. 12.2 that philosophy] the Newtonian philosophy.

28 If it be . . . concerning it] See ¶2 of this section.

Book 1 Part 2 Sect. 6. *Of the idea of existence, and of external existence*

Each of our perceptions is conceived of as existing. Given that all ideas derive ultimately from impressions, and that we have an idea of existence, we can expect to trace this idea to its source. Hume finds, however, that the source is not some distinct impression that accompanies all other perceptions: there is no such distinct and constantly attending impression. Consequently, he concludes that the 'idea of existence . . . is the very same with the idea of what we conceive to be existent' (¶4). We are then told that the idea of external existence can be accounted for in the same manner, and that there is no idea of an external object conceived of as being '*specifically* different from our perceptions'. Such objects may be thought to differ from our perceptions only in so far as objects and perceptions can be thought of as having 'different relations, connexions and durations' (¶9).

1 knowledge and probability] topics treated in *Treatise* 1.3.
2 There is no impression . . . existent] At 1.2.2.8 Hume claims that whatever can be conceived includes the idea of existence. He now claims that every perception, considered as a perception, is conceived as existing. In doing so he tacitly challenges the view, summarized by Chambers, that while *existence* 'necessarily presupposes essence, and cannot be conceived without it', *essence* 'may be conceived without *existence*'. According to Chambers, this difference results from the fact that essence belongs equally to things that are either potential or actual, while existence belongs only to actual things (*Cyclopædia*, 'Existence'). See also Locke, *Essay* 3.3.19.
    being] existence.
3 particular impression] Although each perception is conceived to be existing, there is no one impression that accompanies all other perceptions. Consequently, there is no one impression from which the universal conception of existence is derived.
4 To reflect . . . other] See the maxim mentioned at 1.2.2.8.
5 entity] existence or being.
  n. 13 Part 1. Sect. 7] See 1.1.7.17–18.
7 We may observe . . . occasion] This view is found in Arnauld and Nicole, *Logic* 1, Introduction [25]; Malebranche, *Search* 1.1.1; 3.2.1; Locke, *Essay* 1.1.8; 2.8.8; and 4.1.1; and Chambers, *Cyclopædia*, 'Idea'. Hume repeats his claim at 1.4.2.21, 47; 2.2.2.22; 3.1.1.2.
8 specifically different] of a different kind or species. At 1.4.2.56 Hume says that it is 'impossible for us distinctly to conceive, objects to be in their nature any thing but exactly the same with perceptions'. For more on specific difference, see 1.4.2.2; 1.4.6.13; and esp. 1.4.5.19–20.
  Let us fix . . . possible] Let us focus our attention on what we take to exist outside the mind, on, that is, 'external objects' (¶9 of this section).
  n. 14 Part 4. Sect. 2.] See 1.4.2, esp. ¶¶18–24.

Book 1 Part 3. *Of knowledge and probability*

The seven philosophical relations may be divided into those that do, and those that do not, depend only on the ideas related. The relation of cause and effect is one of the latter and the one relation that enables us to reason beyond present experience. Looking closely at this relation, Hume discovers three things about it: (1) items taken to be causes exist before their effects; (2) causes are contiguous to effects; (3) there is a necessary connection between causes and effects, although from an inspection of sample causes and effects, he can find no impression corresponding to the idea of necessary connection. Satisfied that he will come to understand causation and causal reasoning only by what he takes to be an indirect approach, Hume raises and answers several questions in Sections 3–14. (For a list of these questions, see Ed. Intro., I29.) Section 15 provides eight rules of causal reasoning, while Section 16 considers the reasoning ability of animals. (For further discussion of *Treatise* 1.3, see Ed. Intro., I24–37.)

Book 1 Part 3 Sect. 1. *Of knowledge*

Of the seven philosophical relations (see 1.1.5), four (*resemblance, proportion in quantity or number, degrees in any quality, contrariety*) provide, either by intuition or demonstration, a basis for knowledge. The remaining three (*identity, relations of time and place, causation*) provide a basis for probability or belief. Geometry, by many thought to be a science, is said to be merely an art. The claim that our mathematical ideas are of a subtle, spiritual nature, different from many other ideas, is shown to be false.

1 **These relations . . . ideas**] Hume distinguishes between two kinds of philosophical relation: (1) those (*resemblance, proportion in quantity or number, degrees in any quality*, and *contrariety*) that are unaffected by the order or timing in which the related ideas are presented; and (2) those (*identity, relations of time and place*, and *causation*) that are affected by or depend on the order or timing in which the related ideas are presented. For further discussion of this important difference, see Ed. Intro., I24–6.

relation of equality] a proportion of quantity or number, that is.

relations of *contiguity* **and** *distance*] another way of referring to relations of time and space; *Treatise* 1.2 focuses on certain of these relations.

identity **and** *causation*] Much of *Treatise* 1.3 is taken up with an analysis of the relation of causation, while *Treatise* 1.4 has much to say about the relation of identity.

2 **knowledge and certainty**] At 1.3.11.2 Hume says that by *knowledge* he means 'the assurance arising from the comparison of ideas'. This position is similar to that of Locke, who defines *knowledge* as the perception (or recognition) of the agreement (similarity) or disagreement (dissimilarity) of any ideas compared to one another, and says that we can only have *certainty* when perception of such agreement or disagreement has taken place (*Essay* 4.1.2; 4.4.1).

intuition . . . demonstration] Hume's position is again similar to that of Locke, who defines *intuition* as perception 'at the first sight', or immediately, of the similarity or dissimilarity of two ideas compared to one another. It is in this manner that we perceive that white is not black or 3 is not 2. Locke defines *demonstration* as a way of showing the agreement or disagreement of two ideas by the use of other ideas or proofs that have 'a constant, immutable, and visible connexion one with another'. That is, we show that $A = C$ by showing first that $A = B$ is a constant and intuitively certain relationship; we then show that $B = C$ is also such a constant and intuitively certain relationship; assuming the truth of the principle that things equal to a third thing are equal to each other, we will have demonstrated that $A = C$ (*Essay* 4.2.1–7). Hume later says that, if some conclusion can be demonstrated, its contrary is not only impossible but inconceivable; see 1.3.7.3; 1.3.9.10; and *Abs.* 18. A further important discussion of demonstrative reasoning, and of its relation to probable reasoning, is found at 1.4.1.

3 *artificial* **manner**] Hume's point is that, unless we are dealing with relatively simple sets of numerical ideas ($2 + 5 = 7$, $16{,}356 + 4 = 16{,}360$, for example) our judgements of this sort require demonstration. Few can intuit that $78 \times 69 = 5{,}382$; we must figure this out in ways that we have learned, and that are in that sense *artificial*.

4 **already observ'd**] See esp. 1.2.4.17–18, 29–33.

Our ideas . . . proposition] Hume claims that geometry, although highly precise, cannot be said to give us *knowledge* (as he and Locke understand the term) of reality. The root of this deficiency lies in the fact that the ideas and relations that make up geometry do not correspond perfectly with the impressions of sensation from which they are ultimately derived. The Euclidean geometer will insist that two parallel lines never meet, and that any two straight lines that do meet intersect at a single, indivisible point, and thus have no common segment. But if we look at any two lines supposed to be parallel, and extend these for any distance (imagine a set of railroad tracks), they will appear to run together or to have a common segment. In short, our experience is contrary to the conclusions of the geometers; see also the annotations to 1.2.4.30.

the mathematics] Hume here, and untypically for him, appears to exclude algebra and arithmetic from mathematics. His typical position, that algebra and arithmetic do have precise standards and hence are sciences, is found in ¶6 of this section.

6 chiliagon] a regular plane figure with 1,000 angles. The same point, using the same example, is made by Locke (*Essay* 2.29.13–14). Descartes had argued that so far as images or the ideas of imagination are concerned, the idea of a chiliagon is, in comparison to the idea of a triangle, hopelessly confused (*Meditations* 6).
to run us up to] to reveal to us.

7 'Tis usual . . . capable] Arnauld and Nicole, having accepted a distinction between 'mental ideas' and 'corporeal images', between ideas of the soul and those of the body, argue that there are some corporeal things that cannot be imagined (of which no image can be formed), but that can be conceived in 'a mental form' by the non-corporeal mind. The chiliagon with its 1,000 angles equivalent to 1,996 right angles is said to prove the point well (*Logic*, Discourse 2 [17–18]). See also Malebranche, *Search* 1.4.1; 3.2.1.
destroy this artifice] counter this strategy.
so oft insisted on] See e.g. 1.1.1.7–9; 1.2.3.1; 1.2.5.23.

Book 1 Part 3 Sect. 2. *Of probability; and of the idea of cause and effect*

Identity, relations of time and place, and causation (the three philosophical relations that depend on the manner or order in which ideas or objects come before the mind) provide a basis for probability. Only one of these three, causation, enables us to engage in probable reasoning, to make, that is, inferences beyond present experience. Hume finds that the idea of causation is not derived from an impression of causation, and so undertakes to determine which impressions do give rise to it. He also finds that items believed to be causally connected are contiguous, and that causes are always prior to effects, but these two features of causal relations are not sufficient to explain a third feature, the necessity of the connection between cause and effect. In an effort to explain this idea of necessary connection, Hume sets for himself these questions: Why do we think that everything that begins to exist must have a cause? Why do we think that specific causes have specific effects? What is the nature of the inference we draw from cause to effect or effect to cause? What is the nature of our belief in this inference?

1 science] here, certain knowledge; see 1.3.1.2.
situations in time and place] another way of referring to relations of time and space.
2 When both . . . sensation] The view that the senses are merely passive receptors is found in Malebranche (*Search* 1.1.1) and Locke (*Essay* 2.9.1; 2.22.2). Hume only rarely uses the word *perception*, as he does here, to refer to the process of becoming aware of objects. This process he more typically calls sensation; see e.g. 1.3.6.6.
According . . . objects] Hume argues that neither the relation of identity, nor that of time and place, enables us to make inferences to entities not presently experienced. Only the relation of causation gives rise to inferences of this sort, and thus only this one relation gives rise to the form of probable reasoning Hume goes on to explain; see also 1.3.6.6–7; 1.3.7.5 Note 20; and 1.3.9.2.
We readily . . . perception] We believe an object to have remained the same object even though our experience of it is interrupted; our belief is exactly what it would have

been had we had an unchanging, continuous experience of the object. For Hume's explanation of this fact, see 1.4.2.15–43.

3 **which depend not . . . ideas**] which depend not on ideas alone, but on the order or manner of their appearance.

trac'd beyond] seen to have an effect beyond.

5 **Let us . . . consequence**] The suggestion is that we consider, from every available perspective, any two objects, *A* and *B*, of which one, *A*, is said to be the cause of the other, *B*.

At first sight . . . effect] Hume finds that no one property is a property of every object that is taken to be a cause. As a consequence, he concludes that the idea of cause cannot be traced to impressions of a unique causal property. By a parallel argument, he concludes that the idea of effect has no unique source among the properties of objects.

6 **We may . . . causation**] Hume here argues that there is no direct action at a distance. What seem to be remote causes are in fact part of a causal sequence in which each cause is contiguous to its effect. He also argues that causes and effects must be temporally proximate, but, as we learn in the next paragraph, cannot be simultaneous. See also 1.3.15.3–4.

n. 16 Part 4. Sect. 5.] See 1.4.5.9–14.

7 **Some pretend . . . itself**] Hobbes had said that 'in whatsoever instant the cause is entire, in the same instant the effect is produced' (*Elements of Philosophy* 2.9.5). Hume goes on to argue that a cause cannot be simultaneous with its effect.

'Tis an establish'd . . . cause] The maxim assumes that a cause must precede its effect, but if a putative cause, *A*, has been in existence or operating for any significant or longish time before its putative effect, *C*, comes into existence, then *A* is not the proper or sole cause of *C*. In such circumstances, *C* must also depend on, or be caused by, some additional principle, *B*, acting as a proximate cause. Hume, having said that a thing cannot operate at a time or place even slightly remote from the time and place at which it exists (see ¶6 of this section), takes the maxim to be correct.

Now if . . . cause] Assuming that 'proper cause' is a synonym for the earlier 'sole cause', Hume's argument is that no proper cause can be simultaneous with its effect because, were any such cause in fact exactly simultaneous with its effect, then even all those apparent causes that briefly precede their effects would fail to be proper causes. Why? The established maxim tells us that if *A* has been in existence for some significant or longish time before *C* comes into existence, then *A* is not the proper or sole cause of *C*. But, if even one cause is simultaneous with its effect, then that cause sets the standard: proper causes will be just those that are simultaneous with their effects. In that case, we shall have to conclude that any putative causes that even briefly precede their effects have existed for a significant or longish time before these effects and thus are not proper causes. (The established maxim would have to be changed to say: an object that exists for any time whatsoever in its full perfection without producing another is not the sole cause of that other object.) If we are forced to this conclusion, then we would also be forced to the further unreasonable conclusion that all proper causes are simultaneous not only with their effects, but with each other. If we were to grant that one cause is simultaneous with its effect, we would be forced to conclude that there can be no succession of causes, and by consequence, no time.

8 **preceding case**] See ¶6 of this section.

9 **impulse**] contact. Locke, for example, says that a moving billiard ball sets a second ball in motion 'by impulse' (*Essay* 2.21.4). For Hobbes's similar view, see the second annotation to 1.3.9.10.

When we . . . interval] Malebranche and other Cartesians had for some decades argued that there is no directly sensed causal link or tie between causes and effects; other philosophers had agreed with them. Hume is obviously confident that these earlier philosophers were right about this particular point. As he explains the situation, we see one billiard ball strike another, and the second ball begin to move. We say that the first ball striking the second ball caused the second to move. But we see no actual causal link or tie. Our impressions of sensation are of balls and motion related by priority and location. We have no impression of sensation of a causal link. See Malebranche, *Search* 6.2.3; *Elucidations* 15; *Dialogues on Metaphysics* 7: Boyle, *The Christian Virtuoso* (*Works*, 5:526–8); Glanvill, *Scepsis Scientifica* 23, 25; Locke, *Essay* 2.21.4; Berkeley, *Principles* 1.32.

10 leave this instance] ignore this example.

12 their *relations*] the relations of the objects considered.
already . . . establish'd] See 1.1.1.7; 1.2.3.1; 1.2.5.23; 1.3.1.7.

13 'Tis necessary . . . difficulty] Hume returns to a 'direct survey' of this question at 1.3.14.1.

14 *First* . . . cause?] After examining several existing answers to this question in 1.3.3, Hume puts it aside until 1.3.14. He helpfully summarizes his answer at 2.3.1.4 and *Abs.* 8–16.

15 *Secondly* . . . in it] At 1.3.14.1 Hume indicates that he has answered the first part of this two-part question. For this answer and his account of the inferences we draw between causes and effects and of the nature of our belief in that inference, see esp. 1.3.6–7.

16 Passions . . . together] On this topic, see 2.3.1.5 ff.

Book 1 Part 3 Sect. 3. *Why a cause is always necessary*

Hume argues that, while it is widely held that the maxim '*whatever begins to exist, must have a cause of existence*' is intuitively true, the maxim fails to meet the standard of intuition set out in 1.3.1. Nor can the maxim be demonstrated, for we can conceive of an object beginning to exist without joining to that conception or idea the further idea of a cause. We find, in fact, that every purported demonstration of the principle is fallacious; each such demonstration presupposes exactly what is to be proven, namely, that a cause is always necessary to any beginning of existence. Nor is it satisfactory to claim that, because *cause* and *effect* are relative terms, every effect must have a cause. Given that the maxim does not derive from intuition or demonstration, it must derive from experience. How does experience give rise to it? Hume suggests that we can best answer this question by determining why we think that specific causes have specific effects, and why we draw inferences from causes to effects or effects to causes.

1 This is commonly . . . demanded] Those who appear to take this maxim for granted include Hobbes, *Elements of Philosophy* 2.9; *Leviathan* 1.12; Locke, *Letter*, in *Works*, 4:61–2; Clarke, *Demonstration*, Prop. 1.
intuition] For Hume's view of intuition, see 1.3.1.2.
above-explain'd] See 1.3.1.1–3.

3 the foregoing proposition] the proposition under review in this section, namely, *whatever begins to exist, must have a cause of existence*.
never demonstrate] For Hume's understanding of demonstration, see 1.3.1.2. Hume argues that, because the ideas of cause and effect are distinguishable (because any

apparent effect can be conceived without its associated cause), it is impossible to provide a demonstrative proof that every event or entity that looks like an effect has a cause.

4 n. 17 **Mr.** *Hobbes*] See Hobbes, *Liberty and Necessity* in *English Works*, 4:276. See also *Elements of Philosophy* 2.8.19; 2.9.8; and *Dialogues* (*English Works*, 7:85).

5 n. 18 **Dr.** *Clarke* **and others**] See Clarke, *Demonstration*, Prop. 1; Seth Ward, *Philosophical Essay* 1 [16–17].

6 n. 19 **Mr.** *Locke*] See the *Essay* 4.10.3. The criticized argument is more clearly set out in Clarke, *Demonstration*, Prop. 1.

has nothing for its cause] has for its cause that which is non-existent.

7 **foregoing**] the two preceding arguments.

8 **They are . . . effect**] Possibly a further allusion to Locke, who argued that our idea of 'beginning to be, is necessarily connected with the idea of some operation; and the idea of operation, with the idea of something operating, which we call a cause', and then says that the principle that '*every thing that has a beginning must have a cause*, is a true principle of reason', and known to be certainly true (*Letter*, in *Works*, 4:61–2).

9 **scientific reasoning**] demonstration.

opinion of] belief in.

The next question . . . *another*] For a list of Hume's questions about the causal relation and the locations of his answers, see Ed. Intro., 129–36.

future enquiry] the sections that follow, esp. 1.3.4–7.

Book 1 Part 3 Sect. 4. *Of the component parts of our reasonings concerning cause and effect*

When we reason from causes or effects we go beyond present or remembered experience. From a present cause we infer a yet-to-occur effect, or from a present effect we infer a no-longer-present cause. We also believe in these absent effects or causes. This belief depends ultimately on some impression of the senses or of memory.

1 **immediate perception**] An immediate perception is simply a perception that is at this moment present to the mind. Hume goes on to argue that our causal reasonings are dependent upon immediate perceptions of sense or memory, for, in the absence of such a perception, we would be caught up in an unending chain of thought without belief.

impression of the memory] It is presumably because *ideas* of memory have substantial force and vivacity (see 1.1.3.1), and thus have an effect like that of certain impressions, that Hume now begins to treat them as 'equivalent to impressions' and even to call them *impressions* of memory.

2 **by a visible gradation . . . event**] In rhetoric, *gradation* referred to a series of considerations, 'rising by degrees, and improving on each other' (Chambers, *Cyclopædia*, 'Gradation'). By way of illustrating that the chain of causes must end at some present impression, Hume suggests that the testimony of those closer to an event is noticeably more credible or forceful than the testimony of those who come later.

Book 1 Part 3 Sect. 5. *Of the impressions of the senses and memory*

The three component parts or elements of our reasonings concerning cause and effect are an original impression, an idea, and a transition or inference from the impression to that idea. Hume notes that it is impossible for us to account for our original impressions of sensation. We do not know if these arise from objects, from some creative power of our own minds, or from actions of the deity. Nor does it matter. Whatever the source of these impressions, we can make inferences as a result of the coherent patterns which they are found to have. We are then reminded that the perceptions of memory are more forceful or livelier than those of the imagination. The perceptions of memory generally *feel* different from those of the imagination. From this fact it appears that the belief which accompanies the senses and memory is nothing more than the force or liveliness of the perceptions they present to us.

1 **produc'd by it**] Note that Hume's account of causal reasoning is intended to explain inferences from effects to causes as well as from causes to effects.

2 **they arise . . . object**] This is the position taken by the many philosophers (Locke, for example) who suppose our impressions of sensation are caused by external objects.
produc'd by . . . mind] This possibility is suggested by Descartes in *Meditations* 3.
deriv'd from . . . being] Hume puts in very general terms the view of Malebranche and the Occasionalists. Malebranche lays out the three possibilities mentioned by Hume, but distinguishes two senses in which (what Hume calls) impressions of sensation could be said to derive from the Deity: either 'God has produced them in us while creating the soul or produces them every time we think about a given object' or else (as Malebranche went on to argue) 'the soul is joined to a completely perfect being that contains all . . . the ideas of created beings' (*Search* 3.2.1.2; see also 3.2.6; and *Elucidations* 6, 10, 15).
We may . . . senses] Hume argues that, whatever may be the source of our impressions of sensation (a question that cannot be answered with certainty), the manner or order in which these impressions present themselves enables us to make causal inferences.

3 **feigning . . . adventures**] Feigning here is conscious invention; contrast 1.4.2.40–1.

4 **they become . . . memory**] The ideas come to have, that is, a greater force and vivacity, or intensity, than they had when they were considered fabrications of the imagination.

5 **much decay'd**] Hobbes had defined memory as 'decaying sense'. See *Leviathan* 1.2; see also Locke, *Essay* 2.10.4–5.

7 **first act . . . judgment**] Belief, understood as an act of assent, was widely taken to be the first act of the judgement. Hume offers a revised manner of understanding that act; see also his note to 1.3.7.5.

Book 1 Part 3 Sect. 6. *Of the inference from the impression to the idea*

Our causal inferences are not the effect of reason or of the direct inspection of the qualities of objects. It is by experience only (by the recognition that the behaviour of objects follows uniform patterns or constant conjunctions) that we can come to infer the existence of one object from another. But past uniformities of behaviour cannot provide a secure basis for a demonstrative argument that our future experience will conform to that of the past; neither could past or present intuitions of a causal connection provide such a basis. It is the imagination that enables us to make inferences from a present impression to an absent effect or cause. The inferences in question are brought about by means of the principles of association that guide that faculty. After we have experienced events or objects of one type (*A*) repeatedly followed by events of another type (*B*), the principles of association lead the mind to have an idea of type *B* upon the experience of an impression of type *A*, or an idea of type *A* upon the experience of an impression of type *B*.

1 **this relation**] the relation of cause and effect; see the end of the previous paragraph.
   objects] that is, from those items we identify as causes or effects.
2 **'Tis therefore . . . another**] Hume here sets out to answer the first of the questions posed at 1.3.2.15 (and repeated at 1.3.3.9).
   and infer . . . other] That is, we begin to presume from the present impression of the one kind of event or object (rain, or the cause) that the second kind of event or object (wet streets, or the effect) is or will be available to experience. Or, we begin to presume from the present impression of an event or object of the second type (wet streets, the effect) that an event or object of the first type (rain, or the cause) is or was available to experience. (For further discussion of this aspect of Hume's theory, see Ed. Intro., I29–35).
3 **insensibly**] without at first noticing the fact.
   new relation] See 1.3.2.6–11, where the discovery of the three other relations, contiguity, succession, and necessary connection, is recounted.
   quitting . . . relation] Hume quit the 'direct survey' at 1.3.2.13; see also 1.3.14.1.
   and can only multiply . . . mind] can only repeat existing perceptions but not produce any new ones.
   Perhaps . . . connexion] For more on this possibility, see this section, ¶¶13–15; and 1.3.14.20, 26.
4 *of which . . . no experience*] of which we have had no experience in the sense that these instances have not yet occurred, or have occurred beyond the range of our direct experience. We have had, for example, no experience of tomorrow, nor of its sunrise (should it have one), nor of many past events.
5 **Our foregoing . . . reasoning**] See 1.3.3.3.
6 **discovers not**] here, something like *does not apply to*. Hume goes on to call our attention to a further difference between (1) those relations that depend entirely upon ideas, and (2) those relations that may be changed without any change in ideas or objects (see 1.3.1.1). Relations of the second type produce belief, provided (among other things) that an impression of sense or memory makes up one term of the relation.
   And were . . . reasoning] Compare 1.3.2.2, where 'perception' is described.
7 **just inference . . . another**] Hume repeats the claim that only the causal relation provides a satisfactory ('just') foundation for inferences from 'immediate impressions of our memory and senses' to ideas of absent effects or causes; see also 1.3.2.2–3.
   we thence presume . . . attendant] We conclude, that is, that the object of type *A* that we are presently experiencing will be accompanied by a second object, an object of type *B*, which will resemble those objects that have in the past accompanied objects of type *A*.
   probability . . . probability] Because probability depends on the presumption that previously unexperienced instances will resemble experienced instances, it cannot be that this presumption depends on the probability.
9 **already made**] See 1.3.2.10.
   remark afterwards] See e.g. 1.3.14.
10 **already prov'd**] See 1.3.2.5, 10.
   I ask . . . qualities] Hume's question is: Given that causal power is not among the sensible qualities of an object, why do we presume, as soon as certain sensible qualities are experienced, that the causal power is present? Why do we treat these particular sensible qualities as sure signs that particular effects will follow?
   Your appeal . . . qualities] Even if in the past a given object was perceived to include the causal power that produced a given effect (so that we had perceived a direct causal

link between the object and its effect), it would not follow that the same object (or any other of the same type) has the same power now, or will have that same power in the future. Neither the senses nor reason can provide grounds for concluding that future objects or relations will be like those of the past or present. With this observation Hume lays the groundwork for what has come to be called the problem of induction. See also 1.3.12.20.

foregoing reasoning] the argument considered in this same paragraph.

12 already taken notice] See ¶¶2–3 of this section.

principles . . . imagination] On the association of ideas, see 1.1.4.

matter of fact] In *Treatise* 1.3 Hume typically uses the phrase *matter of fact* in an importantly restricted sense. He uses it to denote whatever absent effects or causes are believed in as a result of inferences from the 'immediate impressions of our memory and senses' to the (enlivened) ideas of these absent effects or causes (see also 1.3.7.2–3, 7; 1.3.8.7; App. 2; *Abs.* 8, 21). Assuming *A* and *B* (or objects or events of type *A* and type *B*) to have been constantly conjoined, so that *A* is taken to be the cause of *B*, a belief in *B* when only *A* is present (or in *A* when only *B* is present) is a belief in matter of fact or existence—a belief in the existence of the absent cause or effect represented by the *idea* to which attention is drawn and vivacity transferred. In so far as Hume uses the phrase 'matter of fact' in this restricted sense, it follows that the present explanation of our belief in matter of fact is not an explanation of why we believe there are external objects corresponding to presently experienced impressions of sensation. Impressions of sensation are by their very nature forceful and thus their force is not in need of further explanation. Moreover, Hume later says that our belief in external objects cannot be accounted for by the causal reasoning that leads to belief in matters of fact (see 1.4.2.14, 21, 47, 54), and then adds that causal reasoning and belief in external and continued existence are 'directly contrary' to one another (1.4.4.15; 1.4.7.4). On this issue, see also Ed. Intro., I38–42.

13 The principles . . . general ones] to, that is, resemblance, contiguity, and cause and effect.

For the thought . . . order] More literally, the mind has great freedom to consider ideas of all kinds in an erratic or unpredictable order. See also 1.1.4.

14 particular idea . . . word] Certain words and ideas are associated with one another in such a way that the use of a particular word calls a particular idea to mind.

The imagination . . . reflection] An act of the imagination, rather than an act of reason, accounts for the fact that a particular sound (or set of characters) immediately calls to mind a particular idea.

16 *philosophical* . . . *natural* relation] For this distinction, see 1.1.4–5.

Book 1 Part 3 Sect. 7. *Of the nature of the idea or belief*

A causal inference carries our attention from a present impression to an associated idea. When we complete such an inference we find ourselves believing in the existence of the object represented by the associated idea that has been brought to mind. Such *belief* is significantly different from mere *conception*, and yet the content of an idea *believed* is no different from that of the same idea merely *conceived*. Belief changes only the *manner* of conceiving. It changes only the force or intensity of an idea. (App. 1–9 directly and usefully supplements this section.)

1 The idea of an object] the conception of anything, whether physical or mental.

assent to] believe to represent real things.

2 'Tis evident . . . qualities] See the final annotation to 1.3.6.12. When we make an inference from the present impression of a cause or effect to the idea of an absent effect or cause, we believe that whatever entity this idea represents exists or is a matter of fact.
likewise maintain] Hume's initial statement of this view is found at 1.2.6.4.
and as this difference . . . conceive it] Hume argues that what might be called the form ('parts or composition') of ideas or conceptions is unchanged by the addition of belief. Our idea of a unicorn, for example, will be the same whether we think unicorns actually exist or are merely imaginary beasts.

3 either immediately . . . ideas] either intuitively or by demonstrative steps; see 1.3.1.2–3 for Hume's understanding of intuition and demonstration.
absolute necessity] the kind of necessity that characterizes those propositions grasped by intuition ($2 + 2 = 4$, for example), or established by demonstration (the angles of a plane triangle are equal to two right angles, for example), which itself relies on intuition. As Hume was later to say, 'When a demonstration convinces me of any proposition, it not only makes me conceive the proposition, but also makes me sensible, that 'tis impossible to conceive any thing contrary. What is demonstratively false implies a contradiction; and what implies a contradiction cannot be conceived' (*Abs.* 18). In contrast, the contraries of propositions taken to represent matter of fact can be conceived. Both 'lead is more fusible than silver' and 'silver is more fusible than lead' make perfectly good sense, as do both 'Caesar died in bed' and 'Caesar did not die in bed'. The *Abstract* is again helpful: 'with regard to any matter of fact, however strong the proof may be from experience, I can always conceive the contrary, tho' I cannot always believe it' (*Abs.* 18; see also 1.3.9.10).

4 principle] here, factor.
precedent ideas] the ideas we have previously entertained but not believed.

5 which differ . . . vivacity] In the Appendix Hume says he made a mistake 'where I say, that two ideas of the same object can only be different by their different degrees of force and vivacity. I believe there are other differences among ideas, which cannot properly be comprehended under these terms. Had I said, that two ideas of the same object can only be different by their different feeling, I shou'd have been nearer the truth' (App. 22; see also 1.3.8.11, 15).
n. 20 This error . . . of them] This commonplace division of the acts of the understanding may be observed in, among many others, Arnauld and Nicole, *Logic* 1 [23], and Watts, *Logick*, Introduction [5].

6 heads . . . arguments] chief points. Hume goes on to summarize the position he had developed in Sects. 1.3.4–7.
run up with] continue.

7 This operation . . . explaining it] At *Abs.* 4 Hume says that the failure of philosophers to address adequately the issue of 'probabilities, and those other measures of evidence on which life and action entirely depend, and which are our guides even in most of our philosophical speculations', had been noted by Leibniz.
This variety . . . unphilosophical] See also 1.3.8.15 and App. 22.
ideas of the judgment] ideas believed, that is.

8 This definition] The definition found at the end of ¶5 of this section.
putting . . . author] imputing the same meaning to the work being read.

Book 1 Part 3 Sect. 8. *Of the causes of belief*

The belief in the existence of absent effects or causes (the belief that characterizes a completed piece of causal reasoning) is ordinarily brought about when the experience of an impression brings to mind an associated idea and enlivens that idea by transferring force or feeling to it. Experiments confirm this hypothesis. Analysis of our experience also shows that this belief is immediate (unreflective); that we ordinarily do not notice the process that produces it; that because we come tacitly to hold the principle *like causes have like effects*, we sometimes come to have beliefs of this sort after only one experience of associated impressions; and that sometimes a mere idea can produce belief of this sort.

2 **spirits**] perhaps mental energies or emotions, which can be elevated (to be in 'good spirits') or depressed (to be in 'low spirits'), or an allusion to animal spirits as explained by e.g. Descartes or Malebranche; see *Principles of Philosophy* 4.190 or *Search* 5.3 [347–8]. **action**] here, operation of the mind. See also 1.4.5.27.

3 **experiment**] For Hume's understanding of this important concept, see Intro. 8 and the Glossary. **intended for him**] intended to be a picture of him.

4 **experiments of the same nature**] further evidence of the same sort. **in excuse of the mummeries**] in explanation of what appear to be fanciful ceremonies or rites that imitate events or objects important to their faith. **shadow out . . . images**] use statues and pictures, for example, as visible, tangible representations of an object of worship. **a resemblance . . . concur**] whenever an *idea* is enlivened by resemblance, a resembling *impression* is on hand. **foregoing principle**] the maxim found in ¶2 of this section.

5 **n. 21 *Naturane . . . disciplina***] Piso, a character in one of Cicero's dialogues, describes how his ideas of ancient philosophers are enlivened as he stands near the site of Plato's original Academy. This illustrates the way in which contiguity enlivens our ideas: 'Thereupon Piso remarked: "Whether it is a natural instinct or a mere illusion, I can't say; but one's emotions are more strongly aroused by seeing the places that tradition records to have been the favourite resort of men of note in former days, than by hearing about their deeds or reading their writings. My own feelings at the present moment are a case in point. I am reminded of Plato, the first philosopher, so we are told, that made a practice of holding discussions in this place; and indeed the garden close at hand yonder not only recalls his memory but seems to bring the actual man before my eyes. This was the haunt of Speusippus, of Xenocrates, and of Xenocrates' pupil Polemo, who used to sit on the very seat we see over there. For my own part even the sight of our senate-house at home (I mean the Curia Hostilia, not the present new building, which looks to my eyes smaller since its enlargement) used to call up to me thoughts of Scipio, Cato, Laelius, and chief of all, my grandfather; such powers of suggestion do places possess. No wonder the scientific training of the memory is based upon locality" ' (*De finibus* 5.1.2).

6 **precedent definition of it**] See 1.3.6.15; 1.3.7.5.

8 **Here 'tis evident . . . producing it**] Hume temporarily adopts the perspective of a natural philosopher who supposes that objects themselves are presented to the senses, and that the experience of one such object results, in the usual way of causal reasoning, in the belief in a second. He then argues that, because the powers and qualities of external objects are unknown to us, it is not these powers that cause this belief. Rather, it is a present impression that causes us to have the relevant idea, and which gives to that idea the intensity or feeling that constitutes belief.

9 **We must . . . impression**] Although it is an impression that causes us to think of a particular idea, and to believe that what that idea represents will come to be, an impression,

occurring only once, would not (typically) cause us to believe in this way. An impression currently being experienced can have the relevant effect only if in the past impressions resembling this one (impressions of a single type, A) have been routinely followed by impressions of another type (type B). If that has happened, then, when I next experience an impression of type A, I will be led to *think* of impressions of type B (I will have an idea of type B) even if I do not actually have an impression of type B. In addition, I will believe that the entity represented by the idea of type B actually exists or is about to exist.

10 from that origin] from custom.

11 correlative idea] The correlative idea is simply the idea usually associated with the idea to which we are presently attending. When impressions of type A and type B have been customarily associated as cause and effect, the thought or idea of an A will bring to mind a thought or idea of the correlative, B; likewise, the idea of a B will bring to mind the idea of the correlative, A.

whole operation] the operation of the mind that results in belief in an absent effect or cause.

12 Thus all probable . . . sensation] Probable reasoning includes all those 'operations of the mind' that begin with a present impression of the senses or memory, and that result, because there is a transfer of force or feeling, in the belief in an idea. When I see that, although the sun is shining, everything outside my window is thoroughly wet (an effect), I have the idea of rain (a cause), and believe that it has recently rained. Reasoning of this sort may be said to be a kind of 'sensation' because the idea that one is brought to believe in has the force or feeling of an impression of sensation. The idea believed *feels* like a sensation. Moreover, the transfer of attention from impression to idea, although sometimes called by Hume an 'inference', is more akin to an act of sensation than to an act of reflective or demonstrative reasoning, a point emphasized in the following paragraph. See also e.g. 1.3.2.2; 1.3.6.6; 1.4.1.8.

13 and not from . . . ideas] not from any direct or perceived link between the idea of sinking and the idea of suffocation.

principle, *that . . . have*] See 1.3.6.5.

14 uniform conjunctions . . . solidity, *&c.*] constant conjunctions that are the subject of the physical sciences, in other words.

reflection] conscious consideration of a single experience.

'Tis certain . . . circumstances] On this point, see also 1.3.15.6.

15 perfect propriety] complete accuracy.

ambiguity . . . *strong and lively*] See also 1.3.7.7 and App. 22.

For as this idea . . . existence] Whatever else may be said of any perception, each one is a real item in the mind. Even a mere idea is an existing entity, and, considered as such, has some force or liveliness that may be transferred to some associated or correlative idea, thus causing that idea to have force and to be believed.

Book 1 Part 3 Sect. 9. *Of the effects of other relations and other habits*

It may seem that the remaining principles of association (resemblance and contiguity) produce belief, and hence that it is a mistake to claim that belief in matter of fact 'arises only from causation' (¶2). We find, however, that while resemblance and contiguity do play an important role in the production of such belief, even to the point of being necessary conditions of it, their role is only a supporting one and one that presupposes causation. Causation, or customary association, connects our impressions with a regularity and necessity the other two relations cannot provide. Only causation can bring us to believe that there are existences beyond our current impressions and memories.

1 foregoing arguments] the arguments of 1.3.5–8.
2 often observ'd] See 1.1.4.1; 1.3.6.13.
also observ'd] See 1.3.8.3–5.
3 **Of these impressions . . . a *reality*]** Our impressions or ideas of memory form a first coherent set of perceptions that are taken to be real.
For finding . . . of *realities*] There is a second coherent set of perceptions that we treat as real. This set, the focus or object of our causal inferences or judgements, is made up of those believed ideas that are unavoidably connected, by causal inferences, to the first set of perceptions mentioned (see previous annotation). The discussion here amplifies Hume's earlier claim that the relation of causation is the only one that enables us to 'discover' real existences beyond those immediately present to us (see 1.3.2.2).
5 presently] in the following paragraph.
Elysian fields] Elysium or the Islands of the Blest, where, according to classical myth, favoured individuals have a blissful afterlife.
6 **when single]** when operating without aid from the relation of causation.
There is . . . objects] While the mind can arbitrarily think of an idea related by resemblance or contiguity to any current impression, there is no determination of mind ('no manner of necessity') that brings this about. In contrast, the relation of causation (as Hume has already argued and argues again in the next paragraph) does determine the mind to pass from impressions to ideas, and even from particular impressions to particular ideas.
9 *Red-Sea . . . Evangelists*] See Exod. 14 for an account of the miraculous separation of the waters of the Red Sea that allowed the Israelites, under the leadership of Moses, to escape the pursuing Egyptians. Two miracles, making water drinkable and the provision of food (manna) in the desert, are described in Exod. 15: 22–5 and 16: 4–36. Matthew, Mark, Luke, and John, traditionally taken to be the authors of the first four books of the New Testament, are called the Evangelists. See John 20: 1–18 for an account of the miracle of Christ's resurrection at Jerusalem. For the miracle of Christ walking on the Sea of Galilee, see John 6: 16–21.
10 have remark'd] See 1.3.2.5 and 1.3.6.1.
yet some philosophers . . . observation] Hobbes takes as an 'axiom' the proposition that 'whatsoever body being at rest is afterwards moved, hath for its immediate movement some other body which is in motion and toucheth it' (*Dialogues*, in *English Works* 7:86).
its rest] the rest of the first or moving body; as the remainder of the sentence reveals, Hume is imagining possible behaviour of the moving object, and not effects on the second, or struck, object.
consistent and natural] within the range of reactions experienced in other circumstances, and hence not abnormal or bizarre.
11 'Tis universally . . . chamber] See Berkeley, *New Theory of Vision* 82. By 'physical points' Hume apparently means what Berkeley called 'visible points' or minimum visibles. On the latter, see 1.2.1.3–4.
13 universal carelessness . . . future state] unconcern and indifference about how or where one will spend eternity, assuming that there is an afterlife. See also 2.3.7.3.
that many eminent . . . souls] Pascal had said: 'Our imagination so magnifies the present, because we are continually thinking about it, and so reduces eternity, because

we do not think about it, that we turn eternity into nothing . . .' (*Pensées* 432; see also 427). Addison had said: 'Nothing can be a greater Disgrace to Reason, than that Men, who are perswaded of these two different States of Being [this life and an afterlife], should be so perpetually employed in providing for a Life of threescore and ten Years, and neglecting to make Provision for that, which after many Myriads of Years, will be still new . . .'. The problem, Addison goes on to say, is that our reason is overcome by the imagination (*Spectator* 575).

13 **strongest figures**] most vivid representations. Hume argues that even the most vivid depictions of hell are inadequate to impress the mind with the enormity of eternal damnation.

inculcated on] to inculcate was to 'repeat and insist on often; as it were to beat a thing into a Person's Brains' (Bailey, *Dictionary*).

14 **want . . . this case**] the lack of resemblance between the experiences of this life and the projections made regarding the forms of life after death.

immortality of the soul] Hume's views on this topic are found in his essay, 'Of the Immortality of the Soul', which he may at one time have intended to include in the *Treatise*.

Gunpowder-treason] the failed plot of a few English Roman Catholics to blow up the Houses of Parliament while the king, Lords, and Commons were assembled on 5 Nov. 1605. The conspirators hoped that the ensuing turmoil would allow them to seize control of the country. The plot was found out, and one of the conspirators, Guy Fawkes (for whom the day still commemorating the event is named), was seized as he entered the cellar of Parliament where thirty-six barrels of gunpowder had been hidden.

massacre of St. *Bartholomew*] In 1572 the festival day (24 Aug.) honouring St Bartholomew marked the beginning of a massacre of French Protestants, first in Paris and then throughout France.

15 **penetrated with the solidity**] affected by the reality.

reposes . . . indolently] considers indifferently, so that the relevant idea is only conceived, not believed.

16 **loose floating . . . fancy**] random, or accidentally associated ideas.

foregoing explication . . . satisfactory] For Hume's earlier account of belief as the effect of transfers of attention and vivacity, see 1.3.5–8, esp. 1.3.5.6–7; 1.3.7.7; 1.3.8.13.

17 **We must . . . same**] We must conclude that vividness and the belief are the same thing.

supply the place of] supplant, take the place of.

19 **n. 22 In general . . . meaning**] This note was prepared after Book 1 of the *Treatise* had been printed. It was added to the text by replacing the original leaf (an original two-sided page) with a revised leaf (called a *cancel*). On the relation of the imagination and understanding, see also 1.4.7.7.

Book 1 Part 3 Sect. 10. *Of the influence of belief*

Pain and pleasure motivate us in one of two ways: when actually felt (directly, through impressions) or when thought of (indirectly, through ideas). It is not every idea that influences our actions, but those that we believe to represent real existences can or do have a motivating influence roughly equivalent to that of an impression. Literary representations can produce enlivened ideas, but however lively these ideas are, they fail to motivate us to action because they *feel* different from those ideas that are believed.

1 education . . . philosophy] The reasons for this rejection of education are found in 1.3.9.13, 16–19.

   passions . . . beauty] The passions are the subject of Book 2. There is no substantial discussion of the sense of beauty in the *Treatise* as published, and the term *sense of beauty* occurs only at 2.1.1.3; 2.2.11.2, 4; 3.3.1.8; and 3.3.6.1. A discussion of the sense of beauty would likely have been a part of the examination of criticism Hume mentions in the Advertisement to Books 1 and 2; see also the final annotation to Note 71.2 (3.2.3.4).

2 Nature . . . actions] A capacity to feel pleasure and pain is a part of human nature, and the principal motivation of our actions.

4 prevailing passion] According to a widely held theory of Hume's time, each human, although subject to many different passions, is most under the influence of a single, predominating passion, or character trait.

   meet with . . . faith] are more easily believed.

   acquainted . . . treatise] Hume may be thinking of his earlier remarks about the enlivening of religious ideas. For these, see 1.3.8.2–7; 1.3.9.8–9. He may also be alluding to an essay, 'Of Miracles', which he at one time thought of including in the *Treatise*. This essay was not published until 1748, in the work now known as *An Enquiry concerning Human Understanding*.

5 poets . . . profession] Johnson says that a poet is 'an inventor; an author of fiction'. Dryden said a poet elevates the elements of poetic inventions (plot, wit, character, and passions) 'as high as the imagination of the poet can carry them' while still maintaining some verisimilitude. Raleigh says simply that 'Poets are lyars' (*History of the World* [2:466]). Much earlier Plato was concerned that poets tell untruths about the gods (*Republic* 377–83c).

6 poetical system of things] the framework provided by established myths and legends.

   MARS, JUPITER, VENUS] the principal deities of the Romans.

7 system] Hume's hypothesis or theory regarding belief.

   so many pipes or canals] Although Hume indicates he is speaking metaphorically, he would have known that some anatomists had argued that the mind does literally include minute pipes or canals 'through which the juices of the body flow' (Johnson, *Dictionary*), and that the operations of mind and body are to be understood by attention to mechanics and hydraulics. See e.g. James Keill, *Essays on several Parts of the Animal Œconomy*. For an alternative metaphor, see 1.2.5.20.

9 they] the operations of the imagination.

   When the imagination . . . passions] Those theories that explained the passions by movement of the animal spirits attributed heightened feeling to an increase in the motion of the blood and these spirits. Hume's discussion here echoes that found in Malebranche, *Search* 2.1.1.1.

10 species of probability] Locke and others had distinguished degrees or levels of knowledge, evidence, and probability. Hume here assumes that there are different degrees or levels of probability having or providing different levels of belief or assurance. Earlier he had indicated that *knowledge* and *probability* constitute distinctive levels of assurance or 'degrees of evidence' (see 1.3.6.4).

10 **apparent agitation of the mind**] degree or level of emotion. The force of belief, although attended with less emotion or feeling, may typically surpass the force of poetic fictions. Hume later argues that a calm passion may be stronger than a violent one, and that a weaker moral sentiment may mark greater virtue than does a stronger sentiment of the same kind. See 2.3.3.8; 2.3.4.1; 3.3.1.16.

11 **afterwards . . . conviction**] This may also be an allusion to the projected examination of criticism. In the *Treatise* as published, there is nothing further on the difference between 'poetical enthusiasm' and 'serious conviction'.
general rules] For more on this topic, see 1.3.13.7–14.

Book 1 Part 3 Sect. 11. *Of the probability of chances*

Varying 'degrees of evidence' or assurance characterize knowledge and probability (¶2). Knowledge was the topic of 1.3.1. The generic type *probability* includes 'proof' (which provides a relatively high level of assurance) and (somewhat confusingly) 'probability' (which provides a weaker level of assurance). A proof is the result of an extensive and uniform experience. Such an experience gives rise to inferences that are merely probable because it is always possible that the course of events will change (some humans might not die, for example). However, such an extensive and uniform experience, because it leaves us with no grounds for doubt or uncertainty, leaves us fully assured. In contrast to proof, 'probability' is the result of a less than uniform experience. Such experience may produce assurance, but in these cases our assurance will be accompanied or moderated by some degree of uncertainty. Probability may also be considered as deriving from chance or from causes. Chance is the negation of cause. To say that an event is the result of chance is to say that no particular cause can be assigned to that event. But, because for even those events for which no particular cause can be assigned, some causal forces appear to be at work, force and vivacity are transferred to our ideas of undetermined outcomes (to our ideas of each of the six sides of a thrown die, for example). Consequently, we believe that one of these seemingly uncaused events will take place (we have a relatively weak belief that any one side of the die will come up). We can also be brought to believe that some such undetermined outcomes are more likely than others.

1 **this system**] the system of belief outlined in 1.3.8–10.
2 **Those philosophers . . . *probability***] Hume apparently has Locke and his followers in mind; for Locke's discussions of knowledge and probability, see the *Essay* 4.1–2 and 4.15. For an earlier version of the distinction between knowledge and probability, see Wilkins, *Principles and Duties of Natural Religion*, ch. 1.
sun will rise to-morrow] Much the same point, regarding the same example, is made by Wilkins, who, granting that there is a possibility of error regarding any matter of fact, none the less asks, 'Who is there so wildly Sceptical as to question whether the Sun shall rise in the East, and not in the North or West, or whether it shall rise at all?' (*Principles and Duties of Natural Religion*, ch. 1; see also Tillotson, 'Wisdom of being Religious'.)
all men must dye] Pascal had asked, 'Who ever proved that it will dawn tomorrow, and that we shall die?' (*Pensées* 821).
knowledge . . . proofs . . . probabilities] This three-part classification had been suggested by a writer Hume knew personally, Andrew Michael Ramsay: 'The source of *Pyrrhonism* is frequently the not distinguishing between *Demonstration, Proof & Probability*. A *Demonstration* is where the contradictory is impossible: A *Proof* where there

are strong reasons for believing, and none against it: a *Probability*, where the reasons for believing are stronger than those for doubting' (*New Cyropædia; or, The Travels of Cyrus* 6).

4 without . . . violence] without feeling that we are acting contrary to the course of nature.

as chance . . . cause] 'For Chance is but a mere Name, and really Nothing in it self' (Bentley, *Sermons*, Sermon 5 [9]); '*Chance* seems to be only a term, by which we express our *ignorance* of the cause of any thing' (William Wollaston, *Religion of Nature Delineated* 5.14).

5 establish'd] hypothesized.

but is acknowledg'd . . . chances] In his *The Doctrine of Chances* De Moivre appears to presuppose, rather than explicitly acknowledge, the 'total indifference' of which Hume speaks. Chambers begins a relatively long discussion of gambling by noting that gamblers begin, or at least are supposed to begin, with equal (or indifferent) chances to win (*Cyclopædia*, 'Gaming').

6 Thus unless . . . hazard] Hume argues that, although the outcome of some events may be entirely contingent, or a matter of chance, we could not calculate probabilities did not certain settled background conditions prevail. If we could not rely on gravity and the continued existence of the die itself, we could not calculate the odds of throwing one of the figures on the die. Our normal probable reasoning leads us to the conclusion that the die will continue to exist, will preserve its form through its fall and motion across the table top, and will come to rest with one face uppermost. If we suppose these causal patterns will prevail, and that no other factors determine the fall of the die (if it is a fair die, fairly thrown), we can then calculate the odds of throwing any given face (see ¶10 of this section). *Hazard*, by the way, was the name of a particular game of chance.

7 arguments we employ'd] arguments found in 1.3.8.

opposition of chances] counterbalancing or contrariety of outcomes; see ¶¶4–5 of this section.

8 The likelihood . . . consequence] On Hume's die (see ¶9 of this section) four sides are marked with one figure (X), and two with another (Y). To say there is 'a superior number of equal chances' (or a greater probability) that one will throw an X rather than a Y is simply to say that there are four chances of throwing an X and two of throwing a Y.

The question . . . assent] Hume now turns to answering the question: How does such a superiority of chances produce a superiority of belief? How does it happen that we believe, and act as though, an X is more likely than a Y?

9 He in . . . contrary] The belief that one of four Xs will come up is balanced by the realization that one of two Ys may come up. If there were five Xs and only one Y, the belief that an X will come up would be even stronger.

11 already observ'd] See 1.3.6.

places . . . table] imagines the die as falling to the table.

12 When therefore . . . possible] In the circumstances described, there is no causal factor that makes one outcome more likely than another.

but it directs . . . them] The imagination supposes it equally likely that any one of the six sides will be uppermost after the die is thrown. Thus, to the possibility that any particular side will be uppermost it apportions one-sixth of the belief that the die is 'necessarily determin'd to fall, and turn up one of its sides'.

the original impulse] here, the initial tendency or disposition to think the die will fall and come to rest. At 1.3.12.10 Hume calls such an impulse a 'determination' of the mind.

13 **and must unite . . . inscrib'd]** Each face marked by an X receives one-sixth of the total belief available, but the imagination (when dealing with Hume's die) notices there are four Xs, and as a consequence unites four of its expectations about particular sides coming up. This creates a four-times stronger belief that the figure X (rather than any particular X) will be uppermost. Each face marked by a Y has a similar effect, but as there are only two such sides, this creates only a two-times stronger belief that the figure Y (rather than any particular Y) will turn up.

But as . . . its strength goes] Hume unexpectedly argues that our stronger expectation that the figure X will be uppermost is related to our weaker expectation that the figure Y will be uppermost as a larger number is related to a smaller number subtracted from it. The two Y-tending impulses destroy or cancel out two X-tending impulses, so that our net expectation in this case is as 4 minus 2. As he later says, 'the mind is determin'd to the superior only with that force, which remains after substracting the inferior' (1.3.12.19). On this account, our expectation that Hume's die will come to rest with an X uppermost will have a strength equivalent to two-sixths of our expectation that the die will fall and come to rest with some one of the six sides uppermost. Even more surprisingly, we would presumably have no expectation that a Y will be thrown.

Book 1 Part 3 Sect. 12. *Of the probability of causes*

Three kinds of probability, derived from (1) imperfect experience, (2) contrary causes, and (3) analogy (¶25), are supposed by philosophers to be acceptable bases of belief (see 1.3.13.1). Hume begins by outlining the process by which we develop a perfect habit of transferring the past to the future. If experience were always uniform it would always (in due course) produce proofs. But experience is not always uniform, and when it is not, the beliefs it produces are weaker or hesitating—either because past experience has produced only a weak expectation of what will follow a given event (imperfect experience), or because a given impression arouses conflicting ideas (contrary causes), and transfers some vivacity to each of these ideas. When there are two such conflicting ideas, each with some measure of force and vivacity, the two cancel one another in the manner of subtraction. The larger, that is, is reduced by the amount of the smaller, with the consequence that the force and vivacity of (or belief in) the larger is reduced and weakened, while (presumably) the smaller loses all force and vivacity.

1 **since 'tis commonly . . . cause]** According to Chambers, 'some vainly imagine, that *Chance* it self can be the cause of any thing . . . *Chance* is frequently personified, and erected into a chimerical being, whom we conceive as acting arbitrarily, and producing all the effects, whose real causes do not appear to us . . .' (*Cyclopædia*, 'Chance').

3 **'Tis worthy . . . with it]** Hume is here focusing on the entrenched habit, acquired early in life, of engaging in causal reasoning, something we do because of a natural tendency to associate ideas with present impressions. Although adults cannot remember when they gained this habit, it has in them reached a level of perfection in the sense that they suppose every event to have a cause, and think they can determine particular causes from a single, appropriately prepared experiment.

another observation] This is the observation that a cause is always necessary, or that every beginning of existence has a cause, or so we have come to believe.

second species . . . observation] the species of probability that never reaches the level of proof or perfect certainty because the relevant experience is not entirely uniform; see also 1.3.11.2.

4 contrariety of events] lack of uniformity among events.

5 The vulgar . . . operation] Ordinary individuals suppose that the course of events is uncertain because, in effect, the course of nature is irregular. In contrast, Hume goes on to say, philosophers suppose that the course of events only appears to be uncertain because we humans lack the ability to detect remote or subtle causes.
they remark] the philosophers notice.

7 this principle] that regarding the imperfect habits.
probable reasonings] those probable reasonings, reflecting an experience less than perfectly uniform, that contrast with proofs; see 1.3.11.2.

10 The first . . . impulse] The initial impulse or determination of mind described in the preceding paragraph is diverted into several conflicting possible outcomes, in the manner described in 1.3.11.9–12. Our basic belief that the future will resemble the past is channelled into two or more outcomes, and our belief in each outcome is proportioned in accordance with our relevant past experience.

11 If our . . . first proportions] Hume is explaining how the force and vivacity produced by past experience function to enliven our judgements (or, in other words, to determine our beliefs) about future events of a like kind. To use his example, if from the many ships that have gone to sea we wish to draw an inference about ships now going to sea, we must overcome a tendency to split and divert the belief (the transferable force and vivacity) experience has produced. If we do so, if we focus this belief on a particular ship now going to sea, we will have, given that 95 per cent of ships have safely returned in the past, a lively belief regarding the safe return of this ship.
fully explain'd] See 1.3.11, esp. ¶13.

13 Just reasoning . . . subtile] Hume interjects a brief justification of refined or abstruse reasoning.

15 been observ'd] See 1.3.11.5–6.

16 *Thirdly* . . . the cause] See 1.3.15.9, rule 7; on causes of a mixed nature, see 2.3.1.17.
Thus because . . . whole] Hume appears to be following Cotes's account of gravity: 'the attractive force of the entire bodies arises from and is composed of the attractive forces of the parts, because . . . if the bulk of the matter be augmented or diminished, its power is proportionately augmented or diminished. We must therefore conclude that the action of the earth is composed of the united actions of its parts' (Cotes, Preface to Newton's *Principia*, 2nd edn [pp. xxii]). On compound effects, see 1.3.15.9.

19 whether . . . entire] whether part of a perfectly uniform experience.
preserves itself entire] remains wholly separate; remains the idea of a single, distinct object.

20 throw them so loose] free them from belief.

22 and their . . . antagonists] and as the number of instances that suggest one outcome is greater than that which suggests the contrary outcome.

23 *undesign'd*] unplanned; not undertaken with an intention of creating belief.
n. 23 Sects. 9, 10] See 1.3.9–10.
better afterwards] See 1.4.2.31–6.

24 above-mention'd] See ¶16 of this section.
explain presently] See 1.3.13.7–13.

25 ANALOGY] Hume is here concerned with that form of probable reasoning that depends on a less than perfect resemblance between the impressions and ideas

involved. His basic theory is that, from repeated experience of events of type *A* followed by events of type *B*, we come, on the experience of another *A*, to infer that another *B* will follow. But suppose that we now experience an event of type *A'*, an event that is importantly like, and yet different from, events of type *A*. From this experience we may infer (believe) that an event of type *B'* (an event that is importantly like, and yet different from, events of type *B*) will follow. *A* and *A'*, and *B* and *B'*, are in such cases only *analogous* (alike in some important respects, but not perfectly resembling). For this reason, Hume concludes, the probability of, and level of belief in, any inference from *A'* to *B'* is less than the probability of, and level of belief in, the inference from any *A* to any *B*.

25 **above-explain'd**] See 1.3.4–8.
above-explain'd] See 1.3.11 and the preceding paragraphs of this section.

Book 1 Part 3 Sect. 13. *Of unphilosophical probability*

This section focuses on factors that have a significant effect on the intensity of beliefs, but that do so for dubious or unsatisfactory ('unphilosophical') reasons. For example, a lively impression or memory produces greater assurance than does a faint one. Long and involved arguments produce beliefs less firm than those produced by shorter and simpler arguments. Our tendency to form and follow general rules leads us to convictions that are stronger than our evidence for them warrants. A single unambiguous impression produces a clearer or stronger opinion than do many ambiguous impressions leading to the same conclusion. Hume argues that each of these unphilosophical ways of behaving is consistent with, and explained by, the theory set out in the *Treatise*.

1 **receiv'd**] judged acceptable.
union] association.
above-explained] See 1.3.12, esp. ¶¶6–12, 25.
foregoing system] See 1.3.7.
3 **long chain . . . esteem'd**] See 1.4.1 for more on this subject.
evidence] here, assurance or feeling of conviction; a quality of evidentness.
4 **Republic of Letters**] See the final annotation to 1.1.7.1.
thousand ages] 100,000 years, an age being equivalent to 100 years.
5 **celebrated argument . . . *Religion***] John Craig had argued that the credibility or persuasive force of the evidence for Christianity, passed from person to person, would be completely exhausted by about AD 3150 (*Rules of Historical Evidence*, 1.18.11 [27]). In opposition, the anonymous author of 'A Calculation of the Credibility of Human Testimony', maintained that a 'written Tradition' preserved by only a single set of successive copies will not lose half its credibility until at least 7,000, perhaps 14,000, years have passed, and if this tradition is preserved by concurrent successive copies, its credibility may by then have actually increased (*Philosophical Transactions*, No. 257 (1699)).
n. 24 Part 4. Sect. 1] See 1.4.1.8–11.
7 **PREJUDICE**] In Hume's time this term was less pejorative than it now is. For Bailey, a *prejudice* is simply a prejudgement, 'a rash Judgement made before a Matter is duly considered' (*Dictionary*), and not an entrenched bias.
solidity] good sense, firmness of purpose, reliability.
dunces or fops] Dunces lack wit or intelligence; fops lack solidity, or seriousness of purpose.
this nation] Great Britain.

8 accounted for] See 1.3.12.25.
10 To illustrate . . . experience] The example is found in Montaigne's *Apology for Raymond Sebond* (*Essays* 2.12 [449]), and is repeated in modified form by Pascal (*Pensées* 44). Malebranche undertakes to explain the phenomenon in *Search* 2.1.5, esp. sect. 2.
11 all reasonings] all reasonings from experience, that is.
   as to render . . . former] as to cause it to reach a conclusion contrary to that of the judgement.
   n. 25 Sect. 15] See 1.3.15.
14 by signs . . . of it] Hume emphasizes that we do not have direct access to the feelings or opinions (the sentiments) of others. For his account of sympathy, the principle of communication that enables us to share such sentiments, see esp. 2.1.11.2–8; 3.3.1.7–14.
16 point of honour] The tacit code or rules which governed the conduct of a particular class of persons; called the 'laws of honour' in the next paragraph. Hume returns to this topic in 3.2.12.
   n. 26 Part 4. Sect. 1] See 1.4.1.10–11.
18 those observations . . . *character*] See Cardinal de Retz, *Memoirs* 3 [1:82; 2:60].
19 The next degree] Hume is listing what he takes to be distinctive levels of probability and assurance; compare 1.3.11.2; and Locke, *Essay* 4.2.
20 The belief . . . memory] See 1.3.5.7.

Book 1 Part 3 Sect. 14. *Of the idea of necessary connexion*

The section begins by raising again the question '*What is our idea of necessity, when we say that two objects are necessarily connected together?*' (see 1.3.2.12). The answer: an idea that derives from or copies a particular impression of reflection, namely, a determination of the mind. The determination in question is the one felt by the mind when, after repeated experiences of two types of contiguous and successive objects or events (of events of type *A* followed by events of type *B*), only one such type of event is experienced. When that happens, we expect an event of the remaining type, or are determined to think of an event of that type. The idea copying this feeling of expectation is the idea of necessary connection. We then go on to project this idea onto objects or events in such a way that events appear to us to be necessarily connected for much the same reason that (according to modern philosophers) objects appear to be coloured or scented. In short, as was predicted at 1.3.6.3, we find that objects appear to be necessarily connected because of an inference of the mind. Suggesting that this is the most shocking of all his 'paradoxes' (¶24), Hume explains why most readers will be biased against his view. Near the end of the section he defines cause and effect when considered as the comparison of two ideas (a philosophical relation) and as an association of two ideas (a natural relation). He concludes that his analysis shows 'all causes are of the same kind'; that 'there is but one kind of *necessity*'; that our belief that every beginning of existence has a cause is not founded 'on any arguments either demonstrative or intuitive'; and that we have no reason to believe in the existence of any object 'of which we cannot form an idea' (¶¶32–6).

1 Having thus . . . *effects*] This issue is raised in 1.3.2.15; Hume's response to it is found throughout 1.3.3–13.
   n. 27 Sect. 2] See 1.3.2.11–13.
   dropt in our way] put aside. The question mentioned is raised in 1.3.2.12–13.
   occasion to observe] See 1.1.1.7; 1.2.3.1; 1.2.5.23; 1.3.1.7.

2 **already establish'd**] See esp. 1.3.4–8.

3 **no question . . . effects**] See the annotations to ¶¶7–8 of this section.

4 **vulgar definitions . . . efficacy**] Those offering such uninformative definitions include Locke: 'whatever is considered by us, to conduce or operate, to the producing any particular simple *Idea*, or Collection of simple *Ideas*, whether Substance or Mode, which did not before exist, hath thereby in our Minds the relation of a Cause, and so is denominated by us' (*Essay* 2.26.1); Berkeley: 'Force is that in bodies which produces motion and other sensible effects' (*Alciphron* 7.9); and Chambers: A cause 'is that which contributes to the production of an effect' (*Cyclopædia*, 'Cause').

5 **n. 28 power**] See Locke's *Essay* 2.21, esp. 1–16.
First . . . original idea] This principle is almost explicit in the discussion at 1.2.3.10, and is presumably a clear implication of the discovery that all our ideas are copies of impressions.
secondly . . . existence] See 1.3.3 and 1.3.6.11–15.

6 **since the principle . . . world**] Chambers reports that 'Mr. Locke seems to have put this matter out of dispute; having made it appear that all our *ideas* are owing to our senses; and that all innate, created, factitious, *ideas*, are mere chimera's' (*Cyclopædia*, 'Idea'). Hume also discusses innate ideas at 1.1.1.12 and *Abs.* 6.

7 **n. 29 upon it**] In addition to *Search* 6.2.3, see *Elucidations* 15.
There are . . . this] This sentence is a paraphrase, in translation, of Malebranche: 'There are some philosophers who assert that secondary causes act . . . through a *substantial form*; others through accidents or *qualities*, and some through *matter* and *form*; of these some through *form* and *accidents*, others through certain *virtues* or *faculties* different from [these]' (*Elucidations* 15 [658]).
negative in philosophy] Hume tacitly recognizes that it is not possible to prove a negative, or, in this case, that an entity of a certain kind does not exist. For further instances of 'defiance', see the final annotation to 1.1.1.5.

8 **fix this power**] determine, that is, what quality in causes 'makes them be follow'd by their effects' (see ¶3 of this section).
oblig'd philosophers . . . matter] Chambers, having noted that Malebranche denies there are any effective natural causes, goes on to say that 'It is certain the philosophers are strangely puzzled, and divided' how such causes operate. Some, he says, borrowing substantially from Malebranche (see the second annotation to ¶7 of this section), say that causes 'act by their matter, figure, and motion . . . others by a substantial form . . . many by accidents, or qualities; some by matter and form; others by certain faculties different from all these' (*Cyclopædia*, 'Cause'). Those who suggest, as Hume puts it, that 'the ultimate force and efficacy of nature is perfectly unknown to us' would include Boyle and other Corpuscularians who are agnostics regarding the issue of ultimate causes (see Boyle, *Essay*), Malebranche and the Occasionalists in so far as they deny that there are any true powers or forces in nature (see the following annotation), and Newton (see *Principia* 3 [2:546–7]).
As the essence . . . extension] Malebranche and the Cartesians held that extension is the essence of matter. Accepting the distinction between a First Cause, the Deity, and second causes, or powers or forces in nature itself, Malebranche denies that second causes are real causes. On this theory, as Hume goes on to note in the following paragraph, everything that takes place in nature does so because of the active intervention of the Deity. It follows, then, that no actual causes can be found in nature. See e.g. Malebranche, *Search* 6.2.3, 9; and *Elucidations* 15.

10 **the *Cartesians* . . . matter**] Hume argues that the Cartesians, supposing that there are

innate ideas, and in particular, an innate idea of the Deity, assume they find in this idea the source of the idea of power or causal efficacy.

12 **Some have asserted . . . mind**] Locke, *Essay* 2.21.1, 4, Lee, *Anti-Scepticism* 2.19.3, and Browne, *Procedure* 3.2, are among those who argue that attention to the operations of the mind provides the clearest available basis (direct access to the power of the mind as it begins to act and to bring about an action, for example) for forming our idea of power. Watts, *Philosophical Essays* 12.4, objects to this view, while Malebranche, *Search* 6.2.7 [495], notes that in our confusion we falsely suppose that the mind has a power capable of motivating thought and action.

13 **establish'd**] See 1.1.7.1–16.
    been rejected] See 1.3.6.10; 1.3.7.3.

16 **been observ'd**] See 1.3.6.2–3.
    our ideas . . . instance] We might add to the gross number of our ideas, but not add to the number of *kinds* of idea.

17 **n. 31 Sect. 6**] 1.3.6.2–3.

20 **This determination . . . resemblance**] Hume emphasizes that this particular determination of mind is in effect the same thing as power and what we mean by the term *power*. We may project onto the world the content of the idea that copies this determination, but it none the less remains the case that this idea represents an impression of the mind, and nothing more.

22 **has any relation**] is in any way relevant.

23 **Thus as . . . other**] Hume distinguishes the necessity of demonstration from that of causal inference, but at once goes on to claim that the two kinds of necessity are alike in having their foundations in the mind.

25 **'Tis a common . . . senses**] Modern philosophers since Galileo and Descartes (and some ancient philosophers) had argued that objects *per se* are not coloured, odiferous, warm, etc., but that such features are produced in our minds and then projected onto objects. Malebranche noted the mind's tendency 'to spread itself onto the objects it considers by clothing them with what it has stripped from itself' (*Search* 1.12.5; see also Rohault, *System of Natural Philosophy* 1.32.12). Hume suggests that the idea of necessity is similarly produced and projected.
    n. 32 Part 4. Sect. 5] See esp. 1.4.5.8–14.

26 **above-mention'd**] See ¶¶24–5 of this section.
    of the mind] This conclusion is forecast at 1.3.6.3. In the remainder of this paragraph Hume sketches the argument of those who will treat his opinions as 'extravagant and ridiculous'.

27 **scarlet . . . solidity**] These examples are also found in Locke's *Essay* 2.4.5; 3.4.11. A generic version of them is found in Arnauld and Nicole, *Logic* 1.1 [28].

28 **have observ'd**] See 1.3.2.6–7; 1.3.6.2–3.

30 **preposterous manner**] literally, putting back to front; putting the cart before the horse.

31 *philosophical . . . natural* **relation**] See 1.1.4–5; 1.3.1.1–2; 1.3.6.16.
    persons . . . delicacy] those who think the definitions given are inadequate or crude.

32 **that distinction . . . final causes**] According to Hobbes, that feature or quality of an 'agent or patient [the entity in which an effect takes place], without which the effect could not be produced, is called *causa sine qua non*' (*Elements of Philosophy* 2.9.3). Chambers had succinctly defined the five remaining kinds of cause mentioned by Hume: 'Causes, in the [Scholastic] philosophy, are distinguished into, *Efficient* Causes,

which are the agents that produce any thing . . . *Material* Causes, the subjects whereon the agent works, or whereof the thing is formed: thus, marble is the matter or *material cause* of the statue . . . *Final* Causes, the motives which induced a man to act; or the end for which the thing is done: thus, victory and peace are the *final causes* of war . . . Some add the *Exemplary* Cause, which is the model the agent forms, or proposes, and by which he conducts himself in the action; but this is not properly any cause at all . . . *Formal* Cause, the change resulting from the action; or that which determines a thing to be this, and distinguishes it from every thing else: thus, the soul is held the form, or *formal cause* of man, *&c.*' (*Cyclopædia*, 'Cause').

32 distinction betwixt *cause* and *occasion*] This distinction was made, or at least pre-supposed, by Malebranche and the Occasionalists (La Forge, Cordemoy, Geulincx, for example), philosophers who denied that there are real causes in nature. Events or objects in the world provide an 'occasion' for the power of the Deity to cause whatever changes take place. See also the annotations to 1.3.14.8.

33 *Secondly . . . in nature*] Chambers provides one account of the distinction between physical and moral necessity: Entities (physical objects, for example) subject to physi-cal necessity are said to be completely devoid of the power to determine the course of events. On the other hand, entities (persons, for example) subject to moral necessity, although in the grip of established habits or strong desires, are said to have some power to resist these forces. Consequently, a person could in some respects be subject only to moral necessity, and thus be in a state between being completely free and com-pletely determined (Chambers, *Cyclopædia*, 'Necessity'). Hume argues that necessity has only one foundation, and thus that the putative distinction between physical and moral necessity is meaningless; for an elaboration of his view, see 2.3.1.

34 The distinction . . . foundation] For Hume's further discussion of the distinction between power and the exercise of power, see 2.1.10.4–12; 2.2.5.7.

35 foregoing reasoning] See 1.3.3.
  foregoing definitions] See ¶31 of this section.

36 following reasonings] See 1.4.3, esp. ¶¶4–6.

Book 1 Part 3 Sect. 15. *Rules by which to judge of causes and effects*

Although there are no objects that cannot, prior to experience, be thought to be causes or effects of any other objects, it is possible to articulate general rules for determining which objects 'really are' the causes or effects of other objects (¶2). Eight such rules are offered. These rules, Hume says, are easy to invent, but difficult to apply well, and even more difficult to apply in moral philosophy than in natural philosophy.

1 precedent doctrine] See esp. 1.3.2.5; 1.3.6.1.
  explain'd above] See 1.3.6.2–3; 1.3.14.31. It is at the latter location that Hume argues that the 'idea of the one [object] determines the mind to form the idea of the other [object]'. See also 1.3.14.14–21, 29.
  n. 33 Part 1. Sect. 5] See 1.1.5.8.
  totally depends] Hume clarifies this claim at ¶5 (rule 3) of this section.

6 The same . . . cause] See also 2.1.3.5–7; 2.1.4.1. For applications of this rule, see 2.1.12.6; 2.2.7.3; 2.3.1.5; 3.1.2.6; and 3.3.1.10.

7 There . . . amongst them] For applications of this rule, see 2.1.12.1; 2.2.4.5.

8 The difference . . . differ] For an application of this rule, see 2.1.8.3.

9 When any . . . cause] For applications of this rule, see 1.3.12.16; 2.2.8.4.

10 The eighth . . . operation] See also 1.3.2.7; this rule is applied at 2.2.6.5.

11 LOGIC] the eight 'general rules' Hume has just established.

long system . . . philosophy] Edmunde Mariotte's *Essay on Logic* begins with a list of ninety-nine 'Fundamental Principles and Propositions of Reasoning'. Watts's *Logick* contains, as its subtitle indicates, a 'Variety of Rules to guard against *Error*' in religion, human life, and the sciences.

experimental philosophy] here, experimental *natural* philosophy.

Book 1 Part 3 Sect. 16. *Of the reason of animals*

Having in the previous sections expanded the conception of reason to include causal reasoning, Hume now argues that the behaviour of animals shows that they too are able to reason in this way. Humans consciously adapt means to ends as they strive for self-preservation. Animals equally adapt means to ends, and hence it is only reasonable that we should believe that they too are guided by 'reason and design' (¶2). Moreover, having concluded that animals reason like humans, Hume argues that they do so because their faculties operate as ours do. This suggests that certain elaborate explanations of the human mind and its operations (those typical of many philosophical theories) are considerably off the mark. In short, we are like animals, and our minds and theirs respond to experience in the manner outlined in the preceding sections. Hume concludes by providing examples illustrating how well his account of causal reasoning and belief fits, and thus explains, the behaviour of animals.

1 The arguments . . . ignorant] Hume's seemingly innocuous comment is in fact highly contentious and surely ironical, for it suggests that the ignorant could see that animals reason even though many of the learned could not. As he would have known, the issue of the intellectual capacity of animals had been actively debated by his predecessors. Moreover, Descartes, Malebranche, and the Cartesians had argued that animals are devoid of mind and incapable of both thought and feeling. The contrary view, that animals have some intellectual capacities, was during the early modern period defended by both Aristotelians and Corpuscularians. For an introduction to the issue, see Bayle, *Dictionary*, 'Rorarius', nn. B–H, K–L; 'Pereira', nn. G–I. The issue is also raised by, among others, Montaigne, *Apology for Raymond Sebond* (*Essays* 2.12 [see esp. 330–58]); Malebranche, *Search* 2.3.5 [189–90]; 5.3 [351–3]; 6.2.7 [492–5]; and Locke, *Essay* 2.10.10; 2.11.5; 2.27.12.

3 The common defect . . . species] Bayle had argued that, on Descartes's account of how we come to *know* that we are not deceived when we affirm the existence of external objects, it is apparent that children, the mentally subnormal, and the vast majority of ordinary adults could never come to know that they are not deceived and that there are such bodies (see Descartes, *Meditations*, 6; Bayle, *Dictionary*, 'Pyrrho', n. B). Hume here (and at 1.4.2.14) makes use of a generalized version of Bayle's argument.

8 They can . . . they have] Hume takes advantage of the fact that not even the staunchest defenders of animal intelligence were prepared to credit animals with the ability to understand abstractions or to perceive necessary connections. On the inability of animals to form abstract ideas, see e.g. Locke, *Essay* 2.11.10–11.

9 reason . . . souls] As becomes apparent, Hume is speaking of the form of reason that he has explained in *Treatise* 1.3.3–14, namely, causal reasoning.

Book 1 Part 4. *Of the sceptical and other systems of philosophy*

Treatise 1.4 takes up a wide range of topics: an assessment of demonstrative reason; an account of what causes us to believe in the existence of external objects; brief discussions of several key characteristics of ancient and modern philosophy; a discussion of the vexed issue of the materiality or immateriality of the soul; and an account of our conception and belief in personal identity. In the conclusion to *Treatise* 1, Hume comments on the nature and function of the imagination and the value of philosophy. Running through these diverse discussions is a unifying theme: Recognizing that his philosophical predecessors had collectively shown that neither reason nor the senses can provide certain knowledge of the existence of external objects and enduring selves, Hume articulates a further scep-tical insight. Although we have deeply rooted beliefs in objects and selves, these beliefs are the product of the imagination. Our other faculties, especially the senses, may contribute something to the formation of these fundamental beliefs, but Hume argues that it is the faculty of imagination that unites otherwise isolated capabilities and materials into vital, action-guiding beliefs. He concludes Part 4 and Book 1 with a reflection on what he has accomplished and on the dilemmas he, and philosophy itself, face as he continues to develop his science of human nature. (For further discussion of *Treatise* 1.4, see Ed. Intro., I38–46.)

Book 1 Part 4 Sect. 1. *Of scepticism with regard to reason*

The rules of the demonstrative sciences (algebra and arithmetic, for example) are 'certain and infallible' (¶1), but, because any application of these rules can be mistaken, demon-strative reasoning can produce only probable truths. This gives us further grounds for examining probable reasoning. Such reasoning is shown to have a different and weaker foundation. Our probable reasoning begins, at best, with a highly probable judgement. Our confidence in this judgement must be tempered by the recognition that human facul-ties are fallible, and that we have made mistakes in the past. But then our confidence in this second judgement must be tempered for these same reasons. And then our confidence in our third judgement must be tempered. And then our confidence, etc. By this process, our original belief would be entirely eroded. The actual outcome, however, is very different. Hume insists he is not one of those sceptics who claim that everything is uncertain—nor are there in fact any such sceptics. Nature does not permit us to doubt everything. Belief is more properly a matter of sensation than of cogitation or thinking. Cogitation would completely subvert belief, and hence cannot be the foundation of it. Belief, then, must be a form of sensation. Hume concludes the section by explaining how we escape from the open-ended regress of doubt that he has depicted, and by insisting that his response to extreme scepticism is more compelling than that of some other philosophers.

1 **By this means . . . question]** Locke had argued that the certainty of our knowledge depends on intuition, or the immediate realization that two ideas are either similar or dissimilar. He went on to say that while each step of a demonstration (the process of showing that particular ideas either agree or disagree) depends on intuition, the results of demonstration are less certain than those of intuition. Demonstration demands attention and effort, and even repetition of the steps required. If a demonstration is lengthy, we need to be sure that we have not omitted steps, and that we have remem-bered correctly the steps that we have taken. At best, then, demonstration is 'more imperfect than intuitive Knowledge', and as a result, we often take 'Falshoods for Demonstrations' (*Essay* 4.2.1–13; see also 1.3.1.2). Hume suggests that demonstrations

are even less reliable than Locke had thought: the fact that our reason does often arrive at false conclusions means that we must treat demonstrative reasoning as only a probable cause of truth, and that what we think are demonstrative truths are in fact only probable truths (see also *Abs.* 27). The remainder of this section first illustrates this conclusion, and then considers both its theoretical and its practical consequences.

3 **and that because . . . absent**] and that because they must be perfect of their kind. A proposition is either certain or probable, but not both.

5 **a reflex act . . . mind**] an act of reflection or thought, namely, the realization that any of our judgements or conclusions may be mistaken. Hume is suggesting that, because we find that we have been mistaken in the past, and may again be mistaken at any time, we should moderate our assurance in our conclusions.

6 **add a new doubt . . . faculties**] take into account a further ground of uncertainty. Hume's position is apparently this: (1) We know from *Treatise* 1.3 that our probable reasonings about objects (entities or events), based as they are on experience or observation, are never absolutely certain. The relevant experience of these objects may not have been uniform, or may yet prove to be less than uniform. For this reason the conclusions of all probable reasoning are indeed only probable. (2) We have since seen (¶¶1–5 of this section) that uncertainty attends the operation of our reasoning faculty. Experience reveals that this faculty has in the past failed to act uniformly (to the extent of producing contradictory results), and may in the future fail to act uniformly. Those who are sensible moderate their assurance accordingly. (3) It now appears that we must moderate our moderation. If our reasoning faculty is less than perfectly reliable, then its estimate of its own reliability is suspect. Our confidence ('evidence') in our previous conclusion will be reduced by the realization that all our reasonings are fallible. (4) But it now appears we must moderate our further moderated moderation. If our reasoning faculty is less than perfectly reliable, then its further estimate of its own liability is suspect. (5) But it now appears . . . and so on, until all assurance or belief is eroded—or would be completely eroded if we followed only the 'rules of logic' mentioned at the end of this paragraph (see also ¶¶9–10 of this section; 1.3.13.5).

7 **those sceptics . . . falshood**] During the early modern period it was widely supposed that a sceptic was, as one reference work put it, a 'Person who maintains there is nothing Certain, and no real Knowledge at all to be had; but that a Man ought to Doubt of, and Disbelieve every thing' (Harris, *Lexicon Technicum* 1, 'Sceptick'). Chambers said much the same thing; he associated scepticism with those (Pyrrho and his followers) 'whose distinguishing tenet was, that all things are uncertain and incomprehensible; contraries equally true; that the mind is never to assent to any thing; but to keep up an absolute hesitancy or indifference' (*Cyclopædia*, 'Scepticks'). A discussion of scepticism, reaching much the same conclusion, is found in Berkeley's *Three Dialogues* 1 [2:171–2]. Hume, although he calls himself a sceptic (see 1.4.7.15), goes on explain why it is that neither he nor anyone else is or could be that kind of extreme or unmitigated sceptic; see also *Abs.* 27.

8 **fantastic sect**] imaginary sect. That is, there are in fact no '*total*' sceptics (¶7 of this section), and those who claim to refute them are only knocking over imaginary opponents.
my hypothesis . . . natures] For Hume's account of belief, see 1.3.7; App. 2–9 and *Abs.* 18–22. Belief, Hume argues, is more properly an act of feeling than an act of thought or cogitation; see also 1.3.8.12.
genius and capacity] abilities as rational beings.
foregoing arguments] See this section, ¶¶3–6.

10 **and the spirits . . . channel**] On spirits gone off course, see 1.2.5.20.

11 **touch the passions**] produce the expected emotional response, catharsis, in his or her audience.

so these latter . . . former] Subtle reasoning and reflection affect the emotions just as the emotions affect reasoning and reflection.

12 **expeditious way . . . sceptics**] The argument Hume goes on to summarize is found in Bayle (*Dictionary*, 'Pyrrho', n. C), and in Chambers, who, although he grants that Pyrrhonian scepticism has some plausibility, concludes by claiming that it 'destroys itself: for if there be nothing certain, then must that dogma itself be precarious; and if no one thing be more probable, or liker to truth than another, why shall the principle of the *Pyrrhonians* be believed preferably to the opposite one?' (*Cyclopædia*, 'Pyrrhonian'). This 'expeditious way' with the sceptics dates from ancient times; see Sextus Empiricus, *Pyrrhonism* 1.7, 10.

enemy] scepticism, that is.

patent under her hand and seal] The allusion is to letters patent. These were documents bearing the seal of some authority (that of the king, for example) and authorizing a person to do or use something that was not otherwise legal to do or use.

sceptical and dogmatical reasons] The reference is to reason as it supports doubt, and reason as it supports belief.

Book 1 Part 4 Sect. 2. *Of scepticism with regard to the senses*

At the outset of this, the longest section in the *Treatise*, Hume says that it is pointless to ask if objects exist. That they do is something 'we must take for granted in all our reasonings'. But it is useful to consider '*What causes induce us to believe in the existence of body?*' (¶1). What causes lead us to believe that objects exist continuously and independently of the mind that perceives them? The possible causes considered are the senses, reason, and the imagination. Neither the senses nor reason can account for this belief; the imagination can, and Hume, at considerable length, shows how this happens. Near the end of the section he contrasts and criticizes the view of the 'vulgar', who fail to distinguish between perceptions and objects (they take perceptions to be objects with a continued existence), and that of modern philosophers, who inconsistently champion a theory that distinguishes between perceptions and objects. In the final two paragraphs of the section Hume reconsiders his claim that we must always take the existence of objects for granted: profound reflection may lead to sceptical doubt about their existence. This doubt, although it is beyond permanent cure, can be treated or controlled by inattention or indifference. (For further discussion of *Treatise* 1.4.2, see Ed. Intro., I38–42.)

2 *viz. why . . . perception*] Hume's questions could be rephrased: Why do we think objects continue to exist even when no one is actually witnessing or experiencing them? And, why do we think, given that we are only ever aware of perceptions in the mind, that objects are physically separate from us, and that their existence is in no way dependent on us? See also 1.2.6.4–8.

vice versa . . . perceiv'd] That is, if objects are separate from the mind, their continued existence is not dependent upon the mind's perception of them.

n. 34 **Part 2. Sect. 6**] See 1.2.6.8–9.

3 **contradiction in terms**] It is a contradiction in terms to say that the senses, which operate only intermittently, are responsible for a belief in things that are continuous. In addition, impressions of sensation, which appear to be the products of the senses,

are of a relatively short duration, while the vast majority of the objects in which we believe are supposed to exist for relatively long durations.

must present . . . existences] If the senses alone could give us the idea of continued existence, they could perhaps do so by conveying to us two things: impressions (images) that depict or copy objects, and, at the same time, the separate object depicted by the image, or at least clear indications (representations) that there are objects separate from the impressions. (This possibility is considered in ¶¶4–9 of this section; ¶11 summarizes Hume's conclusions.) Alternatively, if the senses alone could give us the idea of continued existence, they could perhaps do so by presenting external and distinct objects directly to the mind. (This possibility is discussed in ¶¶10–11, and again in ¶¶44–5 of this section.)

4 of a double existence] of an object and of the perception (image) that supposedly represents it.

put to the account of] attributed to the activity of.

and it certainly . . . betwixt them] Hume emphasizes that any theory that distinguishes between perceptions and objects must rely upon more than the senses, for their operation can produce only perceptions.

5 Upon this . . . situation] Hume is canvassing thoroughly the options open to those who attribute to the senses our belief in the external existence of objects. Here he argues that the character of sensations *qua* sensations is fully known to each person who feels or experiences them. The only questions, then, concern how sensations relate to us and our experience of them. Do they, for example, have causes independent of us? Do these causes outlast the sensations? See also ¶7 of this section.

6 'Tis certain . . . person] This question is the subject of 1.4.6 and App. 10–22.

7 known . . . by consciousness] known to us introspectively and directly.

9 n. 35 Sect. 5] See esp. 1.4.5.8–16.

acknowledg'd . . . philosophers] See at 1.2.5.8 the annotation regarding the question raised by Molyneux.

10 *independency . . . senses*] that our perceptions are independent of the mind is not something the senses can perceive or establish.

see afterwards] See ¶¶14, 21, and 44–7 of this section.

has a sufficient reality] is a real, external object.

incessant revolutions] continual changes in our impressions and ideas.

12 by the senses] Hume goes on to summarize a key component of the distinction between (as Locke put it) primary and secondary qualities, or between those qualities of objects (extension, figure, and motion, for example) that were said to be reliably represented by our ideas, and those qualities of objects (qualities giving rise to the ideas of colour, sound, and warmth, for example) that were said not to be reliably represented by our ideas. In the early modern period the distinction began to be made as early as Galileo, and is found in many subsequent philosophers. (For Galileo's contribution of 1623, see his *Assayer* [273–4]; for Locke's discussion, see *Essay* 2.8; for criticisms of the distinction, see Bayle, *Dictionary*, 'Pyrrho', n. B; Berkeley, *Principles* 1.9–15; *Three Dialogues* 1 [2:187–93].) Hume treats the issue as a question about the distinct and continued existence of three apparently different kinds of impression (those of figure and motion, etc.; those of colour and sound, etc.; and those of pain and pleasure), and to argue that these apparent kinds of impression are, as impressions, indistinguishable. They are all internal (mind-dependent or not distinct from the mind) and fleeting (fail to have continuous existence).

Both philosophers . . . beings] All agree that pains and pleasures are mind-dependent and exist only as feelings. For the present Hume allows us to suppose that the same perception may be experienced at different times. At ¶24 of this section he emphasizes that there are, strictly speaking, no interrupted perceptions: each temporally distinct experience of what may seem to be the same perception is in fact an experience of an entirely distinct perception.

13 **Now 'tis evident . . . perception]** The primary–secondary quality distinction cannot be derived from an analysis of the relevant perceptions, for these perceptions have, as perceptions, exactly the same characteristics.

contrary opinion] the opinion that objects themselves include nothing like colour, sound, heat or cold, etc.

14 **And indeed . . . others]** Hume may well have in mind the proof of the existence of external objects found in Descartes's *Meditations* 6. The counter-argument used here, that because the unlearned and even children believe in the existence of external objects, we can see that this belief does not depend upon philosophical principle or reason, is also found in Bayle (*Dictionary*, 'Pyrrho', n. B; see also 1.3.16.3).

very things . . . see] The 'very things' the vulgar experience, although they do not realize it, are perceptions.

unreasonable] here, contrary to the universally allowed opinion of philosophers, itself the product of reason.

appear presently] in this section, esp. ¶¶46–55.

That opinion . . . IMAGINATION] Hume's argument has been a simple one: our belief in the continuing and independent existence of external objects must be due to the senses, or to reason, or to the imagination. He has shown that this belief is not due to the senses or to reason. Therefore, it must be due to the imagination.

16 **involuntariness . . . violence]** Locke had argued that our belief in the existence of external objects is confirmed by the involuntariness and the greater force of the relevant perceptions; see *Essay* 4.11.5.

heat of a fire] This example is also found in Locke, *Essay* 2.2.8.16.

18 **peculiar *constancy*]** Hume's attention to constancy and then, in the following paragraph, coherence, may reflect Berkeley's suggestion that the ideas of our senses are not only stronger and livelier than those of the imagination, but that they manifest a notable 'steadiness, order, and coherence' (*Principles* 1.30).

mountains . . . houses . . . trees] Exactly the items mentioned by Berkeley, *Three Dialogues* 1 [2:200].

20 **I now proceed . . . opinion]** In this paragraph Hume argues that some of our internal and perishing impressions have a coherence that others lack. If we believe the objects–impressions we are currently experiencing are real, it is because we take them to form a coherent set with countless other objects–impressions, some of which we only remember, and some of which we may never have experienced.

internal impressions . . . perishing] according to ¶16 of this section, the impressions of 'pains and pleasures, passions and affections'.

posts] the mail system or some part thereof (a mail carrier, the stations between which he travelled, the road on which he travelled, or the horse or horses and carriage which conveyed him).

contradictions to] inconsistent with. Hume typically experiences together the sight and the sound of the door. When he experiences only the sound of the door, he has an experience that is unlike these typical experiences. In such circumstances, it might be thought that he should believe the door is no longer there to be seen, or that the world has become significantly different from (contrary to) its former state. But supposing

that the door is still there to be seen eliminates any reason to entertain this 'contradiction' and any impetus to believe the world has changed in this particular way.
at first . . . hypothetical] was only one of many that could have been made.
reconcile these contradictions] make sense out of the seemingly inconsistent experiences just described.

21 But tho' . . . effects] See 1.3.2.2, where Hume suggests that causal reasoning accounts for our belief in the identity of objects.
we shall find] See esp. ¶¶47, 54 of this section, and 1.4.7.4.

22 n. 36 Part 2. Sect. 4] See esp. 1.2.4.24; see also 1.3.13.9–10.
have assign'd] See 1.2.4.18–32.

23 *constancy*] This principle is first discussed in ¶¶18–19 of this section.

24 precedent reasoning] the reasoning of 1.3.7.

25 *First . . . identity*] See ¶¶26–30 of this section.
Secondly . . . them] See ¶¶31–6 of this section.
Thirdly . . . existence] See ¶¶37–40 of this section.
Fourthly . . . propensity] See ¶¶41–2 of this section.

26 principle of individuation] Generally speaking, the feature of a thing that makes that thing what it distinctly is, and hence makes it at each moment of its existence the same thing that it was before. Hume is concerned to determine what it is about certain perceptions that leads us to identify them as perceptions of the same object and thus to suppose that we are experiencing only one thing. Hobbes had said that 'Some place *individuity* in the unity of *matter*; others, in the unity of *form*; and one says it consists in the unity of the *aggregate of all the accidents together*' (*Elements of Philosophy* 2.11.7).
we really . . . affirmation] To say 'an object is the same with itself' is to say no more than 'A = A', and thus is uninformative.
One single . . . identity] It is Hume's contention that a single, continuous experience of the same object–perception fails to give rise to the idea or concept of identity (it gives rise to the idea of unity; see ¶28 of this section). He supposes that the concept of identity is necessarily relational, or necessarily incorporates the understanding that some entity M is one and the same as some other entity N, such that $M = N$. Experience of a single object–perception (of M only) cannot, he argues, give rise to this relational concept.

27 On the other . . . suppos'd] We cannot derive the idea of identity from an assembly of resembling objects (a bag of new and indistinguishable tennis balls, say) because the mind always considers the assembled balls as separate entities even though they are virtually indistinguishable.

28 Since then . . . them] For Hume, the concept of number applies to two or more distinct entities (which may very well be, like new tennis balls, virtually indistinguishable) experienced together. The concept of unity applies to a single entity experienced without interruption and recognized to be a single entity. The concept of identity is like neither number or unity. The concept of identity applies to two or more perceptions, experienced on two or more distinct occasions, and then taken to be perceptions of the same object. The problem, addressed in the next paragraph, is to explain how this concept is derived.

29 n. 37 Part 2. Sect. 5] See 1.2.5.28–9; see also 1.2.3.6–11.
this time] the time during which the single object is viewed.
must be multiply'd] must be thought of as two objects, one for each moment of time conceived.
identity] Hume here goes on to suggest something along these lines: imagine that

you experience a single object–perception B (an unchanging tennis ball, say) uninterruptedly for 100 successive moments. Hume's conception of time is such that each of these moments is a discrete unit and that each must be occupied with something. In this case, each moment is occupied with B. Now, in retrospect, imagine any two of the 100 moments, moments 37 and 38, let us say. These can be imagined in two temporal settings: as (1) existing simultaneously, or (2) existing successively. (1) If the two moments are imagined as existing simultaneously, we obtain 'the idea of number' (of multiple existing things) because each of the two simultaneous moments is occupied with a distinct object–perception. (2) If the two moments are imagined as existing successively, and if we suppose that while we pass from one moment to the next we attend to the same object–perception, we then obtain 'the idea of identity' or the notion of a single object–perception invariant through distinct moments.

29 without . . . number] without thinking there are many objects that are yet somehow a single identical object. Should we do that, we would be saying, unintelligibly, that 'the objects are itself'.

without . . . unity] without limiting ourselves to an uninformative statement ($A = A$) of merely logical or analytical identity. The discovery that two identical but seemingly distinct objects seen at two different times are in fact only one object seen at two different times is informative.

30 *invariableness* and *uninterruptedness*] As Hume indicates in ¶31 of this section, these are the two 'essential qualities of identity'.

without any . . . view] abstracting from any interruptions in its view.

31 *second* part . . . system] See ¶25 of this section.

already observ'd] See ¶¶12–13 of this section.

can never . . . representation] can never be supposed to believe that there are both objects and perceptions, and that the latter represent the former; see also ¶4 of this section.

I shall . . . warning] This warning is given in ¶46 of this section.

32 n. 38 Part 2. Sect. 5] See 1.2.5.20–1.

have observ'd] Hume refers again to the discussion at 1.2.5.20–1.

33 perfect identity] perfect constancy through a succession of moments. Hume goes on to describe the disposition of mind created by the experience of perfect identity.

34 foregoing principle] See ¶32 of this section.

35 afterwards] See e.g. 1.4.3.3; 1.4.6.6.

n. 39 But let us . . . argument] If we carefully distinguish the two forms of resemblance that produce the same disposition, we will understand the argument of ¶¶33–5 of this section.

36 *third* . . . to explain] See ¶25 of this section.

37 n. 40 Sect. 6] See 1.4.6.6–10.

38 *Secondly* . . . image] Hume apparently hopes to explain why it is that we take a subsequent set of resembling impressions to be repetitions of a first impression, and not new and different impressions. Why do we suppose there is an *object*, and not merely a set of resembling, but distinct, impressions? He provides an answer in ¶40 of this section.

39 we may observe . . . identity] The nature of the mind and its identity are the subject of 1.4.6.

41 *fourth* . . . system] See ¶25 of this section.

prov'd already] See 1.3.7; see also *App.* 1–10; *Abs.* 17–23.

43 all philosophers] Here, philosophers just are those who suppose that nothing is ever

really present to the mind but perceptions (see 1.2.6.7) and that 'interrupted perceptions' are really different entities. Having accepted these views, these philosophers must then acknowledge that their beliefs in the continued existence of objects and the identity of resembling perceptions are both fictions, or notions unsupported by the evidence available to them.

44 **already observ'd]** See ¶2 of this section.

45 **When we press . . . position]** The experiment and effect Hume describes were well known to his early modern predecessors. See e.g. Hobbes, *Human Nature* 2.5; Rohault, *System of Natural Philosophy* 1.2.25, 31; and Collier, *Clavis Universalis* 1.1.1–2[24,30]. The experiment is also found in classical writers; see e.g. Aristotle, *Problems* 874ª; Lucretius, *Nature of Things* 4.447–52; Sextus, *Against the Logicians* 1.192.

experiments . . . kind] Hume briefly summarizes some of the arguments used, by both sceptics and rationalists, to show the unreliability of the senses. These may be found in Sextus Empiricus (see e.g. *Pyrrhonism* 1.14, esp. lines 100–23), are repeated and embellished in Montaigne's *Apology for Raymond Sebond* (*Essays* 2.12 [see esp. 443–55]), and are succinctly presented by Rohault, *System of Natural Philosophy* 1.2.9–35.

46 **for the future]** Hume began speaking like the vulgar, or ordinary people, at ¶31 of this section. In the balance of 1.4.2 he again distinguishes between objects and perceptions, and thus speaks like the learned, or philosophers.

betwixt perceptions . . . return] Hume reminds us that, strictly speaking, perceptions are 'perishing'; they do not 'return', but only appear to do so.

48 **first supposition]** the supposition that each perception is a different and distinct entity.

50 **extravagant sceptics]** likely an allusion to Berkeley and perhaps also to Arthur Collier, two early 18th-c. immaterialists. Hume was later to say that Berkeley's writings 'form the best lessons of scepticism . . . to be found among the ancient or modern philosophers' (*EHU* n. 32).

52 **intermediate . . . mind]** the mind as caught between two of its sub-features, the imagination and reason.

54 **already shown]** See ¶¶21, 47 of this section.

above-explain'd] See 1.1.3.2.

55 **n. 41 Sect. 5]** See 1.4.5.12; see also ¶¶32, 35–40 of this section, and 1.4.3.3; 1.4.6.6.

56 **I begun]** See ¶1 of this section.

qualities of the fancy] features or propensities of the imagination.

They . . . existence] Although the coherence and constancy of perceptions give rise to the belief in the continued existence of objects, these qualities provide, strictly speaking, no satisfactory evidence for that belief.

For we may . . . perceptions] We can formulate the hypothesis that there are, over and above perceptions, *objects*, but we cannot conceive of these objects as being significantly or specifically different from our perceptions of them. What we experience determines what we can conceive. See also 1.2.6.8–9; 1.4.5.19–20; 1.4.6.13.

57 **Carelessness . . . remedy]** Descartes and others had, in contrast, explicitly argued that careful attention is the remedy for scepticism; see e.g. *Meditations* 5, and Arnauld and Nicole, *Logic*, Discourse 1 [7–8].

I intend . . . modern] in 1.4.3–6.

enquiry . . . impressions] in Book 2.

This will not . . . purpose] Given the range of topics that follow in *Treatise* 1.4, it is unlikely that by 'present purpose' Hume means the purpose set for 1.4.2 (see ¶2 of this section). At 1.1.2.1 Hume says that *Treatise* 1, 'in order to explain the nature and principles of the human mind', is to 'give a particular account of ideas'. He may here be referring to this broader purpose.

Book 1 Part 4 Sect. 3. *Of the antient philosophy*

Continuing his discussion of issues raised in 1.4.2, Hume undertakes to see what we can learn from a review of the 'fictions of the antient philosophy', the Aristotelian doctrines of substance, substantial form, and accident (¶1). Why, he asks, given that our ideas of bodies appear to be only collections of qualities formed by the mind, do we none the less think objects are simple or identical with themselves? The answer lies in the way our perceptions affect the mind. At any given moment, a close similarity among perceived qualities produces an easy transition which leads us to suppose these qualities are collected together or linked by an underlying identity or simplicity. But, over time, the qualities taken to be part of a single object may show significant variation. The ancient philosophers accounted for such change by appeal to a '*substance, or original and first matter*' (¶4) that they supposed perfectly homogeneous but capable of transformation into the four elements, earth, water, air, and fire. They accounted for identity and simplicity by appeal to substantial form, a principle capable of organizing substance into distinct individuals. Particular qualities (colours, sounds, shape, etc.) were understood as so many accidents inhering in formed substance. Such explanatory notions are the result of the operation of natural principles of the mind very like those explained in 1.4.2, but the resulting Aristotelian system is essentially incomprehensible because the terms *substance, substantial form*, and *accident* are unintelligible, while talk of sympathies, antipathies, and the horrors of a vacuum merely projects human emotions onto external objects.

1 **Several moralists . . . actions**] Plutarch discusses the suggestion that from our dreams we can determine whether or not we are making progress in virtue. He attributes the suggestion to Zeno and Plato. See *Moralia*, 'How a Man may become Aware of his Progress in Virtue' 12.
2 **'Tis confest . . . other**] See Locke, *Essay* 2.13.18–19; 2.23.1–4, 37; Hume outlines the Lockean position at 1.1.6.2.
   It may . . . them] Here and in the following paragraphs Hume attempts to explain how or why the imagination produces an idea of an 'unintelligible something' called *substance*; cf. 1.1.6.1.
3 **the succession**] the succession of impressions and ideas produced by, so we believe, enduring objects; Hume goes on to repeat in brief form his previous finding (see 1.4.2, esp. ¶35), namely, that the relations between perceptions lead us to ascribe identity to what are in fact different perceptions.
4 **survey at once . . . qualities**] Imagine an apple freshly picked. If we were to view this apple daily for six months, the changes we would witness would occur gradually, and we would have no difficulty realizing that we were seeing the same apple throughout the period. But if we view the apple only twice, the day it is picked, and six months later, its appearance upon the two occasions may be so greatly altered that we will fail to attribute identity to it. Such diverse appearances or perceptions will not alone support the notion that only a single apple has been experienced. To 'reconcile' this diversity of appearances and thus enable us both to conceive and to believe that we have experienced only a single apple, the imagination produces the notion of substance, the notion, that is, of something essentially featureless and indistinct, in which the changing qualities of the apple inhere.

6 peripatetic philosophy] 'And nowadays by the *Peripatetick Philosophy* we understand that which was founded on the Principles of *Aristotle* and his Commentators' (Harris, *Lexicon Technicum* 1, 'Peripateticks'). Theophrastus, Boethius, Thomas Aquinas, Duns Scotus, and Ockham are among the commentators mentioned.

substantial form . . . species] a form independent of '*original* matter' but that, when united with matter, causes it to become a specific kind of entity (a human, an oak tree, gold), and also accounts for many of the changes the entity may undergo, as when a single human changes from infant to child to adult.

look along . . . bodies] reflect on changes not initially noticeable by means of the senses.

7 *accidents . . .* forms] Accidents are qualities or features (colours, sounds, tastes, locations) that are supposed not to be essential to a thing being what it is, but that are supposed to inhere in the thing (in a substance) and to depend for their existence upon that substance.

above-mention'd] See ¶¶2–5 of this section.

8 *occult qualities*] See also ¶10 of this section. 'Weak philosophers,' says Chambers, 'when unable to discover the cause of an effect, and unwilling to own their ignorance, say it arises from an *occult virtue*, an *occult cause*, an *occult quality.*' Such qualities are 'secret, hidden, or invisible' (*Cyclopædia*, 'Occult'). For a typical and more extensive attack on Aristotelianism, see Hobbes, *Leviathan* 4.46.

9 *Sisyphus* and *Tantalus*] In Greek myth the gods of the underworld punished Sisyphus for various offences by ordering him to roll a rock to the top of a hill. On each attempt, just as he reached the summit, the rock escaped from his hold and rolled back down again. When Tantalus, a son of Zeus, offended the gods, he was compelled to stand, underneath the branches of a fruit tree, in a pool of water up to his chin. The water receded when he tried to drink, and the wind blew the fruit out of his reach when he tried to eat.

11 *sympathies, antipathies,* and *horrors of a vacuum*] A sympathy was said to be produced by two natural things thought to have an affinity or preference for one another and thus to influence one another positively in such a way that the two things work together or cooperate. An antipathy was said to be produced by two natural things having a disaffinity or aversion for one another. Thus the natural antipathy between foxes and chickens was said to make chickens fly in terror at the sound of a harp strung with fox-gut strings (Chambers, *Cyclopædia*, 'Sympathy', 'Antipathy'). Some writers account for this terror by suggesting that, by the sight or sound of specific objects, 'certain Impressions are transmitted thro' the Fibres of the Nerves into the Brains, which convey the animal Spirits into the Nerves; which upon the Blood being rarified after another manner than is usual, sends into the Brains those Spirits, which are adapted to the Fomenting or Cherishing of Terror' (Bailey, *Dictionary*, 'Antipathy'; on sympathy, see also the Ed. Intro., 155–7, and the Glossary). The Aristotelians taught that it was because nature or natural things had a horror of a vacuum that no vacuum could be found in nature. Hume goes on to criticize these philosophers for incorporating features of human psychology into their explanations of the physical world.

Book 1 Part 4 Sect. 4. *Of the modern philosophy*

The principles directing the imagination are of two kinds. There are those that are permanent, irresistible, consistent, solid, and universal and which are the foundation of thought, action, and human life. There are also those that are changeable, weak, irregular, and avoidable and which are natural only in the sense that illnesses are natural. The system of the ancient philosophers (see 1.4.3) is a consequence of relying on such weak and irregular principles. Modern philosophy claims to be based only on permanent and solid principles of the imagination. A fundamental feature of modern philosophy is its apparently well-founded claim that colours, sounds, tastes, smells, and sensations of touch are only impressions or ideas in the mind. Such perceptions, although said to be caused by the secondary qualities of external objects, fail to resemble or represent these qualities. On the other hand, modern philosophers claim that we do have resembling or representative perceptions of extension, solidity, and motion, three primary qualities of objects. Hume objects that this theory introduces 'the most extravagant scepticism' (¶6) regarding objects. He shows that the allegedly representative ideas of the primary qualities of extension and solidity are inextricably bound up with our unrepresentative ideas of secondary qualities. In brief, the modern philosophers' distinction between primary and secondary qualities collapses. As it does so, it leaves us with the 'extravagant scepticism' mentioned: it leaves us with no grounds for believing there are objects having 'continu'd and independent existence' (¶15).

1 **I must distinguish . . . notice of**] See esp. 1.4.3.11.
2 *modern philosophy*] the philosophy, principally, of Galileo, Descartes and his followers, and such writers as Gassendi, Hobbes, Boyle, and Locke.
3 **A man . . . most**] The examples Hume mentions were widely used. For this particular one, see Malebranche, *Search* 1.13.5; Berkeley, *Three Dialogues* 1 [2:185]. Many of the arguments mentioned here are found in Sextus Empiricus, *Pyrrhonism*; see esp. 1.14.79–91, 100–23.

complexions . . . men] In Hume's time the terms *complexion* and *constitution* were used interchangeably to mean the temperament or physical and mental qualities and propensities of a person. According to Galen and the medieval medical tradition, a person's temperament depended on the relative strength of the four humours, phlegm, blood, choler, or melancholy, in the composition of a person. The person was said to be phlegmatic (calm), sanguine (confident), choleric (irascible), or melancholic (sad), depending on which humour dominated. Although Hume talks about the 'mixture of humours' at 2.1.12.2, by his time few physicians were using Galen's categories. The newer theory divided the humours, now meaning the fluid parts of the body, into nutritious, natural, and morbid. See Malebranche, *Search* 1.13.5, for a brief discussion of the effect of such varied constitutions.

Colours . . . body] See Berkeley, *Three Dialogues* 1 [2:184–6] for a discussion of this phenomenon.

pleasure . . . pain at another] See Locke, *Essay* 2.8.16.
4 **archetype**] This is Locke's preferred name (see *Essay* 2.30.1) for the original entities that are supposed to give rise to, and be represented by, certain perceptions. As we saw at 1.2.2.1, adequate ideas are those that conform exactly to the archetypes from which they are supposed to derive. Among the best-known versions of the argument Hume is recapitulating is that found in Locke's *Essay* (see 2.8).

Now from . . . causes] See rule 4 at 1.3.15.6.

to be nothing . . . existences] to exist only in the mind. Note that while Locke is often said to have claimed that secondary qualities themselves are nothing but perceptions in the mind, he in fact makes a significantly different claim: he argues that while our *ideas* of secondary qualities fail to *resemble* any feature of objects, *secondary qualities* themselves are actually powers or dispositions of objects. Locke's view owes much to Robert Boyle; see Boyle's *Origins of Forms and Qualities*.

5 of fire . . . nature] earth, water, air, and fire, the four elements of the ancient and
medieval philosophers, were proposed by Empedocles as the ultimate matter or principle of all things; by a mixture or separation of these four substances everything came
into being, and into them everything was at last resolved. This theory was widely
attacked during the early modern period.

6 utterly annihilate . . . them] This objection had been formulated by Simon Foucher,
repeated by Bayle, and developed more fully by Berkeley: the very same reasons that
lead us to conclude that the colours, sounds, tastes, etc. attributed to objects are only
perceptions or modifications of the mind will equally lead to the conclusion that
primary qualities (extension, motion, and solidity) are nothing but perceptions or
modifications of the mind. See Foucher, *Critique*, Supposition 7; Bayle, *Dictionary*,
'Pyrrho', n. B; Berkeley, *Principles* 1.9–15; *Three Dialogues* 1 [2:187–93].

8 have prov'd] See 1.2, esp. Sect. 3.4–5.

10 never possess any place] are never in any location.
run on *in infinitum*] be caught in an infinite regress.

11 n. 42 Part 2. Sect. 4] See 1.2.4.4–7.

12 The impressions . . . objects] See ¶4 of this section, and the annotation regarding
Locke and secondary qualities.

13 the palsey] a disease of the nervous system, the symptoms of which may include the
loss of the sensation of touch.
but it does not . . . resembling] It does not follow that the sensation, motion, and
resistance produced in an observer in any way resemble qualities of the object that
produces these responses.

14 except when . . . purpose] The exception noted has no bearing on the present
argument.
And from this simplicity . . . object] The aim of the argument that follows is to show
that, because impressions of touch are simple impressions, they cannot represent
solidity or an external object. This result is obtained by pointing out (1) that our experience of solidity is inseparable from a sensation (a subjective experience) that is not
itself a part of the notion of solidity (a notion or idea having to do only with objects
and their impenetrability); (2) solidity is an idea made up of several component ideas
(those of two objects and of contiguity and motion) and thus cannot be represented
by a simple impression of touch; and (3) solidity is constant while our impressions of
touch are constantly changing.

Book 1 Part 4 Sect. 5. *Of the immateriality of the soul*

Hypotheses about the nature of the mind are not necessarily more obscure and uncertain
than those concerning external objects. The 'intellectual world' is unredeemably puzzling,
but it does not present us with the 'contradictions' that mark hypotheses about the physical world (¶1). Some philosophers have argued that the soul or mind is fundamentally
either a material or an immaterial substance, but the term *substance* is essentially devoid of
meaning. Those who say the soul is immaterial commonly claim that whatever is material
has parts and is divisible; that thought is indivisible; and that the indivisible cannot be
joined to the divisible. These claims are shown to be mistaken. Some perceptions derived
from sight and touch are divisible and are yet joined to indivisible perceptions. The fact that
some perceptions are unextended and indivisible while others are extended and divisible
shows that both materialists and immaterialists are mistaken. In addition, the immaterialist theory of mind and thought is open to the same objection that some immaterialists

have made against Spinoza's metaphysics: individuated entities (things, thought) are said to be modifications of what is alleged to be an indivisible substance (the Deity, mind). If Spinoza's view is absurd, so too is the immaterialist theory of mind.

Some argue that matter and motion can never produce thoughts or passions. Hume argues that we do find matter and motion related to thoughts and passions in just the way that causes are found to be related to effects. We have, then, a choice: we can say either (1) that nothing is a cause unless a causal link is directly perceived, or (2) that things we find appropriately and constantly conjoined 'are upon that account to be regarded as causes and effects' (¶31). If we choose (1), we must conclude there are no causes; if (2), then we must grant that motion may be a cause of thought. Hume notes that to treat the question of the materiality or immateriality of the soul as unintelligible is to remain neutral with respect to the question of the soul's immortality.

1 **The intellectual . . . natural]** Hume suggests that it may be less difficult to explain the 'nature of the mind' than it has been to explain 'external objects'. At App. 10 he concludes that this optimistic assessment of the situation was mistaken; see also Intro. 8–10; 1.4.2.6.

2 **'Tis true . . . ignorance]** Many philosophers had claimed to know the nature of the soul or mind. Descartes and his followers maintained that the soul is an immaterial substance. In contrast, Hobbes argued that the soul is material (*Leviathan*, 3.34; 4.46). Clarke and Collins carried on an extensive debate on the nature of the soul (Clarke, *Works*, 3:749–913).

3 **For how . . . resembling it]** Hume's argument here is reminiscent of that used by Berkeley to show that an idea cannot be like anything but an idea. See *Principles* 1.8–9, 137–8; *Three Dialogues* 1 [2:205–6].

5 **that the definition . . . itself]** This was a commonplace definition of substance during the early modern period. It is found, for example, in Descartes (*Meditations*, *Replies* 4), Spinoza (*Ethics* 1), and Rohault (*System of Natural Philosophy* 1.4.3–4). Chambers gives only one definition of substance, saying that it is 'something that we conceive to subsist of itself, independently of any created being, or any particular mode or accident' (*Cyclopædia*, 'Substance').
already acknowledg'd] See 1.2.2.8; 1.2.6.4.
another principle] See 1.1.3.4; 1.1.7.3.

7 **argument . . . remarkable]** Variations on this argument are found in, for example, Cudworth, *System*, 827–9 and Clarke, *Works*, 2:562–3; 3:731.

8 *local conjunction]* 'conjunction in place', according to ¶11 of this section. Hume goes on to ask what kinds of thing have locations.

9 **relish]** the sensation of taste.
none . . . agree to a desire] none of which can be said of a desire.

10 **several metaphysicians]** In his correspondence with Leibniz, Clarke insists that any object that acts or exists must have a place: 'Nothing can any more *Act*, or *be Acted upon*, where it is not present; than it can *Be*, where it is not' (*Works*, 4:598). A clear anticipation of Hume's maxim '*an object may exist, and yet be no where*' is found in Watts, who denied the ancient axiom 'That which is nowhere, has no Being', and insisted that spirits, because they have 'have no such Relation to *Place* as Bodies have', may be said to '*exist and reside nowhere*', or to 'have a real Existence, and yet have *no proper Place*' (*Philosophical Essays* 6.4; see also *Brief Scheme of Ontology* 12).
objects] objects of thought.
already establish'd] See 1.2, esp. Sect. 3.

11 **n. 43 Part 1. Sect. 5]** See 1.1.5.1.

12 **Tho' an extended . . . relations**] Hume argues that, because tastes exist, and yet exist nowhere, they cannot be related by contiguity or distance to objects that do have spatial location. But these same tastes can be related to such objects in other ways. A taste and an object can be contiguous in time or causally related, for example.

proper place] See 1.4.6.6. The phenomenon to be explained has already been discussed at 1.4.2.32, 35–40; and 1.4.3.3.

n. 44 Sect. 2 towards the end] See 1.4.2.35–7, 42–3.

13 **that *inclination* . . . object**] that propensity to suppose the taste to be joined to an extended object and extended with it.

scholastic principle . . . *parte*] a principle maintained by medieval philosophers. The principle in question, *the whole in the whole, and the whole in every part* (as Hume translates it in the next paragraph) is found in Augustine (*On the Trinity* 6.6) and cited by Aquinas in his discussion of the relation of the soul to the body (*Summa Theologiae* 1a.76.8). Discussions of this principle are also found in the texts of those who debated whether the soul is material or immaterial; see the annotations to ¶¶2, 7, 10 of this section.

14 **For as to . . . points**] Cudworth, citing Plotinus, suggests this possibility; see *System* 824.

15 **materialists . . . extension**] The materialists, Hobbes and Collins, for example, suppose that a material and extended soul could entertain all thoughts, some of which are unextended.

their antagonists] The immaterialists, Cudworth and Clarke, for example, suppose that an immaterial and unextended soul would be compatible with all perceptions, even the extended ones of sight and feeling.

vulgar philosophy] the then most common philosophical theory. Hume has several times noted that modern philosophers are unified in their acceptance of the view that the mind is immediately aware only of perceptions. See 1.2.6.7.

To say the idea . . . extended] Hume confirms that he holds the unusual view that some of our perceptions (our idea of space, for example) are extended. For his account of the origin of this idea, see 1.2.3.4–5, 12–16.

16 **free-thinker**] The 'materialists' mentioned in the previous paragraph would have been called free-thinkers for suggesting that the mind could be composed of matter or for, in other words, speculating about philosophical matters without deference to religious orthodoxy.

theologians] here, the antagonists of the materialists or free-thinkers.

'Tis impossible . . . substance] Any theory that could provide a solution to the questions raised would equally show, for example, how taste is spread through an extended object.

17 **have condemn'd**] See ¶¶2–5 of this section.

atheism] In Hume's time this term was used in a broader sense than it is now. Atheists were taken to include not only those who explicitly denied the existence of a deity or deities, but also those who denied that the Deity is concerned with the affairs of the world, denied that there is an afterlife in which virtue or vice is rewarded or punished, or who had no religion, either true or false.

for which *Spinoza* . . . infamous] Spinoza was widely seen to have tried to overthrow all religion and to have demeaned the Deity, representing him as an imperfect being lacking understanding or intelligence (see e.g. Moreri, *Great Historical Dictionary*, 'Spinosa'). Bayle calls Spinoza a 'systematical Atheist', meaning, apparently, that the principles of his system necessarily lead to atheism (*Dictionary*, 'Spinoza', n. A).

17 I hope . . . retorted on them] Hume, recognizing that his analyses could leave him open to the charge of irreligion, suggests that his opponents (presumably the immaterialists or theologians) will themselves be open to the very objections that they would level against him.

19 n. 45 Part 2. Sect. 6] See 1.2.6.8–9.

a relation without a relative] Relationships hold between two or more *relata* or things; what is proposed is a relationship having only one *relatum* or one thing—in other words, no relationship at all.

20 connexion and repugnance] similarity and dissimilarity.

n. 46 Sect. 2] See 1.4.2.19–22.

21 there are two . . . inhesion] Assuming that there are objects and perceptions, we must give an account, so to speak, of two kinds of inherence and modification: (1) of the qualities or modifications of objects, and (2) of the qualities or modifications of minds. Hume's claim is that these two accounts are, structurally speaking, indistinguishable. Consequently, the objections the theologians bring against Spinoza's view of objects tell equally against their own view of minds.

22 sensible] here, comprehensible.

n. 47 of *Spinoza*] esp. nn. N and CC. The arguments offered in ¶¶23–5 of this section include highly abbreviated forms of Bayle's commentary.

23 scholastic . . . thinking] See 1.4.3.10.

that a mode . . . inhere] If, this argument goes, extension is merely a mode, then, given that modes cannot be different from the substances of which they are modes, the indivisible substance of which Spinoza's universe is made up must be extended. But this is impossible—it is contradictory—because it would require either that the indivisible substance expand itself to conform to its extended modes, or else the extended mode would have to become unextended in order to conform with the simple and indivisible substance. Hume claims that the same kind of inconsistency infects the argument of those who say that extended perceptions are modes of an immaterial substance.

24 *Secondly . . . matter*] According to Spinoza, matter cannot be conceived as something distinct from substance. Consequently, his critics note, whatever we conceive substance to be, that too will matter be. In short, matter is substance and, because each simple and indivisible point making up matter satisfies these critics' definition of a substance (a thing that can exist by itself), each such point is a distinct substance. By parity of reasoning, Hume argues, Spinoza's critics must conclude that each distinct part of a perception is a distinct substance.

already prov'd] See 1.1.6.1–2; 1.4.3.4; this section, ¶¶2–5.

25 *Thirdly . . . incompatible*] If, as Spinoza claims, there is only one substance out of which all things are made, then it follows that this one thing has, at one and the same time, contradictory modifications (is, for example, both round and square at the same time). If, as the theologians claim, there is one immaterial substance, mind, in which all perceptions inhere, then it follows that this one thing has contradictory modifications (has, for example, ideas of circles and squares at the same time).

26 It appears . . . atheism] Hume argues that those who hold that the mind is immaterial are, as much as Spinoza, systematic atheists; see the annotations to ¶17 of this section.

more antient . . . *action*] Among early modern philosophers, the view that thought or ideas are actions of the mind may be found in Descartes (see e.g. *Meditations* Preface; 3; *Replies* 4) and Arnauld (see e.g. *On True and False Ideas* 5–6).

By an action . . . abstraction] For Hume's discussion of distinctions of reason, see 1.1.7.17–18.

27 *First* . . . thinking substance] In this paragraph Hume argues that the proposed theory, according to which modifications of the mind (perceptions) are explained as actions of the substance mind, is inconsistent with what we know to be true of these modifications. We cannot conceive of actions that are separate from a substance acting, while we can conceive of perceptions separate from any mind. The suggestion that actions relate to mental substance as motion relates to material substance is not helpful. Motion alters only the relative positions of objects, not the objects themselves, while the changing perceptions of the mind (whether impressions and ideas) result in significant changes to the mind itself.

precedent reasoning] the principle that our perceptions are different, distinguishable, and separable from one another; on this principle, see also 1.1.3.4; 1.1.7.17; 1.2.1.3; 1.4.6.16.

28 above-explain'd] See esp. ¶¶15–16 of this section.

29 'tis commonly said . . . objects] It is commonly argued, that is, that matter and motion are different in kind from thoughts or feelings, and hence cannot be the cause of thoughts and feelings. Those who offer this argument include the immaterialists mentioned in the annotation to ¶7 of this section. Hume goes on to suggest the kinds of argument used to reach this conclusion. For a further discussion of causation and mental phenomena, see 2.3.1.

30 prov'd at large] proved in detail, and generally; see 1.3.4–6.

n. 48 Part 3. Sect 15] See 1.3.15.1.

precedent reasoning] See ¶27 of this section. Hume here reminds us that, prior to experience, we have no information about what can or cannot cause anything. See 1.3.15.1.

31 But, *secondly* . . . causes] Suppose, as Malebranche and others had argued, that no form of matter includes any causal powers, and that the Deity supplies the power that matter lacks.

n. 49 *Malebranche* . . . *Cartesians*] See Malebranche, *Search* 6.2.3, 9; and *Elucidations* 15. Other Cartesians Hume might have had in mind include La Forge, Cordemoy, and Geulincx.

dangerous . . . doctrine] If created minds have not the power of willing, then the Deity is responsible for the actions of these beings. Given that some of these actions are immoral, the Deity would then be responsible for immorality. To suggest this would be dangerous in two senses: it would tend to undermine religious belief, and it would put those making the suggestion at risk of prosecution for heresy.

33 All our perceptions . . . other] Hume's point is that perceptions occur in the mind without being regularly associated with anything either unextended or extended. Consequently, there is nothing regularly associated with perceptions that can be taken to be the substance in which perceptions inhere or are grounded.

very essence] Hume typically uses the phrase *very essence* to indicate the most important or most striking of several features essential to an entity or effect, and not, as one could think, to indicate a single feature which, in the absence of all other features, would make up the entity or effect. For more on Hume's use of this phrase, see Ed. Intro., 152–3.

34 I hope . . . apprehensions] Prior to publishing Books 1 and 2 of the *Treatise* Hume undertook to remove from his manuscript any passages that he thought might 'give Offence to religious People' (letter of 4 Mar. 1740, *Letters*, 1:37; see also

1:24–5). The present apology, or explanation, may be a part of that same effort to avoid offence.

35 **In both cases . . . inconclusive]** Hume notes that his arguments leave open the possibility that the soul is immortal, as much as the possibility that it is mortal. Only experience can determine the correct answer to the questions: Does the human mind ever become entirely inactive? Is a human mind ever annihilated? A priori reasoning (reasoning in advance of experience) is of no use regarding such questions of fact.

Book 1 Part 4 Sect. 6. *Of personal identity*

Hume explains how we come to have an idea of the self, or of personal identity. This idea cannot be copied from a direct impression of the self because there is no such impression. When we turn our attention inward, trying to catch a glimpse of some simple self or mind that underlies and unifies our diverse experience, we encounter only a succession of perceptions, never such a simple self or mind. After a review of the concept and kinds of identity, Hume explains how the relations of causation and resemblance affect the imagination so as to make us feel as if our perceptions are united or bonded together, thus providing the basis for the idea (a 'fiction') of personal identity. Nothing we experience really unites our different perceptions; we only suppose them united because we find them united in the imagination. (App. 10–21 supplement this section; see also Ed. Intro., 143–5.)

1 **some philosophers . . . simplicity]** In the brief discussion of personal identity found in the *Abstract* Hume notes that Descartes held 'that thought was the essence of the mind' (*Abs.* 28), thus suggesting that it may be Descartes and the Cartesians that he has in mind here; see also Malebranche, *Search* 3.2.7.4. In addition, Locke, although he says that our idea of immaterial substance is a complex one (*Essay* 2.23.15), argues that our own existence is as certain as our pains or thoughts, and 'neither needs, nor is capable of any proof' because in 'every Act of Sensation, Reasoning, or Thinking, we are conscious to our selves of our own Being; and, in this Matter, come not short of the highest degree of *Certainty*' (*Essay* 4.9.3; see also 2.1.10, 19). At *Treatise* 2.2.2.15 Hume himself says that 'we are at all times intimately conscious of ourselves, our sentiments and passions' (see also 2.1.2.2–3; 2.1.11.4). An extensive discussion of consciousness is found in the anonymous *An Essay on Consciousness*. There consciousness is described as 'that inward Sense and Knowledge which the Mind hath of its own Being and Existence', and is said to give us 'infallible Assurance of the Reality of our own Being and Existence' (pp. 144, 182). See also Berkeley, *Three Dialogues* 3 [2:233] and *De Motu* 21; Browne, *Procedure* 1.2, 3.5; Law, notes to King's *Essay on the Origin of Evil* [7]; and, among French authors, La Forge, *Traitté de l'esprit de l'homme* [134]; Arnauld, *On True and False Ideas* 2, 6 [11, 46]; and Bayle, *Dictionary*, 'Rorarius' n. E.

2 **It cannot . . . idea]** Given that Hume goes on to explain how we come to form the notion or idea of self-identity, and assumes there is such an idea throughout the later books of the *Treatise*, he apparently here means that there is 'no such idea' of the self as would be formed by copying some invariant *impression* of the self. A similar rhetoric is employed at 1.3.14.14; on ideas indirectly formed, see 1.1.1.10–11; 1.2.3.4–7.

3 **For my part . . . pleasure]** Hume can never see behind, as it were, individual perceptions to the self in which these perceptions are alleged to inhere or to which they are 'suppos'd to have a reference' (¶2 of this section). The situation is analogous to that regarding physical objects, whereof we seem to experience (at most) particular qualities, but never any underlying substance in which these qualities allegedly inhere. See 1.4.2.24, 31–40.

When my perceptions . . . exist] Compare Locke, *Essay* 2.1.10–19.

4 **metaphysicians . . . kind**] See the annotation to ¶1 of this section.

5 **The first . . . subject**] The second subject, personal identity as it relates to the passions and self-concern, is dealt with in Book 2 of the *Treatise*; see e.g. 2.1.2.2–3; 2.1.11.4; 2.2.2.15.

6 *identity* or *sameness*] For an earlier discussion of identity and perfect identity, see 1.4.2.26–36.

yet we cannot . . . imagination] We cannot for very long believe and act as our philosophical reflections suggest we should.

run into] devise, although not necessarily voluntarily. Compare the discussion at 1.4.2.36–40.

n. 50 *Philosophical Rhapsody*] See *The Moralists, a Philosophical Rhapsody*, in Shaftesbury's *Characteristics* [esp. 2:99–106].

7 **dispute of words**] Locke had said that the 'difficulty or obscurity' regarding the identity of substances arises from 'Names ill used' (*Essay* 2.27.28). Hume goes on to argue that the dispute is not merely one of words because there is an idea, albeit a fiction, based on 'a mistake', to explain; but see also ¶21 of this section. Hume's views on meaning are revealed by his comments at 1.1.7.14; 1.2.5.21; 1.3.6.14; 1.3.14.14; App. 11.

9 *proportion . . . whole*] See also the discussion of comparison in 2.2.8.

11 **A ship . . . another**] A ship, frequently repaired until at last nothing remained of the original, is a common example of such a thing. See Seneca, *Epistles* 102.6; Plutarch, *Lives* 22–3; Grotius, *Rights of War and Peace* 2.9.3; Hobbes, *Elements of Philosophy* 2.11.7; and Clarke, *Works*, 3:844. Locke argues that a machine, a watch, for example, is 'nothing but a fit Organization, or Construction of Parts, to a certain end', and that in this respect it is very much like the body of an animal (*Essay* 2.27.5).

12 *sympathy*] here, a 'reciprocal relation'. In Books 2 and 3 Hume discusses a significantly different form of sympathy; see esp. 2.1.11.2–8; 3.3.1.7–14.

13 **numerical and specific identity**] For more on numerical and specific difference or identity, see 1.2.6.8–9; 1.4.2.3, 56; and esp. 1.4.5.19–20.

15 **We now proceed . . . *England***] In the preceding fifty years the issue of personal identity had been discussed by, among others, Locke, *Essay* 2.27; Shaftesbury, *Characteristics* [2:100–6, 275–6]; Clarke, *Letter* and three defences thereof; Collins, four works: *A Letter*, *A Reply*, *Reflections*, and *An Answer*; Berkeley, *Alciphron* 7.8; Butler, 'Of Personal Identity'; *Spectator* 578; Chambers, *Cyclopædia*, 'Identity'; Watts, *Philosophical Essays* 12.7; Perronet, *Second Vindication*; and, although not published until 1741, Arbuthnot, *Memoirs of Martinus Scriblerius*.

16 **prov'd at large**] See esp. 1.3.3–7, 14.

above-mention'd] See ¶7 of this section.

ideal world] the world of ideas; the mental or intellectual world. See 1.1.4.6; 1.4.5.1; and App. 10.

above-explain'd] See ¶¶9–10 of this section; see also 1.4.2.34; 1.4.3.3–4; and App. 20.

19 **As to *causation* . . . other**] Compare App. 20–1.

20 **'Twill be . . . memory**] Locke (*Essay* 2.27.9–10) and Collins (Clarke, *Works* [3:875]) maintain that personal identity depends on consciousness and the extension of consciousness by memory. Butler criticizes this view in his brief essay, 'Of Personal Identity'. Hume's account makes use of memory, but in an indirect fashion. He gives to memory a key role in developing those inclinations of mind that allow us (or cause us) to fill gaps in our experience by supposing that things not currently experienced (or events not currently remembered) none the less exist. Memory can fill this role despite

the fact that it is erratic and provides only an incomplete or discontinuous record of the relevant activities. See 1.4.2.20 for a parallel discussion.

21 **already observ'd**] See ¶7 of this section.

23 **anatomy of human nature**] This is the first of several occasions on which Hume describes the *Treatise* as being concerned with the anatomy of human nature, or more specifically, of the human mind. See also 2.1.12.2; 3.3.6.6; *Abs.* 2; *Letters*, 1:32–3.

Book 1 Part 4 Sect. 7. *Conclusion of this book*

Before continuing with the science of human nature, Hume pauses to reflect on the task ahead of him, and the tools available to perform it. He is close to despair about his chance of success. His philosophy has reduced him to a state of 'forlorn solitude'. Through his criticism of others, he has left himself open to the hostility 'of all metaphysicians, logicians, mathematicians, and even theologians' (¶2). And what reason does he have to think his own conclusions are more accurate than those he would replace? He has only a '*strong* propensity to consider objects *strongly* in that view, under which they appear' to him (¶3). Experience and habit, not reason, shape and enliven his own views as much as those of others. Everything rests on the imagination, an unreliable principle that leads us, inconsistently, to rely on causal reasoning and to believe in enduring objects. But if we were to reject these natural but illusory effects of the imagination and rely instead on reason alone, the consequences would be fatal: We would believe nothing and literally perish (¶7).

We face a dilemma: shall we follow reason or the imagination. There is no solution, but there is something to be said for letting nature take charge. Philosophize, follow reason into doubt when that is your mood, but relax when nature dispels these doubts, which she is sure to do. Although some philosophical conclusions may have only a fleeting influence, the philosophical attitude is the foundation of all science, and a valuable weapon against the rash claims of superstition or religion. The errors of philosophy may be ridiculous, but those of religion are dangerous. Hume hopes that he can contribute something to the advancement of knowledge by encouraging philosophers to focus on the science of human nature, and by showing them the advantages of conducting their researches in the unruffled manner that he recommends. The volume closes with his apology for sometimes appearing more positive and dogmatic than he really is. (For a further brief discussion of 1.4.7, see Ed. Intro., I45–6.)

2 **commerce**] social interaction.

to mix . . . deformity] to join in when so deformed. It is Hume, imagining himself as 'some strange uncouth monster', who is, metaphorically speaking, deformed.

3 **quality**] that quality of the imagination which is operated on by habit and custom in such a way as to make us 'form ideas in a more intense and lively manner'. When Hume describes this quality as 'trivial' he means that it is such a commonplace part of the operation of our minds as to be generally unnoticed.

4 **principle**] the imagination.

n. 51 Sect. 4] See 1.4.4.15.

that glorious title] the title of philosopher.

5 **n. 52 Part 3. Sect. 14**] See also 1.3.2–7.

6 **sensible**] aware.

this] this lack of awareness.

nothing . . . philosophers] See 1.4.3–4.

angels . . . wings] Angels are so represented at Isa. 6: 2.

7 the understanding . . . imagination] Hume's discussion is slightly complicated by the fact that he here treats reason or the understanding as a form of the imagination, a rhetorical turn of events we are not entirely prepared for by Note 22.

n. 53 Sect. 1] See 1.4.1.3–10.

If we embrace . . . absurdities] Relying only on the imagination, without any limitation from refined reasoning, leads one to hold absurd opinions.

10 affairs of life] Compare 1.4.1.7 and *Abs.* 4.

indolent belief . . . world] acceptance of ordinary, common-sense opinions, including the existence of external objects and enduring selves, and the reality of causes.

splenetic humour] melancholy; a despondent mood.

sceptical disposition and principles] When he earlier indicated that he is not one of those sceptics who holds that everything is uncertain, Hume left open the possibility that there are other and more moderate forms of scepticism. Here he argues that allowing his understanding to be ruled by nature is consistent with his scepticism. The Pyrrhonists whom he attacks (implicitly at 1.4.1.7, openly at *Abs.* 27) would not disagree; see Sextus Empiricus, *Pyrrhonism* 1.10.

12 mind . . . itself] composed and reflective.

I cannot forbear . . . govern me] These subjects are discussed in Books 2 and 3.

13 scenes . . . new] scenes, beings, and objects for which there is little or no basis in experience.

Cynics] The Cynics were a group of ancient philosophers generally united in their disdain of material possessions and social convention. The most famous of them, Diogenes of Sinope, reputedly carried this disdain to the extreme of living in a tub.

14 earthy mixture] an allusion to the four elements and the corresponding humours and temperaments. On that account, increasing the proportion of the 'gross earthy mixture' would moderate fiery excesses; see the second annotation to 1.4.4.3.

BOOK 2. OF THE PASSIONS

Title-page

Rara . . . licet] The rare good fortune of an age in which we may feel what we wish and say what we feel (Tacitus, *Histories* 1.1).

Book 2 Part 1. *Of pride and humility*

Hume begins *Treatise* 2.1 by classifying the several kinds of passion. He then explains how, by means of the principles of association and, more specifically, from a double relation of impressions and ideas, the indirect passions of pride and humility are formed. He next explains why certain qualities of individuals (virtue and beauty, for example) serve as causes of pride, while their contraries (vice and deformity, for example) serve as causes of humility. Sect. 11 introduces and explains sympathy, a principle of communication inherent in human nature; the final section discusses pride and humility in animals. (For further discussion of *Treatise* 2.1, see Ed. Intro., I46–73.)

Book 2 Part 1 Sect. 1. *Division of the Subject*

There are two kinds of perception, impressions and ideas, and also two kinds of impression. These are '*original*' impressions (also called impressions of sensation) and '*secondary*' impressions (also called impressions of reflection). Original impressions (sensations and bodily pains or pleasures, for example) are independent of prior perceptions. Secondary impressions (most passions and emotions) depend on previously experienced impressions or ideas. Saying that he has no interest in determining the causes of original impressions, Hume indicates that his present goal is to account for secondary impressions. He notes that the reflective impressions or passions are commonly but inexactly divided into two types, calm and violent. A closer look at the passions reveals that they can be more accurately divided between the '*direct*' (those that arise directly from pain and pleasure; desire, aversion, grief, and fear are examples) and the '*indirect*' (those that arise from pain and pleasure in conjunction with other qualities; pride, humility, love, and hatred are examples of such indirect passions). For further discussion of the kinds of passion, see Ed. Intro., I48–9.

1 n. 54 **Book 1. Part 1. Sect. 2**] See also *Abs.* 5–7.
   animal spirits] On animal spirits, see the final annotation to 1.2.5.20.
   Original . . . organs] Possible causes of impressions of sensation are also mentioned at 1.3.5.2.
   its idea] by the idea, that is, of one of the original impressions when recalled by either memory or imagination.
2 **into the sciences . . . philosophy**] Hume makes a similar disclaimer at 1.1.2.1.
   affection] here, impression.
3 **commonly distinguish'd . . . other**] The distinction between calm and violent passions may have been commonly made, but not in just these terms. Descartes had contrasted lesser passions with stronger or more violent ones, but did not use the term *calm* (*Passions of the Soul* 1.46 [1:345]; 2.85 [1:358]), while Malebranche had distinguished between calm, general desires or natural inclinations and those 'sensible emotions' that 'affect the soul upon occasion of extraordinary motion in the animal spirits' (*Search* 5.1). Hutcheson generally followed Malebranche (see *Inquiry* 2.6.4–6; *Essay* 1.2.2). Butler contrasted 'cool or settled' general desire with 'passionate or sensual' and 'particular' passions (*Sermons*, Preface; Sermon 11). See also 1.3.10.10.
   having said . . . ideas] Book 1 focuses on the nature and origin of ideas.
4 **By indirect . . . qualities**] The arousal of the indirect passions depends upon the three associative principles, cause and effect, contiguity, and resemblance (and especially the latter). It is apparently for this reason that Hume calls pride, humility, love, and hatred 'indirect passions'.
   This distinction . . . any farther] The direct passions are the subject of 2.3.9; four indirect passions, pride and humility, and love and hatred, are the subjects, respectively, of 2.1 and 2.2.

Book 2 Part 1 Sect. 2. *Of pride and humility; their objects and causes*

Because pride and humility are simple and uniform impressions, they are indefinable, but it is possible to describe the conditions in which they arise. Although directly contrary to one another, these two passions have the same *object*, namely, the self. If we are pleased with some aspect of ourselves, we feel the passion of pride; if displeased, we experience humility. Pride and humility are caused by a combination of a *subject* related to me and some distinctive *quality* of that subject—by, for example, my mind and such qualities as courage or cowardice, my body and such qualities as strength or weakness, or one of my possessions and such qualities as beauty or ugliness. My own mind or house will give rise to pride only if each appears to me to have positive qualities; they will give rise to humility only if each appears to have negative qualities. In contrast, a mind or house unconnected to me, whether distinguished by positive or negative qualities, will never produce pride or humility in me.

1 'tis impossible . . . passions] Hume here, as well as at 2.2.1.1 and 2.3.1.2, applies to the passions the view, found earlier in Locke, that simple ideas cannot be defined (*Essay* 3.4.4, 7; see also 3.3.10).

2 This object . . . consciousness] For Hume's views on the self and our awareness of it or our idea of it, see also 1.4.6.1–2; 2.1.11.4; 2.2.2.15.

3 the one annihilates . . . mind] Hume holds much the same view regarding conflicting beliefs; see 1.3.12.19. For more on contrary passions, see 2.3.9.10–17.

4 The first idea] the first idea in a complex chain of ideas and impressions that results in pride or humility. The idea of the cause (the beautiful house, for example) initiates this process.

5 *subjects*] To avoid confusion, Hume here speaks of *subjects* (rather than *objects*) that have qualities that cause pride or humility. The subjects in question may be one's mind or body, one's relatives and friends, or one's possessions.

6 Both . . . chimerical] Hume anticipates the objection that beauty or other qualities that cause pride are always found in a subject, and hence that the distinction between subject and quality is meaningless. Although he could well agree with the view that qualities cannot be conceived of independently of the subject of which they are qualities, Hume sees that we can intelligibly think of beauty as unrelated to any particular subject (see the discussion of distinctions of reason at 1.1.7.17). Neither beauty nor any other quality can be, in this unrelated form, the source of pride. To be the source of pride, a quality must be the quality of some particular subject that is closely related to the individual who feels that pride.

Book 2 Part 1 Sect. 3. *Whence these objects and causes are deriv'd*

Because the self is always the object of pride and humility, we can say that it is 'natural' that this should be the case (¶2). We can also infer that this constant effect is the result of some original and universal ('inseparable') feature of the mind. The causes of pride and humility are equally natural: the causes of these passions have been the same 'in all nations and ages' (¶4). Neither can we conceive, while human nature remains as we find it, that we will find humans whose pride is unaffected by their personal qualities or possessions. But, although the causes of pride and humility are clearly natural, they are not 'original' (¶5). That is, it is not necessary, in order to account for our pride, to suppose that we have implanted in us an original principle corresponding to each of the virtually unlimited causes of pride. Just as the modern astronomer can account for the diverse motions of the planets and stars by means of a few fundamental principles, so can we account for the nature, origin, causes, and effects of our passions by means of only a few such principles.

2 determin'd] made or structured so as.

a natural . . . original property] a natural and original property of human nature. In the *Abstract* (¶6), Hume suggests that 'all our passions are a kind of natural instinct, derived from nothing but the original constitution of the human mind', and that, in so far as they 'arise immediately from nature', they are innate. See also 2.1.5.3.

3 **That this . . . impulse]** Although Hume is explaining how pride arises, he is also pointing out that our passions are produced by original features of human nature—that our passions are natural, rather than unnatural, as some of his predecessors had maintained. On this issue, see Ed. Intro., 146–8.

4 **We may . . . mind]** Hume goes on to argue that the observed regularity of effects shows that pride and humility are the effects of natural (invariant) principles of human nature.

5 **But tho' . . . nature]** It is not necessary to suppose that those subjects that cause pride do so because each one activates an original instinct or propensity suited only to that one subject. Rather, the subjects that are the causes of pride have features in common, and as a consequence each of a wide variety of such subjects can arouse pride or humility in the same general way.

6 **quality]** explanatory principle.

7 **maxim . . . vain]** This maxim is found in Aristotle, *De caelo* 2.11, and has been widely repeated since. Accepting the maxim carries with it an implicit commitment to seek the simplest explanation consistent with the phenomena to be explained. See also Hume's fourth rule for judging causes and effects, 1.3.15.6.
intricate systems of the heavens] Hume's reference to pre-Copernican astronomy is to the seemingly *ad hoc* and uneconomical explanations of Ptolemaic astronomy. In order to explain the movement of the planets, this widely held system posited an increasingly complex set of circular movements (cycles and epicycles). What Hume describes as the 'more simple and natural' heliocentric view was first formulated in modern times (in 1543) by Copernicus.

Book 2 Part 1 Sect. 4. *Of the relations of impressions and ideas*

Having concluded that the principles that produce pride and humility are both natural and relatively few in number, Hume now undertakes to specify those features that are common to the causes of these passions. Reflecting on human nature, he recalls our propensity to associate together the ideas of resembling, contiguous, and causally related objects. He then notes that we have a similar propensity to associate resembling impressions. Consequently, one passion is likely to give rise to another: grief to anger, anger to envy, envy to malice, malice to grief, for example. A tendency to such change is a fundamental feature of human nature. The associations of ideas and impressions are found to reinforce one another and to give the mind 'a double impulse' towards a further passion (¶4). A passage from Addison illustrates this reinforcing tendency.

2 **often . . . explain'd]** See esp. 1.1.4; also 1.3.6.12–15; 1.3.9.2; *Abs.* 35.

3 **All . . . impressions]** all impressions of reflection, that is.

4 **two kinds of association]** association of ideas (by resemblance, contiguity, cause and effect) and association of impressions (by resemblance).

5 **elegant writer]** Joseph Addison, *Spectator* 412.
fancy] Addison, like Hume, uses *fancy* interchangeably with *imagination*.

Book 2 Part 1 Sect. 5. *Of the influence of these relations on pride and humility*

Hume explains how the several factors previously identified, and especially the relations of impressions and ideas, work together to produce the passions of pride and humility.

Imagine that I feel pride in consequence of owning a beautiful house. The house is the subject in which the quality of beauty is found, and, because of this quality, is the cause of the pride of which I am the object: (1) The beautiful house produces in me an impression and then an idea of itself. (2) This idea, because it is an idea of my house, also gives rise to a related idea, the idea of my self. (3) At the same time, this idea of a beautiful house produces in me an impression, a feeling of pleasure. (4) This first impression gives rise to a second impression to which the first is related by resemblance (both impressions are pleasant). (5) This second impression of pleasure has the second idea (the idea of my self) as its object and is the impression or feeling that constitutes the core of the passion of pride. In short, by means of a double relation of impressions and ideas, the pleasant feeling associated with pride is itself associated with an idea of the constant object of pride, namely, the self. (For a schematic representation of this theory, see Ed. Intro., I51–2.) Hume emphasizes that 'nature has bestow'd a kind of attraction on certain impressions and ideas', so that the experience of some one of these 'naturally introduces its correlative' (¶10). As a consequence, our passions must be understood as effects produced only after we have encountered the appropriate causes. Our passions, very much like our causal judgements, depend upon the operation of a prior, associating disposition of the mind, and on an appropriate present experience.

1 **These principles**] The principles discussed in 2.1.2–4.
 as the qualities . . . subjects] See 2.1.2.6 for the distinction between quality and subject.
2 **virtue and vice**] For a fuller account of how virtue and vice give rise to pride, see 2.1.7.
 beauty or deformity] For a fuller account of how beauty and deformity give rise to pride, see 2.1.8.
3 **look beyond self**] take as their object anything other than the self.
4 **sensations . . . emotions**] the pains or pleasures, that is.
 very being and essence] For a discussion of Hume's use of the phrases 'very essence' and 'very being and essence', see Ed. Intro., I52–3.
5 **That cause . . . deriv'd**] On Hume's account of the phenomenon, my feeling of pride in my beautiful house arises when a particular subject (my house) and quality (beauty) together excite an idea, A, of a beautiful house related to an idea of my self, or idea B. Idea A also produces impression A, a distinct pleasure that, because it resembles impression B, the pleasurable sensation or feeling associated with pride, leads me to have impression B. Idea B is connected to impression B as the object of this impression. For a schematic representation of this account, see Ed. Intro., I51–2.
 double impulse] This notion is introduced at 2.1.4.4.
6 **organs of the human mind**] Elsewhere Hume uses this phrase as a synonym for 'the particular fabric or structure of the mind' ('The Sceptic' 14) and for 'faculties of the mind' ('Of the Standard of Taste' 7). See also 2.2.11.6.
 needs no proof] needs, that is, no formal argument, as it is obvious from a review of the experience of pride.
8 **the very principle**] The principle of *relation*, operating through the association of impressions and ideas, is fundamental to the production of pride.
9 **separate sensation . . . revers'd**] The sensation that triggers humility is displeasure or pain, not pleasure.
 change . . . impressions] It is the set of related impressions, and not the relation between the impressions, that alters. The idea of the now ugly house produces impression A', displeasure, a feeling related to impression B', the passion of humility. But the

relation between impressions *A'* and *B'*, like that between impressions *A* and *B*, is resemblance.

10 **In a word . . . correlative**] The present paragraph summarizes Hume's account of the production of pride and humility. On attraction, see 1.1.4.6.

11 **already explain'd . . . causation**] See 1.3.5–8, esp. 1.3.7.5–7; 1.3.8.2–5.
   nor the spirits excited] nor force and vivacity produced.

Book 2 Part 1 Sect. 6. *Limitations of this system*

The conclusion '*that all agreeable objects, related to ourselves, by an association of ideas and of impressions, produce pride, and disagreeable ones, humility*' is now qualified in five ways: (1) To produce pride, agreeable objects must be closely related to ourselves. (2) To produce pride, the closely related objects must be thought to be relatively scarce. Even so important a quality as good health will often not (especially among the young) be the source of pride. (3) To produce pride, the closely related and agreeable objects must be noticeable to others. (4) To produce pride, the related objects must remain related to us for a significant period of time. (5) General rules have a substantial effect on all the passions. In addition, those who are proudest are not always the most happy; evils or misfortunes can make us unhappy without diminishing our pride.

2 **the first passion . . . joy**] Note that joy is a direct passion and that it may be produced by an object that gives observers pleasure but is not otherwise related to them. See ¶5 of this section.
   pride and vain-glory] In this paragraph Hume appears to treat *pride, vain-glory, self-applause*, and *vanity* as synonyms.
   As it] as relation in general.
   n. 55 Part 2. Sect. 4] See 2.2.4.10–13 and also 2.2.8.

4 **to explain afterwards**] See 2.3.5.
   We likewise . . . merit] A fuller account of our tendency to judge by comparison, rather than from intrinsic worth, is found at 2.2.8. See also 2.1.10.12; 2.1.11.18; 2.2.10.8; 3.2.10.5.

6 **to explain afterwards**] See esp. 2.1.11.1–2, 9–19.

8 **that explain'd**] See 1.3.13.7–14; the effect of general rules is also discussed at 2.1.9.13 and 2.2.5.12–13.

9 **person full-grown . . . world**] Compare Hume's suggestions regarding Adam, 'created in the full vigour of understanding, without experience', found at *Abs.* 11.
   The passions . . . principles] See e.g. 2.2.2.24–8; 2.2.4.9–13; 2.2.9.11–12.
   hereafter ascribe] See e.g. 2.1.10.9; 2.2.5.6–7.

10 **An evil**] a pain. Hume often equates good and evil with pleasure and pain (see e.g. 1.3.10.2; 2.1.1.4; 2.3.1.1; and 2.3.9.8). It is important to note that in doing so he does not commit himself to the view that every good or evil is a *moral* quality. A pleasure that has its source in a beautiful house, for example, is a non-moral or *natural good*; a pain that has its source in ugliness is a non-moral or *natural evil*. In this regard, Hume's position is similar to that of Hutcheson, who explicitly distinguishes between such *natural goods* as possessions and such *moral goods* as benevolent motives. For Hutcheson's position, see his *Inquiry* 2.1.

Book 2 Part 1 Sect. 7. *Of vice and virtue*

Hume considers specific causes of pride and humility with the intent of testing his claim that these passions depend upon a double relation of impressions and ideas. He avoids involving himself in the widespread debate about the question, Are moral distinctions *'founded on natural and original principles, or [do they] arise from interest and education'* (¶2). However one answers this question (whatever one takes to be the foundation of virtue), it is clear that supposing oneself to be virtuous is a cause of pride, while supposing oneself to be vicious is a cause of humility. The perception of virtue gives pleasure; if the virtue in question is appropriately related to me (is my virtue), it will stimulate both the ideas and the impressions that result in the experience of pride. If I have other positive qualities of mind (wit or good humour, for example), my perception of these also produces pride. My perception of any vice I have produces humility. Hume notes that those who think pride is a vice and humility a virtue may find it strange to suppose that we take pride in virtue. Rather than dispute about what may be only a choice of words, he offers a brief description of pride and humility, and insists that feeling the agreeable impression of pride is not always a sign of vice, nor is having the disagreeable feeling associated with humility always a sign of virtue.

2 **the controversy . . . education**] In the two decades prior to the publication of the *Treatise*, contributions to this controversy regarding the foundations of morality were made by, among others, Wollaston, *Religion of Nature Delineated*; Mandeville, *Enquiry into the Origin of Moral Virtue*; Hutcheson, *Inquiry into the Original of our Ideas of Beauty and Virtue*; John Clarke, *Foundation of Morality in Theory and Practice*; Butler, *Sermons*; Archibald Campbell, *Enquiry into the Original of Moral Virtue*; and Balguy, *Foundation of Moral Goodness*. Earlier contributions to this debate include portions of Montaigne's *Apology for Raymond Sebond*; the Preliminary Discourse to *The Rights of War and Peace* by Grotius; *Leviathan* and other writings by Hobbes; the *Maxims* of La Rochefoucauld; *Law of Nature* by Pufendorf; *Treatise Concerning Eternal and Immutable Morality* by Cudworth; *Discourse concerning the Unchangeable Obligations of Natural Religion* by Samuel Clarke; and *An Inquiry concerning Virtue or Merit* by Shaftesbury.
   The examination . . . book] See esp. *Treatise* 3.2 and 3.3, which show Hume to suppose some moral distinctions rest on *'natural and original principles'* and some rest on *'interest and education'*.

3 **defenders of that hypothesis**] Hume most likely alludes to Hobbes and Mandeville, who, arguing that humans are motivated only by self-interest, maintain that the distinction between virtue and vice is merely conventional, not natural. See e.g. Hobbes, *Leviathan* 1.6, 13–14; Mandeville, *Fable* [1:39–57].

5 **those, who . . . nature**] Hume alludes to a disparate group of writers who suppose that the distinction between virtue and vice has a secure, extra-human foundation, and thus is not merely conventional. See e.g. Grotius, *Rights of War and Peace*, Preliminary Discourse; Cudworth, *Treatise* 1.1.5–1.2.3; Hutcheson, *Inquiry*, Preface; Balguy, *Foundation* 1 [1–39].
   The most probable . . . pleasure] Hume alludes to the moral sense theory suggested by Shaftesbury, and more fully developed by Hutcheson, in the works mentioned in the annotation to ¶2 of this section. Hume himself adopts one version of this theory; see *Treatise* 3.1.
   constitute . . . essence] For a discussion of Hume's use of this phrase, see Ed. Intro., 152–3.
   To approve . . . uneasiness] For a brief elaboration of this point, see 3.1.2.1–3.

6 **undeniable proof . . . system**] proof that pride and humility depend on the double relation of impressions and ideas.

7 **vulgar systems of ethics**] common accounts of morality, including those that are a part of religious views. Hume goes on to argue that we respond with pride not only to

those qualities of mind that we are said to have a duty to cultivate (a 'generous and noble character', for example), but also to such natural or uncultivated intellectual abilities as wit and good humour. For his extensive discussion of these 'natural abilities', see 3.3.4–5.

7 **very essence . . . wit**] We do not know what wit is, but we do know that whatever is witty pleases, and what does not please is not witty. Pleasure, in short, is a necessary condition of wit.

8 **There may . . . virtue**] Pride had long been viewed as a sin, and sometimes as one of the seven deadly sins. Consequently, it was portrayed as reprehensible in both sermons that Hume would have heard, and in written works with which he would have been familiar, *The Whole Duty of Man*, for example. But not all popular moralists supposed pride is necessarily a vice. Steele wrote of 'what we may call a vertuous and laudable Pride' (*Spectator* 462; see also No. 512). At 3.3.2.13 Hume suggests that '*heroic virtue*' is, or is at least largely made up of, a 'well-establish'd pride'.

Book 2 Part 1 Sect. 8. *Of beauty and deformity*

Beauty and deformity produce pride and humility. These qualities are closely related to those who have them, and thus they give rise to the idea of self. All forms of beauty give pleasure, as all forms of deformity give pain. Thus beauty and deformity produce precisely those mental elements that trigger the double relation of impressions and ideas that produces pride or humility. Whatever account may be given of the nature of beauty, beauty obviously gives us pleasure (as deformity gives displeasure). Indeed, beauty is essentially that form of things which has a tendency to produce a sensation of pleasure, but even if pleasure is not the essence of beauty, pleasure is inseparable from the experience of beauty. It is clear that it is the pleasure beauty gives that produces the passion of pride. Hume also notes that the only relevant difference between our own beauty and that of external objects lies in the relations these qualities have to us. External things, unrelated to us, give us pleasure, but they do not produce pride, thus confirming that a double relation of impressions and ideas is essential to the production of pride. Should it be argued that beauty is not merely the power of producing pleasure, it can still be shown that other, clearly response-dependent qualities (the quality of being surprising, for example) are capable of producing an impression of pleasure and, by consequence, the passion of pride. This fact confirms that pride and humility are dependent on nothing more than appropriately related impressions and ideas. In closing, Hume explains why the general failure to take pride in one's good health poses no difficulty for his theory.

1 **Whether . . . external**] Many writers had suggested that the body is distinct from, and thus in effect external to, 'ourselves' or the mind. Although Descartes saw the mind as 'residing in the brain', he thought it only 'closely conjoined' to the body (*Principles of Philosophy* 2.2; 4.189, 196). Malebranche argued that only because of a mistaken instinct of sensation do 'we regard our body and all sensible things to which we are joined as part of ourselves' (*Search* 5.5 [366]; see also Preface [p. xix]; 1.10.1; 3.2.10 [253]). Even Berkeley, although he says that a body is 'nothing but a complexion [combination] of such qualities or ideas, as have no existence distinct from being perceived by a mind', had said that 'we are chained to a body' (*Three Dialogues* 3 [2:241]). Hume could also have had in mind theories of metempsychosis (at *EPM* 6.11 he refers to Plato's views on this topic), the view of Aristotle that we are constituted of a soul plus a body (see *De anima* 413ᵃ2), or even the view, discussed by Bayle, that there is a single intellect (or

intellectual soul) 'which serves all Mankind, as the Light of the Sun does the Universe', and which must in consequence be external to the body (*Dictionary*, 'Averroës', n. E).

If . . . ideas] If the conditions Hume has specified are met, pride or humility will necessarily result. If I have an idea of some quality closely related to myself (an idea of my own deformity, for example), this idea will make me uneasy and necessarily lead to the feeling or passion of humility. It should not be forgotten, however, that Hume has suggested a number of limitations that affect this outcome; see 2.1.6.

2 all the hypotheses . . . soul] Those who had noted that beauty is pleasing and satisfying included Shaftesbury (see *Characteristics* [1:251–2, 2:267–9]) and Addison (see *Spectator* 411–21).

This is the distinguishing . . . uneasiness] For a similar argument regarding wit, see 2.1.7.7.

Pleasure . . . essence] This is Hume's way of saying that pleasure is an unfailing and distinguishing feature or effect of beauty, and pain (or uneasiness) is an unfailing and distinguishing feature or effect of deformity. See Ed. Intro., 152–3, for a discussion of the phrase *very essence*.

is deriv'd . . . utility] Berkeley had noted the connection between convenience and beauty: 'architects judge a door to be of a beautiful proportion, when its height is double of the breadth. But if you should invert a well-proportioned door, making its breadth become the height, and its height the breadth, the figure would still be the same, but without that beauty in one situation, which it had in another. What can be the cause of this, but that [the inverted door] would not yield a convenient entrance to creatures of a human figure' (*Alciphron* 3.9).

rules of architecture . . . uneasy] Claude Perrault says that 'To give Satisfaction in two Points that are the most important in Architecture, namely, Solidity or Strength, and the Appearance of Solidity, which, as has been already said, makes a very principal Part in the Beauty of Buildings; all Architects have made their Columns lesser above than below, which is call'd Diminution' (*Treatise of the Five Orders of Columns* [24]). Vitruvius, the Roman architect from whom this rule is derived, recommends what Perrault calls *diminution* because it imitates nature: 'for the purpose of bearing the load, what is below ought to be stronger than what is above, and also, because we ought to imitate nature as seen in the case of things growing; for example, in round smooth-stemmed trees' (*On Architecture* 5.1.3); see also 3.3.1.23.

3 and as a common effect . . . cause] Hume argues that natural and moral beauty are alike only in that both give pleasure and cause pride. Given the rule that like effects have like causes (rule 4 at 1.3.15.6), it must be that the pleasure given by these forms of beauty is the cause of the pride felt by those possessing them. He then notes that the beauty of our bodies differs from the beauty of other things in two ways: our own beauty is closely related to us and it gives rise to pride, while unrelated beauty gives us only pleasure. Given that different effects are the result of differences in causes (rule 6 at 1.3.15.8), it follows that the pride taken in beauty is caused by the fact that the quality (beauty) giving pleasure is closely related to the person feeling the pride. Taking these two findings together provides confirmation of the claim that pride and humility are produced by a double relation of impressions and ideas. Another version of this argument is found in ¶7 of this section.

4 *ambition*] the general desire for power.

present phænomenon] that bodily strength is a source of pride; see also ¶7 of this section.

6 beauty . . . surprise . . . soul] While some might claim that beauty is in fact objective,

no one will dispute the suggestion that surprise ('a pleasure arising from novelty') is merely subjective. Consequently, given that qualities of ourselves that are surprising always produce pride, it is clear that it is the pleasure of surprise that causes this pride. Where surprise of this kind is concerned, nothing lying beyond the pleasure it gives— nothing objective—is ever supposed to exist, and hence nothing other than the requisite pleasure is needed to give rise to pride.

7 **known rules**] For Hume's version of these rules, see 1.3.15.3–10.

above-mention'd] For Hume's initial account of his system of double relations, see 2.1.5, esp. 5, 8–10.

8 *second . . . limitations*] See 2.1.6.4, 7; and the summary annotation for 2.1.6.

9 **Of the epilepsy . . . present**] Some of Hume's predecessors and contemporaries associated epilepsy with divine punishment or possession by evil spirits. See e.g. Hobbes, *Leviathan* 3.34; Chambers, *Cyclopædia*, 'Epilepsy'.

itch . . . infectious] The name for a disease caused by a mite which penetrates the skin and causes pustules that itch intensely. The pest could move from person to person, and thus was said to be 'infectious'. According to Chambers, microscopic examination of this mite showed it to be shaped like a tortoise, with six feet, a sharp head, and two little horns at the end of its snout (*Cyclopædia*, 'Itch'). Itch was also a name for venereal disease, likewise infectious.

king's-evil] This disease, also known as *scrofula* or *struma*, is at present classified as a tuberculosis of the lymphatic system and thought to be genetically transmitted. The popular name, *king's-evil*, derived from the belief that a sovereign's touch could cure the sufferer. In England this superstition can be traced to the time of Edward the Confessor (d. 1066).

evidently appear'd] been evident in. See e.g. 2.1.6.6; 2.1.7.7; and ¶6 of this section.

explain'd afterwards] See 2.1.11, esp. ¶¶1–2 and 9–19.

Book 2 Part 1 Sect. 9. *Of external advantages and disadvantages*

We experience pride in response to the things we own, but not in response to the same kinds of thing if they belong to others. This fact is said to confirm the claim that only a double relation of impressions and ideas can produce pride and humility. Hume notes that it is typically contiguity and causation, rather than resemblance, that relate pride and humility to those things that produce them. He also emphasizes that pride and humility are not produced directly (they are not the first feeling aroused by the relevant causes), but are produced only when a relation of ideas has supplied the proper object of these passions, namely, the idea of the self. In further confirmation of his theory, Hume discusses the pride we take in our country or locality and their characteristics; the tendency some have to disparage their own countries; and our pride in friends and relatives. He also considers the pride we take in the antiquity of our families, and attempts to explain why greater pride is taken in a family sustained entirely by a succession of males.

1 **primary one**] the self with its qualities.

4 **It produces . . . kind**] Hume is making again the point that a double relation, one of impressions and another of ideas, is necessary to produce pride or humility. This assertion is distinct from, and apparently consistent with, his earlier claim (see 1.3.14.1, 20) that a customary association of *impressions* produces a determination of the mind, or a new impression.

5 **affections**] impressions, as at 2.1.1.2.
6 **parish**] in Britain, a unit of local government, either political or ecclesiastical.
  by the supposition] according to the system of double relations.
7 **transition above-explain'd**] another reference to the double relation of impressions and ideas; the previous paragraph provides an illustration of this transition.
10 **collaterals**] relatives in a different line, uncles, aunts, cousins, for example, in contrast to 'forefathers' or those (a grandparent of one's mother, for example) from whom one directly descends.
11 **uninterrupted . . . land**] Hume's own ancestors had occupied Ninewells, a small agricultural holding in the Scottish Borders, since the early 16th c., or through twelve generations over a period of 200 years (Mossner, *The Life of David Hume*, 6–8).
  foregoing system] system of double relations, that is.
12 **identity of the possession**] continuity of ownership in one family.
13 **n. 56 Part 2. Sect. 2**] See 2.2.2.19–26.
  As in the society . . . female] Hume's example reflects the fact that both the state and the church elevated husbands above wives.
  all relations] all relations of ideas, that is. That we also have a propensity to pass from one impression to another is established at 2.1.4.3 and 2.1.5.10.
  doctrine above-explain'd] On the effect of *general rules*, see 1.3.13.7–14 and 2.1.6.8–9.

Book 2 Part 1 Sect. 10. *Of property and riches*

Property is defined as a relationship between a particular person and an object. This relationship gives to that person, and withholds from all other persons, the right to possess and use the object in question. Hume argues that the association between property and its owner is such that the mention of either property or owner will bring to mind the idea of the other. As a result, any property of our own that gives us an impression of pleasure can be expected to produce pride. In fact, although the distinction between a power and its exercise had been said to be unintelligible, Hume shows how past experience makes it possible for us to speak intelligibly about unexercised powers and human freedom. This in turn accounts for the fact that wealth, understood as the power to acquire property, is able to cause pride. In a similar fashion, other forms of unexercised power (authority, for example) produce pride, while a lack of power, in the form of poverty or servitude, produces humility. For further discussion of the status of unexercised powers, see Ed. Intro., I54.

1 **justice . . . virtues**] For Hume's account of justice, see 3.2.2–6; for his account of the other moral virtues, see 3.2.7–12 and 3.3.1–5.
  that property . . . equity] Hume's definition may well be a development of that proposed by Pufendorf: '*Property or Dominion, is a Right, by which the very Substance, as it were, of a Thing, so belongs to one Person, that it doth not in Whole belong, after the same manner, to any other*' (*Law of Nature* 4.4.1). See also 3.2.6.3, 7.
  species of *causation*] an example of the relation of cause and effect.
  if justice . . . virtue] For Hume, an artificial virtue is any virtue that has come into being and developed as a consequence of human activity or practice, any virtue that arises 'from the circumstances and necessities of mankind', as he says at 3.2.1.1. In *Treatise* 3 he argues that justice, promise-keeping, and allegiance, for example, are artificial virtues. Others who argue that these virtues are artificial include Hobbes and Mandeville, two philosophers who suppose that all virtues are artificial in Hume's

sense of that term. For further discussion of this distinction, see esp. 3.2.1 and 3.3.1, and Ed. Intro., I81–2.

1 **foregoing system]** Hume's theory that pride and humility result from a double relation of impressions and ideas; see 2.1.5.5–10.

3 **Paper]** negotiable notes such as bonds, deeds, and securities.

4 **been observ'd]** See 1.3.14.34; see also 2.2.5.7–9. An additional form of the distinction between a power and its exercise, and one that Hume may suppose intelligible, is made by Hobbes, who distinguishes between the *right* of supreme authority and the *exercise* of this authority (*De Cive* 13.1).

5 **scholastic doctrine of *free-will*]** Hume takes this to be the doctrine that the human will is free to make uncaused choices (to make choices independently of all prior conditions or possible influences), from which it would follow that the will always has unexercised powers available. Hume returns to the will and the question of its freedom in 2.3.1–2; see also 1.3.14.32–3 and Ed. Intro., I65–72.

6 **foregoing book]** *Treatise* 1; see esp. 1.3.6.

that the person . . . perform it] We can reasonably infer that one person never will perform an act of type *A* because she has never done so in the past. We can reasonably infer that another person may perform an act of type *A* because he has in the past occasionally performed such an act, or reasonably infer that he is likely to perform such an act because he has regularly performed such acts in the past.

and tho' in general . . . passions] Although I suppose you always to act from some motivating principle or consideration, I may well wonder which of these motivations will have effect on any given occasion.

And indeed . . . objects] The passions are not actuated by what are only mere possibilities. We might think that the person who has never performed an act of type *A* could perform such an act, but our experience gives us no grounds for thinking she can actually do it. In the language of the first book of the *Treatise*, Hume would say that we can conceive of this agent performing an act of type *A*, but we do not believe that she will perform such an act, and that what is only conceived is not a 'real existence'. On Hume's distinction between conceiving and believing, see 1.3.7; *App.* 2–9; *Abs.* 17–23.

8 **actual existence]** Hume repeats this central claim at 2.2.5.7.

9 **A miser . . . possessions]** The miser appears to present the perfect example of the person about whom we reasonably infer that he will never perform some action because he has never done so in the past. As such, he appears to be a counter-example to the claim that wealth gives us pleasure because it is seen to be the means of securing possessions that will give pleasure. Hume meets this implicit objection by saying that the miser imagines that his wealth is making the pleasure of possessions more likely. Given that Hume has just said (¶6 of this section) that a mere conception of possibilities cannot actuate the passions, the imagination of the miser must do more than conceive of mere possibilities. His imagination must mimic a belief—it must have the degree of force and vivacity that is associated with real existences, or with those perceptions in which we believe. For more on the miser, see 2.2.5.7.

n. 57 Part 3. Sect. 2] See 2.3.2.2.

The will . . . settle] Hume argues that prior to acting we imagine ourselves able to do what we do not choose to do even while we choose that which we do choose to do, and that after acting we imagine that we could have selected any of those actions we did not select. The miser imagines that he could have used, or can use, his money to secure possessions that would give him pleasure even though his past experience gives no basis for

500

so imagining. In this way he manages to derive pleasure from his wealth, and to feel pride in consequence.

10 **The very essence . . . life]** This is Hume's way of saying that an unfailing and distinguishing feature or effect of wealth is the power it gives us. On Hume's use of the phrase 'very essence', see also 1.4.5.33; 2.1.5.4; 2.1.7.7; 2.1.8.2; and Ed. Intro., 152–3.

The very essence . . . pleasure] Hume now argues that the power of wealth is unfailingly accompanied by two things: (1) some likelihood of the use of that power, and (2) a degree of pleasure, commensurate with that likelihood, as one anticipates the exercise of this power to obtain desirable items of various sorts. His fuller argument is, then, that wealth gives power; that anticipations of the use of this power give pleasure; and that this pleasure contributes to the production of the passion of pride. Thus one can be proud in response to one's wealth even though that wealth is, strictly speaking, nothing more than pieces of metal, or paper representations of such metal.

foregoing system] system of double relations, that is. See 2.1.5.5.

11 **power . . . the latter]** Note that Hume is now speaking of authority over others, and not the kind of power discussed in the previous paragraph.

12 **Comparison . . . any thing]** The important role of comparison in the production of the passions is also noted at 2.1.11.18; 2.2.10.8; 3.2.10.5; see also Ed. Intro., 162.

appear afterwards] See 2.2.8.7–20.

Book 2 Part 1 Sect. 11. *Of the love of fame*

The pleasure we receive from being famous, and thus being praised, arises '*from a communication of sentiments*' (¶19). Such praise and the pleasure associated with it constitute a secondary source of pride. To understand this fact we must understand sympathy. Hume describes sympathy as a principle of communication, a deep-seated human propensity to share in the sentiments and opinions of others. If I encounter someone who is grieving, the external signs of that grief (facial expressions, tears, or words, for example) convey to me the idea of grief. This idea is then changed into an impression and I thus feel the grief of the person I have encountered. More generally, if suitable circumstances obtain, the observation of another human feeling any passion results in that same passion being felt by the observer. This transfer of passions by means of impressions and ideas is automatic and more or less instantaneous. Hume's reflections on it convince him that it takes place because a lively 'impression of ourselves is always intimately present with us' (¶4). Given that sympathy works in this way, we can see why praise by others causes pride in the person praised. Those who praise another are themselves experiencing the passion of love or esteem. The external signs of this passion convey an idea of it to the person praised. She who is praised then converts that idea of esteem into an impression of pleasure while at the same time she has new grounds for entertaining the idea of herself (the praise is praise of her). Hume concludes by drawing attention to additional features of experience that appear to confirm his view of sympathy. (For further discussion of sympathy, see Ed. Intro., 155–7.)

3 **When any . . . idea of it]** Many of Hume's contemporaries would have agreed that each of the several passions (hatred, love, courage, for example) is sufficiently distinct to produce unique physical effects: 'Nature her self has assigned, to every Emotion of the Soul, its peculiar Cast of the Countenance, Tone of Voice, and Manner of Gesture; and the whole Person, all the Features of the Face and Tones of the Voice answer, like

Strings upon musical Instruments, to the Impressions made on them by the Mind' (Hughes, *Spectator* 541, paraphrasing Cicero, *De oratore* 3.57.216–17).

3 This idea . . . affection] For a description of sympathy at work in a particular case, with the identifiable steps or stages by which a sentiment is communicated and a passion produced, see 2.2.5.14.

4 'Tis evident . . . beyond it] On this point, see also 1.4.6.1–2; 2.1.2.2–3; 2.2.2.15.
foregoing principles] the principles reviewed in the previous paragraph; see also 2.1.12.1.

6 n. 58 Part 2. Sect. 4] See 2.2.4.3.

7 been remark'd] See 1.1.1.1.
approaches its impression] comes nearer to, in intensity or degree of force and vivacity, the impression to which it is related.
opinions and affections] Note that Hume says that sympathy results in shared opinions as well as shared feelings; see also ¶9 of this section.

8 foregoing system] See 1.3.5–7, esp. Sect. 7.
'Tis also evident . . . represent] See 3.3.1.7 for useful enlargement of this point.
Let us compare . . . extraordinary] The correspondences to which Hume alludes have principally to do with the association of ideas and the three relations, resemblance, contiguity, and cause and effect, that dominate these associations. We learned in *Treatise* 1.3 that these associations play an indispensable role in the formation of belief. They enliven ideas to the point that these are indistinguishable from, and function like, impressions. Now we learn that sympathy makes use of these same associative principles, with the result that an observer's idea of another person's passion is transformed into a specifically resembling passion. Whereas belief, according to *Treatise* 1.3, merely enlivens ideas, sympathy actually transforms ideas into impressions (see also ¶16 of this section). Hume may allude to this transforming capability when he says that there is something 'surprizing and extraordinary' about sympathy.

9 already . . . accounted for] in 2.1.7, 9, 10.
hypothesis above-explain'd] Hume's hypothesis concerning the role of a double relation of impressions and ideas in the formation of pride and humility; see e.g. 2.1.5.5.
authority] As the previous sentence indicates, *authority* here denotes that form of reasoning which leads us to take the judgements of others 'as a kind of argument for what they affirm'.
n. 59 Book 1. Part 3. Sect. 10] See 1.3.10, esp. ¶¶4, 9.

13 A mere soldier . . . courage] A soldier of the ranks, in his capacity of soldier, would take little pleasure in being told he is eloquent, for this quality does not form part of his notion of what makes an exemplary soldier. A gownman was someone who, because of his office or profession (law, for example), wore a robe or gown. Baltasar Gracián, citing Tacitus, had written: 'Soldiers have not much Occasion for Wit, because . . . they make more use of their Hands than their Heads. . . . On the contrary, Gown-Men require a great deal of Quickness and Circumspection by reason of the many Impositions and Shifts which are frequent at the Bar' (*Art of Prudence* 2 [119]).

14 We shall . . . easy upon us] Hume's own experience followed the 'usual' pattern he describes: 'I was of a good family. . . . My family, however, was not rich, and being myself a younger brother, my patrimony, according to the mode of my country, was of course very slender. . . . In 1734, I went to Bristol, with some recommendations to eminent merchants, but in a few months found that scene totally unsuitable to me. I went over to France, with a view of prosecuting my studies in a country retreat' (*My Own Life*).

15 **separating these relations**] In this discussion 'relations' may refer to relations of ideas, or to kindred, the members of one's extended family.
16 **relations . . . both subsist**] If while in 'narrow circumstances' (¶14 of this section) a person's family is near, his humility will be greater because those to whom he is related are nearby. But if he is remote from his family, the effect of the close familial relation will be overshadowed by the effect of those to whom he is now near. Hume has already suggested (¶6 of this section) that family or kinship relations are a form of the relation of causation. Thus when physically near one's family, two of the fundamental relations (contiguity, causation) will be in play and affect one's passions.
17 **the separation of relations**] being distant from relatives.
    contempt . . . countrymen] About a year before publishing the *Treatise*, Hume wrote from London to a Scottish kinsman, 'But here I must tell you one of my Foibles. I have a great Inclination to go down to Scotland this Spring to see my Friends, & have your Advice concerning my philosophical Discoveries; but cannot over-come a certain Shamefacedness I have to appear among you at my Years [Hume was then 26], without having yet a Settlement or so much as attempted any' (letter of Dec. 1737, to Henry Home, later Lord Kames; *New Letters of David Hume*, 2).
    above-explain'd] At 2.1.2–6; see esp. 2.1.5.3–5.
19 **but this . . . castle-building**] Castle-building of the kind mentioned is the subject of *Spectator* 167.
    violent lover] one intensely in love.

Book 2 Part 1 Sect. 12. *Of the pride and humility of animals*

The hypothesis that nothing can arouse either pride or humility 'unless it be both related to ourselves, and produces a pleasure or pain independent of the passion' has been established (¶1). To confirm further this view, Hume now focuses on similarities between human and animal anatomy, especially those of the mind. Although the range of animal responses is more limited than that of humans ('animals have little or no sense of virtue or vice' (¶5), for example), some animals show evident signs of feeling pride and humility. In animals as in humans the causes of these passions are specific impressions and ideas: impressions of pleasure and ideas of the self. Experience confirms that the associating principles, cause and effect, contiguity, and resemblance, operate in animal minds much as they do in humans, and thus we may safely conclude these principles are the operating causes of pride, and that they 'operate after the same *manner* thro' the whole animal creation' (¶9).

1 **We have . . . operate**] In drawing his conclusion, Hume relies on the fifth of his rules by which to judge of causes and effects; see 1.3.15.7.
2 **'Tis usual . . . beasts**] Anatomists whose writings were available to Hume and who make this commonplace comparison include Douglas, *A Comparative Description of the Muscles in a Man and Quadruped*, and James Keill, *Essays on several Parts of the Animal Œconomy*.
    humours] here, bodily fluids.
    muscular motion] At the time Hume was writing, it was generally accepted that muscles acted by contraction and extension, but the cause of such movements was very much at issue. Chambers says that most anatomists say that muscular motion is due to an 'influx of some fluid into the muscular fibres', while others say it is due to 'the natural elasticity of those fibres'. Keill in company with others argued that the influx of a fluid composed of a mixture of animal spirits and blood produced muscular

movement. In contrast, Boerhaave was among those who thought the animal spirits alone caused this movement. Chambers reports that the 'latest writers' on this subject dismiss these theories and account 'for *muscular motion* from the intrinsic elasticity of the nervous fibrillæ contracting and restoring themselves against the stretching force of the circulating blood' (*Cyclopædia*, 'Muscular *motion*').

2 **progress of the chyle**] *Chylification*, or the movement of the chyle, is the process whereby food is converted into a fluid (chyle) suited for movement into the intestines and from thence into the blood stream (Chambers, *Cyclopædia*, 'Chylification').

4 **nobler kind**] What for Hume makes an animal nobler is not specified independently of the marks of pride such animals are said to show.

The vanity . . . excellency] Hume was far from alone in supposing that animals have passions. The proverbial pride of the peacock was mentioned in ancient times; see Ovid, *Metamorphoses* 13.801. Addison remarks 'that all Beasts and Birds of Prey are wonderfully subject to Anger, Malice, Revenge, and all the Passions that may animate them in search of their proper Food; as those . . . whose safety lies chiefly in their Flight, are suspicious, fearful, and apprehensive' (*Spectator* 121).

5 **Thus animals . . . vice**] On this topic, see also 3.1.1.25.

and are incapable . . . property] Hume might well grant that animals show a territorial instinct, and yet insist that they are incapable of understanding the notion of property. For Hume the concept of property is dependent on the concept of justice, a concept that humans alone among animals have been able to develop and use. On the inability of animals to form abstract notions such as property and justice, see 1.3.16.8; for Hume's definition of property, see 2.1.10.1.

For which reason . . . objects] For Hume's account of the way in which bodily qualities (beauty or strength, for example) give rise to pride in humans, see 2.1.8.1–4. The other animals, because they cannot form the requisite concepts, can take pride only in their bodies.

6 **rules of analogy**] The relevant rules of analogy suggest that things alike in certain respects are alike in other respects; for Hume's assessment of analogy, see 1.3.12.25.

7 **In like manner . . . present danger**] The example is intended to illustrate the effects of the relation of causation.

8 **love and kindness**] Hume's explanation of these passions follows in 2.2; on the love shown by animals, see 2.2.12.

the sex] the female of the species, that is.

Book 2 Part 2. *Of love and hatred*

In *Treatise* 2.2 Hume argues first that the same double relation of impressions and ideas that produces pride and humility produces, when actuated by a different set of causes, the indirect passions of love and hatred. Sect. 2 describes a set of eight 'experiments' that are said to confirm this theory. After addressing potential objections (Sect. 3), and explaining our tendencies to feel love for family and friends (Sect. 4) and love or esteem for the wealthy and powerful (Sect. 5), Hume turns his attention to eight compound passions. These are benevolence and anger, compassion or pity, malice, envy, respect, contempt, and love between the sexes. The twelfth and final section discusses love and hatred in animals. In the course of discussing these passions Hume explains the principle of comparison as well as other inherent features of human nature—our tendency to rely on general rules and to project our passions onto the future, for example. (For further discussion of *Treatise* 2.2, see Ed. Intro., 157–65.)

Book 2 Part 2 Sect. 1. *Of the objects and causes of love and hatred*

Hume emphasizes the many ways in which love and hatred are like pride and humility, the two indirect passions already explained in *Treatise* 2.1. None of these passions can be defined, although all are familiar through experience. All have *objects* in the form of an idea of a person. All have *causes* that consist of a *subject* and a *quality* of this subject, and that produce in us a pleasure or pain distinct from, but resembling, the passions themselves. All depend upon relations of ideas and impressions: relations of ideas that carry our thought to the idea of the person who is the object of one of these passions; relations of impressions that carry our feeling from a distinct pleasure or pain to the feeling of one of these four passions. Moreover, the same causes that produce pride also produce love, while those that produce humility also produce hatred. On the other hand, there is one essential difference: whereas pride and humility have always the self for their object, love and hatred have always for their object some 'person or thinking being' (¶7) other than the self. It may also be more difficult to see that an association of impressions has a role to play in producing love and hatred, but that it does play this role will be shown later. In the meantime, Hume notes that we expect to be loved by others for exactly those things that give us pride in ourselves, and this fact suggests that love is caused by the same qualities, and in the same manner, as pride.

1 already observ'd] See 2.1.2.1.
2 As the immediate . . . conscious] This point is established at 2.1.2.2.
   some sensible being] This remark leaves open the possibility that humans can love or hate animals. Hume later in this section seems to close off that possibility by saying that the object of the passions of love and hatred is 'always some other person' (¶3 of this section), and that their object is 'evidently some thinking person' (¶6 of this section).
   self-love . . . sense] In arguing that, because the *object* of love is always some other person, it is improper to speak of *'self-love'*, Hume sets himself apart from many of his predecessors (but see 3.3.2.11). La Rochefoucauld had suggested that self-love (*amour-propre*) is the source of all virtues as well as all vices (*Maxims*, 'Of Self-Love'); Butler claimed that 'Every body makes a distinction between self-love and the several particular passions, appetites, and affections' (*Sermons* 1 [6 n.]); Pope had said that self-love is the motive of all our actions: 'Self-love, the spring of motion, acts [activates] the soul' (*Essay* 2.59).
3 the *cause* . . . them] For similar remarks about pride, see 2.1.2.3–4.
4 If we consider . . . common] For similar remarks about pride, see 2.1.2.5.
   love and esteem . . . hatred and contempt] On several occasions Hume uses the term *esteem* as a synonym for *love*, and *contempt* as a synonym for *hatred*, or says that esteem and contempt are 'at bottom' the same as love and hatred. (See e.g. 2.2.2.10; 3.3.4.2 Note 88; see also 2.2.5.1.) No single term seems adequate for naming all the 'passions' Hume discusses under the headings of love and hatred. What he calls *love* or *esteem* appears to include *admiration* (see 2.2.7.5), *friendship* (see 2.2.2.2; 2.2.5.15; 2.2.7.1), *honour* (see 2.2.2.20), *regard* (see 2.2.4.5), and *respect* (see 2.2.1.7; 2.2.2.20; 2.2.5.4, 6, 9); what he calls *hatred* or *contempt* appears to include *aversion* (see 2.2.3.4), *disesteem* (as we might call it), and *enmity* (see 2.2.2.2; 2.2.3.6; 2.2.7.1).
5 a new distinction . . . plac'd] This further distinction between quality and subject is first made at 2.1.2.6, in the discussion of pride and humility. In the example that follows, the *quality* is the beauty; the *subject* is the palace that the prince owns.
6 observations . . . form'd] See 2.1.3–11.
   We may . . . *uneasiness*] These suppositions are probable because they parallel conclu-

sions established by the earlier analysis of pride and humility. See 2.1.2.4–5; 2.1.3.1; and 2.1.5.1.

8 **relation of impressions**] The relation, or association of impressions, is first discussed at 2.1.4.3–4.

But as . . . pleasure] On the distinct or separate pleasures that resemble and are related to pride, see esp. 2.1.5.1–5, 10.

I delay . . . moment] The delayed examination begins in 2.2.2 and continues throughout the remainder of *Treatise* 2.2.

9 *presensation*] pre-sensation or instinct, that is. Shaftesbury had noted that animals 'have instincts which man has not . . . they have indeed perceptions, sensations, and presensations (if I may use the expression) which man, for his part, has not in any proportionable degree. Their females, newly pregnant, and before they have bore young, have a clear prospect or pre-sensation of their state which is to follow; know what to provide, and how, in what manner and at what time. . . . and all this as perfectly at first, and when inexperienced, as at any time of their life afterwards' (*Characteristics* [2:76]).

have been employ'd] Again, see 2.1.5.1–5, 10.

Book 2 Part 2 Sect. 2. *Experiments to confirm this system*

While pride has the self for its object and love has another person for its object, these two passions are both pleasant or agreeable. While humility and hatred also differ in their objects, these two passions are both unpleasant or disagreeable. These parallels are said to support the view that a double relation of impressions and ideas produces the indirect passions, but Hume presents eight 'experiments' that further support his theory. Imagine me in the company of another person for whom I have no feeling of either love or hatred. Experiment (1) shows that an object unrelated to me or my companion produces none of the indirect passions in either of us. Experiment (2) shows that an object belonging either to me or to my companion, but producing no pleasure, produces no passion in either of us. Experiment (3) shows that an object causing pleasure in me or my companion, but belonging to neither of us, produces no pride or love in either of us. We see, then, that when there is no relation of the relevant sort, or only one such relation, neither pride nor love (nor humility or hatred) are produced. Experiment (4) shows that a pleasing quality, belonging to me, causes pride in me and esteem in my companion, or, if belonging to my companion, causes pride in him and esteem in me. A displeasing quality, related to us in these same ways, causes either my humility and my companion's contempt, or my contempt and his humility. The effects of these double relations confirm Hume's theory. Experiment (5) shows that if I have as my companion a different and more closely related individual (a brother, for example), then the pleasing qualities of this person will cause me to feel esteem for him, and pride in myself. I take pride in myself because I esteem my brother, or, more generally, because the positive qualities of a relative, by a transition of passion, produce pride as well as esteem. Experiment (6) shows that if these same positive qualities are mine alone they will not cause me to esteem my brother. Because my idea of myself is more vivid than my idea of my brother, I do not esteem my brother when I take pride in myself. Experiment (7) shows why we typically extend our esteem from such greater objects as princes, masters, and fathers to such lesser objects as subjects, servants, and sons, but do not extend it from these lesser objects to the greater ones. Experiment (8) shows why the pride produced in us by the praise of others leads us to esteem these others. In the final paragraph of the section Hume provides his own review of the results of seven of his eight experiments.

1 **those observations . . . upon]** those observations made throughout the discussion of pride and humility.

3 **Upon the whole . . . impressions]** Hume suggests that pride, humility, esteem, and contempt are related like the corners of a square. This highlights the fact that pride and love resemble one another in feeling, as do humility and contempt. On the other hand, pride and humility have one kind of object, while love and hatred have another kind. Notice that the passions on opposite corners, pride and hatred, humility and love, have no relevant features in common. A diagram may be helpful:

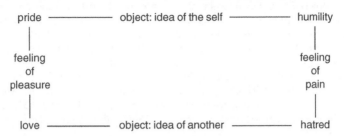

6 **operates secretly . . . mind]** operates unconsciously or without being noticed.
it bestows . . . emotion] This point is argued in more detail at 2.1.2.3 and repeated at 2.2.1.3.

7 **not a cold . . . one]** not without feeling and hence unnoticed, as a relation of ideas may be.
objects] here, the objects causing the pleasure or pain.
may give . . . affections] Objects that give us pleasure or pain may predispose us to love, hatred, pride, or humility, but we will have such a passion only if there is a cause (subject plus quality) that gives rise to the double relation of impressions and ideas. Hume illustrates his point in the following paragraph.

9 **compleated the round]** completed the range of possibilities schematized by the square of the passions discussed at ¶3 of this section. By changing one relation at a time, we are brought to feel in turn each of the indirect passions. Here and in the following paragraph Hume has, in effect, circled the square.

10 **explain afterwards]** See 2.2.5; 3.3.4.2 Note 88; the second annotation to 2.2.1.4 may also be helpful.

11 **relations above-mention'd]** the relations tested in ¶9 of this section.

12 **But to judge . . . impression]** Hume goes on to predict that he will find that, in some circumstances, experiencing one of the indirect passions (love, for example) will result in experiencing a second indirect passion (pride, for example) that resembles the feeling of the first. In the following paragraph experience is shown to confirm this prediction: the love of a close relative is found to change into pride.

14 **Experience . . . instance]** This experiment reveals that pride or humility do not readily change into esteem or contempt. I take pride in my own virtue or other qualities, but do not love my close relatives as a result. In the following paragraphs Hume explains this difference by saying, in effect, that our awareness of our own feelings overshadows our awareness of others. Consequently, we are less likely to transfer our attention from the self to others than from others to the self. But if I do not transfer my attention to some other person—if I do not have an idea of that person—I cannot, for just that reason, experience esteem or contempt for that person. Why? Because it is just that idea that serves as the object of esteem or contempt.

15 ourselves] On this matter, see also 1.4.6.1–2; 2.1.2.2–3; 2.1.11.4.

16 have observ'd] See 2.1.4.4.

17 Some may . . . to us] Hume is continuing to consider the question, Why do pride and humility not change into love or hatred? With this general question in mind, he takes up an objection that can be posed as a more particular issue. In spite of the fact that (1) the imagination and the passions sometimes work together to transfuse passions, and (2) sympathy might be thought to do the same thing, we are none the less easily distracted from our passions by objects around us and thus fail to transfuse pride into love. Why is this so? His answer is also in two parts. First, forget about sympathy. Sympathy does nothing to focus attention on the self. Secondly, the idea of the self is in effect constituted by perceptions of other objects. Consequently, it is not surprising that we should turn our attention from the self to other perceptions or objects. As long as pride or humility continue to be felt, we think of the self, but when these passions cease to be felt, the double relation of impressions and ideas no longer serves to focus attention on the self. This happens readily and naturally in accordance with principles basic to the system, and hence there is nothing strange in the fact that pride does not change into esteem or humility into hatred. Sympathy is first explained at 2.1.11.2–8. See also 3.3.1.7–12.

Ourself . . . nothing] See 1.4.6, esp. ¶¶1–4.

18 already seen] See experiments 4 to 6.

20 *Satellites of Jupiter*] the moons of Jupiter, four of which were described by Galileo in 1609.

reproach of *Cornelia . . . Gracchi*] The Gracchi are Tiberius Sempronius Gracchus (d. 133 BC) and Gaius Sempronius Gracchus (d. 121 BC). According to Plutarch, their mother, Cornelia, upbraided her sons because she was known as the daughter of Scipio rather than as their mother (*Lives*, Tiberius Gracchus).

common custom . . . wives] See also 2.1.9.13.

ceremony of . . . respect] the convention of asking the most honoured or respected member of a group to lead the way, speak first, etc.

21 Now since . . . latter] Hume now must explain why, given the tendency of the imagination to move from the lesser to the greater and from remote to contiguous, we do not, for example, esteem a prince simply because we esteem some subjects or citizens of his realm. In the previous paragraph he argued that, typically, thinking of a prince will not lead us to think of his subjects (thought does not move easily from greater to lesser), but esteeming a prince does (contrary to the usual movement of thought) lead us to esteem his subjects. Furthermore, while thinking of a subject causes us to think of the prince, loving a subject does not lead us to love the prince. In short, actual extensions or transitions of the passions seem contrary to principles already shown to govern the association of ideas. Hume resolves this issue in ¶24 of this section.

22 been observ'd] See 2.1.4.3–4; 2.1.5.10.

A man . . . unlike] A similar point is made at 2.1.4.3 and 2.3.3.10. Montaigne had said that 'there is as much difference between us and ourselves as between us and others' (*Of the Inconsistency of our Actions*, in *Essays* 2.1 [244]).

23 The difficulty . . . once] Having in the preceding paragraph argued that a strong and a weak passion of the same kind may be as repellent to one another as two weak passions of different kinds, Hume now argues that a strong passion may completely extinguish a weak one, or a strong and a weak passion of the same kind may unite to produce an even stronger passion.

24 The degree . . . consequence] Hume notes that the greater in our view a person is, the stronger will be our love or hatred of that person, and then in the remainder of the paragraph explains the puzzling phenomenon noted in ¶21 of this section.
The strongest passion . . . precedence] A strong passion overcomes not only the influence of the association of ideas, but also weaker passions. The passion felt for the master will or may determine what is felt for the servant even if it is contrary to what is felt for the servant. My hatred for a master may lead me to feel a weaker hatred for his servant even though, independently of the master, I might feel a weak love for the servant.

25 foregoing experiment] the sixth experiment, ¶¶14–17 of this section.

26 if we consider . . . contradiction] We need not think the mind consciously undertakes this reconciliation. The discussion that follows indicates that the mind is actuated by contrary principles or tendencies, and that our passions as experienced are consistent with the operation of these contrary principles.
than that . . . violent] than does a feeble passion produce a violent passion.

27 have observ'd] See esp. ¶¶14–15, 20 of this section.
when the very cause . . . person] as when, for example, I feel esteem for a person because she has praised me. When this happens, we pass, notwithstanding that we ordinarily do not do so, from the contiguous (the self as object), to the remote (the other as object). This reversal of the ordinary course of events happens because the other person involved is in fact the cause of the pride we feel.
already establish'd] See ¶¶20–1 of this section.

28 the rule] The rule mentioned in the previous paragraph, namely, '*that the imagination passes with difficulty from contiguous to remote*', or, to put the rule in a positive form: the imagination passes relatively easily from the remote to the contiguous.

Book 2 Part 2 Sect. 3. *Difficulties solv'd*

The love or hatred we feel for others depends on the pleasure or pain their actions cause. But these responses are modified by our views of an agent's intentions and character traits. If the harm that befalls us is the result of a consciously intended act or of an agent's settled traits, we will feel not only pain, but also hatred. If, in contrast, the harm that befalls us is unintended or, given the agent's settled traits, unexpected, we will feel pain, but are much less likely to feel hatred. Hatred typically follows only when the action giving pain is so related to an agent that our attention is directed to this agent as the object of the resulting passion. There are exceptions to this pattern. We may become angry at an agent who involuntarily and accidentally causes us pain, but such a passion is typically short-lived. Our responses may also be moderated if we know that an agent has harmed us intentionally, but from necessity or as a consequence of performing her duty. It may also happen that we first feel a passion, and only afterward ask whether it is justified. Pain alone may make us angry with an agent, but only when we see that this pain was intended will we have a sense of injury. We should not be surprised by the fact that anger produces the sense of injury that is so much a part of the passion of hatred, for the passions have a tendency to remain as strong and lively as possible.

1 *First* . . . passions] These difficulties are the topics of this and the following two sections (2.2.3–5).
Secondly . . . emotions] Hume's discussion of the compound passions occupies 2.2.6–11.

2 acquires . . . ill-will] more simply, is the object of our love or hatred.
Whoever . . . hatred] Hume goes on in this section to show that this claim has to be modified when we consider an agent's intention.
If the general . . . man] At 3.1.2.4 Hume is more optimistic about our ability to assess our enemies fairly.
Oliver Cromwell] Oliver Cromwell (1599–1658), leader of the Parliamentary party and army during the English Civil War, and Lord Protector of England from 1653 until his death in 1658. Works on Cromwell that illustrate Hume's point include: *The Devil's Cabinet-Counsell Discovered . . . Laying Open all the Plots . . . of Oliver Cromwell and the Long Parliament* (1660); *The English Devil; or, Cromwell and his Monstrous Witch Discover'd at White-Hall . . .* (1660); and *A True and Faithful narrative of Oliver Cromwell's Compact with the Devil for Seven Years . . .* (1720).
Duke of *Luxembourg*] The reference is to François Henri de Montmorency-Bouteville, Duke of Luxembourg (1628–95), a French general who defeated the Confederate armies (and William of Orange) in 1672, 1678, 1690, 1691, 1692, and 1693. *The Bargain which the Duke of Luxembourg . . . Made with the Devil, to Win Battles* was published in 1692.

3 There are some . . . intention] Such a view was common among Hume's more immediate predecessors; for further details, see the annotation to 3.1.1.2.

4 But here . . . distinction] The important distinction Hume makes here is that between (1) actions that derive from some relatively lasting mental feature of an agent (her conscious and informed intentions or her settled character), and (2) actions that are unintended (have come about by accident) or are atypical (contrary to the agent's settled character). Hume argues that unintended or atypical actions lack a firm relational connection to agents, and hence do not give rise to the passions of love and hatred. On the other hand, actions deriving from conscious intent or settled character, because they are firmly related to the agent, do give rise to love or hatred. In ¶¶7–8 of this section Hume qualifies the position sketched here.
deformity] moral deformity, that is.

6 operate . . . of ideas] have an effect, and produce short-lived love or hatred, even when we find that an agent has done by accident that action which has produced this love or hatred.

9 opinion of iniquity] the opinion that the agent has intended harm; a sense of injury. Hume's claim is that pain alone may make us angry with an agent, and that once this passion is aroused, we look for grounds to justify it. If these grounds are found, we are not only angry, but also feel *injured*—we feel that the agent has intended to harm us.

10 since otherwise . . . possible] Although Hume elsewhere suggests that the mind, once itself in motion, tends to remain in motion (see 1.3.13.9–10; 1.4.2.22; 2.2.9.2), he appears to offer no further explanation of or support for the claim made here.
The removal . . . injury] Showing that the pain caused by an agent was caused without intent to injure may extinguish our anger, but it does not follow that this anger first arose because the agent was perceived as intending to injure. Building on the previous paragraph, Hume is arguing that (1) the experience of pain may make us angry with the agent who causes it; (2) once angry, we may look for and suppose we have found grounds for thinking the agent intended to cause this pain, in which case our anger is supplemented by a sense of injury; (3) we may then learn that the pain was not intentionally caused and in consequence of this knowledge, may cease to feel both the sense of injury and the anger.
The harm . . . objects] The harm or pain caused is a fact having one effect—it causes

enmity (hatred). Justice, or the realization that the harm was unintentional, is a fact having another effect—it causes goodwill (love).

Book 2 Part 2 Sect. 4. *Of the love of relations*

Individuals (parents or close friends, for example) who are closely associated with us are more likely to be loved than are those not closely associated with us. Several factors account for this phenomenon: (1) the operation of the usual associative principles ensures that individuals closely associated with us are conceived in a lively manner; (2) people tend to associate with those whose temperament or disposition resembles their own; (3) sympathy, where such dispositions are shared, operates more readily, and enhances both our feelings and our passions; (4) in general we prefer those things with which we are familiar. Hume also tries to explain why the children of a widowed mother believe their relation to her weakened if she remarries, while the children of a similarly placed father find that his remarriage has little effect on their relation to him.

1 **Having given**] in the previous section.
  objects] persons who are the objects of the passions of love or hatred.
2 **preceding system**] For an abbreviated statement of the system, see 2.2.2.3–4; see also 2.1.5.3–5.
  object] again, the person who is the object of the passion.
  that this relation . . . others] Hume is discussing two kinds of relation: those between individuals who are relatives or closely associated, and those between impressions and ideas. An experience of a person with whom we are closely associated always produces a double relation of impressions and ideas.
3 **without . . . relation**] without blood relationship.
4 **Those, who . . . emotion**] Pascal had said: 'The only good thing for men therefore is to be diverted from thinking of what they are, either by some occupation which takes their mind off it, or by some novel and agreeable passion which keeps them busy, like gambling, hunting, some absorbing show, in short by what is called diversion' (*Pensées* 136; see also 132).
5 **reasonings . . . effect**] See esp. 1.3.4–8. See also 2.2.9.20, where it is suggested that 'double sympathy' may also contribute to the special relationship we have with relatives and acquaintances.
  second to education] See 1.3.9.16–19.
  This must . . . effects] Hume's conclusion presupposes the fifth of his rules for judging causes and effects; see 1.3.15.7.
6 **foregoing reasoning**] that found in the previous paragraph.
7 **our natural temper**] A reference to sympathy and its operation; for more on this subject, see 2.1.11.2–8 and 3.3.1.7–12.
8 **The great propensity . . . phænomenon**] Our propensity to pride, that is, causes us to prefer those things to which we are accustomed, and to take a greater pleasure in them than we otherwise would. Thus we again find that things to which we are customarily related produce more and stronger passions than do other, less familiar things.
9 **widow-hood**] Hume's own mother was a widow at age 30 and did not remarry. Of her he wrote: 'My father . . . died when I was an infant, leaving me, with an elder brother and a sister, under the care of our mother, a woman of singular merit, who, though young and handsome, devoted herself entirely to the rearing and educating of her children' (*My Own Life*).

11 **challenge its regard**] make it difficult for the imagination to maintain the usual regard for the mother.

vibration] A term borrowed from accounts of sensation and the operation of the nerves. Chambers notes that 'Sensation is supposed to be performed, by means of the *vibratory* motion of the nerves, begun by external objects, and propagated to the brain' (*Cyclopædia*, 'Vibration').

12 **prov'd already**] See 2.1.9.13; 2.2.2.19–26.

Book 2 Part 2 Sect. 5. *Of our esteem for the rich and powerful*

Three different causes may account for our esteem for the wealthy and powerful: (1) mere regard for their possessions; (2) expectation that we will have a share of these possessions; and (3) sympathy. Each of these causes produces in us a pleasure that may be converted into esteem, and thus could in principle account for our widespread regard for these privileged individuals, but sympathy plays the largest role. We do receive pleasure merely from experiencing or thinking about the possessions of the wealthy. But if we esteem those who possess these agreeable objects, sympathy must in its usual way convert mere ideas of agreeable possessions into livelier ideas and then into those impressions or feelings that are the essential components of esteem. Moreover, while it is true that the wealth or power of strangers gives them in principle the power of benefiting us, we have no grounds for supposing that they will share these advantages with us. The expectation of such benefits is too weak to account for the esteem we feel because we do not typically have the kind of experience that gives rise to a general rule indicating that wealthy individuals are likely to help us. It is only sympathy that enables us so fully to share the sentiments of the wealthy that their pleasures produce esteem in us. Hume adds that, because humans are gregarious, social creatures, no person completely isolated from all human society can ever be happy, and that this fact confirms his views about sympathy. He provides further examples of the operation of sympathy, and notes that our passions and opinions 'reverberate' back and forth from one person to another (¶21).

3 **Mr. *Philips* . . . poem**] John Philips's blank verse poem *Cyder* is concerned with the cultivation, manufacture, and virtues of cider.

5 **derivative passion**] the passion derived or produced by the double relation of impressions and ideas.

third principle . . . *first*] The relevant principles are listed in ¶2 of this section.

7 **already observ'd**] See 2.1.10.4–10.

also observ'd] See 2.1.10.8.

An avaritious . . . life] For Hume's account of the miser, see 2.1.10.9.

9 **Self-love**] See 2.2.1.2 for the restriction Hume puts on the meaning of this term.

10 **their condition**] that is, their position in society.

12 ***general rules***] On general rules, see also 1.3.13.7–14 and 2.1.6.8–9.

16 **Most kinds . . . creatures**] On the relation of convenience or utility and beauty, see also 2.1.8.2.

apartments] rooms.

the little room . . . passages] the little space wasted on stairways and halls.

17 **every work of art**] every thing of human construction.

19 **There is . . . gravity**] Several precepts concerned with the disposition of figures are found in Dufresnoy's *De Arte Graphica* (*The Art of Painting*). All figures, according to Precept 7, are to be 'balanc'd on their Centre[s]' (trans. John Dryden; see his *Works*, 20:88–9).

21 **and may decay . . . degrees**] See also 1.3.5.5. Hume elsewhere offers a more specific version of the comparison made here: 'Now, if we consider the human mind, we shall observe, that, with regard to the passions, it is not like a wind instrument of music, which, in running over all the notes, immediately loses the sound when the breath ceases; but rather resembles a string-instrument, where, after each stroke, the vibrations still retain some sound, which gradually and insensibly decays' (*Dissertation of the Passions* 1.2.3; see also 2.3.9.16).

thrown upon] transferred to, by sympathy.

Book 2 Part 2 Sect. 6. *Of benevolence and anger*

Benevolence (desire of another's happiness) and anger (desire of another's misery) are two of the 'compound affections' or passions. They are compound because they (like the other compound passions Hume discusses) are in some way mixed with the simple passions of love and hatred (see 2.2.10.1). While ideas may be conjoined to make one kind of compound, only impressions may compound by forming new wholes in which the identity of the constituent parts is lost. Hume notes that the adequacy of every philosophical theory is tested by some phenomena. Benevolence and anger put the theory of double relations to the test because they invariably accompany love and hatred. That is, if whenever we love someone we invariably desire the happiness of that person, or whenever we hate someone we invariably desire the misery of that person, we may conclude that these constantly conjoined desires for happiness or misery 'constitute the very nature of love and hatred' (¶4). This conclusion would be mistaken. While it is true that love and hatred are always accompanied by benevolence and anger, these latter are by no means the only sentiments that accompany love and hatred, nor do these accompanying passions always arise at the very moment that love and hatred arise. We see, then, that benevolence and anger, although constantly conjoined with love and hatred because of the nature of the mind, are in fact distinct from them, and sufficiently distinct to allow us to imagine that nature could have formed us to desire the unhappiness of those we love, and the happiness of those we hate.

1 **Ideas never . . . mixture**] Ideas may form what Hume calls *compounds*, but only by *conjunction*. In such conjunctions each idea retains its identity. Impressions, in contrast, may form compounds in either of two ways, by conjunction or by *mixture*. The component parts of such mixtures lose their individual identities, thereby producing a new and unified whole. Benevolence and anger compound with love and hatred by conjunction.

2 **'Tis commonly . . . purpose**] Newton proposed a rule for dealing with such resistant phenomena; for this rule, see the final annotation to 1.1.1.10.

 But as the perceptions . . . known] For a fuller version of this claim, see 1.4.2.7.

 contradictions . . . system] A similar attitude is expressed at 1.4.5.1; compare App. 10.

3 **For pride and humility . . . action**] For an example of humility exciting us to action, but perhaps only mediately, see 2.1.11.14–18.

4 **two . . . hypotheses**] Note that in the next paragraph Hume rejects, as contrary to experience, the first of these hypotheses.

 The first is . . . being] See 2.2.1.2–7 for Hume's earlier discussion of the causes and objects of love and hatred.

5 **The passions may . . . objects**] Compare at 1.3.15.10 the eighth of Hume's rules for judging causes and effects.

6 **We may . . . mind]** This is the second of the two hypotheses, and the one that Hume endorses.

Book 2 Part 2 Sect. 7. *Of compassion*

Some passions are themselves the effects of original principles of human nature, and in that sense may be thought of as 'original'. Other passions derive from these original ones, and are in that sense 'secondary' (¶1). Compassion or pity (including a concern for the well-being of those not our friends) and malice (including pleasure in the misery of those not our enemies) are two secondary passions. Pity arises when affliction or grief is presented to us either in real life, or by the writer of a tragedy. Unless we suppose that this one passion is due to some unique and original instinct, thereby unnecessarily multiplying the number of explanatory principles to which appeal is made, it is reasonable to conclude that pity is aroused when, by the operation of sympathy, we come to feel the affliction or grief of other beings like ourselves. Hume also explains (1) how it happens that a 'partial' sympathy can cause us to feel the passion typically associated with a given kind of situation even though the person we observe to be in that situation fails, at the time of observation, to feel the appropriate passion, and (2) how sympathy can cause observers to feel pity for individuals who never themselves feel any grief or pain.

1 **counterfeited]** imitated, without intent to deceive; see 2.2.8.1. As we learn, these imitations have effects very much like the originals they imitate.
Pity . . . malice] At 2.2.9.1 Hume summarizes the account of pity found in 2.2.7 and the account of malice found in 2.2.8.

2 **reasoning . . . sympathy]** Sympathy is first explained at 2.1.11.2–8; see also 2.2.5.14 and 3.3.1.7–12.

3 **above-explain'd]** See 2.1.11.2–8 for this explanation.
To except . . . unreasonable] To suppose that one of many passions is due to a unique and original instinct is to violate the notion that our explanations should invoke no more principles than are absolutely necessary. See 2.1.3.5–7, where Hume warns against positing a 'new principle to every new phænomenon'.

4 **women . . . pity]** Malebranche had said that the 'transport of spirits in the parts of our bodies that correspond to those parts one sees injured in others causes an acute impression in sensitive people with a vivid imagination and very soft and tender flesh. . . . Thus. . . . women and children . . . suffer much pain from the wounds they see others receive. They instinctively have much more compassion for the miserable' (*Search* 2.1.7.2; for Malebranche's further views on the relationship of soft tissue and gender differences, see *Search* 2.2.1). Mandeville maintained a similar view: 'Pity, tho' it is the most gentle and the least mischievous of all our Passions, is yet as much a Frailty of our Nature, as Anger, Pride, or Fear. The weakest Minds have generally the greatest Share of it, for which Reason none are more Compassionate than Women and Children' (Mandeville, *Fable* [1:56]). See also Hobbes, *Human Nature* 9.14 [4:47].
that faculty] the imagination.
Those philosophers] Hobbes and Mandeville fit Hume's description. Hobbes says that 'Pity is *imagination* or *fiction* of *future* calamity to *ourselves*, proceeding from the sense of *another* man's calamity. But when it lighteth on such as we think have not deserved the same, the compassion is greater, because then there appeareth more probability that the same may happen to us' (*Human Nature* 9.10 [4:44]). Mandeville's view is less subtle, but still accounts for pity as a form of self-love; see *Fable* [1:254–9].

5 **communicated passion of sympathy**] the passion communicated by sympathy, that is. Hume goes on to explain that sympathy sometimes causes us to feel the passion that we only expect another to have. Although one person we observe shows or has no joy upon good fortune, another has no misery as the result of misfortune, or a third no shame from foolish conduct, we who observe these individuals in these situations do feel the appropriate passion. Because the imagination follows general rules (treating like cases as like, for example), a 'partial' form of sympathy leads us to feel the passions that are normally appropriate to individuals in the situations we observe, even though these individuals actually feel inappropriate and even contrary passions.

views . . . side] sees, for example, only the external circumstances of an individual.

6 **aggravation**] a term of law referring to the circumstances 'which increase the guilt of a crime' (Johnson), as in our 'aggravated assault'.

historians . . . prince] Thomas More accuses Richard III of beginning his reign with the 'most piteous and wicked' of murders, namely 'the lamentable murder of his innocent nephewes, the young king and his tender brother', whom Richard had held captive (More, *History of Richard III* [82]).

As we ourselves . . . person] In the circumstances described, it is only the observer who is able to recognize the wretchedness of the person who is harmed. A sleeping infant prince, for example, is entirely oblivious of any danger he may face, and feels no passion. In such cases, then, there is no passion for sympathy to communicate. Nevertheless, because the situation the harmed person is in is objectively wretched and associated with the wretchedness of others who have felt misery in similar circumstances, sympathy still induces pity or grief in us.

imagination . . . depends] Hume originally ended this paragraph with a footnote about the different senses in which he uses the word *imagination*. He then apparently thought this note inadequate, for he expanded it substantially and arranged to have it removed from this location and added to the end of 1.3.9.19, where it is now found. An explanation of how this change was effected is found in the annotation to 1.3.9.19 Note 22. The text of the note originally printed here reads: 'To prevent all ambiguity, I must observe, that where I oppose the imagination to the memory, I mean in general the faculty that presents our fainter ideas. In all other places, and particularly when it is oppos'd to the understanding, I understand the same faculty, excluding only our demonstrative and probable reasonings.'

Book 2 Part 2 Sect. 8. *Of malice and envy*

Malice, or a pleasure derived from the misery of those who have done us no injury, is another secondary passion that depends on the way in which we consider the sentiments of others. Because the imagination leads us to judge objects more by comparison than by real worth, some intrinsically pleasing quality of another person may cause pain in those who observe this person and quality. We also find that each impression or idea of sensation is accompanied by a feeling of pleasure or pain. Putting these two facts together, we can understand how malice is produced: I observe another person, and consider, for example, her wealth. At the same time I compare her wealth to my own. Because I often judge things by comparison rather than by intrinsic worth, my recognition of her greater wealth may be accompanied by a feeling of displeasure. When compared with my own pleasure, her pleasure, which normally gives me pleasure, causes pain. As a result, I am also ready to take pleasure in her pain or even in the prospect of her pain. When I do that, I feel malice or 'the unprovok'd desire of producing evil to another, in order to reap a pleasure from the comparison' (¶12). Envy, in many ways like malice, is aroused when my own pleasure is diminished by my recognition that another person is presently feeling greater pleasure. That we are more likely to envy those whose status is like our own, rather than a person very much our superior, is due to the effects of resemblance and contiguity. In conclusion, Hume notes several phenomena that show that the effects of comparison depend on a certain facility of imagination.

1 *malice*] At 2.2.9.1 Hume helpfully summarizes the account of malice found in this section.

2 *original . . . soul*] On such original qualities of the soul, see 2.1.3.3–5.

4 **two principles . . . accounted for**] The principle already accounted for is our tendency to adopt and follow general rules; see esp. 1.3.13.7–14 and 2.1.6.8–9. The remaining principle, the maxim articulated in the next sentence, is one of the subjects of this section; see also 2.2.10.9 and 2.3.3.3–4.

n. 65 **Book 1. Part 3. Sect. 15**] See in particular Hume's seventh rule by which to judge causes and effects, at 1.3.15.9.

6 **above-mention'd**] See ¶¶2–3 of this section.

when . . . likewise encreas'd] Hume notes a further natural tendency to error.

metaphysical part of optics] On the metaphysical aspect of optics (on why the human eye is as it is, and how the understanding corrects the senses, for example) see Malebranche, *Elucidations*, Elucidation on Optics, esp. 27–43.

12 **But even . . . ourself**] We desire that there be a greater difference between ourselves and the allegedly inferior persons with whom we compare ourselves.

14 **have observ'd**] See 2.1.10.12.

16 *Flemish . . . together*] The Flemish horse is a large draft animal; the Welsh horse is much smaller.

17 *Guicciardini . . . Italy*] Guicciardini, writing about early 15th-c. Italy, suggests that 'it is a common human failing to prefer serving foreigners to one's own people' (*History* 3.4 [299]).

18 **Shou'd . . . criticism**] Horace had said: 'If a painter chose to join a human head to the neck of a horse, and to spread feathers of many a hue over limbs picked up now here and now there, so that what at the top is a lovely woman ends below in a black and ugly fish, could you, my friends, if favoured with a private view, refrain from laughing? Believe me . . . quite like such pictures would be a book, whose idle fancies shall be shaped like a sick man's dreams, so that neither head nor foot can be assigned to a single shape. . . . In short, be the work what you will, let it at least be simple and uniform' (*The Art of Poetry* 2.1–9.23). Addison describes 'tragi-comedy' as 'one of the most monstrous Inventions that ever entered into a Poet's Thoughts. An Author might as well think of weaving the Adventures of *Æneas* and *Hudibras* into one Poem, as of writing such a motly Piece of Mirth and Sorrow' (*Spectator* 40).

Yet this . . . volume] Prior's *Poems on Several Occasions* (1718) contains the witty *Alma; or, The Progress of the Mind* and the weighty *Solomon on the Vanity of the World*, as well as widely dissimilar shorter poems.

20 **have observ'd**] See 1.4.6.16; 2.1.5.10–11; 2.1.11.8.

Book 2 Part 2 Sect. 9. *Of the mixture of benevolence and anger with compassion and malice*

Further phenomena test Hume's theory. Love and benevolence give rise to pity, while hatred and anger give rise to malice. But if pity is an uneasy feeling, and malice is a pleasure, then, given the theory of double relations, these results are reversed: pity should give rise to hatred, malice to love. This unexpected result is a consequence of the fact that love and hatred depend not only on a double relation of impressions and ideas, but also on the tendency or drift of the feelings they arouse. If, for example, I observe the financial ruin of another person, whether I feel a form of hatred or a form of love will depend on other, parallel passions that I feel and that depend on such predisposing conditions as duties or interests. If I share interests with the bankrupted person, her pain on the loss of her wealth can be expected to arouse in me pity and benevolence, two distinct passions that incorporate similar desires for the good of any one person who is their object. If the bankrupt person is a commercial foe, his pain on the loss of his wealth can be expected to arouse in me malice and anger, two distinct passions that incorporate similar desires for the misery of any one person who is their object. In both cases the resulting passions are those that incorporate desires that parallel or follow the direction of the desire produced by my interests. Concerned that he may seem to 'run from one principle to its contrary' (¶11), Hume further explains why the communication of pain by sympathy can lead sometimes to one passion and sometimes to its contrary. This apparent inconsistency is also the consequence of the strength or force of the pain communicated. Sympathy, to have effect, must begin with an impression in the person who comes to feel what an observed person feels. Only impressions have the liveliness required to initiate this process of communication. This means that the present circumstances of the person who is the object of our sympathetically derived passion are of central importance. If these circumstances are such that we as observers have an appropriately lively (neither too weak nor too strong) impression of misery, we feel pity for the person who is in painful circumstances. But if this impression is weak, the result is contempt. If it is exceptionally strong, the horror we feel drives out all other thoughts and feelings.

1 have endeavour'd] See 2.2.7 and 2.2.8.
   But it must . . . my system] A fundamental claim of the theory of double relations is that the impression or feeling that is part of any given indirect passion resembles the impression or feeling that the cause of that passion arouses (for a schematic representation of this theory, see Ed. Intro., 151–2). Consequently, if in response to one such cause, the grief of another, we ourselves also feel pain, we would expect to go on to feel for this other person some form of hatred, a passion that resembles this pain. In fact, we sometimes go on to feel pity or benevolence, passions that are unlike, or contrary to, pain. It is this apparent 'contradiction' that Hume's account of pity tries to explain.
2 tendency of it] tendency of the present sensation. Hume goes on to say that, in the right circumstances, the present impression of pain or pleasure carries us to consider the larger story of which the person's present condition is only one part. We are led to consider this larger story by relations and motives associated with the relevant impressions or passions. If I independently desire the well-being of another person, then the pain I feel on observing the ill fortune of that person will be directed along the path of that desire. As a consequence, the pain I feel will lead me to feel pity, which resembles love, rather than hatred.
   impulses . . . correspondent] For earlier discussions of the impulses or directions of the mind itself, see 1.3.13.9–10; 1.4.2.22.
   This cannot . . . action] That pride and humility are not accompanied by a tendency to immediate action was the subject of 2.2.6.3.
3 already found] See 2.2.6.6.
4 As to the connexion . . . primary] See 2.2.6.3–6 for Hume's earlier discussion of this point.

5 another experiment] The first 'experiment' is the 'experience' outlined in the previous paragraph.

7 For taking . . . satisfaction] The success or failure of my rival produces both pain and pleasure. If he fails, for example, I feel pleasure because my interests are served by his failure. And yet I feel for this rival *hatred*, which does not resemble pleasure, rather than *love*, which does resemble pleasure. As initially sketched, the theory of double relations cannot explain this outcome.

8 relation or connexion] On the kind of relation mentioned here, see 2.2.4.2.

9 above-mention'd] See ¶2 of this section. From this earlier discussion we see that the movement Hume has in mind is both parallel, and in the same direction: 'similar and correspondent' is his phrase; see also ¶15 of this section.

11 have endeavour'd] See 2.2.5, esp. ¶¶6–14, 21, for this proof.

maxim . . . establish'd] The maxim is quoted, with modest changes, from ¶2 of this section.

secondary . . . primary] Although in this particular case it is another person's *pain* that is communicated to us, the effect is to produce pity (a 'primary' sensation) and a desire for the well-being of this person (a 'secondary' sensation) in just the way that a communicated pleasure would be expected to produce love and then benevolence. See also ¶15 of this section.

12 have mention'd] See ¶2 of this section.

seems so urgent] seems to threaten the credibility of the theory of double relations and ideas. See ¶1 of this section.

14 extensive sympathy] the sympathy that extends beyond the present to, as Hume has just said, 'all the circumstances of that person, whether past, present, or future'. See also ¶18 of this section.

15 original pleasure] See ¶3 of this section.

But as the extensive . . . sympathy] The strength of the first feeling communicated to us determines the outcome. If that feeling is relatively strong, then it carries us beyond the present, causing us to have the 'extensive sympathy' mentioned in the previous paragraph. If this first feeling is relatively weak, then it becomes the focus of our attention and the crucial determinant of the passion we feel. A strong feeling carries us in the same direction as love and benevolence and produces passions similar to these. A weak feeling resembles hatred and anger and, carrying us no further, produces passions similar to these.

16 The passions . . . degrees] The passions depend on principles (sympathy, for example) whose effects may be moderated or tempered by circumstances and conditions.

17 already observ'd] See 2.2.5.18.

18 compleat sympathy] a synonym for 'extensive sympathy'; see ¶14 of this section.

above-mention'd] See ¶15 of this section.

especially women] On the special susceptibility of women to pity, see also the first annotation to 2.2.7.4.

yet one . . . horror] If we extend Hume's analogy of pipes and fountains (¶14 of this section), we can imagine water rushing into a small reservoir with such force that it overflows before it can reach any exit pipes. By analogy, our response to the use of the rack is so overpowering that the victim's pain produces neither contempt nor pity, but only horror.

20 relations and acquaintance] See 2.2.4, esp. ¶¶6–9.

Book 2 Part 2 Sect. 10. *Of respect and contempt*

Respect is a passion compounded of love and humility; contempt is a passion compounded of hatred and pride. Both result from a (typically tacit) comparison of another person, the object of a passion, with ourselves. Because we have a stronger propensity to pride than to humility, contempt includes a relatively high proportion of pride, while respect includes a lesser proportion of humility. But why do some objects (persons) sometimes produce only uncompounded love or hatred, and sometimes respect or contempt? Because those qualities that give rise to love, pride, hatred, or humility, the elements from which respect and contempt are constituted, may produce these elements in different intensities or quantities. If, for example, a quality produces strong pride but only weak love, contempt, but not respect, will also be produced. And why do some qualities excite only love or hatred unmixed with respect or contempt? Because of our marked tendency to judge some things by comparison. As a consequence, certain qualities (good nature, generosity, for example) are well suited to produce love but not to produce pride. If one of these qualities is observed to belong to another person, it will directly produce substantial love, but little or no humility, in the observer. As there is in this case so little humility to mix with love, the likelihood of producing respect, which depends on the combination of love and humility, is greatly reduced. Hume also notes that our feelings in response to the wealthy and poor differ. Consequently, we not only keep our distance from those judged to be superior or inferior, but are also led by natural principles of the imagination to form the notion of social distance.

1 **passions . . . *contempt*]** Hume uses the term *contempt* to denote both an uncompounded passion, namely, hatred or dislike, and a compound passion made up of hatred and pride. In this section *contempt* is used in this second sense.
   ***amorous* affection]** or 'love betwixt the sexes', the topic of the next section.

4 **already observ'd]** Although Hume earlier notes that pride is a pleasant, and humility an unpleasant sensation, he appears not to have explicitly said that the mind has a stronger propensity to pride than to humility. He does, however, note that we have a 'great propensity' to pride; see 2.2.4.8.

5 **objects]** Here and elsewhere in this section the things or qualities, rather than the person who is object of an indirect passion. For Hume's prescribed vocabulary, see 2.1.2.2–4 and 2.2.1.2–5.

6 **have suppos'd]** See 2.2.2.3.

8 **above-mention'd]** See ¶5 of this section.

9 **been observ'd]** See 2.2.8.4.
   contiguous] On the effect of contiguity and distance on the passions, see 2.3.7–8.

10 ***distance . . . common metaphor*]** The metaphor of distance is discussed in *Spectator* 590, but is not there applied to social differences.
   observe afterwards] See 2.3.7.

Book 2 Part 2 Sect. 11. *Of the amorous passion, or love betwixt the sexes*

Three cooperating factors give rise to love between the sexes. These are the pleasure derived from beauty, from sexual appetite, and from a tendency to benevolence. We have seen that beauty gives rise to love and benevolence. Beauty also gives rise to sexual desire. This desire is pleasant and is enhanced by other pleasant situations and emotions, diminished by unpleasant ones. Just as attractive food supports the hungry person's desire to come close to food and enhances her principal desire, hunger, so too does beauty support and enhance sexual desire. In general, we find that resembling, parallel desires fuse and work together to produce new passions. More particularly, beauty, sexual desire, and benevolence give rise to resembling feelings (pleasures) and move us in the same direction. When combined with the idea of a particular person, these three feelings fuse to produce the compound passion of amorous love. That this is so confirms that the indirect passions arise only on the occasion of the double relation of impressions and ideas described at the beginning of *Treatise* 2.1 and 2.2.

1 **foregoing reasoning**] See 2.1.8.1; 2.2.3.2; also 2.2.2.9–10.
3 **have observ'd**] See 2.2.9.2–3, 9, 15.
   inclination of the soul] Recall that, so far as his discussion of the passions is concerned, Hume does not attempt to distinguish between soul or mind and body; see 2.1.1.1–2.
   meat] food.
   Now 'tis plain . . . second] Exquisitely presented food will increase our appetite; the same food on a fly-infested paper will diminish it.
5 **and has each . . . object**] Our sexual appetite and senses of beauty and kindness each responds to different qualities of the person loved.
6 **have observ'd**] See 2.1.2.2–4; 2.2.1.3–7.
   already describ'd it] See 2.1.5.6.
   Sex . . . appetite] When sexual desire arises we focus on a person having certain (sexual) qualities. Alternatively, thinking about a person with these qualities is enough to arouse sexual desire. By itself, however, this cause of desire cannot sustain the amorous passion. To sustain this passion the lover must also take pleasure in the beauty of the person loved.

Book 2 Part 2 Sect. 12. *Of the love and hatred of animals*

Love and hatred are commonly found among animals. This behaviour can readily be explained by the same 'springs and principles' that operate in humans. Animals are seen to love both other animals and humans. Although animals have relatively small and inactive imaginations, they are none the less able to regulate their affections in response to pleasure and pain, to show an instinctive love of their young, and to communicate by sympathy such passions as fear, anger, courage, and grief. They also evince malice and pity.

1 **above-explain'd**] See 2.2.1.3–4 for a summary, and 2.2.4–11 for extended discussions, of these causes and their varying effects.
   Every thing . . . animals] See 2.1.12.2, 9 for earlier expressions of this claim. Animal reasoning is the subject of 1.3.16.
4 **relation . . . species**] On relation or kinship and love among humans, see 2.2.4.2.

Book 2 Part 3. *Of the will and direct passions*

Understanding the passions, Hume says, depends on understanding the will. Having first described the will as the impression we feel when we consciously bring about a new action or thought, he then argues (1) that there are no good grounds for supposing the will is able to be free of (indifferent to) causal influence and thus capable of making uncaused choices (choices determined only by the will itself). He goes on to explain (2) why it is widely but mistakenly thought that the will is capable of making such uncaused choices, and (3) why it is always the passions, and not the understanding or reason, that function as the proximate and effective influence on the will. In Sect. 4 we learn why some passions are violent and others calm, and that a calm passion may in fact have more influence on actions than does a violent one. Sects. 5–8 inform us of the effects of custom, the imagination, and contiguity and distance (of space and time) on the direct passions. Sect. 9 distinguishes two kinds of direct passion, those (joy, hope, grief, fear, for example) produced by pleasure and pain, and those (hunger, thirst, sexual appetite, for example) whose instinctive operation produces pleasure and pain. Sect. 10 focuses on curiosity, or the love of truth, the distinctive intellectual passion that has motivated Hume's concern for the science of human nature. (For further discussion of *Treatise* 2.3, see Ed. Intro., l65–73.)

Book 2 Part 3 Sect. 1. *Of liberty and necessity*

The will, although not one of the passions, must be understood if the passions are to be understood. The term *will* is taken to refer to nothing more than the impression we feel as we consciously bring about a new bodily motion or a new perception of mind. Because this impression is indefinable, Hume focuses attention on the issue of *'liberty and necessity'*—on the question, that is, of whether or not our actions and thoughts are free or causally determined. It is widely agreed that the actions or motions of *bodies* are absolutely determined or necessary effects. Hume argues that the grounds for supposing the *will* is causally determined are precisely those for supposing that bodies are. Only after we have experienced two objects in constant conjunction do we form the idea that they are necessarily connected, and then only because the constant conjunction has produced 'a determination of the mind to pass from one object to its usual attendant' (¶4). A review of the relevant evidence shows that the moral world is also characterized by constant conjunctions, by the constant conjunction of kinds of motive and circumstance with kinds of volition and action. It follows, then, that the moral world is subject to the same necessity, and the same levels of probability, that characterize the natural world. In support of this conclusion Hume notes that moral and natural evidence are widely mixed together to form a single unbroken chain of causal reasoning. (For additional discussion of the issues raised here, see Ed. Intro., l65–9.)

1 *direct* **passions**] The direct passions are introduced at 2.1.1.4.
2 **impossible to define**] On this point, see 2.1.2.1. Locke had also remarked on the 'difficulty of explaining, and giving clear notions of' the will through the use of words, and had recommended introspection as the best means of understanding its actions; see *Essay* 2.21.15.
   definitions and distinctions . . . will] Chambers provides a helpful 18th-c. perspective on earlier aspects of this debate. Necessity, he notes, is usually confused with constraint. Plato and Epictetus had distinguished between *violent* and *spontaneous* necessity, while the scholastics distinguish between *physical*, *moral*, *absolute*, and *relative* necessity. Aristotle distinguished between *willing* (choosing an end) and *election* (choosing a means), while some of his followers divided acts of the will into the *elicit*, or those produced by the will itself, and the *commanded*, or those produced by sensitive, locomotive, or intellective powers acting on the will. Chambers also suggests that the scholastic philosophers confused will and liberty, and used one definition for both (*Cyclopædia*, 'Necessity'; 'Will'; 'Liberty').
3 **'Tis universally . . . liberty**] Locke had said that 'A Tennis-ball . . . is not by any one taken to be a *free Agent* . . . because we conceive not a Tennis-ball to think, and consequently not to have any Volition . . . [we conclude that it] therefore has not *Liberty*, is

not a free Agent; but all its both Motion and Rest, come under our *Idea* of *Necessary*, and are so call'd'. And 'Where-ever Thought is wholly wanting, or the power to act or forbear according to the direction of Thought, there *Necessity* takes place' (*Essay* 2.21.9, 13). Earlier, Malebranche had said that 'It is clear that no body, large or small, has the power to move itself' (*Search* 6.2.3 [448]; see also 6.2.5 [473]; 6.2.9 [514–16].

4 **been observ'd**] The paragraph that follows recapitulates and builds on discussions found principally in *Treatise* 1.3, esp. Sects. 2, 6, 14. See also 1.4.5.29–32; *Abs.* 10–13, 25–6; and Ed. Intro., I27–37.

constant union . . . mind] Hume anticipates this point at 1.3.2.16.

5 **Like causes . . . effects**] This is the fourth of Hume's rules by which to judge of causes and effects; see 1.3.15.6.

6 *Guienne . . . Champagne*] Guyenne and Champagne are two regions of France where grape 'trees' or vines flourish. Bordeaux is the capital city of Guyenne, a region known for its red wine, while Champagne is known for the white wine that bears its name.

8 **explain the principles . . . founded**] Society will necessarily arise because of a 'natural appetite betwixt the sexes' (3.2.2.4). Even those Hume calls savages (individuals who 'keep no fix'd Habitation, [and] have no Religion, Law, or Policy', Bailey, *Dictionary*), are motivated by this appetite and consequently form a society or at least a proto-society.

9 **stations of life**] social positions, and especially as viewed comparatively so as to reveal rank in a social hierarchy. See also 3.3.2.11.

Men . . . government] In his later and fuller treatment of this issue Hume says that a small, simple society may be maintained without government; see 3.2.8.1–3.

Government . . . of men] For a fuller discussion of the origin of government, see 3.2.7.

10 *Plato's Republic*] This work sketches an ideal city-state. Hume may have declared the *Republic* to be unbelievable because in it Plato suggests that reason is the superior and guiding principle of human nature, and portrays the ideal society as one in which reason, embodied in philosopher-kings, organizes and rules. For Hume's view about the relation of reason and the passions, see 2.3.3.1–7.

Hobbes's Leviathan] This work also sketches a model state, but one very different from that found in Plato's *Republic*. Hobbes portrayed humans as motivated entirely by selfish passions; the model society is one in which these passions are controlled by an arbitrary and all-powerful sovereign. In contrast, Hume supposes we have both selfish and other-regarding passions; see 2.3.3.8–10.

The knowledge . . . actions] On the effect of general rules on our views about national characteristics, see 1.3.13.7.

very essence] For a discussion of Hume's use of this phrase, see Ed. Intro., I52–3.

11 **Human . . . uncertain**] On this subject, see also 2.1.4.3 and 2.3.8.13.

12 **same maxims . . . objects**] Maxims of the sort mentioned are found in 1.3.15.

But below . . . reasoning] Hume discusses degrees and kinds of evidence and probability in 1.3.11–13. On not abandoning a conclusion in the face of one contrary phenomenon, see the final annotation to 1.1.1.10; 2.2.6.2.

13 **mad-men . . . liberty**] Bramhall, who defends human liberty, grants that 'children, fools, mad-men, and beasts' lack liberty (*Defence of True Liberty* [34, 40]). Locke argues that if to act erratically ('to break loose from the conduct of Reason') is to be free, then 'mad Men and Fools are the only Freemen' (*Essay* 2.21.50. See also *Essay* 2.21.13, cited in the annotation to 2.3.1.3; and Bayle, *Dictionary*, 'Rorarius', n. F).

14 **We must now . . . another**] Hume undertakes to show that motives and actions are

constantly conjoined in just the way that objects are conjoined in those cases in which we come to call one kind of object, *A*, a cause, and a second kind of object, *B*, an effect, and to find ourselves determined to believe, upon the experience of some *A*, that some *B* will follow, or upon the experience of some *B*, that some *A* has already occurred. For more on this subject, see Ed. Intro., I29–35.

15 the death of *Caesar . . . Augustus . . . Nero*] Gaius Julius Caesar was assassinated on 15 Mar. 44 BC; Gaius Octavius, later Augustus, was the first Roman emperor; Nero, a later emperor, is remembered for his persecution of the early Christians.

16 All those objects . . . other] On the distinctness of causes and effects, see e.g. 1.3.3.3; 1.3.14.12; 1.3.15.1.
necessary connexion . . . mind] Similar remarks are found at 1.3.14.20–2.

17 And indeed . . . principles] On the supposed distinction between physical and moral necessity, see 1.3.14.33.

18 As chance . . . experience] Chance implies a contradiction when, although thought to be merely the absence of cause or nothing real, it is none the less taken to be the cause of certain effects. At 1.3.11.4 Hume describes chance as the 'negation of a cause' and says that it has an influence 'contrary to that of causation'; see also the second annotation to 1.3.11.4.

Book 2 Part 3 Sect. 2. *The same subject continu'd*

The will is widely held to be free of causal influences for three reasons: (1) People confuse constraint and necessity. (2) There is a *'false sensation'* of the liberty of indifference. (3) Religious writers claim that the contrary view subverts morality and religion. Hume argues that none of these reasons is sound. Whether necessity is revealed by the constant union of two objects, or by the mind's determination to infer one such object from another, we find that it is universally attributed to the operations of the will. Particular motives are constantly associated with particular actions. On the experience of either motive or action, we are led to think of the other as either effect or cause. As we have an unimpeded view of what is going on in our minds, we can see that the present account of the will must be satisfactory. The necessity he attributes to the will is, Hume says, 'essential to religion and morality' (¶5). Only if actions are necessarily connected to motives and character will moral assessments and reward and punishment make sense. It is the theory that the will is free (that its choices are uncaused) that subverts morality. A review of our attributions of blame lends support to this claim by showing, among other things, that even those who maintain there is liberty of indifference presuppose a necessary connection between motives and choices. (For additional discussion of the issues raised here, see Ed. Intro., I69–70.)

1 liberty of *spontaneity*] freedom from constraint. According to Chambers, 'those actions performed from an inward and natural principle, conformable to our own inclinations, excluding all constraint, but not excluding necessity; are called *spontaneous actions*' (*Cyclopædia*, 'Spontaneous').
liberty of *indifference*] freedom from all causal influence. Those who hold that there is such freedom argue that actions may be performed as a consequence of nothing more than an indifferent will, of a will, that is, whose choices or volitions are determined only by itself and are in that sense uncaused or undetermined. Hume goes on to attack the view that there are uncaused choices or that, 'the will itself is subject to nothing' (see ¶2 of this section).
violence] constraint, both moral and physical.

2 **agent]** the object or person taken to be the cause of the action.

intuitive proof of human liberty] Descartes says that he knows 'by experience' that the will is 'not restricted in any way' (*Meditations* 4 [39]); that one 'ought to know by experience' that the will is indifferent to influence (*Meditations, Replies* 5 [259]; and that the 'freedom of the will is self-evident' from the inner experience we have of it (*Principles of Philosophy* 1.39 [205–6]). Bramhall says that 'our own and other mens experience doth teach us, that the will hath a dominion over its own acts to will, or nill without extrinsical necessitation' (*Defence of True Liberty* [221]).

it . . . it] human liberty . . . the will.

as the desire . . . necessity] In order to show that we were free, we do the second time what we did not do the first time. As a result, we find that our second choice is motivated by our desire to show that we were free, and thus find that there was no unmotivated or uncaused choice.

foregoing doctrine] The theory set out in the previous section; see esp. 2.3.1.10–12.

3 **pretext . . . morality]** Chambers notes that 'It is held a grievous and dangerous error, with regard both to religion and morality, to hold that human liberty only consists in *spontaneity*' (*Cyclopædia*, 'Spontaneous').

Such topics] such arguments or concerns.

6 **But according to . . . nothing]** Those who argue that the will is free from causal influence hold, in effect, that our volitions and actions are uncaused, and hence that they have no significant moral relation to us. If, Hume argues, the will is indifferent to influences, so that its volitions are unconnected to motives, then our moral assessments would be very different from what they actually are. We would not assess individuals as agents who are or are not *responsible* for certain actions; we would consider actions only, and treat an accidental injury as morally indistinguishable from a carefully premeditated one. In the next paragraph our practice in these matters is reviewed and shown to contradict (and hence overturn) the view that the will is free from causal influence or undetermined.

8 **have advanc'd]** These subjects are dealt with in 2.3.1.

having prov'd] Recall that Hume describes the will as an '*internal impression*' (2.3.1.2), and not as a faculty. He believes he has shown that each particular feeling of this impression will always have been preceded by some particular cause. Each such impression is conjoined with a motive or some motivating aspect of the subject's character or physical make-up. In the language of *Treatise* 1 he has not only shown that a cause (of the will and volition) is always necessary, but that each particular effect has a particular cause.

proceed to explain] This explanation is found in the following six sections.

Book 2 Part 3 Sect. 3. *Of the influencing motives of the will*

Reason and the passions are commonly thought to be in conflict. Most moral philosophy has taken the view that reason is the superior principle in humans, and that we ought to regulate our actions by it. To prove that this widely held view is mistaken, Hume undertakes to show that reason cannot alone provide the will with motives, nor can it effectively oppose the motives provided by the passions. Neither of the two forms of reasoning, demonstrative and probable, can either produce or prevent an action. Given that it is only the passions that influence the will, reason and the passions cannot be in conflict over governance of the will. In fact, reason is rightly governed by the passions. Reason can, however, by changing our beliefs, effectively extinguish our passions. The widespread view that reason and passion are in conflict arises from a pervasive misunderstanding:

certain calm passions (benevolence, for example) that do conflict with other passions are mistakenly supposed to be determinations of reason. (For additional discussion of the issues raised here, see Ed. Intro., I72.)

1 Nothing . . . dictates] By Hume's time dozens of philosophers had alluded to the struggle between reason and the passions. Those whose works we suppose Hume knew include Pascal, who spoke of 'the internal war of reason against the passions' (*Pensées* 410); Bayle, who said that 'human life is hardly anything else but a continual combat' between the passions and reason in the form of conscience (*Dictionary*, 'Helen', n. ʏ); Steele, who says that the 'entire conquest of the Passions is so difficult a Task' that it ought not to be attempted (*Spectator* 71 [1 : 304]); and Pope, who gives the struggle a domestic and classical turn: 'What Reason weaves, by Passion is undone' (*Essay* 2.1.42).

   Those who gave the preference to reason included Cicero, who said that 'reason commands, appetite obeys' (*De officiis* 1.28.101) and the neo-Stoics. Among the latter, Du Vair argued that we 'must (as necessary to our happiness) purge the Mind from Passions' and be guided by reason (*Moral Philosophy of the Stoics* [15]), while Le Grand said 'that *Passions* are not natural', but 'the diseases of Fools', and insisted that 'Reason composeth Mans real good, that his Felicity consisteth in the use of it, and that to live happily, a man need but be conformable to the Councels of Reason' (*Man without Passion*, x, 22, 69). Other writers were more moderate. Balguy, noting that all moralists agree in saying we ought to follow nature, sees this as meaning that 'we ought primarily and principally to regard our *Reason*; because it is our governing Principle, our Supreme Guide' (*Foundation* 2.35 [85–91]). And some argued that, while reason and passion are in conflict, the passions may be brought to contribute to the practice of virtue: 'there is no passion which is not serviceable to vertue, when they are governed by reason' (Senault, *Use of the Passions*, Discourse 1).

2 The understanding . . . probability] On judgements depending on demonstration and probability, see 1.3.1; 1.3.2.1–3; 1.3.12; and Ed. Intro., I24–6.

3 emotion . . . propensity] a desire to avoid the painful or obtain the pleasurable. Hume goes on to argue that, upon desiring an end, we at once begin to engage in probable reasoning in so far as we consider the means to this end.

4 Since reason . . . emotion] Hume's argument, in brief, is that turning off a desire is no different from turning one on. As reason cannot turn desires on, it follows that it cannot turn them off.

   Reason . . . extraordinary] Many writers had lamented the fact that human reason had come to be enslaved by the passions. Some of these supposed, as Bayle put it, that since the sin of Adam and Eve, 'reason, philosophy, the idea of virtue, the knowledge of the true interest of self-love', all the features of human nature, have been corrupted and 'unable to resist the passions' (*Dictionary*, 'Helen', n. ʏ). Bayle also suggests that this enslavement to reason was familiar to such classical writers as Euripides, Cicero, and Ovid, the latter of whom penned the familiar line, 'I see and approve the good, and yet pursue the evil' ('*video meliora, proboque deteriosa sequor*'). But not all moralists accepted the view that the passions and their control of the will are unfortunate. One sizeable group maintained that the passions are a far more positive feature of human nature than the Stoics and many Christians supposed. The anonymous author of *Spectator* 408, for example, argued that because reason is 'too slow and lazy' to exert itself or move us to action, it is the passions that must provide this motive force. Consequently, he says, we must try to manage the passions 'so as to retain their Vigour . . . we must govern them rather like free Subjects than Slaves, lest while we intend to make them obedient, they become abject, and unfit for those great Purposes to which they were designed'.

Watts agreed, saying that 'the Passions were given us to assist the feeble Influences of our Reason in the Practice of Duty. . . . Reason is too slow, and too weak, to excite a sudden and vigorous Activity in many Cases' (*Doctrine of the Passions* 1.14 [74]). One earlier writer whose work Hume knew and who came close to expressing the view Hume calls 'extraordinary' was Nicole, who said: 'It is not reason that is served by the passions, but the passions, in order to achieve their purposes, that are served by reason; this is the only use that we ordinarily make of reason' ('De la faiblesse de l'homme' 11, in *Œuvres* [91]).

5 'Tis impossible . . . represent] It is a characteristic of some of our perceptions to be representative. Truth is attained when these perceptions accurately copy the objects that they represent; to be false, a perception must be by nature representative, and yet fail to represent accurately. Passions cannot be true or false because they do not meet the fundamental condition: they are not representative. See also *3.1.1.9*.

6 that passions . . . opinion] Imagine a child who desires to play with the silvery moon. This child thinks the moon is about the size of a small ball, really shiny (intrinsically luminescent, that is), and positioned near the top of the house. These opinions accompany the child's desire for the moon. They also, as Hume shows, allow us to say that, in an extended sense of the term, the child's desire is unreasonable: it is unreasonable in the sense that it presupposes or rests on mistaken opinions. No ball-sized and really shiny moon exists, nor can the moon be secured by climbing to the top of the house. In contrast, a desire that is not accompanied by mistaken opinions about what exists or how to secure what exists is not unreasonable.

'Tis not contrary . . . finger] Reason, Hume is arguing, has nothing to do with the choice of moral ends.

9 violent emotions . . . kind] Some violent passions may also be mistaken for determinations of reason. These passions have this effect because the feelings they arouse are strong enough to motivate us to action independently of a concern for pleasure or pain. The distinction between calm and violent passions is introduced at 2.1.1.3.

10 metaphysicians] See the first annotation to 2.1.7.2 for the names of some of these philosophers.

passion and desire] here, the violent passions, in contrast to the calm passions.

Book 2 Part 3 Sect. 4. *Of the causes of the violent passions*

The circumstances that cause a passion to be calm or violent are considered, but we are first told that a well-established calm passion, although operating unconsciously, may have a great influence on a person's behaviour. A calm passion is not necessarily a weak one. Granted, to control another person's behaviour it may be more effective to rely on violent passions, but both calm and violent passions motivate us to obtain good or avoid evil and both kinds are influenced by the amount of good or evil we foresee. In general, the violent passions are more likely to be produced by a proximate good, the calm passions by remote good. Passions may be strengthened in other ways: (1) Any feeling that accompanies a passion is likely to be converted into that passion, thereby adding strength to those passions or desires that are already stronger and more dominating. (2) Conflicting passions, whether their source is internal or external, produce an additional feeling that is incorporated into the dominant passion. This explains why we feel strong desires for that which is forbidden or contrary to our duty: the conflict of desire and principle produces additional feeling, and this feeling and its force is taken over by and strengthens the desire. (3) That which is uncertain in outcome (because novel, for example) has an augmenting effect, while that which is sure and predictable tends to diminish the passions. (4) The partial concealment of an object of desire increases desire, while absence of the object tends to extinguish weak passions and increase strong ones.

1 **'Tis evident . . . violence**] La Rochefoucauld, whom Hume cites at ¶10 of this section, says that it is 'a Mistake to believe that none but the Violent Passions, such as Ambition and Love, are able to Triumph over the other Passions. Laziness . . . insensibly destroys and consumes both Passions and Vertues' (*Maxims* 266).

 vulgarly . . . reason] At 2.3.3.8 Hume argues that the calm passions are commonly mistaken for reason.

 pursue . . . evil] On the identification of good with pleasure, and evil with pain, see e.g. 1.3.10.2; 2.1.1.4; 2.3.1.1; 2.3.9.1–2, 8.

3 **the uniformity . . . allies**] The splendour of uniforms and the patterns and habits instilled by repeated drill increase courage.

10 **Duc de la *Rochefoucault* . . . fire**] 'Absence lessens Moderate Passions, but increases great ones, like the Wind which blows out Tapers, but kindles Fires' (La Rochefoucauld, *Maxims* 276).

Book 2 Part 3 Sect. 5. *Of the effects of custom*

Custom diversely affects the strength or weakness of passions. Some actions or thoughts produce, as they become customary, stronger passions; as others become customary they produce weaker passions. Custom typically creates facility, making certain actions or thoughts easier to produce, and then gives us an inclination towards these same actions and thoughts. In contrast, novelty may be a source of pleasant feelings, or may augment painful ones, and has these effects because it agitates the spirits. Within limits, the facility produced by custom is a source of pleasure, but it also orders or calms the spirits and may thus cause an action or thought that was initially pleasurable to produce feelings so faint and languid as to be painful. For similar reasons, custom or repetition can also make pleasurable what was once painful, diminish the force of passive habits, and increase the force of active ones.

1 **a *facility* . . . object**] Joseph Butler, to whom Hume refers in ¶5 of this section, says that 'by accustoming ourselves to any course of action, we get an aptness to go on, a facility, readiness, and often pleasure in it. The inclinations which rendered us averse to it grow weaker . . .' (*Analogy of Religion* 1.5.2).

2 **foregoing principle**] See 2.3.4.2.

4 **But when . . . affection**] That is, when we become indifferent to or bored with things that once gave us pleasure, these same things produce displeasure or pain.

5 **eminent philosopher**] The eminent philosopher was Joseph Butler, who distinguished between passive habits (merely understanding a language, for example) and *active habits* (being able to speak or write a language, for example). Butler then argued that 'practical habits are formed and strengthened by repeated acts, and that passive impressions grow weaker by being repeated upon us; it must follow that active habits may be gradually forming and strengthening by a course of acting upon such and such motives' (*Analogy of Religion* 1.5.2).

Book 2 Part 3 Sect. 6. *Of the influence of the imagination on the passions*

The imagination and the passions are so closely related that whatever affects the former also affects the latter. More specifically, when our ideas of prospective pleasure and pain are enlivened by the imagination, the related passions increase in strength. It happens, however, that the passions are influenced more by a particular idea of a lesser pleasure than by a merely general idea of a greater pleasure. Because remembered ideas transfer vivacity to the conceptions of the imagination, more recent pleasures have a greater influence than older ones, and prospective pleasures consistent with our way of life have a greater influence than do exotic ones. Hume also reports that eloquence and belief, because they serve to enliven ideas, augment the passions; that neither the calm nor the violent passions can be excited without belief; and that the character of an individual's imagination has a significant effect on the liveliness of her or his passions.

1 **principle above-mention'd**] See 2.3.4.2; 2.3.5.2.
2 **A general idea . . . view**] For Hume's account of abstract or general ideas, see 1.1.7.1–3, 10, 16.
3 **rejected the project**] This story, which is to illustrate the superior influence of particular ideas, is found in Plutarch's lives of Themistocles and of Aristides. The first says that Themistocles' design was 'to burn the Grecian fleet' in the harbour at Pagasae, while the life of Aristides reports that 'On Themistocles telling the people in assembly that he had some advice for them, which could not be given in public, but was most important for the advantage and security of the city, they appointed Aristides alone to hear and consider it with him. And on his acquainting Aristides that his intent was to set fire to the arsenal of the Greeks, for by that means should the Athenians become supreme masters of all Greece, Aristides, returning to the assembly, told them, that nothing was more advantageous than what Themistocles designed, and nothing more unjust. The Athenians, hearing this, gave Themistocles orders to desist; such was the love of justice felt by the people, and such the credit and confidence they reposed in Aristides' (Plutarch, *Lives*).
4 n. 66 **Mons.** *Rollin*] That is, Charles Rollin, in his *Ancient History of the Egyptians, Carthaginians, Babylonians, Medes and Persians, Grecians, and Macedonians* 6.2.13.
8 **already observ'd**] See 2.1.11.7–8.
10 **already observ'd**] See 1.3.7.5–7; 1.3.10.3.

Book 2 Part 3 Sect. 7. *Of contiguity and distance in space and time*

Because we are intimately aware of ourselves, things spatially and temporally near to us significantly influence the imagination and the passions. In contrast, when an already remote object becomes more remote, our idea of that object becomes more faint and obscure than it initially was. Such 'distance' weakens our conceptions and passions because the conception of objects remote in time and space is made difficult by our awareness of (1) our self, (2) the present time and place, and (3) the objects that lie between us and the remote object conceived. The imagination, will, and passions are affected by ideas of contiguous objects (which have an effect like that of impressions) and by those of remote objects (which have a weaker effect). But because space and time have different properties, distance in time has a greater effect on us than distance in space. That is, because the parts of space are contiguous to one another, many parts of space can be experienced at one time; the parts of time are successive, and hence can only be experienced one at a time. Hume then argues that the future influences us more than the past. The future has greater influence because a given amount of past time weakens an idea more than does the same amount of future time, and that because past times recede while we move nearer to future times. Moreover, we have no motivation to act on past time.

1 Ourself . . . to us] For additional comments on this issue, see 1.4.6.1–2; 2.1.11.4; 2.2.2.15.
3 Accordingly . . . fortune] On this point, see also 1.3.9.13–14.
5 Without having . . . co-existent] On the origin of our ideas of space and time, see 1.2.3.
8 have before observ'd] ¶¶1–3 of this section.
9 above-mention'd] See ¶6 of this section.

Book 2 Part 3 Sect. 8. *The same subject continu'd*

Because we appear to admire remote objects in patterns that run contrary to the principles previously established, three questions need to be answered: (1) Why does a great distance increase our admiration for objects? (2) Why does a distance in time increase admiration more than does a like one of space? (3) And why does a given past distance increase admiration more than a like future distance? The answer to (1) is that the mere experience of vast things 'enlarges the soul' (¶2) and produces admiration. A great distance is a vast thing that produces admiration, admiration that is transferred to the object that is far distant from us, or to any thing or person, such as an artefact or a traveller associated with that distant place or time. The answer to (2) involves a 'digression' (¶3). Any opposition that does not simply overwhelm us inspires and invigorates us; great souls even seek out such challenges. In addition, anything that enhances the passions, as challenges do, is pleasing, while whatever diminishes them, as ease of access does, is displeasing. The imagination is affected in the same way, which not only explains why we associate elevation with good, and lowness with evil, but also accounts for the pleasure and vigour we derive from imagining ourselves accepting the challenge of moving, contrary to nature, from the lower to the higher. Consequently, a considerable distance in time increases admiration more than a similar distance in space because it is more difficult for the imagination to move through the essentially broken parts of time than through the united parts of space. Thus, although moving a small distance through time weakens the passions, moving a vast distance through time elevates them by means of the vastness itself and because of the relative difficulty of such movement. The invigorated passion so produced mingles with, and enhances, our admiration of the distant object. The answer to question (3) is similar. We are in the middle between the past and the future. The imagination finds it easier to move into the future with time than into the past against it. Thus, conceiving things remotely past is more challenging, and hence more elevating and pleasurable, than conceiving things remotely future.

3 *Japan* tables] Japan is a form of varnish originating in the country after which both the varnish and tables coated with it were named; by Hume's time, many Japanned items were made elsewhere.
   and bestow more fruitless . . . former] Chronology remained a popular topic in the early 18th c.; see e.g. Newton's *Chronology of Ancient Kingdoms Amended*. Malebranche complained of scholars who 'do not know the genealogy of currently reigning princes, but [who] carefully research those of men who have been dead for four thousand years' (*Search* 4.7 [297–8]).
5 *Spumantemque . . . leonem*] Virgil writes about a boy, Ascanius, who, riding through the valleys, hopes for an opportunity to prove himself. He 'prays that amid the timorous herds a foaming boar may be granted to [test] his vows or a tawny lion come down from the mountain' (*Aeneid* 4.158–9).

7 *Atque . . . penna*] 'And damp earth it spurns on fleeting wing.' The line occurs at the end of a passage in Horace's *Odes* (3.2.23–4), translated thus: 'True worth, opening Heaven wide for those deserving not to die, essays its course by a path denied to others, and spurns the vulgar crowd and damp earth on fleeting [wing].'

8 the idea of facility . . . facility] Musical or poetic compositions attain a sense of closure by ending on a note lower than those preceding. This downward cadence is called a *fall*.

9 *Milton . . . inverted*] See *Paradise Lost* 2.70–7.

13 By *reason . . . faculties*] On the fallacious way of speaking that calls reason what is in fact a calm passion, see 2.3.3.8.

Upon the whole . . . call'd] At 2.3.3.4 Hume argues that, although we speak improperly when we speak of a conflict or struggle between reason and the passions, we do none the less speak of such a struggle, and when we do so we are referring to the struggle between the violent passions on the one hand, and the calm passions (which we mistake for reason) on the other.

Book 2 Part 3 Sect. 9. *Of the direct passions*

Many passions are dependent upon 'good and evil, or in other words, pain and pleasure' (¶8). We instinctively seek good, the source of pleasure, and avoid evil, the source of pain. Consideration of good is enough to produce desire; consideration of evil produces aversion. Eliminate the good–pleasure or evil–pain and the passions or desires will also be eliminated. Of the two forms of passion, direct and indirect, the direct are produced 'most naturally' (¶2) or with the least complication, although, in some circumstances, they also give rise to the indirect passions, and may as a result be strengthened. In addition, some direct passions arise from instincts or natural impulses for such things as the happiness of our friends or hunger. These passions produce, rather than derive from, good or evil, pain or pleasure.

As some passions depend on the probability of events, the same event may, depending on its probability, give rise to different passions. Probability is the effect of contrary experience which causes uncertainty of mind. An object is first thought to exist, then not to exist, as the mind vacillates between contrary possibilities. When a probable outcome is the object of desire, the mind will feel joy (or hope) if this outcome seems likely, grief (or fear) if it seems unlikely. Just as the understanding may be divided between opinions, so may our passions be divided between different feelings. Also, because the passions linger after they are aroused, grief and joy may mingle to produce fear or hope. In general, Hume concludes that (1) when distinct objects cause contrary passions, these passions occur alternately; (2) when different aspects of the same object cause contrary passions, these passions mutually destroy or cancel each other; and (3) when contrary possibilities cause contrary passions, these passions coalesce to form a compound passion. Further discussion reveals that hope and fear can also be caused in other ways—by, for example, the mere conception of a great good or evil. The event imagined may not be likely, but is of such magnitude that merely thinking of it causes fear or hope. Hume also explains why surprise so often turns into fear. Surprise produces 'commotion in the mind', and this in turn produces a violent curiosity that, because of its strength and uncertainty, resembles fear and in due course is converted into fear (¶26). In general, any doubt produces the passion of fear, and whatever mixture or vacillation of the passions causes uneasiness will produce fear, of which there are several forms, just as there are several forms of love. The will and the direct passions of animals are reported to be 'of the same nature, and excited by the same causes as in human creatures' (¶32).

3 **That propensity . . . ideas**] The fact that certain objects are so related to us as to produce the indirect passions does not prevent these same objects from producing, at the same time, desire or aversion, two direct passions.

8 **These passions . . . affections**] Hume here implicitly disagrees with those egoists (Hobbes and Mandeville, for example) who say that we are motivated only by the prospect of our own pleasure. If we have a natural instinct that directs us to the happiness of others, and if this instinct is not motivated by, but produces, good or pleasure, it will be clear that a desire for happiness need not be motivated by the prospect of our own pleasure. Such a pleasure may arise after our goal is obtained, but for all that it is only a concomitant of our fundamental goal.

9 **have already advanc'd**] See 1.3.12.

11 **An object . . . consideration**] If we think of the causes that produce a pleasurable object or outcome, and also think these are relatively probable, then we feel pleasure in anticipation of this outcome. If we think of the causes that produce an unpleasant object or outcome, and also think this outcome is relatively probable, then we feel pain in anticipation of it.

12 **For which . . . other**] When an outcome is uncertain and the imagination vacillates, leaving us to feel different passions in succession, these changes will not be exactly synchronized. As a consequence, the passions felt will tend to mix or coalesce, thus forming new passions.

13 **already explain'd**] See 2.3.4.2–5.

14 **want of relation**] lack of similarity or associating connections. Because of this lack, we feel first one passion and then another, with neither moderating or modifying the other.

16 **in that case . . . union**] The passions of hope and fear are produced when these conditions obtain: (1) a single object may be affected in two contrary ways (for example, a friend who is ill may either recover or not recover); (2) each of the two outcomes is probable, perhaps even to the same degree; (3) one of the outcomes would give pleasure, the other pain. In these circumstances, the imagination considers first one outcome, then the second, then the first again, and so on. As it does so, two different passions are produced: first joy, then grief, then joy again, and so on. But, because passions linger after their initial production, joy and grief are present in the mind at the same time. When that happens, joy and grief coalesce to produce hope (if the pleasing outcome is more probable) or fear (if the painful outcome is more probable).
Each view . . . stroke] Each time we imaginatively consider one outcome, a passion (joy or grief) is felt. This passion, although it gradually subsides, continues to be felt, just as when a violin string is plucked there is for some time afterward a sound or detectable vibration.

22 **A man . . . them**] On this point, see also 3.3.1.7.

23 **as when we tremble . . . security**] On this point, see also 1.3.13.10.

28 **Ut assidens . . . præsentibus**] An excerpt from Horace's *Epodes* (1.19–20): 'just as a brooding mother-bird more keenly dreads attacks of gliding serpents on her unfledged nestlings when she has left them, though she could lend them no more aid were she at hand'. The two preceding lines of the poem help us see why Hume chose

this illustration of his point: 'I shall have less fear, attending thee, for fear lays hold with greater power on those away—'.

Book 2 Part 3 Sect. 10. *Of curiosity, or the love of truth*

Given that the love of truth first motivates our intellectual enquiries, the origin and nature of this distinctive passion merits attention. There are two kinds of truth: the discovery of the relations of ideas, and the discovery of 'the conformity of our ideas of objects' to these objects themselves (¶2). Our love of truth is variable: a simple arithmetical calculation provides truth as much as the most profound enquiry in higher mathematics, but only the latter is likely to give pleasure. We value truth in proportion to: (1) the extent to which we must exercise our genius or capacity to discover it; (2) the extent to which the truth discovered is in one sense useful and important. It is not that either the enquiry or the truth sought is expected to result in obvious practical benefit, but, rather, that any enquiry must seem to be important, while at the same time its outcome is a matter of practical indifference to those who pursue it. This is possible because these relatively weak desires for truth are motivated by sympathy and by the pleasure that arises from the exercise of a mind engaged in a potentially successful enquiry. In this respect, intellectual pursuits are like hunting or wagering. The hunter supposes his efforts have some utility, real or imagined; the gambler takes pleasure in his winnings, but seems not to be motivated merely by the prospect of such winnings. Hume also says that we have an 'implanted' curiosity of another kind, and that this innate principle explains other aspects of our behaviour. It explains, for example, why some individuals are insatiably curious about their neighbours (¶11).

2 **proportions of ideas**] What Hume usually calls 'relations of ideas'.
   For these conclusions . . . other] We can discover that the two objects are equal either by simple and uninteresting measurements, or by means of a challenging mathematical reasoning. Hume goes on to argue that, although the two methods arrive at the same result (truth and assurance), we take pleasure only when we learn the truth by the more challenging means or only when more challenging results are obtained. In short, it is the process, not the product, that gives pleasure.
6 **already remark'd**] See ¶3 of this section.
7 **Upon this head . . . of it**] Our passionate concern for some ends arises not from these ends themselves, but from the interest created by the activity of pursuing these ends.
   above-mention'd] See 2.2.9.2–3, 9, 15.
8 **To make the parallel . . . reasoning**] Pascal, speaking of diversions and hunting in particular, says that what 'people want is . . . the agitation that takes our mind off [our unhappy condition] and diverts us. That is why we prefer the hunt to the capture' (*Pensées* 136; see also 132). Erasmus draws explicit parallels between hunting and philosophy (*Praise of Folly* [124–8, 133–4]).
9 **It has been remark'd . . . effect**] Erasmus has Folly say that when gamblers 'hear the dice rattle, their hearts jump and beat faster. The hope of winning always lures them on until their means are gone' (*Praise of Folly* [129]). Pascal disagreed. No one imagines that gaming and hunting are popular because of 'the money to be won at gaming or the hare to be hunted: no one would take it as a gift'. It might be thought that what the gambler wants is entertainment, but make him then 'play for nothing; his interest will not be fired and he will become bored, so it is not just entertainment he wants. . . . He must have excitement. . . . He must create some target for his passions and then arouse his desire, anger, fear, for this object he has created' (*Pensées* 136).

10 Human life . . . pleasure] 'Being unable to cure death, wretchedness and ignorance, men have decided, in order to be happy, not to think about such things', but to divert themselves (Pascal, *Pensées* 133).
11 curiosity . . . human nature] Men 'have a secret instinct driving them to seek external diversion and occupation' (Pascal, *Pensées* 136). Malebranche also argues that curiosity is natural; see *Search* 4.3.1.
12 prov'd at large] See 1.3.7.5–7.

BOOK 3. OF MORALS

Title-page

Duræ . . . honesti] A lover of austere virtue, you should at least ask now what Virtue is and demand to see Goodness in her visible shape (Lucan, *Civil Wars* 9.562–3).

Advertisement

abstract reasonings . . . them] These would include Hume's accounts, in *Treatise* 1, of how the understanding works to produce, among other elements of the mental world, our ideas of necessary connection, external objects, and an enduring self, and, in *Treatise* 2, of how the several kinds of passion are produced. Some early readers of Books 1 and 2 had complained that they were so abstruse as to be unintelligible; see the Preface to the *Abstract*.
same sense as formerly] See 1.1.1–4; 2.1.1.1–2.

Book 3 Part 1. *Of virtue and vice in general*

In this part of the *Treatise* Hume argues that because only perceptions are present to the mind, morality, the distinction between virtue and vice, must derive either from ideas and their relations, or from impressions. He concludes that morality is founded on a set of distinctive impressions called the moral sentiments. (For further discussion of *Treatise* 3.1, see Ed. Intro., I75–97.)

Book 3 Part 1 Sect. 1. *Moral distinctions not deriv'd from reason*

Hume hopes that his account of morality will add force to what he has said about the understanding and the passions. After reminding us that 'nothing is ever present to the mind but its perceptions' (¶2), and that there are only two kinds of perception, impressions and ideas, he begins his enquiry into morals by asking a single, precise question: Is it by means of our ideas or of our impressions that we discover the difference between vice and virtue? He argues first that those who claim that virtue consists in a conformity to reason and certain unchanging relations of things are in effect saying that moral distinctions can be traced to ideas and their relations, and that reason alone enables us to make moral distinctions. He then devotes the balance of the section to showing that these claims are unconvincing and mistaken. He attempts to show, for example, that: (1) while moral distinctions influence behaviour, reason alone, as was shown in Book 2, 'can never have any such influence' (¶6); (2) while reason is concerned with truth and falsehood (two important features of the relations between ideas) morality is concerned with such non-relational entities as passions, volitions, and actions; (3) while our moral assessments show great sensitivity to differences of degree and kind, the judgements of reason are in this regard inflexible and thus are clearly no foundation for these assessments; (4) there are no relations of ideas that apply uniquely to the real volitions and actions of rational beings, and yet it is only such real volitions and actions, and such beings, that are the object of moral assessment; (5) morality is not some matter-of-fact feature of actions capable of being discovered by the understanding—it is only when we attend to our own feelings that we are able to distinguish virtue and vice; (6) normative conclusions, or, more specifically, claims about what ought or ought not to be the case, cannot be legitimately derived from the ideas of a deity and gratitude. (For additional discussion of the material found in this section, see Ed. Intro., 175–8.)

1 I am not . . . *passions*] The 'present system' is the system Hume sets out in the *Treatise*. The third book of the *Treatise* corroborates the two earlier ones in so far as it makes use of explanatory principles (sympathy, for example) and arguments (the argument showing that reason is unable to influence the will, for example) presented in these books. Such corroborating connections are noted as they occur.
 in an age . . . comprehended] Jonathan Swift, one of Hume's favourite authors, had complained of the 'superficial Vein among many Readers of the present Age, who will by no means be persuaded to inspect beyond the Surface . . . of Things' (*Tale of a Tub* 1).

2 has been observ'd] See 1.2.6.7.

3 Now as perceptions . . . *ideas*] See 1.1.1.1; 2.1.1.1.

4 Those who . . . himself] Samuel Clarke is one of the best-known moralists who held views of the sort Hume is analysing. For Clarke's discussion of eternal fitnesses, conformity to reason, and the relation of morality to the Deity himself, see his *Discourse* 1.1–3 (in *Works*, 2:608–18). Hume later (*EPM* n. 12) suggests that the view that morality depends on certain relations can be traced to Malebranche, and that it was afterwards adopted by Cudworth, Clarke, and others. Locke also argues that it is from the conformity or disconformity of actions to rules that we derive the ideas of moral good and evil, but he does not insist that the rules in question must be eternal or immutable; see *Essay* 2.28.14–15.
 reason alone] Throughout the discussion that follows Hume typically limits himself to claiming that it is not reason *alone* that enables us to distinguish between virtue and vice. In other words, reason may play some role, but is not by itself able to establish or recognize the distinction between virtue and vice.

5 Philosophy . . . understanding] The division of philosophy into the speculative and the practical dates from classical times (see e.g. Aristotle, *Metaphysics* 993^b). Among the moderns, Locke makes the distinction at the beginning and again at the end of the *Essay* (see 1.2.2; 1.3.1–3; 4.21.2–3). Chambers describes speculative philosophy as 'that employed in mere contemplation, and which terminates therein'; practical philosophy he describes as 'that which lays down the rules of [a] virtuous and happy life; and excites us to the practice thereof. *Practical philosophy*, is properly Ethics, alone' (*Cyclopædia*, 'Philosophy').

6 already prov'd] See 2.3.3, esp. ¶¶3–4.

8 only recal] See 2.3.3, esp. ¶¶2, 6–7.

9 Now 'tis evident . . . reason] For a similar remark, see 2.3.3.5.

10 **For it proves** *directly . . .* **to it]** Reason deals only with ideas and their relations. Consequently, reason cannot be the proximate cause of the moral merit assigned to passions and actions because these are not ideas.

and it proves . . . *indirectly . . .* **influence]** Hume's second claim presupposes an assumption regarding the transitivity of influence: that which influences our actions must itself derive from a source which can influence actions. As on Hume's account reason alone cannot influence actions, while moral distinctions do have such an influence, it follows that reason cannot be a remote cause of moral distinctions.

11 **But perhaps . . . action]** It may be objected, Hume grants, that there are extended (and misleading) senses in which it can be said that the causes or effects of volitions and actions appear to contradict reason. An action could, for example, cause an observer of it to form a false conclusion about the agent and her relation to some item. Imagine someone taking a suitcase from a baggage carousel. This action will make us think the bag is hers, that she has a right to it. That would be a reasonable thing to think in such circumstances. But this particular person has no right to the bag. She means to steal it. In these circumstances we may be inclined to say, misleadingly, that the action of taking the bag was contrary to reason.

12 **been observ'd]** See 2.3.3.2–3.

13 **And here . . . equal]** This paragraph points out that the rationalists' account of morality cannot account for several observed facts of our experience: (1) that we see many agreements or disagreements of ideas that are unaccompanied by moral assessment; (2) that we take some crimes to be greater than others; (3) that we judge actions that are avoidable differently from those that were unavoidable. Given these shortcomings, the account must be mistaken.

14 **Shou'd . . . to it]** Hume grants that there may be morally reprehensible mistakes, but he insists that such mistakes presuppose some more fundamental form or source of moral distinctions.

15 **As to those . . . immorality]** Hume in this paragraph grants that an agent's actions may lead observers of those actions to form mistaken judgements about the agent and his relation to other individuals or objects. He doubts, however, that the actions in question are performed with the *intent* to cause false judgements and that moral distinctions have their origin in such mistakes.

n. 68.1 One might . . . deformity] William Wollaston had argued that '*A true proposition may be denied, or things may be denied to be what they are, by deeds, as well as by express words or another proposition.*' He also said that every act or omission that serves to deny true propositions or the truth of things is '*morally evil, in some degree or other*'. It is not obvious, however, that Wollaston claimed (as Hume alleges) that denial or falsehood arising from acts is 'the foundation of all guilt and moral deformity'. Note, too, that Wollaston explicitly says that 'neither all evil, nor all good actions are equal' (*Religion of Nature Delineated* 1.3–9). Francis Hutcheson, with whom Hume discussed the manuscript of *Treatise* 3, had devoted sect. 3 of his *Illustrations on the Moral Sense* to criticisms of Wollaston's theory.

that a false conclusion . . . variable] More generally put, we often make mistakes about the significance of actions simply because we do not know enough about their causes.

n. 68.2 'Tis in vain . . . choice] Wollaston had argued that acts denying the truth of things are morally wrong only when performed by beings '*to whom moral good and evil are imputable*', and then indicated that liberty (the ability to act voluntarily) would be a prerequisite of such a being (*Religion of Nature Delineated* 1.4–5).

15 n. 68.5 squint-sighted] having the condition of one eye not matching the direction of
the other, strabismus.

n. 68.6 **Besides . . . morality**] In this and the following paragraphs Hume poses a
more fundamental objection, namely, that Wollaston begs the question regarding the
foundation of morality. To say, for example, that stealing is wrong because it amounts
to treating another's goods as though these are one's own presupposes that there are
morally relevant property relations just when it is the origin and existence of precisely
those relations that is to be explained.

16 **Reason . . . passion**] See 2.3.3.6–7 for an amplification of this claim.

18 **There has been an opinion . . . algebra**] That morality is capable of demonstration
(that moral conclusions may be established by the same processes that establish mathematical conclusions) had been asserted by Hobbes (*De Cive* 10.5 [42–3]), Pufendorf
(*Law of Nature* 1.2.1–11), and Locke (*Essay* 3.11.16; 4.3.18). Samuel Clarke suggests that
morality is as certain as geometry and algebra. He and Balguy also insisted that some
moral propositions are self-evident, and assumed that still other propositions may be
deduced from these self-evident ones (see Clarke, *Discourse* 1.1; Balguy, *Foundation* 2.5
[9–11]).

'tis allow'd . . . demonstrated] Pufendorf, for example, had argued that regarding
matters of fact we never attain the level of certainty provided by demonstration, but
only 'a strong Presumption grounded on probable Reasons' (*Law of Nature* 1.2.1.11).
Locke had argued that, although the existence of God is known by reason, the '*Knowledge of the Existence* of any other thing we can have only by *Sensation*' (*Essay* 4.11.1–2).
For Hume's views on what may or may not be demonstrated, see 1.3.1.

19 *Resemblance . . . number*] For a fuller account of these relations, see 1.1.5; 1.3.1, esp.
¶¶1–3; and Ed. Intro., I24–6.

n. 69 **They only say . . . purpose or not**] Balguy claimed that reason can discover
that an action is virtuous or vicious just in so far as the action conforms to certain
relationships between things or individuals. See *Foundation* 1 [30–4].

21 *First,* **As moral . . . objects**] In short, the relations must be found to hold between
some durable feature of the mind (character or motive, as we later learn) and some
feature of the world (an action), and not simply between two features of mind or two
features of the world. In setting this condition Hume may appear to accept the view
that motives, if not acted on, are always morally neutral; in contrast, see 3.2.1.2;
3.3.1.19.

22 **but their *effects* . . . species**] Hume is again criticizing a position of Clarke (*Discourse*
1.1) and other rationalists. Hume wrote to Hutcheson: 'I wish from my Heart, I coud
avoid concluding, that since Morality, according to your Opinion as well as mine, is
determin'd merely by Sentiment, it regards only human Nature & human Life.' If
morality were determined by reason, he goes on to say, then we could conclude that it
would be the same for 'all rational Beings', the Deity included. But morality is determined by sentiment, and 'nothing but Experience can assure us, that the Sentiments
are the same [in all Beings]. What Experience have we with regard to superior Beings?
How can we ascribe to them any Sentiments at all?' The most we can say is that,
although these superior beings do not have these sentiments, they have arranged for us
to have them to guide our conduct—just as they have for the same reason arranged for
us to have 'bodily Sensations, which they possess not themselves' (letter of 16 Mar.
1740; *Letters*, 1:40).

already prov'd] See again 2.3.3.2, 6–7 and ¶8 of this section.

has been shown] See 1.3.2–7, 14.

24 **Of all crimes . . . death**] 'Homicides, tyrants, thieves, adulterers, robbers, sacri-
legious men, and traitors there will always be; but worse than all these is the crime of
ingratitude' (Seneca, *Of Benefits* 1.10.4). 'Therefore if ingratitude to others be hateful,
that which is shewn to parents must certainly be the most horrid and detestable'
(Gassendi, *Epicurus* 19 [934]). See also Cicero, *De officiis* 2.18.63; Pufendorf, *Law of
Nature* 3.3.17; Balguy, *Foundation* 2.4 [8–9]).

25 **why incest . . . deformity**] Ovid graphically notes that only humans treat incest as
morally wrong (*Metamorphoses* 10.323). Hutcheson had argued that, without a moral
sense, 'we should only look upon *Incest* as hurtful to ourselves, and shun it, and never
disapprove other *incestuous Persons*, more than we do a [*bankrupt*] *Merchant*' (*Inquiry*
2.4.6). The moral status of animals had been a topic of much interest since ancient
times; for brief early modern discussions, see Pufendorf, *Law of Nature* 2.3.2–3; Bayle,
Dictionary, 'Barbara', n. c.

26 **In which-ever way . . . action**] Hume goes on to indicate that the sentiment felt by
the observer is causally dependent upon, ultimately, the 'motives, volitions, and
thoughts', or, more generally, the character, of the agent who performs the action.
These features of the agent are not found as a part of those actions said to be virtuous
or vicious, but they do determine the moral character of those actions. See esp.
3.1.2.3–4 and 3.2.1.2–7.

Vice and virtue . . . mind] Hume had some doubts about his initial articulation of
this point. To Hutcheson he wrote: 'I must consult you in a Point of Prudence. I have
concluded a Reasoning with these two Sentences. *When you pronounce any Action or
Character to be vicious, you mean nothing but that from the particular Constitution of your
Nature you have a Feeling or Sentiment of Blame from the Contemplation of it. Vice & Virtue,
therefore, may be compar'd to Sounds, Colours, Heat & Cold, which, according to modern Philosophy, are not Qualitys in Objects but Perceptions in the Mind: And this Discovery in Morals,
like that other in Physicks, is to be regarded as a mighty Advancement of the speculative Sciences; tho' like that too, it has little or no Influence on Practice.* Is not this laid a little [too
stro]ng? I desire your Opinion of it, tho I cannot entirely promise to conform myself to
it' (letter of 16 Mar. 1740; *Letters*, 1:39–40). As these are not the concluding sentences of
the published version of Hume's discussion of this topic, it may be that he attempted
to moderate his rhetoric by the addition of the sentence that does end the paragraph.
For Hume's earlier discussion of the view of modern philosophers regarding sounds,
colours, and the other secondary qualities, see 1.4.4.

27 **In every system . . . ought not**] Notwithstanding Hume's claim, it is difficult to locate
moralists who openly proceed in the manner he describes. We can say, however, that
some rationalists, including Clarke and Balguy, did suppose that, from the fact that
God exists and is our creator, it follows that each of us owes him a debt of gratitude. If
it is taken for granted that a debt ought to be repaid, that one owes a debt to one's
creator, and that this debt obliges us to conform to the rules of morality, then establishing the being or existence of an omnificent deity would directly entail claims about
what we ought or ought not to do. We can also say that those who traced morality to
divine commands (moral voluntarists such as Pufendorf is taken to be) did suppose
that, from the fact that an omnipotent God exists and has decreed what is to be right
and wrong, it follows that each of us is obliged to obey these decrees or laws. If it is
assumed that a divine law just is a command that obliges those to whom it applies, that
a deity has proclaimed such laws, and that these laws apply to all of us, then establishing the being or existence of an omnipotent deity does directly entail claims about
what we ought or ought not to do.

This change . . . different from it] Hume's objection is importantly like one raised a few years earlier by an anonymous critic of Balguy's *Foundation*. Seeing that Balguy had traced the idea of obligation to gratitude, this critic challenged him to show how from such moral ideas as that of gratitude the idea of obligation could be derived. If we did not already have an idea of obligation, this critic argued, such ideas 'could never so much as afford us a general Idea of Obligation it self; or inform us what is meant by that Term; much less could we be able to *deduce* the particular Obligation to Gratitude from these Ideas'. Later, this critic argues that obligation is not merely some form of idea or perception; it also includes 'some Proposition, or Affirmation; as that a Man *ought to* be grateful, or that he *ought to* desire the Good of others. But I do not see any such Propositions as these included in those Ideas'. Thus even if reason is capable of having moral perceptions, 'it will not follow . . . that Obligation is *deducible* merely from our Moral Ideas, without supposing any Sentiment'. (These objections were published, with Balguy's replies, as the second part of *Foundation*; see 2.4 [8]; 2.18 [54]; 2.6 [11–12]; italics added.) Note that neither this critic nor Hume deny that we have a meaningful notion of obligation, and that both explicitly trace that notion to certain distinctive impressions or sentiments.

Book 3 Part 1 Sect. 2. *Moral distinctions deriv'd from a moral sense*

Having shown that it cannot be merely reason and ideas that give rise to moral distinctions, Hume concludes that these distinctions must be founded on impressions or sentiments. The experience of virtue produces a distinctive, calm pleasure (*approbation*); experience of vice produces a distinctive calm pain (*disapprobation*). These distinctive sentiments or feelings arise only when we as observers are able to view agents impartially or 'without reference to our particular interest' (¶4). Moreover, they are invariably accompanied by one of the four indirect passions, pride and humility or love and hatred. Hume adds that it would be absurd to suppose that each of our many moral sentiments derives from a distinct and original principle in human nature, for nature is typically economical in the matter of principles. It is, however, reasonable to suppose that these sentiments are in some important senses *natural*. Hume's larger goal, revealed in the final paragraph of the section, is to discover those principles and circumstances that cause us to feel approbation or disapprobation in response to certain characters and actions. (For additional discussion of the material found in this section, see Ed. Intro., 179–80.)

1 Our decisions . . . other] See also 1.1.1.1; 1.2.6.7; 3.1.1.2.
   Morality . . . judg'd of] Compare this claim with Hume's remarks about belief at 1.4.1.8 and App. 3.
   tho' this feeling . . . other] For comments on our tendency to confound resembling phenomena, see 1.2.5.21; 1.4.6.6; 2.3.3.8.
2 A very play . . . vice] According to Hutcheson, even children, in response to the stories they are told, approve what is benevolent and disapprove the selfish or cruel. This fact, he argues, shows the moral sense to be a universal feature of human nature (*Inquiry* 2.4.7).
3 An action . . . admiration] If we can explain why we experience the particular feelings of approbation and disapprobation, Hume argues, we will in effect explain virtue and vice. Given that these particular feelings arise in response to an agent's motives (her passions, intentions, or character) and actions, we can conclude that virtue and vice are to be traced to these motives and actions, while the feelings they cause provide the

foundation of our assessments of these same features. See also ¶11 of this section; and 3.2.8.8.

We go . . . satisfaction] See Intro. 8 for Hume's reason for limiting his explanations.

We do not . . . virtuous] Hume emphasizes that it is our distinctive feeling itself that constitutes our evaluation, so that no reasoning or inference is required.

The case . . . sensations] On this issue, see also 2.1.8.1–2; 3.2.8.8.

4 **I have objected]** See 3.1.1.21.

For, *first* . . . other] Hutcheson had argued that the pleasures and pains produced by natural things (a field, for example) are noticeably different from those produced by moral things (a benevolent motive, for example); see *Inquiry* 2.1.

5 *Secondly*, **We . . . passion]** For Hume, the object of the indirect passions is always oneself or some other person; for his account of these passions, see 2.1.2–6, esp. 2.1.5.5, 8, and 2.2.1–3; see also 3.3.1.3, 26.

6 **To this I reply, *first* . . . constitution]** For further evidence of Hume's concern to appeal to the fewest possible explanatory principles, see 1.3.15.6 and 2.1.3.5–7.

7 **I wou'd reply . . . equivocal]** On the meanings of *nature* and *natural*, see also 3.2.1.19. Earlier writers who had drawn attention to the many meanings of *nature* include Aristotle (see *Metaphysics* 1014^{b}16–1015^{a}19) and Boyle, who distinguished eight different senses of the term, and mentions an unidentified Latin writer who 'reckons up no less than fourteen or fifteen' (*Free Enquiry* [176–82]).

8 **manners]** here, moral behaviour.

9 **But *nature* . . . artifice]** Chambers reports that *natural* 'is also used for something coming immediately out of the hands of nature,' and contrasts this with that which is *artificial*—that which depends on art or contrivance (*Cyclopædia*, 'Natural'; see also 'Nature'). Hume goes on in the next paragraph to suggest that the artificial is that which is 'perform'd with a certain design and intention'.

appear afterwards] *Treatise* 3.2 shows that some virtues are artificial, while *Treatise* 3.3 discusses the natural virtues. For more on the difference between the two types, see 3.2.5.6 and Ed. Intro., 181–2.

n. 70 In the following . . . *moral*] These two contrasts are between natural law and civil law, and between the natural world (the order of physical nature) and the moral world. On this second contrast, see also Intro. 4–7.

10 **Mean while . . . unnatural]** Seneca, for example, had said that 'Virtue is according to nature; vice is opposed to it' (*Epistles* 50.8). Among the moderns, Shaftesbury says much the same thing, although much less succinctly; see *Inquiry* 1.2 [1:243–80].

cou'd never . . . denominations] Hume argues that actions performed without design or intention are devoid of moral character or quality, a point to which he returns in 3.2.1.

Book 3 Part 2. *Of justice and injustice*

In *Treatise* 3.2 Hume explains the artificial virtues. Five of these are analysed: justice, promise-keeping, allegiance, treaty-keeping, and chastity. These virtues are *artificial* in so far as they are in effect moral conventions that did not exist in humanity's original state, but developed gradually and implicitly along with or after the development of society (of social groups larger and more diverse than the extended family). They are also founded on a notable feature of human nature, the concern of each individual for her or his own interests, and thus are in that further sense *natural*. The discussion of justice, or the rules of property, the first of the artificial virtues to develop, occupies about half of *Treatise* 3.2, and provides the paradigm for understanding the remaining four virtues of this type. For Hume's own brief statement of this paradigm, see 3.2.11.4. (For further discussion of *Treatise* 3.2, see Ed. Intro., I74–97.)

Book 3 Part 2 Sect. 1. *Justice, whether a natural or artificial virtue?*

Justice is an artificial virtue, or one of those sources of approbation and disapprobation that arise from 'the circumstances and necessities of mankind' (¶1). Although Hume has previously suggested that certain actions may be the objects of moral praise or blame (3.1.1.26), he now says that actions are in fact only the external signs of motives and that moral assessment always has as its object the motives that produce actions. He grants that we may be motivated to perform a given action because we suppose it to be our duty, but insists that this action could have come to be supposed a duty only if some natural and virtuous motive had regularly caused actions of the same kind to be performed. He then argues that humans in their original state had no natural and virtuous motive capable of influencing them to act justly (of influencing them to repay a debt in a timely manner, for example). In humanity's rude and original state none of the three natural motives (self-interest, public benevolence, and private benevolence) could have been counted on to motivate such an act of justice. But if there is naturally no motive adequate to serve as the foundation of justice, then it must be that our sense of justice (our approbation of justice and our disapprobation of injustice) 'arises artificially, tho' necessarily from education, and human conventions' (¶17). (For additional discussion of these issues, see Ed. Intro., I82–4.)

1 **already hinted**] See 3.1.2.9.
  before I examine] See 3.2.2.
2 **'Tis evident . . . temper**] Hume's claim that the moral character of actions depends on the motives that produce them was also held by such dissimilar early modern moralists as Mandeville, Hutcheson, and John Gay. Mandeville had said that 'it is impossible to judge of a Man's Performance, unless we are th[o]roughly acquainted with the Principle and Motive from which he acts' (*Fable* [1:56]); Hutcheson that 'Actions which in Fact are exceedingly useful' will be void of *moral* character 'if we know they proceeded from no kind Intentions towards others' (*Inquiry* 2.3.1); Gay that whenever the 'End of any Action is the Happiness of another . . . that Action is [morally] meritorious . . . But when an Agent has a view to any particular Action distinct from my Happiness, and that view is his *only Motive* to that Action, tho' that Action promote my Happiness', neither the action nor the agent are morally meritorious (*Preliminary Dissertation* 4 [pp. xxvi]). Hume also addresses this issue at 2.2.3.3–5; 2.3.2.6; see also the annotation to ¶4 of this section.
  look within] look within the agent, that is.
4 **From this principle . . . the action**] There can be no *moral* motive to undertake something that is itself entirely lacking in moral character or that is morally neutral. Moreover, it is only when an action is undertaken because of a virtuous motive that that action becomes, by extension, virtuous—only then can the action be said to be virtuous. Hume traced this view to Cicero. To Hutcheson he wrote that Cicero had argued that it is 'on the Goodness or Badness of the Motives that the Virtue of the Action depends. This proves, that to every virtuous Action there must be a Motive or impelling Passion distinct from the Virtue, & that Virtue can never be the sole Motive to any Action. . . . there is no Proposition more certain or important' (letter of 17 Sept. 1739;

Letters, 1:35; Cicero's argument is found at *De finibus* 4.17.46–8). At ¶6 of this section Hume suggests that one such virtuous motive would be a humane concern for the well-being of others.

5 have the duty in our eye] take duty into account. For more on the sense of duty, see 3.2.5.6.

8 Actions are at . . . meritorious] Having in the preceding paragraphs established to his own satisfaction that no action is intrinsically virtuous (virtuous independently of the motive that produces it), Hume now argues that an individual cannot desire to perform some particular action, *A*, merely because this action seems intrinsically virtuous unless actions resembling *A* (actions of type *A*) have previously been taken to be virtuous. He insists, however, that actions of type *A* can be taken to be virtuous only if there is in human nature some distinct motive that, prior to the time that actions of type *A* are taken to be virtuous, produces actions of this type. It follows, then, that the desire to perform a particular action *A* merely because it seems intrinsically virtuous presupposes the existence and earlier operation of a distinct and natural motive to perform actions of this same type. Thus motives account for the virtue of even those actions that seem to be intrinsically virtuous.

9 But in his rude . . . natural] Hobbes had described the 'state of nature' as 'the ill condition, which man by meer Nature is actually placed in' (*Leviathan* 1.13). Pufendorf calls 'the state of men outside of civil society' a 'natural state' (*Natural State* 2). In the balance of this section Hume argues that in our original state we humans would have had no motive to conform to any rule of justice, not least because such rules would be unintelligible even if they should have been (as is unlikely) articulated; see also 3.2.2.8. Note that Hume's grounds for saying there could be no justice and injustice in the state of nature are significantly different from those of Hobbes; see *Leviathan* 1.13.

For one in . . . others?] Seneca explicitly argues that justice and the other virtues were unknown to early humans. He also says that early humans had within them 'the stuff of virtue', so that, through the refinement of instruction, they were able to develop justice and the other virtues (*Epistles* 90.46).

10 For shou'd . . . appetite] Hume argues first that, in our original condition, self-interest would be at best an erratic or intermittent motive of just acts. He then notes that, acting in its original and uncontrolled manner, such interest inclines us not to justice, but to injustice.

11 shown . . . hereafter] See 3.2.2.2–22.

Secondly . . . borrower] A secret loan would need to be secretly repaid; in such a case the public at large would not know the loan had been made or repaid, and the public interest would be unaffected.

12 sympathy] On sympathy, see esp. 2.1.11.2–8; 3.3.1.7–12; and Ed. Intro., 155–7.

double relation . . . passions] On this double relation, see 2.1.4–5 (esp. 2.1.5.5, 8–10); 2.2.1–3.

13 In all these . . . obligation] A concern for the interest of a particular individual runs the risk of being overpowered by some other concern, and thus is not a reliable motive to justice.

14 Were private . . . justice] Hume begins an argument showing that a concern for private benevolence would fail to provide the motivation to protect private property, and yet the rules of justice, as Hume understands them, have as their goal exactly this protection. In addition, we are generally more concerned to protect what we possess than to gain what we do not have. (This fact is explained at 3.2.3.4.) For two more

reasons, then, a concern for private benevolence cannot be the source of the artificial virtue of justice.

15 **But this . . . property]** The motive appealed to is not a fundamental motive of the kind needed to account for the fact that justice is a virtue, but a secondary motive that is dependent upon the very notion (justice) that is to be explained.

16 **A man's property . . . justice]** Hume sums up his argument regarding private benevolence: according to the rules of justice, the property of all individuals is equally inviolable; private benevolence cannot account for this fact; consequently it is not the original motive to justice.

17 **naturally]** in our rude and uncultivated state, that is.

18 **I shall add . . . morals]** On this point, see ¶¶2–7 of this section.
Our sense . . . passions] Hume suggests that our sense of duty derives from expectations created by the operation of certain passions inherent in human nature; see also ¶5 of this section and 3.2.2.6.

19 **word,** *natural . . . artificial]* On the meaning of the word *natural*, see also 3.1.2.7–10.
rules of justice . . . *Laws of Nature]* Even though the rules of justice are artificial or conventional, Hume consistently uses the term 'laws of nature' to refer to them. See e.g. 3.2.4.2; 3.2.5.8; 3.2.6.1, 10; 3.2.8.3–5; 3.2.11.2.

Book 3 Part 2 Sect. 2. *Of the origin of justice and property*

In this section Hume undertakes to answer two questions: (1) How does artifice lead to the establishment of the rules of justice? (2) Why do we suppose that conforming to or violating these rules is a *moral* matter? In answer to (1) he notes that of all animals, individual humans have the fewest natural advantages in proportion to their needs and desires, and that it is only by uniting in societies that this deficiency can be remedied. By joining together we increase our strength, our capabilities, and our security. Hume suggests that the development of society owed its origin to the deep-seated sexual desire that brings parents together, yet an equally deep-seated selfishness and the scarcity of essential external goods (food, clothing, and shelter, for example) presented a substantial barrier to this development. But humans soon saw that it was in the interest of each individual to eliminate selfishly motivated disputes over these essential goods; they saw that only if these disputes were eliminated or controlled could society survive. Consequently, they gradually developed conventions that stabilized the possession of these scarce items. Once these conventions were established, there arose the ideas of justice and injustice (the ideas of conforming to or violating the conventions), and, along with these, the ideas of property, of property rights, and of the obligation to respect property. In this way, self-interest in its initial, heedless form was brought under control by an enlightened version of this same interest. At the end of his answer to this first question Hume explains how it is that a single act of justice may be contrary to the interests of society or any given individual, and yet the operation of the whole system of justice may benefit society in general and every individual.

Hume defers most of his answer to his second question to *Treatise* 3.3. He has, he says, explained our *natural* obligation to justice; our *moral* obligation to this same virtue can only be explained after the natural virtues have been understood. But he does here say that it is sympathy, in conjunction with our propensity to form general rules, that enables us to feel approbation in response to the just actions of others, and disapprobation in response to their unjust actions. In other words, sympathy enables us to feel exactly those moral sentiments that enable us to recognize virtue and vice. (For additional discussion of these issues, see Ed. Intro., 184–9.)

1 **We shall . . . former**] Hume turns to the second question at ¶23 of this section.

2 **Of all the animals . . . necessities**] Hume and his contemporaries would have been familiar with classical writers who had emphasized the comparative weakness of individual humans. As Seneca put it, individual humans are the prey of other creatures, 'while other creatures possess a strength that is adequate for their self-protection, and [while] those that are born to be wanderers and to lead an isolated life have been given weapons, the covering of man is a frail skin; no might of claws or of teeth makes him a terror to others; naked and weak as he is, his safety lies in fellowship [society]' (*Of Benefits* 4.18). There were also familiar classical accounts of the developments needed for human well-being. Lucretius had claimed that early humans knew nothing of agriculture and building nor of the use of fire and clothing, were unable to communicate by speech, and had no understanding of morals and the common good. These diverse skills, the skills that have enabled our species to survive and thrive, were only developed gradually over the course of ages (*Nature of Things* 5.837–1160).

3 **'Tis by society . . . advantageous**] Hume reiterates a familiar theme. The classical writers cited above agreed in supposing society essential to human well-being and even survival. As Seneca said, 'Take away the Disposition to Society, and you will at the same Time destroy the Union of Mankind, on which the Preservation and Happiness of Life depend' (*Of Benefits* 4.18, quoted from Grotius, *Rights of War and Peace*, Preliminary Discourse 17). Well-known writers of Hume's age, although disagreeing among themselves about the fundamental motivation to form societies, made similar claims. Hobbes said, 'Out of Society we are defended only by our single Strength; in Society, by the Strength of all. Out of Society no Man is sure to keep Possession of what his Industry has gain'd; in Society every Body is secure from that Danger' (*De Cive* 10.1, as paraphrased by Pufendorf, *Law of Nature* 2.2.2). Locke said, 'God having made Man such a Creature, that, in his own Judgment, it was not good for him to be alone, put him under strong Obligations of Necessity, Convenience, and Inclination to drive him into *Society*, as well as fitted him with Understanding and Language to continue and enjoy it' (*Two Treatises* 2.7.77).

4 **This necessity . . . union**] Lucretius traced such social skills as language and morals, and society itself, to the fact that 'Venus coupled the bodies of lovers' (*Nature of Things* 5.962).

till a new tye . . . offspring] Pufendorf says that 'it pleas'd the most wise GOD' to imbue 'the two different Sexes with a natural Power of Propagating their Kind. . . . he implanted in each sex a passionate Love, a most ardent Propension towards the other, with a most deep and tender Affection for their Common Issue, that so they might not only willingly, but joyfully contribute their Service to the Preservation and the continuance of [the] Human Race (*Law of Nature* 6.1.2; see also Locke, *Two Treatises* 2.7.77).

5 **certain philosophers**] Hobbes, La Rochefoucauld, and Mandeville, among others. Criticisms similar to Hume's are found in Pufendorf (*Natural State* 17–18), Shaftesbury (*Sensus Communis* 3.3, in *Characteristics* [1:77]) and Hutcheson (*Inquiry* 2.1.4).

6 **dangerous . . . union**] Our natural generosity is in fact a form of private benevolence (see 3.2.1.13–16) which, if left uncontrolled, will produce conflicts that undermine newly developed societies.

7 There are three . . . fortune] Similar accounts of the kinds of good—of soul, of body, and of external goods or property—are found in Plato (*Laws* 743e), Aristotle (*Nicomachean Ethics* 1098^{b}9–17), and Seneca (*Epistles* 66.29).

As the improvement . . . impediment] Hume articulates a paradox at the heart of society: The formation of society enables individuals to expand the range of their possessions, but this very expansion increases the likelihood that individuals will have possessions that are attractive enough to be seized by others.

8 That virtue . . . men] This claim is first made at 3.2.1.9.

Now it appears . . . immoral] In humanity's rude and uncultivated state, selfish or biased behaviour would be the norm, the accepted way of acting. In those circumstances, Hume argues, we would take behaviour (including unselfish behaviour) that failed to conform to this norm as immoral, while behaviour conforming to this norm (appropriately biased or selfish behaviour) would be taken to be virtuous.

10 This conventions . . . conventions] For Hume's account of promises, see 3.2.5. Hume in this paragraph implicitly attacks those who trace the origin of justice to an explicit promise or contract, a view that can be traced at least to Cicero and which is the basis of the social contract theories of Hobbes and Locke. Cicero said that 'The foundation of justice, moreover, is good faith—that is truth and fidelity to promises and agreements' (*De officiis* 1.7.23). Hume returns to this topic in 3.2.8.8–9.

11 Those . . . solid foundation] As we later learn, Hume is here criticizing the view, dating from ancient times and widely repeated by early modern moralists and lexicographers, that justice is the '*constant and perpetual will of giving every one his due*' (3.2.6.2). See e.g. Plato, *Republic* 331e; Cicero, *De re publica* 3.11.18; Justinian, *Institutes* 1.1.1; Hobbes, *Leviathan* 2.24; Pufendorf, *Law of Nature* 1.7.6; Bailey, *Dictionary*, 'Justice'. On the view Hume criticizes, the concept of justice depends on the notion of property just because it is the appropriate distribution of property that constitutes justice. In contrast, Hume maintains that the notion of property depends on the concept of justice because it is only as the conventions of justice are established that the notion of property becomes intelligible.

13 The question . . . same effect] Hume alludes here to the dispute between those who emphasized our wicked or selfish nature (Hobbes, La Rochefoucauld, Mandeville, for example) and those who emphasized our goodness or social nature (Grotius, Shaftesbury, and Hutcheson, for example). Hume was later to say that, 'Whoever desires to see this Question treated at large, with the greatest Force of Argument and Eloquence, may consult Lord Shaftesbury's *Enquiry concerning Virtue*' (*Essays*, 'Of the Dignity or Meanness of Human Nature' 2 [1741–8 edns. only]).

14 this passion] self-interest.

state of nature] See 3.2.1.9.

15 *golden age*] The metaphor of a Golden Age is typically traced to Hesiod, whose golden race of men lived at a time when life on earth was idyllic. Later Roman poets recast Hesiod's notion of a golden race into that of a Golden Age; see e.g. Virgil, *Georgics* 2.536; Ovid, *Metamorphoses* 1.76–150.

The rivers . . . delicacies] 'Then spring was everlasting, and gentle zephyrs with warm breath played with the flowers that sprang unplanted. . . . Streams of milk and streams of sweet nectar flowed, and yellow honey was distilled from the verdant oak' (Ovid, *Metamorphoses* 1.106–12).

19 First . . . justice] See 3.2.1.11–12.

20 Secondly . . . obligatory] See 3.1.1.4, 10, 17–23. Notice that Hume goes on to call the system that claims to derive morality from reason 'the common system'.

23 *second* question . . . *injustice*] This question is first posed, in a different form, in ¶1 of this section. Although the full answer to the question is deferred to *Treatise* 3.3, which examines the natural virtues, a summary answer follows in ¶¶24–8 of this section.
already establish'd] See 3.2.1.7; 3.2.2.18–21.
The *natural* . . . account of it] Natural obligation has been explained in this section. Although the natural virtues are not explained until *Treatise* 3.3, Hume goes on here to give a brief account of our moral obligation to justice.

25 This, no doubt . . . *blameable*] Mandeville is a likely target here. He had argued that, although we humans have no natural moral dispositions or sentiments, a few cunning politicians were able to induce us to adopt the practices, including the language, of morality. See *Fable* [1:41–9]; Hume repeats his criticism at 3.3.1.11.

28 *state of nature* . . . others] Hume here attempts to distinguish his view from that associated with Hobbes, who had said that, in the state of nature (before the establishment of civil society), humans were in a state of continual war of each against each, that each individual had the right to use his or her power as each saw fit, and that in consequence there were no moral constraints on the seizure of the goods of others (see esp. *Leviathan* 1.13).
promises . . . them] See 3.2.5.

Book 3 Part 2 Sect. 3. *Of the rules, which determine property*

Hume argues that in order to stabilize property and eliminate disorder, the rules of justice (the rules by which ownership of property is determined) must be both general and specific. They must, that is, apply, without regard to need or suitability, to every member of society. As societies begin *present possession* provides the obvious criterion of ownership. As time passes other such criteria are needed. These are *occupation, prescription, accession,* and *succession*. In a series of notes Hume argues that the imagination has considerable influence in determining the precise form taken by these criteria or rules.

2 Justice, in her decisions . . . to him] Elsewhere Hume illustrates this point with a story about the 'young and unexperienced' Cyrus, who mistakenly supposed that, as judge in a dispute over the ownership of coats, he should base his decision on what seemed fit and convenient in a particular case. He should instead have based his decision on 'the general, inflexible rules, necessary to support the general peace and order in society' (*EPM*, App. 3.4); see also 3.2.6.9.

3 I say, 'tis . . . themselves] Hume returns to this issue at 3.2.8.3–6.

4 n. 71.2 n. a Book 1. Part 4. Sect. 5] See 1.4.5.12.
n. 71.2 Many . . . position] On perceptions that exist and yet are nowhere, see 1.4.5.10–14.
n. 71.2 And this is . . . human nature] Hume is alluding to our tendency to associate certain kinds of idea; see 1.1.4.
n. 71.2 afterwards . . . *beauty*] Beauty is again discussed at 3.3.1.8–10, 15, 20, and at 3.3.5.3–4, but the issue raised here is not mentioned. In the Advertisement to *Treatise* 1 and 2 Hume says that he hopes to extend his work to include an examination of 'criticism'. Such a study would have been a likely place to discuss beauty.

5 *occupation*] In civil law *occupation* denoted (among other things) taking initial possession of such things as are presently not the property of anyone, but which are capable of being made property. The catching of a wild animal or the finding of something previously undiscovered would constitute such occupation (Chambers, *Cyclopædia*, 'Occupation').

6 n. 72 **Some philosophers . . . whole**] That a person's labour gives him property in the object of that labour (the labour theory of property, as it is now known) is clearly set out in Locke, *Two Treatises* 2.5.25–51.

n. 72 **This accounts . . . circuit**] Hume suggests that, on Locke's theory of property (see the previous annotation), it is in fact not *labour*, but *accession* (the joining of an item to something already existing), that accounts for property. Locke seems to say as much at *Two Treatises* 2.5.32.

n. 72 **preceding principles**] See Note 71.2.

7 **and as property . . . possession**] Hume also defines property at 2.1.10.1.

n. 73.1 **hare . . . apple**] Locke's examples include hares and apples. See *Two Treatises* 2.5.28, 30.

n. 73.3 **almost every writer**] This story is told by Plutarch (*Moralia*, 'Greek Questions' 30) and retold by, among others, Grotius, *Rights of War and Peace* 2.8.6, and Pufendorf, *Law of Nature* 4.6.8. Hume's version appears to derive from that of Pufendorf.

8 **A person . . . debarkment**] On taking possession of deserted and uncultivated places, see Grotius, *Rights of War and Peace* 2.2, 8; and Pufendorf, *Law of Nature* 4.6.

9 *prescription*] in this context, a right of ownership acquired by use and time, and especially if one's right to use the item is not contested during the time in question. See Pufendorf, *Law of Nature* 4.12.1.

Any considerable . . . being] For Hume's detailed account of the effect of time on the passions, see 2.3.7.

The same facts . . . time] On the effects of time on arguments or proofs, see 1.3.13.1–6.

preceding doctrine . . . justice] the doctrine set out in the preceding section.

But as . . . influence] Hume first argues that property is nothing real in objects at 3.2.2.11; see also ¶7 of this section; 3.2.4.2; and, most importantly, 3.2.6.3.

n. 74 **distance**] distance in time, that is.

n. 75.2 **observ'd above**] See Note 71.2.

n. 75.3 **a principle**] Hume goes on to suggest that this principle is merely a natural association of ideas.

n. 75.4 **already observ'd**] See 2.2.2.19–26.

n. 75.4 **foregoing hypothesis**] The hypothesis articulated in ¶10 of this section, the paragraph to which this note is attached.

n. 75.6 **philosophers and civilians**] A civilian is an authority or writer on the laws of such political entities as cities and countries. For an early statement of the claim that the seas cannot legitimately be made property, see Grotius, *Freedom of the Seas* and *Rights of War and Peace* 2.3. Pufendorf, *Law of Nature* 4.5, reviews the reasons for saying the seas cannot be owned and also discusses the ownership of 'friths and bays' at the sea's edge.

n. 75.7 **rivers . . . nations**] On this subject, see Grotius, *Rights of War and Peace* 2.2.2–12; 2.3.4–18; and Pufendorf, *Law of Nature* 4.7.11–12.

n. 75.8 **The accessions . . . *alluvion***] Alluvion, the gradual forming of new land (alluvial deposits) by the virtually imperceptible action of flowing water, was supposed a lawful means of acquisition. On the topics of this paragraph, see Grotius, *Rights of War and Peace* 2.3.16–17; 2.8.8–17; Pufendorf, *Law of Nature* 4.7.11–12.

n. 75.10 *division . . . separation*] If the owners of two quantities of indistinguishable things (two bushels of wheat, for example) mix their property together, it becomes *inseparable* in the sense that it is not possible to restore to the two owners the precise set of individual items he or she has contributed to the resulting mass. It is, however, possible to *divide* the resulting mass into quantities corresponding to those with which the owners began.

n. 75.11 **Quod si . . . fuerit**] But if the corn of Titius has become mixed with yours, and this by mutual consent, the whole will belong to you in common, because the separate bodies or grains, which before belonged to one or the other of you in severalty, have by consent on both sides been made your joint property. If, however, the mixture was accidental, or if Titius mixed the two parcels of corn without your consent, they do not belong to you in common, because the separate grains remain distinct, and their substance is unaltered; and in such cases the corn no more becomes common property than does a flock formed by the accidental mixture of Titius' sheep with yours. But if either of you keeps the whole of the mixed corn, the other can bring a real action for the recovery of such part of it as belongs to him, it being part of the province of the judge to determine the quantity of the corn which belonged to each (Justinian, *Institutes* 2.1.28).

n. 75.14 **The superficies . . . picture**] Hume alludes to principles found in civil law. The first maintains that ownership of land takes precedence over ownership of buildings or other things ('superficies') on that land, so that if for some reason *X* builds on the land of *Y*, the resulting building becomes the property of *Y*. The second principle maintains that if one person writes on the paper of another, the writing is owned by the person who owns the paper. The third principle maintains that if a painter paints on the canvas of another, the resulting painting is the property of the painter. These conventions are set out in Justinian, *Institutes* 2.1.29–34.

n. 75.15 *Proculus* **and** *Sabinus*] Two Roman jurists of the first century AD. Grotius reports that 'If any Body had formed a Thing out of another's Materials, the *Sabinians* gave the Property to him whose the materials were, but Proculus [gave it to the craftsman] who had given the Form, because he gave to a Thing an Existence which it had not before' (*Rights of War and Peace* 2.8.19).

n. 75.15 *Tribonian*] Roman jurist (d. *c.*AD 545) who collaborated in the preparation of Justinian's *Institutes*.

11 **right of** *succession*] According to Chambers, the 'right to the whole effects left by a defunct' or deceased person (*Cyclopædia*, 'Succession'). Hume again suggests that it is the association of ideas, and thus ultimately the imagination, that leads us to adopt a particular convention for the transfer of property.

Book 3 Part 2 Sect. 4. *Of the transference of property by consent*

The interests of society are served by rules permitting the transfer of property. Given that ownership adds nothing perceptible to an object, the particular forms these rules take, and the manner in which a transfer is signalled, are limited only by the imagination.

1 *present* **possession . . .** *succession*] These concepts are the subject of 3.2.3.5–11.
   law of nature] rule of justice.

2 **that** *delivery* **. . .** *property*] On delivery, see Grotius, *Rights of War and Peace* 2.6.1–2; 2.8.25; and Pufendorf, *Law of Nature* 4.9.5. As Hume indicates near the end of this paragraph, certain acts—handing over keys or bits of stone and earth—were symbolic representations of the transfer of ownership.
   Now as . . . idea] For more on this important claim regarding the role of present impressions in enlivening ideas and producing belief, see 1.3.7.5–7 and App. 9.

Book 3 Part 2 Sect. 5. *Of the obligation of promises*

Promises would be neither intelligible nor produce obligations were it not for certain conventions. Promising is, like justice, an artificial virtue, a human invention 'founded on the necessities and interests of society' (¶7). Those who claim that keeping promises ('fidelity') is a natural virtue must be able to show not only that some distinct act of mind is associated with every act of promising, but also that this act, independently of any sense of duty, obliges agents to keep their promises. This two-part condition cannot be met. *Resolution* and *desire* may seem to be essential to promising, but are not; promises once made are binding even if resolve or desire is lacking. *Willing* may seem to have an important role in promising, but it is clear that we cannot create the new obligation of a promise simply by an act of will. To be effective—to create an obligation—a promise must be expressed in one of many conventional forms ('I promise that . . .', for example) and in the appropriate circumstances (the person promising must comprehend what she does and must not be speaking in jest, for example). When such an expression is made in such circumstances, both a promise and the obligation to fulfil that promise are immediately created.

3 **For a promise . . . actions**] Or, in other words, while the will has effect only in the present, a promise may oblige in the future.

It follows . . . promise] If promising does depend on an act of mind, and if it does not depend on resolution, desire, or a simple act of will, then it must depend on willing the duty or obligation the promise creates, as this is (presumably) the only remaining alternative. But, Hume goes on to argue, this conclusion is absurd and false for it presupposes that we can, contrary to fact, determine our own sentiments by an act of the will.

6 **that reasoning . . . artificial virtue**] Hume goes on to summarize the argument he presents at 3.2.1.2–8.

natural virtues] The natural virtues are defined at 3.3.1.1; see also Ed. Intro., I81.

8 **already found**] See 3.2.2.2–8, 12–14, 18–22.

delivery] On the importance of delivery, see 3.2.4.2.

Here then . . . security] Unless, that is, a remedy (in the form of promising or contracting) is found.

9 **And indeed . . . articles**] On the seemingly immutable character of human nature, see also 3.2.7.6; 3.3.6.5.

11 **and interest . . . promises**] Hume also says that interest produces the first obligation to justice; see 3.2.2.23.

12 **prov'd already**] See ¶3 of this section.

13 **'Tis evident . . . man**] Although promises are not the effect of willing an obligation (¶¶3–4 of this section), Hume appears to grant that they begin with words or other signs that are expressions of the will.

14 *transubstantiation*] According to the Roman Catholic faith, the bread and the wine which are part of a sacrament are transformed into different substances, namely, the body and blood of Christ, but continue to display the qualities or appearances of bread and wine.

n. 78 holy orders . . . *indelible character*] In the Roman Catholic faith, the taking of holy orders is a sacrament which is said to give to an otherwise ordinary person a distinctive and ineradicable spiritual character.

Theologians . . . holy orders] In a later work (*EPM* n. 13) Hume associates this criticism with the Jesuit theologians discussed in Bayle's *Dictionary* (see 'Loyola', n. T). The issue of the intention of priests administering sacraments was a much-discussed topic from the late middle ages to the 17th c. (at the Council of Trent, 1545–63, for example), with many Roman Catholic theologians arguing that a sacramental rite would be invalid should a priest secretly withhold the appropriate intention.

The terrible . . . place] The doctrine Hume describes was not accepted by all Roman Catholic theologians; see e.g. Thomas Aquinas, *Summa Theologiae* 3.60.8; 3.64.8, 10.

Men . . . future] Hume attempts to explain this phenomenon at 1.3.9.13–14.

Book 3 Part 2 Sect. 6. *Some farther reflections concerning justice and injustice*

Hume has completed his discussion of the conventions having to do with stability of possession, transfer of property by consent, and the keeping of promises, or what he interchangeably denominates 'the three fundamental laws of nature' or 'the three fundamental rules of justice' (3.2.11.2). He now offers three additional arguments showing that justice is an artificial virtue. First, although justice is traditionally defined as '*a constant and perpetual will of giving every one his due*' (as though property and the right to it exist independently of the practice of justice), this is a mistake. It is not the existence of property that gives rise to justice, but the development of the conventions of justice that produces the institution of property. Consequently, there can be no original or natural motive to respect property. Secondly, while virtue and vice in their natural forms admit of degrees, justice and injustice admit of no such gradation; actions are either just or unjust. Thirdly, while our natural motives are marked by flexibility, the rules of justice are entirely inflexible, permitting no exceptions whatever. In conclusion Hume says that the distinction between justice and injustice has two foundations: that of *self-interest*, which leads us to devise the rules of justice, and, once these rules are established, that of *morality*, or the feelings of approbation or disapprobation that arise when we observe actions tending to the good or ill of society.

1 We have . . . *promises*] These are, in order, the topics of the three previous sections.
2 already observ'd] See 3.2.2.11.
3 imaginary qualities . . . philosophy] For Hume's more general view of the imaginary inventions of the scholastic or peripatetic philosophers, see 1.4.3.10–11.

Property . . . object] Similar claims about the relational nature of property are made at 3.2.2.11; 3.2.3.7; see also 2.1.10.1.

'Tis, therefore . . . actions] Pufendorf had said that property is a 'moral' quality that does not affect the intrinsic nature of things, but only produces 'a moral Effect with regard to other Persons. . . . the natural Substance of things suffers no alteration, whether Property be added to them or taken from them' (*Law of Nature* 4.4.1).

6 They . . . nature] Grounds for this claim are found at 2.1.3.5–7.

Secondly . . . rules] Hume repeats a point first made at 3.2.2.18–19.

7 foregoing principle] the principle that justice is an artificial virtue.

perfect *dominion* . . . imperfect] Perfect dominion was the exclusive right to something. Dominion was rendered imperfect by e.g. servitude or mortgage, for then some aspect of the right of ownership had to be shared with someone else.

8 moral relations] property and obligation, that is.

references . . . referees] when, that is, disputed matters have been referred to arbitrators who are to settle the issues.

9 No action . . . from it] On this point, see 3.2.1.2–7.

Here are . . . friend] On this contrast and its significance, see also 3.2.3.2.

11 Upon the whole . . . others] On the several points made in this paragraph, see also 3.2.2.23–6.

Book 3 Part 2 Sect. 7. *Of the origin of government*

Although conforming to the rules of justice is in our real or long-term interest, we are typically led to gratify more immediate or short-term interests, and thereby to violate the rules of justice. This deep-seated tendency threatens the very existence of society. It also appears to be irremediable: if we are inherently inclined to prefer short-term interests, we cannot always be made to pursue our remote ones. But we are inclined to try to correct what we perceive to be weaknesses, and this one we correct by changing our circumstances: we arrange things so that conformity to the rules of justice will be in our short-term interest. In short, we institute government. We put one or a few individuals in charge of the administration of justice (thus making conformity to the rules of justice to be in both their short-term and long-term interests), and allow them to have those civil and military aids required to constrain others to conform to the rules of justice. These same rulers or magistrates can adjudicate disputes over property, and enable their societies to carry out new and complex projects that contribute to the public good. (Hume briefly summarizes his view of the origin of government at 3.2.10.2.)

1 Nothing is . . . acquaintance] On the crucial role of natural selfishness and limited generosity, see esp. 3.2.2.5–6, 8, 16–20, 24.
2 been observ'd] See esp. 2.3.6 and the discussions of comparison at 2.2.8.2–8.
Now as every . . . light] On this point see 2.2.2.20–6; 2.3.7.
5 improper sense . . . *reason*] On the confusion that gives rise to this improper sense of the term *reason*, see 2.3.3.8–10.
6 impossible to change . . . nature] Other allusions to the seemingly fixed character of human nature are found at 3.2.5.9 and 3.3.6.5.
7 manner . . . above-mention'd] in the previous paragraph.

Book 3 Part 2 Sect. 8. *Of the source of allegiance*

Allegiance, understood as our sense that we are obliged to obey our government, is founded on more than a (typically remote) promise or original contract. Hume begins by arguing that societies can and do survive for a time before the institution of government. In fact, he suggests, many governments can probably be traced to times of conflict—to wars—between societies. Such external conflicts provided an occasion for a breakdown of internal order, and also produced a need for a military leader. In consequence, one person was given authority to manage affairs during hostilities, and the success of this arrangement led to its continuation once hostilities had ended. Hume then goes on to argue that (1) although societies can exist without government, they cannot be maintained unless the rules of justice are observed; (2) we have an obligation to obey the rules of justice prior to the institution of government; (3) government is instituted just in order to ensure that the rules of justice are obeyed; and, thus, (4) the ultimate source of our obligation to obey our government is our prior obligation to obey the rules of justice. It may be that at least some governments are initially formed by explicit promises, and that those who so promise owe obedience because of their promises. But the obligation of these promises is soon enough replaced by a new obligation, a sense of allegiance. Governments derive ultimately from self-interest and convention, and the duty to obey them derives, ultimately, from that same foundation. After outlining further theoretical grounds for concluding that the obligations associated with promise-keeping and allegiance are distinct, Hume appeals to popular opinion to make the same point: Those bound by a promise or contract, he notes, must know about that contract. But the vast majority of those who feel themselves bound to obey their government know nothing about any such contract, nor do rulers and magistrates suppose that only those who have promised owe allegiance. Allegiance does not, it follows, depend on promises.

1 **An *Indian* . . . society]** Seneca makes similar suggestions about early humans; see *Epistles* 90.40–1.

some philosophers . . . government] Hobbes had said 'that the state of men without civil society [government] . . . is nothing else but a mere war of all against all' (*De Cive*, Preface; see also chs. 1, 5). At *EPM* n. 11 Hume says that Hobbes was not the first to maintain that the state of nature was a state of war, and refers to discussions in Plato (*Republic* 358e ff.) and Cicero (*Pro Sestio* 42.91–2).

2 **American tribes . . . tribes]** Hobbes had claimed that the 'people in many places of America, except the government of small Families . . . have no government at all' (*Leviathan* 1.13). Locke cites Acosta, who reported 'that in many parts of America there was no Government at all' and that the natives of Peru 'for a long time had neither Kings nor Common-wealths, but lived in Troops, as they do this day in Florida, the Cheriquanas [an Andean tribe], those of Brasil, and many other Nations, which have no certain Kings, but as occasion is offered in Peace or War, they choose their Captains as they please' (*Two Treatises* 2.8.102, quoting Acosta's *Naturall and Morall Historie of the Indies*).

Camps . . . cities] Machiavelli argued that cities begin as armed camps, thus suggesting that war is the foundation of government (*Discourses* 1.1). La Bruyère said that 'An injustice committed by the first men was the primary occasion of wars, and made the people feel the necessity of giving themselves masters to settle their rights and pretensions' (*Characters* [245–6]). In contrast, Pufendorf, citing also the opinion of Grotius, says there is no reason to suppose that war is the source or foundation of government; see *Law of Nature* 7.3.5.

And this reason . . . person] The foremost early modern exponent of the patriarchal basis of government was Robert Filmer, whose *Patriarcha; or, The Natural Power of Kings* is criticized throughout Locke's *Two Treatises of Government*. Filmer, who traced the authority of governments to the powers conferred on Adam at creation and then passed on to his male descendants, insisted for just that reason that society without government is impossible: all humans are descendants of Adam and are in consequence subject to the authority passed on by him.

The state . . . generation] Society, Hume has argued, is dependent upon the development and employment of the rules of justice. He now grants that in some circumstances these rules may be employed, and society maintained, prior to the instantiation of government even though it is the purpose of government to enforce these rules and maintain society.

3 **creed of a party]** the creed of the Whigs, a political party which sought to increase parliamentary authority at the expense of royal authority, and which maintained that the authority of government derives from consent and contractual arrangements.

All men . . . duty] Hume here summarizes the position taken by Locke; see *Two Treatises* 2.8.95–9. On natural equality, see also Hobbes (*Leviathan* 1.13) and Pufendorf (*Law of Nature* 3.2).

This conclusion . . . erroneous] Note that Hume implicitly grants that, in its initial stages, government (but not society) may *sometimes* (but only sometimes) depend on an explicit promise or contract.

4 **'Tis reasonable . . . magistracy]** See e.g. Grotius, *Rights of War and Peace*, Preliminary Discourse 16; and Locke, *Two Treatises* 2.8.100–12.

5 already shown] As Hume intimates at 3.2.6.1, the three fundamental laws of nature or justice are discussed in 3.2.3–5; see also 3.2.2.8–18.

7 *natural . . . moral* obligations] On the distinction between natural and moral obligations, see also 3.2.2.23–4.

Education . . . particularly concern'd] On the role of education and the artifice of politicians, see also 3.2.2.25; 3.2.6.11; 3.3.1.11. The industrious efforts of politicians had been highlighted by Mandeville; see *Fable* [1:41–57]).

8 n. 80 consider'd afterwards] No further discussion of this topic is found in the *Treatise*; see the final annotation to 3.2.3.4 for a possible explanation of this fact.

9 In consequence . . . choose] Hume may be referring to, among others, James Francis Edward Stuart (1688–1766), son of James II. After the death (1701) of his deposed father, Stuart was proclaimed king of England in exile; he retained loyal followers in Britain at least until the rebellion of 1745.

Book 3 Part 2 Sect. 9. *Of the measures of allegiance*

The aim of those who trace allegiance to a promise is to show that our duty to obey our government is not absolute and that tyranny can be legitimately resisted. This, Hume grants, is a reasonable aim, but the underlying theory is mistaken. In contrast, he argues that government and allegiance derive ultimately from an interested desire for the security found within civil society, but lacking outside it. Given that this interest provides the 'immediate sanction' of government, the failure of a government to satisfy it is itself enough to put an immediate end to our *natural* obligation to obey that government. There is also, however, a *moral* obligation to allegiance, and this, because of the influence of general rules and our recognition that rulers are only human, does not cease to have effect the moment we find our interests are not being served. Nevertheless, no nation that could possibly overthrow a tyrannous government has failed to do so, or been blamed for the effort. Ordinary persons may not be able to produce theoretical arguments supporting the right to resistance, but they recognize the absurdity of the doctrine of passive obedience.

1 Those political writers . . . allegiance] See Locke, *Two Treatises* 2.17–19 (chapters on usurpation, tyranny, and the dissolution of government). On these issues, Locke himself was influenced by Hooker, Grotius, Hobbes, and Pufendorf.

2 I perceive . . . interest] For Hume's account of promises, see 3.2.5.

This interest . . . independent] For Hume's views on the relations of interest, the origins of government, and the sources of allegiance, see esp. 3.2.7.1–2, 6–8; 3.2.8.5–7.

3 addicted to *general rules*] On the influence of general rules, see 1.3.13.7–14; 2.2.5.12–13; 2.2.8.5; and Ed. Intro., 162–3.

4 Accordingly . . . resistance] Locke notes that, whatever may be the foundation of government, oppressed peoples have routinely rebelled against the tyrants who oppressed them (*Two Treatises* 2.19.224–6; see also Grotius, *Rights of War and Peace* 1.4.1; Pufendorf, *Law of Nature* 7.8.6 n.1).

Dionysius] Dionysius II (*fl.* 360 BC), despotic ruler of Syracuse (Sicily), who in 344 BC was successfully overthrown after his subjects appealed to their mother city, Corinth, for assistance.

Nero] Nero (AD 37–68) was a despotic Roman emperor remembered for, among other things, his persecution of the Christians, whom he blamed for the burning of Rome in AD 64. Boadicea (Boudicca) of Britain was one of those who took up arms against Nero's abusive rule; other rebellions followed until Nero fled from Rome and committed suicide in 68.

Philip the Second] Philip II (1527–98), king of Spain and the Netherlands. The persecution of non-Catholics reached its height during Philip's reign, and was among the causes of the rebellion in the Netherlands.

passive obedience] the doctrine that, no matter how inhumane, unjust, or incompetent any given government may seem to be, it is immoral to resist or attempt to overthrow this government. The view that there is 'an absolute unlimited non-resistance or passive obedience due to the supreme civil power' was defended by Berkeley (*Passive Obedience*, in *Works*, 6:17). In Britain the doctrine was associated with those who favoured a strong hereditary monarchy.

If the sense . . . submission] That our sense of interest is the only motive capable of controlling our passions, and particularly the passion of interest itself, is first noted at 3.2.2.12–13.

Book 3 Part 2 Sect. 10. *Of the objects of allegiance*

Hume begins this section by noting that, while rebellion can be justifiable, it should be used only in response to great tyranny. Otherwise it will tend to undermine the institution of government. He then turns to the main issue of the section: To whom is obedience due? After a government has been in place long enough for allegiance to have become distinct from any initial promises made (see 3.2.8.6–9), allegiance will be accorded those who hold supreme power by right of one or more titles or sources of authority. These include original contract, long possession, present possession, conquest, succession, and positive law, with the strongest title arising from some combination of these sources. Why each of these sources has the effect it does is the subject of the middle half of the section. In conclusion, Hume addresses the question of when a revolution is justified, and offers 'philosophical reflections, which naturally arise' from the English revolution of 1688 (¶17).

2 origin of . . . political society] the topic of 3.2.7.
  that the authority . . . subjects] On this point, see 3.2.8.3; 3.2.9.2.
3 The case . . . possession] Hume alludes to his discussion, found at 3.2.3–4, of the rules determining property and of the transference of property by consent; see esp. 3.2.4.1.
5 The kings of *France* . . . reigns] The Bourbon dynasty began with Henri IV (1553–1610), but, on Hume's account, fully consolidated its power only during the reign of Louis XIV (1638–1715).
  If we . . . *accession*] See 3.2.3.10.
6 principles above-mention'd] those regarding stability and general interests, mentioned in ¶3 of this section.
  a contrary interest] Hume here and in the following paragraph argues that, while the principle of present possession is of no use in disputes about ownership (because a thief might have present possession of some property, but is not for that reason the owner of it), this same principle may serve to identify an appropriate object of allegiance. Because it is only by acts of violence and the creation of disorder that we can strip political authority from those who hold that authority, it may well be better to allow a usurper to retain the power he has seized.
7 Any one . . . mankind] None the less, Locke had argued that a 'Usurper can never have Right on his side' (*Two Treatises* 2.17.197).
  from the dissolution . . . *Turks*] The period from the end of the Roman republic, *c.*40 BC, to the capture of Byzantium or Constantinople by the Ottoman Turks in 1453.

10 principles of the imagination] On these principles and succession, see 3.2.3.11.

12 *Artaxerxes . . . Cyrus*] The two sons of Darius II, king of Persia, 424–405 BC. Artaxerxes ruled Persia from 404–358 BC. Cyrus, the younger brother, died (401 BC) in a struggle to depose Artaxerxes.

above-mention'd] ¶¶4, 10, 11 of this section; see also 2.2.8.2–8; 2.3.6.

13 The interest . . . fix'd] The good of a nation demands that the manner in which power is transferred be fixed, but the precise way in which it is fixed is immaterial. In other words, the detailed conventions for determining the object of allegiance, like the detailed conventions regarding the transfer of property, are the work of the imagination.

14 *Salic* law] a rule of succession which forbids females and those descended in the female line from succeeding to the titles or offices in the family. The rule was most prominently enforced by the French house of Valois (1328–1589) and the succeeding house of Bourbon (1589–1792).

15 *Germanicus, or Drusus . . . Tiberius*] Tiberius, Roman emperor from AD 14 to 37, adopted Germanicus (15 BC–AD 19) in AD 4. Drusus was born to Tiberius and his first wife, Agrippina, c.13 BC. Thus Germanicus was older than Drusus, but was adopted when Drusus was about 17. As it happens, both Germanicus and Drusus died (probably from poison) before Tiberius did.

16 famous *revolution*] Hume is referring to the so-called Glorious Revolution. In 1688 the English Parliament asked William of Orange, a staunch protestant whose wife, Mary, was the daughter of the reigning king, James II (a Roman Catholic), to save the laws and religion of England. James, eventually deserted even by his own army, fled to France. Parliament, declaring his flight as equivalent to abdication, in 1689 formally offered the crown to William. From this time on, ultimate authority in Britain has rested with Parliament rather than the crown. In ¶18 of this section Hume offers a justification for such a transfer of power.

already remark'd] See 3.2.9.

Not only . . . rebellious] For a more detailed discussion of this issue, see Locke, *Two Treatises* 2.19.

18 *lords* and *commons*] the House of Lords and the House of Commons.

The mind . . . begun] On the tendency of the mind to continue a course of action once begun, see 1.2.4.24; 1.3.13.9–10; 1.4.2.22.

19 three princes . . . title] The three were Queen Anne, who ruled from 1702 to 1714; George I, the Elector of Hanover, who was proclaimed king in 1715; and his son George II, who succeeded to the throne on his father's death in 1727.

Julius Cæsar . . . Marius . . . usurpers] Caesar (100–44 BC) formed about 60 BC the 'first triumvirate' with Pompey and Crassus. Caesar eventually assumed dictatorial power, putting an end to the Roman republic, and is by many regarded as the first of the Roman emperors. Earlier Lucius Cornelius Sulla (c.138–78 BC), Roman general and leader of forces supported by the Senate and noble families of Rome, had been elected dictator after a brutal civil war, largely between forces loyal to him and those led by Gaius Marius (157–86 BC), a leader of the popular party who was six times elected a consul by the Roman Senate. With his allies, Marius seized power in Rome in 87 BC, and proceeded to execute those whom he perceived to be his enemies. A year later Sulla regained control and, once in power, set about ruthlessly exterminating his enemies. Although Marius and Sulla may have been no more tyrannical than was Julius Caesar, their rule has not been legitimized by time.

present king of *France . . . Hugh Capet . . . Cromwell*] Louis XV of the house of

Bourbon ruled France in 1740. Hugh Capet (*c*.938–96), who had been a powerful vassal of the last Carolingian kings, Lothair and Louis V, displaced the next Carolingian in line, Charles of Lorraine. The direct Capetian line ended in 1328, but the Bourbons who ruled France in the 17th and 18th cs. were a branch of that line. Oliver Cromwell, Protector from 1653 to 1658, may have been no more a usurper than Caesar or Hugh Capet, but because he failed to found a surviving form of government, he is often taken to have been an illegitimate ruler.

as the establish'd . . . *Philip* the Second] Because the northern Dutch provinces were successful in defending their civil and religious liberties against Philip II, their defence of these liberties takes on a legitimacy it would not otherwise have had.

Book 3 Part 2 Sect. 11. *Of the laws of nations*

Nations have an obligation to govern their interactions by international law and explicit treaties. They are like individuals in important ways: they need one another's assistance, and they increase their own insecurity when they break the rules of justice. But nations are also different from individuals, and so have developed an additional set of rules, the *laws of nations*, that guide behaviour regarding ambassadors, the conduct of war, or use of the seas. Hume insists that the use of rules of both kinds in international matters is motivated by self-interest, just as it is in intranational matters. Unless nations constrain themselves by these rules, peace, commerce, and alliances will suffer. Satisfied that the morality of rulers and nations has the same *scope* as does private morality, Hume explains why international law has a weaker *force*. The obligation to honour treaties and conform to international law derives ultimately from the self-interest of nations and rulers, but because the interaction between nations is not so important to their well-being as is private interaction to the well-being of individuals, both the natural and moral obligations to the laws of nations are (indeterminately) weaker than are the obligations of private individuals to the comparable rules of justice.

1 **Political writers . . . one person**] Hobbes had said that individuals, in submitting themselves to the sovereign, create a 'civil society; and also a civil person. For when there is one will for all men, it is to be esteemed for one person . . . having its own rights and properties' (*De Cive* 5.9). Pufendorf said that by means of 'Covenants . . . a Multitude of Men are so united and incorporated, as to form a civil State; which is conceived to exist like one *Person*, endued with Understanding and Will, and performing other particular Acts, distinct from those of the private Members. . . . So that the most proper Definition of a civil State seems to be . . . "a compound moral Person"' (*Law of Nature* 7.2.13; see also 4.2.17; 7.4.2; and Locke, *Two Treatises* 2.8.95–6).

laws of nations] Hobbes says that the '*natural law* may be divided into that of *men*, which alone hath obtained the title of *law of Nature*; and that of cities, which may be called that of *nations*' (*De Cive* 14.4; see also *Leviathan* 2.30; and Grotius, *Rights of War and Peace* 1.1.14).

Under this head . . . kind] Pufendorf (*Law of Nature* 2.3.23) reports on what others have said about laws of nations or the rules regarding embassies and ambassadors and the conduct of war. On poisoned arms, see Grotius, *Rights of War and Peace* 3.4.15–16.

3 **There is a maxim . . . *persons***] Machiavelli says that 'a prudent ruler ought not to keep faith when by so doing it would be against his interest, and when the reasons which made him bind himself no longer exist' and that 'it must be understood that a prince . . . cannot observe all those things which are considered good in men, being

often obliged, in order to maintain the state, to act against faith, against charity, against humanity, and against religion' (*Prince* 18). Pufendorf says that a prince, because he is supposed the *supreme* ruler, must for that very reason 'be suppos'd exempt from human Laws, or, to speak more properly, *above* them' (*Law of Nature* 7.6.3 [688]; see also 4.2.17). For the views of Grotius, see *Rights of War and Peace*, Preliminary Discourse; 2.15–16; 3.19–21; for those of Locke, *Two Treatises* 2.18.199.

'Tis evident . . . princes] Notwithstanding his view that the prince is above the law and that governments may lie for the good of the state, Pufendorf insists that all governments, and especially princes, should scrupulously observe treaties; see *Law of Nature* 4.1.17–19; 4.2.17.

4 *laws of justice*] also called the *laws of nature* (3.2.1.19) or rules of justice (¶2 of this section).

This obligation . . . duty] On the two kinds or sources of obligation, see also 3.2.2.23; 3.2.5.11–12; 3.2.8.7.

Book 3 Part 2 Sect. 12. *Of chastity and modesty*

Hume is concerned that his account of the laws of nature (the rules of justice) and the laws of nations may seem not to account for the universality with which approbation is associated with the observance, and disapprobation with the transgression, of these laws. Hoping to remove all doubts on this matter, he focuses on chastity and modesty, two closely linked artificial virtues derived from the interests of society, convention, and education. Human infancy is long and thus best managed if parents work together in the care and upbringing of their children. But if males are to be persuaded to contribute to this enterprise, they must be satisfied that the children in question are their own. The connection of women to their children is naturally or physically obvious; for men it is not, and hence an artificial link must be forged. The virtues of modesty and chastity provide just this link. Females are, universally, from their infancy to old age, taught that they must at all times shun every sign of immodesty of thought or behaviour, and so too must all females, even those beyond child-bearing age, avoid all sexual promiscuity. With these virtues established, males can be reasonably certain they are the fathers of those children said to be theirs, and thus are the interests of society served. Hume notes that, because the interest of society in male chastity is relatively weak, so too is the obligation to this virtue weak. In closing, he mentions courage, a largely artificial virtue.

2 **There are some . . . sex**] Mandeville had argued with some vigour that chastity and modesty are artificial virtues: 'the Modesty of Women is the Result of Custom and Education, by which all unfashionable Denudations and filthy Expressions are render'd frightful and abominable to them' (*Fable* [1:65]). Grotius says that it is 'the *Opinion* of the *World*' that has made chastity and reputation a matter of life and death (*Rights of War and Peace* 2.1.7).

5 **All human creatures . . . temptation**] See 2.2.2.20–6; 2.3.7; 3.2.7.2–8; 3.2.8.1, 7, for Hume's earlier discussions of our tendency to overlook remote motives. These discussions themselves provide no basis for the claim he here makes about women, but at 2.2.7.4 he claims that women and children are 'most guided' by the imagination and nearby objects.

8 **see afterwards**] Courage is again discussed at 3.3.2.13–14 and 3.3.3.3–4.

9 **they bear nearly . . . nature**] See 3.2.11.4–5.

Book 3 Part 3. *Of the other virtues and vices*

Treatise 3.3 is principally concerned with the natural virtues, or those virtues that 'have no dependance on the artifice and contrivance of men' (3.3.1.1). Section 1 opens with a review of some basic features of morality, including remarks on the artificial virtues and the role of sympathy in the development of morality, then addresses possible objections to Hume's theory. Sections 2–5 continue the discussion of the role of sympathy and also explore the alleged distinction between natural virtues and natural abilities. Section 6 provides a brief overview of Book 3 and a few concluding remarks. (For further discussion of *Treatise* 3.3, see Ed. Intro., I91–7.)

Book 3 Part 3 Sect. 1. *Of the origin of the natural virtues and vices*

As a prelude to his discussion of the natural virtues, Hume reviews the fundamentals of his moral theory. He reminds us that (1) the human mind is motivated principally by pleasure and pain, which give rise to the direct, and, in certain circumstances, the indirect, passions; (2) moral distinctions depend on certain unique feelings of pleasure and pain, the moral sentiments; (3) the qualities of persons that evoke the moral sentiments also evoke the indirect passions (love and pride, hatred and humility); (4) actions are virtuous or vicious only in so far as they are the consequences of durable features of the mind; (5) sympathy has a central part to play in the origin and operation of morality: it enables us to communicate our sentiments to one another. As a consequence, the artificial virtues, because they serve the public interest, become *moral* virtues—their observance or non-observance arouses, by means of sympathy, the distinctive moral sentiments. Sympathy plays the same role in our response to the observance or non-observance of the natural virtues, but some natural virtues contribute only to the well-being of those who possess them and yet meet with approbation. This fact shows that morality goes beyond self-interested approval. The natural and artificial virtues differ in an additional, important respect: every naturally virtuous act produces good, while some artificially virtuous acts may be, in themselves, contrary to the public good. It is only the systematic and universal observance of the artificial virtues that is certain to produce public good.

Near the middle of the section Hume responds to possible objections to his theory: (1) it may be said that, because the strength of our moral sentiments varies according to the proximity of the persons assessed, our moral assessments must also vary in this way; (2) we in fact count as virtuous those who, though disposed to act for the public good, are prevented from doing so; (3) there may seem to be an insurmountable conflict between the effects of sympathy, on which moral sentiments depend, and the natural selfishness that gives rise to the artificial virtues. Hume's reply to this third concern confirms that our moral sentiments enable us to give moral approval to those qualities of others that contribute only to their private good, and also explains why qualities that produce pride and love or humility and hatred are *morally* assessed. Near the end of the section we are reminded that it is obvious that moral distinctions depend on moral sentiments, and that these sentiments may arise in response to certain durable qualities of mind or to reflections on the likely effects of these same qualities. Thus assessments of virtue derive ultimately from mental qualities of four kinds: (1) those useful to others; (2) those useful to the person who possesses them; (3) those agreeable to others; (4) those agreeable to the person who possesses them.

2 The chief spring . . . pain] Hume first endorses this widely held view at 1.3.10.2.
  The most immediate . . . moment] The effects mentioned are the principal topics of
  Hume's discussion of the direct passions; see esp. 2.3.9.
  But when . . . pleasure] The distinction between direct and indirect passions is first
  noted at 2.1.1.4; the four indirect passions mentioned are the principal topic of *Treatise*
  2.1–2. The theory regarding the double relation of impressions and ideas is developed
  in 2.1.2–6 (see esp. 2.1.5.5, 8) and 2.2.1–3 (see esp. 2.2.2.9).
3 already observ'd] See 3.1.2.1–4.
  Now since . . . humility] Much the same point is made at 3.1.2.5
4 If any *action* . . . morality] For earlier discussions of these points, see 2.2.3.4–5;
  3.2.1.2–8.
7 *sympathy*] On sympathy, see esp. 2.1.11.2–8; 2.2.5.14–21; and Ed. Intro., 155–7.
  irons] metal instruments used for cauterizing or searing tissue to stop haemorrhag-
  ing or to destroy gangrenous cells.
8 Our sense . . . beautiful] On beauty and pleasure, see esp. 2.1.8.
  n. 83 Decentior . . . judicii est] A horse whose flanks are compact are not only better
  to look upon, but swifter in speed. The athlete whose muscles have been formed by
  exercise is a joy to the eye, but he is also better fitted for the contests in which he must
  engage. In fact true beauty and usefulness always go hand in hand. It does not,
  however, require any special ability to discern the truth of this (Quintilian, *Institutes*
  8.3.10–11).
9 allegiance . . . good-manners] Allegiance, the laws of nations, and modesty are the
  subjects of, respectively, 3.2.8–10, 3.2.11, and 3.2.12. There is a further passing reference to good manners at 3.3.6.1; at 3.3.2.10 the rules of good breeding are said to have
  an origin like that of the rules of justice.
  It follows . . . virtues] The role of sympathy in the development of justice is first
  noted at 3.2.2.24.
10 it being an inviolable maxim . . . necessity] Hume affirms this rule at 1.3.15.6 and
  again at 2.1.3.6–7.
  attained experiments] gained experience of, observed; each of the five artificial
  virtues discussed in *Treatise* 3.2 appears to fit the description that follows.
11 some philosophers] Mandeville best fits Hume's description; see *Fable* [1:41–9].
  already observ'd] See 3.2.2.25.
12 After it . . . society] This position is first set out at 3.2.2.23–4.
13 'Tis certain . . . general] On why this is so, see 1.1.5.3; 2.3.6.2.
  In any number . . . by it] See the first annotation to ¶10 of this section.
15 Now 'tis evident . . . objects] The effect on the passions of distance and contiguity is
  explained at 2.3.7–8.
16 Our servant . . . *Marcus Brutus* . . . admiration] Hume judged Brutus to be a moral
  hero because he tried to preserve the liberty of the Roman republic from the dictatorial ambitions of his friend Julius Caesar. In Hume's view, the fact that Brutus failed in
  this effort did not diminish his virtue. See Hume's letter of 17 Sept. 1739, to Hutcheson
  (*Letters*, 1:35).
17 By this reflection . . . opposition] See 3.1.2.4 for a similar claim.
18 Here we are . . . judgment] At 2.2.8.2–6 Hume offers an explanation of why we
  respond as we do.
  formerly said] See 2.3.3.8.
  Being thus loosen'd . . . position] Hume begins by noting that, once we cease assess-
  ing others merely with regard to their tendency to benefit ourselves, we can best assess

them by relying on sympathy. He then argues that, although sympathy produces relatively weak sentiments, we find that these are at least of sufficient force to influence our calm passions. When that happens we see that, were the actions or characters to which we are responding in close proximity to us, they would provoke much livelier sentiments than they actually do. In short, because even a remote Brutus produces weak but still noticeable moral sentiments, we can see that a proximate Brutus would produce extremely lively ones. Much the same point is made in ¶21 of this section.

19 **Virtue in rags . . . virtue**] Hume alludes to Dryden's translation of Horace:

> Content with poverty, my soul I arm;
> And virtue, though in rags, will keep me warm.
>
> (*Odes* 3.29.53–6)

20 **To this we . . . effectual**] Hume's reply is, in effect, that we respond principally to the tendencies of those qualities that arouse the moral sentiments, not to actual effects, and it is for this reason that a person physically constrained may still be virtuous. He makes this point clearly in his correspondence with Hutcheson, where, having noted that the only qualities that are taken to be virtuous are those that have 'a Tendency either to the public Good or to the Good of the Person, who possesses' them, he went on to say: 'I desire you wou'd only consider the Tendencys of Qualitys, not their actual Operation, which depends on Chance' (letter of 17 Sept. 1739; *Letters*, 1:34–5).

General rules . . . imagination] Hume's fullest explanation of the influence of general rules on the imagination is found at 1.3.13.7–14; see also 2.2.5.12–13; 2.2.7.5; and Ed. Intro., 162–3.

22 **'Tis observ'd by critics . . . ear**] 'Nothing can penetrate to the emotions that stumbles at the portals of the ear' (Quintilian, *Institutes* 9.4.10). 'Indeed, let a thought be ever so beautiful in itself, if the words which express it are ill placed, the delicacy of the ear is shocked . . . if there is any thing heavy and superfluous, [the ear] cannot bear it. In a word, nothing can give it pleasure but a copious and harmonious turn of words' (Charles Rollin, *Method of Teaching and Studying* [2:149]).

23 **when oblig'd . . . insecure**] Architecture and the apprehension of danger are discussed more fully at 2.1.8.2.

The *seeming tendencies . . . different*] This issue is discussed more fully at 2.2.9.11–14; see also 1.3.13.10.

26 **This theory . . . himself**] See also 3.1.2.5.

27 **Moral good . . . reason**] That this is the case is the subject of *Treatise* 3.1; see esp. 3.1.2.

There have . . . persons] Hume argues that the only moral theories to be taken seriously are those that trace moral distinctions to moral sentiments (as do his own and that of Hutcheson, for example), then goes on to suggest that his theory differs from Hutcheson's in important ways. See also 3.3.6.3.

29 **foregoing principles**] The several principles or features of human nature discussed in this section, beginning with ¶2.

31 **As to the good . . . occasion**] Hume means to explain why it is that we reward virtue and punish vice. To do so he refers us to his explanation, found in 2.2.6, of what he calls benevolence and anger.

Book 3 Part 3 Sect. 2. *Of greatness of mind*

To illustrate his theory that moral distinctions arise in response to those qualities of mind that are useful or agreeable to their possessors or to others, Hume considers the virtue or vice derived from either an appropriate level, or an excess, of pride and humility. Centring his discussion on greatness of mind or 'a steady and well-establish'd pride and self-esteem' (¶13), he argues that excessive pride is disagreeable to others and thus regarded as vicious, while modesty is agreeable to others, and thus regarded as virtuous. The principles of sympathy and comparison account for these differing responses. Excessive pride is found to be vicious because it causes, by comparison, uneasiness in those who observe it. In contrast, a modest or appropriate valuation of ourselves, when we have genuinely valuable qualities, is taken to be virtuous because sympathy enables observers to feel the pleasure of our well-founded pride. A genuine but discreet pride is a necessary component of a virtuous individual, and thus can also please others because of its usefulness to its possessor.

1 **four sources here explain'd**] See 3.3.1.30. The four sources are mental qualities either useful to their possessors or to others, or mental qualities pleasing to their possessors or to others.

2 *sympathy . . . above-mention'd*] See in the previous section ¶¶7–12 and also 2.1.11.2–8; 2.2.5.14–21.

4 **n. 84 Book 2. Part 2. Sect. 8**] Hume quotes from 2.2.8.9, an earlier discussion of comparison. In doing so, he omits four sentences following the words 'immediate survey', and the words 'to us' (here restored) from the last sentence quoted.

5 **n. 85** *Suave . . . suav' est*] What joy it is, when out at sea the storm winds are lashing the waters, to gaze from the shore at the heavy stress some other man is enduring! Not that anyone's afflictions are in themselves a source of delight; but to realize from what troubles you yourself are free is joy indeed (Lucretius, *Nature of Things* 2.1–4).
'Tis evident . . . comparison] Any idea (or experience) that influences us by comparison must be of middle strength. If an idea is too weak it will not reveal to us our position in relation to others, and hence we will not take note of that position. If an idea is too strong, comparison has no role at all because sympathy accounts for the entire effect on us.

7 **'Tis a trite observation . . . are vain**] La Rochefoucauld had said that 'If we were not Proud our selves, we shou'd not complain of the Pride of others' (*Maxims* 34), while Mandeville suggested that the fact that pride is 'odious to all the World' is a good sign that all the world is proud (*Fable* [1:124]).

9 **been observ'd**] See 3.1.2.1–4; 3.3.1.3.

12 **This passage . . . subjects**] Hume paraphrases a passage from Saint-Evremond, *Works* [1:67–8].

13 **Accordingly we find . . . ambition**] See e.g. Nicole, 'De la faiblesse de l'homme'; Law, *Serious Call to a Devout and Holy Life* 16–17; cf. Prov. 8: 3: 'Pride, and arrogancy . . . do I [the Lord] hate'; Matt. 5: 5: 'Blessed are the meek, for they shall inherit the earth.'
Whether . . . determine] See 2.1.7.8 for an earlier comment on this issue.

17 **n. 87 Book 2. Part 2. Sect. 5**] See 2.2.5.21.

Book 3 Part 3 Sect. 3. *Of goodness and benevolence*

Hume explains how certain qualities of mind come to be regarded as morally good. The generosity of individuals is normally confined to a narrow circle of family and friends. If an agent is generous to those beyond that circle, sympathy enables us to feel approbation in response to her actions even if we ourselves obtain no benefit from the generosity we observe, nor is our *moral* assessment affected by her proximity or the relative strength of our response. A disposition to be generous, because it makes a person both agreeable and useful to others, gives rise to approbation. Sympathy also enables us to experience the *'immediately agreeable'* feeling that love or benevolence produces in those agents who manifest it (¶4). In short, we warmly approve of generosity, and take it to be a sign of virtue. It does not follow, however, that, because hatred and anger are disagreeable, they are always vicious. A hatred that produces cruelty is a detestable vice, but in some circumstances a lack of hatred may be seen as a moral weakness. In general, Hume concludes, we blame those whose dispositions cause them to disturb or injure others, and praise those whose agreeable qualities contribute to the good of those around them.

2 **The case . . . bodies**] On the distance of bodies and judgements of size, see esp. 2.2.8.3–6.
on the theatre] on the stage, that is.

Book 3 Part 3 Sect. 4. *Of natural abilities*

Hume examines the claim that *natural abilities* of the mind are on a par with physical characteristics, and hence are not *moral virtues*. Some have argued that natural abilities are not virtues because they arouse a feeling different from those aroused by the moral virtues, and others, that as the natural abilities are entirely involuntary, no merit can attach to them. Hume grants there may be differences between the kinds of approbation aroused by natural abilities and by natural virtues, but insists that this difference is no greater than that between different kinds of virtue. Moreover, although natural abilities are on the whole unchangeable by 'art or industry' (¶4), while the actions that proceed from moral qualities may be changed by the motives of reward and punishment or praise and blame, ordinary people none the less praise or blame both abilities and virtues according to what pleases them. Thus the usefulness of a distinction between abilities and virtues is of doubtful value: both natural abilities and natural virtues are mental qualities; both are the source of pleasure and esteem in ourselves and others. Thus many natural abilities (perseverance, wisdom, vigilance, temperance, and frugality, for example) arouse approbation because they are *useful* to their possessors; others (wit and eloquence, for example) have this effect because they are agreeable to others; still others (good humour, for example) are agreeable to the person who possesses them. In addition, the natural abilities are a source of approbation because they give individuals an added importance, and thereby bring them to our attention.

1 **No distinction . . . them**] Aristotle distinguishes moral from intellectual virtues; see *Nicomachean Ethics* 1138^{b}18–1139^{b}13; 1143^{b}17–1145^{a}12. Eighteenth-c. writers who explicitly distinguish between virtues and abilities include Wollaston, *Religion of Nature Delineated* 10.4, and Hutcheson, *Inquiry* 2.3.10.
dispute of words] Hume had earlier written to Hutcheson on this issue, saying, 'Whether natural Abilitys be Virtues is a Dispute of Words. I think I follow the common Use of Language. *Virtus* signify'd chiefly Courage among the *Romans*. . . . Upon the whole, I desire to take my Catalogue of Virtues from *Cicero's Offices* [*De officiis*], not from the *Whole Duty of Man*. I had, indeed, the former Book in my Eye in all my Reasonings' (letter of 17 Sept. 1739; *Letters*, 1:33–4). Hume returns to this subject in App. 4 of *EPM*, and there cites Cicero's *De oratore* 2.84.343–4, as well as such other ancient writers as Aristotle, Epictetus, Solomon, and Plutarch who (he says) blur the distinction between virtues and abilities. *The Whole Duty of Man*, an anonymous work first published in 1658, presents the virtues in a stern, puritanical light. Hume read this work as a boy.

2 *Cæsar*] On Julius Caesar, see 3.2.10.19.
Cato] Cato of Utica (95–46 BC), Stoic and rigid moralist, supporter of the Roman republic against the triumvirate of Caesar, Pompey, and Crassus.
Sallust] Gaius Sallustius Crispus (86–35 BC), Roman historian and politician. According to Sallust, Caesar was compassionate and good-natured, while Cato was austere and even forbidding (*War with Catiline* 53–4).
amiable . . . awful] Addison had said 'Cato's character . . . is rather awful than amiable' (*Spectator* 169).
n. 88 Love . . . causes] On the causes and nature of love or esteem, see 2.2.1–3, esp. 2.2.1.3–8.

3 Those, who . . . free-will] Clarke argues that it is not in our power to withhold assent to a 'plain, speculative truth', but that we do have a 'natural liberty' to act contrary to our perceived duty (*Discourse* 1.1). Balguy objected that instinctive or involuntary faculties are 'utterly inconsistent with our Ideas of Goodness' (*Foundation* 1 [10; see also 12–20]).
first . . . *imagination*] Ten years later Hume said that the ancients, when discussing whether virtue can or can not be taught, 'little regarded' the distinction between voluntary and involuntary. He then cites, among others, Plato (*Meno* 70a ff.), Seneca (*Moral Essays* 8.4), and Horace (*Epistles* 1.18.100); see *EPM*, App. 4.20.
Thirdly . . . of men] See 2.3.1–2 and Ed. Intro., 165–9.

4 Men have observ'd . . . blame] See e.g. Balguy, *Foundation* 1 [60]. In contrast, Butler argued that we can 'adjust, manage, and preside over' our instincts or natural abilities; see *Sermons* 3.
Nay . . . cardinal virtues] This view is found in Cicero; see e.g. *De officiis* 1.5.15; 1.43.152. Among Hume's contemporaries, Butler argues that 'prudence is a species of virtue', but grants that the matter is controversial ('On the Nature of Virtue', in *Works*).
philosophers . . . *grammarians*] Hume suggests that philosophers are to explain the causes and conditions associated with the development or recognition of virtue and vice. In contrast, grammarians are assigned the merely linguistic or semantic task of determining consistent and proper ways of speaking about the virtues and the natural abilities. See also 1.4.6.21.

5 Men are superior . . . reason] Cicero had suggested that humans are superior to the animals largely because animals have little perception of the past or future, while humans are able to relate past, present, and future, and thus to plan their conduct (see *De officiis* 1.3.11). Hume discusses the reason of animals at *Treatise* 1.3.16.

9 consider afterwards] The *Treatise* includes no further discussion of this point; see the final annotation to 3.2.3.4 Note 71.2.

11 a certain sense] the moral sense, that is.
Some moralists . . . sense] Shaftesbury, Hutcheson, and Hume are the principal moral sense philosophers.
particular tendencies . . . approbation] The argument here is at least superficially puzzling. Three sentences earlier Hume says that the moral sense responds without needing to reflect on the tendencies of the qualities of which it approves. He now emphasizes that the virtues do have tendencies and that these alone can arouse the moral sentiments. His point appears to be that, although the moral sense does not depend on reason or reflection (it responds immediately), when we do reflect we find that a person's qualities are approved in proportion to their tendency to be useful or agreeable to their possessor or others.

12 *decorum* or *indecorum*] suitability or unsuitability.
　　praise or blame] Cicero had suggested that our duties vary with 'character, circumstance, and age' (*De officiis* 1.34.125).
13 **that men . . . bad one**] This tendency is noted by Steele; see *Spectator* 284. La Rochefoucauld had earlier said 'Every Body complains of his Memory, but not of his Judgment' (*Maxims* 89).

Book 3 Part 3 Sect. 5. *Some farther reflections concerning the natural abilities*

Hume recalls his conclusions regarding the four sources of approbation, namely, those *qualities of mind* that are *useful* or *pleasing* to their possessor or *useful* or *pleasing* to others. He notes that physical assets (strength, beauty of form, for example) and 'advantages of *fortune*' (wealth, power, for example) have much the same effect: they arouse the esteem and approbation of those who observe them. These assets or advantages are agreeable or useful to those who observe them, or to their possessors. In so far as they are, they are pleasing and approved by those who observe them. This fact, Hume argues, serves to confirm his hypothesis about the four sources of approbation. This same fact is also seen to confirm that sympathy has a central role to play in our approvals and disapprovals. In conclusion, Hume notes that the sentiments of approval produced by any one kind of cause are much alike even though these causes may be found among distinctly different sources. On the other hand, the sentiments of approval produced by different kinds of cause (by beautiful objects rather than by virtuous characters, for example) are distinctly different even when the causes are associated with the same individual, and even though all these approvals are the effect of agreeable or useful qualities and the operation of sympathy. This difference cannot be fully explained, but we have ample experience of it.

1 **been observ'd**] See 2.1.7–11; 2.2.4–5.
　　constitutes] here, contributes to the making of. See the discussion of 'very essence' in Ed. Intro., I52–3.
　　We have assign'd] See e.g. 3.3.1.30; 3.3.2.16.
2 *women's men*] Steele devoted *Spectator* 156 to women's men, whom he described as persons whose 'Air and Behaviour [are] quite different from the rest of our Species'. Steele does not, however, claim that these men are well received even by those women whose virtue is proof against their designs.
3 **'Tis certain . . . exercise**] On beauty and utility, see also 2.1.8.2; 3.3.1.8–10.
5 **have observ'd**] See 2.2.5.2.
　　my hypothesis . . . possessions] For Hume's hypothesis, see 2.2.5.5–6, 14–16, 21.
6 **All the sentiments . . . same source**] Hume here argues that the sentiments produced by a single *kind* of object (by beautiful objects, for example) are resembling even though the processes involved may differ. In contrast, the sentiments produced by different kinds of object (by beautiful objects, in contrast to virtuous characters, for example) are distinctly different even though our approbation of them may be the result of the operation of a single principle such as sympathy. See 3.1.2.4 for an earlier discussion of this point.

Book 3 Part 3 Sect. 6. *Conclusion of this book*

Looking back at his theory of morality, Hume concludes that sympathy is 'the chief source of moral distinctions' (¶1). Sympathy fills this important role because it enables us to be concerned with the public good, or the object of the artificial virtues, as well as with the good of individuals. It is generally agreed, for example, that the useful qualities of mind are virtuous because they contribute to the good of others. It is sympathy that brings about the moral approval of those qualities that have this beneficial effect. Hume goes on to suggest that his moral theory, relying as it does on sympathy, provides a further defence of the cause of virtue. His theory agrees with those others who find that our ability to make moral distinctions derives from original features of the human mind; it goes beyond such theories in so far as it shows that the most important of these features, sympathy, is itself morally praiseworthy. Justice, too, Hume notes, although an artificial virtue, is founded on inherent features of human nature: on, first, our deeply rooted self-interest, and then on our tendency to approve actions that contribute to the common good. These same considerations would, if pressed, show that human happiness is dependent upon the practice of virtue, but further remarks of that sort would be out of place in the kind of anatomy of human nature the *Treatise* represents. None the less, such an anatomy may be of great help to the practical moralist.

1 **We are certain . . . good-manners]** Hume here paraphrases the first sentence of 3.3.1.10, a paragraph that itself summarizes much of 3.3.1; see esp. 3.3.1.7–13.

  They must derive . . . with him] Hume discussed with Hutcheson the sense in which sympathy is the chief source of moral distinctions: 'Now I desire you to consider, if there be any Quality, that is virtuous, without having a Tendency either to the public Good or to the Good of the Person, who possesses it. If there be none without these Tendencys, we may conclude, that their Merit is derivd from Sympathy' (letter of 17 Sept. 1739; *Letters*, 1:34).

3 **Those who . . . authority]** Shaftesbury and Hutcheson, for example. Hume himself accepts this view, as far as it goes, as correct.

  who account . . . mankind] Hume is now describing the important addition made by his theory.

4 **Tho' justice . . . approve of it]** On this point, see in particular 3.2.2.23–4; 3.2.6.11.

6 **The anatomist ought . . . painter]** Hume first suggests that the *Treatise* is an anatomy of human nature at 1.4.6.23. He also draws the contrast between the moral anatomist and the moral painter in a letter to Hutcheson: 'There are different ways of examining the Mind as well as the Body. One may consider it either as an Anatomist or as a Painter; either to discover its most secret Springs & Principles or to describe the Grace & Beauty of its Actions. I imagine it impossible to conjoin these two Views. Where you pull off the Skin, & display all the minute Parts, there appears something trivial, even in the noblest Attitudes & most vigorous Actions: Nor can you ever render the object graceful or engaging but by cloathing the Parts again with Skin & Flesh, & presenting only their bare Outside. An Anatomist, however, can give very good Advice to a Painter or Statuary: And in like manner, I am perswaded, that a Metaphysician [a moral anatomist] may be very helpful to a Moralist; tho' I cannot easily conceive these two Characters united in the same Work. Any warm Sentiment of Morals, I am afraid, wou'd have the Air of Declamation amidst abstract Reasonings, & wou'd be esteem'd contrary to good Taste. And tho' I am much more ambitious of being esteem'd a Friend to Virtue, than a Writer of Taste; yet I must always carry the latter in my Eye, otherwise I must despair of ever being servic[e]able to Virtue. I hope these reasons will satisfy you; tho at the same time, I intend to make a new Tryal, if it be possible to make the Moralist & Metaphysician agree a little better' (letter of 17 Sept. 1739; *Letters*, 1:32–3). Hume's two *Enquiries* (*EHU*, *EPM*) may represent his attempt to combine the work of the moral anatomist and the moralist; see esp. *EHU* 1.

Appendix

The Appendix as originally published included nine relatively brief passages, with directions for inserting these into the text of Book 1. In this edition, these passages have been inserted, as directed, at Note 5; 1.2.4.22; 1.2.4.31; Note 12; 1.3.5.4; 1.3.7.7; Note 21; 1.3.10.10–12; 1.3.14.12, with Note 30. Each such insertion is marked by a superscript ^App. at its beginning and end.

In addition, the Appendix contained the remarks on belief and personal identity which are found at pp. 396–401. For further discussion of Hume's views on these topics, see Ed. Intro., I31–3, I43–5.)

1 preceding volumes] On the title-page of *Treatise* 3 Hume describes the Appendix as illustrating and explaining passages in the two volumes of the *Treatise* published in 1739. These volumes contained the Introduction and Books 1 and 2.
except on one article] The one important issue about which Hume admits to making a mistake is that of personal identity: see ¶¶10, 20–1 of this Appendix.

2 *First . . . objects*] See 1.2.6.2–7.
Secondly . . . pleases] See 1.1.3.2, 4; 1.1.4.1.

4 In this case . . . conception] Hume grants that in unusual circumstances a belief may arise in a manner different from that he has described. In those circumstances, there may be an additional feeling of satisfaction distinct from the idea or conception believed.

5 Why . . . necessity] There is no point in positing a further, distinct impression in order to explain belief. The simpler account, in which belief is said to be merely a manner of conceiving, is satisfactory.

9 at large] See 1.3.4–8, 10, 14.
I have added . . . necessary] In accordance with Hume's instructions, the illustrations mentioned have been added to the text of Book 1. For the location of these additions to the text, see the remarks on the Appendix above.

10 I had entertain'd . . . world] See 1.4.5.1.
personal identity] See 1.4.6.
thinking being] See 1.4.6.2–4.

16 Suppose it . . . hunger] A mind that had the simplest sort of perceptual experience (a mind that is not a bundle of varied perceptions because it experiences only one unchanging perception) would still have no impression of the self or substance underlying this perception.

18 If it be . . . substance] Hume suggests that, if the self is identical with an immaterial substance in which perceptions inhere, then it would make no sense to ask whether or not the self always remains the same. Why? Because, according to that hypothesis, the substance-self is unchanging. But, as it does make sense to ask this question, we can conclude that the self is not in fact identical with an unchanging substance.

20 But having . . . perceptions] Hume has argued that our perceptions are distinguishable and separable from one another, and not found to be related to any underlying substance of which we have experience.
n. 89 Book 1 p. 170] 1.4.6.16ff.
precedent reasonings] The arguments summarized in ¶11–19 of this section, and first set out in *Treatise* 1.
It follows . . . other] We only conclude there is personal identity when we feel that the past perceptions of a mind have been associated together in such a way that the thought of one leads naturally to a second, the second to a third, and so on.

21 Most philosophers . . . perception] For philosophers who held this view, see the annotation to 1.4.6.1.
22 two other errors] The errors mentioned are to be found at 1.2.5.12 and 1.3.7.5.

Annotations to the *Abstract*

When readers complained that the first two volumes of the *Treatise* were difficult to understand, Hume wrote and arranged for the publication of the *Abstract*, a work written in the third person and published anonymously in the spring of 1740, several months before Book 3 of the *Treatise*. Not intended to be an abridgement of the *Treatise*, the *Abstract* undertakes to illustrate and explain the 'CHIEF ARGUMENT' of that much longer work. This turns out to be the argument about belief and the idea of necessary connection (see Ed. Intro., I29–33) to which all but a few paragraphs of the *Abstract* are devoted. Hume also mentions his views on personal identity (¶28), geometry (¶29), the passions (¶30), and freedom of the will (¶¶31–4). In the concluding paragraph he notes that the *Treatise* makes 'great pretensions to new discoveries in philosophy', but then adds that if any one thing entitles its author to be thought 'an *inventor*, 'tis the use he makes of the principle of the association of ideas, which enters into most of his philosophy' (¶35).

Preface

1 *My expectations . . . abridging it*] Two years before publishing the *Abstract* Hume had said that he was unable to abridge the *Treatise*: 'I am very sorry I am not able to satisfy your Curiosity by giving you some general Notion of the Plan upon which I proceed. But my Opinions are so new, & even some Terms I am oblig'd to make Use of, that I cou'd not propose by any Abridgement to give my System an Air of Likelyhood, or so much as make it intelligible. Tis a thing I have in vain attempted already' (letter of 2 Dec. 1737, to Henry Home (later Lord Kames); *New Letters of David Hume*, 1).
2 *obscure . . . comprehended*] Hume explained to Hutcheson that he had not sent the *Abstract* for publication in *The History of the Works of the Learned* because there had already 'been an Article with regard to my Book, somewhat abusive, printed in that Work' (letter of 4 Mar. 1740; *Letters*, 1:37–8). For further information about the use and publication of the *Abstract*, see Ed. Intro., I97.
   the Author] Hume himself. Because the *Abstract* is a kind of self-advertisement, Hume chose to write in the third person. Although the work was published anonymously, that he was the author of the work was known to at least some of his acquaintances.
3 *The Author . . . relinquish*] Hume had made similar remarks in a letter to Henry Home (letter of 13 Feb. 1739; *New Letters of David Hume*, 3–4).

Abstract

1 This book . . . fourscore years] In the Introduction to the *Treatise* Hume associates his method with the new experimental natural philosophy of Boyle, Newton, and other members of the Royal Society (founded 1662), and with the observational moral philosophy of Locke, Shaftesbury, and others. See Intro. 7.

And tho' we . . . ultimate principles] See Intro. 8.

2 anatomize human nature] Hume first uses the phrase 'anatomy of human nature' at 1.4.6.23; see also Intro. 4; 3.3.6.6 and the annotation to it.

He talks . . . experience] See Intro. 7–8.

3 *The sole end . . . other*] Hume quotes from Intro. 5.

The author . . . passions] In the Advertisement to the first volume of the *Treatise* Hume envisages his new science as examining five subjects: the understanding, the passions, morals, politics, and criticism.

4 *Leibnitz* has observed] Leibniz makes this observation in the *Theodicy*; see the 'Preliminary Dissertation on the Conformity of Faith with Reason' 31.

probabilities . . . depend] Butler had said that, for humans, 'probability is the very guide of life' (*Analogy of Religion*, Intro.).

the *Essay . . . Penser*] The *Essay concerning Human Understanding*, by Locke; *Le Recherche de la Verité (The Search after Truth)*, by Malebranche; and *Logique; ou, L'Art de penser (Logic; or, The Art of Thinking)* by Arnauld and Nicole. For further details, see the References.

5 Our author . . . definitions] Hume goes on to paraphrase 1.1.1.1.

6 The first proposition . . . minds] See 1.1.1.7–9, 11.

This proposition . . . *innate*] See 1.1.1.1 Note 2, and 1.1.1.12.

Father Malebranche . . . sources] Malebranche is apparently mentioned as a representative of those who maintain that there are innate ideas. Hume argues that even Malebranche would be forced to grant that there is no thought (no *idea* in the sense that Hume uses this term) that does not derive from some prior perception, and hence that there are no innate ideas.

7 Our author thinks . . . composition] Hume quotes, with minor alterations, 1.2.3.1, which itself refers to 1.1.1.7, 11.

Accordingly . . . debates] This approach to philosophical issues is implicit in 1.1.6, Hume's initial discussion of substance. It may also be seen in operation at 1.3.2.4; 1.3.14.4, 27; 1.4.3.10; App. 11. An explicit form of the question '*From what impression that pretended idea is derived?*' is found at 1.4.6.2.

8 matter of fact] On this phrase, see Ed. Intro., I33, Note 38.

In order . . . another] Hume goes on to summarize material found at 1.3.2.4–12 and 1.3.6.

9 billiard-ball] Billiard balls are mentioned, but to illustrate a different point, at 1.3.14.18.

Contiguity . . . cause] See 1.3.2.6–7.

constant conjunction . . . effect] See 1.3.6, esp. 2–4; 1.3.14.12.

10 Let us now . . . exist] For discussions of this inference, see 1.3.2.15 and 1.3.6.

geometry and arithmetic] These subjects are discussed at 1.2.4.10, 17, 29–32; 1.3.1.4–7; see also ¶29 below.

11 demonstration . . . ideas] For Hume's views on demonstration, and how it differs from probable reasoning, see 1.3.1.2, 7; 1.3.4.3; and ¶18 of this work.

whatever we *conceive* is possible] On conceiving and how it differs from belief, see 1.3.7.

12 if . . . not inspired] if not prompted by divine or supernatural powers.

13 It follows . . . consequence] This one paragraph summarizes much of 1.3.6. That all reasonings concerning cause and effect depend on experience is also noted at 1.3.4.3; 1.3.14.36; 1.4.1.8. On the conclusion that like causes produce like effects, see also 1.3.8.14; 1.3.15.7–8, 10.

14 All probable . . . prove it] On 'probable reasonings' and the supposition that the future must resemble the past, see 1.3.12, esp. 7 ff.

15 We are determined . . . past] Hume explains what he means by *custom* at 1.3.8.10, and then goes on to explain how custom influences belief; see also 1.3.13.9–11.

16 'Tis not . . . custom] Cf. ¶4 of this work.

17 What then . . . philosophers] Belief is defined at 1.3.7.5. Hume points out the originality of his effort to understand belief in 1.3.7.5 Note 20.

18 When a demonstration . . . conceived] See 1.2.4.11 and 1.3.6.1.
I can . . . contrary] See 1.3.7.3.

19 To account . . . hypotheses] Although consistent with the account of belief found in Book 1, the argument that follows is not found there. A variant of it is found in the Appendix (¶2) published along with Book 3.

21 MANNER of conceiving] This phrase is first used at 1.3.7.4; see also 1.3.8.7.

22 He seems sensible . . . conception] See 1.3.7.5–8 and 1.3.8.7, 11, 15.
And indeed . . . for such] See 1.3.10.3–5; 1.4.1.11; 2.3.6.10.
Poetry . . . opinion] See 1.3.10.10–11 (a passage first published in the Appendix to Book 3) and 2.1.1.3.

23 Our author . . . mind] Perhaps an allusion to 1.3.8, 'Of the causes of belief'.

24 Our past . . . common] 1.3.12, 'Of the probability of causes', discusses irregularities of experience and, building on an analysis offered in 1.3.11, explains why we put greater faith in that outcome which occurred most often in the past. The example that follows is not found in the *Treatise*.
I lay my account] I put my money on.

25 But the same . . . mind] See 1.3.14.12; 2.3.1.3–4, 14; and ¶33 below.

26 Having dispatched . . . relation] Hume puts aside questions about the relation of cause and effect at 1.3.2.13, and returns to them at 1.3.14.
'tis commonly . . . *energy*] See 1.3.2.11; 1.3.14.5,11.
But so little . . . minds] See 1.3.14.8–10.
Now our own . . . conjoined] See 1.3.14.12.
Upon the whole . . . effect] See 1.3.14.14, 27.

27 Almost all . . . experience] See e.g. 1.3.14.36; 1.3.15.6. At 1.4.1.1–5 Hume argues that all demonstrative reasoning 'resolves itself' into probable reasoning—into reasoning based on experience.
When we . . . kind] See 1.4.2.14, 24, 41–3.
Our author . . . topics] See 1.4.3–6, where doubts are raised about material and immaterial substance, the primary–secondary quality distinction, and personal identity.
Philosophy . . . for it] Cf. 1.4.1.7–8.

28 He asserts . . . identity] See 1.4.6.4.
Des Cartes . . . mind] Cf. 1.4.6.1.
That notion . . . spiritual] Cf. 1.1.6.1–2; 1.4.3; 1.4.5.3–6, 24; 1.4.6.3; App. 19.
We know . . . perceptions] Cf. 1.1.7.4.

29 Having denied . . . for it] See 1.2.1.2; 1.2.2.2–10; 1.2.4–5.
This he does . . . divisibility] See 1.2.4.17–33.
All geometry . . . exactness] Hume makes explicit the point of the discussion of equality found in 1.2.4.18–24.
Now there . . . against it] Hume paraphrases a part of 1.2.4.19.
Two lines . . . equality] Cf. 1.2.4.20.

The greatest . . . term] A similar claim was made in the Appendix to Book 3, and, following Hume's instructions, now forms the first half of 1.2.4.22.

Now this . . . judges of it] Cf. 1.2.4.23, 29.

30 Pride . . . cloaths] Cf. 2.1.2.5.

He afterwards . . . passions] These objects or qualities are alike in causing pleasure in those who possess them; see, for a start, 2.1.3–5.

His theory . . . affections] Love, hatred, and a set of related passions are the subject of *Treatise* 2.2.

31 above-explained] See ¶25 of this work.

31–2 'Tis universally . . . necessity] Hume quotes, with some omissions and relatively insignificant changes, parts of 2.3.1.3–4.

32 Thirty grains . . . purge him] Chambers reports that opium was prescribed to stop vomiting and diarrhoea and that the usual dose was $^1/_2$ to 2 grains, although those habituated to it could take 50 to 60 grains. A form of rhubarb was used as a laxative ('purge').

34 Our author . . . necessity] Cf. 2.3.1.18; 2.3.2.4.

35 imagination . . . fiction] Although the relative freedom of the imagination is noted at 1.1.3.2, 4, it was only in the Appendix to the *Treatise* that Hume spoke as he does here. See App. 2 and 1.3.7.7, a paragraph first published in the Appendix.

apropos of discourse] having each part of the treatment of a subject lead pertinently to the following part.

St. Denis . . . occurs] St Denis is a district adjacent to Paris.

These principles . . . father] The principles of association are introduced at 1.1.4. Resemblance is illustrated by the example of a portrait and the person portrayed at 1.3.8.3. The example of St Denis and Paris, used here to illustrate the relation of contiguity, is not found in the *Treatise*. The causal relation between child and parent is noted at 1.1.4.3.

Glossary

This Glossary explains potentially puzzling words and phrases found in the *Treatise* and *Abstract*. These include archaic expressions, familiar words used or spelled in unfamiliar ways, unusual or obsolete metaphors and idioms, as well as specialized terminology. Our explanations may incorporate meanings Hume provided in the *Treatise* and *Abstract*, or elsewhere in his writings. We have also cited definitions that appear in other early modern sources.

Our explanations often include synonyms as well as definitions. Many of these synonyms are borrowed from the *Treatise*, where they play an important stylistic and rhetorical role. Hume used a commonplace rhetorical device called 'synonymy'. By means of this device, in which synonyms or synonymous phrases were conjoined, an author undertook to amplify meaning (see force for examples). Hume also, in common with other writers of his time, and more often than twentieth-century philosophers, used synonyms to avoid repetition when a particular word or idea was under discussion (see **fancy**, for example). In the matter of synonyms, the comment of Hugh Blair, one of Hume's friends is apropos: synonyms 'are like different shades of the same colour, an accurate writer can employ them to great advantage, by using them so as to heighten and to finish the picture which he gives us. He supplies by one, what was wanting in the other, to the force, or to the lustre of the image which he means to exhibit' (*Rhetoric*, Lecture 10).

For a formal record of historical meanings, we have consulted the *Oxford English Dictionary* (*OED*), both the electronic version (Oxford University Press, 1993) and the compact edition (Oxford University Press, 1971; 2nd edn. 1992). We have also used four reference works published earlier than the *Treatise*, and a fifth, Johnson's *Dictionary*, published in 1755.

BAILEY, NATHAN, *Dictionarium Britannicum*, 2nd edn. (London, 1730; fac. Hildesheim: Georg Olms, 1969).

BAYLE, PIERRE, *Historical and Critical Dictionary*, ed. Pierre Desmaizeaux, 2nd edn. 5 vols. (London, 1734–8; facs. New York: Garland Press, 1984).

CHAMBERS, EPHRAIM, *Cyclopædia* (London, 1728; 2nd edn. 1742).

HARRIS, JOHN, *Lexicon Technicum* (London, 1704–10; fac. New York: Johnson Reprint, 1966).

JOHNSON, SAMUEL, *A Dictionary of the English Language*, 1755 (London, 1832).

To compare Hume's usage with our own, we have relied on, in addition to the *OED*, two recent dictionaries. These are:

The Concise Oxford Dictionary of Current English, 7th edn. (Oxford: Oxford University Press, 1973; repr. 1987).

Merriam Webster's Collegiate Dictionary, 10th edn. (Springfield, Mass., 1993).

When Hume uses a word to mean several different things, we explain *only those uses that might be perplexing*. For example, the entry for *accident* indicates that Hume sometimes used this term to mean *a property of a thing* (colour, for example), but it does not say that he also used *accident* to mean, as we often do, *mishap*.

The textual locations listed in glossary entries were chosen to illustrate Hume's usage. Although in those instances in which a word is used only a few times we may have provided the location of every use, the Glossary is not intended to be an index of uses. On the other hand, the Index to this volume does serve as a supplement to the Glossary. Index entries report the locations of Hume's explanations of terms and also indicate annotations that include such explanations.

Although a word or phrase may take several forms in Hume's text, it will usually appear in the Glossary in its simplest form. Thus substantives (*sb.*) are given in the singular unless the plural usage is a distinct one; verbs (*vb.*) appear in the singular and in the present tense, adjectives (*adj.*) and adverbs (*adv.*) in their non-comparative forms. From the explanation for the entry word the meaning of variants can be inferred.

Each glossed word or phrase is printed in bold and followed by a colon. If it is relevant to indicate the part of speech, this information is found immediately after the colon. Explanations, definitions, and synonyms follow. If a synonym is another entry in this glossary, it is printed in bold. Quotations from Hume or other writers, when these are included, come next, with sources given in parentheses. References without author are to book, part, section, and paragraph of the *Treatise*, to a paragraph in Hume's Introduction (Intro.) to the *Treatise*, the Appendix (App.) or *Abstract* (*Abs.*) of the *Treatise*, or to the Advertisements (Adv.) in Book 1 and Book 3. There are also references to Hume's letters (*Letters*), to his *Essays* and *History of England* (*History*), and to his 'Memoranda'. (See Supplementary Reading at the end of the Editor's Introduction for information about the last four items.) Writers other than Hume are cited by surname, along with a short-title of the work cited. Consult the References for full names, titles, and dates. If a dictionary is given as a source, the quotation or definition, unless otherwise noted, will have been taken from an entry in that dictionary with the same headword (or variant thereof) as our entry. We have given dictionary sources only for direct quotations or for technical, unusual, or conceivably controversial definitions. When a word has two or more distinct usages, these are distinguished by numbers in parentheses. Words mentioned as words are printed in italic.

REMINDER: *This Glossary does not provide common or unproblematic meanings. It follows that the explanations found here are not relevant to every use of a word by Hume.*

abstract ideas: ideas that have become general in their representation (e.g. triangle, horse), even though the idea itself, the image in the mind, 'is only that of a particular object' (1.1.7.6). We may not be able to think of a triangle or of a horse without thinking of a particular triangle or horse; none the less the abstract ideas (triangle, horse) have a 'more extensive signification' which 'makes them recal upon occasion other individuals, which are similar to them' (1.1.7.1). 1.2.3.6; 1.3.1.7; 1.3.14.13.

absurd: contrary to reason, unintelligible. 1.1.7.6; 1.3.7.3.

abusive way of speaking: a 'perversion of terms from their natural meaning' (*Essays*, 'Of the Standard of Taste' 9). 3.1.1.11.

accident: A quality, feature, or property (colour, taste, form, for example) of a thing, supposed not to be essential to the thing, and unable to exist apart from it (Harris); also called a **mode**. 1.1.6.1–3; 1.3.14.7; 1.4.3.7.

accompt, accomptant: account, accountant. 1.4.1.3.

accurate: careful, meticulous. 1.1.1.5; 1.4.7.3; 3.3.6.6.

address: skill. 2.1.2.5; 2.1.9.9; 3.3.1.24.

adequate: a logical term signifying that some thing fully answers to or represents some other thing: 'Those [Ideas] I call *Adequate*, which perfectly represent those Archetypes, which the Mind supposes them taken from; which it intends them to stand for' (Locke, *Essay*, 2.31.1). 1.1.7.12; 1.2.1.5; 1.2.2.1; 1.4.4.5.

admiration: sense of wonder; reaction to something extraordinary, surprize. 1.3.10.4; 2.1.9.1.

advertisement: an explanatory notice, often printed at the beginning of a book in the early modern period. Adv., Bk. 1, Bk. 3.

affection: (1) a feeling or an emotion. 1.2.3.10; 1.4.2.7; 2.1.4.3; 2.2.2.6. (2) passion. 1.3.12.24; 2.1.2.2; 2.1.3.1; 2.2.6.24.

age: a length of time equivalent to 100 years. 1.3.13.4.

air: manner. 1.3.7.8; 2.1.9.3.

alienation: transfer of property. 3.2.4.1.

all a case: all the same. 3.2.2.13.

and that: may have the sense of *so that*. 1.2.3.10.

animal spirits: presumed to be the fluid matter inside nerve passages, the source of sensation and voluntary movement (may also be referred to by the abbreviated form *spirits*). 'There is reason to believe that nerve filaments are hollow like little canals and are completely filled with animal spirits . . . the spirits contained in them transmit to the brain the vibrations they have received from without' (Malebranche, *Search* 1.10.2). Chambers suggests his contemporaries continued to use the notion of animal spirits because they were at a loss for any better explanation for sensation and motion (*Cyclopædia*, 'Animal spirits'). 1.2.5.20; 1.4.2.45; 1.4.4.13. See also the final annotation to 1.2.5.20.

antipathy: a supposedly natural aversion of one body or object for another, resulting from the occult qualities found in each. 1.4.3.11. See also the annotation to 1.4.3.11.

application: assiduous attention to something, careful study. Hume acknowledges in *My Own Life* that his health was 'a little broken by [his] ardent application'. 1.4.6.15; 2.3.10.6.

aqua regia: A mixture of nitric and hydrochloric acids, so-called because it could dissolve gold, the 'king' of metals. 1.1.6.2.

article: point, part. 3.2.8.8; 3.3.4.3; App. 1.

artificial: something 'purposely contriv'd and directed to a certain end' (3.2.6.6), as opposed to something natural or instinctive. 3.2.1.19.

artizan: a skilled worker, with varying degrees of skill from the least or meanest (see mean), to the most skilful; to be distinguished from an unskilled labourer. Intro. 10; 1.3.12.5.

at first: at once. Intro. 8; 2.3.1.2.

atheism: a term used to refer to the views of those who did not believe, in an approved manner, in God or in providence or an afterlife. In the 'Memoranda', Hume notes that some writers have distinguished three kinds of atheist: those who (1) 'deny the Existence of a God. Such as Diagoras, Theodorus'; (2) 'deny a Providence, Such as the Epicureans & Ionic Sect'; (3) 'deny the Free will of the Deity; Such as Aristotle, the Stoics'. See also the second annotation to 1.4.5.17.

at large: at length or in detail. 1.4.5.30; 3.2.1.11.

atom: 'a Corpuscle, or Part, or Particle of Matter so minute or small as to be indivisible' (Bailey). 1.2.1.5; 1.2.4.4.

at pleasure: at will, when wanted. 1.4.3.10.

attraction: The property or force (magnetism, gravitation, for example). whereby a particle of matter draws towards itself another particle not materially attached to it (*OED*). 'Attraction, according to the true sense of the word, supposes one body to act upon another at a distance, or where it is not' (Wollaston, *Religion of Nature* 5.79). 1.2.5.17; 2.3.1.3. Hume also uses the word metaphorically to characterize the relations of ideas and the association of impressions and ideas. 1.1.4.6; 2.1.4.3; 2.1.5.10.

auditor, auditory: listener(s). 1.4.7.14; *Abs*. Pref. 3.

avocation: distraction, diversion. 1.4.7.9.

birth: rank, station, or position in society. 2.1.11.14, 18.

breast: mind or soul, that part of the body in which thought and emotion are located. 1.4.6.18; 3.1.1.26.

but: After a phrase such as 'it is not impossible' Hume may use *but* where we would use *that* (see *OED* 16b). 1.1.1.1. He also occasionally uses *but* instead of *that* after *deny* and *doubt*; thus 'I doubt but' or 'I doubt not but' should be understood as 'I doubt that' or 'I doubt not that'. 1.2.2.6; 1.2.4.30; 1.3.8.6. On other occasions, *but* has the sense of *but that* (1.3.12.7) or simply of *that*.

career: course or procedure being followed. 1.4.2.51.

careless: dispassionate; detached. 1.4.3.9; 1.4.7.14.

carelessness: inattention, indifference. 1.4.2.57.

cast an eye on, cast a view on: consider. 1.3.2.5; 2.3.3.3.

castle-builder, castle-building: daydreamer, daydreaming. 1.3.7.8; 2.1.11.19; App. 3–4.

cavil: *sb.* frivolous or trivial argument, a sophism. 1.2.4.15; 1.4.1.7; 1.4.5.2.

chace: chase, follow. 1.2.6.8; 1.4.2.57; 1.4.6.19.

change on: change in. 1.2.5.16; 1.3.1.1. See also on.

character: (1) the aggregate of personal attributes, features, or qualities that distinguish a person. 2.3.3.10; 3.3.1.19; 3.3.4.2. (2) a particular attribute or quality. 2.1.11.13; 3.3.3.3. (3) a graphic symbol, a letter used in writing or printing. 1.3.4.2; 2.3.1.15.

chymist: chemist. 1.3.16.5.

cloaths: clothes, wearing apparel. 1.3.8.6; 2.1.10.2.

closet: a private place for study, a place for theorizing rather than acting. Hume tells a correspondent that he had 'frequently, in the course of my life, met with interruptions . . . yet always returned to my closet with pleasure' (*Letters*, 1:451). 1.4.2.53; 3.1.1.1.

commerce: social interchange. 1.4.7.2, 10; 3.3.1.18.

commodious: useful, convenient. 3.1.2.11; 3.2.2.24; 3.3.1.18.

common: *adj.* ordinary, general, vulgar. 1.1.3.3; 1.2.1.5; 2.1.8.2.

compass: *sb.* extent, range. 1.1.7.9–10; 1.4.2.23; *Abs.* 23.

complaisance: readiness to submit to the judgement of another, deference. 1.2.1.1.

complexion: temperament, disposition. 1.4.4.3; 2.1.3.4; 2.3.2.2. See also the second annotation to 1.4.4.3.

composition: a compounded object, made up of parts; a mixture. 1.2.3.5; 2.2.1.1.

comprehend: include. 1.1.1.1; 2.1.1.4; 3.1.1.2.

concur: of lines, to converge. 1.2.4.30, 33; 1.3.1.6.

condition: social standing or position. 2.2.5.10–11; 2.2.8.8.

conformable to: consistent with. 1.2.2.9; 1.2.4.1, 16.

confound: confuse, jumble together. 1.2.5.21; 1.3.14.27; 1.4.2.34.

constitution: human nature. 3.1.2.8; 3.3.1.17. For additional connotations, see also the second annotation to 1.4.4.3.

contemn: treat with disregard, consider inferior. 1.3.13.15; 3.1.2.2.

contrivance: something purposefully produced as the result of thought or design. 2.1.2.6; 2.3.10.5; 3.2.5.15.

convenient: fitting, appropriate. 1.3.3.9; 1.3.11.2.

copist: copyist, one who copied or transcribed manuscripts. 1.3.13.6.

correspondent: corresponding. 1.1.1.5–6; 1.3.6.14; 1.3.12.19.

credit: reputation. 2.1.9.9.

criticism: the art or practice of interpreting and making judgements about literature and the fine arts. Intro. 5; 2.2.8.18.

custom: repetition, repeated experience, and the associations of ideas or habits of mind resulting therefrom. 1.3.8.10; 2.3.5.1; 3.2.2.4; *Abs.* 15–16. By extension, a principle of association. 1.3.7.6.

decorum: what is expected of one, the rules of accepted social practice. 1.3.13.18; 3.3.2.14; 3.3.4.12.

delicate: keen, finely sensitive, subtle. 1.2.4.24; 1.3.13.15; 3.3.1.24.

demonstration: a kind and level of proof, one that provides certainty in contrast to probability; 'When a demonstration convinces me of any proposition, it not only makes me conceive the proposition, but also makes me sensible, that 'tis impossible to conceive any thing contrary' (*Abs.* 18). 1.2.2.6; 1.4.1.1; 3.1.1.19. See also the second annotation to 1.3.1.2.

dervise: dervish, member of a Muslim religious order. 1.4.7.13.

desart: *adj.* deserted. 3.2.3.8; *sb.* an uninhabited place. 2.1.9.1

determination of the mind: disposition or tendency of the mind to transfer attention unthinkingly from one object–perception to another; movement of the mind from one perception to a second customarily associated with the first. 1.3.12.7; 1.3.14.20, 23, 29; 1.4.7.5; 2.3.1.4.

discover: to make known, reveal. Intro. 2, 8; 1.3.6.6.

disposition: (1) inclination, temperament. 1.3.9.1; 1.3.10.4; 2.1.5.6. (2) arrangement. 1.2.3.5, 7.

distemper: disease of the human mind or body. 1.4.2.45.

draughts: drafts, preliminary notes. 1.2.4.33.

education: ways of thinking acquired by acculturation, habituation, instruction, and repetition, that is, by those processes that produce 'All those opinions and notions of things, to which we have been accustom'd from our infancy' (1.3.9.17). 1.2.7.2; 1.3.9.19; 1.3.10.1; 3.2.3.26. See also the second annotation to 1.3.9.13.

elevate: *adj.* elevated, uplifted, inspired. 2.2.2.8. *vb.* to be enlivened, stimulated, aroused. 2.3.8.10.

elevation of mind: distinguished by superior moral or intellectual qualities. 3.3.2.13; 3.3.3.4.

ell: in England, 45 inches, or 114.3 centimetres; in Scotland, 37.2 inches, or 94.5 centimetres. 1.2.4.19.

elogium: eulogy; a brief, usually favourable, summary of a person's qualities and accomplishments. 2.1.11.9.

embarrass: perplex, distress. 1.2.4.18; 2.1.6.9.

emergence: emergency, unexpected circumstance. 3.2.8.2.

emotion: a feeling that may attend a **passion**, resemble a passion, be related to a passion, or be produced by a passion. 1.1.1.1; 1.3.12.24; 2.1.1.1; 2.1.4.3; 2.1.5.4; 2.1.9.5; 2.2.6.3; 2.3.3.8; 2.3.5.2.

empire: authority. 1.3.14.12; *Abs.* 35.

entire: realized to its fullest extent, complete, perfect. 1.3.12.18; 1.4.2.40; 2.2.5.7; 2.2.6.1; 3.2.6.7. See also **yet entire.**

equipage: horses and carriages with attendants. 2.1.5.2; 2.2.5.2, 11.

evidence: (1) quality or condition of being **evident** in varying degrees (1.3.13.19; 1.3.6.4; 1.4.7.7), from the assurance of 'irresistible evidence' (2.1.5.5) or unevadable evidence (1.2.1.2), to evidence attended with uncertainty (1.3.11.2) or 'inferior' evidence (2.3.1.12), to that 'seeming evidence' which is refutable (1.4.5.30) or the 'lowest degree of evidence' (1.4.7.7). (2) may be combined with 'force' (1.2.2.6; 1.3.4.2; 1.3.11.1; 1.3.13.5), 'firmness' (1.3.8.4), '**solidity**' (1.3.14.7), 'certainty' (3.2.3.9), and 'belief' (1.3.4.2; 1.3.13.6; 1.4.1.6).

evident: (1) certain, undeniable (1.4.7.15), clear to the understanding (1.2.3.1), obvious 'at first sight' (1.1.3.1) 'from the plainest observation and experience' (1.2.1.2). (2) susceptible to degrees: 'more evident' (3.2.8.6); 'sufficiently evident' (2.2.1.2); 'too evident to be contested' (2.2.1.7).

evidently: on the basis of the **evidence.** 3.2.1.12; 3.2.6.10.

excite: arouse, induce, or bring about. 1.3.10.4; 2.1.7.5; 3.1.1.6.

experience: *sb.* participation in events as a basis for beliefs or conclusions; observation, including observation of one's own thoughts and actions; may be used as a synonym for **experiment.** Intro. 7, 10; 1.2.5.24, 25; 1.3.6.2; 1.3.8.3, 13. See also the first annotation to Intro. 8.

experiment: 'observation of those particular effects, which result from . . . different circumstances and situations' (Intro. 8); finding something out by trial; **experience** and *observation* may be used as synonyms for *experiment.* 1.3.8.3; 1.3.12.11; 1.3.15.6; 3.3.1.10.

experimental: based on **experiment, experience,** or observation. Title-pages; Intro. 7; 1.3.15.11.

extension: space or the property of having extent or of occupying space. For things to appear extended, they must be 'either visible or tangible' (1.2.3.15). 1.2.3.4; 1.2.5.1, 21; 1.4.5.9, 15.

fable: a fiction or a story. 1.1.3.4; 1.3.10.6–7.

fabulous: fictional, imagined. 1.3.9.5.

facility: (1) ease, moving without difficulty. 1.3.13.6; 2.1.5.10; 2.3.5.1. (2) quickness of mind. 2.2.10.8.

faculty: (1) a natural feature or capacity of the mind, e.g. the understanding, reason, or imagination. Intro. 5; 1.1.3.1; Note 22; 1.3.12.20; 1.4.2.14. (2) a meaningless scholastic term. 1.4.5.10.

fain: earnestly desire to, in phrases such as 'I wou'd fain ask' (1.1.6.1). 1.2.4.30; 1.4.7.2.

fancy: the imagination; the faculty of the mind which constructs fictions or that forms and combines and separates internal images. Like many writers of his period, Hume uses *fancy* and *imagination* interchangeably. 1.1.3.4; 1.1.4.2; 1.3.9.5; 1.4.7.6, 7.

feign: imagine, invent either consciously or unconsciously. 1.3.5.3; 1.3.9.5–6; 1.4.3.4.

fiction: a construction of the imagination, arrived at consciously (e.g. 1.3.5.4–5, the fictions of poets) and thus **artificial**; or unconsciously (e.g. 1.4.2.29) and thus **natural**. 1.2.3.11; 1.2.4.24; 1.4.6.6–7.

figure: (1) form, shape. 1.1.7.9–10, 17–18; 1.2.4.21. (2) a rhetorical expression, such as a metaphor or simile. 1.2.5.21. (3) a symbol on a die ('dye'). 1.3.11.13.

fop: a foolish or silly person. 1.3.13.7.

force: *sb.* strength or intensity; used to characterize the feeling conveyed by an **impression** in contrast to that conveyed by an **idea** (1.1.1.1, 3), or the feeling of an idea of the memory in contrast to one of the **imagination**, or the feeling of belief in a matter of fact in contrast to that of a mere conception. Used frequently in conjuction with *vivacity, liveliness, firmness, steadiness, influence, vigour, intensity*. See also **violence, solidity**. 1.3.5.3–6; 1.3.7.7.; 1.3.13.19; 2.1.11.7.

found: to base or build on. 1.1.6.1; 1.3.13.1; 2.1.9.1.

frith: a word used in Scotland, Bailey says, for an 'arm of the sea or the mouth of a river', a firth. 1.4.7.1.

gay: cheerful, lighthearted. 2.2.4.6; 3.3.2.7.

genius: natural ability or capacity. *Genius* began to take on the meaning of *exceptional* natural intelligence or ability only after 1750 (*OED*). 1.1.7.15; 1.3.10.6; 2.2.1.9; 2.2.10.7; 2.3.10.3–4, 6; 3.3.2.6.

greatness: size. 1.3.9.11; 1.4.6.9.

grimace: an expression or gesture (bowing the head reverently, closing the eyes, for example) used to demonstrate one's piety. 3.2.4.2.

habit: (1) **custom**, mode of behaviour acquired by repetition. 1.3.5.6; 1.3.9.17; 1.3.11.11; 1.3.16.9. (2) military or clerical dress. 2.3.4.3; 3.2.4.2.

hackney scriblers: second-rate writers, hacks. 2.2.8.13.

head: (1) heading. 1.1.1.1; 1.1.5.2. (2) point. 1.1.7.16; 1.3.7.6.

head-pieces: intellects, thinkers, used ironically. 1.3.15.11.

humanity: benevolence, one of the **natural** virtues (3.2.5.6); an inclination to treat others with consideration and compassion. 1.3.13.15; 3.3.1.12, 24; 3.3.3.3.

idea: one of the two kinds of **perception**, the other being **impressions**, from which ideas are derived (1.1.1.1; 1.3.8.15). Perceptions (i.e. ideas and impressions) are 'whatever can be present to the mind, whether we employ our senses, or are actuated with passion, or exercise our thought and reflection. . . . When we reflect on a passion or an object which is not present, this perception is an *idea*' (*Abs*. 5). 1.1.3.1–2; 2.1.1.2; 2.1.4.3; 2.1.11.7; Adv. Bk. 3; *Abs*. 5–7.

imagination: one of the two faculties, memory being the other, by which an **impression** is copied in the mind to produce an **idea**. The memory preserves the 'original order and position of its ideas, while the imagination transposes and changes them, as it pleases' (1.3.5.3). In practice this difference does not allow us to distinguish between the two; what does distinguish them is that the ideas of the imagination are 'fainter and more obscure' than those of memory (1.3.5.3). Used interchangeably with **fancy**. 1.1.3.1–4; 1.2.6.8; 1.3.5.4–7; 1.3.7.3, 7; Note 22.

imbecility: feebleness, weakness. 1.4.1.12; 3.3.3.7.

immediate: direct, unmediated, without any intervening perception or operation of the mind, without any intervening agency. 1.3.9.10–11; 1.3.14.10; 2.2.8.9; 3.3.1.27–9. The contrary of mediated and remote, present. 1.3.4.1; 1.3.6.7; 1.3.8.4–5; 1.3.14.1; 3.2.7.8; 3.2.9.3.

impression: one of the two kinds of **perception**, **ideas** being the other; impressions are 'all our sensations, passions and emotions, as they make their first appearance' in the mind (1.1.1.1; see also Adv. Bk. 3). There are two kinds of impression: (1) impressions of sensation that 'without any antecedent perception' arise in the mind; and (2) impressions of reflection, or secondary impressions, those that 'proceed from some of these original ones, either immediately or by the interposition' of ideas (2.1.1.1; see also 1.1.2.1). 'Of the first kind are all the impressions of the senses, and all bodily pains and pleasures: Of the second are the passions, and other emotions resembling them' (2.1.1.1). 1.1.1.8; 1.3.5.2; 1.4.2.7; *Abs.* 5–7.

impudence: lack of modesty. 3.2.12.7

impulse: (1) physical contact, the effect of one body acting on another, a synonym for shock in this sense. 1.3.2.9; 1.3.14.18. (2) force or influence exerted on the mind. 2.1.3.3; 2.1.5.5; 2.3.9.8.

inconvenience; inconveniencies: disadvantage(s). 3.1.1.1; 3.2.2.3; 3.2.4.1.

independency . . . on: independence from. 1.4.2.10.

indolence: passivity, indifference, tranquillity. 1.4.3.9; 1.4.7.10; 3.3.1.24.

inflexion: a geometrical term meaning 'that Point or Place where [a] Curve begins to bend back again a contrary way' (Bailey). 1.2.4.29.

in order to this, in order to that: in order to do this or that. 1.2.3.16; 1.3.14.1; 1.4.2.3.

in our eye: in mind, in view. 1.4.2.10; 3.2.1.5.

insensibly: without being noticed, imperceptibly. 1.1.1.10; 1.3.6.3; 1.3.13.3; 1.4.6.10.

inventor: 'a finder out of something new' (Bailey). *Abs.* 35.

inviron'd: surrounded. 1.4.7.8.

je-ne-sçai-quoi: something indescribable or inexpressible; literally, that *I know not what.* 1.3.8.16; 3.3.4.11.

knowledge: certainty; 'assurance arising from the comparison of ideas' (1.3.11.2). 1.3.1.2; 1.3.13.19; 1.4.1.1. See also the first annotation to 1.3.1.2.

landskip: landscape. 2.1.4.5.

last importance, last consequence: greatest importance or consequence. 1.4.2.34; 3.1.1.27.

late: recent. Intro. 7; 1.1.7.1; 1.4.6.15.

latest posterity: future generations, descendants far distant in time. 1.3.13.6; 1.4.7.14.

literature: learning (Bailey); the whole body of written works, including philosophy, history, fiction, poetry, criticism. Intro. 3.

logic: systematic explanation of 'the principles and operations of our reasoning faculty, and the nature of our ideas' (Intro. 5). 1.3.15.11; 1.4.1.6; *Abs.* 3–4.

lust: the 'natural appetite between the sexes' (3.2.2.4). 2.1.5.6; 2.3.9.8; 3.2.2.5.

luxury: excessive pursuit of pleasure. 3.3.4.7.

manners: (1) behaviour, general way of life, habits. 1.3.9.4; 2.1.11.5; 2.3.1.9; 3.3.3.2. (2) conduct in its moral aspect (*OED* 4b). 3.1.2.8.

mannor: manor, a territorial unit, originating in lands granted to a subject by a monarch or feudal lord. 3.2.4.2.

maxim: an axiom, proposition, or principle supposed to express some general truth or assumed as a premiss. 1.1.1.10; 1.2.2.8; 1.2.4.26; 1.2.5.19. Cf. Locke, *Essay* 4.7.1.

mean: inferior in quality, rank, occupation, or possessions. Intro. 10; 2.1.9.10; 3.3.2.4.

mechanic: a skilled worker, an artisan. 2.1.3.5; 2.3.3.6.

mechanical: requiring manual labour. 2.1.11.14.

mechanics: 'Mechanics are the art of regulating the motions of bodies *to some design'd end or purpose*' (2.3.3.2). 1.2.4.24.

mein: mien, air, or bearing, demeanour. 2.1.2.5; *Abs.* 30.

members: body parts. 1.4.2.9; 3.3.5.3; App. 4.

mobility: capacity for movement. 1.3.14.8; 1.4.4.10; 1.4.5.15.

mode: attribute or quality of a substance; accident. 1.1.6.2–3. See also the first annotation to 1.1.6.2.

natural philosophy: what we now call the sciences, both physical and biological. Intro. 4–5; 1.2.5.4.

natural religion: the science that uses reason or our natural abilities to discover the nature of the deity or deities and of our related religious and moral duties. Intro. 4–5.

nature, natural: See Hume's discussion of the different senses of *nature* at 3.1.2.7–10 and 3.2.1.19.

nay: used to introduce a more correct, precise, or emphatic claim than the one previously stated. 1.1.7.9; 1.2.3.5; 1.3.16.9.

never so: ever so. 1.4.1.6.

nice: exact, subtle. 1.3.8.15; 1.4.6.21; 2.3.4.1.

non-entities: non-existent things. 1.2.3.14; 1.4.4.8.

occult: a name for qualities whose nature was unknown or unexplained. 1.4.3.1. See also the annotation to 1.4.3.8.

offices: (1) 'in a civil sense, denotes the mutual aid, and assistance, which men owe to one another' (Chambers). 2.2.3.5; 3.2.5.9–10. (2) 'in a moral sense, denotes a duty; or that which virtue, and right reason directs a man to do' (Chambers). 3.2.8.5.

on: may have the sense of *in* or *of*; see change on, independency . . . on.

opinion: belief: 'An opinion, therefore, or belief may be most accurately defin'd, A LIVELY IDEA RELATED TO OR ASSOCIATED WITH A PRESENT IMPRESSION' (1.3.7.5). 1.3.7.7; 1.3.8.15; 1.3.9.17; *Abs.* 22.

original: instinctive, prior to experience. 1.1.4.6; 2.1.1.1; 2.1.3.3.

outness: externality, separateness from the mind. 1.4.2.9.

paint, paint out: depict, represent. 1.1.3.1; 1.3.9.4; 3.2.2.15.

paradox: a proposition contrary to the common opinion (Bailey); 1.2.1.1; 3.2.10.7.

participate of: share the nature of, have some of the qualities or characteristics of. 1.4.2.29.

parts: abilities, talent. 3.3.2.7; 3.3.4.1.

passion: a secondary **impression**, that is, an impression of reflection 'arising either from the original impressions [of sensation], or from their **ideas**' (2.1.1.2), or arising from certain natural instincts (2.3.9.8). The passions include, among others, love, hate, pride, humility, hope, fear, desire, aversion (2.1.1.4). 1.4.2.7; 2.1.1.3; 2.3.8.13; 2.3.9.1. See also **emotion** and **affection**.

passionate: easily moved to strong feeling, irascible, prone to anger or impatience. 3.2.3.2; 3.3.4.3.

patridge: partridge. 2.3.10.8.

peculiar: distinctive, particular. 1.1.1.1; 2.3.1.10; *Abs.* 28.

penetration: (1) supposed occupation of the same space by two bodies at the same time; a 'Philosophical way of expressing, That two bodies are in the same Place, so that the Parts of one do every where penetrate into, and adequately fill up the Dimensions or Places of the Parts of the other; which is manifestly impossible and contradictory to Reason' (Harris). 1.2.4.4–6; 1.4.4.10. (2) keenness of perception, insight, discernment. 2.2.12.1; 3.3.4.4.

perception: 'Every thing that enters the mind' (1.4.2.7), the general name for **impressions** and **ideas** (1.1.1.1). 1.4.2.39; *Abs.* 5.

perfect: complete, fixed, without exception. 1.1.3.1; 1.1.7.10, 1.3.12.9; 1.4.2.40; 3.2.6.7.

period: in rhetoric, the term for a unit or a segment, such as a sentence, a paragraph, a stanza, whose elements are integrally connected. 1.1.7.13; 2.3.8.8.

pitch on: consider, focus on. 1.3.2.5; 1.3.16.2.

plagiaries: those who plagiarize. 2.1.11.19.

plenum: the contrary of a vacuum or a void. 1.2.5.2, 27.

policy: design, strategy. 1.4.3.1; 2.2.3.2.

positive: absolute, certain. 1.1.5.10; 1.4.6.2; 1.4.7.15; 2.3.1.18.

pound: a pound sterling equalled twenty shillings; a Scottish pound, twenty pence, or one-twelfth of a pound sterling (Bailey). 1.3.12.24.

power: capacity for producing an effect or for performing an act. 1.3.6.8; 1.3.14.4, 12; 2.1.10.6.

preposterous: literally, back to front; putting the cart before the horse. 1.3.14.30; 3.2.2.11.

presently: (1) a little later, shortly. 1.3.9.5. (2) immediately (a meaning common in Scottish writers: *OED*). App. 4.

present with: present in or to. 1.1.3.1; 1.2.6.7, 8.

pretend, pretension: claim, to presume an ability to do something; cf. French *prétendre*. Intro. 1, 8; 1.1.4.6; 3.2.10.12; *Abs.* 34.

principle: This word occurs frequently with varying and overlapping connotations. Two basic and broad meanings: (1) a cause of, source of, or reason for an action, event, or state of affairs; a fundamental force including such things as laws of nature, natural dispositions, the mind, original tendencies, and faculties. 1.3.8.1; 1.3.9.6, 17; 1.3.10.2; 1.3.12.7; 1.4.6.18; 1.4.7.3; 2.1.4.1; 2.1.7.2; 2.2.5.14; 2.2.10.4; 3.2.7.5. (2) a tenet, proposition, or component of a system of thought, or that system of thought itself. 1.2.3.12; 1.3.14.2, 8; 1.4.5.19; 3.1.1.7.

probability: a degree of assurance or evidence, that is, evidence 'which is still attended with uncertainty' (1.3.11.2). 1.3.6.6, 7; 1.3.12.1, 2, 17, 25.

projection: a technical term in chemistry for the process of putting any substance that was 'to be calcined or fulminated [heated or melted] into a Crucible, Spoonful by Spoonful' (Bailey). 1.3.16.5.

projector: inventor, one who forms rash schemes. Hume told Henry Home, Lord Kames, 'My fondness for what I imagined new discoveries, made me overlook all common rules of prudence; and having enjoyed the usual satisfaction of projectors, 'tis but just I should meet with their disappointments' (*Letters*, 1:31). 1.3.10.4.

propension: propensity. 1.4.2.36, 42; 1.4.6.5; 3.2.7.3.

prosecution: application, pursuit. 1.2.5.20; 2.3.3.10.

quack: a charlatan, especially one whose medical skill is of uncertain origin or who offers wondrous remedies. Hume remembered Addison writing about 'a quack that advertised pills for an earthquake' (*Letters*, 1:141). 1.3.10.4.

quadrate: agree; correspond. 2.2.6.2.

radical cure: a remedy that operates by completely eradicating (rooting out, that is) some quality. 1.4.2.57; 3.2.7.6.

radicated: rooted, established. 3.2.2.26.

receive: *vb*. accept as true. 1.3.9.1, 12; 1.3.13.1.

receiv'd: *adj*. accepted. 1.1.7.1; 1.4.7.7.

refin'd: *adj*. abstract, raised to a high degree of subtlety. Intro. 9; 1.3.1.7; 1.4.7.7.

regular figure: having all sides and all angles equal. 1.1.7.9.

regularly: taking things in their proper order. 1.3.2.4.

relish: *sb*. a flavour, taste. 1.4.5.9, 11, 13; 2.3.1.6.

remarkable: worthy of remark, deserving notice. 1.1.1.3; 1.4.5.7; 2.1.11.2; 2.2.4.9.

rencounter: an encounter between two opposing forces. 2.3.9.13, 16; 3.3.2.3.

repugnance: (1) contradiction, disagreement, opposition. 1.1.7.14; 1.4.5.20–1; 2.2.2.22. (2) aversion. 1.3.14.35.

resume: *vb*. summarize, provide a résumé of. 1.4.2.11; 2.3.8.13; *Abs*. 21.

returns in a circle, runs in a circle: uses a circular or question-begging argument. 1.2.4.28; 1.3.2.10; 1.4.4.9–10.

ridicule: ridiculousness. 1.3.16.1.

right line: a straight line. 1.2.4.25–6; 1.3.1.4.

rouze, rouze up: arouse. 1.3.14.2; 2.2.10.4; 3.3.2.3.

run into: (1) tend towards. 1.1.7.8; 2.1.12.8; 3.1.1.19. (2) merge with, blend or coalesce with. 1.1.1.10; 1.3.12.19; 1.4.1.3; 3.1.2.4. (3) to favour or have a fancy for. 1.4.2.52; 2.2.9.4; 3.2.4.2.

run up, run up to: to trace or follow up in some way. 1.2.1.2; 1.2.4.21; 1.3.1.6; 1.3.7.6.

scalenum: scalene, a triangle whose three sides are of unequal length. 1.1.7.8.

scholastic, scholastics: pertaining to theological and philosophical views deriving in large part from Aristotle and the medieval Roman Catholic writers. Also, the teachers of these views. 1.3.15.11; 1.4.5.13, 23; 2.1.10.5.

schools: the medieval and early modern European universities or the subject-matter taught therein. 1.1.7.17; 1.2.4.3; 1.4.5.29; 2.3.2.1. 2.3.3.8.

scritoire: Anglicization of the French *escritoire*, 'a great sort of cabinet with Drawers, and the conveniency of a Table to write upon' (*OED*, citing G. Miege, *Great French Dictionary*, 1687–8). 2.1.3.5; 2.2.5.17.

scruple: (1) *sb*. hesitation, difficulty with some thing or idea. 1.3.9.14; 2.1.3.7; 2.2.8.19. Also, to *make a scruple*. 1.1.1.1; 1.4.6.11; 2.2.2.1. (2) *vb*. to hesitate, raise doubts about. 1.4.6.8.

secret: something unknown, undiscovered. 1.3.8.13; 1.3.14.7; 1.4.3.10.

secretly: operating without notice or observation. 1.3.13.1; 2.2.2.6.

sensible: *adj*. (1) perceivable by the senses, discernible. 1.1.3.1; 1.2.1.4; 1.2.5.17; 1.3.8.4; 1.4.4.5. (2) in a verb phrase: to be or become aware of or be made aware of. 1.2.5.25; 1.4.1.8; *Abs*. 22.

sensibly: observably, perceptibly. 2.2.8.11; 3.3.4.13.

sentiment: (1) used to convey various connotations of *feeling* and **opinion**; cf. French *sentiment*. 1.3.13.9; 1.3.14.8; 1.4.1.5; 2.1.11.1–2; 2.2.8.2; 2.3.1.9 (2) **passion, affection, emotion**, or a thought or feeling prompted by a passion. 1.4.1.11; 1.4.2.37; 2.1.11.7; 2.2.6.5; 2.3.9.4.

sentiments of morality/morals: the moral sense; the unique feeling of approbation or disapprobation felt in response to the character or motives of other persons. 3.1.2.8; 3.2.2.11; 3.2.5.12, 15; 3.2.10.3, 5.

several: distinct. 1.1.1.10; 1.3.9.16; 1.3.12.6.

shock: (1) *vb*. make contact; put into motion; cf. French *choquer*. *Abs*. 10. (2) *sb*. collision, encounter. 1.3.14.18; 1.4.5.29; 2.3.9.13.

signal: significant. 1.3.13.12; 1.4.3.11; *Abs*. 2.

simple, simplicity: not compounded or composite; frequently, in Hume's usage, indivisible. 1.1.1.2, 7; 1.1.7.18; 1.2.1.2, 4; 1.4.4.8.

singly: singularly. 1.3.1.6.

solidity: (1) of a compelling nature; **force** or **vivacity**; used to describe the feeling by which we distinguish 'the ideas of the judgment from the fictions of the imagination' (1.3.7.7). 1.3.8.15; 1.3.10.6. (2) serious, not frivolous. 1.3.9.15; 1.3.13.7.

soul: (1) the seat of thought and action in man, distinct from the body. Hume and his contemporaries often used *soul* interchangeably with *mind*. Intro. 9; 1.1.1.1; 1.3.10.2; 1.3.14.23; 1.3.16.9; *Abs*. 28. (2) a spritual essence, that component of a human which many believe will survive death. 1.4.5.35.

specious: apparently sound or convincing, fashioned to make a favourable impression. 1.2.5.20; 1.4.7.14; 2.1.1.3; 2.1.12.6.

spirit: in the singular, the immaterial element of life in contrast to the body or material element. 1.3.14.20; 1.4.5.35.

spleen: melancholy, dejection. 1.4.7.11, 14.

splenetic: impatient, irritable, irascible. 1.4.7.10; 3.3.4.3.

spread out in the mind: imagine, picture. 1.1.7.14; 1.4.2.20.

springs and principles: causes, things that arouse to action or produce effects. 1.3.10.2; 1.3.12.5; 3.3.1.2.

station: rank or standing in society. 2.3.1.9; 2.3.8.7; 3.3.2.11.

strikes (not) in with: is (not) consistent with. 1.3.12.20; 1.4.2.37.

stupidity: ignorance; incomprehension. 1.3.9.13; 1.4.3.10.

subscription: signature at the end of a letter. 1.4.2.20.

substracting: subtracting. 1.3.12.19.

super-add: to add over and above. 1.3.8.7; 3.2.8.6; 3.2.11.2.

super-cargo: someone who superintends a merchant's business in a foreign country, or, who, serving as an officer on board ship, supervises the cargo and commercial transactions during a voyage. 2.3.1.15.

superstition: inexplicable or irrational beliefs or systems of belief. 1.3.8.4; 1.4.7.13; 3.2.4.2.

surprize: an agreeable wonder. Surprise is, Hume says, a 'pleasure arising from novelty' (2.1.8.6). Often paired with **admiration**. 1.2.1.1; 1.3.10.4; 2.3.5.2.

sympathy: (1) that feature of the mind by which 'we enter into the sentiments' of others, and 'partake of their pleasure and uneasiness' (2.2.5.14); thus a means of 'communication' (2.2.12.6; 3.3.2.2). 2.1.11.2–3, 8, 19; 2.2.9.13; 2.3.6.8; 3.3.1.7, 10. (2) an occult quality in a body or object which is supposed to explain the natural inclination of one body or object for another. 1.4.3.11. See also the annotation to 1.4.3.11.

system: a comprehensive body of principles, a theory. Intro. 1; 1.2.4.1; 1.3.11.5; 1.4.6.23.

table: *sb.* provision of food and entertainment. 2.1.10.2.

take place: have effect, be produced, occur. 1.1.6.2; 2.2.4.9; 3.1.1.13; 3.2.2.4; 3.2.8.1.

taper: (1) *sb.* a type of wax candle used chiefly for devotional or penitential purposes (*OED*). 3.2.4.2. (2) *adj.* tapering, that is, narrowing in breadth or thickness towards one end. 3.3.5.3.

temper: disposition. App. 1; 2.1.3.4.

tierce: the harmonic combination of two tones a third apart. 1.2.4.24.

topic: a kind or class of considerations suitable to the purposes of a rhetorician or disputant (*OED* 2), an argument. 'These strong topics, in favour of the house of Lancaster, were opposed by arguments no less convincing on the side of the house of York' (*History* 21 [2:437]). 1.2.4.29; 1.3.13.5; 2.3.2.3; *Abs.* 27.

traces: paths, channels. 1.2.5.20.

train: (1) retinue, group of attendants. 2.2.5.11. (2) sequence or succession of perceptions, causes, etc. 1.3.12.9; 2.2.7.3; 2.3.1.17.

translation: transference (of property). 3.2.4.1; 3.2.8.3.

unite, unity: one. 1.2.2.3.

unsteadiness: inconsistency, variableness. 1.2.4.7; 1.3.10.2.

vacuum: void, or a space devoid of all matter. 1.2.5.2–4.

violence: (1) intensity of some condition or influence; a marked or powerful effect; force. 1.1.1.1; 1.4.2.16; 2.1.4.4. (2) distortion. 1.3.11.4.

violent: (1) moving to action or arousing strongly felt desire; 1.4.2.18; 1.4.6.1; 2.3.8.13. (2) a kind of passion, contrasted with calm. 2.1.1.3; 2.3.4.1.

vulgar: (1) *sb.* common, ordinary people (not a pejorative term). 1.2.3.11; 1.3.12.5; 1.4.2.53. (2) *adj.* common or ordinary, usual. 1.1.3.3; 1.2.4.30; 1.3.14.4, 7; 2.1.10.5.

vulgarly: *adv.* ordinarily, in everyday speech. 2.2.7.5; 2.3.4.1.

will: '*the internal impression we feel and are conscious of, when we knowingly give rise to any new motion of our body, or new perception of our mind*' (2.3.1.2). 1.1.4.5; 2.3.9.7; 3.1.1.24–5.

without: outside. Intro. 2; 1.4.7.13.

yet entire: unexamined (*OED* 4d). 2.3.7.6.

References

THIS list provides a succinct description of the persons mentioned but not identified in Hume's text or the annotations to it. It also provides a more complete title of, and bibliographical details about, each book mentioned by Hume or by the editors in the annotations. Should you want more information about the individuals listed here, we suggest you begin by consulting such standard reference books as *The Oxford Companion to Classical Literature*, *The Dictionary of National Biography*, *The Oxford Companion to English Literature*, *The Oxford Companion to French Literature*, or *The Encyclopedia of Philosophy*. From these resources you can go on to such bibliographical aids as *The Philosopher's Index* or *The Humanities Index*. In many libraries such aids are now accessible by computer. Unless otherwise noted, classical works are cited from Loeb Library editions (London: Heinemann, v.d.). A date in parentheses (1690) following a title indicates date of first publication of the work in question; place and date in parentheses (London, 1733) following a title identify the particular edition of the work cited in the annotations.

'A Calculation of the Credibility of Human Testimony', *Philosophical Transactions of the Royal Society*, No. 257 (Oct. 1699).

ACOSTA, JOSÉ DE (c.1539–1600). Spanish Jesuit missionary to Peru, author of *The Naturall and Morall Historie of the Indies* (1590), trans. anon. (London, 1604).

ADDISON, JOSEPH (1672–1719). English writer and politician. Work cited: articles from *The Spectator* (with others, esp. Richard Steele), ed. D. F. Bond, 5 vols. (Oxford: Clarendon Press, 1965).

An Essay on Consciousness (London, 1728; fac. New York: Garland Press, 1976); this work is tentatively attributed to Charles Mayne (d. 1737), English civil servant.

AQUINAS, ST THOMAS (c.1224–1274). Roman Catholic theologian and philosopher. Work cited: *Summa Theologiae*.

ARBUTHNOT, JOHN (1667–1735). English physician and writer. Work mentioned: *The Memoirs of Martinus Scriblerius*, written with Pope, Swift, and others before 1720 (London, 1741).

ARISTOTLE (384–322 BC). Greek philosopher. Works cited:
—— *De caelo* [*On the Heavens*].
—— *Metaphysics*.
—— *Nicomachean Ethics*.
—— *Problems*.

ARNAULD, ANTOINE (1612–94). French philosopher and theologian. Works cited:
—— *On True and False Ideas* (1683), trans. E. J. Kremer (Lewiston, NY: Edwin Mellen Press, 1990).
—— *Logic*, i.e. *Logic; or, The Art of Thinking* (1662), trans. J. V. Buroker (Cambridge: Cambridge University Press, 1996). Pierre Nicole collaborated with Arnauld on this work.

AUGUSTINE, ST (354–430). Roman Catholic philosopher and theologian. Work cited: *On the Trinity*.

AUGUSTUS (b. Gaius Octavius; 63 BC–AD 14). First Roman emperor.

BACON, FRANCIS (1561–1626). English philosopher and statesman. Work cited: *The Advancement of Learning* (London, 1605).

References

BAILEY, NATHAN (d. 1742). English lexicographer. Work cited: *Dictionary*, i.e. *Dictionarium Britannicum*, 2nd edn. (London, 1730; fac. Hildesheim: Georg Olms, 1969).

BALGUY, JOHN (1686–1741). English clergyman. Work cited: *Foundation*, i.e. *The Foundation of Moral Goodness*, in 2 pts. (London, 1728–9; fac. New York: Garland Press, 1976).

BARROW, ISAAC (1630–77). English mathematician and theologian. Work cited: *The Usefulness of Mathematical Learning Explained and Demonstrated, being Mathematical Lectures . . .* (London, 1734; fac. London: Frank Cass, 1970); 1st pub. as *Mathematicae Lectiones . . .* (1683).

BAYLE, PIERRE (1647–1706). French protestant philosopher and historian. Work cited: *Dictionary*, i.e. *Mr. Bayle's Historical and Critical Dictionary* (1697), ed. Pierre Desmaizeaux, 2nd edn., 5 vols. (London, 1734–8; fac. New York: Garland Press, 1984).

BENTLEY, RICHARD (1662–1742). English clergyman and classical scholar. Work cited: *Sermons*, i.e. *Eight Boyle Lectures on Atheism* (London, 1692–3; fac. New York: Garland Press, 1976).

BERKELEY, GEORGE (1685–1753). Irish philosopher and Anglican bishop. Works cited are from *The Works of George Berkeley, Bishop of Cloyne*, ed. A. A. Luce and T. E. Jessop, 9 vols. (Edinburgh: Thomas Nelson, 1948–57):

—— *Alciphron*, i.e. *Alciphron; or, The Minute Philosopher. In Seven Dialogues. Containing an Apology for the Christian Religion, against those who are called Free-thinkers* (1732).

—— *De Motu*, i.e. *Of Motion; or, The Principle and Nature of Motion and the Cause of the Communication of Motions* (1721).

—— *New Theory of Vision*, i.e. *An Essay towards a New Theory of Vision* (1709).

—— *Passive Obedience* (1712).

—— *Principles*, i.e. *A Treatise concerning the Principles of Human Knowledge* (1710).

—— *Three Dialogues*, i.e. *Three Dialogues between Hylas and Philonous* (1713).

BLAIR, HUGH (1718–1800). Scottish clergyman and rhetorician. Work cited: *Rhetoric*, i.e. *Lectures on Rhetoric and Belles Lettres* (Edinburgh, 1818).

BOETHIUS, ANICIUS MANLIUS SEVERINUS (c.480–524). Roman statesman and philosopher.

BOYLE, ROBERT (1627–91). English natural philosopher. Works cited are from *Selected Philosophical Papers of Robert Boyle*, ed. M. A. Stewart (Manchester: Manchester University Press, 1979):

—— *Essay*, i.e. *An Essay, Containing a Requisite Digression, concerning those that would Exclude the Deity from Intermeddling with Matter* (1663).

—— *Free Enquiry*, i.e. *Free Enquiry into the Vulgarly Received Notion of Nature* (1686).

—— *Origins of Forms and Qualities*, i.e. *Origins of Forms and Qualities according to the Corpuscular Philosophy* (1666).

BRAMHALL, JOHN (1594–1663). Archbishop of Armagh. Work cited: *A Defence of True Liberty from Antecedent and Extrinsecall Necessity* (London, 1655; fac. New York: Garland Press, 1977).

BROWNE, PETER (d. 1735). Bishop of Cork and Ross. Work cited: *Procedure*, i.e. *The Procedure, Extent, and Limits of Human Understanding* (London, 1728; fac. New York: Garland Press, 1976).

BRUTUS, MARCUS JUNIUS (c.85–42 BC). Roman patriot and assassin of Julius Caesar.

BUTLER, JOSEPH (1692–1752). English philosopher and bishop. Works cited are from *Works*, ed. W. E. Gladstone, 2 vols. (Oxford: Clarendon Press, 1896):

—— *Analogy of Religion*, i.e. *The Analogy of Religion, Natural and Revealed, to the Constitution and Course of Nature* (1736).

—— *Sermons*, i.e. *Fifteen Sermons Preached at the Rolls Chapel* (1726).

—— 'On the Nature of Virtue', essay pub. with *Analogy of Religion*.

—— 'Of Personal Identity', essay pub. with *Analogy of Religion*.

CAESAR, GAIUS JULIUS. See the annotation to 3.2.10.19.

CAMPBELL, ARCHIBALD (1691–1756). Scottish clergyman. Work cited: *An Enquiry into the Original of Moral Virtue* (London, 1728).

CHAMBERS, EPHRAIM (d. 1740). English encyclopaedist. Work cited: *Cyclopædia*, i.e. *Cyclopædia; or, An Universal Dictionary of Arts and Sciences; containing an Explication of the Terms, and an Account of the Things Signified thereby, in the several Arts, both Liberal and Mechanical; and the several Sciences, Human and Divine* . . . (1728; 2nd edn. London, 1742).

CHEYNE, GEORGE (1671–1743). Scottish physician and moralist. Work cited: *The English Malady* (London, 1733; fac. London: Routledge, 1991).

CICERO, MARCUS TULLIUS (106–43 BC). Roman philosopher, orator, and statesman.

—— *Academica* (*The Academy*), trans. H. Rackham.

—— *De finibus*, i.e. *De finibus bonorum et malorum* (*About the Ends of Goods and Evils*), trans. H. Rackham.

—— *De officiis* (*Of Duties*), trans. W. Smith.

—— *De oratore* (*Of Oratory*), trans. E. W. Sutton and H. Rackham, 2 vols.

—— *Pro Sestio* (*Defence of P. Sestius*), trans. R. Gardner.

—— *De re publica* (*The Republic*), trans. C. W. Keyes.

CLARKE, JOHN (1706–61). English schoolmaster and philosopher. Work cited: *The Foundation of Morality in Theory and Practice* (York, [1726]).

CLARKE, SAMUEL (1675–1729). English philosopher and theologian. Works cited are from *The Works of Samuel Clarke*, 4 vols. (London, 1738; fac. New York: Garland Press, 1978):

—— *Demonstration*, i.e. *A Demonstration of the Being and Attributes of God. More particularly in Answer to Mr. Hobbes, Spinoza, and their Followers* (1705), in *Works*, 2:518–77.

—— *Discourse*, i.e. *Discourse concerning the Unchangeable Obligations of Natural Religion* . . . (1706), in *Works*, 2:579–733.

—— *A Letter to Mr. Dodwell; wherein All the Arguments in his Epistolary Discourse against the Immortality of the Soul are particularly answered* . . . (1706), in *Works*, 3:725–47.

—— *A Defence of an Argument Made use of in a Letter to Mr. Dodwell, to prove the Immateriality and natural Immortality of the Soul* (1706), in *Works*, 3:755–63.

—— *A Second Defence of an Argument Made use of in a Letter to Mr. Dodwell* . . . (1707), in *Works*, 3:781–99.

—— *A Third Defence of an Argument Made use of in a Letter to Mr. Dodwell* . . . (1708), in *Works*, 3:823–53.

—— *A Fourth Defence of an Argument Made use of in a Letter to Mr. Dodwell* . . . (1708), in *Works*, 3:889–913.

—— *A Collection of Papers, which passed between the late Learned Mr. Leibnitz, and Dr. Clarke* . . . *Relating to the Principles of Natural Philosophy and Religion* (1717), in *Works*, 4:575–710.

COLLIER, ARTHUR (1680–1732). English clergyman and philosopher. Work cited: *Clavis Universalis; or, A New Inquiry after Truth, being a Demonstration of the Non-Existence, or Impossibility, of an External World* (London, 1713; fac. New York: Garland Press, 1978).

COLLINS, ANTHONY (1676–1729). English free-thinking philosopher. Works cited:

—— *An Answer*, i.e. *An Answer to Mr. Clarke's Third Defence of his Letter to Mr. Dodwell* (1708); repr. in Samuel Clarke, *Works*, vol. 3.

—— *A Letter*, i.e. *A Letter to the Learned Mr. Henry Dodwell; containing some Remarks on a (pre-*

tended) Demonstration of the Immateriality and Natural Immortality of the Soul, in Mr. Clarke's Answer (1707); repr. in Samuel Clarke, *Works*, vol. 3.

——*Reflections*, i.e. *Reflections on Mr. Clarke's Second Defence of his Letter to Mr. Dodwell* (1707); repr. in Samuel Clarke, *Works*, vol. 3.

——*Free-Thinking*, i.e. *A Discourse of Free-Thinking, Occasion'd by the Rise and Growth of a Sect call'd Free-Thinkers* (London, 1713; fac. New York: Garland Press, 1978).

——*Philosophical Inquiry*, i.e. *A Philosophical Inquiry concerning Human Liberty* (London, 1717; fac. New York: Garland Press, 1978).

——*A Reply*, i.e. *A Reply to Mr. Clarke's Defence of his Letter to Mr. Dodwell* (1707); repr. in Samuel Clarke, *Works*, vol. 3.

COPERNICUS, NICOLAUS (1473–1543). Polish clergyman and astronomer.

CORDEMOY, GÉRAUD DE (*c*.1610–84). French philosopher and historian, author of *Le Discernement du corps et de l'âme* (*The Distinction of Body and Mind*) (1666).

COTES, ROGER (1682–1716). English mathematician. Work cited: Preface, to Newton's *Mathematical Principles of Natural Philosophy*, 2nd edn. (1713). Cited from I. Newton, *Principia*, trans. A. Motte, rev. F. Cajori, 2 vols. (Berkeley: University of California Press, 1971).

CRAIG, JOHN (d. 1731). English mathematician. Work cited: *Craig's Rules of Historical Evidence*, trans. anon. (The Hague: Mouton, 1964).

CUDWORTH, RALPH (1617–88). English philosopher-theologian. Works cited:

——*System*, i.e. *The True Intellectual System of the Universe . . . Wherein, All the Reason and Philosophy of Atheism is Confuted and Its Impossibility Demonstrated* (London, 1678; fac. New York: Garland Press, 1978).

——*Treatise*, i.e. *Treatise concerning Eternal and Immutable Morality* (London, 1731; fac. New York: Garland Press, 1976).

DE MOIVRE, ABRAHAM (1667–1754). French mathematician, settled in England in 1688. Work cited: *The Doctrine of Chances; or, A Method of Calculating the Probabilities of Events in Play* (1718; fac. of the 1738 edn. New York: Chelsea Publishing, 1967).

DESCARTES, RENÉ (1596–1650). French philosopher. Works cited are from *The Philosophical Writings of Descartes*, trans. J. Cottingham, R. Stoothoff, D. Murdoch, and A. Kenny, 3 vols. (Cambridge: Cambridge University Press, 1985–91):

——*Meditations*, i.e. *Meditations on First Philosophy* (1641).

——*Optics* (1637).

——*The Passions of the Soul* (1649).

——*Principles of Philosophy* (1644).

DIOGENES OF SINOPE (4th c. BC). Greek philosopher, a Cynic.

DOUGLAS, JAMES (1675–1742). English physician. Work cited: *A Comparative Description of the Muscles in a Man and Quadruped* (London, 1707).

DRYDEN, JOHN (1631–1700). English poet and critic. Works cited are from *The Works of John Dryden*, ed. H. T. Swedenberg (Berkeley: University of California Press, 1956–).

——(trans.), *The Art of Painting*, by Charles Alphonse Dufresnoy (1695); 1st pub. as *De Arte Graphica* (1668).

——*Dramatic Poetry* (1668).

——*Odes* (1684).

DUFRESNOY, CHARLES ALPHONSE (1611–65). French poet and painter. Work cited: *The Art of Painting* (*De Arte Graphica*) (1668), trans. J. Dryden (1695).

DUNS SCOTUS, JOHN (*c*.1266–1308). Scottish philosopher.

DU VAIR, GUILLAUME (1556–1621). French statesman and moral philosopher. Work cited: *The Moral Philosophy of the Stoics*, trans. T. J[ames] (London, 1598).

References

EMPEDOCLES (*c.*495–435 BC). Early Greek philosopher.

ERASMUS, DESIDERIUS (*c.*1469–1536). Dutch scholar and theologian. Work cited: *The Praise of Folly*, from *The Essential Erasmus*, ed. J. P. Dolan (New York: New American Library, 1964).

EURIPIDES (*c.*485–406 BC). Athenian dramatist.

FILMER, ROBERT (*c.*1590–1653). English political writer. Work cited: *Patriarcha; or, The Natural Power of Kings* (1680).

FOUCHER, SIMON (1644–96). French philosopher. Work cited: *Critique*, i.e. *Critique de la Recherche de la vérité ou l'on examine en même-tem une partie des Principes de Mr Descartes* (*A Critique of the* Search after Truth, *with an Examination of One Part of Descartes's Principles*) (1675).

GALEN OF PERGAMUM (129–99 BC). Greek physician.

GALILEI, GALILEO (1564–1642). Italian natural philosopher. Work cited: *The Assayer* (Rome, 1623), in *Discoveries and Opinions of Galileo*, ed. S. Drake (Garden City, NY: Doubleday, 1957).

GASSENDI, PIERRE (1592–1655). French priest and philosopher. Works cited:
—— *Epicurus*, i.e. *De Vita et Moribus Epicuri* (1647). Cited from Thomas Stanley, *A History of Philosophy* (London, 1687; fac. New York: Garland Press, 1978).
—— *Logic*, i.e. *Institutio Logica* (1658), trans. H. Jones (Assen: Van Gorcum, 1981).

GAY, JOHN (1699–1745). English clergyman and philosopher. Work cited: *Preliminary Dissertation concerning the Fundamental Principle of Virtue or Morality* (London, 1731; fac. New York: Garland Press, 1978).

GEULINCX, ARNOLD (1624–69). Flemish philosopher. Relevant work: *Metaphysica Vera* (*True Metaphysics*) (1691).

GLANVILL, JOSEPH (1636–80). Anglican theologian. Championed experimental research of the Royal Society. Work mentioned: *Scepsis Scientifica* or, *Confest Ignorance, The Way to Science* (London, 1665).

GRACIÁN Y MORALES, BALTASAR (1601–58). Spanish Jesuit and writer. Work cited: *Art of Prudence*, trans. J. Savage, 3rd edn. (London, 1714).

GROTIUS, HUGO (1583–1645). Dutch jurist-philosopher. Works cited:
—— *Freedom of the Seas* (1609).
—— *The Rights of War and Peace* (1625), trans. anon. (London, 1739).

GUICCIARDINI, FRANCESCO (1483–1540). Italian statesman and historian. Work cited: *History of Italy*, trans. G. Grayson (London: Sadler & Brown, 1966).

HARRIS, JOHN (*c.*1667–1719). Clergyman, compiled first English dictionary of the arts and sciences. Work cited: *Lexicon Technicum; or, An Universal English Dictionary of the Arts and Sciences: Explaining not only the Terms of Art, but the Arts Themselves* (London, 1704–10; fac. New York: Johnson Reprint, 1966).

HESIOD (*c.*700 BC). Early Greek poet.

HOBBES, THOMAS (1588–1679). English philosopher. Unless otherwise noted, works cited are from *The English Works of Thomas Hobbes*, ed. W. Molesworth, 11 vols. (London, 1839–45; repr. Darmstadt: Scientia Verlag, 1962):
—— *De Cive* (1642). Cited from *Man and Citizen*, ed. B. Gert (Indianapolis: Hackett, 1991).
—— *Dialogues*, i.e. *Decameron Physiologicum; or, Ten Dialogues of Natural Philosophy* (1678), in *English Works*, vol. 7.
—— *Elements of Philosophy . . . concerning Body* (1656), in *English Works*, vol. 1.
—— *Human Nature*, i.e. *Human Nature; or, The Fundamental Elements of Policy* (1650) in *English Works*, vol. 4.

——*Leviathan*, i.e. *Leviathan, or the Matter, Forme, and Power of a Commonwealth Ecclesiastical and Civil* (1651). Cited from the edn. of R. Tuck (Cambridge: Cambridge University Press, 1991).

——*Of Liberty and Necessity* (1654), in *English Works*, vol. 4.

HOME, HENRY, LORD KAMES (1696–1782). Scottish lawyer, judge, philosopher.

HOOKE, ROBERT (1635–1703). English natural philosopher. Work cited:

——*Micrographia; or, Some Physiological Descriptions of Minute Bodies made by Magnifying Glasses* (London, 1665; fac. Lincolnwood: Science Heritage, 1987).

HORACE (Quintus Horatius Flaccus; 65–8 BC). Roman poet.

——*Ars poetica* (*The Art of Poetry*), trans. H. R. Fairclough.

——*Epodes*, trans. C. E. Bennett.

——*Odes*, trans. C. E. Bennett.

HUGHES, JOHN (1677–1720). English poet and essayist. Work cited: *The Spectator*; see Addison, above.

HUTCHESON, FRANCIS (1694–1747). Irish philosopher, professor of moral philosophy at Glasgow University, 1729–47. Works cited:

——*Essay*, i.e. *An Essay on the Nature and Conduct of the Passions and Affections. With Illustrations on the Moral Sense* (1728; fac. of 3rd edn., Gainesville, Fla.: Scholars Facsimiles, 1969).

——*Inquiry*, i.e. *An Inquiry into the Original of our Ideas of Beauty and Virtue; in Two Treatises. I. Concerning Beauty, Order, Harmony, Design. II. Concerning Moral Good and Evil* (1726; fac. of 4th edn., Westmead, Hants: Gregg International Publishers, 1969).

JOHNSON, SAMUEL (1709–84). English poet, critic, and lexicographer. Work cited: *A Dictionary of the English Language* (1755; London, 1832).

JUSTINIAN (Flavius Justinianus; c.482–565). Roman emperor at Constantinople, responsible for codifying Roman law. Work cited: *The Institutes of Justinian* (Oxford: Clarendon Press, 1913).

KEILL, JAMES (1673–1719). Scottish physician and anatomist. Work cited: *Essays on several Parts of the Animal Œconomy* (London, 1717).

KEILL, JOHN (1671–1721). Scottish natural philosopher. Work cited: *An Introduction to Natural Philosophy; or, Philosophical Lectures Read in the University of Oxford, Anno Dom. 1700* (Eng. trans. London, 1720).

KING, WILLIAM (1650–1729). Archbishop of Dublin. Work cited: *Essay on the Origin of Evil* (1702), trans., with copious notes, Edmund Law (London, 1731; fac. New York: Garland Press, 1978).

LA BRUYÈRE, JEAN DE (1645–96). French moralist. Work cited: *The Characters of Jean de la Bruyère* (1688), trans. Henri van Laun (London: Routledge, 1929).

LA CHAMBRE, MARIN CUREAU DE (1595–1669). French physician and moralist, author, c. 1640, of *Les caractères des passions*.

LA FORGE, LOUIS DE (*fl.* 1660–75). French protestant philosopher. Work cited: *Traitté de l'esprit de l'homme* (*Treatise on the Human Mind*) (1666).

LA ROCHEFOUCAULD, FRANÇOIS DUC DE (1613–80). French moralist. Work cited: *Maxims*, i.e. *Réflexions ou Sentences et Maximes* (1678); anon. trans. (London, 1706).

LAW, WILLIAM (1686–1761). English religious writer. Work cited: *A Serious Call to a Devout and Holy Life* (1729), ed. J. C. Reid (London: Collins, 1965).

LEE, HENRY (d. 1713). English clergyman. Work cited: *Anti-Scepticism; or, Notes upon each Chapter of Mr. Lock's Essay concerning Humane Understanding. With an Explication of all the Particulars of which he Treats* . . . (London, 1702; fac. New York: Garland Press, 1978).

References

Le Grand, Antoine (c.1620–99). French philosopher. Work cited: *Man without Passion; or, The wise Stoick, according to the sentiments of Seneca* (London, 1675).

Leibniz, Gottfried Wilhelm (1646–1716). German philosopher and mathematician. Work cited: *Theodicy: Essays on the Goodness of God, the Freedom of Man and the Origin of Evil* (1710), ed. A. Farrer, trans. E. M. Huggard (London: Routledge, 1951).

Locke, John (1632–1704). English philosopher. Works cited:

—— *Essay*, i.e. *An Essay concerning Human Understanding* (1690), ed. P. H. Nidditch (Oxford: Clarendon Press, 1975).

—— *Letter*, i.e. *A Letter to the . . . Bishop of Worcester, concerning . . . Mr. Locke's Essay* (1697), in *The Works of John Locke*, 10 vols. (London, 1823; fac. Darmstadt: Scientia Verlag, 1963), vol. 4.

—— *Two Treatises*, i.e. *Two Treatises of Government* (1690), ed. P. Laslett (Cambridge: Cambridge University Press, 1963).

Lucan (Marcus Lucanus; 39–65). Latin poet. Work cited: *The Civil Wars*, from *Lucan*, trans. J. D. Duff.

Lucretius (Titus Lucretius Carus; 98–c.55 bc). Roman poet and philosopher. Work cited: *Nature of Things* (*De rerum natura*), trans. R. E. Latham (Harmondsworth: Penguin, 1958).

Machiavelli, Niccolò (1467–1527). Italian politician and political philosopher. Works cited:

—— *Discourses*, i.e. *Discourses on the First Ten Books of Titus Livius* (1517), trans. C. Detmold (New York: Modern Library, 1950).

—— *The Prince* (1513), ed. Q. Skinner and R. Price (Cambridge: Cambridge University Press, 1988).

Malebranche, Nicolas (1638–1715). French philosopher-theologian. Works cited:

—— *Dialogues on Metaphysics* (*Entretiens sur la métaphysique et sur la religion*) (1688), trans. W. Doney (New York: Abaris Books, 1980).

—— *Elucidations*, i.e. *Elucidations of the Search after Truth* (1677–8), trans. T. M. Lennon and P. J. Olscamp (Columbus: Ohio State University Press, 1980).

—— *Search*, i.e. *The Search after Truth* (1674–5), trans. T. M. Lennon and P. J. Olscamp (Columbus: Ohio State University Press, 1980).

Malezieu, Nicholas de (1650–1727). French mathematician, tutor to Louis, duke of Burgundy. Work cited: *Elements of Geometry* (*Elemens de Geometrie de Monseigneur le Duc de Bourgogne*) (1706). Excerpts from this work are found in Norman Kemp Smith, *The Philosophy of David Hume* (London: Macmillan, 1964), ch. 14, app. D.

Mandeville, Bernard de (1670–1733). Dutch physician, settled in London. Work cited: *Fable*, i.e. *The Fable of the Bees; or, Private Vices, Publick Benefits* (1705–23), ed. F. B. Kaye, 2 vols. (Oxford: Clarendon Press, 1966). *An Enquiry into the Origin of Moral Virtue* is a part of the *Fable*.

Mariotte, Edmund (d. 1684). French natural philosopher. Work cited: *Essay on Logic* (*Essai de Logique*) from *Œuvres de Mr. Mariotte* (Leiden, 1717).

Milton, John (1608–74). English poet. Work cited: *Paradise Lost* (1667).

Molyneux, William (1656–98). Irish writer on optics and politics. Corresponded with Locke. See Locke, *Essays* 2.9.8.

Monro, Alexander (1697–1767). Scottish anatomist and physician.

Montaigne, Michel Eyquem de (1533–92). French essayist. Works cited are from *The Complete Essays of Montaigne* (1580–95), trans. D. M. Frame, 3 vols. in 1 (Palo Alto, Calif.: Stanford University Press, 1989):

—— *Apology*, i.e. *Apology for Raymond Sebonde*.

—— *Of the Inconsistency of our Actions.*

MORE, THOMAS (*c.*1477–1535). English writer and politician. Work cited: *History of King Richard III*, ed. R. S. Sylvester (New Haven: Yale University Press, 1976).

MORERI, LOUIS (1643–80). French clergyman and historian. Work cited: *The Great Historical Dictionary* (*Le Grand Dictionnaire historique*) (Lyons, 1674).

NERO. See the annotation to 2.3.1.15.

NEWTON, ISAAC (1642–1727). English natural philosopher and mathematician. Works cited:

—— *Chronology of Ancient Kingdoms Amended* (London, 1728).

—— *Principia*, i.e. *Mathematical Principles of Natural Philosophy and his System of the World* (1687), trans. A. Motte, rev. F. Cajori, 2 vols. (Berkeley: University of California Press, 1971).

NICOLE, PIERRE (1625–95). French moralist and theologian. Works cited:

—— *Logic*, i.e. *Logic; or, The Art of Thinking* (1662), trans. J. V. Buroker (Cambridge: Cambridge University Press, 1996). Nicole collaborated with Antoine Arnauld on this work.

—— 'De la faiblesse de l'homme' ('On the Weakness of Man'), in *Œuvres philosophiques et morales* (*Philosophical and Moral Works*) (Paris, 1845; fac. Hildesheim: Georg Olms, 1970).

OCKHAM, WILLIAM (1285–1349). English philosopher-theologian.

OVID (Publius Ovidus Naso; 43 BC–AD 17). Roman poet. Work cited: *Metamorphoses*, trans. F. J. Miller, 2 vols.

PASCAL, BLAISE (1623–62). French mathematician and philosopher-theologian. Work cited: *Pensées*, trans. A. J. Krailsheimer (Harmondsworth: Penguin, 1966). This translation uses the Lafuma arrangement of texts.

PERRAULT, CLAUDE (1613–88). French architect and physician. Work cited: *A Treatise of the Five Orders of Columns in Architecture*, trans. J. James, 2nd edn. (London, 1722).

PERRONET, VINCENT (1693–1785). English clergyman. Work cited: *A Second Vindication of Mr. Locke, Wherein his Sentiments relating to Personal Identity are clear'd from some Mistakes of the Rev. Dr. Butler in his Dissertation on that Subject* (London, 1738; fac. Bristol: Thoemmes Press, 1991).

PHILIPS, JOHN (1676–1709). English poet. Work cited: *Cyder* (1708).

Philosophical Transactions of the Royal Society (London, 1699).

PLATO (427–347 BC). Greek philosopher. Works cited:

—— *Meno.*

—— *Laws.*

—— *Republic.*

PLOTINUS (*c.*205–70). Greek philosopher, author of the *Enneads*.

PLUTARCH (*c.*46–120). Greek philosopher and biographer. Works cited:

—— 'Greek Questions', from *Moralia*, trans. F. C. Babbitt.

—— 'How a Man may become Aware of his Progress in Virtue', from *Moralia*, trans. F. C. Babbitt.

—— *Lives*, trans. B. Perrin.

POPE, ALEXANDER (1688–1744). English poet. Work cited: *Essay on Man* (1733–4).

PRIOR, MATTHEW (1664–1721). English poet. Works cited are from *The Literary Works of Matthew Prior*, ed. H. B. Wright and M. K. Spears, 2nd edn. (Oxford: Clarendon Press, 1971):

—— *Alma; or, The Progress of the Mind* (1718).

—— *Solomon on the Vanity of the World* (1709).

PUFENDORF, SAMUEL VON (1632–94). German statesman and political philosopher. Works cited:

—— *Law of Nature*, i.e. *Of the Law of Nature and Nations* (1672), trans. B. Kennett *et al.*, 4th edn. (London, 1729).

—— *Natural State*, i.e. *On the Natural State of Men* (1678), trans. M. Seidler (Lewiston, NY: Edwin Mellen Press, 1990).

QUINTILIAN (Marcus Fabius Quintilianus; *c.*35–*c.*95). Roman rhetorician. Work cited: *Institutes* (*Institutio oratoria*), trans. H. E. Butler, 4 vols.

RALEIGH, WALTER (*c.*1554–1618). English mariner and writer. Work cited: *History of the World* (London, 1634).

RAMSAY, ANDREW MICHAEL (1686–1743). Expatriate Scottish philosopher. Work cited: *A New Cyropædia; or, The Travels of Cyrus* (1727).

RETZ, JEAN-FRANÇOIS-PAUL DE GONDI (1613–79). French clergyman and politician. Work cited: *Memoirs of Jean François Paul de Gondi, Cardinal de Retz*, trans. P. Davall (London: Dutton, 1917).

ROHAULT, JACQUES (1620–72). French natural philosopher. Work cited: *Rohault's System of Natural Philosophy, Illustrated with Dr. Samuel Clarke's Notes, Taken mostly out of Sir Isaac Newton's Philosophy*, trans. J. Clarke, 2 vols. (London, 1723; fac. New York: Johnson Reprint, 1969).

ROLLIN, CHARLES (1661–1741). French historian. Works cited:

—— *Histoire ancienne*, i.e. *The Ancient History of the Egyptians, Carthaginians, Babylonians, Medes and Persians, Grecians, and Macedonians*, 8 vols. (Edinburgh, 1775).

—— *The Method of Teaching and Studying* (*Belles-lettres*), 4 vols. (London, 1734).

SAINT-EVREMOND, CHARLES MARGUETEL DE SAINT-DENIS, SEIUR DE (1613–1703). French literary figure. Work cited: *The Works of Saint-Evremond*, trans. Pierre Desmaizeaux, 3 vols. (London, 1714).

SALLUST (Gaius Sallustius Crispus). Roman historian and politician (86–35 BC). Work cited: *War with Catiline*.

SENAULT, JEAN-FRANÇOIS (*c.*1601–1672). French clergyman and philosopher. Work cited: *The Use of the Passions*, trans. H. Carey (London, 1649).

SENECA, LUCIUS ANNAEUS (4 BC–AD 65). Roman philosopher and politician. Works cited:

—— *Epistles*, i.e. *Ad Lucilium epistulae morales*, trans. R. M. Gummere, 3 vols.

—— *Of Benefits*, from *Moral Essays*, trans. J. W. Basore, 3 vols.

SEXTUS EMPIRICUS (*fl.* AD 200). Greek physician, important source of information about ancient scepticism. Work cited: *Pyrrhonism*, i.e. *Outlines of Pyrrhonism*, trans. R. G. Bury.

SHAFTESBURY, ANTHONY ASHLEY, LORD (1671–1713). English philosopher. Works cited:

—— *Characteristics of Men, Manners, Opinions, Times* (1711), ed. J. M. Robertson, 2 vols. (Indianapolis: Bobbs-Merrill, 1964).

—— *Inquiry*, i.e. *An Inquiry concerning Virtue or Merit*, included in *Characteristics*.

—— *The Moralists, a Philosophical Rhapsody*, included in *Characteristics*.

Spectator (1711–12, 1714), by J. Addison, R. Steele, *et al.*, ed. D. F. Bond, 5 vols. (Oxford: Clarendon Press, 1965).

SPINOZA, BARUCH (1632–77). Dutch philosopher. Works cited are from *The Collected Works of Spinoza*, vol. 1, ed. E. Curley (Princeton: Princeton University Press, 1985).

—— *Descartes' Principles*, i.e. *Parts I and II of Descartes' Principles of Philosophy Demonstrated in the Geometric Manner* (1663).

—— *Ethics* (1677).

STEELE, RICHARD (1672–1729). English playwright and essayist.

SWIFT, JONATHAN (1667–1745). Irish writer and Anglican clergyman. Work cited: *A Tale of a Tub* (1704).

TACITUS (*c*.56–*c*.120). Roman historian. Work cited: *Histories*, in *Tacitus*, trans. C. H. Moore, 5 vols., vol. 2.

THEOPHRASTUS (*c*.379–*c*.287 BC). Greek philosopher, student and successor of Aristotle.

THOMAS, AQUINAS, ST. See Aquinas.

TILLOTSON, JOHN (1630–94). English theologian, archbishop of Canterbury. Work cited: 'The Wisdom of being Religious', in *The Works of John Tillotson*, 7th edn. (London, 1714).

VIRGIL (Publius Vergilius Maro; 70–19 BC). Roman poet. Works cited:
——*Aeneid*, from *Virgil*, trans. H. R. Fairclough, 2 vols.
——*Georgics*, from *Virgil*, trans. H. R. Fairclough, 2 vols.

VITRUVIUS POLLIO (*fl*. 50–25 BC). Roman engineer and architect. Work cited: *On Architecture*, trans. F. Granger.

WARD, SETH (1617–89). English churchman and mathematician. Work cited: *Essay*, i.e. *A Philosophical Essay toward the Eviction of the Being and Attributes of God; Immortality of the Souls* . . . (London, 1752).

WATTS, ISAAC (1674–1748). English clergyman and philosopher. Works cited:
——*A Brief Scheme of Ontology; or, The Science of Being in General*, in *Philosophical Essays*.
——*The Doctrine of the Passions Explain'd and Improv'd; or, A Brief and Comprehensive Scheme of the Natural Affections of Mankind* (London, 1729).
——*Logick; or, The Right Use of Reason in the Enquiry after Truth* (London, 1725).
——*Philosophical Essays on Various Subjects, viz. Space, Substance, Body, Spirit, the Operations of the Soul in Union with the Body, Innate Ideas, Perpetual Consciousness, Place and Motion of Spirits* (London, 1733).

The Whole Duty of Man (1658). English devotional work, perhaps written by Richard Allestree (1619–81).

WILKINS, JOHN (1614–72). English clergyman and philosopher. Work cited: *Of the Principles and Duties of Natural Religion* (1675).

WILLIAM OF ORANGE (1650–1702), later William III, king of England, Scotland, and Ireland (1690–1702).

WOLLASTON, WILLIAM (1660–1724). English philosopher. Work cited: *The Religion of Nature Delineated* (London, 1724; fac. New York: Garland Press, 1978).

ZENO OF CITIUM (*c*.333–*c*.262 BC). Greek philosopher, founder of the Stoic school, not to be confused with Zeno of Elea (*c*.490–*c*.445 BC), a disciple of Parmenides.

INDEX

This is an index to the texts of the *Treatise* and *Abstract*, to the Editor's Introduction, and to the Editors' Annotations. The Supplementary Reading, the Glossary, and the References, materials already organized for easy access, are not indexed. The index treats a substantial number of key concepts or issues in an analytical manner. For more general guidance on the contents of Hume's texts or the Editor's Introduction, consult the Contents pages (v–ix). Numbers preceded by I (I9–I99) refer to the Editor's Introduction. Hume's texts are found on pages 1–417. References to pages 423–569 are to the Editors' Annotations.

Index

Index

Philip II 353, 362, 553, 555
Philips, John 232, 512
philosophers; *see also* Cartesians; philosophy;
  scholastic philosophy
  common opinions or maxims of 29–30, 49,
    52, 67n, 90–1, 95, 102, 106–7, 113, 129,
    134, 137, 139–44, 145, 161, 164, 194, 202,
    328n, 338, 347, 350, 399, 400, 408, 410,
    415, 483
  dispositions of 23, 74
  disputes among 3, 106, 193, 325n
  failure to address probability 408, 454
  false or unlikely opinions of 77, 106–9, 113,
    145–8, 149, 150–2, 152–63, 164–5, 239,
    257, 260, 262–5, 268, 296–7, 297n, 298n,
    302, 305, 313, 316–17, 332, 338–9,
    347–52, 357, 361, 370, 408
  join the vulgar 143
  motivation of 287
  nature's consolation for 147–8
  obscure ideas of 52, 257
  role of 389
  Stoics 148
*Philosophical Essay Toward the Eviction of the
  Being and Attributes of God* (Ward) 450
Philosophical Essays on Various Subjects (Watts)
  482, 487
A Philosophical Inquiry concerning Human Liberty
  (Collins) 166–7
philosophical relations
  as basis of knowledge or probability 50–3
  and the causal maxim 56
  identified, characterized 120–1, 124–5, 14–15,
    50, 429–30, 445–6
philosophy; *see also* philosophers
  abstruseness of Hume's 3–4, 151, 405
  advantages of 176–8
  analogous to hunting, gaming 288–9, 532
  ancient 110–11, 111n, 144–9, 265, 389, 407,
    478–9
  and belief in external objects 129
  a contradiction in Hume's 173
  disgraceful state of 3
  easy and obvious 95
  likely reception of Hume's 81
  limitations of 280
  modern 111, 148–52, 265, 480
  and objects of the mind 49, 127, 129, 131,
    140–1, 157, 223, 293, 399, 408, 472,
    476–7
  pleasures of 102, 176, 267–8, 288–9
  and religion 113, 163–4, 263–4
  as speculative or practical 294, 395, 534
  subversion of 102

  true 14, 147, 185, 359, 369
  unnecessary, ineffectual 208, 216, 278, 364
physical points 31, 77
Physiological Library 110
pilgrims 76–7
pity or compassion (compound passion) 160,
    316, 386
  in animals 256
  characterized 238, 240, 246
  and contiguity 239
  as a contrary phenomenon 242, 245–50, 517,
    518
  and the imagination 239–40, 245, 256, 514
  as related to love 245–6
  and sympathy 238–9, 247–50, 518
  and tendency or drift 246–50, 517
Plato 148, 259, 455, 459, 478, 496, 522, 544, 551,
    562
pleasure and pain; *see also* good or evil
  and comparison 205–6, 242–3, 247
  distinctive kinds of 179
  ideas of 81–2
  as impressions of sensation 81–2, 181
  as mind dependent 128, 473–4
  as a source of passions 152–3, 153n, 181, 265,
    272, 280, 367
  universally motivate 81, 181, 204, 265–8,
    367, 458–9
plenum 40, 47, 441–2; *see also* vacuum
Plotinus 483
Plutarch 112n, 478, 487, 508, 528, 546, 561
poet(s), poetry 76, 317
  effects of 83–5
  and the passions 84–5, 124, 181, 194, 231–2,
    238, 244, 278, 412
  and philosophy 45, 72, 147
  and verisimilitude 83–4, 459
politicians
  and artifice 269, 321, 370
politics 2, 4, 424
Pope, Alexander 112n, 505, 525
The Port-Royal Logic; *see Logic; or, The Art of
  Thinking* (Arnauld and Nicole)
power; *see also* necessary or causal connection
  unexercised 154, 13–14, 19, 115, 203–5,
    232–3, 429, 433, 500, 501
The Praise of Folly (Erasmus) 532
Preface to Newton's *Principles of Natural
  Philosophy* (Cotes) 463
*Preliminary Dissertation concerning the
  Fundamental Principle of Virtue or
  Morality* (Gay) 183n, 540
prescription; *see under* property
presensation 216, 506

Index

resemblance
  of acts, dispositions of mind 45, 135, 145,
    166–7
  among humans 207
  assists in the production of belief 69–70,
    75–79, 456
  as an associating quality 13, 65, 74, 416, 430
  and belief in external objects 132–3, 134–9
  and choice of associates 229
  as contrariety 247
  effects of 69–70, 74–81, 97, 100, 136–7,
    138–9, 156, 166–7, 331
  facilitates sympathy 207–8
  as a fertile source of error 44–5, 134–6, 136n,
    443–4
  as a natural relation 13–14
  and the passions 198–9, 229–30, 234, 243,
    253, 282
  as a philosophical relation 124–5, 15, 50, 298,
    446
respect and contempt (compound passions)
    160–1, 505
  comparison as cause of 250–1
  a difficulty solved 251–2
  and love, pride 251
  and social distance 252–3
responsive passions; *see under* passions
Retz, Jean-François-Paul de Gondi (Cardinal de
    Retz) 103, 465
Revolution of 1688 360, 554
right(s) 310, 315, 329n, 338–41, 355–61
The Rights of War and Peace (Grotius) 487, 495,
    546, 547, 551, 552, 555, 556
Rohault, Jacques 112n, 434, 435, 444, 467, 477,
    482
  on vacuum and plenum 441, 442
  wheel of fire 437
Rollin, Charles 272–3, 528, 559
Roman Catholics, Catholicism 70, 79, 331,
    336–7, 458, 548–9
Rome, Romans 75, 277, 357, 360, 362
Royal Society 566
rules for judging causes and effects 116–17,
    468–9
  application(s) 117–18, 197, 238, 241, 369,
    371, 398
  corollaries 54, 352–3

Sabinus 329n, 547
Saint-Evremond, Charles de Margeutel de Saint
    Denis, Sieur de 382, 560
  The Works of Saint-Evremond, 560
Salic law 359, 554
Sallust 387, 562

Scepsis Scientifica (Glanvill) 449
'The Sceptic' (Hume, *Essays*) 493
scepticism
  about ultimate principles 5–6, 46, 46–7n, 173
  and belief 123–5
  early modern definitions 112, 471
  and external existence 125, 143–4, 150
  extreme or unjustified versions 3, 123, 142,
    150, 174, 471, 472, 477
  Hume's 112–14, 146, 175–8, 399, 400, 413–14,
    471, 489
  inadequate responses to 124–5
  moderate, true 148, 176–8
  a natural, incurable form 144
  pleasures of 102
  Pyrrhonian 414, 460, 472, 489
  and reason 121–5
  regarding causes 107–8
  remedies for 144, 177, 477
  and the senses 126–8, 143–4, 477
scholastic philosophy, Peripatetics 263, 267–8
  arguments of 27
  and free-will 203, 500, 521
  and mathematical points 31, 34
  metaphysics of 16, 146–8, 156, 478–9, 483
  unintelligible terms, distinctions of 106–7,
    338, 430–1, 478, 479
science of human nature 424
  as anatomy of human nature 171, 395, 407,
    564
  foundation of 4–6, 425
  the foundational science 114–15, 4, 407–8
  limitations 5–6, 413–14
  neglected 177
  principles and maxims of 10, 29, 44, 69, 93,
    95, 416–17; *see also* maxims, Hume's
sciences 114n, 4, 51, 423; *see also* mathematics;
    natural philosophy
Scipio Africanus 222, 508
The Search after Truth (Malebranche) 408, 428,
    433, 434, 442, 443, 445, 447, 449, 451,
    459, 465, 466, 467, 469, 480, 485, 486,
    490, 496, 514, 522, 529, 533, 567
A Second Vindication of Mr. Locke (Perronet) 487
secondary qualities, impressions or ideas of
    127–9, 149–52; *see also* primary qualities
  bodies unknowable without 151–2
  have no model or archetype 149, 151, 480
  and impressions of primary qualities 128,
    151–2
  and moral sentiments 301–2, 537
  and pleasures, pains 128, 149
  projected onto objects 137, 112–13, 467
  variations of 140, 149, 240

618